Most recent ed. as of Ja. 2014

FANTASY LITERATURE FOR CHILDREN AND YOUNG ADULTS

A Comprehensive Guide

Fifth Edition

RUTH NADELMAN LYNN

LIBRARIES
UNLIMITED
A Member of the Greenwood Publishing Group

Westport, Connecticut · London

Recent Titles in the Children's and Young Adult Literature Reference Series
Catherine Barr, Series Editor

Best Books for Middle School and Junior High Readers, Grades 6-9
John T. Gillespie and Catherine Barr

Best Books for High School Readers, Grades 9-12
John T. Gillespie and Catherine Barr

Popular Series Fiction for K-6 Readers: A Reading and Selection Guide
Rebecca L. Thomas and Catherine Barr

Popular Series Fiction for Middle School and Teen Readers: A Reading and Selection Guide
Rebecca L. Thomas and Catherine Barr

Library of Congress Cataloging-in-Publication Data

Lynn, Ruth Nadelman, 1948-
  Fantasy literature for children and young adults : a comprehensive guide. --5th
edition / by Ruth Nadelman Lynn.
    p. cm.
  Includes bibliographical references and index.
  ISBN 1-59158-050-1 (alk. paper)
  1. Children--Books and reading. 2. Children's literature--Bibliography. 3. Young
adult literature--Bibliography. 4. Fantasy literature--Bibliography. I. Title.
Z1037.L97 2005
016.80883'8766--dc22   2004063247

British Library Cataloguing in Publication Data is available.

Library of Congress Catalog Card Number: 2004063247
ISBN: 1-59158-050-1

First published in 2005

Libraries Unlimited, 88 Post Road West, Westport, CT 06881
A Member of the Greenwood Publishing Group, Inc.
www.lu.com

Printed in the United States of America

The paper used in this book complies with the
Permanent Paper Standard issued by the National
Information Standards Organization (Z39.48-1984).

10   9   8   7   6   5   4   3   2   1

With love to Bruce, to Josh, and to Noah,
who always illuminate my reality with
delight and with joy.

CONTENTS

PREFACE

The fifth edition of *Fantasy Literature for Children and Young Adults* is a comprehensive annotated guide to more than 7,600 fantasy novels and story collections for children and young adults in grades 3 through 12. This edition continues to include hundreds of "crossover" adult fantasy titles of interest to young adult readers. Such books are indicated by the grade-level designation Gr. 10 up. *Fantasy Literature for Children and Young Adults* is intended for use by librarians, teachers, parents, and those studying children's and young adult literature.

Significant improvements have been made in this edition. A total of 2,880 books have been added to the 4,800 books included in the previous (1995) edition and 80 have been deleted, for a total of 7,600 books—a 62 percent increase. This edition features nearly 4,500 numbered main entry titles. Additionally, nearly 3,150 sequels and related works are cited in the main entry annotations.

The books included in this comprehensive guide are novels and story collections published in English in the United States (including translations) between 1900 and 2004. A few 19th-century classics such as Lewis Carroll's *Alice's Adventures in Wonderland* (1865) and Mark Twain's *A Connecticut Yankee in King Arthur's Court* (1889) have also been included. Careful attention has been given to original publication dates and to recommended (by professional review sources discussed below) 20th- and 21st-century U.S. editions of these significant works. The same can be said for works originally published abroad, both in English and in foreign languages that were translated into English. Review citations from professional journals continue to be given in each entry, and only books recommended in two or more sources have been included. Neither science fiction nor horror literature is featured in this bibliography, although a number of "science-fantasies" with more fantasy elements than science fiction (e.g., McCaffrey's Dragonriders of Pern series) and some anthologies containing both fantasy and science fiction or horror short stories will be found.

Chapter Title Changes. In this edition, the three sections devoted to high fantasy have been separated into three chapters: Chapter 5, High Fantasy: Alternate Worlds or Histories; Chapter 6, High Fantasy: Myth and Legend Fantasy; and Chapter 7, High Fantasy: Travel to Other Worlds.

Award-Winning Fantasy Literature. Hundreds of works of fantasy and authors of fantasy have won international and national literary awards. The list of award winners has been greatly expanded in this edition, and can be found following the Introduction.

Out-of-Print Entries. Recommended but out-of-print works of fantasy continue to appear in this bibliography. Such books deserve inclusion since many are available in library collections, and librarians often use this guide as an aid in making choices while weeding their collections. The out-of-print status is noted in the publication information. Fortunately, many outstanding fantasy novels have been brought back into print during the past decade.

The Research Guide. In order to allow space for the addition of more than 2,800 new works of fantasy literature to this edition, the Research Guide section found in the fourth edition (1995) has been eliminated. This decision allows the fifth edition to remain a comprehensive guide to recommended fantasy literature for children and young adults. It is hoped that an updated guide to critical and historical studies of fantasy literature and its authors can be published at a later date.

GUIDE TO USE

Entries contain, where applicable, the following bibliographic information:

- Entry numbers: chapter numbers have been added to the beginning of each entry number (e.g., 1-37, 12-104)
- Author name and/or pseudonym (the real names of pseudonymous authors are included in parentheses)
- Title
- Series title in parentheses
- Suggested grade level: All books, whether for children or young adults, have been interfiled and arranged in 12 topical chapters, with numerous cross-references. Each entry has been given a specific grade-level designation (for example, Gr. 3–5 or Gr. 8–10). Adult books read by young adults are indicated by the designation Gr. 10 up.
- Original country of publication if other than the United States, and alternate or British title
- Annotation
- Bibliographic information
- Review citations

Recommendation Symbols. In this edition, two stars (✮✮) denote books of outstanding quality that have been recommended in five or more professional review sources or are generally regarded as "classics" by librarians who work with children and young adults; a single star (✮) denotes books that have been recommended in four review sources. These stars, if applicable, will be found directly under the entry number. Note that all the books included in this comprehensive guide have received at least two professional recommendations.

Annotations. Annotations provide a brief description of each title. A list of sequels or related works, including publisher and date, follows the annotation. If the publisher of a series title or related work is the same as that for the main entry title, only the date of publication is given. Sequels or related works judged to be important and significantly different from the main entry have also been given brief descriptive annotations within the main entry. When applicable, annotations conclude with a notation of major awards won.

Bibliographic Information and Review Citations. The information following the annotation includes the illustrator, translator, and adaptor; publisher and date of publication; pagination of the most recent edition; ISBN number(s); or an o.p. (out-of-print) designation if applicable; and a list of review citations. Each main entry must have been recommended by at least two professional reviewing sources to be considered for inclusion. Reviews cited pertain to all editions listed in the entry, including out-of-print editions. (For a complete list of the review sources used see "Abbreviations of Books and Review Journals Cited" below.)

In cases where a book fits into two or more categories (for example, time travel and ghost fantasy), it is placed in the chapter that best fits it, and a cross-reference is entered in the alternate chapter(s). Cross-references are interfiled alphabetically with the main entries and are listed by author's surname, first name, title of book, and chapter where the main entry is found.

Title Entries for Anthologies. It is accepted library practice to use title entries for anthologies of stories written by many authors and/or compiled by an editor. Such anthologies continue to be listed by title in this edition.

Reviewing Sources Cited. Ten contemporary and 10 historical professional reviewing sources and review journals have been consulted and may be cited in each entry (see "Abbreviations of Books and Review Journals Cited," below, following the "Guide to Use"). All of the books included in this comprehensive guide have been recommended in at least 2 of the 20 professional reviewing sources.

Indexes. The Subject Index has been expanded once again. It includes topical headings on the major fantasy worlds (e.g., *Narnia*) and headings on imaginary beings (for example, lilliputians, dragons, and merpeople). The Subject Index also includes historical periods such as the Middle Ages and World War II, folklore from various countries and cultures (e.g., *France—Folklore* and *Native American folklore*), and adaptations of classic folktales (for example, *"The Frog Prince," adaptations of*). This edition contains a new index of series titles. The titles listed in the Title Index and the Author Index include titles of main entry listings and titles of sequels and related works noted in the main entry annotation. The numbers in each of the four indexes (Author and Illustrator, Title, Series, and Subject) refer to entry numbers, not page numbers.

ABBREVIATIONS OF BOOKS AND REVIEW JOURNALS CITED

In this edition, reviews have been cited from 10 contemporary journals and 10 books and journals of historic importance. Reviews from most journals have been cited by volume and page number. The exceptions are those reviews from the *Bulletin of the Center for Children's Books* prior to December 1949, *Horn Book Magazine* prior to 1930, *Library Journal* beginning in 1985, the [London] *Times Literary Supplement* for those few years when Roman numerals were used for page numbers, and *VOYA* prior to April 1983. Since these five journals were not given consecutive paging throughout the year, reviews are cited by month, year, and page number. For the same reason, all reviews from *Kliatt* and *School Library Journal* are also cited by month, year, and page number.

BL *Booklist*. Chicago: American Library Association, 1904–.

Bookshelf *The Bookshelf for Boys and Girls*. Edited by Clara W. Hunt and others. New York: R. R. Bowker, 1918–1935.

CCBB *Center for Children's Books, Bulletin*. Chicago: University of Chicago Press, 1948–1992. Urbana: University of Illinois Press, 1992–.

Eakin Eakin, Mary. *Good Books for Children, 1950–1965*, 3rd ed. Chicago: University of Chicago Press, 1966.

HB *The Horn Book Magazine*. Boston: Horn Book, 1924–.

HBG *The Horn Book Guide to Children's and Young Adult Books*. Boston: Horn Book, 1990–.

Kirkus *Kirkus Reviews*. New York: Kirkus Service, 1932–.

Kliatt *Kliatt Young Adult Paperback Book Guide*. Newton, MA: Kliatt Paperback Book Guide, 1966–.

LJ *Library Journal*. New York: Reed Business Information, 1875–.

Mahony 1 Mahony, Bertha E. *Books for Boys and Girls: A Suggestive Purchase List*. Boston: Woman's Educational and Industrial Union, Bookshop for Boys and Girls, 1914–1922.

Mahony 2 Mahony, Bertha E., and Elinor Whitney. *Realms of Gold in Children's Books*. Garden City, NY: Doubleday, 1929.

Mahony 3 Mahony, Bertha E., and Elinor Whitney. *Five Years of Children's Books: A Supplement to "Realms of Gold."* Garden City, NY: Doubleday, 1936.

Moore Moore, Anne Carroll. *The Three Owls*, Vol. 3. New York: Macmillan, 1931.

SLJ   *School Library Journal*. New York: Reed Business Information, 1953–.

Suth   Sutherland, Zena. *The Best in Children's Books, 1966–1972*. Chicago: University of Chicago Press, 1973.

Suth 2   Sutherland, Zena. *The Best in Children's Books, 1973–1978*. Chicago: University of Chicago Press, 1980.

Suth 3   Sutherland, Zena. *The Best in Children's Books; The University of Chicago Guide to Children's Literature, 1979–1984*. Chicago: University of Chicago Press, 1986.

Suth 4   Sutherland, Zena, Betsy Hearne, and Roger Sutton. *The Best in Children's Books: The University of Chicago Guide to Children's Literature, 1985–1990*. Chicago: University of Chicago Press, 1991.

TLS   [London] *Times Literary Supplement*, London, England: Times Newspapers, Ltd, 1938–.

VOYA   *VOYA: Voice of Youth Advocates*. Lanham, MD: Scarecrow Press, 1977–.

INTRODUCTION

Fantasy literature for children and young adults has long been considered to be "the richest and most varied of all the genres,"[1] and "the most wrenching, depth-provoking kind of fiction available to our children,"[2] according to authors and critics Sheila Egoff and Jane Yolen. As critic Elizabeth Nesbit writes, "[I]t is probable that no other type of book has done more to give genuine distinction to children's literature than has fantasy."[3]

And since the publication of J. K. Rowling's first Harry Potter novel in 1997, fantasy literature has also become the most popular genre of children's and young adult fiction. According to the January 2004 issue of *School Library Journal*, "[T]eens prefer reading fantasy books more than anything else, according to the first Teens' Top Ten list, sponsored by the Young Adult Library Services Association (YALSA). Some 1,700 12- to 18-year-olds from across the nation had a chance to vote online for their favorite books as part of YALSA's Teen Read Week, October 19–25, 2003."[4]

Rowling's fantasy novels have been credited with igniting a love of reading in an entire generation of children, and the Harry Potter books are also being read by nearly as many adults. According to the November 17, 2003, BBC News: World Edition, 250 million copies of the Harry Potter books had been sold in more than 200 countries, and the books had been translated into more than 60 languages.[5] Their popularity has led to a series of feature-length Harry Potter films, which, in turn have encouraged filmmakers to create live-action films of other classic fantasy novels, including J. R. R. Tolkien's The Lord of the Rings trilogy and Natalie Babbitt's *Tuck Everlasting*. In 2004 alone, film versions of *Ella Enchanted* and Lemony Snicket's A Series of Unfortunate Events were released, along with *Finding Neverland*, a film for adults about J. M. Barrie's creation of *Peter Pan*. And film versions of C. S. Lewis's Chronicles of Narnia, beginning with *The Lion, the Witch, and the Wardrobe*, and of Philip Pullman's His Dark Materials trilogy, beginning with *The Golden Compass*, are due to be released in 2005.

Critic Michael Cart discussed "the emergence of fantasy as one of the hottest genres in publishing for children and young adults," in his April 15, 2004, *Booklist* column. He points out that 50 percent of the titles on two newly established YALSA "Teens' Top 10 Lists" are fantasy. "The one-two publicity punch delivered by the Rowling-Tolkien combination has captured the imaginations of readers—and viewers—the world over, and the result has been a sudden renaissance of interest in a form that has been with us since Alice went down that rabbit hole in 1865. Though fantasy has traditionally belonged to the world of children's literature . . . it is also the quintessential crossover genre with inherent appeal to readers and dreamers of all ages."[6]

Defining Fantasy

Natalie Babbitt has said:

> True fantasy . . . is not so much created as it is distilled and interpreted—from impressions that go far back into pre-history, impressions that, so far as we can tell from the study of folk tales, are common to us all, no matter what our age or nationality. True fantasy . . . aims to define the universe. Fantasy offers a system of symbols everyone of every age understands; it enriches and simplifies our lives and makes them bearable.[7]

"Fantasy literature" is a broad term used to describe books in which magic causes impossible, and often wondrous, events to occur. Either a quest or a struggle between good and evil is often central to the plot of contemporary fantasy novels, and many of these works are steeped in myth or legend. Fantasy tales can be set in our own everyday world or in a "secondary" world somewhat like our own. The existence of the magic cannot be explained. Tales of fantasy should not be confused with science fiction stories, which involve a future made more or less possible by scientific or technological advances.

Paradoxically, imaginative fantasies, especially those written for young people over the past four decades, often contain the most serious of underlying themes. Such themes as the conflict between good and evil, the struggle to preserve joy and hope in a cruel and frightening world, and the acceptance of the inevitability of death have led some critics to suggest that fantasies may portray a truer version of reality than many or most realistic novels.

What is fantasy literature for children and young adults? How does it differ from fantasy written for adults? What is the appeal of fantasy? How does the development of fantasy fit into the development of children's and young adult literature in general? Why do authors write fantasy? Hundreds of articles and books have attempted to answer these questions. This introduction surveys the important critical literature on these topics and contains an updated historical overview of the outstanding fantasy literature for children and young adults.

The Oxford English Dictionary, Second Edition (1989), states that the two forms of the word fantasy, spelled "fantasy" and "phantasy," come from the Latin *phantasia* and the Greek *φavraoia*, the sense of which combines spectral apparitions or phantoms with the faculties of "sensuous perception" and imagination. The predominant modern sense of *fantasy* is described as "caprice, whim, fanciful invention," and that of *phantasy* as "imagination, visionary notion." Fantasy as a genre of literary composition "deals with things that are not and cannot be," [while] science fiction deals with things that can be, that some day may be.[8]

The Random House Dictionary of the English Language, Second Edition, Unabridged, defines fantasy literature as "an imaginative or fanciful work, especially one dealing with supernatural or unnatural events or characters."[9] Literary critics and fantasists have enlarged upon these definitions.

Critical definitions of fantasy vary from the ambiguous—for example, "Fantasy may be almost all things to all men" and "Fantasy . . . is so many different things that attempts to define it seem rather pointless"—to the obscure: "[In fantasy] the perspectives enforced by the ground rules of the narrative world must be diametrically contradicted." Between these poles lies a great variety of interpretations.[10]

The two elements of fantastic literature given the greatest weight by critics and fantasists alike are the presence of magic[11] and of the impossible or inexplicable.[12] Critic Jane Mobley has observed that within a fantasy narrative no attempt is made to explain the origin of the magic, it simply exists; and she suggests that the narrative itself is in a sense magical in its ability to enchant readers, drawing them into another world where they demand no explanation as to how they got there.[13]

Many critics have written of fantasy's violation of natural laws,[14] and others give the element of "wonder"[15] prime importance in defining fantasy literature. Still others point to fantasy literature's propensity for pushing past the boundaries of the realities of our own world, the so-called primary world, into secondary otherworlds. Ann Swinfen describes modern fantasy as "a serious form of the modern novel, often characterized by notable literary merit, and concerned both with heightened awareness of the complex nature of primary reality and with the exploration beyond empirical experience into the transcendent reality embodied in imaginative and spiritual otherworlds."[16]

Critic Sheila Egoff and fantasist Eleanor Cameron have pointed out the paradoxes inherent in fantasy. According to Egoff:

> Fantasy is a literature of paradox. It is the discovery of the real within the unreal, the credible within the incredible, the believable within the unbelievable. . . . The creators of fantasy may use the most fantastic, weird and bizarre images and happenings but their basic concern is with the wholesomeness of the human soul, or to use a more contemporary term, the integrity of the self. . . . The tenet of the fantasist is "there is another kind of real, one that is truer to the human spirit, demanding a pilgrim's progress to find it."[17]

To Cameron, the paradox of fantasy is that all fantasy that works has a sense of reality; that within the everyday world of the novel there exists a pool of magic possessing a strange but powerful and convincing reality of its own.[18]

It should come as no surprise that fantasists should have their own unique visions of the nature of fantasy. To J. R. R. Tolkien, in *Tree and Leaf* (Houghton, 1965), fantasy is the making or glimpsing of otherworlds. For Jane Langton, fantasy novels are "waking dreams. They make up to us for the sense of loss we feel when we wake up and find our dreams shrinking out of memory. A literary fantasy gives us a dream back to keep." Lloyd Alexander also speaks of dreams, as he succinctly calls attention to the psychological depths that fantasy probes and the fact that even so-called realistic novels are an author's invention: "I suppose you might define realism as fantasy pretending to be true; and fantasy as reality pretending to be a dream." And Mollie Hunter explains that her vision of fantasy comes from her memories of childhood: "As a writer . . . I find that the form of children's literature which best exemplifies both the fascinated terror [of childhood memory] and the yearning [for a sudden glimpse of something strange and wonderful] is what—for lack of a more exact name—we refer to as fantasy."[19]

Fantasy has been variously described as imaginative, fanciful, visionary, strange, otherworldly, supernatural, mysterious, frightening, magical, inexplicable, wondrous, dreamlike, and, paradoxically, realistic. It has been termed an awareness of the inexplicable existence of "magic" in the everyday world, a yearning for a sudden glimpse of something strange and wonderful, and a different and perhaps truer version of reality.

If it is difficult to encapsulate the entire genre of fantasy literature into a single definition; we can, nevertheless, acknowledge the powerful effect that fantasy can have on its readers. As Ursula K. Le Guin asserts:

> [Fantasy] is a different approach to reality, an alternative technique for apprehending and coping with existence. It is not antirational, but pararational; not realistic, but surrealistic, superrealistic; a heightening of reality. . . . Fantasy is nearer to poetry, to mysticism, and to insanity than naturalistic fiction is. . . . A fantasy is a journey. It is a journey into the subconscious mind, just as psychoanalysis is. Like psychoanalysis, it can be dangerous; and it will change you.[20]

The Purpose of Fantasy

Does fantasy have any function beyond entertainment? Certainly, it can be entertaining. It can also provide the reader with insights into himself or herself through identification with or rejection of a particular character. In these ways it parallels the literature of other genres. But critics and fantasists agree that good fantasy does more. Jane Mobley writes in *Phantasmagoria* (Anchor, 1977) that fantasy's purpose is to evoke wonder and mystery, and Lloyd Alexander tells readers in a *Library Journal* article (December 15, 1966) that its purpose is to refresh the heart through escape or "liberation."

Sheila Egoff and Ursula K. Le Guin have pointed out fantasy's unique way of helping us to better understand our own world. Unlike other genres, which tend to offer either a total escape from or total immersion in reality, fantasy can meet both needs. Egoff puts it this way: "The purpose of fantasy is not to escape reality, but to illuminate it: to transport us to a world different from the real world, yet to demonstrate certain immutable truths that persist even there—and in every possible world."[21]

Critic Swinfen agrees that "the fundamental purpose of serious fantasy is to comment upon the real world and to explore the moral, philosophical and other dilemmas posed by it."[22] According to Egoff, "What distinguishes fine fantasy from other fine literature is not merely its framework or its view of life, but its inner core. The writer of fantasy goes beyond realism to disclose that we do not live entirely in a world of the perceived senses, that we also inhabit an inner world of the mind and spirit where the creative imagination is permanently struggling to expand vision and perception. . . . It is from the 'worlds within' created by fantasists that the faculty of the imagination can be seen at its most powerful and stimulating."[23]

The Images of Fantasy

Some authors assert that they begin their writing with a mental image, rather than specific characters or a completely developed plot. It is interesting, therefore, to compare the variety of images that some fantasists have used to describe fantasy itself. These images range from onions to soap bubbles.

Alan Garner likens the many layers of meaning found in a serious fantasy to an onion:

> In order to connect, the book must be written for all levels of experience. This means that any given piece of text must work at simple plot level . . . and it must also work for me, and for every stage between. . . . An onion can be peeled down through its layers, but it is always, at every layer, an onion, whole in itself. I try to write onions.[24]

Jane Louise Curry also uses a spherical image in her analogy between the structure of a "visionary" fantasy and that of a pearl:

> The fantasy of the lost "ph" . . . is rarely, if ever, simply a picaresque series of adventures like bright Venetian beads on a string. More often—if it approaches real excellence—it is shaped as a single pearl is shaped: a whole built up around a theme, or person, or place, or relationship.[25]

Susan Cooper compares the ephemeral nature of fantasy to a soap bubble:

> [Fantasy is] the most magnificent bubble I have ever seen, iridescent, gleaming . . . and in the sunlight all the colors in the world were swimming over that gleaming sphere—swirling, glowing, achingly beautiful. Like a dancing rainbow the bubble hung there for a long moment; then it was gone.[26]

French literary scholar Paul Hazard describes the nature of fairy tales as a deep pool: "Fairy tales are like beautiful mirrors of water, so deep and crystal clear! In their depth we sense the mysterious experience of a thousand years. Their contents date from the primeval ages of humanity."[27]

A final example of descriptive imagery comes from the *Green and Burning Tree* (Little, Brown, 1969), in which Eleanor Cameron likens fantasists to wizards, whose imaginative virtuosity allows them to toss up ideas like dazzling, brilliantly colored balls; wizards able to juggle past, present, and future with a deftness that almost defies analysis.[28]

Children's and Young Adult Fantasy Versus Adult Fantasy

Before the advent of Harry Potter, novels for children and young adults could usually be distinguished from novels for adults on the superficial levels of length and format: children's and young adult novels were usually much shorter than adult novels. Of course, children's novels are often printed in a larger typeface with wider margins, some children's and young adult novels are illustrated, and most, but not all, of the human protagonists in children's and young adult novels tend to be young people.

Fantasist Natalie Babbitt maintains that although children's literature deals with all of the so-called adult emotions of love, pride, grief, fear of death, violence, and the yearning for success, there is one emotion to be found only in children's books, and that is joy.[29]

Although overt sexuality is usually avoided in books for children, children's and young adult fantasies can be as complex in terms of plot, theme, and writing style as "adult" fantasies. According to Swinfen: "It is quite clear from any prolonged study of what might be termed 'high fantasy,' that to label them as children's books is grossly misleading. They operate on an adult level of meaning and the issue of deciding the dividing line, if such could ever exist, between worthwhile literature for children and for adults seems to be a futile exercise."[30] Indeed, Sheila Egoff asserts in *Thursday's Child* that "fantasy written for children is far superior to that written for adults."

In the not-too-distant past, however, critical agreement seemed to be quite the opposite. "Adult" literary critics tended to lump children's fantasies under the heading "light entertainment." *Peter Pan* was frequently offered as an example of the frivolousness of fantasy literature for children.[31]

Even librarian Donnarae MacCann, a proponent of children's fantasy, concluded that

The only notable difference in an author's stylistic treatment when he writes for the child audience is the overall tone of gaiety or sympathetic understanding pervading the story. The same writer, perhaps, may allow some bitterness to colour his communications with his peers.[32]

And as recently as 1973, "adult" fantasy author Lin Carter maintained that "A fantasy is a book or story . . . in which magic really works—not a fairy tale, not a story for children, like *Peter Pan* or *The Wizard of Oz*, but a work of fiction for adults—a story which challenges the mind, which sets it working."[33]

Obviously, Carter was unaware that such powerful "children's" fantasies as William Mayne's *Earthfasts*, Alan Garner's *The Owl Service*, Ursula K. Le Guin's *A Wizard of Earthsea*, and Susan Cooper's *The Dark Is Rising* had already been published by 1973. Certainly, none of these "children's" fantasies could be characterized as whimsical, or lighthearted, and it is even more certain that reading any of these novels would "challenge the mind."

What, then, does differentiate a "children's" fantasy from an "adult" fantasy, if it is not lightness of tone or the absence of substance? Natalie Babbitt feels that the one tangible difference is that all the children's stories we remember longest and love best have "happy endings."

Not, please . . . a simple "happily ever after," or . . . the kind of contrived final sugar coating that seems to be tacked on . . . but . . . something which goes much deeper, something which turns a story ultimately toward hope rather than resignation and contains within it a difference not only between the two literatures but also between youth and age.[34]

J. K. Rowling has told interviewers that her seven Harry Potter novels will become darker as the series continues. It remains to be seen whether the final two volumes of the series, in which Harry will be portrayed as age sixteen and seventeen, will continue to appeal to children, as well as to young adults and adults.

Youth Response Versus Adult Response

Some critics and fantasists have turned the question of the difference between children's and adult fantasy around, proposing that it is not the books that are different, but the level of response to the story that separates adult readers from child readers. "A fantasy," says Sheila Egoff, "may often be read on two levels. It may be only an adventure story for some children; others will have—at once, or on later reflection—the richer experience of sensing the inner truths behind the exciting and entertaining tale."[35]

Critic Neil Philip proposes that children respond to what they read on an emotional level, whereas adults are more analytical. Adults, according to Philip, think like philosophers, using a logical progression of ideas to produce a solution. Whereas children think like poets, gaining insight from a condensation of images, allowing them to experience emotions they may not be able to explain or to completely understand.[36]

Fantasist Susan Cooper feels that children are more open to accepting the fantastic than are adults:

[It is not] surprising that we [fantasists] should be read, today, mainly by children . . . children are the natural audience for fantasy. They aren't a different species. They're us, a little while ago. It's just that they are still able to accept mystery. . . . They still know the essence of wonder, which is to live without ever being quite sure what to expect. And therefore, quite often, to encounter delight.[37]

According to Ursula K. Le Guin, "Fantasy is the great age-equalizer, if it's good when you're twelve, it's quite likely to be just as good, or better when you're thirty-six."[38]

In the genre of fantasy as a whole, there are great variations in tone and complexity, both in literature written for children and young adults and that written for adults. It seems clear, however, that as in all literature, it is the level of the reader's understanding and his or her willingness to accept the presence of magic and impossibility that determine an individual's choice of reading material.

The Appeal of Fantasy

Of course, long before the appearance of Harry Potter, fantasy literature appealed to adults as well as children and young adults. Adults find it "a source of marvel and mystery and wonder and joy that [they] find nowhere else." It brings "a sense of the strange, the numinous, the totally Other, . . . [into their lives, as well as something that] cannot be found in any human relationship . . . queer pricklings of delight, excitement and terror . . . magic."[39]

Young people can find adventure, humor, and nonsense in fantasy, while their emotions are being touched and their imaginations stretched. Susan Cooper explains fantasy's appeal for children:

Very young children, their conscious minds not yet developed, are all feeling and instinct. Closer to the unconscious than they will ever be again, they respond naturally to the archetypes and the deep echoes of fairy story, ritual, and myth. . . .

Some children . . . go on seeking out fantasy all their lives, instinctively aware that far from being babyish, it is probably the most complex form of fiction they will ever find.[40]

For fantasist Jane Langton ("The Weak Place . . ."), fantasy "feeds a hunger we didn't know we had," and for critic Jane Mobley (*Phantasmagoria*), it satisfies "the human craving to be carried or enchanted to worlds beyond the one we know, or to have revealed to us here in this world some glimpse of the other."

Fantasy can also provide a fresh perspective on our own world. C. S. Lewis observed that

fairyland arouses a longing [in the reader] for he knows not what. It stirs and troubles him (to his lifelong enrichment) with the dim sense of something beyond his reach and, far from dulling or emptying the actual world, gives it a new dimension of depth. He does not despise the real woods because he has read of enchanted woods: the reading makes all real woods a little enchanted. This is a special kind of longing.[41]

The concept of time is one aspect of contemporary fantasy that many readers find particularly intriguing. According to Jane Louise Curry: "There is great force in the recognition that today holds yesterday and tomorrow within it: that 'past,' 'present,' and 'future' are not labels to put on isolated pigeonholes . . . [that] the same moment does contain the mundane and the marvellous."[42] And Tolkien emphasizes the profound emotional effect great fantasy can have on its readers: "in a serious tale of faerie . . . when the sudden 'turn' comes, we get a piercing glimpse of joy, and heart's desire, that for a moment passes outside the frame, rends indeed the very web of the story, and lets a gleam come through."[43]

Critics Francis J. Molson and Susan G. Miles have written that:

YA fantasy flourishes today because it satisfies two genuine needs of the audience it is designed to reach. The first is aesthetic. YA fantasy at its best is very effective storytelling, providing believable characters, stimulating description, original setting, and distinctive writing. . . . The second need is psychological, . . . Youth do need and deserve assistance as they confront the central concerns of adolescence. YA fantasy, like most YA literature, speaks to those in passage from childhood to adulthood. . . . YA fantasy provides imaginative and vicarious opportunities to identify and empathize; to try out different roles or assume new faces; or to pursue different options or to take off in new directions. As an especially effective medium of dramatizing the journey of self-discovery or coming of age, YA fantasy assists in revealing to adolescents that they are not immortal, that evil exists both within and outside, that they are capable of great evil as well as great good, and that they must make choices or render judgments if they are to grow into authentic adulthood.[44]

Fantasist Tamora Pierce has written that the idealism and imagination in fantasy literature are especially appealing to young people, who have the time and emotional energy
to devote to social and political causes,

> but they need fuel to spark and refine ideas, the same kind of fuel that fires ideal-
> ism. That fuel can be found—according to the writings of Jung, Bettelheim, M.
> Ester Harding, and Joseph Campbell—in the mighty symbols of myth, fairy tales,
> dreams, legends—and fantasy. . . . [F]antasy, in its fresh and modern (i.e., post-
> 1900) forms, using contemporary sensibilities and characters youngsters identify
> with, reigns supreme. Here the symbols of meaningful struggle and of truth as an
> inner constant exist in their most undiluted form outside myth and fairy tale. . . .
> These stories appear to have little to do with reality, but they do provide readers
> with the impetus to challenge the way things are, something YAs respond to
> wholeheartedly. Young people are drawn to battles for a discernable higher good:
> the images of such battles evoke their passion. . . .
>   Fantasy, more than any other genre, is a literature of empowerment. In the real
> world, kids have little say. This is a given; it is the nature of childhood. In fantasy,
> however short, fat, unbeautiful, weak, dreamy or unlearned individuals may be,
> they find a realm in which those things are negated by strength. . . . Young readers
> seem to come away from the characters' mishaps not depressed but energized, as if
> the protagonist's struggle was something they survived as well.
>   Most important of all in fantasy is that great equalizer between the powerful and
> the powerless: magic, the thing that keeps young children captivated by fairy tales
> and older ones enthralled by wizards. . . . Fantasy creates hope and optimism in
> readers. It is the pure stuff of wonder, the kind that carries over into everyday life
> and colors the way readers perceive things around them.[45]

Fantasy's direct relationship to our own lives is explained by Lloyd Alexander:

> If a work of fantasy delights, refreshes, or gloriously terrifies us, it also encourages
> us on our own adventures, richer and more exciting than any fiction. . . . [W]hether
> we're children or grownups, fantasy can move us because it suggests a world
> where all we value as human beings—courage, justice, love—really work.[46]

According to editor Sharyn November,

> Out of all the genres of fiction—with perhaps the exception of the graphic novel—
> fantasy seems to have the highest crossover readership. Both teenagers and adults
> eagerly pick up books by Diana Wynne Jones, Orson Scott Card, Philip Pullman,
> J. R. R. Tolkien, and of course, J. K. Rowling. Why is this? Well, it's not hard to
> explain. . . .
>   Unlike other genres, fantasy "translates up." One can read the work of Lloyd
> Alexander as a child, a teenager, or an adult without compromising its (or one's)

literary integrity. The writing is clear and grounded; the narrative has a mythic feel; the characters seem real; and there is nothing "young" about the books at all. These books, and many other examples of good fantasy, remain satisfying, no matter what the reader's age.

Try saying that about most children's mysteries, teen romances, historicals, or even "realistic" contemporary fiction. If you develop a fondness for any of those genres, you're quickly going to "age out" of books for younger readers, and search for their adult analogues. But there is no adult analogue for Lloyd Alexander, Madeleine L'Engle, Ursula K. Le Guin, Robin McKinley, Garth Nix, and so many others—they are *sui generis*.

That is why you find discerning adult readers in the children's or YA fantasy and science fiction sections of bookstores and libraries—and not pretending to get these books for imaginary children, either. When the mass media "discovered"(as it periodically does) that books for younger readers were terrific, these long-time readers were unsurprised and unimpressed. They had known it for years.[47]

It is interesting to note that the selection of Seamus Heaney's translation of *Beowulf* over J. K. Rowling's *Harry Potter and the Prisoner of Azakaban* for the 1999 British Whitbread Book of the Year literary prize engendered much public debate. Rowling's book was criticized both for its popularity (in other words, "lack of literary quality") and because it was written for children. As in previous years, the rules barred children's books from consideration for the overall best book of the year prize, on the assumption that they were not worth considering. Yet, only two years later, two "children's" fantasy novels were awarded prestigious "adult" awards. Rowling's *Harry Potter and the Goblet of Fire* won the 2001 Hugo Award for Best Novel, and Philip Pullman's *The Amber Spyglass* won the 2001 Whitbread Book of the Year Award. As Sharyn November puts it, "Not best 'children's novel,' or 'best teen novel'—Best Novel, period."

The Effect of Fantasy on Children and Young Adults

It seems clear that reading fantasy is beneficial as well as enjoyable. According to Kornei Chukovskii, Soviet literary critic and children's author:

> Fantasy is the most valuable attribute of the human mind and it should be diligently nurtured from earliest childhood, as one nurtures musical sensitivity—and not crushed. . . . Without imaginative fantasy there would be complete stagnation in both physics and chemistry . . . the value of such tales [is] in developing, strengthening, enriching, and directing children's thinking and emotional responses.[48]

Psychologist Bruno Bettelheim and others have explored the therapeutic value of fairy tales in defusing children's anxieties and resolving their emotional conflicts. And fantasist Lloyd Alexander feels that "Fantasy, by its power to move us so deeply, to dramatize, even melodramatize, morality, can be one of the most effective means of establishing a capacity for adult values."[49]

It is logical to presume that an exposure to fairy tales and fantasy as a child will aid the adult in appreciating more-sophisticated literature. Indeed, the lack of exposure to imaginative tales as a child may preclude an adult's interest in epic, allegory, and folklore; at the very least it may make a "suspension of belief" difficult to achieve. Fantasist Penelope Lively contends that fantasy helps children learn about human nature and develop a sense of place and time.

> Children need to sense that we live in a permanent world that reaches away and behind and ahead of us, and that the span of a lifetime is something to be wondered at, and thought about, and that—above all—people evolve during their own lives . . . [They] end up a curious irrational blend of experience and memory. . . . Perhaps books can help, just a little.[50]

Eleanor Cameron finds hope for adult perceptions in children's response to fantasy:

> [Fantasy is] a form of literature which . . . [helps] young children to orient themselves in the surrounding world, that enriches their spiritual development, that enables them to regard themselves as fearless participants in imaginary struggles for justice, goodness, and freedom. . . . I feel that in a child's longing for what cannot be expressed, in his love of what cannot be proved, his cherishing of a vision, there lies a kind of hope. If he guards it and has faith in it, there is nothing more powerful. It may even be the beginning of illumination, and this is to me the precious element in any work of art.[51]

In a 1993 *Journal of Youth Services in Libraries* article on gender bias in young adult fiction, Linda Forrest cites studies showing that as recently as 1986 "the cultural stereotype of the dependent female, 'the perennial damsel in distress,' needing a man's protection, was still being reflected." She urges librarians to "help counteract gender bias by deliberately selecting and promoting materials that help young people develop positive views of females and an awareness of the obstacles women face in overcoming sexual stereotypes. . . . Fantasy is one area of young adult literature that offers a rich source of gender-fair fiction. It is popular with both male and female adolescents and has traditionally been a genre in which women escape the standard cultural roles. Portrayals of passive females can certainly be found; nevertheless, readers are often offered a chance to experience what females could be instead of what they are. . . . Well-written fantasy novels . . . shatter the 'dependent damsel' stereotype [with characters who] develop into fully fleshed people who struggle, grow, [and] change in their attempts to conquer evil."[52]

Negative Criticism of Fantasy Literature

Critics who feel that fantasy has little value as a literary genre often dismiss such works as "escapist." According to Ursula K. Le Guin:

> There is still, in this country, a deep puritanical distrust of fantasy. . . . Fantasy, to [its critics] is escapism. . . . They confuse fantasy, which in the psychological sense is a universal and essential faculty of the human mind, with infantilism and pathological regression. . . . [On the contrary,] fantasy is the natural, the appropri-

ate language for the recounting of the spiritual journey and the struggle of good and evil in the soul.[53]

Donnarae MacCann points out that

Some adults distrust fantasies as being somehow "unhealthy." They raise the question, "Won't these dwarfs and talking beasts encourage unwholesome fantasizing on the part of children or make them withdraw from the real world?" These fears result from a confusion of terms: confusion of the word fantasy when it refers to a *literary form* with fantasy as a *psychological illness*.[54]

Fantasists Alan Garner and Susan Cooper have refuted such suspicions. According to Garner: "Mythology is not an escape, it is not an entertainment. It is an attempt to come to terms with reality, and therefore I would say that fantasy that works is not an escape from life. . . . It is a coming to terms with reality, it is a clarification . . ."; and Cooper contends: "When we depart from our own reality into the reality of the book . . . we're going out of time, out of space, into the unconscious. . . . We aren't escaping out, we're escaping in, without any idea of what we may encounter. Fantasy is the metaphor through which we discover ourselves."[55]

It is interesting to note that two otherwise valuable and scholarly works on children's literature, psychologist Bruno Bettelheim's *The Uses of Enchantment* and French literary critic Isabelle Jan's *On Children's Literature*, disparage contemporary fantasy for young people. Both authors, it would seem, have based their criticisms on an outdated reading of the genre. In 1969, Jan wrote: "Apart from [Kipling and de Ségur] the modern fairy tale has definitely had its day," and proceeds to accuse children's fantasy novels of static settings, a lack of character development, and stereotypical protagonists. She concluded that: "Children who are not brought up by nurses in a nursery and for whom [boarding] school lore is something they know only by hearsay or from books, find it difficult to appreciate fantasy. . . . To be successful, children's stories must correspond to real experiences."[56]

That final sentence is most important. "Real experience" always underlies the fantasies written by Alan Garner, William Mayne, Ursula K. Le Guin, Susan Cooper, and Philippa Pearce, to name but a few outstanding children's and young adult fantasists. A reading of even one or two of these authors' novels would demonstrate that such criticisms are unfounded. In spite of their lack of a "nursery upbringing" or a "boarding school education," it is obvious that contemporary children and young adults not only read and enjoy, but love fantasy fiction.

A second example of what appears to be unfounded criticism of modern fantasy is found in Bruno Bettelheim's *The Uses of Enchantment*. Bettelheim devoted only 5 of the 328 pages of his analysis of the effects of fairy tales on children to the thousands of "modern" fantasy novels for children. In these 5 pages, he makes two questionable judgments. The first is that "Many of these modern tales have sad endings, which fail to provide the escape and consolation which the fearsome events in the fairy tale make necessary, to strengthen the child for meeting the vagaries of his life."[57] Oddly enough, the only "modern" tale Bettelheim mentions by name is *The Blue Bird*, a play written by Maurice Maeterlinck in 1909. A more up-to-date reading of children's fantasy novels would seem warranted. In this light, fantasist Natalie Babbitt's remarks about hope and happy endings are particularly to the point (see notes 29 and 65).

In his second criticism, Bettelheim dismisses "modern" fantasy because "when children are asked to name their favorite fairy tales, hardly any modern tales are among their choices." To back up this statement, he cites a 1958 study in which 264 college students were asked to recall their favorite children's stories. The study found that 59 percent of the women and 30 percent of the men preferred "fairy tales" (including "new tales of magic like *The Wizard of Oz*, *Brer Rabbit*, and *Little Black Sambo*") to "fiction."[58]

Putting aside the fact that *The Wizard of Oz* is a fantasy novel, not a fairy tale, and that the study's findings do not seem to support Bettelheim's thesis, one obvious question arises: What "modern" tales could students who read children's books before 1950 be expected to mention? A study of adult recollections of books read more than 50 years ago could not possibly render relevant information about the reading habits of contemporary children. To dismiss the entire genre of children's fantasy on such a basis is indefensible.

More recently, the publication of J. K. Rowling's Harry Potter novels has drawn the ire of conservative critics and theologians, who feel that the positive portrayal of witchcraft in these books may entice children to seek out satanism in the real world. Critic Alison Lurie discusses one such work, *Harry Potter and the Bible: The Menace Behind the Magick (And the Bible Series)* by Richard Abanes (Horizon Books, 2001), in which the author states that "[T]he Harry Potter series is not morally compatible with Christianity," and that the books are "filled with potentially harmful messages exalting occultism and moral relativism."[59] Lurie points out that conservative critics often decry the "un-Christian" or "unbiblical" behavior of the main characters, who rebel against rules and sometimes tell lies and disobey orders. And she describes the difficulty these critics have with the ambiguity of good and evil in the Potter books, where even the "good" characters have weaknesses, and it is not always easy or obvious to discern which characters are good and which are evil.

In conclusion, Lurie makes an interesting point about what adults want children to learn from the books we choose for them: "The world of Harry Potter is complex and ambiguous and fluid. And in this, of course, it is far more like our own world, in which it is not always easy to tell the ogres from the giants. When we choose books for our children, do we want them to teach obedience to authority or skepticism, acceptance of the status quo or a determination to change what needs to be changed?"

Why Write Fantasy?

Why do writers create fantasy and what makes their work successful? Critics Sheila Egoff, Jane Mobley, and Ann Swinfen express their views as follows. According to Egoff: "Modern fantasists . . . engender a sense of wonder in readers, not so much by making us realize that the fantastic and the real can coexist, as by convincing us that they already do so."[60] Elsewhere she has written: "Fantasists . . . respect the qualities of children—curiosity, a sense of wonder, a love of the fabulous, and an ability to see to the heart of things with courage and honesty. Fantasists recognize that such assets should not be lost with the ending of childhood, but are ones that are necessary for all mature and sensitive human beings." Mobley writes: "The skillful fantasist is the true wizard. Through the magic of naming he makes reality, he calls things into being. As namer, the wonder-storyteller is a poet, and his is the oldest form of poetry: incantation, the making of magic through words."[61] According to Swinfen:

> It is noteworthy that fantasy, which some might expect to be a literature of "withdrawal," since it is so often carelessly dismissed as "escapist," is in reality employed to condemn [the temptation toward violence and withdrawal]. . . . Those views of society which are expressed with such remarkable consistency by so many of the writers of serious modern fantasy arise from a desperate dissatisfaction with contemporary life, a need to break free and realize full human potential. These writers of fantasy are thus amongst the latest voices in the long tradition of liberal humanism in English literature.[62]

Each fantasist has, of course, his or her own answers to these questions. According to Andre Norton in *The Book of Andre Norton* (DAW, 1975), "You cannot write fantasy unless you love it, unless you yourself can believe in what you're telling." Helen Cresswell asserts: "I write fantasy . . . because I have always had a very strong sense of the miraculous being about to erupt into the everyday."[63] And Roger W. Drury writes fantasy stories "because they make children creative; because children reared on such stories grow into resourceful adults, who are never bored or cornered. . . . I write such tales because I like them that way. My realism comes naturally with a wide fringe."[64] In his well-known article "On Three Ways of Writing for Children," C. S. Lewis states that he writes "a children's story because a children's story is the best art-form for something you have to say . . . of course readers who want to hear that will read the story or reread it at any age."[65] Natalie Babbitt writes that children's fantasists are people who have not settled for compromise in their lives, who have retained their childlike hope that in the end, everything will turn out all right.[66]

Like any artist, a fantasist must draw his or her creations from within, both from his or her conscious experiences and from the unconscious. According to Susan Cooper, "I think those of us who write fantasy are dedicated to making impossible things seem likely, making dreams seem real. . . . Our writing is haunted by those parts of our experience which we do not understand, or even consciously remember."[67] Ursula K. Le Guin carries this one step further. She proposes that writers of fantasy inevitably draw on the "collective unconscious" for their inspiration, whether they intend to or not.

> The artist who goes into himself most deeply—and it is a painful journey—is the artist who touches us most closely, speaks to us most clearly. . . . So it would seem that true myth arises only in the process of connecting the conscious and the unconscious realms. . . . The writer who draws not upon the works and thoughts of others, but upon his own thoughts and his own deep being, will inevitably hit upon common material. The more original his work, the more imperiously recognizable it will be. "Yes, of course!" says the reader, recognizing himself, his dreams, his nightmares.[68]

Mollie Hunter concurs: "[N]o such thing as pure fantasy exists. There is only a succession of folk memories filtered through the storyteller's imagination, and since all mankind shares in these memories, they are the common store on which the modern storyteller must draw in his attempts to create fantasy."[69]

Whether or not a fantasist realizes that his or her works are rooted in "the collective unconscious," good fantasy must have all of the elements of good fiction—unique style, memorable plot and characters, and deep meaning. The additional element needed to ensure the creation of lasting works of fantasy is the author's ability to share his or her wholehearted belief that the impossible is possible.

Patricia Wrightson describes her craft: "What it is that writers do . . . they drop stones into pools: finding a visionary stone, handling and weighing it; dropping it into a pool of another mind; watching for the ripples to spread, and perhaps for the stirred water to give something back."[70]

Women as Fantasists

As recently as 40 years ago, the idea that great fantasies could be written by women as well as by men was called into question. In an article published in *New Society* in 1962, critic Helen Lourie characterizes Hans Christian Andersen, Lewis Carroll, George MacDonald, and J. M. Barrie as writers of genius, and concludes:

> Is it an accident that all these writers, and those in the same group who are writing today are men? No. . . . Women can be excellent storytellers: their powers of invention and fancy are not inferior to that of men. But what they lack is the wholehearted abandonment to their inspiration: the power to enter the other world . . . without keeping some conscious hold on normality.[71]

Aside from the antifeminist bias of Lourie's conclusions, she seems to have overlooked a few authors. E. Nesbit and Selma Lagerlöf were both writing during the early years of children's fantasy. As for writers of Lourie's day, L. M. Boston, Rumer Godden, Carol Kendall, Mary Norton, Philippa Pearce, and Rosemary Sutcliff had already produced unquestionable literary masterpieces. And more recently, Natalie Babbitt, Franny Billingsley, Eleanor Cameron, Susan Cooper, Diana Wynne Jones, Ursula K. Le Guin, Lois Lowry, Anne McCaffrey, Robin McKinley, Margaret Mahy, Tamora Pierce, J. K. Rowling, Nancy Springer, Megan Whalen Turner, Cynthia Voigt, Sylvia Waugh, Patricia Wrightson, and Jane Yolen are only a few of the female masters of young people's fantasy.

Classifying Fantasy

In an effort to analyze the many works grouped under the heading Fantasy Literature, the genre has often been subdivided. Fantasies have been categorized by subject matter, by setting, by degree of seriousness of treatment, and by the sex of the author. Psychologist Ravenna Helson, writing in *Horn Book Magazine* (April 1970), feels that fantasies written by men differ from those written by women. Her categories for men's novels are "wish fulfillment and humor," "heroism," and "tender feelings"; and for women's novels, "independence and self-expression," "transformation," and "inner mystery and awe."

In his essay "On Fairy-Stories," J. R. R. Tolkien separated stories that are set in, or involve, a world other than our own from those tales set in the real world. He called the otherworlds "Secondary Worlds," and our world the "Primary World." Tolkien concluded that only those stories involving secondary worlds were "true" fairy stories. In addition, he outlined four essential elements of a good fairy story: "Fantasy, Recovery, Escape, and Consolation." He described Fantasy as the author's "image-making" or "subcreation"; Recovery as insight or renewal; Escape as a liberation from life's evils, rather than an evasion of reality; and Consolation as a happy ending or "eucatastrophe."

Like Tolkien, critics Tymn, Zahorski, and Boyer, in their *Fantasy Literature* (Bowker, 1979), use setting to distinguish various types of fantasy written for adults. They label stories set in the real world as Low Fantasy and those set in secondary worlds as High Fantasy. Their High Fantasy category included "myth fantasy" (interpreted retellings of myth), "faery tales," "gothic fantasy" (weird tales with no rational explanation), and "science fantasy" (tales offering a scientific explanation for the existence of the secondary world, but that use magic during the remainder of the story).

Fantasist Jane Louise Curry divides fantasy stories into two categories, whimsical and visionary.

There are excellences and excellences. I would suggest, always with qualifications and reservations in mind, that the two broad types of fantasy differ in focus, tone, technique, and quality of insight in much the same way that fairy tale differs from myth. In one, our attention is focused primarily on the story or action, itself; in the other it is the feeling, the emotional dimension, that holds us.[72]

Although both types of fantasy story can be well written, they appeal to the reader in different ways. For example, Norton's *The Borrowers* and Grahame's *The Wind in the Willows* and *The Reluctant Dragon* "are 'dear' to us," writes Curry, whereas Boston's Green Knowe books, Mayne's Earthfasts, Lewis's Chronicles of Narnia, Tolkien's Lord of the Rings, Garner's *Elidor* and *The Owl Service*, and Pearce's *Tom's Midnight Garden*

are not "dear" to us. It may be nearer the truth to say that they are a power over us. . . . Our feeling for them is of quite a different quality. . . . Fantasy offers on one hand entertainment, reassurance, and—yes—escape: on the other, involvement, provocative ideas and insights, consolation, and the intensification of feeling. . . . Whimsical fantasy may give us deep delight, but "visionary" fantasy can give us joy.[73]

The Mythic Element in Contemporary Fantasy

Critics Sheila Egoff and Ralph Lavender have noted that children's novels that relive or reinterpret myth or legend and those that "cast fantasy within the structure of legend" were a notable development of the 1970s.[74] Ursula K. Le Guin, Alan Garner, William

Mayne, Susan Cooper, and others have written fantasies of great seriousness and depth. These books, which usually center around a battle of good versus evil, are of two types. Some involve modern-day characters in dangerous encounters with the mythological past—and a magic that breaks into their everyday world. In others, entirely new mythologies are created. Egoff has observed that

> the mythic element in modern fantasy gives a quasi-religious tone to the narrative; we are persuaded that we are concerned with major moral issues, that the very stability and continuity of our world is at stake. This is in contrast to the magical, almost capricious supernatural efforts of older fantasies [such as *Mary Poppins*, *Peter Pan*, or E. Nesbit's stories of magic].[75]

A Historical Overview of Children's and Young Adult Fantasy

Most children's classics that have lasted from earlier times are fantasies, mainly because they are a literature least dependent upon the immediacy of time and surroundings.[76]

In *Thursday's Child: Trends and Patterns in Contemporary Children's Literature* (Chicago: American Library Association, 1981), Sheila Egoff did an impressive job of relating the historical development of children's literature to the evolution of Western society's attitude toward children. The following is an attempt to relate her theory to the development of European and American children's fantasy as a genre. I have inserted additional information about the history and development of young adult fantasy.

THE NINETEENTH CENTURY

Original fantasy stories written for children and young adults are a fairly recent phenomenon. Invented tales of wonder and magic began appearing in English only around the middle of the 19th century, and fantasies written specifically for young adults did not really proliferate until after the middle of the 20th century. A number of earlier books written for adults and containing elements of fantasy were later adopted by young people, including John Bunyan's *The Pilgrim's Progress* (1671) and Jonathan Swift's *Gulliver's Travels* (1726).

According to Gillian Avery and Margaret Kinnell, the first fantasy novel published in the English language was *Glenowen; or, the Fairy Palace*, written by Eleanor Sleath, and published in England by Black and Co. and John Harris in 1815.[77] F. E. Paget's *The Hope of the Katzekopfs*, cited in *The Oxford Companion to Children's Literature* and by Roger Lancelyn Green in *Tellers of Tales: British Authors of Children's Books from 1800 to 1964* as the first English children's fantasy novel, was published nearly 30 years later, in 1844.[78]

Hans Christian Andersen's tales were published in Denmark in 1835, and were translated into English eleven years later, in 1846. Andersen was the first great writer of original fantasy for children. His memorable tales are still among the most loved of all children's stories. Critic Margery Fisher describes Andersen's genius:

> There are plenty of writers since Andersen who have animated tin soldiers. . . . But to draw tears and smiles, quite spontaneous and genuine, on account of a lead soldier with one leg and a paper doll—that takes genius. Not cleverness or wit or

ingenuity, but the power to compel truth out of yourself that has grown slowly out of childhood impressions. This is how writers of fairy tale work.[79]

Some critics consider "Uncle David's Nonsensical Story of Giants and Fairies" to be the first literary fairy tale written in the English language. It was contained in an otherwise realistic novel, *Holiday House*, written by Catherine Sinclair, published in 1839. Early collections of literary fairy tales for American children included James Kirk Paulding's anonymously published *A Christmas Gift from Fairy Land* (Appleton, 1838), which contained the first American fairy tale, "The Nameless Old Woman," according to critic Gillian Avery.[80] Two more early American collections were Jane Goodwin Austin's *Fairy Dreams; or Wanderings in Elf-Land* (Tilton, 1859), and Mary Wentworth Newman's *Fairy Tales from Gold Lands* (Roman, 1867 and 1870).

In England, William Morris published seven fantasy tales for adults in 1856, in *Oxford and Cambridge Magazine*. According to Wendy Mass and Stuart P. Levine, Morris "is considered by purists to be the father of 'modern fantasy' because his were some of the first works to contain the familiar characteristics of modern fantasy. . . . In much of his work, Morris explored England's mythology and retold the stories in modernized tales."[81]

These collections of literary fairy tales were, of course, preceded by a rich tradition of oral folklore, anonymous tales of magical creatures and occurrences, passed from one generation to the next. Before 1850, however, most books written specifically for children tended to be didactic, moralistic tales, and the children themselves were regarded as miniature adults who were constantly admonished to be "good." Children were given stories written for the purpose of saving them from damnation. There were no "teenagers" or "teenage literature" in the 19th century; young people in their teens were considered to be adults, and those who could read were given adult books.

The latter half of the 19th century has been called the first "golden age" of children's literature and it was during this period, the Victorian era, that Western European and American children were finally deemed worthy of a literature of their own. Children were now seen as basically good, but needing to be guided onto the path of conformity. They were looked at as mischievous but perceptive, and they were finally given books with interesting characters and exciting plots, books written specifically for them, whose authors wanted to amuse them, rather than to subdue them.

Many of the Victorian fantasies are now considered classics. They include John Ruskin's *The King of the Golden River* (written in 1841, published in 1851), Mrs. Fairstar's *Memoirs of a London Doll* (1846 in England; 1852 in the United States), which was the first talking doll fantasy, William Makepeace Thackeray's *The Rose and the Ring* (1855), Frances Browne's *Granny's Wonderful Chair* (1856 in England; 1892 in the United States), the Comtesse de Ségur's *The Enchanted Forest* (1856 in France; 1869 in the United States), Charles Kingsley's *The Water Babies* (1863), Lewis Carroll's *Alice's Adventures in Wonderland* (1865), Jean Ingelow's *Mopsa the Fairy* (1869), and George MacDonald's *At the Back of the North Wind* (1871, 1875) and *The Princess and the Goblin* (1872).

These books were followed by Mary L. Molesworth's *The Cuckoo Clock* (1877); Carlo Collodi's *The Adventures of Pinocchio* (written in Italy in 1880; published in the United States in 1892); Lucretia P. Hale's *The Peterkin Papers* (1880); Frank R.

Stockton's *The Floating Prince and Other Fairy Tales* (1881); Richard Jeffries's *Wood Magic* (1881), which is considered the first animal fantasy novel written for children; Louise de la Ramée's *The Nürnberg Stove* (1882 in France; 1901 in the United States); Howard Pyle's *The Merry Adventures of Robin Hood* (1883); Frank R. Stockton's *The Bee-Man of Orn and Other Fanciful Tales* (1884); Howard Pyle's *Pepper and Salt* (1886) and *The Wonder Clock* (1887); Oscar Wilde's *The Happy Prince and Other Tales* (1888); Andrew Lang's *Prince Prigio* (1889); Rudyard Kipling's *The Jungle Book* (1894); Laurence Housman's *A Doorway in Fairyland* (1894–1904 in England; 1905 in the United States); and Kenneth Grahame's *The Reluctant Dragon* (1898 in England; 1938 in the United States).

"An interesting fact," notes critic Naomi Lewis, "is that the fantasy genre was attracting (if briefly) most of the leading adult novelists. Ruskin, Thackeray, Dickens, Kingsley—MacDonald too—were all basically writers for adults when they turned to this new kind [of literature]; and though they chose themes of magic, they did not temper their manner or approach, so their books interest adults too."[82]

As a matter of fact, some of the "adult" fantasy works of this period are still read today, both by adults and young adults. This list might include Edward Bellamy's *Looking Backward: 2000–1887* (1888), Mark Twain's *A Connecticut Yankee in King Arthur's Court* (1889), Oscar Wilde's *The Picture of Dorian Gray* (1891), and William Morris's *The Well at the World's End* (1896). As mentioned above, William Morris has been called the father of modern high fantasy, and his work influenced many others, including Lord Dunsany, J. R. R. Tolkien, and C. S. Lewis.

THE TWENTIETH CENTURY

During the first half of the 20th century, childhood was still considered an idyllic time, a period to be prolonged and kept separate from adulthood. This attitude was, of course, reflected in the books written for children. In spite of the fact that "most of the major writers of the [Edwardian] period—Nesbit, Potter, Kipling, and Grahame—had far from idyllic childhoods," writes Egoff, "these writers drew a curtain firmly down on the adult world, and therefore on pain and distress."[83]

A decade-by-decade examination of the development of 20th-century children's fantasy shows the surprising number of "old" books that are still being read.

The early years of the century produced a number of memorable books, beginning with the first truly American children's fantasy, L. Frank Baum's *The Wonderful Wizard of Oz* (1900). According to Sheila Egoff, *The Wonderful Wizard of Oz* was "not only the first other world fantasy in American children's literature; it [was] the first fully created imaginative world in the whole of children's literature."[84] Those that followed include E. Nesbit's *Five Children and It* (1902 in England; 1905 in the United States) and *The Story of the Amulet* (1906 in England; 1906 in the United States), which was the first time travel fantasy written for children; Howard Pyle's *The Story of King Arthur and His Knights* (1903); J. M. Barrie's *Peter Pan* (1904; 1911); W. H. Hudson's *A Little Boy Lost* (1905 in England; 1918 in the United States); Frances Hodgson Burnett's *Racketty-Packetty House* (1906); Rudyard Kipling's *Puck of Pook's Hill* (1906); Kenneth Grahame's *The Wind in the Willows* (1907 in England; 1908 in the United States); Selma Lagerlöf's *The Wonderful Adventures of Nils* (1907 in Sweden; 1908 in the United States); Friedrich de la Motte Fouqué's *Undine* (written in

1811; published in the United States in 1908); Walter de la Mare's *The Three Mulla-Mulgars* (1910 in England; 1919 in the United States); and E. F. Benson's *David Blaize and the Blue Door* (1918 in England; 1919 in the United States).

THE 1920S AND 1930S

During and following World War I, there was an understandable lull in the writing and publishing of all types of children's books; other needs were more pressing. In contrast, the 1920s, a period of relative prosperity, produced a number of lighthearted fantasies, including talking toy and animal stories and tales of voyages to wondrous lands. Some of the better-known books from this period are W. W. Tarn's *Treasure of the Isle of Mist* (1919, 1920), which contained the first real-world villain in children's fantasy literature; Padraic Colum's *The Boy Apprenticed to an Enchanter* (1920); Hugh Lofting's *The Story of Doctor Dolittle* (1920); Margery Williams Bianco's *The Velveteen Rabbit* (1922), which was the first toy animal fantasy novel written for children; Carl Sandburg's *Rootabaga Stories* (1922); Stewart Edward White's *The Magic Forest* (1923); A. A. Milne's *Winnie-the-Pooh* (1926); Walter Brooks's Freddy books (1927–1958); John Masefield's *The Midnight Folk* (1927), which, according to Egoff, included "the first feisty girl character in children's literature"; Paul Fenimore Cooper's *Tal* (1929); Rachel Field's *Hitty* (1929); and Beatrix Potter's *The Fairy Caravan* (1929). Laurence Housman's gentle tales of fairies and princesses, first published during the 1890s, were reissued in new collections in the 1920s, and Walter De La Mare's memorable short story collections began appearing in 1925.

The years of the Great Depression produced two of the best-loved English fantasies—P. L. Travers's *Mary Poppins* (1931) and J. R. R. Tolkien's *The Hobbit* (1937)—as well as Elizabeth Coatsworth's *The Cat Who Went to Heaven* (1930), Anne Parrish's *Floating Island* (1930), Eleanor Farjeon's *The Little Book Room* (1931 in England; 1956 in the United States), Ella Young's *The Unicorn with Silver Shoes* (1932), Kate Seredy's *The White Stag* (1937), Richard and Florence Atwater's *Mr. Popper's Penguins* (1938), Dr. Seuss's *The 500 Hats of Bartholomew Cubbins* (1938), Robert Lawson's *Ben and Me* (1939), and Alison Uttley's *A Traveller in Time* (1939, 1940).

During the 1920s and 1930s, teenagers were expected to read the classics, and school reading lists of this period often included Tennyson's Arthurian poem, "Idylls of the King," written in 1859. Westerns, mysteries, and adventure stories, rather than fantasies, seem to have been the recreational reading of young people at this time, although we should note that a number of the fantasies written for adults during the 1920s and 1930s are still read today by both adults and young adults. These include E. R. Eddison's *The Worm Ouroboros* (1922 in England; 1926 in the United States), James Stephens's *Deirdre* (1923), Lord Dunsany's *The King of Elfland's Daughter* (1924), Robert Nathan's *Portrait of Jenny* (1929), James Hilton's *Lost Horizon* (1933), Evangeline Walton's *The Virgin and the Swine* (1936, later retitled *The Island of the Mighty*), Stephen Vincent Benét's *The Devil and Daniel Webster* (1937), J. R. R. Tolkien's *The Hobbit* (1937), and T. H. White's *A Sword in the Stone* (1938, 1939). *The Hobbit*, with its richly detailed other-world and its imaginative tribe of small people called "hobbits" broke new ground in the world of fantasy literature. Tolkien's ability to meld an exciting plot, a memorable setting, and a strong sense of a moral code, with characters who are changed by their experiences had an impact on the genre that is still felt today. Ironically, the importance of *The Hobbit* to modern fantasy literature was not recognized for nearly 30 years, until the novel's reissue in 1966.

THE 1940S AND 1950S

In contrast to the World War I period, a number of noteworthy children's fantasies were published during World War II. These include B. B.'s (D. J. Watkins-Pitchford) *The Little Grey Men* (1942 in England; 1949 in the United States), Enys Tregarthen's *The Doll Who Came Alive* (1942), Mary Norton's *The Magic Bedknob* (1943 in England; 1957 in the United States), Antoine de Saint-Exupéry's *The Little Prince* (1943), Julia L. Sauer's *Fog Magic* (1943), James Thurber's *Many Moons* (1943), Robert Lawson's *Rabbit Hill* (1944), Eric Linklater's *The Wind on the Moon* (1944), Astrid Lindgren's *Pippi Longstocking* (1945 in Sweden; 1950 in the United States), Carolyn Bailey's *Miss Hickory* (1946), Eleanor Farjeon's *The Glass Slipper* (1946 in England; 1956 in the United States), Elizabeth Goudge's *The Little White Horse* (1946, 1947), T. H. White's *Mistress Masham's Repose* (1946), William Pène du Bois's *The Twenty-One Balloons* (1947), Rumer Godden's *The Doll's House* (1947), Ruth Stiles Gannett's *My Father's Dragon* (1948), Tove Jansson's *Finn Family Moomintroll* (1949 in Finland; 1958 in the United States), and Rumer Godden's *The Mousewife* (1951).

According to Sheila Egoff,

In general . . . [the fantasies] of the 1940s have a sense of children at play, but with play used as a metaphor for experiencing life. . . . Play is not seen as a trivial, time-filling activity. . . . Chiefly, there is a scenario of mini-war. Tyranny is fought and defeated. Might goes down before courage and cunning, goodness and generosity. The writers of this decade present their ideas quite plainly and endow their young heroes and heroines with a kind of stylized innocence. . . . [These fantasies] are halfway houses to those stories of the 1960s and 1970s where time and distance from real battles resulted in a highly mythic and symbolic approach to the struggle between good and evil."[85]

Following World War II, childhood came to be seen as preparation for adulthood. Adults were peripheral characters in the books of this era, and the children were depicted as resourceful and imaginative. The 1950s were again golden years for children's fantasy. Included among the many outstanding works published during this decade were, according to critics,[86] three "perfect" fantasies: E. B. White's *Charlotte's Web* (1952), L. M. Boston's *The Children of Green Knowe* (1954, 1955), and Philippa Pearce's *Tom's Midnight Garden* (1958 in England; 1959 in the United States).

In addition to those three books, many of the memorable children's fantasies from the 1950s and early 1960s were magic adventure tales: C. S. Lewis's Chronicles of Narnia (1951–1956), Edward Eager's *Half Magic* (1954), K. M. Briggs's *Hobberdy Dick* (1955 in England; 1977 in the United States), Barbara Sleigh's *Carbonel* (1955, 1956), William Mayne's *A Grass Rope* (1957 in England; 1962 in the United States), Mary Chase's *Loretta Mason Potts* (1958), Elizabeth Marie Pope's *The Sherwood Ring* (1958), Agnes Smith's *An Edge of the Forest* (1959), and Norton Juster's *The Phantom Tollbooth* (1961).

A number of others involved miniature worlds, including Mary Norton's The Borrowers series (1952–1982), Carol Kendall's *The Gammage Cup* (1959), and Pauline Clarke's *The Return of the Twelves* (1962, 1963).

Still others involved humorous exaggeration or were lighthearted talking animal tales: Oliver Butterworth's *The Enormous Egg* (1956), Dodie Smith's *The Hundred and One Dalmatians* (1956, 1957), Eve Titus's Basil of Baker Street series (1958–1982), Margery Sharp's Miss Bianca books (1959–1978), Michael Bond's Paddington series (1960–1982), George Selden's *The Cricket in Times Square* (1960), Mary Stolz's *Belling the Tiger* (1961), Beverly Cleary's Ralph Mouse trilogy (1965–1982), and Maurice Sendak's *Higglety Pigglety Pop!* (1967).

One criticism could be leveled at many of the children's fantasies written during the 1950s: In spite of their fantastic adventures, the children in most of these stories never grew or changed. With the exception of a few books, notably Philippa Pearce's *Tom's Midnight Garden* (1958), L. M. Boston's *The Children of Green Knowe* (1959), and Mary Chase's *Loretta Mason Potts*, children with "problems" did not appear in literature during the 1950s; the children were almost repetitiously pictured as happy and safe.

According to Egoff, "Simplicity combined with depth of feeling is one of the chief hallmarks of the fantasy novels of the 1950s. . . . These are all child-centered books and childhood is seen as a very natural state. . . . The emphasis was on the family and family life. The children's books of the period all have this sense of security and hope. . . . The greatest triumph of these writers lay in their ability to present such concepts [as empathy with others and with the natural world] in a clear, lucid style and with memorable images."[87]

Most of the books popular with teenagers during the two decades following World War II were not fantasies, but rather were war stories, sports stories, car stories, and romances, beginning with Maureen Daly's *Seventeenth Summer* (1942). The immediate popularity of J. D. Salinger's realistic novel *The Catcher in the Rye* (1951) marked the beginning of a new body of literature written with the teenage reader in mind, although the term "young adult literature" did not come into use for more than 20 years.

In spite of the development of this "new" category of books aimed at teenagers, the fantasy novels written between 1945 and 1965 were still mainly "adult" works that only later gained popularity with young people. These works include George Orwell's *Animal Farm* (1945), Valentine Davies's *The Miracle on 34th Street* (1947), John Myers Myers's *Silverlock* (1949), Jack Vance's *Dying Earth* (1950), J. R. R. Tolkien's Lord of the Rings trilogy (1954–1956), Leonard Wibberley's *The Mouse That Roared* (1955), Mary Renault's *The King Must Die* (1958), T. H. White's *The Once and Future King* (1958), Peter Beagle's *A Fine and Private Place* (1960), Ray Bradbury's *Something Wicked This Way Comes* (1962), Marion Zimmer Bradley's first Darkover novel (*The Sword of Aldones*, 1962), and Andre Norton's *Witch World* (1963).

THE 1960S

By the mid-1960s, children, particularly in the United States and England, were thought to be more mature than their earlier counterparts, and capable of handling many heretofore "adult" problems. As a consequence, children's and young adult novels of all genres written during the past four decades have become much more open about the realities of parental conflict, divorce, death, child abuse, love, and sexual identity. The protagonists of contemporary fantasy novels also deal with these issues. In addition, the magic in these stories is now seen to have serious consequences if misused, and those characters whose lives are touched by magic are themselves changed by the experience.

It was not until the reissue of J. R. R. Tolkien's *The Hobbit* in 1966 and Lord of the Rings trilogy in 1967 that young adults began to find fantasy novels written specifically for them. Indeed, the term "young adult literature" first came into use in the early 1970s, along with the rise of realistic problem novels aimed at young people, the first of which was S. E. Hinton's *The Outsiders* (1967).

Two types of fantasy have gained special prominence during the last four decades: stories in which characters in the real world become involved with forces of myth and legend, sometimes called myth fantasy, and stories set in imaginary worlds, variously called epic fantasy, high fantasy, heroic fantasy, other-world fantasy, and alternate world fantasy. In these "high fantasy" novels of both types, the fate of the world often hangs in the balance, as the forces of good and evil, or the Light and the Dark, battle for control of humanity and of the entire earth.

The prime example of the latter type of fantasy written for young people during the 1960s was Ursula K. Le Guin's Earthsea quintet, begun in 1968 with *A Wizard of Earthsea*, which Egoff calls "the most intellectual and quotable of modern fantasies written for the young."[88] Two well-known other-world fantasy series written for adults and read by young adults arrived on the scene during the 1960s: Marion Zimmer Bradley's Darkover series (beginning in 1962) and Anne McCaffrey's Dragonriders of Pern series (beginning in 1968).

One variation on the other-world fantasy novel is the alternate-history fantasy, which is a story set in an alternate version of real-world history, such as Joan Aiken's Wolves Chronicles, which began in 1962 with *The Wolves of Willoughby Chase*, and Peter Dickinson's Changes trilogy, begun in 1968 with *The Weathermonger*. A second variation on the other-world theme is the story of real-world protagonists who visit another world, best exemplified during the 1960s by Alan Garner's *Elidor* (1965, 1967).

In the category of contemporary involvement with myth, the three outstanding examples from the 1960s are William Mayne's *Earthfasts* (1966, 1967), Susan Cooper's The Dark Is Rising sequence, which began with *Over Sea, Under Stone* in 1966, and Alan Garner's *The Owl Service* (1967, 1968). Garner's story brought the Welsh legends of "The Mabinogion" to life, while Mayne and Cooper used Arthurian themes, which have become increasingly important in contemporary fantasy literature.

Other authors began to expand mythical and legendary tales into novel-length, or even saga-length stories during the 1960s, including K. M. Briggs's *Kate Crackernuts* (1963); Lloyd Alexander's Chronicles of Prydain, which began with *The Book of Three* (1964); and Rosemary Harris's Reuben trilogy, which began with *The Moon in the Cloud* (1968).

During the 1960s, adolescent main characters became much more common in fantasy literature. As in the realistic fiction being written for young people after 1960, an important aspect of these "new" fantasies is the coming of age of their protagonists, who deal with serious problems and mature from childhood through adolescence into adulthood. These young women and men grapple with the complexity and ambiguity of their own characters, learning that they have the potential for both good and evil actions.

There were also, of course, outstanding fantasies with child protagonists being written during the 1960s, many of which were magic adventure and time travel stories. These books included Penelope Farmer's *The Summer Birds* (1962), John Lawson's *You Better Come Home with Me* (1966), Leon Garfield's *Mister Corbett's Ghost* (1968), Antonia Barber's *The Ghosts* (1969), Helen Cresswell's *A Game of Catch* (1969, 1977), and Penelope Farmer's *Charlotte Sometimes* (1969).

A number of memorable animal fantasies were written during the 1960s, including George Selden's *A Cricket in Times Square* (1960), Beverly Cleary's *The Mouse and the Motorcycle* (1965), Randall Jarrell's *The Animal Family* (1965, 1985), and Russell Hoban's multi-leveled masterpiece *The Mouse and His Child* (1967), which describes a father and son's attempts to create a family for themselves, while satirizing American society.

THE 1970S

The genre of fantasy literature for children and young adults expanded immensely during the 1970s. In addition to already prominent fantasy authors such as Joan Aiken, Lloyd Alexander, Susan Cooper, Helen Cresswell, Peter Dickinson, Penelope Farmer, Leon Garfield, Alan Garner, Mollie Hunter, Ursula K. Le Guin, and William Mayne, a number of important new fantasy authors appeared, including Richard Adams, Natalie Babbitt, Diana Wynne Jones, Penelope Lively, Robin McKinley, Robert Westall, and Patricia Wrightson.

"High fantasy" novels, including both stories set in other-worlds and those involving myth and legend, proliferated during this decade. Outstanding examples of alternate world fantasy written during the 1970s include Joy Chant's *Red Moon and Black Mountain* (1970, 1971, 1976), Patricia McKillip's *The Forgotten Beasts of Eld* (1974), Elizabeth Pope's *The Perilous Gard* (1974), Diana Wynne Jones's *Cart and Cwidder* (1975, 1977), Peter Dickinson's *The Blue Hawk* (1976), Anne McCaffrey's Harper Hall trilogy (which began with *Dragonsong* in 1976), and Lloyd Alexander's *The First Two Lives of Lukas-Kasha* (1978).

A number of so-called adult other-world fantasy series also began appearing during the 1970s: Katherine Kurtz's Chronicles of Deryni (beginning in 1970), Roger Zelazny's Amber series (beginning in 1970), Gordon R. Dickson's Dragon Knight series (beginning in 1976), Stephen R. Donaldson's Chronicles of Thomas Covenant, the Unbeliever (beginning in 1977), Piers Anthony's Magic of Xanth series (beginning in 1977), and Robert L. Asprin's Myth Adventure series (beginning in 1978).

Critically acclaimed "myth fantasies" written for young people during the 1970s included Penelope Lively's *The Wild Hunt of the Ghost Hounds* (1971, 1972), Dahlov Ipcar's *The Queen of Spells* (1973), Patricia Wrightson's *The Nargun and the Stars* (1973), and Natalie Babbitt's *Tuck Everlasting* (1975), which Sheila Egoff called "one of the simplest yet most profound fantasies in children's literature. In asking—and answering—questions about morality, it takes its place alongside E. B. White's *Charlotte's Web*." [89]

Other outstanding myth fantasies of the decade were Susan Cooper's *The Grey King* (1975), Mollie Hunter's *A Stranger Came Ashore* (1975), Robin McKinley's *Beauty*

(1978), and Rosemary Sutcliff's The Sword and the Circle trilogy (1979–1982). Cooper used Arthurian themes in her The Dark Is Rising series, and Sutcliff retold the Arthurian legends themselves, while Mary Stewart re-created the King Arthur stories by telling them from Merlin's point of view in her "adult" quartet that began with *The Crystal Cave* (1970).

Memorable animal fantasies written for young people during the 1970s included Robert C. O'Brien's *Mrs. Frisby and the Rats of NIMH* (1971) and Richard Adams's *Watership Down* (1972, 1974). Ghost fantasies included Eleanor Cameron's *The Court of the Stone Children* (1973), Penelope Lively's *The Ghost of Thomas Kempe* (1973), Richard Peck's Blossom Culp trilogy (1975–1986), and Robert Westall's *The Watch House* (1977, 1978). Humorous fantasies included Mary Rogers's *Freaky Friday* (1972), Natalie Babbitt's *The Devil's Storybook* (1974), and Christine Nöstlinger's *Konrad* (1977). Magic adventure and time travel fantasies from this decade included Otfried Preussler's *The Satanic Mill* (1971, 1973), Diana Wynne Jones's *The Ogre Downstairs* (1974, 1990), and Andrew Davies's *Conrad's War* (1978, 1980). Two well-received adult time travel novels were published during this decade: Jack Finney's *Time and Again* (1970) and Richard Matheson's *Bid Time Return* (1975).

Sheila Egoff has one criticism for the authors of contemporary fantasy for young people to consider: "Modern writers who endow their young characters with supernatural powers (that is beyond the use of talismans) deprive us of a chance to deal with our own humanity. The best fantasies remind us of our humanity, not allowing us to fantasize beyond our innate capabilities, but encouraging us to use these capabilities to the utmost."[90]

During the past 30 years, alternate-world or epic fantasy has become the fastest-growing category of fantasy literature, along with the publication of numerous derivative "adult" fantasy novels and series, often referred to as "sword-and-sorcery fantasy," whose popularity is perhaps tied to the popularity of fantasy role-playing games such as "Dungeons and Dragons," "Magic Cards," and online fantasy games. Some feel that this trend is a problem plaguing the genre of contemporary young adult fantasy: In a 1990 *New York Times Book Review* front-page article, editor David G. Hartwell decried the proliferation of formulaic mass-market fantasy novels written for adults, a literary sub-genre that, according to him, accounted for nearly 10 percent of all fiction sales in the United States. He deplored the authors' "slavish imitation of Tolkien" and outlined the criteria for these formula books that were set up by Bantam editor Lester del Rey in the late 1970s:

> The books would be original novels set in invented worlds in which magic works.
> Each would have a male central character who triumphed over the forces of evil
> (usually associated with technical knowledge of some variety) by innate virtue,
> and with the help of a tutor or tutelary spirit. . . . The covers would be rich,
> detailed illustrations of a colorful scene. . . . Mr. del Rey had codified a children's
> literature that could be sold as adult. It was nostalgic, conservative, pastoral and
> optimistic. . . . By the late '70s, the success of the Del Rey formula was so con-
> firmed that many other publishers had begun to publish in imitation. Dragons and
> unicorns began to appear all over the mass-market racks. . . . In the '80s most
> mass-market publishers [got into this new market]. Trilogies were the order of the

day. Some authors complained that publishers often requested revisions in the endings of their fantasy works so that a single novel, if popular, might be extended by
two more volumes. . . . Unquestionably, [mass-market publishers] created an enormous wave of trash writing [for] an audience trained . . . to accept tiny nuances
and gestures overlaying mediocrity and repetition as true originality.

Mr. Hartwell concluded on an optimistic note by commending a number of distinguished examples of contemporary fantasy literature, which have "rich artistic possibil-
ities when properly executed, especially when in the hands of the finest writers working
in fantasy today. . . . These works have individual excellences that are expanding the
literary boundaries of stylistic and imaginative achievement in fantasy and in contemporary literature."[91]

CONTEMPORARY FANTASY, 1980 TO THE PRESENT

During the past 25 years, numerous outstanding fantasies for children and young adults
have appeared. Well-respected fantasy authors such as Lloyd Alexander, Susan
Cooper, Peter Dickinson, Diana Wynne Jones, Ursula K. Le Guin, Robin McKinley,
Margaret Mahy, Tamora Pierce, Cynthia Voigt, and Jane Yolen have added to their
oeuvre, while new and talented authors began writing fantasy, including David
Almond, Hilari Bell, Lois Lowry, Hilary McKay, Garth Nix, Philip Pullman, J. K.
Rowling, Jonathan Stroud, Megan Whalen Turner, and Sylvia Waugh.

Some of these contemporary classics include animal fantasies such as Clare Bell's
Ratha's Creature (1983), Brian Jacques's Redwall saga (1986–1994), Ursula K. Le
Guin's Catwings books (1988–1994), Avi's Dimwood Forest Tales (1995–2000),
Robin Jarvis's Deptford Mice trilogy (1989–2002), and Kate DiCamillo's *The Tale of
Despereaux* (2003). Sylvia Waugh's Mennyms series (1993, 1994–1996, 1997) are
unusual and memorable novels about life-sized, living dolls.

Outstanding ghost fantasies of the past two and a half decades include Virginia
Hamilton's *Sweet Whispers, Brother Rush* (1982), Sylvia Cassedy's *Behind the Attic
Wall* (1983), Margaret Mahy's *The Tricksters* (1986, 1987), Nicholas Wilde's *Into the
Dark* (1987, 1990), Hilary McKay's *The Amber Cat* (1996, 1997), and David Almond's
Kit's Wilderness (1999, 2000). Well-written humorous fantasies include Roald Dahl's
Matilda (1988), and humor and witchcraft are effectively combined in Kate Gilmore's
Enter Three Witches (1990) and Patrice Kindl's *Owl in Love* (1993).

Notable tales of magic adventure include Jane Langton's *The Fledgling* (1980);
Lynne Reid Banks's Indian in the Cupboard quartet (1980–1993); Bill Brittain's Coven
Tree saga, which began with *The Devil's Donkey* (1981); Chris Van Allsburg's *Jumanji*
(1981); Margaret Mahy's *The Haunting* (1982); Mary Norton's *The Borrowers
Avenged* (1982); Luli Gray's *Falcon's Egg* (1995); Corneila Funke's *The Thief Lord*
(2000, 2002); and Eoin Colfer's *Artemis Fowl* (2001).

Magic and witchcraft continue to be an extremely popular combination, particularly
in Diana Wynne Jones's Chrestomanci series (1978–2001); Margaret Mahy's *The
Changeover* (1984); J. K. Rowling's Harry Potter series (1997, 1998–); Tamora
Pierce's Circle of Magic quartet (1997–1999), beginning with *Sandry's Book*; Diana
Wynne Jones's *The Dark Lord of Derkholm* (1998), and Jonathan Stroud's *The Amulet
of Samarkand* (2003).

Time travel fantasy has been enriched by David Wiseman's *Jeremy Visick* (1981), Ruth Park's *Playing Beatie Bow* (1982), Jane Yolen's *The Devil's Arithmetic* (1988), Pam Conrad's *Stonewords* (1990), Mary Downing Hahn's *Time for Andrew* (1994), and Susan Cooper's *King of Shadows* (1999).

There have been numerous well-written novels set in alternate worlds written for young people during the past two and a half decades, including Lloyd Alexander's Westmark trilogy (1981–1984); Robin McKinley's *The Blue Sword* (1982); Meredith Ann Pierce's *The Darkangel* (1982); Patricia McKillip's *Moon-Flash* (1984); Cynthia Voigt's The Kingdom saga (1985–1999), including *On Fortune's Wheel* (1990); Sid Fleischman's *The Whipping Boy* (1986); Monica Furlong's *Wise Child* (1987); Susan Fletcher's *Dragon's Milk* (1989); William Mayne's *Antar and the Eagles* (1989, 1990); Terry Pratchett's Bromeliad trilogy, which began with *Truckers* (1989); Ursula K. Le Guin's *Tehanu* (1990) and *The Other Wind* (2001); Patricia C. Wrede's Enchanted Forest Chronicles (1990–1993); Gillian Bradshaw's *The Dragon and the Thief* (1991); Grace Chetwin's *Child of the Air* (1991); Vivian Vande Velde's *Dragon's Bait* (1992); Lois Lowry's *The Giver* (1993); Sherryl Jordan's *Winter of Fire* (1993) and *Secret Sacrament* (1996, 2001); Garth Nix's Abhorsen trilogy, beginning with *Sabriel* (1995, 1996); Megan Whalen Turner's *The Thief* (1996); Franny Billingsley's *The Folk Keeper* (1999); Tamora Pierce's Protector of the Small quartet (1999–2002); Philip Pullman's His Dark Materials trilogy (1995–2000), beginning with *The Golden Compass* (1995, 1996), and Hilari Bell's *Flame* (2003).

Notable stories of travel from our world to another include Diana Wynne Jones's *The Lives of Christopher Chant* (1988), Pauline Fisk's *Midnight Blue* (1990, 2003), Eloise McGraw's *The Moorchild* (1996), and Sally Prue's *Cold Tom* (2002, 2003).

Outstanding fantasy novels involving mythology and folklore include Vivien Alcock's *Singer to the Sea God* (1992), Elizabeth E. Wein's *The Winter Prince* (1993), Donna Jo Napoli's *Zel* (1996) and *Crazy Jack* (1999), David Almond's *Skellig* (1998, 1999), Nancy Springer's *I Am Mordred* (1998), Kevin Crossley-Holland's *The Seeing Stone* (2000, 2001), Caroline Cooney's *Goddess of Yesterday* (2002), Shannon Hale's *The Goose Girl*, and Jane Yolen's *Sword of the Rightful King* (2003).

The past two decades have also seen the growth in popularity of two newer types of young adult and adult fantasy: graphic novels, which are not covered in this book, and darker, grittier tales, sometimes referred to as "urban fantasy." Will Shetterly's *Elsewhere* (1991) and Emma Bull's *Finder: A Novel of the Borderlands* (1994) are both set in the shadowy world of Borderland, as are the short stories in *Borderland, No. 1* edited by Terri Windling and Mark Arnold (1986). Charles de Lint's stories and novels set in Newford, including *Someplace to Be Flying* (1998) and *Waifs and Strays* (2002), Holly Black's *Tithe: A Modern Faerie Tale* (2002), Neil Gaiman's *Coraline* (2002), Sally Prue's *Cold Tom* (2002, 2003), and Sarah Zettel's *A Sorcerer's Treason: A Novel of Isavalta* (2002) are also examples of this "darker" fantasy, which can border on horror fiction.

Well-written "crossover" adult fantasy novels of the past 25 years read by young adults include Terry Pratchett's Discworld series (beginning in 1980), Marion Zimmer Bradley's *The Mists of Avalon* (1982), Diana Wynne Jones's *Fire and Hemlock* (1984), Nancy Willard's *Things Invisible to See* (1985), Barbara Hambley's *Dragonsbane* (1986), Patricia Wrede and Caroline Stevermer's *Sorcery and Cecelia* (1988, 2003),

Neil Gaiman's *Stardust* (1998), and Juliet Marillier's *Daughter of the Forest* (2000), the first volume in her Sevenwaters trilogy (2000–2002).

A particularly welcome development in the genre of fantasy literature for young people written during the past 25 years has been the growing number of strong female protagonists, including Dido Twite in Joan Aiken's Wolves Chronicles; Zoe in Pam Conrad's *Stonewords*; Anaxandra in Caroline Cooney's *Goddess of Yesterday*; Kaeldra in Susan Fletcher's *Dragon's Milk*; Juniper in Monica Furlong's *Wise Child*; Polly in Diana Wynne Jones's *Fire and Hemlock*; Tenar in Ursula K. Le Guin's *Tehanu*; Menolly in Anne McCaffrey's *Dragonsong*; Sybel in Patricia McKillip's *The Forgotten Beasts of Eld*; Harry Crew in Robin McKinley's *The Blue Sword*; Laura in Margaret Mahy's *The Changeover*; Sabriel and Liriel in Garth Nix's Abhorsen trilogy; Aeriel in Meredith Ann Pierce's *The Darkangel*; Alanna, Sandry, and others in Tamora Pierce's various series; Kate in Elizabeth Marie Pope's *The Perilous Gard*; Lyra in Philip Pullman's His Dark Materials trilogy; Gwyn and Birle in Cynthia Voigt's The Kingdom saga; Cimorene in Patricia Wrede's The Enchanted Forest Chronicles; and Hannah in Jane Yolen's *The Devil's Arithmetic*.

Conclusion

Fantasy literature has become during the past decade the most popular genre of children's and young adult literature, and books written in series continue to be extremely popular, in both fantasy and realistic fiction. Younger children want to read another book "just like" their favorites; older children and young adults want to find out "what happens next" in their favorite characters' lives; and publishers like to bet on a sure thing. Of course, fantasy series are not a new phenomenon—L. Frank Baum's *The Wonderful Wizard of Oz*, written in 1900, was followed by 53 sequels. However, it is interesting to note that one third (1,650) of the 4,800 titles included in the fourth edition (1995) of *Fantasy Literature for Children and Young Adults* were sequels, yet 54 percent (1,496) of the 2,877 recommended new titles added to this fifth edition are sequels.

J. K. Rowling's Harry Potter books and Philip Pullman's His Dark Materials trilogy are two notable examples of contemporary fantasy series that have attained the status of classics. Interestingly, although the Harry Potter books were not critically acclaimed when first published, opinions have changed. As Roger Sutton, editor in chief of *The Horn Book Magazine* writes: "[L]et's take a moment to acknowledge both His Dark Materials and Harry Potter as classics in the making. I was wrong three years ago (September/October 1999) when I wrote that Harry Potter was "likable but critically insignificant." I'll still cite you chapter and verse of where I think the series flounders, but one man's opinion does not a classic make or unmake, and at some level textual criticism is beside the point. A classic isn't necessarily a masterpiece. It's instead a book that won't go away, one whose presence demands continued reckoning by readers and writers alike . . . Great and small, dismal and brilliant, most books come and go. Others quietly stick around, gathering readers and reputation over time. And while "instant classics" tend to last just about that long, some books, Harry Potter and His Dark Materials among them, arrive bold as paint and demand from the start that we keep looking."[92]

This edition of *Fantasy Literature for Children and Young Adults* retains an updated listing of national and international "Award-Winning Fantasy Literature," following an updated list of "Outstanding Fantasy, 1960–2004." I have retained and updated this "Outstanding" list, which includes many of the titles discussed above, because so many well-written books don't win awards. As Jane Langton put it in a *New York Times* review of the 1992 Newbery award-winning book: "Did *Shiloh* really deserve the prize? Surely there must have been a book more important than this agreeable but slight story. Like the Oscar, the Newbery has sometimes passed over the good and the great. There have been embarrassing omissions. Where were the prizes for Ursula K. Le Guin's *A Wizard of Earthsea* [and] Natalie Babbitt's *Tuck Everlasting* . . . ? Possibly the greatest children's book ever written in the English language, E. B. White's *Charlotte's Web*, ran second to an otherwise forgotten wonder, *Secret of the Andes*, by Ann Nolan Clark. . . . The Newbery judges . . . are all members of the American Library Association, good workers in the vineyard. . . . Can a committee of 15 do anything but compromise?"[93]

Natalie Babbitt has written that one of the special qualities of fantasy literature is that it not only lets us share the hero's hopes and triumphs but that it ends on a note of hope. She feels that fantasy "is not a sop for the terminally optimistic, but an affirmation of one of the things that makes us, as a species, unique: the always present hope that something will happen to change everything, once and for all, for the better."[94]

It is my hope that the authors of fantasy literature will continue to create stories that illuminate reality, delight us, refresh our hearts, provide us with hope for the future, and give us joy.

Notes

1. Sheila Egoff, *Thursday's Child: Trends and Patterns in Contemporary Children's Literature* (Chicago: American Library Association, 1981), p. 82.
2. Jane Yolen, "Tough Magic," *Top of the News* 35 (Winter, 1979): 186.
3. Elizabeth Nesbit, *A Critical History of Children's Literature: A Survey of Children's Books in English*, rev. ed. by Cornelia Meigs, Anne Thaxter Eaton, Elizabeth Nesbit, and Ruth Hill Viguers (New York: Macmillan, 1969), p. 347.
4. "Fantasy Books Top the List for Teens: Young Adults Choose Their Favorite Books as Part of YALSA Teen Read Week." *School Library Journal*, January 2004, vol. 50, p. 23.
5. BBC News: World Edition, 17 November 2003 (http://news.bbc.co.uk/1/hi/entertainment/arts/2996578.stm)
6. Cart, Michael. "Carte Blanche: What Rowling Has Wrought." *Booklist* 100 (April 15, 2004): 1438.
7. Natalie Babbitt, "The Purposes of Fantasy." In *Proceedings of the Ninth Annual Conference of the Children's Literature Association* (Ypsilanti, Mich: Children's Literature Association, 1983), pp. 22, 29. Reprinted with permission, in *Innocence and Experience*, ed. by Barbara Harrison and Gregory Maguire (New York: Lothrop, 1987), pp. 174–181.
8. *The Oxford English Dictionary*, Second Edition (Oxford, England: Clarendon Press, 1989), Vol. V, pp. 722–723.
9. *The Random House Dictionary of the English Language*, Second Edition, Unabridged (New York: Random House, 1987), p. 698.
10. Everett F. Bleiler, *The Checklist of Fantastic Literature: A Bibliography of Fantasy, Weird and Science Fiction Published in the English Language* (Chicago: Shasta, 1948), p. 3; Perry Nodelman, "Defining Children's Literature," in *Children's Literature* 8 (New Haven, Conn.: Yale University Press, 1980), p. 187; Eric S. Rabkin, *The Fantastic in Literature* (Princeton, N.J.: Princeton University Press, 1976), p. 8; and Tsvetan Todorov, *The Fantastic: A Structural*

Approach to a Literary Genre (Cleveland, Ohio: Case Western Reserve University Press, 1973), p. 25. "[Fantasy is] that hesitation experienced by a person . . . confronting an apparently supernatural event." See also Pierre Castex, *Le Conte Fantastique en France de Nodier à Maupassant* (Paris: Corti, 1951), quoted in Todorov, *The Fantastic*, p. 26. "[Fantasy is] the brutal intrusion of mystery [into real life]"; H. P. Lovecraft, quoted in Todorov, *The Fantastic*, p. 34; Peter Penzoldt, *The Supernatural in Fiction* (Atlantic Highlands, N.J.: Humanities Press, 1965), quoted in Todorov, *The Fantastic*, p. 35. "A fantasy is a tale of fear and terror"; and Julius Kagarlitski, "Realism and Fantasy," in *Science Fiction: The Other Side of Realism—Essays in Modern Fantasy and Science Fiction*, ed. by Thomas D. Clareson (Bowling Green, Ohio: Bowling Green University Popular Press, 1971), p. 29. "[Fantasy is a tale in which] disbelief arises side by side with belief."

11. Lin Carter, *Imaginary Worlds: The Art of Fantasy* (New York: Ballantine, 1973), p. 6. See also James E. Higgins, *Beyond Words: Mystical Fancy in Children's Literature* (New York: Columbia University Press, 1970), p. 5; Naomi Lewis, *Fantasy Books for Children*, rev. ed. (London: National Book League, 1977), p. 5; and Patrick Merla, "'What Is Real?' Asked the Rabbit One Day; Realism vs. Fantasy in Children's and Adult Literature," in *Only Connect*, 2nd ed., ed. by Sheila Egoff, G. T. Stubbs, and L. F. Ashley (New York: Oxford University Press, 1980), p. 348. ". . . the essential element of any true work of fantasy is magic—a force that affects the lives and actions of all the creatures that inhabit the fantastic world. . . . Always it is a supernatural force whose use, misuse, or disuse irrevocably changes the lives of those it touches. . . . Real magic cannot be explained in material terms, nor manufactured with mechanical devices, nor achieved through ingested substances."

12. Louis Vax, *L'Art et la Littérature Fantastiques* (Paris: Presses Universitaires de France, 1960), quoted in Todorov, *The Fantastic*, p. 26. "The fantastic narrative generally describes men like ourselves, inhabiting the real world, suddenly confronted by the inexplicable." See also: Roger Caillois, *Au Coeur de Fantastique* (Paris), quoted in Todorov, *The Fantastic*, p. 26. "The fantastic is always a break in the acknowledged order, an irruption of the inadmissible, within the changeless everyday legality."

13. Jane Mobley, ed., *Phantasmagoria: Tales of Fantasy and the Supernatural* (New York: Anchor Press, 1977), pp. 17, 23.

14. Brian Attebery, *The Fantasy Tradition in American Literature from Irving to Le Guin* (Bloomington: Indiana University Press, 1980), p. 2. "Any narrative which includes as a significant part of its make-up some violation of what the author clearly believes to be natural law—that is fantasy." See also: W. R. Irwin, *The Game of the Impossible: A Rhetoric of Fantasy* (Champaign: University of Illinois Press, 1976), pp. 4, 9. "[The primary feature of fantasy is] an overt violation of what is generally accepted as possibility . . . a narrative is fantasy if it presents the persuasive establishment and development of an impossibility"; Leo P. Kelley, ed., *Fantasy: The Literature of the Marvelous* (New York: McGraw-Hill, 1974), p. v. "[Fantasy] tells us of events which could not occur in a universe whose major physical laws are known and necessarily obeyed"; and Marshall B. Tymn, Kenneth J. Zahorski, and Robert H. Boyer, *Fantasy Literature: A Core Collection and Reference Guide* (New York: Bowker, 1979), pp. 3, 4. "[Fantasies are] works in which events occur, or places or creatures exist that could not exist according to rational standards or scientific explanations. . . . Fantasy . . . has its own vision of reality."

15. Attebery, *Fantasy Tradition*, p. 3. "The most important thing [works of fantasy] share is a sense of wonder . . . invoke[d] . . . by making the impossible seem familiar and the familiar seem new and strange." See also: C. N. Manlove, *Modern Fantasy: Five Studies* (New York: Cambridge University Press, 1975), p. 1. "A fantasy is 'A fiction evoking wonder and containing a substantial and irreducible element of the supernatural with which the mortal characters in the story or the readers become on at least partly familiar terms.'"

16. Ann Swinfen, *In Defense of Fantasy: A Study of the Genre in English and American Literature Since 1945* (Boston: Routledge, 1984), p. 234. Reprinted with permission of the publisher.

17. Egoff, *Thursday's Child*, p. 80. Reprinted with permission of the American Library Association, excerpt taken from *Thursday's Child: Trends and Patterns in Contemporary Children's Literature* by Sheila Egoff (Chicago: ALA, 1981).

18. Eleanor Cameron, *The Green and Burning Tree: On the Writing and Enjoyment of Children's Books* (Boston: Little, Brown, 1969), p. 16.

19. Jane Langton, "The Weak Place in the Cloth: A Study of Fantasy for Children," *Horn Book Magazine* 49 (October 1973): 433; Lloyd Alexander, "Wishful Thinking—Or Hopeful Dreaming?" *Horn Book Magazine* 44 (August 1968): 386; and Mollie Hunter, "One World," *Horn Book Magazine* 51 (December 1975): 557.

20. Ursula K. Le Guin, "From Elfland to Poughkeepsie," in *The Language of the Night: Essays on Fantasy and Science Fiction*, edited by Susan Wood. (New York: Putnam, 1979), pp. 84, 93. Reprinted with the permission of the editor's Estate, the Author, and their joint agent, Virginia Kidd.

21. Sheila Egoff, *The Republic of Childhood*, 2nd ed. (New York: Oxford University Press, 1975), p. 134.

22. Swinfen, *In Defense of Fantasy*, p. 231. Reprinted with permission of the publisher.

23. Sheila Egoff, *Worlds Within: Children's Fantasy from the Middle Ages to Today.* (Chicago: American Library Association, 1988), p. 19.

24. Alan Garner, "A Bit More Practice," [London] *Times Literary Supplement*, June 6, 1968, p. 577.

25. Jane Louise Curry, "On the Elvish Craft," *Signal* 2 (May 1970): 44.

26. Susan Cooper, "Escaping into Ourselves," in Betsy Hearne and Marilyn Kaye, *Celebrating Children's Books* (New York: Lothrop, 1981), pp. 22–23.

27. Paul Hazard, *Books, Children and Men*, 4th ed. (Boston: Horn Book, 1960), p. 157.

28. Cameron, *Green and Burning Tree*, pp. 15–16.

29. Natalie Babbitt, "Happy Endings? Of Course, and Also Joy," *New York Times Book Review*, Nov. 8, 1970, p. 1.

30. Swinfen, *In Defense of Fantasy*, p. 2. Reprinted with permission of the publisher.

31. See, for example, Carter, *Imaginary Worlds*, p. 1; Louis Macneice, *Varieties of Parable* (New York: Cambridge University Press, 1965), p. 102. "When we reach the twentieth century, children's fantasy is represented, I suppose, typically by *Peter Pan*, a work which is not only frivolous but perverse"; and Isabelle Jan, *On Children's Literature* (New York: Schocken, 1974), pp. 67–68.

32. Donnarae MacCann, "Wells of Fancy, 1865–1965," *Wilson Library Bulletin* 40 (December 1965): 403.

33. Carter, Imaginary Worlds, p. 1.

34. Babbitt, "Happy Endings?" p. 50.

35. Egoff, *The Republic of Childhood*, p. 134. See also Cameron, *Green and Burning Tree*, pp. 87–88. "A writer, it seems to me, should feel himself no more under necessity to restrict the complexity of his plotting because of differences in child understanding . . . than he feels the necessity of restricting his vocabulary. What is important is not, I think, that a child shall have understood each turn of the author's thinking, but that his excitement be set simmering as vista after vista of mental and spiritual distances, hitherto unguessed at, open before him. [These implications and overtones of meaning] will haunt the child long after he has forgotten the plot. . . . [These stories] are satisfying to [an adult] in ways which the child is not yet aware of . . . but the child can experience a very deep sense of satisfaction without in the least knowing why."

36. Neil Philip, "Fantasy: Double Cream or Instant Whip?" *Signal* 35 (May 1981): 83.

37. Susan Cooper, "Newbery Award Acceptance Address," *Horn Book Magazine* 52 (August 1976): 362.

38. Le Guin, "Dreams Must Explain Themselves," in *Language of the Night*, p. 55. See also C. S. Lewis, "On Three Ways of Writing for Children," in *Of Other Worlds: Essays and Stories* (New York: Harcourt, 1967), p. 24. "I am almost inclined to set it up as a canon that a children's story which is enjoyed only by children is a bad children's story. The good ones last."

39. Carter, *Imaginary Worlds*, p. 1; Elizabeth Cook, *The Ordinary and the Fabulous* (New York: Cambridge University Press, 1969), p. 5.

40. Cooper, "Escaping into Ourselves," pp. 15–16.

41. Lewis, "On Three Ways," pp. 29–30.

42. Curry, "On the Elvish Craft," p. 47.

43. J. R. R. Tolkien, *Tree and Leaf* (Boston: Houghton Mifflin, 1965), pp. 46–55.

44. Neil Barron, *Fantasy Literature: A Reader's Guide* (New York: Garland, 1990), pp. 309–310.

45. Tamora Pierce, "Fantasy: Why Kids Read It, Why Kids Need It," *School Library Journal* 39 (October 1993): 50–51.

46. Lloyd Alexander, "Substance and Fantasy," *Library Journal* 91 (December 15, 1966): 6159; and Lloyd Alexander, "The Truth About Fantasy," *Top of the News* 24 (January 1968): 174.
47. Sharyn November, "Crossing Over: Fantasy and Its Readers," *CBC Features*, Spring 2004, vol. 57, pp. 6–8.
48. Kornei Chukovskii, *From Two to Five* (Berkeley: University of California Press, 1963), pp. 116–117, 124.
49. Alexander, "Wishful Thinking," p. 389.
50. Penelope Lively, "Children and Memory," *Horn Book Magazine* 49 (August 1973): 407.
51. Eleanor Cameron, "The Dearest Freshness Deep Down Things." Reprinted with the permission of Eleanor Cameron, *The Green and Burning Tree: On the Writing and Enjoyment of Children's Books* (Boston: Atlantic-Little, 1969), pp. 272–273; also in *Horn Book Magazine* 40 (October 1964): pp. 471–472.
52. Linda A. Forrest, "Young Adult Fantasy and the Search for Gender-Fair Genres," *Journal of Youth Services in Libraries* 7 (Fall 1993): 37–42.
53. Le Guin, "The Child and the Shadow," in *The Language of the Night*, pp. 68–69. See also Swinfen, *In Defense of Fantasy*, p. 229.
54. MacCann, "Wells of Fancy," p. 334.
55. Alan Garner, "Coming to Terms," *Children's Literature in Education* 2 (July 1970): 17; and Cooper, "Escaping into Ourselves," p. 16.
56. Isabelle Jan, *On Children's Literature* (New York: Schocken, 1974, published in France in 1969), pp. 44, 67, 75.
57. Bruno Bettleheim, *The Uses of Enchantment* (New York: Knopf, 1976), p. 144.
58. Mary J. Collier and Eugene L. Gaier, "Adult Reactions to Preferred Childhood Stories," *Child Development* 29 (March 1958): 97–103.
59. Alison Lurie, *Boys and Girls Forever: Children's Classics from Cinderella to Harry Potter* (New York: Penguin, 2003), pp. 119–121, 137, 260.
60. Egoff, *Worlds Within*, p. 20.
61. Egoff, *Thursday's Child*, p. 87; and Mobley, *Phantasmagoria*, p. 35.
62. Swinfen, *In Defense of Fantasy*, p. 229. Reprinted with permission of the publisher.
63. Helen Cresswell, "If It's Someone from Porlock, Don't Answer the Door," *Children's Literature in Education* 4 (March 1971): 37.
64. Roger W. Drury, "Realism Plus Fantasy Equals Magic," *Horn Book Magazine* 48 (April 1972): 119.
65. Lewis, "On Three Ways," p. 23.
66. Babbitt, "Happy Endings?" p. 50.
67. Cooper, "Escaping into Ourselves," p. 22.
68. Le Guin, "Myth and Archetype in Science Fiction," in *The Language of the Night*, pp. 78–79, edited by Susan Wood. Reprinted with permission of the editor's estate, the author, and their joint agent, Virginia Kidd. See also Attebery, *Fantasy Traditions*, p. 15. "The materials of fantasy, the things that call forth feelings of wonder . . . are partly individual invention and partly community property."
69. Mollie Hunter, "One World," *Horn Book Magazine* 51 (December 1975): 562 (continued in 52 [January 1976]: 32–38).
70. Patricia Wrightson, "Stones into Pools," *Top of the News* 41 (Spring 1985): 286.
71. Helen Lourie, "Where Is Fancy Bred?" in Egoff, *Only Connect*, p. 110.
72. Curry, "On the Elvish Craft," pp. 42–43.
73. Ibid., pp. 43, 49. Other critics who divide fantasy into two basic categories are Frank Eyre, *British Children's Books in the Twentieth Century* (New York: Dutton, 1971), pp. 116–117. "[The first kind is] a story of ordinary life but with some extra quality added—wishes granted, time travel, talking animals, fairy creatures—the adventures happen in the real world. . . . [The second kind is] either about a different world altogether, or about our own world but in a completely different time in which everything is different"; Göte Klingberg, "The Fantastic and the Mythical as Reading for Modern Children and Young People," in *How Can Children's Literature Meet the Needs of Modern Children* (15th IBBY conference, 1976), p. 32. "I will call here a novel where some strange world is united with an everyday world . . . a fantastic tale, and a novel telling only of a mystical country wholly outside our ordinary world, a mythical tale"; Manlove, *Modern Fantasy*, p. 11. "The two broad classes of fantasy are 'comic' or 'escapist' or 'fanciful' [in which]

the point of the work . . . is the reader's pleasure in the invented characters or situations, [and] 'imaginative fantasy' [in which] the object is to enlist [the author's] experience and invention into giving a total version of reality transformed: that is to make their fantastic worlds as real as our own"; and Diana Waggoner, *The Hills of Faraway: A Guide to Fantasy* (New York: Atheneum, 1978). Waggoner uses the term "Magic in Operation" for tales set in our world and "Magic of Situation" for tales that take place in a magical world.

74. Egoff, *Thursday's Child*, p. 82; Ralph Lavender, "Other Worlds: Myth and Fantasy, 1970–1980," *Children's Literature in Education* 12, no. 3 (Autumn 1981): 141–142.

75. Egoff, *Thursday's Child*, p. 92.

76. Egoff, *Thursday's Child*, p. 83.

77. Hunt, Peter. *Children's Literature: An Illustrated History* (New York: Oxford University Press, 1995), pp. 71–72.

78. Carpenter, Humphrey, and Mari Prichard, *Oxford Companion to Children's Literature* (New York: Oxford University Press, 1984), p. 259. "This book has been judged to be the first full-length children's fantasy written in English." Green, Roger Lancelyn, *Tellers of Tales: British Authors of Children's Books from 1800 to 1964*, rev. ed. (New York: Ward, 1965), pp. 24–26, 235, describes it as "the first literary fairy story."

79. Margery Fisher, *Intent upon Reading* (New York: Watts, 1962), p. 100.

80. Avery, Gillian. *Behold the Child: American Children and Their Books, 1621–1922* (Baltimore: Johns Hopkins University Press, 1994), pp. 131–133.

81. *Fantasy (The Greenhaven Press Companion to Literary Movements and Genres)*. Ed. by Wendy Mass and Stuart P. Levine. San Diego: Greenhaven Press, 2002, pp. 17–18, 159.

82. Lewis, *Fantasy Books*, p. 5.

83. Egoff, *Worlds Within*, p. 78.

84. Ibid, p. 73.

85. Ibid, p. 150.

86. Frank Eyre, *British Children's Books in the Twentieth Century* (New York: Dutton, 1971), p. 128. "[*Tom's Midnight Garden* and *The Children of Green Knowe* are the two] perfect fantasies of our time." See also John Rowe Townsend, *Written for Children* (New York: Lothrop, 1967), pp. 127–128. "*Tom's Midnight Garden* . . . has not a flaw . . . it is as near to being perfect in its construction and its writing as any book I know. . . . If I were asked to name a single masterpiece of English children's literature since the last war . . . it would be this outstandingly beautiful and absorbing book"; and Eudora Welty, "Life in the Barn Was Very Good," *New York Times Book Review*, October 19, 1952, p. 49. "As a piece of work [*Charlotte's Web*] is just about perfect, and just about magical in the way it is done."

87. Egoff, *Worlds Within*, pp. 171–172.

88. Ibid., p. 182.

89. Ibid., p. 248.

90. Ibid., p. 310.

91. David G. Hartwell, "Dollars and Dragons: The Truth About Fantasy." *New York Times Book Review*, April 29, 1990, pp. 1, 40–41.

92. Roger Sutton, "Editorial: Classic Reckoning." *The Horn Book Magazine* 78 (July/August 2002): 371.

93. Jane Langton, Review of *Shiloh* by Phyllis Reynolds Naylor (Atheneum, 1991), *New York Times Book Review*, May 10, 1992, p. 21.

94. Babbitt, "The Purposes of Fantasy," p. 28.

OUTSTANDING FANTASY, 1960–2004

The following alphabetical lists of books and series published since 1960 make up a core list of outstanding examples of fantasy literature for children and young adults. The titles on these lists were chosen based on personal opinion as well as that expressed in professional review sources. For a list of the professional review sources used, see Abbreviations of Books and Review Journals Cited (above). The first twelve headings in this section correspond to Chapters 1 through 12 of this book. The final list, Crossover Books Read by Young Adults, includes adult fantasy works that have become popular with young adults. Occasionally, a title will fit into two or more categories and will appear on more than one list. To locate complete information on a specific book, see the Title Index, or the Author and Illustrator Index.

Allegorical Fantasy and Literary Fairy Tales

A number of fine contemporary allegorical stories and literary fairy tales have been written in the tradition of the classic stories by Hans Christian Andersen, Saavedra Miguel de Cervantes, Padraic Colum, Charles Dickens, Rudyard Kipling, Andrew Lang, George MacDonald, Antoine de Saint-Exupéry, Frank R. Stockton, William Makepeace Thackeray, James Thurber, and Oscar Wilde, including:

Adams, Richard. *Watership Down*. 1972, 1974
Alexander, Lloyd. *The Remarkable Journey of Prince Jen*. 1991
Almond, David. *Heaven Eyes*. 2000, 2001
Beagle, Peter S. *The Last Unicorn*. 1968, 1988
Brittain, Bill. *Dr. Dredd's Wagon of Wonders*. 1987
Fleischman, Paul. *Coming-and-Going Men*. 1985
Fleischman, Sid. *The Whipping Boy*. 1986
Garfield, Leon. *The Wedding Ghost*. 1985, 1987
Hoban, Russell. *The Mouse and His Child*. 1967, 2001
Lawson, John. *You Better Come Home with Me*. 1966
Le Vert, John. *The Flight of the Cassowary*. 1986
Moeri, Louise. *Star Mother's Youngest Child*. 1975
Paterson, Katharine. *The King's Equal*. 1992
Price, Susan. *The Ghost Drum*. 1987
Pullman, Philip. *The Golden Compass*. 1995, 1996 (His Dark Materials trilogy, 1995–2000)
Stockton, Frank R. *The Bee-Man of Orn*. 1964, 1987, 2003
Thurber, James. *Many Moons*. 1943, 1990
Wangerin, Walter. *The Book of the Dun Cow*. 1978

Animal Fantasy

Two types of animal fantasy novels are represented in this chapter and on this list: allegorical tales of animals attempting to escape human evils and more lighthearted talking animal stories. George Orwell's *Animal Farm* (1945), in the first category, and E. B. White's *Charlotte's Web* (1952), in the second category, are classic animal fantasy novels written before 1960 that set the standard for those that have followed.

Adams, Richard. *Watership Down*. 1972, 1974

Avi. *Poppy*. 1995 (Dimwood Forest Tales, 1995–2000)

Bell, Clare. Ratha quartet. 1983–994

Bond, Michael. Paddington series. 1960–1984

Cleary, Beverly. Ralph S. Mouse trilogy. 1965–1982

Corbett, W. J. *The Song of Pentecost*. 1982, 1983

DiCamillo, Kate. *The Tale of Despereaux*. 2003

Erickson, Russell E. Warton and Morton series. 1974–1986

Hoban, Russell. *The Mouse and His Child*. 1967, 2001

Hoeye, Michael. *Time Stops for No Mouse*. 2000 (Hermux Tantamoq Adventure Series, 2000–2004)

Howe, James. Bunnicula series. 1979–2004

Jacques, Brian. Redwall saga. 1986–2004

Jarrell, Randall. *The Animal Family*. 1965, 1985

Jarvis, Robin. *The Dark Porta*l. 1989, 2000 (The Deptford Mice trilogy, 1989–2002)

King-Smith, Dick. *Babe: The Gallant Pig*. 1983, 1985; *Martin's Mice*. 1988; *Three Terrible Trins*. 1994

Lasky, Kathry. *The Captive*. 2003 (Guardians of Ga'Hoole series, 2003–2004)

Le Guin, Ursula K. Catwings quartet. 1988–1999

Lively, Penelope. *The Voyage of QV66*. 1978, 1979

Marshall, James. *Rats on the Roof and Other Stories*. 1991

O'Brien, Robert C. *Mrs. Frisby and the Rats of NIMH*. 1971 (and the sequels by Jane Leslie Conly, 1986–1990)

Oppel, Kenneth. Silverwing trilogy. 1997–2003

Seidler, Tor. *Mean Margaret*. 1997

Selden, George. The Cricket in Times Square series. 1960–1987

Sendak, Maurice. *Higglety Pigglety Pop! Or, There Must Be More to Life*. 1967

Sharp, Margery. Miss Bianca series. 1959–1978

Steig, William. *Abel's Island*. 1976

Stolz, Mary. *Belling the Tiger*. 1961, 1989

Fantasy Story Collections

During the so-called golden age of the fantasy short story genre—the latter half of the 19th and the early years of the 20th centuries—classic stories were created by Hans Christian Andersen, Arthur Bowie Chrisman, Padraic Colum, Walter de la Mare, Eleanor Farjeon, Laurence Housman, Rudyard Kipling, E. Nesbit, Barbara Leonie

Picard, Howard Pyle, Carl Sandburg, Frank R. Stockton, and Oscar Wilde. Since the early 1970s there has been a renewed interest in the fantasy short story, leading to the publication of a number of excellent collections. These include:

Aiken, Joan. *Up the Chimney Down and Other Stories*. 1984, 1985
Babbitt, Natalie. The Devil's Storybook duology. 1974, 1987
Beware! Beware! Chilling Tales. Ed. by Jean Richardson. 1989
Black, Francesca Lia. *The Rose and the Beast: Fairy Tales Retold*. 2000
Brooke, William J. *A Telling of the Tales*. 1990
Dickinson, Peter. *The Lion-Tamer's Daughter and Other Stories*. 1997
Ellis, Sarah. *Back of Beyond: Stories of the Supernatural*. 1996, 1997
The Faery Reel: Tales from the Twilight Realm. Ed. by Ellen Datlow and Terri
    Windling. 2004
Firebirds: An Anthology of Original Fantasy and Science Fiction. Ed. by Sharyn
    November. 2003
Galloway, Priscilla. *Truly Grim Tales*. 1995
Gothic! Ten Original Dark Tales. Ed. by Deborah Noyes. 2004
Harris, Rosemary. *Sea Magic and Other Stories of Enchantment*. 1974
Housman, Laurence. *The Rat Catcher's Daughter*. 1974
Jones, Diana Wynne. *Warlock at the Wheel and Other Stories*. 1984, 1985
Kennedy, Richard. *Richard Kennedy: Collected Stories*. 1987
Le Guin, Ursula K. *The Wind's Twelve Quarters*. 1975
Lively, Penelope. *Uninvited Ghosts and Other Stories*. 1984, 1985
McKinley, Robin. *Imaginary Lands*. 1985; *A Knot in the Grain and Other Stories*.
    1994
McKinley, Robin, and Peter Dickinson. *Water: Tales of the Elemental Spirits*. 2002
McKissack, Patricia C. *The Dark-Thirty: Southern Tales of the Supernatural*. 1992
Mahy, Margaret. *The Girl with the Green Ear*. 1992
Pearce, Philippa. *Lion at School: And Other Stories*. 1985, 1986; *Familiar and
    Haunting: Collected Stories*. 1977, 1977, 1987, 2002
Singer, Isaac Bashevis. *Stories for Children*. 1984
Things That Go Bump in the Night. Ed. by Jane Yolen and Martin H. Greenberg.
    1989
Turner, Megan Whalen. *Instead of Three Wishes*. 1995
Westall, Robert. *The Haunting of Chas McGill and Other Stories*. 1983
Williams, Jay. *The Practical Princess and Other Liberating Fairy Tales*. 1978
Yolen, Jane. *The Girl Who Cried Flowers and Other Tales*. 1974; *The Faery Flag*.
    1989; *Here There Be Witches*. 1995

Ghost Fantasy

The most memorable recent books in the category of ghost fantasy include:

Aiken, Joan. *The Shadow Guests*. 1980
Almond, David. *Kit's Wilderness*. 1999, 2000
Beware! Beware! Chilling Tales. Ed. by Jean Richardson. 1989

Boston, Lucy. The Children of Green Knowe series, 1955, 1967
Burgess, Barbara Hood. *Oren Bell.* 1991
Cameron, Eleanor. *The Court of the Stone Children.* 1973
Cassedy, Sylvia. *Behind the Attic Wall.* 1983
Collier, James Lincoln. *The Empty Mirror.* 2004
Cresswell, Helen. *A Game of Catch.* 1969, 1977
Fleischman, Sid. *The Midnight Horse.* 1990; *The Thirteenth Floor: A Ghost Story.*
   1995
Garfield, Leon. *Mister Corbett's Ghost.* 1968; *The Empty Sleeve.* 1988
Hahn, Mary Downing. *Wait Till Helen Comes.* 1986; *Time for Andrew: A Ghost
   Story.* 1994
Hamilton, Virginia. *Sweet Whispers, Brother Rush.* 1982
Lively, Penelope. *The Ghost of Thomas Kempe.* 1973
Lunn, Janet. *Shadow in Hawthorne Bay.* 1986, 1987
McKay, Hilary. *The Amber Cat.* 1996, 1997
McKissack, Patricia C. *The Dark-Thirty: Southern Tales of the Supernatural.* 1992
Mahy, Margaret. *The Tricksters.* 1986, 1987
Pearce, Philippa. *The Shadow Cage and Other Tales of the Supernatural.* 1977;
   Familiar and Haunting: Collected Stories. 2002
Peck, Richard. *The Ghost Belonged to Me.* 1975 (The Blossom Culp quartet.
   1975–1986)
Schnur, Steven. *The Shadow Children.* 1994
Things That Go Bump in the Night. Ed. by Jane Yolen and Martin H. Greenberg.
   1989
Westall, Robert. *The Watch House.* 1977, 1978; *The Scarecrows.* 1981
Wilde, Nicholas. *Into the Dark.* 1987, 1990
Wright, Betty Ren. *A Ghost in the House.* 1991

High Fantasy

The late 1960s and the 1970s were marked by the development of a relatively new type
of children's and young adult novel-high fantasy, also called heroic fantasy or secondary world fantasy. The numerous books of high fantasy published during the last 35
years have been divided into three chapters in this bibliography: Alternate Worlds or
Histories, stories set entirely in a secondary world; Myth and Legend Fantasy,
retellings of myth and stories of contemporary involvement in myth; and Travel to
Other Worlds, stories in which a character from the real or primary world visits a secondary world.

High Fantasy: Alternate Worlds or Histories

The outstanding alternate world fantasy novels written since Tolkien's *The Hobbit*
(1937) include:

Aiken, Joan. The Wolves Chronicles. 1962–2003; *The Whispering Mountain.* 1969
Alexander, Lloyd. Westmark trilogy. 1981–1984; *The Iron Ring.* 1997

Bath, K. P. *The Secret of Castle Cant.* 2004
Beagle, Peter S. *The Last Unicorn.* 1968, 1988
Bell, Hilari. *Flame.* 2003. (The Book of Sorahb trilogy, 2003–)
Billingsley, Franny. *Well Wished.* 1997; *The Folk Keeper.* 1999
Bradshaw, Gillian. The Dragon and the Thief duology. 1991, 1992
Calhoun, Dia. *Firegold.* 1999
Chetwin, Grace. Tales of Gom series. 1986–1989; *Child of the Air.* 1991
Christopher, John. Winchester trilogy. 1970–1972
Dickinson, John. *The Cup of the World.* 2004
Dickinson, Peter. *The Blue Hawk.* 1976; The Changes trilogy. 1968–1970; *The Ropemaker.* 2001
Downer, Ann. Caitlin and Badger series. 1987–1993
Fisher, Catherine. *The Oracle Betrayed.* 2004 (The Oracle Prophecies trilogy)
Fleischman, Sid. *The Whipping Boy.* 1986
Fletcher, Susan. *Dragon's Milk.* 1989; *Flight of the Dragon Kyn.* 1993
Funke, Cornelia. *Dragon Rider.* 2004
Furlong, Monica. *Wise Child.* 1987; *Juniper.* 1990, 1991
Gloss, Molly. *Outside the Gates.* 1986
Halam, Ann. *The Daymaker.* 1987
Harris, Geraldine. Seven Citadels quartet. 1982–1984
James, Betsy. *Long Night Dance.* 1989
Jones, Diana Wynne. *Cart and Cwidder.* 1975, 1977; *Howl's Moving Castle.* 1986; *The Dark Lord of Derkholm.* 1998
Jordan, Sherryl. *Winter of Fire*, 1993; *Secret Sacrament.* 1996, 2001
King, Stephen. *The Eyes of the Dragon.* 1987
Kisling, Lee. *Fool's War.* 1992
Lee, Tanith. *Black Unicorn.* 1991
Le Guin, Ursula K. Earthsea Cycle. 1968–2003
Levin, Betty. *The Ice Bear.* 1986
Levine, Gail Carson. *The Two Princesses of Bamarre.* 2001
Lovett, Margaret. *The Great and Terrible Quest.* 1967
Lowry, Lois. *The Giver.* 1993; *Gathering Blue.* 2000; *Messenger.* 2004
McCaffrey, Anne. Harper Hall trilogy. 1976–1979
McKillip, Patricia. *The Forgotten Beasts of Eld.* 1974; *Moon-Flash.* 1984; Star-Bearer trilogy. 1976–1979; *The Changeling Sea.* 1988
McKinley, Robin. *The Blue Sword.* 1982; *The Hero and the Crown.* 1984
Mark, Jan. *Aquarius.* 1982, 1984
Mayne, William. *Antar and the Eagles.* 1989, 1990
Murphy, Shirley Rousseau. Nightpool trilogy. 1985–1988
Nix, Garth. *Sabriel.* 1995, 1996 (Abhorsen trilogy, 1995–2003)
Norton, Andre. *The Crystal Gryphon.* 1972
Oppel, Kenneth. *Airborn.* 2004
Pierce, Meredith Ann. The Darkangel trilogy. 1982–1990; *Treasure at the Heart of the Tanglewood.* 2001
Pierce, Tamora. Song of the Lioness series. 1983–1988; *Wild Magic: The Immortals.* 1992; *Sandry's Book.* 1997 (Circle of Magic quartet, 1997–1999);

First Test. 1999 (Protector of the Small quartet, 1999–2002); *Trickster's Choice.* 2003 (Daughter of the Lioness series, 2003–)

Pratchett, Terry. *Truckers* (1989) (The Bromeliad trilogy. 1989–1991); *The Amazing Maurice and His Educated Rodents.* 2001; *The Wee Free Men.* 2003

Pullman, Philip. *The Golden Compass.* 1995, 1996 (His Dark Materials trilogy, 1995–2000)

Rodda, Emily. *Rowan of Rin.* 2001 (Rowan of Rin series, 2001–2003)

Shinn, Sharon. *The Safe-Keeper's Secret.* 2004

Smith, Sherwood. *Crown Duel.* 1997, 2002 (The Crown and Court Duet, 1997, 1998, 2002)

Snicket, Lemony. *The Bad Beginning.* 1999. (A Series of Unfortunate Events, 1999–)

Stroud, Jonathan. *The Amulet of Samarkand.* 2003 (The Bartimaeus trilogy, 2003–)

Turner, Megan Whalen. *The Thief.* 1996

Vande Velde, Vivian. *Dragon's Bait.* 1992

Voigt, Cynthia. *On Fortune's Wheel.* 1990; *Elske.* 1999 (The Kingdom saga, 1985–1999)

Wilder, Cherry. Rulers of Hylor trilogy. 1984–1986

Wooding, Chris. *The Haunting of Alaizabel Cray.* 2004

Wrede, Patricia C. *Dealing with Dragons,* 1990 (Enchanted Forest Chronicles. 1990–1993)

Wrede, Patricia, and Caroline Stevermer. *Sorcery and Cecelia.* 1988, 2003

Yep, Laurence M. Dragon quartet. 1982–1992

Yolen, Jane. Pit Dragons trilogy. 1982–1987

Zettner, Pat. *The Shadow Warrior.* 1990

High Fantasy: Myth and Legend Fantasy

T. H. White's *The Sword in the Stone* (1938, 1939) was the forerunner of the retold-myth type of fantasy, represented more recently by:

Alcock, Vivien. *Singer to the Sea God.* 1992

Alexander, Lloyd. Chronicles of Prydain series. 1964–1968

Bradshaw, Gillian. *Hawk of May.* 1980

Briggs, K. M. *Kate Crackernuts.* 1963, 1979, 1980

Coolidge, Olivia. *The King of Men.* 1966

Cooney, Caroline B. *Goddess of Yesterday.* 2002

Crossley-Holland, Kevin. *The Seeing Stone.* 2000, 2001 (Arthur Trilogy 2000–2004)

Curry, Jane Louise. *The Sleepers.* 1968

Farjeon, Eleanor. *The Glass Slipper.* 1945, 1956, 1986

Farmer, Nancy. *The Sea of Trolls.* 2004

Gardner, John C. *Grendel.* 1971

Garfield, Leon, and Blishen, Edward. *The God Beneath the Sea.* 1970, 1971

Hale, Shannon. The Goose Girl trilogy. 2003–

Hamilton, Virginia. *The Magical Adventures of Pretty Pearl.* 1983
Harris, Rosemary. *The Moon in the Cloud.* 1968 (The Reuben trilogy. 1968–1972)
Ipcar, Dahlov. *The Queen of Spells.* 1973
Johnston, Norma. *Strangers Dark and Gold.* 1975
Langrish, Katherine. *Troll Fell.* 2004
Levine, Gail Carson. *Ella Enchanted.* 1997
McKinley, Robin. *Beauty.* 1978; *The Outlaws of Sherwood.* 1988; *Rose Daughter.* 1997; *Spindle's End.* 2000
Maguire, Gregory. *Confessions of an Ugly Stepsister.* 1999
Morris, Gerald. *The Squire's Tale.* 1998 (Denizens of Camelot series, 1998–2004)
Napoli, Donna Jo. *Zel.* 1996; *Sirena.* 1998; *Crazy Jack.* 1999; *Beast.* 2000; *Bound.* 2004
Orgel, Doris. *Ariadne, Awake!* 1994
Pattou, Edith. *East.* 2003
Seraillier, Ian. *The Challenge of the Green Knight.* 1967
Springer, Nancy. *I Am Mordred: A Tale from Camelot.* 1998; *I Am Morgan Le Fay: A Tale from Camelot.* 2001
Sutcliff, Rosemary. The Sword and the Circle trilogy. 1979–1982; *Black Ships Before Troy: The Story of the Iliad.* 1993
Thomson, Sarah L. *The Dragon's Son.* 2001
Wein, Elizabeth E. *The Winter Prince.* 1993 (Medrault trilogy, 1993–2004)
Yolen, Jane. *The Dragon's Boy.* 1990; The Young Merlin trilogy. 1996–1997; *Sword of the Rightful King: A Novel of King Arthur.* 2003

Outstanding stories of contemporary involvement with myth include:

Alcock, Vivien. *The Stonewalkers.* 1983
Almond, David. *Skellig.* 1998, 1999
Babbitt, Natalie. *Tuck Everlasting.* 1975
Black, Holly. *Tithe: A Modern Faerie Tale.* 2002
Cooper, Susan. The Dark Is Rising sequence. 1966–1977
Curry, Jane Louise. *The Sleepers.* 1968
Dunlop, Eileen. *Clementina.* 1985, 1987
Farmer, Penelope. *A Castle of Bone.* 1972
Garfield, Leon. *The Wedding Ghost.* 1985, 1987
Garner, Alan. *The Owl Service.* 1967, 1968; *The Weirdstone of Brisingamen.* 1960
Harris, Rosemary. *The Seal-Singing.* 1971
Hunter, Mollie. *A Stranger Came Ashore.* 1975
Lawrence, Louise. *Star Lord.* 1978
Lively, Penelope. *The Wild Hunt of the Ghost Hounds.* 1971, 1972
Mayne, William. *Earthfasts.* 1966, 1967
O'Shea, Pat. *The Hounds of the Morrigan.* 1985, 1986
Service, Pamela. *Winter of Magic's Return.* 1985
Wangerin, Water, Jr. *The Crying for a Vision.* 1994
Wrightson, Patricia. *The Ice Is Coming.* 1977 (The Wirrun trilogy. 1977–1981); *Balyet.* 1989

High Fantasy: Travel to Other Worlds

The best contemporary children's and young adult books in the category of travel to other worlds include:

Alexander, Lloyd. *The First Two Lives of Lukas-Kasha.* 1978
Chabon, Michael. *Summerland.* 2002
Chant, Joy. *Red Moon and Black Mountain.* 1970, 1971, 1976
Christopher, John. Fireball trilogy. 1981–1986
Collins, Suzanne. *Gregor the Overlander.* 2003 (The Underland Chronicles, 2003–)
Cooper, Susan. *Seaward.* 1983
Dalton, Annie. *Out of the Ordinary.* 1988, 1990
Duane, Diane. *So You Want to Be a Wizard.* 1983 (Young Wizards series, 1983–2003)
Ende, Michael. *The Neverending Story.* 1983
Fisk, Pauline. *Midnight Blue.* 1990, 2003
Gaiman, Neil. *Stardust.* 1998; *Coraline.* 2002
Garner, Alan. *Elidor.* 1965, 1967
Hilgartner, Beth. *Colors of the Dreamweaver's Loom.* 1989
Jones, Diana Wynne. *The Lives of Christopher Chant.* 1988 (Chrestomanci series, 1978–2000, 2001)
Lawrence, Michael. *A Crack in the Line.* 2004 (The Withern Rise trilogy, 2004–)
Le Guin, Ursula K. *The Beginning Place.* 1980
McGraw, Eloise. *The Moorchild.* 1996
Mahy, Margaret. *Dangerous Spaces.* 1991
Naylor, Phyllis Reynolds. *Sang Spell.* 1998
Nodelman, Perry. *The Same Place But Different.* 1995
Pope, Elizabeth. *The Perilous Gard.* 1974
Prue, Sally. *Cold Tom.* 2002, 2003
Pullman, Philip. *The Golden Compass.* 1995, 1996 (His Dark Materials trilogy, 1995–2000)
Rowling, J. K. *Harry Potter and the Sorcerer's Stone.* 1997, 1998 (Harry Potter series, 1997–)
Westall, Robert. *The Devil on the Road.* 1979
Winthrop, Elizabeth. The Castle in the Attic series. 1985, 1993

Humorous Fantasy

Humorous fantasy continues to be popular, although more humorous stories seem to be written for children than for young adults. The well-loved stories by Dr. Seuss, Richard and Florence Atwater, William Pène du Bois, and Oliver Butterworth have been followed by:

Babbitt, Natalie. The Devil's Storybook duology. 1974, 1987
Cresswell, Helen. *The Piemakers.* 1967, 1980
Dahl, Roald. *Matilda.* 1988

Dickinson, Peter. *Chuck and Danielle*. 1996
Fleischman, Sid. Numerous tall tales. 1962–1990
Gilmore, Kate. *Enter Three Witches*. 1990
Horvath, Polly. *The Pepins and Their Problems*. 2004
Kindl, Patrice. *Owl in Love*. 1993; *Goose Chase*. 2001
King-Smith, Dick. *Harry's Mad*. 1986
Le Vert, John. *The Flight of the Cassowary*. 1986
Mahy, Margaret. *The Great White Man-Eating Shark*. 1989, 1990
Napoli, Donna Jo. *The Prince of the Pond*. 1992 (The Frog Prince trilogy, 1992–2004)
Nöstlinger, Christine. *Konrad*. 1977
Peck, Richard. *The Ghost Belonged to Me*. 1975 (The Blossom Culp quartet 1975–1986)
Pinkwater, Daniel Manus. Numerous offbeat stories. 1976–1986
Raskin, Ellen. *Figgs and Phantoms*. 1974
Rodgers, Mary. Freaky Friday trilogy. 1972–1983
Scieszka, Jon. *The Stinky Cheese Man and Other Fairly Stupid Tales*. 1992

Magic Adventure Fantasy

The magic adventure tradition of E. Nesbit, P. L. Travers, and C. S. Lewis has been continued in:

Brittain, Bill. *The Wish Giver*. 1983
Cassedy, Sylvia. *Behind the Attic Wall*. 1983
Colfer, Eoin. Artemis Fowl series. 2001–
Cresswell, Helen. *The Secret World of Polly Flint*. 1982
Curry, Jane Louise. *Mindy's Mysterious Miniature*. 1970
Dickinson, Peter. *Inside Grandad*. 2004
Duane, Diane. *So You Want to Be a Wizard*. 1983 (Young Wizards series, 1983–2003)
Farmer, Penelope. *The Summer Birds*. 1962
Funke, Cornelia Caroline. *The Thief Lord*. 2000, 2002; *Inkheart*. 2003
Gray, Luli. *Falcon's Egg*. 1995
Jones, Diana Wynne. *The Ogre Downstairs*. 1974, 1990
Konigsburg, E. L. *Up from Jericho Tel*. 1986
Langton, Jane. *The Fledgling*. 1980
Lisle, Janet Taylor. *The Lost Flower Children*. 1999
McCaughrean, Geraldine. *A Pack of Lies*. 1988, 1989
McEwan, Ian. *The Daydreamer*. 1994
McKay, Hilary. *Saffy's Angel*. 2001, 2002
Mahy, Margaret. *The Changeover*. 1984; *The Haunting*. 1982; *Alchemy*. 2003
Murphy, Rita. *Night Flying*. 2000
Norton, Mary. *The Borrowers Avenged*. 1982 (The Borrowers series, 1952, 1953–1982)
Pearce, Philippa. *The Little Gentleman*. 2004

Pullman, Philip. *Clockwork*. 1997, 1998

Reid Banks, Lynne. The Indian in the Cupboard quartet. 1980–1993

Rowling, J. K. *Harry Potter and the Sorcerer's Stone*. 1997, 1998 (Harry Potter series, 1997–)

Rylant, Cynthia. *The Islander*. 1998

Selden, George. *The Genie of Sutton Place*. 1973

Snyder, Zilpha Keatley. *Black and Blue Magic*. 1966

Townsend, John Rowe. *The Persuading Stick*. 1986, 1987

Van Allsburg, Chris. *Jumanji*. 1981

Waugh, Sylvia. The Mennyms series. 1993, 1994 – 1996, 1997

Wells, Rosemary. *Through the Hidden Door*. 1987

Winthrop, Elizabeth. The Castle in the Attic series. 1985–1993

Time Travel Fantasy

The concept of time travel continues to fascinate readers of all ages, although its complexities are best understood by young people from about age 10 up. Outstanding books that have followed in the footsteps of E. Nesbit's *The Story of the Amulet*, Alison Uttley's *A Traveller in Time*, and Philippa Pearce's *Tom's Midnight Garden* include:

Barber, Antonia. *The Ghosts*. 1969

Bond, Nancy. *A String in the Harp*. 1976

Buffie, Margaret. *The Haunting of Frances Rain*. 1987, 1989

Cameron, Eleanor. *Beyond Silence*. 1980

Conrad, Pan. *Stonewords*. 1990

Cooper, Susan. *King of Shadows*. 1999

Cresswell, Helen. *Moondial*. 1987; *Up the Pier*. 1971

Curry, Jane Louise. *Over the Sea's Edge*. 1971

Davies, Andrew. *Conrad's War*. 1978, 1980

Dexter, Catherine. *Mazemaker*. 1989

Farmer, Penelope. *Charlotte Sometimes*. 1969

Fleischman, Sid. *The Thirteenth Floor: A Ghost Story*. 1995

Garner, Alan. *The Red Shift*. 1973

Hahn, Mary Downing. *Time for Andrew: A Ghost Story*. 1994

Heneghan, James. *The Grave*. 2000

James, J. Alison. *Sing for a Gentle Rain*. 1990

Jones, Diana Wynne. *A Charmed Life*. 1977, 1978

Lyon, George Ella. *Here and Then*. 1994

Mayne, William. *A Game of Dark*. 1971

Naylor, Phyllis Reynolds. *Shadows on the Wall*. 1980 (The York trilogy. 1980–1981)

Park, Ruth. *Playing Beatie Bow*. 1982

Parker, Richard. *The Old Powder Line*. 1971

Paton Walsh, Jill. *A Chance Child*. 1978

Peck, Richard. *Voices After Midnight*. 1989

Reiss, Kathryn. *Time Windows*. 1991; *Dreadful Sorry*. 1993

Stolz, Mary. *Cat in the Mirror*. 1975
Wesley, Mary. *Haphazard House*. 1983, 1993
Westall, Robert. *The Devil on the Road*. 1978, 1980; *The Wind Eye*. 1976, 1977
Wiseman, David. *Jeremy Visick*. 1981
Yolen, Jane. *The Devil's Arithmetic*. 1988

Toy Fantasy

Novels about toys or other inanimate objects that come to life are published less frequently than they were in the past, although such old favorites as E. T. A. Hoffmann's *The Nutcracker* (1819), Margery Williams Bianco's *The Velveteen Rabbit* (1922), A. A. Milne's *Winnie-the-Pooh* (1926), Rachel Field's *Hitty, Her First Hundred Years* (1929), Anne Parrish's *Floating Island* (1930), Carolyn Sherwin Bailey's *Miss Hickory* (1946), and Rumer Godden's numerous doll stories (1947–1964) are still popular and frequently reprinted. The most memorable contemporary toy fantasies include:

Cassedy, Sylvia. *Behind the Attic Wall*. 1983
Gardam, Jane. *Through the Doll's House Door*. 1987
Kennedy, Richard. *Amy's Eyes*. 1985
Mahy, Margaret. *The Five Sisters*. 1996, 1997
Martin, Ann M., and Laura Godwin. *The Doll People*. 2000
Nabb, Magdalen. *The Enchanted Horse*. 1992, 1993
O'Connell, Jean. *The Dollhouse Caper*. 1976
Reid Banks, Lynne. The Indian in the Cupboard quartet. 1980–1993
Sleator, William. *Among the Dolls*. 1975, 1985
Waugh, Sylvia. The Mennyms series. 1993, 1994–1996, 1997
Wright, Betty Ren. *The Dollhouse Murders*. 1983

Witchcraft and Sorcery Fantasy

The best of the contemporary witchcraft and sorcery novels for young people include the Harry Potter books and many others:

Bedard, Michael. *A Darker Magic*. 1987
Bell, Hilari. *The Goblin Wood*. 2003
Bellairs, John. *The Curse of the Blue Figurine*. 1983
Brittain, Bill. *The Devil's Donkey*. 1981 (The Coven Tree saga. 1981–1990)
Dickinson, Peter. *The Tears of the Salamander*. 2003
Duane, Diane. *So You Want to Be a Wizard*. 1983 (Young Wizards series, 1983–2003)
Furlong, Monica. *Wise Child*. 1987; *Juniper*. 1990, 1991
Gilmore, Kate. *Enter Three Witches*. 1990
Harris, Deborah Turner. *The Burning Stone*. 1987
Hunter, Mollie. *Thomas and the Warlock*. 1967, 1986

Jones, Diana Wynne. *Howl's Moving Castle*. 1986; *The Lives of Christopher Chant*. 1988 (Chrestomanci series, 1978–2000, 2001); *The Dark Lord of Derkholm*. 1998; *The Merlin Conspiracy*. 2003

Kindl, Patrice. *Owl in Love*. 1993

Mahy, Margaret. *The Changeover*. 1984; *The Haunting*. 1982; *Alchemy*. 2003

Nix, Garth. *Sabriel*. 1995, 1996 (Abhorsen trilogy, 1995–2003)

Pierce, Tamora. *Sandry's Book*. 1997. (Circle of Magic quartet, 1997–1999)

Preussler, Otfried. *The Satanic Mill*. 1971, 1973

Rowling, J. K. *Harry Potter and the Sorcerer's Stone*. 1997, 1998 (Harry Potter series, 1997–)

Sedgwick, Marcus. The Book of Dead Days series. 2004

Stroud, Jonathan. *The Amulet of Samarkand*. 2003 (The Bartimaeus trilogy, 2003–)

Turner, Ann. *Rosemary's Witch*. 1991

Wrede, Patricia, and Caroline Stevermer. *Sorcery and Cecelia*. 1988, 2003

Zambreno, Mary Frances. *A Plague of Sorcerers*. 1991

Crossover Fantasy: Adult Fantasy Read by Young Adults

Many readers who devoured children's and young adult fantasy novels have discovered the ever-expanding genre of adult fantasy. These crossover novels, frequently part of a series, include:

Anthony, Piers. The Magic of Xanth series. 1977–1994

Asimov, Isaac, Charles G. Waugh, and Martin H. Greenberg. *Dragon Tales*. 1982

Asprin, Robert L. Myth Adventure series. 1978–1987

Beagle, Peter S. *The Last Unicorn*. 1968

Bradley, Marion Zimmer. Darkover series. 1962–1994; *Hawkmistress!* 1982; *The Mists of Avalon*. 1982

Brust, Steven. *The Paths of the Dead*. 2002

Bull, Emma. *Finder: A Novel of the Borderlands*. 1994, 2003

Bujold, Lois McMaster. *The Curse of Chalion*. 2001

Butler, Octavia E. *Kindred*. 1979

Card, Orson Scott. *Seventh Son*. 1987 (Tales of Alvin Maker series, 1987–2003)

Cherryh, C. J. *Angel with the Sword*. 1985

Clarke, Susanna. *Jonathan Strange and Mr. Norrell*. 2004

Dart-Thornton, Cecilia. *The Ill-Made Mute*. 2001

De Lint, Charles. *Someplace to Be Flying*. 1998 (Newford stories, 1990–)

Dickson, Gordon R. *The Dragon and the George*. 1976 (Dragon Knight series. 1976–2000)

Donaldson, Stephen R. Chronicles of Thomas Covenant, the Unbeliever. 1977–1983

Egan, Doris. *The Gate of Ivory*. 1989

Feist, Raymond E. *Silverthorn*. 1985

Finney, Jack. *Time and Again*. 1970

Goldstein, Lisa. *The Red Magician*. 1982, 1993

Hambley, Barbara. *Dragonsbane*. 1986

Jones, Diana Wynne. *Fire and Hemlock*. 1984

Keyes, J. Gregory. *The Waterborn.* 1996
Kurtz, Katherine. The Chronicles of Deryni. 1970–1991
Kushner, Ellen, and Delia Sherman. *The Fall of the Kings.* 2002
Lackey, Mercedes. Mage Wind trilogy. 1991–1993; *Sacred Ground.* 1994
MacAvoy, R. A. *The Book of Kells.* 1985
McCaffrey, Anne. Dragonriders of Pern series. 1968–1994
McKinley, Robin. *Deerskin.* 1993
Mahfouz, Naguib. *Arabian Nights and Days.* 1979, 1995
Marillier, Juliet. *Daughter of the Forest.* 2000 (Sevenwaters trilogy, 2000–2002)
Matheson, Richard. *Bid Time Return.* 1975
Norton, Andre, and Mercedes Lackey. *The Elvenbane.* 1991.
Odom, Mel. *The Rover.* 2001
Orwell, George. *Animal Farm.* 1945, 1982
The Pendragon Chronicles. Ed. by Mike Ashley. 1989, 1990
Pratchett, Terry. Discworld series. 1980–2003
Shwartz, Susan. *Moonsinger's Friends.* 1985
Silverberg, Robert. *Lord Valentine's Castle.* 1980
Springer, Nancy. *Chains of Gold.* 1986
Stewart, Mary. *The Crystal Cave.* 1970 (The Merlin quartet. 1970–1979)
Stewart. Sean. *Galveston.* 2000
Tarr, Judith. The Hounds of God cycle. 1985–1991; *A Fall of Princes.* 1988
Tolkien, J. R. R. Lord of the Rings trilogy. 1954, 1967, 1992
Volsky, Paula. *The Grand Ellipse.* 2000
Warner, Sylvia Townsend. *Kingdoms of Elfin.* 1976
Wellman, Manly Wade. Silver John series. 1963–1984
Windling, Terri. *The Wood Wife.* 1996
Willard, Nancy. *Things Invisible to See.* 1985
Wolfe, Gene. The Book of the New Sun series. 1980–1983
Zelazny, Roger. *Nine Princes in Amber* (The Amber series. 1970–1991)

AWARD-WINNING FANTASY LITERATURE

This list includes international and national literary awards won by children's and young adult fantasy novels, story collections, authors, and illustrators. State and provincial award winners are not listed.

The American Book Award

Awarded between 1980 and 1986 by the Association of American Publishers for the most distinguished books of the preceding year published in the United States, in a number of categories. It replaced the National Book Award (see below), and was renamed the National Book Award in 1987. The Children's Book categories were discontinued in 1984.

1980 Science Fiction. *The Book of the Dun Cow*. Walter Wangerin

1982 Children's Fiction. *Westmark*. Lloyd Alexander

1982 Graphic Design. *Jumanji*. Chris Van Allsburg

1983 Pictorial Design. *Alice's Adventures in Wonderland*, illus. by Barry Moser. Lewis Carroll

1983 Original Paperback. *The Red Magician*. Lisa Goldstein

Hans Christian Andersen Medal

Awarded biennially by the International Board on Books for Young People (IBBY) to an author and an illustrator in recognition of his or her entire body of work.

1956 Author. Eleanor Farjeon (Great Britain)

1958 Author. Astrid Lindgren (Sweden)

1960 Author. Erich Kästner (Germany)

1964 Author. René Guillot (France)

1966 Author. Tove Jansson (Finland)

1968 Author. José Maria Sanchez-Silva (Spain)

1968 Author. James Krüss (Germany)

1968 Highly Commended Author. Elizabeth Coatsworth (United States)

1970 Highly Commended Author. E. B. White (United States)

1970 Illustrator. Maurice Sendak (United States)

1972 Highly Commended Author. Otfried Preussler (Germany)

1972 Highly Commended Author. Maria Gripe (Sweden)

1974 Author. Maria Gripe (Sweden)

1974 Highly Commended Author. Rosemary Sutcliff (Great Britain)

1976 Highly Commended Author. E. B. White (United States)

1978 Highly Commended Author. Alan Garner (Great Britain)

1984 Author. Christine Nöstlinger (Austria)

1986 Author. Patricia Wrightson (Australia)

1992 Author. Virginia Hamilton (United States)

1998 Auhor: Katherine Paterson (United States)

May Hill Arbuthnot Honor Lecture Award

Awarded annually by the Association for Library Service to Children, American Library Association, to an individual of distinction in the field of children's literature, who will write and deliver a lecture that will make a significant contribution to the world of children's literature.

1975 Mollie Hunter

1985 Patricia Wrightson

1989 Margaret Mahy

1993 Virginia Hamilton

1997 Katherine Paterson

2001 Susan Cooper

2002 Philip Pullman

2003 Maurice Sendak

2004 Ursula K. LeGuin

Australian Children's Book of the Year Award

See Children's Book Council of Australia Book of the Year Award.

Mildred L. Batchelder Award

Awarded by the Association for Library Service to Children, American Library Association, to a U.S. publisher for the most outstanding English translation of a children's book originally published in a foreign language in a foreign country during the preceding year.

1968 *The Little Man* (Harcourt). Erich Kästner

1978 *Konrad* (Watts). Christine Nöstlinger

1979 *Rabbit Island* (Harcourt). Jörg Steiner

1984 *Ronia, the Robber's Daughter* (Viking). Astrid Lindgren

1998 Honor Book. *Nero Corleone: A Cat's Story* (Viking). Elke Heidenreich

2003 *The Thief Lord* (Chicken House/Scholastic). Corneila Funke

Boston Globe-Horn Book Award

Cosponsored by *The Boston Globe* and *The Horn Book Magazine*, for outstanding fiction, nonfiction, and illustration.

1968 Text. *The Spring Rider*. John Lawson

1969 Text. *A Wizard of Earthsea*. Ursula K. Le Guin

1971 Text Honor. *Mrs. Frisby and the Rats of NIMH*. Robert C. O'Brien

1972 Text. *Tristan and Iseult*. Rosemary Sutcliff

1973 Text. *The Dark Is Rising*. Susan Cooper

1973 Illustration. *King Stork*, illus. by Trina Schart Hyman. Howard Pyle

1976 Fiction Honor. *A Stranger Came Ashore*. Mollie Hunter

1976 Fiction Honor. *A String in the Harp*. Nancy Bond

1979 Fiction. *Humbug Mountain*. Sid Fleischman

1980 Fiction. *Conrad's War*. Andrew Davies

1980 Illustration. *The Garden of Abdul Gasazi*. Chris Van Allsburg

1981 Illustration Honor. *Jumanji*. Chris Van Allsburg

1982 Fiction. *Playing Beatie Bow*. Ruth Park

1982 Fiction Honor. *The Scarecrows*. Robert Westall

1983 Fiction. *Sweet Whispers, Brother Rush*. Virginia Hamilton

1983 Fiction Honor. *The Road to Camlann*. Rosemary Sutcliff

1984 Fiction. *A Little Fear*. Patricia Wrightson

1984 Fiction Honor. *Archer's Goon*. Diana Wynne Jones

1985 Fiction Honor. *The Changeover*. Margaret Many

1986 Fiction Honor. *Howl's Moving Castle*. Diana Wynne Jones

1990 Fiction Honor. *Stonewords*. Pam Conrad

1993 Fiction Honor. *The Giver*. Lois Lowry

1996 Fiction. *Poppy*. Avi

1996 Fiction Honor. *The Moorchild*. Eloise McGraw

2000 Fiction. *The Folk Keeper*. Franny Billingsley

2000 Fiction Honor. *King of Shadows*. Susan Cooper

2002 Fiction Honor. *Saffy's Angel*. Hilary McKay

British Book Award, Children's Book of the Year

Awarded annually and chosen by more than 150 representatives from all areas of the book trade.

1996 *Northern Lights* (U.S. title: *The Golden Compass*). Philip Pullman

1997 *Harry Potter and the Philosopher's Stone*. J. K. Rowling

1998 *Harry Potter and the Chamber of Secrets*. J. K. Rowling

2000 *The Amber Spyglass*. Philip Pullman

2001 *Artemis Fowl*. Eoin Colfer

2001 Author of the Year. Philip Pullman

2002 *Artemis Fowl: The Arctic Incident*. Eoin Colfer

British Fantasy Award

Awarded annually by the British Fantasy Society. Not limited to British authors. Named the August Derleth Fantasy Award from 1971 to 1976. From 1977 on, the August Derleth Fantasy Award has been given in the best novel category. Winners in the remaining categories receive the British Fantasy Award.

1976 Best Novel. *The Dragon and the George*. Gordon R. Dickson

1977 Best Novel. *A Spell for Chameleon*. Piers Anthony

1978 Best Novel. The Chronicles of Thomas Covenant (trilogy). Stephen Donaldson

1982 Best Novel. *The Sword of the Lictor*. Gene Wolfe

1984 Special Award. Manley Wade Wellman

1993 Committee Award: Michael Moorcock

1999 Karl Edward Wagner Award (Special Award): Diana Wynne Jones

2000 Karl Edward Wagner Award (Special Award): Anne McCaffrey

Randolph Caldecott Medal

Awarded by the Association for Library Service to Children, American Library Association, to the artist of the most distinguished American picture book for children published in the United States during the preceding year.

1944 *Many Moons*, illus. by Louis Slobodkin. James Thurber

1950 Honor. *Bartholomew and the Oobleck*. Dr. Seuss

1954 Honor. *The Steadfast Tin Soldier*, illus. by Marcia Brown. Hans Christian Andersen

1980 Honor. *The Garden of Abdul Gazasi*. Chris Van Allsburg

1982 *Jumanji*. Chris Van Allsburg

1993 Honor. *The Stinky Cheese Man and Other Fairly Stupid Tales*, illus. by Lane Smith. Jon Scieszka

Canadian Governor General's Award for Children's Literature

See Governor General's Literary Award for Children's Literature

Canadian Library Association Book of the Year for Children Award

Awarded by the Canadian Library Association to an outstanding children's book by a Canadian author.

1973 *Marrow of the World*. Ruth Nichols

1976 *Jacob Two-Two Meets the Hooded Fang*. Mordecai Richler

1980 *Uncle Jacob's Ghost Story*. Don Kushner

1981 *The Violin-Maker's Gift*. Don Kushner

1982 *The Root Cellar*. Janet Lunn

1987 *Shadow in Hawthorn Bay*. Janet Lunn

1988 *A Handful of Time*. Kit Pearson

1989 Runner-Up. *The Third Magic*. Welwyn W.Katz

1991 *Redwork*. Michael Bedard

1994 Illustration. *The Dragon's Pearl*. Julie Lawson; illus. by Paul Morin

1998 *Silverwing*. Kenneth Oppel

2000 *Sunwing*. Kenneth Oppel

Canadian Science Fiction and Fantasy Prix Aurora Award

Awarded annually to English- or French-speaking Canadian writers of science fiction and fantasy novels.

1987 *The Wandering Fire*. Guy Gavriel Kay

1988 *Jack the Giant Killer*. Charles de Lint

Carnegie Medal

Awarded by The [British] Library Association to the outstanding book for children written in English and published in the United Kingdom.

1942 *The Little Grey Men*. B.B. [Denys Watkins-Pitchford]

1944 *The Wind on the Moon*. Eric Linklater

1946 *The Little White Horse*. Elizabeth Goudge

1947 *Collected Stories for Children*. Walter De La Mare

1952 *The Borrowers*. Mary Norton

1954 Commended. *The Children of Green Knowe*. L. M. Boston

1954 Commended. *The Horse and His Boy*. C. S. Lewis

1954 Commended. *The Lady of the Linden Tree*. Barbara Picard

1955 *The Little Bookroom*. Eleanor Farjeon

1956 *The Last Battle*. C. S. Lewis

1956 Commended. *The Fairy Doll*. Rumer Godden

1957 *A Grass Rope*. William Mayne

1957 Commended. *The Blue Boat*. William Mayne

1958 *Tom's Midnight Garden*. Philippa Pearce

1958 Commended. *The Chimneys of Green Knowe*. L.M.Boston

1959 Commended. *The Borrowers Afloat*. Mary Norton

1959 Commended. *The Rescuers*. Marjorie Sharp

1961 Commended. *Miss Happiness and Miss Flower*. Rumer Godden

1962 *The Twelve and the Genii.* Pauline Clarke

1962 Commended. *The Summer Birds.* Penelope Farmer

1965 Commended. *Elidor.* Alan Garner

1967 *The Owl Service.* Alan Garner

1967 Commended. *The Piemakers.* Helen Cresswell

1968 *The Moon in the Cloud.* Rosemary Harris

1968 Honour. *The Whispering Mountain.* Joan Aiken

1969 Honour. *The Night Watchmen.* Helen Cresswell

1970 *The God Beneath the Sea.* Leon Garfield and Edward Blishen

1970 Honour. *The Devil's Children.* Peter Dickinson

1971 Highly Commended. *Tristan and Iseult.* Rosemary Sutcliff

1971 Highly Commended. *Up the Pier.* Helen Cresswell

1972 *Watership Down.* Richard Adams

1973 *The Ghost of Thomas Kempe.* Penelope Lively

1973 Commended. *The Bongleweed.* Helen Cresswell

1973 Commended. *The Dark Is Rising.* Susan Cooper

1975 Commended. *Dogsbody.* Diana Wynne Jones

1975 Commended. *The Grey King.* Susan Cooper

1976 Commended. *The Blue Hawk.* Peter Dickinson

1977 Commended. *Charmed Life.* Diana Wynne Jones

1977 Commended. *The Shadow-Cage and Other Tales.* Philippa Pearce

1978 Commended. *The Devil on the Road.* Robert Westall

1981 *The Scarecrows.* Robert Westall

1982 *The Haunting.* Margaret Mahy

1984 *The Changeover.* Margaret Mahy

1987 *The Ghost Drum.* Christine Price

1987 Commended. *Wise Child.* Monica Furlong

1987 Commended. *The House on the Hill.* Eileen Dunlop

1987 Commended. *King of the Cloud Forest.* Michael Morpurgo

1988 *A Pack of Lies.* Geraldine McCaughrean

1988 Commended. *The Monster Garden.* Vivien Alcock

1988 Commended. *The Lives of Christopher Chant.* Diana Wynne Jones

1995 *Northern Lights* (U.S. title, *The Golden Compass*). Philip Pullman.

1996 Commended. *Clockwork, or All Wound Up.* Philip Pullman.

1997 Commended. *Harry Potter and the Philosopher's Stone.* J. K. Rowling

1998 *Skellig.* David Almond

1999 Highly Commended. *Kit's Wilderness.* David Almond

2000 Highly Commended. *The Amber Spyglass.* Philip Pullman.

2001 *Amazing Maurice and His Educated Rodents.* Terry Pratchett.

Children's Book Council of Australia Children's Book of the Year Award

Awarded annually by the Children's Book Council of Australia.

1974 *The Nargun and the Stars*. Patricia Wrightson

1978 *The Ice Is Coming*. Patricia Wrightson

1981 *Playing Beatie Bow*. Ruth Park

1983 *Master of the Grove*. Victor Kelleher

1984 *A Little Fear*. Patricia Wrightson

1987 *Pigs Might Fly*. Entity Rodda

1989 *The Best-Kept Secret*. Emily Rodda

1991 Older Readers. *Strange Objects*. Gary Crew

1991 Younger Readers. *Finders Keepers*. Emily Rodda

1994 Younger Readers. *Rowan of Rin*. Emily Rodda

1995 Older Readers. *Foxspell*. Gillian Rubinstein

1995 Honour Book. *Somewhere Around the Corner*. Jackie French

2004 Honour Book. *Mister Monday*. Garth Nix

Margaret A. Edwards Award

Formerly called the YASD/SLJ Young Adult Author Award (1988–1990). Awarded by the Young Adult Library Services Association, American Library Association, to an outstanding U.S. author for lifetime achievement in young adult literature, and a lifetime contribution to young adult readers.

1989 Richard Peck

1993 M. E. Kerr (pseudonym of Marijane Meaker; uses the pseudonym Mary James for her fantasy novels)

1995 Cynthia Voigt

1998 Madeleine L'Engle

1999 Anne McCaffrey

2004 Ursula K. Le Guin

Esther Glen Award

Awarded by the Library and Information Association of New Zealand Aoteaora to a New Zealand citizen or resident for a book that is considered to be the most distinguished contribution of the year to literature for children or young adults.

1959 Winner. *Falter Tom and the Water Boy*. Maurice Duggan

1983 Winner. *The Haunting*. Margaret Mahy

1985 Winner. *The Changeover*. Margaret Mahy

1990 Short List. *The Blood-and-Thunder Adventure on Hurricane Peak*. Margaret Mahy

1992 Short List. *The Juniper Game*. Sherryl Jordan

1992 Short List. *The Wednesday Wizard*. Sherryl Jordan (continued by *Denzil's Dilemma*)

1995 Short List. *Tanith*. (U.S. title *Wolf-Woman*). Sherryl Jordan

1996 Short List. *Tingleberries, Tuckertubs and Telephones: A Tale of Love and Ice-Cream*. Margaret Mahy

2003 Short List. *Alchemy*. Margaret Mahy

Golden Cat Award

International award given by the Swedish Publishers' Association (Stockholm, Sweden) to an author of any nationality who has created works of distinction and quality in fiction for children and young adults.

1984 Lloyd Alexander (United States)

1985 Leon Garfield (Great Britain)

1986 Patricia Wrightson (Australia)

1988 Philippa Pearce (Great Britain)

1990 Peter Dickinson (Great Britain)

Golden Kite Award

Awarded by the Society of Children's Book Writers and Illustrators to works of fiction, nonfiction, and illustration that exhibit excellence in writing and genuinely appeal to the interests and concerns of children.

1973 Fiction Honor. *McBroom the Rainmaker*. Sid Fleischman

1974 Fiction. *The Girl Who Cried Flowers and Other Tales*. Jane Yolen

1975 Fiction Honor. *The Transfigured Hart*. Jane Yolen

1976 Fiction Honor. *The Moon Ribbon and Other Tales*. Jane Yolen

1980 Fiction Honor. *The Half-a-Moon Inn*. Paul Fleischman

1982 Fiction. *Ralph S. Mouse*. Beverly Cleary

1987 Fiction Honor. *The Great Dimpole Oak*. Janet Taylor Lisle

1988 Fiction Honor. *The Reluctant God*. Pamela F. Service

1993 Fiction Honor. *Owl in Love*. Patrice Kindl

1996 Fiction. *The Moorchild*. Eloise McGraw

2003 Fiction Honor. *Breath*. Donna Jo Napoli

Governor General's Literary Award for Children's Literature

Awarded by the Canada Council for the Arts to outstanding books for young people written in English and in French and/or illustrated by Canadians during the preceding year.

1986 Text. *Shadow in Hawthorn Bay*. Janet Lunn

1988 Text. *The Third Magic*. Welwyn W. Katz

1990 Text. *Redwork*. Michael Bedard

2001 Text. *Dust*. Arthur Slade

2004 Text. *Airborn*. Kenneth Oppel

Grand Master of Fantasy Award

See Hugo Award.

Great Prize of the Swedish Academy

1994 Tove Jansson

Kate Greenaway Medal

Awarded by the Library Association (London, UK) to an artist who has produced the most distinguished work in the illustration of a children's book published in the previous year.

1970 Honors List. *The God Beneath the Sea*. Edward Blishen and Leon Garfield

1972 Commended. *The Ghost Downstairs*, illus. by Antony Maitland. Leon Garfield

1976 Highly Commended. *The Church Mice Adrift*. Graham Oakley

1982 Highly Commended. *The Church Mice in Action*. Graham Oakley

1985 *Sir Gawain and the Loathly Lady*, illus. by Juan Wijngaard. Selina Hastings

1987 Commended. *The Enchanter's Daughter*, illus. by Errol LeCain. Antonia Barber

1988 Highly Commended. *Alice's Adventures in Wonderland*, illus. by Anthony Browne. Lewis Carroll

1988 Highly Commended. *The Adventures of Pinocchio*, illus. by Roberto Innocenti. Carlo Collodi

1988 Highly Commended. *Merlin Dreams*, illus. by Alan Lee. Peter Dickinson

1990 Commended. *A Christmas Carol*, illus. by Roberto Innocenti. Charles Dickens

1999 *Alice's Adventures in Wonderland*, illus. by Helen Oxenbury. Lewis Carroll

The Guardian Children's Fiction Prize

Awarded by *The Guardian* (London, UK) to the best novel for children published in Britain by a British or Commonwealth author.

1968 *The Owl Service*. Alan Garner

1969 *The Whispering Mountain*. Joan Aiken

1973 *Watership Down*. Richard Adams

1977 *The Blue Hawk*. Peter Dickinson

1977 Commended. *The Power of Three*. Diana Wynne Jones

1978 *Charmed Life*. Diana Wynne Jones

1978 Commended. *The Ice is Coming*. Patricia Wrightson

1979 *Conrad's War*. Andrew Davies

1981 Runner-up. *Daggie Dogfoot*. Dick King-Smith

1982 Runner-up. *Playing Beatie Bow*. Ruth Park

1984 *The Sheep-Pig*. Dick King-Smith

1989 *A Pack of Lies*. Geraldine McCaughrean

1994 *The Mennyms*. Sylvia Waugh

1996 *Northern Lights*. Philip Pullman

1999 First Book Award. *The Sterkarm Handshake*. Susan Price

2001 *Arthur: The Seeing Stone*. Kevin Crossley-Holland

Nils Holgersson Award

Awarded by the Swedish Library Association (Stockholm, Sweden) to the best Swedish children's book published during the previous year, or to the collected works of an author.

1953 *Moomin, Mymble and Little My*. Tove Jansson

1965 *The White Stone*. Gunnel Linde

Hugo Award

Presented annually by the World Science Fiction Society. The Grand Master of Fantasy Award, unofficially known as the Gandalf Award, is presented for a writer's lifetime contribution to fantasy literature.

1974 Gandalf Award (Grand Master of Fantasy). J. R. R. Tolkien

1975 Gandalf Award (Grand Master). L. Sprague de Camp

1977 Gandalf Award (Grand Master). Andre Norton

1978 Gandalf Award (Grand Master). Poul Anderson

1978 Best Book-Length Fantasy. *The Silmarillion*. J. R. R. Tolkien

1979 Gandalf Award (Grand Master).   Ursula K. Le Guin

1979 Best Book-Length Fantasy. *The White Dragon*. Anne McCaffrey

1980 Gandalf Award (Grand Master). Ray Bradbury

2001 Best Novel. *Harry Potter and the Goblet of Fire*. J. K. Rowling

2003 Best Novella. *Coraline*. Neil Gaiman

I.R.A. Children's Book Award

Awarded by the International Reading Association for an author's first or second work of fiction or nonfiction for children or young adolescents.

1977 *A String in the Harp*. Nancy Bond

1983 *The Darkangel*. Meredith Ann Pierce

1984 *Ratha's Creature*. Clare Bell

Kerlan Award

Awarded by the Kerlan Award Committee, Children's Literature Research Collections, University of Minnesota, in recognition of singular attainments in the creation of children's literature.

1975 Elizabeth Coatsworth

1978 Carol Ryrie Brink

1980 Glen Rounds

1985 Eleanor Cameron

1986 Charlotte Zolotow

1988 Jane Yolen

1990 Madeleine L'Engle

1993 Mary Stolz

1995 Phyllis Reynolds Naylor

1998 Dahlov Ipcar

2001 Jane Resh Thomas

2002 Joan Lowery Nixon

2004 Lois Lowry

Coretta Scott King Award

Awarded annually by the Association of Library Services for Children of the American Library Association to an African American author and illustrator whose works encourage and promote the cause of peace and brotherhood, and inspire children and youth to dedicate their talents and energies to help achieve these goals.

1983 Fiction. *Sweet Whispers, Brother Rush*. Virginia Hamilton

1993 Fiction. *The Dark-Thirty: Southern Tales of the Supernatural*. Patricia C. McKissack

Anne Spencer Lindbergh Prize in Children's Literature

Awarded biennially, beginning in 1996, by the Charles A. and Anne Morrow Lindbergh Foundation to recognize the best children's fantasy novel published in the English language in the award years.

1995–1996 Winner. *Cold Shoulder Road*. Joan Aiken

1995–1996 Honor Books. *Wren's War*. Sherwood Smith; *Out of Time*. Caroline B. Cooney

1997–1998 Winner. *Harry Potter and the Sorcerer's Stone*. J. K. Rowling

1997–1998 Honor Book. *Well Wished*. Franny Billingsley

1999–2000 Winner. *Which Witch?* Eva Ibbotson

1999–2000	Honor Books. *The Power of Un*. Nancy Etchemendy; *Spindle's End*. Robin McKinley
1999–2000	Special Commendation for Outstanding Contribution to Children's Fantasy Literature. Harry Potter series. J. K. Rowling
2001–2002	Winner. *Heir Apparent*. Vivian Vande Velde
2001–2002	Special Commendation. Young Wizards series. Diane Duane

Astrid Lindgren Memorial Award for Children's Literature

Awarded annually, an international prize established by the Swedish government in 2003 to recognize authors and illustrators whose work reflects the spirit of Lindgren's books.

2003 Maurice Sendak, Christine Nöstlinger

John D. and Catherine T. MacArthur Foundation Fellows Genius Award

The MacArthur Fellows Program awards unrestricted fellowships to talented individuals who have shown extraordinary originality and dedication in their creative pursuits and a marked capacity for self-direction.

1995 Virginia Hamilton

Mythopoeic Fantasy Award for Adult Literature

Awarded annually by the Mythopoeic Society, for a book-length work of fantasy in the spirit of the Inklings: J. R. R. Tolkien, C. S. Lewis, and Charles Williams. No awards were given from 1976 to 1980. The Children's Literature category was created in 1992.

1971 *The Crystal Cave*. Mary Stewart

1972 *Red Moon and Black Mountain*. Joy Chant

1973 *The Song of Rhiannon*. Evangeline Walton

1974 *The Hollow Hills*. Mary Stewart

1975 *A Midsummer Tempest*. Poul Anderson

1981 *Unfinished Tales*. J. R. R. Tolkien

1983 *The Firelings*. Carol Kendall

1984 *When Voiha Wakes*. Joy Chant

1987 *The Folk of the Air*. Peter Beagle

1988 *Seventh Son*. Orson Scott Card

1990 *The Stress of Her Regard*. Tim Powers

1991 *Thomas the Rhymer*. Ellen Kushner

1993 *Briar Rose*. Jane Yolen

1999 *Stardust*. Neil Gaiman and Charles Vess

2000 *Tamsin*. Peter S. Beagle

2002 *The Curse of Chalion*. Lois McMaster Bujold

2004 *Sunshine*. Robin McKinley

Mythopoeic Fantasy Award for Children's Literature

1992 *Haroun and the Sea of Stories*. Salman Rushdie

1993 *Knight's Wyrd*. Debra Doyle and James D. Macdonald

1994 *The Kingdom of Kevin Malone*. Suzy McKee Charnas

1995 *Owl in Love*. Patrice Kindl

1996 *The Crown of Dalemark*. Diana Wynne Jones

1997 *The Wood Wife*. Terry Windling

1998 Young Merlin trilogy (consisting of *Passager*, *Hobby*, and *Merlin*). Jane Yolen

1999 *Dark Lord of Derkholm*. Diana Wynne Jones

2000 *The Folk Keeper*. Franny Billingsley

2001 *Aria of the Sea*. Dia Calhoun

2002 *The Ropemaker*. Peter Dickinson

2003 *Summerland*. Michael Chabon

2004 *The Hollow Kingdom*. Clare B. Dunkle.

National Book Award, Children's Fiction Category

Awarded by the National Book Committee (1969–1974), the American Academy of Arts and Letters (1975–1977), the Association of American Publishers (1978–1979), and the National Book Foundation (1987–) to the most distinguished book published in the United States during the preceding year. This award was replaced by the American Book Award (see above) between 1980 and 1986. In 1984 the children's book category was discontinued.

1969 Finalist. *The High King*. Lloyd Alexander

1971 *The Marvelous Misadventures of Sebastian*. Lloyd Alexander

1971 Finalist. *Trumpet of the Swan*. E. B. White

1972 Finalist. *Mrs. Frisby and the Rats of NIMH*. Robert C. O'Brien

1972 Finalist. *The Tombs of Atuan*. Ursula K. Le Guin

1973 *The Farthest Shore*. Ursula K. Le Guin

1973 Finalist. *Dominic*. William Steig

1974 *The Court of the Stone Children*. Eleanor Cameron

1975 Finalist. *The Devil's Storybook*. Natalie Babbitt

1975 Finalist. *The Girl Who Cried Flowers and Other Tales*. Jane Yolen

1979 Finalist. *The First Two Lives of Lukas-Kasha*. Lloyd Alexander

1979 Finalist. *Humbug Mountain*. Sid Fleischman

Nebula Award

Awarded by the Science Fiction Writers of America to the best novel published in the previous year in the field of science fiction, and to a grand master of science fiction writing.

1977 Grand Master. Clifford D. Simak

1979 Grand Master. L. Sprague de Camp

1984 Grand Master. Andre Norton

1987 Grand Master. Isaac Asimov

1988 Best Novel. *The Falling Woman*. Pat Murphy

1989 Grand Master. Ray Bradbury

1990 Best Novel. *The Healer's War*. Elizabeth Ann Scarborough

1991 Best Novel. *Tehanu*. Ursula K. Le Guin

2002 Grand Master. Ursula K. Le Guin

2003 Damon Knight Grand Master of Fantasy Award. Robert Silverberg

The Nestlé Smarties Book Prize

Awarded annually since 1985 by the Book Trust (London, UK), an independent educational charity, and sponsored by Nestlé, to a work of children's fiction or poetry written in English by a citizen or resident of the United Kingdom and published in the United Kingdom, to encourage high standards and stimulate interest in books for children. Before 1996, a Grand Prix was given each year to one of the three age-category winners. Since 1996, gold, silver, and bronze awards have been given in each age category.

1986 Grand Prix. *The Snow Spider*. Jenny Nimmo

1986 7–11 years. *The Snow Spider*. Jenny Nimmo

1987 6–8 years. *Tangle and the Firesticks*. Benedict Blathwayt

1990 Grand Prix. *Midnight Blue*. Pauline Fisk

1990 9–11 years. *Midnight Blue*. Pauline Fisk

1990 6–8 years. *Essio Trott*. Roald Dahl

1991 9–11 years. *Krindlekrax*. Philip Ridley

1996 Silver Award, 6–8 years. *Harry the Poisonous Centipede*. Lynne Reid Banks

1997 Gold Award, 9–11 years. *The Firework Maker's Daughter*. Philip Pullman

1997 Gold Award, 9–11 years. *Harry Potter and the Philosopher's Stone*. J. K. Rowling

1997 Silver Award, 9–11 years. *Clockwork, or All Wound Up*. Philip Pullman

1997 Bronze Award, 9–11 years. *Fire, Bed, and Bone*. Henrietta Branford

1998 Gold Award, 9–11 years. *Harry Potter and the Chamber of Secrets*. J. K. Rowling.

1999 Gold Award, 9–11 years. *Harry Potter and the Prisoner of Azkaban*. J. K. Rowling

1999 Silver Award, 9–11 years. *Kit's Wilderness*. David Almond

2000 Gold Award, 9–11 years. *The Wind Singer*. William Nicholson

2000 Bronze Award, 9–11 years. *The Seeing Stone*. Kevin Crossley-Holland

2002 Silver Award, 9–11 years. *Cold Tom*. Sally Prue

2003 Gold Award, 9–11 years. *The Fire Eaters*. David Almond

2003 Bronze Award, 9–11 years. *The Various*. Steve Augarde

2003 Gold Award, 6–8 years. *Varjak Paw*. S. F. Said

2003 Bronze Award, 6–8 years. *The Countess's Calamity*. Sally Gardner

2004 Silver Award, 9–11 years. *The Star of Kazan*. Eva Ibbotson

John Newbery Medal

Awarded by the Association for Library Service to Children, American Library Association, to the author of the most distinguished contribution to American literature for children published in the United States by a citizen or resident during the preceding year.

1922 *The Old Tobacco Shop*. William A. Bowen

1923 *The Voyages of Doctor Dolittle*. Hugh Lofting

1925 Honor. *The Dream Coach*. Anne and Dilwyn Parrish

1925 Honor. *Nicholas*. Anne Carroll Moore

1926 *Shen of the Sea*. Arthur Bowie Chrisman

1929 Honor. *The Pigtail of Ah Lee Ben Loo*. John Bennett

1930 *Hitty, Her First Hundred Years*. Rachel Lyman Field

1931 *The Cat Who Went to Heaven*. Elizabeth Coatsworth

1931 Honor. *Floating Island*. Anne Parrish

1932 Honor. *The Fairy Circus*. Dorothy P. Lathrop

1938 *The White Stag*. Kate Seredy

1939 Honor. *Mr. Popper's Penguins*. Richard and Florence Atwater

1944 Honor. *Fog Magic*. Julia L. Sauer

1945 *Rabbit Hill*. Robert Lawson

1947 *Miss Hickory*. Carolyn Sherwyn Bailey

1948 *The Twenty-One Balloons*. William Pene Du Bois

1948 Honor. *The Quaint and Curious Quest of Johnny Longfoot*. Catherine Besterman

1949 Honor. *My Father's Dragon*. Ruth Stiles Gannett

1950 Honor. *The Blue Cat of Castle Town*. Catherine Cate Coblentz

1951 Honor. *The Story of Appleby Capple*. Anne Parrish

1953 Honor. *Charlotte's Web*. E. B. White

1960 Honor. *The Gammage Cup*. Carol Kendall

1961 Honor. *The Cricket in Times Square*. George Selden

1962 Honor. *Belling the Tiger*. Mary Stolz

1966 Honor. *The Animal Family*. Randall Jarrell

1966 Honor. *The Black Cauldron*. Lloyd Alexander

1967 Honor. *Zlateh the Goat and Other Stories*. Isaac Bashevis Singer

1968 Honor. *The Fearsome Inn*. Isaac Bashevis Singer

1969 *The High King*. Lloyd Alexander

1970 Honor. *Journey Outside*. Mary Q. Steele

1971 Honor. *Knee-Knock Rise*. Natalie Babbitt

1972 *Mrs. Frisby and the Rats of NIMH*. Robert C. O'Brien

1972 Honor. *The Tombs of Atuan*. Ursula K. Le Guin

1974 Honor. *The Dark Is Rising*. Susan Cooper

1975 Honor. *Figgs and Phantoms*. Ellen Raskin

1975 Honor. *The Perilous Gard*. Elizabeth Pope

1976 *The Grey King*. Susan Cooper

1977 Honor. *Abel's Island*. William Steig

1977 Honor. *A String in the Harp*. Nancy Bond

1981 Honor. *The Fledgling*. Jane Langton

1983 Honor. *The Blue Sword*. Robin McKinley

1983 Honor. *Graven Images*. Paul Fleischman

1983 Honor. *Sweet Whispers, Brother Rush*. Virginia Hamilton

1984 Honor. *The Wish Giver*. Bill Brittain

1985 *The Hero and the Crown*. Robin McKinley

1987 *The Whipping Boy*. Paul Fleischman

1993 Honor. *The Dark-Thirty*. Patricia C.McKissack

1994 *The Giver*. Lois Lowry

1997 Honor. *The Moorchild*. Eloise Jarvis McGraw

      The Thief. Megan Whalen Turner

1998 Honor. *Ella Enchanted*. Gail Carson Levine

2004 *The Tale of Despereaux*. Kate DiCamillo.

Order of New Zealand

New Zealand's highest honor, held by only 20 living people at any one time.

1992 Margaret Mahy, for her internationally acclaimed contribution to children's
      literature

Phoenix Award

Awarded by the Children's Literature Association to an author of a book for children first published exactly 20 years earlier, which did not win a major literary award at the time of its publication, but which has passed the test of time and is deemed to be of high literary quality.

1989 *The Night Watchmen*. Helen Cresswell

1991 Honor. *A Game of Dark*. William Mayne

1991 Honor. *The Tombs of Atuan*. Ursula K. Le Guin

1995 Honor. *Tuck Everlasting*. Natalie Babbitt

1996 Honor. *Abel's Island*. William Steig

1998 *A Chance Child*. Jill Paton Walsh

1998 Honor. *Beauty*. Robin McKinley

2000 Honor. *The Fledgling*. Jane Langton

Michael L. Printz Award

Presented annually by the American Library Association, for literary excellence in young adult literature. The Printz Award is sponsored by *Booklist* magazine and administered by the Young Adult Library Services Association.

1999 Honor. *Skellig*. David Almond

2000 Winner. *Kit's Wilderness*. David Almond

2002 Honor. *The Ropemaker*. Peter Dickinson

The Regina Medal

Awarded annually since 1959 by the Catholic Library Association to honor an individual's continued distinguished contribution to children's literature.

1959 Eleanor Farjeon

1961 Padraic Colum

1980 Beverly Cleary

1982 Theodor Seuss Geisel

1986 Lloyd Alexander

1987 Katherine Paterson

1990 Virginia Hamilton

1992 Jane Yolen

1993 Chris Van Allsburg

1994 Lois Lowry

Tir Na N-Og Award

Awarded by the Welsh Books Council in three categories: to original Welsh-language novels, stories, and picture books; to other Welsh-language books published during the relevant year; and to the best English-language children's book published in the preceding year with an authentic Welsh background. Fantasy winners in this third category are:

1976 *The Grey King*. Susan Cooper

1977 *A String in the Harp*. Nancy Bond

1978 *Silver on the Tree*. Susan Cooper

1987 *The Snow Spider*. Jenny Nimmo

2001 *The Seeing Stone*. Kevin Crossley-Holland

Whitbread Children's Book of the Year Award

Awarded by the Booksellers Association of Great Britain and Ireland (London, UK) to books first published in the United Kingdom or Ireland within the previous year, by authors who have lived in Great Britain or Ireland for three or more years, to promote a high standard of English literature.

1974 *How Tom Beat Captain Najork*. Russell Hoban

1976 *A Stitch in Time*. Penelope Lively

1982 *The Song of Pentecost*. W. J. Corbett

1982 Runner-up. *The Secret World of Polly Flint*. Helen Cresswell.

1983 *The Witches*. Roald Dahl

1998 *Skellig*. David Almond

1999 *Harry Potter and the Prisoner of Azkaban*. J. K. Rowling

2001 *The Amber Spyglass*. Philip Pullman

2002 *Saffy's Angel*. Hilary McKay

Whitbread Book of the Year Award

Awarded by the Booksellers Association of Great Britain and Ireland, chosen from all of the winners in each year's various literary categories. *The Amber Spyglass* is the first children's book ever chosen to be Book of the Year.

2001 Winner. *The Amber Spyglass*. Philip Pullman

Laura Ingalls Wilder Award

Awarded by the Association for Library Service to Children, American Library Association, every five years from 1954 to 1980, and every three years since 1980, to an author or illustrator whose books, published in the United States, have made a substantial and lasting contribution to literature for children.

1965 Ruth Sawyer

1970 E. B. White

1975 Beverly Cleary

1980 Theodor Geisel (Dr. Seuss)

1983 Maurice Sendak

1995 Virginia Hamilton

World Fantasy Award

Awarded annually at the World Fantasy Convention. Categories include: Best Novel, Best Anthology, and a Life Achievement Award.

1975 Novel. *The Forgotten Beasts of Eld*. Patricia McKillip

1976 Novel. *Bid Time Return*. Richard Matheson

1980 Novel. *Watchtower*. Elizabeth A. Lynn

1980 Anthology. *Amazons!* Ed. by Jessica A. Salmonson

1980 Life Achievement. Manly Wade Wellman

1981 Novel. *The Shadow of the Torturer*. Gene Wolfe

1982 Anthology. *Elsewhere*. Ed. by Terri Windling and Mark Arnold

1983 Life Achievement. Roald Dahl

1984 Life Achievement. L. Sprague de Camp

1984 Life Achievement. Richard Matheson

1984 Life Achievement. Jack Vance

1985 Novel. *Mythago Wood*. Robert Holdstock

1986 Anthology. *Imaginary Lands*. Ed. by Robin McKinley

1987 Life Achievement. Jack Finney

1989 Anthology. *The Year's Best Fantasy, First Annual Collection*. Ed. by Ellen Datlow and Terri Windling

1989 Life Achievement. Evangeline Walton

1990 Anthology. *The Year's Best Fantasy, Second Annual Collection*. Ed. by Ellen Datlow and Terri Windling

1991 Novel. *Thomas the Rhymer*. Ellen Kushner

1992 Novel. *The White Mists of Power*. Kathryn K. Rusch

1995 Life Achievement Award. Ursula K. Le Guin

1996 Life Achievement Award. Gene Wolfe

1997 Best Novella. *A City in Winter*. Mark Helprin

1998 Life Achievement Award. Andre Norton

2000 Life Achievement Award. Marion Zimmer Bradley

2000 Life Achievement Award. Michael Moorcock

2000 Best Collection. *Moonlight and Vines*. Charles de Lint

2002 Best Novel. *The Other Wind*. Ursula K. Le Guin

2003 Life Achievement Award. Lloyd Alexander

2003 Best Novel. *Ombria in Shadow*. Patricia A. McKillip

2003 Best Anthology. *The Green Man: Tales from the Mythic Forest*. Ed. by Ellen Datlow and Terri Windling.

2004 Best Novel. *Tooth and Claw*. Jo Walton

2004 Life Achievement Award. Stephen King

2004 Life Achievement Award. Gahan Wilson

YALSA Top Ten Best Books for Young Adults

Presented annually since 1997 by the Young Adult Library Services Association, American Library Association.

1997 *The Golden Compass*. Philip Pullman

1999 *Harry Potter and the Sorcerer's Stone*. J. K. Rowling

2002 *Liriel: Daughter of the Clayr*. Garth Nix

2004 *East*. Edith Pattou

2004 *The Amulet of Samarkand*. Jonathan Stroud

YASD/SLJ Young Adult Author Award

See Margaret A. Edwards Award.

Young Adult Canadian Book Award

Awarded by the Young Adult Services Interest Group, Canadian Library Association, to the best Canadian book of the year for young adults.

1989 Runner-up. *Blood Red Ochre*. Kevin Major

2001 Winner. *Before Wings*. Beth Goobie

1

Allegorical Fantasy
and Literary Fairy Tales

The books in this chapter are individual tales with both simple and abstract levels of meaning. Literary fairy tales are short stories written by modern authors in the style of traditional folktales, often utilizing such elements as kings, princesses, dragons, and fairies. Modern allegorical fantasies, unlike traditional allegorical fables, frequently involve characters other than animals, and the full significance of the stories may not be obvious. Collections of literary fairy tales are found in Chapter 3, Fantasy Collections. Retellings of legends and myths, which often have allegorical elements, are found in Chapter 6, High Fantasy: Myth or Legend Fantasy.

1-1   ABELL, Kathleen. *King Orville and the Bullfrogs.* Gr. 2–4.
Three young princes are transformed into frogs and banished after they outdo their father-in-law, King Orville, in a bagpipe contest.
Illus. by Errol Le Cain, Little, Brown, 1974, 48 pp., o.p.
(BL 70:871; Kirkus 42:239; LJ 99:1463)

ADAMS, Hazard. *The Truth About Dragons: An Anti-Romance.*
See Chapter 5, High Fantasy: Alternate Worlds or Histories.

ADAMS, Richard (George). *Shardik.*
See Chapter 5, High Fantasy: Alternate Worlds or Histories.

ADAMS, Richard (George). *Watership Down.*
See Chapter 2, Animal Fantasy.

AHLBERG, Allan. *Ten in a Bed.*
See Chapter 9, Magic Adventure Fantasy.

AHLBERG, Janet. *Jeremiah in the Dark Woods.*
See Chapter 8, Humorous Fantasy.

AIKEN, Joan (Delano). *A Harp of Fishbones and Other Stories.*
See Chapter 3, Fantasy Collections.

1-2 **AIKEN, Joan (Delano).** *The Moon's Revenge.* Gr. 2–5.
Young Sep angers the moon when he uses magic to learn to play the fiddle, but his musical ability is what breaks the moon's curse on his town.
Illus. by Alan Lee, Knopf, 1987, 32 pp., o.p.
(BL 84:929; HB 64:199; Kirkus 55:1623; SLJ Feb 1988 p. 57)

AIKEN, Joan (Delano). *A Necklace of Raindrops and Other Stories.*
See Chapter 3, Fantasy Collections.

AIKEN, Joan (Delano). *Past Eight O'Clock: Goodnight Stories.*
See Chapter 3, Fantasy Collections.

1-3 **AIKEN, Joan (Delano).** *The Shoemaker's Boy.* Gr. 2–5. (Orig. pub. in England.)
While his father is away on a pilgrimage to pray for Jem's mother's recovery, the boy has a magical encounter with two knights who represent good and evil.
Illus. by Victor G. Ambrus, Simon, 1994, 32 pp. (0-671-86647-8)
(BL 90:1815; Kirkus 62:839; HBG 5:298; SLJ June 1994 p. 94)

AIKEN, Joan (Delano). *Smoke from Cromwell's Time and Other Stories.*
See Chapter 3, Fantasy Collections.

1-4 **AIKEN, Joan (Delano).** *Street: A Play for Children.* Gr. 5–8.
☆ In the town of Street, the theft of the toll bridge key by the village witch's eldest son causes deep hostilities between the inhabitants of the river side, and those of the forest side of Street's only thoroughfare. Only the love between the witch's younger son, Toomy, and Meg, a girl from the other side of the street, can heal the town's animosities and restore safety and justice.
Illus. by Arvis Stewart, Viking, 1978, 128 pp., o.p.
(BL 74:1247, 1251; HB 55:527; Kirkus 46:696; SLJ May 1978 p. 62)

ALDEN, Raymond Macdonald. *Why the Chimes Rang and Other Stories.*
See Chapter 3, Fantasy Collections.

ALEXANDER, Lloyd (Chudley). *The Cat Who Wished to Be a Man.*
See Chapter 2, Animal Fantasy.

1-5 **ALEXANDER, Lloyd (Chudley).** *The Remarkable Journey of Prince Jen.*
☆ Gr. 5–9.
Prince Jen wanders from adventure to adventure through the Chinese countryside, accompanied by a flute girl named Voyaging Moon, while learning how to be a good ruler and a good man.
Dutton, 1991, 288 pp., o.p.; Puffin, 2004, pap., 273 pp. (0-14-240225-7)
(BL 88:696, 865, 872; CCBB 45:55; HB 68:200; HBG 3:62; Kirkus 60:1219; SLJ Dec 1991 pp. 28, 113; VOYA 14:378)

ALEXANDER, Lloyd (Chudley). *The Town Cats, and Other Tales.*
See Chapter 2, Animal Fantasy.

ALEXANDER, Lloyd (Chudley). *The Truthful Harp.*
See Chapter 5, High Fantasy: Alternate Worlds or Histories.

ALLEN, Judy. *The Lord of the Dance.*
See Chapter 6, High Fantasy: Myth or Legend Fantasy.

1-6   **ALLEN, Judy.** *The Spring on the Mountain.* Gr. 5–8.
An old woman sends Peter, Emma, and Michael in search of a magical, knowl-edge-giving spring that she, herself, once found.
Farrar, 1973, 153 pp., o.p.
(BL 70:653; LJ 98:3142; TLS 1973 p. 1114)

1-7   **ALMOND, David.** *Heaven Eyes.* Gr. 5–9. (Orig. British pub. 2000.)
★   Erin, January, and Mouse run away from a home for "damaged" children, raft-ing down the River Tyne into the Black Middens, where they meet Heaven Eyes, a dreamy girl searching for her family.
Delacorte, 2001, 240 pp. (0-385-32770-6); Dell, 2003, pap., 234 pp. (0-440-22910-3)
(BL 97:950; CCBB 54:295; HB 77:205; HBG 12:298; Kirkus 69:254; Kliatt Mar 2001 p. 8; SLJ Mar 2001 p. 245; VOYA 24:34)

1-8   **ALMOND, David.** *Secret Heart.* Gr. 5 up. (Orig. British pub. 2001.)
Joe Maloney is inexplicably drawn to the circus briefly stopping in his village, particularly to a strangely familiar girl name Corrina, and a tiger that first appeared to him in a dream.
Delacorte, 2002, 208 pp. (0-385-72947-2)
(BL 99:322; CCBB 56:140; HB 78:745; HBG 14:74; Kirkus 70:1300; Kliatt Nov 2002 p. 5; SLJ Oct 2002 p. 154; VOYA 25:393)

AMADO, Jorge. *The Swallow and the Tom Cat: A Grown-Up Love Story.*
See Chapter 2, Animal Fantasy.

ANDERSEN, Hans Christian. *Andersen's Fairy Tales.*
See Chapter 3, Fantasy Collections.

1-9   **ANDERSEN, Hans Christian.** *The Emperor's New Clothes.* Gr. K–4.
★   (Written in Denmark, 1837, orig. U.S. pub. as a separate tale, 1848.)
Thieves pretending to create a magnificent new suit for the vain Emperor fool everyone in the kingdom except one small boy.
Illus. by Virginia Lee Burton, Houghton, 1949, 44 pp., o.p., 1979, pap. (0-395-28594-1); tr. and illus. by Erik Blegvad, Harcourt, 1959, 32 pp., o.p.; trans. by H. W. Dulcken, adapt. and illus. by Anne Rockwell, Harper, 1982, 1987, pap., 32 pp., o.p.; retold and illus. by Nadine Bernard Westcott, Little, Brown, 1984, 32 pp., o.p.; adapt. and illus. by Janet Stevens, Holiday, 1979, 32 pp., o.p.; retold by Anthea Bell, illus. by Dorothée Duntze, North-South, 1986, 24 pp., o.p.; retold by Riki Levinson, illus. by Robert Byrd, Dutton, 1991, 40 pp., o.p.; retold and illus. by S. T. Mendelson, Stewart, 1992, 32 pp., o.p.; trans. by Naomi Lewis, illus. by Angela Barrett, Candlewick, 1997, 32 pp., o.p.; adapt. by Christine San Jose, illus. by Anastassija Archipowa, Boyds Mills, 1998, 28 pp. (1-56397-699-4); adapt. and illus. by Eve Tharlet, trans. by Rosemary Lan-ning, North-South, 2000, 32 pp. (0-7358-1340-X); Neugebauer, 2002, pap., 32

pp. (0-735-81701-4); illus. by Virginia Lee Burton, Houghton, 2004, 48 pp. (0-618-34421-7); adapt. by Marcus Sedgwick, illus. by Alison Jay, Chronicle, 2004, 32 pp. (0-8118-4569-9)

(BL 46:51, 70:336, 78:1155, 81:214, 82:341, 83:346, 88:770, 94:701, 1334, 96:1751; CCBB 2[Nov 1949]:1, 13:25; HB 25:523, 73:688; HBG 3:23, 9:283; Kirkus 41:961; LJ 74:1533, 1612, 99:197; SLJ Apr 1982 p. 54, Dec 1984 p. 66, Jan 1987 p. 57, Nov 1991 p. 89, Dec 1992 p. 76, Nov 1997 p. 76, Oct 2000, p. 110, Apr 2004 p. 137; TLS 1973 pp. 384, 1121, Dec 1986 p. 1458)

ANDERSEN, Hans Christian. *Fairy Tales.*
See Chapter 3, Fantasy Collections.

1-10 **ANDERSEN, Hans Christian.** *The Fir Tree.* Gr. K–4. (Orig. Danish pub.
✮ 1837, U.S. 1849.)
A little fir tree glories in becoming a Christmas tree, and then mourns the fate that awaits him after Christmas.
Illus. by Nancy Ekholm Burkert, Harper, 1970, o.p., 1986, pap., 48 pp., o.p.; illus. by Svend Otto S., Van Nostrand, 1971, 30 pp., o.p.; adapt. and illus. by Bernadette Watts, North-South, 1990, 32 pp., o.p.
(BL 67:375, 87:929; CCBB 24:53; HB 47:66; HBG 2:35; Kirkus 38:1142, 58:1256; LJ 96:3487; Suth:13; TLS 1971 p. 1343)

1-11 **ANDERSEN, Hans Christian.** *Little Ida's Flowers.* Gr. K–3. (Orig. pub. in Denmark.)
Ida awakens to music and finds cut flowers from the garden waltzing in her playroom, in one of Andersen's lesser known tales.
Illus. by Linda Allen, Putnam, 1989, 32 pp., o.p.
(BL 86:1081; HBG 1:61; SLJ Feb 1990 p. 68)

1-12 **ANDERSEN, Hans Christian.** *The Little Match Girl.* Gr. K–5. (Orig. Dan-
✮ ish pub. 1846, U.S. 1870.)
A penniless little match-seller burns the last of her matches to keep warm on Christmas Eve, and sees wondrous visions in the flames.
Illus. by Gustaf Tenggren, Grosset, 1944, 28 pp., o.p.; illus. by Blair Lent, Houghton, 1968, 43 pp., o.p.; illus. by Rachel Isadora, Putnam, 1987, 30 pp. (0-399-21336-8), 1990, pap., 30 pp. (0-399-22007-0); retold by Christine San Jose, illus. by Anastassija Archipowa, Caroline House, 1995, 32 pp., o.p.; illus. by Jerry Pinkney, Puffin, 2002, pap., 32 pp. (0-14-230188-4); adapt. by Christine San Jose, illus. by Kestutis Kasparavicius, Boyds Mills, 2002, 32 pp. (1-59078-000-0)
(BL 84:387, 96:443 and 99:329; CCBB 22:121, 51:385; HB 63:716, 718; HBG 9:58, 14:23; Kirkus 36:1039, 55:1387, 57:1601; LJ 93:3953; SLJ Oct 1987 p. 30, Nov 1995 p. 64, Oct 1999 p. 102; Suth:14; TLS 1987 p. 1284)

1-13 **ANDERSEN, Hans Christian.** *The Little Mermaid.* Gr. K–5. (Written 1837,
✮ orig. Danish pub. 1846.)
A young mermaid in love with a human makes the tragic decision to give up her undersea home and live as a mortal. *My Love, My Love, or The Peasant Girl,* by Rosa Guy (Holt, 1985; see Chapter 6, High Fantasy: Myth or Legend Fantasy) is a contemporary version of this story, written for young adults.
Trans. by M. R. James, illus. by Pamela Bianco, Holiday, 1935, 55 pp., o.p.; retold and illus. by Dorothy P. Lathrop, Macmillan, 1939, 48 pp., o.p.; trans. by

Eva Le Gallienne, illus. by Edward Frascino, Harper, 1971, 50 pp., o.p.; trans. by M. R. James, illus. by Josef Palacek, Faber, 1981, 26 pp., o.p.; adapt. by Anthea Bell, illus. by Chihiro Iwasaki, Picture Book Studio, 1984, 33 pp., o.p.; adapt. and illus. by Katie Thamer Treherne, Harcourt, 1989, 48 pp. (0-15-246320-8); retold by Deborah Hautzig, illus. by Darcy May, Random, 1991, 48 pp. (0-679-92241-5), pap. (0-679-82241-0); illus. by Charles Santore, Random, 1993, 48 pp. (0-679-88757-1); illus. by Michael (R.) Hague, Holt, 1994, 48 pp., o.p.; retold and illus. by Rachel Isadora, Putnam, 1998, 32 pp. (0-399-22813-6); 2001, pap., 32 pp. (0-698-11829-4); illus. by Lisbeth Zwerger; trans. by Anthea Bell, Putnam, 2004, 48 pp. (0-698-40001-1)

(BL 32:80, 36:157, 202, 68:468, 81:585, 86:921, 90:149, 90:1814, 101:328; Bookshelf 1935 p. 2; CCBB 45:116, 58:159; HB 16:43, 109, 48:142; HBG 1:47, 3:56, 5:298, 9:283; Kirkus 39:1124, 57:1601; LJ 97:771; Mahony 3:200; SLJ Apr 1982 p. 65, Feb 1985 p. 70, Nov 1989 p. 102, Oct 1993 p. 123, June 1994 p. 124, Aug 1998 p. 132)

1-14   **ANDERSEN, Hans Christian.** *The Nightingale.* Gr. K–5. (Written in Den-
✮   mark, 1844, orig. U.S. pub. 1896.)
A selfish Emperor prefers a bejeweled mechanical bird to the faithful nightingale who loves him. Kara Dalkey's *The Nightingale* (Berkley, 1988; see Chapter 6, High Fantasy: Myth or Legend Fantasy) is a novel-length adaptation of this story.
Trans. by Eva Le Gallienne, illus. by Nancy Ekholm Burkert, Harper, 1965, 32 pp., LB (0-06-023781-3); trans. by Erik Haugaard, illus. by Lemoine, Schocken, 1981 (entitled *The Emperor's Nightingale*), 34 pp., o.p.; trans. by Anthea Bell, illus. by Lisbeth Zwerger, Picture Book Studio, 1991 (0-907234-57-7); trans. and adapt. by Alan Benjamin, illus. by Beni Montresor, Crown, 1985, o.p.; adapt. by Anna Bier, illus. by Demi, Harcourt, 1988, 30 pp., o.p.; illus. by Alison Claire Darke, Doubleday, 1989, 28 pp., o.p.; trans. by Naomi Lewis, illus. by Josef Palacek, North-South, 1990, 40 pp., o.p.; adapt. by Michael Bedard, illus. by Regolo Ricci, Houghton, 1992, 32 pp., o.p.; retold and illus. by Meilo So, Macmillan, 1992 (entitled *The Emperor and the Nightingale*), 32 pp. (0-02-786045-0); illus. by Lisbeth Zwerger, trans. by Anthea Bell, North-South, 1999, 24 pp. (0-7358-1118-0); adapt. by Fiona Walters, illus. by Paul Birkbeck, Bloomsbury, 2000, 26 pp. (0-7475-3559-0); adapt. by Stephen Mitchell, illus. by Bagram Ibatoulline, Candlewick, 2002, 48 pp. (0-7636-1521-8); adapt. and illus. by Jerry Pinkney, Penguin Putnam, 2002, 40 pp. (0-8037-2464-0)

(BL 31:385, 34:78, 59:113, 61:995, 78:705, 81:585, 82:564, 86:1081, 87:929, 97:645, 99:488; CCBB 16:89, 18:157, 38:59, 39:41, 56:97, 98; HB 38:601, 41:389, 61:172, 62:78; HBG 1:83, 2:35, 10:274, 14:23, 64; Kirkus 33:373, 60:320; LJ 90:2393; Mahony 3:200; SLJ Mar 1982 pp. 116, 126, Feb 1985 p. 61, Oct 1985 p. 166, May 1992 p. 85, Oct 1992, p. 78, Sep 2002 p. 180, Nov 2002 p. 11)

1-15   **ANDERSEN, Hans Christian.** *The Old House.* Gr. 2–5. (Orig. pub. in Denmark, orig. British pub. in this edition 1984.)
The tin soldier once given to a lonely old man by a neighbor boy reappears in a new house built for the now grown-up boy, on the site of the original house.
Trans. and adapt. by Anthea Bell, illus. by Jean Claverie, North-South, 1986, o.p.
(HB 68:364365; SLJ Mar 1987 p. 139)

1-16   **ANDERSEN, Hans Christian.** *The Red Shoes.* Gr. 1–4. (Orig. pub. in Denmark, this ed. orig. pub. in Austria.)
A young girl is punished for her vanity by a stern angel who decrees that she must never stop dancing in her new red shoes.
Trans. by Anthea Bell, illus. by Chihiro Iwasaki, Neugebauer, 1983, 34 pp., o.p.; Picture Book Studio, 1988, pap., 36 pp., o.p.; adapt. and illus. by Barbara Bazilian, Whispering Coyote, 1997, 40 pp. (1-87908-556-9); Charlesbridge, 2001, 40 pp. (1-580890-69-5)
(BL 79:1461; SLJ Sep 1983, p. 100)

1-17   **ANDERSEN, Hans Christian.** *The Snow Queen.* Gr. 2–5. (Written in Den-
★   mark, 1845, orig. U.S. pub. 1849.)
Gerda faces many perils as she tries to save her friend, Kay, imprisoned in the Snow Queen's ice palace.
Trans. by R. P. Keigwin, illus. by June Corwin, Atheneum, 1968, o.p.; illus. by Marcia Brown, Scribner, 1972, 95 pp., o.p.; adapt. by Naomi Lewis, illus. by Errol Le Cain, Viking, 1979, o.p.; Puffin, 1982, pap. (0-14-050294-7); adapt. by Amy Ehrlich, illus. by Susan Jeffers, Dial, 1982, 40 pp. (0-8037-8029-X), pap. (0-8037-0692-8); trans. by Eva Le Gallienne, illus. by Arieh Zeldich, Harper, 1985, o.p.; adapt. and illus. by Richard Hess, Macmillan, 1985, o.p.; trans. and adapt. by Anthea Bell, illus. by Bernadette Watts, North-South, 1987, 32 pp., o.p.; trans. by Naomi Lewis, illus. by Angela Barrett, Holt, 1988, 42 pp., o.p.; trans. by Naomi Lewis, illus. by Angela Barrett, Candlewick, 1993, 32 pp., o.p.; adapt. by Caroline Peachey, illus. by P. J. Lynch, Harcourt, 1994, 48 pp., o.p.; adapt. by Richard Kennedy, illus. by Edward S. Gazsi, entitled *The Snow Queen: A Christmas Pageant*, HarperCollins, 1996, 88 pp., o.p.; (entitled *Hans Christian Andersen's The Snow Queen*) adapt. by Ken Setterington, illus. by Nelly and Ernst Hofer, Tundra, 2000, 48 pp. (0-88776-497-5)
(BL 39:37, 65:650, 69:531, 75:1627, 79:672, 684, 82:977, 84:470, 85:569, 90:521, 91:135, 97:815; Bookshelf 1921–1922 p. 8; CCBB 22:21, 73, 36:121; 50:162; HB 49:141; HBG 1:82; 5:72, 5, 6:64; 12:31; 298; Kirkus 36:820, 40:1307, 47:1205, 62:1403; LJ 67:884, 910, 93:3753, 3964, 98:999; SLJ Jan 1980 p. 64, Mar 1983 p. 154, Jan 1986 p. 53, Oct 1987 p. 109, Feb 1994 p. 76, Nov 1994 p. 102, Feb 1997 p. 74, Mar 2001 p. 192; Suth 3:16; TLS 1968 p. 586)

1-18   **ANDERSEN, Hans Christian.** *The Steadfast Tin Soldier.* Gr. K–5. (Written
★   in Denmark, 1838, orig. U.S. pub. 1927.)
A malevolent jack-in-the-box tries to separate two lovers, a tin soldier and a paper ballerina. The 1953 Scribner edition illustrated by Marcia Brown was awarded a Randolph Caldecott Honor Book Medal in 1954.
Trans. by M. R. James, illus. by Marcia Brown, Scribner, 1953, o.p.; illus. by Monika Laimgruber, Atheneum, 1971 (orig. pub. 1970), o.p.; illus. by Paul Galdone, Houghton, 1979, o.p.; adapt. and illus. by Thomas Di Grazia, Prentice, 1981, 32 pp. (0-13-846295-X); illus. by Alain Vaës, Little, Brown, 1983, o.p.; illus. by David Jorgensen, Knopf, 1986, 48 pp., o.p.; trans. by Naomi Lewis, illus. by P. J. Lynch, Harcourt, 1992, 32 pp., o.p.; adapt. by Tor Seidler, illus. by Fred Marcellino, Harper, 1992, 32 pp., o.p., 1997, pap., 32 pp. (0-06-2059009).; adapt. and illus. by Rachel Isadora, Putnam, 1996, 32 pp. (0-399-22676-1); adapt. by Adrian Mitchell, illus. by Jonathan Heale, DK, 1996, 32 pp., o.p.
(BL 50:18, 76:498, 78:595, 80:853, 89:665, 92:1440; 93:509; CCBB 7:1, 50:163; HB 29:347, 58:151; HBG 8:17, 14:23; Kirkus 21:532, 48:61, 60:1138, 1371; LJ 78:1544, 96:2373; SLJ Dec 1979 p. 71, Jan 1982 p. 58, Mar 1984 p. 137, Feb 1993 p. 68, Jan 1997 p. 75; Suth:216)

1-19   **ANDERSEN, Hans Christian.** *The Swineherd.* Gr. K–5. (Orig. Danish pub.
☆   1841, U.S. 1924.)
Scorned by a self-centered princess, a prince decides to make a fool of her by
wooing her, disguised as a swineherd.
Trans. and illus. by Erik Blegvad, Harcourt, 1958, o.p.; trans. by Anthea Bell,
illus. by Lisbeth Zwerger, Morrow, 1982, o.p.; Picture Book Studio, 1986, pap.,
o.p.; trans. by Naomi Lewis, illus. by Dorothée Duntze, North-South, 1987, 32
pp., o.p.; adapt. and illus. by Deborah Hahn, Lothrop, 1991, 32 pp., o.p.; trans.
by Anthea Bell, illus. by Lisbeth Zwerger, Neugebauer, 1995 (reissue of Morrow, 1982 ed.), 32 pp. (1-55858-428-5)
(BL 55:27, 78:951, 83:1280; CCBB 12:93; HB 34:38, 58:277; HBG 3:23, 6:256; Kirkus
26:605, 59:1085; LJ 55:27, 83:3004; SLJ Mar 1982 p. 127, June/July 1987 p. 75)

1-20   **ANDERSEN, Hans Christian.** *Thumbelina.* Gr. K–5. (Written in Denmark,
☆   1835, orig. U.S. pub. Macmillan, 1928.)
A tiny, thumb-sized girl named Thumbelina is carried off by a frog, saved by a
field mouse, and is nearly married to a mole before reaching the land of the
flower people.
Trans. by R. P. Keigwin, illus. by Adrienne Adams, Scribner, 1961, o.p.; adapt.
by Amy Ehrlich, illus. by Susan Jeffers, Dial, 1979, LB (0-8037-8814-2); trans.
by Richard Winston and Clara Winston, illus. by Lisbeth Zwerger, Morrow,
1980 (entitled *Thumbeline*), o.p.; trans. by Anthea Bell, illus. by Lisbeth
Zwerger, Picture Book, 1985 (entitled *Thumbeline*), 29 pp., o.p.; adapt. and
illus. by Demi, Putnam, 1989, 32 pp., o.p.; retold by Deborah Hautzig, illus. by
Kaarina Kaila, Knopf, 1990, 32 pp., o.p.; illus. by Alison Claire Darke, Doubleday, 1991, o.p.; illus. by Wayne Anderson, retold by James Riordan, Putnam,
1991, 32 pp. (0-399-21756-8); retold by Jane Falloon, illus. by Emma Chichester Clark, Simon, 1997, 48 pp., o.p.; trans. by Erik Haugaard, illus. by Arlene
Graston, Doubleday, 1997, 32 pp., o.p.; illus. by Eva Montanari, McGraw-Hill,
2002, 32 pp. (1-58845-478-9); illus. by Brian Pinkney, Greenwillow/Harper-
Collins, 2003, 40 pp. (0-688-17477-9); illus. by Brad Sneed, Dial, 2004, 40 pp.
(0-8037-2812-3); Little, Brown, 2005, 42 pp. (0-316-57359-0)
(BL 58:228, 76:554, 77:112, 82:681, 87:1494, 85:1189, 93:1435, 94:565, 101:254; CCBB
15:90, 33:145, 56:4, 57:139; HB 4[Aug 1928]:9, 38:41; HBG 2:43, 2:241, 3:23, 9:58; Kirkus
29:953, 48:209, 49:55, 58:1332, 59:326; LJ 86:4357; SLJ Jan 1980 p. 53, Mar 1980 p. 116,
Sep 1980 p. 55, Feb 1986 p. 70, Apr 1989 p. 75, Sep 1990 p. 192, June 1991 p. 89, Feb 1992
p. 70, June 1997 p. 78; Sep 1997 p. 72)

1-21   **ANDERSEN, Hans Christian.** *The Tinderbox.* Gr. K–4. (Orig. Danish pub.
☆   1835.)
A soldier's fortune is made when he steals a magical tinderbox from a witch;
striking it brings three huge dogs to grant their master's wishes. In the Little,
Brown, 1990, edition retold by Moser, the story is set in the post-Civil War Tennessee mountains, and the witch has been replaced by a wily mountain man.
Illus. by Warwick Hutton, Macmillan, 1988, 32 pp., o.p.; adapt. and illus. by
Barry Moser, Little, Brown, 1990, 32 pp., o.p.; adapt. by Peggy Thomson, illus.
by James Warhola, Simon & Schuster, 1991, 40 pp., o.p.
(BL 85:263, 87:438, 971, 88:64; HB 64:768, 67:65; HBG 2:70, 3:24; Kirkus 56:1145,
58:1165; SLJ Dec 1988 p. 96, Oct 1990 p. 113, Nov 1991 p. 89)

1-22   **ANDERSEN, Hans Christian.** *The Ugly Duckling.* Gr. K–5. (Written in
✶   Denmark, 1842, orig. U.S. pub. 1850.)
Mistreated by the other ducks, an "ugly duckling" runs away to spend a terrible
winter on his own. But when spring arrives he has become a beautiful swan.
Trans. by R. P. Keigwin, illus. by Adrienne Adams, Scribner, 1965, o.p.; retold
and illus. by Lorinda Bryan Cauley, Harcourt, 1979, o.p., 1989, pap. (0-15-
692528-1); trans. by Anne Stewart, illus. by Monika Laimgruber, Greenwillow,
1985, o.p.; adapt. by Joel Tuber and Clara Stites, illus. by Robert Van Nutt,
Knopf, 1986 (0-394-88298-9); adapt. by Marianna Mayer, illus. by Thomas
Locker, Macmillan, 1987, 38 pp. (0-02-765130-4); illus. by Troy Howell, Put-
nam, 1990, 38 pp., o.p.; illus. by Alan Marks, trans. by Anthea Bell, Picture
Book Studio, 1991, 44 pp., o.p.; adapt. by Adrian Mitchell, illus. by Jonathan
Heale, Dorling Kindersley, 1994, 32 pp., o.p.; adapt. and illus. by Jerry
Pinkney, Morrow, 1999, 40 pp. (0-688-15933-8); illus. by Bernadette Watts,
North-South, 2000 (0-7358-1389-2); adapt. by Kevin Crossley-Holland, illus.
by Meilo So, Knopf, 2001, 32 pp. (0-375-91319-X); trans. by Anthea Bell,
illus. by Robert Ingpen, Putnam, 2005, 32 pp. (0-698-40010-0)
(BL 62:270, 76:499, 82:681, 83:706, 1280, 86:1337, 95:1207, 96:1751, 101:657; CCBB 5:64,
19:141, 40:141, 43:179, 52:231, 55:128; HB 41:627, 62:188; HBG 5:298, 10:275; Kirkus
33:899, 47:1206, 54:1719, 55:133, 58:348, 62:839; LJ 90:4602; SLJ Jan 1980 p. 54, Jan 1986
p. 53, Feb 1987 p. 63, Apr 1990 p. 86, July 1994 p.73, May 99 p. 79; Suth:216)

1-23   **ANDERSEN, Hans Christian.** *The Wild Swans.* Gr. K–5. (Orig. pub. in
✶   Denmark, orig. U.S. pub. 1922.)
A young princess tries to break the spell that changed her 11 brothers into
swans. *Swan's Wing* by Ursula Synge (see Chapter 6, High Fantasy: Myth or
Legend Fantasy) and *Daughter of the Forest* by Juliet Marillier (see Chapter 6,
High Fantasy: Myth or Legend Fantasy) are novelized versions of this story,
written for older readers.
Trans. by M. R. James, illus. by Marcia Brown, Scribner, 1963, o.p.; adapt. by
Amy Ehrlich, illus. by Susan Jeffers, Dial, 1976, 1990, 40 pp. (0-8037-9391-
X); trans. by Naomi Lewis, illus. by Angela Barrett, Bedrick, 1984, 33 pp.,
o.p.; retold by Deborah Hautzig, illus. by Kaarina Kaila, Knopf, 1992, 32 pp.,
o.p.; adapt. by Ken Setterington, illus. by Nelly Hofer and Ernst Hofer, Tundra,
2003, 40 pp. (0-88776-615-3)
(BL 60:416, 78:646, 81:585; CCBB 35:102; HB 39:601, 40:487; HBG 4:54; SLJ Jan 1982 p.
58, Dec 1984 p. 67)

1-24   **ANDERSON, Mildred Napier.** *A Gift for Merimond.* Gr. 4–6. (Orig. pub. in
England.)
Prince Merimond's gift of having all his wishes granted leads to unexpected
problems.
Illus. by J. Paget-Fredericks, Oxford University Press, 1953, 84 pp., o.p.
(BL 49:273; CCBB 7:19; HB 29:119; Kirkus 21:114; LJ 78:737)

1-25   **ANDERSON, Mildred Napier.** *Sandra and the Right Prince.* Gr. 3–5.
(Orig. pub. in England.)
Princess Sandra rules out jousting and dragon-slaying as criteria in selecting
her future husband.
Illus. by J. Paget-Fredericks, Oxford University Press, 1951, 72 pp., o.p.
(BL 47:369; CCBB 4:40; HB 27:179, 238; LJ 76:781)

ANDREWS, Allen. *The Pig Plantagenet.*
See Chapter 2, Animal Fantasy.

ARKIN, Alan (Wolf). *The Lemming Condition.*
See Chapter 2, Animal Fantasy.

AULNOY, Marie Catherine Jumelle de Berneville, Comtesse d'. *The Children's Fairyland.*
See Chapter 3, Fantasy Collections.

AULNOY, Marie Catherine Jumelle de Berneville, Comtesse d'. *The White Cat and Other Old French Fairy Tales.*
See Chapter 3, Fantasy Collections.

1-26 **AVI (Avi Wortis).** *Tom, Babette, and Simon: Three Tales of Transformation.* Gr. 4–7.
Three stories about a boy who trades bodies with his cat, a princess who is perfect but invisible, and a man who becomes a bird from the neck up.
Illus. by Alexi Natchev, Simon, 1995, 100 pp., o.p.
(BL 901:1643; CCBB 48:376; HBG 6:294; Kirkus 63:776; SLJ June 1995 p. 108)

1-27 **BABBITT, Natalie (Zane Moore).** *Knee-Knock Rise.* Gr. 3–5.
☆ The people living closest to Knee-Knock Rise hill are both proud and fearful of the noisy monster said to live there, until a boy named Egan discovers the real cause of the terrible noise. John Newbery Medal Honor Book, 1971.
Illus. by the author, Farrar, 1970, 117 pp. (0-374-34257-1), 1984, pap. (0-374-44260-6)
(BL 67:99, 659; CCBB 24:53; HB 46:295; Kirkus 38:551; LJ 95:2306; Suth:24)

1-28 **BABBITT, Natalie (Zane Moore).** *The Search for Delicious.* Gr. 3–6.
☆ While polling inhabitants on the exact definition of "delicious," Gaylen uncovers a plot by the queen's brother to take over the kingdom.
Farrar, 1969, 176 pp. (0-374-36534-2), 2005, pap., 176 pp. (0-374-46536-3)
(BL 66:53; CCBB 23:21; HB 45:407; Kirkus 37:373; LJ 95:3603; TLS 1975 p. 365)

BABBITT, Natalie (Zane Moore). *Tuck Everlasting.*
See Chapter 6, High Fantasy: Myth or Legend Fantasy.

1-29 **BACH, Richard (David).** *Jonathan Livingston Seagull.* Gr. 10 up.
Exiled from his flock for daring to fly for the joy of it, rather than following in the dignified Gull family tradition, Jonathan discovers that his purpose in life is to help others find perfection.
Macmillan, 1970, 93 pp. (0-02-504540-7); Avon, 1973, pap. (0-380-01286-3)
(BL 67:553; LJ 95:4187, 97:4093)

BACON, Martha (Sherman). *Moth Manor: A Gothic Tale.*
See Chapter 11, Toy Fantasy.

BAKER, Betty (Lou). *Dupper.*
See Chapter 2, Animal Fantasy.

1-30   **BAKER, Betty (Lou).** *Save Sirrushany! (Also Agotha, Princess Gwyn and All the Fearsome Beasts).* Gr. 4–6.
A dragon, a rare snail, and a girl named Agotha restore the fortunes of the Kingdom of Sirrushany.
Illus. by Erick Ingraham, Macmillan, 1978, 134 pp., o.p.
(CCBB 32:22; Kirkus 46:496; SLJ May 1978 p. 62)

1-31   **BAKER, Betty (Lou).** *Seven Spells to Farewell.* Gr. 4–6.
Orphaned Drucilla runs away from her uncle's inn with a talking raven and a performing pig, and crosses the mountain to the town of Farewell to become a sorceress.
Macmillan, 1982, 123 pp., o.p.
(CCBB 35:162; SLJ Apr 1982, p. 65)

1-32   **BAKER, Margaret.** *The Black Cats and the Tinker's Wife.* Gr. K–4.
The tinker's wife works magic with her good wishes.
Illus. by Mary Baker, Dodd, 1939, 1951, 120 pp., o.p.
(BL 20:104; Bookshelf 1923–1924 Suppl., p. 1; CCBB 5:42; LJ 77:71)

1-33   **BAKER, Margaret.** *Cat's-Cradles for His Majesty.* Gr. 2–4.
Pete, his mother, and Cinders the cat introduce the king to the game of cat's cradle.
Illus. by Mary Baker, Dodd, 1933, 115 pp., o.p.
(BL 30:157, Bookshelf 1933 p. 6; HB 9:204; LJ 59:403)

1-34   **BAKER, Margaret.** *The Lost Merbaby.* Gr. 2–4.
The fisherman and his wife adopt a mischievous merbaby placed in the fisherman's basket by the mermaids.
Illus. by Mary Baker, Duffield, 1927, o.p.; Dodd, 1941, 85 pp., o.p.
(BL 23:388; HB 3[Aug 1927]:26-27; Mahony 2:130; Moore:345; TLS 1927 p. 873)

1-35   **BAKER, Margaret.** *Noddy Goes A-Plowing.* Gr. 3–4.
A young man named Noddy wins a plowing match and the hand of the Princess.
Illus. by Mary Baker, Duffield, 1930, 104 pp., o.p.
(BL 27:211; HB 6:319, 7:115; Mahony 3:104; TLS 1930 p. 982)

1-36   **BANCROFT, Alberta.** *The Goblins of Haubeck.* Gr. 3–5.
A mischievous changeling makes trouble for the good goblins who help the housewives of Haubeck.
Illus. by Harold Sichel, McBride, 1925, 1933, 117 pp., o.p.
(BL 22:167; HB 2[Nov 1925]:18; LJ 58:806; Mahony 2:272)

BANKS, Lynne Reid. *The Fairy Rebel.*
See Chapter 9, Magic Adventure Fantasy.

1-37   **BANKS, Lynne Reid.** *The Farthest-Away Mountain.* Gr. 5–7. (Orig. British pub. 1976.)
Dakin and a prince-turned-frog set off for an unreachable mountain in order to break a witch's spell.

Illus. by Victor G. Ambrus, Doubleday, 1977, 140 pp., o.p.; illus. by Dave Henderson, Doubleday, 1991, 128 pp. (0-385-41534-6); Delacorte, 2003, 153 pp. (0-385-90117-8)

(BL 74:809; CCBB 31:122; HBG 2:270, 15:87; Kirkus 46:2; SLJ Feb 1978 p. 54, Mar 1991 p. 192; TLS 1976 p. 1553)

BANKS, Lynne Reid. *The Magic Hare.*
See Chapter 2, Animal Fantasy.

1-38 **BANKS, Richard.** *The Mysterious Leaf.* Gr. 2–5.
A mysterious girl convinces three college professors to care for a tiny leaf that must never touch anything but the flesh of their hands.
Illus. by Irene Haas, Harcourt, 1954, 53 pp., o.p.

(BL 51:251; CCBB 8:74; HB 31:111; Kirkus 22:633; LJ 79:2253)

1-39 **BARBER, Antonia.** *The Enchanter's Daughter.* Gr. K–4. (Orig. British pub.
✬ 1987.)
The enchanter's beautiful young daughter has vague memories of another life, far from the lonely, cold white land at the top of the world. Kate Greenaway Medal Commended Book, 1987.
Illus. by Errol Le Cain, Farrar, 1988, 32 pp. (0-374-32170-1)

(BL 85:478; CCBB 42:64; Kirkus 56:1319; SLJ Dec 1988 p. 79; Suth 4:21)

BARRETT, Nicholas. *Fledger.*
See Chapter 2, Animal Fantasy.

1-40 **BARRIE, Sir J(ames) M(atthew).** *Peter Pan in Kensington Gardens.* Gr. 4–6. (Orig. British pub. in *The Little White Bird; or, Adventures in Kensington Gardens*, 1902; U.S. pub. Scribner, 1906, 1934.)
A very young Peter Pan comes to live among the birds and fairies in Kensington Gardens. This story, abridged from *The Little White Bird; or, Adventures in Kensington Gardens* (1892, 1902), is a forerunner to the author's classic tale, *Peter Pan* (1911; see Chapter 7, High Fantasy: Travel to Other Worlds). Both tales are published together in the Oxford University Press edition.
Illus. by Arthur Rackham, Oxford University Press, 1999, pap., entitled *Peter Pan in Kensington Gardens; Peter and Wendy*, 240 pp. (0-19-283929-2)

(BL 7:173)

BATO, Joseph. *The Sorcerer.*
See Chapter 12, Witchcraft and Sorcery Fantasy.

BAUM, L(yman) Frank. *The Surprising Adventures of the Magical Monarch of Mo and His People.*
See Chapter 3, Fantasy Collections.

BAXTER, Lorna. *The Eggchild.*
See Chapter 12, Witchcraft and Sorcery Fantasy.

BEAGLE, Peter S(oyer). *The Last Unicorn.*
See Chapter 5, High Fantasy: Alternate Worlds or Histories.

1-41 **BEHN, Harry.** *The Faraway Lurs.* Gr. 5–8.
Heather, a girl from a peaceful forest tribe, falls in love with the son of the enemy chief, who plans to cut down the sacred tree of the forest people, in this tragic love story set in prehistoric time.
Collins World, 1963, 190 pp., o.p.
(BL 59:893, 896; HB 39:165; LJ 88:2140)

1-42 **BENARY-ISBERT, Margot.** *The Wicked Enchantment.* Gr. 5–7. (Orig.
✰ pub. in Germany.)
Anemone and her dog Winnie run away after an evil spell is cast over their town.
Trans. by Richard Winston and Clara Winston, illus. by Enrico Arno, Harcourt, 1955, o.p.
(BL 52:18; CCBB 9:18; Eakin:29; HB 31:374; 60:223; Kirkus 23:538; LJ 80:2644)

BENCHLEY, Nathaniel (Goddard). *Feldman Fieldmouse: A Fable.*
See Chapter 2, Animal Fantasy.

BENÉT, Stephen Vincent. *The Devil and Daniel Webster.*
See Chapter 6, High Fantasy: Myth or Legend Fantasy.

1-43 **BENJAMIN, Alan.** *Appointment.* Gr. 4–7.
Death, disguised as an old woman, stalks Abdulah, an elderly servant, through the marketplace of Baghdad, in this story adapted from W. Somerset Maugham's novel *Appointment in Samarra*, adapted from his play *Sheppey* (1934).
Illus. by Roger Essley, Simon, 1993, 32 pp. (0-671-75887-X)
(BL 89:1692; HBG 4:269)

1-44 **BERGER, Barbara Helen.** *Gwinna.* Gr. 4–7.
The Mother of the Owls grants a childless couple's wish for a baby, but they are horrified when their daughter, Gwinna, grows wings.
Illus. by the author, Putnam, 1980, 127 pp. (0-399-21738-X)
(BL 87:441; CCBB 44:111; HBG 2:66; Kirkus 58:1391; SLJ Dec 1990 p. 98)

1-45 **BIANCO, Margery (Winifred) Williams.** *The Apple Tree.* Gr. 2–4.
An allegorical tale about spring and the renewal of life.
Illus. by Boris Artzybasheff, Doran, 1926, 47 pp., o.p.
(BL 22:425)

1-46 **BIANCO, Margery (Winifred) Williams.** *The House That Grew Smaller.*
Gr. 2–4.
An uninhabited hillside house blows away and grows steadily smaller, until it is just the right size for a special inhabitant.
Illus. by Rachel Lyman Field, Macmillan, 1931, 40 pp., o.p.
(BL 28:107; HB 7:317; Mahony 3:105)

BIANCO, Margery (Winifred) Williams. *The Velveteen Rabbit; or, How Toys Became Real.*
See Chapter 11, Toy Fantasy.

1-47 **BIANCO, Pamela.** *The Starlit Journey, a Story.* Gr. 2–4.
A little princess begins her betrothal journey.

Illus. by the author, Macmillan, 1933, 46 pp., o.p.
(Bookshelf 1933 p. 6; LJ 58:898)

1-48 **BIEGEL, Paul.** *The King of the Copper Mountains.* Gr. 4–6. (Orig. Dutch pub. 1965.)
While awaiting the arrival of a doctor to save the king's life, several animals tell stories to distract the king.
Trans. by Gillian Hume and Paul Biegel, illus. by Babs Van Wely, Dent, 1977 (repr. of 1968 ed.), 176 pp., o.p.
(CCBB 23:141; LJ 95:1632; Suth:38; TLS 1968 p. 1373)

Black Water: The Book of Fantastic Literature. **Ed. by Alberto Manguelo.**
See Chapter 3, Fantasy Collections.

BLACKWOOD, Gary L. *Beyond the Door.*
See Chapter 7, High Fantasy: Travel to Other Worlds.

1-49 **BLISS, Corinne Demas.** *Matthew's Meadow.* Gr. 3–6.
Matthew returns each summer to a secret meadow cleared by his late grandmother, where he learns about preserving the natural world from a red-tailed hawk.
Illus. by Ted Lewin, Harcourt, 1992, 40 pp. (0-15-200759-8)
(BL 88:1356; HBG 3:253; Kirkus 60:250; SLJ Aug 1992 p. 132)

1-50 **BODGER, Joan (Mercer).** *Clever-Lazy, the Girl Who Invented Herself.* Gr. 5–8.
Clever-Lazy and her husband flee the Emperor's Court to keep the gunpowder she invented from falling into the wrong hands.
Atheneum, 1979, 201 pp., o.p.
(BL 76:663; HB 56:53; SLJ Jan 1980 p. 77; VOYA 3:26)

BOMANS, Godfried (Jan Arnold). *Eric in the Land of the Insects.*
See Chapter 7, High Fantasy: Travel to Other Worlds.

BOMANS, Godfried (Jan Arnold). *The Wily Witch and All the Other Fairy Tales and Fables.*
See Chapter 3, Fantasy Collections.

BOURLIAGUET, Léonce. *The Giant Who Drank from His Shoe and Other Stories.*
See Chapter 3, Fantasy Collections.

1-51 **BOWEN, Vernon.** *The Wonderful Adventures of Ting Ling.* Gr. 3–5.
★ Ting Ling, a juggler's assistant in ancient China, manages to accomplish five impossible tasks set by the cruel emperor and wins the hand of the princess.
Illus. by Kurt Wiese, McKay, 1952, 49 pp., o.p.
(BL 49:18; HB 28:319; Kirkus 20:403; LJ 77:1412)

1-52 **BOWEN, William A(lvin).** *The Enchanted Forest.* Gr. 3–5.
Six tales about the adventures of two young boys, Bojohn and Bildad, who meet elves, fairies, princesses, and princes. *Solario the Tailor* (1922) is the sequel.

Illus. by Maud and Miska Petersham, Macmillan, 1920, 1926, 197 pp., o.p.
(BL 17:220; Bookshelf 1923–192 p. 8)

1-53   BOYLE, Kay. *The Youngest Camel.* Gr. 3–4. (Orig. pub. 1939.)
A lonely young camel wanders without purpose until he meets a caravan of
white camels that circles the earth.
Illus. by Ronni Solbert, Harper, 1959, 96 pp., o.p.
(HB 15:295, 380, 35:387; LJ 64:870)

BRADBURY, Ray (Douglas). *Something Wicked This Way Comes.*
See Chapter 12, Witchcraft and Sorcery Fantasy.

BRADLEY, Marion Zimmer. *Night's Daughter.*
See Chapter 6, High Fantasy: Myth or Legend Fantasy.

1-54   BRANCH, M(ary) L(ydia) (Bolles). *Guld the Cavern King.* Gr. 3–5. (Orig.
British pub. 1917.)
Little Guld leads his people up into the light from the Koboldland caverns
beneath the earth.
Bookshop for Boys and Girls, 1918, 175 pp., o.p.
(BL 15:189; Mahony 2:274)

1-55   BRENTANO, Clemens Maria. *Schoolmaster Whackwell's Wonderful
Sons.* Gr. 3–6. (Orig. pub. in Germany.)
The schoolmaster's five sons spend a year seeking their separate fortunes, and
then join forces to rescue a princess held captive by a giant.
Trans. by Doris Orgel, illus. by Maurice (Bernard) Sendak, Random, 1962, 88
pp., o.p.
(BL 59:490; HB 39:58; LJ 87:4618)

1-56   BRENTANO, Clemens Maria. *The Tale of Gockel, Hinkel and Gackeliah.*
(Orig. U.S. title: *Gockel, Hinkel and Gackeleia,* **1914).** Gr. 4–6. (Orig. Ger-
man pub. 1838, orig. U.S. pub. Silver, 1914.)
A magic ring brings good fortune to Gockel and his family, until his daughter is
deceived into giving it to a stranger.
Trans. by Doris Orgel, illus. by Maurice (Bernard) Sendak, Random, 1961, 143
pp., o.p.
(BL 58:444; HB 38:49; Kirkus 29:504; LJ 86:2532)

BRIGGS, K(atharine) M(ary). *Kate Crackernuts.*
See Chapter 6, High Fantasy: Myth or Legend Fantasy.

BRIGHT, Robert. *Richard Brown and the Dragon.*
See Chapter 8, Humorous Fantasy.

BROOKE, William J. *A Telling of the Tales: Five Stories.*
See Chapter 3, Fantasy Collections.

1-57   BROWN, Judith Gwyn. *The Mask of the Dancing Princess.* Gr. 3–6.
Selfish Princess Rosamund spends seven years living with a band of gypsies,
learning how to be a kind and fair ruler.

Illus. by the author, Macmillan, 1989, 48 pp. (0-689-31427-2)
(BL 86:660; HBG 1:82; Kirkus 57:1400; SLJ Nov 1989 p. 104)

BRYHER, Winifred. *A Visa for Avalon.*
See Chapter 6, High Fantasy: Myth or Legend Fantasy.

BUCHWALD, Emilie. *Gildaen: The Heroic Adventures of a Most Unusual Rabbit.*
See Chapter 2, Animal Fantasy.

1-58 **BULLA, Clyde Robert.** *The Moon Singer.* Gr. 3–5.
Torr, a foundling who sings unearthly songs to the moon, is taken from his foster parents to be raised as a prince.
Illus. by Trina Schart Hyman, Harper, 1969, 48 pp., o.p.
(HB 45:671; Kirkus 37:1111; LJ 95:2307)

1-59 **BULLA, Clyde Robert.** *My Friend the Monster.* Gr. 3–5.
☆ Young Prince Hal rescues a monster named Humbert and the two become fast, but secret, friends.
Illus. by Michele Chessare, Harper, 1980, 75 pp., o.p.
(BL 77:455; CCBB 34:107; HB 56:639; Kirkus 49:6; SLJ Dec 1980 p. 58)

1-60 **BULLA, Clyde Robert.** *The Sword in the Tree.* Gr. 3–5.
☆ Young Shan becomes a knight to avenge his father's loss of all rights to his uncle, Lord Weldon.
Illus. by Paul Galdone, Harper, 1962, 113 pp., o.p.; illus. by Bruce Bowles, HarperTrophy, 2000, pap., 112 pp. (0-06-442132-5)
(HB 32:184; Kirkus 21:1; LJ 81:764)

1-61 **BUNYAN, John.** *The Pilgrim's Progress.* **(Orig. title:** *The Pilgrim's Progress; from This World to That Which Is to Come, 1671*). Gr. 5 up.
A simplified retelling of Christian's allegorical journey from the City of Destruction to the Eternal City.
Ed. by Mary Godolphin, illus. by Robert Lawson, Lippincott, 1939, 1976, o.p.; illus. by Frank C. Pape, Dutton, 1954, 1979 (repr. of 1954 ed.), o.p.; adapt. by James Reeves, illus. by Joanna Troughton, Bedrick, 1987, 160 pp. (0-87226-148-4); adapt. by Gary D. Schmidt, illus. by Barry Moser (entitled *Pilgrim's Progress: A Retelling*), Eerdmans, 1994, 78 pp. (0-8028-5080-4)
(BL 36:76, 91:501; HB 15:305, 16:17, 26, 126; HBG 6:86; Kirkus 55:861; LJ 64:712; SLJ Dec 1994 p. 130)

BURCH, Robert. *The Jolly Witch.*
See Chapter 12, Witchcraft and Sorcery Fantasy.

1-62 **BURTON, Philip.** *The Green Isle.* Gr. 2–4.
After Geraint, a Welsh shepherd, is imprisoned by the Normans as punishment for his love for her, Lady Eleanor escapes with him to a mysterious emerald island.
Illus. by Robert Andrew Parker, Dial, 1974, 32 pp., o.p.
(BL 71:98; Kirkus 42:876; SLJ Jan 1975 p. 37)

BYFIELD, Barbara Ninde. *Andrew and the Alchemist.*
See Chapter 12, Witchcraft and Sorcery Fantasy.

1-63 CAMERON, Eleanor (Frances Butler). *The Beast with the Magical Horn.*
Gr. 3–5.
Alison saves a unicorn and captures seven fabulous creatures for an evil queen.
Illus. by Beth Krush and Joe Krush, Little, Brown, 1963, 73 pp., o.p.
(BL 60:313; CCBB 17:75; HB 39:602; LJ 88:4471)

ČAPEK, Karel. *Nine Fairy Tales and One More Thrown In for Good Measure.*
See Chapter 3, Fantasy Collections.

1-64 CAREW, Jan (Rynveld). *Children of the Sun.* Gr. 3–5.
The two sons of an earth woman and the sun set out to answer their father's
query: "Would you like to be good men or great men?"
Illus. by Leo Dillon and Diane Dillon, Little, Brown, 1980, 40 pp., o.p.
(BL 76:1122; CCBB 33:187; Kirkus 48:774; SLJ May 1980 p. 65)

CAREY, Valerie Soho. *The Devil and Mother Crump.*
See Chapter 8, Humorous Fantasy.

CARROLL, Lewis. *Alice's Adventures in Wonderland.*
See Chapter 7, High Fantasy: Travel to Other Worlds.

CARTER, Robert. *The Collectors.*
See Chapter 2, Animal Fantasy.

A Cavalcade of Dragons. **Ed. by Roger (Gilbert) Lancelyn Green.**
See Chapter 3, Fantasy Collections.

1-65 CAYLUS, Anne Claude Philippe, Comte de. *Heart of Ice.* Gr. 2–3.
Kidnapped by a vengeful fairy at his christening, a tiny prince manages to scale
the slopes of the Ice Mountain to win the hand of Princess Sabella.
Adapt. by Benjamin Appel, illus. by J. K. Lambert, Pantheon, 1977, 58 pp., o.p.
(BL 74:158; CCBB 31:76; Kirkus 45:669; SLJ Oct 1977 p. 109)

1-66 CERVANTES, Saavedra Miguel de. *The Adventures of Don Quixote de la*
✯ *Mancha.* Gr. 5 up. (Orig. Spanish pub. in two parts, 1605 and 1615; first English ed. 1612.)
Don Quixote and Sancho Panza, knight and page, ride off to defend the poor
and rescue ladies in distress.
Adapt. by Leighton Barret, illus. by Warren Chappell, Knopf, 1960, o.p.; adapt.
by James Reeves, illus. by Edward Ardizzone (entitled *Exploits of Don
Quixote*), Walck, 1960, o.p.; illus. by W. Heath Robinson, Dent, 1983 (repr. of
1953 ed.), o.p.; retold by James Reeves, illus. by Edward Ardizzone, Bedrick,
1985 (entitled *The Exploits of Don Quixote;* orig. British pub. in this ed. 1959),
219 pp. (0-87226-025-9); adapt. and trans. by Magda Bogin, illus. by Manuel
Boix, Stewart, 1991, 144 pp., o.p.; adapt. by Margaret Hodges, illus. by
Stephen Marchesi, Macmillan, 1992, 72 pp. (entitled *Don Quixote and Sancho
Panza*) (0-684-19235-7); retold and illus. by Marcia Williams, Candlewick,
1993, 32 pp. (1-56402-174-2); adapt. by Michael Harrison, illus. by Victor G.

Ambrus, Oxford University Press, 1999, 95 pp. (0-19-274182-9); adapt. by Eric A. Kimmel, illus. by Leonard Everett Fisher (entitled *Don Quixote and the Windmills*) Farrar, 2004, 32 pp. (0-374-31825-5)

(BL 46:47, 57:130, 88:758, 100:1446; Bookshelf 1932 p. 8; CCBB 11:51, 46:171; HB 36:308, 69:227; HBG 4:66, 4:285, 7:59; Kirkus 28:621; LJ 85:3869; SLJ Jan 1981 p. 67, Jan 1992 p. 108, Nov 1992 p. 92, May 1993 p. 103; TLS Dec 4, 1951 p. xii, 1980 p. 1032)

CHARLES, Prince of Wales. *The Old Man of Lochnagar.*
See Chapter 8, Humorous Fantasy.

CHERRYH, C. J. (pseud. of Carolyn Janice Cherry). *The Dreamstone.*
See Chapter 6, High Fantasy: Myth or Legend Fantasy.

1-67 **CLÉMENT, Claude.** *The Man Who Lit the Stars.* Gr. 3–5. (Orig. pub. in Belgium and France, 1992.)
A lonely orphan follows a mysterious man who claims to be a star-polisher up a great ladder into the heavens.
Illus. by John Howe, Little, Brown, 1992, 32 pp., o.p.
(BL 89:984; Kirkus 60:987; SLJ Oct 1992 p. 114)

1-68 **COATSWORTH, Elizabeth (Jane).** *The Cat Who Went to Heaven.* Gr.
✫ 4–6. (Orig. pub. 1930.)
When a poor Japanese artist paints his little white cat into a picture of the dying Buddha, his pet is allowed into heaven. John Newbery Medal, 1931.
Illus. by Lynd Ward, Macmillan, 1967, 62 pp. (0-02-719710-7), 1990, pap. (0-689-71433-5)
(BL 27:107, 55:191; Bookshelf 1932 p.8; CCBB 12:60; HB 6:214, 7:119, 36:146, 62:344; LJ 56:279, 598; Moore:409, 431)

1-69 **COATSWORTH, Elizabeth (Jane).** *Cricket and the Emperor's Son.* Gr.
✫ 3–6. (Orig. pub. 1932.)
A little prince with insomnia is entertained each night by Cricket, an apprentice with an endless number of stories to tell.
Illus. by Juliette Palmer, Norton, 1965, 126 pp., o.p.
(BL 29:118, 61:873; Bookshelf 1933 p. 6; CCBB 18:144; Eakin:77; HB 8:157, 41:275; Kirkus 33:310; LJ 58:899, 90:2042)

COATSWORTH, Elizabeth (Jane). *Marra's World.*
See Chapter 6, High Fantasy: Myth or Legend Fantasy.

1-70 **COATSWORTH, Elizabeth (Jane).** *The Princess and the Lion.* Gr. 4–6.
✫ After the king surprises his court by naming Prince Michael heir to the throne, Princess Miriam journeys to the Prison of Princes to prevent Michael's escape.
Illus. by Evaline Ness, Pantheon, 1963, 77 pp., o.p.
(BL 60:39; Eakin:77; HB 39:281; LJ 88:2549)

1-71 **COATSWORTH, Elizabeth (Jane).** *Pure Magic.* **(pap. title:** *The Were-fox*). Gr. 4–5.
Johnny's new friend Giles has a secret: he can change into a fox, which proves dangerous when fox-hunting season begins.
Illus. by Ingrid Fetz, Macmillan, 1973, 68 pp., o.p.
(BL 70:385; HB 49:464; Kirkus 41:642; LJ 98:2649)

1-72 COEHLO, Paulo. *The Alchemist: A Fable About Following Your Dream.* Gr. 10 up. (Orig. Brazilian pub. 1988.)
After a seer advises young shepherd Santiago to follow his dream about hidden treasure by leaving Spain for Egypt, he travels to Tangier and joins a caravan bound for the East.
Trans. by Alan R. Clark and Paulo Coehlo, Harper, 1993, 192 pp. (0-06-250217-4)
(BL 89:1547, 1548; Kirkus 61:545; LJ June 15, 1993 p. 94; SLJ July 1993 p. 110)

COLLINS, Meghan. *The Willow Maiden.*
See Chapter 6, High Fantasy: Myth or Legend Fantasy.

COLLODI, Carlo. *The Adventures of Pinocchio.*
See Chapter 11, Toy Fantasy.

COLUM, Padraic. *The Boy Apprenticed to an Enchanter.*
See Chapter 12, Witchcraft and Sorcery Fantasy.

1-73 COLUM, Padraic. *The Children Who Followed the Piper.* Gr. 3–5.
John Ball, the miller's son, Golden Hood, the milk-woman's daughter, and Valentine, son of the Emperor, follow the Piper into adventure.
Illus. by Dugald Stewart Walker, Macmillan, 1922, 1935, 1944, 152 pp., o.p.
(BL 19:91; Mahony 2:134)

1-74 COLUM, Padraic. *The Girl Who Sat by the Ashes.* Gr. 3–5. (Orig. U.S. pub.
✶ 1919, 1939.)
An expanded version of the traditional "Cinderella" story.
Illus. by Imero Gobbato, Macmillan, 1968, 117 pp., o.p.
(BL 16:174; Bookshelf 1923–1924 p. 8; Kirkus 36:336; LJ 45:980; Mahony 1:25, 2:134)

1-75 COLUM, Padraic. *The King of Ireland's Son.* Gr. 5–7. (Orig. pub. Holt 1916.)
The king's son falls in love with the daughter of Fedelma, the Enchanter.
Illus. by Willy Pogány, Macmillan, 1921, 1962, 275 pp., o.p.
(BL 13:269, 18:95, 59:84; HB 39:75; Mahony 2:277)

COLUM, Padraic. *The Stone of Victory and Other Tales.*
See Chapter 3, Fantasy Collections.

1-76 CONRAD, Pam. *Blue Willow.* Gr. 3–5.
In this story of doomed love, Kung Shi Fair's merchant father forbids her marriage to fisherman Chang the Good, but after his daughter drowns and Chang is killed, the merchant commissions a Blue Willow plate to commemorate their love.
Illus. by S. Saelig Gallagher, Putnam, 1999, 32 pp. (0-399-22904-3)
(BL 96:441; CCBB 53:126; Kirkus 67:1414; SLJ Aug 1999 p. 131)

1-77 COOKE, Donald Edwin. *The Firebird.* Gr. 3–5.
A magical firebird helps the Red Prince pass through an enchanted land and defeat the evil Black Prince. This tale is taken from the same Russian source as Stravinski's "Firebird Suite."

Illus. by the author, Winston, 1939, 144 pp., o.p.
(BL 36:347; LJ 65:37)

1-78   COOPER, Gale. *Unicorn Moon.* Gr. 3–5.
A princess must solve the riddle of true love before she can separate the young
man imprisoned in her dreams from a real man she can love.
Illus. by the author, Dutton, 1984, 32 pp., o.p.
(BL 81:786; CCBB 38:103; SLJ Dec 1984 p. 79)

COOPER (Grant), Susan (Mary). *Tam Lin.*
See Chapter 6, High Fantasy: Myth or Legend Fantasy.

1-79   COOPER, Margaret. *The Ice Palace.* Gr. 3–5.
Princess Kasha is given a palace of ice, especially built to keep her cool.
Illus. by Harold Leland Goodwin, Macmillan, 1966, 50 pp., o.p.
(CCBB 20:136; Kirkus 34:574; LJ 91:4329)

1-80   COOPER, Paul Fenimore. *Dindle.* Gr. 3–5.
A rug-weaver named Dindle longs to rid the kingdom of the terrible white
dragon whose tail turns living things to stone.
Illus. by Marion Cooper, Putnam, 1963, 64 pp., o.p.
(HB 40:174; LJ 89:951)

CORBETT, W(illiam) J(esse). *The Song of Pentecost.*
See Chapter 2, Animal Fantasy.

1-81   CRANCH, Christopher P(earse). *The Last of the Huggermuggers, a Giant
Story.* Gr. 4–6. (Orig. British pub. 1855; U.S. 1856.)
Shipwrecked on an island in the East Indies, a young sailor named Jacket is
befriended by two kindly giants, or Huggermuggers. On his second visit,
described in the sequel, *Kobboltozo* (orig. British pub. 1856; U.S. 1857), Jacket
finds that a race of dwarfs is trying to take over the island. The books were
published together in a now out-of-print edition by University of Georgia Press
in 1993.
Illus. by J. Watson Davis, Burt, 1901(?), 170 pp., o.p.
(HB 20:172–175)

1-82   CRESSWELL (Rowe), Helen. *The Night Watchmen.* Gr. 4–6. (Orig. British
✫   pub. 1969.)
Two tramps named Josh and Caleb tell a boy named Henry the secret of the
Night Train. Carnegie Medal Honour Book, 1969; Phoenix Award, 1989.
Illus. by Gareth Floyd, Macmillan, 1970, 122 pp., o.p., 1989, pap., o.p.
(BL 67:371; CCBB 24:121; HB 46:615; Kirkus 38:1146; LJ 96:2128; Suth:94)

CRESSWELL (Rowe), Helen. *Up the Pier.*
See Chapter 10, Time Travel Fantasy.

1-83   CRESSWELL (Rowe), Helen. *The Winter of the Birds.* Gr. 5–8. (Orig.
✫   British pub. 1975.)
Neighbors unite when old Mr. Rudge foretells the coming of "terrible steel
birds" that kill live birds and bring evil to the town.
Macmillan, 1976, 243 pp., o.p.

(BL 72:1404; CCBB 30:80; HB 52:404; Kirkus 44:482; SLJ Sep 1976 p. 130; TLS 1975 p. 1457)

1-84 CROTHERS, Samuel McChord. *Miss Muffet's Christmas Party.* Gr. 4–6.
(Written 1891, orig. U.S. pub. 1902.)
Miss Muffet and the spider invite all of her favorite literary characters to their Christmas party.
Illus. by Olive M. Long, Houghton, 1929, 106 pp., o.p.
(BL 25:401; LJ 53:810; Mahony 2:278)

1-85 CROWNFIELD, Gertrude. *Princess Whiteflame.* Gr. 4–6.
Princess Radiance breaks the spell that had transformed Princess Whiteflame into a tiny flame.
Illus. by Anne Merriman Peck, Dutton, 1920, 229 pp., o.p.
(BL 17:352; Mahony 1:39)

CUMMINGS, e(dward) e(stlin). *Fairy Tales.*
See Chapter 3, Fantasy Collections.

1-86 CUNNINGHAM, Julia (Woolfolk). *Come to the Edge.* Gr. 5–7.
Unable to trust adults after his father's betrayal and the loss of his friend, Gravel Winter continually runs away from foster homes.
Pantheon, 1977, 79 pp., o.p.
(BL 74:37; CCBB 31:11; HB 53:449; Kirkus 45:4; SLJ May 1977 p. 60)

1-87 CUNNINGHAM, Julia (Woolfolk). *Dorp Dead.* Gr. 5 up.
✷   Gilly is taken from an unhappy life in an orphanage to an even more miserable foster home, from which he escapes to avoid being kept in a cage.
Illus. by James J. Spanfeller, Pantheon, 1965, o.p.; Knopf, 1993, pap., 96 pp. (0-679-84718-9); illus. by James J. Spanfeller, Knopf, 2002, 104 pp. (0-375-92255-5)
(CCBB 19:30; Eakin:87; HBG 14:93; LJ 90:2018)

CUNNINGHAM, Julia (Woolfolk). *Maybe, a Mole.*
See Chapter 2, Animal Fantasy.

1-88 CUNNINGHAM, Julia (Woolfolk). *Oaf.* Gr. 4–6.
Oaf, who has inherited three magic gifts, shares a dangerous adventure with a crow, a dog, a cat, and a rat.
Illus. by Peter Sís, Knopf, 1986, 86 pp., o.p.
(BL 82:1016; CCBB 39:144; Kirkus 54:544; SLJ Apr 1986 p. 86)

1-89 CUNNINGHAM, Julia (Woolfolk). *Tuppenny.* Gr. 5–8.
✷   The appearance of a young girl named Tuppenny changes the lives of three families: one whose daughter ran away from home, one whose retarded daughter is institutionalized, and one whose daughter was murdered.
Dutton, 1978, o.p.
(BL 75:371; CCBB 32:112; HB 55:639; Kirkus 46:1309; SLJ Nov 1978 p. 72; Suth 2:111)

CUNNINGHAM, Julia (Woolfolk). *Viollet.*
See Chapter 2, Animal Fantasy.

1-90 CUNNINGHAM, Julia (Woolfolk). *Wolf Roland.* Gr. 6–8.
A medieval peddler hunts down the huge yellow-eyed wolf that devoured his donkey friend, and this talking wolf agrees to take the donkey's place.
Pantheon, 1983, 108 pp., o.p.
(BL 79:1214; Kirkus 51:522; SLJ May 1983 p. 80)

CURLEY, Daniel. *Ann's Spring.*
See Chapter 6, High Fantasy: Myth or Legend Fantasy.

CURLEY, Daniel. *Billy Beg and the Bull.*
See Chapter 6, High Fantasy: Myth or Legend Fantasy.

1-91 CURRY, Jane Louise. *Little Little Sister.* Gr. K–3.
★ A forgetful older brother is saved three times by a sister so tiny that she can stow away in his pocket.
Illus. by Erik Blegvad, Macmillan, 1989, 32 pp., o.p.
(BL 86:741; CCBB 43:53; HB 65:767; HBG 1:81; Kirkus 57:1472; SLJ Nov 1989 p. 78)

1-92 DAHL, Borghild (Margarethe). *The Cloud Shoes.* Gr. 3–5.
King Brynne saves his kingdom of Brydalen from famine by using the gift of magical cloud shoes to travel to other lands for help.
Illus. by Hans Helweg, Dutton, 1957, 60 pp., o.p.
(BL 54:256; Kirkus 25:690; LJ 82:3246)

1-93 DAHL, Roald. *Two Fables.* Gr. 10 up. (Orig. British pub. 1986.)
Two adult fairy tales: "The Princess and the Poacher" and "Princess Mammalia," the former about a man rewarded by a king with the choice of any woman in the kingdom, and the latter about a plain princess turned pretty who misuses her power.
Illus. by Graham Dean, Viking, 1986, 61 pp. (0-670-81530-6)
(BL 84:26, 54)

DALKEY, Kara. *The Nightingale.*
See Chapter 6, High Fantasy: Myth or Legend Fantasy.

1-94 DAMJAN, Mischa (pseud.). *December's Travels.* Gr. 2–4. (Orig. German pub. 1986.)
The North Wind gives the boy, December, the magic gift of being able to visit March, June, and October. These visits give him a new appreciation of his winter home.
Illus. by Dušan Kállay, trans. by Anthea Bell, Dial, 1986, 32 pp., o.p.
(BL 83:127,138; CCBB 40:103; SLJ Nov 1986 p. 74)

1-95 DANK, Gloria Rand. *The Forest of App.* Gr. 4–6.
A young Rhymer, or storyteller, named Nob runs away and gets lost in an enchanted forest, where he helps the creatures recover their lost magic.
Greenwillow, 1983, 154 pp., o.p.
(CCBB 37:84; Kirkus 51:202; SLJ Feb 1984 p. 67)

DANN, Colin (Michael). *The Animals of Farthing Wood.*
See Chapter 2, Animal Fantasy.

D'AULAIRE, Ingri Mortenson, and D'AULAIRE, Edgar Parin.
D'Aulaires' Trolls.
See Chapter 3, Fantasy Collections.

1-96   DAVIES, Valentine. *The Miracle on 34th Street.* Gr. 4–7. (Orig. pub. 1947.)
Old Mr. Kringle tries to convince skeptics that he is Santa Claus, and gets a job
as Macy's Christmas Santa to prove it.
Harcourt, 1947, o.p.; illus. by Tomie dePaola, Harcourt, 1984, 116 pp., o.p.,
1987, pap. (0-15-254528-X); Harcourt, 2001 (reissue of 1947 ed.), 128 pp. (0-
15-216377-8)
(BL 43:359, 81:190, 211, 245, 247; CCBB 38:43; HBG 13:83; Kirkus 15:316; LJ 72:1033;
SLJ Oct 1984 p. 175)

1-97   DAY, David. *The Emperor's Panda.* Gr. 3–5. (Orig. Canadian pub. 1986.)
Wise and magical Lord Beishung, the Master Panda, helps young Kung, a poor
flute player, gain wisdom, a princess, and an empire.
Illus. by Eric Beddows, Dodd, 1987, 111 pp., o.p.
(BL 83:1599; SLJ Aug 1987 p. 81)

DEAN, Pamela. *Juniper, Gentian & Rosemary.*
See Chapter 6, High Fantasy: Myth or Legend Fantasy.

DEAN, Pamela. *Tam Lin.*
See Chapter 6, High Fantasy: Myth or Legend Fantasy.

1-98   DEFELICE, Cynthia. *The Strange Night Writing of Jessamine Colter.* Gr.
★   5–8.
Jessie Colter's calligraphic talent has enabled her to record most of her hometown's important events over the years, but even she is surprised that she can
see into the future, and discovers that everything she involuntarily writes at
night actually comes to pass.
Calligraphy by Leah Palmer Preiss, Macmillan, 1988, 51 pp. (0-02-726451-3)
(BL 85:264; CCBB 42:5; Kirkus 56:1058; SLJ Nov 1988 p. 124; VOYA 12:26)

DE LA MARE, Walter (John). *The Three Royal Monkeys.*
See Chapter 2, Animal Fantasy.

DE LINT, Charles. *Dreams Underfoot: The Newford Collection.*
See Chapter 5, High Fantasy: Alternate Worlds or Histories.

DE LINT, Charles. *Jack the Giant-Killer.*
See Chapter 6, High Fantasy: Myth or Legend Fantasy.

DELL, Joan. *The Missing Boy.*
See Chapter 7, High Fantasy: Travel to Other Worlds.

DE MORGAN, Mary (Augusta). *The Necklace of Princess Fiorimonde;
and Other Stories.*
See Chapter 3, Fantasy Collections.

DE REGNIERS, Beatrice Schenk (Freedman). *The Boy, the Rat, and the Butterfly.*
See Chapter 9, Magic Adventure Fantasy.

1-99 **DE REGNIERS, Beatrice Schenk (Freedman).** *Penny.* Gr. 1–4.
✫ Penny is a tiny girl "no bigger than a penny" who is adopted and raised by an elderly couple, marries a young man just her size, and goes to live in the land of tiny people.
Illus. by Marvin Bileck, Viking, 1966, 62 pp., o.p.; illus. by Betsy Lewin, Lothrop, 1987, 59 pp., o.p.
(BL 83:1204; CCBB 20:107; HB 42:705; Kirkus 34:1096, 55:135; LJ 91:6184)

1-100 **DIAMOND, Donna, adapt.** *Swan Lake.* Gr. 3 up.
Prince Siegfried falls in love with the Swan Queen Odette but is fooled by a sorcerer into pledging his love to her look-alike, Odille, in this retelling of the ballet story.
Illus. by the adapter, Holiday, 1981, 32 pp., o.p.
(BL 76:1289; Kirkus 48:1082; SLJ May 1980 p. 66)

1-101 **DICKENS, Charles (John Huffam).** *A Christmas Carol.* Gr. 3 up. (Orig.
✫ British pub. 1843.)
Mean old Ebenezer Scrooge is cured of his miserliness after he is visited by the ghosts of Christmases Past, Present, and Yet to Come.
Illus. by Arthur Rackham, Lippincott, 1915, 1952, o.p.; illus. by John Groth, Macmillan, 1963, o.p.; illus. by Michael Foreman, Dial, 1983, 128 pp. (0-8037-0032-6); illus. by Trina Schart Hyman, Holiday, 1983, 128 pp. (0-8234-0486-2); illus. by Greg Hildebrandt, Simon, 1983, 122 pp., o.p.; illus. by Lisbeth Zwerger, Picture Book Studio, 1988, pap., 65 pp. (0-88708-069-3); illus. by Roberto Innocenti, Stewart, 1990, 152 pp., o.p.; illus. by Quentin Blake, Simon, 1995, 144 pp., o.p.; illus. by Roberto Innocenti, Harcourt, 1995 (reissue of 1990 ed.), 152 pp. (0-15-100200-2); illus. by Carter Goodrich, Morrow, 1996, 56 pp., o.p.; illus. by William Geldart, Viking, 2000 [orig. pub. in France], 112 pp., o.p., 2000, pap., 107 pp. (0-670-88879-6); adapt. by Stephen Krensky, illus. by Dean Morrissey, HarperCollins, 2001, 62 pp. (0-06-028578-8); illus. by Lisbeth Zwerger, North-South, 2001, 67 pp. (0-7358-1259-4); illus. by Quentin Blake, Chrysalis, 2004, pap., 144 pp. (1-84365-063-0).
(BL 49:147, 58:194, 80:169, 406, 630, 633, 87:817; Bookshelf 1928 p. 35; CCBB 37:46; HB 59:731, 64:762, 67:198; HBG 2:65, 5:64, 65, 7:60, 8:65,12:83, 13:72 and 83; Kirkus 29:564; LJ 86:4046; SLJ Oct 1983 p. 179, Mar 1984 p. 172, Oct 1990 p. 36, Oct 1996 p. 34

1-102 **DICKENS, Charles (John Huffam).** *The Magic Fishbone.* Gr. 3–5. (Orig.
✫ British pub. 1868.)
Exhausted from caring for her 19 brothers and sisters, Princess Alice is given a magic fishbone that will grant one wish.
Illus. by Louis Slobodkin, Vanguard, 1953, 36 pp., o.p.; illus. by Robert Florczak, Harcourt, 2000, 40 pp. (0-15-201080-7)
(BL 97:958; Bookshelf 1923–1924 p. 8; Eakin:99; HB 1[June 1925]:45, 12:60; LJ 78:2226; Mahony 1:38; SLJ Nov 2000, p. 113; TLS 1971 p. 774)

DICKINSON, Peter (pseud. of Malcolm de Brissac). *The Blue Hawk.*
See Chapter 5, High Fantasy: Alternate Worlds or Histories.

1-103 DICKINSON, Peter (pseud. of Malcolm de Brissac). *Giant Cold.* Gr. 4–6.
(Orig. British pub. 1983.)
Giant Cold has awakened and turned tropical Apple Island to ice, and when
"you" try to stop the Giant, "you" are reduced to Lilliputian size.
Illus. by Alan E. Cober, Dutton, 1984, 69 pp., o.p.
(CCBB 37:184; HB 60:50; SLJ Apr 1984 p. 122; TLS May 1984 p. 558)

1-104 DICKINSON, Peter (pseud. of Malcolm de Brissac). *The Iron Lion.* Gr.
✴   2–4.
Princess Yasmin challenges Prince Mustapha to bring her the Iron Lion of Fer-
dustan, in order to win her hand in marriage.
Illus. by Marc Brown, Little, Brown, 1972, o.p.; illus. by Pauline Baynes,
Bedrick, 1984 (orig. British pub. in this ed. 1983), 32 pp., o.p.
(CCBB 25:120; HB 60:591; Kirkus 40:135; LJ 97:1594; SLJ Nov 1984 p. 106; TLS 1973 p.
1431)

1-105 DOBBS, Rose. *The Discontented Village.* Gr. 4–6.
A thick fog of gloom hangs over a pleasant town until a mysterious stranger
teaches the villagers about contentment.
Illus. by Beatrice Tobias, Coward, 1946, 31 pp., o.p.
(BL 43:173; HB 23:108; LJ 71:1466)

1-106 DOBBS, Rose. *No Room: An Old Story Retold.* Gr. 3–5.
✴   An old man who wishes to avoid sharing his house with his daughter's family
is given some unexpected advice.
Illus. by Fritz Eichenberg, McKay, 1944, 44 pp., o.p.
(BL 41:61; HB 20:375; Kirkus 12:429; LJ 69:763, 865)

DOLBIER, Maurice (Wyman). *A Lion in the Woods.*
See Chapter 8, Humorous Fantasy.

1-107 DOLBIER, Maurice (Wyman). *Torten's Christmas Secret.* Gr. 2–4.
✴   Torten, one of Santa's elves, decides to make his own gifts for the not-so-good
children overlooked by Santa.
Illus. by Robert Henneberger, Little, Brown, 1951, 61 pp., o.p.
(BL 48:51; CCBB 5:28; HB 27:401, 415; Kirkus 19:388; LJ 76:1342)

1-108 DONEHOWER, Bruce. *Miko, Little Hunter of the North.* Gr. 3–5.
Young Miko takes his reindeer through the freezing winter-long night to rescue
Ravna, daughter of the sun and the moon, whose release will bring the sun back
to Lapland.
Illus. by Tom Pohrt, Farrar, 1990, 89 pp., o.p.
(BL 86:1799, 87:637; CCBB 43:236; HBG 1:257; SLJ Aug 1990 p. 146)

DONOVAN, John. *Family: A Novel.*
See Chapter 2, Animal Fantasy.

***Don't Bet on the Prince: Contemporary Feminist Fairy Tales in North
America and England.* Ed. by Jack Zipes.**
See Chapter 3, Fantasy Collections.

1-109 DRUON, Maurice (Samuel Roger Charles). *Tistou of the Green Thumbs.*
✶ **(British title:** *Tistou of the Green Fingers***).** Gr. 4–6. (Orig. French pub.
1957.)
Tistou makes flowers bloom, bringing beauty and happiness into the world, and
stopping a war.
Trans. by Humphrey Hare, illus. by Jacqueline Duhème, Scribner, 1958, 178
pp., o.p.
(BL 55:221; CCBB 12:130; HB 34:382, 61:84; Kirkus 26:659; LJ 83:3006; TLS Nov 21, 1958
p. x)

DU BOIS, William (Sherman) Pène. *Lazy Tommy Pumpkinhead.*
See Chapter 8, Humorous Fantasy.

DU BOIS, William (Sherman) Pène. *Otto and the Magic Potatoes.*
See Chapter 8, Humorous Fantasy.

1-110 DUNBAR, Aldis. *Once There Was a Prince.* Gr. 5–7. (Orig. pub. in Eng-
land.)
Opposed to the oppression of his people, a young prince escapes in disguise to
a neighboring land to learn how to rule fairly and wisely.
Illus. by Maurice Day, Little, Brown, 1928, 302 pp., o.p.
(BL 25:216; HB 4:27)

1-111 DUNBAR, Aldis. *The Sons O'Cormac an' Tales of Other Men's Sons.* Gr.
5–7. (Orig. pub. in England, 1904.)
A Celtic fantasy about the adventures of the son of the High King of Ireland,
Cormac Mac Art, who ruled in Tara in the 3rd century A.D.
Illus. by Myra Luxmoore, Longmans, 1904; illus. by Ferdinand Hussszti-Hor-
vath, Dutton, 1920, 1929, 302 pp., o.p.
(BL 17:235, 26:77; Mahony 1:40)

DUNSANY, Lord (pseud. of Edward John Morton Drax Plunkett). *The
Charwoman's Shadow.*
See Chapter 12, Witchcraft and Sorcery Fantasy.

DUNSANY, Lord (pseud. of Edward John Morton Drax Plunkett). *The
King of Elfland's Daughter.*
See Chapter 5, High Fantasy: Alternate Worlds or Histories.

EDMONDS, Walter D(umaux). *Beaver Valley.*
See Chapter 2, Animal Fantasy.

EHRLICH, Amy. *Lucy's Winter Tale.*
See Chapter 9, Magic Adventure Fantasy.

1-112 ELIOT, Ethel (Augusta) Cook. *The Wind Boy.* Gr. 5–6. (Orig. pub. 1923.)
✶ A winged boy from the Clear Land comes to play with two refugee children
awaiting their father's return from war.
Illus. by Robert Hallock, Viking, 1945, 244 pp., o.p.
(BL 20:105, 42:61; Bookshelf 1927 p. 7; HB 22:213; Kirkus 13:370; LJ 70:980; Mahony
2:278)

The Enchanter's Spell: Five Famous Tales. **Adapt. by Gennady Spirin.**
See Chapter 3, Fantasy Collections.

ENDE, Michael. *Momo.*
See Chapter 5, High Fantasy: Alternate Worlds or Histories.

1-113 ENRIGHT, Elizabeth (Wright). *Tatsinda.* Gr. K–4.
✭ In love with an outcast girl named Tatsinda, Prince Tackatan of Tatrajan deter-
mines to rescue her from the horrible giant who has kidnapped her.
Illus. by Irene Haas, Harcourt, 1963, 80 pp., o.p.; illus. by Katie Thamer Treherne, Harcourt, 1991, 64 pp. (0-15-284280-2)
(BL 59:896, 89:1830; CCBB 16:159; Eakin:109; HB 39:382; HBG 2:257; Kirkus 61:454; LJ
88:2774; SLJ July 1991 p. 56; TLS 1964 p. 1081)

1-114 ERSHOV, Petr Pavlovich. *The Little Hump-backed Horse: A Russian*
✭ *Tale.* Gr. 3–5. (Orig. U.S. pub. Harper, 1931, entitled *Humpy,* o.p.; Macmillan,
1942, entitled *Little Magic Horse,* o.p.; Putnam, 1942, entitled *The Little
Hunchback Horse,* o.p.)
Ivan the Fool's magical horse helps him defeat his enemies, win a bride, and
become Tsar of Russia.
Adapt. by Margaret Hodges from a poem by Petr Pavlovich Ershov, trans. by
Gina Kovarsky, illus. by Chris Conover, Farrar, 1980, 25 pp., o.p., 1987, pap.,
32 pp. (0-374-44495-1); adapt. by Elizabeth Winthrop, illus. by Alexander
Koshkin, Clarion, 1997, 24 pp. (0-395-65361-4)
(BL 28:354, 39:298, 77:513, 93:1159; CCBB 34:172, 50:337; HB 19:34, 57:61; Kirkus
48:1461; LJ 56:1058, 67:883, 68:38, 173; SLJ Dec 1980 p. 44, Apr 1997 p. 132)

1-115 ESSEX, Rosamund (Sibyl). *Into the Forest.* Gr. 5–7. (Orig. British pub.
1963.)
Five children abandoned during the Great Destruction undertake a dangerous
journey through the forest in search of a better world.
Coward-McCann, 1965, 156 pp., o.p.
(BL 62:716; Kirkus 33:907; LJ 90:5512)

EUSTIS, Helen. *Mr. Death and the Redheaded Woman.*
See Chapter 8, Humorous Fantasy.

Faery! **Ed. by Terri Windling.**
See Chapter 3, Fantasy Collections.

1-116 FALKBERGET, Johan (Petter). *Broomstick and Snowflake.* Gr. 2–4.
(Orig. pub. in Norway.)
Broomstick, the tanner's son, meets the North Mountain Giant's daughter,
Snowflake.
Illus. by Helen Sewell, Macmillan, 1933, 88 pp., o.p.
(BL 30:123; Bookshelf 1933 p. 5; HB 9:205; Mahony 3:172)

The Fantastic Imagination: An Anthology of High Fantasy. **Ed. by
Robert H. Boyer and Kenneth J. Zohorski.**
See Chapter 5, High Fantasy: Alternate Worlds or Histories.

FARBER, Norma (Holzman). *Six Impossible Things Before Breakfast.*
See Chapter 3, Fantasy Collections.

FARJEON, Eleanor. *The Glass Slipper.*
See Chapter 6, High Fantasy: Myth or Legend Fantasy.

FARJEON, Eleanor. *The Little Bookroom: Eleanor Farjeon's Short Stories for Children, Chosen by Herself.*
See Chapter 3, Fantasy Collections.

1-117   FARJEON, Eleanor. *Martin Pippin in the Apple Orchard.* Gr. 5–7. (Orig. British pub. 1921.)
A minstrel named Martin Pippin frees an imprisoned farm girl by entertaining her six guards with his tales. The sequel is *Martin Pippin in the Daisy Field* (1937, 1963).
Stokes, 1922, o.p.; illus. by Richard Kennedy, Lippincott, 1949, 1961, 305 pp., o.p.
(BL 19:53, 58:112; HB 37:557; Kirkus 29:670; Mahony 2:279)

FARJEON, Eleanor. *The Silver Curlew.*
See Chapter 6, High Fantasy: Myth or Legend Fantasy.

FARMER (Mockridge), Penelope. *A Castle of Bone.*
See Chapter 6, High Fantasy: Myth or Legend Fantasy.

FARMER (Mockridge), Penelope. *The Summer Birds.*
See Chapter 9, Magic Adventure Fantasy.

FAST, Howard (Melvin). *The General Zapped an Angel: New Stories of Fantasy and Science Fiction.*
See Chapter 3, Fantasy Collections.

1-118   FENTON, Edward. *The Nine Questions.* Gr. 5–7.
✫   Willy and Gabriella use a magical silver whistle and hunting cap to rescue Willy's father, the king.
Illus. by C(yril) Walter Hodges, Doubleday, 1959, 235 pp., o.p.
(BL 56:125; HB 36:129; Kirkus 27:495; LJ 85:1302)

1-119   FENWICK, Elizabeth. *Cockleberry Castle.* Gr. 3–5.
When the Prince throws a banquet for the other palace children, they are afraid they are about to be punished.
Illus. by Fabio Rieti, Pantheon, 1963, 74 pp., o.p.
(Kirkus 32:3; LJ 88:2550)

1-120   FLEISCHMAN, (Albert) Sid(ney). *The Hey Hey Man.* Gr. 2–4.
✫   A wood spirit called the Hey Hey Man magically punishes a thief who has stolen a farmer's gold.
Illus. by Nadine Bernard Westcott, Atlantic, 1979, 32 pp., o.p.
(BL 76:42; HB 55:527; Kirkus 47:1141; SLJ Sep 1979 p. 135)

FLEISCHMAN, (Albert) Sid(ney). *The Whipping Boy.*
See Chapter 5, High Fantasy: Alternate Worlds or Histories.

1-121 FLEISCHMAN, Paul (Taylor). *The Birthday Tree.* Gr. 3–4.
✭ An ex-sailor and his wife try to avoid losing a fourth son to the sea by moving inland and planting a Birthday Tree in honor of his birth.
Illus. by Marcia Sewall, Harper, 1979, 32 pp., o.p.
(BL 75:1535; Kirkus 47:573; SLJ Sep 1979 p. 110)

1-122 FLEISCHMAN, Paul (Taylor). *Coming-and-Going Men: Four Tales.* Gr.
✭ 6–9.
Four interconnected stories involving artisans and tradesmen passing through the town of New Canaan, Vermont, in 1800: a silhouette cutter who battles the devil, a poet who saves a man's soul, three artists whose works are destroyed, and a peddler who gives a woman back her life.
Illus. by Randy Gaul, Harper, 1985, 160 pp., o.p.
(BL 81:1390, 1399; CCBB 39:7; HB 61:315; Kirkus 53:J32; SLJ Aug 1985 p. 75; Suth 4:117; VOYA 8:184)

FLEISCHMAN, Paul (Taylor). *Finzel the Farsighted.*
See Chapter 8, Humorous Fantasy.

FLEISCHMAN, Paul (Taylor). *The Half-a-Moon Inn.*
See Chapter 12, Witchcraft and Sorcery Fantasy.

FLORA, James (Royer). *Wanda and the Bumbly Wizard.*
See Chapter 12, Witchcraft and Sorcery Fantasy.

1-123 FLORY, Jane Trescott. *The Lost and Found Princess.* Gr. 2–4.
Clues dropped by three robbers enable a cat, a dragon, and an old woman to rescue a captive princess.
Illus. by the author, Houghton, 1979, 48 pp., o.p.
(BL 75:1156; Kirkus 47:518; SLJ Apr 1979 p. 42)

1-124 FOLLETT, Barbara Newhall. *The House Without Windows and Eepersip's Life There.* Gr. 4–6.
In this story written by a 9-year-old, a lonely little girl runs away to the woods, where she becomes a dryad.
Knopf, 1927, 166 pp., o.p.
(BL 23:347; HB 3:41; Mahony 2:279; Moore:427)

FORD, Richard. *Quest for the Faradawn.*
See Chapter 2, Animal Fantasy.

1-125 FORST, S. *Pipkin.* Gr. 1–4.
Pipkin, the lost prince of the gnomes, is cared for by an old woman until he is able to find his way back into the Ladybug Kingdom.
Illus. by Robin Jacques, Delacorte, 1970, 144 pp., o.p.
(HB 46:476; LJ 96:1007)

FORWARD, Toby. *Traveling Backward.*
See Chapter 9, Magic Adventure Fantasy.

1-126 FOSTER, Malcolm (Burton). *The Prince with a Hundred Dragons.* Gr. 2–4.

A gentle dragon agrees to help Prince Guy fool his father into thinking that Guy is a fearless dragon slayer.
Illus. by Barbara Remington, Doubleday, 1963, 60 pp., o.p.
(CCBB 17:138; Kirkus 31:656; LJ 88:4083)

FOX (Greenberg), Paula. *The Little Swineherd and Other Tales.*
See Chapter 3, Fantasy Collections.

FRANCE, Anatole. *Bee, the Princess of the Dwarfs.*
See Chapter 7, High Fantasy: Travel to Other Worlds.

FRANKO, Ivan, and MELNYK, Bohdan. *Fox Mykyta.*
See Chapter 2, Animal Fantasy.

1-127 FREEMAN, Barbara C(onstance). *Broom-Adelaide.* Gr. 4–6. (Orig. British pub. 1963.)
No one at the castle suspects that the governess, Madame Crowberry, is actually a witch.
Illus. by the author, Little, Brown, 1965, 124 pp., o.p.
(BL 62:219; HB 41:490; Kirkus 33:626; LJ 90:3790; TLS 1963 p. 980)

1-128 FRENCH, Vivian. *Under the Moon.* Gr. 2–5. (Orig. British pub. 1993.)
✯ Three folktale-like stories about a kindly tree spirit, a boy whose clever grandmother rescues him from a wolf, and a woman asked to dust the cobwebs from the sky.
Illus. by Chris Fisher, Candlewick, 1994, 96 pp., o.p.
(BL 90:1365; HBG 5:376; Kirkus 62:479; SLJ June 1994 p. 98)

GACKENBACH, Dick. *Beauty, Brave and Beautiful.*
See Chapter 2, Animal Fantasy.

1-129 GALLICO, Paul (William). *The Snow Goose.* Gr. 6–12. (Orig. pub. 1940.)
The wounded snow goose he nursed back to health watches over Rhayader as he braves the German bombardment to rescue English soldiers from the sea during the Battle of Dunkirk.
Knopf, 1941, 57 pp. (0-394-44593-7); illus. by Beth Peck, 1992, 32 pp., o.p.
(BL 89:137; HBG 4:68; SLJ Feb 1993 p. 93)

GARDNER, John (Champlin) (Jr.). *Dragon, Dragon, and Other Timeless Tales.*
See Chapter 3, Fantasy Collections.

GARDNER, John (Champlin) (Jr.). *In the Suicide Mountains.*
See Chapter 5, High Fantasy: Alternate Worlds or Histories.

GARFIELD, Leon. *The Wedding Ghost.*
See Chapter 6, High Fantasy: Myth or Legend Fantasy.

GARNER, Alan. *Alan Garner's Fairytales of Gold.*
See Chapter 3, Fantasy Collections.

GARNER, Alan. *Once Upon a Time: Though It Wasn't in Your Time, and It Wasn't in My Time, and It Wasn't in Anybody Else's Time . . .*
See Chapter 3, Fantasy Collections.

GARNETT, David. *Two by Two: A Story of Survival.*
See Chapter 6, High Fantasy: Myth or Legend Fantasy.

GATE, Ethel M(ay). *The Fortunate Days.*
See Chapter 3, Fantasy Collections.

1-130 GERSTEIN, Mordicai. *The Giant.* Gr. 3–5.
A lonely giant reaches out to three young girls who live on the other side of a ravine.
Illus. by the author, Hyperion, 1995, 36 pp., o.p.
(BL 93:401; HBG 7:54; Kirkus 63:1350)

1-131 GIBSON, Katharine. *Cinders.* Gr. 3–5.
Overlooked when Cinderella's fairy godmother turned the other servants back into animals, Cinders the coachman decides to go into service to the king.
Illus. by Vera Bock, Longman, 1939, 133 pp., o.p.
(BL 36:17; HB 15:296; LJ 64:712)

1-132 GIBSON, Katharine. *Jock's Castle.* Gr. 4–5.
The hunter rescued by Jock the miller turns out to be Crown Prince Henry.
Illus. by Vera Bock, Longman, 1940, 139 pp., o.p.
(BL 37:18; HB 16:343; LJ 65:714, 849)

GILMAN, Dorothy. *The Maze in the Heart of the Castle.*
See Chapter 7, High Fantasy: Travel to Other Worlds.

1-133 GODDEN (Dixon), (Margaret) Rumer. *The Dragon of Og.* Gr. 3–5. (Orig.
✭ pub. in England.)
The stubborn new Lord of Og wants to get rid of the gentle local dragon, against the advice of his wife and his chief minister.
Illus. by Pauline Baynes, Viking, 1981, 60 pp., o.p.
(BL 78:706; CCBB 55:106; SLJ Nov 1981 p. 75; Suth 3:154)

1-134 GODDEN (Dixon), (Margaret) Rumer. *The Mousewife.* Gr. 2–4.
✭ A little mouse sets a caged dove free in return for wondrous descriptions of the outside world.
Illus. by William (Sherman) Pène du Bois, Viking, 1951, o.p.; illus. by Heidi Holder, Viking, 1982, 31 pp., o.p.
(BL 47:297, 79:777; CCBB 4:50, 36:46; Eakin:143; HB 27:93, 102; Kirkus 19:61; LJ 76:781; TLS 1951 p. 9)

GOGOL, Nikolai. *The Nose.*
See Chapter 8, Humorous Fantasy.

GOLDMAN, William W. *The Princess Bride.*
See Chapter 5, High Fantasy: Alternate Worlds or Histories.

GOLDSTEIN, Lisa. *The Red Magician.*
See Chapter 12, Witchcraft and Sorcery Fantasy.

GOODWIN, Harold Leland. *Magic Number.*
See Chapter 2, Animal Fantasy.

1-135 **GOUDGE, Elizabeth (de Beauchamp).** *The Valley of Song.* Gr. 5–8. (Orig.
☆ British pub. 1951.)
Tabitha lifts the spirits of her town's disheartened shipbuilders by leading them
into the Valley of Song.
Illus. by Richard Floethe, Coward, 1952, 281 pp., o.p.
(BL 49:92; CCBB 6:67; HB 28:395, 405; Kirkus 20:552; LJ 77:1822; TLS 1951 p. 15)

1-136 **GRAHAME, Kenneth.** *The Reluctant Dragon.* Gr. 4–6. (Orig. British pub.
☆ 1898 in *Dream Days*.)
St. George and his young friend find a dragon that is not at all like the one they
had intended to slay.
Illus. by Ernest H. Shepard, Holiday, 1938, 58 pp. (0-8234-0093-X), 1989,
pap., 57 pp. (0-8234-0755-1); illus. by Michael (R.) Hague, Holt, 1983, 48 pp.
(0-8050-1112-9); Holt, 1989, pap., 48 pp. (0-8050-0802-0); adapt. by Robert D.
San Souci, illus. by John Segal, Scholastic/Orchard, 2004, 39 pp. (0-439-
45581-2); adapt. and illus. by Inga Moore, Candlewick, 2004, 64 pp. (0-763-
62199-4)
(BL 35:143, 80:680, 100:1942; CCBB 7:29; Eakin:146; HB 15:29, 80:483–484, 490; LJ 64:1
18; SLJ Nov 1983 p. 77, Nov 2004 p. 104)

GRAHAME, Kenneth. *The Wind in the Willows.*
See Chapter 2, Animal Fantasy.

GRAY, Nicholas Stuart. *Mainly in Moonlight: Ten Stories of Sorcery and
the Supernatural.*
See Chapter 3, Fantasy Collections.

GRAY, Nicholas Stuart. *A Wind from Nowhere.*
See Chapter 3, Fantasy Collections.

1-137 **GREAVES, Margaret.** *A Net to Catch the Wind.* Gr. 2–4.
A king uses his young daughter to trap a unicorn, causing both the girl and the
unicorn to fall ill.
Illus. by Stephen Gammell, Harper, 1979, 40 pp., o.p.
(BL 75:1438; Kirkus 47:451; SLJ Sep 1979 p. 110)

GREENE, Jacqueline Dembar. *The Leveller.*
See Chapter 6, High Fantasy: Myth or Legend Fantasy.

1-138 **GREGORY, Philippa.** *Florizella and the Wolves.* Gr. 3–5. (Orig. British
☆ pub. 1991.)
Princess Florizella's parents insist that her four orphaned wolf cubs must be
returned to the wild, but one keeps finding its way back to the palace.
Illus. by Patrice Aggs, Candlewick, 1993, 80 pp., o.p.
(BL 89:1588; HBG 4:285; Kirkus 61:371; SLJ May 1993 p. 105)

1-139 GREGORY, Valiska. *Through the Mickle Woods.* Gr. 2–5.
Despondent after the death of his queen, a king follows his wife's written instructions to find a bear in the snowy mickle woods, give him her ring, and listen to the three stories he tells.
Illus. by Barry Moser, Little, Brown, 1992, 32 pp., o.p.
(BL 89:675; HB 69:202; HBG 4:57; Kirkus 60:1130; SLJ Dec 1992 p. 113)

GRIPARI, Pierre. *Tales of the Rue Broca.*
See Chapter 3, Fantasy Collections.

GRIPE, Maria (Kristina). *The Glassblower's Children.*
See Chapter 12, Witchcraft and Sorcery Fantasy.

GRIPE, Maria (Kristina). *In the Time of the Bells.*
See Chapter 5, High Fantasy: Alternate Worlds or Histories.

GRIPE, Maria (Kristina). *The Land Beyond.*
See Chapter 7, High Fantasy: Travel to Other Worlds.

1-140 GUILLOT, René. *The Three Hundred Ninety-Seventh White Elephant.* Gr.
✷   3–6. (Orig. pub. in France.)
The young king is cured of his illness by Hong-Mo the Magnificent, a mysterious white elephant who becomes leader of the royal herd. The sequel is *The Elephants of Sargabel* (1957). The British sequels are *Master of the Elephants* and *Great Land of the Elephant*.
Trans. by Gwen Marsh, illus. by Moyra Leatham, Phillips, 1957, 94 pp., o.p.
(BL 53:434; HB 33:221; Kirkus 25:176; LJ 82:1102)

GUNN, Neil Miller. *The Green Isle of the Great Deep.*
See Chapter 7, High Fantasy: Travel to Other Worlds.

GUY, Rosa (Cuthbert). *My Love, My Love, or the Peasant Girl.*
See Chapter 6, High Fantasy: Myth or Legend Fantasy.

1-141 HACKETT, Walter Anthony. *The Swans of Ballycastle.* Gr. 3–5.
✷   Three children who were driven from home by their stepmother are changed into swans and find refuge on an island where time stands still.
Illus. by Bettina, Ariel, 1954, 63 pp., o.p.
(BL 51:179; CCBB 8:51; HB 30:435; Kirkus 22:479; LJ 79:2491)

1-142 HALLOWELL, Priscilla. *The Long-Nosed Princess: A Fairy Tale.* Gr.
✷   3–5.
No one notices Princess Felicity's long nose until her self-centered fiancé brings it up.
Illus. by Rita Fava, Viking, 1959, 61 pp., o.p.
(BL 55:633; CCBB 12:168; HB 35:299; Kirkus 27:88; LJ 84:2086)

HAMILTON, Virginia (Esther). *The Magical Adventures of Pretty Pearl.*
See Chapter 6, High Fantasy: Myth or Legend Fantasy.

HAMLEY, Dennis. *Hare's Choice.*
See Chapter 2, Animal Fantasy.

HANCOCK, Neil (Anderson). *Dragon Winter.*
See Chapter 2, Animal Fantasy.

HANSEN, Ron. *The Shadowmaker.*
See Chapter 9, Magic Adventure Fantasy.

HASELEY, Dennis. *Ghost Catcher.*
See Chapter 4, Ghost Fantasy.

1-143 HAUFF, Wilhelm. *The Adventures of Little Mouk.* Gr. 3–4. (Orig. pub. in Germany.)
Even Little Mouk's magic shoes and walking stick can't keep him out of the king's dungeon.
Trans. and adapt. by Elizabeth Shub, illus. by Monika Laimgruber, Macmillan, 1975, 36 pp., o.p.
(BL 71:866; CCBB 29:10; HB 51:257; Kirkus 43:18; SLJ Apr 1975 p. 53, July 2004 p. 77)

HAUFF, Wilhelm. *The Caravan.*
See Chapter 3, Fantasy Collections.

1-144 HAUFF, Wilhelm. *Dwarf Long-Nose.* Gr. 3–5. (Orig. pub. in Germany; orig.
★ U.S. pub. 1881, 1916.)
Transformed into an ugly dwarf by a wicked fairy, Long-Nose becomes a chef in the Duke's kitchen and searches for a special herb to break the spell.
Trans. by Doris Orgel, illus. by Maurice (Bernard) Sendak, Random, 1960, 60 pp., o.p.; trans. by Anthea Bell, illus. by Lisbeth Zwerger, North-South, 1994 (entitled *Dwarf Nose*), 47 pp. (1-55858-261-4) (Orig. Swiss pub. in this ed., 1993); illus. by Laura Stoddart, Candlewick, 1997, 95 pp. (entitled *Little Long-Nose*) (0-7636-0327-9)
(BL 57:128, 91:1575; Eakin:151; HB 36:510; HBG 6:77, 9:60; Kirkus 63:1564; LJ 85:3862; SLJ Jan 1995 p. 118, July 2004 p. 77)

HAUFF, Wilhelm. *The Fairy Tales of Wilhelm Hauff.*
See Chapter 3, Fantasy Collections.

1-145 HAUGAARD, Erik Christian. *Princess Horrid.* Gr. K–5.
A spoiled princess learns how to behave properly after she is transformed into a cat and adopted by the scullery maid.
Illus. by Dawson Hearn, Macmillan, 1990, 48 pp., o.p.
(BL 87:855; HBG 2:65; Kirkus 58:1085; SLJ Nov 1990 p. 93)

HAWDON, Robin. *A Rustle in the Grass.*
See Chapter 2, Animal Fantasy.

1-146 HAWTHORNE, Julian. *Rumpty-Dudget's Tower: A Fairy Tale.* Gr. K–4. (Orig. pub. in *St. Nicholas* magazine, 1879; orig. pub. in book form, illus. by George W. Hood, Stokes, 1924, o.p.)
An evil dwarf named Rumpty-Dudget kidnaps Prince Henry and locks him in a tower in order to turn the world into a desert, in this story written by Nathaniel Hawthorne's son.
Adapt. and illus. by Diane Goode, Knopf, 1987, 48 pp., o.p.

(BL 21:237, 84:862; Bookshelf 1924–1925 Suppl. p. 1; HB 1[Nov 1924]:7; Kirkus 55:1515; LJ 50:803; Mahony 2:281)

HAWTHORNE, Nathaniel. *The Snow Image.*
See Chapter 3, Fantasy Collections.

HAZEL, Paul. *Yearwood.*
See Chapter 5, High Fantasy: Alternate Worlds or Histories.

HEARNE, Betsy (Gould). *South Star.*
See Chapter 5, High Fantasy: Alternate Worlds or Histories.

1-147   HEATH, W(illiam) L. *The Earthquake Man.* Gr. 4–6.
Sinn Fein, a troll-catching tinsmith, convinces Rafe and Ansel O'Grady that he can rid their farm of the troll living under the footbridge.
Beaufort, 1980, 95 pp., o.p.
(Kirkus 49:213; SLJ Jan 1981, p. 61)

HELPRIN, Mark. *Swan Lake.*
See Chapter 6, High Fantasy: Myth or Legend Fantasy.

HELPRIN, Mark. *Winter's Tale.*
See Chapter 5, High Fantasy: Alternate Worlds or Histories.

HESSE, Hermann. *Pictor's Metamorphoses, and Other Fantasies.*
See Chapter 3, Fantasy Collections.

HEWETT, Anita. *The Bull Beneath the Walnut Tree and Other Stories.*
See Chapter 3, Fantasy Collections.

1-148   HILGARTNER, Beth. *A Necklace of Fallen Stars.* Gr. 6–8.
Princess Kaela runs away rather than marry the man her father has chosen for her.
Illus. by Michael (R.) Hague, Little, Brown, 1979, 209 pp., o.p.
(BL 76:558; Kirkus 48:222; SLJ Oct 1979 p. 150)

HIRSCH, Odo. *Bartlett and the Ice Voyage.*
See Chapter 5, High Fantasy: Alternate Worlds or Histories.

HIRSCH, Odo. *Yoss.*
See Chapter 5, High Fantasy: Alternate Worlds or Histories.

1-149   HOBAN, Russell C(onwell). *The Marzipan Pig.* Gr. 3–5.
After a marzipan pig falls behind the sofa, his sweetness and loving thoughts are absorbed by the mouse that eats him, and by the owl that eats the mouse, in this gentle and whimsical tale.
Illus. by Quentin Blake, Farrar, 1987, 40 pp. (0-374-34859-6)
(CCBB 40:210; Kirkus 55:719; SLJ Sep 1987 p. 164; TLS Apr 3, 1987 p. 356)

1-150   HOBAN, Russell C(onwell). *The Mouse and His Child.* Gr. 4 up.
✫   A broken windup mouse and his son set out to find happiness but are pursued by an evil rat intent on enslaving them. This story can also be read as a satire on American society.

Illus. by Lillian Hoban, Harper, 1967, o.p.; illus. by David Small, Scholastic, 2001, 246 pp. (0-439-09826-2)

(BL 64:593, 98:642; CCBB 21:143; HBG 13:86; Kirkus 35:1134; LJ 92:4612; Suth:185; TLS 1969 p. 357)

HOBAN, Russell C(onwell). *The Sea-Thing Child.*
See Chapter 2, Animal Fantasy.

1-151 HODGES, Elizabeth Jamison. *The Three Princes of Serendip.* Gr. 4–6.
The King of Serendip's sons search throughout India and Persia for a dragon-killing potion to save their kingdom. The sequel is *Serendipity Tales* (1966).
Illus. by Joan Berg, Atheneum, 1964, 158 pp., o.p.

(BL 60:1002; HB 40:281; Kirkus 32:108; LJ 89:2219)

1-152 HODGES, Margaret, ed. *Comus.* Gr. 2–5. (From the poem written by John Milton in 1634.)
Young Alice is rescued from a spell cast by an evil magician in this story based on John Milton's "Masque at Ludlow Castle," the theatrical version of the English folktale "Childe Roland."
Illus. by Trina Schart Hyman, Holiday, 1996, 32 pp. (0-8234-1146-X)

(BL 92:1182; CCBB 49:266; HBG 7:260; Kirkus 64:135; SLJ Mar 1996 p. 196)

HOFFMANN, E(rnst) T(heodor) A(madeus). *The Nutcracker.*
See Chapter 11, Toy Fantasy.

1-153 HOFFMANN, E(rnst) T(heodor) A(madeus). *The Strange Child.* Gr. 4–6.
(Orig. German pub. as part of a collection, 1857; orig. Austrian pub. in this edition, 1981.)
A mysterious child, the daughter of the queen of fairies, helps two human children get rid of their evil tutor.
Trans. and adapt. by Anthea Bell, illus. by Lisbeth Zwerger, Picture Book Studio, 1984, 1991, 31 pp., o.p.

(BL 81:520; CCBB 38:87; HB 61:177; SLJ Apr 1985 p. 88)

1-154 HOLLANDER, John. *The Quest of the Gole.* Gr. 6–8.
✶ Three princes search for the "Gole" to break the curse of darkness on their kingdom.
Illus. by Reginald Pollack, Atheneum, 1966, 116 pp., o.p.

(BL 63:418; HB 42:562; Kirkus 34:982; LJ 91:4352)

HOLMAN (Valen), Felice. *The Blackmail Machine.*
See Chapter 8, Humorous Fantasy.

1-155 HOLT, Isabella. *The Adventures of Rinaldo.* Gr. 4–6.
✶ Knight Rinaldo wins a bear, a stag, and a pig while searching for a wife and a castle.
Illus. by Erik Blegvad, Little, Brown, 1959, 142 pp., o.p.

(BL 55:458; HB 35:131; Kirkus 27:7; LJ 84:643)

1-156 HOOKS, William H(arris). *The Ballad of Belle Dorcas.* Gr. 2–5.
✷   A conjure woman turns Belle's husband into a cedar tree to avoid his being
        sold to another master, in this retelling of an African American slave tale from
        the Carolina coast.
        Illus. by Brian Pinkney, Knopf, 1990, 40 pp., o.p.
        (BL 87:51; CCBB 44:87; HB 67:208; HBG 2:101; Kirkus 58:1087; SLJ Oct 1990 p. 116; Suth
        4:184)

        HORWITZ, Elinor Lander. *The Strange Story of the Frog Who Became a
        Prince.*
        See Chapter 12, Witchcraft and Sorcery Fantasy.

        HORWOOD, William. *Duncton Wood.*
        See Chapter 2, Animal Fantasy.

1-157 HOUSMAN, Laurence. *Cotton-Wooleena.* Gr. 2–4. (Orig. British pub. in
        this format, 1967.)
        A newly crowned king discovers that a haughty fairy named Cotton-Wooleena
        has been ruling his country for the past 300 years.
        Illus. by Robert Binks, Doubleday, 1974, 58 pp., o.p.
        (BL 70:1056; Kirkus 42:425; LJ 99:2270)

        HOUSMAN, Laurence. *The Rat-Catcher's Daughter: A Collection of Sto-
        ries.*
        See Chapter 3, Fantasy Collections.

1-158 HOWARD, Alice (Woodbury). *Ching-Li and the Dragons.* Gr. 2–4. ·
        Young King Ching Wong's magical jade flute sends him off to rescue a mighty
        dragon.
        Illus. by Lynd Ward, Macmillan, 1931, 55 pp., o.p.
        (BL 28:265; HB 7:322; Mahony 3:205)

        HUDSON, W(illiam) H(enry). *Green Mansions: A Romance of the Tropi-
        cal Forest.*
        See Chapter 7, High Fantasy: Travel to Other Worlds.

1-159 HUDSON, W(illiam) H(enry). *A Little Boy Lost: A Tale for Children.* Gr.
✷   4–6. (Orig. British pub. 1905.)
        A little boy following a mirage becomes lost in the wilds of South America,
        much to his delight.
        Knopf, 1918, 1922, 222 pp., o.p.; illus. by A. D. McCormick, Knopf, 1923,
        1946, 1951, o.p.; illus. by Dorothy P. Lathrop, Knopf, 1920, 1939, o.p.
        (BL 15:15, 35:70; Bookshelf 1932 p. 8; HB 14:147; LJ 63:817, 847, 76:660; Mahony 2:281)

        HUGHES, Shirley. *Enchantment in the Garden.*
        See Chapter 9, Magic Adventure Fantasy.

        HUGHES, Ted (Edward James). *How the Whale Became.*
        See Chapter 2, Animal Fantasy.

1-160 HUGHES, Ted (Edward James). *The Iron Giant: A Story in Five Nights.*
        Gr. 3–6. (British title: *The Iron Man*, 1968.)

The people ask the Iron Giant for help against the hungry space-bat-angel-dragon who is terrorizing them. The sequel is *The Iron Woman* (Dial, 1995).
Illus. by Robert Nadler, Harper, 1968, 1988, 58 pp., o.p.; illus. by Andrew Davidson, Knopf, 1999, 83 pp. (0-375-90167-1); Random, 1999, pap. (0-375-80153-7)
(BL 65:496; CCBB 41:208; Kirkus 36:114; Suth 4:194; TLS 1968 p. 256)

1-161 **HUNTER, Mollie (pseud. of Maureen Mollie Hunter McVeigh McIl-**
☆ **wraith).** *The Kelpie's Pearls.* Gr. 4–6. (Orig. British pub. 1964.)
The pearl necklace that a water sprite gives to Morag MacLeod causes the old woman to be accused of witchcraft.
Funk, 1966, 112 pp., o.p.; Harper, 1976, 134 pp., o.p.
(BL 63:451; CCBB 20:109; HB 42:710; Kirkus 34:688; LJ 91:5231; TLS 1964 p. 1081)

1-162 **HUNTER, Mollie (pseud. of Maureen Mollie Hunter McVeigh McIl-**
☆ **wraith).** *The Knight of the Golden Plain.* **(Sir Dauntless trilogy, bk. 1).** Gr. 1–4.
Daydreaming, a young boy is transformed into Sir Dauntless, Knight of the Golden Plain, who battles dragons, witches, and a nasty wizard to save the maiden Dorabella. The sequels are *The Three-Day Enchantment* (1985) and *Day of the Unicorn* (1994).
Illus. by Marc Simont, Harper, 1983, 48 pp., o.p.
(BL 80:86; CCBB 37:51; HB 60:54; Kirkus 51:162; SLJ Sep 1983 p. 108)

1-163 **INGRAM, Tom (Thomas Henry).** *Garranane.* Gr. 4–6. (Orig. British pub. 1971, entitled *The Hungry Cloud*.)
Prince Kai and Princess Flor flee after discovering that the mysterious Miss Fenrir has trapped the king and queen within her drawings.
Illus. by Bill Geldart, Bradbury, 1972, 191 pp., o.p.
(BL 69:302; Kirkus 40:623; LJ 98:261; TLS 1971 p. 767)

IPCAR, Dahlov (Zorach). *The Queen of Spells.*
See Chapter 6, High Fantasy: Myth or Legend Fantasy.

IPCAR, Dahlov (Zorach). *The Warlock of Night.*
See Chapter 12, Witchcraft and Sorcery Fantasy.

IRVING, Washington. *The Legend of Sleepy Hollow.*
See Chapter 6, High Fantasy: Myth or Legend Fantasy.

IRVING, Washington. *Rip Van Winkle.*
See Chapter 6, High Fantasy: Myth or Legend Fantasy.

Isaac Asimov's Magical Worlds of Fantasy: Faeries. **Ed. by Isaac Asimov, Martin H. Greenberg, and Charles G. Waugh.**
See Chapter 3, Fantasy Collections.

ISH-KISHOR, Sulamith. *The Master of Miracle: A New Novel of the Golem.*
See Chapter 6, High Fantasy: Myth or Legend Fantasy.

JACKSON, Shelley. *Sophia, the Alchemist's Dog.*
See Chapter 2, Animal Fantasy.

JACQUES, Brian. *Redwall.*
See Chapter 2, Animal Fantasy.

1-164 **JARRELL, Randall.** *The Animal Family.* Gr. 4–6.
✩ A lonely hunter and a mermaid fall in love and acquire a family consisting of a bear cub, a lynx kitten, and a shipwrecked boy. John Newbery Medal Honor Book, 1966.
Illus. by Maurice (Bernard) Sendak, Pantheon, 1965, 1985, 200 pp. (0-685-10494-X)
(BL 62:487; CCBB 19:100; Eakin:171; HB 42:45, 61:714716, 737; LJ 90:5516; TLS 1976 p. 392)

1-165 **JARRELL, Randall.** *The Gingerbread Rabbit.* Gr. K–2.
The gingerbread rabbit cookie a mother bakes for her little girl comes to life and escapes into the forest, chased by the mother and a hungry fox.
Illus. by Garth (Montgomery) Williams, Macmillan, 1964, 1972, 1978, 55 pp., all o.p.; illus. by Garth (Montgomery) Williams, HarperCollins, 2003, 55 pp. (0-06-052768-4); HarperTrophy, 2004, pap. (0-06-053302-1)
(HB 79:583; HBG 16:355; Kirkus 32:232 (J-70); LJ 89:2210)

1-166 **JOHNSON, Elizabeth.** *The Little Knight.* Gr. 3–5.
✩ To avoid marrying a stranger, Princess Lenora dons armor and sets out to win the title of the bravest knight in the land.
Illus. by Ronni Solbert, Little, Brown, 1957, 56 pp., o.p.
(BL 54:28; HB 33:400; Kirkus 25:412; LJ 82:2191)

1-167 **JOHNSON, Elizabeth.** *The Three-in-One Prince.* Gr. 3–4.
✩ All three of King Frederick's sons enter the competition for Princess Alicia Anastasia Alfreda Anne's hand, but only Prince John, the middle son, can prove he is "three in one."
Illus. by Ronni Solbert, Little, Brown, 1961, 58 pp., o.p.
(BL 57:498; HB 37:261; Kirkus 29:102; LJ 86:1689)

JONES, Adrienne. *The Hawks of Chelney.*
See Chapter 5, High Fantasy: Alternate Worlds or Histories.

JONES, David Lee. *Unicorn Highway.*
See Chapter 9, Magic Adventure Fantasy.

JONES, Diana Wynne. *Cart and Cwidder.*
See Chapter 5, High Fantasy: Alternate Worlds or Histories.

JONES, Terry. *Fantastic Stories.*
See Chapter 8, Humorous Fantasy.

1-168 **JONES, Terry.** *The Saga of Erik the Viking.* Gr. 4–6. (Orig. British pub. 1983.)
A band of Vikings has a series of fantastic adventures while searching for the land where the sun goes at night.

Illus. by Michael Foreman, Schocken, 1983, o.p.; Puffin, 1993, pap., 192 pp. (0-14-032261-2)
(CCBB 37:149; SLJ Jan 1984 p. 78)

JUSTER, Norton. *Alberic the Wise and Other Journeys.*
See Chapter 3, Fantasy Collections.

JUSTER, Norton. *The Phantom Tollbooth.*
See Chapter 7, High Fantasy: Travel to Other Worlds.

KÄSTNER, Erich. *The Animal's Conference.*
See Chapter 2, Animal Fantasy.

1-169 KAVANAUGH, James. *A Fable.* Gr. 6 up.
A parable about the effect of greed on the contented villagers of Harmony, after a stranger seduces them with gold.
Illus. by Daniel Biamonte, Dutton, 1980, 64 pp., o.p.
(BL 77:394, 400; Kirkus 48:1179; SLJ Mar 1981 p. 157)

1-170 KAYE, M(argaret) M(ary). *The Ordinary Princess.* Gr. 3–6. (Orig. British
✭ pub. 1981.)
Tired of suitors who consider her too ordinary to marry, Princess Amy runs away to find a prince who will like her just the way she is.
Illus. by the author, Doubleday, 1984, o.p.; Viking, 2002 (0-670-03544-0); Puffin, 2002, pap., 112 pp. (0-142-30085-3)
(BL 81:641; CCBB 38:8; HB 60:758, 78:432; HBG 13:375; SLJ Mar 1985 p. 168; TLS 1980 p. 1326)

1-171 KELLER, Beverly (Lou). *A Small, Elderly Dragon.* Gr. 4–6.
✭ Terrorized by a feeble old dragon named Blystfylyl, the peasants of Minervia enlist the aid of the king, a princess, the Black Knight of Doum, and a sorcerer whose sister turns the dragon into a parrot.
Illus. by Nola Langner Malone, Lothrop, 1984, 144 pp., o.p.
(BL 80:1248; CCBB 37:188; HB 60:466; SLJ May 1984 p. 81; VOYA 7:147)

KENDALL, Carol (Seeger). *The Gammage Cup.*
See Chapter 5, High Fantasy: Alternate Worlds or Histories.

1-172 KENNEDY, (Jerome) Richard. *The Blue Stone.* Gr. 3–6.
✭ The blue stone that fell from the sky brings magic into the peaceful lives of Bertie and Jack by turning people into animals, making poems come true, and changing a sparrow into a baby angel.
Illus. by Ronald (Norbert) Himler, Holiday, 1976, 93 pp., o.p.
(BL 73:323; CCBB 30:127; Kirkus 44:1094; SLJ Nov 1976 p. 60)

1-173 KENNEDY, (Jerome) Richard. *The Boxcar at the Center of the Universe.*
Gr. 7–10.
An elderly bum who calls himself Ali meets a lost 16-year-old boy aboard a traveling boxcar, and tells him the fabulous story of his search for the center of the universe.
Illus. by Jeff Kronen, Harper, 1982, 89 pp., o.p.
(BL 78:1307, 1314; CCBB 36:70; Kirkus 50:496; SLJ Aug 1982 p. 126; VOYA 5:33)

1-174 KENNEDY, (Jerome) Richard. *Come Again in the Spring.* Gr. 4–6.
✶ Old Hark is afraid to die and leave his birds to fend for themselves in midwinter, so he strikes a bargain with Death: If Hark can answer three questions, Death will wait until spring to take him.
Illus. by Marcia Sewall, Harper, 1976, 47 pp., o.p.
(BL 73:253; HB 53:154; Kirkus 44:904; SLJ Feb 1977 p. 56)

1-175 KENNEDY, (Jerome) Richard. *The Dark Princess.* Gr. 5–7.
A princess's blinding beauty serves as a test for prospective suitors, and prevents her from finding love, until the court fool risks blindness to declare his love for her.
Illus. by Donna Diamond, Holiday, 1978, 32 pp., o.p.
(HB 55:641; Kirkus 46:1137; SLJ Dec 1978 p. 53)

1-176 KENNEDY, (Jerome) Richard. *Inside My Feet: The Story of a Giant.* Gr.
✶ 4–6.
After his parents are carried off by a giant, a boy frantically prepares for the giant's return.
Illus. by Ronald (Norbert) Himler, Harper, 1979, 71 pp. (0-06-023118-1)
(BL 76:449; CCBB 33:155; Kirkus 47:1210; SLJ Sep 1979 p. 141)

KENNEDY, (Jerome) Richard. *The Mouse God.*
See Chapter 2, Animal Fantasy.

KENNEDY, (Jerome) Richard. *Richard Kennedy: Collected Stories.*
See Chapter 3, Fantasy Collections.

KILWORTH, Garry. *The Foxes of Firstdark.*
See Chapter 2, Animal Fantasy.

KING-SMITH, Dick. *Godhanger.*
See Chapter 2, Animal Fantasy.

1-177 KING-SMITH, Dick. *Lady Lollypop.* Gr. 3–5. (Orig. pub. in England.)
✶ Spoiled Princess Penelope insists on the gift of Lollipop the pig for her birthday, despite the fact that Lollipop is the only possession of her keeper, Johnny Skinner. The sequel is *Clever Lollipop* (2003).
Illus. by Jill Barton, Candlewick, 2001, 125 pp. (0-7636-1269-3), 2003, pap., 128 pp. (0-7636-2181-1)
(BL 97:1552; CCBB 55:22; HB 77:327; HBG 12:292; Kirkus 69:662; SLJ June 2001 p. 121)

1-178 KINGSLEY, Charles. *The Water Babies: A Fairy Tale for a Land Baby.*
✶ Gr. 4–6. (Orig. British pub. 1863, U.S. 1864.)
An apprentice chimney sweep named Tom runs away from his cruel master and is taken in by fairies who transform him into a tiny water baby.
Illus. by Rosalie K(ingsmill) Fry, Dutton, 1905, 1957, o.p.; illus. by Jessie Willcox Smith, Dodd, 1910, 1937, o.p.; illus. by W. Heath Robinson, Houghton, 1915, 1923, o.p.; illus. by Maria Louise Kirk, Lippincott, 1917, o.p.; adapt. by Kathleen Lines, illus. by Harold Jones, Watts, 1961, o.p.; illus. by Linley Sambourne, Garland, 1976 (repr. of 1864 ed.), o.p.; illus. by Jessie Willcox

Smith, Morrow, 1997, 369 pp. (0-688-14831-X); adapt. by Josephine Poole,
illus. by Jan Omerod, Millbrook, 1998, 96 pp. (0-7613-0411-8)
(BL 1:74, 5:63, 10:253, 12:204, 14:141, 53:538, 58:352; Bookshelf 1928 p. 10; HB 1[June
1925]:32, 37:549; HBG 8:314, 9:336; LJ 45:980; Mahony 2:282)

1-179 KIPLING, (Joseph) Rudyard. *The Beginning of the Armadilloes.* Gr. 1–4.
✶   (Orig. British pub. in *Just So Stories,* 1902; in this edition, 1982.)
In this tale from the *Just So Stories* (1897–1902; see Chapter 2, Animal Fanta-
sy), a hedgehog and a tortoise turn into armadillos while tricking a young
jaguar out of his dinner.
Illus. by Charles Keeping, Bedrick, 1983, o.p.; illus. by Lorinda Bryan Cauley,
Harcourt, 1985, 43 pp. (0-15-206380-3); illus. by John A. Rowe, North-South,
1995, o.p.
(BL 80:859, 82:262; HB 60:357; SLJ Feb 1984 p. 60, Dec 1985 p. 75, Jan 1996 p. 83)

1-180 KIPLING, (Joseph) Rudyard. *The Butterfly That Stamped.* Gr. 2–4. (Orig.
British pub. in *Just So Stories,* 1902; in this edition, 1982.)
This tale from Kipling's *Just So Stories* (1897–1902; see Chapter 2, Animal
Fantasy) explains the nature of butterflies.
Illus. by Alan Baker, Bedrick, 1983, 31 pp., o.p.
(BL 80:859; SLJ Feb 1984 p. 60)

1-181 KIPLING, (Joseph) Rudyard. *The Cat That Walked by Himself.* Gr. 2–4.
(Orig. British pub. in *Just So Stories,* 1902; in this edition, 1982.)
A tale from Kipling's *Just So Stories* (1897–1902; see Chapter 2, Animal Fan-
tasy), in which cats learn to be independent.
Illus. by William Stobbs, Bedrick, 1983, 31 pp., o.p.
(BL 80:859; SLJ Feb 1984 p. 60)

1-182 KIPLING, (Joseph) Rudyard. *The Crab That Played with the Sea.* Gr. 2–4.
✶   (Orig. British pub. in *Just So Stories,* 1902; in this edition, 1982.)
One of Kipling's *Just So Stories* (1897–1902; see Chapter 2, Animal Fantasy),
in which Eldest Magician creates huge ocean creatures that come into conflict
with human beings.
Illus. by Michael Foreman, Bedrick, 1983, 31 pp., o.p.
(BL 80:859; HB 60:358; SLJ Feb 1984 p. 60)

1-183 KIPLING, (Joseph) Rudyard. *The Elephant's Child.* Gr. K–4. (Orig.
✶   British pub. in *Just So Stories,* 1902.)
A classic tale from the *Just So Stories* (1897–1902; see Chapter 2, Animal Fan-
tasy) that explains how the elephant got his long trunk.
Illus. by Leonard Weisgard, Walker, 1971, 32 pp., o.p.; illus. by Lorinda Bryan
Cauley, Harcourt, 1983, 44 pp., o.p.; illus. by Louise Brierly, Bedrick, 1985, 31
pp., o.p.; illus. by Jan Mogensen, Crocodile, 1989 (orig. pub. in Denmark), 48
pp., o.p.; illus. by Emily Bolam, Dutton, 1992, 24 pp., o.p.; illus. by John A.
Rowe, North-South, 1995, 28 pp., o.p.; adapt. by Jean Richards; illus. by Norman Gorbaty; Holt, 2003, 32 pp. (0-8050-6699-3)
(BL 80:87, 82:496; CCBB 37:130, 56:376; HBG 1:237, 6:292; Kirkus 58:660, 71:477; LJ
96:258; SLJ Oct 1983 p. 150, Feb 1986 p. 76, Jan 1992 p. 92, Feb 1992 p. 74, May 1995 p. 86)

1-184 KIPLING, (Joseph) Rudyard. *How the Camel Got His Hump.* Gr. K–4.
(Orig. British pub. in *Just So Stories,* 1902; in this edition, 1984.)
A lazy camel who refuses all work with a "Humph!" is given a hump on his
back by the magical Djinn in charge of all deserts, in this tale from the *Just So
Stories* (1897–1902; see Chapter 2, Animal Fantasy).
Illus. by Quentin Blake, Bedrick, 1985, 32 pp., o.p.; illus. by Lisbeth Zwerger,
North-South, 2001, 24 pp. (0-7358-1483-X)
(BL 82:496, 98:649; SLJ Feb 1986 p. 76, Dec 2001 p. 105)

1-185 KIPLING, (Joseph) Rudyard. *How the Leopard Got His Spots.* Gr. 1–4.
✫   (Orig. British pub. in *Just So Stories,* 1902.)
The leopard and the Ethiopian change their skins to improve their hunting abili-
ties in this tale from the *Just So Stories* (1897–1902; see Chapter 2, Animal
Fantasy).
Illus. by Leonard Weisgard, Walker, 1973, o.p.; illus. by Caroline Ebborn,
Bedrick, 1986, 32 pp. (0-8722-6072-0); illus. by Lori Lohstoeter, Picture Book
Studio, 1991, o.p.
(BL 69:948; Kirkus 41:381; LJ 98:3139; TLS 1972 p. 1333)

1-186 KIPLING, (Joseph) Rudyard. *How the Rhinoceros Got His Skin.* Gr. 2–4.
✫   (Orig. British pub. in *Just So Stories,* 1902.)
In this tale from the *Just So Stories* (1897–1902; see Chapter 2, Animal Fanta-
sy), a cake-thieving rhinoceros is punished by the Parsee who puts itchy cake
crumbs inside the rhino's skin.
Illus. by Leonard Weisgard, Walker, 1974, o.p.; illus. by Jenny Thorne,
Bedrick, 1987 (British pub. 1985), 31 pp., o.p.; illus. by Tim Raglin, Picture
Book Studio, 1991, 28 pp., o.p.
(BL 70:1154, 83:1749; CCBB 28:45; LJ 99:2250; Suth 2:257; TLS 1973 p. 1431)

1-187 KIPLING, (Joseph) Rudyard. *How the Whale Got His Throat.* Gr. 2–4.
(Orig. British pub. in *Just So Stories,* 1902; in this edition 1983.)
A shipwrecked mariner swallowed by a whale convinces the creature to take
him home.
Illus. by Pauline Baynes, Bedrick, 1987, 32 pp., o.p.
(BL 83:1749)

KIPLING, (Joseph) Rudyard. *Just So Stories.*
See Chapter 2, Animal Fantasy.

KOONTZ, Dean R(ay). *Oddkins: A Fable for All Ages.*
See Chapter 11, Toy Fantasy.

KORTUM, Jeanie. *Ghost Vision.*
See Chapter 12, Witchcraft and Sorcery Fantasy.

KOTZWINKLE, William. *Doctor Rat.*
See Chapter 2, Animal Fantasy.

KOTZWINKLE, William. *Hearts of Wood: And Other Timeless Tales.*
See Chapter 3, Fantasy Collections.

1-188 KRENSKY, Stephen (Alan). *A Big Day for Scepters.* Gr. 4–6.

A boy named Corey teams up with Calandar, a magician, to oppose the villain-ous Prince Grogol in a race for possession of a powerful evil scepter.
Illus. by Bruce Degen, Atheneum, 1977, 112 pp., o.p.
(BL 73:1576; Kirkus 45:352; SLJ Apr 1977 p. 68)

KRENSKY, Stephen (Alan). *Castles in the Air and Other Tales.*
See Chapter 3, Fantasy Collections.

1-189 **KRENSKY, Stephen (Alan).** *The Perils of Putney.* Gr. 4–6.
A peace-loving giant, pressed into a search for a missing Fair Damsel and cap-tured by a band of dwarfs, encounters a dragon, a witch, and a wizard.
Illus. by Jürg Obrist, Atheneum, 1978, 116 pp., o.p.
(BL 75:477; Kirkus 46:1189; SLJ Oct 1978 p. 146)

1-190 **KRENSKY, Stephen (Alan).** *A Troll in Passing.* Gr. 4–6.
✮ Morgan, dissatisfied with troll life, saves his people from a band of giant trolls and sets off to see the world.
Atheneum, 1980, 128 pp., o.p.
(BL 76:1424; CCBB 33:175; Kirkus 48:440; SLJ May 1980 p. 68; Suth 3:245)

KROPP, Lloyd. *The Drift.*
See Chapter 7, High Fantasy: Travel to Other Worlds.

1-191 **KUSHNER, Donn.** *Uncle Jacob's Ghost Story.* Gr. 6–10. (Orig. Canadian pub. 1980.)
Uncle Jacob is reunited with the ghosts of his best friends, Simon and Esther, who died of typhus long ago, in this touching and sophisticated story. Canadian Library Association Best Book of the Year for Children, 1980.
Holt, 1986, 132 pp., o.p.
(BL 82:1605, 1614; CCBB 39:170; Kirkus 54:550; SLJ May 1986 p. 94)

1-192 **KUSHNER, Donn.** *The Violin-Maker's Gift.* Gr. 5–7. (Orig. Canadian pub.
✮ 1981.)
Gaspard the violin-maker rescues a beautiful bird and sets it free. As a reward, the bird tells him a secret that causes all of Gaspard's instruments to sing as though they had souls. Canadian Library Association Best Book of the Year for Children, 1981.
Illus. by Doug Panton, Farrar, 1982, 74 pp., o.p.
(BL 78:1145; CCBB 35:191; SLJ Sep 1982 p. 123; Suth 3:246)

1-193 **LAGERLÖF, Selma (Ottiliana Lovisa).** *The Changeling.* Gr. K–4. (Orig.
✮ Swedish pub. in this ed. 1989.)
A grieving mother risks her life and her marriage to protect the ugly troll baby left in exchange for her own stolen infant.
Trans. by Susanna Stevens, illus. by Jeanette Winter, Knopf, 1992, 40 pp. (0-679-81035-8)
(BL 88:826; CCBB 45:183; HB 68:337; HBG 3:257; Kirkus 60:53; SLJ Apr 1992 p. 118)

LALLY, Soinbhe. *A Hive for the Honeybee.*
See Chapter 2, Animal Fantasy.

1-194 **LA MOTTE FOUQUÉ, Baron Friedrich Heinrich Karl de.** *Sintram and His Companions, a Northern Romance.* Gr. 6 up. (Written in France, 1814; orig. U.S. pub. 1869; Lippincott, 1901.)
A knight named Sintram struggles against the powers of evil. Also published as part of *Sintram and His Companions, and Undine* (Stokes, 189?, 1909, 1912, 1930).
Illus. by Gordon Browne, Wildside, 2002, 168 pp. (1-587-15687-3), pap. (1-587-15688-1)
(BL 6:420; Mahony 1:31, 2:669)

1-195 **LA MOTTE FOUQUÉ, Baron Friedrich Heinrich Karl de.** *Undine.* Gr. 5 up. (Written in 1811, orig. U.S. pub. 1908.)
Huldbrand, a knight married to the water nymph Undine, is threatened with death if he should ever betray her. *Haunted Waters* (Candlewick, 1994; see Chapter 6, High Fantasy: Myth or Legend Fantasy) is a retelling of the Undine story written for readers in grades 7–10.
Trans. by Edmund Gosse, illus. by Arthur Rackham, R.West, 1978, o.p.; Hyperion, 1985 (repr. of 1912 ed.), 136 pp., o.p.; Wildside, 2002, pap., 128 pp. (1-58715-689-X)
(BL 5:195; Bookshelf 1923–1924 p. 15; CCBB 25:5; Kirkus 39:236; Mahony 2:283; TLS 1929 p. 180; Tymn:105)

1-196 **LANCASTER, Osbert.** *The Saracen's Head; or, the Reluctant Crusader.* Gr. 4–6. (Orig. British pub. 1948.)
Cowardly Sir William de Littlehampton becomes a hero after he fights El Babooni.
Illus. by the author, Houghton, 1949, 67 pp., o.p.
(BL 46:101; CCBB 3:7; HB 25:533; Kirkus 17:302; LJ 74:1466; TLS 1948 p. 712)

LANG, Andrew. *My Own Fairy Book.*
See Chapter 3, Fantasy Collections.

1-197 **LANG, Andrew.** *Prince Prigio and Prince Ricardo: The Chronicles of*
✮ *Pantouflia.* Gr. 4–6. (Orig. British pub. 1889, 1893; orig. U.S. pub. in *My Own Fairy Book,* McKay, 1895, 1927.)
Prince Prigio and its sequel, *Prince Ricardo*, were originally published separately. *Prince Prigio*, the lighter of the two tales, is the story of an overly clever prince cursed by a fairy not invited to his christening. *Tales of a Fairy Court* (1906) is a related work.
Illus. by Robert Lawson, Little, Brown, 1942, o.p.; illus. by D. J. Watkins-Pitchford, Dutton, 1961, 171 pp., o.p.; illus. by Jeanne Titherington, Godine, 1981 (entitled *The Chronicles of Pantouflia: Prince Prigio and Prince Ricardo of Pantouflia*), 1984, 191 pp., o.p.
(BL 24:75; HB 18:423, 60:613; LJ 67:1069; SLJ Nov 1981 p. 94; TLS 1972 p. 795)

1-198 **LARSON, Jean (Russell).** *The Silkspinners.* Gr. 3–5.
✮ Li Po battles a sea monster and a sorcerer while searching for the lost silk spinners of China.
Illus. by Uri Shulevitz, Scribner, 1967, 93 pp., o.p.
(BL 64:448; CCBB 21:112; Kirkus 35:1047; LJ 92:3852; Suth:239)

LATHROP, Dorothy P(ulis). *The Colt from Moon Mountain.*
See Chapter 9, Magic Adventure Fantasy.

1-199 LATHROP, Dorothy P(ulis). *The Fairy Circus.* Gr. 2–4.
The fairies and the small woodland creatures stage a circus. John Newbery
Medal Honor Book, 1932.
Illus. by the author, Macmillan, 1931, 66 pp., o.p.
(BL 28:205; HB 7:315; Mahony 3:107)

1-200 LATTIMORE, Deborah Nourse. *The Fool and the Phoenix: A Tale of
Ancient Japan.* Gr. 2–5.
Mute Hideo falls in love with the human form of the phoenix he trapped in his
net, in this tale set in ancient Japan.
Illus. by the author, HarperCollins, 1997, 40 pp. (0-06-026211-7)
(BL 93:1901; Kirkus 65:951; SLJ Sep 1997 p. 185)

LAURENCE, (Jean) Margaret (Wemyss). *Jason's Quest.*
See Chapter 2, Animal Fantasy.

LAWRENCE, Ann (Margaret). *The Half Brothers.*
See Chapter 5, High Fantasy: Alternate Worlds or Histories.

LAWSON, Amy. *Star Baby.*
See Chapter 9, Magic Adventure Fantasy.

1-201 LAWSON, John S(hults). *You Better Come Home with Me.* Gr. 5 up.
✲   The lyrical tale of an orphaned boy searching for love, and the scarecrow who
takes him home to stay.
Illus. by Arnold Spilka, Crowell, 1966, 125 pp., o.p.; Harper, 1990, 136 pp., o.p.
(BL 63:419; CCBB 20:92; HB 42:711; LJ 91:5232; Suth:241)

1-202 LAWSON, Marie (Abrams). *Dragon John.* Gr. 2–4.
A small, unhappy dragon turns out to be an enchanted prince.
Illus. by the author, Viking, 1943, 52 pp., o.p.
(BL 40:64; HB 19:409; LJ 68:894)

1-203 LEE, Tanith. *Animal Castle.* Gr. 2–4.
Prince Rimtheed invites animals to live in his kingdom, but regrets his invita-
tion when they take advantage of their hosts.
Illus. by Helen Craig, Farrar, 1972, 37 pp., o.p.
(BL 69:948; Kirkus 40:1094; LJ 97:3797; TLS 1972 p. 808)

LEE, Tanith. *The Dragon Hoard.*
See Chapter 5, High Fantasy: Alternate Worlds or Histories.

LEE, Tanith. *Princess Hynchatti and Some Other Surprises.*
See Chapter 3, Fantasy Collections.

LEE, Tanith. *Red as Blood; or Tales from the Sisters Grimmer.*
See Chapter 6, High Fantasy: Myth or Legend Fantasy.

1-204 **LE GUIN, Ursula K(roeber).** *Fish Soup.* Gr. 1–3.
The children imagined by the Thinking Man and the Writing Woman come to life, but they are not quite as their parents had pictured them.
Illus. by Patrick Wynne, Macmillan, 1992, 32 pp. (0-689-31733-6)
(HBG 4:59; Kirkus 60:1257; SLJ Jan 1993 p. 80)

LE GUIN, Ursula K(roeber). *Gifts.*
See Chapter 5, High Fantasy: Alternate Worlds or Histories.

1-205 **LE GUIN, Ursula K(roeber).** *A Ride on the Red Mare's Back.* Gr. K–4.
★ A brave girl fills her pockets with treasures, including a small red wooden horse, and sets off through the snowy woods to rescue her little brother, who was stolen by trolls.
Illus. by Julie Downing, Orchard, 1992, 48 pp., o.p.; Orchard, 1996, pap., 48 pp. (0-531-07079-4)
(BL 88:1847; CCBB 46:47; HB 69:204; HBG 4:59; Kirkus 60:851; SLJ Sep 1992 p. 207)

LE GUIN, Ursula K(roeber). *A Wizard of Earthsea.*
See Chapter 5, High Fantasy: Alternate Worlds or Histories.

L'ENGLE, Madeleine. *Many Waters.*
See Chapter 10, Time Travel Fantasy.

1-206 **LESKOV, Nikolai.** *The Steel Flea, a Story.* Gr. 3–5. (Orig. U.S. pub. 1943.)
The czar challenges his friend Platov to create something even more ingenious than the dancing steel flea he was sent as a gift from England.
Adapt. by Babette Deutsch and Avrahm Yarmolinsky, illus. by Janina Domanska, Harper, 1964 (rev. ed.), 56 pp., o.p.
(BL 40:167, 60:1004, CCBB 19:65; HB 40:178; LJ 69:73, 89:1452)

1-207 **LE VERT, John.** *The Flight of the Cassowary.* Gr. 8–12.
★ John's high school classmates label him as crazy after he tells them about the intense moments during which he feels as though he has turned into an animal.
Atlantic, 1986, 288 pp., o.p.
(BL 82:1136, 1142, 83:1592; CCBB 39:172; HB 62:332; Kirkus 54:869; SLJ May 1986 p. 105, Mar 1987 p. 120; TLS 1987 p. 1028; VOYA 9:80)

1-208 **LEVIN, Meyer.** *The Spell of Time: A Tale of Love in Jerusalem.* Gr. 10 up.
Two scientists working at an Israeli research institute fall in love with a young French colleague, and make a mystical pact to exchange bodies but retain their own personalities in order to test the young woman's ability to find her true love.
Praeger, 1974, 127 pp., o.p.
(BL 71:268, 285; HB 51:77; Kirkus 42:829; LJ 99:2620)

1-209 **LEWIS, Beth (pseud. of Beth Lipkin).** *The Blue Mountain.* Gr. 2–4.
Prince Desmond agrees to hold a mountain-climbing contest to choose his bride, even though he is in love with Princess Noreen.
Illus. by Adrienne Adams, Knopf, 1956, 59 pp., o.p.
(CCBB 10:52; HB 32:351; Kirkus 24:519)

LEWIS, C(live) S(taples). *The Lion, the Witch, and the Wardrobe.*
See Chapter 7, High Fantasy: Travel to Other Worlds.

1-210 LEY, Madeleine. *The Enchanted Eve.* Gr. 3 up. (Orig. French pub. 1935.)
On Saint Sylvain's Eve, Barbara, the crippled daughter of a Flemish painter, is
granted her wish for freedom, enabling her to skate wherever she wishes to go.
Trans. by Willard Trask, illus. by Edy LeGrand, Howell, 1946, 48 pp., o.p.
(HB 23:263, 438; LJ 72:894)

LEZRA, Giggy (Grizzella Paull). *The Cat, the Horse, and the Miracle.*
See Chapter 2, Animal Fantasy.

1-211 LIFTON, Betty Jean (Kirschner). *The Dwarf Pine Tree.* Gr. 3–5.
☆ To save the dying princess's life, a young pine tree agrees to undergo painful
binding in order to become a dwarf-sized tree.
Illus. by Fuku Akino, Atheneum, 1963, 37 pp., o.p.
(BL 60:262; Eakin:210; HB 39:499; LJ 88:116)

LINDGREN, Astrid. *The Brothers Lionheart.*
See Chapter 7, High Fantasy: Travel to Other Worlds.

1-212 LISLE, Janet Taylor. *Forest.* Gr. 4–7.
☆ Twelve-year-old Amber and a squirrel named Woodbine are branded as traitors
because they want to prevent a war between the humans of Lower Forest and
the squirrels of Upper Forest.
Orchard, 1993, 150 pp., o.p.; Puffin, 1999, pap., 135 pp. (0-689-811805-7)
(BL 90:443; CCBB 47:160; HB 70:199; HBG 5:79; Kirkus 61:1205; SLJ Nov 1993 p. 109)

1-213 LISLE, Janet Taylor. *The Great Dimpole Oak.* Gr. 4–7.
The majestic old oak in the town of Dimpole has a mythic presence that draws
both local inhabitants and the followers of an Indian swami. Golden Kite
Award Honor Book, 1987.
Illus. by Stephen Gammell, Orchard, 1987, 144 pp., LB (0-531-08316-0)
(BL 84:150, 873; CCBB 41:121; HB 64:64; Kirkus 55:1518; SLJ Dec 1987 p. 86)

LIVELY, Penelope (Margaret Low). *Astercote.*
See Chapter 6, High Fantasy: Myth or Legend Fantasy.

1-214 LLOYD, (Mary) Norris. *The Desperate Dragons.* Gr. 2–4.
☆ A young cowherd puts the knights of Rondo to shame by ridding the kingdom
of the last 12 dragons on earth.
Illus. by Joan Balfour (Dicks) Payne, Hastings, 1960, 64 pp., o.p.
(CCBB 13:151; HB 36:289; Kirkus 28:88; LJ 85:2041)

1-215 LLYWELYN, Morgan. *The Elementals.* Gr. 10 up.
Four stories whose main characters—Kesair, Meriones, Annie, and George—
live in different times and places, but whose respect for the earth helps them
and their peoples to survive.
Tor, 1993, 304 pp., o.p.
(BL 89:1678, 1682; Kirkus 61:493; LJ June 15, 1993 p. 104; VOYA 16:311)

LOVETT, Margaret (Rose). *The Great and Terrible Quest.*
See Chapter 5, High Fantasy: Alternate Worlds or Histories.

1-216 LOWREY, Janette Sebring. *The Lavender Cat.* Gr. 4–6.
⭐ The little wild cat tamed by a lost boy named Jemmy eventually leads the boy home.
Illus. by Rafaello Busoni, Harper, 1944, 180 pp., o.p.
(BL 41:127; HB 21:33; Kirkus 12:431; LJ 69:1050)

LOWRY, Lois. *Messenger.*
See Chapter 5, High Fantasy: Alternate Worlds or Histories.

LUENN, Nancy. *Arctic Unicorn.*
See Chapter 12, Witchcraft and Sorcery Fantasy.

1-217 LUENN, Nancy. *The Ugly Princess.* Gr. 3–5.
The veiled Princess Saralinde has difficulty choosing between the handsome but vain Prince Phillip, and the kind but unattractive Dragonlord.
Illus. by David Wiesner, Little, Brown, 1981, 27 pp., o.p.
(CCBB 35:90; HB 57:659; Kirkus 50:201; SLJ Oct 1981 p. 144)

LUENN, Nancy. *Unicorn Crossing.*
See Chapter 9, Magic Adventure Fantasy.

1-218 LYNCH, Patricia (Nora). ***Brogeen Follows the Magic Tune.*** **(Brogeen series, bk. 4).** Gr. 4–6. (Orig. British pub. 1952.)
Brogeen the leprechaun is determined to retrieve the fairies' magic tune, stolen by a human fiddler. This story is preceded by *Brogeen and the Lost Castle* (British), *Brogeen and the Black Enchanter* (British), and *Brogeen and the Little Wind* (1963), and the sequels are *Brogeen and the Bronze Lizard* (1970), *Brogeen and the Red Fez* (British), and *Guests at the Beech Tree* (British).
Illus. by Ralph Pinto, Macmillan, 1968, 165 pp., o.p.
(BL 65:837; Kirkus 36:1163; LJ 94:302)

1-219 MACAULAY, David. *BAAA.* Gr. 6 up.
⭐ After humans disappear from the earth, sheep take up human clothing, possessions, and thoughts, become consumers, and eventually destroy themselves, rioting over inequities.
Illus. by the author, Houghton, 1985, 64 pp. (0-395-38948-8)
(BL 82:53; CCBB 31:13; SLJ Oct 1985 p. 183)

1-220 MacDONALD, George. *At the Back of the North Wind.* Gr. 5–8. (Orig.
⭐ British pub. 1871, U.S. 1875.)
A beautiful lady takes a boy named Diamond on fabulous travels, and the final journey is to the land at the back of the North Wind. One of the chapters in this story has been published separately as *Little Daylight* (1987, 1988; see below).
Illus. by Maria Louise Kirk, Lippincott, 1909, o.p.; illus. by Jessie Willcox Smith, McKay, 1919, o.p.; illus. by D. Bedford, Macmillan, 1924, o.p.; illus. by Gertrude A. Kay, McKay, 1926, 1934, o.p.; illus. by George Hauman and Doris Hauman, Macmillan, 1950, 1964, o.p.; Puffin, 1996, pap., 352 pp. (0-14-

036768-3); illus. by Jessie Willcox Smith, Morrow, 1989 (facsimile of 1919
ed.), 347 pp. (0-688-07808-7); Tor, 1998, pap., 305 pp. (0-8125-6712-9)
(BL 6:146, 47:162; Bookshelf 1923–1924 p. 15; CCBB 11:61; HB 1[Nov 1924]:7, 26:490,
34:122; LJ 26[no. 8]:67, 45:980, 50:803; Mahony 2:286, SLJ Feb 1989 p. 119)

1-221 MacDONALD, George. *The Fairy Fleet.* Gr. 2–4. (Orig. British pub. in *The
Carasoyn, Light Princess and Other Fairy Tales.*)
Young Colin rescues a changeling child from the fairy fleet,
Illus. by Stuyvesant Van Veen, Holiday, 1936, 52 pp., o.p.
(BL 33:30; HB 12:289; LJ 61:733)

1-222 MacDONALD, George. *The Golden Key.* Gr. 4 up. (Orig. British and U.S.
pub. in *Dealings with the Fairies,* 1867; as a separate tale, 1906.)
After Tangle discovers the key to the door at the end of the rainbow, he and his
sister search for the mystical land beyond the door.
Crowell, 1906, o.p.; illus. by Maurice (Bernard) Sendak, Farrar, 1976, rev. ed.
1984, 96 pp. (0-374-32706-8), pap. (0-374-42590-6)
(HB 43:464; Kirkus 35:609; LJ 92:3187)

1-223 MacDONALD, George. *The Light Princess.* Gr. 3–6. (Orig. British pub. in
☆   *Dealings with the Fairies,* 1867; orig. British pub. as a separate tale, 1872; U.S.
1926.)
Angry Aunt Makemnort's curse removes all of the princess's gravity, leaving
her to laugh but never cry, and to float but never walk on the ground.
Illus. by Dorothy P. Lathrop, Macmillan, 1926, 1940, 1952, o.p.; illus. by
William Pène du Bois, Crowell, 1962, o.p.; illus. by Maurice (Bernard) Sendak,
Farrar, 1969, rev. ed. 1984, 120 pp. (0-374-34455-8), 1992, pap. (0-374-44458-
7); adapt. by Robin McKinley, illus. by Katie Thamer Treherne, Harcourt,
1988, 44 pp. (0-15-245300-8)
(BL 59:499, 66:623, 84:1838; Bookshelf 1926–1927 Suppl. p. 3; CCBB 23:162; HB 2[Nov
1928]:45, 28:422, 38:605, 46:41; Kirkus 37:1257, 56:365, LJ 87:427, 95:1640; Mahony 2:288;
SLJ Aug 1988 p. 83; Suth:262)

1-224 MacDONALD, George. *Little Daylight.* Gr. 3–6.
Princess Daylight was cursed at her christening to sleep all day and remain
awake all night, while her youth and beauty waxed and waned with the moon.
This story was adapted from a chapter in *At the Back of the North Wind* (1871;
see above).
Adapt. by Anthea Bell, illus. by Dorothée Duntze, North-South, 1987, 26 pp.,
o.p.; illus. by Erick Ingraham, Morrow, 1988, 40 pp., o.p.
(BL 84:787, 85:81; CCBB 42:47; SLJ Nov 1988 p. 92)

1-225 MacDONALD, George. *Phantastes: A Faerie Romance for Men and
Women.* Gr. 10 up. (Orig. British pub. 1858; U.S. 1871; McKay 1911, o.p.;
Dutton, 1916, 1923, 1940, o.p.)
On the morning of the hero's 21st birthday, his bedroom turns into a woodland
glade, and he sets out on a series of fantastic and dangerous adventures.
Eerdmans, 1981, pap. (0-8028-6060-5); Johannesen, 1998 (1-881084-22-1)
(HB May 1927, pp. 17B22; TLS 1982 p. 1175)

1-226   MacDONALD, George. *The Princess and the Goblin.* Gr. 5–7. (Orig.
★★   British and U.S. pub. 1872.)
Curdie, a miner's son, overhears a Goblin plot to flood the mines and take over
the kingdom. The sequel is *The Princess and Curdie* (Orig. British pub. 1882;
U.S. 1883; Macmillan, 1954, o.p.; Puffin, 1996, pap.).
Illus. by Maria Louise Kirk and Arthur Hughes, Lippincott, 1907, 1910, 1913,
1934, o.p.; illus. by Jessie Willcox Smith, McKay, 1920, 1934, o.p.; illus. by
F(rancis) D(onkin) Bedford, Macmillan, 1926, 1930, o.p.; illus. by Elizabeth
MacKinstry, Doubleday, 1928, 1937, o.p.; illus. by Nora S(picer) Unwin,
Macmillan, 1951, o.p.; illus. by Dorothy Lathrop, Atheneum, 1967 (0-02-
761850-1); Dell, 1985, pap. (0-440-47189-3); illus. by Jessie Willcox Smith,
Morrow, 1986, 208 pp. (0-688-06604-6); illus. by Arthur Hughes, Puffin, 1997,
pap., 256 pp. (0-14-036746-2); Dover, 1999, pap., 165 pp. (0-486-10787-X)
(BL 5:64, 83:354, 84:67; Bookshelf 1932 p. 8; CCBB 4:45; HB 27:261, 63:84; LJ 26:67;
Mahony 2:287; Moore:290; SLJ Oct 1987 p. 116)

1-227   MacDONALD, George. *The Wise Woman and Other Fantasy Stories.* Gr.
5–7. (Orig. British and U.S. pub. 1875; retitled *The Lost Princess: A Double
Story,* 1895.)
The paths of two little girls, a princess and a shepherd's daughter, converge at
the home of the wise woman, who changes both their lives.
Harcourt, 1924 (entitled *The Lost Princess: A Double Story*), o.p.; Dutton,
1965, 142 pp. (entitled *The Lost Princess*), o.p.; Eerdmans, 1980, pap., 176 pp.,
o.p.; illus. by D(enys) J(ames) Watkins-Pitchford, Zondervan, 1981, o.p.; ed.
by Glenn Edward Sadler, illus. by Bernhard Oberdieck (entitled *The Lost
Princess: A Double Story*), Eerdmans, 1992, 148 pp. (0-8028-5070-7)
(BL 89:908; HB 42:306; HBG 1:239, 4:73; SLJ Apr 1981 p. 129; TLS 1965 p. 1150)

1-228   McGINLEY, Phyllis (Louise). *The Plain Princess.* Gr. 2–4.
★   Dame Goodwit teaches a selfish young princess to be kind and helpful,
Illus. by Helen Stone, Lippincott, 1945, 64 pp., o.p.
(BL 42:133; HB 21:454, 447; Kirkus 13:297; LJ 70:950, 1138)

1-229   McKENZIE, Ellen Kindt. *The King, the Princess, and the Tinker.* Gr. 2–5.
★   None of his subjects recognize the king after his crown falls off, because,
unlike the beloved Princess Rosilla, he has spent his entire life inside his mir-
rored throne room, watching his own reflection and that of his treasure.
Illus. by William Low, Henry Holt, 1992, 70 pp., o.p., 1993, pap., 64 pp. (0-
8050-2951-6)
(BL 88:1280; CCBB 45:168; HBG 3:267; Kirkus 60:54; SLJ May 1992 p. 91)

McKILLIP, Patricia A(nne). *The Forgotten Beasts of Eld.*
See Chapter 5, High Fantasy: Alternate Worlds or Histories.

McKINLEY, (Jennifer Carolyn) Robin (Turrell). *Beauty: A Retelling of
the Story of Beauty and the Beast.*
See Chapter 6, High Fantasy: Myth or Legend Fantasy.

McKINLEY, (Jennifer Carolyn) Robin (Turrell). *The Door in the Hedge.*
See Chapter 3, Fantasy Collections.

MacLACHLAN, Patricia. *Tomorrow's Wizard.*
See Chapter 12, Witchcraft and Sorcery Fantasy.

1-230 MAETERLINCK, Maurice. *The Children's Blue Bird.* **(Orig. title:** *The Blue Bird: A Fairy Play in Five Acts,* **1909; prose version, 1913).** Gr. 3–5.
Two children search for the blue bird of happiness. Maeterlinck also published a sequel: *The Betrothal: A Sequel to the Blue Bird* (Dodd, 1918).
Adapt. by Georgette Leblanc (Maeterlinck), trans. by Alexander De Mattos, illus. by Herbert Paus, Dodd, 1950, 1962, 182 pp., o.p.; Philos, 1985 (entitled *The Blue Bird*, bound with *The Betrothal*), 304 pp., o.p.
(BL 5:174, 10:163; Bookshelf 1927 Suppl. p. 26; Mahony 1:34; Mahony 2:26; Mahony 3:37)

MAGUIRE, Gregory. *The Dream Stealer.*
See Chapter 12, Witchcraft and Sorcery Fantasy.

MAHY, Margaret (May). *The Door in the Air and Other Stories.*
See Chapter 9, Magic Adventure Fantasy.

MAHY, Margaret (May). *The Five Sisters.*
See Chapter 11, Toy Fantasy.

1-231 MARIA, Consort of Ferdinand, King of Rumania. *The Story of Naughty Kildeen.* Gr. 2–4. (Orig. British pub. 1921.)
A spoiled young princess learns to control her temper, and becomes more considerate of others.
Illus. by Job, Harcourt, 1926, 95 pp., o.p.
(BL 24:169; Bookshelf, 1923–1924, p. 2)

1-232 MARKS, Alan. *The Thief's Daughter.* Gr. 2–4. (Orig. British pub. 1993.)
Magpie clears her father's name after a mysterious woman gives her a golden key that opens a mysterious box given to her father long ago.
Illus. by the author, Farrar, 1994, 46 pp., o.p.
(HBG 5:302; Kirkus 62:633; SLJ Apr 1994 p. 110)

1-233 MAUGHAM, W(illiam) Somerset. *Princess September.* **(Alternate title:** *Princess September and the Nightingale*). Gr. 3–5. (Orig. pub. as part of *The Gentleman in the Parlour,* 1930.)
A nightingale caged by Princess September nearly dies.
Illus. by Jacqueline Ayer, Harcourt, 1969, 33 pp., o.p.; entitled *Princess September and the Nightingale*, illus. by Richard C. Jones (illus. first pub. 1939), Oxford University Press, 1998, 48 pp. (0-19-512480-4)
(BL 95:597; CCBB 22:31; HB 45:308; HBG 10:58; LJ 94:2104; TLS 1970 p. 420)

1-234 MAYER, Marianna. *The Little Jewel Box.* Gr. K–3.
✯ Isabel proves herself to be "brave, outspoken, and intelligent besides," as she performs the arduous tasks needed to win John for her husband.
Illus. by Margot Tomes, Dial, 1968, 32 pp., o.p.
(BL 82:1086; CCBB 39:154; HB 62:443; Kirkus 54:793; SLJ May 1986 p. 82)

MAYER, Marianna. *Noble-Hearted Kate: A Celtic Tale.*
See Chapter 6, High Fantasy: Myth or Legend Fantasy.

MAYER, Marianna. *The Sorcerer's Apprentice; A Greek Fable.*
See Chapter 6, High Fantasy: Myth or Legend Fantasy.

1-235 MAYER, Marianna. *Turandot.* Gr. 4–7.
After he answers her three riddles correctly, Princess Turandot breaks her
promise to marry the Persian prince, Calaf, in this retelling of an Italian fairy
tale first dramatized by 18th-century Venetian playwright Carlo Gozzi, and
later made into an opera by Giacomo Puccini.
Illus. by Winslow Pels, Morrow, 1995, 48 pp. (0-688-09073-7)
(HBG 7:56; Kirkus 63:1191; SLJ Oct 1995 p. 149)

MAYHAR, Ardath. *The Saga of Grittel Sundotha.*
See Chapter 5, High Fantasy: Alternate Worlds or Histories.

1-236 MAYNE, William (James Carter). *A Year and a Day.* Gr. 4–6. (Orig.
✫   British pub. 1976.)
Sara and Rebecca find a fairy changeling boy who brings happiness to their
family, but only for a year and a day.
Dutton, 1976, 86 pp., o.p.; Candlewick, 2000, illus. by John Lawrence, 126 pp.
(0-7636-0850-5)
(BL 72:1528; CCBB 29:178; HB 52:398, 60:223; Kirkus 44:391; SLJ Apr 1976 p. 76; TLS
1976 p. 1241)

1-237 MAZER, Anne. *The Oxboy.* Gr. 4–7.
Oxboy, the mixed-blood son of a human mother and a banished ox father, is
forced to pretend to be a "pure-blood human," and hide his friendship with an
otter.
Knopf, 1993, 109 pp. (0-679-84191-1)
(BL 90:523; CCBB 47:52; HBG 5:80; Kirkus 61:1526; SLJ Nov 1993 p. 110)

MEIGS, Cornelia (Lynde). *The Kingdom of the Winding Road.*
See Chapter 3, Fantasy Collections.

1-238 MELLECKER, Judith. *Randolph's Dream.* Gr. K–4.
Seven-year-old Randolph, staying with relatives while his father fights in North
Africa during World War II, flies in his dreams to the desert where his father
lies wounded, and leads him to safety.
Illus. by Robert Andrew Parker, Knopf, 1991, 40 pp. (0-679-91115-4)
(BL 87:1037, 1128; CCBB 44:269; HBG 2:257; Kirkus 58:1741; SLJ May 1991 p. 81)

MENOTTI, Gian Carlo. *Amahl and the Night Visitors.*
See Chapter 6, High Fantasy: Myth or Legend Fantasy.

MERRILL, Jean (Fairbanks). *The Black Sheep.*
See Chapter 2, Animal Fantasy.

MERRILL, Jean (Fairbanks). *The Pushcart War.*
See Chapter 8, Humorous Fantasy.

1-239 MERRILL, Jean (Fairbanks). *The Superlative Horse: A Tale of Ancient*
✫   *China.* Gr. 4–6.

When Hankan, a lowly stable boy, finds a wonderful horse for Duke Mu, the boy is made chief groom.

Illus. by Ronni Solbert, Addison-Wesley, 1961, 79 pp., o.p.

(BL 58:287; Eakin:234; HB 38:48; LJ 87:334)

1-240 MEYER, Zoe. *The Little Green Door.* Gr. 2–4.

A collection of tales describing how the Fairy of the Green Forest helped the robin get his spotted breast, the hermit thrush get his song, and the owl learn to fly at night.

Illus. by Clara E. Atwood, Little, Brown, 1921, 157 pp., o.p.

(BL 18:161; Bookshelf, 1923–1924, p. 8)

1-241 MILES, (Mary) Patricia. *The Gods in Winter.* Gr. 5–8.

☆ Strange things begin happening when Mrs. Korngold moves in as the Brambles' housekeeper: she changes cousin Crispin into a lizard, saves Lottie's life, and seems to be the cause of an extremely severe winter.

Dutton, 1978, 140 pp., o.p.

(BL 75:51; CCBB 32:48; HB 55:518; Kirkus 46:750; SLJ Oct 1978 p. 147; Suth 2:319; TLS 1978 p. 764)

1-242 MILNE, A(lan) A(lexander). *Once on a Time.* Gr. 5–7. (Orig. British and

☆ U.S. pub. 1917.)

When their kings go to war, the kingdoms of Euralia and Barodia are ruled by women.

Illus. by Charles Robinson, Putnam, 1922, o.p.; illus. by Susan Perl, New York Graphic Society, 1962, 242 pp., o.p.

(BL 19:87; Bookshelf 1928 p. 23; HB 2[Nov 1928]:45; Kirkus 29:1086; LJ 87:842)

1-243 MILNE, A(lan) A(lexander). *Prince Rabbit and the Princess Who Could Not Laugh.* Gr. 2–4.

Two humorous tales about an enchanted prince in rabbit-form and a contest to make a princess laugh.

Illus. by Mary Shepard, Dutton, 1966, 72 pp., o.p.

(CCBB 20:61; LJ 92:329)

MODESITT, L(eland) E(xton), Jr. *The Magic of Recluce.*

See Chapter 5, High Fantasy: Alternate Worlds or Histories.

1-244 MOERI, Louise. *Star Mother's Youngest Child.* Gr. 2 up.

☆☆ A crotchety old woman and Star Mother's Ugly Child spend Christmas together, turning that previously lonely day into a warm and memorable one.

Illus. by Trina Schart Hyman, Houghton, 1975, 48 pp., o.p., 1980, pap. (0-395-29929-2)

(BL 72:304; CCBB 29:115; HB 51:582; Kirkus 43:1180; SLJ Oct 1975 p. 81)

1-245 MOERI, Louise. *The Unicorn and the Plow.* Gr. 2–4.

A unicorn plows a starving farmer's field, turning it into a flourishing vegetable garden overnight.

Illus. by Diane Goode, Dutton, 1982, 31 pp., o.p.

(BL 78:1527; CCBB 36:16; Kirkus 50:419; SLJ Apr 1982 p. 60)

MOLESWORTH, Mary Louisa (Stewart). *Fairy Stories.*
See Chapter 3, Fantasy Collections.

MOLESWORTH, Mary Louisa (Stewart). *Stories by Mrs. Molesworth.*
See Chapter 3, Fantasy Collections.

MONSELL, Mary Elise. *Toohy and Wood.*
See Chapter 2, Animal Fantasy.

MONTROSE, Anne. *The Winter Flower, and Other Fairy Stories.*
See Chapter 3, Fantasy Collections.

MOON, Sheila (Elizabeth). *Knee-Deep in Thunder.*
See Chapter 7, High Fantasy: Travel to Other Worlds.

MOORCOCK, Michael (John). *The Ice Schooner: A Tale.*
See Chapter 5, High Fantasy: Alternate Worlds or Histories.

1-246 MOORCOCK, Michael (John). *The War Hound and the World's Pain: A Fable.* Gr. 10 up.
Heartsick at the atrocities he has seen perpetrated in the name of God during the Thirty Years' War (1618–1648), Captain Von Beck is sent by Satan to find the "Cure for the World's Pain," in order to free his soul from the Devil's grip. The sequel is *The City in the Autumn Stars* (1987). *Lunching with the Antichrist: A Family History: 1925–2015* (1995) is a related work.
Simon, 1981, o.p.; Ultramarine, 1981, 239 pp., o.p.
(Kirkus 49:1100; LJ 106:2052; SLJ Jan 1982 p. 92)

1-247 MORGAN, Robin. *The Mer-Child: A Legend for Children and Other Adults.* Gr. 4–6.
A lonely mer-child, scorned because he is half-human, begins a lifelong friendship with a paralyzed bi-racial girl who, because of his friendship, grows up to become an oceanographer.
Illus. by Jessie Spicer Zerner, Talman, 1991, 55 pp. (1-55861-053-7)
(HBG 3:70; Kirkus 59:1537; SLJ Aug 1992 p. 156)

1-248 MORPURGO, Michael. *Jo-Jo the Melon Donkey.* Gr. 3–5. (Orig. British pub. 1987.)
A little donkey who longs for a better life saves the citizens of 16th-century Venice by braying loudly to warn them that the sea is coming in.
Illus. by Chris Molan, Prentice-Hall, 1988, 32 pp., o.p.
(Kirkus 55:1677; SLJ Apr 1988 p. 87)

1-249 MOZART, Wolfgang Amadeus. *The Magic Flute.* Gr. 3–6.
✫   In Mozart's opera retold for children, Prince Tamino battles the Queen of Night for the hand of his beloved Pamina. *Night's Daughter* by Marion Zimmer Bradley (Ballantine, 1985; see Chapter 6, High Fantasy: Myth or Legend Fantasy) is a contemporary version of this story, written for young adults.
Adapt. and illus. by John Updike and Warren Chappell, Knopf, 1962, o.p.; adapt. by Stephen Spender, illus. by Beni Montresor, Putnam, 1966, 40 pp., o.p.
(BL 59:615; HB 43:196; LJ 87:3896, 92:337)

1-250 **MULLER, Robin.** *The Magic Paintbrush.* Gr. 3–5.
A magic paintbrush that brings to life whatever Nib paints, becomes especially useful after the king imprisons Nib.
Illus. by the author, Viking, 1990, 32 pp., o.p.
(BL 86:1634, 2000; HBG 1:229; Kirkus 58:344; SLJ July 1990 p. 79)

1-251 **MULOCK, Diana (pseud. of Dinah Craik).** *The Little Lame Prince and*
✫ *His Travelling Cloak.* Gr. 4–6. (Orig. British pub. 1874.)
Prince Dolor, lame from an accident in infancy, uses magic to escape his greedy uncle and to gain his rightful throne.
Grossett, 1948, o.p.; adapt. and illus. by Rosemary Wells, Dial, 1990 (entitled *The Little Lame Prince*), 32 pp., o.p.
(BL 6:142, 45:145, 87:174, Bookshelf 1932 p. 8; CCBB 2[Jan 1949]:2; HB 7:116; LJ 26[no. 8]:67, 74:69; Mahony 2:278)

MURPHY, Rita. *Night Flying.*
See Chapter 9, Magic Adventure Fantasy.

1-252 **MURPHY, Shirley Rousseau.** *Silver Woven in My Hair.* Gr. 4–6.
✫ In an extended version of the Cinderella story, orphaned Thursey is ill-treated by her stepmother and stepsisters until her friend, the goatherd, turns out to be a long-lost prince.
Illus. by Alan Tiegreen, Atheneum, 1977, 121 pp., o.p.
(BL 73:1355; CCBB 31:51, 44:19; HB 53:316; Kirkus 45:224; SLJ Sep 1977 p. 134)

1-253 **MURPHY, Shirley Rousseau.** *Valentine for a Dragon.* Gr. K–4.
A shy demon's gifts to a lovely lady dragon keep going up in smoke until he finds the perfect gift and wins her heart.
Illus. by Kay Chorao, Atheneum, 1984, 48 pp., o.p.
(BL 80:1550, 83:360; CCBB 37:171; SLJ Aug 1984 p. 63)

1-254 **MYERS, Walter Dean.** *The Golden Serpent.* Gr. 3–5.
A wise man finds the answer to the mystery of the golden serpent, but the king does not understand this answer.
Illus. by Alice Provensen and Martin Provensen, Viking, 1980, 40 pp., o.p.
(BL 77:575; CCBB 34:157; HB 56:636; SLJ Jan 1981 p. 53; TLS 1981 p. 343)

1-255 **NATHAN, Robert (Gruntal).** *Portrait of Jennie.* Gr. 10 up.
Each time a struggling artist meets Jennie, she has mysteriously grown older "in order to catch up with him," but tragedy intervenes after they fall in love.
Knopf, 1929, 1940, 1949, 212 pp. (0-394-44093-5)
(BL 36:198; TLS 1940 p. 85)

NESBIT (Bland), E(dith). *The Complete Book of Dragons.*
See Chapter 3, Fantasy Collections.

1-256 **NESBIT (Bland), E(dith).** *The Last of the Dragons.* Gr. 4–6. (Orig. British and U.S. pub. in *The Book of Dragons,* 1901; as a separate tale, 1925.)
Faced with a Cornish princess and her suitor, England's last dragon reveals that he wants only to be loved.

Illus. by Peter Firmin, McGraw-Hill, 1980, 25 pp., o.p.; illus. by Erik Blegvad, Puffin, 1985, pap. (0-14-035069-1)
(CCBB 34:115; SLJ Feb 1981 p. 69)

NESBIT (Bland), E(dith). *The Magic World.*
See Chapter 9, Magic Adventure Fantasy.

1-257 **NESBIT (Bland), E(dith).** *Melisande.* Gr. K–4. (Orig. British pub. in *Nine*
☆   *Unlikely Tales,* 1901.)
A spell of baldness is cast over Princess Melisande by a fairy who was not invited to her christening party, but when she grows up and makes a wish, Melisande suddenly has hair that will not stop growing.
Illus. by P. J. Lynch, Harcourt, 1989, 48 pp. (0-15-253164-5); illus. by P. J. Lynch, Candlewick, 1999, pap., 45 pp. (0-7636-0717-7)
(BL 86:353; HB 65:763; HBG 1:81; Kirkus 57:1478; SLJ Jan 1990 p. 87)

NEWMAN, Robert (Howard). *Merlin's Mistake.*
See Chapter 6, High Fantasy: Myth or Legend Fantasy.

NORTH, Joan. *The Cloud Forest.*
See Chapter 9, Magic Adventure Fantasy.

NYE, Robert. *The Mathematical Princess and Other Stories.*
See Chapter 3, Fantasy Collections.

1-258 **NYE, Robert.** *Wishing Gold.* Gr. 3–5. (Orig. British pub. 1970.)
Wishing Gold, the lost son of the King of Ireland, battles an evil queen and her three sons and saves his father's life.
Illus. by Helen Craig, Hill, 1971, 109 pp., o.p.
(Kirkus 39:52; LJ 96:1507; TLS 1970 p. 714)

OAKLEY, Graham. *Henry's Quest.*
See Chapter 8, Humorous Fantasy.

O'BRIEN, Robert C. *Mrs. Frisby and the Rats of NIMH.*
See Chapter 2, Animal Fantasy.

Once upon a Time: A Treasury of Modern Fairy Tales. **Ed. by Lester Del Rey and Risa Kessler.**
See Chapter 3, Fantasy Collections.

ORWELL, George. *Animal Farm.*
See Chapter 2, Animal Fantasy.

OSBORNE, M(aurice) M(achado) (Jr.). *Ondine: The Story of a Bird Who Was Different.*
See Chapter 2, Animal Fantasy.

The Oxford Book of Modern Fairy Tales. **Ed. by Alison Lurie.**
See Chapter 3, Fantasy Collections.

1-259 **PAGE, P(atricia) K(athleen) (pseud. of Patricia Kathleen Page Irwin).** *A*
☆   *Flask of Sea Water.* Gr. 2–5. (Orig. Canadian pub. 1989.)

A goatherd in love with a princess may win her hand only by bringing a flask of special seawater to the king.
Illus. by Laszlo Gal, Oxford University Press, 1989, 32 pp., o.p.
(BL 86:834, 87:178; HB 66:60, 367; HBG 1:81; Kirkus 57:1675)

1-260 PAGET, (Reverend) F(rancis) (pseud. of William Churne of Stafford-shire). *The Hope of the Katzekopfs; or, the Sorrow of Selfishness: A Fairy Tale.* **(Alternate title:** *The Self-Willed Prince; or, The Hope of the Katzekopfs, a Fairy Tale Retold in Short Words***).** Gr. 5–6. (Orig. British pub. 1844.)
Abracadabra, the uninvited fairy guest at the christening of the Fairy King and Queen's son, gives him the gift of "self-will," causing him to become selfish and mischievous. When the fairy is called back to take charge of him, she draws him out into a long elastic string, turns him into a ball, and bounces him all over the country. This book is considered to be one of the first English children's fantasy novels, and critics have noted its influence on Thackeray's *The Rose and the Ring* (1855; see below) and Kipling's *Rewards and Fairies* (1910; see discussion of *Puck of Pook's Hill* in Chapter 10, Time Travel Fantasy).
Adapt. and retitled: *The Self-Willed Prince; or, The Hope of the Katzekopfs, a Fairy Tale Retold in Short Words*, illus. by J. L. Gilmour, Stokes, 1917, o.p.; Johnson, 1968 (repr. of 1844 ed.), 211 pp., o.p.

1-261 PALMER, Mary. *The Magic Knight.* Gr. 3–5.
Prince Gillian's page, Quist, helps him to slay a dragon and tame a sea serpent.
Illus. by Bill Sokol, Hale, 1964, 93 pp., o.p.
(CCBB 18:91; Kirkus 32:955; LJ 90:382)

1-262 PARKER, (James) Edgar (Jr.). *The Enchantress.* Gr. 3–5.
✭   An enchantress-princess decides to help the young knight she loves to accomplish the three impossible tasks she had set for prospective suitors.
Illus. by the author, Pantheon, 1960, 36 pp., o.p.
(BL 57:249; CCBB 14:99; HB 36:407; Kirkus 28:816; LJ 85:3866)

PARKER, (James) Edgar (Jr.). *The Flower of the Realm.*
See Chapter 2, Animal Fantasy.

1-263 PATERSON, Katherine. *The King's Equal.* Gr. 2–5.
✭   A wolf transforms Rosamund the goatherd into the perfect wife for a king, but she refuses the arrogant king's hand and sends him off to learn humility while she rules the land.
Illus. by Vladimir Vagin, Harper, 1992, 64 pp., o.p.
(BL 88:1944; CCBB 46:154; HB 68:583; HBG 4:60; Kirkus 60:1066; SLJ Sep 1992 p. 255)

PATON WALSH, Jill (Gillian Bliss). *Birdy and the Ghosties.*
See Chapter 4, Ghost Fantasy.

1-264 PATON WALSH, Jill (Gillian Bliss). *Matthew and the Sea Singer.* Gr.
✭   2–5. (Orig. British pub. 1992.)
Orphaned Matthew is stolen by the seal-queen, who carries him to the bottom of the sea to teach her own child how to sing beautifully. This is a companion story to *Birdy and the Ghosties* (1990; see Chapter 4, Ghost Fantasy).

Illus. by Alan Marks, Farrar, 1993, 46 pp. (0-374-34869-3)

(BL 89:1518; CCBB 46:297; HBG 4:292; Kirkus 61:535; SLJ May 1993 p. 90)

1-265   **PEARCE, (Ann) Philippa.** *The Squirrel Wife.* Gr. 2–4. (Orig. British pub.
⋆   1971.)
Jealous of Jack's magic ring and fairy wife, Jack's brother has him imprisoned.
Illus. by Derek Collard, Crowell, 1972, 61 pp., o.p.

(BL 68:822; CCBB 26:14; HB 48:265; Kirkus 40:194, 1412; LJ 97:2479; Suth:307)

1-266   **PELGROM, Els.** *Little Sophie and Lanky Flop.* Gr. 3–6. (Orig. Dutch pub.
1987.)
Gravely ill and confined to her bed, Sophie joins her doll, Lanky Flop, on a
series of dreamlike adventures.
Trans. by Arnold Pomerans, illus. by The Tjong Khing, Farrar, 1988, 88 pp.,
o.p.

(CCBB 42:131; Kirkus 56:1744; SLJ Feb 1989 p. 81)

1-267   **PENDERGRAFT, Patricia.** *The Legend of Daisy Flowerdew.* Gr. 6–9.
Daisy is sold into an unhappy marriage by her selfish mother and cruel stepfather, but she is rescued by the wish-granting traveling salesman who once gave
her some magical paper dolls. This book can be read as a tragic realistic novel
with a fantasy ending or as a contemporary fairy tale.
Putnam, 1990, 192 pp., o.p.

(BL 86:1694, 1709; CCBB 44:42; HBG 1:252; Kirkus 58:801; SLJ Dec 1990 p. 106; VOYA
13:109)

1-268   **PENNAC, Daniel.** *Eye of the Wolf.* Gr. 5–8. (Orig. French pub. 1982.)
An Alaskan wolf caged in a zoo and an orphaned African boy trade life stories
as they stare into each other's eyes in this allegorical tale.
Trans. by Sarah Adams, illus. by Max Grafe, Candlewick, 2003, 112 pp. (0-
7636-1896-9)

(BL 99:1199; CCBB 56:284; HBG 14:373; Kirkus 70:1855; SLJ Feb 2003 p. 146; VOYA
26:152)

1-269   **PHIPSON, Joan (pseud. of Joan Margaret Fitzhardinge).** *The Watcher in
the Garden.* Gr. 6–9. (Orig. Australian pub. 1982.)
Blind Mr. Lovett's beautiful hilltop garden seems to sense the peaceful intentions toward its elderly owner of 15-year-old Kitty—as well as the violent plans
of 17-year-old Terry—in this story told from both of the young people's points
of view.
Macmillan, 1982, 203 pp., o.p.

(BL 79:199, 248; CCBB 36:75; HB 58:522; Kirkus 50:1159; SLJ Nov 1982 p. 89)

PICARD, Barbara Leonie. *The Faun and the Woodcutter's Daughter.*
See Chapter 3, Fantasy Collections.

PICARD, Barbara Leonie. *The Goldfinch Garden: Seven Tales.*
See Chapter 3, Fantasy Collections.

PICARD, Barbara Leonie. *The Lady of the Linden Tree.*
See Chapter 3, Fantasy Collections.

PICARD, Barbara Leonie. *The Mermaid and the Simpleton.*
See Chapter 3, Fantasy Collections.

1-270 PIERCE, Meredith Ann. *Where the Wild Geese Go.* Gr. 1–4.
Truzjka must go on a magical search for the wild geese in order to save her grandmother's life.
Illus. by Jamichael Henterly, Dutton, 1988, 64 pp., o.p.
(HB 64:349; Kirkus 56:205; SLJ June 1988 p. 94)

1-271 PIKE, Christopher. *Sati.* Gr. 10 up.
When truck driver Michael meets Sati, a girl who claims to be God reborn, in the Arizona desert, he struggles to decide whether he believes her story or not.
Tor, 1990, 256 pp., o.p.
(BL 87:601, 610; Kirkus 58:1198; SLJ Apr 1991 p. 154)

POLLAND, Madeleine A(ngela Cahill). *Deirdre.*
See Chapter 6, High Fantasy: Myth or Legend Fantasy.

POPE, Elizabeth Marie. *The Perilous Gard.*
See Chapter 7, High Fantasy: Travel to Other Worlds.

PRICE, Susan. *The Ghost Drum.*
See Chapter 12, Witchcraft and Sorcery Fantasy.

Princesses and Peasant Boys: Tales of Enchantment. **Ed. by Phyllis Reid Fenner.**
See Chapter 3, Fantasy Collections.

The Princesses: Sixteen Stories About Princesses. **Ed. by Sally Patrick Johnson.**
See Chapter 3, Fantasy Collections.

PULLMAN, Philip. *The Golden Compass.*
See Chapter 5, High Fantasy: Alternate Worlds or Histories.

PUSHKIN, Alexander Sergeevich. *The Golden Cockerel and Other Stories.*
See Chapter 3, Fantasy Collections.

1-272 PUSHKIN, Alexander Sergeevich. *The Tale of Czar Saltan, or the Prince and the Swan Princess.* **(British title:** *The Tale of Tsar Saltan***).** Gr. 3–5.
(Orig. pub. in Russia; British title: *The Tale of Tsar Saltan,* 1974.)
Abandoned in a foreign land, czar Saltan's son is reunited with his family by an enchanted swan.
Trans. by Patricia Lowe, illus. by I. Bilbin, Crowell, 1975, 24 pp., o.p.; trans. by Pauline Hehl; illus. by Gennady Spirin, Dial, 1996, 32 pp., o.p.
(BL 72:167, 93:427; CCBB 50:110; HBG 8:104; SLJ Nov 1975 p. 82, Oct 1996 p. 116; TLS 1974 p. 1382)

1-273 PUSHKIN, Alexander Sergeevich. *The Tale of the Golden Cockerel.* Gr.
☆ 3–5. (Orig. pub. in Russia; Orig. U.S. pub. 1938.)

The czar's magic cockerel warns him of enemy invasions, but cannot save him from the wiles of an enchantress.

Trans. and retold by Patricia Tracy Lowe, illus. by I. Bilbin, Crowell, 1975, 24 pp., o.p.

(BL 35:51, 72:167; CCBB 29:18; HB 14:298, 51:455; SLJ Oct 1975 p. 101; Suth 2:372)

1-274 **PYLE, Howard.** *Bearskin.* Gr. 1–4. (Orig. pub. in *The Wonder Clock,* 1987.)
★★ Set adrift in a basket after the king orders the miner's baby's death, Bearskin is raised by a she-bear and grows up to rescue the princess from a dragon, and to marry her, following the prophecy.

Illus. by Trina Schart Hyman, Morrow, 1997, 48 pp. (0-688-09837-1)

(BL 94:468, 734; CCBB 51:98; HB 73:588; HBG 9:79; SLJ Aug 1997 p. 139, Dec 1997 p. 27)

1-275 **PYLE, Howard.** *The Garden Behind the Moon: A Real Story of the Moon Angel.* Gr. 3–6. (Orig. U.S. pub. 1895.)
The mysterious Moon Angel convinces Davy to follow the moonpath all the way up to the moon.

Illus. by the author, Scribner, 1929, o.p.; Parabola, 1988 (repr. of 1895 ed.), 176 pp., o.p.; Starscape, 2002, pap., 132 pp. (0-765-34242-1)

(BL 85:713; Bookshelf 1921–1922 p. 15; Mahony 2:292; SLJ Feb 1989 p. 119)

PYLE, Howard. *King Stork.*
See Chapter 12, Witchcraft and Sorcery Fantasy.

1-276 **PYLE, Howard.** *Twilight Land.* Gr. 4–6. (Orig. U.S. pub. 1894.)
The narrator visits Mother Goose's Inn, where he meets a number of well-known fairy-tale characters, each of whom tells a tale.

Illus. by the author, Harper, 1922, o.p.

(Mahony 2:292; TLS 1968 p. 1120)

PYLE, Howard. *The Wonder Clock; or, Four & Twenty Marvelous Tales.*
See Chapter 3, Fantasy Collections.

1-277 **RAMACHANDER, Akumal.** *Little Pig.* Gr. 4–6. (Orig. British pub. 1992.)
Mary, a pig farmer who tricks Little Pig onto a van bound for the slaughterhouse, finds the tables are turned when she herself is transformed into a pig, in this disturbing story illustrated with eerie photographs of masks held in place by human hands.

Illus. by Stasys Eidrigevicius, Viking, 1992, 32 pp., o.p.

(BL 89:593; CCBB 46:85; SLJ Jan 1993 p. 102)

REEVES, James (pseud. of John Morris Reeves). *The Cold Flame.*
See Chapter 5, High Fantasy: Alternate Worlds or Histories.

REEVES, James (pseud. of John Morris Reeves). *Maildun the Voyager.*
See Chapter 6, High Fantasy: Myth or Legend Fantasy.

REEVES, James (pseud. of John Morris Reeves). *Sailor Rumbelow and Other Stories.*
See Chapter 3, Fantasy Collections.

1-278 **REID, Alastair.** *Fairwater.* Gr. 3–5.

A stone-cutter named Garth is barred from the Kingdom of Fairwater when he tries to rescue an enchanted princess. In the sequel, *Allth* (1958), a young minstrel named Prin attempts to rescue Princess Ailin and recover the stolen Song of Allth.

Illus. by Walter Lorraine, Houghton, 1957, 47 pp., o.p.

(CCBB 11:85; Eakin:269; HB 33:222; Kirkus 25:330; LJ 82:2192)

ROBINSON, Joan (Mary) G(ale Thomas). *When Marnie Was There.*
See Chapter 4, Ghost Fantasy.

ROCCA, Guido. *Gaetano the Pheasant: A Hunting Fable.*
See Chapter 2, Animal Fantasy.

Rocking Horse Land and Other Classic Tales of Dolls and Toys. **Comp. by Naomi Lewis.**
See Chapter 11, Toy Fantasy.

RODDA, Emily. *The Best-Kept Secret.*
See Chapter 10, Time Travel Fantasy.

ROSS, Ramon Royal. *Prune.*
See Chapter 2, Animal Fantasy.

ROSS, Tony. *A Fairy Tale.*
See Chapter 9, Magic Adventure Fantasy.

RUSHDIE, Salman. *Haroun and the Sea of Stories.*
See Chapter 5, High Fantasy: Alternate Worlds or Histories.

1-279 RUSKIN, John. *The King of the Golden River, or the Black Brothers: A*
☆ *Legend of Stiria.* Gr. 2–5. (Written 1841, orig. British pub. 1851, U.S. 1900.)
Little Gluck's cruel older brothers torment him until the King of the Golden River and the South-West Wind come to his aid.
Illus. by Fritz Kredel, World, 1946, 111 pp., o.p.; Watts, 1958, 60 pp., o.p.;
illus. by Krystyna Turska, Greenwillow, 1978, 40 pp., o.p.; Putnam, 1988, o.p.;
illus. by Juan Wijngaard, Candlewick, 2000, 96 pp. (0-7636-0845-9)
(BL 42:304; Bookshelf 1921–1922 p. 9; CCBB 13:120; HB 22:213, 28:422, 55:520; HBG 12:78; Kirkus 46:1017; Mahony 2:296; SLJ Oct 1978 p. 138)

1-280 SAINT-EXUPÉRY, Antoine (Jean-Baptiste-Marie-Roger) de. *The Little*
☆ *Prince.* Gr. 5 up. (Orig. pub. in France; orig. U.S. pub. 1943.)
A pilot stranded in the Sahara meets a strange boy who tells him about his travels through the universe.
Trans. by Katherine Woods, illus. by the author, Harcourt, 1943, 91 pp., o.p.;
trans. by Richard Howard, illus. by the author, Harcourt, 2003, 96 pp. (0-15-202398-4)
(BL 39:354; HB 70:95; HBG 5:74, 14:365; LJ 68:248; SLJ Sep 2000 p. 258)

1-281 SANCHEZ-SILVA, José. *The Boy and the Whale.* Gr. 3–5. (Orig. Spanish pub. 1962.)
An imaginary whale helps a young boy deal with his grandmother's approaching death.

Trans. by Michael Heron, illus. by Margery Gill, McGraw-Hill, 1964, 80 pp., o.p.
(HB 40:376; Kirkus 32:453; LJ 89:2662)

1-282 SAND, George (pseud. of Amandine Lucile Aurore Dupin). *The Castle of Pictures and Other Stories: A Grandmother's Tales, vol. 1.* Gr. 4–7. (Orig. French pub. 1873, entitled *Tales of a Grandmother.*)
Three fairy tales and a novella written for her grandchildren by this well-known 19th-century French author.
Trans. by Holly Eskine Hirko, illus. by Mary Warshaw, Feminist Press, 1995, pap., 176 pp. (1-55861-092-8)
(BL 91:1648; HBG 6:303; SJL May 1995 p. 108)

1-283 SAND, George (pseud. of Amandine Lucile Aurore Dupin). *The Mysterious Tale of Gentle Jack and Lord Bumblebee.* Gr. 2–4. (Orig. French pub. 1873, in *Tales of a Grandmother*; orig. U.S. pub 1930; orig. Austrian pub. in this ed., 1986.)
Unloved by his parents and tempted by the evil Lord Bumblebee, Jack escapes to the fairy kingdom, where he learns how to redeem the people of his world, in this story originally published in France in 1873 in the author's *Tales of a Grandmother.*
Trans. by Gela Jacobson, illus. by Gennady Spirin, Dial, 1988, 75 pp., o.p.
(BL 85:655; Kirkus 56:1247; SLJ Feb 1989 p. 75; TLS Aug 19, 1988 p. 917)

1-284 SANDERSON, Ruth. *The Enchanted Wood: An Original Fairy Tale.* Gr. K–5.
Galen, the youngest of the king's three sons, succeeds in finding the Heart of the World, needed to end the drought holding their kingdom in its grip.
Illus. by the author, Little, Brown, 1991, 32 pp., o.p.
(HBG 3:47; Kirkus 59:1232; SLJ Oct 1991 p. 103)

SAN SOUCI, Robert D. *Feathertop: Based on the Tale by Nathaniel Hawthorne.*
See Chapter 12, Witchcraft and Sorcery Fantasy.

SARGENT, Sarah. *Watermusic.*
See Chapter 6, High Fantasy: Myth or Legend Fantasy.

1-285 SAWYER, Ruth. *This Way to Christmas.* Gr. 3–5. (Orig. pub. 1916.)
A lonely boy and a fairy spend Christmas together listening to Christmas tales from around the world.
Illus. by Maginel Barney, Harper, 1944, 1952, 175 pp., o.p.; HarperCollins, rev. ed., 2000, 175 pp. (0-06-025212-X)
(BL 13:185)

SCARBOROUGH, Elizabeth Ann. *The Harem of Aman Akbar; or The Djinn Decanted.*
See Chapter 8, Humorous Fantasy.

1-286 SCHLEIN, Miriam. *The Raggle Taggle Fellow.* Gr. 2–4.
✯ Dick's father disapproves of his third and youngest son's ambition to become a minstrel,

Illus. by Harvey Weiss, Abelard-Schuman, 1959, 62 pp., o.p.
(BL 55:544; Eakin:286; HB 35:286; Kirkus 27:134; LJ 84:1690)

1-287 SCHMIDT, Werner (Felix). *The Forests of Adventure.* Gr. 3–6.
Eric's adventure-filled search for his missing guardian, Black Otto, includes
archery battles with outlaws, escape from imprisonment, the rescue of a fair
lady, and a king's coronation.
Illus. by Artur Marokvia, Little, Brown, 1963, 161 pp., o.p.
(HB 39:174; LJ 88:2554)

1-288 SCHRANK, Joseph. *The Plain Princess and the Lazy Prince.* Gr. 2–4.
In an attempt to marry off their unattractive daughter, the king and queen
advertise for a dragon, but it is the princess who ends up rescuing a prince.
Illus. by Mircea Vasiliu, Day, 1958, 57 pp., o.p.
(CCBB 12:74; Kirkus 26:498; LJ 83:3012)

1-289 SCHWARZ, Eugene M. *Two Brothers.* Gr. 1–4. (Orig. pub. in the Soviet
Union.)
After he locks Little Brother out in the cold, Big Brother must save him from
Great-grandfather Frost.
Trans. by Elizabeth Hapgood, illus. by Gabriel Lisowski, Harper, 1973, 44 pp.,
o.p.
(Kirkus 41:559; LJ 98:2644)

SCIESZKA, Jon. *The Stinky Cheese Man and Other Fairly Stupid Tales.*
See Chapter 8, Humorous Fantasy.

SCIESZKA, Jon. *The True Story of the 3 Little Pigs: By A. Wolf.*
See Chapter 8, Humorous Fantasy.

1-290 SÉGUR, Comtesse Sophie (Rostopchine) de. *The Enchanted Forest.*
✳ **(Alternate titles:** *Blondine and Bear-Cub*; *Forest of Lilacs*). Gr. 2–4. (Orig.
French pub. 1856, U.S. 1869 in *Fairy Tales for Little Folks*.)
A wicked queen banishes little Princess Blondine to the enchanted Forest of
Lilacs, where she is imprisoned by wicked fairies and rescued by good fairies
and a young prince.
British Book Service, 1957, entitled *Blondine and Bear-Cub*, o.p.; illus. by
Nicole Claveloux, Harlin Quist, 1969, entitled *Forest of Lilacs*, 40 pp., o.p.;
adapt. by Beatrice Schenk de Regniers, illus. by Gustave Doré, Atheneum,
1974, 87 pp., o.p.
(BL 17:127; Bookshelf 1932 p. 23; HB 51:54; Kirkus 42:1251; LJ 83:649; SLJ Mar 1975 p.
86; TLS 1970 p. 419)

1-291 SEIDLER, Tor, and SELZNICK, Brian. *The Dulcimer Boy.* Gr. 3–5.
Mr. and Mrs. Carbuncle unwillingly take in their infant nephews, William and
Jules, who arrive on the doorstep inside a wicker chest, along with a silver-
stringed dulcimer.
Illus. by David Hockney, Viking, 1979, 83 pp., o.p.; HarperCollins, 2003, 153
pp. (0-06-623610-X), pap. (0-06-623609-6)
(CCBB 33:118; HBG 16:375; Kirkus 47:819; SLJ Nov 1979 p. 81, June 2003 p. 152)

1-292 SELFRIDGE, Oliver. *The Trouble with Dragons.* Gr. 4–6.
Although her older sisters' attempts at dragon slaying failed, Princess Celia succeeds and wins a prince's love in the bargain.
Illus. by Shirley Hughes, Addison-Wesley, 1978, 86 pp., o.p.
(BL 74:1556; CCBB 31:184; SLJ Sep 1978 p. 148; Suth 2:402)

1-293 SENDAK, Jack. *Circus Girl.* Gr. 2–3. (Orig. pub. Harper, 1957.)
Born and raised in a circus, young Flora slips out of the tent one night to find out what the people outside the circus are really like.
Illus. by Maurice (Bernard) Sendak, HarperCollins, 2002, 32 pp. (0-06-028784-5)
(HB 33:483; Kirkus 25:739; LJ 83:233)

1-294 SENDAK, Philip. *In Grandpa's House.* Gr. 4 up. (Orig. written in Yiddish.)
A young boy flying on the back of a large bird encounters giants, monsters, and wild beasts while searching for his parents.
Trans. and adapt. by Seymour Barofsky, illus. by Maurice (Bernard) Sendak, Harper, 1985, 42 pp., o.p.; Di Capua, 2003, 48 pp. (0-06-028787-X)
(HB 62:60; SLJ Oct 1985 p. 177; TLS 1986 p. 389)

1-295 SEREDY, Kate. *Lazy Tinka.* Gr. 3–4.
After Tinka is befriended by the forest animals, she learns to be more helpful at home.
Illus. by the author, Viking, 1962, 56 pp., o.p.
(BL 59:450; Kirkus 62:683; LJ 88:98; TLS 1964 p. 605)

SEREDY, Kate. *The White Stag.*
See Chapter 6, High Fantasy: Myth or Legend Fantasy.

1-296 SEUSS (Geisel), Dr. (Theodore). *The 500 Hats of Bartholomew Cubbins.*
✮   Gr. 1–4.
Even the King of Didd's most able wise men and sorcerers cannot take off all 500 of Bartholomew's hats. In the sequel, *Bartholomew and the Oobleck* (Random, 1949), Bartholomew saves the kingdom from sticky green oobleck that falls from the sky. *Bartholomew and the Oobleck* was a Randolph Caldecott Medal Honor Book, 1950.
Illus. by the author, Random, 1938, 45 pp., LB (0-394-84484-X)
(BL 35:102; HB 14:365, 377; LJ 63:818, 890)

1-297 SHAPIRO, Irwin. *Twice upon a Time.* Gr. 2–4.
Since the King of Gib-Gib has decreed that everything must be twice as much or twice as many, ought there to be two kings?
Illus. by Adrienne Adams, Scribner, 1973, 35 pp., o.p.
(CCBB 27:86; HB 50:40; Kirkus 41:1032; LJ 98:3703)

1-298 SHARMA, Partap. *The Surangini Tales.* Gr. 4–6.
✮   Beautiful Surangini refuses to reappear from within the carpet woven by her suitor, Kalu, until 17 tales have been told.
Illus. by Demi Hitz, Harcourt, 1973, 125 pp., o.p.
(BL 70:125; CCBB 26:176; HB 49:463; Kirkus 41:386, 1351; LJ 98:2657; TLS 1974 p. 716)

1-299 **SHURA, Mary Francis (pseud. of Mary Francis Craig).** *The Nearsighted Knight.* Gr. 4–6.
After learning that his sister must marry before he can leave home, Prince Todd decides to help the Knight Before Glasses kill a dragon and win his sister's hand.
Illus. by Adrienne Adams, Knopf, 1964, 111 pp., o.p.
(CCBB 17:130; HB 40:284; Kirkus 32:61; LJ 89:1454)

1-300 **SILVERMAN, Maida.** *The Magic Well.* Gr. K–4.
The Fairy Queen lures young Janet down into the fairy realm, but her mother saves her on the night of the Fairy Ride, in this story reminiscent of the ballad "Tam Lin."
Illus. by Manuel Boix, Simon & Schuster, 1989, 40 pp., o.p.
(HBG 1:100; Kirkus 57:1537; SLJ Feb 1990 p. 79)

SIMAK, Clifford D(onald). *Enchanted Pilgrimage.*
See Chapter 5, High Fantasy: Alternate Worlds or Histories.

1-301 **SINGER, Isaac Bashevis.** *Alone in the Wild Forest.* Gr. 4–6.
Orphaned Joseph dreams of meeting and winning Princess Chassidah, but wicked Bal Makane plots against him.
Trans. by the author and Elizabeth Shub, illus. by Margot Zemach, Farrar, 1971, 79 pp., o.p.
(CCBB 25:97; Kirkus 39:1015; LJ 97:285)

1-302 **SINGER, Isaac Bashevis.** *The Fearsome Inn.* Gr. 4–6.
☆ With his piece of magic chalk, Liebel, a young Cabala student, rescues three young girls held captive by a witch and a devil. John Newbery Medal Honor Book, 1968.
Trans. by the author and Elizabeth Shub, illus. by Nonny Hogrogian, Scribner, 1967, 45 pp., o.p.
(BL 64:338; CCBB 21:67; HB 43:751, 61:595; Kirkus 35:880; LJ 92:3190; Suth:367)

1-303 **SINGER, Isaac Bashevis.** *A Tale of Three Wishes.* Gr. 2–4.
Three children make wishes that cause unexpected problems on the night of Hoshanah Rabbah.
Illus. by Irene Lieblich, Farrar, 1976, 30 pp., o.p.
(BL 72:1118; CCBB 30:18; Kirkus 44:201; SLJ Apr 1976 p. 65)

1-304 **SINGER, Isaac Bashevis.** *The Topsy-Turvy Emperor of China.* Gr. 2–4.
The crown prince of ancient China joins the revolutionaries attempting to overthrow the rule of his cruel father, the emperor.
Trans. by the author and Elizabeth Shub, illus. by William Pène du Bois, Harper, 1971, 32 pp., o.p.; illus. by Julian Jussim, Farrar, 1996, 32 pp. (0-374-37681-6)
(CCBB 25:51; HBG 7:288; Kirkus 39:1015, 64:607; LJ Feb 15, 1972 p. 779; SLJ June 1996 p. 124)

SINGER, Isaac Bashevis. *Zlateh the Goat and Other Stories.*
See Chapter 3, Fantasy Collections.

1-305 SINGER, Marilyn. *The Golden Heart of Winter.* Gr. 1–4.
A raven gives young Half a riddle to help him find the Golden Heart of Winter, which ensures that life will return to the earth each spring, but Half's older brothers try to steal the treasure.
Illus. by Robert Rayevsky, Morrow, 1991, 40 pp., o.p.
(BL 88:166; HBG 3:61; Kirkus 59:861; SLJ Dec 1991 p. 102)

1-306 SLOBODKIN, Louis. *The Amiable Giant.* Gr. 1–3.
A wizard tries to frighten the villagers with terrifying tales about the friendly local giant, but Gwendolyn discovers the truth.
Illus. by the author, Macmillan, 1955, 36 pp., o.p.; Vanguard, 1966 (c. 1955), 36 pp., o.p.
(BL 52:173; HB 32:27; Kirkus 23:784)

1-307 SLOBODKIN, Louis. *The Little Mermaid Who Could Not Sing.* Gr. 1–3.
A young mermaid named Cynthia discovers that her gigantic voice becomes vitally important whenever fog covers the Blue Rocks in the great Southern Sea.
Macmillan, 1956, 38 pp., o.p.
(BL 53:253; HB 32:330; Kirkus 24:783)

1-308 SMITH, Agnes. *An Edge of the Forest.* Gr. 5–9. (Orig. pub. Viking, 1959.)
☆ An orphaned lamb who accidentally wanders into the forest is saved from death and adopted by a black leopardess.
Illus. by Roberta Moynihan, Viking, 1959, 192 pp., o.p.
(BL 55:578; CCBB 13:21; Eakin:301; HB 35:10; Kirkus 27:91; LJ 84:1700)

SNYDER, Zilpha Keatley. *Below the Root.*
See Chapter 5, High Fantasy: Alternate Worlds or Histories.

1-309 SNYDER, Zilpha Keatley. *The Changing Maze.* Gr. 2–4.
☆ A shepherd boy lost in a maze created by an evil wizard searches for his stray pet lamb, ignoring the gold at the heart of the maze.
Illus. by Charles Mikolaycak, Macmillan, 1985, o.p.
(BL 82:269; CCBB 39:57; HB 62:52; SLJ Dec 1985 p. 83)

SOYER, Abraham. *The Adventures of Yemina.*
See Chapter 3, Fantasy Collections.

STANTON, Mary. *The Heavenly Horse from the Outermost West.*
See Chapter 2, Animal Fantasy.

STEARNS, Pamela (Fujimoto). *The Fool and the Dancing Bear.*
See Chapter 5, High Fantasy: Alternate Worlds or Histories.

1-310 STEARNS, Pamela (Fujimoto). *The Mechanical Doll.* Gr. 4–6.
Jealous of the life-sized mechanical doll that has captured the king's fancy, Hulon, the court musician, breaks it and is banished from the court.
Illus. by Trina Schart Hyman, Houghton, 1979, 45 pp., o.p.
(BL 75:1160; CCBB 32:184; Kirkus 47:519; SLJ Nov 1979 p. 82)

STEELE, Mary Q(uintard Govan). *Journey Outside.*
See Chapter 5, High Fantasy: Alternate Worlds or Histories.

STEELE, Mary Q(uintard Govan). *The Owl's Kiss: Three Stories.*
See Chapter 3, Fantasy Collections.

STEELE, Mary Q(uintard Govan). *The True Men.*
See Chapter 5, High Fantasy: Alternate Worlds or Histories.

1-311 STEIN, Gertrude. *The World Is Round.* Gr. 1–4. (Orig. pub. 1939.)
A reissue of famed writer/philosopher Gertrude Stein's children's story about Rose, Willie, and Willie's pet lion. In this story, the author experimented with rhythm and word patterns.
Illus. by Clement Hurd, Young Scott, 1966, o.p.; Farrar, 1988 (0-865-47326-9)
(BL 36:180; HB 15:294; LJ 92:330; TLS 1939 p. 758)

STEINER, Jörg. *Rabbit Island.*
See Chapter 2, Animal Fantasy.

1-312 STEINER, Jörg. *The Sea People.* Gr. 3–6. (Orig. German pub. 1981.)
Two neighboring island communities with vastly different customs must learn to cooperate after one island is virtually destroyed by its people's greed for gold.
Trans. by Victor Gollancz, illus. by Jörg Müller, Schocken, 1982, 35 pp., o.p.
(CCBB 36:135; SLJ Apr 1983 p. 119; TLS 1982 p. 1305)

1-313 STEPHENS, James. *The Crock of Gold.* Gr. 6–9. (Orig. U.S. pub. Macmillan, 1912.)
Seumas and Brigid, children of two philosophers, meet extraordinary creatures in the woods, including leprechauns and the god Pan.
Illus. by Thomas MacKenzie, Telegraph Books, 1980 (repr. of 1912 ed.), 312 pp., o.p.; North Books, 1992, 273 pp. (0-93949-534-1); Dover, 1998, pap., 227 pp. (0-486-29931-7)
(BL 10:245; TLS 1981 p. 348)

STEVENS, Eden Vale. *Abba.*
See Chapter 2, Animal Fantasy.

1-314 STEVENSON, Robert Louis. *The Bottle Imp.* Gr. 5–8. (Orig. pub. in Samoa, 1891.)
The magic bottle Keawe buys brings him his heart's desires, as well as disaster, each time he makes a wish.
Illus. by Jacqueline Mair, Clarion, 1996, 60 pp., o.p.
(BL 92:1023; CCBB 49:206; HBG 7:298; SLJ May 1996 p. 135)

1-315 STEVENSON, Robert Louis. *The Touchstone: A Fable.* Gr. 5–7.
Two rival princes searching for the "touchstone of truth," in order to win the hand of a princess, complete their quests in very different fashions.
Illus. by Uri Shulevitz, Greenwillow, 1976, 47 pp., o.p.
(Kirkus 44:844; SLJ Nov 1976 p. 63)

1-316 STEWART, Mary (Florence Elinor). *Ludo and the Star Horse.* Gr. 5–8.
(Orig. British pub. 1974.)
Ludo and his old horse fall into a hidden pit and journey through the 12 houses
of the zodiac.
Illus. by Gino D'Achille, Morrow, 1975, 191 pp., o.p.
(BL 71:967; Kirkus 43:376; SLJ Sep 1975 p. 112; TLS 1974 p. 1380)

1-317 STOCKTON, Frank (Francis) R(ichard). *The Bee-Man of Orn.* Gr. 4–6.
✫ (Orig. pub. in *Fanciful Tales* 1884; as a separate tale, Holt, 1964.)
An old beekeeper, told by a sorcerer that he was transformed from another sort
of being, decides to uncover his origins.
Illus. by Maurice (Bernard) Sendak, Harper, 1987, 48 pp., o.p.; illus. by P. J.
Lynch, Candlewick, 2004, 48 pp. (0-7636-2239-7); Di Capua, 2004, 56 pp. (0-
06-029729-8)
(BL 61:528, 100:1056; Eakin:312; HB 40:611, 63:491; 80:483, 490; LJ 89:4643; Mahony
1:27; SLJ Mar 2004 p. 182; TLS 1976 p. 376)

1-318 STOCKTON, Frank (Francis) R(ichard). *The Griffin and the Minor Canon.*
✫ Gr. 3–5. (Orig. pub. in *Fanciful Tales,* 1884; as a separate tale, Holt, 1963.)
The last of the griffins threatens to remain in a terrified village because it so
admires its likeness carved above the church door.
Illus. by Maurice (Bernard) Sendak, Harper, 1986, 56 pp., o.p., 1987, pap. (0-
06-443126-6); Di Capua, 2003, 56 pp. (0-06-029731-X)
(BL 59:900, 83:357; Eakin:313; HB 39:384, 63:84; LJ 88:2555)

STOCKTON, Frank (Francis) R(ichard). *The Queen's Museum and
Other Fanciful Tales.*
See Chapter 3, Fantasy Collections.

1-319 STOLP, Hans. *The Golden Bird.* Gr. 3 up. (Orig. Dutch pub. 1987.)
✫ Three birds teach Daniel, dying of cancer, that he will blossom like a cherry
tree blooms after the deathlike winter season when he is reunited with his father
in heaven.
Illus. by Lidia Postma, Dial, 1990, 56 pp., o.p.
(BL 56:1639; HBG 1:246; Kirkus 58:432; SLJ Apr 1990 p. 124; VOYA 13:35)

1-320 STOLZ, Mary (Slattery). *The Cuckoo Clock.* Gr. 4–6.
✫ Ula, the old clockmaker, makes one final marvelous cuckoo clock before he
dies, as part of a magical legacy for his assistant, a young foundling named
Erich.
Illus. by Pamela Johnson, Godine, 1986, 84 pp., o.p., 1993, 84 pp. (0-8792-
3819-4)
(BL 83:652; CCBB 40:179; Kirkus 55:376; SLJ Apr 1987 p. 105; Suth 4:399)

1-321 STOLZ, Mary (Slattery). *The Leftover Elf.* Gr. 3–5.
✫ The survival of the last elf in the world depends on his finding someone who
believes in him.
Illus. by Peggy Bacon, Harper, 1952, 57 pp., o.p.
(CCBB 5:69; HB 28:172; Kirkus 20:188; LJ 77:653)

1-322 STOLZ, Mary (Slattery). *The Scarecrows and Their Child.* Gr. 3–5.
Two unemployed scarecrows, Handy and Blossom, marry and live peacefully
with their cat child, Bohel, until they are kidnapped, whereupon Bohel sets out
to find them.
Illus. by Amy Schwartz, Harper, 1987, 67 pp., o.p.
(BL 54:572; CCBB 41:77; Kirkus 53:1467; SLJ Jan 1988 p. 76)

1-323 STRANGER, Joyce (pseud. of Joyce Muriel Judson Wilson). *The Fox at
Drummer's Darkness.* Gr. 6–9. (Orig. British pub. 1976.)
Poisoned by toxic chemicals in the water, a night watchman's ghost rises from
his grave to warn the townspeople.
Illus. by William Geldart, Farrar, 1977, 108 pp., o.p.
(BL 73:1731; HB 53:534; Kirkus 45:540; SLJ May 1977 p. 72)

1-324 SUTCLIFF, Rosemary. *Chess-Dream in a Garden.* Gr. 3 up. (Orig. British
pub. 1993.)
A sophisticated illustrated tale combining chess and fable, about a queen who
goes into battle to save her kingdom from the enemy Red Horde.
Illus. by Ralph Thompson, Candlewick, 1993, 48 pp. (1-56402-192-0)
(BL 90:52; CCBB 47:102; HBG 5:70; Kirkus 61:943; SLJ Nov 1993 p. 110)

1-325 SUTCLIFF, Rosemary. *The Minstrel and the Dragon Pup.* Gr. K–4. (Orig.
☆ British pub. 1993.)
A wandering minstrel must cure a young prince's illness to win back the baby
dragon stolen from him.
Illus. by Emma Chichester Clark, Candlewick, 1993, 45 pp., o.p.; Candlewick,
1996, pap., 46 pp. (1-56402-603-5)
(BL 89:1238; CCBB 46:226; HB 69:455; HBG 4:292; Kirkus 61:380; SLJ Apr 1993 p. 103)

SUTCLIFF, Rosemary. *The Sword and the Circle: King Arthur and the
Knights of the Round Table.*
See Chapter 6, High Fantasy: Myth or Legend Fantasy.

SWIFT, Jonathan. *Gulliver's Travels.*
See Chapter 7, High Fantasy: Travel to Other Worlds.

SYNGE, (Phyllis) Ursula. *Swan's Wing.*
See Chapter 6, High Fantasy: Myth or Legend Fantasy.

Tales Before Tolkien: The Roots of Modern Fantasy. **Ed. by Douglas A.
Anderson.**
See Chapter 3, Fantasy Collections.

TASSIN, Algernon de Vivier. *The Rainbow String.*
See Chapter 3, Fantasy Collections.

TAYLOR, G. P. *Shadowmancer.*
See Chapter 9, Magic Adventure Fantasy.

1-326 TENNYSON, Noel. *The Lady's Chair and the Ottoman.* Gr. 1–4.
☆ True love and loyalty win out in the end when an ottoman becomes separated
from the lady's chair he loves when their owner's home is sold.

Illus. by the author, Lothrop, 1987, 32 pp., o.p.

(BL 84:324; CCBB 41:79; Kirkus 56:1326; SLJ Sep 1987 p. 183)

TEPPER, Sheri S. *Beauty: A Novel.*
See Chapter 6, High Fantasy: Myth or Legend Fantasy.

1-327 **TERLOUW, Jan (Cornelis).** *How to Become King.* Gr. 6–8. (Orig. British pub. 1976.)
Seventeen-year-old Stark demands to know how he can become king, so the Ministers of Katoren devise seven impossible tasks for him, including silencing the Birds of Decibel, destroying the Dragon of Smog, and outwitting the Wizard of Equilibrium.
Hastings, 1977, 128 pp., o.p.

(BL 74:1111; CCBB 31:135; SLJ Mar 1978 p. 134; Suth 2:445; VOYA 1[Apr 1978]:65)

1-328 **THACKERAY, William Makepeace.** *The Rose and the Ring; or the History of Prince Giglio and Prince Bulbo: A Fireside Pantomime for Great and Small Children.* Gr. 5–8. (Orig. British pub. 1855.)
✫ Princess Rosealba and Prince Giglio are restored to their rightful thrones through the good offices of Fairy Blackstick.
Illus. by the author, John Gilbert, and Paul Hogarth, Pierpont Morgan, 1947, 212 pp., o.p.; Viking, 1989, pap., 144 pp., o.p.; Yestermorrow, 1999 (1-567-23171-3)

(BL 5:124, 6:230, 20:65; Bookshelf 1932 p. 23; HB 23:14, 35:480; Mahony 1:38)

1-329 **THEROUX, Paul.** *A Christmas Card.* Gr. 5 up.
Lost in a blizzard on Christmas Eve, Marcel and his family are welcomed into the house of a man called Pappy, whose magic helps them find their way home.
Illus. by John Lawrence, Houghton, 1978, 96 pp., o.p.

(BL 75:227; Kirkus 46:1358; SLJ Oct 1978 p. 113)

1-330 **THURBER, James (Grover).** *The Great Quillow.* Gr. 3–4.
✫ Quillow the toymaker saves the town by outwitting an unruly giant named Hunder.
Illus. by Doris Lee, Harcourt, 1944, 1975, o.p.; illus. by Steven Kellogg, Harcourt, 1994, 56 pp., o.p.

(BL 41:95, 91:667; HB 20:469, 482, 70:727; HBG 6:71; Kirkus 12:449; LJ 69:866, 1004, SLJ Nov 1994 p. 91)

1-331 **THURBER, James (Grover).** *Many Moons.* Gr. K–4.
✫ Only the court jester is wise enough to cure Princess Lenore's illness by "giving" her the moon. Randolph Caldecott Medal for Illustration, 1944.
Illus. by Louis Slobodkin, Harcourt, 1943, 1981, 46 pp. (0-15-251873-8); illus. by Marc Simont, Harcourt, 1990, 48 pp. (0-15-251872-X); Voyager, 1998, pap., 48 pp. (0-15-201895-6)

(BL 40:20, 87:174; HB 19:318, 422, 20:21, 67:60; HBG 2:29; Kirkus 58:1096; LJ 68:672, 818; SLJ Jan 1991 p. 82)

1-332 **THURBER, James (Grover).** *The 13 Clocks.* Gr. 5 up.
To marry the princess, Prince Zorn must find a thousand jewels to start all of the stilled clocks in the land.

Illus. by Marc Simont, Simon, 1950, 124 pp., o.p.; Dutton, 1990, o.p.; Dell, 1992, pap. (0-440-40582-3)
(BL 47:174)

1-333 THURBER, James (Grover). *The White Deer.* Gr. 5 up.
✫ Since he once married a princess who appeared from the enchanted forest in the guise of a white deer, King Clode and his three sons are tempted to hunt in the forest when another white deer is sighted.
Illus. by the author and Don Freeman, Harcourt, 1945, o.p.; Harcourt, 1984, 116 pp. (0-15-69264-5), pap. (0-15-96119-0)
(BL 42:57; HB 21:447; Kirkus 13:43)

1-334 THURBER, James (Grover). *The Wonderful O.* Gr. 5 up.
✫ Wicked Black and his pirate crew decide to destroy everything spelled with the letter "O."
Illus. by Marc Simont, Simon, 1957, 72 pp., o.p.; Dutton, 1990 (1-55611-189-4)
(BL 53:559; Kirkus 25:308; LJ 82:1780)

1-335 TILLSTROM, Burr. *The Dragon Who Lived Downstairs.* Gr. 2–4.
A friendly dragon releases the princess and her parents from an enchantment, and helps a non-royal knight win the princess's hand.
Illus. by David Small, Morrow, 1984, 44 pp., o.p.
(CCBB 37:157; SLJ Aug 1984 p. 66)

1-336 TOLKIEN, J(ohn) R(onald) R(euel). *Farmer Giles of Ham: The Rise and*
✫ *Wonderful Adventures of Farmer Giles, Lord of Tame, Count of Worming-hall, and King of the Little Kingdom.* Gr. 5–8. (Orig. pub. 1949.)
Farmer Giles leads a simple life until the day he finds himself protecting his village from dragons.
Illus. by Pauline Baynes, Houghton, 1978, 78 pp., o.p.; illus. by Roger Garland, Houghton, 1991, 82 pp., o.p.; Houghton, 1999, 128 pp. (0-618-00936-1); HarperCollins, 1990 (0-04-440723-8)
(CCBB 4:23; HB 26:287; HBG 2:267; LJ 75:2084)

TOLKIEN, J(ohn) R(onald) R(euel). *Fellowship of the Ring.*
See Chapter 5, High Fantasy: Alternate Worlds or Histories.

TOLKIEN, J(ohn) R(onald) R(euel). *The Hobbit; Or, There and Back Again.*
See Chapter 5, High Fantasy: Alternate Worlds or Histories.

1-337 TOLKIEN, J(ohn) R(onald) R(euel). *Smith of Wootton Major.* Gr. 5–8. (Orig. pub. Houghton, 1967.)
When the blacksmith's son finds a magical star buried in a piece of cake, his life is completely changed.
Illus. by Pauline Baynes, Houghton, 1978, o.p.; illus. by Roger Garland, Houghton, 1991, 96 pp. (0-395-57646-6)
(HB 44:63; HBG 2:267; Kirkus 35:1164; LJ 92:4175; TLS 1967 p. 1153)

1-338 TORREY, Marjorie (Chanslor Hood). *Artie and the Princess.* Gr. 2–4.
Artie the lonely dragon child searches for a playmate and finds a princess.

Illus. by the author, Howell, 1945, 107 pp., o.p.
(BL 41:344; Kirkus 13:181; LJ 70:343, 492)

1-339 TURKLE, Brinton (Cassaday). *The Fiddler of High Lonesome.* Gr. 3–6.
When the magic of Lysander's fiddle-playing draws wild animals into a moon-light dance, his cruel cousins attempt to hunt the helpless creatures down.
Illus. by the author, Viking, 1968, 47 pp., o.p.
(BL 64:1189; CCBB:21:166; HB 44:424; Kirkus 36:338; LJ 93:2117)

1-340 TWAIN, Mark (pseud. of Samuel Clemens). *Legend of Sagenfeld.* Gr. 2–8.
(Orig. Australian pub. in this edition, 1987.)
In an attempt to avoid the disaster prophesied for his kingdom, King Hubert chooses a donkey as the animal whose music sounds the sweetest.
Illus. by George Molnar, Publishers Group, 1988, 26 pp., o.p.
(BL 84:1531; Kirkus 55:1739; SLJ Mar 1988 p. 177)

1-341 URQUHART, Elizabeth. *Horace.* Gr. 3–5.
A little girl named Miriam and a young dragon named Horace save the drag-on's father from St. George.
Illus. by Rosita Pastor, Dutton, 1951, 116 pp., o.p.
(BL 48:38; CCBB 5:25; HB 27:325; Kirkus 19:387; LJ 76:1433)

1-342 VAN ALLSBURG, Chris. *The Sweetest Fig.* Gr. 3 up.
✶ Despite self-centered Monsieur Bibot's mistreatment of his dog, the Parisian dentist's dreams literally come true when he eats a magic fig given to him by a poor old woman.
Illus. by the author, Houghton, 1993, 32 pp. (0-395-67346-1)
(BL 90:343; CCBB 47:104; HBG 5:58; Kirkus 61:1339; SLJ Nov 1993 p. 110)

VAN ALLSBURG, Chris. *The Widow's Broom.*
See Chapter 12, Witchcraft and Sorcery Fantasy.

Visions of Wonder: An Anthology of Christian Fantasy. **Ed. by Robert H. Boyer and Kenneth J. Zahorski.**
See Chapter 3, Fantasy Collections.

VOEGELI, Max. *The Wonderful Lamp.*
See Chapter 6, High Fantasy: Myth or Legend Fantasy.

1-343 WAECHTER, Friedrich, and EILERT, Bernd. *The Crown Snatchers.* Gr. 4–6. (Orig. German pub. 1972.)
Three children who help bring about the downfall of the Pig King are disap-pointed to find that the new king is also a tyrant.
Trans. by Edite Kroll, illus. by the authors, Pantheon, 1975, 160 pp., o.p.
(BL 71:697; Kirkus 43:377; SLJ Apr 1975 p. 60)

1-344 WAHL, Jan (Boyer). *How the Children Stopped the Wars.* Gr. 4–6.
A shepherd boy envisions terrible wars, gathers children from all the surround-ing villages, and marches them to the battlefield to stop the fighting.
Illus. by Mitchell Miller, Farrar, 1969, o.p.
(CCBB 23:136; HB 46:164; Kirkus 37:1260; LJ 95:782, 3610)

1-345 WANGERIN, Walter, Jr. *The Book of the Dun Cow.* Gr. 8 up.

✭ In this complex Christian allegory, Chaunticleer the rooster and Mundo Cani Dog save the world from the evils of the giant Wyrm and his "minion" Cockatrice. The American Book Award, Science Fiction Category, 1980. The sequel is *The Book of Sorrows* (1985).
Harper, 1978, 241 pp., o.p.
(BL 75:927; CCBB 32:92; Kirkus 46:1255; SLJ Oct 1978 p. 160; Suth 2:469; TLS 1980 p. 368; VOYA 1[Feb 1979]:43, 3[Oct 1980]:49)

1-346 WANGERIN, Walter, Jr. *Branta and the Golden Stone.* Gr. 3–6.
Branta's father, who was once one of the three Magi, reveals on his deathbed that the Golden Stone he's kept for himself has the power to permanently transform her into another creature.
Illus. by Deborah Healy, Simon, 1993, 35 pp., o.p.
(BL 890:524; SLJ Oct 1993 p. 134)

1-347 WANGERIN, Walter, Jr. *Elisabeth and the Water-Troll.* Gr. 3–5.
Elisabeth's despair over her mother's death awakens the sympathy of a water troll who hopes to make her happy at the bottom of his well.
Illus. by Deborah Healy, Harper, 1991, 64 pp., o.p.
(BL 87:1800; HBG 2:272; Kirkus 59:325; SLJ May 1991 p. 96)

1-348 WANGERIN, Walter, Jr. *Potter, Come Fly to the First of the Earth.* Gr. 4–6.
An oriole takes a boy named Potter out of his sickbed on a journey that helps him come to terms with his best friend's death.
Illus. by Daniel San Souci, Cook, 1985, 52 pp., o.p.
(BL 82:874; SLJ Apr 1986 p. 93)

1-349 WANGERIN, Walter, Jr. *Thistle.* Gr. 2–4.
Thistle, the youngest child, dares to kiss an ugly witch in order to save her family from being eaten by a giant potato.
Illus. by Marcia Sewall, Harper, 1983, 47 pp., o.p.
(CCBB 37:80; Kirkus 51J156; SLJ Nov 1983 p. 84)

WARBURG, Sandol Stoddard. *On the Way Home.*
See Chapter 5, High Fantasy: Alternate Worlds or Histories.

1-350 WEIR, Rosemary (Green). *Albert the Dragon.* **(Albert the Dragon series, bk. 1).** Gr. 4–6.
As a favor for a friend, Albert the vegetarian dragon pretends to let a knight defeat him in battle. The sequels are *Further Adventures of Albert the Dragon* (1964), *Albert the Dragon and the Centaur* (1968), and *Albert and the Dragonettes* (British).
Illus. by Quentin Blake, Abelard-Schuman, 1961, 107 pp., o.p.
(CCBB 15:68; Kirkus 29:669; LJ 86:4043)

1-351 WERSBA, Barbara. *Let Me Fall Before I Fly.* Gr. 3–5.
A young boy finds a two-inch-high circus giving daily performances in his garden.
Illus. by Mercer Mayer, Atheneum, 1971, o.p.; illus. by James Hoys, Creative, 1986, 48 pp., o.p.
(CCBB 26:66; HB 47:616; Kirkus 39:1124; LJ 97:1611)

1-352   WERSBA, Barbara. *A Song for Clowns.* Gr. 4–6.
Humphrey the minstrel resents the fact that the king has abolished sheriffs, the color blue, love, hope, puddings, and minstrels.
Illus. by Mario Rivoli, Atheneum, 1965, 100 pp., o.p.
(CCBB 19:53; HB 41:629; Kirkus 33:677; LJ 90:3797; TLS 1966 p. 1087)

1-353   WESTON, John (Harrison). *The Boy Who Sang the Birds.* Gr. 4–6.
Two boys try to stop a flock of strange birds from causing a catastrophic winter in their village.
Illus. by Donna Diamond, Scribner, 1976, 106 pp., o.p.
(BL 72:1272; Kirkus 44:257; SLJ Apr 1976 p. 79)

1-354   WETTERER, Margaret K. *The Giant's Apprentice.* Gr. 2–4.
When Liam McGowen, apprentice blacksmith, is kidnapped by a giant, only his uncle can save him.
Illus. by Elise Primavera, Atheneum, 1982, 40 pp., o.p.
(BL 78:1261; HB 58:410; Kirkus 50:492; SLJ May 1982 p. 67)

1-355   WETTERER, Margaret K. *The Mermaid's Cape.* Gr. 2–4.
A mermaid, trapped into marriage and human form by a lonely fisherman, is freed when their beloved young son finds her magical cape.
Illus. by Elise Primavera, Atheneum, 1981, 32 pp., o.p.
(BL 77:1302; HB 57:427; Kirkus 49:506; SLJ May 1981 p. 60)

WHITE, E(lwyn) B(rooks). *Charlotte's Web.*
See Chapter 2, Animal Fantasy.

WHITE, Eliza Orne. *The Enchanted Mountain.*
See Chapter 7, High Fantasy: Travel to Other Worlds.

WHITE, T(erence) H(anbury). *The Sword in the Stone.*
See Chapter 6, High Fantasy: Myth or Legend Fantasy.

1-356   WIGGIN, Kate Douglas (Smith). *The Bird's Christmas Carol.* Gr. 3–5.
(Orig. pub. 1888.)
Carol Bird saves the Ruggles's Christmas. The sequel is *Polly Oliver's Problem* (1896).
Illus. by Jessie Gillespie, Houghton, 1941, 84 pp., o.p.; Houghton, 1997, 80 pp. (0-395-07205-0)
(BL 38:137; Bookshelf 1925–1926 p. 4; HBG 9:83)

1-357   WILDE, Oscar (Fingal O'Flahertie Wills). *The Birthday of the Infanta.*
Gr. 3–5. (Orig. British pub. 1891; U.S. 1905.)
An ugly dwarf entertains the Princess of Spain on her birthday. This story was originally published in the U.S. in *A House of Pomegranates* (1906).
Illus. by Pamela Bianco, Macmillan, 1929, 57 pp., o.p.; illus. by P. Craig Russell, Nantier, 1998, 32 pp. (1-56163-213-9)
(BL 26:170; Mahony 3:486)

WILDE, Oscar (Fingal O'Flahertie Wills). *The Birthday of the Infanta and Other Tales.*
See *The Fairy Tales of Oscar Wilde* in Chapter 3, Fantasy Collections.

1-358 WILDE, Oscar (Fingal O'Flahertie Wills). *The Happy Prince.* Gr. 3–5.
✮ (Orig. British pub. in *The Happy Prince and Other Tales,* 1888.)
A bejeweled statue of a prince, unhappy at the misery of the people around him, persuades a swallow to carry his riches to the needy.
Illus. by Kaj Beckman, Methuen, 1977, o.p.; illus. by Jean Claverie, Oxford University Press, 1981, 40 pp., o.p.; illus. by Ed Young, Simon, 1989, pap., 48 pp., o.p.; illus. by Jane Ray, Dutton, 1995, 32 pp., o.p.; Orchard, 1996, pap., 32 pp. (1-8603-9092-7); illus. by Robin Muller, Stoddart Kids, 2002, 24 pp. (0-7737-3218-3)
(BL 78:444, 91:760, 98:1258; Bookshelf 1932 p. 24; HB 41:630; Kirkus 45:1320, 63:235; LJ 91:430; Mahony 1:37; SLJ Jan 1978 p. 92, Mar 1982 p. 153, July 1989 p. 78, Mar 1999 p. 189; TLS 1981 p. 343, Mar 1995 p. 189, May 2002 p. 131)

WILDE, Oscar (Fingal O'Flahertie Wills). *The Happy Prince and Other Tales.*
See *The Fairy Tales of Oscar Wilde* in Chapter 3, Fantasy Collections.

1-359 WILDE, Oscar (Fingal O'Flahertie Wills). *The Picture of Dorian Gray.* Gr.
✮ 10 up. (Orig. British pub. 1891, orig. U.S. pub. in an unauthorized ed. 1890.)
Granted eternal youth, Dorian Gray lives a wild, dissipated life while his portrait grows old and haggard.
Putnam, 1909, 1916, 337 pp., o.p.; Random, 1926, 1954, 1985, 1992, 248 pp. (0-679-60001-9); Dutton, 1930, 186 pp., o.p.; Harper, 1965, o.p.; ed. by Isobel Murray, Oxford University Press, 1974, 249 pp., o.p.; Modern Library, 1998, 304 pp. (0-3757-5151-3); illus. by Tony Ross, Viking, 2001, 272 pp. (0-670-89494-X)
(BL 28:113; HBG 12:327; Kliatt 16[Spring 1982]:18; TLS 1974 p. 811; VOYA 24:210)

1-360 WILDE, Oscar (Fingal O'Flahertie Wills). *The Selfish Giant.* Gr. 1–4.
✮ (Orig. British pub. in *The Happy Prince and Other Tales,* 1888.)
A giant has a change of heart, allows children to play in his garden, and assures himself a place in heaven.
Illus. by Gertrude Reiner and Walter Reiner, Harvey, 1967, 72 pp., o.p.; illus. by Michael Foreman and Freire Wright, Methuen, 1978, 30 pp., o.p.; illus. by Lisbeth Zwerger, Picture Book Studio, 1984, pap., 28 pp., o.p.; illus. by Dom Mansell, Prentice, 1986, 32 pp., o.p.; illus. by S. Saelig Gallagher, Putnam, 1995, 32 pp. (0-399-22448-3)
(BL 75:551, 80:1631; CCBB 8:56, 37:196; HB 60:463, 71:349; HBG 6:293; Kirkus 46:1242; LJ 93:2117; SLJ Jan 1979 p. 49, Jan 1980 p. 63, Sep 1984 p. 122, Apr 1987 p. 91, July 1995 p. 70; Suth 3:444; TLS 1967 p. 1137)

1-361 WILDE, Oscar (Fingal O'Flahertie Wills). *The Star Child: A Fairy Tale.*
Gr. 2–4. (Orig. British pub. 1891, U.S. 1906 in *A House of Pomegranates.*)
A selfish orphaned boy searching for his mother learns compassion and self-sacrifice before he discovers his true identity.
Adapt. by Jennifer Westwood, illus. by Fiona French, Macmillan, 1979, 30 pp., o.p.; illus. by Jindra Capek, Floris, 1999, 32 pp. (0-8631-5303-8); adapt. by Stella Maidment, illus. by Olyyn Whelan, Chrysalis, 2004, 40 pp. (1-8445-8039-3)
(BL 76:670; CCBB 33:123; SLJ Jan 1980 p. 63)

1-362 WILKINS (Freeman), Mary E(leanor). *Princess Rosetta and the Popcorn Man.* Gr. 2–4. (Orig. pub. in *The Pot of Gold,* 1892, 1970.)
After the infant Princess of Romalia disappears during the annual bee festival, a wandering popcorn man finds her in a neighboring kingdom.
Adapt. by Ellin Greene, illus. by Trina Schart Hyman, Lothrop, 1971, 40 pp., o.p.
(Kirkus 39:94; LJ 97:1174)

1-363 WILKINS (Freeman), Mary E(leanor). *The Pumpkin Giant.* Gr. 2–4.
✯ (Orig. pub. in *The Pot of Gold,* 1892, 1970.)
A brave father kills the dreadful pumpkin-headed giant so that his plump son can marry the king's plump daughter, and they all feast on pumpkin pie.
Retold by Ellin Greene, illus. by Trina Schart Hyman, Lothrop, 1970, 40 pp., o.p.
(BL 67:192; CCBB 24:68; HB 46:607; Kirkus 38:870)

WILLARD, Nancy (Margaret). *Beauty and the Beast.*
See Chapter 6, High Fantasy: Myth or Legend Fantasy.

1-364 WILLARD, Nancy (Margaret). *The Marzipan Moon.* Gr. 4–5.
A hungry parish priest wishes for a marzipan moon to appear in his old crock every morning. When his wish is granted, an officious bishop steps in and tries to take charge of this miracle.
Illus. by Marcia Sewall, Harcourt, 1981, o.p.
(BL 77:1302; HB 57:418; Kirkus 49:428; SLJ Aug 1981 p. 72)

WILLARD, Nancy (Margaret). *Sailing to Cythera, and Other Anatole Stories.*
See Chapter 7, High Fantasy: Travel to Other Worlds.

1-365 WILLARD, Nancy (Margaret). *Things Invisible to See.* Gr. 10 up.
✯ Ruth and young neighborhood baseball star Ben fall in love after a ball hit by Ben strikes Ruth in the head and paralyzes her.
Knopf, 1984, 263 pp., o.p.; Universe, 2000, pap., 272 pp. (0-595-13850-2)
(BL 81:484, 82:753, 86:907; Kirkus 52:1020; Kliatt 20[Spring 1986]:26; LJ 109:2301; SLJ May 1985 p. 115, Jan 1986 p. 50, Apr 1986 p. 31; VOYA 8:190)

WILLETT, John (William Mills). *The Singer in the Stone.*
See Chapter 5, High Fantasy: Alternate Worlds or Histories.

1-366 WILLIAMS, Anne. *Secret of the Round Tower.* Gr. 4–6.
Melisande and Galpin must keep their discovery of a pure white unicorn secret from the king.
Illus. by J. C. Kocsis, Random, 1968, 87 pp., o.p.
(HB 45:47; Kirkus 36:820; LJ 94:880)

1-367 WILLIAMS, Jay. *Petronella.* Gr. 2–4.
On her way to seek her fortune, Princess Petronella rescues an enchanted prince. This story has been republished in *The Practical Princess and Other Liberating Fairy Tales* (1978; see Chapter 3, Fantasy Collections).
Illus. by Friso Henstra, Parents, 1973, 33 pp., o.p.
(BL 70:176; Kirkus 41:454; LJ 98:2646)

1-368 WILLIAMS, Jay. *The Practical Princess.* Gr. 2–4.

The fairy gift of common sense helps a princess defeat a dragon and find her own prince. This story has been republished in *The Practical Princess and Other Liberating Fairy Tales* (1978; see Chapter 3, Fantasy Collections).
Illus. by Friso Henstra, Parents, 1969, 40 pp., o.p.
(BL 65:1129; CCBB 23:68; Kirkus 37:1774, 2073, 4583)

WILLIAMS, Jay. *The Practical Princess and Other Liberating Fairy Tales.*
See Chapter 3, Fantasy Collections.

WILLIAMS (John), Ursula Moray. *Adventures of a Little Wooden Horse.*
See Chapter 11, Toy Fantasy.

1-369 WILLIAMS, Kit. *Masquerade.* Gr. 4–6. (Orig. British pub. 1979.)
The moon, in love with the sun, gives him the gift of a jeweled hare. This book contains clues that touched off a real-life three-year treasure hunt in England.
Illus. by the author, Schocken, 1980, o.p.
(BL 77:6; CCBB 34:103; SLJ Nov 1980 p. 80)

WILLIAMS, Tad. *Tailchaser's Song.*
See Chapter 2, Animal Fantasy.

WILSON, A. N. *Stray.*
See Chapter 2, Animal Fantasy.

WILSON, David Henry. *The Coachman Rat.*
See Chapter 6, High Fantasy: Myth or Legend Fantasy.

WILSON, Willie. *Up Mountain One Time.*
See Chapter 2, Animal Fantasy.

A Wizard's Dozen: Stories of the Fantastic. **Ed. by Michael Stearns.**
See Chapter 3, Fantasy Collections.

WOLITZER, Meg. *The Dream Book.*
See Chapter 9, Magic Adventure Fantasy.

WREDE, Patricia C(ollins). *Snow White and Rose Red.*
See Chapter 6, High Fantasy: Myth or Legend Fantasy.

WRIGGINS, Sally. *The White Monkey King: A Chinese Fable.*
See Chapter 6, High Fantasy: Myth or Legend Fantasy.

WRIGHTSON, (Alice) Patricia (Furlonger). *Moon Dark.*
See Chapter 2, Animal Fantasy.

YEP, Laurence M(ichael). *Dragon of the Lost Sea.*
See Chapter 5, High Fantasy: Alternate Worlds or Histories.

YOLEN (Stemple), Jane (Hyatt). *The Acorn Quest.*
See Chapter 2, Animal Fantasy.

1-370 YOLEN (Stemple), Jane (Hyatt). *The Bird of Time.* Gr. 2–4.
Pieter and the magic of the Bird of Time rescue a captive princess from a giant.

Illus. by Mercer Mayer, Crowell, 1971, 32 pp., o.p.
(BL 68:509; CCBB 25:83; LJ 97:770)

1-371   YOLEN (Stemple), Jane (Hyatt). *The Boy Who Had Wings.* Gr. K–4.
Aetos uses his forbidden wings to rescue his father from a mountain blizzard.
Illus. by Helga Aichinger, Crowell, 1974, 25 pp., o.p.
(BL 71:296; HB 50:687; LJ 99:3270)

YOLEN (Stemple), Jane (Hyatt). *Briar Rose.*
See Chapter 6, High Fantasy: Myth or Legend Fantasy.

1-372   YOLEN (Stemple), Jane (Hyatt). *Dove Isabeau.* Gr. 3–6.
When her jealous stepmother turns Princess Dove Isabeau into a huge dragon,
she is forced to eat her 99 suitors to survive.
Illus. by Dennis Nolan, Harcourt, 1989, 32 pp., o.p.
(BL 86:750; HBG 1:83; Kirkus 57:1483; SLJ July 1990p. 79)

YOLEN (Stemple), Jane (Hyatt). *Dragonfield and Other Stories.*
See Chapter 3, Fantasy Collections.

YOLEN (Stemple), Jane (Hyatt). *The Giants' Farm.*
See Chapter 8, Humorous Fantasy.

1-373   YOLEN (Stemple), Jane (Hyatt). *The Girl in the Golden Bower.* Gr. K–4.
✶   Aurea's animal friends protect the girl from a sorceress who poisoned her
mother to steal her magic comb.
Illus. by Jane Dyer, Little, Brown, 1994, 32 pp., o.p.
(BL 91:440; CCBB 48:71; HBG 6:71; Kirkus 62:1581; SLJ Oct 1994 p. 106)

YOLEN (Stemple), Jane (Hyatt). *The Girl Who Cried Flowers and Other Tales.*
See Chapter 3, Fantasy Collections.

1-374   YOLEN (Stemple), Jane (Hyatt). *The Girl Who Loved the Wind.* Gr. 1–4.
✶   A wealthy merchant tries to protect his beautiful daughter from unhappiness by
keeping her a prisoner in their palace, but a whispering wind makes the girl dis-
contented with her life.
Illus. by Ed Young, Harper, 1972, 1982, 32 pp., o.p.
(BL 69:575; CCBB 26:100; HB 48:585; Kirkus 40:1353; LJ 98:998; TLS 1973 p. 1431)

1-375   YOLEN (Stemple), Jane (Hyatt). *Good Griselle.* Gr. 2–4.
✶   Attempting to prove that a young woman named Griselle is not as good as she
seems, the gargoyles carved on an old cathedral send her an unlovable
changeling child, whom she takes in and refuses to abandon.
Illus. by David Christiana, Harcourt, 1994, 40 pp., o.p.
(BL 91:335; HB 70:761; HBG 6:71; Kirkus 62:1419; SLJ Oct 1994 p. 45.)

YOLEN (Stemple), Jane (Hyatt). *Greyling: A Picture Story from the Islands of Shetland.*
See Chapter 6, High Fantasy: Myth or Legend Fantasy.

YOLEN (Stemple), Jane (Hyatt). *Here There Be Dragons.*
See Chapter 3, Fantasy Collections.

YOLEN (Stemple), Jane (Hyatt). *The Hundredth Dove and Other Tales.*
See Chapter 3, Fantasy Collections.

YOLEN (Stemple), Jane (Hyatt). *Merlin's Booke.*
See Chapter 6, High Fantasy: Myth or Legend Fantasy.

YOLEN (Stemple), Jane (Hyatt). *The Moon Ribbon and Other Tales.*
See Chapter 3, Fantasy Collections.

YOLEN (Stemple), Jane (Hyatt). *Sleeping Ugly.*
See Chapter 8, Humorous Fantasy.

YOLEN (Stemple), Jane (Hyatt). *Tam Lin: An Old Ballad.*
See Chapter 6, High Fantasy: Myth or Legend Fantasy.

1-376 **YOLEN (Stemple), Jane (Hyatt).** *The Transfigured Hart.* Gr. 5–7.
Richard and Heather discover an albino hart living near a pool in the woods and
protect it from her hunter brothers. Golden Kite Award Honor Book, 1975.
Illus. by Donna Diamond, Crowell, 1975, 96 pp., o.p.
(Kirkus 43:662; SLJ Sep 1975 p. 115; VOYA 21:64)

YOLEN (Stemple), Jane (Hyatt). *The Wild Hunt.*
See Chapter 6, High Fantasy: Myth or Legend Fantasy.

YOUNG, Ella. *The Unicorn with Silver Shoes.*
See Chapter 7, High Fantasy: Travel to Other Worlds.

1-377 **ZARING, Jane T(homas).** *The Return of the Dragon.* Gr. 3–6.
Caradoc, the last Welsh dragon, decides to go home to Wales in spite of the
fact that the people do not want him to return.
Illus. by Polly Broman, Houghton, 1981, 146 pp., o.p.
(HB 57:541; SLJ Feb 1982 p. 84)

1-378 **ZEMACH, Harve(y Fischtrom).** *The Tricks of Master Dabble.* Gr. 1–3.
★ Playing upon the vanity of the castle inhabitants, Master Dabble tricks them
into believing he is a painter, and that his mirror is a masterpiece.
Illus. by Margot Zemach, Holt, 1965, 32 pp., o.p.
(BL 62:164; HB 41:166; Kirkus 33:3; LJ 90:1546)

ZIMNIK, Reiner. *The Bear and the People.*
See Chapter 5, High Fantasy: Alternate Worlds or Histories.

ZINDEL, Paul. *Let Me Hear You Whisper: A Play.*
See Chapter 2, Animal Fantasy.

ZOLOTOW, Charlotte S(hapiro). *The Man with Purple Eyes.*
See Chapter 9, Magic Adventure Fantasy.

2

Animal Fantasy

There is sometimes only a fine line between realistic and fantastic portrayal of animals in literature. Thus, any tales in which animal characters think or talk in a humanlike manner have been placed in this chapter, including both "beast tales," which are rather serious stories about "realistic" animals fleeing human evils, and talking animal tales, which are lighter in tone and feature dressed-up, anthropomorphic animals.

2-1   **ADAMS, Richard (George).** *The Plague Dogs.* Gr. 10 up.
After escaping from an animal research lab, two dogs run free in England's Lake District. They are befriended by a fox, but are hunted by humans as possible carriers of bubonic plague.
Knopf, 1978, 390 pp., o.p.; Fawcett, 1986, pap. (0-449-21182-7)
(BL 74:975; Kirkus 46:54, 115; Kliatt 13:4; LJ 103:773; SLJ Sep 1978 p. 168)

ADAMS, Richard (George). *Shardik.*
See Chapter 5, High Fantasy: Alternate Worlds or Histories.

2-2   **ADAMS, Richard (George).** *Watership Down.* Gr. 6 up. (Orig. British pub.
★★   1972.)
Premonitions of destruction drive a small band of rabbits from their peaceful hillside warren into the wilderness. Carnegie Medal, 1972; Guardian Award for Children's Fiction, 1973. *Tales from Watership Down* (1996, 1998) contains 15 tales, including five about the rabbit folk hero El-ahrairah and eight stories about Hazel, Fiver, Bigwig, and the other characters from *Watership Down.*
Macmillan, 1974, 429 pp., o.p.; Avon, 1976, pap. (0-380-00293-0); Scribner, 1996, 448 pp. (0-6848-3605-X); Perennia, 2001, pap., 512 pp. (0-06-093545-6)
(BL 70:852, 71:747, 72:1096, 1107, 80:351; CCBB 27:121; HB 50:365, 405; LJ 99:1148, 1235; Suth 2:2)

AIKEN, Joan (Delano). *The Kingdom and the Cave.*
See Chapter 5, High Fantasy: Alternate Worlds or Histories.

AIKEN, Joan (Delano). *A Necklace of Raindrops and Other Stories.*
See Chapter 3, Fantasy Collections.

AINSWORTH (Gilbert), Ruth (Gallard). *The Bear Who Liked Hugging People and Other Stories.*
See Chapter 3, Fantasy Collections.

2-3 **ALEXANDER, Lloyd (Chudley).** *The Cat Who Wished to Be a Man.* Gr.
✭ 4–6.
Lionel nags the wizard Stephanus to change him from a cat into a human. Stephanus grants his wish, only to find that he cannot reverse the process.
Dutton, 1973, 107 pp., o.p.; Puffin, 2000, pap. (0-41-30704-8)
(BBC:67; BL 70:168; CCBB 27:21; HB 49:463; Kirkus 41:639; LJ 98:2647; Suth 2:8)

2-4 **ALEXANDER, Lloyd (Chudley).** *The Town Cats, and Other Tales.* Gr.
✭ 4–6.
Eight fairy tales about wise and heroic cats.
Illus. by Laszlo Kubinyi, Dutton, 1977, 144 pp., o.p.; Puffin, 1988, pap. (0-14-130122-8)
(BL 74:472; CCBB 31:89; HB 54:42; Kirkus 45:1096; SLJ Nov 1977 p. 52; Suth 2:9)

2-5 **ALLAN, Ted.** *Willie the Squowse.* Gr. 3–5. (Orig. British pub. 1977.)
Willie, the son of a mouse and a squirrel, gives a poor family the money stored in their wealthy neighbors' walls.
Illus. by Quentin Blake, Hastings, 1991, 57 pp., o.p.
(BBC:197; CCBB 32:57; SLJ Nov 1978 p. 39; TLS 1977 p. 1414)

ALTON, Andrea I. *Demon of Undoing.*
See Chapter 5, High Fantasy: Alternate Worlds or Histories.

2-6 **AMADO, Jorge.** *The Swallow and the Tom Cat: A Grown-Up Love Story.*
Gr. 10 up. (Written in Brazil, 1952.)
A fable by a major Brazilian novelist about star-crossed lovers, a swallow and a tom cat, whose families force them to marry others.
Trans. by Barbara Shelby Merello, illus. by Carybé, Delacorte, 1982, 96 pp., o.p.
(BL 79:90, 104; Kirkus 50:943; LJ 107:1767)

ANDERSEN, Hans Christian. *Thumbelina.*
See Chapter 1, Allegorical Fantasy and Literary Fairy Tales.

ANDERSEN, Hans Christian. *The Ugly Duckling.*
See Chapter 1, Allegorical Fantasy and Literary Fairy Tales.

2-7 **ANDERSON, Mary.** *F*T*C* Superstar.* Gr. 4–6.
Freddie the cat dreams of becoming an actor, but when Emma, his pigeon friend, helps him attain his dream, stardom goes to his head. The sequel is *F*T*C* & Company* (1979).
Illus. by Gail Owens, Atheneum, 1976, 156 pp., o.p.
(BL 73:140; Kirkus 44:320; SLJ Apr 1976 p. 68)

2-8 **ANDREWS, Allen.** *The Pig Plantagenet.* Gr. 10 up.
✭ A domesticated 13th-century French pig becomes embroiled in a plot to save a family of wild boars from a massacre by the lord of the chateau. The sequel is *Castle Crespin* (1984).

(Adapted from the French *Le Roman de Fulbert* by Michel Héloin.) Illus. by Michael Foreman, Viking, 1980, 188 pp., o.p.

(BL 77:286, 287; Kirkus 48:1406; LJ 105:2513; TLS 1980 p. 1329; VOYA 4:27)

2-9   ANNETT (Pipitone Scott), Cora. *How the Witch Got Alf.* **Gr. 3–5.**
Alf, the old folks' donkey, feels unloved and decides to run away.
Illus. by Steven Kellogg, Watts, 1975, 47 pp., o.p.

(BL 71:864; CCBB 29:1; Kirkus 43:70; SLJ Mar 1975 p. 84; Suth 2:16)

2-10   ANNETT (Pipitone Scott), Cora. *When the Porcupine Moved In.* **Gr. 1–4.**
Porcupine disrupts Rabbit's comfortable life by moving into Rabbit's house and bringing all of his relatives with him.
Illus. by Peter Parnall, Watts, 1971, 40 pp., o.p.

(BL 68:626; CCBB 25:70; LJ 97:1593)

2-11   ANNIXTER, Paul (pseud. of Howard Allison Sturtzel). *The Cat That Clumped.* **Gr. 1–4.**
Unhappy with his life as a cat, Herbert decides to become a horse.
Illus. by Brinton (Cassaday) Turkle, Holiday, 1966, 35 pp., o.p.

(CCBB 19:157; Kirkus 34:240; LJ 91:1694)

2-12   ARKIN, Alan (Wolf). *The Lemming Condition.* **Gr. 4–5.**
✴   When Bubber's family and friends undertake an unquestioning journey toward the sea and death, Bubber must battle his own instincts in order to survive. The sequel is *The Clearing* (1986).
Illus. by Joan Sandin, Harper, 1976, 64 pp., o.p.

(BL 72:1182; HB 52:394; Kirkus 44:389; SLJ Apr 1976 p. 68)

2-13   ARUNDEL, Honor. *The Amazing Mr. Prothero.* **Gr. 3–5.** (Orig. British pub. 1968.)
Scamp, a dog who prefers to be called Mr. Prothero, rescues Julia's baby brother from a runaway carriage.
Illus. by Jane Paton, Nelson, 1972, 80 pp., o.p.

(BL 69:200; CCBB 26:101; Kirkus 40:30; LJ 97:2928)

2-14   ASCH, Frank. *Class Pets: The Ghost of PS 42.* **(Class Pets series, bk. 1). Gr. 2–4.**
Sibling mice Molly and Jake search for a safe new home, she in a third-grade classroom, and he on a playground threatened by Big Gray the cat and Hooter the barn owl. The sequels are *Battle in a Bottle* (2003) and *Survival School* (2003).
Illus. by John Kanzler, Simon, 2002, 96 pp. (0-689-84653-3); Aladdin, 2003, pap. (0-689-84652-5)

(BL 99:759; Kirkus 70:1121; SLJ Oct 2002 p. 98)

2-15   ASCH, Frank. *Pearl's Promise.* **Gr. 3–5.**
Pearl mouse is horrified when her little brother, Tony, is given to the Pet Shop's new python for dinner, and she vows to rescue him. The sequel is *Pearl's Pirates* (1987).
Illus. by the author, Delacorte, 1984, 160 pp., o.p.

(BL 81:60; CCBB 37:160; HB 60:193; SLJ Apr 1984 p. 111)

2-16 **ATTWOOD, Frederic.** *Vavache, the Cow Who Painted Pictures.* Gr. 3–5.
A young American boy visiting Normandy meets Vavache, a talking cow who paints with her tail.
Illus. by Roger Duvoisin, Aladdin, 1950, 77 pp., o.p.
(BL 46:291; CCBB 3:39; HB 26:193; LJ 75:632, 1054)

AUCH, Mary Jane. *I Was a Third Grade Science Fair Project.*
See Chapter 8, Humorous Fantasy.

2-17 **AVERILL, Esther (Holden).** *Captains of the City Streets: A Story of the*
☆ *Cat Club.* **(Jenny and the Cat Club series, bk. 9).** Gr. 3–4.
Two tramp cats named Sinbad and the Duke move to New York City and become involved in a club run by the local cats. This is the sequel to *The Cat Club: Or, The Life and Times of Jenny Linsky* (1944), *The School for Cats* (1947), *Jenny's First Party* (1948), *Jenny's Moonlight Adventure* (1949), *When Jenny Lost Her Scarf* (1951), *Jenny's Adopted Brothers* (1952), *How the Brothers Joined the Cat Club* (1953), and *The Hotel Cat* (1969). *Jenny and the Cat Club: A Collection of Favorite Stories about Jenny Linsky* (New York Review of Books, 2003) includes *The Cat Club, Jenny's First Party, When Jenny Lost Her Scarf, Jenny's Adopted Brothers,* and *How the Brothers Joined the Cat Club.*
Illus. by the author, Harper, 1972, 147 pp., o.p.
(BL 69:809; CCBB 26:149; HB 48:47, 80:154–155; Kirkus 40:1354; LJ 98:1678)

2-18 **AVI (Avi Wortis).** *The End of the Beginning: Being the Adventures of a*
☆ *Small Snail (and an Even Smaller Ant).* Gr. 3–5.
Having read all about adventurous quests, Avon the Snail and Edward the Ant set out on a journey to the end of their branch in this expanded version of the author's *Snail Tale: The Adventures of a Rather Small Snail* (Pantheon, 1972).
Illus. by Tricia Tusa, Harcourt, 2004, 144 pp. (0-15-204968-1)
(BL 101:242; CCBB 58:113; Kirkus 72:956; SLJ Oct 2004 pp. 104, 154)

2-19 **AVI (Avi Wortis).** *The Good Dog.* Gr. 3–6.
☆ Malamute McKinley enjoys life as head dog in his Colorado town and looking after his "human pup" Jack, but everything changes when a wolf named Lupin arrives to recruit local dogs for her wild pack.
Atheneum, 2001, 243 pp. (0-689-83824-7); Aladdin/Simon, 2003, pap., 243 pp. (0-689-83825-5)
(BL 98:102; HB 78:75; HBG 13:81; Kirkus 69:1418; SLJ Dec 2001 p. 132; VOYA 24:366)

2-20 **AVI (Avi Wortis).** *The Mayor of Central Park.* Gr. 4–7.
Oscar Westerwit, squirrel manager of the Central Park Green Sox baseball team, must contend with a missing star pitcher and the invasion of an army of rats in this tale set in New York City in 1900.
Illus. by Brian Floca, HarperCollins, 2003, 208 pp. (0-06-051556-2); Harper-Collins, 2005, pap. (0-06-051557-0)
(BL 99:1976; CCBB 57:140; HBG 15:75; Kirkus 71:1012; SLJ Dec 2003 p. 144)

2-21 **AVI (Avi Wortis).** *Perloo the Bold.* Gr. 5–7.
☆ After the death of the rabbit-like Montmer leader, scholar Perloo is accused of murdering her. He flees and is taken in by the Montmers' traditional enemies, the coyote-like Felbarts.

Scholastic, 1998, 240 pp. (0-590-11002-0), 1999, pap., 225 pp. (0-590-11003-9)

(BL 95:749; CCBB 52:87; HB 75:58; HBG 10:62; Kirkus 66:1528; SLJ Nov 1998 p. 116; VOYA 21:362, 22:12)

2-22   **AVI (Avi Wortis).** *Poppy.* **(Dimwood Forest Tales, bk. 1).** Gr. 4–6.
★★   Poppy the deer mouse is determined to find a new home for her family after her friend Ragweed is killed by Mr. Ocax, the owl who rules their territory. Boston Globe Horn Book Award, 1996. In the prequel, *Ragweed: A Tale from Dimwood Forest* (1999), country mouse Ragweed hops a freight train to the city where he hangs out with hipster mice musicians Clutch, Dipstick, and Lugnut, and helps them battle cat members of F.E.A.R. (Felines Enraged About Rodents). In the sequel, *Poppy and Rye* (1998), Poppy and her porcupine friend Ereth travel to "The Brook" only to find that beavers have flooded Ragweed's family's home. In *Ereth's Birthday: A Tale from Dimwood Forest* (2000), Poppy and Rye's grouchy friend Ereth adopts three young foxes after their mother dies in a trap.
Illus. by Brian Floca, Orchard, 1995, 147 pp. (0-531-09483-9); HarperCollins, 2005, pap., 176 pp. (0-380-72769-2)

(BL 92:402, 741, 1288; CCBB 49:154; HB 72:71; HBG 7:58; Kirkus 63:1346; SLJ Dec 1995 pp. 20 and 102, June 1996 p. 55; VOYA 19:104)

2-23   **AYMÉ, Marcel (André).** *The Wonderful Farm.* Gr. 4–6. (Orig. pub. in France.)
Marinette and Delphine don't know how to get around their parents' strict rules until the farm animals give the girls some unusual ideas. The sequel is *The Magic Pictures: More About the Wonderful Farm* (1954, British title: *Return to the Wonderful Farm*, 1954).
Trans. by Norman Denny, illus. by Maurice (Bernard) Sendak, Harper, 1951, 182 pp., o.p.

(BL 48:161; CCBB 5:35; HB 27:406; LJ 76:2009)

BABCOCK (Thompson), Betty (Elizabeth S.). *The Expandable Pig.*
See Chapter 9, Magic Adventure Fantasy.

BACH, Richard (David). *Jonathan Livingston Seagull.*
See Chapter 1, Allegorical Fantasy and Literary Fairy Tales.

BACON, Peggy. *The Ghost of Opalina, or Nine Lives.*
See Chapter 4, Ghost Fantasy.

2-24   **BACON, Peggy.** *The Lion-Hearted Kitten and Other Stories.* Gr. 3–4.
A collection of short, humorous, folktale-like animal stories.
Illus. by the author, Macmillan, 1927, 102 pp., o.p.

(BL 24:124; Bookshelf 1929 p. 9; HB 3:19; LJ 53:484)

2-25   **BACON, Peggy.** *Mercy and the Mouse and Other Stories.* Gr. 2–4.
In the first of these animal stories, an ambitious young cellar cat becomes a household pet.
Illus. by the author, Macmillan, 1928, 85 pp., o.p.

(BL 25:289; HB 4:20, 4:76; Mahony 2:117; Moore:35)

2-26   **BAILEY, Carolyn Sherwin.** *Finnegan II: His Nine Lives.* Gr. 4–6.
Finnegan the cat proves to have more than nine lives.
Illus. by Kate Seredy, Viking, 1953, 95 pp., o.p.
(BL 50:150; HB 29:455, 64:516; LJ 78:2225)

2-27   **BAKER, Betty (Lou).** *Danby and George.* Gr. 3–4.
A wood rat and a deer mouse make a home for themselves at the zoo.
Illus. by Adrienne Lobel, Greenwillow, 1981, 64 pp., o.p.
(BL 77:1025; CCBB 35:4; Kirkus 49:283; SLJ Jan 1982 p. 72)

2-28   **BAKER, Betty (Lou).** *Dupper.* Gr. 5–7.
Dupper is an outcast in the prairie dog world until his search for the Great Ants
leads to a solution to the killer rattlesnake problem.
Illus. by Chuck Eckart, Greenwillow/Morrow, 1976, 147 pp., o.p.
(BL 73:140; CCBB 30:38; Kirkus 44:684; SLJ Feb 1977 p. 60; Suth 2:24)

2-29   **BAKER, Elizabeth Whitemore.** *Sonny-Boy Sim.* Gr. 1–4.
The woodland animals decide to turn the tables on Sonny-Boy Sim and his
hound dog.
Illus. by Susanne Suba, Rand, 1948, 31 pp., o.p.
(BL 45:320; CCBB 2:1; HB 25:285; Kirkus 17:177; LJ 74:666)

2-30   **BAKER, Margaret.** *Three for an Acorn.* Gr. 1–4.
☆   Mrs. Squirrel's shop sells dandelion lollipops, three for an acorn.
Illus. by Mary Baker, Dodd, 1935, 96 pp., o.p.
(BL 32:45; Bookshelf 1935 p. 2; HB 11:289; LJ 60:857; Mahony 3:78)

2-31   **BAKER, Margaret Joyce.** *Homer the Tortoise.* Gr. 4–6. (Orig. British pub.
1949, entitled *"Nonsense!" Said the Tortoise.*)
Homer the educated tortoise comes to live with the Brown family. The sequels
are *Homer Goes to Stratford* (1958) and *Homer Sees the Queen* (British).
Illus. by Leo Bates, McGraw-Hill, 1950, 149 pp., o.p.
(BL 46:278; CCBB 3:33; Kirkus 18:97; LJ 75:629, 986)

BAKER, Margaret Joyce. *Porterhouse Major.*
See Chapter 9, Magic Adventure Fantasy.

BAKER, Olaf. *Bengey and the Beast.*
See Chapter 9, Magic Adventure Fantasy.

2-32   **BALABAN, John.** *The Hawk's Tale.* Gr. 4–6.
Glister the water snake, Mirais the toad, and Mr. Trembly the deermouse search
for the fierce white eagle in order to rescue a boy named James and Mr. Trem-
bly's niece Lilac.
Illus. by David Delamare, Harcourt, 1988, 148 pp., o.p.
(BL 84:1918; Kirkus 51:614; SLJ Sep 1988 p. 182)

2-33   **BALL, Duncan.** *Selby: The Secret Adventures of a Talking Dog.* Gr. 3–6.
(Orig. Australian pub. 1996, entitled *Selby, Spacedog.*)
As the only talking dog in Australia, Selby keeps his talents a secret from his
owners while winning contests, solving mysteries, and preventing crimes. The
sequel is *Selby Speaks: More Adventures of a Talking Dog* (1997).

Illus. by M. K. Brown, HarperCollins, 1997, pap., 102 pp., o.p.

(BL 83:939; SLJ Mar 1997 p. 148)

BANKS, Lynne Reid. *The Farthest-Away Mountain.*
See Chapter 1, Allegorical Fantasy and Literary Fairy Tales.

2-34 BANKS, Lynne Reid. *Harry the Poisonous Centipede: A Story to Make You Squirm.* Gr. 3–5. (Orig. British pub. 1996.)
Harry and his friend George keep getting into trouble while learning about the dangers of the Hoo-Min world. Nestlé Smarties Book Prize, Silver Award, 1996. The sequel is *Harry the Poisonous Centipede's Big Adventure: Another Story to Make You Squirm* (2001).
Illus. by Tony Ross, Morrow, 1997, 153 pp., o.p.; Harper, 1998, pap. (0-380-72734-X)

(BL 94:234; HBB 9:67; Kirkus 65:946; SLJ Sep 1997 p. 172)

2-35 BANKS, Lynne Reid. *I Houdini: The Autobiography of a Self-Educated Hamster.* Gr. 3–6. (Orig. British pub. 1978.)
Houdini the hamster takes after his namesake in his unrelenting attempts to escape from his cage, explore the out-of-doors, and find himself a wife.
Illus. by Terry Riley, Doubleday, 1988, 127 pp., o.p.; Delacorte, 2003 (0-385-90118-6); Dell, 2003, pap. (0-440-41924-7)

(BL 85:70; HB 64:493; Kirkus 56:688; SLJ June 1988 p. 100)

2-36 BANKS, Lynne Reid. *The Magic Hare.* Gr. 3–6. (Orig. British pub. 1993.)
✫ Ten contemporary fables about a magic hare's encounters with a dragon, a witch, a selfish queen, a prince with hiccups, and two giants.
Illus. by Barry Moser, Morrow, 1993, 49 pp. (0-688-10895-4); Avon, 1994, pap.

(BL 90:149; CCBB 47:37; HB 69:743; HBG 5:63; Kirkus 61:930; SLJ Nov 1993 p. 104)

2-37 BARKLEM, Jill. *Autumn Story.* **(Brambly Hedge series, bk. 1).** Gr. K–3. (Orig. British and U.S. pub. 1980.)
The mice of Brambly Hedge plan a surprise birthday party for Wilfred Toad-flax in this book set in a cozy world of elaborately dressed mice. The sequels are *Winter Story* (1980, 1986), *Spring Story* (1980, 1982, 1989), *Summer Story* (1980, 1989), *The Secret Staircase* (1983, 1986), *The High Hills* (1986), and *Sea Story* (1990, 1991). The first four books have been combined in *The Four Seasons of Brambly Hedge* (1988, 1990).
Illus. by the author, Putnam, 1986, c. 1980, 32 pp., o.p.

(BL 77:695; SLJ Mar 1981 p. 128; TLS Sep 19, 1980, p. 1029)

2-38 BARRETT, Nicholas. *Fledger.* Gr. 10 up.
Goldie, a young puffin, leads his flock's struggle against the deadly island rats who have destroyed the puffins' breeding grounds.
Macmillan, 1985, 207 pp., o.p.

(Kirkus 53:647; LJ Oct 1, 1985 p. 110; SLJ Jan 1986 p. 83; VOYA 9:37)

BASE, Graeme. *TruckDogs.*
See Chapter 5, High Fantasy: Alternate Worlds or Histories.

BAUER, Marion Dane. *Ghost Eye.*
See Chapter 4, Ghost Fantasy.

2-39 **BAUER, Steven.** *A Cat of a Different Color.* Gr. 3–6.
The new mayor of Felicity-by-the-Lake has terrified its citizens, and Ulwazzer the cat and his human friend Daria attempt to improve things.
Illus. by Tim Raglin, Delacorte, 2000, 197 pp., o.p.
(BL 96:1890; CCBB 53:390; HB 76:450; HBG 11:299; Kirkus 68:791; SLJ Aug 2000 p. 177)

BAUER, Steven. *Satyrday: A Fable.*
See Chapter 5, High Fantasy: Alternate Worlds or Histories.

BEAGLE, Peter S(oyer). *A Fine and Private Place.*
See Chapter 4, Ghost Fantasy.

2-40 **BECHDOLT, Jack (pseud. of John Ernest Bechdolt).** *Bandmaster's Holiday.* Gr. 2–4.
Barko the circus sea lion decides to try living in the ocean,
Illus. by Decie Merwin, Oxford University Press, 1938, 71 pp., o.p.
(HB 14:159; LJ 63:284, 690)

BEEKS, Graydon. *Hosea Globe and the Fantastical Peg-Legged Chu.*
See Chapter 8, Humorous Fantasy.

2-41 **BEHN, Harry.** *Roderick.* Gr. 4–6.
A thoughtful, loving crow named Roderick unexpectedly becomes the leader of his flock.
Illus. by Mel Silverman, Harcourt, 1961, 64 pp., o.p.
(HB 37:340; LJ 86:2353)

BELL, Clare E. *The Jaguar Princess.*
See Chapter 5, High Fantasy: Alternate Worlds or Histories.

2-42 **BELL, Clare E.** *Ratha's Creature.* **(Ratha quartet, bk. 1).** Gr. 7–12.
☆☆ Ratha, a yearling from a clan of intelligent cats living in an alternate prehistoric time, is exiled for learning to handle fire and then caught up in a war between her clan and the Un-Named, a band of hunter cats. International Reading Association Children's Book Award, 1984. The sequels are *Clan Ground* (1984, 1987), *Ratha and Thistle-Chaser* (1990), in which Ratha is forced to confront Thistle-Chaser, the maimed daughter she abandoned as a cub, and *Ratha's Challenge* (1994).
Atheneum, 1983, 248 pp., o.p.
(BL 79:956, 962; CCBB 36:202; SLJ Sep 1983 p. 130; VOYA 6:196)

2-43 **BELL, Clare E.** *Tomorrow's Sphinx.* Gr. 7–12.
☆ Kichebo, a black-and-gold cheetah living in a post-ecological-disaster future time, is able to link minds with an ancient Egyptian cheetah who teaches her to accept a young human companion.
Atheneum, 1986, 312 pp., o.p.
(BL 83:344, 346, 83:776; CCBB 40:42; Kirkus 54:1372; SLJ Nov 1986 p. 96)

BENCHLEY, Nathaniel (Goddard). *Demo and the Dolphin.*
See Chapter 6, High Fantasy: Myth or Legend Fantasy.

2-44 BENCHLEY, Nathaniel (Goddard). *Feldman Fieldmouse: A Fable.* Gr.
✭ 3–6.
Uncle Feldman's lessons in wild mouse survival are quite a change for Fendall
after his pampered life as a household pet.
Illus. by Hilary Knight, Harper, 1971, 96 pp., o.p.
(BL 68:55; CCBB 25:54; HB 47:285; Kirkus 39:500; LJ 96:2128; Suth:33)

2-45 BENCHLEY, Nathaniel (Goddard). *Kilroy and the Gull.* Gr. 5–7.
Kilroy the killer whale and a seagull friend escape from an aquarium after frus-
trating attempts to communicate with humans, and search the sea for Kilroy's
family.
Illus. by John Schoenherr, Harper, 1977, 118 pp., o.p.
(BL 73:1086; CCBB 30:138; HB 53:309; Kirkus 45:3; SLJ Oct 1977 p. 109; Suth 2:41)

2-46 BERESFORD, Elizabeth. *The Wombles.* **(The Wombles series, bk. 1).** Gr.
4–6. (Orig. pub. in England.)
Wombles are furry, subterranean creatures who survive by "collecting" things
from human beings. The British sequels are *MacWomble's Pipe Band; The
Invisible Womble; The Snow Womble; The Wandering Wombles; The Wombles
at Work; The Wombles Book; The Wombles Go Round the World; The Wombles
in Danger; The Wombles Make a Clean Sweep; The Wombles of Wimbledon;*
and *The Wombles to the Rescue.*
Illus. by Margaret Gordon, Meredith, 1968, 183 pp., o.p.
(Kirkus 37:1147; LJ 95:1192; TLS 1968 p. 1376, 1973 p. 386)

BERGENGREN, Ralph Wilhelm. *David the Dreamer: His Book of
Dreams.*
See Chapter 7, High Fantasy: Travel to Other Worlds.

2-47 BEST, (Oswald) Herbert. *Desmond's First Case.* **(Desmond Dog Detective
series, bk. 1).** Gr. 3–5.
A dog detective named Desmond and his boy, Gus, solve the mystery of a
missing banker. The sequels are *Desmond the Dog Detective: The Case of the
Lone Stranger* (1962), *Desmond and the Peppermint Ghost: The Dog Detec-
tive's Third Case* (1965), and *Desmond and Dog Friday* (1968).
Illus. by Ezra Jack Keats, Viking, 1961, 96 pp., o.p.
(Kirkus 29:55; LJ 86:1980)

2-48 BESTERMAN, Catherine. *The Quaint and Curious Quest of Johnny
Longfoot, the Shoe King's Son.* Gr. 4–6.
Johnny Longfoot and a group of animals search for buried treasure. John New-
bery Medal Honor Book, 1948. The sequel is *The Extraordinary Education of
Johnny Longfoot in His Search for the Magic Hat* (1949).
Bobbs-Merrill, 1947, 147 pp., o.p.
(BL 44:116; HB 23:435; 24:36; LJ 72:1618)

BETHANCOURT, T(homas) Ernesto (pseud. of Tom Paisley). *The Dog Days of Arthur Cane.*
See Chapter 9, Magic Adventure Fantasy.

2-49 **BIANCO, Margery (Winifred) Williams.** *The Good Friends.* Gr. 4–6.
The animals on Farmer Hicks's farm must care for themselves after he goes into the hospital.
Illus. by Grace Paull, Viking, 1934, 142 pp., o.p.
(BL 31:67; Bookshelf 1934–1935 p. 5; HB 10:296; LJ 60:304; Mahony 3:200)

BIANCO, Margery (Winifred) Williams. *Poor Cecco: the Wonderful Story of a Wonderful Wooden Dog Who Was the Jolliest Toy in the House Until He Went Out to Explore the World.*
See Chapter 11, Toy Fantasy.

BIANCO, Margery (Winifred) Williams. *The Velveteen Rabbit; or, How Toys Became Real.*
See Chapter 11, Toy Fantasy.

BIEGEL, Paul. *The King of the Copper Mountains.*
See Chapter 1, Allegorical Fantasy and Literary Fairy Tales.

2-50 **BIRNEY, Betty G.** *The World According to Humphrey.* Gr. 2–5.
Weekend visits to the homes of students and school staff members entertain Humphrey, Room 26's classroom hamster, and partially make up for the fact that the teacher, Mrs. Brisbane, dislikes him.
Putnam, 2004, 136 pp. (0-399-24198-1)
(BL 100:1188; CCBB 57:316; Kirkus 72:33; SLJ Apr 2004 p. 102)

2-51 **BLACKWOOD, Algernon (Henry).** *The Adventures of Dudley and Gilderoy.* Gr. 1–4. (Orig. British and U.S. title: *Dudley and Gilderoy: A Nonsense*, 1929.)
An aristocratic parrot and a ginger cat travel to London in search of adventure.
Adapt. by Marion Cothren, illus. by Feodor Rojankovsky, Dutton, 1941, 32 pp., o.p.
(BL 26:159; HB 17:99; TLS 1929 p. 1030)

2-52 **BLAISDELL, Mary Frances.** *Bunny Rabbit's Diary.* Gr. 2–4. (Orig. pub. 1915.)
Eight tales about Bunny Rabbit and his friends, as recorded by Bunny Rabbit in his maple-leaf book.
Illus. by Anne Jauss, Little, Brown, 1960 (rev. ed.), 92 pp., o.p.
(Kirkus 28:29; LJ 85:2025; Mahony 2:162)

2-53 **BLATHWAYT, Benedict.** *Stories from Firefly Island.* Gr. 2–4. (Orig.
☆ British pub. 1992.)
Storyteller Tortoise explains the mysteries of life to the other animal inhabitants of Firefly Island.
Illus. by the author, Greenwillow, 1993, 120 pp. (0-688-12487-9)
(BL 90:935; HBG 5:73; Kirkus 61:1269; SLJ Dec 1993 p. 80)

BLISS, Corinne Demas. *Matthew's Meadow.*
See Chapter 1, Allegorical Fantasy and Literary Fairy Tales.

BLUNT, Wilfrid (Jasper Walter). *Omar; a Fantasy for Animal Lovers.*
See Chapter 8, Humorous Fantasy.

2-54 **BODECKER, N(iels) M(ogens).** *The Mushroom Center Disaster.* Gr. 2–4.
When the insect inhabitants of Mushroom Center find their peaceful community threatened by littering humans, William Beetle creates a Garbage Emergency Plan to recycle the debris.
Illus. by Erik Blegvad, Atheneum, 1974, 48 pp., o.p.
(BL 70:1054; CCBB 28:24; Kirkus 42:421; LJ 99:1464)

2-55 **BOND, (Thomas) Michael.** *A Bear Called Paddington.* **(Paddington Bear**
⋆⋆ **series, bk. 1).** Gr. 3–5. (Orig. British pub. 1958.)
The Brown family decides to adopt a little Peruvian bear they find at Paddington railroad station, but life with Paddington isn't always easy. The sequels are *Paddington Helps Out* (1961, 1999), *More About Paddington* (1962, 1997, pap., 2001), *Paddington at Large* (1963, 1998), *Paddington Marches On* (1965), *Paddington at Work* (1967, 2001), *Paddington Goes to Town* (1968, 2000), *Paddington Takes the Air* (1971, 2003), *Paddington Abroad* (1972), *Paddington's Garden* (Random, 1973), *Paddington at the Circus* (Random, 1974), *Paddington's Lucky Day* (1974), *Paddington Takes to TV* (1974, 2000), *Paddington on Top* (1975, 2001), *Paddington on Stage* (1977), *Paddington at the Seaside* (Random, 1978), *Paddington at the Tower* (Random, 1978), *Paddington Takes the Test* (1980, 2002), and *Paddington on Screen* (1982). *Paddington's Storybook* (1984) and *Paddington Treasury* (1999) are collections of stories from the original books. *Paddington Bear at the Circus* (2000) and *Paddington Bear in the Garden* (2002) are picture-book versions of Paddington stories. The British sequels are *The Adventures of Paddington, Fun and Games with Paddington, Paddington Does It Himself, Paddington Goes Shopping, Paddington Goes to the Sales, Paddington Hits Out, Paddington in the Kitchen*, and *Paddington's Birthday Party.*
Illus. by Peggy Fortnum, Houghton, 1960, 128 pp., o.p.; Houghton, 1998 (0-395-92951-2), 2001, pap. (0-618-15071-4)
(BL 80:95; CCBB 14:106; HB 37:53; Kirkus 28:676; LJ 85:3856; Suth:42; TLS Nov 21, 1958 p. xiv)

2-56 **BOND, (Thomas) Michael.** *Here Comes Thursday.* **(Thursday Mouse series, bk. 1).** Gr. 3–5. (Orig. British pub. 1966.)
The "Help Yourself" sign posted by Thursday Mouse almost puts his family's store out of business. The sequels are *Thursday Rides Again* (1969), *Thursday Ahoy!* (1970), and *Thursday in Paris* (British).
Illus. by Daphne Rowles, Lothrop, 1967, 126 pp., o.p.
(BL 64:541; CCBB 21:106; HB 43:748; Kirkus 35:1204; LJ 93:1301; TLS 1966 p. 1087)

2-57 **BOND, (Thomas) Michael.** *Tales of Olga Da Polga.* **(Olga Da Polga series,**
⋆ **bk. 1).** Gr. 3–5. (Orig. British pub. 1971.)
Olga the guinea pig thinks very highly of herself, especially after she wins a pet show prize: Fattest Guinea Pig in the Show. The sequels are *Olga Meets Her Match* (Hastings, 1975), *Olga Carries On* (Hastings, 1977), *Olga Counts Her*

Blessings (EMC, 1977, pap.), *Olga Makes a Friend* (EMC, 1977, pap.), *Olga Makes Her Mark* (EMC, 1977, pap.), *Olga Takes a Bite* (EMC, 1977, pap.), *Olga's New Home* (EMC, 1977, pap.), *Olga's Second Home* (EMC, 1977, pap.), *Olga's Special Day* (EMC, 1977, pap.), *Olga Makes a Wish* (EMC, 1977, pap.), and *The Complete Adventures of Olga Da Polga* (Delacorte, 1983). Illus. by Hans Helweg, Macmillan, 1972, 1989, 113 pp., o.p.

(BL 69:987, 70:826; CCBB 27:38; HB 49:268; Kirkus 41:60, 1349; LJ 98:1384; SLJ Feb 1989 p. 118; Suth 2:52)

2-58 BOS, Burny. *Meet the Molesons.* Gr. 2–3. (Orig. Swiss pub. 1994.)
The five members of the Moleson mole family lead ordinary lives, but their activities never seem to go as planned. The sequels are *More from the Molesons* (1995), *Leave It to the Molesons!* (1995), and *Fun with the Molesons* (2000). Trans. by J. Alison James, illus. by Hans de Beer, North-South, 1994, 46 pp. (1-55858-257-6)

(BL 90:2042; HBG 5:299; SLJ June 1994 p. 96)

2-59 BOSHINSKI, Blanche. *Aha and the Jewel of Mystery.* Gr. 4–6.
Self-centered Aha the cat learns the value of friendship after he is rescued by an Egyptian slave who is searching for his true identity.
Illus. by Shirley Pulido, Parents, 1968, 155 pp., o.p.

(HB 45:168; LJ 94:868)

BOYLE, Kay. *The Youngest Camel.*
See Chapter 1, Allegorical Fantasy and Literary Fairy Tales.

2-60 BRANFORD, Henrietta. *Fire, Bed, and Bone.* Gr. 5–9. (Orig. British pub.
☆   1997.)
A nameless old hunting hound narrates this story of life in 14th-century England, detailing the difficulties her master's family faces during the 1381 Peasant Revolt. Nestlé Smarties Book Prize, Bronze Award, 1997.
Candlewick, 1998, 122 pp. (0-7636-0338-4)

(BL 894:1240; CCBB 51:314; HBG 9:326; Kliatt July 1998 p. 4; SLJ May 1998 p. 138; VOYA 21:282)

2-61 BRENNER, Barbara (Johnes). *Hemi: A Mule.* Gr. 4–6.
Hemionus, ex-farm mule and official mascot of West Point, runs away from army life to look for the farmhand who once befriended him.
Illus. by J(effrey) Winslow Higginbottom, Harper, 1973, 120 pp., o.p.

(BL 70:539; Kirkus 41:1263; LJ 98:3142)

BRENTANO, Clemens Maria. *The Tale of Gockel, Hinkel and Gackeliah.*
See Chapter 1, Allegorical Fantasy and Literary Fairy Tales.

2-62 BRIGGS, Anita. *Hobart.* Gr. 2–4.
Violet, Byron, Wilfred, and Hobart pig run away from their farmyard home to perfect their artistry in acrobatics, poetry, singing, and tap dancing, and to avoid being sent to the butcher.
Illus. by Mary (Yoma, née Grigson) Rayner, Simon, 2002, 57 pp. (0-689-84129-9)

(BL 98:1525; CCBB 55:356; HBG 13:355; Kirkus 70:563; SLJ June 2002 p. 88)

2-63   BRO, Margueritte (Harmon). *The Animal Friends of Peng-U.* Gr. 1–4.
Chickens, a fox, and a rabbit help farmer Peng-U find a wife.
Illus. by Seong Moy, Doubleday, 1965, 96 pp., o.p.
(BL 61:956; HB 41:274; Kirkus 33:173)

2-64   BROOKS, Walter Rollin. *Freddy Goes to Florida.* **(Freddy the Pig series,**
✰   **bk. 1).** Gr. 4–6. (Orig. title *To and Again,* 1927; British title *Freddy's First*
Adventure.)
Charles the Rooster suggests migration to avoid the cold, and Freddy the Pig
goes along with the other farmyard animals. The other books in this series are
Freddy Goes to the North Pole (1951, 2001; orig. title: *More To and Again,*
1930), *Freddy the Detective* (1932, 1987, 1997), *The Story of Freginald* (1936,
2003), *The Clockwork Twin* (1937, 2003), *Freddy the Politician* (1948, 1986,
2000; orig. title: *Wiggins for President,* 1939), *Freddy's Cousin Weedly* (1940,
2002), *Freddy and the Ignormus* (1941, 1998, Penguin, pap. 2001), *Freddy and*
the Perilous Adventure (1942, 1986), *Freddy and the Bean Home News* (1943,
2000), *Freddy and Mr. Camphor* (1944, 2000, 2003), *Freddy and the Popinjay*
(1945, 2001), *Freddy the Pied Piper* (1946, 2002), *Freddy the Magician* (1947,
2002), *Freddy Goes Camping* (1948, 1986), *Freddy Plays Football* (1949,
2000), *Freddy Rides Again* (1951, 2002), *Freddy the Cowboy* (1951, 1987),
Freddy and Freginald (1952), *Freddy the Pilot* (1952, 1986, 1999), *Collected*
Poems of Freddy the Pig (1953, 2001), *Freddy and the Space Ship* (1953,
2001), *Freddy and the Men from Mars* (1954, 2000), *Freddy and the Baseball*
Team from Mars (1955, 1987, 1998), *Freddy and the Dragon* (1955, 2003),
Freddy and Simon the Dictator (1956, 2003), and *Freddy and the Flying*
Saucer Plans (1958, 1998). *The Freddy Anniversary Collection* (Overlook,
2002) contains *Freddy Goes to Florida, Freddy Goes to the North Pole,* and
Freddy the Detective.
Illus. by Kurt Wiese, Knopf, 1949, 196 pp., o.p.; Overlook, 1997 (0-87951-
808-1)
(BL 24:30, 45:248; Bookshelf 1933 p. 8; CCBB 2:1; HB 3:46, 3:11, 7:116, 25:115; HBG
9:68; Kirkus 17:58; LJ 74:559; Mahony 2:112; TLS 1927 p. 883)

2-65   BROOME, Errol. *Magnus Maybe.* Gr. 2–4. (Orig. Australian pub. 1998.)
After shy Magnus, a pet white mouse, nibbles a hole in his cage and escapes, he
discovers a new world of wild mice.
Illus. by Ann James, Simon, 2002, pap., 144 pp. (0-7434-3796-9)
(BL 98:1955; SLJ Aug 2002 p. 147)

2-66   BROWN, Palmer. *Hickory.* Gr. 3–5.
Hickory the field mouse's youthful home inside a grandfather clock does not
prepare him for life in the fields, but a friendly grasshopper helps him to over-
come his loneliness.
Illus. by the author, Harper, 1978, 42 pp., o.p.
(HB 55:513; Kirkus 46:1137; SLJ Sep 1978 p. 104)

2-67   BROWN, Rita Mae, and BROWN, Sneaky Pie. *Wish You Were Here.*
(Mrs. Murphy Mystery series, bk. 1). Gr. 10 up.
Small town postmistress Mary ("Harry") Haristeen, her unusually intelligent
gray tiger cat, Mrs. Murphy, and her Welsh corgi, Tee Tucker, solve a number

of grisly murders, each preceded by a strange postcard. The sequels are *Rest in Pieces* (1992, 1993), *Murder at Monticello, or, Old Sins* (1994, 1995), *Pay Dirt, or, Adventures at Ash Lawn* (1995, 1996), *Murder, She Meowed* (1996, 1998), *Murder on the Prowl* (1998, 1999), *Cat on the Scent* (1999, 2000), *Pawing Through the Past* (2000, 2001), *Claws and Effect* (2001, 2002), *Catch as Cat Can* (2002, 2003), *Tail of the Tip-Off* (2003), and *Whisker of Evil* (2004). Illus. by Wendy Wray, Bantam, 1990, 243 pp., o.p.

(BL 87:258, 321; Kirkus 58:1269; LJ Nov 1, 1990 p. 128; SLJ Apr 1991 p. 153)

BUCHWALD, Art. *The Bollo Caper: A Fable for All Ages.*
See Chapter 8, Humorous Fantasy.

2-68   BUCHWALD, Emilie. *Floramel and Esteban.* Gr. 3–5.
Lonely Floramel, a Caribbean cow, gets all her news from her friend Esteban, a cattle egret. After she learns to play music on conch shells, the president makes her a National Treasure.
Illus. by Charles Robinson, Harcourt, 1982, 72 pp., o.p.

(BL 79:976; CCBB 36:3; SLJ Sep 1982 p. 104)

2-69   BUCHWALD, Emilie. *Gildaen: The Heroic Adventures of a Most Unusual*
☆   *Rabbit.* Gr. 4–6.
Gildaen Rabbit sets out on a quest to save the kingdom and to restore the memory of his friend, who is transformed from an owl to a prince to a peasant woman.
Illus. by Barbara Flynn, Harcourt, 1973, 189 pp., o.p.; Milkweed, 1993, 184 pp. (0-915943-38-7)

(BL 69:1019; CCBB 26:167; HBG 5:307; Kirkus 41:455; LJ 98:2191; Suth 2:63)

2-70   BURGESS, Thornton W(aldo). *Old Mother West Wind.* **(Mother West Wind series, bk. 1).** Gr. 2–4. (Orig. pub. 1910.)
Tales of Johnny Chuck, Reddy Fox, and the other animals living near the Green Meadows, the Smiling Pool, the Laughing Brook, and the Lone Little Path through the woods. Other books in the series are *Mother West Wind's Children* (1911; Little, 1962), *Mother West Wind's Animal Friends* (1912; Grosset, 1940), *Mother West Wind's Neighbors* (1913; Little, 1968), *The Adventures of Johnny Chuck* (1913; Grosset, 1952), *The Adventures of Reddy Fox* (1913; Grosset, 1950), *Mother West Wind's "Why" Stories* (1915; Grosset, 1941), *Mother West Wind's "How" Stories* (1916; Grosset, 1941), *The Adventures of Buster Bear* (1916; Grosset, 1941), *Mother West Wind's "When" Stories* (1917; Grosset, 1941), *Mother West Wind's "Where" Stories* (1918; Grosset, 1941), *The Adventures of Old Granny Fox* (Grosset, 1943), *The Adventures of Lightfoot the Deer* (Grosset, 1944), *The Adventures of Whitefoot the Wood-mouse* (Grosset, 1944), *The Adventures of Chatterer the Red Squirrel* (Grosset, 1949), *The Adventures of Prickly Porky* (Grosset, 1949), *The Adventures of Sammy Jay* (Grosset, 1949), *The Adventures of Danny Meadowmouse* (Grosset, 1950), *The Adventures of Peter Cottontail* (Grosset, 1950), *The Adventures of Jerry Muskrat* (Grosset, 1951), *The Adventures of Unc' Billy Possum* (Grosset, 1951), *The Adventures of Grandfather Frog* (Grosset, 1952), *The Adventures of Old Man Coyote* (Grosset, 1952), *The Adventures of Poor Mrs. Quack* (Grosset, 1953), *The Adventures of Bob White* (Grosset, 1954), *The Adventures of*

Bobby Coon (Grosset, 1954), *The Adventures of Jimmy Skunk* (Grosset, 1954), and *The Adventures of Ol' Mistah Buzzard* (Grosset, 1957).
Illus. by Harrison Cady, Little, Brown, 1960, 1985, 140 pp., o.p., 1985, pap. (0-316-11655-6); illus. by Harrison Cady and George Kerr, Grossett, 1976, o.p.; illus. by Harrison Cady, Grossett, 1990 (entitled *Thornton W. Burgess Animal Tales*), 96 pp., o.p.; illus. by Michael (R.) Hague, Holt, 1990, 90 pp., o.p.; Holt, 2003, 96 pp. (0-8050-7238-1)
(BL 7:168, 86:1976; HB 36:526; HBG 1:234)

2-71 **BURMAN, Ben Lucien.** *High Water at Catfish Bend.* **(Catfish Bend series, bk. 1).** Gr. 5–7.
The animals of Catfish Bend persuade the Army Corps of Engineers to build levees along the Mississippi River. The sequels are *Seven Stars for Catfish Bend* (1956, 1977), *The Owl Hoots Twice at Catfish Bend* (1961, 1977), *Blow a Wild Bugle for Catfish Bend* (1967, 1979), and *High Treason at Catfish Bend* (Vanguard, 1977). A collection called *Three from Catfish Bend* was published by Taplinger in 1967.
Illus. by Alice Caddy, Messner, 1952, 121 pp., o.p.
(BL 48:344; HB 28:174; Kirkus 20:224; LJ 77:1018)

2-72 **BUTTERS, Dorothy G(ilman).** *Papa Dolphin's Table.* Gr. 4–6.
It was crowded enough in the Dolphins' apartment without the enormous table Papa brought home.
Illus. by Kurt Werth, Knopf, 1955, 88 pp., o.p.
(BL 52:171; CCBB 9:82; Eakin:56; Kirkus 23:597; LJ 80:2640)

2-73 **BUZZATI, Dino.** *The Bears' Famous Invasion of Sicily.* Gr. 4–6.
King Leander's bear army conquers the island of Sicily.
Illus. by the author, trans. by Frances Lobb, Pantheon, 1947, 146 pp., o.p.; illus. by the author, trans. by Frances Lobb, New York Review of Books, 2003, 148 pp. (1-59017-076-8); HarperCollins, 2005, pap., 192 pp. (0-06-072608-3)
(BL 44:189; CCBB 1:2; HB 24:36; Kirkus 15:625; LJ 72:1473)

2-74 **BYARS, Betsy (Cromer).** *Little Horse.* Gr. 1–4.
☆ Miniature Little Horse falls into a river and is swept away into the dangerous human-sized world. The sequel is *Little Horse on His Own* (2004).
Illus. by (Michael) David McPhail, Holt, 2002, 454 pp. (0-8050-6413-3)
(BL 98:1255; CCBB 55:357; HB 78:325; HBG 13:355; Kirkus 70:407; SLJ Apr 2002 p. 101)

2-75 **CAIRE, Helen.** *Señor Castillo, Cock of the Island.* Gr. 3–4.
Castillo the old rooster boards a fishing boat to fulfill his dream of seeing the sea.
Illus. by Christine Price, Rinehart, 1948, 76 pp., o.p.
(HB 24:195; LJ 73:604, 656)

CALLANDER, Don. *Aquamancer.*
See Chapter 12, Witchcraft and Sorcery Fantasy.

2-76 **CAMPBELL, Hope.** *Peter's Angel: A Story About Monsters.* Gr. 3–5. (Pap. title: *The Monster's Room.*)

After the monster posters in Peter's room come to life, his two mouse friends decide that an angel is needed to exorcise the creatures.
Illus. by Lilian Obligado, Four Winds, 1976, 151 pp., o.p.; (entitled *The Monster's Room*) Scholastic, 1979, pap., o.p.
(BL 72:1525; Kirkus 44:467; SLJ Sep 1976 p. 112)

CARLSON, Natalie Savage. *Alphonse, That Bearded One.*
See Chapter 8, Humorous Fantasy.

2-77 **CARLSON, Natalie Savage.** *Evangeline, Pigeon of Paris.* Gr. 4–6. (British
☆ title: *Pigeon of Paris.*)
Evangeline and her mate, Gabriel, become separated when the Paris chief of police orders all pigeons trapped and deported.
Illus. by Nicolas Mordvinoff, Harcourt, 1960, 72 pp., o.p.
(BL 56:632; HB 36:215; Kirkus 28:184; LJ 85:2475)

CARRIS, Joan Davenport. *Witch-Cat.*
See Chapter 12, Witchcraft and Sorcery Fantasy.

2-78 **CARTER, Angela.** *Sea-Cat and Dragon King.* Gr. 2–4. (Orig. British pub.
2001.)
Captured by the Dragon King, ruler of the sea, because of his beautiful seaweed suit, young Sea-Cat suggests that his mother knit a dragon-sized suit for the king.
Illus. by Eva Tatcheva, Bloomsbury, 2002, 96 pp. (1-58234-768-9)
(BL 98:1955; CCBB 55:877; Kirkus 70:877; SLJ Apr 1995 p. 100)

2-79 **CARTER, Robert.** *The Collectors.* Gr. 6–8. (Orig. pub. in Australia.)
After rebellious Edwud K. challenges the rigid organization of his insect colony, he and his friends go on an adventure-filled quest to search for the legendary moonocal.
Lothrop, 1994, 288 pp. (0-688-13763-6)
(BL 91:491; CCBB 48:82; HBG 6:73; SLJ Sep 1994 p. 238)

2-80 **CASSERLEY, Anne Thomasine.** *Barney the Donkey.* Gr. 3–5.
Twelve humorous tales about a mischievous Irish donkey,
Illus. by the author, Harper, 1938, 145 pp., o.p.
(BL 34:304; HB 14:163; LJ 63:385)

2-81 **CASSERLEY, Anne Thomasine.** *Roseen.* Gr. 2–4.
Twelve Irish tales about a little black pig named Roseen, a wild goat, Brock the badger, and Kerry the cow. The sequel is *Brian of the Mountain* (1931).
Illus. by the author, Harper, 1929, 152 pp., o.p.
(BL 26:165; HB 5:44–45, 49, 7:115; Mahony 3:105)

CASSERLEY, Anne Thomasine. *The Whins on Knockattan.*
See Chapter 3, Fantasy Collections.

2-82 **CAUFIELD, Don, and CAUFIELD, Joan.** *The Incredible Detectives.* Gr.
4–6.
Reginald Bulldog, Madam Chang the Siamese cat, and Hennessy Crow solve their master's mysterious kidnapping.

Illus. by Kiyo Komoda, Harper, 1966, 75 pp., o.p.

(CCBB 20:71; HB 42:708; Kirkus 343:830; LJ 91:5771; Suth:67)

2-83   **CAZET, Denys.** *Saturday.* Gr. 2–3.

Barney spends a few days visiting his grandparents, the Spanielsons, who love him in spite of the mischief he causes. The sequel is *Sunday* (1988).

Illus. by the author, Bradbury, 1985, 60 pp., o.p.

(BL 82:402; CCBB 39:3; SLJ Nov 1985 p. 67)

CHAN, Gillian. *The Carved Box.*

See Chapter 6, High Fantasy: Myth or Legend Fantasy.

CHASE, Mary (Coyle). *Harvey, a Play.*

See Chapter 8, Humorous Fantasy.

2-84   **CHEKHOV, Anton.** *Kashtanka.* Gr. 3–5. (Orig. Russian pub. 1889.)

★   Accidentally separated from her master, a dog named Kashtanka is adopted by a circus clown and the pig, goose, and cat who perform in his act.

Trans. by Richard Pevear, illus. by Barry Moser, Putnam, 1991, 48 pp. (0-399-21905-6)

(CCBB 45:85; HBG 3:63; Kirkus 59:1468; SLJ Nov 1991 p. 116)

2-85   **CHENOWETH, Russ.** *Shadow Walkers.* Gr. 5–7.

Brother and sister water rats Peter and Sara travel across Cape Cod to deliver insulin to needy relatives.

Macmillan, 1993, 176 pp. (0-684-19447-3)

(BL 89:1965; HBG 4:295; Kirkus 61:526; SLJ May 1993 p. 103)

2-86   **CHOCOLATE, Debbie.** *Pigs Can Fly! The Adventures of Harriet Pig and Friends.* Gr. 2–4.

Four tales about Harriet the potbellied pig, who stars as a flying fairy in her school play, competes in a swimming contest, helps a friend who is afraid of heights, and nearly drives another friend to distraction.

Illus. by Leslie Tryon, Cricket, 2004, 64 pp. (0-8126-2706-7)

(BL 100:161; Kirkus 72:219; SLJ May 2004 p. 108)

CHRISTIAN, Mary Blount. *Sebastian (Super-Sleuth) and the Crummy Yummies Caper.*

See Chapter 8, Humorous Fantasy.

CHRISTOPHER, Matt(hew F.). *The Dog That Stole Football Plays.*

See Chapter 9, Magic Adventure Fantasy.

2-87   **CLARK, Ann Nolan.** *Looking-for-Something: The Story of a Stray Burro of Ecuador.* Gr. 1–4.

Grey Burro searches for someone to belong to.

Illus. by Leo Politi, Viking, 1952, 53 pp., o.p.

(BL 48:236; HB 28:96; Kirkus 20:123; LJ 77:725)

2-88   CLEARY, Beverly (Bunn). *The Mouse and the Motorcycle.* **(Ralph S.**
★★   **Mouse series, bk. 1).** Gr. 2–4.
A boy named Keith shows a mouse named Ralph the joys of cycling on a toy
motorcycle. The sequels are *Runaway Ralph* (1970; Avon, pap., 1991) and
Ralph S. Mouse (1982; Avon, 1993, pap.). *Ralph S. Mouse* won the Golden
Kite Award in 1982.
Illus. by Louis Darling, Morrow, 1965, 158 pp., LB (0-688-31698-0); Avon,
1990, pap. (0-380-70924-4)
(BL 62:270; CCBB 19:60; Eakin:76; HB 41:628; Kirkus 33:905; LJ 90:5510)

2-89   CLEARY, Beverly (Bunn). *Socks.* Gr. 3–5.
The Brickers' new baby deprives a kitten named Socks of the family's undivid-
ed attention.
Illus. by Beatrice Darwin, Morrow, 1973, 160 pp., o.p.
(CCBB 27:23; Kirkus 41:599; LJ 98:2185)

2-90   CLEMENT, Aeron. *The Cold Moons.* Gr. 10 up. (Orig. British pub. 1988.)
A clan of badgers flees threatened extermination toward a safe haven called
Elysia.
Delacorte, 1989, 336 pp., o.p.
(BL 85:898, 899; Kirkus 57:142; LJ Mar 15, 1989 p. 84; SLJ Nov 1989 p. 136, Dec 1990 p.
216; VOYA 12:273)

2-91   CLEMENT-DAVIES, David. *Fire Bringer.* Gr. 7 up. (Orig. British pub.
★   1999.)
Born with the mark of an oak leaf on his forehead, young Rannoch escapes with
a small band of other deer from the dreaded stag Drail and his minions, gaining
time to mature before he and his friends return to battle Drail to the death.
Dutton, 2000, 512 pp. (0-525-46492-1); Pan Macmillan, 2000, pap., 560 pp., o.p.
(BL 97:114, 692, 1561; HB 77:89; HBG 12:82; Kirkus 68:1353; SLJ Dec 2000 p. 142; VOYA
23:272, 24:10)

2-92   CLEMENT-DAVIES, David. *The Sight.* Gr. 6 up. (Orig. British pub. 2001.)
★   Two young wolf cub siblings live out a fearsome prophecy involving the outcast Mongra, whose powers force other wolves to give her their newborn cubs
in this dark story set in Transylvania.
Dutton, 2002, 465 pp. (0-525-46723-8); Firebird, 2003, pap., 480 pp. (0-14-
250047-X)
(BL 98:1133, 1417; CCBB 55:274; HB 78:455; HBG 13:389; Kirkus 70:251; Kliatt Mar 2002
p. 7; SLJ June 2002 p. 134; VOYA 25:125)

2-93   CLIFFORD, Eth. *Flatfoot Fox and the Case of the Missing Eye.* **(Flatfoot**
Fox Mystery series, bk. 1). Gr. 1–4.
Fat Cat's glass eye is missing, and the smartest detective in the world, Flatfoot
Fox, is called in to crack the case. The sequels are *Flatfoot Fox and the Case of
the Noisy Otter* (1992), *Flatfoot Fox and the Case of the Missing Whoooo*
(1993), *Flatfoot Fox and the Case of the Bashful Beaver* (1995), and *Flatfoot
Fox and the Case of the Missing Schoolhouse* (1997).
Illus. by Brian Lies, Houghton, 1990, 48 pp., o.p.; Scholastic, 1992, pap. (0-
590-45812-4)
(BL 87:861; HBG 2:69; SLJ Mar 1991 p. 170)

2-94   **CLIFFORD, Sandy.** *The Roquefort Gang.* Gr. 2–4.
Nicole mouse joins forces with the Roquefort Gang to rescue hundreds of mice
destined for laboratory experiments.
Illus. by the author, Parnassus, 1981, 79 pp., o.p.
(BL 77:1251; CCBB 34:189; Kirkus 49:283; SLJ Apr 1981 p. 122)

2-95   **CLINE, Linda.** *The Miracle Season.* Gr. 10 up.
Crow discovers that mercury poisoning is the cause of his friends' mysterious
deaths.
Berkley, 1976, 182 pp., o.p.
(Kirkus 44:748; Kliatt 11:4; LJ 101:2084; SLJ Dec 1976 p. 74)

2-96   **COATES, Anna.** *Dog Magic.* Gr. 3–6.
Matt and Katie's dog, Toby, tells them that his pups have been adopted by
someone bad, and they find the pups in an illegal cosmetics-testing laboratory.
Bantam, 1991, pap., 135 pp. (0-553-15910-0)
(BL 88:829; SLJ Jan 1992, p. 108)

2-97   **COATSWORTH, Elizabeth (Jane).** *The Cat and the Captain.* Gr. 2–4.
★   (Orig. pub. 1927.)
The captain's cat saves his master's house from burglary and earns a place in
the housekeeper's heart.
Illus. by Bernice Loewenstein, Macmillan, 1974, 95 pp., o.p.
(BL 24:210; CCBB 28:40; HB 3:12, 28:421, 50:395; Kirkus 42:364; LJ 53:484, 99:2242)

COATSWORTH, Elizabeth (Jane). *The Cat Who Went to Heaven.*
See Chapter 1, Allegorical Fantasy and Literary Fairy Tales.

COATSWORTH, Elizabeth (Jane). *The Enchanted: An Incredible Tale.*
See Chapter 6, High Fantasy: Myth or Legend Fantasy.

COATSWORTH, Elizabeth (Jane). *Pure Magic.*
See Chapter 1, Allegorical Fantasy and Literary Fairy Tales.

COBLENTZ, Catherine Cate. *The Blue Cat of Castle Town.*
See Chapter 9, Magic Adventure Fantasy.

2-98   **COLE, Joanna, and CALMENSON, Stephanie.** *The Gator Girls.* Gr. 2–4.
Best friends Allie and Amy Gator try to fit all their summer plans into the few
days before Allie leaves for overnight camp. The sequels are *Rockin' Reptiles*
(1997) and *Get Well, Gators!* (1998).
Illus. by Lynn Munsinger, Morrow, 1995, 89 pp. (0-688-12120-9)
(BL 91:1497; HBG 6:290; SLJ Apr 1997 p. 91)

2-99   **COLEMAN, Janet Wyman.** *Fast Eddie.* Gr. 3–6.
Fast Eddie Raccoon's friends—a squirrel, dog, and cat—try to save him from
the wrath of Mr. Plotkin, whose family has intruded into raccoon territory.
Illus. by Alec Gillman, Macmillan, 1993, 144 pp., o.p.
(HBG 4:296; Kirkus 61:595; SLJ June 1993 p. 104)

2-100 **COLOMA, Padre Luis.** *Perez, the Mouse.* Gr. 1–4. (Orig. pub. in Spain;
orig. U.S. pub. 1915.)

King Bube and Perez the Mouse travel throughout the kingdom.
Adapt. by Lady Moreton, illus. by George Howard Vyse, Dodd, 1950, 63 pp.,
o.p.
(BL 46:206; HB 26:99, 112; Mahony 2:112)

2-101 COLUM, Padraic. *The Boy Who Knew What the Birds Said.* Gr. 3–5.
After an old crow teaches a boy how to speak with the birds, each has a story to
tell him.
Illus. by Dugald Stewart Walker, Macmillan, 1918, 176 pp., o.p.
(BL 15:113; HB 1:30; Mahony 1:39)

2-102 COLUM, Padraic. *Where the Winds Never Blew and the Cocks Never Crew.* Gr. 3–5.
Tibbie the cat and seven other animals live peacefully by an old woman's
hearth until a beautiful swan's song lures each of them away.
Illus. by Richard Bennett, Macmillan, 1940, 96 pp., o.p.
(BL 37:157; HB 16:429, 17:31)

2-103 COLUM, Padraic. *The White Sparrow.* Gr. 3–5. (Orig. British pub. 1933,
entitled *Sparrow Alone.*)
Rescued from a street vendor, Jimmy the sparrow goes to work for a crocodile.
Illus. by Joseph Low, McGraw-Hill, 1972, 61 pp., o.p.
(BL 29:344; Bookshelf 1933 p. 6; Kirkus 40:1097; LJ 58:805, 98:259)

2-104 CONLY, Jane Leslie. *Racso and the Rats of NIMH.* **(The Rats of NIMH**
☆ **series, bk. 2).** Gr. 5–8.
Two young rodents, Timothy Frisby mouse and Racso rat, meet on their way to
begin their education with the rats of NIMH, and quickly become involved in
the rats' plan to destroy the dam that threatens their valley. This is the sequel to
Robert C. O'Brien's *Mrs Frisby and the Rats of NIMH* (1971, 1999; see this
chapter). Jane Conly is Robert C. O'Brien's daughter. In Conly's second
sequel, *R-T, Margaret, and the Rats of NIMH* (1990, 1991), Artie and Margaret, two human children lost in the North Woods, are rescued by Christopher
Rat, and soon become involved in the lives of the residents of Thorn Valley.
Illus. by Leonard Lubin, Harper, 1986, 278 pp. (0-06-021362-0); Harper-
Collins, 1988, pap., 288 pp. (0-06-440245-2)
(BL 82:1458; 83:794, 84:1441; CCBB 39:182; HB 62:588; SLJ Apr 1986 p. 85; TLS 1986 p.
1042; VOYA 9:86, 10:23)

2-105 COOK, Glen. *Doomstalker.* **(Darkwar trilogy, vol. 1).** Gr. 10 up.
Marika, a young female member of an intelligent, canine-like race, survives the
massacre of her tribe by nomads only to be captured by Silth Witches who want
to use her psychic powers for their own battles with the nomads. The sequels
are *Warlock* (1985) and *Ceremony* (1986).
Warner, 1985, pap., 272 pp., o.p.
(BL 82:31, 52; VOYA 8:393)

COOPER, Paul Fenimore. *Tal: His Marvelous Adventures with Noom-
Zor-Noom.*
See Chapter 7, High Fantasy: Travel to Other Worlds.

2-106 CORBETT, W(illiam) J(esse). *The Song of Pentecost.* Gr. 5–9. (Orig.
✭ British pub. 1982.)
A clan of harvest mice and their leader, Pentecost, leave their polluted home in
search of utopia and truth. Whitbread Literary Award, Children's Book Catego-
ry, 1982. The sequel is *Pentecost and the Chosen One* (1987).
Illus. by Martin Ursell, Dutton, 1983, 216 pp., o.p.
(BL 79:1463, 84:1441; CCBB 37:3; HB 59:450; SLJ Aug 1983 p. 63; TLS 1982 p. 1302)

CORDER, Zizou (pseud. of Louisa Young and Isabel Adomakoh Young).
Lionboy.
See Chapter 9, Magic Adventure Fantasy.

2-107 CREGAN, Maírín. *Old John.* Gr. 4–6. (Orig. pub. in Ireland.)
A fairy doctor disguised as a cat comes to live with the old shoemaker of Tir
Aulin.
Illus. by Helen Sewell, Macmillan, 1936, 184 pp., o.p.
(BL 32:330; HB 12:153; LJ 61:457, 809)

2-108 CROCKER, Carter. *The Tale of the Swamp Rat.* Gr. 4–8.
✭ After his family is eaten by a rattlesnake named Mr. Took, a young swamp rat
named Ossie is taken in by Uncle Will, an ancient alligator who teaches him
how to survive in their Florida swamplands home.
Illus. by the author, Philomel, 2003, 240 pp. (0-399-23964-2)
(BL 100:608; CCBB 57:147; HBG 15:89; Kirkus 71:1172; SLJ Oct 2003 p. 162; VOYA
27:140)

2-109 CROWLEY, Maude. *Azor and the Blue-Eyed Cow: A Christmas Story.*
✭ **(Azor series, bk. 3).** Gr. 1–4.
A young boy named Azor decides to prove the existence of Santa Claus. This is
a sequel to *Azor* (1948) and *Azor and the Haddock* (1949); it is followed by *Tor
and Azor* (1955).
Illus. by Helen Sewell, Walck, 1951, 70 pp., o.p.
(BL 48:70; CCBB 5:13; HB 27:414; Kirkus 19:530; LJ 76:2120)

2-110 CULLEN, Countee (Porter). *The Lost Zoo (A Rhyme for the Young, but
✭ Not Too Young) by Christopher Cat and Countee Cullen.* Gr. 3–6.
Christopher Cat tells a tale in verse about some extraordinary beasts that Noah
forgot to take on his ark. *My Lives and How I Lost Them, by Christopher Cat
and Countee Cullen* (1942, 1964) is Christopher's second literary effort.
Illus. by Joseph Low, Harper, 1940, 95 pp., o.p.; Follett, 1969, 95 pp., o.p.;
illus. by Brian Pinkney, Silver Burdett, 1992, 95 pp., o.p.
(BL 37:292, 66:140; CCBB 23:157, 45:292; HB 45:542, 62:78; LJ 94:4276)

2-111 CUNNINGHAM, Julia (Woolfolk). *Candle Tales.* Gr. 3–4.
Six animals tell a kind old man stories for his birthday,
Illus. by Evaline Ness, Pantheon, 1964, 57 pp., o.p.
(BL 60:876; HB 40:376; Kirkus 32:51; LJ 89:1448)

2-112 CUNNINGHAM, Julia (Woolfolk). *Macaroon.* Gr. 3–5.
Macaroon, a raccoon who spends his winters in children's homes, decides to choose the home of a selfish, surly child one winter, so that it won't be so hard to leave in the spring.
Illus. by Evaline Ness, Pantheon, 1962, 63 pp., o.p.
(BL 59:288; HB 38:480; LJ 87:4266; TLS 1963 p. 980)

2-113 CUNNINGHAM, Julia (Woolfolk). *Maybe, a Mole.* Gr. 3–5.
Five episodes about a mole named Maybe who is rejected by his own kind because he is not blind, but is befriended by a fox, a mouse, and a turtle.
Illus. by Cyndy Szekeres, Pantheon, 1974, 81 pp., o.p.
(BL 71:506; CCBB 28:109; HB 51:51; Kirkus 42:1303)

CUNNINGHAM, Julia (Woolfolk). *OAF.*
See Chapter 1, Allegorical Fantasy and Literary Fairy Tales.

2-114 CUNNINGHAM, Julia (Woolfolk). *Viollet.* Gr. 4–6.
Oxford the dog, Warwicke the fox, and Viollet the thrush band together to save the life of Oxford's master.
Illus. by Alan E. Cober, Pantheon, 1966, 82 pp., o.p.
(CCBB 20:86; Kirkus 34:1054; LJ 91:6190)

2-115 CUNNINGHAM, Julia (Woolfolk). *The Vision of François the Fox.* Gr. 1–4.
François is inspired by a vision to give up his greedy ways and become a saint.
Illus. by Nicholas Angelo, Houghton, 1960, 35 pp., o.p.
(HB 36:406; Kirkus 28:617)

CUNNINGHAM, Julia (Woolfolk). *Wolf Roland.*
See Chapter 1, Allegorical Fantasy and Literary Fairy Tales.

2-116 DAHL, Roald. *Fantastic Mr. Fox.* Gr. 3–5. (Orig. British pub. 1970.)
Mr. Fox, his wife, and four children out-fox three of the meanest and stupidest farmers around.
Illus. by Donald Chaffin, Knopf, 1970, 1986, 72 pp., o.p.; Knopf, 2002, 88 pp. (0-375-82207-0)
(BL 82:1538; CCBB 24:89; HBG 14:77; LJ 96:1106)

DAHL, Roald. *James and the Giant Peach: A Children's Story.*
See Chapter 9, Magic Adventure Fantasy.

DAHL, Roald. *The Twits.*
See Chapter 8, Humorous Fantasy.

DAHL, Tessa. *Gwenda and the Animals.*
See Chapter 9, Magic Adventure Fantasy.

DAHL, Tessa. *School Can Wait.*
See Chapter 8, Humorous Fantasy.

2-117 DALLAS-SMITH, Peter. *Trouble for Trumpets.* Gr. 2–4. (Orig. British pub. 1982.)

Pod, a little animal called a Trumpet, tells the story of the Trumpets' war against the hostile Grumpets. The sequel is *Trumpets in Grumpetland* (1985). Illus. by Peter Cross, Random, 1984, 30 pp., o.p.
(CCBB 38:104; SLJ Jan 1985 p. 73; Suth 3:112)

2-118 DANA, Barbara. *Rutgers and the Watersnouts.* Gr. 3–5.
Rutgers the bulldog and his friends search for more of the prickly creatures he found on the beach.
Illus. by Fred Brenner, Harper, 1969, 149 pp., o.p.
(BL 65:1075; Kirkus 37:53; LJ 94:1324)

2-119 DANA, Barbara. *Zucchini.* Gr. 3–5.
☆   Zucchini, a runaway ferret from the Bronx Zoo, is taken to an ASPCA shelter where he meets Billy, a boy who loves him, and has to choose between escape and a real home. In *Zucchini Out West* (1997) Billy, his family, and Zucchini travel to Wyoming to find out whether he is an endangered black-footed ferret.
Illus. by Eileen Christelow, Harper, 1982, 128 pp., o.p.
(BL 79:443; CCBB 36:64; Kirkus 50:1105; SLJ Oct 1982 p. 150)

2-120 DANN, Colin (Michael). *The Animals of Farthing Wood.* **(White Deer Park series, bk. 1).** **Gr. 7–10.** (Orig. British pub. 1979.)
Led by Fox and Toad, the animal inhabitants of Farthing Wood unite and flee to a safer life in a nature preserve. The British sequels are *Escape from Danger* (1979), *The Way to White Deer Park* (1979), *In the Grip of Winter* (1982), and *Siege of White Deer Park* (1985; U.S. pub. 1986).
Elsevier, 1980, 255 pp., o.p.
(BL 77:110; LJ 105:2104)

DAVIES, Andrew (Wynford). *Marmalade and Rufus.*
See Chapter 8, Humorous Fantasy.

2-121 DAVIS, Mary Gould. *The Handsome Donkey.* Gr. 3–4.
Baldasarre the donkey becomes famous in this story told through the eyes of a dachshund named Tedesco.
Illus. by Emma L(illian) Brock, Harcourt, 1933, 67 pp., o.p.
(BL 30:51; HB 9:205; Mahony 3:242)

2-122 DAVIS, Robert. *Padre Porko: The Gentlemanly Pig.* Gr. 4–6. (Orig. pub. 1939.)
Twelve tales about a pig who helps people and animals in distress.
Illus. by Fritz Eichenberg, Holiday, 1948, 197 pp., o.p.
(BL 36:308; 45:17; CCBB 1:2; HB 24:379; LJ 65:123, 74:134)

DAWNAY, Romayne. *The Champions of Appledore.*
See Chapter 8, Humorous Fantasy.

2-123 DE LA MARE, Walter (John). *Mr. Bumps and His Monkey.* Gr. 4–6. (Orig. British pub. as "The Old Lion" in the children's annual *Joy Street* [1923–1938].)
Jasper the English-speaking monkey is stolen from Mr. Bumps.

Illus. by Dorothy P. Lathrop, Holt, 1942, 69 pp., o.p.
(BL 39:73; HB 18:426; LJ 67:884, 955)

2-124 **DE LA MARE, Walter (John).** *The Three Royal Monkeys.* Gr. 5–7. (Orig.
✰ British title, 1910: *The Three Mula Mulgars.*)
Three Mulgars, or monkeys, search for their father, the prince, using a magic
wonderstone.
Illus. by Mildred Eldridge, Knopf, 1919, 1941, 1948, 1966, 277 pp., o.p.
(BL 45:110; CCBB 2:3; HB 14:143; LJ 74:69; Mahony 2:278)

2-125 **DELANEY, M(ichael) C(lark).** *Birdbrain Amos.* Gr. 2–4.
Kindhearted Amos the hippo hires Kumba the tick bird to eat the bugs that are
bothering him, but can't assert himself when Kumba builds a net on his head
and throws a baby shower on his back.
Illus. by the author, Philomel, 2002, 160 pp. (0-399-23614-7)
(BL 98:1323; CCBB 55:278; HB 78:211; HBG 13:356; Kirkus 70:179; SLJ Apr 2002 p. 103)

DELANEY, M(ichael) C(lark). *Henry's Special Delivery.*
See Chapter 8, Humorous Fantasy.

DE LEEUW, Adele Louise. *Nobody's Doll.*
See Chapter 11, Toy Fantasy.

2-126 **DE LINT, Charles.** *A Circle of Cats.* Gr. 3–5.
Lillian's life is saved by a circle of magical cats who transform her from a girl
into a kitten after she is bitten by a poisonous snake. This story is related to a
tale in de Lint's young adult novel *Seven Wild Sisters* (Subterranean, 2002).
Illus. by Charles Vess, Viking, 2003, 48 pp. (0-670-03647-1)
(CCBB 57:10; HBG 14:353; Kirkus 71:802; SLJ Oct 2003 p. 116)

DE REGNIERS, Beatrice Schenk (Freedman). *The Boy, the Rat, and the
Butterfly.*
See Chapter 9, Magic Adventure Fantasy.

2-127 **DICAMILLO, Kate.** *The Tale of Despereaux: Being the Story of a Mouse,
✰✰ a Princess, Some Soup, and a Spool of Thread.* Gr. 3–6.
Young Despereaux's un-mouselike behavior includes falling in love with a
princess and results in his banishment to a dungeon ruled by killer rats. New-
bery Medal, 2004.
Illus. by Timothy Basil Ering, Candlewick, 2003, 272 pp. (0-7636-1722-9)
(BL 99:1886; CCBB 57:99; HB 79:607; HBG 15:90; Kirkus 71:962; SLJ Aug 2003 p. 126;
VOYA 26:322)

DICKINSON, Peter. *Chuck and Danielle.*
See Chapter 8, Humorous Fantasy.

2-128 **DICKINSON, Peter.** *Time and the Clock Mice, Etcetera.* Gr. 3–5. (Orig.
✰ pub. in England.)
An old clockmaker discovers three families of intelligent mice living inside the
Branton Town Hall clock, a "wonder of the world" built by his grandfather.
Illus. by Emma Chichester Clark, Delacorte, 1994, 128 pp., o.p.
(BL 90:2042; HBG 5:309; Kirkus 62:773; SLJ June 1994 p. 126)

2-129 DIGGS, Lucy. *Selene Goes Home.* Gr. 2–4.
Angry at her owner for moving to a houseboat, a cat named Selene talks a gull into flying her back home, where an unpleasant surprise is waiting.
Illus. by Emily Arnold McCully, Macmillan, 1989, 64 pp., o.p.
(BL 85:1721; CCBB 42:192; HB 65:368; Kirkus 57:122; SLJ June 1989 p. 87)

DOLBIER, Maurice (Wyman). *A Lion in the Woods.*
See Chapter 8, Humorous Fantasy.

2-130 DONOVAN, John. *Family: A Novel.* Gr. 6–9.
✫   Four apes escape from a scientific laboratory only to find that survival in the wild is impossible for them.
Harper, 1976, 1986, 128 pp., o.p.
(BL 72:112, 80:95; CCBB 29:173; HB 52:404; Kirkus 44:405; SLJ Sep 1976 p. 131; Suth 2:127)

2-131 DRURY, Roger W(olcott). *The Champion of Merrimack County.* Gr. 3–5.
O Crispin is the champion mouse bicyclist until a sliver of soap on the Berryfields' bathtub causes a bicycle wreck and a dislocated tail.
Illus. by Fritz Wegner, Little, Brown, 1976, 198 pp., o.p.
(BL 73:1265; CCBB 30:104; HB 53:50; Kirkus 44:1092; SLJ Jan 1977 p. 91)

DUANE, Diane (Elizabeth). *The Book of Night with Moon.*
See Chapter 12, Witchcraft and Sorcery Fantasy.

DU BOIS, William (Sherman) Pène. *Elisabeth the Cow Ghost.*
See Chapter 4, Ghost Fantasy.

DU BOIS, William (Sherman) Pène. *The Forbidden Forest.*
See Chapter 8, Humorous Fantasy.

DU BOIS, William (Sherman) Pène. *The Great Geppy.*
See Chapter 8, Humorous Fantasy.

DU BOIS, William (Sherman) Pène. *Otto and the Magic Potatoes.*
See Chapter 8, Humorous Fantasy.

DU BOIS, William (Sherman) Pène. *The Squirrel Hotel.*
See Chapter 8, Humorous Fantasy.

2-132 DUFFEY, Betsy. *A Boy in the Doghouse.* Gr. 2–4.
In alternating chapters, George and his new puppy, Lucky, describe their ultimately successful master- and pet-training program.
Illus. by Leslie Morrill, Simon & Schuster, 1991, 84 pp., o.p.
(BL 88:703; HBG 3:58; SLJ Sep 1991 p. 232)

2-133 DUFFY, James. *The Revolt of the Teddy Bears.* (**May Gray Mystery series, bk. 1**). Gr. 3–5.
May Gray, poodle detective, comes out of retirement to solve a rash of attacks by teddy bears on the animal inhabitants of Paris. The sequel is *The Christmas Gang* (1989).
Illus. by Barbara McClintock, Macmillan, 1985, 80 pp., o.p.
(BL 81:949; SLJ May 1985, p. 109)

2-134 DUGGAN, Alice. *Violet's Finest Hour.* Gr. 2–5.
A magical purple cape that enables a cat named Violet to fly and to make a new friend helps the cats foil a bank robbery.
Illus. by Harvey Stevenson, Lothrop, 1991, 64 pp., o.p.
(BL 88:438; HBG 3:58; Kirkus 59:1294; SLJ Jan 1992 p. 109)

2-135 DUMAS, Gerald J. *Rabbits Rafferty.* Gr. 4–6.
Rabbits Rafferty stumbles into a fight with Mink Mumsey's tough gang that wants to destroy the other animals' homes.
Illus. by Wallace Tripp, Houghton, 1968, 196 pp., o.p.
(CCBB 22:25; Kirkus 36:510; LJ 93:2733; TLS 1970 p. 414)

DURRELL, Gerald (Malcolm). *The Talking Parcel.*
See Chapter 7, High Fantasy: Travel to Other Worlds.

2-136 EAGER, Edward (McMaken). *Mouse Manor.* Gr. 2–4.
✻ Myrtilla, a poor but genteel country mouse, travels to London to see the queen.
Illus. by Beryl Bailey-Jones, Ariel, 1952, 50 pp., o.p.
(BL 49:19; CCBB 6:4; HB 28:399; Kirkus 20:451; LJ 77:1310)

2-137 EDMONDS, Walter D(umaux). *Beaver Valley.* Gr. 4–6.
A young deermouse watches helplessly as the dams built by an ambitious beaver family destroy or displace the other wild creatures of the valley.
Illus. by Leslie Morrill, Little, Brown, 1971, 70 pp., o.p.
(BL 67:797; HB 47:286; Kirkus 39:432; LJ 96:2363)

2-138 EDMONDS, Walter D(umaux). *Time to Go House.* Gr. 4–6.
After her family's move to a vacant human house, Smalleata the field mouse falls in love with Raffles the house mouse.
Illus. by Joan Victor, Little, Brown, 1969, 137 pp., o.p.
(BL 66:296; HB 45:535; Kirkus 37:776; LJ 94:4284)

EDMONDSON, Madeline. *The Witch's Egg.*
See Chapter 12, Witchcraft and Sorcery Fantasy.

2-139 ELISH, Dan. *The Great Squirrel Uprising.* Gr. 4–6.
The squirrels and other wild animals of New York City's Central Park unite to keep humans out of their territory, permanently.
Illus. by Denys Cazet, Orchard, 1992, 128 pp., o.p.
(BL 88:1277; CCBB 45:203; HBG 3:262; Kirkus 60:252)

2-140 ELISH, Dan. *Jason and the Baseball Bear.* Gr. 3–6.
The coach of Jason's Little League baseball team is Whitney, an elderly polar bear from the zoo, and only Jason can communicate with him.
Illus. by John Stadler, Orchard, 1990, 131 pp., o.p.
(BL 86:1548; HB 66:600; HBG 1:255; Kirkus 58:422; SLJ June 1990 p. 118)

2-141 EMSHWILLER, Carol. *Carmen Dog.* Gr. 10 up.
In some future time, the men of the world are astounded when women begin turning into animals, and animals into women, including Pooch, a setter who longs to become an opera singer.

Mercury, 1990, 161 pp., o.p.

(BL 86:1070, 1078; Kirkus 58:7; LJ Apr 15, 1990 p. 122)

ENDE, Michael. *The Night of Wishes, or The Satanarcheolidealcohellish Notion Potion.*
See Chapter 8, Humorous Fantasy.

2-142 **ERICKSON, Russell E(verett).** *A Toad for Tuesday.* **(Warton and Morton**
★★ **series, bk. 1).** Gr. 3–4.
Captured by an owl, Warton the toad becomes his housekeeper to avoid being eaten as birthday dinner. The sequels are *Warton and Morton* (1976), *Warton's Christmas Eve Adventure* (1977), *Warton and the King of the Skies* (1978), *Warton and the Traders* (1979), *Warton and the Castaways* (1982), and *Warton and the Contest* (1986).
Illus. by Lawrence Di Fiori, Lothrop, 1974, 64 pp., o.p.
(BL 71:98; CCBB 28:76; HB 51:48; Kirkus 42:681; LJ 99:2244)

2-143 **ERWIN, John.** *Mrs. Fox.* Gr. 5–6.
Mrs. Fox raises a baby monkey she has stolen from a circus and gets the best of Mrs. Wildcat and the local wolves.
Illus. by Wallace Tripp, Simon, 1969, 127 pp., o.p.
(CCBB 23:6; Kirkus 37:99; LJ 94:1780)

2-144 **ESTES, Eleanor (Ruth Rosenfeld).** *Miranda the Great.* Gr. 3–5.
A Roman cat named Miranda, lost by her human family, gathers other strays and proclaims herself Queen of the Colosseum.
Illus. by Edward Ardizzone, Harcourt, 1967, 79 pp., o.p.
(BL 63:948; CCBB 20:120; HB 43:201; Kirkus 35:130; LJ 92:1315)

2-145 **EVANS, Sanford.** *Naomi's Geese.* Gr. 5–7.
★ A story told alternately from the points of view of a girl named Naomi and a pair of Canada geese she is trying to protect from environmental poisoning.
Simon, 1993, 192 pp. (0-671-75623-0)
(BL 90:690; CCBB 47:43; HBG 5:75; Kirkus 61:1328; SLJ Nov 1993 p. 106; VOYA 17:26)

2-146 **EZO (pseud.).** *Avril.* Gr. 4–6. (Orig. pub. in France.)
When Avril runs away from her foster family, she is accompanied by a lamb, a cat, a bear, and a baby ghost.
Trans. by John Buchanan-Brown, illus. by Douglas Bissot, Abelard-Schuman, 1967, 94 pp., o.p.
(Kirkus 35:1046; LJ 92:4612)

EZO (pseud.). *My Son-in-Law, the Hippopotamus.*
See Chapter 8, Humorous Fantasy.

FARALLA, Dana. *The Singing Cupboard.*
See Chapter 9, Magic Adventure Fantasy.

2-147 **FARMER, Nancy.** *The Warm Place.* Gr. 4–7.
★ Ruva, an African giraffe incarcerated in a California zoo, finds her way home with the help of a chameleon, a rat, and a boy named Jabila.

Orchard, 1995, 152 pp., o.p.; Puffin, 1996, pap., 152 pp. (0-14-037956-8)

(BL 91:1391; CCBB 48:304; HB 71:597; HBG 6:296; Kirkus 63:555; SLJ Mar 1995 p. 204)

FAST, Howard (Melvin). *The General Zapped an Angel: New Stories of Fantasy and Science Fiction.*
See Chapter 3, Fantasy Collections.

2-148 FEAGLES, Anita MacRae. *Casey, the Utterly Impossible Horse.* Gr. 2–4.
Mike is not exactly pleased that Casey the talking horse has chosen him as a pet.
Illus. by Dagmar Wilson, Addison-Wesley, 1960, 95 pp., o.p.; Shoe String, 1989, o.p.

(CCBB 14:78; LJ 85:4566)

2-149 FIELD, Rachel (Lyman). *Little Dog Toby.* Gr. 3–5.
Toby performs in a Punch and Judy show during a Christmas party at Buckingham Palace.
Illus. by the author, Macmillan, 1928, 1952, 116 pp., o.p.

(BL 25:127, 49:147; Bookshelf 1929 p. 18; HB 4:9, 4:78, 7:115, 28:421; Mahony 2:118)

FIENBERG, Anna. *The Magnificent Nose (and Other Marvels).*
See Chapter 9, Magic Adventure Fantasy.

2-150 FINE, Anne. *The Chicken Gave It to Me.* Gr. 4–6. (Orig. British pub. 1992.)
"The True Story of Harrowing Farm," a book written by a chicken, reveals to Gemma and Andrew that people-eating aliens are taking over the world.
Illus. by Cynthia Fisher, Little, Brown, 1993, 78 pp. (0-316-28316-9)

(BL 89:1966; CCBB 46:343; HBG 4:297; Kirkus 61:660; SLJ Aug 1993 p. 163)

2-151 FINNEY, Patricia. *I, Jack.* Gr. 3–6. (Orig. British pub. 2000.)
✫   A yellow Labrador named Jack tells the story of his life, with some snide help from the three cats that share his den, in this humorous tale of love for the Samoyed next door.
Illus. by Peter Bailey, HarperCollins, 2004, 192 pp. (0-06-052208-9)

(BL 100:750; CCBB 57:311–312, 325; Kirkus 72:82; SLJ May 2004 p. 147)

2-152 FLACK, Marjorie. *Walter the Lazy Mouse.* Gr. 2–4. (Orig. pub. Hale, 1937.)
Left behind during his family's move, Walter is befriended by Turtle and three Frogs while he searches for his family.
Illus. by Cyndy Szekeres, Doubleday, 1963, 95 pp., o.p.

(HB 13:284; LJ 62:782)

2-153 FLEISCHMAN, (Albert) Sid(ney). *A Carnival of Animals.* Gr. 2–4.
✫   A collection of tall tales set on Barefoot Mountain after a tornado transforms Yellercat into a lion and Floyd rooster into a glowing light, and causes J. J. Jones the hog to frighten himself with his own scary stories.
Illus. by Marylin Hafner, Greenwillow, 2000, 48 pp. (0-688-16948-1)

(BL 97:113; CCBB 54:180; HBG 12:61; Kirkus 68:1281; SLJ Oct 2000 p. 124)

FLORY, Jane Trescott. *The Lost and Found Princess.*
See Chapter 1, Allegorical Fantasy and Literary Fairy Tales.

2-154 **FOOTE, Timothy (Gilson).** *The Great Ringtail Garbage Caper.* Gr. 4–6.
Oldest Raccoon and his gang heist a garbage truck to keep their friends in food.
Illus. by Normand Chartier, Houghton, 1980, 66 pp., o.p.
(BL 76:1363, 84:1441; HB 56:294; Kirkus 48:583; SLJ May 1980 p. 66)

FORBUS, Ina B(ell). *The Magic Pin.*
See Chapter 9, Magic Adventure Fantasy.

2-155 **FORD, Richard.** *Quest for the Faradawn.* Gr. 10 up.
Abandoned in the woods by his parents, a human baby is taken in by badgers
who raise him in fulfillment of a legend that foretold the coming of the savior
of the world.
Illus. by Owain Bell, Delacorte, 1982, 310 pp., o.p.
(BL 78:1068, 1082; Kirkus 50:374; LJ 107:1014; SLJ Sep 1982 p. 148; VOYA 5:39)

FORST, S. *Pipkin.*
See Chapter 1, Allegorical Fantasy and Literary Fairy Tales.

2-156 **FORT, John.** *June the Tiger.* Gr. 4–6.
✭   Mrs. Pinckney's feisty dog June and her friend Billy the Bull declare war on a
bear named Scratch who has ravaged Mrs. Pinckney's house.
Illus. by Bernice Loewenstein, Little, Brown, 1975, 59 pp., o.p.
(BL 72:855, 84:1441; CCBB 29:143; HB 52:48; Kirkus 43:1397; SLJ Mar 1976 p. 102)

FOSBURGH, Liza. *Bella Arabella.*
See Chapter 9, Magic Adventure Fantasy.

2-157 **FOX, Denise P.** *Through Tempest Trails.* Gr. 3–5.
Burr the raccoon, Minkley the mink, a peacock, and three shrews escape from
outlaws and journey to Harbor Town, only to be captured by pirates.
Illus. by Judith Gwyn Brown, Atheneum, 1987, 116 pp., o.p.
(BL 84:705, 1441; Kirkus 55:1574; SLJ Dec 1987 p. 85)

2-158 **FOX (Greenberg), Paula.** *Dear Prosper.* Gr. 3–5.
A dog named Chien writes his life story in a letter to the boy who was his first
master.
Illus. by Steve McLachlin, White, 1968, 67 pp., o.p.
(Kirkus 36:393; LJ 93:2733)

FOX (Greenberg), Paula. *The Little Swineherd and Other Tales.*
See Chapter 3, Fantasy Collections.

2-159 **FRANKO, Ivan, and MELNYK, Bohdan.** *Fox Mykyta.* Gr. 4–5. (Orig.
Ukrainian pub. 1890.)
The animals in Lion's court never manage to hurt wily Fox Mykyta.
Trans. by Bodhan Melnyk, illus. by William Kurelek, Tundra, 1978, 148 pp., o.p.
(BL 75:933; HB 55:191)

2-160 **FREDDI, Cris.** *Pork, and Other Stories.* Gr. 10 up.
A collection of connected animal tales set in a forest ruled by a magical stag.
Knopf, 1981, o.p.; Dutton, 1983, pap., 224 pp., o.p.
(BL 78:28, 36; Kirkus 49:819; LJ 106:2048; SLJ Dec 1981 p. 88)

FREEMAN, Barbara C(onstance). *Broom-Adelaide.*
See Chapter 1, Allegorical Fantasy and Literary Fairy Tales.

2-161 FREMLIN, Robert. *Three Friends.* Gr. 1–3.
The friendship of Cat, Pig, and Squirrel is tested in three stories about Pig threatening to run away, demonstrating his acrobatic "tricks," and giving Squirrel bad advice on a new suit.
Illus. by Wallace Tripp, Little, Brown, 1975, 64 pp., o.p.
(BL 71:965; CCBB 29:44; Kirkus 43:374; SLJ Oct 1975, p. 90)

2-162 FRESCHET, Bernice (Louise Speck). *Bernard of Scotland Yard.* **(Bernard**
★ **series, bk. 1).** Gr. 2–3.
Bernard the mouse helps his cousin Foster of Scotland Yard to break up a gang of robber moles who are planning a heist of the crown jewels. This is the sequel to *Bernard Sees the World* (1976) and is followed by *Bernard and the Catnip Caper* (1981).
Illus. by Gina Freschet, Scribner, 1978, 48 pp., o.p.
(BL 75:750; CCBB 32:135; Kirkus 47:3; SLJ Mar 1979 p. 121; Suth 2:156)

2-163 FRESCHET, Gina. *Winnie and Ernst.* Gr. K–3.
Four short stories about best friends Ernst the otter and Winnie the possum, who find a lost gift for a friend's birthday, bake a cake, and host a spring celebration.
Illus. by the author, Farrar, 2003, 48 pp. (0-374-38452-5)
(BL 100:327; Kirkus 71:1224; SLJ Nov 2003 p. 94)

2-164 FRY, Rosalie K(ingsmill). *The Wind Call.* Gr. 2–4.
Mother Blackcap finds a lost baby of the Little People, names him Pierello, and raises him along with her three baby birds.
Illus. by the author, Dutton, 1955, 115 pp., o.p.
(CCBB 10:50; HB 32:30; LJ 80:2916)

2-165 GACKENBACH, Dick. *Beauty, Brave and Beautiful.* Gr. 2–4.
A homeless, ugly little mutt finds a loving home with two children after she saves them from an attack by a bear.
Illus. by the author, Houghton, 1990, 48 pp. (0-395-52000-2)
(BL 86:1341; HBG 1:237; SLJ May 1990 p. 84)

2-166 GALLICO, Paul (William). *The Abandoned.* Gr. 8 up. (British title: *Jennie*,
★ 1950.)
Injured in an automobile accident, Peter imagines his transformation into a homeless cat.
Knopf, 1950, 307 pp., o.p.; International Polygonics, 1987, 1995, pap., 250 pp. (1-55882-097-3)
(BL 47:2, 39; HB 26:501; Kirkus 18:394; LJ 75:2161)

2-167 GANGLOFF, Deborah. *Albert and Victoria.* Gr. 3–5.
Albert misses his best friend and fellow insect, Victoria, after she climbs to the top of the Empire State Building for the winter months, so he undertakes a perilous journey to follow her.
Illus. by Bill Woodman, Crown, 1989, 80 pp., o.p.
(BL 85:1294; Kirkus 56:1810; SLJ July 1989 p. 64)

GARDNER, Sally. *The Countess's Calamity.*
See Chapter 11, Toy Fantasy.

2-168 GATES, Doris. *The Cat and Mrs. Cary.* Gr. 5–7.
Mrs. Cary is able to solve a mystery because she can understand cat language.
Illus. by Peggy Bacon, Viking, 1962, 216 pp., o.p.
(Eakin:135; HB 38:598; LJ 88:864)

2-169 GAUNT, Michael (pseud. of [James] Dennis Robertshaw). *Brim's Boat.*
(Brim trilogy, bk. 1). Gr. 4–6. (Orig. British pub. 1964.)
A terrier named Brim finds an abandoned boat and decides to become a sailor.
The sequels are *Brim Sails Out* (1966) and *Brim's Valley* (British).
Illus. by Stuart Tresilian, Coward, 1966, 128 pp., o.p.
(BL 62:831; HB 42:305; Kirkus 34:56; LJ 91:1063)

2-170 GAUTIER, (Louise) Judith. *The Memoirs of a White Elephant.* Gr. 5–6.
(Orig. pub. in France.)
A royal Indian elephant describes how he once saved his master's life and
became the guardian of the baby princess of Golconda.
Trans. by S. A. B. Harvey, illus. by L. H. Smith and S. B. Kite, Duffield, 1916,
233 pp., o.p.
(BL 13:269; Bookshelf 1921–1922 p. 13; Mahony 2:343)

2-171 GERAS, Adèle. *The Cats of Cuckoo Square: Two Stories.* Gr. 2–4. (Orig.
✭   British pub. 1997.)
Two related stories told from a cat's point of view. In "Blossom's Revenge," a
cat and her 6-year-old owner are tormented by angelic cousin Prissy, and in
"Picasso Perkins," Blossom's friend tries to avoid posing for his owner's art
project. The stories were later published separately as part of the Cats of Cuck-
oo Square paperback series: *Blossom's Revenge* (Dell, 2002) and *Picasso
Perkins* (Dell, 2002). The sequels are *Geejay the Hero* (Dell, 2003) and *Cal-
lie's Kitten* (Dell, 2003).
Illus. by Tony Ross, Delacorte, 2001, 190 pp., o.p.
(BL 98:104; CCBB 55:139; HBG 13:73; Kirkus 69:1423; SLJ Dec 2002 p. 102)

GERAS, Adèle. *The Fabulous Fantoras: Book One: Family Files.*
See Chapter 8, Humorous Fantasy.

GERSTEIN, Mordicai. *Fox Eyes.*
See Chapter 9, Magic Adventure Fantasy.

GIFALDI, David. *Gregory, Maw and the Mean One.*
See Chapter 8, Humorous Fantasy.

2-172 GLEITZMAN, Morris. *Toad Rage.* Gr. 3–6. (Orig. Australian pub. 2000.)
✭   Australian cane toad Limpy and his cousin Goliath hitch a ride to the city,
where they hope to become "goodwill ambassadors" from their species to the
human race. The sequel is *Toad Heaven* (2001, 2005).
Random, 2004, 176 pp. (0-375-92762-X)
(BL 100:1188; CCBB 57:405–406, 418; Kirkus 72:329; SLJ Apr 2004 p. 154)

2-173 GODDEN (Dixon), (Margaret) Rumer. *Mouse House.* Gr. K–3. (Orig.
☆ British pub. 1952.)
Mary makes sure that her miniature house gets the right kind of tenants: a family of mice.
Illus. by Adrienne Adams, Viking, 1957, 63 pp., o.p.
(BL 54:28; CCBB 11:80; HB 33:483; Kirkus 25:480; LJ 82:2693)

GODDEN (Dixon), (Margaret) Rumer. *The Mousewife.*
See Chapter 1, Allegorical Fantasy and Literary Fairy Tales.

2-174 GOLDMAN, Kelly, and DAVIDSON, Ronnie. *Sherlick Hound and the
Valentine Mystery.* Gr. 2–4.
Who stole Princess Penelope Poodle's new ruby-studded collar? "Dog-Honest
Detective" Sherlick Hound and his reporter friend Scoop Schnauzer solve the
case.
Illus. by Don Madden, Whitman, 1989, 40 pp., o.p.
(BL 85:1466; SLJ June 1989 p.88)

2-175 GOODWIN, Harold Leland. *Magic Number.* Gr. 4–6.
In a bid for equal rights, the garden-dwelling animals declare war on the house
pets at a veterinarian's home.
Illus. by the author, Bradbury, 1969, 97 pp., o.p.
(BL 66:206; CCBB 23:8; Kirkus 37:559; LJ 95:3603)

2-176 GOODWIN, Murray. *Alonzo and the Army of Ants.* Gr. 4–6.
Alonzo the anteater must save his village from an invasion of army ants.
Illus. by Kiyo Komoda, Harper, 1966, 104 pp., o.p.
(Kirkus 34:419; LJ 91:3258)

GRAHAM, Harriet. *A Boy and His Bear.*
See Chapter 9, Magic Adventure Fantasy.

2-177 GRAHAME, Kenneth. *Bertie's Escapade.* Gr. 1–3. (Orig. pub. as part of
☆ *First Whispers of the Wind in the Willows,* 1944 in England; 1945 in the U.S.
Orig. U.S. pub. in this format, Lippincott, 1949.)
Bertie Pig, Peter Rabbit, and Benjie Rabbit's Christmas caroling efforts disturb
Mr. Stone, who sets his dogs on them.
Illus. by Ernest H. Shepard, Harper, 1977, 28 pp., o.p.
(BL 41:223; CCBB 2:4; HB 21:200, 25:413, 552; Kirkus 13:31, 45:1094; LJ 70:264, 74:1533,
1681; TLS 1944 p. 369)

2-178 GRAHAME, Kenneth. *The Wind in the Willows.* Gr. 4–8. (Orig. British
☆☆ pub. 1907, U.S. Scribner, 1908, 302 pp., o.p.)
Ratty, Mole, and Toad battle the weasels and stoats that have taken over Toad
Hall. A. A. Milne used this story as a basis for a play entitled *Toad of Toad
Hall* (Scribner, 1929, 1957). Picture-book versions of four chapters from the
novel have been published by Scribner: *The River Bank* (1977), *The Open Road*
(1980), *Wayfarers All* (1981), and *Mole's Christmas, or, Home Sweet Home*
(1983, pap., 1986). Dixon Scott has written a sequel for a slightly older audience entitled *A Fresh Wind in the Willows* (orig. British pub. 1983, Dell, 1987,
pap.; see this chapter). William Horwood has written a series of sequels for

young adults and adults entitled *The Willows in Winter* (orig. British pub. 1993; St. Martin's, 1994; see this chapter), *Toad Triumphant* (Dunne, 1996), *The Willows and Beyond* (Dunne, 1998), and *The Willows at Christmas* (St. Martin's/ Dunne, 2001).

Illus. by Arthur Rackham, Heritage, 1940, 190 pp., o.p.; illus. by Ernest H. Shepard, Macmillan, 1933, 1983, 1991, 264 pp. (0-684-19345-0), 1989, pap. (0-689-71310-X); illus. by Michael Hague, Ariel, 1982, 205 pp., o.p.; illus. by John Burningham, Viking, 1983, 240 pp., o.p.; illus. by Patrick Benson, St. Martin's, 1995, 272 pp. (0-312-13624-2); illus. by Inga Moore, Candlewick, 1996, entitled *The River Bank: And Other Stories from "The Wind in the Willows,"* 96 pp. (0-7636-0059-8); illus. by Inga Moore, Candlewick, 1998, entitled *The Adventures of Mr. Toad from "The Wind in the Willows,"* 86 pp. (0-7636-0581-6); illus. by Michael Hague, *A Wind in the Willows Christmas*, North-South, 2000, o.p.; illus. by Mary Jane Begin, North-South, 2002, 208 pp. (1-58717-204-6); illus. by Michael Foreman, Harcourt, 2002, 240 pp. (0-15-216807-9); illus. by Michael (R.) Hague, Holt, 2003, 208 pp. (0-8050-7237-3); illus. by Inga Moore, Candlewick, 2003, 184 pp. (orig. pub as *The River Bank* [1996] and *The Adventures of Mr. Toad* [1998]) (0-7636-2242-7)

(BL 50:20, 77:1250, 80:85, 680, 85:1188, 99:664; CCBB 7:4, 34:111, 36:209; HB 1:34, 46, 7:118, 9:205, 30:83, 59:733, 60:357; HBG 8:58, 12:61, 14:67, 15:78; Mahony 2:280; SLJ Nov 1980 p. 74, Sep 1983 p. 122, Jan 1997 p. 77, Jan 2003 p. 96, Nov 2003 p. 138; Suth 3:158, 159)

GRAY, Nicholas Stuart. *Grimbold's Other World.*
See Chapter 7, High Fantasy: Travel to Other Worlds.

GREGORY, Valiska. *Through the Mickle Woods.*
See Chapter 1, Allegorical Fantasy and Literary Fairy Tales.

2-179 **GRIFFITH, Helen V(irginia).** *Alex and the Cat.* Gr. 1–3.
Seven short adventures of a dog named Alex and his family's cat, originally published separately as *Alex and the Cat* (1982), *More Alex and the Cat* (1983), and *Alex Remembers* (1983).
Illus. by Sonja Lamut, Greenwillow, 1997, 50 pp. (0-688-15241-4)
(BL 94:406; CCBB 51:126; HBG 9:60)

GUILLOT, René. *Nicolette and the Mill.*
See Chapter 9, Magic Adventure Fantasy.

GUILLOT, René. *The Three Hundred Ninety-Seventh White Elephant.*
See Chapter 1, Allegorical Fantasy and Literary Fairy Tales.

2-180 **HAAS, Dorothy F. (Dee Francis).** *The Bears Up Stairs.* Gr. 5–7.
Wendy befriends Otto and Ursula Ma'am, two bears hiding in her apartment building while they wait for transportation to the planet Brun.
Greenwillow, 1978, 192 pp., o.p.
(BL 75:49; CCBB 32:44; Kirkus 46:1248; SLJ Oct 1978 p. 144)

HABER, Melissa Glenn. *The Heroic Adventures of Hercules Amsterdam.*
See Chapter 9, Magic Adventure Fantasy.

2-181 HAHN, Harriet. *James, the Connoisseur Cat.* Gr. 10 up.
An American fine arts agent in London is befriended by James, a large gray feline art expert, who manages to unmask forgeries, find stolen jewels, impersonate an Egyptian cat goddess, and star in a TV show. The sequel is *James, Fabulous Feline: Further Adventures of a Connoisseur Cat* (1993).
St. Martin's, 1991, 169 pp., o.p.
(BL 88:120, 131; Kirkus 59:1031)

2-182 HALE, Bruce. *The Chameleon Wore Chartreuse: From the Tattered Casebook of Chet Gecko, Private Eye.* **(Chet Gecko series, bk. 1).** Gr. 3–5.
Fourth-grade lizard detective Chet Gecko solves a case involving a classmate's missing brother and reveals a plot to steal the football team's mascot. The sequels are *The Mystery of Mr. Nice* (2000), *Farewell, My Lunchbag* (2001), *The Big Nap* (2001), *The Hamster of the Baskervilles* (2002), *This Gum for Hire* (2002), *The Malted Falcon* (2003), *Trouble Is My Beeswax* (2003), *Give My Regrets to Broadway* (2004), and *Murder, My Tweet* (2004).
Illus. by the author, Harcourt, 2000, 97 pp. (0-15-202281-3), 2001, pap., 97 pp. (0-15-202485-9)
(BL 96:1744; CCBB 53:357; Kirkus 68:475; SLJ Aug 2000 p. 155)

HALL, Lynn. *The Mystery of the Caramel Cat.*
See Chapter 4, Ghost Fantasy.

2-183 HAMILTON, Carol. *The Dawn Seekers.* Gr. 4–6.
Nocturnal young kangaroo rat Quentin joins forces with a bossy jerboa and a poetic centipede to venture out into the desert by day.
Illus. by Jeremy Guitar, Whitman, 1987, 160 pp., o.p.
(BL 83:1446, 84:1441; Kirkus 55:56; SLJ Mar 1987 p. 160)

2-184 HAMLEY, Dennis. *Hare's Choice.* Gr. 4–6. (Orig. British pub. 1988.)
A dead hare is given the choice of going to an eternally peaceful valley to become the Queen of Hares or living on eternally by becoming a character in a children's story.
Illus. by Meg Rutherford, Delacorte, 1990, 88 pp., o.p.
(CCBB 43:214; HBG 1:257; Kirkus 58:424; SLJ May 1990 p. 106)

2-185 HANCOCK, Neil (Anderson). *Dragon Winter.* Gr. 8–12.
A mysterious voice unites a group of otters, beavers, squirrels, badgers, a muskrat, and a mole, all of whom have been driven from their homes. The voice convinces them to go on a magic quest to find a great silver bear. The sequel is *The Fires of Windameir* (Warner, 1985), and both books are related to Hancock's The Wilderness of Four series (*Across the Far Mountain, The Plains of the Sea, On the Boundaries of Darkness,* and *The Road to the Middle Islands,* all 1982).
Popular Library, 1978, 351 pp., o.p.
(Kliatt 12:7; VOYA 7:56)

2-186 HANSEN, Brooks. *Caesar's Antlers.* Gr. 5–7.
★ Caesar the reindeer carries Bette the sparrow and her children on his antlers while searching for his human friends and her missing mate.

Illus. by the author, Farrar, 1997, 218 pp. (0-374-31024-6); Sunburst, 2001, pap., 224 pp. (0-374-41072-0)

(BL 94:329; CCBB 51:204; HB 74:73; HBG 9:72; Kirkus 65:1305; SLJ Nov 1997 p. 118)

HARPER, Tara K. *Wolfwalker.*
See Chapter 5, High Fantasy: Alternate Worlds or Histories.

2-187 HARRIS, Dorothy Joan. *The House Mouse.* Gr. K–2.
All winter long, Jonathan shares cookies and conversation with the mouse who lives in his sister's dollhouse. The sequel is *The School Mouse* (1977).
Illus. by Barbara Cooney, Warne, 1973, 48 pp., o.p.

(CCBB 27:27; Kirkus 41:559; LJ 98:2640)

HARVEY, Dean. *The Secret Elephant of Harlan Kooter.*
See Chapter 9, Magic Adventure Fantasy.

2-188 HASS, E. A. *Incognito Mosquito, Private Insective.* **(Incognito Mosquito series, bk. 1).** Gr. 3–5.
A mosquito detective describes five of his most serious cases, including the capture of the "bug napper" of baseball star Mickie Mantis. The sequels are *Incognito Mosquito Flies Again* (1985) and *Incognito Mosquito Takes to the Air* (1986).
Illus. by the author, Lothrop, 1982, 96 pp., o.p.

(CCBB 36:108; Kirkus 50:1105; SLJ Dec 1982 p. 79)

2-189 HATCH, Richard Warren. *The Lobster Books.* Gr. 4–6. (Orig. pub. separately as *The Curious Lobster*, Harcourt, 1937, and *The Curious Lobster's Island*, Dodd, 1939.)
An old lobster meets a badger and a bear while exploring unknown territory upriver.
Illus. by Marion Freeman Wakeman, Houghton, 1951, 347 pp., o.p.

(BL 34:132; CCBB 4:50; HB 13:288, 15:383, 27:260; LJ 62:809, 881, 64:840, 904; TLS 1937 p. 948)

2-190 HAWDON, Robin. *A Rustle in the Grass.* Gr. 10 up. (Orig. British pub.
✭ 1984.)
A young soldier ant named Dreamer, struggling to work out his purpose in life, scouts the brutal red ant army and plays a key role in the war to defend his territory and his queen.
Dodd, 1985, 244 pp., o.p.

(BL 81:1029, 1050; Kirkus 53:150; LJ Apr 1, 1985 p. 158; SLJ Aug 1985 p. 86; VOYA 8:394, 10:23)

2-191 HAWKINS, Laura. *Figment, Your Dog, Speaking.* Gr. 3–6.
A talking dog plays an important role in the lives of three unrelated people: lonely 10-year-old Marcella; her frightened, developmentally delayed neighbor, Benny; and an elderly judge with a guilty secret.
Houghton, 1991, 155 pp., o.p.

(BL 88:1029; CCBB 45:63; HBG 3:66; Kirkus 59:1403; SLJ Mar 1992 p. 237)

2-192 HAYES, Geoffrey. *The Alligator and His Uncle Tooth: A Novel of the Sea.*
Gr. 3–5.

Uncle Tooth's adventure-filled tales convince an old sea captain to sail again, with Corduroy as mate. Two sequels written for younger readers are *The Mystery of the Pirate Ghost* (Random, 1985) and *The Secret of Foghorn Island* (Random, 1988).
Illus. by the author, Harper, 1977, 88 pp., o.p.
(BL 73:1420; CCBB 31:33; HB 53:441; Kirkus 45:350; SLJ Sep 1977 p. 109; TLS 1977 p. 1414)

HAYES, Sarah. *Crumbling Castle.*
See Chapter 12, Witchcraft and Sorcery Fantasy.

HEAL (Berrien), Edith. *What Happened to Jenny.*
See Chapter 9, Magic Adventure Fantasy.

2-193   **HEIDENRIECH, Elke.** *Nero Corleone: A Cat's Story.* Gr. 3–5. (Orig. pub.
☆   in Germany.)
Italian farm cat Don Nero Corleone convinces his shy sister, Rosa, to move in with a vacationing German couple in order to return with them to Cologne. Mildred L. Batchelder Award Honor Book, 1998.
Trans. by Doris Orgel, illus. by Quint Buchholz, Viking, 1997, 89 pp. (0-670-87395-0)
(BL 94:235; CCBB 51:127; HBG 9:73; Kirkus 65:1306 SLJ Dec 1997 p. 92)

HENDRY, Diana. *A Camel Called April.*
See Chapter 9, Magic Adventure Fantasy.

HESS, Fjeril. *The Magic Switch.*
See Chapter 9, Magic Adventure Fantasy.

HEWETT, Anita. *The Bull Beneath the Walnut Tree and Other Stories.*
See Chapter 3, Fantasy Collections.

HILLER, Catherine. *Abracatabby.*
See Chapter 9, Magic Adventure Fantasy.

2-194   **HIMLER, Ronald (Norbert), and HIMLER, Ann.** *Little Owl, Keeper of the Trees.* Gr. K–3.
Although Little Owl is afraid of high places, his favorite spot is the highest branch of the Old Sycamore Tree, where he dreams of being the mighty guardian of the forest.
Illus. by Ronald (Norbert) Himler, Harper, 1974, 63 pp., o.p.
(BL 71:570; CCBB 28:148; Kirkus 42:1103; SLJ Jan 1975 p. 39)

2-195   **HOBAN, Lillian.** *It's Really Christmas.* Gr. K–3.
The family of a lame baby mouse named Gamey Joe cheers him up by creating Christmas in July while he recovers from a bad fall.
Illus. by the author, Greenwillow, 1982, 39 pp., o.p.
(BL 79:116; CCBB 36:27; Kirkus 50:995; SLJ Oct 1982 p. 165)

2-196   **HOBAN, Russell C(onwell).** *Dinner at Alberta's.* Gr. 2–4.
☆   Arthur Crocodile decides to learn table manners in preparation for dinner at Alberta Saurian's house. The sequel is *Arthur's New Power* (1978).

Illus. by James (Edward) Marshall, Crowell, 1975, 40 pp., o.p.

(BL 72:302; CCBB 29:98; HB 52:46; Kirkus 42:993; SLJ Dec 1975 pp. 31, 64; Suth 2:216)

2-197 HOBAN, Russell C(onwell). *Jim Hedgehog and the Lonesome Tower.* Gr. 2–4.

Heavy metal fan Jim Hedgehog accidentally drops his recorder into a stream and follows it to a mysterious castle, where he teaches a female singer to read music. The sequel is *Jim Hedgehog's Supernatural Christmas* (1992).

Illus. by Betsy Lewin, Houghton, 1992, 44 pp., o.p.

(BL 88:1680; HBG 3:256; Kirkus 60:256; SLJ June 1992 p. 95)

HOBAN, Russell C(onwell). *The Mouse and His Child.*
See Chapter 1, Allegorical Fantasy and Literary Fairy Tales.

2-198 HOBAN, Russell C(onwell). *The Sea-Thing Child.* Gr. 2–4.

Friendly shore creatures help a newborn sea-thing to overcome its fear of flying.

Illus. by Abrom Hoban, Harper, 1972, 35 pp., o.p.; slightly abridged ed.: illus. by Patrick Benson, Candlewick, 1999, 48 pp. (0-7636-0847-5)

(CCBB 26:92; HBG 11:66; Kirkus 40:1188, 1412; LJ 98:644; SLJ Dec 1999 p. 98; TLS 1972 p. 1323)

2-199 HOBAN, Russell C(onwell). *Trouble on Thunder Mountain.* Gr. 2–4. (Orig. British pub. 1999.)

The O'Saurus dinosaur family outwits developer J. M. Flatbrain, who plans to turn their Thunder Mountain home into an amusement park called Megafright Mountain.

Illus. by Quentin Blake, Orchard, 2000, 40 pp. (0-531-30206-7)

(BL 96:1892; CCBB 54:21; HBG 11:293; SLJ July 2000, p. 80)

2-200 HOEYE, Michael. *Time Stops for No Mouse.* **(Hermux Tantamoq Adven-**
✮ **ture series, bk. 1).** Gr. 5–8. (Originally self-published, 2000.)

Mouse watchmaker Hermux Tantamoq searches for the missing daredevil aviatrix Linka Perflinger, whom he suspects may have been a victim of foul play. In the sequel, *The Sands of Time* (2001, 2002), Hermux, Linka, and chipmunk Birch Tentintrotter follow an ancient map in search of the tomb of Ka Narsh-Pa in the lost Kingdom of Cats. The third book in the series is *No Time like Show Time* (2004).

Illus. by Dale Champlin, Putnam, 2002, 250 pp. (0-399-23878-6); SPEAK, 2003, pap., 250 pp. (0-698-11991-6)

(BL 98:1257, 1461; HB 78:462; HBG 13:374; SLJ May 2002 p. 154; VOYA 25:128, 26:12)

HOFFMAN, Mary. *The Four-Legged Ghosts.*
See Chapter 9, Magic Adventure Fantasy.

2-201 HOFFMANN, Eleanor. *The Four Friends.* Gr. 3–5.
✮ To avoid becoming Christmas dinner, a pig runs away in a rental car, along with a dog, a parrot, and a hen.

Illus. by Kurt Wiese, Macmillan, 1946, 105 pp., o.p.

(BL 43:173; HB 22:349; Kirkus 14:422; LJ 71:1808)

HOFFMANN, E(rnst) T(heodor) A(madeus). *The Nutcracker.*
See Chapter 11, Toy Fantasy.

2-202   **HOLM, Jennifer L., and HAMEL, Jonathan.** *The Postman Always Brings Mice.* **(The Stink Files, Dossier 001).** Gr. 4–6.
After his beloved owner—the director of a secret British spy agency—is poisoned, James Edward Bristlefur is shipped from London to the United States to become a house pet. Dossier 002 is *To Scratch a Thief* (2004).
Illus. by Brad Weinman, HarperCollins, 2004, 144 pp. (0-06-052980-6)
(BL 100:1498; Kirkus 72:492)

2-203   **HOLMAN (Valen), Felice.** *The Cricket Winter.* Gr. 3–5.
A boy and a cricket communicate in Morse code to save a mouse family from a thieving rat.
Illus. by Ralph Pinto, Norton, 1967, 107 pp., o.p.
(BL 64:784; CCBB 21:111; LJ 92:3849; Suth:193)

2-204   **HOREJS, Vít.** *Pig and Bear.* Gr. 1–4.
Pig and Bear open a pawn shop, but run into trouble because they have no idea how to run such a business.
Illus. by Friso Henstra, Macmillan, 1989, 40 pp., o.p.
(CCBB 43:60; HBG 1:66; Kirkus 57:1246; SLJ Feb 1990 p. 75)

HORNE, Richard Henry. *The Good-Natured Bear: A Story for Children of All Ages.*
See Chapter 8, Humorous Fantasy.

2-205   **HORNE, Richard Henry.** *King Penguin: A Legend of the South Sea Isles.*
☆   Gr. 3–5. (Orig. British pub. 1848.)
A remorseful sailor sets out to free the captive King of the Penguins.
Macmillan, 1925, 95 pp., o.p.; illus. by James Daugherty, Macmillan, 1952, 68 pp., o.p.
(BL 22:122; HB 2:19, 28:421; LJ 51:836; Mahony 2:148; Moore:42)

HORNIK, Laurie Miller. *Zoo School.*
See Chapter 8, Humorous Fantasy.

HORWITZ, Elinor Lander. *The Strange Story of the Frog Who Became a Prince.*
See Chapter 12, Witchcraft and Sorcery Fantasy.

2-206   **HORWOOD, William.** *Duncton Wood.* Gr. 10 up.
The moles of Duncton Wood, and all of southern England, are saved by a pair of star-crossed lovers and an epic battle between the forces of good and evil.
McGraw-Hill, 1980, 736 pp., o.p.
(BL 76:1410, Kirkus 48:152; LJ 105:1409; VOYA 4:32, 4:48)

HOUGH, (Helen) Charlotte (Woodyatt). *Red Biddy and Other Stories.*
See Chapter 3, Fantasy Collections.

2-207   **HOWARD, Joan (pseud. of Patricia Gordon).** *The Taming of Giants.* Gr. 1–4.

A field mouse searching for a new home encounters a classroom full of "giants."

Illus. by Garry MacKenzie, Viking, 1950, 57 pp., o.p.

(BL 47:16; CCBB 4:3; HB 26:375; Kirkus 18:512)

2-208 HOWARD, Joan (pseud. of Patricia Gordon). *Uncle Sylvester.* Gr. 2–4.
In order to save their homes from destruction by erosion, Uncle Sylvester mole and his nephew Digger move the entire colony across the river to the Green Forest.

Illus. by Garry MacKenzie, Oxford University Press, 1950, 48 pp., o.p.

(CCBB 3:35; HB 26:194; Kirkus 18:176; LJ 75:629, 987)

2-209 HOWE, Deborah, and HOWE, James. *Bunnicula: A Rabbit Tale of Mys-*
★ *tery.* **(Bunnicula series, bk. 1).** Gr. 3–5.
Family pets Chester and Harold suspect that the bunny rabbit brought home from a Dracula movie is actually a vampire. The sequels, all written by James Howe, are *Howliday Inn* (1982, pap., 2001), *The Celery Stalks at Midnight* (1983, pap., 1989), *Nighty-Nightmare* (1987, pap., 1988), *The Fright Before Christmas* (1988, pap., 1990), *Scared Silly: A Halloween Treat* (Morrow, 1989, pap., 1990), *Harold and Chester in Hot Fudge* (1990, pap., 1999), *Return to Howliday Inn* (1992, pap., 2004), *Rabbit-Cadabra!* (1993, pap., 1999), and *Bunnicula Strikes Again!* (1999, pap., 2001). Related stories, written by Howie the dachshund, in the Tales from the House of Bunnicula series include *It Came from Beneath the Bed!* (Simon, 2002), *Invasion of the Mind Swappers from Asteroid 6!* (2002), *Howie Monroe and the Doghouse of Doom* (2002), *Howie Monroe and the Screaming Mummies of the Pharoah's Tomb II* (2003), *Bud Barking, Private Eye* (2003), and *The Amazing Odorous Adventures of Stinky Dog* (2003). James Howe has adapted *Bunnicula* into a beginning chapter book called *The Vampire Bunny* (2004), the first book in the Bunnicula and Friends series. The sequels are *Hot Fudge* (2004) and *Scared Silly* (2005).

Illus. by Alan Daniel, Atheneum, 1979, 112 pp., o.p.; Aladdin, 1996, pap., 98 pp. (0-689-80659-0); illus. by Alan Daniel, Atheneum, 1999, 148 pp. (0-689-83219-2); Atheneum, 2004, 112 pp. (0-689-86775-1)

(BL 75:1439; CCBB 32:192; HBG 11:80; Kirkus 47:741; SLJ May 1979 p. 81; Suth 3:200)

2-210 HOWE, James. *Morgan's Zoo.* Gr. 3–5.
Morgan the zookeeper, two children, and all of the animals join forces to save their zoo from closing.

Illus. by Leslie Morrill, Atheneum, 1984, 192 pp., o.p.

(BL 81:448; SLJ Sep 1984 p. 119)

2-211 HUGHES, Ted (Edward James). *How the Whale Became.* Gr. 2–5. (Orig.
★ British pub. 1963.)
A collection of stories describing how the whale, the owl, the hare, the polar bear, and the hyena developed their individual personalities.

Illus. by Rick Schreiter, Atheneum, 1964, 100 pp., o.p.; illus. by Jackie Morris, Orchard, 2000, 96 pp. (0-531-30303-9)

(BL 61:482; CCBB 54:147; HB 40:498; HBG 12:307; Kirkus 32:650; LJ 89:4196; SLJ Nov 2000 p. 123)

2-212 HUNTER, Erin. *Into the Wild.* **(Warriors series, bk. 1).** Gr. 6 up.
☆   Rusty runs away from his comfortable home to join the ThunderClan, feral cats
      who rename him Firepaw, teach him to hunt and fight, and enlist his help when
      the ShadowClaw clan attacks. The sequels are *Fire and Ice* (2003), *Forest of
      Secrets* (2003), *Rising Storm* (2004), and *A Dangerous Path* (2004).
      HarperCollins, 2003, 256 pp. (0-06-052548-7), 2004, pap., 336 pp. (0-06-
      052550-9)
      (BL 99:1064, 1465; CCBB 56:277; HBG 16:368; Kirkus 71:61; SLJ May 2003 p. 154)

2-213 HURWITZ, Johanna. *PeeWee's Tale.* **(Park Pals Adventure series, bk. 1).**
      Gr. 2–4.
      PeeWee the guinea pig's reading abilities come in handy after he is left in a
      park and befriended by a squirrel named Lexi. The sequels are *Lexi's Tale*
      (2001) and *PeeWee and Plush* (2002).
      Illus. by Patience Brewster, North-South, 2000, 96 pp. (1-58717-027-2)
      (BL 97:339; Kirkus 68:1424; SLJ Oct 2000 p. 127)

2-214 JACKSON, Shelley. *Sophia, the Alchemist's Dog.* Gr. 2–5.
      When her master proves unable to create gold for the king, Sophia, the
      alchemist's dog, does it herself, with the help of an angel and an imp.
      Illus. by the author, Atheneum, 2002, 48 pp. (0-689-84279-1)
      (BL 99:336; HBG 14:68; Kirkus 70:1226; SLJ Oct 2002 p. 166)

2-215 JACQUES, Brian. *Redwall.* **(Redwall Saga, bk. 1).** Gr. 5–9. (Orig. British
☆   pub. 1986.)
      Young Matthias Mouse helps defend Redwall Abbey against marauding rats
      bent on enslaving the peaceful mice who have taken refuge there. The follow-
      ing sequels are arranged in the chronological order of events, with *Redwall*
      falling in the middle, between *Salamandastron* and *Mattimeo.* In *Lord Brock-
      tree* (2000), young haremaid Dotti and the great badger Lord Brocktree join
      forces with moles, otters, squirrels, and hares to battle the Blue Hordes of wild-
      cat Ungatt Trunn threatening Salamandastron fortress. In *Martin the Warrior*
      (1993, 1994), young Martin escapes enslavement by the stoat Badrang the
      Tyrant. In *Mossflower* (1988, 1998), Martin battles the evil wildcat Tsarmina to
      bring peace to the Mossflower Woodlands. In *The Legend of Luke* (1999) Mar-
      tin, Trimp the hedgehog, and Gonff the mousethief set out to follow the words
      of an old ballad to discover the fate of Martin's father, Luke, who had vowed to
      avenge the massacre of his wife and his tribe by Vilu Daskar. In *Outcast of
      Redwall* (1995, 1996), Sunflash is rescued by Skarlath the kestrel from captivi-
      ty by ferret warlord Swartt Sixclaw, and becomes badger lord of the mountain
      fort of Salamandastron. In *Mariel of Redwall* (1991, 1992), Mariel, the daugh-
      ter of Joseph the bellmaker, becomes a warrior after Gabool the Wild, a pirate
      rat, steals the Joseph Bell and tries to drown her. In *The Bellmaker* (1994,
      1995), Mariel's father, Joseph, sails to Southward with a band of friends to res-
      cue Mariel from Foxwolf Nagru. In *Salamandastron* (1992, 1993), Martin's
      sword has been stolen and Salamandastron Castle is attacked by Feragho the
      Assassin. *Redwall* falls here in chronological order of events. In *Mattimeo*
      (1989, 1990), Matthias's son Mattimeo is enslaved by Slager the Fox and
      Matthias attempts a rescue, while Mattimeo's mother, Cornflower, defends
      Redwall Abbey from other enemies. In *The Pearls of Lutra* (1996, 1997),

mouse warrior Martin, grandson of Matthias, leads a band of warriors against the enemy forces of pine marten Mad Eyes, while hedgehog Tansy searches for some mysterious pink pearls. In *The Long Patrol* (1997, 1998), Lady Cregga Rose Eyes sends out the Long Patrol, a crack unit of hares, to follow the vermin Rapscallion warriors plotting to capture Redwall Abbey. In *Marlfox* (1998, 1999), four young heroes search for the stolen tapestry depicting Martin the Warrior, while evil Marlfoxes besiege Redwall Abbey. In *Taggerung* (2001, 2002), Taggerung the otter, kidnapped from Redwall in infancy and raised by Sawny Rath, the savage ferret leader, grows to detest his adoptive father and his murderous band. In *Triss* (2002), three slaves, including a young squirrel named Triss, manage to escape their captors at about the same time that Sagax, son of the badger ruler of Salamandastron, and his friend Scarum the hare, son of the leader of the Long Patrol, decide to run away in search of adventure. In *Loamhedge* (2003), two Redwall warriors search for the legendary Abbey of Loamhedge, leaving Redwall Abbey vulnerable to attack. In the seventeenth sequel, *Rakkety Tam* (2004), warrior squirrels Rakkety Tam and Wild Doogy Plumm join the Long Patrol to battle the murderous wolverine Gulo the Savage. Jacques has also written two illustrated books for younger readers in grades 2–5 that do not fall at a particular time in the chronology. In *The Great Redwall Feast* (illus. by Christopher Denise; 1996), Matthias, Constance, Cornflower, and other familiar Redwall characters prepare a surprise feast for Father Abbott. In *A Redwall Winter's Tale* (illus. by Christopher Denise; 2001), Matthias mouse and his wife Cornflower welcome a troupe of traveling players to Redwall Abbey on the last day of autumn.

Illus. by Gary Chalk, Putnam, 1987, 351 pp. (0-399-21424-0); Avon, 1990, pap. (0-380-70827-2); illus. by Troy Howell, Philomel, 1997, 351 pp. (0-399-23160-9)

(BL 83:1519, 1522, 84:1248, 1441, 91:415; CCBB 40:211; HB 64:71; HBG 9:74; Kirkus 55:858; SLJ Aug 1987 p. 96, Dec 1987 p. 37)

2-216 JAFFREY, Madhur. *Robi Dobi: The Marvelous Adventures of an Indian Elephant.* Gr. 3–5. (Orig. British pub. 1997.)

Robi Dobi the elephant allows some small creatures, a mouse, a butterfly, and parrots, to take shelter in his warm ear while he helps them solve their problems.

Illus. by Amanda Hall, Dial, 1997, 76 pp. (1-86205-160-7); Pavilion, 1998, 2001, pap., 76 pp. (1-86205-160-7)

(HB 73:456; HBG 9:61; Kirkus 65:1222; SLJ Sep 1997 p. 184)

2-217 JAMES, Mary (pseud. of Marijane Meaker, a.k.a. M. E. Kerr). *Shoebag.*
★ Gr. 3–7.

After his sudden transformation from Shoebag the cockroach into a little boy named Stewart Bagg, Shoebag is adopted by the Biddle family and must deal with a school bully, a TV-commercial-star sister, and the increasing hostility of his cockroach father. The sequel is *Shoebag Returns* (1996).

Scholastic, 1990, 144 pp., o.p.

(BL 86:1632; CCBB 43:164; HBG 1:255; Kirkus 58:264; SLJ June 1990 p. 124, Dec 1990 p. 22; VOYA 13:219)

2-218 JARRELL, Randall. *The Bat-Poet.* Gr. 3–5.

A young bat writes poetry about day-creatures to convince his nocturnal friends to stay awake during the day.
Illus. by Maurice (Bernard) Sendak, Macmillan, 1964, 44 pp., o.p.
(HB 57:453; LJ 89:2210)

JARRELL, Randall. *Fly by Night.*
See Chapter 9, Magic Adventure Fantasy.

JARRELL, Randall. *The Gingerbread Rabbit.*
See Chapter 1, Allegorical Fantasy and Literary Fairy Tales.

2-219   **JARVIS, Robin.** *The Dark Portal.* **(The Deptford Mice trilogy, bk. 1).** Gr.
☆   5–9. (Orig. British pub. 1989.)
Audrey mouse and her young friends search the sewers beneath their home after her father disappears through the grill into the dangerous world ruled by Jupiter the rat. In *The Crystal Prison* (1989, 2002), the Starwife, a squirrel mystic, summons Audrey to save the life of albino mouse Oswald and orders her to accompany the evil rat Madam Akkikyu to Fennywold and stay with her until her death. In *The Final Reckoning* (1990, 2002), Jupiter returns to steal the Starwife's Starstone, enabling him to bring on a fiercely icy winter that endangers the lives of all of the mice and bats. The Deptford Mice Histories are prequels to *The Dark Portal*, including *The Alchemist's Cat* (England, 1991, entitled *The Alchymist's Cat*; U.S., 2003), *The Oaken Throne* (England, 1993), and *Thomas* (England, 1995).
North-South, 2000, 240 pp. (1-58717-021-3); Seastar, 2001, pap. (1-58717-112-0)
(BL 98:1949; HBG 14:83; Kirkus 700:1034; SLJ Sep 2002 p. 226; VOYA 26:12, 26:65)

2-220   **JEFFERIES, (John) Richard.** *Wood Magic; a Fable.* Gr. 7 up. (Orig. British and U.S. pub. 1881.)
A battle by the animal inhabitants of an English meadow over dwelling rights, dominance, and survival is observed by a little boy named Bevis. This book is considered to be the first animal fantasy novel written for children. The sequel is *Bevis: The Story of a Boy* (orig. British pub. 1882, U.S. Dutton, 1966).
Introduction by Richard Adams, Third Press, 1974, 271 pp., o.p.
(BL 71:792; LJ 100:409; SLJ Apr 1975 p. 74)

2-221   **JEKEL, Pamela.** *The Third Jungle Book.* Gr. 5 up.
This contemporary sequel to Rudyard Kipling's *The Jungle Book* (1894; see this chapter) and *The Second Jungle Book* (1895) contains ten further adventures of Mowgli the wolf-boy and his friends Baloo the bear, Bagheera the panther, and Akela the wolf.
Illus. by Nancy Malick, Rinehart, 1992, 219 pp., o.p.
(HBG 4:71; SLJ Nov 1992 p. 94)

2-222   **JENNINGS, Patrick.** *Faith and the Electric Dogs.* Gr. 3–6.
After a stray Mexican dog adopts 10-year-old Faith, she names him Edison, and he joins her on a rocket journey to a desert island. The sequel is *Faith and the Rocket Cat* (1998).
Scholastic, 1996, 146 pp., o.p.
(BL 93:653 and 93:766; CCBB 50:176; HBG 8:68; Kirkus 64:1402; SLJ Dec 1996 p. 122)

2-223 JOHANSEN, Hannah. *7 X 7 Tales of a Sevensleeper.* Gr. 2–4. (Orig. Swiss pub. 1985.)
Sevensleepers are squirrel-like animals that hibernate for seven months of the year, eat things in multiples of seven, and like seven of anything.
Trans. by Christopher Franceschelli, illus. by Käthi Bhend, Dutton, 1989, 95 pp., o.p.
(BL 86:1344; HBG 1:84; SLJ July 1990 p. 61)

2-224 JOHANSEN, Hannah. *A Tomcat's Tale.* Gr. 4–7. (Orig. Swiss pub. 1987.)
✭   Felis, an orange tabby cat, runs away from home and lives a dangerous life in the out-of-doors.
Trans. by Susanna Fox, illus. by Käthi Bhend, Dutton, 1991, 142 pp. (0-525-44583-8)
(BL 87:1967; CCBB 45:13; Kirkus 59:605; HBG 2:266; SLJ Jan 1991 p. 113)

2-225 JOHNSON, Annabel. *I Am Leaper.* Gr. 3–5.
A talking kangaroo mouse named Leaper tries to contact laboratory scientists to warn them that a monster is destroying her territory in the California desert.
Illus. by Stella Ormai, Scholastic, 1990, 128 pp., o.p.
(BL 87:657, 1037; HBG 2:81; Kirkus 58:1326; SLJ Jan 1991 p. 92)

2-226 JOHNSTON, Johanna. *Great Gravity the Cat.* Gr. 3–5.
Gravity is jealous of the new baby in the house and runs away to seek his fortune.
Illus. by Kurt Wiese, Knopf, 1958, 66 pp., o.p.; illus. by Melissa Bay Mathis, Linnet, 1989, 64 pp., o.p.
(CCBB 111:120; HB 34:195; Kirkus 26:74; LJ 83:1602; SLJ Oct 1989 p. 89)

JONES, Diana Wynne. *Dogsbody.*
See Chapter 7, High Fantasy: Travel to Other Worlds.

2-227 JOUBERT, Jean. *White Owl and Blue Mouse.* Gr. 2–3. (Orig. French pub. 1978.)
A mouse who feels responsible for an owl's capture spends each night telling him about her daily explorations of the countryside.
Trans. by Denise Levertov, illus. by Michel Gay, Zoland, 1990, 63 pp., o.p.
(BL 87:755; CCBB 44:122; HBG 2:67)

2-228 KARAZIN, Nikolaí Nikoleavich. *Cranes Flying South.* Gr. 4–6. (Orig. pub. in the Soviet Union.)
A young Russian crane describes his summer of training with Longnose the Wise One before his first flight south.
Trans. by M. Pokrovsky, illus. by Vera Bock, Doubleday, 1931, 235 pp., o.p.
(BL 27:506; HB 7:237, 238; Mahony 3:206)

2-229 KARR, Kathleen. *Exiled: Memoirs of a Camel.* Gr. 5–8.
✭   Ali the Egyptian camel tells the story of his life after he is shipped to Texas in 1856 to join the U.S. Camel Corps.
Marshall Cavendish, 2004, 240 pp. (0-7614-5164-1)
(BL 100:1559; CCBB 57:378; Kirkus 72:271; SLJ May 2004 p. 150; VOYA 27:230)

2-230 KÄSTNER, Erich. *The Animals' Conference.* Gr. 4–6. (Orig. Swiss pub. 1949.)
The animals of the world unite and force the humans to make peace.
Trans. by Zita de Schauensee, illus. by Walter Trier, McKay, 1953, 62 pp., o.p.
(BL 49:380; CCBB 7:5; HB 29:271; Kirkus 21:333)

KATZ, Welwyn Wilton. *Whalesinger.*
See Chapter 9, Magic Adventure Fantasy.

2-231 KAUFMAN, Charles. *The Frog and the Beanpole.* Gr. 5–6.
Wesley, an invisible research laboratory frog, and a girl named Holly run away to join a traveling circus.
Illus. by Troy Howell, Lothrop, 1980, 189 pp., o.p.
(BL 76:1608; CCBB 33:174; Kirkus 48:836; SLJ Aug 1980 p. 64)

2-232 KEHRET, Peg, and PETE THE CAT. *The Stranger Next Door.* **(Pete the**
☆ **Cat series, bk. 1).** Gr. 4–7.
Alex's observant cat, Pete, knows who is behind the rash of vandalism and arson in their new housing development, but he has trouble convincing his humans. In the sequel, *Spy Cat* (2003), Pete solves a string of burglaries by leading his family to missing 7-year-old Benjie, who had followed the burglars.
Dutton, 2002, 160 pp. (0-525-46829-3); Puffin, 2003, pap., 176 pp. (0-14-250178-6)
(BL 98:938; HBG 13:375; Kirkus 70:415; SLJ Mar 2002 p. 232; VOYA 24:447)

KELLER, Gottfried. *The Fat of the Cat and Other Stories.*
See Chapter 3, Fantasy Collections.

2-233 KELLEY, Ellen A. *The Lucky Lizard.* Gr. 2–4.
Bima the pet lizard tells the story of his young owner's adventures at school and at home.
Illus. by Kevin O'Malley, Dutton, 2000, 96 pp. (0-525-46142-6)
(BL 97:340; HBG 12:63; SLJ Oct 2000 p. 128)

2-234 KELLEY, True Adelaide, and LINDBLOM, Steven (Winther). *The Mouses' Terrible Christmas.* Gr. 2–3.
Santa gets into a sticky situation when he falls through a hole in the Mouse family's roof and lands on last year's recycled Christmas tree. The sequel is *The Mouses' Terrible Halloween* (1980).
Illus. by True Adelaide Kelley, Lothrop, 1978, 63 pp., o.p.
(BL 75:552; CCBB 32:64; Kirkus 46:1187; SLJ Oct 1978 p. 114)

KENEALLY, Thomas (Michael). *Ned Kelly and the City of the Bees.*
See Chapter 7, High Fantasy: Travel to Other Worlds.

2-235 KENNEDY, (Jerome) Richard. *The Mouse God.* Gr. 2–5.
☆ Too lazy to catch his own meals, a cat dresses up as a mouse god and convinces the mice to enter a special cage (mouse church) so he can catch them at his leisure.
Illus. by Stephen Harvard, Atlantic-Little, 1979, 32 pp., o.p.
(BL 75:1440; HB 55:407; Kirkus 47:385; SLJ May 1979 p. 52)

KENNEDY, X. J. (pseud. of Joseph Charles Kennedy). *The Owlstone Crown.*
See Chapter 7, High Fantasy: Travel to Other Worlds.

2-236   **KERR, M. E. (pseud. of Marijane Meaker).** *Snakes Don't Miss Their Mothers.* Gr. 4–7.
A king snake named Marshall and a dog named Irving are two of the residents of an animal shelter called Critters; their first-person narratives describe their loneliness and longing to be loved.
HarperCollins, 2003, 208 pp. (0-06-052625-4)
(BL 100:257; CCBB 57:110; HBG 15:96; Kirkus 71:1225; SLJ Oct 2003 p. 169; VOYA 26:312)

2-237   **KESEY, Ken.** *Little Tricker the Squirrel Meets Big Double the Bear.* Gr.
✰   3–6.
Little Tricker the tree squirrel confronts horrible, huge, hairy, hateful, and hungry Big Double the bear and cuts him down to size.
Illus. by Barry Moser, Viking, 1990, 32 pp. (0-670-81136-X); Puffin, 1992, pap. (0-14-050623-3)
(BL 87:924, 1484; CCBB 44:34; HBG 2:65; Kirkus 58:1457; SLJ Dec 1990 p. 104; Suth 4:215)

2-238   **KILWORTH, Garry.** *The Foxes of Firstdark.* Gr. 10 up. (Orig. British pub. 1989.)
After O-ha, the vixen, sees her first love killed in a fox hunt, she creates a family with Camio, another male fox, and tries to rear their three cubs in the face of food shortages and human cruelty.
Doubleday, 1990, 304 pp., o.p.
(BL 86:1526, 1540; Kirkus 58:294; LJ May 15, 1990 p. 99)

KINDL, Patrice. *Owl in Love.*
See Chapter 12, Witchcraft and Sorcery Fantasy.

2-239   **KING, (David) Clive.** *The Town That Went South.* Gr. 4–6.
A great storm sends the town of Ramsley drifting off across the ocean toward the South Pole.
Illus. by Maurice Bartlett, Macmillan, 1959, 117 pp., o.p.
(HB 36:130; LJ 85:1305; TLS May 20, 1960 p. xv, 1969 p. 352)

2-240   **KING, Gabriel.** *The Wild Road.* Gr. 7–12.
Tag must rescue the king and queen of cats from an evil sorcerer who has been torturing generations of cats to gain control of The Wild Road, a dimension containing the memories of all animals. The sequel is *The Golden Cat* (1999).
Ballantine, 1998, 384 pp., o.p.
(LJ Apr 15, 1998 p. 119; SLJ Feb 1999 p. 142; VOYA 21:130 and 22:14)

2-241   **KING-SMITH, Dick.** *Ace: The Very Important Pig.* Gr. 4–6. (Orig. British
✰   pub. 1990, entitled *Ace.*)
The great-grandson of *Babe: The Gallant Pig* (1983, 1985; see below), Ace understands human speech and becomes famous after he appears on a television show.

Illus. by Lynette Hemmant, Crown, 1990, 134 pp., o.p.; Knopf, 1997, 136 pp., o.p.; Peter Smith, 1997 (0-8446-6890-7)

(BL 87:442; CCBB 44:88; HB 66:602; HBG 2:70; Kirkus 58:1004; SLJ Nov 1990 p. 115, Dec 1990 p. 23; Suth 4:218)

2-242 KING-SMITH, Dick. *Animal Stories.* Gr. K–5. (Orig. British pub. 1997.)
Eight stories about heroic animals, including Max the hedgehog, Fat Lawrence the cat, and Babe the pig.
Illus. by Michael Terry, Orchard, 1998, 121 pp. (0-531-30099-4)

(BL 95:119; HBG 10:56; SLJ Nov 1998 p. 88)

2-243 KING-SMITH, Dick. *Babe: The Gallant Pig.* Gr. 4–6. (Orig. British pub.
✮ 1983, entitled *The Sheep-Pig*.)
Farmer Hogget's sheep dog, Fly, trains Babe the pig to become a champion sheepherder. Guardian Award for Children's Fiction, 1984.
Illus. by Mary (Yoma, née Grigson) Rayner, Crown, 1985, 1993, 176 pp. (0-517-55556-5)

(BL 81:1666, 82:1232; HB 61:449, 70:345; HBG 5:78; SLJ Aug 1985 p. 66)

2-244 KING-SMITH, Dick. *The Cuckoo Child.* Gr. 3–6. (Orig. British pub. 1991.)
✮ The ostrich egg that Jack steals from Wildlife Park and hides under the barn-yard goose hatches into a chick named Oliver, who grows to be 9 feet tall.
Illus. by Leslie W. Bowman, Hyperion, 1993, 128 pp. (1-56282-350-7)

(BL 89:1514; HBG 4:300; Kirkus 61:229; SLJ Apr 1993 p. 121)

2-245 KING-SMITH, Dick. *The Fox-Busters.* Gr. 3–6. (Orig. British pub. 1978.)
✮ Three high-flying chickens strike back when four young foxes raid their chick-en coop.
Illus. by Jon Miller, Delacorte, 1988, 117 pp., o.p.

(BL 85:711; CCBB 42:43; HB 65:210; Kirkus 56:1605; SLJ Dec 1988 p. 104; Suth 4:218)

2-246 KING-SMITH, Dick. *Funny Frank.* Gr. 3–5. (Orig. British pub. 2001.)
✮ Jemima, the farmer's daughter, helps a baby chick named Frank achieve his dream of swimming like a duck.
Illus. by John Eastwood, Knopf, 2002, 112 pp. (0-375-91460-9); Yearling, 2003, pap., 108 pp. (0-440-41880-1)

(BL 98:858; HBG 13:359; Kirkus 70:47; SLJ Mar 2002 p. 190)

2-247 KING-SMITH, Dick. *Godhanger.* Gr. 5–8. (Orig. British pub. 1996.)
Skymaster, a huge golden bird, and his 12 woodland bird "apostles" try to pro-tect the animals of Godhanger Wood from a vicious gamekeeper.
Illus. by Andrew Davidson, Crown, 1999, 156 pp., o.p.

(BL 95:1202; HB 75:467; HBG 10:294; Kirkus 66:1735; SLJ Feb 1999 p. 108)

KING-SMITH, Dick. *Harriet's Hare.*
See Chapter 9, Magic Adventure Fantasy.

KING-SMITH, Dick. *Harry's Mad.*
See Chapter 8, Humorous Fantasy.

KING-SMITH, Dick. *Hogsel and Gruntel and Other Animal Stories.*
See Chapter 6, High Fantasy: Myth or Legend Fantasy.

2-248 KING-SMITH, Dick. *The Jenius.* Gr. 2–4. (Orig. British pub. 1988.)
Judy's parents find it hard to believe her stories about the amazing tricks she has taught her baby guinea pig, Jenius.
Illus. by Peter Firmin, Trafalgar Sq./David & Charles, 1990, 44 pp., o.p.; illus. by Brian Floca, Hyperion, 1996, 52 pp. (entitled *Jenius: The Amazing Guinea Pig*), o.p.
(CCBB 44:10; HB 73:60; HBG 8:58; Kirkus 58:877; SLJ Sep 1990 p. 206, Nov 1996 p. 87)

2-249 KING-SMITH, Dick. *Magnus Powermouse.* Gr. 4–6. (Orig. British pub.
☆ 1982.)
Life with Magnus, the giant-sized mouse baby, proves to be somewhat difficult for his parents, in spite of his victory over a local cat.
Illus. by Mary (Yoma, née Grigson) Rayner, Harper, 1984, 120 pp., o.p.
(BL 80:1191; CCBB 37:207; HB 60:329; Kirkus 52:40; SLJ Aug 1984 p. 74; Suth 3:235)

2-250 KING-SMITH, Dick. *Martin's Mice.* Gr. 4–6. (Orig. British pub. 1988.)
☆ After Martin—a barn cat who would rather keep mice as pets than eat them—captures Drusilla Mouse, he is kept busy protecting her and her 12 children from his feline relatives.
Illus. by Jez Alborough, Crown, 1988, 122 pp., o.p.
(BL 85:939; HB 65:71; Kirkus 56:1740; SLJ Jan 1989 p. 78, Dec 1989 p. 39)

2-251 KING-SMITH, Dick. *The Mouse Butcher.* Gr. 4–6. (Orig. British pub.
☆ 1981.)
A cat named Tom Plug is hired by a wealthy Persian cat family to be their mouse butcher, but his life is endangered by a killer cat named Great Mog.
Illus. by Margot Apple, Viking, 1982, 132 pp., o.p.
(BL 78:1526; CCBB 36:71; HB 58:404; Kirkus 50:605; SLJ Apr 1982 p. 71; Suth 3:236)

2-252 KING-SMITH, Dick. *A Mouse Called Wolf.* Gr. 2–4. (Orig. British pub.
1997.)
Tiny Wolfgang Amadeus Mouse's musical talents amaze his family and the elderly woman in whose house they live.
Illus. by Jon Goodell, Crown, 1997, 98 pp. (0-517-70973-2)
(BL 94:329; HBG 9:62)

KING-SMITH, Dick. *Mr. Potter's Pet.*
See Chapter 8, Humorous Fantasy.

2-253 KING-SMITH, Dick. *The Nine Lives of Aristotle.* Gr. 2–4. (Orig. British
☆ pub. 2003, entitled *Aristotle*.)
Witch's kitten Aristotle uses up eight of his nine lives in a series of dangerous adventures, and then settles down for a peaceful life as a witch's familiar.
Illus. by Bob Graham, Candlewick, 2003, 80 pp. (0-7636-2260-5)
(BL 100:667; CCBB 57:111; HBG 15:81; Kirkus 71:1176; SLJ Oct 2003 p. 128)

2-254 KING-SMITH, Dick. *Pigs Might Fly.* Gr. 4–6. (Orig. British pub. 1980, enti-
☆ tled *Daggie Dogfoot*.)
Daggie, the dog-footed runt of the pig litter, learns to swim and rescues the other pigs during a flash flood. Runner-up, Guardian Award for Children's Fiction, 1981.

Illus. by Mary (Yoma, née Grigson) Rayner, Viking, 1982, 158 pp., o.p.
(BL 78:1368, 79:685, 978, 84:1441; CCBB 36:29; HB 58:405; Kirkus 50:419; SLJ Aug 1982 p. 99; Suth 3:236)

KING-SMITH, Dick. *Pretty Polly.*
See Chapter 8, Humorous Fantasy.

2-255 **KING-SMITH, Dick.** *The School Mouse.* Gr. 3–5. (Orig. British pub. 1995.)
✮ Flora mouse puts her reading skills to use as she saves her parents from eating poison and teaches the other mice how to read.
Illus. by Cynthia Fisher, Hyperion, 1995, 124 pp. (0-7868-0036-4); Disney, 1997, pap., 124 pp. (0-7868-1156-0)
(BL 92:404; CCBB 49:164; HBG 7:64; Kirkus 63:1494; SLJ Dec 1995 p. 82)

2-256 **KING-SMITH, Dick.** *The Swoose.* Gr. 3–5. (Orig. British pub. 1993.)
Fitzherbert—part goose, part swan—sets off down the River Thames to search for his father, a swan from Windsor Castle.
Illus. by Marie Corner, Hyperion, 1994, 45 pp., o.p.
(BL 91:929; CCBB 48:133; HBG 6:67; SLJ Jan 1995 p. 108)

2-257 **KING-SMITH, Dick.** *Three Terrible Trins.* Gr. 3–5. (Orig. British pub.
✮ 1994.)
Mrs. Gray, a mouse, raises her triplets to hate cats and urges them to avenge their father's death.
Illus. by Mark Teague, Crown, 1994, 105 pp., o.p.; Knopf, 1997, pap., 106 pp. (0-679-88552-8)
(BL 91:594, 861, and 1411; CCBB 48:203; HB 790:733; HBG 6:78; Kirkus 62:1409; SLJ Nov 1994 p. 105)

2-258 **KING-SMITH, Dick.** *Titus Rules!* Gr. 4–6. (Orig. British pub. 2002, entitled *Titus Rules OK!*.)
Royal pet Corgie puppy Titus manages to stop a jewel thief and summon help to put out a fire in this humorous story.
Illus. by John Eastwood, Knopf, 2003, 128 pp. (0-375-91461-7)
(BL 99:995; HBG 14:355; Kirkus 70:1769; SLJ Mar 2003 p. 235)

2-259 **KING-SMITH, Dick.** *The Toby Man.* Gr. 3–5. (Orig. British pub. 1989.)
✮ Tod fulfills his dream of becoming a highway robber like his father, with the help of a talking donkey named Matilda, a mastiff named Digby, Loudmouth the magpie, and Evil the ferret, in this story set in 18th-century England.
Illus. by Lynette Hemmant, Crown, 1991, 83 pp., o.p.
(BL 88:440; CCBB 45:14; HB 68:736; HBG 3:68; Kirkus 59:1224; SLJ Sep 1991 p. 254)

2-260 **KIPLING, (Joseph) Rudyard.** *All the Mowgli Stories.* Gr. 4–7.
Mowgli is a human boy raised by jungle animals. His stories were originally told in *The Jungle Books* (1893, 1895; see below).
Illus. by Kurt Wiese, Doubleday, 1936, 299 pp., o.p.
(BL 32:333; HB 12:158; LJ 61:733)

KIPLING, (Joseph) Rudyard. *The Beginning of the Armadilloes.*
See Chapter 1, Allegorical Fantasy and Literary Fairy Tales.

KIPLING, (Joseph) Rudyard. *The Elephant's Child.*
See Chapter 1, Allegorical Fantasy and Literary Fairy Tales.

KIPLING, (Joseph) Rudyard. *How the Camel Got His Hump.*
See Chapter 1, Allegorical Fantasy and Literary Fairy Tales.

KIPLING, (Joseph) Rudyard. *How the Leopard Got His Spots.*
See Chapter 1, Allegorical Fantasy and Literary Fairy Tales.

KIPLING, (Joseph) Rudyard. *How the Rhinoceros Got His Skin.*
See Chapter 1, Allegorical Fantasy and Literary Fairy Tales.

2-261 KIPLING, (Joseph) Rudyard. *The Jungle Book.* Gr. 3–7. (Orig. British and
✭ U.S. pub. 1894.)
Tales of Mowgli, a boy adopted by wolves; Kotik the seal; Rikki-Tikki-Tavi,
the mongoose; and other jungle animals. The sequel is *The Second Jungle Book*
(Scribner, 1895; Doubleday, 1923; Puffin, 1987). Pamela Jekel has written a
contemporary sequel entitled *The Third Jungle Book* (Roberts, 1992; see this
chapter).
Illus. by J(ohn) L(ockwood) Kipling, Doubleday, 1928, 1946, 212 pp., o.p.;
illus. by Kurt Wiese, Doubleday, 1932, o.p.; illus. by Fritz Eichenberg, Grosset,
1950, 279 pp., o.p.; illus. by Robert Shore, Macmillan, 1964, 371 pp., o.p.;
adapt. by Robin McKinley, Random, 1985 (entitled *Tales from "The Jungle
Book"*), 64 pp., o.p.; illus. by Gregory Alexander, Arcade, 1991, 128 pp. (1-
55970-127-7); illus. by Inga Moore, Simon, 1992, 98 pp. (entitled *The Favorite
Mowgli Stories from The Jungle Book*), o.p.; illus. by Jerry Pinkney, Morrow,
1995, 272 pp. (entitled *The Jungle Book: The Mowgli Stories*) (0-688-09979-3);
illus. by Christian Broutin, Viking, 1996, 210 pp. (0-670-86919-8)
(BL 47:162, 82:135, 89:737, 93:404; Bookshelf 1933 p. 9; CCBB 5:15; HB 1:34; HBG 4:72,
7:64; Kirkus 32:1014; LJ 75:2085; SLJ Nov 1991 p. 118)

2-262 KIPLING, (Joseph) Rudyard. *Just So Stories.* Gr. 1–5. (Orig. British pub.
✭ 1897–1902.)
Twelve classic animal fables, including "How the Camel Got His Hump,"
"How the Leopard Got His Spots," and "How the Rhinoceros Got His Skin."
Many of these tales have been published in individual volumes, and can be
found in Chapter 1, Allegorical Fantasy and Literary Fairy Tales.
Illus. by the author, Doubleday, 1902, 1952, 249 pp., o.p.; illus. by Feodor
Rojankovsky (entitled *The Elephant's Child and Other Just So Stories*), Doubleday, 1942, o.p.; illus. by Etienne Delessert, Doubleday, 1946 (anniversary
ed.), 1972, o.p.; illus. by Victor G. Ambrus, Rand, 1982, 64 pp., o.p.; illus. by
Meg Rutherford, Silver, 1986, 76 pp., o.p.; illus. by Safaya Salter, Holt, 1987,
96 pp. (0-8050-0439-4); illus. by Michael Foreman, Viking, 1987, 127 pp. (0-
670-80242-5); illus. by David Frampton, Harper, 1991, 122 pp., LB (0-06-
023294-3); illus. by the author, Knopf, 1992, 192 pp. (0-679-41797-4); illus. by
Isabelle Brent, Viking, 1993 (entitled *The Complete Just So Stories*), 160 pp.
(0-670-85196-5); illus. by Barry Moser, Morrow, 1996, 160 pp. (0-688-13957-
4); Candlewick, 2004 (entitled *A Collection of Rudyard Kipling's Just So Stories*), 128 pp. (0-7636-2629-5)
(BL 77:327, 79:778, 83:512, 84:709, 88:625, 90:755; Bookshelf 1928 p. 9; CCBB 6:17, 26:93;
Eakin:188; HB 1:45, 58:565, 68:97, 70:199; HBG 3:68, 5:78, 8:69; Kirkus 40:940, 1413,

54:1450, 55:1159, 59:1412, 61:1393; LJ 98:1682; SLJ Nov 1987 p. 105, Nov 1991 p. 118, Dec 1993 p. 112)

2-263 KIPLING, (Joseph) Rudyard. *Rikki-Tikki-Tavi.* Gr. 1–4. (Orig. British pub. as part of *The Jungle Book*, 1894.)

Rikki-Tikki-Tavi, a young mongoose who adopts an English family living in India, saves their little boy's life by killing poisonous snakes in their garden in this story from *The Jungle Book* (1894; see entry above).

Illus. by Lambert Davis, Harcourt, 1992, 37 pp., o.p.; adapt. and illus. by Jerry Pinkney, Morrow, 1997, 40 pp. (0-688-14320-2); illus. by Danuta Mayer; Candlewick, 1997, 64 pp. (0-7636-0132-2)

(BL 89:155, 94:117, and 734; CCBB 51:163; HBG 4:58, 9:60 and 62; Kirkus 60:1 131; SLJ Dec 1992 p. 85, Aug 1997 p. 136)

2-264 KIRBY, Mansfield. *The Secret of Thut-Mouse III; or Basil Beandesert's Revenge.* Gr. 3–5. (Orig. Dutch pub. 1987.)

A group of educated mice living in an art museum take revenge on the museum director for buying a cat by producing fake Egyptian artifacts that convince the director to write a book on his fabulous find.

Illus. by Mance Post, Farrar, 1985, 64 pp., o.p.

(BL 82:496; CCBB 39:70; SLJ Dec 1985 p. 90)

2-265 KIRK, Daniel. *Rex Tabby: Cat Detective.* Gr. 3–5.

After feline detective Rex Tabby sends fish thief Ma Manx to the slammer, her kittens, Rumpy and Stumpy, start causing trouble.

Illus. by the author, Orchard, 2004, 144 pp. (0-439-45286-4)

(BL 100:1935; Kirkus 72:578; SLJ Aug 2004 p. 89)

2-266 KOLLER, Jackie French. *Mole and Shrew: All Year Through.* Gr. 2–3.

Best friends Mole and Shrew enjoy a year full of fun. Other books about Mole and Shrew include two picture books, *Mole and Shrew* (1991) and *Mole and Shrew Step Out* (1992), and three short novels, *Mole and Shrew Are Two* (2000), *Mole and Shrew Find a Clue* (2001), and *Mole and Shrew Have Jobs to Do* (2001).

Illus. by John Beder, Random, 1997, 80 pp., o.p.

(BL 94:918; HBG 9:62)

KORSCHUNOW, Irina. *Small Fur.*
See Chapter 9, Magic Adventure Fantasy.

2-267 KOTZWINKLE, William. *Doctor Rat.* Gr. 10 up.

The free animals of the world unite to liberate those trapped in scientific laboratories by human researchers and by Doctor Rat, a rodent collaborator. World Fantasy Award, 1976.

Knopf, 1976, 243 pp., o.p.; Marlowe, 1997, pap., 243 pp., o.p.

(BL 72:1570; Kirkus 44:273, 336; LJ 101:1556; TLS 1976 p. 815)

KOTZWINKLE, William. *Trouble in Bugland: A Collection of Inspector Mantis Mysteries.*
See Chapter 8, Humorous Fantasy.

2-268 KOVACS, Deborah. *Brewster's Courage.* Gr. 3–6.
Having fallen in love with bayou music, Brewster, a black-footed ferret from South Dakota, decides to move to the Moustafaya Swamp in Louisiana and set up a bicycle messenger service.
Illus. by Joseph Mathieu, Simon & Schuster, 1992, 104 pp., o.p.
(Kirkus 60:780; HBG 3:266; SLJ Sep 1992 p. 254)

2-269 KRENSKY, Stephen (Alan). *Woodland Crossings.* Gr. 3–5.
Five tales about a proud Flower King brought low, a worm who fools his blackbird captor, and other forest creatures.
Illus. by Jan Brett Bowler, Macmillan, 1978, 43 pp., o.p.
(Kirkus 46:497; SLJ May 1978 p. 69)

2-270 KRÜSS, James (Jacob Heinrich). *Eagle and Dove.* Gr. 3–5. (Orig. German pub. 1963.)
Trapped by an eagle, a dove distracts him by telling stories while she digs an escape hole.
Trans. by Edelgard von Heydekampf Brühl, illus. by Pat Kent, Atheneum, 1965, 69 pp., o.p.
(BL 62:364; Kirkus 33:624; LJ 90:3792)

KRÜSS, James (Jacob Heinrich). *The Happy Islands Behind the Winds.*
See Chapter 7, High Fantasy: Travel to Other Worlds.

2-271 KWITZ, Mary DeBall. *Shadow Over Mousehaven Manor.* Gr. 3–5.
Minabel Mouse makes a treacherous journey across snow-covered prairies to rescue her elderly Aunt Pitty Pat from gang leader Magnus Rat. The sequel is *The Bell Tolls at Mousehaven Manor* (1991).
Illus. by Stella Ormai, Scholastic, 1989, 160 pp., o.p.
(BL 86:743; HBG 1:83; Kirkus 57:1672; SLJ Nov 1989 p. 112)

2-272 LABATT, Mary. *Strange Neighbors.* **(Sam, Dog Detective series, bk. 3).** Gr. 3–5.
Sam the sheepdog convinces Jennie that their new neighbors are witches making the neighborhood animals sick. This book is preceded by *The Ghost of Captain Briggs* (1999) and *Spying on Dracula* (1999); sequels are *Aliens in Woodford* (2000), *A Weekend at the Grand Hotel* (2001), *The Secret of Sagawa Lake* (2001), *The Mummy Lives!* (2002), and *One Terrible Halloween* (2002).
Illus. by Troy Hill-Jackson, Kids Can, 2000, 110 pp. (1-55074-603-0), 2000, pap., 110 pp. (1-55074-605-7)
(BL 96:1668; HBG 11:306:SLJ Sep 2000 p. 202)

LAGERLÖF, Selma (Ottiliana Lovisa). *The Wonderful Adventures of Nils.*
See Chapter 9, Magic Adventure Fantasy.

2-273 LALLY, Soinbhe. *A Hive for the Honeybee.* Gr. 7–12.
☆ Life is busy inside the honeybee hive, particularly for worker bees Thora and Belle, and for Mo, the radical drone who dreams of equality for the workers.
Illus. by Patience Brewster, Scholastic, 1999, 224 pp. (0-590-51038-X), 2001, pap., 224 pp. (0-590-51045-2)

(BL 95:969; CCBB 52:884; HB 75:209; HBG 10:304; Kirkus 66:1736; Kliatt Jan 1999 p. 7; SLJ May 1999 p. 127; VOYA 22:48)

LAMPMAN, Evelyn Sibley. *The City Under the Back Steps.*
See Chapter 7, High Fantasy: Travel to Other Worlds.

2-274 LANDSMAN, Sandy. *Castaways on Chimp Island.* Gr. 6–8.
Exiled to an island with other "unteachable" laboratory chimps, Danny and three friends hatch a plan for getting home.
Atheneum, 1986, 202 pp., o.p.
(BL 82:1614; CCBB 39:171; HB 62:597; Kirkus 54:869; SLJ Aug 1986 p. 94; VOYA 9:220)

2-275 LANIER, Sterling E(dmund). *The War for the Lot: A Tale of Fantasy and Terror.* Gr. 4–6.
Alec helps the woodland creatures living around his grandfather's farm to fight off the tyrannical rats.
Illus. by Robert Baumgartner, Follett, 1969, 256 pp., o.p.
(BL 66:928; CCBB 24:61; HB 46:162; LJ 95:1945, 3603)

2-276 LASKY (Knight), Kathryn. *The Capture.* **(Guardians of Ga'Hoole series,**
☆ **bk. 1).** Gr. 5–9.
When Soren, a young barn owl, falls from his nest, he is captured by evil owls and placed in St. Aegolius Academy for Orphaned Owls, where ancient owl legends about the Guardians of Ga'Hoole help him and his new friend Gylfie to survive and escape. The sequels are *The Journey* (2003), and *The Rescue* (2004).
Scholastic, 2003, pap., 226 pp. (0-439-40557-2)
(BL 100:240; Kliatt Sep 2003 p. 26; SLJ Oct 2003 p. 170; VOYA 26:414)

2-277 LASSIG, Jurgen. *Spiny.* Gr. K–4. (Orig. Swiss pub. 1995.)
Spiny, a newly hatched spinosaurus, wanders away from his nest, but his iguanodon babysitter saves him from Tyroar, the fearsome tyrannosaurus.
Trans. by J. Alison James, illus. by Uli Waas, North-South, 1995, 58 pp., o.p.
(BL 91:1575; HBG 6:292; SLJ June 1995 p. 90)

LATHROP, Dorothy P(ulis). *The Fairy Circus.*
See Chapter 1, Allegorical Fantasy and Literary Fairy Tales.

LATHROP, Dorothy P(ulis). *The Little White Goat.*
See Chapter 9, Magic Adventure Fantasy.

2-278 LATHROP, Dorothy P(ulis). *The Snail Who Ran.* Gr. 3–4.
A moonbeam fairy gives one wish each to a mouse and a snail.
Illus. by the author, Stokes, 1934, 57 pp., o.p.
(BL 31:177; Bookshelf 1935 p. 2; HB 10:357; LJ 59:854; Mahony 3:80)

2-279 LAUBER, Patricia (Grace). *Home at Last! A Young Cat's Tale.* Gr. 2–4.
Two kittens raised in a library set off to find a new home, fortified for their adventures by reading heroic books.
Illus. by Mary Chalmers, Coward, 1980, 47 pp., o.p.
(BL 77:406; HB 57:47; Kirkus 49:7; SLJ Feb 1981 p. 58)

2-280 LAUBER, Patricia (Grace). *Purrfectly Purrfect.* Gr. 2–4.
Kittens Bo, Tiffany, and Dudley enter The Acatemy, a finishing school for
"purrfect" cats.
Illus. by Betsy Lewin, HarperCollins, 2000, 80 pp. (0-688-17299-7)
(CCBB 54:153; HBG 12:64; Kirkus 68:1120; SLJ Dec 2000 p. 113)

2-281 LAURENCE, (Jean) Margaret (Wemyss). *Jason's Quest.* Gr. 5–7. (Orig.
British pub. 1970.)
Searching for a cure for his hometown's illness, Jason Mole travels to the city
of Londinium and is captured by a gang of rats.
Illus. by Staffen Torell, Knopf, 1970, 211 pp., o.p.
(CCBB 24:29; LJ 96:3050; Suth:240; TLS 1970 p. 1458)

LAWSON, John S(hults). *You Better Come Home with Me.*
See Chapter 1, Allegorical Fantasy and Literary Fairy Tales.

2-282 LAWSON, Robert. *Ben and Me: A New and Astonishing Life of Benjamin*
✶ *Franklin as Written by His Good Mouse, Amos: Lately Discovered.* Gr. 4–7.
(Orig. pub. 1939.)
Amos Mouse discloses the fact that most of Ben Franklin's inventions were
actually Amos's ideas, and describes their adventures together.
Illus. by the author, Little, Brown, 1951, 1988, 114 pp., o.p.
(BL 36:117; HB 15:388, 16:28; LJ 65:125)

2-283 LAWSON, Robert. *Captain Kidd's Cat: Being the True and Dolorous*
✶ *Chronicle of Wm. Kidd, Gentleman and Merchant of New York; Late Cap-*
tain of the Adventure Galley; Of the Vicissitudes Attending His Unfortu-
nate Cruise in Eastern Waters, Of His Unjust Trial and Execution, as
Narrated by His Faithful Cat, McDermot, Who Ought to Know. Gr. 4–7.
McDermot Cat doesn't think Captain Kidd deserves to be called a pirate.
Illus. by the author, Little, Brown, 1956, 151 pp., o.p.
(BL 52:282; CCBB 9:115; Eakin:203; HB 32:121, 61:78; Kirkus 24:3; LJ 81:767)

2-284 LAWSON, Robert. *Edward, Hoppy and Joe.* Gr. 3–5.
Father Rabbit struggles to educate his son Edward and friends Hoppy Toad and
Joe Possum.
Illus. by the author, Knopf, 1952, 122 pp., o.p.
(BL 48:303; HB 28:107; Kirkus 20:224; LJ 77:907)

2-285 LAWSON, Robert. *I Discover Columbus: A True Chronicle of the Great*
Admiral and His Finding of the New World, Narrated by the Venerable
Parrot Aurelio, Who Shared in the Glorious Venture. Gr. 4–7.
It is Aurelio, a Caribbean parrot stranded in Spain, who convinces Columbus to
make his voyage to the New World.
Illus. by the author, Little, Brown, 1941, 110 pp., o.p.
(BL 38:58; HB 17:366, 453; LJ 66:908)

2-286 LAWSON, Robert. *Mr. Revere and I: Being an Account of Certain*
✶ *Episodes in the Career of Paul Revere, Esq., as Recently Revealed by His*
Horse, Scheherazade, Late Pride of His Royal Majesty's 14th Regiment of
Foot. Gr. 5–7.

Scheherazade, a former cavalry horse rescued by Sam Adams from the glue factory, tells of her subsequent life with Paul Revere's family.
Illus. by the author, Little, Brown, 1953, 152 pp., o.p.
(BL 50:84; CCBB 7:31; Eakin:204; HB 29:464; Kirkus 21:357; LJ 78:1858)

2-287 LAWSON, Robert. *Mr. Twigg's Mistake.* Gr. 4–6.
✳   Super-vitamin-laced cereal transforms Mr. Twigg's pet mole.
Illus. by the author, Little, Brown, 1947, 141 pp., o.p.
(BL 44:117; CCBB 2:4; Kirkus 15:467; LJ 72:1543)

LAWSON, Robert. *Mr. Wilmer.*
See Chapter 8, Humorous Fantasy.

2-288 LAWSON, Robert. *Rabbit Hill.* **(Rabbit Hill trilogy, bk. 1).** Gr. 3–6.
✳   Although they are happy that a new family is moving into the empty farm-house, the animals on Rabbit Hill fear the newcomers may bring traps and guns. John Newbery Medal, 1945. The sequels are *Robbut: A Tale of Tails* (1948; Linnet, 1990) and *The Tough Winter* (1954).
Illus. by the author, Viking, 1944, 127 pp., o.p.; Puffin, 1982, pap. (0-14-031010-X)
(BL 41:62; HB 20:487, 66:481; Kirkus 12:403; LJ 69:866, 886)

LAZARUS, Keo Felker. *The Shark in the Window.*
See Chapter 8, Humorous Fantasy.

LEE, Tanith. *Animal Castle.*
See Chapter 1, Allegorical Fantasy and Literary Fairy Tales.

2-289 LE GUIN, Ursula K(roeber). *Buffalo Gals and Other Animal Presences.*
✳   Gr. 10 up.
Ten stories and 19 poems, many of which have been published previously, on the theme of the oneness of life, told mainly from the point of view of animals attempting to open the eyes of humans to the larger community of life.
Illus. by Margaret Chodos-Irvine, Capra, 1987, 196 pp., o.p.; NAL, 1988, pap., 236 pp. (0-452-26480-4), 1990, pap. (0-451-45049-3)
(Kliatt Jan 1991 p. 22; LJ Nov 1, 1987 p. 112; TLS 1990 p. 534; VOYA 13:364)

2-290 LE GUIN, Ursula K(roeber). *Catwings.* **(Catwings series, bk. 1).** Gr. K–4.
✳   Four winged kittens escape from a dangerous city neighborhood to a forest, where they find friends and a safe home. In *Catwings Return* (1989), two of the kittens fly back to the city in hopes of rescuing their mother and a sister they've never met. In *Wonderful Alexander and the Catwings* (1994), Jane, one of the flying cats, rescues a lost kitten named Alexander who helps her to regain her ability to speak. In *Jane on Her Own* (1999), Jane, lonely for her mother, flies back to the city from Overhill Farm, searching for adventure and new friends.
Illus. by S. D. Schindler, Orchard, 1988, 40 pp. (0-531-05759-3); Scholastic, 1992, pap. (0-5904-6072-2)
(BL 84:1928; CCBB 42:13; HB 64:781; Kirkus 56:976; SLJ Nov 1988 p. 91; Suth 4:240)

2-291 LE GUIN, Ursula K(roeber). *Solomon Leviathan's Nine Hundred and Thirty-First Trip Around the World.* Gr. 3–5.

Two philosopher friends—a giraffe and a boa constrictor—are swallowed by a whale named Simon Leviathan after they set off across the sea in search of the horizon.

Illus. by Alicia Austin, Putnam, 1988, 32 pp., o.p.

(Kirkus 56:1676; SLJ Dec 1988 p. 88)

2-292 LEONARD, Elmore. *A Coyote's in the House.* Gr. 4–8.

☆ Antwan, leader of a Hollywood Hills coyote pack, gets himself adopted into the human family of retired German shepherd movie star Buddy and champion poodle Miss Betty, but Buddy resents sharing the limelight.

HarperEntertainment, 2004, 160 pp. (0-06-054404-X)

2-293 LEONARD, Nellie Mabel. *The Graymouse Family.* Gr. 4–6. (Orig. pub. 1916; retitled *The Mouse Book,* 1926.)

Mother Graymouse and her six children live in the walls of a human family's house. The sequel is *Grandfather Whiskers, M.D., a Graymouse Story* (1953; orig. title: *Grand-Daddy Whiskers, M.D.*, 1919).

Illus. by Barbara Cooney, Crowell, 1950, 209 pp., o.p.

(CCBB 4:44; Kirkus 18:330; LJ 75:2162)

LEROE, Ellen. *Ghost Dog.*
See Chapter 4, Ghost Fantasy.

2-294 LEROY, Gen. *Taxi Cat and Huey.* Gr. 3–6.

Life changes dramatically for Huey, the Walton family basset hound, after the arrival of Taxi, a part-Siamese cat who thinks he's a Ninja warrior.

Illus. by Karen Ritz, Harper, 1992, 140 pp. LB (0-06-021769-3)

(BL 88:1451; HBG 3:266; Kirkus 60:721; SLJ July 1992 p. 73)

2-295 LEVY, Elizabeth. *A Hare-Raising Tail: A Fletcher Mystery.* **(Fletcher Mystery series, bk. 1).** Gr. 2–5.

Fletcher the basset hound detective solves the case of a rabbit missing from his owner's classroom. The sequels are *The Principal's on the Roof* (2002), *The Mixed-Up Mask Mystery* (2003), *The Mystery of the Too Many Elvises* (2003), and *The Cool Ghoul Mystery* (2004). Fletcher began as a character in the author's Something Queer mystery series (Hyperion).

Illus. by Mordicai Gerstein, Aladdin, 2000, 80 pp. (0-689-84631-2); Simon, 2002, pap., 71 pp. (0-689-84626-6)

(BL 99:124; HBG 13:360)

LEWIS, C(live) S(taples). *The Lion, the Witch, and the Wardrobe.*
See Chapter 7, High Fantasy: Travel to Other Worlds.

2-296 LEZRA, Giggy (Grizzella Paull). *The Cat, the Horse, and the Miracle.* Gr. 4–6.

A lady in blue gives an unhappy cat and horse a golden thread that will lead them into their future.

Illus. by Zena Bernstein, Atheneum, 1967, 114 pp., o.p.

(CCBB 20:155; Kirkus 35:198; LJ 92:1317; Suth:250)

2-297 **LINDOP, Audrey E.** *The Adventures of the Wuffle.* Gr. 4–6. (Orig. British pub. 1966.)
Wuffle's grandmother advises him to become important, so he and his friend Norrie the tortoise decide to become lawyers.
Illus. by William Stobbs, McGraw-Hill, 1968, 126 pp., o.p.
(Kirkus 36:150; LJ 93:2730; TLS 1966 p. 1087)

LINDSAY, Norman (Alfred William). *The Magic Pudding: Being the Adventures of Bunyip Bluegum and His Friends Bill Barnacle and Sam Sawnoff.*
See Chapter 8, Humorous Fantasy.

LISLE, Janet Taylor. *Forest.*
See Chapter 1, Allegorical Fantasy and Literary Fairy Tales.

LITTLE, Jane. *Sneaker Hill.*
See Chapter 12, Witchcraft and Sorcery Fantasy.

2-298 **LIVELY, Penelope (Margaret Low).** *A House Inside Out.* Gr. 3–6. (Orig.
☆ British pub. 1987.)
The Dixon family share their home with 39 animals and several thousand insects. Each chapter is told through the eyes of one of the nonhuman inhabitants of 54 Pavilion Road.
Illus. by David Parkins, Dutton, 1987, 127 pp., o.p.
(BL 84:1265, 1441; CCBB 41:95; Kirkus 55:1630; SLJ Feb 1988 p. 73; Suth 4:250; TLS 1987 p. 1176)

2-299 **LIVELY, Penelope (Margaret Low).** *The Voyage of Q V 66.* Gr. 6–8. (Orig.
☆ British pub. 1978.)
In a future time when animals are the only survivors of a great flood, six creatures travel to London in hope of discovering Stanley's true identity.
Illus. by Harold Jones, Dutton, 1979, 172 pp., o.p.
(BL 75:1627; CCBB 32:195; HB 55:415; Kirkus 47:637; SLJ Dec 1979 p. 152; Suth 3:269)

LOFTING, Hugh. *The Story of Doctor Dolittle.*
See Chapter 8, Humorous Fantasy.

2-300 **LOFTING, Hugh.** *The Story of Mrs. Tubbs.* Gr. 2–4. (Orig. British pub. 1923.)
A dog, a duck, and a pig care for old Mrs. Tubbs until she is strong enough to go home to her farm.
Illus. by the author, Stokes, 1923, 91 pp., o.p.; Lippincott, 1951, 1968, 91 pp., o.p.
(BL 20:63; Bookshelf 1927 p. 7; Kirkus 36:393)

2-301 *The Lonely Little Pig and Other Animal Tales.* **Ed. by Wilhelmina Harper.**
Gr. 2–4.
Thirteen short, humorous animal stories.
Illus. by Vera Neville, McKay, 1938, 108 pp., o.p.
(BL 35:160; HB 15:31)

LOWREY, Janette Sebring. *The Lavender Cat.*
See Chapter 1, Allegorical Fantasy and Literary Fairy Tales.

2-302 **LOWRY, Lois.** *Stay! Keeper's Story.* Gr. 5–8.
✻ Keeper, an orphaned pup, tells the story of his life with three owners: a homeless man, a photographer, and a little girl.
Illus. by True Adelaide Kelley, Houghton, 1997, 128 pp. (0-395-87048-8);
Yearling, 1999, pap., 128 pp. (0-440-41524-1)
(BL 94:472; CCBB 51:165; HB 74:76; HBG 9:75; Kirkus 65:1584; SLJ Oct 1997 p. 134)

2-303 **LURIE, Morris.** *The Twenty-Seventh Annual African Hippopotamus Race.*
Gr. 3–5.
Edward Day, an 8-year-old African hippo, competes in the annual 14-mile race up the Zamboola River, with guidance from his former-champion grandfather.
Illus. by Richard Sawers, Simon, 1969, 56 pp., o.p.
(HB 46:381; LJ 95:3229)

MACAULAY, David. *BAAA.*
See Chapter 1, Allegorical Fantasy and Literary Fairy Tales.

McCAFFREY, Anne (Inez). *No One Noticed the Cat.*
See Chapter 5, High Fantasy: Alternate Worlds or Histories.

2-304 **McCOY, Neely.** *The Tale of the Good Cat Jupie.* Gr. 2–4.
A talking cat and a little girl set up housekeeping together. The sequels are *Jupie Follows His Tale* (1928) and *Jupie and the Wise Old Owl* (1931).
Illus. by the author, Macmillan, 1926, 1932, 99 pp., o.p.
(BL 23:276; HB 2:45; LJ 53:484)

2-305 **McGOWEN, Tom (Thomas E.).** *Odyssey from River Bend.* Gr. 4–6.
✻ Kip the badger leads a group of animals from River Bend into the Haunted Land to search for the secrets of the ancients.
Little, Brown, 1975, 166 pp., o.p.
(BL 72:44; CCBB 29:82; Kirkus 43:513; SLJ Sep 1975 p. 107; Suth 2:300)

2-306 **McHUGH, Elizabet.** *Beethoven's Cat.* Gr. 3–6.
After the Carter's cat, Wiggie, becomes convinced that he is the direct descendant of Beethoven's cat, Ludwig, only a visit to an animal psychiatrist can relieve his haunted spirit. The sequel is *Wiggie Wins the West* (1989).
Illus. by Anita Riggio, Macmillan, 1988, 53 pp., o.p.
(BL 84:1265; CCBB 41:162; Kirkus 56:541; SLJ Apr 1988 p. 103; VOYA 11:133)

2-307 **McINERNEY, Judith Whitelock.** *Judge Benjamin: Superdog.* **(Judge Benjamin: Superdog series, bk. 1).** Gr. 4–6.
The O'Rileys' St. Bernard, Judge Benjamin, describes his busy life as family protector. The sequels are *Judge Benjamin: The Superdog Secret* (1983), *Judge Benjamin: The Superdog Rescue* (1984), *Judge Benjamin: The Superdog Surprise* (1985; 1990), *Judge Benjamin: The Superdog Gift* (1986), and *Judge Benjamin and the Purloined Sirloin* (1986).
Illus. by Leslie Morrill, Holiday, 1982, 142 pp., o.p.
(BL 78:1315; SLJ Aug 1982 p. 118)

McINERNY, Ralph M. *Quick As a Dodo.*
See Chapter 8, Humorous Fantasy.

2-308 **McPHAIL, (Michael) David.** *Henry Bear's Park.* Gr. 2–4.
During the long wait for his balloonist father's return, Henry Bear devotes himself to beautifying their park. Stanley Raccoon's life story is told in the companion volume, *Stanley, Henry Bear's Friend* (1979).
Illus. by the author, Little, Brown, 1976, 48 pp., o.p.; illus. by the author, Atheneum, 2003, 48 pp. (0-689-83967-7)
(BL 72:1408; Kirkus 44:589; SLJ Sep 1976 p. 102)

2-309 **McPHAIL, (Michael) David.** *Piggy's Pancake Parlor.* Gr. 2–3.
✶ Piggy and his new friend Fox open a pancake parlor featuring Mrs. Farmer Todd's delicious secret pancake recipe.
Illus. by the author, Dutton, 2002, 48 pp. (0-525-45930-8)
(BL 98:1974; CCBB 55:411; HBG 13:361; Kirkus 70:737; SLJ June 2002 p. 103)

2-310 *Magicats!* **Ed. by Jack Dann and Gardner Dozois.** Gr. 10 up.
✶ Eighteen fantasy and science fiction tales involving cats, whose authors include Ursula K. Le Guin, Pamela Sargent, and Gene Wolfe.
Ace, 1984, pap., 270 pp., o.p.
(BL 80:1599, 1609; Kliatt 18:25; SLJ Sep 1984 p. 140; VOYA 7:267)

MAGUIRE, Gregory. *Leaping Beauty: And Other Animal Fairy Tales.*
See Chapter 8, Humorous Fantasy.

MAGUIRE, Gregory. *Seven Spiders Spinning.*
See Chapter 8, Humorous Fantasy.

2-311 **MAJOR, Beverly.** *Porcupine Stew.* Gr. 2–4.
Thomas gives up his favorite silver whistle for admission to the Perpetu-annual Porcupine Parade and Picnic, where he watches a quill-throwing contest and eats "porcupine stew."
Illus. by Erick Ingraham, Morrow, 1982, 39 pp., o.p.
(BL 79:724, 1283; CCBB 36:93; Kirkus 50:1057; SLJ Nov 1982 p. 70)

2-312 **MAMIN-SIBERIAK (pseud. of Dmitrii Narkisovich Mamin).** *Verotchka's Tales.* Gr. 3–5. (Orig. pub. in Russia.)
A collection of Russian stories about animals, birds, and insects.
Trans. by Ray Davidson, illus. by Boris Artzybasheff, Dutton, 1922, 190 pp., o.p.
(BL 19:129; Mahony 2:290)

MANES, Stephen. *Some of the Adventures of Rhode Island Red.*
See Chapter 8, Humorous Fantasy.

2-313 **MARCIANO, John Bemelmans.** *Harold's Tail.* Gr. 3–6.
After a rat talks him into shaving the fur off his tail, Harold the squirrel must learn how to live like a rat to survive in Manhattan.
Illus. by the author, Viking, 2003, 160 pp. (0-670-03660-9)
(BL 11:119; HBG 15:98; Kirkus 71:1020; SLJ Nov 2003 p. 108)

2-314 MARSHALL, James (Edward). *Rats on the Roof and Other Stories.* Gr.
☆   1–5.
Seven humorous stories about a near-sighted goose who doesn't recognize a
wolf masquerading as a canary, a tall mouse bride who saves the wedding party
from a cat, and a dog couple who hire a very ratlike cat to rid their house of
mice. The sequel, *Rats on the Range and Other Stories* (1993), contains eight
more humorous animal stories.
Illus. by the author, Dial, 1991, 80 pp., o.p.; illus. by the author, Puffin, 1997,
pap., 79 pp. (0-14-038646-7)
(BL 87:1879; CCBB 44:244; HB 67:453; HBG 2:257; Kirkus 59:790; SLJ July 1991 p. 61)

2-315 MARSHALL, James (Edward). *A Summer in the South.* Gr. 2–4.
Eleanor Owl, famous detective, solves the case of the ghostly figure frightening
Marietta Chicken.
Illus. by the author, Houghton, 1977, 97 pp., o.p.; illus. by the author, Hough-
ton, 1999, pap., 112 pp. (0-395-91361-6)
(Kirkus 45:1144; SLJ Dec 1977 p. 61)

2-316 MARSHALL, James (Edward). *Taking Care of Carruthers.* Gr. 3–4.
Carruthers the bear, Eugene the turtle, and Emily the pig take a sightseeing trip
downriver in a rowboat, traveling through skunk country to Stupendousberg
where Carruthers stars in a production of "Goldilocks." This is the sequel to the
picture book *What's the Matter with Carruthers?* (1972).
Illus. by the author, Houghton, 1981, 128 pp., o.p.
(BL 78:598; Kirkus 50:3; SLJ Jan 1981 p. 80)

MASEFIELD, John (Edward). *The Midnight Folk: A Novel.*
See Chapter 9, Magic Adventure Fantasy.

2-317 MASON, Miriam E(vangeline). *Hoppity.* Gr. 2–4. (Orig. pub. 1947.)
Hoppity the goat eats everything from crayons to ladies' hats, until the day he
tastes the bee on a baby's nose.
Illus. by Cyndy Szekeres, Macmillan, 1962, 66 pp., o.p.
(BL 44:117; HB 23:34; Kirkus 15:427)

2-318 MATTHIESSEN, Peter. *The Seal Pool.* Gr. 3–5.
While being transported to the Bronx Zoo, a Great Auk escapes and hides near
the seal pool in Central Park.
Illus. by William (Sherman) Pène du Bois, Doubleday, 1972, 78 pp., o.p.
(CCBB 25:80; Kirkus 40:724; LJ 98:645)

MAYNE, William (James Carter). *Antar and the Eagles.*
See Chapter 5, High Fantasy: Alternate Worlds or Histories.

MAYNE, William (James Carter). *The Blue Boat.*
See Chapter 9, Magic Adventure Fantasy.

MAZER, Anne. *The Oxboy.*
See Chapter 1, Allegorical Fantasy and Literary Fairy Tales.

2-319 MAZER, Harry. *The Dog in the Freezer: Three Novellas.* Gr. 6–9.

Three novellas about boys and dogs, including one about a dog who trades bodies with his master, just as the most important basketball game of the year is about to begin.
Simon, 1997, 170 pp. (0-689-80753-8)
(Bl 93:1236; Kirkus 65:466; SLJ July 1997 p. 96)

2-320 MERRILL, Jean (Fairbanks). *The Black Sheep.* Gr. 4–6.
A black sheep born into a community of white ones refuses to conform. Instead of knitting sweaters, he wears his own shaggy coat and spends his time gardening.
Illus. by Ronni Solbert, Pantheon, 1969, 73 pp., o.p.
(CCBB 23:131; LJ 95:1641, 1912, 3603; Suth:279)

MEYER, Zoe. *The Little Green Door.*
See Chapter 1, Allegorical Fantasy and Literary Fairy Tales.

2-321 MICHELS, Tilde. *Rabbit Spring.* Gr. 2–4. (Orig. Swiss pub. 1986.)
Two litters of babies are born in the spring, one to wild rabbits Silla and Rahn in the meadow, the other to the hares in the field.
Trans. by J. Alison James, illus. by Käthi Bhend, Harcourt, 1988, 96 pp., o.p.
(BL 84:1352, 1441; HB 64:491; SLJ Sep 1988 p. 184)

MILNE, A(lan) A(lexander). *Prince Rabbit and the Princess Who Could Not Laugh.*
See Chapter 1, Allegorical Fantasy and Literary Fairy Tales.

2-322 MITCHARD, Jacquelyn. *Starring Prima! The Mouse of the Ballet Jolie.* Gr. 2–5.
Mouse ballerina Prima is befriended by a girl named Kristen, who helps her to become a star but whose cat, Meowsky, threatens to eat her.
Illus. by Tricia Tusa, HarperCollins, 2004, 160 pp. (0-06-057357-0)
(BL 100:1844; Kirkus 72:445; SLJ Sep 2004 p. 175)

2-323 MITTON, Tony. *A Tale of Tales.* Gr. 1–4. (Orig. British pub. 2003.)
Monkey, Elephant, Spider, Bear, Cat, Owl, and Worm entertain each other with rhyming tales on their journey to Volcano Valley to hear ancient Baboon tell the greatest story ever told, the Tale of Tales.
Illus. by Peter Bailey, Fickling, 2004, 112 pp. (0-385-75038-2)
(BL 100:1443; CCBB 57:341; SLJ Apr 2004 p. 140)

MOLESWORTH, Mary Louisa (Stewart). *The Cuckoo Clock.*
See Chapter 7, High Fantasy: Travel to Other Worlds.

MOLESWORTH, Mary Louisa (Stewart). *The Tapestry Room: A Child's Romance.*
See Chapter 9, Magic Adventure Fantasy.

2-324 MONSELL, Mary Elise. *Crackle Creek.* Gr. 2–5.
Douglas and Rosemary Mouse run rival newspapers in Crackle Creek until a storm destroys much of the community and they are forced to work together.
Illus. by Kathleen Garry McCord, Macmillan, 1990, 56 pp., o.p.
(BL 86:1900; HBG 1:245; Kirkus 58:267; SLJ July 1990 p. 63)

2-325 MONSELL, Mary Elise. *The Mysterious Cases of Mr. Pin.* **(Mr. Pin Mystery series, bk. 1).** Gr. 2–4.
Mr. Pin, a penguin detective, solves his cases from the back room of the Smiling Sally Diner in Chicago. The sequels are *Mr. Pin: The Chocolate Files* (1990), *The Spy Who Came North from the Pole* (1993), and *A Fish Named Yum* (1994).
Illus. by Eileen Christelow, Macmillan, 1989, 53 pp. (0-689-31435-3)
(BL 85:1652; Kirkus 57:627; SLJ June 1989 p. 91)

2-326 MONSELL, Mary Elise. *Toohy and Wood.* Gr. 3–5.
✯ Wood, a poetic turtle, helps lizard Toohy accept the death of his best friend, a dove named Pearl.
Illus. by Leslie Tryon, Macmillan, 1992, 80 pp., o.p.
(BL 89:327; CCBB 46:117; HBG 4:74; Kirkus 60:1064; SLJ Oct 1992 p. 118)

MOON, Sheila (Elizabeth). *Knee-Deep in Thunder.*
See Chapter 7, High Fantasy: Travel to Other Worlds.

2-327 MOORE, Lilian. *I'll Meet You at the Cucumbers.* Gr. 2–5.
✯ Adam Mouse comes to the city to meet Amanda Mouse on her birthday and, during the course of a day of wondrous discovery, realizes that he is a poet. In the sequel, *Don't Be Afraid, Amanda* (1992), Amanda visits her penpal, Adam, in the country, despite her fears about life outside the city. *Adam Mouse's Book of Poems* (1992) is a related work.
Illus. by Sharon Wooding, Atheneum, 1988, 72 pp. (0-689-31243-1)
(BL 84:1266, 1441; CCBB 41:142; HB 64:492; Kirkus 51:622; SLJ Apr 1988 p. 82; Suth 4:296)

2-328 MOORE, Lilian. *Little Raccoon.* Gr. 2–4.
Three stories about the adventures of a young raccoon, originally published separately in *Little Raccoon and the Thing in the Pool* (McGraw-Hill, 1963), *Little Raccoon and the Outside World* (1965), and *Little Raccoon and No Trouble at All* (1972).
Illus. by Doug Cushman, Holt, 2002, 64 pp. (0-8050-6543-1)
(BL 98:1328; HBG 13:362)

2-329 MOORE, Margaret Eileen. *Willie Without.* Gr. 1–4. (Orig. British pub. 1951.)
Willy the poetic worm makes many new friends as he searches for a new hat.
Illus. by Nora S(picer) Unwin, Coward, 1952, 85 pp., o.p.
(CCBB 5:81; HB 28:108; Kirkus 20:124; LJ 77:444)

2-330 MORANVILLE, Sharelle Byars. *The Purple Ribbon.* Gr. 1–4.
A field mouse named Spring raises her family inside an old automobile as she dreams of being reunited with Gran Dora, who raised her and gave her a special purple ribbon.
Illus. by Anna Alter, Holt, 2003, 80 pp. (0-8050-6659-4)
(BL 99:12327; HBG 14:357; Kirkus 71:537; SLJ May 3002 p. 126)

2-331 MORGAN, Alison (Mary Raikes). *River Song.* Gr. 4–6.
Timothy Wagtail adopts a young flycatcher who has lost his family.
Illus. by John Schoenherr, Harper, 1975, 160 pp., o.p.
(BL 72:457; HB 52:52; Kirkus 43:1131; SLJ Sep 1975 p. 108)

2-332 MORGAN, Clay. *The Boy Who Spoke Dog.* Gr. 5–8.
Thrown overboard and washed up on a deserted New Zealand island, young Jack finds that he can communicate with the island's shepherd dogs and helps them to fight against the wild fango dogs.
Dutton, 2003, 166 pp. (0-525-47159-6)
(BL 100:860; SLJ Jan 2004 p. 133; VOYA 27:145)

2-333 MORRIS, Gilbert. *Journey to Freedom.* Gr. 4–8.
Chip, youngest child in a white-foot mouse family, is chosen by a prophet named Silver to lead a brigade of farm mice to battle the brown rat invaders.
Crossway, 2000, 256 pp. (1-58134-191-1)
(BL 97:820; HBG 12:312; VOYA 23:434)

2-334 MURPHY, Shirley Rousseau. *Cat in the Dark.* **(Joe Grey Mystery series, bk. 4).** Gr. 9 up.
Feline detectives Joe Grey and Dulcie try to solve a string of burglaries and discover another sentient cat, Azrael, who foresees three human corpses. The first three books in the series are *Cat on the Edge* (1996), *Cat Under Fire* (1997), and *Cat Raise the Dead* (1997). The sequels are *Cat to the Dogs* (2000), *Cat Spitting Mad* (2001), *Cat Laughing Last* (2002), and *Cat Seeing Double* (2003). HarperPrism, 1999, 272 pp. (0-06-105096-2), 1999, pap., 314 pp. (0-06-105947-1)
(BL 95:728; Kirkus 66:1698; LJ Dec 1998 p. 160; SLJ May 1999 p. 158)

MURPHY, Shirley Rousseau. *The Catswold Portal.*
See Chapter 7, High Fantasy: Travel to Other Worlds.

2-335 MURPHY, Shirley Rousseau. *Flight of the Fox.* Gr. 5–7.
A kangaroo rat and a pet lemming ask a boy named Charlie to help them pilot a motorized model airplane.
Illus. by Donald Sibley, based on original designs by Richard Cuffari, Atheneum, 1978, 164 pp., o.p.
(BL 75:384; CCBB 32:142; Kirkus 46:1358; SLJ Jan 1979 p. 56)

MURPHY, Shirley Rousseau. *Nightpool.*
See Chapter 5, High Fantasy: Alternate Worlds or Histories.

MURPHY, Shirley Rousseau. *The Pig Who Could Conjure the Wind.*
See Chapter 12, Witchcraft and Sorcery Fantasy.

2-336 MYERS, Anna. *Flying Blind.* Gr. 5–9.
Murphy the psychic macaw and Ben, 13, adopted son of "magic elixer"-selling "Professor" Riley, narrate this adventure-filled story set in Florida during the early 1900s, where egrets, hunted for their feathers, are fast becoming extinct.
Walker, 2003, 192 pp. (0-8027-8879-3)
(BL 100:240; Kirkus 71:1076; SLJ Nov 2003 p. 49; VOYA 26:326, 27:13)

2-337 MYERS, Walter Dean. *Three Swords for Grenada.* Gr. 3–6.
Three swashbuckling cats save the town of Grenada by outwitting the dogs of the Fidorean Guard in this action-packed parody set in 1420 Spain.
Illus. by John Speirs, Holiday, 2002, 80 pp. (0-8234-1676-3)
(BL 98:1848; HBG 16:357; Kirkus 70:886; SLJ Sep 2002 p. 230)

NAPOLI, Donna Jo. *The Prince of the Pond: Otherwise Known as De Fawg Pin.*
See Chapter 8, Humorous Fantasy.

2-338 **NAYLOR, Phyllis Reynolds.** *The Grand Escape.* **(Club of Mysteries series, bk. 1).** Gr. 4–7.
Marco and Polo, house cats who set off to find adventure, must solve three "great mysteries" in order to join the neighborhood cats' Club of Mysteries. The sequels are *The Healing of Texas Jake* (1997, 1998) and *Carlotta's Kittens and the Club of Mysteries* (2000, 2002).
Illus. by Alan Daniel, Macmillan, 1993, 148 pp., o.p.; Dell, 1994, pap., 148 pp. (0-44-040968-3)
(BL 89:1967; HBG 4:302; Kirkus 61:534; SLJ Aug 1993 p. 166)

2-339 **NEWELL, Averil.** *The Fly-By-Nights.* Gr. 2–4.
A mouse family sets up housekeeping in a vacant house conveniently located between a toyshop and a bakery.
Illus. by Kathleen Hiken, Macmillan, 1948, 48 pp., o.p.
(BL 44:253; CCBB 2:5; HB 24:190; Kirkus 16:109; LJ 73:485)

NEWMAN, Robert (Howard). *The Shattered Stone.*
See Chapter 5, High Fantasy: Alternate Worlds or Histories.

2-340 **NICKLESS, Will.** *Owlglass.* **(The Owlglass Chronicles, vol. 1).** Gr. 4–6.
(Orig. British pub. 1964.)
Old Beak and Claws the owl is losing his vision, so the forest animals steal the villagers' eyeglasses for him. The British sequels are *The Nitehood, Molepie,* and *Dotted Lines.*
Illus. by the author, Day, 1966, 158 pp., o.p.
(BL 62:833; HB 42:307; LJ 91:2696)

2-341 **NIXON, Joan Lowery.** *Gus and Gertie and the Missing Pearl.* Gr. 2–4.
Vacationing on a tropical island, Gus and Gertie penguin are caught up in a party of the Bad Guys Club and help solve the crime of Gertie's stolen necklace.
Illus. by Diane DeGroat, North-South, 2000, 48 pp., o.p.
(BL 97:540; Kirkus 68:1288; SLJ Oct 2000 p. 132)

2-342 **NIXON, Joan Lowery.** *Magnolia's Mixed-Up Magic.* Gr. 2–4.
Magnolia Possum and her grandmother try out a few spells from an old magic book but can't seem to undo them when Magnolia begins flying around the house and the mailman disappears.
Illus. by Linda Bucholtz-Ross, Putnam, 1983, 43 pp., o.p.
(BL 79:1403; CCBB 37:14; Kirkus 51:618; SLJ Oct 1983 p. 152)

NORTON, Andre (pseud. of Alice Mary Norton). *Fur Magic.*
See Chapter 9, Magic Adventure Fantasy.

NORTON, Andre (pseud. of Alice Mary Norton). *The Mark of the Cat.*
See Chapter 5, High Fantasy: Alternate Worlds or Histories.

2-343 NYGAARD, Jacob Been. *Tobias the Magic Mouse.* Gr. 2–4. (Orig. Danish pub. 1961.)
Elected to the position of magic mouse, Tobias travels to the Moon to eat magic cheese in preparation for solving animal and human problems on Earth. Trans. by Edith Joan McCormick, illus. by Ib Spang Olsen, Harcourt, 1968, 52 pp., o.p.
(Kirkus 36:1049; HB 45:167; LJ 94:288)

2-344 OAKLEY, Graham. *The Church Mouse.* **(The Church Mice series, bk. 1).**
☆ Gr. 2–4.
Despite his friendship with Sampson the cat, Arthur the church mouse was lonely, so he decided to fill the church with friendly mice. The sequels are *The Church Cat Abroad* (1973), *The Church Mice and the Moon* (1974), *The Church Mice Spread Their Wings* (1976), *The Church Mice Adrift* (1977; a Kate Greenaway Medal Highly Commended Book, 1976), *The Church Mice at Bay* (1979), *The Church Mice at Christmas* (1980), *The Church Mice in Action* (1983; a Kate Greenaway Medal Highly Commended Book, 1982), *Diary of a Churchmouse* (1987), and *The Church Mice and the Ring* (1992).
Illus. by the author, Atheneum, 1972, 33 pp., o.p.
(CCBB 26:130; HB 49:132; LJ 98:1675; Kirkus 40:1187; TLS 1972 p. 1327)

2-345 O'BRIEN, Robert C. (pseud. of Robert Leslie Conly). *Mrs. Frisby and the*
☆ *Rats of NIMH.* **(The Rats of NIMH series, bk. 1).** Gr. 4–7.
Mrs. Frisby, a field mouse with a problem, is befriended by a group of super-intelligent laboratory rats and manages to save their lives. John Newbery Medal, 1972; Boston Globe Horn Book Award Honor Book, 1971; National Book Award finalist, 1972. O'Brien's daughter, Jane Leslie Conly, has written two sequels entitled *Racso and the Rats of NIMH* (Harper, 1986; see this chapter) and *R-T, Margaret, and the Rats of NIMH* (Harper, 1990).
Illus. by Edward S. Gazi, Atheneum, 1971, 240 pp. (0-689-20651-8); Scholastic, 1982 (entitled *The Secret of NIMH*), o.p.; Aladdin, 1999, pap., 233 pp. (0-689-82966-3)
(BL 67:955, 68:670, 80:96; CCBB 25:29; HB 47:385; LJ 96:4159, 4186; Suth:298; TLS 1972 p. 1317)

2-346 OPPEL, Kenneth. *Silverwing.* Gr. 5–8. (Orig. pub. in Canada.)
☆ Shade, a young silverwing bat, gets lost during migration to the bats' winter roost and has many adventures. Canadian Library Association Best Book of the Year for Children, 1998. In a sequel, *Sunwing* (2000, 2001), Shade and his friends become trapped in a military research facility where bats fitted with bombs are sent out as living weapons. Canadian Library Association Best Book of the Year for Children, 2000. In *Firewing* (2003), Shade's son, Griffin, is sucked into the world of the dead, where he is threatened by Goth, his father's mortal enemy, who plans to return to life by killing the young bat.
Simon, 1997, 217 pp. (0-689-81529-8); Aladdin, 2002, pap., 216 pp. (0-689-81529-8)
(CCBB 51:170; HB 73:684; Kirkus 65:1394; SLJ Oct 1997 p. 137; VOYA 21:14, 21:58)

2-347 O'ROURKE, Frank. *Burton and Stanley.* Gr. 3–6.
When two Kenyan marabou storks named Burton and Stanley arrive via tornado at his railroad station in the American Midwest in 1935, Mr. Kraft discovers that they can communicate in Morse code and helps them return to Africa.
Illus. by Jonathan Allen, Godine, 1993, 64 pp. (0-87923-824-0)
(BL 89:1693; HBG 4:302; Kirkus 61:151; SLJ May 1993 p. 108)

2-348 ORWELL, George (pseud. of Eric Hugh Blair). *Animal Farm.* Gr. 7 up.
✶ (Orig. British pub. 1945.)
At Farmer Jones's farm, the pigs lead a successful revolt to drive out the humans and put themselves in charge in this classic satire of communism.
Harcourt, 1946, 118 pp., o.p.; illus. by Joy Batchelor and John Halas, Harcourt, 1954, 160 pp., o.p.; Everyman's Library, 1993 (0-679-42039-8); Signet, 2004, pap., 144 pp. (0-451-52634-1)
(BL 43:18, 83:1592; Kirkus 14:351; LJ 7:1048; TLS 1945 p. 401)

2-349 OSBORNE, M(aurice) M(achado) (Jr.). *Ondine: The Story of a Bird Who*
✶ *Was Different.* Gr. 4–6.
Ondine, a nonconformist sandpiper, is befriended by a seagull, an owl, and a hermit.
Illus. by Evaline Ness, Houghton, 1960, 75 pp., o.p.
(BL 56:690; Eakin:251; HB 36:290; LJ 85:2683)

2-350 OSBORNE, M(aurice) M(achado) (Jr.). *Rudi and the Mayor of Naples.*
Gr. 2–4.
It takes a very special cake to make Rudi the donkey stand up and pull his cart again.
Illus. by Joseph Low, Houghton, 1958, 48 pp., o.p.
(HB 35:33; LJ 84:641)

2-351 OSBORNE, Mary Pope. *Spider Kane and the Mystery Under the May*
✶ *Apple.* (Spider Kane Mystery series, bk. 1). Gr. 3–5.
After the kidnapping of his true love, Mimi, butterfly Leon Leafwing and detective Spider Kane follow her into the Dark Swamp, realm of the evil Emperor Moth. The sequel is *Spider Kane and the Mystery at Jumbo Nightcrawler's* (1993).
Illus. by Victoria Chess, Knopf, 1992, 28 pp. (0-679-80855-8), 1999, pap. (0-679-80855-8)
(BL 88:1602; CCBB 45:244; HBG 3:268; Kirkus 60:541; SLJ Apr 1992 p. 118)

2-352 OTTO, Margaret G(lover). *The Tiny Man.* Gr. 3–4.
Two sea gulls find a tiny man carved from the heart of an oak tree and help him to find a home.
Illus. by Peter Burchard, Holt, 1955, 122 pp., o.p.
(Kirkus 23:647; LJ 81:240)

2-353 PAINE, Albert Bigelow. *The Hollow Tree and Deep Woods Book.* Gr. 4–6.
(Orig. pub. separately as *The Hollow Tree*, 1898, and *In the Deep Woods*, 1899.)
A Coon, a Possum, and a Big Black Crow live together in a hollow tree. The sequels are *Hollow Tree Nights and Days* (1916), *The Hollow Tree Snowed-In Book* (1910, 1937, 1938), *How Mr. Dog Got Even* (1915), *How Mr. Rabbit Lost*

His Tail (1910, 1915), *Making Up with Mr. Dog* (1915), *Mr. Crow and the Whitewash* (1917), *Mr. Possum's Great Balloon Trip* (1915), *Mr. Rabbit's Big Dinner* (1901, 1915), *Mr. Rabbit's Wedding* (1917), *Mr. Turtle's Flying Adventure* (1917), and *When Jack Rabbit Was a Little Boy* (1910, 1915).
Illus. by J. M. Conde, Harper, 1898-1900, 1929, 1938, 272 pp., o.p.
(Bookshelf 1928 p. 9; HB 7:116; Mahony 2:113)

2-354 PALMER, Robin (Riggs). *Wise House.* Gr. 3–5.
A cat and a crow move a family of children to a pirate's island, along with their house.
Illus. by Decie Merwin, Harper, 1951, 138 pp., o.p.
(Kirkus 19:387; LJ 76:2124)

2-355 PARKER, (James) Edgar (Jr.). *The Dream of the Dormouse.* Gr. 2–4.
Hibernating Dormouse is sure he must be dreaming when he is kidnapped by a pirate bulldog.
Illus. by the author, Houghton, 1963, 48 pp., o.p.
(CCBB 17:144; HB 39:286; Kirkus 3:53; LJ 88:2553)

2-356 PARKER, (James) Edgar (Jr.). *The Duke of Sycamore.* Gr. 1–4.
When the Lion King announces an upcoming visit, a group of forest friends search frantically for a castle to borrow.
Illus. by the author, Houghton, 1959, 38 pp., o.p.
(BL 55:488; CCBB 12:154; HB 35:214; Kirkus 27:264; LJ 84:1699)

2-357 PARKER, (James) Edgar (Jr.). *The Flower of the Realm.* Gr. 3–5.
Sir Stephen Stag and Baron Roebuck duel for the love of a beautiful doe.
Illus. by the author, Houghton, 1966, 60 pp., o.p.
(HB 42:564; Kirkus 34:831; LJ 91:5236)

2-358 PARKER, (James) Edgar (Jr.). *The Question of a Dragon.* Gr. 3–5.
A raccoon, a cat, and a frog are commanded to rid the forest of a dreadful dragon.
Illus. by the author, Pantheon, 1964, 43 pp., o.p.
(CCBB 19:16; HB 40:283; Kirkus 32:232; LJ 89:2661)

PARKER, (James) Edgar (Jr.). *Rogue's Gallery.*
See Chapter 8, Humorous Fantasy.

PARRISH, Anne, and PARRISH, Dillwyn. *Knee-High to a Grasshopper.*
See Chapter 9, Magic Adventure Fantasy.

2-359 PAYNE, Joan Balfour (Dicks). *Ambrose.* Gr. 2–4.
A spoiled dog named Ambrose searches for a family with children that is willing to adopt him.
Illus. by the author, Hastings, 1956, 48 pp., o.p.
(CCBB 11:17; HB 32:445; Kirkus 24:627)

2-360 PAYNE, Joan Balfour (Dicks). *The Piebald Princess.* Gr. 3–5.
A Siamese cat claiming to be a princess makes life difficult for witch Molly Pippin.
Illus. by the author, Farrar, 1954, 79 pp., o.p.
(BL 50:327; CCBB 7:77; HB 30:95; Kirkus 22:229; LJ 79:702, 865)

2-361 PEABODY, Paul. *Blackberry Hollow.* Gr. 1–4.
It's always springtime in Blackberry Hollow, home of Jeremy fieldmouse, Major the horse, Tom McPaddy the Scottish frog, Mr. Kip the raccoon, and Parnassus the bear.
Illus. by the author, Putnam, 1993, 147 pp., o.p.
(BL 90:833; HBG 5:81; Kirkus 61:938; SLJ Jan 1994 p. 96)

PEARCE, (Ann) Philippa. *The Little Gentleman.*
See Chapter 9, Magic Adventure Fantasy.

2-362 PENNAC, Daniel. *Dog.* Gr. 3–7. (Orig. French pub. 1982.)
Dog narrates his own story of life as a stray who lives in a dump and longs for a human owner but is disappointed by the one he finds.
Trans. by Sarah Adams, illus. by Britta Teckentrup, Candlewick, 2004, 192 pp. (0-7636-2421-7)
(BL 100:1620; CCBB 57:347; Kirkus 72:1453; SLJ Aug 2004 p. 92; VOYA 27:145)

PENNAC, Daniel. *Eye of the Wolf.*
See Chapter 1, Allegorical Fantasy and Literary Fairy Tales.

2-363 **PINKWATER, D(aniel) Manus.** *Blue Moose.* **(Blue Moose trilogy, bk. 1).**
⭐ Gr. 1–4.
The maitre d' of Mr. Breton's gourmet restaurant in the wild is a talking blue moose. The sequels are *Return of the Moose* (1979) and *The Moospire* (1986).
Illus. by the author, Dodd, 1975, 47 pp., o.p.
(BL 72:45; CCBB 29:84; HB 52:46; Kirkus 43:661; SLJ Sep 1975 p. 88; Suth 2:365)

PINKWATER, D(aniel) Manus. *The Hoboken Chicken Emergency.*
See Chapter 8, Humorous Fantasy.

PINKWATER, D(aniel) Manus. *Jolly Roger: A Dog of Hoboken.*
See Chapter 8, Humorous Fantasy.

PINKWATER, D(aniel) Manus. *Lizard Music.*
See Chapter 8, Humorous Fantasy.

2-364 PLENN, Doris. *The Green Song.* Gr. 4–6. (Orig. pub. 1954.)
Pepe, a green tree frog from Puerto Rico, comes to New York City,
Illus. by Paul Galdone, McKay, 1969, 126 pp., o.p.
(HB 30:137; Kirkus 22:152; LJ 79:1238)

2-365 POCHOCKI, Ethel. *The Attic Mice.* Gr. 3–5.
A family of mice who live in an old doll farmhouse stored in the attic have a series of adventures.
Illus. by David Catrow, Henry Holt, 1990, 113 pp., o.p.; Dell, 1993, pap. (0-440-40745-1)
(BL 87:743; HBG 2:80; Kirkus 58:459; SLJ Oct 1990 p. 118)

2-366 POLLOCK, Penny. *Stall Buddies.* Gr. 3–4.
Scarlett, a skittish filly bought by a young man who desperately needs her to win races, is befriended by Rufus rooster and Merabel goat, who boost her self-confidence.

Putnam, 1984, 63 pp., o.p.
(BL 81:848; CCBB 38:115; SLJ Mar 1985 p. 170)

PORTE, Barbara Ann. *Beauty and the Serpent: Thirteen Tales of Unnatural Animals.*
See Chapter 4, Ghost Fantasy.

2-367 POTTER, (Helen) Beatrix (Heelis). *The Fairy Caravan.* Gr. 4–6. (Orig.
✫   British and U.S. pub. 1929.)
The animal caravan traveling through the English countryside includes Tuppeny the long-haired guinea pig, Pony Billy, Jenny Ferret, and Princess Xarifa the dormouse.
Warne, 1951, 1985, 225 pp., o.p.; Warne, new ed., 1992, 192 pp. (0-7232-4044-2)
(BL 47:278; CCBB 4:37; HB 5:9, 47–49, 28:163; LJ 76:660; Mahony 3:209; Moore:120)

2-368 POTTER, (Helen) Beatrix (Heelis). *The Tale of Little Pig Robinson.* Gr.
K–4. (Orig. British pub. 1930.)
Sent to market by his aunts, Dorcas and Porcas, Little Pig Robinson gets lost and ends up aboard a ship bound for Robinson Crusoe's island.
Illus. by the author, Warne, 1930, 1987, 123 pp., o.p.; Warne, new ed., 2002, 128 pp. (0-7232-4788-9)
(BL 27:266; TLS Nov 1930 p. 986)

2-369 POTTER, (Helen) Beatrix (Heelis). *The Tale of the Faithful Dove.* Gr.
2–4. (Orig. British and U.S. pub. 1955.)
A mother dove fleeing a falcon becomes trapped in a chimney, but a mouse family and a boy help her to escape.
Illus. by Marie Angel, Warne, 1970 (2nd ed.), 47 pp., o.p.
(CCBB 24:112; HB 46:604; Kirkus 38:1141; LJ 96:1498; TLS 1971 p. 768)

PRICE, Susan. *The Ghost Drum: A Cat's Tale.*
See Chapter 12, Witchcraft and Sorcery Fantasy.

PRICE, Susan. *Ghost Song.*
See Chapter 12, Witchcraft and Sorcery Fantasy.

2-370 PRICEMAN, Marjorie. *My Nine Lives: By Clio.* Gr. 2–6.
Cleo the cat keeps an illustrated journal of her lives in Mesopotamia, ancient China, ancient Rome, Renaissance Italy, Viking America, and modern-day Wisconsin.
Illus. by the author, Simon, 1998, 48 pp. (0-689-81135-7)
(BL 95:591:Kirkus 66:1388; SLJ Oct 1998 p. 110)

PUSHKIN, Alexander Sergeevich. *The Tale of Czar Saltan, or the Prince and the Swan Princess.*
See Chapter 1, Allegorical Fantasy and Literary Fairy Tales.

2-371 QUACKENBUSH, Robert M(ead). *Express Train to Trouble: A Miss Mallard Mystery.* **(Miss Mallard Mystery series, bk. 1).** Gr. 2–4.
A humorous takeoff on Agatha Christie's *Murder on the Orient Express*, in which all of the characters are animals, including the detective, Miss Mallard. The sequels are *Dig to Disaster* (1982), *Stairway to Doom* (1983), *Gondola to*

Danger (1983), *Rickshaw to Horror* (1984), *Taxi to Intrigue* (1984), *Stage Door to Terror* (1985), *Bicycle to Treachery* (1985), *Dogsled to Dread* (1987), *Danger in Tibet* (Pippen, 1989), *Lost in the Amazon* (1990), and *Evil Under the Sea* (1992).

Illus. by the author, Prentice, 1981, 48 pp., o.p.

(BL 78:758; SLJ Aug 1982 p. 104)

2-372 RAYNER, Mary (Yoma, née Grigson). *Mrs. Pig Gets Cross; and Other*
✫ *Stories.* Gr. K–3. (Orig. British pub. 1986.)
Seven short, humorous stories about Mrs. Pig and her untidy but clever piglets who always manage to outwit fox and wolf. This is the sequel to four books for a slightly younger audience: *Mr. and Mrs. Pig's Evening Out* (Atheneum, 1976), *Garth Pig and the Ice-Cream Lady* (Atheneum, 1977), *Mrs. Pig's Bulk Buy* (Atheneum, 1981), and *Garth Pig Steals the Show* (1993).

Illus. by the author, Dutton, 1987, 64 pp., o.p.

(BL 83:1209, 84:873; CCBB 40:154; HB 58:338; Kirkus 55:137; SLJ Mar 1987 p. 149, Dec 1987 p. 39)

2-373 RAZZI, Jim (James), and RAZZI, Mary. *The Search for King Pup's Tomb.* Gr. 3–5.
Sherluck Bones, master canine detective, finds the lost treasure of King Pup's tomb in his first full-length exploit. Bantam has also published six short-mystery-episode books in the related Sherluck Bones Mystery-Detective Book series.

Illus. by Ted Enik, Bantam, 1985, 64 pp., pap., o.p.

(BL 81:1337; SLJ May 1985 p. 110)

2-374 REICHE, Dietlof. *I, Freddy.* **(The Golden Hamster saga, bk. 1).** Gr. 3–6.
(Orig. German pub. 1998.)
Golden Hamster Freddy makes sure he'll be adopted by young Sophie in order to accomplish his real ambition—to learn to read. The sequel is *Freddy in Peril* (2004).

Trans. by John Brownjohn, illus. by Joe Cepeda, Scholastic, 2003, 208 pp. (0-439-28356-6)

(BL 99:1398; CCBB 56:459; HBG 14:358; Kirkus 71:756; SLJ Nov 2003 p. 113)

Ribbiting Tales: Original Stories About Frogs. **Ed. by Nancy Springer.**
See Chapter 8, Humorous Fantasy.

2-375 ROACH, Marilynne K(athleen). *Presto: Or, the Adventures of a Turnspit Dog.* Gr. 5–7.
Rescued by a traveling puppeteer, a dog named Presto finds adventure in the streets of 18th-century London.

Illus. by the author, Houghton, 1979, 148 pp., o.p.

(BL 76:560; CCBB 33:117; HB 56:56; Suth 3:361)

2-376 ROBERTSON, Mary Elsie. *Jemimalee.* Gr. 4–6.
Jemimalee, an internationally acclaimed cat poet, types inspiring verses on her master's typewriter, watches over the family by night, and defends her family's farm from rats by day.

Illus. by Judith Gwyn Brown, McGraw-Hill, 1977, 122 pp., o.p.

(Kirkus 45:991; SLJ Dec 1977 p. 50)

2-377 ROBINSON, Mabel L(ouise). *Back-Seat Driver.* **(Riley trilogy, bk. 1).** Gr. 3–5.
A wirehair terrier who delights in giving his master backseat driving tips is given a car of his own. The sequels are *Skipper Riley* (1955) and *Riley Goes to Obedience School* (1956).
Illus. by Leonard Shortall, Random, 1949, 68 pp., o.p.

(CCBB 3:18; Kirkus 17:360; LJ 74:1918)

2-378 ROBINSON, Marileta. *Mr. Goat's Bad Good Idea.* Gr. 2–4.
Three Navajo tales concerning Mr. Goat, Grandfather Sheep, and Jerry the prairie dog.
Illus. by Arthur Getz, Crowell, 1979, 39 pp., o.p.

(BL 75:1160; CCBB 33:17; Kirkus 47:329; SLJ Apr 1979 p. 47)

2-379 ROCCA, Guido. *Gaetano the Pheasant: A Hunting Fable.* Gr. 3–5. (Orig.
✮ Italian pub. 1961.)
Gaetano and his mate decide to escape from the threat of hunters' guns,
Illus. by Giulio Cingoli and Giancarlo Carloni, Harper, 1966, 60 pp., o.p.

(CCBB 20:115; HB 42:431; Kirkus 34:418; LJ 91:3252; Suth:335)

2-380 ROGERS, Mark E. *The Adventures of Samurai Cat.* **(Samurai Cat series, bk. 1).** Gr. 10 up.
A satirical fantasy starring Miaowara Tomokato, the Samurai Cat, who embarks on a quest for vengeance against the killers of his master. The sequels are *More Adventures of Samurai Cat* (1986), *Samurai Cat in the Real World* (1989), *Samurai Cat Goes to the Movies* (1994), *Samurai Cat Goes to Hell* (1998), and *Sword of the Samurai Cat* (2003).
Illus. by the author, Grant, 1984, 124 pp., pap., o.p.; Tor, 1986, pap. (0-8125-5246-6)

(BL 81:483; SLJ Feb 1985 p. 91)

2-381 ROSS, Ramon Royal. *Prune.* Gr. 5–7.
Two lonely animals, a magpie and a muskrat, befriend a talking prune who desperately wishes to return to his orchard.
Atheneum, 1984, 175 pp., o.p.

(BL 81:848, 84:1441; Kirkus 52:98; SLJ Dec 1984 p. 94)

2-382 RUCH, Sandi Barrett. *Junkyard Dog.* Gr. 2–4.
Toad, living under an old stove in the junkyard, describes Slobber the junkyard watch-dog's rescue of 5-year-old Huey, son of the junkman.
Illus. by Marjorie Wunsch, Orchard, 1990, 96 pp. (0-531-05842-5)

(BL 87:162; HB 66:451; HBG 1:236; Kirkus 58:802; SLJ Aug 1990 p. 149)

RUFF, Matt. *Fool on the Hill.*
See Chapter 9, Magic Adventure Fantasy.

2-383 RYLANT, Cynthia. *Gooseberry Park.* Gr. 3–6.
After Stumpy the squirrel disappears during an ice storm, her friends Kona the Labrador, Murray the bat, and Gwendolyn the hermit crab rescue and care for her babies.
Illus. by Arthur Howard, Harcourt, 1995, 133 pp. (0-15-232242-6)
(BL 92:320; CCBB 49:201; HBG 7:68; Kirkus 63:1500; SLJ Dec 1995 p. 108)

2-384 RYLANT, Cynthia. *The Lighthouse Family: The Storm.* **(The Lighthouse Family series, bk. 1).** Gr. 2–4.
Lighthouse keeper Pandora the cat saves sailor Seabold the dog when his boat is destroyed in a storm; they become a family when they take in three orphaned mice. The sequel is *The Whale* (2003).
Illus. by Preston McDaniels, Simon, 2002, 80 pp. (0-689-84880-3); Aladdin, 2003, pap., 80 pp. (0-689-84882-X)
(BL 99:612; Kirkus 70:1141; SLJ Nov 2002 p. 134)

2-385 SAID, S. F. *Varjak Paw.* Gr. 4–7. (Orig. British pub. 2003.)
✷ Young Varjak Paw, an aristocratic "Mesopotamian Blue" kitten, leaves his family for the excitement and dangers of the city streets, encouraged by dreams of his mythic ancestor Jahal Paw. Nestlé Smarties Book Prize Gold Award, 2003. The upcoming sequel is *Outlaw Varjak Paw* (2005; entitled *The Outlaw Varjak Paw* in Britain, 2005).
Illus. by Dave McKean, Random, 2003, 256 pp. (0-385-75030-7)
(BL 99:1779; CCBB 57:32; HB 79:467; HBG 16:374; Kirkus 71:683; SLJ June 2003 p. 151)

2-386 SAINTSBURY (Green), Dana. *The Squirrel That Remembered.* Gr. 2–4.
Grandma Nutcracker, an English squirrel living in New York's Central Park, tries to help a homesick English girl.
Illus. by the author, Viking, 1951, 60 pp., o.p.
(CCBB 5:54; HB 27:331; Kirkus 19:388; LJ 76:1572)

SAMPSON, Fay. *Pangur Ban: The White Cat.*
See Chapter 6, High Fantasy: Myth or Legend Fantasy.

SANCHEZ-SILVA, José. *The Boy and the Whale.*
See Chapter 1, Allegorical Fantasy and Literary Fairy Tales.

SATHRE, Vivian. *Slender Ella and Her Fairy Hogfather.*
See Chapter 6, High Fantasy: Myth or Legend Fantasy.

2-387 SAYERS, Frances Clarke. *Mr. Tidy Paws.* Gr. 2–4.
A cat named Mr. Tidy Paws comes to the deserted village of Bear Blossom to help Christopher and his grandmother.
Illus. by Zhenya Gay, Viking, 1935, 64 pp., o.p.
(BL 32:78; Bookshelf 1935 p. 3; HB 11:197, 351; LJ 61:35; Mahony 3:209)

2-388 SCHAEFFER, Susan Fromberg. *The Autobiography of Foudini M. Cat.* Gr. 10 up.
Foudini the cat writes his memoirs for the edification of young Grace, the new cat who has joined the family.

Knopf, 1997, 160 pp. (0-679-45474-8)

(BL 94:60; Kirkus 65:1058; LJ Sep 15, 1997 p. 103; SLJ Mar 1998 p. 244)

2-389 SCHEFFLER, Ursel. *Rinaldo, the Sly Fox.* **(Rinaldo trilogy, bk. 1).** Gr. 2–4. (Orig. Swiss pub. 1992.)

Rinaldo the fox is a thieving, swindling trickster whose nemesis, Bruno the Duck, is always one step behind him. The sequels are *The Return of Rinaldo, the Sly Fox* (1993), and *Rinaldo on the Run* (1995).

Trans. by J. Alison James, illus. by Iskender Gider, North-South, 1992, 62 pp. (1-55858-181-2)

(BL 89:1061; HBG 4:62; Kirkus 60:1193; SLJ Nov 1992 p. 78)

SCHMIDT, Annie M. G. *Minnie.*
See Chapter 9, Magic Adventure Fantasy.

SCHOLES, Katherine. *The Landing: A Night of Birds.*
See Chapter 9, Magic Adventure Fantasy.

2-390 SCHWED, Antonia Holding. *Noah and Me: A Novel.* Gr. 10 up.

All of psychotherapist Nathaniel Danzon's patients are animals, including a butterfly with multiple personality disorder and a praying mantis who feels guilty about eating her mate.

Evans, 1991, 168 pp., o.p.

(BL 88:241, 311; Kirkus 59:967; LJ Oct 1991 p. 122)

SCIESZKA, Jon. *The Frog Prince, Continued.*
See Chapter 8, Humorous Fantasy.

SCIESZKA, Jon. *The True Story of the Three Little Pigs: By A. Wolf.*
See Chapter 8, Humorous Fantasy.

2-391 SCOTT, Dixon. *A Fresh Wind in the Willows.* Gr. 5–7. (Orig. British pub. 1983.)

The inhabitants of Riverbank still find Toad's misbehavior to be trying in this contemporary sequel to Kenneth Grahame's *The Wind in the Willows* (1908; see this chapter) written for a slightly older audience.

Illus. by Jonathon Coudrille, Dell, 1987, pap., 111 pp., o.p.

(Kliatt 21:29; SLJ Nov 1987 p. 107)

2-392 SEEMAN, Elizabeth (Brickel). *The Talking Dog and the Barking Man.* Gr. 3–5.

Candido the talking dog runs away from home and joins a traveling ventriloquist's show.

Illus. by James (Royer) Flora, Watts, 1960, 186 pp., o.p.

(HB 36:291; LJ 85:2043)

2-393 SÉGUR, Comtesse Sophie (Rostopchine) de. *The Wise Little Donkey.* Gr. 3–5. (Orig. French pub. 1860; orig. U.S. pub. 1880, entitled *The Adventures of a Donkey;* 1901, entitled *The Story of a Donkey.*)

Cadichon the learned donkey tells the story of his life.

Trans. by Marguerite Fellows Melcher, illus. by Lauren Ford, Macmillan, 1924, entitled *Memoirs of a Donkey*; trans. by Louis Auguste Loiseaux, illus. by Emma L(illian) Brock, Whitman, 1931, 191 pp., o.p.

(BL 21:161, 28:313; Mahony 2:114)

2-394 SEIDLER, Tor. *Mean Margaret.* Gr. 3–6.

✮ Fred and Phoebe woodchuck find their marital bliss threatened after they adopt Margaret, an ill-tempered 2-year-old human dumped at their burrow by her exasperated older siblings.

Illus. by Jon Agee, HarperCollins, 1997, 165 pp. (0-06-205091-5); HarperTrophy, 2001, pap. (0-06-441039-0)

(BL 94:619; CCBB 51:218; HB 74:80; HBG 9:80; Kirkus 65:1395; SLJ Nov 1997 p. 99, Dec 1997 p. 27)

2-395 SEIDLER, Tor. *A Rat's Tale.* Gr. 4–6.

✮ An artistic young rat named Montague earns a fortune, brings honor to his family, and wins his girlfriend's heart, all by creating and selling miniature shell paintings. In the sequel, *The Revenge of Randal Reese-Rat* (2001), Randal—former suitor of Montague's true love, Isabel—vows to take revenge on them and is suspected of setting a fire that destroys their home

Illus. by Fred Marcellino, Farrar, 1986, 187 pp., o.p.; HarperTrophy, 1999, pap., 192 pp. (0-06-440779-9)

(BL 83:788, 84:1441; CCBB 40:118; HB 63:212; Kirkus 54:1511; SLJ Jan 1986 p. 79)

2-396 SEIDLER, Tor. *Toes.* Gr. 4–6.

After learning about the human world from television, a kitten with seven toes on each foot becomes lost and is taken in by a lonely young musician.

Illus. by Eric Beddows, HarperCollins, 2004, 176 pp. (0-06-054100-8)

(BL 100:1729; CCBB 58:38; Kirkus 72:497; SLJ July 2004 p. 112)

2-397 SEIDLER, Tor. *The Wainscott Weasel.* Gr. 4–6.

✮ In this romantic tale set at the weasels' Spring Cotillion, Zeke Whitebelly falls in love with newcomer Wendy Blackish, who falls for the dashing Bagley Brown, Jr., who falls in love with a beautiful fish whose life is threatened by an osprey.

Illus. by Fred Marcellino, Harper, 1993, 193 pp. (0-06-205032-X)

(BL 90:519; CCBB 47:99; HBG 5:82; Kirkus 61:1151; SLJ Dec 1993 p. 116)

2-398 SELDEN (Thompson), George. *The Cricket in Times Square.* **(The Cricket in Times Square series, bk. 1).** Gr. 3–6.

✮ Chester Cricket's beautiful music (as managed by Tucker Mouse) brings fame to Chester and fortune to the subway-station newspaper stand where they live. John Newbery Medal Honor Book, 1961. The sequels are *Tucker's Countryside* (1969), *Harry Cat's Pet Puppy* (1974), *Chester Cricket's Pigeon Ride* (1981), *Chester Cricket's New Home* (1983), *Harry Kitten and Tucker Mouse* (1986), and *The Old Meadow* (1987).

Illus. by Garth (Montgomery) Williams, Farrar, 1960, 160 pp. (0-374-31650-3); Dell, 1999, pap. (0-440-70015-9)

(BL 57:250, 80:96; CCBB 14:86; Eakin:288; HB 36:407; LJ 85:4570; TLS 1982 p. 798)

2-399 SELDEN (Thompson), George. *Irma and Jerry.* Gr. 4–6.

Newly arrived in Greenwich Village, a proper cocker spaniel named Jerry meets a runaway cat named Irma, and the two manage to prevent a robbery and become actors in an off-Broadway play.

Illus. by Leslie Morrill, Avon, 1982, pap., 207 pp., o.p.

(BL 79:780; HB 59:167; SLJ Nov 1982 p. 104)

2-400 SELDEN (Thompson), George. *Oscar Lobster's Fair Exchange.* Gr. 3–5. (Orig. pub. Viking, 1957, entitled *The Garden Under the Sea.*)

Oscar Lobster and his friends decide to retaliate for the humans' annual thievery of shells and rocks by creating their own undersea garden using items stolen from the humans.

Illus. by Peter Lippman, Harper, 1966, 174 pp., o.p.

(BL 53:508; CCBB 11:85; Kirkus 25:37; LJ 82:1802, 91:3538)

2-401 SENDAK, Maurice (Bernard). *Higglety Pigglety Pop! Or, There Must Be*
☆ *More to Life.* Gr. 2–4.

Bored by life at home, a sheepdog named Jenny packs her bag and sets off to find happiness as the leading lady at the World Mother Goose Theater.

Illus. by the author, Harper, 1967, 80 pp. (0-06-025487-4); HarperCollins, 2001, 69 pp. (0-06-028479-X)

(BL 64:451; CCBB 21:66; HB 44:151, 161; HBG 12:295; Kirkus 35:1209; LJ 92:4618; Suth:354)

2-402 SEPULVEDA, Luis. *The Story of a Seagull and the Cat Who Taught Her to Fly.* Gr. 3–6. (Orig. pub. in Spanish.)

A large black cat named Zorba adopts the egg of a dying seagull, cares for the chick with his feline friends, and teaches her to fly.

Trans. by Margaret Sayers Peden, illus. by Chris Sheban, Scholastic, 2003, 128 pp. (0-439-40186-0)

(BL 100:121; HBG 15:102; SLJ Dec 2003 p. 125)

SEREDY, Kate. *Lazy Tinka.*

See Chapter 1, Allegorical Fantasy and Literary Fairy Tales.

2-403 SHACHTMAN, Tom. *Driftwhistler: A Story of Daniel au Fond.* **(Daniel au Fond trilogy, bk. 3).** Gr. 5–8.

Sea lion Daniel au Fond gathers together members of the 13 tribes of seagoing mammals, finds the legendary island of Pacifica where humans and sea mammals once lived harmoniously, and hopes to teach humans to cease their pollution of the environment. This is the sequel to *Beachmaster* (1988) and *Wavebender* (1989).

Henry Holt, 1991, 176 pp., o.p.

(BL 88:698; HBG 3:73; Kirkus 59:1475; SLJ Feb 1992 p. 89)

2-404 SHALANT, Phyllis. *Bartleby of the Mighty Mississippi.* Gr. 3–6.

Bartleby the red-eared turtle decides to leave his 5-year-old owner behind and swim to the Mississippi River, accompanied by Mother Wak the duck, Zip the peeper, and Seezer the former pet alligator.

Illus. by Anna Vojtech, Dutton, 2000, 160 pp. (0-525-46033-0)

(BL 96:1744; HBG 11:312; Kirkus 68:803; SLJ Aug 2000 p. 189)

2-405 **SHARP (Castle), Margery.** *The Rescuers.* **(Miss Bianca series, bk. 1).** Gr.
★★ 3–6. (Orig. British pub. 1959.)
Miss Bianca and two other mice go on a dangerous mission to rescue a human
poet from imprisonment in a deep dungeon. Carnegie Medal Commended Book,
1959. The sequels are *Miss Bianca* (1962), *The Turret* (1963), *Miss Bianca in
the Salt Mines* (1966), *Miss Bianca in the Orient* (1970), *Miss Bianca in the
Antarctic* (1971), *Miss Bianca and the Bridesmaid* (1972), *Bernard the Brave*
(1977), *Bernard into Battle* (1978), and *Miss Bianca in the Arctic* (British).
Illus. by Garth (Montgomery) Williams, Little, Brown, 1959, 149 pp. (0-316-
78314-5); Dell, 1982, pap. (entitled *Miss Bianca and the Rescuers*), o.p.; Little,
Brown, 2006, 160 pp. (0-316-00055-8)
(BL 56:274; CCBB 13:105; Eakin:295; HB 36:38; Kirkus 27:617; LJ 84:3153; TLS Dec 4,
1959 p. xv)

2-406 **SHEEDY, Alexandra E.** *She Was Nice to Mice: The Other Side of Eliza-
beth I's Character Never Before Revealed by Previous Historians.* Gr. 3–5.
Esther Long Whiskers Gray Hair Wallgate the 42nd, a mouse with a literary
mind, finds the memoirs of one of her ancestors who lived at the court of Queen
Elizabeth I in this story written and illustrated by two young adolescents.
Illus. by Jessica Levy, McGraw-Hill, 1975, 95 pp., o.p.
(CCBB 29:86; Kirkus 43:849; SLJ Oct 1975 p. 108)

2-407 **SHEEHAN, Carolyn, and SHEEHAN, Edmond.** *Magnifi-Cat.* Gr. 6 up.
The arrival at the Pearly Gates of a small gray cat with a saint's halo jams
Heaven's soul-processing computer.
Doubleday, 1972, 229 pp., o.p.
(BL 69:551, 570, 767; Kirkus 40:887; LJ 97:2756)

2-408 **SHIPTON, Paul.** *Bug Muldoon: The Garden of Fear.* Gr. 4–6. (Orig. British
pub. 1995.)
After private eye Bug Muldoon takes on a missing-insect case, he is drawn into
a garden-wide conspiracy involving a plot to assassinate the reigning ant queen.
Bug Muldoon and the Killer in the Rain (2000) is the British sequel.
Illus. by Elwood H. Smith, Viking, 2001, 138 pp. (0-670-89687-X)
(BL 88:224; HBG 12:315; SLJ Oct 2001 p. 170)

2-409 **SHIPTON, Paul.** *The Mighty Skink.* Gr. 5–8.
A fearful young rhesus monkey named Kaz and a risk-taking newcomer named
Skink escape from the zoo to explore the outside world.
HarperCollins, 2000, 192 pp. (0-688-17420-5)
(BL 96:2142; CCBB 53:331; HBG 11:312; Kirkus 68:720; SLJ June 2000 p. 154)

2-410 **SHREEVE, Elizabeth.** *Hector Springs Loose.* **(The Adventures of Hector
Fuller, bk. 1).** Gr. 2–4.
After Hector the wumblebug is evicted by a flea circus, he has a series of
adventures while searching for a new home. The sequels are *Hector Finds a
Fortune* (2004), *Hector Afloat* (2004), and *Hector on Thin Ice* (2004).
Illus. by Pamela R. Levy, Simon/Aladdin, 2004, 67 pp. (0-689-86418-3);
Aladdin, pap., 2004, 67 pp. (0-689-86414-0)
(Kirkus 71:1454; SLJ Mar 2004 p. 181)

2-411 SHULEVITZ, Uri. *The Strange and Exciting Adventures of Jeremiah Hush.* Gr. 3–6.
A middle-aged monkey named Jeremiah Hush leaves his quiet home to visit the Shake 'n' Roll Dancin' Hole and to enter a chocolate-banana-pecan-cream pie-eating contest.
Illus. by the author, Farrar, 1986, 90 pp., o.p.
(BL 83:846; CCBB 40:135; Kirkus 54:1795; SLJ Feb 1987 p. 84)

2-412 SHURA, Mary Francis (pseud. of Mary Francis Craig). *A Tale of Middle*
✮ *Length.* Gr. 5–6.
Dominic and Alec mouse discover that the strange object near their mouse colony is a mouse trap.
Illus. by Peter Parnall, Atheneum, 1966, 105 pp., o.p.
(BL 63:268; CCBB 20:48; HB 42:566; Kirkus 34:687; LJ 91:4343)

SILVERSTEIN, Shel(by). *Uncle Shelby's Story of Lafcadio, the Lion Who Shot Back.*
See Chapter 8, Humorous Fantasy.

2-413 SIMONT, Marc. *Mimi.* Gr. 3–5.
A mouse named Mimi is secretly trained to run across the stage every time a famous concert singer needs to hit a high note.
Illus. by the author, Harper, 1954, 56 pp., o.p.
(HB 31:111; Kirkus 22:726; LJ 80:193)

SINCIC, Alan. *Edward Is Only a Fish.*
See Chapter 8, Humorous Fantasy.

2-414 SINCLAIR, Tom. *Tales of a Wandering Warthog.* Gr. 4–6.
Wart the warthog flees his African homeland and goes to New York City, where he and his teenage friends solve numerous local and world crises.
Illus. by John C. Wallner, Whitman, 1985, 134 pp., o.p.
(BL 81:1404; SLJ Aug 1985 p. 69)

SINGER, Marilyn. *Charmed.*
See Chapter 7, High Fantasy: Travel to Other Worlds.

2-415 SINGER, Marilyn. *The Fido Frame-Up.* **(The Sam Spayed series, bk. 1).** Gr. 4–6.
In this detective novel spoof, Samantha Spayed, dog detective, is the brains behind her master Philip Barlowe's solutions to his dangerous cases. The sequels are *A Nose for Trouble* (1985) and *Where There's a Will, There's a Wag* (1986).
Illus. by Andrew Glass, Warne, 1983, 90 pp., o.p.
(BL 80:576; HB 59:712; SLJ Dec 1983 p. 83)

2-416 SISSON, Rosemary Anne. *The Adventures of Ambrose.* Gr. 2–4. (Orig. British pub. 1951.)
Ambrose and Simon mouse travel to London to meet the king and queen.
Illus. by Astrid Walford, Dutton, 1952, 118 pp., o.p.
(HB 28:406; Kirkus 20:598; LJ 77:1662)

SLEIGH, Barbara (de Riemer). *Carbonel: The King of the Cats.*
See Chapter 9, Magic Adventure Fantasy.

SMITH, Agnes. *An Edge of the Forest.*
See Chapter 1, Allegorical Fantasy and Literary Fairy Tales.

2-417 **SMITH, Alison.** *Come Away Home.* Gr. 3–5.
Trapped in a Scottish loch by a storm and unable to get back to the ocean, a young sea monster named Angus is befriended by Fiona and her dog, James.
Illus. by Deborah Haeffele, Macmillan, 1991, 105 pp., o.p.
(BL 87:1800; CCBB 44:276; HBG 2:271; Kirkus 59:539; SLJ July 1991 p. 74)

2-418 **SMITH, Dodie (Dorothy Gladys).** *The Hundred and One Dalmatians.* Gr.
✶ 4–6. (Orig. British pub. 1956.)
Pongo and Missis rescue their 15 puppies from Cruella DeVil, who dognapped them to make into fur coats. The sequel is *The Starlight Barking* (1967, 1997).
Illus. by Janet Grahame-Johnstone and Anne Grahame-Johnstone, Viking, 1957, 199 pp., o.p.; illus. by Michael Dooling, Viking, 1989, pap., 184 pp., o.p.; Puffin, 1989, pap., 184 pp. (0-14-034034-3)
(BL 53:588; HB 33:222; Kirkus 25:75; LJ 82:1802)

2-419 **SMITH, Emma.** *Emily: The Traveling Guinea Pig.* Gr. 3–5.
Emily Guinea Pig sets off to see the ocean, leaving her brother Arthur behind to look after her tidy little house. The sequel is *Emily's Voyage* (Harcourt, 1966).
Illus. by Katherine Wigglesworth, Astor-Honor, 1960, 76 pp., o.p.
(HB 36:287; Kirkus 28:232)

SONENKLAR, Carol. *Bug Boy.*
See Chapter 9, Magic Adventure Fantasy.

2-420 **SOTO, Gary.** *The Cat's Meow.* Gr. 2–4.
No one believes third-grader Graciela when she reports that her white cat, Pip, has begun speaking in Spanish.
Illus. by Joe Cepeda, Scholastic, 1995, 78 pp. (0-590-47001-9)
(BL 92:637; HBG 7:57; SLJ Oct 1995 p. 120)

SPINNER, Stephanie, and WEISS, Ellen. *Gerbilitis.*
See Chapter 8, Humorous Fantasy.

2-421 **SPIRES, Elizabeth.** *The Mouse of Amherst.* Gr. 2–5.
Emmaline mouse moves into a hole in poet Emily Dickinson's bedroom wall and falls in love with the poetry she writes.
Illus. by Claire A. Nivola, Farrar, 1999, 64 pp. (0-374-35083-3)
(BL 95:1330; HBG 10:285; Kirkus 64:306; SLJ May 1999 p. 98)

2-422 **STANTON, Mary.** *The Heavenly Horse from the Outermost West.* Gr. 10 up.
✶ The Appaloosa breed faces extinction because of an evil bargain made by the Lead Mare, until the horse god, Dancer, gives up his immortality and returns from the land of the Outermost West. The sequel is *Piper at the Gate* (1989).
Baen, 1988, pap., 344 pp., o.p.
(BL 84:1575, 1598, 86:907; Kliatt Sep 1988 p. 27; LJ June 15, 1988 p. 71; VOYA 11:296, 12:14)

STEARNS, Pamela (Fujimoto). *Into the Painted Bear Lair.*
See Chapter 7, High Fantasy: Travel to Other Worlds.

2-423 STEFANEC-OGREN, Cathy. *Sly, P.I.: The Case of the Missing Shoes.* Gr. 1–4.
Sly Fox, private investigator, solves his first case when his old friend ballerina Loretta Oink's toe shoes disappear on the opening night of "Sleeping Beauty."
Illus. by Priscilla Posey Circolo, Harper, 1989, 48 pp., o.p.
(BL 85:1554; CCBB 42:206; SLJ Jan 1989 p. 95)

2-424 STEIG, William. *Abel's Island.* Gr. 3–6.
✯✯ A storm sweeps Abel the mouse away from his new bride, Amanda, to a deserted island, where he develops a talent for sculpting. John Newbery Medal Honor Book, 1977; Phoenix Award Honor Book, 1996.
Illus. by the author, Farrar, 1976, 128 pp. (0-374-30010-0), 1985, pap. (0-374-40016-4)
(BL 73:181, 80:46; CCBB 30:33; HB 52:500; Kirkus 44:686; SLJ Oct 1976 p. 101; Suth 2:429; TLS 1977 p. 1248)

2-425 STEIG, William. *Dominic.* Gr. 4–6.
✯ An adventurous dog named Dominic finds an enchanted garden, is given a fortune by an old pig, and helps fight the Doomsday Gang. National Book Award Finalist, 1973.
Illus. by the author, Farrar, 1972, 145 pp., o.p., 1984, pap. (0-374-41826-8)
(BL 69:531; CCBB 26:31; HB 48:470; Kirkus 40:1414; LJ 97:2954; SLJ Aug 1992 p. 99; Suth 378; TLS 1973 p. 386)

2-426 STEIG, William. *The Real Thief.* Gr. 2–5.
✯ Angry over the theft of his jewels, the king accuses his loyal guard, Gawain the goose, despite Gawain's pleas of innocence.
Illus. by the author, Farrar, 1976, 64 pp., o.p., 1984, pap. (0-374-46208-9)
(BL 70:242, 827; CCBB 27:102; HB 49:595; Kirkus 41:756; LJ 98:3446; Suth 2:431)

2-427 STEINER, Jörg. *Rabbit Island.* Gr. 3–5. (Orig. Swiss pub. 1977.)
Big Gray and Little Brown escape from the rabbit factory where they are being fattened for slaughter. Mildred L. Batchelder Award, 1978.
Trans. by Ann Conrad Lammers, illus. by Jörg Müller, Harcourt, 1978, 32 pp., o.p.; Bergh, 1984 (repr. of 1978 ed.), o.p.
(HB 54:634; Kirkus 46:1135; SLJ Oct 1978 p. 139; TLS 1978 p. 763)

2-428 STEVENS, Carla. *Stories from a Snowy Meadow.* Gr. 2–3.
✯ Old Vole entertains her young friends Mole, Shrew, and Mouse with three final tales before her peaceful death.
Illus. by Eve Rice, Seabury, 1976, 48 pp., o.p.
(Bl 73:329; CCBB 30:82; Kirkus 44:975; SLJ Dec 1976 p. 64)

2-429 STEVENS, Eden Vale. *Abba.* Gr. 3–6.
Abba, an orphaned elephant, searches for Einhorn, the Great White Buffalo, to help rescue another elephant held captive by hunters.
Illus. by Anthony Stevens, Atheneum, 1962, 116 pp., o.p.
(BL 59:576; LJ 87:190)

2-430 STEVENSON, James. *Here Comes Herb's Hurricane!* Gr. 2–4.
Herb Rabbit develops a hurricane warning system that refuses to work until a real hurricane comes along.
Illus. by the author, Harper, 1973, 149 pp., o.p.
(CCBB 27:150; Kirkus 41:1310, 1351; LJ 98:3709)

2-431 STEVENSON, James. *Oliver, Clarence, and Violet.* Gr. 2–4.
Oliver Beaver's round-the-world boat trip is complicated by the numerous friends who decide to go with him, including a toad, a turkey, a turtle, and two bats.
Illus. by the author, Greenwillow, 1982, 96 pp., o.p.
(BL 78:1370; Kirkus 50:347; SLJ May 1952 p. 65)

2-432 STEVENSON, James. *The Supreme Souvenir Factory.* Gr. 2–4.
✴ Chester the dog and his bat friend Wendy join forces to save the factory from the weasely plans of Mr. Sashwayte.
Illus. by the author, Greenwillow, 1988, 56 pp. (0-688-07782-X)
(BL 85:487; HB 65:206; Kirkus 56:1408; SLJ Dec 1989 p. 94)

STOLP, Hans. *The Golden Bird.*
See Chapter 1, Allegorical Fantasy and Literary Fairy Tales.

2-433 STOLZ, Mary (Slattery). *Belling the Tiger.* Gr. 2–4.
✴ Asa and Rambo mouse are selected to put a bell on Siri, the tigerlike housecat, bringing about an unexpected trip to the land of elephants and real tigers. John Newbery Medal Honor Book, 1962. The sequels are *The Great Rebellion* (1961), *Siri the Conquistador* (1963), and *Maximilian's World* (1966). The three sequels have been published together as *Tales at the Mousehole* (Godine, 1992, see entry below) with new illustrations and renamed main characters.
Illus. by Beni Montresor, Harper, 1961, 1989, 64 pp., o.p.; illus. by Pierre Pratt, Running Pr., 2004, 31 pp. (0-7624-1889-3)
(BL 57:644, 101:125; CCBB 14:149; Eakin:314; HB 37:339, 80:482–483, 490; Kirkus 29:326; LJ 86:1989; SLJ Sep 2004 p. 181)

2-434 STOLZ, Mary (Slattery). *Casebook of a Private (Cat's) Eye.* Gr. 3–6.
✴ Eileen O'Kelly, the only feline detective in 1912 Boston, solves a number of mysteries, including that of a missing kitten and the murder of a talented chef.
Illus. by Pamela R. Levy, Front Street, 1999, 118 pp. (0-8126-2650-8)
(BL 95:1532; CCBB 52:367; HBG 10:300; Kirkus 67:636; SLJ June 1999 p. 137)

2-435 STOLZ, Mary (Slattery). *Cat Walk.* Gr. 3–6.
✴ A six-toed black barn kitten runs away from the home where a little girl has dressed him up and named him Tootsie Wootsie, and searches for a home where he will be loved for himself.
Illus. by Erik Blegvad, Harper, 1983, 120 pp., o.p.
(BL 79:1223; CCBB 36:218; HB 59:306; Kirkus 51:307; SLJ Aug 1983 p. 71; Suth 3:412)

2-436 STOLZ, Mary (Slattery). *Deputy Shep.* Gr. 2–5.
✴ Slow-moving Jack Shep, deputy sheriff, reluctantly tries to solve the rash of robberies at canine homes throughout Canoville in this humorous animal detective story.

Illus. by Pamela Johnson, Harper, 1991, 96 pp., o.p.
(BL 87:2148; CCBB 45:51; HBG 3:74; Kirkus 59:1094; SLJ Oct 1991 p. 105)

2-437 **STOLZ, Mary (Slattery).** *Frédou.* Gr. 4–6.
☆ Runaway Paul is taken in by a hotel-owning Parisian cat.
Illus. by Tomi Ungerer, Harper, 1962, 118 pp., o.p.
(BL 59:84; CCBB 15:166; HB 38:370; Kirkus 30:386; LJ 87:2625)

2-438 **STOLZ, Mary (Slattery).** *Pigeon Flight.* Gr. 2–4.
Mr. and Mrs. Pigeon decide to leave New York City and move to New England.
Illus. by Murray Tinkelman, Harper, 1962, 54 pp., o.p.
(CCBB 16:16; Eakin:317; HB 38:607; LJ 87:3206)

2-439 **STOLZ, Mary (Slattery).** *Quentin Corn.* Gr. 4–6.
☆ Bored with life as a pig, Quentin Corn decides to live as a man; but though he
is accepted by adults, the children are not all so accepting.
Illus. by Pamela Johnson, Godine, 1985, 128 pp. (0-87923-553-5)
(BL 82:270, 84:1441; CCBB 39:80; HB 61:737; SLJ Sep 1985 p. 140, Dec 1985 p. 34; Suth
4:401)

2-440 **STOLZ, Mary (Slattery).** *Tales at the Mousehole.* Gr. 3–5.
These three stories about the adventures of two tiny house mice were originally
published separately as *The Great Rebellion* (Harper, 1961), *Siri the Conquistador* (Harper, 1963), and *Maximilian's World* (Harper, 1966). The names of the
main characters have been changed in this edition. This is the sequel to *Belling
the Tiger* (Harper, 1961; 1989; see entry above).
Illus. by Pamela Johnson, Godine, 1992, 102 pp. (0-87923-789-9)
(BL 89:671; HBG 4:77)

2-441 **STONG, Phil(ip Duffield).** *Prince and the Porker.* Gr. 4–6.
☆ A boy and a pig help a harness trotter named Prince to win blue ribbons.
Illus. by Kurt Wiese, Dodd, 1950, 67 pp., o.p.
(BL 47:226; CCBB 3:71; HB 26:477; LJ 75:2083)

2-442 **SYMONDS, John.** *Elfrida and the Pig.* Gr. 2–4. (Orig. British pub. 1959.)
Elfrida's secret friend, the pig next door, helps her find a doll of her very own.
Illus. by Edward Ardizzone, Watts, 1959, 48 pp., o.p.
(CCBB 14:18; HB 36:292; LJ 85:2044; TLS Dec 4, 1959 p. xv)

TARN, (Sir) W(illiam) W(oodthorpe). *The Treasure of the Isle of Mist: A
Tale of the Isle of Skye.*
See Chapter 9, Magic Adventure Fantasy.

2-443 **TITUS, Eve.** *Basil of Baker Street.* **(Basil of Baker Street series, bk. 1).**
☆ Gr. 3–5.
Basil, an English mouse detective who idolizes Sherlock Holmes, solves one of
Mouse-dom's most baffling and mysterious kidnapping cases. The sequels are
Basil and the Lost Colony (1964), *Basil and the Pygmy Cats* (1971; 1989,
pap.), *Basil in Mexico* (1975), and *Basil in the Wild West* (1982).
Illus. by Paul Galdone, McGraw-Hill, 1958, 128 pp., o.p.
(BL 54:593; CCBB 11:124; HB 34:266; Kirkus 26:335; LJ 83:1947)

2-444 TODD, Ruthven. *Space Cat.* **(Space Cat series, bk. 1).** Gr. 3–5.
Flyball the cat not only makes an important scientific discovery on his way to the moon but also saves the pilot's life. The sequels are *Space Cat Visits Venus* (1955), *Space Cat Meets Mars* (1957), and *Space Cat and the Kittens* (1959). Illus. by Paul Galdone, Scribner, 1952, 69 pp., o.p.
(CCBB 6:28; HB 28:320; Kirkus 20:657; LJ 77:1819)

TOLKIEN, J(ohn) R(onald) R(euel). *Roverandom.*
See Chapter 11, Toy Fantasy.

2-445 TOMLINSON, Jill. *Hilda the Hen Who Wouldn't Give Up.* Gr. 2–4.
Hilda the hen is so enamored of her Aunt Emma's chicks that she decides to have a brood of her own, against Farmer Biddick's wishes.
Illus. by Fernando Krahn, Harcourt, 1967, 1980, 96 pp., o.p.
(BL 76:1612; Kirkus 48:838; SLJ Aug 1980 p. 58)

2-446 TREVOR, Elleston. *Deep Wood.* **(Deep Wood series, bk. 1).** Gr. 4–6.
Five friends—Badger, Otter, Owl, Squirrel, and Fox—live along the Wild River in Deep Wood. The sequels are *Heather Hill* (1948) and *Badger's Wood* (1958, 1959).
Illus. by Stephen Voorhis, Longman, 1947, 282 pp., o.p.
(BL 44:138; CCBB 1:7; HB 23:358; Kirkus 45:394; LJ 73:126)

TURKLE, Brinton (Cassaday). *Mooncoin Castle; or Skulduggery Rewarded.*
See Chapter 4, Ghost Fantasy.

TURNBULL, Agnes Sligh. *George.*
See Chapter 9, Magic Adventure Fantasy.

2-447 UNWIN, Nora S(picer). *Two Too Many.* Gr. 2–4.
On Halloween night, two lost kittens are taken for a ride on a witch's broom.
Illus. by the author, McKay, 1962, 54 pp., o.p.
(Eakin:339; HB 38:473; LJ 87:4615; TLS 1965 p. 1141)

UPENSKY, Eduard. *Uncle Fedya, His Dog, and His Cat.*
See Chapter 9, Magic Adventure Fantasy.

2-448 UTTLEY, Alison (Jane [Taylor]). *Foxglove Tales.* Gr. K–3. (Orig. British pub. 1984.)
Cozy animal stories from Uttley's British story collections, *Moonshine and Magic* (1932), *Candlelight Tales* (1936), and *Lavender Shoes* (1970).
Chosen by Lucy Meredith, illus. by Shirley Felts, Faber, 1984, 107 pp., o.p.
(BL 81:1671; SLJ Feb 1985 p. 69)

VAMBA. *The Prince and His Ants.*
See Chapter 9, Magic Adventure Fantasy.

VANDE VELDE, Vivian. *Smart Dog.*
See Chapter 8, Humorous Fantasy.

2-449   VAN DE WETERING, Janwillem. *Hugh Pine.* **(Hugh Pine trilogy, bk. 1).**
Gr. 2–4.
Hugh Porcupine decides to walk upright, wearing a hat and coat, in order to
cross roads safely. The sequels are *Hugh Pine and the Good Place* (1986) and
Hugh Pine and Something Else (1989).
Illus. by Lynn Munsinger, Houghton, 1980, 96 pp. (0-395-29459-2)
(BL 77:122; CCBB 34:102; Kirkus 48:1518; SLJ Mar 1981 p. 152)

2-450   VAN LEEUWEN, Jean. *The Great Christmas Kidnapping Caper.* **(Marvin**
☆   **the Magnificent Mouse series, bk. 2).** Gr. 3–5.
The disappearance of Santa Claus mobilizes Marvin the Magnificent Mouse
and his gang to the rescue. This is the sequel to *The Great Cheese Conspiracy*
(Random, 1969, pap., 2001) and is followed by *The Great Rescue Operation*
(1982, 1985), *The Great Summer Camp Catastrophe* (1992), and *The Great
Googlestein Museum Mystery* (2003), in which mice heroes Marvin, Raymond,
and Fats spend a week inside New York City's Guggenheim Museum.
Illus. by Steven Kellogg, Dial, 1975, 133 pp., o.p.; Volo/Hyperion, 2002, pap.
(0-7868-1469-1)
(BL 72:169; CCBB 29:54; HB 78:430; Kirkus 43:778; SLJ Oct 1975 p. 81; Suth 2:459)

2-451   WABER, Bernard. *Dear Hildegarde.* Gr. 2–4.
Hildegarde Owl is an advice columnist who tries to solve the problems of her
fellow creatures.
Illus. by the author, Houghton, 1980, 64 pp., o.p.
(CCBB 34:141; HB 57:54; Kirkus 49:4; SLJ Feb 1981 p. 60)

2-452   WABER, Bernard. *Mice on My Mind.* Gr. 2–5.
Suffering from an obsession with mice, a cat finally finds a cure for his malady.
Illus. by the author, Houghton, 1977, 48 pp., o.p.
(CCBB 31:103; HB 53:526; Kirkus 45:1045; SLJ Sep 1977 p. 117; Suth 2:464)

WAECHTER, Friedrich, and EILERT, Bernd. *The Crown Snatchers.*
See Chapter 1, Allegorical Fantasy and Literary Fairy Tales.

2-453   WAHL, Jan (Boyer). *Pleasant Fieldmouse.* **(Pleasant Fieldmouse series,**
bk. 1). Gr. 2–4.
Pleasant Fieldmouse becomes a firefighter and courageously rescues Anxious
Squirrel's mother and Mrs. Worrywind Hedgehog. The sequels are *The Six
Voyages of Pleasant Fieldmouse* (Delacorte, 1971), *Pleasant Fieldmouse's
Halloween Party* (Putnam, 1974), *The Pleasant Fieldmouse Storybook* (Pren-
tice, 1977), and *Pleasant Fieldmouse's Valentine Trick* (Dutton, 1977).
Illus. by Maurice (Bernard) Sendak, Harper, 1964, 80 pp., o.p.; Harper, 1992
(0-06-026331-8)
(CCBB 18:94; HB 40:373; LJ 89:3477; TLS 1969 p. 1387)

2-454   WALLACE, Barbara Brooks. *Palmer Patch.* Gr. 4–6.
Thinking they are no longer wanted, the Patch family's pets run away from
home.
Illus. by Lawrence Di Fiori, Follett, 1976, 128 pp., o.p.
(BL 73:671; CCBB 30:116; SLJ Apr 1977 p. 72)

2-455 WALLACE, Bill. *Snot Stew.* Gr. 3–5.
Adopted by a farm family, brother and sister kittens Kikki and Toby enjoy the cuddling and good food, but try to avoid Butch, the family's dangerous dog.
Illus. by Lisa McCue, Holiday, 1989, 81 pp., o.p.
(BL 85:1657; SLJ Apr 1989 p. 109)

2-456 WALLACE, Bill. *Upchuck and the Rotten Willy.* **(Upchuck and the Rotten Willy books, # 1).** Gr. 3–6.
Lonely Chuck the cat, whose best friend has moved away, spends two nights trapped in a tree until his rescue by a kind rottweiler named Willy. The sequels are *Running Wild* (2000) and *The Great Escape* (2001).
Illus. by David Slonim, Minstrel/Pocket, 1998, 101 pp. (0-671-01769-1)
(Kirkus 66:201; SLJ Mar 1998 p. 189)

2-457 WALLACE, Bill. *Watchdog and the Coyotes.* Gr. 3–5.
A timid Great Dane called Sweetie learns to defend himself, his owners, and his Irish setter and beagle friends from bullying coyotes.
Illus. by David Slonim, Simon, 1995, 105 pp. (0-671-53620-6); Pocket, 1995, pap. (0-671-89075-1)
(Bl 92:706; HBG 7:70; SLJ Nov 1995 p. 107)

2-458 WALLACE, Carol, and WALLACE, Bill. *The Meanest Hound Around.* Gr. 2–5.
Abandoned by his beloved boy's father, a dog named Freddie befriends Spike, a mistreated junkyard watchdog, and helps Spike escape his master.
Illus. by John Steven Gurney, Simon, 2003, 160 pp. (0-7434-3785-3)
(HBG 14:359; Kirkus 71:148; SLJ Apr 2003 p. 142)

WANGERIN, Walter, Jr. *The Book of the Dun Cow.*
See Chapter 1, Allegorical Fantasy and Literary Fairy Tales.

2-459 WATKINS, Will. *Sid Seal, Houseman.* Gr. 3–5.
Sid Seal—waiter, musician, and companion to young Waltham de Swine—adds spice to the stuffy de Swine family's lives.
Illus. by Toni Goffe, Orchard, 1989, 89 pp. (0-531-00384-5)
(BL 85:1908; CCBB 42:285; SLJ Sep 1989 p. 235)

2-460 WATSON, Wendy. *Tales for a Winter's Eve.* Gr. K–3.
★ Freddie Fox's family and friends cheer him up after a skiing accident by telling him stories.
Illus. by the author, Farrar, 1988, 32 pp., o.p.
(BL 85:588, 880; CCBB 42:88; HB 65:64; Kirkus 56:1746; SLJ Feb 1989 p. 76)

2-461 WEIR, Rosemary (Green). *Pyewacket.* Gr. 3–5.
Pyewacket leads the neighborhood cats in revolt against their owners.
Illus. by Charles Pickard, Abelard-Schuman, 1967, 123 pp., o.p.
(Kirkus 35:1210; LJ 93:297; TLS 1967 p. 1153)

2-462 WENNING, Elisabeth. *The Christmas Mouse.* Gr. K–4. (Orig. British pub. 1961, entitled *The Christmas Churchmouse.*)

Hungry little Kaspar Kleinmause helps Herr Gruber write the carol "Silent Night."
Illus. by Barbara Remington, Holt, 1959, 44 pp., o.p.
(BL 56:225; HB 35:471; Kirkus 27:756; LJ 84:3627)

WERBER, Bernard. *Empire of the Ants.*
See Chapter 7, High Fantasy: Travel to Other Worlds.

WESTALL, Robert (Atkinson). *The Cats of Seroster.*
See Chapter 5, High Fantasy: Alternate Worlds or Histories.

2-463 **WHAYNE, Susanne Santoro.** *Watch the House.* Gr. 2–5.
The family pets—a guinea pig, two cats, a dog, a canary, and two guppies—decide to explore the outdoor world while their masters are away.
Illus. by Leslie Morrill, Simon & Schuster, 1992, 80 pp., o.p.
(BL 88:1940; HBG 3:272; Kirkus 60:856; SLJ July 1992 p. 66)

WHINNEM, Reade Scott. *Utten and Plumley.*
See Chapter 10, Time Travel Fantasy.

2-464 **WHITE, Anne Hitchcock.** *Junket.* Gr. 4–6.
✯ It takes an entire summer for an Airedale named Junket to teach his new owners about farm life.
Illus. by Robert McCloskey, Viking, 1955, 183 pp., o.p.
(BL 51:287; CCBB 9:31; Eakin:348; HB 31:114; Kirkus 23:81; LJ 80:1259)

2-465 **WHITE, Anne Hitchcock.** *The Story of Serapina.* Gr. 3–5.
✯ Serapina the cat adopts the Salinus family, although they are not sure they want her.
Illus. by Tony Palazzo, Viking, 1951, 128 pp., o.p.
(BL 47:333; CCBB 4:47; Eakin:348; HB 27:180; LJ 76:970)

2-466 **WHITE, E(lwyn) B(rooks).** *Charlotte's Web.* Gr. 3 up.
✯✯ Wilbur the pig is destined for the annual fall slaughtering, but his resourceful friend, a spider named Charlotte, tries to save him. John Newbery Medal Honor Book, 1953. *The E. B. White Collection* (Avon, 2003) contains *Charlotte's Web*, *Stuart Little*, and *The Trumpet of the Swan*.
Illus. by Garth (Montgomery) Williams, Harper, 1952, 184 pp., LB (0-06-026385-7), 1974, pap. (0-06-440055-7); HarperCollins, 1999, illus. by Garth (Montgomery) Williams and Rosemary Wells, 184 pp. (0-06-028298-3), 2001, pap. (0-06-441093-5); illus. by Garth (Montgomery) Williams, HarperCollins, 2002, 224 pp. (0-06-000698-6).
(BL 49:2, 80:96; CCBB 6:36; Eakin:348; HB 28:394, 407; HBG 14:89; Kirkus 20:501; LJ 77:2185; TLS 1952 p. 7)

2-467 **WHITE, E(lwyn) B(rooks).** *Stuart Little.* Gr. 4–6.
Stuart Little is the second son of a normal American family, except that Stuart turns out to be a mouse instead of a boy. *The E. B. White Collection* (Avon, 2003) contains *Charlotte's Web*, *Stuart Little*, and *The Trumpet of the Swan*.
Illus. by Garth (Montgomery) Williams, Harper, 1945, 131 pp., LB (0-06-026395-4), 1974, pap. (0-06-440056-5); HarperCollins, 1999, illus. by Garth

(Montgomery) Williams and Rosemary Wells, 131 pp. (0-06-028297-5), 2001, pap. (0-06-441092-7)

(HB 21:455; Kirkus 13:314)

2-468 **WHITE, E(lwyn) B(rooks).** *The Trumpet of the Swan.* Gr. 4–6.
☆ Lewis's father buys him a trumpet to overcome his speech defect and starts the young swan on a career as a nightclub entertainer. Finalist, National Book Award, 1971. *The E. B. White Collection* (Avon, 2003) contains *Charlotte's Web*, *Stuart Little*, and *The Trumpet of the Swan*.
Illus. by Edward Frascino, Harper, 1970, 210 pp., LB (0-06-026397-0), pap. (0-06-440048-4); illus. by Fred Marcellino, HarperCollins, 2000, 257 pp. (0-06-028936-8); HarperTrophy, 2001, pap. (0-06-441094-3); HarperCollins, 2004 (0-06-028410-2)

(BL 67:59, 661; CCBB 24:35; HB 46:391; HBG 12:318; Kirkus 38:455; LJ 95:2537, 4327; TLS 1970 p. 1458)

2-469 **WHITELAW, Stella, GARDINER, Judith, and RONSON, Mark.** *Grimalkin's Tales.* Gr. 10 up.
Twelve tales about cats, some of which are fantasy, including one about Leopold, a large cat who can fly.
St. Martin's, 1985, 160 pp., o.p.

(Kirkus 53:830; SLJ Jan 1986 p. 84)

WHYBROW, Ian. *Little Wolf's Book of Badness.*
See Chapter 8, Humorous Fantasy.

WIGGIN, Kate Douglas (Smith). *The Bird's Christmas Carol.*
See Chapter 1, Allegorical Fantasy and Literary Fairy Tales.

WILDE, Oscar (Fingal O'Flahertie Wills). *The Happy Prince.*
See Chapter 1, Allegorical Fantasy and Literary Fairy Tales.

2-470 **WILLARD, Dale C.** *The Linnet's Tale.* Gr. 6–12.
Raised by a family of field mice who taught him to fly, orphaned linnet Waterford Hopstep describes his comfortable life in the mouse community, Tottensea Burrows.
Scribner, 2002, pap., 208 pp. (0-7432-2498-1)

(BL 98:1214; Kirkus 70:71; VOYA 25:299, 26:14)

2-471 **WILLIAMS, Garth (Montgomery).** *The Adventures of Benjamin Pink.* Gr. 2–4.
A rabbit named Benjamin Pink is shipwrecked while on a fishing trip.
Illus. by the author, Harper, 1952, 152 pp., o.p.

(HB 27:400; 28:27; Kirkus 19:347; LJ 76:1710)

2-472 **WILLIAMS (John), Ursula Moray.** *Bogwoppit.* Gr. 5–7. (Orig. British pub.
☆ 1978.)
Samantha's crusade to save the furry creatures who live in the drains of her aunt's mansion takes a new turn when her aunt is kidnapped by the Bogwoppits.
Nelson, 1978, 128 pp., o.p.

(BL 75:54; CCBB 32:128; Kirkus 46:879; SLJ Sep 1978 p. 152; Suth 2:481; TLS 1978 p. 765)

2-473 WILLIAMS (John), Ursula Moray. *Gobbolino the Witch's Cat.* Gr. 3–5. (Orig. British pub. 1942.)
Witch kitten Gobbolino dreams of finding a loving home with an ordinary family. The sequel is *The Further Adventures of Gobbolino and The Little Wooden Horse* (2002), which is related to the author's *Adventures of a Little Wooden Horse* (1938, 1939; see Chapter 11, Toy Fantasy).
Illus. by Paul Howard, Kingfisher, 2002, 220 pp. (0-7534-5405-X)
(HBG 13:366)

2-474 WILLIAMS (John), Ursula Moray. *The Nine Lives of Island MacKenzie.*
☆   Gr. 4–6. (Orig. British pub. 1959; orig. U.S. title *Island MacKenzie*.)
MacKenzie the cat and a cat-hating woman named Miss Pettifer survive shipwreck, sharks, and crocodiles to be cast up together on a desert island.
Illus. by Edward Ardizzone, Morrow, 1960, 128 pp., o.p.; Chatto, 1980, 128 pp., o.p.
(BL 57:157; CCBB 14:88; HB 36:503, 56:664; Kirkus 28:498; LJ 85:3228; TLS Dec 4, 1959 p. xv)

WILLIAMS (John), Ursula Moray. *Tiger Nanny.*
See Chapter 8, Humorous Fantasy.

2-475 WILLIAMS, Tad. *Tailchaser's Song.* Gr. 10 up.
The quest saga of a young ginger cat, Fritti Tailchaser, who is captured and enslaved by an evil cat-god while on a journey to find his lost mate.
NAL, 1985, o.p.; DAW, 1986, pap., 320 pp., o.p.
(BL 82:317, 332, 86:907; Kirkus 53:980; LJ Nov 15, 1985 p. 112; SLJ Nov 1985 p. 106)

WILLIS, Paul J. *No Clock in the Forest.*
See Chapter 7, High Fantasy: Travel to Other Worlds.

2-476 WILSON, A. N. *Hazel the Guinea Pig.* Gr. 1–4. (Orig. British pub. 1989.)
Three stories about Hazel, the pet guinea pig, getting stuck in a rubber boot, finding a mate named Tobacco, and starting a family.
Illus. by Jonathan Heale, Candlewick, 1992, 92 pp., o.p.
(CCBB 45:250; HBG 3:259; Kirkus 60:473; SLJ June 1992 p. 104)

2-477 WILSON, A. N. *Stray.* Gr. 6–10. (Orig. British pub. 1987.)
Pufftail, an independent cat, tells his grandkitten the story of his adventurous life, his search for love, and his attempts to understand human behavior. *Tabitha* (U.K. 1988, U.S. 1989; see below) is a book about Pufftail's daughter, written for younger children.
Orchard, 1989, 256 pp., o.p.
(BL 86:902, 922; HBG 1:79; Kirkus 57:1170; SLJ Oct 1989 p. 138; VOYA 12:285)

2-478 WILSON, A. N. *Tabitha.* Gr. 1–4. (Orig. British pub. 1988, entitled *The Tabitha Stories*.)
The daughter of Pufftail the alleycat who told his story in the young adult book *Stray* (U.K. 1987, U.S. 1988; see above), Tabitha describes her life with a family of "two-footers."
Illus. by Sarah Fox-Davies, Orchard, 1989, 48 pp., o.p.
(HB 56:480; Kirkus 57:218; SLJ Aug 1989 p. 133)

WILSON, David Henry. *The Coachman Rat.*
See Chapter 6, High Fantasy: Myth or Legend Fantasy.

2-479 **WILSON, Gahan.** *Harry, the Fat Bear Spy.* Gr. 4–6.
Harry would rather be a chef or a tap dancer than a bumbling spy, but he does manage to solve the case of the great Bearmania macaroons. The sequel is *Harry and the Sea Serpent* (1976).
Illus. by the author, Scribner, 1973, 120 pp., o.p.
(Kirkus 41:698; LJ 99:2281)

2-480 **WILSON, Willie.** *Up Mountain One Time.* Gr. 4–7.
A young shantytown-dwelling mongoose named Viggo decides to search for a better life in the bush country that his late mother longingly described to him.
Illus. by Karen Bertrand, Orchard, 1987, 133 pp., o.p.
(BL 84:154, 1442; CCBB 41:40; Kirkus 55:1076; SLJ Sep 1987 p. 184)

2-481 **WINTHROP (Mahony), Elizabeth.** *The Red-Hot Rattoons.* Gr. 5–7.
Five orphaned rats—Ella, Benny, Fletcher, Woody, and Monk—travel to Manhattan to fulfill their tap-dancing dreams and follow the legacy of their jazz trumpeter and dancer parents.
Illus. by Betsy Lewin, Holt, 2003, 224 pp. (0-8050-7229-2)
(HBG 15:105; SLJ Oct 2003 p. 180; VOYA 26:420)

2-482 **WISE, William.** *Christopher Mouse: The Tale of a Small Traveler.* Gr. 3–5. (Orig. British pub. 2004.)
Christopher Mouse chronicles his life, from his brothers' departure for a medical laboratory, to his and his sister's stay in a pet store, to his subsequent travels from owner to owner.
Illus. by Patrick Benson, Bloomsbury, 2004, 152 pp. (1-58234-878-2)
(BL 100:365; CCBB 57:396; Kirkus 72:403; SLJ June 2004 p. 122)

WOOD, James Playsted. *An Elephant in the Family.*
See Chapter 8, Humorous Fantasy.

WRIGGINS, Sally. *The White Monkey King: A Chinese Fable.*
See Chapter 6, High Fantasy: Myth or Legend Fantasy.

2-483 **WRIGHTSON, (Alice) Patricia (Furlonger).** *Moon-Dark.* Gr. 5–8. (Orig.
★ Australian pub. 1987.)
One dark night, a dog named Blue and the other animal inhabitants of a remote section of Australia call on Keeting, an ancient moon spirit, to save their territory from encroaching human beings who have upset the natural balance.
Illus. by Noela Young, Macmillan, 1988, 163 pp. (0-689-50451-9)
(CCBB 41:194; HB 64:637; Kirkus 56:462; SLJ Apr 1988 p. 106; Suth 4:447; VOYA 11:92)

2-484 **WYNDHAM, Lee (pseud. of Jane Andrews Hyndman).** *Mourka, the Mighty Cat.* Gr. 2–4.
Mourka the village cat pretends to be the mighty ruler of the forest.
Illus. by Charles Mikolaycak, Parents, 1969, 41 pp., o.p.
(HB 45:529; LJ 95:1192)

2-485 YEP, Laurence M(ichael). *The Curse of the Squirrel.* Gr. 2–4.
Farmer Johnson's hunting dog, Howie—under a curse by Shag, the monster squirrel—becomes a squirrel by night so that he can understand how it feels to be "treed like a possum."
Illus. by Dirk Zimmer, Random, 1987, 45 pp., o.p.
(BL 84:325; CCBB 41:60, Kirkus 55:1582; SLJ Dec 1987 p. 76)

2-486 YOLEN (Stemple), Jane (Hyatt). *The Acorn Quest.* Gr. 3–5.
✮ King Earthor Owl of Woodland sends his wizard, Squirrelin, and his knights— a groundhog, a turtle, a rabbit, and a mouse—on a quest for the Golden Acorn in this takeoff on an Arthurian legend.
Illus. by Susanna Natti, Crowell, 1981, 57 pp., o.p.
(BL 78:444; HB 58:48; Kirkus 49:1346; SLJ Dec 1981 p. 59)

2-487 YOLEN (Stemple), Jane (Hyatt). *Hobo Toad and the Motorcycle Gang.* Gr. 3–5.
Hobo and his gang foil an attempted bank robbery and kidnapping,
Illus. by Emily Arnold McCully, Collins+World, 1970, 62 pp., o.p.
(BL 67:149; HB 46:391; Kirkus 38:455; LJ 95:3056)

2-488 YOLEN (Stemple), Jane (Hyatt). *Piggins.* **(Piggins trilogy, bk. 1).** Gr.
✮✮ K–3.
Mr. and Mrs. Reynard's butler, Piggins, solves the mystery of Mrs. Reynard's stolen diamond lavaliere. The sequels are *Picnic with Piggins* (1988) and *Piggins and the Royal Wedding* (1989).
Illus. by Jane Dyer, Harcourt, 1987, 32 pp., o.p.
(BL 83:1132; CCBB 40:160; HB 63:459; Kirkus 55:304; SLJ Apr 1987 p. 91; Suth 4:449)

ZARING, Jane T(homas). *The Return of the Dragon.*
See Chapter 1, Allegorical Fantasy and Literary Fairy Tales.

ZIMNIK, Reiner. *The Bear and the People.*
See Chapter 5, High Fantasy: Alternate Worlds or Histories.

2-489 ZINDEL, Paul. *Let Me Hear You Whisper: A Play.* Gr. 7 up.
A short but moving play about a laboratory cleaning woman who discovers that a dolphin being used in an experiment can talk, and tries to save him from being killed.
Illus. by Stephen Gammell, Harper, 1974, 44 pp., o.p.
(CCBB 27:188; Kirkus 42:124; LJ 99:1234)

2-490 *Zoo 2000: Twelve Stories of Science Fiction and Fantasy Beasts.* Ed. by Jane (Hyatt) Yolen (Stemple). Gr. 6–9.
A collection of 12 science fiction and fantasy tales about animals of the future, including James Thurber's "Interview with a Lemming" and Andre Norton's "All Cats Are Gray."
Seabury, 1973, 224 pp., o.p.
(BL 70:538, 546; CCBB 27:167; Kirkus 41:1162; LJ 98:3715)

3

Fantasy Collections

Collections of literary fairy tales, which often resemble traditional folktales in style, and of fantastic short stories are listed in this chapter.

3-1　*After the King: Stories in Honor of J. R. R. Tolkien.* **Ed. by Martin H. Greenberg.** Gr. 10 up.

An anthology of fantasy stories written in honor of the 100th anniversary of J. R. R. Tolkien's birth by 19 authors, including Jane Yolen, Emma Bull, Judith Tarr, Charles de Lint, Terry Pratchett, and Andre Norton. Some of these stories were republished in *Shadows and Moonshine: Stories* (Godine, 2002).

Tor, 1992, 448 pp. (0-312-85175-8), 1993, pap. (0-312-85353-X)

(BL 88:915, 921; Kirkus 59:1503; LJ Dec 1991 p. 203; VOYA 15:171, 16:9)

AHLBERG, Allan. *The Clothes Horse and Other Stories.*
See Chapter 8, Humorous Fantasy.

3-2　**AIKEN, Joan (Delano).** *The Faithless Lollybird.* Gr. 5–8. (Orig. British pub.
☆　1977, entitled *The Faithless Lollybird and Other Stories*.)

These 13 modern fairy tales include stories about a witch, a haunted tower, and a mermaid.

Illus. by Eros Keith, Doubleday, 1978, 255 pp., o.p.

(BL 74:1614; CCBB 31:153; HB 54:281; Kirkus 46:594; SLJ Apr 1978 p. 90; Suth 2:6; TLS 1977 p. 863)

3-3　**AIKEN, Joan (Delano).** *The Far Forests: Tales of Romance, Fantasy and Suspense.* Gr. 8 up. (Orig. British pub. 1977.)

Fifteen sophisticated tales touched with humor, magic, and the macabre, including "As Gay as Cheese," "A Taxi to Solitude," "Furry Night," and "The Cold Flame."

Viking, 1977, 154 pp., o.p.

(CCBB 31:25; HB 53:536; Kirkus 45:233, 363; LJ 102:827; Suth 2:6)

AIKEN, Joan (Delano). *A Foot in the Grave.*
See Chapter 4, Ghost Fantasy.

3-4 **AIKEN, Joan (Delano).** *Give Yourself a Fright: Thirteen Stories of the Supernatural.* Gr. 7 up. (Stories originally published in England in 1980, 1984, 1985, 1987, and 1988.)
Thirteen tales of ghosts, magic, the devil, and the macabre.
Delacorte, 1989, 192 pp. (0-440-50120-2)
(CCBB 42:141; HB 65:213; Kirkus 57:119; SLJ Apr 1989 p. 116; VOYA 12:113)

3-5 **AIKEN, Joan (Delano).** *The Green Flash and Other Tales of Horror, Suspense, and Fantasy.* Gr. 6–9. (Orig. British pubs. 1957, 1969.)
Fourteen tales, including "Marmalade Wine," "The Dead Language Master," and "The Windshield Weepers."
Holt, 1971, 163 pp., o.p.
(BL 68:428; HB 48:54; Kirkus 39:1131; LJ 96:4200)

3-6 **AIKEN, Joan (Delano).** *A Harp of Fishbones and Other Stories.* Gr. 5 up. (Orig. British pub. 1972.)
Thirteen fantasy tales, including "The Boy with a Wolf's Foot," "The Lost Five Minutes," and "The Prince of Darkness."
Puffin, 1975, pap., 229 pp., o.p.
(TLS 1972 p. 474)

3-7 **AIKEN, Joan (Delano).** *The Last Slice of Rainbow: And Other Stories.* Gr.
✮ 3–6. (Orig. British pub. 1985.)
Nine short fantasy stories, including one about a boy who wants to keep a rainbow.
Illus. by Alix Berenzy, Harper, 1988, 144 pp. (0-06-020043-X), 1989, pap., o.p.
(BL 84:1338; CCBB 41:129; Kirkus 56:613; SLJ May 1988 p. 94; TLS 1985 p. 1360)

3-8 **AIKEN, Joan (Delano).** *A Necklace of Raindrops and Other Stories.* Gr.
3–5. (Orig. British pub. 1968.)
Eight stories, including "There's Some Sky in This Pie," "The Elves in the Shelves," and "The Patchwork Quilt."
Illus. by Jan Pienkowski, Doubleday, 1969, 96 pp., o.p.; illus. by Kevin Hawkes, Knopf, 2001, 88 pp., o.p.
(CCBB 23:37; HB 45:530; HBG 13:70; Kirkus 37:631; LJ 95:238)

3-9 **AIKEN, Joan (Delano).** *Not What You Expected: A Collection of Short*
✮ *Stories.* Gr. 6–9. (Orig. British pub. 1974.)
Twenty-one tales, including "The Boy with a Wolf's Foot," "The Lost Five Minutes," and "The Third Wish." These stories were published in Britain in three collections: *A Small Pinch of Weather* (1969), *A Harp of Fishbones* (1971), and *All and More* (1971). Some of these stories were republished in *Shadows and Moonshine: Stories* (Godine, 2002).
Doubleday, 1974, 320 pp., o.p.
(BL 71:377; CCBB 28:73; HB 51:151; Kirkus 42:1258; SLJ Jan 1975 p. 42; TLS 1969 p. 689)

3-10 **AIKEN, Joan (Delano).** *Past Eight O'Clock: Goodnight Stories.* Gr. 3–5. (Orig. British pub. 1986.)
Eight magical tales about dreams, sleep, and the night.

Illus. by Jan Pienkowski, Viking, 1987, 128 pp., o.p.
(CCBB 40:201; SLJ Oct 1987 p. 124)

3-11 AIKEN, Joan (Delano). *Shadows and Moonshine Stories.* Gr. 4–8. (Orig. British pub. 2001.)
Thirteen stories previously published in *Smoke from Cromwell's Time* (1970), *Not What You Expected* (1974), and *The Faithless Lollybird* (1978).
Illus. by Pamela Johnson, Godine, 2002, 171 pp. (1-56792-167-1)
(HB 78:431–432; HBG 13:367; SLJ Feb 2002 p. 129)

3-12 AIKEN, Joan (Delano). *Smoke from Cromwell's Time and Other Stories.*
☆ Gr. 4–7. (Orig. British pubs. 1959, 1966, 1969.)
Fourteen tales including "The King Who Stood All Night," "The Wolves and the Mermaids," and "The Parrot Pirate Princess." Some of these stories were republished in *Shadows and Moonshine: Stories* (Godine, 2002).
Doubleday, 1970, 163 pp., o.p.
(BL 67:142; CCBB 24:37; HB 46:476; Kirkus 38:742; LJ 95:3044)

AIKEN, Joan (Delano). *A Touch of Chill: Tales for Sleepless Nights.*
See Chapter 4, Ghost Fantasy.

AIKEN, Joan (Delano). *Up the Chimney Down and Other Stories.*
See Chapter 8, Humorous Fantasy.

AIKEN, Joan (Delano). *A Whisper in the Night: Tales of Terror and Suspense.*
See Chapter 4, Ghost Fantasy.

3-13 AINSWORTH (Gilbert), Ruth (Gallard). *The Bear Who Liked Hugging People and Other Stories.* Gr. K–4. (Orig. British pub. 1976.)
Thirteen stories about witches, animals, and magic.
Illus. by Antony Maitland, Crane Russak, 1978, 102 pp., o.p.
(BL74:1487; SLJ Oct 1978 p. 141)

AINSWORTH (Gilbert), Ruth (Gallard). *The Phantom Carousel and Other Ghostly Tales.*
See Chapter 4, Ghost Fantasy.

3-14 *The Air of Mars: And Other Stories of Time and Space.* **Ed. by Mirra**
☆ **Ginsburg.** Gr. 6–9. (Orig. Russian pub. 1964–1972.)
Nine fantasy and science fiction tales from the former Soviet Union, including one about a woman whose husband turns into a garden.
Trans. by the editor, Macmillan, 1976, 141 pp., o.p.
(BL 72:1592; HB 52:410; Kirkus 44:204; SLJ Apr 1976 p. 74)

ALCOCK, Vivien (Dolores). *Ghostly Companions: A Feast of Chilling Tales.*
See Chapter 4, Ghost Fantasy.

3-15 ALDEN, Raymond Macdonald. *The Boy Who Found the King; a Tournament of Stories.* Gr. 3–5.

A young prince and princess hold a storytelling tournament to choose an official storyteller, and the stories in this collection are told by the contestants. The 1946 edition, illustrated by Evelyn Copelman, was titled *Once There Was a King; a Tournament of Stories.*
Illus. by W. R. Lohse, Bobbs Merrill, 1922, 1946, 176 pp., o.p.
(BL 19:127, 43:90; Mahony 2:269)

3-16 **ALDEN, Raymond Macdonald.** *Why the Chimes Rang and Other Stories.*
Gr. 3–6. (Orig. pub. 1908.)
Eleven tales of kings, knights, giants, and magic.
Illus. by Rafaello Busoni, Bobbs-Merrill, 1954, 146 pp., o.p.
(BL 42:170; LJ 80:188; Mahony 2:269)

3-17 **ALDISS, Brian W(ilson).** *Seasons in Flight.* Gr. 10 up.
Ten tales about the impact of modern cultures on ancient ones, including "The Other Side of the Lake," "The Gods in Flight," and "Incident in a Far Country." Some stories are related to Aldiss's "Helliconia trilogy": *Helliconia Spring* (1982), *Helliconia Summer* (1983), and *Helliconia Winter* (1985).
Atheneum, 1986, 157 pp., o.p.
(BL 82:733, 750; Kirkus 53:1293)

Alternative Histories: Eleven Stories of the World as It Might Have Been.
Ed. by Charles G. Waugh and Martin H. Greenberg.
See Chapter 5, High Fantasy: Alternate Worlds or Histories.

Amazons! **Ed. by Jessica Amanda Salmonson.**
See Chapter 5, High Fantasy: Alternate Worlds or Histories.

3-18 *American Fairy Tales: From "Rip VanWinkle" to "The Rootabaga Sto-*
★ *ries."* **Ed. by Neil Philip.** Gr. 5–8.
Twelve fantasy stories written between 1815 and 1922 by well-known American authors, including Louisa May Alcott, Carl Sandburg, L. Frank Baum, and Nathaniel Hawthorne.
Illus. by Michael McCurdy, Hyperion, 1996, 160 pp. (0-7868-0207-3); Disney, 1998, pap., 160 pp. (0-7868-1093-9)
(BL 93:721; CCBB 50:3 HB 73:66; HBG 8:74 Kirkus 64:1606; SLJ Nov 1996 p. 117)

3-19 *The American Fantasy Tradition.* **Ed. by Brian M. Thomsen.** Gr. 7–12.
More than 40 American fantasy stories written by such writers as Ursula K. Le Guin, Washington Irving, L. Frank Baum, Nathaniel Hawthorne, and Mark Twain.
Tor, 2002, 604 pp. (0-765-30152-0)
(Kirkus 70:1184; VOYA 26:61)

Ancient Enchantresses. **Ed. by Kathleen M. Massie-Ferch, Martin H. Greenberg, and Richard Gilliam.**
See Chapter 12, Witchcraft and Sorcery Fantasy.

3-20 **ANDERSEN, Hans Christian.** *Fairy Tales.* Gr. 3 up. (Orig. Danish pub.
★★ 1835–1845; orig. English translation by Mary Howitt, entitled *Wonderful Stories for Children*, 1846.)

Andersen was the first great writer of original fantasy for children, and his tales are still among the best-loved of all children's stories. There have been numerous editions of Andersen's story collections published in English, under various titles. These include the following collections, arranged alphabetically by title:

Andersen's Fairy Tales. Illus. by W. Heath Robinson, Houghton, 1931, 355 pp., o.p.; Putnam, 1958, 352 pp., o.p.; Wanderer, 1983, 300 pp., o.p.

*Ardizzone's Hans Andersen: Fourteen Classic Tales. Illus. by Edward Ardizzone, Atheneum, 1979, c. 1978, 191 pp., o.p.

The Complete Fairy Tales and Stories. Doubleday, 1974, 1101 pp., o.p.

* Dulac's The Snow Queen and Other Stories from Hans Andersen. Illus. by Edmund Dulac, Doubleday, 1976, 143 pp., o.p.

Eighty Fairy Tales. Trans. by R. P. Keigwin, illus. by Vilhelm Pedersen and Lorenz Frolich, Pantheon, 1982 (c. 1976), 483 pp., o.p.;

* Fairy Tales. Illus. by W. Heath Robinson, Holt, 1913, 288 pp., o.p.; illus. by Kay Nielsen, Garden City, 1924, 1932, o.p.; Viking/Metropolitan Museum of Art, 1981, 155 pp., o.p.; illus. by Arthur Rackham, McKay, 1932, 287 pp., o.p.; illus. by Fritz Kredel, Heritage, 1942, 297 pp., o.p.; illus. by Vilhelm Pedersen, Scribner, 1950, 394 pp., o.p.

Fairy Tales from Hans Christian Andersen. (Orig. British pub. 1901.) Illus. by Thomas H. Robinson, Charles Robinson, and W. Heath Robinson, Dutton, 1903, 1930, o.p.; adapt. by Russell Ash and Bernard Higton, illus. by nine artists, Chronicle, 1992, 128 pp., o.p.

Fairy Tales of Hans Christian Andersen, trans. by Neil Philip, illus. by Isabelle Brent, Viking, 1995, 140 pp. (0-670-85930-3)

Favorite Tales of Hans Andersen. Illus. by Robin Jacques, Faber, 1986 (orig. British pub., 1978), 168 pp., o.p.

* Hans Andersen: His Classic Fairy Tales. Illus. by Michael Foreman, Doubleday, 1978, 196 pp., o.p.

Hans Andersen's Fairy Tales. Illus. by Maria L. Kirk and E. A. Lehmann, Lippincott, 1911, 219 pp., o.p.; illus. by W. Heath Robinson, Doran, 1924, 319 pp., o.p.; illus. by Ernest H. Shepard, Walck, 1962, c. 1959, 327 pp., o.p.; retold by E. Jean Robertson and Caroline Peachey, illus. by Shirley Hughes, Schocken, 1979 (repr. of 1961 Scottish ed.), pap., 264 pp., o.p.; illus. by Sumiko, Schocken, 1980, 96 pp., o.p.; illus. by Philip Gough, Penguin, 1981, pap., 176 pp., o.p.; trans. by Anthea Bell, illus. by Lisbeth Zwerger, Picture Book Studio, 1992, 68 pp. (0-88708-182-7); trans. by Anthea Bell, selected and illus. by Lisbeth Zwerger, new ed., North-South/Neugebauer, 2001, 104 pp. (0-7358-1394-9)

Hans Andersen's Fairy Tales: A Selection. Illus. by Lorenz Frolich and Vilhelm Pedersen, Oxford University Press, 1984, pap., 493 pp. (0-19-281699-3)

It's Perfectly True, and Other Stories. Illus. by Richard Bennett, Harcourt, 1938, 305 pp., o.p.

The Little Mermaid and Other Fairy Tales. Ed. by Neil Philip, illus. by Isabelle Brent, Viking, 1998, 144 pp. (0-670-87840-5)

The Mermaid, and Other Fairy Tales. Illus. by Maxwell Armfield, Dutton, 1914, 1916, 127 pp., o.p.

Little Mermaids and Ugly Ducklings: Favorite Fairy Tales by Hans Christian Andersen. Illus. by Gennady Spirin, Chronicle, 2001, 59 pp. (0-8118-3320-8)

* *Michael Hague's Favorite Hans Christian Andersen Fairy Tales*. Illus. by Michael (R.) Hague, Holt, 1981, 176 pp., o.p.; Holt, 2003, 162 pp. (0-8050-7239-X)

* *Seven Tales*. Adapt. by Eva Le Gallienne, illus. by Maurice (Bernard) Sendak, Harper, 1959, 127 pp., LB (0-06-023790-2), 1991, pap. (0-06-443172-X)

Stories from Hans Andersen. Illus. by Edmund Dulac, Hodder, 1911, 1922; Doran, 1923, 1927, 1930, 250 pp., o.p.

The Stories of Hans Andersen. Illus. by Robin Lawrie, Silver, 1985, 80 pp., o.p.

The Swan's Stories. Illus. by Chris Riddell, Candlewick, 1997, 144 pp. (1-56402-894-1)

Tales of Hans Christian Andersen. Trans. and comp. by Naomi Lewis, illus. by Joel Stewart, Candlewick, 2004, 208 pp. (0-7636-2515-9)

* *Twelve Tales*. Adapt. and illus. by Erik Blegvad, Macmillan, 1994, 96 pp. (0-689-50584-1)

(BL 20:109, 233, 28:110, 396, 34:303, 40:324, 47:241, 55:512, 58:797, 70:738, 73:1159, 74:1730, 75:1216, 78:241, 493, 89:745, 91:328, 95:665, 98:639; Bookshelf 1933 p. 5; CCBB 27:122, 35:101, 58:159; HB 1:6; 7:187–189, 9:152, 10:37, 13:25, 14:153, 20:46, 164, 27:93, 35:297, 50:269, 55:408, 58:539, 67:223, 70:729; HGB 2:64, 4:63, 78, 6:71, 7:67, 10:62, 12:287, 13:70, 14:352; Kirkus 27:264, 30:111, 42:12, 46:879, 47:519, 49:1411, 60:1499, 62:1263; LJ 58:1050, 63:284, 69:72, 76:530, 84:1692, 87:2409, 99:568; Mahony 2:271; SLJ Feb 1977 p. 60, Nov 1978 p. 54, Apr 1979 p. 52, Dec 1981 p. 59, Feb 1993 p. 92, Dec 1995 p. 72, Apr 1999 p. 85, Dec 2001 p. 116; Suth 2:14; Suth 3:15, 16; TLS Dec 1, 1961 p. xii, 1974 p. 1377, 1981 p. 1360)

3-21 **ANDERSON, Poul (William).** *Fantasy.* Gr. 10 up.
A collection of Anderson's short fantasy fiction and essays, plus an introductory essay on Anderson's work by Sandra Miesel.
Tor, 1981, pap., 334 pp., o.p.
(BL 78:425, 434; LJ 106:2409; SLJ Mar 1982 p. 162)

ANDERSON, Poul (William). *The Time Patrol.*
See Chapter 10, Time Travel Fantasy.

3-22 *Another World; Adventures in Otherness: A Science Fiction Anthology.* **Ed. by Gardner Dozois.** Gr. 7–12.
Eleven tales of science fiction and fantasy written by Gene Wolfe, Ursula K. Le Guin, and Robert Silverberg, among others.
Follett, 1977, 282 pp., o.p.
(BL 73:1568; SLJ Oct 1977 p. 122)

3-23 **ANTHONY, Piers (pseud. of Piers A. D. Jacob).** *Alien Plot.* Gr. 10 up.
Eighteen fantasy and science fiction stories plus an essay.
Tor, 1992, 256 pp. (0-312-85394-7), 1993, pap. (0-8125-3072-1)
(BL 89:129, 133; Kirkus 60:1094; LJ Oct 15 1992 p. 104; SLJ Apr 1993 p. 149)

The April Witch and Other Strange Tales. **Ed. by Barbara Ireson.**
See Chapter 4, Ghost Fantasy.

3-24   *Arabesques 2.* **Ed. by Susan Shwartz.** Gr. 10 up.
☆   Eighteen fantasy stories with Arabian settings and themes, written by Judith
Tarr, Diana Paxson, Tanith Lee, and others. This is a companion volume to
Arabesques: More Tales of the Arabian Nights (1988).
Avon, 1989, pap., 384 pp., o.p.
(BL 85:1783; Kliatt Sep 1989, p. 22; LJ June 15, 1989 p. 83; VOYA 12:218)

An Armory of Swords. **Ed. by Fred Saberhagen.**
See Chapter 5, High Fantasy: Alternate Worlds or Histories.

ASIMOV, Isaac. *Azazel.*
See Chapter 9, Magic Adventure Fantasy.

ASPRIN, Robert (Lynn). *Thieves' World.*
See Chapter 5, High Fantasy: Alternate Worlds or Histories.

3-25   *Atlantis.* **Ed. by Isaac Asimov, Martin H. Greenberg, and Charles G.
Waugh.** Gr. 7 up.
Short stories about the legend of Atlantis by Ursula K. Le Guin, Manly Wade
Wellman, L. Sprague de Camp, and others.
NAL, 1988, pap., 349 pp., o.p.
(BL 84:541, 555; VOYA 11:137)

3-26   **AULNOY, Marie Catherine Jumelle de Berneville, Comtesse d'.** *The
Children's Fairy Land.* Gr. 4–6.
Eight illustrated fairy tales.
Illus. by Harriet Mead Olcott, Holt, 1919, 189 pp., o.p.
(BL 16:62; Bookshelf 1928 p. 10; LJ 45:980)

3-27   **AULNOY, Marie Catherine Jumelle de Berneville, Comtesse d'.** *The
☆   White Cat and Other Old French Fairy Tales.* Gr. 3–5. (Orig. pub. in France;
orig. British title *Fairy Tales by the Countess D'Aulnoy*, 1855; orig. U.S. title
D'Aulnoy's Fairy Tales, 1858; McKay, 1923, o.p.; orig. U.S. pub. with this
title, 1928.)
A collection of French folk tales, embroidered and adapted to take place in a
palace, including "The Blue-Bird," "The Hind in the Wood," and "The Yellow
Dwarf."
Adapt. by Rachel Field, illus. by Elizabeth MacKinstry, Macmillan, 1967, 150
pp., o.p.
(BL 20:303, 25:253; HB 4:11; LJ 53:811, 93:866; Mahony 2:195–197; Moore:290, 434)

AVI (Avi Wortis). *Tom, Babette, and Simon: Three Tales of
Transformation.*
See Chapter 1, Allegorical Fantasy and Literary Fairy Tales.

BABBITT, Natalie (Zane Moore). *The Devil's Storybook.*
See Chapter 8, Humorous Fantasy.

BACON, Peggy. *The Lion-Hearted Kitten and Other Stories.*
See Chapter 2, Animal Fantasy.

BACON, Peggy. *Mercy and the Mouse and Other Stories.*
See Chapter 2, Animal Fantasy.

3-28 **BAILEY, Margery.** *The Little Man with One Shoe.* Gr. 3–6.
Six magical fairy tales told by a fairy shoemaker.
Illus. by Alice Bolan Preston, Little, Brown, 1921, 227 pp., o.p.
(BL 18:88; Bookshelf 1923–1924 p. 7; LJ 47:869; Mahony 2:271)

3-29 **BAILEY, Margery.** *Seven Peas in the Pod.* Gr. 3–6.
Seven stories, one for each day of the week.
Illus. by Alice Bolan Preston, Little, Brown, 1919, 201 pp., o.p.
(BL 16:137; Bookshelf 1923–1924 p. 7; LJ 45:980; Mahony 1:39; Mahony 2:272)

3-30 **BAILEY, Margery.** *Whistle for Good Fortune, in Which It Is Shown How Six from Six Makes Six and One to Carry, with Other Riddles Here and There Along the Way.* Gr. 4–6.
Six original fairy tales told in folktale-style.
Illus. by Alice Bolan Preston, Little, Brown, 1940, 237 pp., o.p.
(BL 36:308; LJ 65:260)

3-31 **BAKER, Margaret.** *Fifteen Tales for Lively Children.* Gr. 2–4. (Orig. British pub. 1938, entitled *The Goose Feather Gown.*)
This collection of humorous tales is a companion volume to *Tell Them Again Tales* (1934).
Illus. by Mary Baker, Dodd, 1939, 144 pp., o.p.
(BL 35:292; LJ 64:380; TLS 1938 p. 789)

3-32 **BAKER, Margaret.** *Pedlar's Ware.* Gr. 3–4. (Orig. pub. in England.)
Four fairy tales: "The Sad Princess," "The Leprechaun," "The Ghost and the Shadow," and "The Princess and the Beggar Maid."
Illus. by Mary Baker, Duffield, 1925, 88 pp., o.p.
(BL 21:386)

3-33 **BAKER, Margaret.** *Tell Them Again Tales.* Gr. 2–4. (Orig. pub. in England.)
Eighteen tales about kings, animals, and princesses. *15 Tales for Lively Children* (1939) is a companion volume.
Illus. by Mary Baker, Dodd, 1934, 143 pp., o.p.
(BL 31:67; Bookshelf 1934–1935 p. 4; HB 10:296; LJ 60:403; Mahony 3:85)

3-34 *A Baker's Dozen: Thirteen Stories to Tell and to Read Aloud.* **Comp. by Mary Gould Davis.** Gr. 4–6.
A collection that includes stories by Laurence Housman, Carl Sandburg, Mary E. Wilkins, Frank R. Stockton, and Gottfried Keller.
Illus. by Emma L(illian) Brock, Harcourt, 1930, 207 pp., o.p.
(BL 27:108; HB 6:329; LJ 55:736; Mahony 3:158)

3-35   BAUM, L(yman) Frank. *The Surprising Adventures of the Magical Monarch of Mo and His People.* Gr. 3–6. (Orig. titles *A New Wonderland*, Russell, 1900, and *The Magical Monarch of Mo*, Bobbs-Merrill, 1901, 1947.) Fourteen stories of princes, giants, wizards, and a dragon, set in the magical land of Mo, where anything one wants can be picked from a tree.
Dover, 1968, pap., 237 pp., o.p.; Peter Smith (entitled *The Magical Monarch of Mo*), 1985, o.p.
(LJ 72:1620; TLS 1969 p. 352)

3-36   BEAGLE, Peter S(oyer). *The Fantasy Worlds of Peter S. Beagle.* Gr. 10 up.
This collection includes *A Fine and Private Place* and *The Last Unicorn*, plus two short stories, "Lila the Werewolf" and "Come, Lady Death."
Viking, 1978, 430 pp., o.p.
(BL 75:598, 606; Kirkus 46:977)

BEAGLE, Peter S(oyer). *Giant Bones.*
See Chapter 5, High Fantasy: Alternate Worlds or Histories.

BENNETT, John. *The Pigtail of Ah Lee Ben Loo, with Seventeen Other Laughable Tales.*
See Chapter 8, Humorous Fantasy.

BENSON, E(dward) F(rederic). *The Collected Ghost Stories of E. F. Benson.*
See Chapter 4, Ghost Fantasy.

3-37   *Bestiary!* Ed. by Jack Dann and Gardner Dozois. Gr. 10 up.
An anthology of tales about dragons, giants, unicorns, and other mythical creatures, written by Tanith Lee, Manly Wade Wellman, Gene Wolfe, and others. This is a companion volume to *Unicorns!* (1982) and *Magicats!* (1984).
Ace, 1985, pap., 304 pp., o.p.
(BL 82:195, 216)

3-38   BESTON, Henry B. (pseud. of Henry Beston Sheahan). *Henry Beston's*
✶   *Fairy Tales.* Gr. 4–6.
This collection contains many of the stories from *The Firelight Fairy Book* (1919) and *The Starlight Wonder Book* (1923), including "The Seller of Dreams," "The Lost Half-Hour," and "The City Under the Sea."
Illus. by Fritz Kredel, Aladdin, 1952, 353 pp., o.p.
(BL 16:174, 20:62, 37:364, 49:76; Bookshelf 1932 p. 8; HB 28:311, 420; Kirkus 20:546; LJ 77:1820; Mahony 1:39; Mahony 2:273; Moore:426)

***Beware! Beware! Chilling Tales.* Ed. by Jean Richardson.**
See Chapter 4, Ghost Fantasy.

3-39   BIANCO, Margery (Winifred) Williams. *A Street of Little Shops.* Gr. 3–5.
Seven tales about a street of shops in a small country town, including one about a cigar store Indian who runs away.
Illus. by Grace Paull, Doubleday, 1932, 119 pp., o.p.; Gregg, 1981, 111 pp., o.p.
(Bookshelf 1932 p. 10; HB 21:191; LJ 58:899)

3-40 *Black Water: The Book of Fantastic Literature.* **Ed. by Alberto Manguelo.** Gr. 10 up. (Orig. Canadian pub. 1983.)
Seventy-two stories of fantasy and horror drawn primarily from England, the United States, and Latin America, whose authors include Henry James, D. H. Lawrence, and Tennessee Williams.
Crown, 1984, pap., o.p.
(HB 60:634; LJ 109:824; VOYA 7:262)

BLOCK, Francesca Lia. *The Rose and the Beast: Fairy Tales Retold.*
See Chapter 6, High Fantasy: Myth or Legend Fantasy.

3-41 *The Blue Rose; a Collection of Stories for Girls.* **Ed. by Eulalie Steinmetz**
★ **Ross.** Gr. 4–6.
Stories by Hans Christian Andersen, Laurence Housman, Howard Pyle, Walter de la Mare, Eleanor Farjeon, George MacDonald, and Ruth Sawyer.
Illus. by Enrico Arno, Harcourt, 1966, 186 pp., o.p.
(BL 63:186; HB 42:566; Kirkus 34:106; LJ 91:4342; TLS 1966 p. 1092)

3-42 **BOMANS, Godfried (Jan Arnold).** *The Wily Witch and All the Other*
★ *Fairy Tales and Fables.* Gr. 3–5. (An earlier Dutch ed. of selected tales pub. 1969; this ed. pub. 1975.)
Forty-five fairy tales, including "The Rich Blackberry Picker," "The Princess with Freckles," and "The Curse." Twenty-four of these tales were originally published in *The Wily Wizard and the Wicked Witch and Other Weird Stories* (Watts, 1969).
Trans. by Patricia Crampton, illus. by Wouter Googendijk, Stemmer, 1977, 205 pp., o.p.
(BL 73:1726; CCBB 23:156, 31:6; LJ 95:777; SLJ Sep 1977 p. 121; Suth 2:51; TLS 1969 p. 3521)

Boo! Stories to Make You Jump. **Compiled by Laura Cecil.**
See Chapter 4, Ghost Fantasy.

3-43 *The Book of Dragons.* **Ed. by Michael Hague.** Gr. 4–6.
Seventeen selections from fantasy novels, including C. S. Lewis's *Voyage of the Dawn Treader* and J. R. R. Tolkien's *The Hobbit*, stories such as Kenneth Grahame's novella *The Reluctant Dragon*, and folktales about dragons.
Illus. by Michael (R.) Hague, Morrow, 1995, 146 pp. (0-688-10879-2)
(BL 92:313; HBG 7:134; Kirkus 63:1110; SLJ Oct 1995 p. 148)

3-44 **BORGES, Jorge Luis, with GUERRERO, Margarita.** *The Book of Imaginary Beings.* Gr. 10 up. (Orig. Mexican pub. 1957.)
A treasury of carefully researched descriptions of 120 legendary creatures from all over the world.
Rev., enlarged, and trans. by Norman Thomas di Giovanni in collaboration with the author, Dutton, 1969, 256 pp., o.p.
(HB 46:186; LJ 94:4526; TLS 1971 p. 149)

3-45 **BOUCHER, Anthony (pseud. of William Anthony Parker White).** *The Compleat Werewolf: and Other Stories of Fantasy and Science Fiction.* Gr. 10 up.
Ten short stories and novellas about a werewolf, a demon, ogres, and a ghost.

Simon, 1969, 256 pp., o.p.
(BL 66:823, 837; Kirkus 37:955; LJ 94:3665, 3839, 95:1913)

3-46 BOURLIAGUET, Léonce. *The Giant Who Drank from His Shoe and Other Stories.* Gr. 4–6. (Orig. pub. in France.)
Humorous tales about French villagers, giants, and animals.
Trans. by John Buchanan Brown, illus. by Gerald Rose, Abelard-Schuman, 1966, 93 pp., o.p.
(Kirkus 34:1979; LJ 91:3531; TLS 1965 p. 1140)

3-47 BOURLIAGUET, Léonce. *A Sword to Slice Through Mountains and Other Stories.* Gr. 3–5. (Orig. pub. in France.)
Tales about two smiths who can make a sword capable of slicing mountains in half, but fail to win a princess; a stutterer who gets his revenge on some unkind villagers; and a scarecrow who wants to be rewarded with a medal.
Trans. by John Buchanan-Brown, illus. by Gerald Rose, Abelard-Schuman, 1967, 96 pp., o.p.
(Kirkus 36:117; LJ 93:2732)

3-48 BRADBURY, Ray (Douglas). *Dinosaur Tales.* Gr. 10 up.
A collection of Bradbury's stories and poems about dinosaurs, including "Tyrannosaurus Rex," "The Fog Horn," and "Besides a Dinosaur, Whatta Ya Wanna Be When You Grow Up?"
Illus. by Kenneth Smith, William Stout, Steranko, Moebius, Gahan Wilson, and David Wiesner, Bantam, 1983, pap., 144 pp., o.p.; Sagebrush, rebound, 2003 (0-6139-8767-5)
(Kirkus 51:339; Kliatt 17:21)

3-49 BRADBURY, Ray (Douglas). *The Illustrated Man.* Gr. 9 up.
Eighteen short stories of science fiction, the supernatural, and fantasy.
Doubleday, 1951, 251 pp., o.p.; Bantam, 1969, 1983, pap., 192 pp. (0-553-27449-X); Morrow, 1997, 288 pp. (0-380-97384-7)
(BL 47:255; HB 27:197; Kirkus 18:740)

3-50 BRADBURY, Ray (Douglas). *A Medicine for Melancholy.* Gr. 10 up.
Twenty-two short stories, ranging from fantasy to science fiction and horror.
Doubleday, 1959, 240 pp., o.p.; Perennial, pap., 1998, 320 pp. (0-380-73086-3)
(BL 55:394; Kirkus 26:883)

3-51 BRADBURY, Ray (Douglas). *R Is for Rocket.* Gr. 8 up.
Seventeen science fiction and science-fantasy short stories originally published in magazines, including stories about sea serpents and time travel.
Doubleday, 1962, 233 pp., o.p.; Bantam, 1990, pap., 368 pp. (0-553-28637-4)
(BL 59:488; LJ 88:350)

3-52 BRADBURY, Ray (Douglas). *The Stories of Ray Bradbury.* Gr. 10 up.
✶ One hundred of Bradbury's science fiction, fantasy, horror, and midwestern short stories.
Knopf, 1980, 884 pp., o.p.; Morrow, 2003, 912 pp. (entitled *Bradbury Stories: 100 of His Most Celebrated Tales*) (0-06-054242-X)
(BL 77:4, 7; Kirkus 48:1120; LJ 105:1883; SLJ Dec 1980 p. 79; VOYA 4:36)

3-53   **BRADBURY, Ray (Douglas).** *The Toynbee Convector.* Gr. 10 up.
A collection of 23 fantasy, horror, and science fiction stories, including a number involving ghosts.
Knopf, 1988, 295 pp., o.p.
(BL 84:1458; Kirkus 56:573; LJ June 15, 1988 p. 71; VOYA 11:246)

3-54   **BRENTANO, Clemens Maria.** *Fairy Tales from Brentano.* Gr. 4–6. (Orig. German pub. 1846–1847; U.S. 1886.)
Seven original fairy tales selected from the works of this German storyteller. *More Fairy Tales from Brentano* (1888) is a companion volume.
Trans. by Kate Freiligrath Kroeker, illus. by F. Carruthers Gould, Stokes, 1925, 326 pp., o.p.
(BL 22:425)

BRÖGER, Achim. *Bruno.*
See Chapter 8, Humorous Fantasy.

3-55   **BROOKE, William J.** *A Telling of the Tales: Five Stories.* Gr. 3–6.
★   Five well-known tales expanded and retold from new points of view: "Sleeping Beauty," "Paul Bunyan," "Cinderella," "John Henry," and "Jack and the Beanstalk." This is a companion volume to *Untold Tales* (1992). In the author's *A Telling of Tales* (1990), written for grades 5 up, an old storyteller turns familiar fairy tales into fractured tales with the aid of a little girl who sometimes becomes the main character of the tales.
Illus. by Richard Egielski, Harper, 1990, 32 pp., o.p.
(BL 86:1699; CCBB 43:208; HBG 1:242; Kirkus 58:496; SLJ June 1990 p. 116; Suth 4:43)

BROWNE, Frances. *Granny's Wonderful Chair and Its Tales of Fairy Times.*
See Chapter 9, Magic Adventure Fantasy.

BUCHAN, John. *The Watcher by the Threshold and Other Tales.*
See Chapter 6, High Fantasy: Myth or Legend Fantasy.

BURGESS, Thornton W(aldo). *Old Mother West Wind.*
See Chapter 2, Animal Fantasy.

Camelot: A Collection of Original Arthurian Stories. **Ed. by Jane (Hyatt) Yolen (Stemple).**
See Chapter 6, High Fantasy: Myth or Legend Fantasy.

The Camelot Chronicles. **Ed. by Mike Ashley.**
See Chapter 6, High Fantasy: Myth or Legend Fantasy.

Camelot Fantastic. **Ed. by Lawrence Schimel and Martin H. Greenberg.**
See Chapter 6, High Fantasy: Myth or Legend Fantasy.

3-56   **CANFIELD, Dorothy (pseud. of Dorothea Frances [Canfield] Fisher).** *Made-to-Order Stories.* Gr. 4–6.
The author's 10-year-old son chose the elements used in these humorous stories.
Illus. by Dorothy P. Lathrop, Harcourt, 1925, 263 pp., o.p.
(BL 22:75; Bookshelf 1932 p. 12; HB 2:21, 14:208; LJ 51:836; Mahony 2:606)

3-57 **ČAPEK, Karel.** *Nine Fairy Tales and One More Thrown In for Good Measure.* Gr. 5–9. (Orig. Czech pub. 1932.)
Ten modern tales containing humor, wordplay, mythical creatures, and magic.
Trans. by Dagmar Herrmann, illus. by Josef Čapek, Northwestern University
Press, 1990, 180 pp., o.p.
(BL 86:2166, 2170; Kliatt Jan 1991 p. 25; TLS 1990 p. 1036)

3-58 **CARD, Orson Scott.** *Maps in a Mirror: The Short Fiction of Orson Scott Card.* Gr. 10 up.
Forty-six fantasy, science fiction, and horror stories by this well-known writer.
Tor, 1990, 512 pp., o.p.
(BL 87:143, 148; LJ Nov 15, 1990 p. 95; VOYA 14:40, 15:10)

3-59 **CASSERLEY, Anne Thomasine.** *Michael of Ireland.* Gr. 4–6. (Orig. British pub. 1926.)
The animals tell Michael stories about the fairy people.
Illus. by the author, Harper, 1927, 139 pp., o.p.
(BL 24:124; Bookshelf 1932 p. 8; HB 3:9–10; LJ 53:484, 1033; Mahony 2:132)

3-60 **CASSERLEY, Anne Thomasine.** *The Whins on Knockattan.* Gr. 2–4.
Pandeen and his grandmother share the whin-covered hillside of Knockattan
with Little Black Lamb and Shaughran the red fox.
Illus. by the author, Harper, 1928, 178 pp., o.p.
(BL 25:215; Bookshelf 1929 p. 11; HB 4:30–32; Mahony 2:133; TLS 1929 p. 475)

3-61 *Catfantastic: Nine Lives and Fifteen Tales.* **Ed. by Andre Norton and Martin H. Greenberg.** Gr. 10 up.
Fantasy and science fiction stories about cats by authors including Clare Bell,
Elizabeth H. Boyer, Mercedes Lackey, and Ardath Mayhar. *Catfantastic II*
(1991), *Catfantastic III* (1994), *Catfantastic IV* (1996), and *Catfantastic V*
(1999) are companion volumes.
DAW, 1989, pap., 320 pp., o.p.
(BL 85:1873, 1891; VOYA 12:370)

3-62 *A Cavalcade of Dragons.* **Ed. by Roger (Gilbert) Lancelyn Green.** Gr. 4–7.
✭ (British title: *The Hamish Hamilton Book of Dragons*, 1970.)
Folktales, fantasy, and poetry about dragons, including "The Lady Dragonissa"
by Andrew Lang, "The Fiery Dragon" by E. Nesbit, "The Hoard" by J. R. R.
Tolkien, and "The Dragon Speaks" by C. S. Lewis.
Illus. by Krystyna Turska, Walck, 1970, 256 pp., o.p.
(BL 68:108; HB 47:283; Kirkus 39:297; LJ 96:2130; TLS 1971 p. 388)

3-63 *A Cavalcade of Goblins.* **Ed. by Alan Garner.** Gr. 4–6. (British title: *The*
✭ *Hamish Hamilton Book of Goblins.*)
A collection of myths, folktales, poems, and literary fairy tales about goblins
and other fearsome creatures.
Illus. by Krystyna Turska, Walck, 1969, 227 pp., o.p.
(BL 66:129; CCBB 23:58; HB 45:531; LJ 94:4604; Suth:142)

A Cavalcade of Magicians. **Ed. by Roger (Gilbert) Lancelyn Green.**
See Chapter 12, Witchcraft and Sorcery Fantasy.

3-64 *A Cavalcade of Queens.* **Ed. by Eleanor Farjeon and William Mayne.** Gr.
✯ 4–6. (British title: *The Hamish Hamilton Book of Queens*, 1965.)
A companion volume to *A Cavalcade of Kings* (1965), this collection includes
stories by Andrew Lang, Nathaniel Hawthorne, and Rudyard Kipling.
Illus. by Victor G. Ambrus, Walck, 1965, 243 pp., o.p.
(BL 62:875; HB 42:193; LJ 91:1698; TLS 1965 p. 1136)

CHANT, Joy (pseud. of Eileen Joyce Rutter). *The High Kings.*
See Chapter 6, High Fantasy: Myth or Legend Fantasy.

3-65 **CHERRYH, C. J. (pseud. of Carolyn Janice Cherry).** *The Collected Short
Fiction of C. J. Cherryh.* Gr. 10 up.
Twenty-nine fantasy and science fiction novellas and short stories, including
"Sea Change," "Cassandra," "The Dark King," and "Gwydion and the Drag-
on."
DAW, 2004, 400 pp. (0-7564-0217-4)
(BL 100:1046; LJ Feb 15, 2004 p. 167)

3-66 **CHESNUTT, Charles Waddell.** *Conjure Tales.* Gr. 5–7.
✯ Seven tales of magic and witchcraft drawn from 19th-century African Ameri-
can slave life.
Retold by Ray Shepard, illus. by John Ross and Clare Romano, Dutton, 1973,
99 pp., o.p.
(CCBB 27:126; HB 50:48; Kirkus 41:1035, 1152; LJ 98:3689, 3705; Suth 2:82)

3-67 **CHRISMAN, Arthur Bowie.** *Shen of the Sea: Chinese Stories for Chil-
✯ dren.* Gr. 5–8.
A collection of humorous Chinese fairy tales. John Newbery Medal, 1926. *The
Wind That Wouldn't Blow: Stories of the Merry Middle Kingdom for Children
and Myself* (1927) is a companion volume.
Illus. by Else Hasselriis, Dutton, 1926, 1968 (redesigned), 221 pp., o.p.
(BL 22:167; Bookshelf 1932 p. 8; HB 2:20; LJ 51:836; Mahony 2:277; TLS 1969 p. 1193)

3-68 **CHRISMAN, Arthur Bowie.** *The Wind That Wouldn't Blow: Stories of the
Merry Middle Kingdom for Children and Myself.* Gr. 5–7.
A collection of stories that tell how things came to be as they are in China. This
is a companion volume to *Shen of the Sea: Chinese Stories for Children* (1926,
1968).
Illus. by Else Hasselriis, Dutton, 1927, 355 pp., o.p.
(BL 24:71; Bookshelf 1927 Suppl. p. 5; HB 3:47; Mahony 2:277)

3-69 *Christmas Forever.* **Ed. by David G. Hartwell.** Gr. 10 up.
Twenty-eight fantasy and science fiction Christmas stories written by Joan
Aiken, Charles de Lint, Roger Zelazny, and others.
Tor, 1993, 416 pp. (0-312-85576-1)
(BL 90:258, 262; Kirkus 61:1107; LJ Oct 15, 1993, p. 93)

Christmas Ghosts. **Ed. by Kathryn Cramer and David G. Hartwell.**
See Chapter 4, Ghost Fantasy.

Christmas Ghosts: An Anthology. **Ed. by Seon Manley and Gogo Lewis.**
See Chapter 4, Ghost Fantasy.

3-70 **COATSWORTH, Elizabeth (Jane).** *The Snow Parlor and Other Bedtime Stories.* Gr. 3–4.
Five tales about talking animals, toys that come to life, a walking pine tree, and a boy who enters a mountain to find out where snow comes from.
Illus. by Charles Robinson, Grosset, 1971, 64 pp., o.p.
(CCBB 25:137; Kirkus 39:1011; LJ 97:2476)

COHEN, Daniel. *Great Ghosts.*
See Chapter 4, Ghost Fantasy.

3-71 **COLUM, Padraic.** *The Big Tree of Bunlahy: Stories of My Own Countryside.* Gr. 3–5.
A combination of Irish legends and original tales, including "Our Hen" and "The Three Companions."
Illus. by Jack B. Yeats, Macmillan, 1933, 166 pp., o.p.
(BL 30:87; HB 10:33–36; LJ 59:482; Mahony 3:166)

COLUM, Padraic. *The Boy Who Knew What the Birds Said.*
See Chapter 2, Animal Fantasy.

3-72 **COLUM, Padraic.** *The Fountain of Youth; Stories to Be Told.* Gr. 4–6.
Seventeen of Colum's tales chosen from several of his collections as being particularly good for storytelling.
Illus. by Jay Van Everen, Macmillan, 1927, 206 pp., o.p.
(BL 24:251; LJ 53:485)

3-73 **COLUM, Padraic.** *The Peep-Show Man.* Gr. 1–3.
A peep-show man traveling the roads of Ireland tells a little boy three stories, one each for midsummer-day, Halloween, and Easter.
Illus. by Lois Lenski, Macmillan, 1924, 65 pp., o.p.
(BL 21:71; Bookshelf 1924–1925 Suppl. p. 1; Mahony 3:85)

3-74 **COLUM, Padraic.** *The Stone of Victory and Other Tales.* Gr. 4–6.
✶ Irish tales drawn from Colum's previously published collections, including "The Twelve Silly Sisters," "The Wizard Earl," and "Kat Mary Ellen and the Fairies."
Illus. by Judith Gwyn Brown, McGraw-Hill, 1966, 121 pp., o.p.
(BL 63:794; HB 43:200; Kirkus 34:980; LJ 91:5746; Suth:85)

3-75 **COVILLE, Bruce.** *Oddly Enough: Stories.* Gr. 6–8.
Nine fantasy and horror stories featuring brownies, elves, unicorns, werewolves, and ghosts. The companion volume *Odder Than Ever* (1999) contains nine more stories, including "The Giant's Tooth," "The Stinky Princess," and "There's Nothing Under the Bed."
Illus. by Michael Hussar, Harcourt, 1994, 136 pp., o.p.
(BL 91:318, 1399, 1416; HBG 6:74; Kirkus 62:1525; SLJ Dec 1994 p. 106; VOYA 17:344)

The Crafters. **Ed. by Christopher Stasheff and Bill Fawcett.**
See Chapter 12, Witchcraft and Sorcery Fantasy.

CRAMER, Alexander. *A Night in Moonbeam County.*
See Chapter 4, Ghost Fantasy.

3-76 **CUMMINGS, e(dward) e(stlin).** *Fairy Tales.* Gr. K–3.
Four whimsical tales, originally written for the poet's young daughter, including "The House That Ate Mosquito Pie," "The Old Man Who Said 'Why,'" "The Elephant and the Butterfly," and "The Little Girl Named I."
Illus. by John Eaton, Harcourt, 1950, 1965, 1975, 39 pp., o.p.
(HB 42:52; Kirkus 33:899; LJ 90:4604)

CUNNINGHAM, Julia (Woolfolk). *Candle Tales.*
See Chapter 2, Animal Fantasy.

3-77 **DAHL, Roald.** *The Wonderful Story of Henry Sugar and Six More.* Gr. 5–9. (Orig. British pub. 1977.)
Six short stories, including two with fantasy elements, plus an autobiographical essay.
Knopf, 1977, 225 pp., o.p.; Viking, 1988 (c. 1977), 225 pp., o.p.; Knopf, 2001 (rev. ed.), 231 pp. (0-375-91423-4)
(Kirkus 45:1148; HB 54:52, 78:428–429)

3-78 **DANN, Jack.** *Jubilee.* Gr. 10 up. (Orig. Australian pub. 2001.)
Seventeen science fiction and dark fantasy tales, including "Marilyn," "The Diamond Pit," and the title story, "Jubilee."
Tor, 2003, 448 pp. (0-765-30676-X)
(BL 99:860; LJ Jan 2003 p. 165)

3-79 **D'AULAIRE, Ingri Mortenson, and D'AULAIRE, Edgar Parin.**
★ *D'Aulaires' Trolls.* Gr. 3–5.
In the mountains, forests, and waterways of Norway live bands of little creatures called trolls, gnomes, and hulder-people.
Illus. by the authors, Doubleday, 1972, 62 pp., o.p.
(BL 69:404; CCBB 26:37; HB 48:592; Kirkus 40:1415; Suth:22)

3-80 *David Copperfield's Tales of the Impossible.* **Ed. by David Copperfield and Janet Berliner.** Gr. 10 up.
A collection of 17 fantasy and science fiction stories by Ray Bradbury, Raymond Feist, and others. *David Copperfield's Beyond Imagination* (1996) is a companion volume.
HarperCollins, 1995, 400 pp., o.p.; Harper, 1996, pap., 496 pp. (0-06-105492-5)
(BL 92:138, 541; Kirkus 63:1205; LJ Oct 15, 1995 p. 90)

DAVIS, Robert. *Padre Porko: The Gentlemanly Pig.*
See Chapter 2, Animal Fantasy.

3-81 *DAW 30th Anniversary Fantasy Anthology.* **Ed. by Elizabeth R. Wollheim and Sheila E. Gilbert.** Gr. 10 up.
A collection of fantasy stories by Mercedes Lackey, Tanith Lee, Marion Zimmer Bradley, Andre Norton, and others.
DAW, 2002, 432 pp. (0-7564-0070-8)
(BL 98:1514; LJ May 15, 2002 p. 130; VOYA 25:290)

3-82 **DE LA MARE, Walter (John).** *Broomsticks and Other Tales.* Gr. 5–7.
★ (Orig. British pub. 1925.)
Twelve stories including "The Lovely Myfanwy," "Alice's Godmother," and
"Maria-Fly."
Knopf, 1942, 334 pp., o.p.
(BL 22:252; HB 2:20, 18:180; LJ 67:892; TLS 1925 p. 797)

3-83 **DE LA MARE, Walter (John).** *The Dutch Cheese.* Gr. 3–5. (Orig. British
pub. 1925.)
Two stories from *Broomsticks and Other Tales* (1925, 1942): "The Dutch
Cheese" and "The Lovely Myfanwy."
Illus. by Dorothy P. Lathrop, Knopf, 1931, 75 pp., o.p.
(BL 28:156; HB 7:223; Mahony 3:204)

3-84 **DE LA MARE, Walter (John).** *The Lord Fish.* ((**Orig. British pub. 1933**).
Gr. 5–7.
Seven stories: "The Lord Fish," "A Penny a Day," "The Jacket," "Dick and the
Beanstalk," "Hodmadod," "The Old Lion," and "Sambo and the Snow Moun-
tains." *The Lord Fish* was published as an individual story by Candlewick,
1997 (0-7636-0134-9).
Illus. by Rex Whistler, Faber, 1933, 289 pp., o.p.
(HB 10:232; Mahony 3:204)

3-85 **DE LA MARE, Walter (John).** *The Magic Jacket and Other Stories.* Gr.
★ 5–7. (Orig. British pub. 1943.)
Ten tales of magic, including "The Magic Jacket," "The Riddle," and "Broom-
sticks."
Illus. by Paul Kennedy, Knopf, 1962, 277 pp., o.p.
(BL 58:689; CCBB 16:93; Eakin:97; HB 38:276; Kirkus 30:180; LJ 87:1316)

3-86 **DE LA MARE, Walter (John).** *A Penny a Day.* Gr. 4–7. (Orig. British pub.
★ 1925.)
Six stories, including "The Three Sleeping Boys of Warwickshire," "Dick and
the Beanstalk," and "The Lord Fish."
Illus. by Paul Kennedy, Knopf, 1960, 209 pp., o.p.
(BL 57:219; CCBB 14:78; Eakin:98; HB 36:503; LJ 85:4565)

3-87 **DE LA MARE, Walter (John).** *Tales Told Again.* Gr. 2–5. (Orig. British
★ pub. 1927, entitled *Told Again: Traditional Tales*; orig. U.S. pub., Knopf, 1927,
1943, entitled *Told Again; Old Tales Told Again.*)
This book contains all of the tales from *Broomsticks and Other Tales* (1942), *A
Penny a Day* (1960), and *Animal Stories* (1940), including both traditional and
modern fairy tales. One of these tales, "The Turnip," has been published separately as *The Turnip* (Godine, 1992).
Scribner, 1940, o.p.; Knopf, 1946, 207 pp., o.p.; illus. by Alan Howard, Knopf,
1959, 207 pp., o.p.; Farrar, 1980, 208 pp., o.p.
(BL 24:324, 55:459; CCBB 12:130; HB 35:298; LJ 84:1694; TLS 1927 p. 873, Dec 4, 1959 p.
xvi)

DE LINT, Charles. *Dreams Underfoot: The Newford Collection.*
See Chapter 5, High Fantasy: Alternate Worlds or Histories.

DE LINT, Charles. *Moonlight and Vines: A Newford Collection.*
See Chapter 5, High Fantasy: Alternate Worlds or Histories.

DE LINT, Charles. *Waifs and Strays.*
See Chapter 5, High Fantasy: Alternate Worlds or Histories.

Demons of the Night: Tales of the Fantastic, Madness, and the
Supernatural from Nineteenth-Century France. **Ed. by Joan C. Kessler.**
See Chapter 4, Ghost Fantasy.

3-88　**DE MORGAN, Mary (Augusta).** *The Complete Fairy Tales of Mary De*
Morgan. Gr. 4–7. (Orig. British pubs. 1876, 1880, and 1900.)
Contains the stories from three of De Morgan's collections: *On a Pincushion*
(orig. British pub. 1876, U.S. 1891), *The Necklace of Princess Fiorimonde*
(orig. British pub. 1880, U.S. 1922), and *The Windfairies* (orig. British pub.
1900, U.S. 1901). A facsimile edition of *On a Pincushion* and *The Necklace of*
Princess Fiorimonde was published by Garland, 1977, o.p.
Illus. by William De Morgan, Walter Crane, and Olive Cockerell, Watts, 1963,
412 pp., o.p.
(LJ 88:4081)

3-89　**DE MORGAN, Mary (Augusta).** *The Necklace of Princess Fiorimonde;*
and Other Stories. Gr. 4–6. (Orig. British pub. 1880, U.S. 1922.)
Six Victorian fairy tales, including "The Wanderings of Arasmon," "The Rain
Maiden," and the title story, "The Necklace of Princess Fiorimonde."
Illus. by Sylvie Monti, Hutchinson, 1990, 95 pp., o.p.; Trafalgar Sq., 1992, 96
pp., o.p.
(BL 88:1675; CCBB 45:233; SLJ July 1992 p. 81)

DERMAN, Martha. *Tales from Academy Street.*
See Chapter 9, Magic Adventure Fantasy.

3-90　**DICKINSON, Peter (pseud. of Malcolm de Brissac).** *The Flight of Drag-*
ons. Gr. 6 up. (Orig. British pub. 1979.)
An illustrated collection of dragon lore predicated on the view that dragons
once existed.
Illus. by Wayne Anderson, Harper, 1979, 137 pp., o.p.; Overlook, 1998, pap.,
128 pp. (0-87951-839-1)
(BL 76:311, 344; HB 55:696; LJ 104:2230)

3-91　**DICKINSON, Peter (pseud. of Malcolm de Brissac).** *The Lion-Tamer's*
✫　*Daughter and Other Stories.* Gr. 6–9. (Orig. British pub. 1997.)
Four short stories about contemporary young people who meet their counter-
parts from other worlds and times: "The Spring," "Checkers," "Touch and Go,"
and "The Lion-Tamer's Daughter."
Delacorte, 1997, 298 pp. (0-385-32327-1); Laurel Leaf, 1998, pap., 304 pp. (0-
440-22694-2)
(BL 93:1321; CCBB 50:245; HB 73:197; HBG 8:312; Kirkus 65:58; SLJ Mar 1997 p. 184,
Dec 1997 p. 24; VOYA 20:40)

DICKINSON, Peter (pseud. of Malcolm de Brissac). *Merlin Dreams.*
See Chapter 6, High Fantasy: Myth or Legend Fantasy.

3-92 **DICKSON, Gordon R(upert).** *The Last Dream.* Gr. 7–12.
An anthology of fantasy and science fiction stories about dragons, witches, and magical transformations.
Baen, 1986, pap., 263 pp., o.p.
(VOYA 9:236)

3-93 **DOLBIER, Maurice (Wyman).** *The Half-Pint Jinni, and Other Stories.* Gr. 4–7.
Eight magical tales set in Baghdad.
Illus. by Allan Thomas, Random, 1948, 242 pp., o.p.
(BL 45:36; CCBB 1:2; Kirkus 16:280; LJ 73:1097, 1457)

DONALDSON, Stephen R(upert). *Daughter of Regals and Other Tales.*
See Chapter 5, High Fantasy: Alternate Worlds or Histories.

3-94 **DONALDSON, Stephen R(upert).** *Reave the Just and Other Tales.* Gr. 10
✸ up.
Eight fantasy and horror stories about a warlock, a vampire, a genie, and other fantastic creatures.
Bantam, 1999, 384 pp., o.p., 2000, pap., 496 pp. (0-553-58014-0)
(BL 95:655; Kirkus 66:1637; Kliatt May 2000 p. 22; VOYA 22:190, 23:11)

DONOGHUE, Emma. *Kissing the Witch: Old Tales in New Skins.*
See Chapter 6, High Fantasy: Myth or Legend Fantasy.

3-95 *Don't Bet on the Prince: Contemporary Feminist Fairy Tales in North America and England.* **Ed. by Jack Zipes.** Gr. 10 up.
An anthology of 16 feminist fairy tales written for children and adults, by such authors as Jane Yolen, Judith Viorst, and Tanith Lee, followed by four critical essays about the impact of fairy tales on children.
Routledge, 1986, 270 pp., o.p.
(BL 83:468, 496; Kirkus 54:1199; SLJ Feb 1987 p. 36; TLS Nov 28, 1986 p. 1348)

Don't Give Up the Ghost: The Delacorte Book of Original Ghost Stories. **Ed. by David Gale.**
See Chapter 4, Ghost Fantasy.

3-96 *Dragon Fantastic.* **Ed. by Rosalind M. Greenberg and Martin H. Greenberg.** Gr. 6–12.
Sixteen dragon stories, some set in alternate worlds and others in our contemporary world.
DAW, 1992, pap., 299 pp. (0-88677-511-6)
(LJ Apr 15, 1992 p. 125; VOYA 15:236)

3-97 *The Dragon Quintet.* **Ed. by Marvin Kaye.** Gr. 10 up.
Five dragon tales, including Mercedes Lackey's "Joust," Orson Scott Card's "In the Dragon's House," and Tanith Lee's "Love in a Time of Dragons."
Tor, 2004, 304 pp. (0-765-31035-X)
(BL 100:1431; LJ May 15, 2004 p. 119; VOYA 27:228)

3-98 *Dragon Tales.* **Ed. by Isaac Asimov, Charles G. Waugh, and Martin H.**
✭ **Greenberg.** Gr. 7 up.
Twelve stories about dragons, including Anne McCaffrey's "Weyr Search" and
Gordon Dickson's "The Dragon and the George."
Fawcett, 1982, pap., 318 pp., o.p.
(BL 79:294, 304; SLJ Dec 1982 p. 86; VOYA 5:36)

Dragons & Dreams: A Collection of New Fantasy and Science Fiction
Stories. **Ed. by Jane (Hyatt) Yolen (Stemple), Martin H. Greenberg, and**
Charles G. Waugh.
See Chapter 9, Magic Adventure Fantasy.

3-99 *Dream Time: New Stories by Sixteen Award Winning Authors.* **Ed. by Toss**
Gascoigne, Jo Goodman, and Margot Tyrell. Gr. 6–9. (Orig. Australian
pub. 1989.)
Sixteen stories loosely tied to the theme of Australian Aboriginal "Dream
Time," written by Patricia Wrightson, Victor Kelleher, Mary Steele, Lee Hard-
ing, and others.
Houghton, 1991, 184pp. (0-395-57434-X)
(CCBB 45:89; HBG 3:119; Kirkus 59:930; SLJ Nov 1991, p. 117; VOYA 14:370)

3-100 *Earth, Air, Fire, Water: Tales from the Eternal Archives, Number 2.* **Ed. by**
Margaret Weis. Gr. 7–12.
Thirteen tales about the four elementals and how they affect our world, written
by Tanya Huff, Kristine Kathryn Rusch, Jane Lindskold, and others. This is a
companion volume to *Legends: Tales from the Eternal Archives, Number 1*
(1999), which includes stories by Deborah Turner Harris, Margaret Weis, and
Dennis L. McKiernan, among others.
DAW, 1999, pap., 308 pp. (0-886-77857-3)
(Kliatt Mar 2000 p. 24; VOYA 23:359)

3-101 **EDGEWORTH, Maria.** *Simple Susan and Other Tales.* Gr. 3–5. (Orig. U.S.
pub. 1819.)
Eight of the author's best-known stories, including "The Cherry Orchard,"
"The Orange Man," and "The Purple Jar."
Dutton, 1907, o.p.; illus. by Clara Burd, Macmillan, 1929, 216 pp., o.p.
(BL 26:169; HB 5:53)

3-102 **ELLIS, Sarah.** *Back of Beyond: Stories of the Supernatural.* Gr. 6–10.
✭ (Orig. Canadian pub. 1996.)
Twelve supernatural stories about ordinary people who encounter the extraordi-
nary.
Illus. by Andrew Moore, McElderry/Simon, 1997, 136 pp. (0-689-81484-4)
(BL 94:794; CCBB 51:83; HB 73:680; HBG 9:86; Kirkus 65:1531; SLJ Nov 1997 p. 117, Dec
1997 p. 24; VOYA 20:324, 21:12)

3-103 *Elsewhere, Elsewhen, Elsehow.* **Ed. by Miriam Allen De Ford.** Gr. 10 up.
Eighteen fantasy, science fiction, and horror stories, including "The Old
Woman" and "The Monster."
Walker, 1971, 180 pp., o.p.
(Kirkus 39:465, 567; LJ 96:3641, 4205)

Elsewhere, Vol. I. **Ed. by Terri Windling and Mark Alan Arnold.**
See Chapter 5, High Fantasy: Alternate Worlds or Histories.

3-104 *The Enchanted Book.* **Ed. by Alice Dalgliesh.** Gr. 3–5.
Twenty-one stories of magical enchantment whose authors include Hans Christian Andersen and Marie d'Aulnoy.
Illus. by Concetta Cacciola, Scribner, 1947, 246 pp., o.p.
(BL 44:137; CCBB 1:2; HB 24:37; LJ 72:1436, 1690)

3-105 *The Enchanter's Spell: Five Famous Tales.* **Adapt. by Gennady Spirin.**
✱ Gr. 3–7. (Orig. German pub. 1986.)
This collection of literary fairy tales contains Hans Christian Andersen's "The Emperor's New Clothes," Miguel de Cervantes' "The Beautiful Kitchen Maid," E. T. A. Hoffmann's "The Nutcracker," George MacDonald's "Little Daylight," and Alexander Pushkin's "The Princess and the Seven Brothers."
Illus. by the adapter, Dial, 1988, 96 pp., o.p.
(BL 84:1608; CCBB 41:170; Kirkus 56:128; SLJ Apr 1988 p. 100; Suth 4:391)

3-106 **ESTES, Eleanor (Ruth Rosenfeld).** *The Sleeping Giant and Other Stories.*
✱ Gr. 2–5.
Three tales: "The Sleeping Giant," "The Lost Shadow," and "A Nice Room for Giraffes."
Illus. by the author, Harcourt, 1948, 101 pp., o.p.
(BL 45:123; CCBB 1:4; HB 25:35; Kirkus 16:571; LJ 73:1825)

3-107 **ETCHEMENDY, Nancy.** *Cat in Glass: And Other Tales of the Unnatural.*
✱ Gr. 8 up.
Eight fantasy, horror, ghost, and science fiction tales, previously published in magazines and in an anthology, including "The Lily and the Weaver's Heart," and "The Sailor's Bargain."
Cricket, 2002, 192 pp. (0-8126-2674-5)
(BL 9:588; HBG 14:93; Kirkus 70:1308; SLJ Dec 2002 p. 137; VOYA 26:11, 62)

EVANS, Douglas. *Math Rashes: And Other Classroom Tales.*
See Chapter 8, Humorous Fantasy.

3-108 **EWING, Juliana (Horatia Gatty).** *The Brownies and Other Stories.* Gr. 4–6. (Orig. British pub. 1870, entitled *The Brownies and Other Tales;* orig. U.S. pub. 1910.)
Seven tales, including "The Brownies," "Amelia and the Dwarfs," and "The Land of Lost Toys."
Illus. by Alice B. Woodward, Macmillan, 1910, 176 pp., o.p.; illus. by Ernest H. Shepard, Dutton, 1954, 239 pp., o.p.; Dent, 1975 (repr. of 1954 ed.), 250 pp., o.p.
(BL 7:85, 51:210; CCBB 9:44; Mahony 2:279)

Excalibur. **Ed. by Richard Gilliam.**
See Chapter 6, High Fantasy: Myth or Legend Fantasy.

3-109 *The Faber Book of Modern Fairy Tales.* **Ed. by Sara Corrin and Stephen Corrin.** Gr. 4–6. (Orig. British pub. 1981.)

Fifteen original tales by E. Nesbit, Laurence Housman, James Thurber, A. A. Milne, Philippa Pearce, and others.
Illus. by Ann Strugnell, Faber, 1982, 312 pp., o.p.
(CCBB 36:6; Suth 3:103; TLS 1981 p. 1356)

Faces in the Dark: A Book of Scary Stories. **Ed. by Chris Powling.**
See Chapter 4, Ghost Fantasy.

3-110 *Faerie Tales.* **Ed. by Martin H. Greenberg and Russell Davis.** Gr. 10 up.
An anthology of 12 tales based on Irish and British folklore, whose authors include Elizabeth Ann Scarborough, Charles de Lint, and Tanya Huff.
DAW, 2004, pap., 320 pp. (0-7564-0182-8)
(BL 100:1551; Kliatt July 2004 p. 30)

3-111 *Faery!* **Ed. by Terri Windling.** Gr. 10 up.
An anthology of 23 stories involving the Kingdom of Faery, written by Jane Yolen, Patricia McKillip, Sherri Tepper, Robin McKinley, and others.
Ace, 1985, pap., 308 pp., o.p.
(BL 81:927, 945)

3-112 *The Faery Reel: Tales from the Twilight Realm.* **Ed. by Ellen Datlow and**
☆ **Terri Windling.** Gr. 9–12.
Three poems and 17 tales about the world of Faerie by such authors as Patricia McKillip, Gregory Maguire, Tanith Lee, Nina Kiriki Hoffman, Neil Gaiman, and Delia Sherman. This is a companion volume to *The Green Man: Tales from the Mythic Forest* (2002; see Chapter 6, High Fantasy: Myth or Legend Fantasy).
Viking, 2004, 544 pp. (0-67-005914-5)
(BL 100:1450; CCBB 58:12; Kirkus 72:489; SLJ July 2004 p. 104)

3-113 *Famous Tales of the Fantastic.* **Ed. by Herbert Maurice Van Thal.** Gr. 10 up.
Eleven American and British short stories whose authors include Ray Bradbury, Nathaniel Hawthorne, Washington Irving, and Robert Louis Stevenson.
Illus. by Edward Pagram, Hill, 1965, 208 pp., o.p.
(BL 62:525; LJ 90:5303; TLS 1966 p. 29)

3-114 *Fantastic Creatures: An Anthology of Fantasy and Science Fiction.* **Ed. by Isaac Asimov, Martin H. Greenberg, and Charles G. Waugh.** Gr. 7–10.
A combination of eight fantasy and science fiction stories, including Anne McCaffrey's "The Smallest Dragonboy."
Watts, 1981, 155 pp., o.p.
(BL 78:434, 438; CCBB 35:142; SLJ Aug 1982 p. 123)

The Fantastic Imagination: An Anthology of High Fantasy, Vol. 1. **Ed. by Robert H. Boyer and Kenneth J. Zahorski.**
See Chapter 5, High Fantasy: Alternate Worlds or Histories.

3-115 *Fantastic Tales: Visionary and Everyday.* **Ed. by Italo Calvino.** Gr. 10 up.
(Orig. Italian pub. 1983.)
Twenty-six 19th-century fantasy stories whose authors include E. T. A. Hoffmann, Honoré de Balzac, Nikolai Gogol, Nathaniel Hawthorne, Charles Dickens, Edgar Allan Poe, and Rudyard Kipling.

Pantheon, 1997, 608 pp., o.p.
(BL 94:454; Kirkus 65:1414; LJ Oct 1997 p. 128)

3-116 *Fantasy Annual V.* **Ed. by Terry Carr.** Gr. 10 up.
A sampling of the best short fantasy of 1981, most of which are stories based in reality with a psychological rather than supernatural basis for the fantasy elements. Other books in the series are *The Year's Finest Fantasy, 1978* (Berkley 1978), *The Year's Finest Fantasy, Vol. 2* (1979), *Fantasy Annual III* (1981), and *Fantasy Annual IV* (1981).
Pocket, 1982, 240 pp., o.p.
(BL 79:601; LJ 107:2192)

3-117 *Fantasy Hall of Fame.* **Ed. by Robert Silverberg and Martin H. Greenberg.** Gr. 10 up.
Twenty-three stories chosen as the best of modern fantasy by the 1982 and 1983 World Fantasy Conventions. The authors range from Edgar Allan Poe to Ursula K. Le Guin.
Arbor House, 1983, 414 pp., o.p.
(BL 80:397; LJ 108:1976)

3-118 *Fantasy Stories: A Spellbinding Collection.* **Comp. by Diana Wynne Jones.** Gr. 4–8. (Orig. British pub. 1994.)
An anthology of tales from classic fantasy authors, including C. S. Lewis, Rudyard Kipling, and L. Frank Baum.
Illus. by Robin Lawrie, Kingfisher, 1994, pap., 256 pp. (1-85697-982-2)
(BL 91:1243; SLJ Nov 1994 p. 104)

3-119 **FARBER, Norma (Holzman).** *Six Impossible Things Before Breakfast.* Gr. 3–5.
Four poems and two short stories about magic, a unicorn, and a princess, each illustrated by a different artist.
Illus. by Tomie de Paola, Trina Schart Hyman, Hilary Knight, Friso Henstra, Lydia Dabcovich, and Charles Mikolaycak, Addison-Wesley, 1977, 43 pp., o.p.
(CCBB 30:123; HB 53:307; SLJ Apr 1977 p. 66)

3-120 **FARJEON, Eleanor.** *Italian Peepshow and Other Tales.* Gr. 3–5. (Orig. pub. in England; orig. U.S. pub. 1926.)
Three children visiting Italy listen to a number of stories, including "Oranges and Lemons" and "Nella's Dancing Shoes."
Illus. by Rosalind Thornycroft, Stokes, 1926, 146 pp., o.p.; illus. by Edward Ardizzone, Walck, 1960, 96 pp., o.p.
(BL 24:125, 57:274; Bookshelf 1928 p. 16; HB 3:18, 36:406; Kirkus 28:904; LJ 85:4566; TLS Nov 25, 1960 p. vii)

3-121 **FARJEON, Eleanor.** *Jim at the Corner.* Gr. 3–5. (Orig. pub. in England,
☆ entitled *The Old Sailor's Yarn Box*.)
Old Jim the sailor tells a young boy named Derry eight tales of the sea. This is a companion volume to *The Old Nurse's Stocking Basket* (1931, 1965; see below).
Stokes, 1934, 143 pp. (entitled *The Old Sailor's Yarn Box*), o.p.; illus. by Edward Ardizzone, Walck, 1958, 102 pp., o.p.
(BL 31:244, 55:192; Bookshelf 1935 p. 2; Eakin:113; HB 10:355; 34:473; LJ 60:403)

3-122 **FARJEON, Eleanor.** *The Little Bookroom: Eleanor Farjeon's Short Sto-*
★   *ries for Children, Chosen by Herself.* Gr. 4–7. (Orig. British pub. 1931.)
      Twenty-seven stories, including "The Giant and the Mite," "The Seventh
      Princess," and "The Glass Peacock." Carnegie Medal, 1955.
      Illus. by Edward Ardizzone, Walck, 1956, 302 pp., o.p.; illus. by Edward
      Ardizzone, Oxford University Press, 1979 (repr. of 1931 ed.), o.p.
      (BL 52:415; CCBB 10:5; HB 32:179, 270, 61:77; LJ 81:1719)

FARJEON, Eleanor. *Martin Pippin in the Apple Orchard.*
See Chapter 1, Allegorical Fantasy and Literary Fairy Tales.

3-123 **FARJEON, Eleanor.** *The Old Nurse's Stocking Basket.* Gr. 3–5. (Orig.
      British pub. 1931.)
      The Old Nurse tells stories about caring for Hercules, the Princess of China,
      and the Spanish Infanta. A companion to *Jim at the Corner* (1958, orig. title:
      The Old Sailor's Yarn Box 1934; see above).
      Illus. by Edward Ardizzone, Walck, 1965, 102 pp., o.p.
      (HB 42:193, 80:153–154; LJ 91:2209; Mahony 3:86)

3-124 **FARJEON, Eleanor.** *One Foot in Fairyland: Sixteen Tales.* Gr. 4–6. (Orig.
      British pub. 1938.)
      A collection of original fantasy tales and retellings of fairy tales.
      Illus. by Robert Lawson, Stokes, 1938, 261 pp., o.p.
      (BL 35:121; HB 14:381; LJ 63:978; TLS 1938 p. 789)

3-125 **FARJEON, Eleanor.** *The Tale of Tom Tiddler, with Rhymes of London*
      Town. Gr. 4–6. (Orig. British pub. 1929.)
      Tales set in various parts of London unfold while Tom Tiddler searches the city
      for Jinny Jones.
      Illus. by Norman Tealby, Stokes, 1930, 224 pp., o.p.
      (BL 27:67)

3-126 **FAST, Howard (Melvin).** *The General Zapped an Angel: New Stories of*
      Fantasy and Science Fiction. Gr. 10 up.
      Nine short stories of allegorical fantasy and science fiction.
      Morrow, 1970, 160 pp., o.p.
      (BL 66:955, 968; LJ 95:1047)

3-127 **FAST, Howard (Melvin).** *A Touch of Infinity: Thirteen New Stories of*
      Fantasy and Science Fiction. Gr. 10 up.
      Thirteen satirical fantasy and science fiction tales, including one about a gnat-
      sized man on the back porch, and another about plucking breakfast rolls from
      the air.
      Morrow, 1973, 182 pp., o.p.
      (BL 70:473, 484; Kirkus 41:659; LJ 98:2339, 2678)

Festival Moon. **Ed. by C. J. Cherryh.**
See Chapter 5, High Fantasy: Alternate Worlds or Histories.

FIELD, Rachel (Lyman). *Eliza and the Elves.*
See Chapter 7, High Fantasy: Travel to Other Worlds.

FIENBERG, Anna. *The Magnificent Nose (and Other Marvels).*
See Chapter 9, Magic Adventure Fantasy.

FINNEY, Jack (pseud. of Walter Branden Finney). *About Time: Twelve Stories.*
See Chapter 10, Time Travel Fantasy.

3-128 *Fire and Wings: Dragon Tales from East and West.* **Ed. by Marianne Carus.** Gr. 3–6.
Fifteen stories about dragons, many originally published in *Cricket* magazine, written by E. Nesbit, Patricia MacLachlan, Jane Yolen, Geraldine McCaughrean, and others.
Illus. by Nilesh Mistry, Cricket, 2002, 146 pp. (0-8126-2664-8)
(Kirkus 70:1464; SLJ Dec 2002 p. 86; VOYA 26:11, 63)

3-129 *Firebirds: An Anthology of Original Fantasy and Science Fiction.* **Ed. by**
★★ **Sharyn November.** Gr. 7 up.
Sixteen tales written by well-known fantasy authors including Megan Whalen Turner, Lloyd Alexander, Diana Wynne Jones, Garth Nix, Sherwood Smith, Nancy Springer, and Delia Sherman.
Firebird/Penguin, 2003, 440 pp. (0-14-250142-5)
(BL 100:404; CCBB 57:201; HB 80:89; Kirkus 71:1021; SLJ Oct 2003 p. 172; VOYA 26:411, 27:11)

3-130 *Fires of the Past: Thirteen Contemporary Fantasies About Hometowns.* **Ed. by Anne Devereaux Jordan.** Gr. 10 up.
Twelve fantasy and science fiction stories and one poem, all on the theme of hometowns.
St. Martin's, 1991, 208 pp., o.p.
(BL 87:1322, 1374; LJ Mar 15, 1991 p. 119; VOYA 14:179, 15:9)

FLEISCHMAN, (Albert) Sid(ney). *A Carnival of Animals.*
See Chapter 2, Animal Fantasy.

FLEISCHMAN, (Albert) Sid(ney). *Jim Bridger's Alarm Clock, and Other Tall Tales.*
See Chapter 8, Humorous Fantasy.

FLEISCHMAN, Paul (Taylor). *Graven Images: Three Stories.*
See Chapter 4, Ghost Fantasy.

3-131 *Flights: Extreme Visions of Fantasy.* **Ed. by Al Sarrantonio.** Gr. 11 up.
Twenty-nine tales of fantasy and horror, whose authors include Patricia McKillip, Neil Gaiman, Nina Kiriki Hoffman, Charles de Lint, and Orson Scott Card.
NAL/Roc, 2004, 560 pp. (0-451-45977-6)

FLORA, James (Royer). *Grandpa's Ghost Stories.*
See Chapter 4, Ghost Fantasy.

3-132 **FOX (Greenberg), Paula.** *The Little Swineherd and Other Tales.* Gr. 3–6.
★ Five tales: four fables about a rooster, a pony, an alligator, and a raccoon, and one story about an abandoned swineherd.

Illus. by Leonard Lubin, Dutton, 1978, 104 pp., o.p.; illus. by Robert Byrd, Dutton, 1995, 135pp. (0-525-45398-9)

(BL 75:292; CCBB 32:43; HB 55:516; HBG 7:61; Kirkus 46:1071, 63:1109; SLJ Oct 1978 p. 144)

FRANKO, Ivan, and MELNYK, Bohdan. *Fox Mykyta.*
See Chapter 2, Animal Fantasy.

FREDDI, Cris. *Pork, and Other Stories.*
See Chapter 2, Animal Fantasy.

FRENCH, Vivian. *Under the Moon.*
See Chapter 1, Allegorical Fantasy and Literary Fairy Tales.

Fun Phantoms: Tales of Ghostly Entertainment. **Ed. by Seon Manley and Gogo Lewis.**
See Chapter 4, Ghost Fantasy.

3-133 **FYLEMAN, Rose (Amy).** *Forty Good-Night Tales.* Gr. K–4. (Orig. British pub. 1923.)
Humorous tales and fairy stories to read aloud to young children at bedtime. *Forty Good-Morning Tales* (Doubleday 1929, 1938) is a companion volume.
Illus. by Thelma Cudlipp Grosvenor, Doran, 1924, 131 pp., o.p.
(BL 21:200; HB 1:4; Mahony 2:57)

3-134 **FYLEMAN, Rose (Amy).** *Tea Time Tales.* Gr. 3–5. (Orig. pub. in England.)
Twenty humorous short stories to be read aloud,
Illus. by Erick Berry, Doubleday, 1930, 246 pp., o.p.
(BL 26:401; HB 6:210; LJ 55:995; Mahony 3:86)

GALLOWAY, Priscilla. *Truly Grim Tales.*
See Chapter 6, High Fantasy: Myth or Legend Fantasy.

3-135 **GARDNER, John (Champlin) (Jr.).** *Dragon, Dragon, and Other Timeless Tales.* Gr. 5–7.
Four fairy tale spoofs about dragons, giants, and magic.
Illus. by Charles Shields, Knopf, 1975, 75 pp., o.p.
(BL 72:684; CCBB 29:109; HB 52:154; Kirkus 43:1129)

3-136 **GARNER, Alan.** *Alan Garner's Fairytales of Gold.* Gr. 3–5. (Orig. pub. separately in England in 1979.)
Four original tales in the fairy tale tradition: "The Golden Brothers," "The Girl of the Golden Gate," "The Three Golden Heads of the Well," and "The Princess and the Golden Mane."
Philomel, 1980, 200 pp., o.p.
(BL 77:963; CCBB 34:132; Kirkus 49:357; SLJ Mar 1981 p. 132)

3-137 **GARNER, Alan.** *Once Upon a Time: Though It Wasn't in Your Time, and*
☆ *It Wasn't in My Time, and It Wasn't in Anybody Else's Time . . .* Gr. K–3. (Orig. British pub. 1993.)
Three stories written in folktale style: "The Fox, the Hare, and the Cock," "The Girl and the Geese," and "Battibeth."

Illus. by Norman Messenger, Dorling, 1993, 32 pp. (1-56458-381-3)
(BL 90:694; CCBB 47:153; Kirkus 61:1523; SLJ Mar 1994 p. 215)

3-138 GATE, Ethel M(ay). *The Broom Fairies, and Other Stories.* Gr. 3–5.
Eight original fairy tales.
Illus. by Maud and Miska Petersham, Yale University Press, 1917, 110 pp., o.p.
(BL 14:172; 19:134; Mahony 2:280)

3-139 GATE, Ethel M(ay). *The Fortunate Days.* Gr. 3–5.
Nine fairy tales about a tailor in Constantinople who follows his Persian cat
through its nine lives.
Illus. by Vianna Knowlton, Yale University Press, 1922, 127 pp., o.p.
(BL 19:127; Bookshelf 1923–1924 p. 8; LJ 45:980; Mahony 2:28)

3-140 GATE, Ethel M(ay). *Tales from the Enchanted Isles.* Gr. 3–5.
Seven fairy tales modeled on traditional folklore.
Illus. by Dorothy P. Lathrop, Yale University Press, 1927, 118 pp., o.p.
(BL 23:235; HB 2:44; Mahony 2:280)

3-141 GATE, Ethel M(ay). *Tales from the Secret Kingdom.* Gr. 2–4.
Nine original fairy stories.
Illus. by Katherine Buffum, Yale University Press, 1919, 93 pp., o.p.
(BL 16:138; LJ 45:980; Mahony 1:40)

The Ghost Story Treasury. **Selected by Linda Sonntag.**
See Chapter 4, Ghost Fantasy.

Ghosts: An Anthology. **Ed. by William Mayne.**
See Chapter 4, Ghost Fantasy.

The Ghost's Companion: A Haunting Anthology. **Ed. by Peter Haining.**
See Chapter 4, Ghost Fantasy.

Ghosts for Christmas. **Ed. by Richard Dalby.**
See Chapter 4, Ghost Fantasy.

Ghostwise: A Book of Midnight Stories. **Ed. by Dan Yashinsky.**
See Chapter 4, Ghost Fantasy.

3-142 *A Glory of Unicorns.* **Ed. by Bruce Coville.** Gr. 5–8.
✭   Thirteen unicorn stories written by Bruce Coville, Gregory Maguire, Jessica
Amanda Salmonson, and Katherine Coville, among others.
Illus. by Alix Berenzy, Scholastic, 1998, 198 pp. (0-590-95943-3); Apple,
2000, pap., 198 pp. (0-439-06628-X)
(BL 94:1765; HBG 9:406; SLJ May 1998 p. 138; VOYA 21:210, 22:13)

GODDEN (Dixon), (Margaret) Rumer. *Four Dolls.*
See Chapter 11, Toy Fantasy.

3-143 GOLDSTEIN, Lisa. *Travellers in Magic.* Gr. 6–12.
Fifteen thought-provoking supernatural stories, some with Jewish themes,
including "Ever After," "The Woman in the Painting," and "Infinite Riches."

Tor, 1994, 284 pp. (0-312-86301-2), 1997, pap. (0-312-86301-2)
(Kirkus 62:1317; LJ Nov 15, 1994 p. 90; VOYA 18:104, 19:23)

GORDON, John (William). *The Burning Baby and Other Ghosts.*
See Chapter 4, Ghost Fantasy.

3-144 **GOROG, Judith.** *In a Creepy, Creepy Place, and Other Scary Stories.* Gr.
2–4.
Five stories about ghosts, a talking doll, and angels.
Illus. by Kimberly Bulcken Root, HarperCollins, 1996, 64 pp. (0-06-025131-X)
(BL 93:859; HB 73:65; HBG 8:58; SLJ Feb 1997 p. 81)

3-145 **GOROG, Judith.** *In a Messy, Messy Room, and Other Strange Stories.* Gr.
3–6.
Five eerie stories, including "The Smelly Sneakers Contest," in which Todd
wins the championship but loses his feet.
Illus. by Kimberly Bulcken Root, Putnam, 1990, 48 pp., o.p.
(BL 86:1897; CCBB 43:240; HBG 1:246; Kirkus 58:648; SLJ July 1990 p. 76)

GOROG, Judith. *No Swimming in Dark Pond, and Other Chilling Tales.*
See Chapter 4, Ghost Fantasy.

GOROG, Judith. *On Meeting Witches at Wells.*
See Chapter 4, Ghost Fantasy.

GOROG, Judith. *Please Do Not Touch.*
See Chapter 4, Ghost Fantasy.

GOROG, Judith. *A Taste for Quiet, and Other Disquieting Tales.*
See Chapter 4, Ghost Fantasy.

3-146 **GOROG, Judith.** *Three Dreams and a Nightmare, and Other Tales of the*
✻ *Dark.* Gr. 5–9.
A companion volume to Gorog's *A Taste for Quiet* (1983; see Chapter 4, Ghost
Fantasy) and *No Swimming in Dark Pond* (1987; see Chapter 4, Ghost Fanta-
sy), this is a collection of 14 fantasy and horror stories.
Putnam, 1988, 156 pp., o.p.
(BL 85:258, 318; CCBB 42:71; Kirkus 56:974; SLJ Nov 1988 p. 125; VOYA 12:16, 42)

3-147 *Gothic! Ten Original Dark Tales.* **Ed. by Deborah Noyes.** Gr. 10 up.
✻ Ten dark fantasy tales written by Gregory Maguire, Joan Aiken, Garth Nix,
Vivian Vande Velde, Neil Gaiman, M. T. Anderson, and others.
Illus. by Gary Kelley, Candlewick, 2004, 256 pp. (0-7636-2243-5)
(BL 101:404; CCBB 58:137; HB 80:714; Kirkus 72:871)

GOULART, Ron(ald Joseph). *The Chameleon Corps and Other Shape*
Changers.
See Chapter 5, High Fantasy: Alternate Worlds or Histories.

3-148 **GRAHAME, Kenneth.** *The Golden Age.* Gr. 5–7. (Orig. British and U.S.
pub. 1895.)
Five orphaned children take turns telling the stories in this book and its companion volume, *Dream Days* (orig. pub. 1898; Dodd, 1930; Ten Speed, 1993;

Akadine, 2000). *Dream Days* includes the story "The Reluctant Dragon" (see Chapter 1, Allegorical Fantasy and Literary Fairy Tales).
Illus. by Ernest H. Shepard, Dodd, 1922, 174 pp., o.p.; illus. by Maxfield Parrish, Garland, 1976 (repr. of 1900 ed.), o.p.; Beaufort, 1985 (repr. of 1898 ed.), 288 pp., o.p.; Ten Speed, 1993, 252 pp., o.p.; Akadine, 2000, 174 pp. (1-585790-19-2)
(BL 25:176, 26:77; CCBB 18:129; HB 1:46, 7:324, 30:66; HBG 5:86)

3-149 **GRAY, Nicholas Stuart.** *Mainly in Moonlight: Ten Stories of Sorcery and*
✷ *the Supernatural.* Gr. 4–6. (Orig. British pub. 1965.)
Tales of wizards, princes, and princesses, including "The Sorcerer's Apprentices," "The Reluctant Familiar," and "The Man Who Sold Magic."
Illus. by Charles Keeping, Meredith, 1967, 181 pp., o.p.
(HB 43:462; Kirkus 35:207; LJ 92:2449; SLJ Feb 1980 p. 55; TLS 1965 p. 1130)

3-150 **GRAY, Nicholas Stuart.** *A Wind from Nowhere.* Gr. 5–7. (Orig. pub. in England.)
Humorous fairy tales involving dragons, princes, wizards, and demons.
Faber, 1979, 155 pp., o.p.
(HB 56:55; SLJ Dec 1979 p. 85)

Great Ghost Stories. **Selected by Barry Moser.**
See Chapter 4, Ghost Fantasy.

3-151 **GREEN, Kathleen.** *Leprechaun Tales.* Gr. 3–5.
Irish-inspired tales of leprechauns, foolish human beings, pookas, and banshees.
Illus. by Victoria de Larrea, Lippincott, 1968, 127 pp., o.p.
(BL 64:1042; HB 44:172; Kirkus 36:340; LJ 93:1310)

3-152 **GREEN, Kathleen.** *Philip and the Pooka and Other Irish Fairy Tales.* Gr. 4–6.
Ten tales about Irish fairy folk: the little people, pookas, Lochrimeh, and witches.
Illus. by Victoria de Larrea, Lippincott, 1966, 93 pp., o.p.
(BL 62:831; CCBB 20:25; HB 42:305; LJ 91:2210)

The Green Man: Tales from the Mythic Forest. **Ed. by Ellen Datlow and Terri Windling.**
See Chapter 6, High Fantasy: Myth or Legend Fantasy.

3-153 **GRINDLEY, Sally.** *Breaking the Spell: Tales of Enchantment.* Gr. 3–5.
Seven tales, some original and others based on folklore, whose authors include Jane Yolen, Ann Turnbull, and Joan Aiken.
Illus. by Susan Field, Kingfisher, 1997, 80 pp., o.p.
(BL 94:812; SLJ Dec 1997 p. 90)

3-154 **GRIPARI, Pierre.** *Tales of the Rue Broca.* Gr. 5–7. (Selections from 1967 French edition.)
Six imaginative tales from France, among them tales about a good devil, a pair of shoes in love, and a hero with a ridiculous name.

Trans. by Doriane Grutman, illus. by Emily Arnold McCully, Bobbs-Merrill, 1969, 111 pp., o.p.

(CCBB 23:128; LJ 95:1942; Kirkus 37:1112; Suth:159)

HALDANE, J(ohn) B(urdon) S(anderson). *My Friend Mr. Leakey.*
See Chapter 12, Witchcraft and Sorcery Fantasy.

HALE, Lucretia P(eabody). *The Complete Peterkin Papers.*
See Chapter 8, Humorous Fantasy.

3-155 *Half-Human.* Ed. by Bruce Coville. Gr. 6 up.
☆ Ten stories about mythical creatures in contemporary settings, written by Tamora Pierce, Nancy Springer, Jane Yolen, and others.
Illus. by Marc Tauss, Scholastic, 2001, 224 pp. (0-590-95944-1), 2001, pap., 212 pp. (0-590-95588-8)

(BL 98:723; Kirkus 99:1481; SLJ Dec 2001 p. 133; VOYA 24:369, 25:13)

HAMILTON (Adoff), Virginia (Esther). *The All Jahdu Storybook.*
See Chapter 8, Humorous Fantasy.

3-156 HARRIS, Rosemary (Jeanne). *Sea Magic and Other Stories of Enchant-*
☆ *ment.* Gr. 6–8. (Orig. pub. in England, 1974, entitled *The Lotus and the Grail: Legends from East to West.*)
Ten tales of magic and superstition, including "The Graveyard Rose" and "White Orchid, Red Mountain." The British edition includes eight additional stories.
Macmillan, 1974, 178 pp., o.p.

(BL 70:819; CCBB 28:9; HB 50:145; Kirkus 42:192; LJ 99:2290; Suth 2:203)

3-157 HARRISON, David Lee. *The Book of Giant Stories.* Gr. K–4.
Three tales about boys who use their wits either to escape or to befriend a giant.
Illus. by Philippe Fix, McGraw-Hill, 1972, 44 pp., o.p.

(Kirkus 40:1021; LJ 98:253; TLS 1972 p. 1332)

3-158 HAUFF, Wilhelm. *The Caravan.* Gr. 6 up. (Orig. pub. in Germany, 1855; orig. U.S. pub. Appleton, 1850, entitled *The Caravan: A Collection of Popular Tales;* Stokes, 1912, entitled *Caravan Tales and Some Others.*)
Six suspenseful tales told by merchants traveling in a caravan across the desert.
Trans. by Alma Overholt, illus. by Burt Silverman, Crowell, 1964, 1972, 220 pp., o.p.; Fredonia, 2002 (entitled *Tales of the Caravan, Inn, and Palace*), 400 pp. (1-58963-837-9)

(BL 9:303, 61:656; HB 41:57; Kirkus 32:1011; LJ 90:379)

3-159 HAUFF, Wilhelm. *The Fairy Tales of Wilhelm Hauff.* Gr. 5–7. (Orig. pub. in Germany, 1826; orig. U.S. pub. McKay, 1895; Dutton, 1910, entitled *Fairy Tales.*)
Magical adventure tales with an "Arabian Nights" flavor, including "Snout the Dwarf and "The Inn in the Forest."
Trans. by Anthea Bell, illus. by Ulrik Schramm, Abelard-Schuman, 1969, 223 pp., o.p.; Watts, 1971 (entitled *The Big Book of Stories*), 223 pp., o.p.

(BL 66:1045; Kirkus 37:1199; LJ 95:1638; Mahony 1:21; TLS 1969 p. 688)

The Haunted and the Haunters: Tales of Ghosts and Other Apparitions.
Ed. by Kathleen Lines.
See Chapter 4, Ghost Fantasy.

The Haunted House: A Collection of Original Stories. **Ed. by Jane (Hyatt) Yolen (Stemple) and Martin H. Greenberg.**
See Chapter 4, Ghost Fantasy.

Haunting Tales. **Ed. by Barbara Ireson.**
See Chapter 4, Ghost Fantasy.

3-160 HAWTHORNE, Nathaniel. *The Snow Image and Other Twice-Told Tales.*
Gr. 4 up. (Orig. U.S. pub. 1851, 1899.)
A collection of allegorical and supernatural tales.
Illus. by Dorothy P. Lathrop, Macmillan, 1930, 1944 (entitled *The Snow Image*), 69 pp., o.p.; Ohio State University Press, 1974 (entitled *The Snow Image and Uncollected Tales*), 488 pp., o.p.
(Bookshelf 1932 p. 23)

Hecate's Cauldron. **Ed. by Susan M. Shwartz.**
See Chapter 12, Witchcraft and Sorcery Fantasy.

3-161 HESSE, Hermann. *The Fairy Tales of Hermann Hesse.* Gr. 10 up. (Orig. pub. in Germany.)
Twenty-two fairy tales written for adults between 1900 and 1933, exploring the themes of war and peace, self-discovery, and the cycle of life.
Trans. by Jack Zipes, illus. by David Frampton, Bantam, 1995, 304 pp. (0-553-10023-8)
(BL 932:252, 257; Kirkus 63:1131; Kliatt Jan 1996 p. 19; LJ Sep 15, 1995 p. 95)

3-162 HESSE, Hermann. *Pictor's Metamorphoses, and Other Fantasies.* Gr. 10
✯   up. (Orig. German pub. 1923, 1975.)
Nineteen allegorical fairy tales written by the German Nobel laureate between 1900 and 1951, including "Lulu," "The Merman," and "Conversation with the Stove."
Trans. by Rika Lesser, illus. by the author, ed. by Theodore Ziolkowski, Farrar, 1982, 225 pp., o.p.; Picador, pap., 2003, 240 pp. (0-312-42264-4)
(BL 78:537; LJ Jan 1, 1982 p. 108; TLS Sep 10, 1982 p. 965)

3-163 HEWETT, Anita. *The Bull Beneath the Walnut Tree and Other Stories.*
✯   Gr. K–4. (Orig. British pub. 1966.)
Eighteen short tales including "The Singing Witch" and "The Galloping Hedgehog."
Illus. by Imero Gobbato, McGraw-Hill, 1967, 155 pp., o.p.
(BL 64:501; HB 43:588; Kirkus 35:804; LJ 92:3178; TLS 1966 p. 1092)

3-164 *Hidden Turnings: A Collection of Stories Through Time and Space.* **Ed. by**
✯   **Diana Wynne Jones.** Gr. 7–12. (Orig. British pub. 1989.)
Twelve tales about strange occurrences in everyday life, written by Helen Cresswell, Diana Wynne Jones, Tanith Lee, and others.
Greenwillow, 1990, 182 pp., o.p.

(BL 86:1693, 1704; CCBB 43:242; HBG 1:255; Kirkus 58:730; SLJ Aug 1990 p. 148; VOYA 13:296)

3-165 **HOUGH, (Helen) Charlotte (Woodyatt).** *Red Biddy and Other Stories.* Gr.
☆ 4–5. (Orig. British pub. 1966.)
Ten stories about princesses, dragons, giants, witches, and fairies.
Illus. by the author, Coward, 1967, 127 pp., o.p.
(CCBB 22:8; HB 43:463; Kirkus 35:413; LJ 92:2450)

3-166 **HOUSMAN, Laurence.** *A Doorway in Fairyland.* Gr. 4–7. (Orig. pub. in
England.)
Twelve tales from *A Farm in Fairyland* (1894), *The House of Joy* (1895), *The Field of Clover* (1898), and *The Blue Moon* (1904), including "The Bound Princess" and "The Rat-Catcher's Daughter."
Illus. by the author and Clemence Housman, Harcourt, 1905, 1922, 219 pp., o.p.
(BL 20:24; Mahony 2:281)

3-167 **HOUSMAN, Laurence.** *Moonshine and Clover.* Gr. 4–7. (Orig. British pub.
1922.)
Eighteen stories from *A Farm in Fairyland* (1894), *The House of Joy* (1895), *The Field of Clover* (1898), and *The Blue Moon* (1904), including "A Capful of Moonshine" and "The White Doe."
Illus. by the author and Clemence Housman, Harcourt, 1923, 220 pp., o.p.
(BL 20:24; Mahony 2:281)

3-168 **HOUSMAN, Laurence.** *The Rat-Catcher's Daughter: A Collection of Sto-*
☆ *ries.* Gr. 4–7. (Stories orig. pub. in England.)
Twelve tales of princesses, magic, and little people, including "The White Doe" and "The Cloak of Friendship."
Ed. by Ellin Greene, illus. by Julia Noonan, Atheneum, 1974, 169 pp., o.p.
(BL 70:874; HB 50:379; Kirkus 42:244; LJ 99:1451, 1473)

HOWE, Deborah, and HOWE, James. *Teddy Bear's Scrapbook.*
See Chapter 11, Toy Fantasy.

3-169 **HUGHES, Richard (Arthur Warren).** *Don't Blame Me!* Gr. 3–5. (Orig.
British pub. 1940.)
Humorous stories with a touch of the supernatural, including "The Doll and the Mermaid" and "Don't Blame Me."
Illus. by Fritz Eichenberg, Harper, 1940, 159 pp., o.p.
(LJ 65:849, 926; TLS 1940 p. 634)

3-170 **HUGHES, Richard (Arthur Warren).** *The Wonder-Dog: The Collected*
Stories of Richard Hughes. Gr. 4–6. (Stories orig. pub. in England, 1931; U.S., in *The Spider's Palace and Other Stories* [1932, 1960] and in *Don't Blame Me!* [1940, see above].)
Thirty illogical tales about a doll who owns a child, talking animals, and an evil motorbike.
Illus. by Antony Maitland, Greenwillow, 1977, 180 pp., o.p.
(Bookshelf 1932 p. 10; HB 37:53; Kirkus 45:1197; LJ 65:849, 926; Mahony 3:206; SLJ Apr 1978 p. 84; TLS 1931 p. 957, 1940 p. 634, 1977 p. 1273)

HUGHES, Ted (Edward James). *How the Whale Became.*
See Chapter 2, Animal Fantasy.

3-171 **HUGHES, Ted (Edward James).** *Tales of the Early World.* Gr. 4 up. (Orig.
✭ British pub. 1988.)
Ten stories about God's creation of the world's creatures, written by the British
Poet Laureate in a variety of styles ranging from Kiplingesque to Native Amer-
ican myth.
Illus. by Andrew Davidson, Farrar, 1991, 128 pp. (0-374-37377-9)
(BL 87:1646; CCBB 44:240; HBG 2:275; Kirkus 59:248; SLJ May 1991 p. 93; VOYA
14:124)

3-172 **HUNTER, Mollie (pseud. of Maureen Mollie Hunter McVeigh McIl-**
✭ **wraith).** *A Furl of Fairy Wind: Four Stories.* Gr. 2–4. (Orig. British pub.
1986.)
Four Scottish tales involving the fairy world: "The Brownie," "The Enchanted
Boy," "Hi Johnny," and "A Furl of Fairy Wind."
Illus. by Stephen Gammell, Harper, 1977, 58 pp., o.p.
(BL 74:613; CCBB 31:142; HB 54:47; Kirkus 45:1097; SLJ Sep 1977 p. 109; Suth 2:233)

HUNTER, Norman (George Lorimer). *The Incredible Adventures of*
Professor Branestawm.
See Chapter 8, Humorous Fantasy.

Imaginary Lands. **Ed. by Robin McKinley.**
See Chapter 5, High Fantasy: Alternate Worlds or Histories.

3-173 *Imagine That! Fifteen Fantastic Tales.* **Ed. by Sara Corrin and Stephen**
Corrin. Gr. 4–6.
Twelve folktales, plus three original tales written by James Reeves, E. Nesbit,
and William Hauff.
Illus. by Jill Bennett, Faber, 1986, 175 pp., o.p.
(BL 83:648; Kirkus 54:1648; SLJ Apr 1987 p. 93; TLS 1986 p. 1346)

In Celebration of Lammas Night. **Ed. by Josepha Sherman.**
See Chapter 12, Witchcraft and Sorcery Fantasy.

3-174 *Into the Unknown: Eleven Tales of Imagination.* **Ed. by Terry Carr.** Gr.
7–9.
This collection of tales about unusual phenomena includes Ray Bradbury's
"McGillahee's Brat" and Robert Silverberg's "As Is."
Nelson, 1973, 192 pp., o.p.
(BL 70:649, 654; Kirkus 41:691; LJ 99:216)

3-175 *Isaac Asimov Presents the Best Fantasy of the 19th Century.* **Ed. by Isaac**
Asimov, Charles G. Waugh, and Martin H. Greenberg. Gr. 10 up.
Fourteen tales whose authors include Charles Dickens, Washington Irving, Sir
Arthur Conan Doyle, Oscar Wilde, and H. G. Wells.
Beaufort, 1982, 368 pp., o.p.
(LJ 107:2355)

3-176 *Isaac Asimov's Magical Worlds of Fantasy: Faeries.* **Ed. by Isaac Asimov, Martin H. Greenberg, and Charles G. Waugh.** Gr. 10 up.
Eighteen stories about fairies, elves, and visits to fairyland, written by Andre Norton, Poul Anderson, Lord Dunsany, and others.
Penguin, 1991, pap., 374 pp., o.p.
(Kliatt Apr 1992 p. 12; VOYA 14:383)

3-177 **JACQUES, Brian.** *The Ribbajack and Other Curious Yarns.* Gr. 5–8. (Orig. British pub. 2004.)
Six scary and humorous tales with surprising endings, about ghosts, werewolves and naiads.
Philomel, 2004, 176 pp. (0-399-24220-1)
(BL 100:1935; CCBB 57:422; Kirkus 72:395; SLJ May 2004 p. 150; VOYA 27:230)

JACQUES, Brian. *Seven Strange and Ghostly Tales.*
See Chapter 4, Ghost Fantasy.

JEKEL, Pamela. *The Third Jungle Book.*
See Chapter 2, Animal Fantasy.

3-178 **JENNINGS, Paul.** *Unreal! Eight Surprising Stories.* Gr. 4–8. (Orig. Australian pub. 1985.)
Eight humorous and supernatural stories, each told from a boy's point of view, including one about magic underwear that leaves the protagonist naked at school and another about a pair of ghostly lighthouse keepers who scare visitors away. There are six companion volumes: *Uncanny! Even More Surprising Stories* (1991), *Unmentionable! More Amazing Stories* (1993), *Unbelievable! More Surprising Stories* (published in Australia 1992; U.S. 1995), *Unbearable! More Bizarre Stories* (1995), *Undone! More Mad Endings* (1995), and *Uncovered! Weird, Weird Stories* (1996).
Viking, 1991, 112 pp. (0-670-84175-7); Puffin, 1993, pap. (0-14-034910-3)
(BL 87:2147; CCBB 45:13; HBG 3:67; Kirkus 59:1344; SLJ Dec 1991 p. 117)

3-179 **JONES, Diana Wynne.** *Believing Is Seeing: Seven Stories.* Gr. 6–12. (Orig. British pub. 1999.)
Seven fantasy stories, including "Dragon Reserve, Home Eight," "What the Cat Told Me," and "The Sage of Theare."
Greenwillow, 1999, 165 pp. (0-688-16843-4)
(BL 96:614; HBG 11:95; Kirkus 67:1644)

JONES, Diana Wynne. *Mixed Magics: Four Tales of Chrestomanci.*
See Chapter 12, Witchcraft and Sorcery Fantasy.

JONES, Diana Wynne. *Stopping for a Spell: Three Fantasies.*
See Chapter 9, Magic Adventure Fantasy.

3-180 **JONES, Diana Wynne.** *Unexpected Magic: Collected Stories.* Gr. 5–12.
✶ A collection of 15 magical stories, including "Dragon Reserve, Home Eight" and "The Green Stone," as well as a novella, "Everard's Ride."
HarperCollins, 2004, 504 pp. (0-06-055534-3)
(BL 100:1450; CCBB 57:423; Kirkus 72:395; SLJ Sep 2004 p. 209; VOYA 27:60)

JONES, Diana Wynne. *Warlock at the Wheel and Other Stories.*
See Chapter 12, Witchcraft and Sorcery Fantasy.

JONES, Louis C(lark). *Things That Go Bump in the Night.*
See Chapter 4, Ghost Fantasy.

JONES, Terry. *Fairy Tales.*
See Chapter 8, Humorous Fantasy.

JONES, Terry. *Fantastic Stories.*
See Chapter 8, Humorous Fantasy.

3-181 **JUSTER, Norton.** *Alberic the Wise and Other Journeys.* Gr. 4–8.
☆   Three tales, about a hero searching for wisdom, a boy who enters a painting, and two kings searching for happiness.
Illus. by Domenico Gnoli, Pantheon, 1965, 67 pp., o.p.; illus. by Leonard Baskin, Picture Book Studio, 1992, 28 pp., o.p.
(BL 89:908; CCBB 19:150, 46:180; HB 42:54, 69:231; HBG 4:71; Kirkus 60:1504; LJ 91:1064; SLJ Mar 1993 p. 198)

3-182 **KELLER, Gottfried.** *The Fat of the Cat and Other Stories.* Gr. 4–6. (Orig.
☆   pub. in Switzerland.)
Adaptations of Swiss legends and folktales about animals and witches.
Adapt. by Louis Untermeyer, illus. by Albert Sallak, Harcourt, 1925, 283 pp., o.p.
(BL 22:122; Bookshelf 1928 p. 10; HB 2:20; LJ 51:836; Mahony 2:198; Moore:435)

3-183 **KENNEDY, (Jerome) Richard.** *Richard Kennedy: Collected Stories.* Gr.
☆   4–9.
Sixteen stories originally published separately, including "The Porcelain Man," "The Leprechaun's Story," and "The Dark Princess."
Illus. by Marcia Sewall, Harper, 1987, 274 pp. (0-06-023256-0)
(BL 84:625, 635; HB 64:359; Kirkus 55:1629; SLJ Nov 1987 p. 105; VOYA 10:235)

KING-SMITH, Dick. *Animal Stories.*
See Chapter 2, Animal Fantasy.

KING-SMITH, Dick. *Hogsel and Gruntel and Other Animal Stories.*
See Chapter 6, High Fantasy: Myth or Legend Fantasy.

Kingdoms of Sorcery. **Ed. by Lin Carter.**
See Chapter 5, High Fantasy: Alternate Worlds or Histories.

KIPLING, (Joseph) Rudyard. *All the Mowgli Stories.*
See Chapter 2, Animal Fantasy.

KIPLING, (Joseph) Rudyard. *The Jungle Book.*
See Chapter 2, Animal Fantasy.

KIPLING, (Joseph) Rudyard. *Just So Stories.*
See Chapter 2, Animal Fantasy.

3-184 KIPLING, (Joseph) Rudyard. *Kipling's Fantasy: Stories by Rudyard Kipling.* Gr. 6–12.
Twelve fantasy and horror stories, many of which involve Indian mythology. Ed. by John Bruner, Tor, 1992, 224 pp., o.p., 1993, pap. (entitled *Kipling's Fantasy Stories*), o.p.; Tor, pap., 2005, 224 pp. (entitled *Kipling's Fantasy Stories*) (0-8125-2002-5)
(BL 89:402, 412; VOYA 16:41, 17:8)

KIPLING, (Joseph) Rudyard. *Phantoms and Fantasies: Twenty Tales.*
See Chapter 4, Ghost Fantasy.

Knight Fantastic. **Ed. by Martin H. Greenberg and John Helfers.**
See Chapter 6, High Fantasy: Myth or Legend Fantasy.

3-185 KOTZWINKLE, William. *Hearts of Wood: And Other Timeless Tales.* Gr. 4–6.
Five original fairy tales, including stories about carousel animals that come to life, a man who becomes a butterfly, and a woodsman who becomes King of the Fairies. Four of these tales were originally published as *The Oldest Man and Other Timeless Stories* (Pantheon, 1971).
Illus. by Joe Servello, Godine, 1986, 128 pp., o.p.
(CCBB 26:27, 40:129; Kirkus 39:1013; LJ 97:1914; SLJ May 1987 p. 101)

3-186 KRENSKY, Stephen (Alan). *Castles in the Air and Other Tales.* Gr. 4–6.
Five humorous fairy tales based on familiar phrases: "Castles in the Air," "A Fine Kettle of Fish," "The Last Straw," "Too Clever for Words," and "A Barrel of Fun."
Illus. by Warren Lieberman, Macmillan, 1979, 66 pp., o.p.
(CCBB 33:50; Kirkus 47:637; SLJ Sep 1979 p. 142)

KRENSKY, Stephen (Alan). *Woodland Crossings.*
See Chapter 2, Animal Fantasy.

KRÜSS, James (Jacob Heinrich). *Eagle and Dove.*
See Chapter 2, Animal Fantasy.

3-187 LACKEY, Mercedes. *Fiddler Fair.* Gr. 7–12.
Twelve short stories, including "Cup and Cauldron," "Dragon's Teeth," and "Fiddler Fair," the story that begins the author's Bardic Voices series (see *The Lark and the Wren* in Chapter 5, High Fantasy: Alternate Worlds or Histories).
Baen, 1998, pap., 260 pp. (0-671-87866-2)
(Kliatt Sep 1998 p. 28; VOYA 21:284, 22:14)

3-188 LANG, Andrew. *My Own Fairy Book.* Gr. 5–7. (Orig. British and U.S. pub. 1895, o.p.)
This story collection contains "Prince Prigio," "Prince Ricardo," and "The Gold of Fairnilee."
Illus. by Gertrude A. Kay, McKay, 1927, 402 pp.
(BL 24:75)

LEACH, Maria. *The Thing at the Foot of the Bed and Other Scary Tales.*
See Chapter 4, Ghost Fantasy.

3-189 **LEAMY, Edmund.** *The Fairy Minstrel of Glenmalure: And Other Stories for Children.* Gr. 3–5. (Orig. pub. Warne, 1913.)
Three fanciful tales set in Ireland.
Fitzgerald, 1913, o.p.; illus. by Vera Casseau, Roth, 1976, 92 pp., o.p.
(BL 27:216, 34:271; HB 14:106; Mahony 1:22)

3-190 **LEAMY, Edmund.** *The Golden Spears and Other Fairy Tales.* Gr. 3–5. (Orig. pub. 1890, entitled *Irish Fairy Tales, a Collection of Seven Fairy Tales*.)
Seven tales set in Ireland, including "The Enchanted Cave," "The Fairy Tree of Dooros," and "Princess Finola and the Dwarf."
Fitzgerald, 1911, 1930, o.p.; illus. by Corinne Turner, Roth, 1976, 180 pp., o.p.
(BL 8:278, 27:216, 35:33; HB 10:299; LJ 63:798; Mahony 3:206)

3-191 **LEBERMANN, Norbert.** *New German Fairy Tales.* Gr. 3–6. (Orig. pub. in Germany.)
A combination of traditional and modern tales, including one about an inventor-hero who conquers the goblins of electricity and steam.
Illus. by Margaret Freeman, Knopf, 1930, 247 pp., o.p.
(HB 6:331; LJ 55:1023; Mahony 3:206)

3-192 **LEE, Tanith.** *Dreams of Dark and Light: The Great Short Fiction of Tanith Lee.* Gr. 10 up.
Twenty-three previously published tales written between 1977 and 1984, including "Because Our Skins Are Finer," "Tamastara," and "The Gorgon."
Arkham, 1986, 507 pp., o.p.
(BL 82:1667; Kirkus 54:978; VOYA 9:164, 10:22)

3-193 **LEE, Tanith.** *Princess Hynchatti and Some Other Surprises.* Gr. 4–6. (Orig. ✫ British pub. 1972.)
A collection of 12 humorous fairy tales, including one about a prince who accidentally falls in love with a witch and another about a beautiful swan who is transformed into an awkward, yellow-eyed princess.
Illus. by Velma Ilsley, Farrar, 1973, 183 pp., o.p.
(BL 69:1021; HB 69:948; Kirkus 41:457; LJ 98:2195; TLS 1972 p. 1332)

LEE, Tanith. *Red as Blood; or Tales from the Sisters Grimmer.*
See Chapter 6, High Fantasy: Myth or Legend Fantasy.

LEE, Tanith. *Tamastara; or the Indian Nights.*
See Chapter 6, High Fantasy: Myth or Legend Fantasy.

3-194 *Legends: Stories by the Masters of Modern Fantasy.* **Ed. by Robert Silver-** ✫ **berg.** Gr. 10 up.
Eleven novellas by well-known modern fantasy writers including Ursula K. Le Guin, Anne McCaffrey, Orson Scott Card, Robert Jordan, Terry Pratchett, Robert Silverberg, Raymond Feist, and Stephen King. The companion volumes are *Legends II* (1998, 1999, 2004), and *Legends III: New Short Novels by the Masters of Modern Fantasy* (1998, 2000, 2004).
Tor, 1998, 608 pp. (0-312-86787-5), 2001, pap., 720 pp. (0-765-30035-4)
(BL 94:1924, 95:781, 1401, 1678; Kirkus 66:1076; LJ Oct 15, 1998 p. 103; VOYA 22:14, 48)

LE GUIN, Ursula K(roeber). *Buffalo Gals and Other Animal Presences.*
See Chapter 2, Animal Fantasy.

3-195 **LE GUIN, Ursula K(roeber).** *The Wind's Twelve Quarters: Short Stories.*
✮   Gr. 8 up.
Seventeen stories of fantasy and science fiction, including "Winter's King" and
"The Day Before the Revolution."
Harper, 1975, 303 pp., o.p.
(BL 72:615; Kirkus 43:942; LJ 100:1950; SLJ Mar 1976 p. 120; TLS 1976 p. 950)

Liavek. **Ed. by Will Shetterly and Emma Bull.**
See Chapter 5, High Fantasy: Alternate Worlds or Histories.

3-196 *The Lifted Veil: The Book of Fantastic Literature by Women, 1800–World
War II.* **Ed. by A. Susan Williams.** Gr. 10 up. (Orig. British pub. 1992.)
An anthology of stories from Britain, America, Australia, Ireland, Canada,
South Africa, India, the West Indies, and New Zealand, written by women
between 1806 and 1992.
Carroll & Graf, 1992, 952 pp., o.p.
(BL 89:579, 586; LJ Nov 1, 1992, p. 120; TLS Dec 18, 1992 p. 17)

3-197 *Listen to This.* **Ed. by Laura Cecil.** Gr. K–4. (Orig. British pub. 1987.)
A collection, meant to be read aloud, of familiar folktales plus stories by Mar-
garet Mahy, Rudyard Kipling, and Philippa Pearce, with lively watercolor illus-
trations.
Illus. by Emma Chichester Clark, Greenwillow, 1988, 92 pp., o.p.
(BL 84:1183; Kirkus 56:198; SLJ June 1988 p. 84; TLS 1987 p. 1361)

The Literary Ghost: Great Contemporary Ghost Stories. **Ed. by Larry
Dark.**
See Chapter 4, Ghost Fantasy.

LIVELY, Penelope (Margaret Low). *Uninvited Ghosts and Other Stories.*
See Chapter 8, Humorous Fantasy.

The Lonely Little Pig and Other Animal Tales. **Ed. by Wilhelmina Harper.**
See Chapter 2, Animal Fantasy.

3-198 *The Lost Half-Hour: A Collection of Stories.* **Ed. by Eulalie Steinmetz
Ross.** Gr. 4–6.
Stories by Rudyard Kipling, Ruth Sawyer, Howard Pyle, Barbara Freeman,
Oscar Wilde, Kate Seredy, and others.
Illus. by Enrico Arno, Harcourt, 1963, 191 pp., o.p.
(BL 60:210; HB 39:604; LJ 88:4088)

Lost Worlds, Unknown Horizons: Nine Stories of Science Fiction. **Ed. by
Robert Silverberg.**
See Chapter 7, High Fantasy: Travel to Other Worlds.

LURIE, Alison. *Women and Ghosts.*
See Chapter 4, Ghost Fantasy.

3-199 LYNN, Elizabeth A. *The Woman Who Loved the Moon, and Other Stories.*
Gr. 10 up.
This collection of 16 fantasy and horror short stories includes "Wizard's Domain" and "The Woman Who Loved the Moon," which won a World Fantasy Award in 1980.
Berkley, 1981, pap., 197 pp., o.p.
(BL 78:427, 435; Kliatt 16:22, VOYA 4:39)

3-200 McCAFFREY, Anne (Inez). *The Girl Who Heard Dragons.* Gr. 7–12.
✮ Fifteen fantasy and science fiction stories, including a novella set in Pern and two time-travel stories, "A Flock of Geese" and "The Bones Do Lie."
Tor, 1994, 352 pp. (0-312-93173-5), 1995, pap., 416 pp. (0-8125-1099-2)
(BL 90:1301; Kirkus 62:349; LJ May 15, 1994 p. 103; VOYA 17:224, 18:9)

3-201 MacDONALD, George. *The Complete Fairy Tales of George MacDonald.*
✮ Gr. 4–8. (Orig. pub. in England; orig. U.S. pub. 1893, entitled *The Light Princess and Other Fairy Tales.*)
Eight tales, including "The Light Princess," "The Giant's Heart," "The Golden Key," and "The Day Boy and the Night Girl."
Illus. by Arthur Hughes, Watts, 1961 (entitled *The Light Princess and Other Tales, Being the Complete Fairy Stories of George MacDonald*), 288 pp., o.p.; illus. by Arthur Hughes, Schocken, 1979, o.p.; Penguin, 1999, pap., 254 pp. (0-14-043737-1)
(BL 58:446, 74:1014; CCBB 32:196; HB 38:177, 55:441)

3-202 McKINLEY, (Jennifer Carolyn) Robin (Turrell). *The Door in the Hedge.*
Gr. 5–7.
Two original tales, "The Hunting of the Hind" and "The Stolen Princess," and two traditional folktales, "The Princess and the Frog" and "The Twelve Dancing Princesses."
Greenwillow, 1981, 1996, 216 pp., o.p.; Firebird/Penguin, 2004, pap., 216 pp. (0-698-11960-6)
(BL 77:810; CCBB 35:33; HB 57:433; HBG 7:303; Kirkus 49:876; SLJ Aug 1981 p. 77)

McKINLEY, (Jennifer Carolyn) Robin (Turrell). *A Knot in the Grain and Other Stories.*
See Chapter 5, High Fantasy: Alternate Worlds or Histories.

McKINLEY, (Jennifer Carolyn) Robin (Turrell), and DICKINSON, Peter. *Water: Tales of the Elemental Spirits.*
See Chapter 5, High Fantasy: Alternate Worlds or Histories.

McKISSACK, Patricia C(arwell). *The Dark-Thirty: Southern Tales of the Supernatural.*
See Chapter 4, Ghost Fantasy.

3-203 MACOUREK, Miloš. *Curious Tales.* Gr. 3–5. (Orig. Czech pubs. 1966, 1971.)
Fourteen imaginative tales, including three about a turkey-eating plant, an alarm clock revolt, and an operatic kitchen sink.

Trans. by Marie Burg, illus. by Adolf Born, Oxford University Press, 1980, 88 pp., o.p.
(BL77:45; SLJ Sep 1981 p. 111; TLS Nov 21, 1980 p. 1325)

Magic in Ithkar. **Ed. by Andre Norton and Robert Adams.**
See Chapter 5, High Fantasy: Alternate Worlds or Histories.

Magicats! **Ed. by Jack Dann and Gardner Dozois.**
See Chapter 2, Animal Fantasy.

MAGUIRE, Gregory. *Leaping Beauty: And Other Animal Fairy Tales.*
See Chapter 8, Humorous Fantasy.

MAHY, Margaret (May). *Bubble Trouble and Other Poems and Stories.*
See Chapter 8, Humorous Fantasy.

MAHY, Margaret (May). *The Chewing-Gum Rescue and Other Stories.*
See Chapter 8, Humorous Fantasy.

MAHY, Margaret (May). *The Door in the Air and Other Stories.*
See Chapter 9, Magic Adventure Fantasy.

MAHY, Margaret (May). *The Girl with the Green Ear: Stories About Magic in Nature.*
See Chapter 9, Magic Adventure Fantasy.

MAHY, Margaret (May). *Nonstop Nonsense.*
See Chapter 8, Humorous Fantasy.

MAHY, Margaret (May). *A Tall Story and Other Tales.*
See Chapter 9, Magic Adventure Fantasy.

MAHY, Margaret (May). *Tick Tock Tales: Twelve Stories to Read Around the Clock.*
See Chapter 8, Humorous Fantasy.

MAMIN-SIBERIAK. *Verotchka's Tales.*
See Chapter 2, Animal Fantasy.

3-204 *The Mammoth Book of Fantasy.* **Ed. by Michael Ashley.** Gr. 10 up.
An anthology of 23 fantasy tales by Victorian to contemporary authors, including George MacDonald, Lord Dunsany, Ursula K. Le Guin, Charles de Lint, and Patricia A. McKillip.
Carroll, 2001, pap., 512 pp. (0-7867-0917-0)
(BL 98:306; Kirkus 69:1252)

MANLEY, Seon. *The Ghost in the Far Garden and Other Stories.*
See Chapter 4, Ghost Fantasy.

MARSHALL, James (Edward). *Rats on the Roof and Other Stories.*
See Chapter 2, Talking Animal Fantasy.

3-205 *Masterpieces of Fantasy and Enchantment.* **Comp. by David G. Hartwell and Kathryn Cramer.** Gr. 10 up.

This collection includes tales written both before and after Tolkien's work appeared, including excerpts and stories by Charles Dickens, Nathaniel Hawthorne, Ursula K. Le Guin, and Michael Moorcock.
St. Martin's, 1988, 622 pp., o.p.
(BL 84:1984, 1915; VOYA 12:44)

3-206 *Masterpieces of Fantasy and Wonder*. Ed. by David G. Hartwell and Kathryn Cramer. Gr. 7–12.
Fantasy stories for children and adults by well-known writers including E. Nesbit, L. Frank Baum, Robin McKinley, E. T. A. Hoffmann, Charles Dickens, Mark Twain, and Isaac Bashevis Singer.
St. Martin's 1994, 656 pp. (0-312-11024-3)
(BL 90:1780, 1787; VOYA 17:158)

***Masters of Shades and Shadows: An Anthology of Great Ghost Stories*. Ed. by Seon Manley and Gogo Lewis.**
See Chapter 4, Ghost Fantasy.

MAYNE, William (James Carter). *The Green Book of Hob Stories*.
See Chapter 9, Magic Adventure Fantasy.

3-207 MAZER, Anne. *A Sliver of Glass and Other Uncommon Tales*. Gr. 5–8.
Eleven fantasy and horror short stories, including imaginative retellings of traditional tales about King Midas, "The Princess and the Pea," and "The Wild Swans."
Hyperion, 1996, 70 pp. (0-7868-0197-2)
(BL 93:242; CCBB 50:107; HBG 8:71; Kirkus 64:1404; SLJ Feb 1997 p. 104)

3-208 MEIGS, Cornelia (Lynde). *The Kingdom of the Winding Road*. Gr. 5–7.
Twelve tales in which the same wandering man with bright blue eyes plays on his silver pipe, summoning those he meets to adventure before he vanishes down the winding road.
Illus. by Frances White, Macmillan, 1915, 238 pp., o.p.
(BL 12:296; Bookshelf 1920–1921 p. 15; HB 7:117)

MENDOZA, George. *Gwot! Horribly Funny Hairticklers*.
See Chapter 8, Humorous Fantasy.

***Merlin*. Ed. by Martin H. Greenberg.**
See Chapter 6, High Fantasy: Myth or Legend Fantasy.

***The Merlin Chronicles*. Ed. by Mike Ashley.**
See Chapter 6, High Fantasy: Myth or Legend Fantasy.

MEYER, Zoe. *The Little Green Door*.
See Chapter 1, Allegorical Fantasy and Literary Fairy Tales.

MILNE, A(lan) A(lexander). *Prince Rabbit and the Princess Who Could Not Laugh*.
See Chapter 1, Allegorical Fantasy and Literary Fairy Tales.

MITTON, Tony. *A Tale of Tales*.
See Chapter 2, Animal Fantasy.

3-209 *Modern Classics of Fantasy.* **Ed. by Gardner Dozois.** Gr. 10 up.
Thirty-two American fantasy tales written between 1939 and 1996 by authors
including Ursula K. Le Guin, Tanith Lee, Suzy McKee Charnas, L. Sprague de
Camp, and Judith Tarr.
St. Martin's, 1997, 688 pp. (0-312-15173-X)
(BL 93:643; LJ Dec 1996 p. 152)

3-210 *Modern Fairy Stories.* **Ed. by Roger (Gilbert) Lancelyn Green.** Gr. 5–7.
(Orig. British pub. 1955.)
Sixteen stories written by such authors as Lewis Carroll, Juliana Horatia
Ewing, Andrew Lang, Mary Louise Molesworth, Oscar Wilde, E. Nesbit, and
John Ruskin.
Illus. by Ernest H. Shepard, Dutton, 1956, 270 pp., o.p.
(BL 52:369; HB 30:121)

Modern Ghost Stories by Eminent Women Writers. **Ed. by Richard Dalby.**
See Chapter 4, Ghost Fantasy.

3-211 **MOLESWORTH, Mary Louisa (Stewart).** *Fairy Stories.* Gr. 4–6. (Orig.
pub. in England.)
Eight tales of magic and enchantment, including "The Reel Fairies" and "The
Weather Maiden."
Ed. by Roger (Gilbert) Lancelyn Green, Roy, 1958, 159 pp., o.p.
(BL 19:95; HB 34:478; Kirkus 26:659; LJ 83:3002; Mahony 2:291)

3-212 **MOLESWORTH, Mary Louisa (Stewart).** *Stories by Mrs. Molesworth.*
Comp. by Sidney Baldwin. Gr. 4–6. (Orig. pub. in England.)
Nine tales, including "The Cuckoo Clock," "Six Poor Princesses," "The Reel
Fairies," and "Blue Dwarfs."
Illus. by Edna Cooke, Duffield, 1922, 353 pp., o.p.
(BL 19:95; Mahony 2:292)

3-213 *Monsters, Ghoulies and Creepy Creatures: Fantastic Stories and Poems.*
Comp. by Lee Bennett Hopkins. Gr. 4–6.
Stories by Natalie Babbitt, John Gardner, Natalie Savage Carlson, Tom
McGowen, and Lee Bennett Hopkins, about devils, dragons, monsters, and
demons.
Illus. by Vera Rosenberry, Whitman, 1977, 128 pp., o.p.
(BL 74:1110; CCBB 31:178)

3-214 **MONTROSE, Anne.** *The Winter Flower, and Other Fairy Stories.* Gr. 4–6.
Thirteen tales of princesses, magic, witches, and a dragon.
Illus. by Mircea Vasiliu, Viking, 1964, 143 pp., o.p.
(HB 40:611; LJ 89:4642)

3-215 *Moonsinger's Friends: In Honor of Andre Norton.* **Ed. by Susan M.**
✶ **Shwartz.** Gr. 10 up.
Fourteen fantasy tales by such well-known authors as Marion Zimmer Bradley,
C. J. Cherryh, Katherine Kurtz, Tanith Lee, Anne McCaffrey, Nancy Springer,
and Jane Yolen.
Bluejay, 1985, 342 pp., o.p.
(BL 81:1637, 1657; Kirkus 53:561; LJ Aug 1985 p. 121; SLJ Nov 1985 p. 106; VOYA 8:326)

3-216   MORRIS, Kenneth. *The Dragon Path: Collected Tales of Kenneth Morris.*
Gr. 10 up.
Thirteen fantasy tales, including "A Mermaid's Tragedy" and "The Last
Adventure of Don Quixote."
Tor, 1995, 384 pp. (0-312-85309-2)
(BL 91:1180; LJ Feb 15, 1995 p. 186)

MÜNCHAUSEN, Karl. *The Adventures of Baron Münchausen.*
See Chapter 8, Humorous Fantasy.

3-217   MURPHY, Pat. *Points of Departure.* Gr. 10 up.
Nineteen powerful fantasy and science fiction stories, many of them about
lonely women who escape from abusive relationships, including one about time
travel ("Orange Blossom Time"), two about selkies ("Sweetly the Waves Call
to Me" and "In the Islands"), and one about a witch's black magic ("With Four
Hounds").
Bantam, 1990, 336 pp., o.p.
(BL 86:2077, 2083; VOYA 14:46, 15:10)

3-218   NESBIT (Bland), E(dith). *The Complete Book of Dragons.* Gr. 4–6. (Writ-
★   ten in England, 1899, orig. U.S. pub. 1901, entitled *The Book of Dragons.*)
Nine tales about children confronting dragons, including "The Ice Dragon,"
"The Dragon Tamers," and "The Last of the Dragons."
Illus. by Erik Blegvad, Macmillan, 1973, 198 pp., o.p.; Seastar, 2001, 256 pp.
(1-58717-105-8), pap. (1-58717-106-6), entitled *The Book of Dragons*;
abridged version entitled *The Book of Beasts*, illus. by Inga Moore, 64 pp., Candlewick, 2001 (0-7636-1579-X)
(BL 69:911; CCBB 26:142; HB 49:272; HBG 13:90; Kirkus 41:6; LJ 26:167; SLJ Dec 2001 p.
108)

3-219 *New Magics: An Anthology of Today's Fantasy.* **Ed. by Patrick Nielsen
Hayden.** Gr. 6–12.
Twelve contemporary fantasy tales whose authors include Robin McKinley,
Ursula K. Le Guin, Neil Gaiman, Charles de Lint, Jane Yolen, Orson Scott
Card, Sherwood Smith, and Ellen Kushner.
Tor, 2004, 256 pp. (0-765-30015-X)
(LJ Jan 2004 p. 168; VOYA 27:232)

The New Young Oxford Book of Ghost Stories. **Comp. by Dennis Pepper.**
See Chapter 4, Ghost Fantasy.

Nightshade: Twentieth Century Ghost Stories. **Ed. by Robert Phillips.**
See Chapter 4, Ghost Fantasy.

NIXON, Joan Lowery. *Ghost Town: Seven Ghostly Stories.*
See Chapter 4, Ghost Fantasy.

3-220   NORTON, Andre (pseud. of Alice Mary Norton). *Moon Mirror.* Gr. 10 up.
These nine stories include one from Norton's Witch World saga (see Chapter 7,
High Fantasy: Travel to Other Worlds) and two reworkings of traditional fairy
tales.

Tor, 1988, 250 pp., o.p.
(BL 85:754, 780; Kirkus 56:1646; VOYA 12:116, 13:258)

NORTON, Andre (pseud. of Alice Mary Norton). *Wizards' Worlds.*
See Chapter 12, Witchcraft and Sorcery Fantasy.

3-221 NYE, Robert. *The Mathematical Princess and Other Stories.* Gr. 4–6.
(Orig. British pub, 1971, entitled *Poor Pumpkin.*)
Six stories, including the tale of a princess who puts all of her suitors to sleep
with her lectures on Euclid.
Illus. by Paul Bruner, Hill, 1972, 125 pp., o.p.
(HB 48:468; Kirkus 40:673; LJ 98:646)

3-222 *On Crusade: More Tales of the Knights Templar.* **Ed. by Katherine Kurtz.**
(The Knights Templar series, bk. 2). Gr. 12 up.
Ten historical fantasy stories about the Knights Templar, warrior-monk cru-
saders, written by Andre Norton, Deborah Turner Harris, Diane Duane, Kather-
ine Kurtz, and others. The first book in the series is *Tales of the Knights
Templar* (1995), and the third is *Crusade of Fire: Mystical Tales of the Knights
Templar* (2002). Kurtz and Deborah Harris have also written a series of novels
about the Knights Templar, beginning with *The Temple and the Stone* (1998;
see Chapter 5, High Fantasy: Alternate Worlds or Histories).
Warner, 1998, 256 pp. (0-446-67339-0)
(Kirkus 666:452; Kliatt July 1998 p. 20; VOYA 21:370)

3-223 *Once Upon a Time: A Treasury of Modern Fairy Tales.* **Ed. by Lester Del
Rey and Risa Kessler.** Gr. 10 up.
Ten tales written by Anne McCaffrey, Barbara Hambly, C. J. Cherryh, Kather-
ine Kurtz, and other contemporary authors of fantasy.
Illus. by Michael Pangrazio, Ballantine, 1991, 352 pp. (0-345-36263-2)
(BL 88:608, 611; Kirkus 59:1122; LJ Oct 15 1991 p. 127)

3-224 *100 Great Fantasy Short Stories.* **Ed. by Isaac Asimov, Terry Carr, and
Martin H. Greenberg.** Gr. 10 up.
The stories included here were written by Roger Zelazny, Gene Wolfe, and
Marion Zimmer Bradley, among others.
Doubleday, 1984, 311 pp., o.p.
(Kirkus 52:114; LJ 109:600; TLS 1984 p. 1359; VOYA 7:207)

Orphans of the Night. **Ed. by Josepha Sherman.**
See Chapter 6, High Fantasy: Myth or Legend Fantasy.

OSBORNE, Mary Pope. *Favorite Medieval Tales.*
See Chapter 6, High Fantasy: Myth or Legend Fantasy.

The Other Side of the Clock: Stories Out of Time, Out of Place. **Ed. by
Philip Van Doren Stern.**
See Chapter 10, Time Travel Fantasy.

Out of Avalon: An Anthology of the Old Magic and New Myths. **Ed. by
Jennifer Roberson.**
See Chapter 6, High Fantasy: Myth or Legend Fantasy.

3-225 *The Oxford Book of Fantasy Stories.* **Ed. by Tom Shippey.** Gr. 10 up. (Orig. British pub. 1994.)
A collection of tales written between 1888 and 1992 whose authors include Lord Dunsany and Poul Anderson.
Oxford University Press, 1994, 497 pp. (0-19-214216-X)
(BL 90:1333, 1338; TLS Mar 11, 1994 p. 24)

3-226 *The Oxford Book of Modern Fairy Tales.* **Ed. by Alison Lurie.** Gr. 10 up. (Orig. British pub. 1993.)
An anthology of fantasy short stories written for children and adults by such renowned British and American authors as Joan Aiken, L. Frank Baum, Charles Dickens, Nathaniel Hawthorne, Richard Hughes, Ursula K. Le Guin, E. Nesbit, Isaac Bashevis Singer, James Thurber, Oscar Wilde, and Jay Williams.
Oxford University Press, 1993, 480 pp. (0-19-214218-6)
(BL 89:1572, 1576; TLS July 30, 1993 p. 7)

PAINE, Albert Bigelow. *The Hollow Tree and Deep Woods Book.*
See Chapter 2, Animal Fantasy.

PARK, (Rosina) Ruth (Lucia). *Things in Corners.*
See Chapter 4, Ghost Fantasy.

3-227 **PARRISH, Anne, and PARRISH, Dillwyn.** *The Dream Coach.* Gr. 3–5.
Each night a dream coach travels across the sky, leaving dream stories along its way. John Newbery Medal Honor Book, 1925.
Illus. by the authors, Macmillan, 1924, 143 pp., o.p.
(BL 21:158; HB 1:12, 7:61–67)

PATNEAUDE, David. *Dark Starry Morning: Stories of This World and Beyond.*
See Chapter 4, Ghost Fantasy.

PEARCE, (Ann) Philippa. *Familiar and Haunting: Collected Stories.*
See Chapter 4, Ghost Fantasy.

PEARCE, (Ann) Philippa. *Lion at School: And Other Stories.*
See Chapter 9, Magic Adventure Fantasy.

PEARCE, (Ann) Philippa. *The Shadow-Cage and Other Tales of the Supernatural.*
See Chapter 4, Ghost Fantasy.

PEARCE, (Ann) Philippa. *Who's Afraid? And Other Strange Stories.*
See Chapter 4, Ghost Fantasy.

The Pendragon Chronicles: Heroic Fantasy from the Time of King Arthur. **Ed. by Mike Ashley.**
See Chapter 6, High Fantasy: Myth or Legend Fantasy.

3-228 *The Penguin Book of Modern Fantasy by Women.* **Ed. by A. Susan Williams and Richard Glyn Jones.** Gr. 10 up.
Thirty-eight fantasy short stories written after 1940 whose authors include Ursula K. Le Guin, Kate Wilhelm, and Joanna Russ.

Viking, 1995, 576 pp. (0-670-85907-9)
(BL 92:145, 148; TLS June 30, 1995 p. 23)

3-229 *Peter S. Beagle's Immortal Unicorn.* **Ed. by Peter S. Beagle and Janet Berliner.** Gr. 10 up.
An anthology of unicorn stories written by Judith Tarr, Charles de Lint, and Ellen Kushner, among others.
Harper, 1995, pap., 528 pp. (0-06-105224-8); HarperPrism, 1998, pap., 398 pp. (0-06-105480-1)
(BL 92:389, 392; VOYA 19:42)

3-230 *Phantasmagoria: Tales of Fantasy and the Supernatural.* **Ed. by Jane Mobley.** Gr. 10 up.
An anthology of English and American fantastic and supernatural tales whose authors include Lord Dunsany, George MacDonald, Ursula K. Le Guin, Andre Norton, and Peter Beagle.
Doubleday, 1977, pap., 439 pp., o.p.
(BL 74:463, 470; Kliatt 12:14)

3-231 *Phoenix Feathers: A Collection of Mythical Monsters.* **Ed. by Barbara Silverberg.** Gr. 6–10.
Tales of dragons, griffins, unicorns, and the phoenix.
Illus. with old prints, Dutton, 1973, 206 pp., o.p.
(BL 70:737; Kirkus 41:820; LJ 98:3457)

The Phoenix Tree: An Anthology of Myth Fantasy. **Ed. by Robert H. Boyer and Kenneth J. Zahorski.**
See Chapter 6, High Fantasy: Myth or Legend Fantasy.

3-232 **PICARD, Barbara Leonie.** *The Faun and the Woodcutter's Daughter.* Gr.
✫   5–7. (Orig. British pub. 1951.)
This collection of 14 fairy tales begins with the story of a woodcutter's daughter who meets a faun in the woods and cannot live without him.
Illus. by Charles Stewart, Abelard-Schuman, 1964, 255 pp., o.p.
(BL 61:436; CCBB 18:168; Eakin:261; HB 41:57; LJ 89:5010)

3-233 **PICARD, Barbara Leonie.** *The Goldfinch Garden: Seven Tales.* Gr. 4–6.
✫   (Orig. British pub. 1963.)
Seven original fairy tales about mortals who become involved with a witch, a water sprite, a fairy maiden, and other creatures.
Illus. by Anne Linton, Criterion, 1965, 121 pp., o.p.
(BL 62:532; HB 42:55; Kirkus 33:1042)

3-234 **PICARD, Barbara Leonie.** *The Lady of the Linden Tree.* Gr. 5–7. (Orig.
✫   British pub. 1954.)
Twelve tales of knights, princes, princesses, and enchantment, including "Findings Are Keepings," "The Castle in the Cornfield," and "The Piper with the Hoofs of a Goat." Carnegie Medal Commended Book, 1954.
Illus. by Charles Stewart, Criterion, 1962, 214 pp., o.p.
(BL 58:694; CCBB 16:14; Eakin:261; HB 38:276; Kirkus 30:176; LJ 87:2027)

3-235 PICARD, Barbara Leonie. *The Mermaid and the Simpleton.* Gr. 5–7.
☆ (Orig. British pub. 1949.)
Fifteen tales of princesses, witches, and magic, including "Heart of the Wind," "The Ivory Box," and "Three Wishes."
Illus. by Philip Gough, Criterion, 1970, 253 pp., o.p.
(BL 47:225, 67:150; CCBB 4:15; HB 26:488; Kirkus 18:642, 38:454; LJ 16:55, 95:2535, 4326)

3-236 PIERCE, Meredith Ann. *Waters Luminous and Deep: Shorter Fictions.*
☆ Gr. 6–10.
Seven fantasy tales with a variety of connections to water, including "The Sea Hag," "Icerose," "The Fall of Ys," and "The Frogskin Slippers."
Viking, 2004, 256 pp. (0-670-03687-0)
(BL 100:1450; CCBB 57:387; Kirkus 72:275; SLJ Apr 2004 p. 160; VOYA 27:233)

PORTE, Barbara Ann. *Beauty and the Serpent: Thirteen Tales of Unnatural Animals.*
See Chapter 4, Ghost Fantasy.

3-237 PORTE, Barbara Ann. *Jesse's Ghost and Other Stories.* Gr. 4–6.
☆ A collection of thought-provoking stories told by a storyteller who "sits where three worlds meet, before and now and after."
Greenwillow, 1983, 105 pp., o.p.
(BL 80:366; CCBB 37:134; Kirkus 51:J164; SLJ Nov 1983 p. 82)

PREUSSLER, Otfried. *The Wise Men of Schilda.*
See Chapter 8, Humorous Fantasy.

3-238 *Princesses and Peasant Boys: Tales of Enchantment.* **Ed. by Phyllis Reid Fenner.** Gr. 4–6.
Included in this collection are stories by Hans Christian Andersen, Howard Pyle, and Margery Williams Bianco.
Illus. by Henry C. Pitz, Knopf, 1944, 188 pp., o.p.
(BL41:126; Kirkus 12:430; LJ 69:1049)

3-239 *The Princesses: Sixteen Stories About Princesses.* **Ed. by Sally Patrick**
☆ **Johnson.** Gr. 4–6. (Orig. pub. in England, entitled *The Book of Princesses.*)
One tale each by 16 authors, including Hans Christian Andersen, Mary de Morgan, Somerset Maugham, Walter de la Mare, Eleanor Farjeon, Ruth Sawyer, and Rudyard Kipling. *The Harper Book of Princes* (1964) is the companion volume, containing stories by A. A. Milne, E. Nesbit, Frank R. Stockton, Laurence Housman, and Oscar Wilde.
Illus. by Beni Montresor, Harper, 1962, 318 pp., o.p.
(BL 59:396; CCBB 16:96; Eakin:178; HB 38:603; LJ 87:187)

3-240 *The Provensen Book of Fairy Tales.* **Ed. by Alice Provensen.** Gr. 3–6.
Stories by Hans Christian Andersen, Henry Beston, Ruth Manning-Sanders, A. A. Milne, Barbara Picard, Howard Pyle, and Oscar Wilde.
Illus. by Alice Provensen and Martin Provensen, Random, 1971, 140 pp., o.p.
(CCBB 25:96; Kirkus 39:1130; LJ 97:1916)

3-241 **PUSHKIN, Alexander Sergeevich.** *The Golden Cockerel and Other Stories.* Gr. 3–7. (Orig. pub. in Russia.)
Five poetic retellings of Russian folktales, including "The Tale of Tsar Saltan" and "The Tale of the Fisherman and the Little Golden Fish."
Trans. by James Reeves, illus. by Ján Lebiš, Watts, 1969, 110 pp., o.p.; trans. by Jessie Wood, illus. by Boris Zvorykin, Doubleday, 1990 (orig. pub. in France, 1925), 112 pp. (entitled *The Golden Cockerel and Other Fairy Tales*), o.p.
(BL 87:1125; HB 46:384; Kirkus 58:1605; LJ 95:3631; TLS 1970 p. 420)

3-242 **PYLE, Howard.** *Pepper and Salt; or, Seasoning for Young Folk.* Gr. 4–7.
✫ (Orig. British pub. 1886.)
Eight tales, including "The Skillful Huntsman," "Clever Peter and the Two Bottles," and "The Apple of Contentment."
Illus. by the author, Harper, 1923, 109 pp., o.p.
(BL 20:384; Bookshelf 1932 p. 8; HB 1:29; Mahony 1:37)

PYLE, Howard. *Twilight Land.*
See Chapter 7, High Fantasy: Travel to Other Worlds.

3-243 **PYLE, Howard.** *The Wonder Clock; or, Four and Twenty Marvelous Tales,*
✫ *Being One for Each Hour of the Day.* Gr. 5–7. (Orig. British pub. 1887.)
Twenty-four tales, including "One Good Turn Deserves Another," "The Princess Golden Hair and the Great Black Raven," and "King Stork." Three of the stories in this collection have been published separately: *King Stork* (Little, 1973, Morrow, 1998; see Chapter 12, Witchcraft and Sorcery Fantasy), *Bearskin* (Morrow, 1997; see Chapter 1, Allegorical Fantasy and Literary Fairy Tales), and *The Swan Maiden* (Holiday, 1994).
Verses by Katharine Pyle, illus. by the author, Harper, 1943, 318 pp., o.p.; Dover, 1965, pap. (0-486-21446-X); Peter Smith, 1990, 318 pp. (0-8446-2767-4); Starscape, pap., 2003, 336 pp. (0-7653-4266-9)
(Bookshelf 1932 p. 8; HB 1:31,19:48; Mahony 2:292)

The Random House Book of Ghost Stories. **Ed. by Susan Hill.**
See Chapter 4, Ghost Fantasy.

3-244 **REEVES, James (pseud. of John Morris Reeves).** *Sailor Rumbelow and Other Stories.* Gr. 4–6. (Orig. British pub. in two volumes: *Sailor Rumbelow and Britannia,* 1962, and *Pigeons and Princesses,* 1956.)
Two retellings of traditional tales plus nine original stories, including "The Stonemason of Elphinstone."
Illus. by Edward Ardizzone, Dutton, 1962, 223 pp., o.p.
(BL 59:498; HB 38:605; LJ 87:3898)

REID BANKS, Lynne. *The Magic Hare.*
See Chapter 2, Animal Fantasy.

Ribbiting Tales: Original Stories About Frogs. **Ed. by Nancy Springer.**
See Chapter 8, Humorous Fantasy.

3-245 *A Ring of Tales.* **Ed. by Kathleen Lines.** Gr. 4–7. (Orig. British pub. 1958.)
✮ Tales by Alison Uttley, A. A. Milne, Hans Christian Andersen, Walter de la
Mare, Eleanor Farjeon, and Selma Lagerlöf.
Illus. by Harold Jones, Watts, 1959, 239 pp., o.p.
(BL 55:488; HB 35:299; LJ 84:1698; TLS Nov 21, 1958 p. xvi)

3-246 **RITCHIE, Alice.** *The Treasure of Li-Po.* Gr. 4–7. (Orig. British pub. 1948.)
Six magical stories set in ancient China.
Illus. by T. Ritchie, Harcourt, 1949, 154 pp., o.p.
(BL 46:17; CCBB 2:4; HB 25:416, 436; Kirkus 17:393; LJ 74:1208, 1542)

3-247 **ROACH, Marilynne K(athleen).** *Encounters with the Invisible World;*
✮ *Being Ten Tales of Ghosts, Witches, and the Devil Himself in New Eng-*
land. Gr. 6–10.
Ten supernatural tales set in New England, about ghosts, piracy, witchcraft, and
the devil.
Illus. by the author, Crowell, 1977, 131 pp., o.p.

ROBINSON, Marileta. *Mr. Goat's Bad Good Idea.*
See Chapter 2, Animal Fantasy.

SAND, George. *The Castle of Pictures and Other Stories: A*
Grandmother's Tales, vol. 1.
See Chapter 1, Allegorical Fantasy and Literary Fairy Tales.

SANDBURG, Carl (August). *Rootabaga Stories.*
See Chapter 8, Humorous Fantasy.

3-248 *The Sandman: Book of Dreams.* **Ed. by Neil Gaiman and Edward E.**
Kramer. Gr. 10 up.
A collection of tales related to Gaiman's *Sandman* graphic novels, in which
immortals intervene in human lives, written by Will Shetterly, Lisa Goldstein,
Gene Wolfe, Steven Brust, and others. The sequel is *Sandman: Endless Nights*
(2003).
HarperPrism, 1996, 293 pp. (0-06-100833-8); HarperTorch, 2002, pap., 402 pp.
(0-380-81770-5)
(Kirkus 64:918; SL Aug 1996 p. 120; VOYA 19:340)

SCIESZKA, Jon. *The Stinky Cheese Man and Other Fairly Stupid Tales.*
See Chapter 8, Humorous Fantasy.

Shades of Dark: Stories. **Ed. by Aidan Chambers.**
See Chapter 4, Ghost Fantasy.

3-249 **SHANNON, Monica.** *California Fairy Tales.* Gr. 5–7. (Orig. pub. Doubleday, 1926.)
Tales of the elves, fairies, and goblins living in California's orchards, gardens,
and forests. *More Tales from California* (1960; orig. title: *Eyes for the Dark*,
1928) is the companion volume.
Illus. by C. E. Millard, Stephen Daye, 1957, 298 pp., o.p.
(BL 23:348; 54:310; HB 2:42, 344:124; Mahony 2:297; Moore:429)

3-250 *Shape Shifters: Fantasy and Science Fiction Tales About Humans Who Can Change Their Shapes.* **Ed. by Jane (Hyatt) Yolen (Stemple).** Gr. 6–9.
Twelve tales about people transformed into animals, monsters, and machines, including "The Boy Who Would Be a Wolf," "The Enchanted Village," and "Judas Fish."
Seabury, 1978, 182 pp., o.p.
(BL 74:1259; CCBB 32:40; Kirkus 46:552; SLJ Sep 1978 p. 167)

SHARMA, Partap. *The Surangini Tales.*
See Chapter 1, Allegorical Fantasy and Literary Fairy Tales.

Sherwood: Original Stories from the World of Robin Hood. **Ed. by Jane (Hyatt) Yolen (Stemple).**
See Chapter 6, High Fantasy: Myth or Legend Fantasy.

The Shimmering Door. **Ed. by Katharine Kerr.**
See Chapter 12, Witchcraft and Sorcery Fantasy.

The Silent Playmate: A Collection of Doll Stories. **Ed. by Naomi Lewis.**
See Chapter 11, Toy Fantasy.

3-251 **SINGER, Isaac Bashevis.** *Naftali the Storyteller and His Horse, Sus, and* ✮ *Other Stories.* Gr. 4–7.
Eight tales, including stories about the foolish people of Chelm and an imp called the lantuch.
Trans. by Joseph Singer, Ruth Finkel, and the author, illus. by Margot Zemach, Farrar, 1976, pap., 129 pp., o.p.
(BL 73:670; CCBB 30:98; HB 53:162; Kirkus 44:1139; SLJ Dec 1976 p. 56; Suth 2:415)

3-252 **SINGER, Isaac Bashevis.** *Stories for Children.* Gr. 4–7.
✮ A collection of most of Singer's children's stories, including those about the fools of Chelm, "Zlateh the Goat" and "Mazel and Shlimazel."
Farrar, 1984, 337 pp., o.p., 1985, pap. (0-374-46489-8)
(BL 81:592; CCBB 38:73; HB 61:183; Suth 3:395; SLJ Dec 1984 p. 86)

3-253 **SINGER, Isaac Bashevis.** *Zlateh the Goat and Other Stories.* Gr. 4–7.
✮ Seven stories, including three tall tales about the foolish people of Chelm, two about the devil, and an allegorical tale about a young boy and his goat who are lost in a blizzard. John Newbery Medal Honor Book, 1967.
Illus. by Maurice (Bernard) Sendak, Harper, 1966, 90 pp., o.p.; illus. by Maurice Sendak, HarperCollins, 2001, 90 pp. (0-06-028478-1)
(BL 63:378; CCBB 20:79; HB 42:712; HBG 13:92; Kirkus 34:1045; LJ 91:6197; Suth:368)

3-254 *Sisters in Fantasy, 2.* **Ed. by Susan Shwartz and Martin H. Greenberg.** Gr. 10 up.
An anthology of 23 fantasy stories written by women, among them Patricia McKillip, Mercedes Lackey, and Jane Yolen. *Sisters in Fantasy* (Penguin, 1995) is a companion volume.
Roc, 1996, pap., 347 pp. (0-451-45503-7)
(Kliatt Sep 1996 p. 20; VOYA 19:171)

3-255 SLEIGH, Barbara (de Riemer). *Stirabout Stories, Brewed in Her Own Cauldron.* Gr. 4–6. (Orig. British pub. 1971, entitled *West of Widdershins.*) Fourteen tales of magic, fairies, witches, and sea monsters.
Illus. by Victor G. Ambrus, Bobbs-Merrill, 1971, 143 pp., o.p.
(CCBB 26:49; LJ 97:3808; TLS 1971 p. 1321)

Small Shadows Creep. **Ed. by Andre Norton.**
See Chapter 4, Ghost Fantasy.

Smart Dragons, Foolish Elves. **Ed. by Alan Dean Foster and Martin H. Greenberg.**
See Chapter 8, Humorous Fantasy.

Snow White, Blood Red. **Ed. by Ellen Datlow and Terri Windling.**
See Chapter 6, High Fantasy: Myth or Legend Fantasy.

SOMMER-BODENBURG, Angela. *If You Want to Scare Yourself.*
See Chapter 4, Ghost Fantasy.

3-256 SOYER, Abraham. *The Adventures of Yemima.* Gr. 4–6. (Orig. pub. in Palestine, 1939.)
Six fables, including tales about a gift of flying money, greedy animals, and a brave little girl.
Trans. from Hebrew by Rebecca Beagle and Rebecca Soyer, illus. by Raphael Soyer, Viking, 1979, 80 pp., o.p.
(BL 75:1298; HB 55:305; Kirkus 47:518; SLJ Apr 1979 p. 49)

3-257 *Spaceships and Spells: A Collection of New Fantasy and Science-Fiction Stories.* **Ed. by Jane (Hyatt) Yolen (Stemple), Martin H. Greenberg, and Charles G. Waugh.** Gr. 5–8.
Thirteen fantasy and science fiction tales whose authors include Bruce Coville, Robert Lawson, Jane Yolen, and Charles de Lint.
Harper, 1987, 182 pp., o.p.
(BL 84:868; CCBB 41:40; SLJ Dec 1987 p. 89; VOYA 10:292)

SPINELLI, Jerry. *The Library Card.*
See Chapter 9, Magic Adventure Fantasy.

Spooky Stories for a Dark and Stormy Night. **Ed. by Alice Low.**
See Chapter 4, Ghost Fantasy.

3-258 STEELE, Mary Q(uintard Govan). *The Owl's Kiss: Three Stories.* Gr. 6–8.
In these three tales, a little girl fears owls will kill her for stealing her grandmother's fruit, an older girl longs to become a witch, and a man is falsely accused of theft.
Greenwillow/Morrow, 1978, 99 pp., o.p.
(BL 75:53; HB 55:522; Kirkus 46:878; SLJ Dec 1978 p. 57)

3-259 STOCKTON, Frank (Francis) R(ichard). *The Queen's Museum and Other Fanciful Tales.* Gr. 5–7. (Orig. pub. 1887.)

Ten stories, including "The Griffin and the Minor Canon," "The Bee-Man of Orn," and "Old Pipes and the Dryad."

Illus. by Frederick Richardson, Scribner, 1906, 219 pp., o.p.

(BL 3:23; Bookshelf 1921–1922 p. 15; HB 1:45; Mahony 2:297)

3-260 STOCKTON, Frank (Francis) R(ichard). *The Reformed Pirate: Stories from The Floating Prince, Ting-a-Ling Tales and the Queen's Museum.* Gr. 5–7. (Orig. pub. 1881.)

Twelve imaginative tales about fairies, dragons, pirates, and kings.

Illus. by Reginald B. Birch, Scribner, 1936, 342 pp., o.p.

(BL 33:94; HB 13:36; LJ 62:126)

3-261 STOCKTON, Frank (Francis) R(ichard). *The Storyteller's Pack, a Frank
✮ R. Stockton Reader.* Gr. 5–7. (Orig. pub. 1897, entitled *A Story-Teller's Pack.*)

Seventeen stories, including "The Bee-Man of Orn," "The Griffin and the Minor Canon," and "The Lady or the Tiger."

Illus. by Bernarda Bryson, Scribner, 1968, 358 pp., o.p.

(BL 65:1019; HB 45:60; LJ 94:891)

3-262 STOCKTON, Frank (Francis) R(ichard). *Ting-a-Ling Tales.* Gr. 4–7. (Orig. pub. 1870, entitled *Ting-a-ling.*)

A collection of fanciful tales.

Illus. by Richard Floethe, Scribner, 1955, 161 pp., o.p.

(BL 52:110; CCBB 11:86; HB 31:445, 466)

3-263 *Stories for Nine-Year-Olds and Other Young Readers.* **Ed. by Sara Corrin and Stephen Corrin.** Gr. 4 up. (Orig. British pub. 1979.)

A combination of myths and modern fantasy by such authors as Helen Cresswell, Rudyard Kipling, Joan Aiken, Saki, and James Thurber, all appropriate for reading aloud.

Illus. by Shirley Hughes, Faber, 1979, 160 pp., pap., o.p.

(BL 76:452; SLJ Apr 1980 p. 122; TLS 1979 p. 129)

STORR, Catherine (Cole). *Cold Marble and Other Ghost Stories.*
See Chapter 4, Ghost Fantasy.

3-264 *Strange Dreams: Unforgettable Fantasy.* **Ed. by Stephen R. Donaldson.**
✮ Gr. 10 up.

Twenty-eight short fantasy and science fiction stories by Rudyard Kipling, C. J. Cherryh, Orson Scott Card, and others.

Bantam, 1993, pap., 544 pp., o.p.

(BL 89:1678; Kliatt Sep 1993 p. 16; LJ May 15, 1993 p. 100; VOYA 16:313)

Supernatural Stories: 13 Tales of the Unexpected. **Ed. by Jean Russell.**
See Chapter 4, Ghost Fantasy.

Swan Sister: Fairy Tales Retold. **Ed. by Ellen Datlow and Terri Windling.**
See Chapter 6, High Fantasy: Myth or Legend Fantasy.

Sword and Sorceress: An Anthology of Heroic Fantasy. **Ed. by Marion Zimmer Bradley.**
See Chapter 5, High Fantasy: Alternate Worlds or Histories.

3-265 *Tales Before Tolkien: The Roots of Modern Fantasy.* **Ed. by Douglas A. Anderson.** Gr. 10 up.
Twenty-one early literary fairy tales and a verse play, written by E. Nesbit, George MacDonald, L. Frank Baum, Kenneth Morris, Frank R. Stockton, and others.
Ballantine, 2003, 432 pp. (0-345-45854-0), 2003, pap. (0-345-45855-9)
(BL100:76; LJ July 2003 p. 133; SLJ Feb 2004 p. 172)

3-266 *Tales from the Great Turtle.* **Ed. by Piers Anthony and Richard Gilliam.** Gr. 10 up.
A collection of fantasy tales on Native American themes, some by Native American authors.
Tor, 1994, 352 pp. (0-312-85628-8)
(BL 91:482, 487; LJ Nov 15, 1994 p. 90; VOYA 18:126)

Tales out of Time. **Ed. by Barbara Ireson.**
See Chapter 10, Time Travel Fantasy.

3-267 **TASSIN, Algernon de Vivier.** *The Rainbow String.* Gr. 4–6.
Six humorous adventure tales about the romances of six princesses.
Illus. by Anna Richards Brewster, Macmillan, 1921, 1929, 114 pp., o.p.
(BL 18:291; Bookshelf 1923–1924 p. 8; Mahony 1:40)

3-268 **TATE, Eleanora E.** *Don't Split the Pole: Tales of Down Home Folk Wisdom.* Gr. 3–6.
Seven African American folktale-like stories based on traditional sayings and proverbs.
Illus. by Cornelius Van Wright and Ying-Hwa Hu, Delacorte, 1997, 131 pp. (0-385-32302-6)
(BL 94:474; Kirkus 65:1589; SLJ Nov 1997 p. 124)

That's Ghosts for You! Thirteen Scary Stories. **Ed. by Marianne Carus.**
See Chapter 4, Ghost Fantasy.

Things That Go Bump in the Night: A Collection of Original Stories. **Ed. by Jane (Hyatt) Yolen (Stemple) and Martin H. Greenberg.**
See Chapter 4, Ghost Fantasy.

3-269 *Told Under the Magic Umbrella: Modern Fanciful Stories for Young Children.* **Ed. by the Association for Childhood Education Literature Committee.** Gr. 3–5.
Thirty-three fantasy stories written by Marjorie Williams Bianco, Carl Sandburg, Monica Shannon, Laurence Housman, Eleanor Farjeon, Ted Hughes, Anne Thomasine Casserley, Carol Ryrie Brink, and Betty Brock.
Illus. by Elizabeth Orton Jones, Macmillan, 1939, 1955, 248 pp., o.p.
(BL 35:312; HB 15:166; LJ 64:380)

3-270 *Tomorrow's Children: 18 Tales of Fantasy and Science Fiction.* **Ed. by**
✮ **Isaac Asimov.** Gr. 7–12.
Eighteen fantastic tales whose authors include Ray Bradbury and Clifford Simak.

Illus. by Emanuel Schoengut, Doubleday, 1966, 431 pp., o.p.
(BL 63:843; CCBB 20:69; HB 43:69; Kirkus 34:993; LJ 91:6198)

***Trips in Time: Nine Stories of Science Fiction*. Ed. by Robert Silverberg.**
See Chapter 10, Time Travel Fantasy.

3-271   **TURNER, Megan Whalen.** *Instead of Three Wishes.* Gr. 5–8.
✭   Seven magical stories, including "A Plague of Leprechaun," "Instead of Three
Wishes," and "The Baker King."
Greenwillow, 1995, 132 pp. (0-688-13922-1); Puffin, 1998, pap., 132 pp. (0-
14-038672-6)
(BL 92:309, 742; CCBB 49:72; HB 72:336; HBG 7:76; Kirkus 63:954; SLJ Sep 1995 p. 204)

3-272   *The Unicorn Treasury: Stories, Poems and Unicorn Lore.* **Ed. by Bruce
Coville.** Gr. 5–8.
Unicorn stories by Jane Yolen, C. S. Lewis, Madeleine L'Engle, and others.
Illus. by Tim Hildebrandt, Doubleday, 1988, 166 pp. (0-385-24000-7); Har-
court, 2004, pap. (0-15-205216-X)
(BL 85:942; Kirkus 56:1057; SLJ Nov 1988 p. 118)

3-273   *Unicorns!* **Ed. by Jack Dann and Gardner Dozois.** Gr. 10 up.
An anthology of humorous, mythic, and horror tales about unicorns, written by
Roger Zelazny, Ursula K. Le Guin, Gene Wolfe, Stephen R. Donaldson, and
others. The sequel is *Unicorns II* (1992)
Ace, 1982, pap., 310 pp., o.p.
(BL 79:95, 106; VOYA 5:50)

UTTLEY, Alison (Jane [Taylor]). *Foxglove Tales.*
See Chapter 2, Animal Fantasy.

VANDE VELDE, Vivian. *Being Dead: Stories.*
See Chapter 4, Ghost Fantasy.

3-274   **VANDE VELDE, Vivian.** *Curses, Inc.: And Other Stories.* Gr. 6–10.
✭   Ten tales about magic spells, including "Boy Witch," "Remember Me," and
"Curses, Inc."
Harcourt, 1997, 226 pp. (0-15-201452-7); Laurel Leaf, 1998, pap., 226 pp. (0-
440-22767-4)
(BL 94:1226; CCBB 50:336; HBG 8:316; Kirkus 65:307; SLJ June 1997 p. 128; VOYA
20:121, 21:41)

VANDE VELDE, Vivian. *The Rumpelstiltskin Problem.*
See Chapter 6, High Fantasy: Myth or Legend Fantasy.

VANDE VELDE, Vivian. *Tales from the Brothers Grimm and the Sisters
Weird.*
See Chapter 6, High Fantasy: Myth or Legend Fantasy.

***Victorian Ghost Stories: An Oxford Anthology*. Selected by Michael Cox
and R. A. Gilbert.**
See Chapter 4, Ghost Fantasy.

3-275 *The Viking Treasury of Children's Stories.* **Ed. by Anna Trenter.** Gr. 2–6.
(Orig. pub. in England.)
Thirty-six stories and excerpts from American and English children's classics,
including *The Wizard of Oz, The Hobbit, Winnie the Pooh, Charlotte's Web,*
and *The Lion, the Witch, and the Wardrobe.*
Illus. by various illustrators, Viking 1997, 309 pp. (0-670-87303-9)
(BL 93:1707; HBG 8:374; SLJ July 1997 p. 77)

3-276 *Visions of Wonder: An Anthology of Christian Fantasy.* **Ed. by Robert H.
Boyer and Kenneth J. Zahorski.** Gr. 10 up.
A collection of fables, fairy tales, legends, allegories, and satires drawn from
Christian concepts, including material by George MacDonald.
Avon, 1981, 1986, pap., 240 pp., o.p.
(BL 78:538, 546; Kliatt 16:20)

3-277 *Visions of Wonder: The Science Fiction Research Association Reading
Anthology.* **Ed. by David G. Hartwell and Milton T. Wolf.** Gr. 10 up.
An anthology of 32 short fantasy and science fiction stories, plus nine essays by
Anne McCaffrey, Ursula K. Le Guin, Andre Norton, and others.
Tor, 1996, 798 pp. (0-312-86224-5), pap. (0-312-85287-8)
(LJ Nov, 15, 1996 p. 92; VOYA 20:121)

VIVELO, Jackie. *Chills in the Night: Tales That Will Haunt You.*
See Chapter 4, Ghost Fantasy.

3-278 **VIVELO, Jackie.** *A Trick of the Light: Stories to Read at Dusk.* Gr. 5–8.
Six of these nine stories involve magical events, including "The Fireside Book
of Ghost Stories," in which people disappear after reading stories that affect
their lives.
Putnam, 1987, 124 pp., o.p.; Beyond Words, 1989, pap., o.p.
(BL 84:638; CCBB 41:104; SLJ Feb 1988 p. 76; VOYA 10:284)

3-279 *Wandering Stars: An Anthology of Jewish Fantasy and Science Fiction.*
Ed. by Jack Dann. Gr. 10 up.
Thirteen humorous science fiction and fantasy stories whose authors include
Robert Silverberg, Isaac Asimov, and Isaac Bashevis Singer.
Harper, 1974, 239 pp., o.p.; Jewish Lights, 1998 (1-58023-005-9)
(BL 70:906, 932; Kirkus 41:1287)

3-280 **WATT-EVANS, Lawrence.** *Crosstime Traffic.* Gr. 10 up.
Twenty fantasy and science fiction stories about alternate worlds, demons, and
dragons.
Ballantine, 1992, pap., 247 pp. (0-345-37395-2)
(BL 89:407, 412; Kliatt Jan 1993 p. 20)

WEAVER, Jack. *Mr. O'Hara.*
See Chapter 8, Humorous Fantasy.

3-281 *Weird Tales from Shakespeare.* **Ed. by Katherine Kerr and Martin H.
Greenberg.** Gr. 10 up.
Fantasy and science fiction tales of ghosts, robots, vampires, and fairies, based
on Shakespeare's plays.

DAW, 1994, pap., 318 pp. (0-88677-605-8)
(Kliatt Nov 1994 p. 23; VOYA 17:161)

3-282 WELLS, H(erbert) G(eorge). *The Door in the Wall and Other Stories.* Gr. 10 up. (Orig. British and U.S. pubs. 1911; 1925, 1939.)
Eight short stories, including "The Door in the Wall," "A Moonlight Fable," and "The Country of the Blind."
Photos by Alvin Langdon Coburn, Godine, 1980, 157 pp., o.p.; Wildside, 2004, 156 pp. (0-8095-9660-1), pap., 2004, 156 pp. (0-8095-9307-6)
(BL 77:199, 206; Kliatt 15:19)

WESTALL, Robert (Atkinson). *The Call and Other Stories.*
See Chapter 4, Ghost Fantasy.

WESTALL, Robert (Atkinson). *Demons and Shadows: The Ghostly Best Stories of Robert Westall.*
See Chapter 4, Ghost Fantasy.

WESTALL, Robert (Atkinson). *The Haunting of Chas McGill and Other Stories.*
See Chapter 4, Ghost Fantasy.

WESTALL, Robert (Atkinson). *In Camera and Other Stories.*
See Chapter 4, Ghost Fantasy.

3-283 WESTALL, Robert (Atkinson). *Rachel and the Angel and Other Stories.*
✯ Gr. 8–12. (Orig. British pub. 1986.)
Seven fantasy and science fiction stories, including the title story, in which a vicar's daughter tricks the angel of death into sparing the townspeople, in spite of their faults.
Greenwillow, 1987, 187 pp., o.p.
(BL 84:139, 154; CCBB 41:39; HB 64:74; Kirkus 55:1399; SLJ Dec 1987 p. 106; VOYA 10:239)

WESTALL, Robert (Atkinson). *Shades of Darkness: More of the Ghostly Best Stories of Robert Westall.*
See Chapter 4, Ghost Fantasy.

What Did Miss Darrington See? An Anthology of Feminist Supernatural Fiction. **Ed. by Jessica Amanda Salmonson.**
See Chapter 4, Ghost Fantasy.

3-284 WHITCHER, Susan. *Real Mummies Don't Bleed: Friendly Tales for October Nights.* Gr. 3–6.
Five humorous scary stories, including "Annie's Pet Witch," "The Paper Bag Genie," and "Toad Meets Frankenstein."
Illus. by Andrew Glass, Farrar, 1993, 119 pp. (0-374-36213-0)
(CCBB 47:135; Kirkus 61:1082; SLJ Feb 1994 p. 104)

WHITELAW, Stella, GARDINER, Judith, and RONSON, Mark. *Grimalkin's Tales.*
See Chapter 2, Animal Fantasy.

3-285 **WILDE, Oscar (Fingal O'Flahertie Wills) (pseud. of Fingal O'Flahertie**
✶ **Wills).** *The Fairy Tales of Oscar Wilde.* Gr. 4 up.
There have been many editions of Wilde's collected fairy tales for children,
which include such well-known stories as "The Happy Prince" and "The Self-
ish Giant."
The following collections are arranged alphabetically by title:

The Birthday of the Infanta and Other Tales. Illus. by Beni Montresor, Macmillan, 1982, 73 pp., o.p.

Complete Fairy Tales of Oscar Wilde. NAL, 1990, pap., 221 pp., o.p.

Fairy Tales of Oscar Wilde. (Orig. British pub in *The Happy Prince and Other
Tales*, 1888; *The House of Pomegranates*, 1891, 1906; and *Fairy Tales*, 1913);
illus. by Charles Mozley, Watts, 1960, o.p.; illus. by Craig P. Russell, Nantier,
1992, 48 pp., o.p.; illus. by Michael (R.) Hague, Holt, 1993 (Orig. British pub.
in this ed. 1991), 184 pp., (0-8050-1009-2); illus. by Isabelle Brent, Viking,
1994, 144 pp. (0-670-85585-5).

The Happy Prince and Other Fairy Stories. Putnam, 1909, 1911, o.p.

The Happy Prince and Other Fairy Tales. (Orig. British pub. 1888); illus. by
Charles Robinson, Putnam, 1913, o.p.; illus. by Charles Robinson, Brentanos,
1920, o.p.; illus. by Charles Robinson, Morrow, 1991, 136 pp. (0-688-10390-1).

The Happy Prince and Other Tales. Illus. by Peggy Fortnum, Dent, 1977, o.p.

Stories for Children. (Orig. British pub. in this ed. 1990.) Illus. by P. J. Lynch,
Macmillan, 1991, 96 pp., o.p.
(BL 37:222, 79:782, 88:153, 89:985, 1425, 91:665; Bookshelf 1921–1922 p. 15; CCBB
36:139; HBG 2:257, 3:75, 4:306, 6:85; Kirkus 36:826, 59:1170, 62:1579; Kliatt Sep 1990 p. 5;
SLJ Oct 1980 p. 152, Dec 1991 p. 119, Apr 1993 p. 125, Aug 1993 p. 162, Mar 1995 p. 189;
TLS 1977 p. 352)

3-286 **WILHELM, Kate (Katie Gertrude).** *And the Angels Sing: Stories.* Gr. 10
✶ up.
Twelve fantasy and horror stories, including "The Dragon Seed," "The Look
Alike," and "Forever Yours, Anna."
St. Martin's, 1992, 320 pp. (0-3120-6898-0)
(BL 88:1092, 1095; Kirkus 60:76; LJ Feb 15, 1992 p. 200; SLJ July 1992 p. 98; VOYA 15:49)

3-287 **WILHELM, Kate (Katie Gertrude).** *Children of the Wind: Five Novellas.*
✶ Gr. 10 up.
One of these five novellas, "The Girl Who Fell into the Sky," which won the
1986 Nebula Award for the best novelette, is about an old player piano that
transports two people 100 years into the past where they become involved in a
murder.
St. Martin's, 1989, 256 pp. (0-3120-3303-6), 1991, pap. (0-3120-5400-9)
(BL 86:147, 165; Kirkus 57:1288; LJ Oct 15, 1989 p. 105; VOYA 13:11,40)

3-288 **WILHELM, Kate (Katie Gertrude).** *The Downstairs Room, and Other
Speculative Fiction.* Gr. 10 up.
Fourteen fantastic, realistic, and science fiction short stories, including "The
Unbirthday Party," "Baby You Were Great," and "The Downstairs Room."

Doubleday, 1968, 215 pp., o.p.
(BL 65:440, 445; Kirkus 36:719)

3-289 WILKINS (Freeman), Mary E(leanor). *The Pot of Gold, and Other Stories.* Gr. 4–6. (Orig. pub. Lothrop, 1892.)
Sixteen tales, including "Princess Rosetta and the Popcorn Man," "The Pumpkin Giant," and "The Silver Hen."
Ayer, reprint ed., 1940, 324 pp., o.p.; Books for Libraries, 1970, 324 pp., o.p.
(Mahony 1:27, 2:27)

WILLARD, Nancy (Margaret). *Sailing to Cythera, and Other Anatole Stories.*
See Chapter 7, High Fantasy: Travel to Other Worlds.

3-290 *William Mayne's Book of Giants.* **Ed. by William (James Carter) Mayne.**
✫ Gr. 4–6. (Orig. British pub. 1968, entitled *The Hamish Hamilton Book of Giants.*)
Nineteen tales whose authors include Oscar Wilde, Eleanor Farjeon, and Janet McNeill.
Illus. by Raymond Briggs, Dutton, 1969, 215 pp., o.p.
(BL 65:1078; CCBB 22:179; HB 45:313; Kirkus 37:181; LJ 94:2105; TLS 1968 p. 1373)

3-291 WILLIAMS, Jay. *The Practical Princess and Other Liberating Fairy*
✫ *Tales.* Gr. 3–5.
Six lively tales originally published separately: "The Practical Princess," "Stupid Marco," "The Silver Whistle," "Forgetful Fred," "Petronella," and "Philbert the Fearful."
Illus. by Rick Schreiter, Parents, 1978, 99 pp., o.p.
(BL 75:937; CCBB 32:166; Kirkus 47:7; SLJ Sep 1979 p. 124)

3-292 WILLIS, Connie. *Fire Watch.* Gr. 10 up.
Twelve science fiction and fantasy tales, including the title story in which London's St. Paul's Cathedral is saved by a time traveler during the Blitz.
Bluejay, 1985, 288 pp., o.p.
(BL 81:824; Kirkus 52:1172; LJ Feb 15, 1985 p. 182)

3-293 *The Wishing Penny and Other Fantasy Stories.* Gr. 2–4.
Seven magical tales about a pair of runaway shoes, frozen melodies, a wandering cloud, and an umbrella with portable sunshine.
Illus. by Anita Lobel, Parents, 1967, 71 pp., o.p.
(Kirkus 35:342; LJ 92:2022)

Witches. **Ed. by Isaac Asimov, Martin H. Greenberg, and Charles G. Waugh.**
See Chapter 12, Witchcraft and Sorcery Fantasy.

Witches, Witches, Witches. **Ed. by Helen Hoke.**
See Chapter 12, Witchcraft and Sorcery Fantasy.

With Cap and Bells: Humorous Stories to Tell and to Read Aloud. **Ed. by Mary Gould Davis.**
See Chapter 8, Humorous Fantasy.

The Wizard's Den: Spellbinding Stories of Magic and Madness. **Ed. by Peter Haining.**
See Chapter 12, Witchcraft and Sorcery Fantasy.

3-294 *A Wizard's Dozen: Stories of the Fantastic.* **Ed. by Michael Stearns.** Gr. 6
★ up.
Thirteen short fantasy tales whose authors include Vivian Vande Velde, Will Shetterly, Bruce Coville, and Patricia Wrede.
Harcourt, 1993, 192 pp. (0-15-200965-5)
(BL 90:748; CCBB 47:169; SLJ Dec 1993 p. 138; VOYA 17:42)

A Wolf at the Door, And Other Retold Fairy Tales. **Ed. by Ellen Datlow and Terri Windling.**
See Chapter 6, High Fantasy: Myth or Legend Fantasy.

3-295 *Worlds Near and Far: Nine Stories of Science Fiction.* **Ed. by Terry Carr.**
Gr. 7 up.
Nine science-fantasy tales, including Fritz Lieber's "Four Ghosts from Hamlet," Robert Silverberg's "Dybbuk of Mazel Tov IV," and Gene Wolfe's "Feather Tigers."
Nelson, 1974, 224 pp., o.p.
(BL 71:34; Kirkus 42:808; LJ 99:2744)

3-296 **WREDE, Patricia C(ollins).** *Book of Enchantments.* Gr. 5–8.
★ Some of the short stories in this collection are set in the world of Queen Cimorene's Enchanted Forest Chronicles (see *Dealing with Dragons* in Chapter 5, High Fantasy: Alternate Worlds or Histories) and others include "Roses by Midnight," "The Lorelei," and "Stronger Than Time."
Harcourt, 1996, 234 pp. (0-15-201255-9); Scholastic, 1998, pap., 234 pp. (0-590-97218-9)
(BL 92:1588; CCBB 49:319; HBG 7:306; Kirkus 64:609; SLJ June 1996 p. 130; VOYA 19:173)

3-297 **WURTS, Janny.** *That Way Lies Camelot.* Gr. 10 up.
Fifteen fantasy and science fiction stories, including three set in the world of the Blood of Ten Chiefs series.
HarperPrism, 1996, 275 pp. (0-06-105221-3)
(Kirkus 63:1738; VOYA 19:222)

3-298 *Xanadu.* **Ed. by Jane (Hyatt) Yolen (Stemple).** Gr. 10 up.
★ An anthology of contemporary fantasy stories and poetry written by Ursula K. Le Guin and others. *Xanadu 2* (1994) and *Xanadu 3* (1995, 1997) continue the series.
Tor, 1993, 288 pp. (0-312-85367-X), 1994, pap., o.p.
(BL 89:872, 885; Kirkus 60:1412; LJ Dec 1992 p. 191; SLJ Aug 1993 p. 206; VOYA 16:172)

3-299 *The Year's Best Fantasy: First Annual Collection.* **Ed. by Ellen Datlow and Terri Windling.** Gr. 10 up.
This anthology, which includes stories by Ursula K. Le Guin, Charles de Lint, and Jane Yolen, won the World Fantasy Convention Award, 1989. The succeeding volumes are *The Year's Best Fantasy: Second Annual Collection*

(1989), *The Year's Best Fantasy and Horror: Third Annual Collection* (1990), *The Year's Best Fantasy and Horror: Fourth Annual Collection* (1991), *The Year's Best Fantasy and Horror: Fifth Annual Collection* (1992), *The Year's Best Fantasy and Horror: Sixth Annual Collection* (1993), *The Year's Best Fantasy and Horror: Seventh Annual Collection* (1994), *The Year's Best Fantasy and Horror: 8th Annual Collection* (1995), *The Year's Best Fantasy and Horror: 9th Annual Collection* (1996), *The Year's Best Fantasy and Horror: 10th Annual Collection* (1997), *The Year's Best Fantasy and Horror: 11th Annual Collection* (1998), *The Year's Best Fantasy and Horror: 12th Annual Collection* (1999), *The Year's Best Fantasy and Horror: 13th Annual Collection* (2000), *The Year's Best Fantasy and Horror: 14th Annual Collection* (2001), *The Year's Best Fantasy and Horror: 15th Annual Collection* (2002), *The Year's Best Fantasy and Horror: 16th Annual Collection* (2003), and *The Year's Best Fantasy and Horror: 17th Annual Collection* (2004).
St. Martin's, 1988, 512 pp., o.p.
(BL 85:43; Kirkus 56:1019; LJ Dec 1988 p. 113; VOYA 11:296, 12:16)

3-300 ***The Year's Best Fantasy Stories, 6.* Ed. by Lin Carter.** Gr. 10 up.
This annual anthology of fantasy contains tales by Roger Zelazny, Tanith Lee, and others. There were 14 annual volumes in this series, published between 1975 and 1988. Volumes 10–14 were edited by Arthur W. Saha.
DAW, 1980, pap., 192 pp., o.p.
(BL 77:561; LJ 105:2437; VOYA 4:41)

3-301 YOLEN (Stemple), Jane (Hyatt). *Dragonfield and Other Stories.* Gr. 10 up.
Twenty stories and seven poems about dragons, angels, shape-shifters, mermen, selchies, princesses, and magic.
Ace, 1985, pap., 241 pp., o.p.
(BL 81:1638, 1657; VOYA 8:397)

3-302 YOLEN (Stemple), Jane (Hyatt). *Dream Weaver.* Gr. 5–8.
Seven tales told by a blind old woman to passers-by. Two are somewhat lighter in tone, the other five more somber.
Illus. by Michael (R.) Hague, Collins, 1979, 80 pp., o.p.; Putnam, 1989 (rev. ed.), 80 pp., o.p.
(BL 75:1582, 86:1012:CCBB 33:84; HBG 1:85; Kirkus 47:742)

3-303 YOLEN (Stemple), Jane (Hyatt). *The Faery Flag: Stories and Poems of*
☆ *Fantasy and the Supernatural.* Gr. 5–10.
Five poems and nine fantasy and horror stories, including "The Face in the Cloth," "The Boy Who Drew Unicorns," and "Words of Power."
Illus. by Trina Schart Hyman, Orchard, 1989, 128 pp., o.p.
(BL 86:838; CCBB 43:73; HB 66:90; HBG 1:82; Kirkus 57:1172; SLJ Sep 1989 p. 258; VOYA 12:229)

3-304 YOLEN (Stemple), Jane (Hyatt). *The Girl Who Cried Flowers and Other*
☆ *Tales.* Gr. 4–6.
Five tales, including one about a girl who cries flowers instead of tears. Golden Kite Award, 1974. National Book Award finalist, 1975.
Illus. by David Palladini, Crowell, 1974, 64 pp., o.p.
(BL 71:48, 768; CCBB 28:88; Kirkus 42:741; LJ 99:2744; SLJ Dec 1978 p. 33)

3-305 **YOLEN (Stemple), Jane (Hyatt).** *Here There Be Angels.* Gr. 4–8.
☆ More than a dozen retold tales and poems about angels, set in contemporary times, ancient Greece, biblical, and other times. A companion volume to *Here There Be Unicorns* (1994; see below), *Here There Be Witches* (1995; see Chapter 12, Witchcraft and Sorcery Fantasy), and *Here There Be Ghosts* (1998; see Chapter 4, Ghost Fantasy).
Illus. by David Wilgus, Harcourt, 1996, 92 pp. (0-15-200938-8)
(BL 93:425; HBG 8:77; SLJ Nov 1996 p. 119; VOYA 20:11, 49)

3-306 **YOLEN (Stemple), Jane (Hyatt).** *Here There Be Dragons.* Gr. 4 up.
Eight stories and five poems about dragons, including one story Yolen later developed into *The Dragon's Boy* (Harper, 1990; see Chapter 6, High Fantasy: Myth or Legend Fantasy), and another that formed the basis for her Pit Dragons trilogy (Delacorte, 1982–1987; see Chapter 5, High Fantasy: Alternate Worlds or Histories). The companion volumes are *Here There Be Angels* (1996; see above), *Here There Be Unicorns* (1994; see below) and *Here There Be Witches* (1995; see Chapter 12, Witchcraft and Sorcery Fantasy)
Illus. by David Wilgus, Harcourt, 1993, 160 pp. (0-15-209888-7)
(Kirkus 61:1532; SLJ Dec 1993 p. 118, Jan 1994 p. 117)

3-307 **YOLEN (Stemple), Jane (Hyatt).** *Here There Be Unicorns.* Gr. 4–8.
☆ Eighteen stories and poems about unicorns, including "Unicorn Tapestry," "The Boy Who Drew Unicorns," and "An Infestation of Unicorns." A companion volume to *Here There Be Angels* (1996; see above), *Here There Be Witches* (1995; see Chapter 12, Witchcraft and Sorcery Fantasy), and *Here There Be Ghosts* (1998; see Chapter 4, Ghost Fantasy).
Illus. by David Wilgus, Harcourt, 1994, 115 pp. (0-15-209902-6)
(BL 91:492; HBG 6:143; Kirkus 62:1546; SLJ Jan 1995 p. 110; VOYA 18:9, 40)

3-308 **YOLEN (Stemple), Jane (Hyatt).** *The Hundredth Dove and Other Tales.* Gr. 2–5.
Seven stories, including "The Lady and the Merman," "The White Seal Maid," and "The Wind Cap."
Illus. by David Palladini, Harper, 1977, 64 pp., o.p.; Schocken, 1980, pap., 80 pp., o.p.
(BL 74:817; CCBB 31:168; Kirkus 45:1198; SLJ Jan 1978 p. 83)

3-309 **YOLEN (Stemple), Jane (Hyatt).** *The Moon Ribbon and Other Tales.* Gr. 3–5.
Six tales, including "The Moon Child," "Somewhen," "Rosechild," and "Honey-Stick Boy." Golden Kite Award Honor Book, 1976.
Illus. by David Palladini, Crowell, 1976, 54 pp., o.p.
(BL 73:328; Kirkus 44:792; SLJ Feb 1977 p. 70)

3-310 **YOLEN (Stemple), Jane (Hyatt).** *Sister Emily's Lightship and Other Stories.* Gr. 10 up.
Twenty-eight fantasy and science fiction short stories, including "The Thirteenth Fey," "Lost Girls," and "Memoirs of a Bottle Djinn."
Tor, 2000, 300 pp. (0-312-87378-6), 2001, pap., 300 pp. (0-312-87523-1)
(BL 96:2126; Kliatt Nov 2001 p. 23; VOYA 23:438)

3-311 YOLEN (Stemple), Jane (Hyatt). *Twelve Impossible Things Before Breakfast: Stories.* Gr. 6–9.
Twelve fantasy tales, including a reworking of *Peter Pan* called "Lost Girls" and "The Bridge's Complaint," a version of "The Three Billy-Goats Gruff" told from the bridge's point of view.
Harcourt, 1997, 192 pp. (0-15-201524-8)
(BL 94:463; SLJ Dec 1997 p. 132; VOYA 20:328, 21:15)

YOLEN (Stemple), Jane (Hyatt). *The Wizard Islands.*
See Chapter 4, Ghost Fantasy.

Young Ghosts. **Ed. by Isaac Asimov, Martin H. Greenberg, and Charles G. Waugh.**
See Chapter 4, Ghost Fantasy.

Young Witches and Warlocks. **Ed. by Isaac Asimov, Martin H. Greenberg, and Charles G. Waugh.**
See Chapter 12, Witchcraft and Sorcery Fantasy.

3-312 *A Yuletide Universe: Sixteen Fantastical Tales.* **Ed. by Brian M. Thomsen.**
Gr. 10 up.
Sixteen fantasy and science fiction Christmas stories, written by Anne McCaffrey, Neil Gaiman, L. Frank Baum, and others.
Warner/Aspect, 2003, pap., 256 pp. (0-446-69187-9)
(BL 100:399; LJ Oct 15, 2003 p. 102)

3-313 ZELAZNY, Roger (Joseph Christopher). *Frost and Fire.* Gr. 10 up.
Eleven fantasy and science fiction short stories, plus two essays on writing science fiction.
Morrow, 1989, 224 pp., o.p.
(BL 85:1873, 1895; Kirkus 57:804; Kliatt Sep 1990 p. 25; LJ Jan 15, 1989 p. 84)

3-314 ZELAZNY, Roger (Joseph Christopher). *The Last Defender of Camelot.*
Gr. 10 up.
Fourteen short stories and two novellas, including "He Who Shapes," "The Last Defender of Camelot," and "For Breath of Tarny." Some of the stories were originally published under the pseudonym Harrison Denmark.
Simon, 1980, pap., 308 pp., o.p.; Avon, 1988, pap. (0-380-70316-5)
(BL 77:376, 377; LJ 105:2436; SLJ Mar 1981 p. 162; VOYA 4:55)

Zoo 2000. **Ed. by Jane (Hyatt) Yolen (Stemple).**
See Chapter 2, Animal Fantasy.

4

Ghost Fantasy

Tales about ghosts fascinate readers of all ages. Many, although not all, of the tales listed here have an element of humor, and most are only mildly chilling. Horror stories have not been included in this book, unless they are part of an anthology containing fantasy stories. Novels about contemporary protagonists who become involved with ghosts from the past are listed in this chapter. If the human characters travel back into the past with ghosts, however, the books are listed in Chapter 10, Time Travel Fantasy.

4-1   ADLER, C(arole) S(chwerdtfeger). *Footsteps on the Stairs.* Gr. 5–7.
☆   Dodie, 13, and her stepsister Anne solve a mystery concerning the ghosts of two teenage girls who haunt their summer house.
        Delacorte, 1982, 151 pp., o.p.
        (BL 78:1091; SLJ May 1982 p. 83; VOYA 5:39)

4-2   ADLER, David A. *Jeffrey's Ghost and the Leftover Baseball Team.* Gr. 3–5.
        Jeffrey's baseball team is not having a good season until Bradford, the baseball-playing ghost who lives in Jeffrey's house, joins the team, building up their skills and confidence. The sequels are *Jeffrey's Ghost and the Fifth-Grade Dragon* (1985) and *Jeffrey's Ghost and the Ziffel Fair Mystery* (1987).
        Illus. by Jean Jenkins, Holt, 1984, 58 pp., o.p.
        (BL 80:1546; CCBB 38:39; SLJ Oct 1984 p. 153)

4-3   AHLBERG, Allan. *My Brother's Ghost.* Gr. 5–8. (Orig. British pub. 2000.)
☆   Devastated after their older brother Tom's death in an accident, orphaned Frances and Harry are thrilled to discover that Tom's ghost has returned to take care of them.
        Viking, 2001, 96 pp. (0-670-89290-4); Puffin, 2001, pap., 80 pp. (0-14-130618-1)
        (CCBB 54:294; HBG 12:298; Kirkus 69:178; SLJ July 2001 p. 102)

4-4   AIKEN, Joan (Delano). *A Foot in the Grave.* Gr. 6–10. (Orig. British pub.
☆   1989.)
        A collection of eight ghostly tales, including "Amberland," "Beezlebub's Baby," and the title story, "A Foot in the Grave."

Illus. by Jan Pienkowski, Viking, 1993, 128 pp. (0-670-84169-2)

(BL 88:1349; CCBB 45:197; HB 68:449; HBG 3:260; Kirkus 60:249; SLJ May 1992 p. 130)

AIKEN, Joan (Delano). *Give Yourself a Fright: Thirteen Stories of the Supernatural.*
See Chapter 3, Fantasy Collections.

AIKEN, Joan (Delano). *The Green Flash and Other Tales of Horror, Suspense, and Fantasy.*
See Chapter 3, Fantasy Collections.

4-5   **AIKEN, Joan (Delano).** *The Haunting of Lamb House.* Gr. 10 up. (Orig. British pub. 1992.)
Three interrelated novellas about three 18th- and 19th-century inhabitants of Lamb House in Sussex: Toby Lamb, who leaves a manuscript about his haunted life, and the authors Henry James and E. F. Benson.
St. Martin's, 1993, 208 pp. (0-312-09060-9)
(BL 89:466; LJ Dec 15, 1992 p. 184; SLJ May 1993 p. 141)

4-6   **AIKEN, Joan (Delano).** *Return to Harken House.* Gr. 5–8. (Orig. British pub. 1988, entitled *Voices.*)
Sent to live with her stepmother after her own mother's remarriage, 11-year-old Julia begins hearing angry voices from the past: those of Joshua Harken, a 17th-century alchemist who died tragically, and of her own parents arguing before their divorce.
Delacorte, 1990, 128 pp., o.p.
(BL 86:996; CCBB 43:152; HBG 1:246; Kirkus 57:1821; SLJ Mar 1990 p. 215; VOYA 13:349)

4-7   **AIKEN, Joan (Delano).** *The Shadow Guests.* Gr. 6–8. (Orig. British pub.
✶   1980.)
Cosmo learns of a family curse that may explain the mysterious disappearance of his mother and older brother. According to his cousin Eunice, the eldest sons of the family are fated to die in battle and their mothers to die of grief.
Delacorte, 1980, 150 pp., o.p.; Dell, 1986, pap. (0-440-48226-7)
(BL 77:41; CCBB 34:85; HB 56:644; SLJ Oct 1980 p. 140; Suth 3:7; TLS 1980 p. 357; VOYA 3:27)

4-8   **AIKEN, Joan (Delano).** *A Touch of Chill: Tales for Sleepless Nights.* Gr. 8
✶   up. (Orig. British pub. 1979.)
Fifteen short stories combining realism, comedy, and fantasy, including "The Cat Flap and the Apple Pie" and "Listening."
Delacorte, 1980, 183 pp., o.p.
(BL 76:1416; CCBB 34:25; SLJ May 1980 p. 73; TLS 1979 p. 123)

4-9   **AIKEN, Joan (Delano).** *A Whisper in the Night: Tales of Terror and Sus-*
✶   *pense.* Gr. 6–12. (Orig. British pub. 1982.)
Thirteen stunning stories of fantasy and horror, including "Snow Horse," "Miss Spitfire," and "Lob's Girl."
Delacorte, 1984, 203 pp., o.p.
(BL 81:582, 585; CCBB 38:59; Kirkus 52:J102; SLJ Dec 1984 p. 87; TLS 1982 p. 788; VOYA 7:321, 8:46)

4-10   AINSWORTH (Gilbert), Ruth (Gallard). *The Phantom Carousel and Other Ghostly Tales.* Gr. 4–6. (Orig. British pub. 1977, entitled *The Phantom Roundabout and Other Ghostly Tales.*)
Ten stories about children who meet ghosts.
Illus. by Shirley Hughes, Follett, 1978, 176 pp., o.p.
(BL 74:1489; Kirkus 46:176; SLJ Feb 1978 p. 62; TLS 1977 p. 1414)

ALAMA, Pauline J. *The Eye of Night.*
See Chapter 5, High Fantasy: Alternate Worlds or Histories.

4-11   ALCOCK, Vivien (Dolores). *Ghostly Companions: A Feast of Chilling*
☆   *Tales.* Gr. 6–10. (Orig. British pub. 1984.)
Ten ghostly tales with young protagonists, including "The Sea Bride," "Qwertyuiop," and "The Whisperer."
Delacorte, 1987, 132 pp., o.p.
(BL 83:1596; CCBB 40:161; HB 63:460; Kirkus 55:789; SLJ Sep 1987 p. 194; VOYA 10:118)

4-12   ALCOCK, Vivien (Dolores). *The Haunting of Cassie Palmer.* Gr. 6–8.
☆   (Orig. British pub. 1980.)
A ghost named Deverill who she accidentally raises from the dead makes Cassie's life very difficult.
Delacorte, 1982, pap., 149 pp., o.p.; Houghton, 1997, pap., 192 pp. (0-395-81653-X)
(BL 78:1305, 1308; CCBB 35:161; HB 58:294, 62:616; Kirkus 50:421; SLJ Apr 1982 p. 78; Suth 3:9)

ALCOCK, Vivien (Dolores). *The Red-Eared Ghosts.*
See Chapter 10, Time Travel Fantasy.

4-13   ALMOND, David. *Kit's Wilderness.* Gr. 6–9. (Orig. British pub. 1999.)
☆☆   When Kit, 13, returns to the English coal-mining town of Stonygate to help care for his grandfather, he is drawn into a frightening game called Death, and sees the ghosts of ancestors who died in the mine as boys. Carnegie Medal Highly Commended Book, 1999; Nestlé Smarties Book Prize, Silver Award, 1999; Michael L. Printz Award, 2000.
Delacorte, 2000, 240 pp. (0-385-32665-3); Random, 2001, pap., 229 pp. (0-440-41605-1)
(BL 96:899, 97:860; HB 76:192; HBG 11:316; Kirkus 67:1954; Kliatt Mar 2000 p. 6; SLJ Mar 2000 p. 233, Dec 2000 p. 52; VOYA 23:10, 42)

4-14   ALPHIN, Elaine Marie. *The Ghost Cadet.* Gr. 4–7.
Hugh, the ghost of a military cadet killed during the Civil War, is befriended by Benjy, a boy visiting his grandmother in contemporary Virginia.
Henry Holt, 1991, 182 pp. (0-8050-1614-7)
(BL 87:1714; CCBB 44:184; HBG 2:267; Kirkus 59:667; SLJ May 1991 p. 91)

4-15   ALPHIN, Elaine Marie. *Ghost Soldier.* Gr. 5–8.
Angry about his father's plans to remarry after his mother's departure, Alex Raskin is drawn to the ghost of Richeson Francis Chamblee, who is searching for the family he lost during Sherman's Civil War March to the Sea.
Holt, 2001, 216 pp. (0-8050-6158-4)

(BL 97:2118; CCBB 54:400; HBG 13:367; Kirkus 69:736; SLJ Aug 2001 p. 175; VOYA 24:210)

4-16   ANASTASIO, Dina. *A Question of Time.* Gr. 4–6.
After her unwanted move from Manhattan to Minnesota, Syd discovers a connection between her new friend Laura, some antique dolls, and an all-but-forgotten tragedy.
Illus. by Dale Payson, Dutton, 1978, 90 pp., o.p.
(BL 75:287; CCBB 32:109; Kirkus 46:1246; SLJ Dec 1978 p. 68)

4-17   ANDERSON, Janet S. *The Last Treasure.* Gr. 5–9.
☆   Thirteen-year-old cousins Ellsworth (Zee) and Jess search their ramshackle family homestead for a treasure hidden by their wealthy 19th-century ancestor.
Dutton, 2003, 256 pp. (0-525-46919-2); Puffin, pap., 2004, 257 pp. (0-14-240217-6)
(BL 99:1326; CCBB 56:348; Kirkus 71:530; SLJ June 2003 p. 136; VOYA 26:40)

4-18   ANDERSON, Margaret J(ean). *The Ghost Inside the Monitor.* Gr. 4–6.
The ghost of Pascale, a girl who lived in Sarah's town nearly a century ago, appears on Sarah's computer screen asking for help in finding her lost home.
Knopf, 1990, 119 pp., o.p.
(BL 87:1059; HBG 2:73; Kirkus 58:1001; SLJ Oct 1990 p. 113)

4-19   *The April Witch and Other Strange Tales.* Ed. by Barbara Ireson. Gr. 7–9.
(Orig. British pub. 1977, entitled *Fantasy Tales*.)
Fourteen eerie stories by such well-known authors as Ray Bradbury, H. G. Wells, and Nicholas Stuart Gray.
Illus. by Richard Cuffari, Scribner, 1978, 238 pp., o.p.
(BL 74:1676; Kirkus 46:599; SLJ Sep 1978 p. 159)

4-20   ARTHUR, Ruth M(abel). *The Autumn People.* Gr. 6–10. (Orig. British pub. 1973.)
Ghosts from the year 1901 reveal the truth about the death of Romilly's great-grandmother's suitor.
Illus. by Margery Gill, Atheneum, 1973, 166 pp., o.p.
(BL 69:1071; CCBB 27:21; HB 49:375; Kirkus 41:122; LJ 98:1702; TLS 1973 p. 680)

4-21   ARTHUR, Ruth M(abel). *Miss Ghost.* Gr. 5–7. (Orig. British pub. 1979.)
The ghost that Elphie meets in the tower room of her boarding school encourages her to make real friends.
Atheneum, 1979, 119 pp., o.p.
(BL 76:116; HB 55:53; Kirkus 47:1262; SLJ Nov 1979 p. 73)

4-22   ARTHUR, Ruth M(abel). *The Whistling Boy.* Gr. 6–9. (Orig. British pub. 1969.)
Deeply unhappy over her father's remarriage, Kristy falls in love with a young man haunted by visions of a suicidal ancestor.
Illus. by Margery Gill, Atheneum, 1969, 200 pp., o.p.
(BL 65:1173; HB 45:310; Kirkus 37:244; LJ 94:1789; TLS 1969 p. 1199)

ASCH, Frank. *Class Pets: The Ghost of PS 42.*
See Chapter 2, Animal Fantasy.

AVI (Avi Wortis). *Midnight Magic.*
See Chapter 12, Witchcraft and Sorcery Fantasy.

AVI (Avi Wortis). *Something Upstairs: A Tale of Ghosts.*
See Chapter 10, Time Travel Fantasy.

BACON, Martha (Sherman). *Moth Manor: A Gothic Tale.*
See Chapter 11, Toy Fantasy.

4-23   **BACON, Peggy.** *The Ghost of Opalina, or Nine Lives.* Gr. 4–7.
The talkative ghost of a Persian cat named Opalina haunts the new home of
Philip, Ellen, and Jeb.
Illus. by the author, Little, Brown, 1967, 243 pp., o.p.
(BL 64:866; Kirkus 35:648; LJ 92:4608)

BARBER, Antonia. *The Ghosts.*
See Chapter 10, Time Travel Fantasy.

4-24   **BARRETT, Tracy.** *Cold in Summer.* Gr. 5–9.
☆   Lonely and homesick for her old friends, Ariadne is befriended by the ghost of
Mary Butler, a 12-year-old girl whose body was never found after the valley
was flooded 50 years earlier.
Holt, 2003, 203 pp. (0-8050-7052-4)
(BL 99:1395; CCBB 57:6; HB 79:338; HBG 14:362; Kirkus 71:764; Kliatt May 2003 p. 6;
SLJ July 2003 p. 123; VOYA 26:146, 27:10)

4-25   **BAUER, Marion Dane.** *Ghost Eye.* Gr. 3–6.
Former showcat Purrloom Popcorn resents becoming Melinda's housebound
pet after the death of her elderly owner, despite the companionship of the many
feline ghosts who live in Melinda's old house.
Illus. by Trina Schart Hyman, Scholastic, 1994, 64 pp. (0-590-45298-3)
(BL 89:148; HBG 4:55; Kirkus 60:1184; SLJ Oct 1992 p. 112)

4-26   **BAUER, Marion Dane.** *A Taste of Smoke.* Gr. 5–8.
☆   Angry that her older sister is paying so much attention to her boyfriend on their
camping trip, 13-year-old Caitlin discovers that she can communicate with the
100-year-old ghost of a young boy orphaned by a forest fire.
Houghton, 1993, 106 pp. (0-395-64341-4); Dell, 1995, pap. (0-440-41034-7)
(BL 90:440; CCBB 47:147; HB 70:68; HBG 5:72; Kirkus 61:1326; SLJ Dec 1993 p. 111;
VOYA 16:364)

4-27   **BEAGLE, Peter S(oyer).** *A Dance for Emilia.* Gr. 9 up.
Actor Jacob Holtz realizes that the spirit of his late childhood friend Sam
Kagan has returned—inside the body of Sam's cat, Millament.
Penguin/Roc, 2000, 96 pp. (0-451-45800-1); Roc, 2001, pap., 275 pp. (0-451-
45820-6)
(BL 96:2124; Kirkus 68:1239 VOYA 23:430, 24:10)

4-28   **BEAGLE, Peter S(oyer).** *A Fine and Private Place, A Novel.* Gr. 10 up.
☆   Michael Morgan and Laura Durand, two ghosts in the Yorkchester Cemetery,
decide to force themselves to remember what it was like to be alive in order to
circumvent the oblivious forgetfulness of death.

Viking, 1960, o.p.; NAL, 1992, pap., 304 pp. (0-451-45096-5)
(BL 56:601; Kirkus 28:243; LJ 85:1822)

4-29 **BEAGLE, Peter S(oyer).** *Tamsin.* Gr. 10 up.

☆ Teenager Jenny Gluckstein moves with her mother and new stepfather from New York to an old English farmhouse, where she meets the 300-year-old ghost of Tamsin Willoughby, haunting the house where she died while searching for her lost love. Mythopoeic Fantasy Award, 2000.
Penguin/Roc, 1999, 288 pp. (0-451-45763-3); Puffin, pap., 2004, 335 pp. (0-14-240154-4)
(BL 95:1532, 1984; Kirkus 67:1179; LJ Oct 15, 1999 p. 110; VOYA 22:340)

BEDARD, Michael. *A Darker Magic.*
See Chapter 12, Witchcraft and Sorcery Fantasy.

BELLAIRS, John. *The Curse of the Blue Figurine.*
See Chapter 12, Witchcraft and Sorcery Fantasy.

4-30 **BELLAIRS, John.** *The House with a Clock in Its Walls.* Gr. 5–7.
Lewis is impressed by his warlock uncle's magic abilities, but when he tries some magic himself he unwittingly summons up a sinister ghost. The sequels are *The Figure in the Shadows* (1975); *The Letter, the Witch and the Ring* (1977); *The Ghost in the Mirror* (1993), which was completed by Brad Strickland after John Bellairs's death; *The Vengeance of the Witch-Finder* (1993) and *The Doom of the Haunted Opera* (1995), both completed by Strickland; and *The Specter from the Magician's Museum* (1998), *The Beast Under the Wizard's Bridge* (2000), *The Tower at the End of the World* (2001), and *The Whistle, the Grave and the Ghost* (2003), all written by Strickland.
Illus. by Edward Gorey, Dial, 1984, 179 pp., o.p.; Puffin, 2004, pap., 179 pp. (0-14-240257-5)
(BL 70:227; CCBB 27:37; Kirkus 41:514; LJ 98:1701)

4-31 **BENDICK, Jeanne.** *The Goodknight Ghost.* Gr. 3–5.
Karen and Mike meet a ghostly knight and dragon when they are accidentally locked inside a museum overnight.
Illus. by the author, Watts, 1956, 51 pp., o.p.
(CCBB 10:62; HB 32:446; Kirkus 24:432; LJ 82:584)

4-32 **BENSON, E(dward) F(rederic).** *The Collected Ghost Stories of E. F. Benson.* Gr. 10 up. (Orig. British pub. 1987.)
Fifty-four British ghost stories written between 1890 and 1940.
Carroll & Graf, 1992, pap., 624 pp., o.p.; Carroll & Graf, 2002, 672 pp. (0-7867-0980-4)
(BL 89:578, 586; VOYA 16:98)

4-33 *Beware! Beware! Chilling Tales.* **Ed. by Jean Richardson.** Gr. 6–9. (Orig.

☆ British pub. 1987.)
Nine tales about ghosts and witches, written by Peter Dickinson, Adèle Geras, Vivian Alcock, Jan Mark, and others.
Viking, 1989, 120 pp., o.p.
(BL 85:1717, 1719; CCBB 42:155; HB 65:379; Kirkus 57:127; SLJ Mar 1989 p. 202; VOYA 13:36)

BLAYLOCK, James P(aul). *Land of Dreams.*
See Chapter 7, High Fantasy: Travel to Other Worlds.

BLAYLOCK, James P(aul). *The Paper Grail.*
See Chapter 6, High Fantasy: Myth or Legend Fantasy.

4-34   *Boo! Stories to Make You Jump.* **Comp. by Laura Cecil.** Gr. 2–4. (Orig.
✶   British pub. 1990.)
A collection of familiar and not-so-familiar stories by Margaret Mahy, Diana
Wynne Jones, and others.
Illus. by Emma Chichester Clark, Greenwillow, 1990, 93 pp., o.p.
(BL 87:922; CCBB 44:80; HBG 2:133; SLJ Mar 1991 p. 200)

4-35   **BOSTON, L(ucy) M(aria Wood).** *The Children of Green Knowe.* Gr. 4–7.
✶✶   (Orig. British pub. 1954.)
With the help of three of his ancestors, Tolly lifts the curse on his family's
ancient home, Green Knowe. Carnegie Medal Commended Book, 1954. Tolly
searches for lost family treasure in *The Treasure of Green Knowe* (1958; Peter
Smith, 1987, Harcourt, 2002 [British title: *The Chimneys of Green Knowe*;
Carnegie Medal Commended Book, 1958]), and battles a witch in *An Enemy at
Green Knowe* (1964; Harcourt, 2002). Related stories are *The Stones of Green
Knowe* (Atheneum, 1976; Harcourt, 2002), *The River at Green Knowe* (1959;
Harcourt, 2002), and *A Stranger at Green Knowe* (1961; Harcourt, 2002),
although the latter is not a fantasy.
Illus. by Peter Boston, Harcourt, 1955, 1967, 157 pp., o.p.; illus. by Peter
Boston, Harcourt, 2002, 192 pp. (0-15-202462-X), pap. (0-15-202468-9)
(BL 52:37, 80:95; CCBB 9:33; Eakin:40; HB 31:375, 78:426–427; Kirkus 23:357; LJ
80:1965)

4-36   **BOWLER, Tim.** *River Boy.* Gr. 6–10. (Orig. British pub. 1997.)
✶   Deeply saddened by her grandfather's imminent death, Jess promises to help
him complete his last painting, "River Boy," while a mysterious boy tries to
convince her to swim the local river with him "from source to sea." Carnegie
Medal, 1998.
Illus. by Rafal Olbinski, Simon, 2000, 160 pp. (0-689-82908-6), 2002, pap.,
234 pp. (0-689-84804-8)
(BL 96:1660; CCBB 53:391; Kirkus 68:791; SLJ Aug 2000 p. 177; VOYA 23:185)

4-37   **BOWLER, Tim.** *Storm Catchers.* Gr. 6–10. (Orig. British pub. 2001.)
✶   Young Sam sees a ghostly girl who helps him and his older brother Fin rescue
their kidnapped sister Ella from an abandoned Cornish lighthouse, but dark
secrets threaten to destroy their family.
McElderry, 2003, 208 pp. (0-689-84573-1); Oxford University Press, pap.,
2004, 202 pp. (0-19-275200-6)
(BL 100:112; CCBB 56:437; Kirkus 71:746; Kliatt May 2003 p 6; SLJ May 2003 p. 144;
VOYA 26:216)

BRADBURY, Ray (Douglas). *The Toynbee Convector.*
See Chapter 3, Fantasy Collections.

4-38 **BRANDON, Paul.** *Swim the Moon.* Gr. 10 up.
Richard Brennan returns to his coastal Scottish birthplace after his father's mysterious death to discover that his family has been living under a curse that may also cost him his life.
Tor, 2001, 384 pp. (0-312-87794-3)
(BL 98:58; Kirkus 69:10:73 LJ Sep 15, 2001 p. 115)

4-39 **BRENNER, Anita.** *The Timid Ghost: Or What Would You Do with a Sackful of Gold?* Gr. 3–5.
A man and his wife demand gold in exchange for answering a ghost's questions.
Illus. by Jean Chariot, Addison-Wesley, 1966, 48 pp., o.p.
(BL 62:954; HB 42:193; Kirkus 34:179; LJ 91:2206)

4-40 **BRITTAIN, Bill.** *Who Knew There'd Be Ghosts?* Gr. 4–6.
✫ Tommy Donahue and his friends find allies in two ghosts, Essie and Horace, and recover a mysterious treasure as they try to save the vacant Parnell mansion from destruction. In the sequel, *The Ghost from Beneath the Sea* (1992, 1994), Tommy and his friends try to save their ghostly allies' historic house by attempting to prove that a poker game played on the *Titanic* the night it sank was rigged.
Illus. by Michele Chessare, Harper, 1985, 128 pp., o.p.
(BL 81:1392, 83:585; HB 61:448; Kirkus 53:31; SLJ May 1985 p. 108)

4-41 **BROCK, Betty.** *The Shades.* Gr. 3–5.
✫ In an old walled garden, Hollis meets the Shade family, ghosts of previous visitors to the garden.
Illus. by Victoria de Larrea, Harper, 1971, 128 pp., o.p.
(BL 68:290; HB 48:47; Kirkus 39:1069; LJ 96:4198; TLS 1973 p. 386)

BROCK, Darryl. *If I Never Get Back.*
See Chapter 10, Time Travel Fantasy.

4-42 **BROW, Thea J.** *The Secret Cross of Lorraine.* Gr. 5–7.
Twyla is unable to return a medallion to the elusive old man who lost it until she finds a secret passageway in the former World War II-era bunker where her family lives.
Illus. by Allen Say, Houghton, 1981, 177 pp., o.p.
(BL 77:925, 81:1405; CCBB 34:208; HB 57:299; SLJ Apr 1981 p. 121)

4-43 **BUFFIE, Margaret.** *Angels Turn Their Backs.* Gr. 7–9. (Orig. Canadian pub. 1998.)
Addie's panic attacks and her anger over her parents' divorce confine her to her new apartment building, where she is drawn into the troubles of the house's late owner, a talented tapestry artist named Lotta Engel.
Kids Can, 1998, 239 pp. (1-55074-415-1)
(CCBB 52:90; Kirkus 66:1282; SLJ Nov 1998 p. 119)

4-44 **BUFFIE, Margaret.** *The Dark Garden.* Gr. 6–9. (Orig. Canadian pub. 1995.)
✫ Struggling to recover her memory after an accident, Thea begins hearing the voice of Susannah, a young woman who was murdered in Thea's garden following a tragic affair.

Kids Can, 1997, 237 pp. (1-55074-288-4), 2001, pap., 237 pp. (1-55337-091-0)
(BL 94:397; CCBB 51:44; HB 73:568; HBG 9:84; Kirkus 65:1107; SLJ Oct 1997 p. 128)

BUFFIE, Margaret. *The Haunting of Frances Rain.*
See Chapter 10, Time Travel Fantasy.

4-45   **BUFFIE, Margaret.** *Someone Else's Ghost.* Gr. 7–10. (Orig. Canadian pub. 1992, entitled *My Mother's Ghost.*)
After her brother's accidental death and the family's move to a new home, Jessica and her mother begin to see the ghost of a boy who may have been murdered in the house many years ago.
Scholastic, 1995, 256 pp. (0-590-46922-3)
(BL 91:1235; CCBB 48:193; HBG 6:308; SLJ Mar 1995 p. 222; VOYA 18:19)

BUFFIE, Margaret. *The Warnings.*
See Chapter 9, Magic Adventure Fantasy.

4-46   **BUNTING, (Anne) Eve(lyn Bolton).** *Ghost Behind Me.* Gr. 6–9.
Sixteen-year-old Cinnamon's depression after the deaths of her mother and sister in a plane crash causes her to think she's only imagining the ghostly young man she sees in their rented summer house.
Pocket, 1984, 1986, pap., 69 pp., o.p.
(BL 80:1547; VOYA 7:143)

4-47   **BUNTING, (Anne) Eve(lyn Bolton).** *The Ghosts of Departure Point.* Gr. 7–9.
Vicki and Ted, the ghosts of two teenage auto accident victims, meet and fall in love while they attempt to prove to the town that a safer highway must be built.
Lippincott, 1982, 113 pp., o.p.
(BL 79:362, 365; CCBB 36:43; Kirkus 50:1109; SLJ Apr 1983 p. 110)

4-48   **BUNTING, (Anne) Eve(lyn Bolton).** *The Presence: A Ghost Story.* Gr.
✫   6–10.
Deeply depressed after the death of her best friend in an accident in which she, herself, was injured, 17-year-old Catherine is unsure whether to trust a handsome ghost who appears near her grandmother's church.
Clarion, 2003, 208 pp. (0-618-26919-3)
(BL 100:404; CCBB 57:95; HBG 15:106; Kirkus 71:1121; Kliatt Sep 2003 p. 6; SLJ Oct 2003 p. 162; VOYA 26:500)

4-49   **BURGESS, Barbara Hood.** *Oren Bell.* Gr. 5–9.
✫   Seventh-grade twins Oren and Latonya hope that the ghost of the man who built their condemned house will show them his hidden gold so that they and their family can escape from the dangers of their Detroit neighborhood. The non-fantasy sequel is *The Fred Field* (1994).
Delacorte, 1991, 192 pp. (0-385-30325-4); Dell, 1993, pap. (0-440-40747-8)
(BL 87:1791; CCBB 44:259; HB 67:196; HBG 2:262; Kirkus 59:602; SLJ Apr 1991 p. 116; VOYA 14:26)

4-50   **BURGESS, Melvin.** *The Ghost Behind the Wall.* Gr. 5–8. (Orig. British pub.
✫   2000.)

Secretly exploring the ventilation ducts of his apartment building after his suspension from school, 12-year-old David meets a ghostly boy bent on playing dangerous tricks on another tenant, elderly Mr. Alveston.
Holt, 2003, 176 pp. (0-8050-7149-0)
(BL 99:1470; CCBB 56:227; HBG 14:363; Kirkus 71:460; Kliatt Mar 2003 p. 8; SLJ July 2003 p. 124; VOYA 26:61)

4-51 **BUTTS, Nancy.** *Cheshire Moon.* Gr. 6–9.
Angry over her isolating deafness and the recent death of her friend Timothy, Miranda discovers that she shares recurring dreams of Timothy's ghost with Boone, another angry teen whose father has abandoned the family.
Front Street, 1996, 105 pp., o.p.
(HBG 8:62; Kirkus 64:1320; SLJ Nov 1996 p. 103; VOYA 20:38)

4-52 **CALIF, Ruth.** *The Over-the-Hill Ghost.* Gr. 4–6.
Mystery, buried treasure, and a haunted house become part of Jamie's life after his family's move to the country, where he helps a ghost find the murderer of his house's previous owner.
Illus. by Jean Holub, Pelican, 1988, 144 pp., o.p.
(BL 84:1832; SLJ Dec 1988 p. 102)

4-53 **CAMERON, Eleanor (Frances Butler).** *The Court of the Stone Children.*
★★ Gr. 5–8.
The ghost of a 19th-century French girl whose father was executed for treason begs Nina Harmsworth to help prove her father's innocence. National Book Award, 1974.
Dutton, 1973, 191 pp., o.p.
(BL 70:486, 826, 80:95; CCBB 27:75; HB 50:151; Kirkus 41:1159, 1349; LJ 98:3718; Suth 2:74)

4-54 **CARD, Orson Scott.** *Homebody.* Gr. 10 up.
Builder Don Lark meets the ghost of Sylvie Delaney in the North Carolina house he is renovating and begins hunting for her murderer.
HarperCollins, 1998, 291 pp., o.p.
(Kirkus 66:128; SLJ Aug 1998 p. 196; VOYA 21:206)

4-55 **CARLSON, Natalie Savage.** *The Ghost in the Lagoon.* Gr. 2–4.
★ Timmy Hawkins uses an old scarecrow to frighten off the pirate ghost guarding the treasure in the swamp. This is the sequel to *Spooky Night* (1982), a book for younger children.
Illus. by Andrew Glass, Lothrop, 1984, 40 pp., o.p.
(BL 81:842; CCBB 38:143; SLJ Feb 1985 p. 71)

4-56 **CARRIS, Joan Davenport.** *A Ghost of a Chance.* Gr. 5–7.
Punch and his two new friends decide to search for buried treasure in Blackbeard's home, which is rumored to be haunted.
Little, Brown, 1992, 144 pp. (0-316-13016-8)
(CCBB 45:256; HBG 3:261; VOYA 15:221)

4-57 **CARROLL, Jenny (pseud. of Meg Cabot).** *Darkest Hour.* **(The Mediator series, bk. 4).** Gr. 7–10.

Sixteen-year-old Suze, a "mediator" who can communicate with ghosts, is caught up in a 150-year-old feud between the handsome ghost who lives in her house and the ghost of his wealthy, knife-wielding ex-fiancée. The other books in the series are *Shadowland* (2000), *Ninth Key* (2001), *Reunion* (2001), and *Hunted* (2003).

Pocket, 2001, pap., 244 pp. (0-671-78847-7)

(Kliatt May 2002 p. 24; SLJ Apr 2002 p. 42)

4-58   CASSEDY, Sylvia. *Behind the Attic Wall.* **Gr. 6–8.**

★★   Twelve-year-old Maggie's life with her two unwelcoming great-aunts proves to be as lonely as her previous stays in foster homes and boarding schools until voices draw her to a forgotten attic room where she finds a family of dolls who have lived there since a mysterious tragedy a century before.

Harper, 1983, 320 pp., o.p.; Avon, 1985, pap. (0-380-69843-9)

(BL 80:566; CCBB 37:45; HB 60:49; Kirkus 51:J200; SLJ Oct 1983 p. 156; Suth 3:80; TLS May 1984 p. 506)

4-59   CATES, Emily. *The Ghost in the Attic.* **(Haunting with Louisa trilogy, bk. 1). Gr. 4–6.**

After her mother dies, Dee is sent to spend the winter on Misty Island, where she meets Louisa, a ghostly girl who died in 1897 but must help four living relatives before she can rest peacefully. The sequels are *The Mystery of Misty Island Inn* (1990) and *The Ghost Ferry* (1991).

Bantam, 1990, pap., 160 pp. (0-553-15826-0)

(BL 87:1502; SLJ Oct 1990, p. 113)

4-60   CAVANAGH, Helen. *The Last Piper.* **Gr. 4–7.**

Visiting Scotland after their father's death, 13-year-old Christie and her 5-year-old brother Mikey try to help the ghost of a man wrongly hanged for murder.

Simon, 1996, 123 pp. (0-689-80481-4)

(BL 92:1826; CCBB 49:295; HBG 7:290; Kirkus 64:599; SLJ May 1996 p. 110; VOYA 19:1826)

CAVANAGH, Helen. *Panther Glade.*

See Chapter 6, High Fantasy: Myth or Legend Fantasy.

CHASE, Mary (Coyle). *The Wicked Pigeon Ladies in the Garden.*

See Chapter 10, Time Travel Fantasy.

CHERRYH, C. J. (pseud. of Carolyn Janice Cherry). *Rusalka.*

See Chapter 12, Witchcraft and Sorcery Fantasy.

4-61   *Christmas Ghosts.* Ed. by Kathryn Cramer and David G. Hartwell. Gr. 10 up.

Seventeen classic 19th- and 20th-century ghost stories written by British and American authors.

Arbor House, 1987, 283 pp., o.p.

(BL 84:26, 52; VOYA 10:278)

4-62   *Christmas Ghosts: An Anthology.* Ed. by Seon Manley and Gogo Lewis. Gr. 7 up.

Eleven short stories involving ghosts and Christmas whose authors include Charles Dickens and Lord Dunsany.
Doubleday, 1978, 227 pp., o.p.
(BL 75:53; CCBB 32:68; SLJ Oct 1978 p. 113)

4-63   CHRISTOPHER, Matt(hew F.). *Favor for a Ghost.* Gr. 4–6.
Lennie is haunted by the ghost of Billy Marble, a former school bully, who wants Lennie to dig up Billy's dog's grave and move it next to his own.
Westminster, 1983, 107 pp., o.p.
(BL 80:966; 83:585; SLJ Feb 1984 p. 67)

CHRISTOPHER, Matt(hew F.). *The Kid Who Only Hit Homers.*
See Chapter 9, Magic Adventure Fantasy.

CHRISTOPHER, Matt(hew F.). *Skateboard Tough.*
See Chapter 9, Magic Adventure Fantasy.

4-64   CHURCH, Richard (Thomas). *The French Lieutenant: A Ghost Story.* Gr. 5–7. (Orig. British pub. 1971.)
Robert doesn't believe in the 18th-century ghost said to haunt the castle near his home until he actually sees the ghost himself.
Day, 1972, 153 pp., o.p.
(BL 69:44; Kirkus 40:398; LJ 97:1927; TLS 1971 p. 766)

4-65   CLAPP, Patricia. *Jane-Emily.* Gr. 5–9.
★   No one believes Jane's explanation that the frightening episodes occurring at her grandmother's house are caused by Emily, the ghost of her aunt who died at age 12.
Lothrop, 1969, 160 pp., o.p.; Morrow, 1993, pap., 160 pp. (0-688-04592-8)
(BL 65:1224; CCBB 22:172; HB 45:538; LJ 94:2508)

4-66   CLARKE, Judith. *Starry Nights.* Gr. 5–9. (Orig. Australian pub. 2002.)
Ten-year-old Jess's family is falling apart after her older brother's drowning; her mother retreats into depression, her older sister into occult experimentation, and Jess senses a ghost-like presence in their home.
Front Street, 2003, 152 pp. (1-886910-82-0)
(BL 99:1759; HB 79:608; Kirkus 71:747; VOYA 26:500)

4-67   CLIMO, Shirley. *T. J.'s Ghost.* Gr. 4–6.
On foggy days at the beach, T. J. always meets a strange boy searching for a lost gold ring and gradually comes to understand that the boy is a ghost who drowned in a shipwreck in 1866.
Harper, 1989, 151 pp., o.p.
(BL 85:1721; Kirkus 57:460; SLJ Nov 1989 p. 105; VOYA 12:156)

4-68   COBALT, Martin (pseud. of William Mayne). *Pool of Swallows.* Gr. 5–8.
★   (Orig. British pub. 1972, entitled *Swallows.*)
A family of ghosts causes the ponds on Martin's farm to become an ocean that swallows up a herd of cattle and Martin's father as well.
Nelson, 1974, 139 pp., o.p.
(BL 70:999; CCBB 28:26; LJ 99:2286; Suth 2:91)

4-69 **COHEN, Daniel.** *Great Ghosts.* Gr. 3–5.
Nine ghostly encounters from England, the Netherlands, Greece, and the Middle East.
Illus. by David Linn, Dutton, 1990, 48 pp., o.p.
(BL 87:329; HBG 2:90; SLJ Nov 1990 p. 121)

4-70 **COLLIER, James Lincoln.** *The Empty Mirror.* Gr. 5–9.
✰ Orphaned Nick, 13, notices that his reflection has disappeared when a mysterious trouble-making double appears and Nick is accused of murder.
Bloomsbury, 2004, 192 pp. (1-58234-949-5)
(BL 101:402; CCBB 58:64; Kirkus 72:803; SLJ Oct 2004 p. 159)

CONRAD, Pam. *Stonewords: A Ghost Story.*
See Chapter 10, Time Travel Fantasy.

4-71 **COOKSON, Catherine (McMullen).** *Mrs. Flannagan's Trumpet.* Gr. 6–8.
A ghostly figure and Eddy's stubborn Granny help rescue Eddy's younger sister from white slavers.
Lothrop, 1980, 192 pp., o.p.
(BL 76:1124; CCBB 34:5; Kirkus 48:364; SLJ Oct 1980 p. 144)

COOPER (Grant), Susan (Mary). *Jethro and the Jumbie.*
See Chapter 9, Magic Adventure Fantasy.

4-72 **CORBETT, Scott.** *Captain Butcher's Body.* Gr. 4–6.
✰ The ghost of the legendary pirate Captain Butcher is due to make its once-a-century appearance, and George and Leo don't want to miss seeing it.
Little, Brown, 1976, 168 p., o.p.
(BL 73:1010, 75:305; CCBB 30:139; Kirkus 44:973; SLJ Dec 1976 p. 68)

4-73 **CORBETT, Scott.** *The Discontented Ghost.* Gr. 5–7.
✰ The ghost of Sir Simon de Canterville retells the Oscar Wilde tale *The Canterville Ghost* (orig. pub. 1906; 1997; see this chapter) and sets the record straight about his attempts to rid his home of its new American owners.
Dutton, 1978, 180 pp., o.p.
(BL 75:859, 865, 928; HB 55:190; Kirkus 46:1307; SLJ Feb 1979 p. 62)

4-74 **CRAMER, Alexander.** *A Night in Moonbeam County.* Gr. 6–9.
Ten ghostly stories told to runaway teens Chas and Ran by hoboes around a southern campfire.
Scribners, 1994, 208 pp. (0-684-19704-9)
(BL 90:1674; CCBB 47:315; HBG 5:319; Kirkus 61:553; SLJ June 1994 p. 147; VOYA 17:220)

4-75 **CREECH, Sharon.** *Pleasing the Ghost.* Gr. 3–6.
The ghost of his Uncle Arvie tries to enlist 9-year-old Dennis in a plot to keep Arvie's widow from marrying another man.
Illus. by Stacey Schuett, HarperCollins, 1996, 89 pp. (0-06-026985-5);
HarperTrophy, 1997, pap., 89 pp. (0-06-440686-5)
(BL 93:125; CCBB 50:53; HBG 8:16; Kirkus 64:1046; SLJ Nov 1996 p. 104)

4-76 **CRESSWELL (Rowe), Helen.** *A Game of Catch.* Gr. 4–6. (Orig. British
✫   pub. 1969.)
Kate and Hugh's games of ice-skating, tag, and catch near an old castle bring to
life the children who played there long ago.
Illus. by Ati Forberg, Macmillan, 1977, 48 pp., o.p.; Hodder, 1999, pap., 80 pp.
(0-034-063462-6)
(BL 73:895; CCBB 30:173; HB 53:312; Kirkus 45:4; SLJ Feb 1977 p. 62; Suth 2:109; TLS
1969 p. 1388)

CRESSWELL (Rowe), Helen. *Moondial.*
See Chapter 10, Time Travel Fantasy.

4-77 **CROSS, Gilbert B.** *A Witch Across Time.* Gr. 6–10.
The ghost of a Puritan girl who was hanged as a witch haunts 15-year-old Han-
nah, depressed after her mother's death.
Macmillan, 1990, 192 pp., o.p.
(BL 86:1276, 1338; CCBB 43:134; HBG 1:257; Kirkus 58:103; SLJ Mar 1990 p. 234; VOYA
13:27)

4-78 **CROSS, Gillian (Clare Arnold).** *The Dark Behind the Curtain.* Gr. 6–9.
✫   (Orig. British pub. 1982.)
Only Colin and Ann realize that their rehearsals for the school play, "Sweeney
Todd, the Demon Barber of Fleet Street," have called up miserable ghosts
intent on reenacting the old legend.
Illus. by David Parkins, Oxford University Press, 1987, 159 pp., o.p.
(CCBB 42:118; HB 60:596; Kliatt Jan 1989 p.20; SLJ Aug 1984 p. 83; Suth 4:87; TLS 1982
p. 788; VOYA 7:263)

4-79 **CROWE, Carole.** *Sharp Horns on the Moon.* Gr. 5–8.
Swimming alone on Boneyard Reef, Ivy meets Eleanor, the ghost of a drowned
girl, who leads Ivy into danger and demands that she go back in time to prevent
the shipwreck that killed Eleanor and her family.
Boyds Mills, 1998, 112 pp., o.p.
(CCBB 51:318; HBG 9:328; Kirkus 66:194; SLJ Mar 1998 p. 211)

4-80 **CULLEN, Lynn.** *The Backyard Ghost.* Gr. 5–7.
In the face of rejection by her new school's popular crowd, 12-year-old Eleanor
becomes obsessed with the ghost of a Confederate bugle boy who appears in
her backyard.
Houghton, 1993, 149 pp. (0-395-64527-1)
(BL 89:1830; CCBB 46:342; HBG 4:296; Kirkus 61:526; SLJ May 1993 p. 104)

4-81 **CURRY, Jane Louise.** *The Bassumtyte Treasure.* Gr. 5–7.
✫   Clues to a lost family treasure lie in a cryptic riddle, two ancestral portraits, and
an old medallion, but it is a 16th-century ghost named Lady Margaret who
helps Tommy solve the mystery.
Atheneum, 1978, 129 pp., o.p.
(BL 74:1347; CCBB 32:6; HB 54:393; Kirkus 46:243; SLJ May 1978 p. 84; TLS 1978 p.
1396)

4-82 **CURRY, Jane Louise.** *Poor Tom's Ghost.* Gr. 6–9.
✶ A hidden staircase is not the only secret held by the old house Roger's father inherits; ghostly sobbings and footsteps prove to be caused by Tom Garland, a 17th-century actor who involves Roger's family in danger.
Atheneum, 1977, 178 pp., o.p.
(BL 73:1413, 1419; CCBB 31:12; HB 53:439; Kirkus 45:426; SLJ May 1977 p. 67; TLS 1977 p. 864)

4-83 **CUSICK, Richie Tankersley.** *The House Next Door.* Gr. 6–12.
Dared by her twin brother to spend the night in the haunted house next door, Emma risks her life to help the ghost of a man who lost his life rescuing her in another lifetime.
Simon, 2002, 272 pp. (0-7434-1838-7)
(BL 98:841; Kliatt Mar 2002 p. 20; SLJ Feb 2002 p. 130; VOYA 25:126)

4-84 **CUYLER, Margery.** *The Battlefield Ghost.* Gr. 3–5.
John and Lisa Perkins discover that their 300-year-old house is haunted by the ghost of a Hessian soldier who fought in the Revolutionary War Battle of Princeton.
Illus. by Arthur Howard, Scholastic, 1999, 103 pp. (0-590-10848-4)
(BL 96:626; HBG 11:64; Kirkus 67:1225; SLJ Dec 1999 p. 90)

4-85 **DEANS, Sis.** *Every Day and All the Time.* Gr. 5–8.
Emily Racine, 11, tries to sabotage the sale of her family's house because the ghost of her brother Jon, killed in a car accident, lives in the basement, and she fears she will lose him forever.
Holt, 2003, 240 pp. (0-8050-7337-X)
(BL 100:119; Kirkus 71:1071; SLJ Dec 2003 p. 148; VOYA 26:302)

4-86 **DEEM, James M.** *The Very Real Ghost Book of Christina Rose.* Gr. 4–7.
✶ Christina and Danny's neighbor, a professor of the paranormal, suggests that they record any evidence of ghosts haunting the new home they move into after their mother's death.
Houghton, 1996, 158 pp. (0-395-76128-X); Yearling, 1998, pap., 176 pp. (0-440-41426-1)
(BL 92:1506; CCBB 49:223; HBG 7:291; Kirkus 64:372; SLJ May 1996 p. 112; VOYA 19:208)

4-87 **DEFELICE, Cynthia.** *The Ghost of Fossil Glen.* (Ghost series, bk. 1). Gr.
✶ 4–7.
The ghost of a girl murdered in Fossil Glen guides Allie Nichols to safety after a fall in exchange for Allie's avenging her murder. In the sequel, *The Ghost and Mrs. Hobbs* (2001), Allie realizes that she is a "ghost magnet" who helps spirits come to terms with their former lives when she meets the ghost of a boy who died in a fire. In *The Ghost of Cutler Creek* (2004), Allie's connection to a ghost dog convinces her that the disappearance of Hoover, her teacher's stolen dog, and the deaths of puppies at the town pet store are not a coincidence.
Farrar, 1998, 176 pp. (0-374-31787-9); HarperTrophy, 1999, pap., 160 pp. (0-380-73175-4)
(BL 94:1243; CCBB 51:240; HB 74:606; HBG 9:329; Kirkus 66:195; SLJ July 1998 p. 92, Dec 1998 p. 24)

4-88 **DELANEY, M(ichael) C(lark).** *The Great Sockathon.* Gr. 3–6.
Four best friends entering sixth grade raise money to protect the 275-year-old Balm of Gilead tree on their village green after the ghost of Eliza Baker asks Sabrina for help.
Dutton, 2004, 160 pp. (0-525-46856-0)
(BL 100:1933; Kirkus 72:683; SLJ Aug 2004 p. 120)

4-89 *Demons of the Night: Tales of the Fantastic, Madness, and the Supernatural from Nineteenth-Century France.* **Ed. by Joan C. Kessler.** Gr. 10 up.
Thirteen 19th-century French ghost stories, including tales by Honoré de Balzac, Alexander Dumas, Guy de Maupassant, and Jules Verne.
University of Chicago, 1995, 347 pp. (0-226-43207-6)
(BL 91:1478; Kliatt Sep 1995 p. 22)

4-90 **DEXTER, Catherine.** *The Gilded Cat.* Gr. 5–9.
The ghost of a boy pharaoh tells Maggie that the little cat figure she bought at a yard sale is the stolen mummy of his pet kitten, and that his magician uncle murdered him and has pursued his spirit into the 20th century.
Morrow, 1992, 199 pp. (0-688-09425-2)
(BL 88:1357; CCBB 45:292; HB 68:584; HBG 3:262; Kirkus 60:535; SLJ Apr 1992 p. 113; VOYA 15:222)

DICKENS, Charles (John Huffam). *A Christmas Carol.*
See Chapter 1, Allegorical Fantasy and Literary Fairy Tales.

DICKINSON, Peter. *The Lion-Tamer's Daughter and Other Stories.*
See Chapter 3, Fantasy Collections.

4-91 *Don't Give Up the Ghost: The Delacorte Book of Original Ghost Stories.*
★ **Ed. by David Gale.** Gr. 4–8.
Twelve tales written by well-known children's book authors including Constance Greene, Johanna Hurwitz, Walter Dean Myers, and Mary Downing Hahn.
Delacorte, 1993, pap., 144 pp., o.p.
(BL 89:2062; Kirkus 61:1200; SLJ Sep 1993 p. 232; VOYA 16:308, 17:7)

4-92 **DU BOIS, William (Sherman) Pène.** *Elisabeth the Cow Ghost.* Gr. 3–5.
(Orig. pub. 1936, entitled *Elizabeth the Cow Ghost.*)
The ghost of Elisabeth the cow returns to haunt her former master.
Illus. by the author, Viking, 1964, 41 pp., o.p.
(HB 12:28, 40:120; Kirkus 32:108; LJ 89:2208)

4-93 **DUNLOP, Eileen (Rhona).** *The Ghost by the Sea.* Gr. 4–7. (Orig. British pub. 1996).
The angry ghost of a girl who drowned 80 years ago haunts Robin and John's grandmother's house, Culaloe.
Holiday, 1996, 150 pp. (0-8234-1264-4); Poolbeg, 1998, pap. (1-85371-722-3)
(BL 93:859; CCBB 50:246; HBG 8:298; Kirkus 64:1735; SLJ Mar 1997 p. 187)

4-94 **DUNLOP, Eileen (Rhona).** *Green Willow.* Gr. 5–8. (Orig. British pub. 1993, entitled *Green Willow's Secret.*)

Kojima, the ghostly gardener Kit meets near their rented flat, helps Kit and her mother recover from the death of her sister Juliet.
Holiday, 1993, 160 pp. (0-8234-1021-8)
(BL 90:684; HBG 5:75; Kirkus 61:1328; SLJ Jan 1994 p. 114; VOYA 17:24)

4-95 **DUNLOP, Eileen (Rhona).** *The House on the Hill.* Gr. 6–9. (Orig. British
✷ pub. 1987.)
Cousins Susan and Philip uncover the cause of the mysterious light in Great-Aunt Jane's old house. Carnegie Medal Commended Book, 1987.
Holiday, 1987, 147 pp. (0-8234-0658-X)
(BL 84:392, 1276; CCBB 41:63; Kirkus 55:1461; SLJ Nov 1987 p. 115; Suth 4:105; TLS 1987 p. 529; VOYA 11:22)

4-96 **ERSKINE, Barbara.** *House of Echoes.* Gr. 10 up.
An ancient power threatens the lives of the Grant family after they inherit an old manor house.
Dutton, 1996, 433 pp. (0-525-93867-2); Signet, 1997, pap., 476 pp. (0-451-18195-6)
(BL 92:1801, 1815; Kirkus 64:766)

4-97 **ERWIN, Betty K.** *Who Is Victoria?* Gr. 4–6.
No one seems to know Victoria, the elusive girl in old-fashioned clothes who helps Margaret, Polly, and Emilie solve their problems.
Illus. by Kathleen Anderson, Little, Brown, 1973, 134 pp., o.p.
(BL 70:385; Kirkus 41:1035; LJ 99:208)

EUBANK, Judith. *Crossover.*
See Chapter 10, Time Travel Fantasy.

EZO (pseud.). *Avril.*
See Chapter 2, Animal Fantasy.

4-98 *Faces in the Dark: A Book of Scary Stories.* **Ed. by Chris Powling.** Gr. 4–6.
(Orig. British pub. 1994.)
Ten slightly spooky stories, including Chris Powling's "The Oddment," Vivien Alcock's "Siren Song," and an adaptation of Sid Fleischman's *The Ghost on a Saturday Night.*
Illus. by Peter Bailey, Kingfisher, 1994, 80 pp. (1-85697-986-5)
(BL 91:820; HBG 6:143; SLJ Dec 1994 p. 112)

4-99 **FARMER (Mockridge), Penelope.** *Penelope: A Novel.* Gr. 5–9. (Orig.
✷ British pub. 1996.)
Twelve-year-old Flora, raised by her aunt after her mother's death, begins to believe that she is the reincarnation of an 18th-century ancestor named Penelope.
McElderry, 1996, 184 pp. (0-689-80121-1)
(BL 92:1354; CCBB 49:369; HB 72:339; HBG 7:301; Kirkus 64:373; SLJ May 1996 p. 112; VOYA 19:155)

4-100 **FARMER (Mockridge), Penelope.** *Thicker Than Water.* Gr. 5–9. (Orig.
✷ British pub. 1989.)

Becky's cousin Will is haunted by the voice of a ghostly boy trapped in the shaft of a coal mine near their home.

Candlewick, 1993, 205 pp. (1-56402-178-5)

(BL 89:1229; CCBB 46:209; HBG 4:309; Kirkus 61:659; SLJ Apr 1993 p. 118; TLS Nov 24, 1989 p. 1311)

4-101 FEIL, Hila. *Blue Moon.* Gr. 7–9.

Working as a summer au pair on Cape Cod, 16-year-old Julia comes to believe that the ghost of her charge's dead mother is trying to protect the house and her daughter Molly from Molly's stepmother.

Macmillan, 1990, 193 pp., o.p.

(BL 86:1792; CCBB 43:108; HBG 1:256; Kirkus 58:178; SLJ Mar 1990 p. 235; VOYA 13:29)

4-102 FINNEY, Jack (pseud. of Walter Branden Finney). *Marion's Wall: A Novel.* Gr. 10 up.

Marion Marsh, the ghost of a promising young actress from the 1920s, returns to inhabit Jan Cheyney's body after Jan and her husband uncover a message Marion left on the wall of their San Francisco apartment.

Simon, 1973, 187 pp., o.p.

(BL 70:221; Kirkus 41:137; LJ 98:563)

4-103 FLEISCHMAN, (Albert) Sid(ney). *The Ghost in the Noonday Sun.* Gr. ☆ 4–7.

Pirates kidnap Oliver Finch in the hope that he will be able to see the ghost of Gentleman Jim, guardian of buried treasure.

Illus. by Warren Chappell, Little, Brown, 1965, 173 pp., o.p.; illus. by Peter Sís, Greenwillow, 1989, 131 pp. (0-688-08410-9); Random, 1999, pap. (0-440-41583-7)

(BL 62:54; CCBB 19:43, 42:222; Eakin:121; HB 41:490; Kirkus 33:245, 472; LJ 90:3790; SLJ Feb 1989 p. 118)

4-104 FLEISCHMAN, (Albert) Sid(ney). *The Midnight Horse.* Gr. 3–6.

☆☆ Orphaned Touch and his ghostly friend the Great Chuffalo work together to foil the dastardly plots of Touch's uncle Judge Henry Wigglesforth.

Illus. by Peter Sís, Greenwillow, 1990, 84 pp. (0-688-09441-4); Dell, 1992, pap. (0-440-40614-5)

(BL 86:2171; CCBB 44:83; HB 66:744; HBG 2:71; Kirkus 58:1003; SLJ Sep 1990 p. 226, Dec 1990 p. 22; Suth 4:119)

FLEISCHMAN, (Albert) Sid(ney). *The 13th Floor: A Ghost Story.*
See Chapter 10, Time Travel Fantasy.

4-105 FLEISCHMAN, Paul (Taylor). *Graven Images: Three Stories.* Gr. 7–9.

☆ In the only fantasy story of the three, "The Man of Influence," a poor but arrogant sculptor accepts a ghost's commission to carve a statue of himself committing an infamous murder. John Newbery Medal Honor Book, 1983.

Illus. by Andrew Glass, Harper, 1982, 85 pp., o.p., pap., 96 pp. (0-06-440186-3)

(BL 79:368, 980; CCBB 36:125; HB 58:656; Kirkus 50:937; SLJ Sep 1982 p. 137; Suth 3:135)

4-106   FLORA, James (Royer). *Grandpa's Ghost Stories.* Gr. 2–4.
✯ Grandpa has scary tales to tell: about a screaming skeleton, a ghost, a witch, and a werewolf. The sequel is *Grandpa's Witched-Up Christmas* (1982).
Illus. by the author, Atheneum, 1978, 32 pp., o.p.
(BL 75:216; HB 55:510; Kirkus 46:1066; SLJ Oct 1978 p. 132, Apr 1982 p. 31)

4-107   FREEMAN, Barbara C(onstance). *A Haunting Air.* Gr. 5–7. (Orig. British
✯ pub. 1976.)
Melissa and her neighbor search old letters and newspapers to discover why they keep hearing the ghostly singing of a Victorian child named Hanny.
Illus. by the author, Dutton, 1977, 158 pp., o.p.
(BL 74:811; CCBB 31:141; HB 54:163; Kirkus 45:1270; SLJ Feb 1978 p. 57; Suth 2:155)

4-108   FREEMAN, Barbara C(onstance). *A Pocket of Silence.* Gr. 7–9. (Orig.
British pub. 1977.)
Zilia spins a tale of romance, kidnapping, and murder for Caroline, who discovers that Zilia has come from 200 years in the past to help solve a mystery.
Decorations by the author, Dutton, 1978, 171 pp., o.p.
(BL 75:804, 809; HB 55:192; Kirkus 42:132; SLJ Apr 1979 p. 55; TLS 1977 p. 864)

**4-109   *Fun Phantoms: Tales of Ghostly Entertainment.* Ed. by Seon Manley and
Gogo Lewis.** Gr. 6–10.
Twelve humorous ghost stories by such authors as Frank Stockton, Philippa Pearce, Oscar Wilde, Saki, and James Thurber.
Morrow, 1979, 192 pp., o.p.
(BL 75:860; Kirkus 47:267; SLJ Mar 1979 p. 142)

4-110   GAGE, Wilson (pseud. of Mary Q[uintard] Govan Steele). *The Ghost of
✯ Five Owl Farm.* Gr. 4–6.
Ted's attempts to enliven the summer by creating "ghostly" visitations backfire when a real ghost appears.
Illus. by Paul Galdone, World, 1966, 127 pp., o.p.
(BL 62:1049; CCBB 20:9; HB 42:435; Kirkus 34:245; LJ 91:2716)

GAIMAN, Neil. *Coraline.*
See Chapter 7, High Fantasy: Travel to Other Worlds.

4-111   GARFIELD, Leon. *The Empty Sleeve.* Gr. 6–9. (Orig. British pub. 1988.)
✯ As predicted at his birth, twin Peter Gannet is haunted by ghostly apparitions in this Dickensian tale set in 18th-century England.
Delacorte, 1988, 216 pp., o.p.
(BL 85:149, 158, 879; CCBB 42:34; HB 65:78; Kirkus 56:972; SLJ Oct 1988 p.161; Suth 4:130; TLS 1988 p. 716)

4-112   GARFIELD, Leon. *The Ghost Downstairs.* Gr. 7–9. (Orig. British pub.
1972.)
Dennis Fast eagerly gives up seven years of his life in exchange for a million pounds, but finds, to his dismay, that he is haunted by the ghost of himself as a child because he'd unwittingly given away the *first* seven years of his life. Kate Greenaway Medal Commended Book, 1972.
Illus. by Antony Maitland, Pantheon, 1972, 107 pp., o.p.
(CCBB 25:168; HB 48:599; Kirkus 40:623; LJ 97:4056, 4087)

4-113 **GARFIELD, Leon.** *Mister Corbett's Ghost.* Gr. 5–8. (Orig. British pub.
✶   1968.)
The ghost of his former master, Mr. Corbett, returns to haunt Benjamin after his
idle wish for the man's death is fulfilled.
Pantheon, 1968, 87 pp., o.p.; Viking, 1988, o.p.
(BL 65:450, 84:1189; CCBB 22:92; HB 4:560; Kirkus 36:824; LJ 73:8; Suth:141; TLS 1969
p. 350)

4-114 **GARFIELD, Leon.** *The Restless Ghost: Three Stories.* Gr. 5–7. (Orig. pub.
✶   in England.)
In the title story, a ghost returns to haunt his imitator.
Illus. by Saul Lambert, Pantheon, 1969, 132 pp., o.p.
(CCBB 23:143; HB 46:45; Kirkus 37:1122; LJ 94:4295; Suth:142)

GARFIELD, Leon. *The Wedding Ghost.*
See Chapter 6, High Fantasy: Myth or Legend Fantasy.

4-115 **GARLAND, Sherry.** *Cabin 102.* Gr. 5–9.
The ghostly crying he hears coming from the next cabin on a cruise ship leads
Dusty, 12, to the ghost of an Arawak Indian girl.
Harcourt 1995, 242 pp. (0-15-200663-X)
(BL 92:559; CCBB 49:127; Kirkus 63:1564; Kliatt Mar 1996 p. 16; SLJ Dec 1995 p. 104;
VOYA 18:300)

4-116 **GARRETSON, Jerri.** *The Secret of Whispering Springs.* Gr. 5–8.
Until Cassie's little brother disappears, her parents don't believe in the danger
she senses surrounding their isolated old house. It involves Annie, the ghost of
a child killed by lightning long ago.
Ravenstone, 2002, pap., 206 pp. (0-9659712-4-4)
(Bl 98:1948; Kliatt Nov 2002 p. 24; SLJ Aug 2002 p. 184; VOYA 25:296)

4-117 **GATES, Susan P.** *The Burnhope Wheel.* Gr. 6–9. (Orig. British pub. 1989.)
Fifteen-year-old Ellen and her new friend Dave are drawn into replaying a
tragedy that occurred a hundred years previously at the bottom of the Burnhope
lead mine.
Holiday, 1989, 174 pp., o.p.
(BL 86:735, 742; CCBB 43:84; HBG 1:83; Kirkus 57:1747; SLJ Dec 1989 p. 118; VOYA
13:290)

4-118 *The Ghost Story Treasury.* **Sel. by Linda Sonntag.** Gr. 5–8.
Fifteen ghostly stories and poems by such authors as Virginia Hamilton and
Judith Gorog.
Illus. by Annabel Spenceley, Putnam, 1987, 87 pp., o.p.
(Kirkus 55:1325; SLJ Mar 1988 p. 200)

4-119 *Ghosts: An Anthology.* **Ed. by William (James Carter) Mayne.** Gr. 6–9.
(Orig. British pub. 1971.)
Twenty-five stories and poems about ghosts and goblins, including works by
Rudyard Kipling, Robert Louis Stevenson, and Walter de la Mare.
Nelson, 1971, 187 pp., o.p.
(BL 68:430, 434; CCBB 25:12; HB 47:491; LJ 96:3478)

4-120 *The Ghost's Companion: A Haunting Anthology.* **Ed. by Peter Raining.**
Gr. 10 up.
Fifteen ghostly and supernatural tales whose authors include Ray Bradbury,
M. R. James, and Rudyard Kipling.
Taplinger, 1976, 191 pp., o.p.
(BL 72:1090, 1103; Kirkus 44:159; TLS 1976 p. 561)

4-121 *Ghosts for Christmas.* **Ed. by Richard Dalby.** Gr. 10 up. (Orig. British pub.
1988.)
Thirty ghostly tales set during the Christmas season, written in the 19th and
20th centuries, whose authors include Charles Dickens and Robert Louis
Stevenson.
Carroll & Graf, 1989, 339 pp., o.p.
(BL 86:525, 540; TLS 1988 p. 1351; VOYA 13:38)

4-122 *Ghostwise: A Book of Midnight Stories.* **Ed. by Dan Yashinsky.** Gr. 6–12.
Thirty-five supernatural tales often told by practicing storytellers.
August House, 1997, pap., 223 pp. (0-87483-499-6)
(CCBB 51:263; Kliatt Nov 1997 p. 17; VOYA 20:392)

4-123 **GODDEN (Dixon), (Margaret) Rumer.** *Take Three Tenses; A Fugue in
Time.* Gr. 10 up. (Orig. British pub. 1945, entitled *A Fugue in Time.*)
Ninety-nine years of Dane family history come to life for an American girl vis-
iting her 80-year-old great-uncle's London home.
Little, Brown, 1945, 252 pp., o.p.
(BL 41:225; Kirkus 13:38; TLS 1945 p. 245)

4-124 **GOOBIE, Beth.** *Before Wings.* Gr. 7–12. (Orig. Canadian pub. 2000.)
☆ Working at her aunt's summer camp two years after surviving a brain
aneurysm, Adrien, 15, sees five ghostly spirits on the lake and realizes that they
are connected to a tragedy that haunts her aunt. Young Adult Canadian Book
Award, 2001.
Orca, 2001, 203 pp. (1-55143-161-0), 2001, pap., 176 pp. (1-55143-163-7)
(BL 97:1391; HB 778:207; HBG 12:322; Kliatt Mar 2001 p. 10, Sep 2001 p. 16; SLJ Apr
2001 p. 140; VOYA 24:11, 51)

4-125 **GORDON, John (William).** *The Burning Baby, and Other Ghosts.* Gr.
☆ 8–12. (Orig. British pub. 1992.)
Five tales about ghosts seeking revenge on those who killed them, including
"Under the Ice," "The Eels," and "The Burning Baby."
Candlewick, 1993, 112 pp. (1-56402-067-3)
(BL 90:430; CCBB 47:44; HBG 5:86; Kirkus 61:1273; SLJ Nov 1993 p. 122)

4-126 **GORDON, John (William).** *The Ghost on the Hill.* Gr. 8 up. (Orig. British
pub. 1976.)
The ghost of Tom Goodchild becomes entangled in the lives of three young vil-
lagers—Ralph, Jenny, and Joe.
Viking, 1977, 171 pp., o.p.
(CCBB 31:32; Kirkus 45:290; SLJ May 1977 p. 78)

GOROG, Judith. *In a Creepy, Creepy Place, and Other Scary Stories.*
See Chapter 3, Fantasy Collections.

GOROG, Judith. *In a Messy, Messy Room, and Other Strange Stories.*
See Chapter 3, Fantasy Collections.

4-127 GOROG, Judith. *No Swimming in Dark Pond, and Other Chilling Tales.*
Gr. 6–10.
Thirteen shiver-producing tales, including "Flawless Beauty," "The Sufficient
Prayer," and "No Swimming in Dark Pond."
Philomel, 1987, 111 pp., o.p.
(BL 83:1590, 1601; CCBB 40:207; Kirkus 55:227; SLJ Mar 1987 p. 158; VOYA 10:120)

4-128 GOROG, Judith. *On Meeting Witches at Wells.* Gr. 5–8.
Three teachers and some ghostly visitors tell stories to a group of eighth-
graders, including "An Old, Often Retold, Story of Revenge," "The Silver
Skier," and the title story, "On Meeting Witches at Wells."
Putnam, 1991, 119 pp. (0-399-21803-3)
(BL 88:758; CCBB 45:156; HBG 3:65; Kirkus 59:1222; SLJ Jan 1992 p. 109)

4-129 GOROG, Judith. *Please Do Not Touch.* Gr. 5–9.
Touching an exhibit at an interactive museum sends visitors into the worlds of
11 eerie stories, including those about a shape-shifting brother-in-law, an over-
bearing teapot that takes over its owner's life, and a young DJ whose thoughts
are broadcast on the air.
Scholastic, 1993, 144 pp., o.p.
(BL 90:51; CCBB 47:10; HBG 5:86; Kirkus 61:1001; SLJ Sep 1993 p. 251; VOYA 16 290)

4-130 GOROG, Judith. *A Taste for Quiet, and Other Disquieting Tales.* Gr. 6–10.
Twelve eerie tales, some in fairy tale style and others in contemporary settings,
including "Those Three Wishes," "A Story About Death," and "Critch."
Illus. by Jeanne Titherington, Putnam, 1982, 128 pp., o.p.
(BL 79:906; HB 59:170; Kirkus 50:1295; SLJ Mar 1983 p. 192)

Gothic! Ten Original Dark Tales. **Ed. by Deborah Noyes.**
See Chapter 3, Fantasy Collections.

4-131 GRAY, Genevieve S(tuck). *Ghost Story.* Gr. 3–5.
A ghost family is kept busy haunting the vagrants who have moved into their
house.
Illus. by Greta Matus, Lothrop, 1975, 46 pp., o.p.
(BL 71:690; CCBB 28:177; Kirkus 43:122; SLJ Apr 1975 p. 52; Suth 2:77)

4-132 *Great Ghost Stories.* **Sel. by Barry Moser.** Gr. 6–12.
Thirteen ghost stories by well-known authors, including Philippa Pearce, H. P.
Lovecraft, H. G. Wells, and Madeleine L'Engle.
Illus. by Barry Moser, Morrow, 1998, 240 pp. (0-688-14587-6)
(BL 95:580; SLJ Oct 1998 p. 142; VOYA 21:442)

GREENBERG, Dan. *A Ghost Named Wanda.*
See Chapter 8, Humorous Fantasy.

4-133 GRIFFIN, Adele. *The Other Shepards.* Gr. 6–9.
Annie, a young painter, shakes Holland and Geneva Shepard out of their fearful
obsession with the accidental deaths of their three older siblings.

Hyperion, 1998, 218 pp. (0-7868-0423-8)

(BL 94:1999, 95:782; CCBB 52:85, 97 Kirkus 66:1117; SLJ Sep 1998 p. 203, Dec 1998 p. 25; VOYA 21:273)

4-134 GRIFFIN, Peni R(ae). *The Ghost Sitter.* Gr. 4–6.

✭ Charlotte and her new friend Shannon hold a séance to contact Susie, the ghost haunting Charlotte's new home.

Dutton, 2001, 128 pp. (0-525-46676-2); Puffin, 2002, pap., 144 pp. (0-14-230216-3)

(BL 97:2120; HB 77:323; HBG 12:305; Kirkus 69:659; SLJ June 2001 p. 149)

4-135 GRIFFITH, Helen V(irginia). *Cougar.* Gr. 4–7.

✭ The ghost of Cougar, a half-wild horse that died in a barn fire, takes over orphaned Nickel's bicycle, helping him to cope with his new foster home and a school bully.

Greenwillow, 1999, 112 pp. (0-688-16337-8); HarperTrophy, 2001, 112 pp. (0-380-73240-8)

(BL 95:1414; CCBB 62:229, 239; HB 75:330; HBG 10:292; Kirkus 67:800; SLJ May 1999 p. 125)

4-136 GRIPE, Maria (Kristina). *Agnes Cecilia.* Gr. 6–10. (Orig. Swedish pub.

✭ 1981.)

Lonely Nora's beautiful old doll reveals some sad family secrets involving other orphaned or unloved children from the past.

Trans. by Rika Lesser, Harper, 1990, 288 pp., o.p.

(BL 86:1890, 1898; CCBB 43:161; HBG 1:250; Kirkus 58:727; SLJ Apr 1990 p. 140, Dec 1990 p. 22; VOYA 13:103)

HAHN, Mary Downing. *The Doll in the Garden: A Ghost Story.*
See Chapter 10, Time Travel Fantasy.

4-137 HAHN, Mary Downing. *The Old Willis Place: A Ghost Story.* Gr. 4–7.

Who are the ghosts haunting the old Willis mansion? Lissa, daughter of the new caretaker, Diana, and her younger brother, George, are determined to find out.

Clarion, 2004, 208 pp. (0-618-43018-0)

(BL 101:124; CCBB 58:122; Kirkus 72:866)

HAHN, Mary Downing. *Time for Andrew.*
See Chapter 10, Time Travel Fantasy.

4-138 HAHN, Mary Downing. *Wait Till Helen Comes: A Ghost Story.* Gr. 5–7.

Molly and Michael's miserable stepsister Heather threatens them with punishment by Helen, a ghost only the children can perceive, in this suspenseful story.

Houghton, 1986, 184 pp., o.p.

(BL 83:60; CCBB 40:27; HB 62:744; Kirkus 54:1204; SLJ Oct 1986, p. 176)

HALL, Lynn. *Dagmar Schultz and the Angel Edna.*
See Chapter 8, Humorous Fantasy.

4-139 HALL, Lynn. *The Mystery of the Caramel Cat.* Gr. 3–4.

The ghost of a caramel cat has haunted an abandoned mansion, formerly a stop on the Underground Railroad, ever since the cat accidentally caused the capture of two runaway slaves.

Illus. by Ruth Sanderson, Garrard, 1981, 64 pp., o.p.

(BL 78:438; SLJ Dec 1981 p. 82)

4-140 HAMILTON (Adoff), Virginia (Esther). *Sweet Whispers, Brother Rush.*
★★ Gr. 7–10.

Fifteen-year-old Tree (Teresa) has ghostly visions of the past that enable her to piece together the tragic history of her mother's family. John Newbery Medal Honor Book, 1983; Boston Globe/Horn Book Award, 1983; Coretta Scott King Fiction Award, 1983.

Putnam, 1982, 224 pp. (0-399-20894-1); Avon, 1983, pap. (0-380-65193-9)

(BL 78:1518, 1525; 79:685, 980, 80:352, 86:790; CCBB 35:207; HB 58:505, 59:330; Kirkus 50:801; SLJ Sep 1982 p. 138; Suth 3:172; VOYA 5:31, 5:36)

4-141 HARRIS, Christie (Lucy Irwin). *Secret in the Stlalakum Wild.* Gr. 4–7.
(Orig. pub. in Canada.)

Spirits of the Northwest Coast Salish Indians send a little girl named Morann into the wilderness alone on a quest for treasure.

Illus. by Douglas Tait, Atheneum, 1972, 186 pp., o.p.

(BL 68:908; CCBB 25:169; Kirkus 40:478; LJ 97:1913)

HARRIS, Rosemary (Jeanne). *Sea Magic and Other Stories of Enchantment.*
See Chapter 3, Fantasy Collections.

HARRIS, Rosemary (Jeanne). *The Seal-Singing.*
See Chapter 6, High Fantasy: Myth or Legend Fantasy.

4-142 HASELEY, Dennis. *Ghost Catcher.* Gr. 5–6.

This is an allegorical tale about a man who snatches loved ones back from the land of the dead to give them a second chance at happiness—until the day he himself becomes trapped in the land of the ghosts.

Illus. by Lloyd Bloom, Harper, 1991, 40 pp., LB (0-06-022247-6)

(BL 88:327; HBG 3:34; Kirkus 59:1160; SLJ Nov 1991 p. 117)

**4-143 *The Haunted and the Haunters: Tales of Ghosts and Other Apparitions.*
Ed. by Kathleen Lines.** Gr. 7–10. (Orig. British pub. 1975.)

Spine-tingling tales by Lucy Boston, Joan Aiken, and Walter de la Mare, among others. This is a companion volume to *The House of the Nightmare and Other Eerie Stories* (1968).

Farrar, 1975, 275 pp., o.p.

(BL 72:358; HB 52:60; Kirkus 43:1194; SLJ Dec 1975 p. 68)

4-144 *The Haunted House: A Collection of Original Stories.* Ed. by Jane (Hyatt) Yolen (Stemple) and Martin H. Greenberg. Gr. 3–6.

Each story in this collection is set in a different room in the house at 66 Brown's End, where ghosts drive out a succession of owners.

Illus. by Doron Ben-Ami, HarperCollins, 1995, 88 pp. (0-06-024467-4)

(BL 92:77; HBG 7:135; SLJ Nov 1995 p. 108)

4-145 *Haunting Tales.* **Ed. by Barbara Ireson.** Gr. 6–9. (Orig. British pub. 1973.)
Ghostly tales by E. Nesbit, Joan Aiken, Ray Bradbury, and Eleanor Farjeon.
Illus. by Freda Woolf, Dutton, 1974, 279 pp., o.p.
(BL 71:570; HB 50:697; Kirkus 42:1161)

4-146 **HAWES, Louise.** *Rosey in the Present Tense.* Gr. 7–10.
☆ Seventeen-year-old Franklin is still grieving over the death of his girlfriend,
Rosey, when her ghost returns, worrying his mother and his friends even more.
Walker, 1999, 128 pp. (0-8027-8685-5), 2001, pap., 144 pp. (0-8027-7603-5)
(BL 95:1398; CCBB 52:314; HBG 10:303; Kirkus 67:451; Kliatt May 1999 p. 10; SLJ May
1999 p. 125)

HAYES, Sarah. *Crumbling Castle.*
See Chapter 12, Witchcraft and Sorcery Fantasy.

4-147 **HAYES, Sheila.** *Zoe's Gift.* Gr. 4–6.
On vacation in England, Manhattanite Cory befriends a girl named Zoe who is
kept locked away because her grandmother fears her ability to see into the past.
Dutton, 1994, 156 pp. (0-525-67484-5)
(BL 91:41; HBG 6:77; Kirkus 62:985; SLJ Aug 1994 p. 156)

4-148 **HAYNES, Betsy.** *The Ghost of the Gravestone Hearth.* Gr. 4–6.
Charlie spends the summer searching for buried treasure after an encounter
with the ghosts of a drowned boy and his pirate enemies.
Nelson, 1977, 160 pp., o.p.
(BL 74:41; CCBB 31:60; Kirkus 45:351; SLJ May 1977 p. 77)

4-149 **HEARNE, Betsy (Gould).** *Eli's Ghost.* Gr. 4–7.
A young boy named Eli runs away from his cruel father to search for his moth-
er, almost drowns in a whirlpool, and releases a mischievous ghost.
Illus. by Ronald (Norbert) Himler, Macmillan, 1987, 104 pp. (0-689-50420-9)
(BL 83:1205; CCBB 40:126; HB 63:612; Kirkus 55:56; SLJ Apr 1987 p. 94; Suth 4:170)

HENDRICH, Paula (Griffith). *Who Says So?*
See Chapter 9, Magic Adventure Fantasy.

4-150 **HENRY, Maeve.** *A Gift for Gift: A Ghost Story.* Gr. 6–9. (Orig. British pub.
☆ 1990.)
Michael, a ghostly creature from "the gap between the worlds," promises to
take 15-year-old Fran away from her squalid home and make all her wishes
come true if she agrees to become his eternal companion.
Delacorte, 1992, 106 pp., o.p.
(BL 88:1825; CCBB 45:181; HBG 3:274; Kirkus 60:670; SLJ Mar 1992 p. 256; VOYA
15:28)

4-151 **HILDICK, E(dmund) W(allace).** *The Ghost Squad Breaks Through.* **(The**
☆ **Ghost Squad series, bk. 1).** Gr. 5–7.
Four ghosts and two live teenagers band together to solve crimes. The sequels
are *The Ghost Squad and the Halloween Conspiracy* (1985), *The Ghost Squad
Flies Concorde* (1985), *The Ghost Squad and the Ghoul of Grünberg* (1986),
The Ghost Squad and the Prowling Hermits (1987), and *The Ghost Squad and
the Menace of the Malevs* (1988).

Dutton, 1984, 112 pp., o.p.
(BL 80:1398, 85:585; SLJ 30:101)

HOFFMAN, Mary. *The Four-Legged Ghosts.*
See Chapter 9, Magic Adventure Fantasy.

4-152 HOFFMAN, Nina Kiriki. *A Red Heart of Memories.* Gr. 10 up.

✷ Homeless Matt (Matilda) Black accompanies her new friend Edmund Reynolds to his hometown to meet the ghost of an old friend and to search for a missing friend named Suki. The sequel is *Past the Size of Dreaming* (2001), and *A Stir of Bones* (2003; see below) is the prequel.
Berkley/Ace, 1999, 336 pp., o.p.; Ace, 2000, pap., 329 pp. (0-441-00768-6)
(BL 96:239; Kirkus 67:1354; LJ Oct 15, 1999 p. 110; VOYA 22:414, 23:11)

4-153 HOFFMAN, Nina Kiriki. *A Stir of Bones.* Gr. 7 up.
In this prequel to the author's *A Red Heart of Memories* (1999; see above), 14-year-old Susan Blackstrom uses the power of Nathan Blacksmith, a ghost haunting a nearby house, to help her mother escape from her abusive father.
Viking, 2003, 211 pp. (0-670-03551-3)
(BL 100:310; CCBB 57:192; HBG 15:110; Kirkus 71:1018; SLJ Dec 2003 p. 152; VOYA 26:412, 27:12)

4-154 HOLMAN (Valen), Felice. *Real.* Gr. 5–8.
Exploring in the California desert in 1932, Colly meets Sparrow, an 18th-century Cahuilla Indian boy trapped in time.
Simon, 1997, 176 pp. (0-689-80772-4)
(BL 94:319; CCBB 51:130; HBG 9:73; Kirkus 65:1390; SLJ Nov 1997 p. 119; VOYA 20:386)

4-155 HOTZE, Sollace. *Acquainted with the Night.* Gr. 7–12.

✷ The ghost of Evaline Bloodsworth, a young woman who died on Plum Cove Island in 1824, appears to 17-year-old Molly and her cousin Caleb throughout the summer they spend together on the Maine island.
Houghton, 1992, 230 pp. (0-395-61576-3)
(BL 89:666; CCBB 46:75; Kirkus 60:1377; SLJ Nov 1992 p. 123; VOYA 15:292)

HOWARD, Joan (pseud. of Patricia Gordon). *The Witch of Scrapfaggot Green.*
See Chapter 12, Witchcraft and Sorcery Fantasy.

4-156 HOYLAND, John. *The Ivy Garland.* Gr. 4–6.
Linda, Diane, and Jamie feel compelled to solve the mystery of the ghostly boy in old-fashioned clothes whom they meet in a mountain cave.
Illus. by Richard Vicary, Schocken, 1983, 1987, 96 pp., o.p.
(CCBB 36:211; SLJ Mar 1984 p. 160)

4-157 HUGHES, Dean. *Nutty's Ghost.* Gr. 5–7.
The ghost of a Shakespearean actor whose career was ruined by his appearance in a mediocre film haunts Nutty Nutsell as he prepares for a part in a movie by the same director. This is the sequel to the nonfantasy *Nutty, the Movie Star* (1989).

Macmillan, 1993, 136 pp. (0-689-31743-3)

(BL 89:1054; HBG 4:299; Kirkus 61:148; SLJ May 1993 p. 106)

4-158 HURST, Carol Otis. *The Wrong One.* Gr. 3–6.
A ghost contacts newly adopted 5-year-old Sookan after her mother and siblings move from Brooklyn to an old Massachusetts farmhouse.
Houghton, 2003, 160 pp. (0-618-27599-1)

(BL 99:1198; HBG 14:368; Kirkus 71:678; SLJ May 2003 p. 154)

4-159 IBBOTSON, Eva. *Dial-a-Ghost.* Gr. 4–7. (Orig. British pub. 1996.)
☆ After orphaned Oliver inherits Helton Hall, his enraged relatives Fulton and Frieda Snodde-Brittle hire a ghost placement agency that sends the terrifying Shriekers to frighten Oliver to death.
Illus. by Kevin Hawkes, Dutton, 2001, 256 pp. (0-525-46693-2); Puffin, 2003, pap., 208 pp. (0-14-250018-6)

(BL 98:392; CCBB 55:20; HB 77:586; HBG 13:87; Kirkus 69:741; SLJ Aug 2001 p. 184; VOYA 24:370)

4-160 IBBOTSON, Eva. *The Great Ghost Rescue.* Gr. 5–7. (Orig. British pub. 1983.)
So many of England's great mansions have become unhauntable that Humphrey the Horrible appeals to the prime minister for help.
Illus. by Giulio Maestro, Walck, 1975, 135 pp., o.p.; illus. by Kevin Hawkes, Dutton, 2002, 167 pp. (0-525-46769-6)

(CCBB 56:113; HB 51:593, 78:574; HBG 14:83; Kirkus 43:605; SLJ May 1975 p. 70, Aug 2002 p. 189)

4-161 IBBOTSON, Eva. *The Haunting of Granite Falls.* Gr. 3–7. (Orig. British pub. 1987.)
The Scottish ghosts haunting Castle Cara band together to rescue Hiram C. Hopgood's kidnapped daughter Helen and orphaned Alex MacBuff after Hopgood buys the castle and ships it to Texas.
Illus. by Kevin Hawkes, Dutton, 2004, 224 pp. (0-525-47192-8)

(BL 100:1589; CCBB 58:22; HB 80:453; Kirkus 72:395)

IRVING, Washington. *The Legend of Sleepy Hollow.*
See Chapter 6, High Fantasy: Myth or Legend Fantasy.

4-162 JACQUES, Brian. *Castaways of the Flying Dutchman.* Gr. 5–8. (Orig. British pub. 2001.)
After a mute boy named Ben stows away on the 17th-century pirate ship *Flying Dutchman*, he watches an angel condemn the ship to sail throughout eternity and is given the gifts of freedom, speech, and eternal youth. In *The Angel's Command* (2003), Ben and his black Labrador, Ned, sail the Caribbean with buccaneer Captain Thuran, and then sail to France to rescue a young man named Adamo.
Philomel, 2001, 327 pp. (0-399-23601-5); Ace/Penguin, 2002, pap., 361 pp. (0-441-00914-X)

(BL 97:1271; CCBB 54:266; HB 77:208; HBG 12:308; Kirkus 69:111; SLJ Mar 2001 p. 250; VOYA 24:53)

JACQUES, Brian. *The Ribbajack and Other Curious Yarns.*
See Chapter 3, Fantasy Collections.

4-163 JACQUES, Brian. *Seven Strange and Ghostly Tales.* Gr. 5–7. (Orig. British pub. 1991.)
Humorous and shivery stories set in present-day English neighborhoods and schools, involving ghosts, vampires, and the Devil.
Putnam, 1991, 137 pp. (0-399-22103-4); Avon 1993, pap. (0-380-71906-1); Paper Star, 1999, pap. (0-698-11808-1)
(BL 88:524; CCBB 45:93; HB 68:341; HBG 3:82; SLJ Dec 1991 p. 116)

JAMES, M(ontague) R(hodes). *The Five Jars.*
See Chapter 9, Magic Adventure Fantasy.

JENNINGS, Paul. *Unreal! Eight Surprising Stories.*
See Chapter 3, Fantasy Collections.

4-164 JENSEN, Dorothea. *The Riddle of Penncroft Farm.* Gr. 5–7.
Lars's oddly dressed new friend, Geordie, tells him about meeting General George Washington and taking part in the Revolutionary War encampment at Valley Forge.
Harcourt, 1989, 180 pp. (0-15-200574-9), 1991, pap. (0-15-266908-6)
(BL 86:351; CCBB 43:62; HBG 1:87; Kirkus 57:1328; SLJ Oct 1989 p. 120)

JONES, Diana Wynne. *The Time of the Ghost.*
See Chapter 10, Time Travel Fantasy.

4-165 JONES, Louis C(lark). *Things That Go Bump in the Night.* Gr. 5–8.
Tales of ghosts, witches, and haunted houses.
Illus. by Erwin Austin, Hill, 1959, 208 pp., o.p.
(BL 55:559; Kirkus 27:205; LJ 84:1275)

4-166 KEEHN, Sally M. *Moon of Two Dark Horses.* Gr. 5–9.
The ghost of Coshmoo, a 12-year-old Delaware Indian boy, tells the story of his doomed friendship with Daniel, the son of white settlers on the Susquehanna River, as they try to prevent their peoples from destroying each other during the Revolutionary War.
Putnam, 1995, 218 pp. (0-399-22783-0)
(BL 92:558; CCBB 49:59; HBG 7:64; Kirkus 63:1282; VOYA 18:303)

4-167 KEHRET, Peg. *Horror at the Haunted House.* Gr. 5–7.
✯ Lydia Clayton, the ghost of the original owner of the historic Clayton house, appears to Ellen whenever she examines Mrs. Clayton's priceless collection of Wedgwood china. This is the sequel to *Terror at the Zoo* (1992), which is not a fantasy.
Dutton, 1992, 144 pp. (0-525-65106-3)
(BL 89:56; HBG 4:71; Kirkus 60:991; SLJ Sep 1992 p. 254; VOYA 15:224)

4-168 KELLEHER, Victor (pseud. of Michael Kitchener). *Baily's Bones.* Gr. 6–10. (Orig. Australian pub. 1988.)

Dee and Alex's mentally disabled brother Kenny is taken over by the vengeful ghost of Frank Baily in the remote Australian valley where their mother is doing historical research.

Dial, 1989, 182 pp., o.p.

(BL 86:670; CCBB 43:140; HB 66:204; HBG 1:86; Kirkus 57:1594; SLJ Nov 1989 p. 111; VOYA 13:30)

4-169 KEMP, Gene. *Jason Bodger and the Priory Ghost.* Gr. 4–7. (Orig. British
☆ pub. 1985.)

A medieval ghost that only Jason can see convinces this tough boy to cooperate with his timid teachers.

Illus. by Elaine McGregor Turney, Faber, 1985, 140 pp., o.p.

(BL 82:810; CCBB 39:169; SLJ Sep 1986 p. 136; Suth 4:211; TLS 1985 p. 1460)

4-170 KIMMEL, Elizabeth Cody. *In the Stone Circle.* Gr. 5–8.
☆ Spending the summer in Wales with her researcher father, Cristyn, 14, meets Carwen, a ghostly girl related to the 13th-century ruler of Wales.

Scholastic, 1998, 225 pp. (0-590-21308-3), 2001, pap. (0-439-06259-4)

(BL 94:1448; CCBB 51:248; HBG 9:332; Kirkus 66:583; Kliatt May 1998 p. 6; SLJ Apr 1998 p. 132; VOYA 21:202)

4-171 KING-SMITH, Dick. *The Roundhill.* Gr. 4–7. (Orig. British pub. 1999.)
☆ In the summer of 1936, 14-year-old Evan meets a ghostly girl named Alice on the domed hilltop near his home in the Cotswolds.

Illus. by Sian Bailey, Crown, 2000, 96 pp., o.p.; Random, 2002, pap., 96 pp. (0-440-41845-5)

(BL 97:960; HBG 12:75; Kirkus 68:1546; Kliatt Nov 2000 p. 6; SLJ Dec 2000 p. 145)

4-172 KINSELLA, W(illiam) P(atrick). *Shoeless Joe.* Gr. 10 up.
☆ Baseball fanatic Ray Kinsella joins forces with J. D. Salinger in resurrecting the long-deceased members of the Chicago Black Sox team, including Shoeless Joe Jackson.

Houghton, 1982, 265 pp., o.p.; Ballantine, 1983, pap. (0-345-34256-9)

(BL 78:941; Kirkus 50:159; LJ 107:745; SLJ Aug 1982 p. 131, Dec 1982 p. 291)

4-173 KIPLING, (Joseph) Rudyard. *Phantoms and Fantasies: Twenty Tales.* Gr. 6–8. (Orig. pub. in England.)

Twenty ghostly stories set in India and England.

Illus. by Burt Silverman, Doubleday, 1965, 302 pp., o.p.

(Kirkus 33:533; LJ 90:3133)

4-174 KLAVENESS, Jan O'Donnell. *The Griffin Legacy.* Gr. 6–9.
☆ Amy's resemblance to an 18th-century ancestor, Lucy Griffin, enables her to speak with apparitions of Lucy and of Seth Howes, a Loyalist shot to death by Lucy's father. With the help of friends, Amy solves the mystery of a lost family legacy and brings peace to the souls of Lucy and Seth.

Macmillan, 1983, 184 pp., o.p.

(BL 80:297; CCBB 37:110; HB 60:61; SLJ Dec 1983 p. 85; Suth 3:236; VOYA 7:32)

4-175 KNOWLES, Anne. *The Halcyon Island.* Gr. 5–7.
✶ A ghostly boy named Giles teaches 12-year-old Ken to overcome his fear of the
water.
Harper, 1981, 120 pp., o.p.
(BL 77:1300; CCBB 34:213; HB 57:302; Kirkus 49:571; SLJ Apr 1981 p. 128; Suth 3:240)

KONIGSBURG, E(laine) L(obl). *Up from Jericho Tel.*
See Chapter 9, Magic Adventure Fantasy.

KRENSKY, Stephen (Alan). *A Ghostly Business.*
See *The Dragon Circle* in Chapter 9, Magic Adventure Fantasy.

KUSHNER, Donn. *Uncle Jacob's Ghost Story.*
See Chapter 1, Allegorical Fantasy and Literary Fairy Tales.

LACKEY, Mercedes, and DIXON, Larry. *Born to Run.*
See Chapter 12, Witchcraft and Sorcery Fantasy.

4-176 LAMPMAN, Evelyn Sibley. *Captain Apple's Ghost.* Gr. 5–7.
The ghost of Captain Apple returns to save his former home.
Illus. by Ninon MacKnight, Doubleday, 1952, 249 pp., o.p.
(HB 28:406; Kirkus 20:405; LJ 77:1739, 78:70)

LASKY (Knight), Kathryn. *Blood Secret.*
See Chapter 10, Time Travel Fantasy.

LASKY (Knight), Kathryn. *Home Free.*
See Chapter 10, Time Travel Fantasy.

4-177 LAWRENCE, Louise (pseud. of Elizabeth Rhoda Holden). *Sing and Scat-
ter Daisies.* Gr. 8–10.
Seventeen-year-old Nicky Hennessy's jealousy of the love between his favorite
aunt, Anna, and a ghost named John Hollis nearly blinds him to the fact that
Anna is dying. This is the sequel to *The Wyndcliffe* (1975).
Harper, 1977, 256 pp., o.p.
(BL 73:1084, 1092; CCBB 30:162; HB 53:450; Kirkus 45:358; SLJ Apr 1977 p. 77)

LAWRENCE, Michael. *The Poltergoose: A Jiggy McCue Story.*
See Chapter 8, Humorous Fantasy.

LAWSON, John S(hults). *The Spring Rider.*
See Chapter 10, Time Travel Fantasy.

4-178 LEACH, Christopher. *Rosalinda.* Gr. 7–9.
Rosalinda died in the 1700s at the age of 17, but her anguish over a thwarted
romance causes her to reach into the 20th century to control the life of Anne,
daughter of the curator of the Warrender estate.
Warne, 1978, 124 pp., o.p.
(BL 74:1552; CCBB 32:12; SLJ Sep 1978 p. 142; TLS 1978 p. 765)

4-179 LEACH, Maria (pseud. of Alice Mary Doanne Leach). *The Thing at the
Foot of the Bed and Other Scary Tales.* Gr. 5–7.

A collection of ghost and witch tales, including "The Thing at the Foot of the Bed," "Wait 'til Martin Comes," and "The Golden Arm."
Illus. by Kurt Werth, Putnam, 1959, 1987, 126 pp., o.p.
(BL 55:543; Eakin:204; Kirkus 27:265; LJ 84:1697)

4-180 LEHR, Norma. *The Secret of the Floating Phantom.* Gr. 3–6.
Kathy and her friends find buried pirate treasure with the help of a phantom whom only Kathy can see. This is the sequel to *The Shimmering Ghost of Riversend* (1991).
Lerner, 1994, 178 pp. (0-8225-0736-6)
(BL 61:681, 830; HBG 6:79; SLJ Dec 1994 p. 110)

4-181 LEROE, Ellen. *Ghost Dog.* Gr. 2–4.
Ghost Dog helps 9-year-old Artie protect his grandpa's valuable baseball card from a thief. The sequel is *Racetrack Robbery* (1996).
Hyperion, 1993, 64 pp. (1-56282-268-3), Little, Brown, 1994, pap., o.p.
(BL 89:1431; HBG 4:300; SLJ June 1993 p. 78)

4-182 LEVIN, Betty (Lowenthal). *A Binding Spell.* Gr. 6–8.
✭ Only Wren and an extremely reclusive neighbor, Axel Pederson, can see the ghostly horse that appears in the countryside near their homes.
Dutton, 1984, 179 pp., o.p.
(BL 81:449:CCBB 38:151; HB 60:759; SLJ Dec 1984 p. 101)

4-183 LILLINGTON, Kenneth (James). *Full Moon.* Gr. 8–12. (Orig. British pub. 1986.)
The unhappy ghosts of two sisters possess twins John and Jennifer, whose parents have inherited an old house and an antique shop from Great-Aunt Clara.
Faber, 1986, 136 pp., o.p.
(BL 82:1455, 1462; Kirkus 54:1022)

4-184 LILLINGTON, Kenneth (James). *What Beckoning Ghost?* Gr. 7–10. (Orig. British pub. 1983.)
The sobbing ghost of a young woman appears only to women who have refused to marry men chosen by their parents, and 16-year-old Emma Nash tries to understand the ghost's sadness.
Faber, 1983, 156 pp., o.p.
(BL 80:338, 360; CCBB 37:111; SLJ Dec 1983 p. 85)

4-185 LINDBERGH, Anne Spencer. *The People in Pineapple Place.* Gr. 4–6.
Lonely after his move to a new home, August makes friends with a group of invisible people from the past who take him on wonderful expeditions. The sequel is *The Prisoner of Pineapple Place* (1988, pap., 1990; Candlewick, 2003).
Harcourt, 1982, 156 pp., o.p.; Avon, 1990, pap. (0-380-70766-7); Candlewick, 2003, 184 pp. (0-7636-2131-5); Candlewick, 2003, pap. (0-7636-1739-3)
(BL 79:116; CCBB 36:30; HB 58:650; Kirkus 50:1106; SLJ Oct 1982 p. 153; Suth 3:265)

4-186 LISLE, Janet Taylor. *The Crying Rocks.* Gr. 5–9.
✭ The ghostly voices Joelle, 13, and her friend Carlos hear at the Crying Rocks near their Rhode Island town help them sort out the tragedies in their own lives.

Simon, 2003, 208 pp. (0-689-85319-X); Simon Pulse, 2005, pap., 208 pp. (0-689-85320-3)

(BL 100:405; CCBB 57:157; HB 79:750; Kirkus 71:1227; Kliatt Nov 2003 p. 6; SLJ Dec 2003 p. 156)

4-187 *The Literary Ghost: Great Contemporary Ghost Stories.* **Ed. by Larry Dark.** Gr. 10 up.

Twenty-eight ghost stories from Britain, the United States, South Africa, India, and Canada, whose authors include Isaac Bashevis Singer, Nadine Gordimer, and Joyce Carol Oates.

Atlantic, 1991, 384 pp., o.p.

(BL 88:408, 423)

4-188 **LITTKE, Lael.** *Lake of Secrets.* Gr. 7–10.

✶ Trying to uncover the truth behind her brother's drowning death 18 years earlier, Carlene and her mother visit Lake Isadora where Carlene begins to remember a life she never lived.

Holt, 2002, 208 pp. (0-8050-6730-2)

(Bl 98:1131; CCBB 55:286; HB 78:334; HBG 13:393; Kirkus 70:261; SLJ Mar 2002 p. 232; VOYA 25:120)

4-189 **LIVELY, Penelope (Margaret Low).** *The Driftway.* Gr. 5–7. (Orig. British

✶ pub. 1972.)

Running away from home along the "driftway" after their father's remarriage, Paul and his sister have visions of a Viking raid, a Civil War battle, and an 18th-century highway robbery.

Dutton, 1973, 140 pp., o.p.

(BL 69:813; CCBB 26:172; HB 49:271; Kirkus 41:188; LJ 98:2003; Suth 2:288; TLS 1972 p. 812)

4-190 **LIVELY, Penelope (Margaret Low).** *The Ghost of Thomas Kempe.* Gr.

✶✶ 4–6. (Orig. British pub. 1973.)

James Harrison becomes the unwilling apprentice of a 17th-century sorcerer and ends up taking the blame for the mischief caused when Thomas Kempe decides to start life anew in the 20th century. Carnegie Medal, 1973.

Dutton, 1973, 186 pp. (0-525-30495-9); Puffin, 1995, pap., 186 pp. (0-14-037794-8)

(BL 70:388, 80:96; CCBB 27:81; HB 49:591; Kirkus 41:883; LJ 99:211; Suth 2:288; TLS 1973 p. 380)

4-191 **LIVELY, Penelope (Margaret Low).** *The Revenge of Samuel Stokes.* Gr.

✶ 5–7. (Orig. British pub. 1981.)

Enraged at finding a housing development on the estate he landscaped centuries before, the ghost of Samuel Stokes returns to haunt the residents.

Dutton, 1981, 122 pp., o.p.

(BL 78:549, 550; CCBB 35:175; HB 58:44; SLJ Oct 1981 p. 144; Suth 3:269; TLS 1982 p. 345)

4-192 **LIVELY, Penelope (Margaret Low).** *A Stitch in Time.* Gr. 4–7. (Orig.

✶ British pub. 1976.)

Maria is convinced that Harriet, the girl in a century-old photograph hanging in Maria's summer house, still lives in that house. Whitbread Literary Award, Children's Book Category, 1976.

Dutton, 1976, 140 pp., o.p.

(BL 73:610; CCBB 30:129; HB 53:52; Kirkus 44:1169; SLJ Jan 1977 p. 94; Suth 2:289; TLS 1976 p. 885)

LIVELY, Penelope (Margaret Low). *Uninvited Ghosts and Other Stories.*
See Chapter 8, Humorous Fantasy.

LIVELY, Penelope (Margaret Low). *The Wild Hunt of the Ghost Hounds.*
See Chapter 6, High Fantasy: Myth or Legend Fantasy.

4-193 **LUNN, Janet (Louise Swoboda).** *Shadow in Hawthorn Bay.* Gr. 6–10.
☆ (Orig. Canadian pub. 1986.)
Her cousin's ghost "calls" 15-year-old Mary Urquhart to make the difficult voyage from Scotland to Canada in 1815, but she finds that he is summoning her into the lake where he committed suicide. Governor General's Literary Award for Children's Literature, 1986; Canadian Library Association Best Book of the Year for Children, 1987.

Scribner, 1987, 180 pp., o.p.

(BL 83:1525; CCBB 40:192; HB 63:618, 641; Kirkus 55:796; SLJ Sep 1987 p. 197; VOYA 10:122)

4-194 **LUNN, Janet (Louise Swoboda).** *Twin Spell.* Gr. 5–7. (Orig. Canadian pub. 1968, entitled *Double Spell*.)
An antique doll gives twins Jane and Elizabeth identical nightmares and intertwines their lives with a pair of twins from the past.

Illus. by Emily Arnold McCully, Harper, 1969, 158 pp., o.p.; Puffin, 1986 (entitled *Double Spell*), pap., 144 pp., o.p.

(CCBB 23:101; HB 45:675; Kirkus 37:1064; LJ 94:3821)

4-195 **LURIE, Alison.** *Women and Ghosts.* Gr. 10 up. (Orig. British pub. 1994.)
Nine eerie tales about women faced with ghostly apparitions.

Doubleday, 1994, 192 pp., o.p.

(BL 91:24, 31; Kirkus 62:798; LJ July 1994 p. 131; TLS June 17, 1994 p. 23)

4-196 **LYKKEN, Laurie.** *Little Room of Terror.* Gr. 6–8.
The ghost of a young girl appears in the tower room of the old house that Dianne's recently remarried father is renovating.

Willowisp Pr., 1991, 156 pp., o.p.

(BL 87:1976; Kliatt Apr 1991 p. 10; VOYA 14:173)

LYON, George Ella. *Here and Then.*
See Chapter 10, Time Travel Fantasy.

4-197 **McALLISTER, Margaret.** *Ghost at the Window.* Gr. 4–7. (Orig. British pub. 2001.)
Everyone knows that Ewan's new Scottish home is haunted, but only he can see the ghost of 9-year-old Elspeth, who became stuck in a time-shift when she died.

Dutton, 2002, 160 pp. (0-525-46852-8)

(CCBB 55:373; HBG 14:84; Kirkus 70:958; SLJ Aug 2002 p. 194; VOYA 25:204, 26:13)

4-198   McBAY, Bruce, and HENEGHAN, James. *Waiting for Sarah.* Gr. 6–10.
(Orig. Canadian pub. 2003.)
Bitter and depressed after the deaths of his parents and sister in the car accident
that left him without legs, Vancouver 10th-grader Mike Scott becomes interest-
ed in a local history project after he is encouraged by the ghost of a girl named
Sarah.
Orca, 2003, pap., 176 pp. (1-55143-270-6)
(BL 100:231; SLJ Oct 2003 p. 171; VOYA 26:414)

4-199   McBRATNEY, Sam. *The Ghosts of Hungryhouse Lane.* Gr. 4–6.
A crisis occurs for the ghosts of Hungryhouse Lane after their friend, Mercia
Porterhouse, dies and her house is inherited by the Sweet family and their ram-
bunctious children. The sequel is *The Ghastly Gerty Swindle with the Ghosts of
Hungryhouse Lane* (1994).
Illus. by Lisa Thiesing, Henry Holt, 1989, 118 pp., o.p.
(BL 85:1387; CCBB 42:231; Kirkus 57:380; SLJ May 1989 p. 110)

4-200   McDONALD, Joyce. *Shades of Simon Gray.* Gr. 7 up.
In a coma after his car hits the Liberty Tree, the oldest tree in the country,
Simon meets the ghost of Jessup Wildemere, unjustly accused of murder and
hanged from the tree 200 years earlier.
Delacorte, 2001, 245 pp. (0-385-32659-9)
(CCBB 55:148; HB 78:80; HBG 13:99; Kirkus 69:1362; SLJ Nov 2001 p. 161; VOYA
24:372, 25:15)

4-201   McGINNIS, Lila S(prague). *The Ghost Upstairs.* Gr. 3–6.
Albert Shook has trouble explaining his unusually good grades and tidy room
because they've been caused by Otis White, the ghost of a boy who died 75
years earlier.
Illus. by Amy Rowen, Hastings, 1982, 119 pp., o.p.
(BL 79:314, 83:586; SLJ Sep 1983 p. 124)

McGOWEN, Tom (Thomas E.). *Sir Machinery.*
See Chapter 12, Witchcraft and Sorcery Fantasy.

4-202   McGRAW, Eloise Jarvis. *A Really Weird Summer.* Gr. 6–8.
✭   While trying to cope with his parents' imminent divorce, Nels's secret friend-
ship with Alan, a mysterious boy from the past, hurts his younger brother's
feelings.
Atheneum, 1977, 218 pp., o.p.
(BL 73:1421; CCBB 31:62; HB 53:532; Kirkus 45:427; SLJ Oct 1977 p. 126; VOYA 14:33)

4-203   McGRAW, Eloise Jarvis. *The Trouble with Jacob.* Gr. 5–8.
Andy and his twin, Kat, help the ghost of Jacob, a boy who died in 1876, go to
his eternal rest.
Macmillan, 1988, 288 pp., o.p.
(BL 84:1435; Kirkus 56:365; SLJ Apr 1988 p. 102; VOYA 11:96)

4-204   McKAY, Hilary. *The Amber Cat.* Gr. 4–7. (Orig. British pub. 1996.)
✭✭   Robin's mother tells him and his friends, Dan and Sundance, about the summer
she met a mysterious girl named Harriet on the beach, a ghost who "borrows"

objects from the present and the past. This is the sequel to *Dog Friday* (1995) and is followed by *Dolphin Luck* (1999).

McElderry, 1997, 134 pp. (0-689-81360-0); Aladdin, 1999, pap., 134 pp. (0-689-82557-9)

(BL 94:559, 734, 1618; CCBB 51:91; HB 73:680; HBG 9:76; Kirkus 65:1535; SLJ Nov 1997 p. 12, Dec 1997 p. 26)

4-205 MacKELLAR, William. *Alfie and Me and the Ghost of Peter Stuyvesant.* Gr. 5–7.

Peter Stuyvesant's ghost gives Billy and Alfie a map directing them to treasure buried beneath Times Square.

Illus. by David Stone, Dodd, 1974, 150 pp., o.p.

(Kirkus 42:877; LJ 99:3268)

4-206 MacKELLAR, William. *A Ghost Around the House.* Gr. 4–6.

While exploring Strowan Castle on Halloween night, Jasper meets a 250-year-old ghost.

Illus. by Marilyn Miller, McKay, 1970, 117 pp., o.p.

(Kirkus 38:876; LJ 95:4352)

4-207 MacKELLAR, William. *The Ghost in the Castle.* Gr. 4–6.

✶ A ghost tells Angus Campbell the truth about Bonnie Prince Charlie's secret mission to Dunnach.

Illus. by Richard Bennett, McKay, 1960, 86 pp., o.p.

(BL 57:500; HB 36:396; Kirkus 28:624; LJ 85:4568)

MacKELLAR, William. *The Witch of Glen Gowrie.*

See Chapter 12, Witchcraft and Sorcery Fantasy.

4-208 McKILLIP, Patricia A(nne). *The House on Parchment Street.* Gr. 5–7.

Carol's cousins don't believe that she has seen ghosts from the 17th century in their cellar.

Illus. by Charles Robinson, Atheneum, 1973, 190 pp., o.p.

(BL 69:1093; CCBB 26:173; Kirkus 41:115; LJ 98:1701)

4-209 McKISSACK, Patricia C(arwell). *The Dark-Thirty: Southern Tales of the*
✶ *Supernatural.* Gr. 4–8.

Ten ghostly stories written in the style of traditional folk tales, using themes from African American history and folklore. Newbery Honor Book, 1993; Coretta Scott King Award, 1993.

Illus. by Brian Pinkney, Knopf, 1992, 122 pp. LB (0-679-91863-9)

(BL 89:738; CCBB 46:117; HB 69:209; HBG 4:173; Kirkus 60:1313; SLJ Dec 1992 p. 113)

4-210 McMULLAN, Kate. *Under the Mummy's Spell.* Gr. 5–8.

On a dare, 12-year-old Peter kisses the mummy mask of Egyptian Princess Nephia, thus fulfilling an ancient prophecy by awakening her ghost, who begs him to bring her the mummy of her cat before her sorceress aunt finds it.

Farrar, 1992, 214 pp. (0-374-38033-3)

(BL 88:1936; HBG 3:267; Kirkus 60:781; SLJ July 1992 p. 74; VOYA 15:226)

4-211 MAGUIRE, Gregory. *Lost.* Gr. 10 up.
Having come to England to visit her cousin, John Comestor, children's book writer Winifred Rudge discovers that John is missing, and that his flat is haunted. Regan, 2001, 339 pp. (0-06-039382-3)
(BL 98:383; Kirkus 69:1154; LJ Oct 1, 2001 p. 141; VOYA 24:337)

MAHY, Margaret (May). *Dangerous Spaces.*
See Chapter 7, High Fantasy: Travel to Other Worlds.

4-212 MAHY, Margaret (May). *The Horribly Haunted School.* Gr. 3–6. (Orig. New Zealand pub. 1997.)
At his new school, the Brinsley Codd School for Sensible Thought, Monty meets the ghost of Brinsley Codd himself.
Illus. by Robert Staermose, Viking, 1998, 119 pp. (0-670-87490-6)
(Kirkus 66:814; SLJ July 1998 p. 97)

MAHY, Margaret (May). *A Tall Story and Other Tales.*
See Chapter 9, Magic Adventure Fantasy.

4-213 MAHY, Margaret (May). *The Tricksters.* Gr. 9 up. (Orig. New Zealand pub.
★★ 1986.)
Harry (Ariadne) Hamilton accidentally calls up the spirit of Teddy Carnival, a former inhabitant of her family's vacation home, who appears in the form of triplet brothers claiming to be long-lost Carnival relations.
Macmillan, 1987, 272 pp. (0-689-50400-4); Aladdin, 1999, pap., 266 pp. (0-689-82910-8)
(BL 83:1008, 84:1248; CCBB 40:131; HB 63:471; Kirkus 55:60; SLJ Mar 1987 p. 172, Dec 1987 p. 38; TLS 1988 p. 370; VOYA 10:80)

4-214 *The Mammoth Book of Ghost Stories 2.* **Ed. by Richard Dalby.** Gr. 7–12.
Fifty-nine British and American stories whose authors include Charles Dickens, Rudyard Kipling, E. Nesbit, and Washington Irving. This is a companion volume to *The Mammoth Book of Ghost Stories* (1990).
Carroll & Graf, 1991, pap., 672 pp. (0-88184-701-1)
(BL 87:2099, 2111; LJ Sep 1, 1991 p. 233; VOYA 14:384)

4-215 MANLEY, Seon. *The Ghost in the Far Garden and Other Stories.* Gr. 6–9.
Eleven original ghost stories based on legends, including "The Mistress of Montauk Point," "The Cats Here Speak Only Spanish," and "Evil One."
Illus. by Emanuel Schoengut, Morrow, 1977, 128 pp., o.p.
(BL 74:1094, 1109; Kirkus 45:1049; SLJ Jan 1978 p. 96)

4-216 MANNS, Nick. *Operating Codes.* Gr. 5–9.
In this combination ghost story and spy thriller, Graham and Mattie Hayton begin to suspect that their new home is haunted after they learn that the house was a secret poison gas test site during World War I.
Little, Brown, 2001, 182 pp. (0-316-60465-8)
(BL 98:723; HBG 13:89; SLJ Jan 2002 p. 138)

4-217 *Masters of Shades and Shadows: An Anthology of Great Ghost Stories.* **Ed. by Seon Manley and Gogo Lewis.** Gr. 7 up.

Sixteen ghost stories arranged chronologically, from Charles Dickens to Ray Bradbury.
Doubleday, 1978, 216 pp., o.p.
(BL 74:608; CCBB 31:164; Kirkus 46:112; SLJ Dec 1977 p. 62)

4-218 MAYNE, William (James Carter). *It.* Gr. 6–9. (Orig. British pub. 1977.)
The ghost of a witch's familiar alerts Alice to other supernatural occurrences.
Greenwillow, 1978, 189 pp., o.p.
(CCBB 32:84; HB 55:646; Kirkus 46:1017; SLJ Dec 1978 p. 62; TLS 1978 p. 376; VOYA 1:40)

MIAN, Mary (Lawrence Shipman). *Take Three Witches.*
See Chapter 12, Witchcraft and Sorcery Fantasy.

4-219 MILLER, Judi. *Ghost in My Soup.* Gr. 3–5.
A ghost living in Scottie's century-old house helps the boy make friends in his new neighborhood.
Bantam, 1985, pap., 86 pp., o.p.
(BL 82:811; SLJ Nov 1985 p. 88)

4-220 *Modern Ghost Stories by Eminent Women Writers.* **Ed. by Richard Dalby.**
Gr. 10 up. (Orig. British pub. 1992.)
Twenty-seven chilling ghost stories whose authors include Joan Aiken, E. Nesbit, and Penelope Lively. A companion volume to Dalby's *Victorian Ghost Stories by Eminent Women Writers* (1989).
Carroll & Graf, 1992, 318 pp. (0-88184-864-6)
(LJ Oct 15, 1992 p. 102; VOYA 16:44, 17:10)

MONTES, Marisa. *A Circle of Time.*
See Chapter 10, Time Travel Fantasy.

4-221 MONTES, Marisa. *Something Wicked's in Those Woods.* Gr. 5–7.
Lonely after his parents' deaths and his move to an aunt's house in San Francisco, Nico Cisneros is befriended by Hamish, the ghost of a boy killed in an unsolved crime.
Harcourt, 2000, 224 pp. (0-15-202391-7)
(BL 97:438; CCBB 54:76; Kirkus 68:1287; SLJ Dec 2000 p. 146)

4-222 MONTGOMERY, Hugh. *The Voyage of the Arctic Tern.* Gr. 5–7. (Orig. British pub. 2001.)
Captain Bruno of the *Arctic Tern* spends many centuries searching for a chest of gold stolen from the King of Spain.
Illus. by Nick Poullis, Candlewick, 2002, 212 pp. (0-7636-1902-7)
(CCBB 56:70; Kirkus 70:1038; SLJ Aug 2002 p. 195)

4-223 MORPURGO, Michael. *The Butterfly Lion.* Gr. 4–7. (Orig. British pub. 1996.)
A ghostly old woman shows a runaway 10-year-old boy the likeness of a great white lion carved into the hillside chalk by her son Bertie, in memory of his former pet.
Viking, 1997, 90 pp. (0-670-87461-2)
(BL 93:1704; HBG 8:305; Kirkus 65:645; SLJ Aug 1997 p. 158)

4-224 MORPURGO, Michael. *The Ghost of Grania O'Malley.* Gr. 5–8. (Orig. British pub. 1996.)
The ghost of Irish pirate queen Grania O'Malley returns to Clare Island to fight for the preservation of the hill she loved.
Viking, 1996, 184 pp. (0-670-86861-2)
(BL 92:1720; CCBB 49:309; HBG 8:71; Kirkus 64:749; SLJ July 1996 p. 85)

MOWRY, Jess. *Ghost Train.*
See Chapter 10, Time Travel Fantasy.

MURPHY, Pat. *The Falling Woman: A Fantasy.*
See Chapter 6, High Fantasy: Myth or Legend Fantasy.

MYERS, Walter Dean. *The Black Pearl and the Ghost; or, One Mystery After Another.*
See Chapter 8, Humorous Fantasy.

4-225 NATHAN, Robert (Gruntal). *Mia.* Gr. 10 up.
✫   The ghost of a middle-aged woman's lost youth comes between her and a would-be lover, the retired novelist who tells this story.
Knopf, 1970, 179 pp., o.p.
(BL 67:38; HB 46:502; Kirkus 38:346; LJ 95:2181, 3080)

4-226 NAYLOR, Phyllis Reynolds. *Bernie and the Bessledorf Ghost.* **(Bessledorf**
✫   **Mystery series, bk. 3).** Gr. 4–6.
Bernie discovers that the hotel his father manages is haunted by the ghost of a young boy named Jonathan Bessledorf. This is the sequel to two non-fantasies: *The Mad Gasser of Bessledorf Street* (1983) and *The Bodies in the Bessledorf Hotel* (1986), and is followed by *The Face in the Bessledorf Funeral Parlor* (1993), *The Bomb in the Bessledorf Bus Depot* (1996), *The Treasure of Bessledorf Hill* (1998), *Peril in the Bessledorf Parachute Factory* (1999), and *Bernie Magruder and the Bats in the Belfry* (2003).
Macmillan, 1990, 144 pp., o.p.
(BL 86:1635; HBG 1:259; Kirkus 58:582; SLJ July 1990 p. 78)

NAYLOR, Phyllis Reynolds. *Shadows on the Wall.*
See Chapter 10, Time Travel Fantasy.

4-227 *The New Young Oxford Book of Ghost Stories.* **Comp. by Dennis Pepper.**
Gr. 8 up. (Orig. British pub. 1999.)
Twenty-three chilling stories written by Mary Frances Zambreno, Adèle Geras, and Shirley Jackson, among others. This is a companion volume to *The Young Oxford Book of Ghost Stories* (1994, 1997).
Illus. by Dennis Pepper, Oxford University Press, 1999, 216 pp. (0-19-278154-5)
(BL 96:428; SLJ Dec 1999 p. 138)

4-228 *Nightshade: 20th Century Ghost Stories.* **Ed. by Robert Phillips.** Gr. 10 up.
An anthology of 27 20th-century tales written by Joan Aiken, Shirley Jackson, Rudyard Kipling, and others. This is a companion anthology to Phillips' *Triumph of the Night: 20th Century Ghost Stories* (1989).
Carroll, 1999, 470 pp. (0-7867-0614-7)

4-229 **NIXON, Joan Lowery.** *Ghost Town: Seven Ghostly Stories.* Gr. 4–7.
Seven tales set in American Wild West ghost towns, including "The Magic Eye," "The Shoot-Out," and "Buried."
Delacorte, 2000, 147 pp. (0-385-32681-5); Dell, 2000, pap., 184 pp. (0-440-22008-4)
(BL 97:119, 821; HBG 12:77; Kirkus 68:1202; SLJ Oct 2000 p. 168)

4-230 **NIXON, Joan Lowery.** *Haunted Island.* Gr. 4–6.
While renovating an island inn, Chris Holt and his family discover that the island is haunted by the ghost of Amos Corley, who died 175 years earlier.
Scholastic, 1987, pap., 123 pp., o.p.
(BL 83:1132; Kliatt 21:24; SLJ May 1987 p. 102)

4-231 **NIXON, Joan Lowery.** *The Haunting.* Gr. 6–9.
☆ Anne takes on the challenge of driving away the ghosts haunting Graymoss mansion after her parents decide to take in unwanted foster children.
Delacorte, 1998, 185 pp. (0-385-32247-X); Laurel Leaf, 2000, pap., 192 pp. (0-440-22008-4)
(BL 94:1873; HB 74:737; HBG 10:81; Kirkus 66:898; Kliatt May 1998 p. 7; SLJ Aug 1998 p. 164; VOYA 21:358)

4-232 **NORTON, Andre, and MILLER, Phyllis.** *House of Shadows.* Gr. 5–7.
Mike, Susan, and Tucker Whelan's frightening dreams seem to be connected to an old set of paper dolls, and to the deaths of three ancestors in their 200-year-old house.
Macmillan, 1984, 201 pp., o.p.
(BL 80:1118; CCBB 37:171; HB 60:331; SLJ May 1984, p. 92)

4-233 **ORMONDROYD, Edward.** *Castaways on Long Ago.* Gr. 5–7.
Richard, Linda, and Dudley explore the forbidden Long Ago Island and meet its ghostly inhabitant.
Illus. by Ruth Robbins, Parnassus, 1973, 182 pp., o.p.
(CCBB 27:99; HB 50:150; LJ 99:575; Suth 2:346)

4-234 **PARK, (Rosina) Ruth (Lucia).** *Things in Corners.* Gr. 5–8. (Orig. Australian pub. 1989.)
☆ Five supernatural stories set in Australia, including one about a fur collar that comes alive and bites at night and another about an old car haunted by the ghost of a man who drowned his family in it.
Viking, 1991, 197 pp. (0-670-82225-6); Puffin, 1993, pap. (0-14-032713-4)
(BL 87:1194, 1195; CCBB 44:174; HBG 2:266; Kirkus 59:109; SLJ May 1991 p. 112; VOYA 14:112)

PASSEY, Helen K. *Speak to the Rain.*
See Chapter 6, High Fantasy: Myth or Legend Fantasy.

4-235 **PATNEAUDE, David.** *Dark Starry Morning: Stories of This World and Beyond.* Gr. 6–8.
Six eerie tales about teenagers' encounters with ghosts, monsters, and the unknown.
Whitman, 1995, 123 pp. (0-8075-1474-8)
(BL 92:78; HBG 7:67; Kirkus 63:1115; SLJ Sep 1995 p. 220)

4-236 PATNEAUDE, David. *Haunting at Home Plate.* Gr. 4–7.
Nelson's baseball team is having a bad season until Mike, his older female cousin, takes over as coach and ghostly messages begin appearing on the field. Whitman, 2000, 181 pp. (0-8075-3181-2)
(BL 97:118; CCBB 54:116; HBG 12:77; SLJ Sep 2000 p. 235)

4-237 PATON WALSH, Jill (Gillian Bliss). *Birdy and the Ghosties.* Gr. 1–4.
✭ (Orig. British pub. 1989.)
Birdy's "second sight" doesn't seem extraordinary until the day Papa is asked to ferry three "ghosties" across the sea to a mysterious island. *Matthew and the Sea Singer* (1993; see Chapter 1, Allegorical Fantasy and Literary Fairy Tales) is a companion story.
Illus. by Alan Marks, Farrar, 1989, 46 pp. (0-374-30716-4)
(BL 86:1096; CCBB 43:149; HBG 1:84; Kirkus 57:1675; SLJ Feb 1990 p. 80)

4-238 PAULSEN, Gary. *Canyons.* Gr. 7–10.
After 14-year-old Brennan Cole finds the skull of Coyote Runs, an Apache boy murdered by U.S. soldiers 100 years in the past, the boy's spirit convinces Brennan to return the skull to Apache holy ground.
Delacorte, 1990, 184 pp. (0-385-30153-7); Laurel Leaf, 1991, pap., 192 pp. (0-440-21023-2)
(BL 87:326; HBG 2:86; Kirkus 58:1090; SLJ Sep 1990 p. 256; VOYA 13:355)

PAYNE, Joan Balfour (Dicks). *The Leprechaun of Bayou Luce.*
See Chapter 9, Magic Adventure Fantasy.

4-239 PEARCE, (Ann) Philippa. *Familiar and Haunting: Collected Stories.* Gr.
✭✭ 5–12. (Orig. pub. in England.)
Thirty-seven ghostly stories gathered from three collections previously published in England and the United States (*What the Neighbors Did and Other Stories*, 1973, *The Shadow-Cage and Other Tales of the Supernatural*, 1977, and *Who's Afraid? And Other Strange Stories*, 1987), plus one collection published only in England.
HarperCollins, 2002, 392 pp. (0-06-623965-6)
(BL 98:1527; CCBB 56:73; HB 78:335; HBG 13:379; SLJ July 2002 p. 124; VOYA 25:130, 26:13)

4-240 PEARCE, (Ann) Philippa. *The Shadow-Cage and Other Tales of the*
✭ *Supernatural.* Gr. 5–8. (Orig. British pub. 1977.)
Ten tales of ghostly encounters, including "The Shadow Cage," "The Dog Got Them," and "The Strange Illness of Mr. Arthur Cook." Carnegie Medal Commended Book, 1977.
Illus. by Ted Lewin, Crowell, 1977, 144 pp., o.p.
(BL 74:554; Kirkus 45:934; SLJ Dec 1977 p. 50; TLS 1977 p. 864)

4-241 PEARCE, (Ann) Philippa. *Who's Afraid? And Other Strange Stories.* Gr.
✭ 5–9. (Orig. British pub, 1986.)
Eleven strange tales of ghosts and the supernatural.
Greenwillow, 1987, 152 pp., o.p.
(BL 83:1208; CCBB 40:152; HB 58:344; Kirkus 55:375; SLJ May 1987 p. 116; Suth 4:320:VOYA 10:206)

4-242 PEARSON, Kit. *Awake and Dreaming.* Gr. 4–7. (Orig. Canadian pub. 1996.)
Somehow, in the time between her old life with her immature mother and her new life with an unknown aunt, Theo meets the family of her dreams.
Viking, 1997, 228 pp. (0-670-86954-6)
(BL 93:1705; CCBB 50:332; HBG 8:306; Kirkus 65:647; SLJ June 1997 p. 125)

4-243 PECK, Richard (Wayne). *The Ghost Belonged to Me: A Novel.* (The Blos-
★★   som Culp quartet, bk. 1). Gr. 5–9.
Encounters with the ghost of a girl named Inez Dumaine convince Alexander Armsworth that he has second sight. In *Ghosts I Have Been* (1977; 1979; Puf-fin, 2001), the second sight of Alexander's friend Blossom Culp involves her with a child who drowned on the *Titanic* and earns her an audience with the Queen of England. In *The Dreadful Future of Blossom Culp* (Delacorte, 1983, 1987; Puffin, 2001), Blossom makes an accidental trip from 1918 into the future world of the 1980s. In *Blossom Culp and the Sleep of Death* (Delacorte, 1986, 1987), the angry ghost of Egyptian Princess Sat-Hathor demands that Blossom and Alexander find the missing items plundered from her tomb and protect it from any future defilement.
Viking, 1975, pap., o.p.; Puffin, 1997, pap., 192 pp. (0-14-038671-8)
(BL 71:1129, 80:96; CCBB 28:182; HB 51:471; Kirkus 43:456; SLJ Sep 1975 p. 109, Dec 1976 p. 32; TLS 1977 p. 348)

PENN, Malka. *The Hanukkah Ghosts.*
See Chapter 10, Time Travel Fantasy.

4-244 PEYTON, K. M. (pseud. of Kathleen Wendy Peyton). *A Pattern of Roses.*
★   Gr. 7–9. (Orig. British pub. 1972.)
The old drawings Tim finds signed with his own initials enable him to see the ghost of a young man whose death was never explained.
Illus. by the author, Crowell, 1973, 186 pp., o.p.
(BL 70:124, 827; CCBB 27:49; HB 49:473, 60:361–364; Kirkus 41:819; LJ 98:2667, 3691; Suth 2:361)

Phantasmagoria: Tales of Fantasy and the Supernatural. Ed. by Jane
Mobley.
See Chapter 3, Fantasy Collections.

4-245 PHILLIPS, Ann. *A Haunted Year.* Gr. 5–8. (Orig. British pub. 1991.)
Lonely Florence summons the ghost of her mysterious cousin George, who takes over her life until her new stepbrother helps rid her of the malevolent spirit.
Macmillan, 1994, 175 pp. (0-02-774605-4)
(BL 90:1365; CCBB 47:230; HBG 5:314; Kirkus 62:483; SLJ Apr 1994 p. 130)

POPE, Elizabeth Marie. *The Sherwood Ring.*
See Chapter 10, Time Travel Fantasy.

4-246 PORTE, Barbara Ann. *Beauty and the Serpent: Thirteen Tales of Unnatural Animals.* Gr. 6–10.
Thirteen eerie stories about creatures with supernatural abilities, including "Haunted House," "Snakefeathers," and "Ghost Story."

Illus. by Rosemary Feit Covey, Simon, 2001, 128 pp. (0-689-84147-7)
(Kirkus 69:1365; SLJ Nov 2001 p. 183; VOYA 24:450)

PORTE, Barbara Ann. *Jesse's Ghost and Other Stories.*
See Chapter 3, Fantasy Collections.

POSTMA, Lidia. *The Witch's Garden.*
See Chapter 9, Magic Adventure Fantasy.

4-247 POTTER, Ellen. *Olivia Kidney.* Gr. 4–7.
☆ Lonely and bereft after her brother's death, Olivia discovers that the other residents of her New York apartment building include a ghost, a pirate, and a deposed princess. The sequel is *Olivia Kidney and the Exit Academy* (2005).
Illus. by Peter H. Reynolds, Philomel, 2003, 160 pp. (0-399-23850-6); Puffin, 2004, pap., 155 pp. (0-14-240234-6)
(BL 99:1778; CCBB 56:417; HB 79:617; Kirkus 71:809; SLJ June 2003 p. 150)

4-248 PREUSSLER, Otfried. *The Little Ghost.* Gr. 4–6. (Orig. pub. in Germany.)
A little ghost disregards the advice of his friend Toowhoo the owl and makes a daylight appearance at Town Hall.
Trans. by Anthea Bell, Abelard-Schuman, 1967, 126 pp., o.p.
(Kirkus 35:1271; LJ 92:4617; TLS 1967 p. 445)

PRICE, Susan. *The Ghost Drum: A Cat's Tale.*
See Chapter 12, Witchcraft and Sorcery Fantasy.

4-249 PRYOR, Bonnie. *Marvelous Marvin and the Pioneer Ghost.* Gr. 3–6.
Marvin, his twin sister Sarah, their former enemy Ernie, and a ghost solve the mystery of who is polluting a local creek. This is the sequel to *Marvelous Marvin and the Wolfman Mystery* (1994), which is not a fantasy.
Illus. by Melissa Sweet, Morrow, 1995, 144 pp. (0-688-13886-1)
(BL 91:1575; HBG 6:302; SLJ July 1995 p. 80)

4-250 RABINOWITZ, Ann. *Knight on Horseback.* Gr. 6–8.
While on a tour of England, Eddy Newby meets the ghost of Richard III, who mistakes the 13-year-old American boy for his son Edward.
Macmillan, 1987, 187 pp., o.p.
(BL 84:572; CCBB 41:73; SLJ Oct 1987 p. 142; VOYA 10:245)

RADFORD, Ken. *The Cellar.*
See Chapter 10, Time Travel Fantasy.

4-251 RADFORD, Ken. *Haunting at Mill Lane.* Gr. 5–7. (Orig. British pub. 1983.)
Sally-Anne, the ghost of a young Welsh girl, uses a rag doll to lure 12-year-old Sarah into her own time.
Holiday, 1988, 153 pp., o.p.
(BL 84:1437; SLJ June 1988 p. 106)

4-252 *The Random House Book of Ghost Stories.* **Ed. by Susan Hill.** Gr. 5–8.
(Orig. British pub. 1990, entitled *The Walker Book of Ghost Stories*.)
Sixteen ghost stories by well-known English children's book authors, including Joan Aiken, Leon Garfield, Penelope Lively, and Philippa Pearce.

Illus. by Angela Barrett, Random, 1991, 223 pp. LB (0-679-91234-7)
(BL 88:698; CCBB 45:92; HBG 3:119)

REES, Celia. *City of Shadows.*
See Chapter 10, Time Travel Fantasy.

REISS, Kathryn. *Dreadful Sorry.*
See Chapter 10, Time Travel Fantasy.

REISS, Kathryn. *Paperquake: A Puzzle.*
See Chapter 10, Time Travel Fantasy.

4-253 **REISS, Kathryn.** *Sweet Miss Honeywell's Revenge.* Gr. 5–9.
Two parallel tales alternate, one set in 1919 and the other about a contemporary
girl named Zibby who buys a haunted antique doll house.
Harcourt, 2004, 448 pp. (0-15-216574-6)
(BL 100:1499; CCBB 57:481; Kirkus 72:580; SLJ Aug 2004 p. 128)

ROACH, Marilynne K(athleen). *Encounters with the Invisible World;*
Being Ten Tales of Ghosts, Witches, and the Devil Himself in New
England.
See Chapter 3, Fantasy Collections.

4-254 **ROBINSON, Joan (Mary) G(ale Thomas).** *When Marnie Was There.* Gr.
5–7. (Orig. British pub. 1967.)
Anna, a lonely foster child, is befriended by Marnie, an elusive girl from the
house at the edge of the marsh.
Coward, 1968, 256 pp., o.p.
(CCBB 22:163; HB 45:56; Kirkus 36:979; TLS 1967 p. 1141)

4-255 **RODOWSKY, Colby F.** *The Gathering Room.* Gr. 4–7.
☆ Angered by hints of an impending family move away from their cemetery gate-
house home, Mudge realizes that he will miss the friendship of the cemetery's
ghostly inhabitants.
Farrar, 1981, 185 pp., o.p.
(BL 78:394; CCBB 35:157; HB 57:537; Kirkus 49:1297; SLJ Oct 1981 p. 146; Suth 3:363)

4-256 **ROMAIN, Joseph.** *The Mystery of the Wagner Whacker.* Gr. 5–9. (Orig.
Canadian pub. 1998.)
A blow to the head causes baseball fan Matt Killburn to meet the ghost of leg-
endary player Honus Wagner's brother, inventor of a potentially revolutionary
baseball-bat-making machine.
Firefly, 1998, pap., 173 pp. (1-895629-94-2)
(BL 94:1873; SLJ July 1998 p. 99)

4-257 **RUBY, Laura.** *Lily's Ghosts.* Gr. 5–9.
☆ In this suspenseful tale, Lily, 13, and her new friend Vaz uncover family secrets
involving betrayal, rivalry, and revenge in the haunted house her mother recently inherited.
HarperCollins, 2003, 272 pp. (0-06-051830-8); HarperTrophy, 2005, pap., 272
pp. (0-06-051831-6)
(CCBB 57:31; HBG 15:101; Kirkus 71:914; SLJ Dec 2003 p. 160; VOYA 27:146)

4-258 RUSSELL, Barbara Timberlake. *Blue Lightning.* Gr. 5–7.
The ghost of Rory McKinney, a car accident victim, hitches a ride in Cal Doogan's body when the two cross paths in the emergency room where Cal is recovering from a lightning strike.
Viking, 1997, 122 pp. (0-670-87023-4)
(BL 93:1024; CCBB 50:221; HB 73:328; HBG 8:308; Kirkus 64:1674; SLJ Feb 1997 p. 104)

4-259 ST. JOHN, Wylly Folk. *The Ghost Next Door.* Gr. 4–6.
Lindsey and Tammy discover that their neighbor Sherry can communicate with the ghost of her dead half-sister, Miranda.
Illus. by Trina Schart Hyman, Harper, 1971, 178 pp., o.p.
(BL 68:395; HB 48:147; Kirkus 39:1014; LJ 96:4198)

4-260 SARGENT, Sarah. *Jerry's Ghosts and the Mystery of the Blind Tower.* Gr. 5–7.
In a story told alternately by a 12-year-old ghost named Mattie and by Jerry, a contemporary 11-year-old, Mattie warns Jerry to stay away from her Uncle Ezekiel's apparatus in an old mansion-turned-museum, lest he be used in an immortality experiment.
Macmillan, 1992, 134 pp. (0-02-778035-X)
(BL 88:1380; CCBB 45:277; HBG 3:270; Kirkus 60:398; SLJ Mar 1992 p. 242)

4-261 SAUNDERS, Susan. *The Ghost Who Ate Chocolate.* **(Black Cat Club series, bk. 1).** Gr. 2–4.
Sam, Robert, Belinda, and Andrew form the ghost-busting Black Cat Club to investigate the spirit of a young girl haunting their local public library. The sequels are *The Haunted Skateboard* (1996), *The Curse of the Cat Mummy* (1997), *The Ghost of Spirit Lake* (1997), *The Revenge of the Pirate Ghost* (1997), *The Case of the Eyeball Surprise* (1998), *The Chilling Tale of Crescent Pond* (1998), *The Creature Double Feature* (1998), and *The Creepy Camp-Out* (1998).
Illus. by Jane Manning, HarperCollins, 1996, pap., 80 pp. (0-06-442035-3)
(BL 93:727; SLJ Nov 1996 p. 92)

4-262 SCHNUR, Steven. *The Shadow Children.* Gr. 5–8.
★★ Eleven-year-old Etienne is haunted by the ghosts of Jewish refugee children handed over to the Nazis by his grandfather and other French villagers during World War II.
Illus. by Herbert Tauss, Morrow, 1994, 86 pp. (0-688-13831-4)
(BL 91:603; CCBB 48:144; HB 71:61; HBG 6:83; Kirkus 62:1543; SLJ Oct 1994 p. 128)

4-263 SEABROOKE, Brenda. *The Haunting at Stratton Falls.* Gr. 5–8.
★ Staying with cousins while her father fights in World War II, Abby discovers the truth about the ghost of a young girl haunting their house.
Dutton, 2000, 151 pp. (0-525-46389-5)
(BL 96:2030; CCBB 54:37; Kirkus 68:892; SLJ Aug 2000 p. 189; VOYA 32:278)

4-264 SEABROOKE, Brenda. *The Haunting of Holroyd Hill.* Gr. 5–8.
Melinda and Kevin encounter two ghosts haunting their new home and a neighbor's home and uncover a Civil War-era mystery.
Dutton, 1995, 137 pp. (0-525-65167-5)
(BL 42:66; CCBB 48:357; HBG 6:304; SLJ Apr 1995 p. 136)

4-265 SEABROOKE, Brenda. *The Haunting of Swain's Fancy.* Gr. 4–7.
Forced to share a bedroom for the summer, new stepsisters Taylor, 11, and Nicole, 12, solve the mystery of Civil War-era ghosts haunting their West Virginia home.
Dutton, 2003, 160 pp. (0-525-46938-9)
(BL 99:1662; CCBB 57:34; HBG 15:101; Kirkus 71:864; SLJ Aug 2003 p. 166; VOYA 26:242)

4-266 SEFTON, Catherine (pseud. of Martin Waddell). *The Ghost and Bertie Boggin.* Gr. 3–5. (Orig. British pub. 1980.)
Bertie Boggin meets Ghost in his coal cellar and is overjoyed to have made a friend at last.
Illus. by Jill Bennett, Faber, 1982, 64 pp., o.p.
(BL78:1261; SLJ Aug 1982 p. 105)

4-267 SEFTON, Catherine (pseud. of Martin Waddell). *In a Blue Velvet Dress.* Gr. 4–6. (Orig. British pub. 1972.)
The ghost of Mary Quinton, an orphaned girl who once lived in Jane's house, brings books for 11-year-old Jane to read each night of her stay at 3 Mole Street.
Illus. by Eros Keith, Harper, 1973, 160 pp., o.p.; Volo/Hyperion, 2002, pap., 182 pp. (0-7868-1693-7)
(HB 78:430; Kirkus 41:561; LJ 98:3718; SLJ Oct 2002 p. 95)

4-268 SERVICE, Pamela F. *Phantom Victory.* Gr. 4–7.
Terri and Brian attempt to solve an 85-year-old mystery on South Bass Island after the ghosts of their ancestors appear.
Scribner, 1994, 128 pp. (0-684-19441-4)
(BL 90:1679; CCBB 47:334; HBG 5:315; SLJ July 1994 p. 119; VOYA 17:341)

4-269 SEVERN, David (pseud. of David Unwin). *The Girl in the Grove.* Gr. 7–9.
✫ Jonquil becomes jealous when her friend Paul spends more and more time with a ghostly girl named Laura.
Harper, 1974, 266 pp., o.p.
(BL 71:93,102; Kirkus 42:1111; LJ 99:3277; TLS 1974 p. 717)

4-270 *Shades of Dark: Stories.* **Ed. by Aidan Chambers.** Gr. 7 up. (Orig. British
✫ pub. 1984.)
Eight ghost stories by British authors including Vivian Alcock, Helen Cresswell, and Jan Mark.
Harper, 1986, 126 pp., o.p.
(BL 83:571, 581; CCBB 40:83; HB 63:215; Kirkus 54:1514)

4-271 SHEARER, Alex. *The Great Blue Yonder.* Gr. 5–9. (Orig. British pub. 2001.)
After he is hit and killed by a truck, Harry, 11, wanders through the Other Lands with his new friend Arthur, until the two ghosts decide to return to Earth to search for Harry's grieving family.
Clarion, 2002, 192 pp. (0-618-21257-4)
(CCBB 55:382; HBG 13:382; Kirkus 70:426; SLJ Apr 2002 p. 157; VOYA 25:131)

4-272 SHECTER, Ben. *The Whistling Whirligig.* Gr. 4–6.

✶   While staying with his history teacher, Josh meets Matthew Hubbard, the 100-year-old ghost of a runaway slave, who has been hiding since the Civil War. Harper, 1974, 143 pp., o.p.; Scholastic, pap. (entitled *The Ghost and the Whistling Whirligig*), o.p.

(BL 71:463; CCBB 28:138; HB 50:693; Kirkus 42:1253; LJ 99:2721)

4-273 SHURA, Mary Francis (pseud. of Mary Francis Craig). *Happles and Cinnamunger.* Gr. 3–5.

The Taggert children's new housekeeper, Ilsa, is haunted by a ghost, and it is up to the children to free her from it.

Illus. by Bertram M. Tormey, Dodd, 1981,157 pp., o.p.

(BL 78:655; CCBB 35:116; HB 58:169; SLJ Jan 1982 p. 82)

4-274 SHURA, Mary Francis (pseud. of Mary Francis Craig). *Simple Spigott.* Gr. 3–5.

Simple Spigott is a small ghost searching for lost Irish treasure.

Illus. by Jacqueline Tomes, Knopf, 1960, 90 pp., o.p.

(BL 56:609; CCBB 13:169; Eakin:299; HB 36:291; LJ 85:2043)

4-275 SILVERSTEIN, Herma. *Mad, Mad Monday.* Gr. 5–8.

✶   Miranda Taylor accidentally conjures up the ghost of Monday Newberry, who has returned after 30 years to seek revenge on a former girlfriend who married someone else after his death.

Dutton, 1988, 120 pp., o.p.

(BL 84:1337, 1353; CCBB 41:76; Kirkus 55:1738; Kliatt Apr 1989 p. 17; SLJ Feb 1988 p. 74, VOYA 11:184)

4-276 SINGER, Marilyn. *Deal with a Ghost.* Gr. 6–9.

✶   An expert at the game of attracting boys, 15-year-old Deal isn't prepared for the arrival of a grandmother she barely knows, or for the ghost who arrives with her.

Holt, 1997, 181 pp. (0-8050-4797-2); Avon, 1999, pap., 179 pp. (0-380-73183-5)

(BL 93:1686; CCBB 50:374; HBG 9:91; Kirkus 65:727; SLJ June 1997 p. 128; VOYA 21:290)

4-277 SINGER, Marilyn. *Ghost Host.* Gr. 5–9.

High school football star Bart Hawkins enlists the help of a friendly ghost and of Arvie, a bright classmate, to deal with Stryker, a poltergeist inhabiting Bart's home.

Harper, 1987, 182 pp., o.p.

(CCBB 40:218; Kirkus 55:1076; SLJ Sep 1987 p. 182; VOYA 10:83)

4-278 *Small Shadows Creep.* Ed. by Andre Norton. Gr. 6–10.

✶   Nine ghostly tales involving children or teenagers, including M. R. James's "Lost Hearts" and Eleanor Farjeon's "Faithful Jenny Dove."

Dutton, 1974, 195 pp., o.p.

(BL 71:687, 694; HB 51:279; Kirkus 43:24; SLJ Apr 1975 p. 56)

4-279 SNYDER, Zilpha Keatley. *Eyes in the Fishbowl.* Gr. 6–9.
Dion thinks the strange girl he meets in the Alcott-Simpson Department Store might be a ghost.
Illus. by Alton Raible, Atheneum, 1968, 1970, 168 pp., o.p.
(BL 64:1097; CCBB 21:181; HB 44:182; Kirkus 36:124; LJ 93:1804)

4-280 SNYDER, Zilpha Keatley. *The Ghosts of Rathburn Park.* Gr. 5–7.
Exploring the ruins of an old church, Matt, 11, meets Amelia Rathburn, a secretive girl dressed in old-fashioned clothes who knows how to get into the old Rathburn mansion.
Delacorte, 2002, 191 pp. (0-385-90064-3)
(CCBB 56:250; HBG 14:88; Kirkus 70:40; SLJ Sep 2002 p. 234)

4-281 SNYDER, Zilpha Keatley. *The Trespassers.* Gr. 5–9.
☆ Neely Bradford's 7-year-old brother, Grub, befriends the ghost of a former young resident of Halcyon House.
Delacorte, 1995, 200 pp. (0-385-31055-2); Yearling, 1996, pap., 208 pp. (0-440-41277-3)
(BL 91:1773; CCBB 49:70; HBG 7:69; Kirkus 63:863; SLJ Aug 1995 p. 144; VOYA 18:166)

4-282 SNYDER, Zilpha Keatley. *The Truth About Stone Hollow.* Gr. 6–8.
Jason, new in school, takes Amy to a strange valley where loops of time come together, enabling them to see ghosts from the past.
Illus. by Alton Raible, Atheneum, 1974, 211 pp., o.p.; Dell, 1985, pap. (0-440-48846-X)
(BL 70:825; CCBB 27:164; HB 50:380; Kirkus 42:245; LJ 99:576, 1451)

4-283 SOMMER-BODENBURG, Angela. *If You Want to Scare Yourself.* Gr. 3–5. (Orig. German pub. 1984.)
Freddy's parents and grandmother tell him eerie stories about ghosts and vampires when he gets bored being sick in bed, and he writes a few of his own.
Trans. by Renée Vera Cafiero, illus. by Helga Speiss, Harper, 1989, 105 pp., o.p.
(BL 86:464; HBG 1:87; Kirkus 57:1333; SLJ Dec 1989 p. 103)

4-284 SOTO, Gary. *The Afterlife: A Novel.* Gr. 6–12.
☆ After Chuy, 17, is stabbed to death at a high school dance, his ghost returns to mourn his fate.
Harcourt, 2003, 176 pp. (0-15-204774-3), 2005, pap., 160 pp. (0-15-205220-8)
(BL 99:1981; CCBB 57:77; HB 79:755; HBG 15:117; Kirkus 71:1183; Kliatt Sep 2003 p. 13; SLJ Nov 2003 p. 148; VOYA 26:506, 27:15)

4-285 SPEARING, Judith (Mary Harlow). *The Ghosts Who Went to School.* Gr. 5–7.
Tired of haunting the house, Wilbur and Mortimer Temple decide to go to school. The sequel is *The Museum House Ghosts* (1969).
Illus. by Marvin Glass, Atheneum, 1966, 186 pp., o.p.
(BL 62:920; HB 42:308; LJ 91:1710)

4-286 *Spooky Stories for a Dark and Stormy Night.* Ed. by Alice Low. Gr. 3–6.
An anthology of ghostly folktales as well as stories written by Charles Dickens, Penelope Lively, Bruce Coville, Laurence Yep, and others.

Illus. by Gahan Wilson, Hyperion, 1994, 128 pp., o.p.

(BL 91:321; CCBB 48:171; HBG 6:142; Kirkus 62:1535; SLJ Nov 1994 p. 105)

SPRINGER, Nancy. *The Friendship Song.*
See Chapter 7, High Fantasy: Travel to Other Worlds.

4-287 STAHL, Ben(jamin). *Blackbeard's Ghost.* Gr. 5–8.
J. D. and Hank accidentally summon up the ghost of the pirate Blackbeard, who discovers that the tavern he built 300 years earlier is about to be torn down. The sequel is *The Secret of Red Skull* (1971).
Illus. by the author, Houghton, 1965, 184 pp., o.p.

(HB 41:393; Kirkus 33:244; LJ 90:2897)

4-288 STORR, Catherine (Cole). *Cold Marble and Other Ghost Stories.* Gr. 6–10. (Orig. British pub. 1985.)
Eleven poignant and humorous ghost stories, including "How to Be a Ghost," "Pale Marble," and "Bill's Ghost."
Faber, 1985, 101 pp., o.p.

(BL 82:861, 871; SLJ Mar 1986 p. 179)

STRANGER, Joyce. *The Fox at Drummer's Darkness.*
See Chapter 1, Allegorical Fantasy and Literary Fairy Tales.

4-289 STRASSER, Todd. *Hey Dad, Get a Life!* Gr. 5–7.
☆   Sisters Kelly and Sasha try to convince Mom that the ghost of their late father has come back to help them.
Holiday, 1996, 164 pp., o.p.

(BL 93:1024; CCBB 50:259; HBG 8:309; Kirkus 64:1805; SLJ Mar 1997 p. 193)

STRAUB, Peter (Francis). *Shadowland.*
See Chapter 12, Witchcraft and Sorcery Fantasy.

STRICKLAND, Brad. *Dragon's Plunder, or, The Last Voyage of Captain Deadmon: A Fantasy Adventure.*
See Chapter 9, Magic Adventure Fantasy.

4-290 SUDBERY, Rodie (Tutton). *The Silk and the Skin.* Gr. 6–8. (Orig. British
☆   pub. 1976.)
Guy Carmichael reluctantly joins the class bully's gang. They try to call up the spirit of a long-dead wizard's bat and succeed by tricking Guy's developmentally delayed younger brother into doing the summoning.
Deutsch, 1982, 144 pp., o.p.

(BL 79:316; HB 58:523; SLJ Nov 1982 p. 91; TLS 1976 p. 1554)

4-291 *Supernatural Stories: 13 Tales of the Unexpected.* **Ed. by Jean Russell.** Gr.
☆   5–8.
Thirteen "pleasantly eerie" stories whose authors include Joan Aiken, Joan Phipson, Patricia Miles, and Catherine Storr. Many of these stories were previously published in England.
Orchard, 1987, 156 pp., o.p.

(BL 84:55, 74; CCBB 41:75; HB 63:745; SLJ Sep 1987 p. 182; VOYA 10:283)

SYKES, Pamela. *Mirror of Danger.*
See Chapter 10, Time Travel Fantasy.

4-292 TAPP, Kathy Kennedy. *The Scorpio Ghosts and the Black Hole Gang.* Gr. 4–7.
Ryan, Josh, Carrie, and Brooke help a ghostly bus and its inhabitants break through the time barrier.
Harper, 1987, 192 pp., o.p.
(BL 83:1057; CCBB 40:136; Kirkus 55:225; SLJ Apr 1987 p. 105)

4-293 *That's Ghosts for You! 13 Scary Stories.* **Ed. by Marianne Carus.** Gr. 4–7.
Thirteen ghostly stories written by Eric A. Kimmel, Josepha Sherman, Susan Price, and others.
Illus. by YongSheng Xuan, Front Street, 2000, 131 pp. (0-8126-2675-3); Scholastic, 2002, pap. (entitled *13 Scary Ghost Stories*), 134 pp. (0-439-34021-7)
(BL 97:713; SLJ Dec 2000 p. 142)

4-294 THESMAN, Jean. *Appointment with a Stranger.* Gr. 7–10.
✴ Embarrassed by her asthma, Keller Parish avoids making friends at her new high school and becomes involved instead with Tom, the ghost of a boy who drowned 40 years earlier in an isolated pond.
Houghton, 1989, 155 pp., o.p.
(BL 85:1657; CCBB 43:22; HB 65:380; Kirkus 57:470; SLJ Feb 1989 p. 103; VOYA 12:108)

4-295 THESMAN, Jean. *Cattail Moon.* Gr. 6–9.
✴ After 15-year-old Julia moves in with her father and grandfather, she begins hearing ghostly singing in a nearby marsh.
Houghton, 1994, 197 pp. (0-395-67409-3); Flair, 1995, pap., 176 pp. (0-380-72504-5)
(BL 90:137; CCBB 47:336; HB 70:461; HBG 5:325; Kirkus 62:310; SLJ May 1994 p. 135; VOYA 17:150)

4-296 *Things That Go Bump in the Night: A Collection of Original Stories.* **Ed.**
✴ **by Jane (Hyatt) Yolen (Stemple) and Martin H. Greenberg.** Gr. 5–8.
Eighteen scary stories by Diana Wynne Jones, William Sleator, Jane Yolen, and others.
Harper, 1989, 288 pp., o.p.
(BL 86:356; CCBB 43:23; HB 66:73; HBG 1:82; Kirkus 57:1171; SLJ Oct 1989 p. 139)

4-297 TOLAN, Stephanie S. *The Face in the Mirror.* Gr. 5–9.
✴ The ghost of actor George Marsden tempts Jared, 15, to retaliate against his malicious stepbrother Tad.
Morrow, 1998, 208 pp. (0-688-15394-1); HarperCollins, 2000, pap., 214 pp. (0-380-73263-7)
(BL 95:111; CCBB 52:34; HBG 10:75; Kirkus 66:1391; Kliatt Nov 1998 p. 8; SLJ Nov 1998 p. 130; VOYA 22:42)

4-298 TOLAN, Stephanie S. *Who's There?* Gr. 5–8.
Drew and Evan's new lives with relatives after their parents' deaths are disturbed by encounters with the ghost of their step-grandmother, Amalie.
Morrow, 1994, 235 pp. (0-688-04611-8)
(BL 91:45; CCBB 48:146; HBG 6:84)

4-299 **TOMALIN, Ruth.** *Gone Away.* Gr. 5–7. (Orig. British pub. 1979.)
✫ Francie becomes convinced that her secret friend is actually the ghost of a girl
who lived in her house during the Middle Ages.
Faber, 1979, 158 pp., o.p.
(BL 76:452; CCBB 33:83; Kirkus 47:933; SLJ Dec 1979 p. 89)

4-300 **TUNNELL, Michael O.** *School Spirits.* Gr. 3–7.
Patrick and Nairen discover that their school is haunted by the ghost of a mur-
dered child.
Holiday, 1997, 201 pp. (0-8234-1310-1)
(BL 94:1012; CCBB 51:262; HBG 9:82; Kirkus 65:1843; SLJ Mar 1998 p. 224; VOYA
21:214)

4-301 **TURKLE, Brinton (Cassaday).** *Mooncoin Castle; or Skulduggery Reward-
ed.* Gr. 4–6.
A ghost, a witch, and a jackdaw join forces to save an Irish castle from demoli-
tion.
Viking, 1970, 141 pp., o.p.
(BL 67:149; Kirkus 38:554; LJ 95:3054)

4-302 **URE, Jean.** *The Children Next Door.* Gr. 3–6. (Orig. British pub. 1994.)
Laura's shyness nearly prevents her from trying to meet the children playing in
the garden next door, but she discovers that they may be ghosts.
Scholastic, 1996, 135 pp. (0-590-22293-7)
(BL 92:836; CCBB 49:317; HBG 7:298; Kirkus 63:1706; SLJ Mar 1996 p. 198)

4-303 **VANDE VELDE, Vivian.** *Being Dead: Stories.* Gr. 6–10.
✫ Seven ghost stories, including "Shadow Brother," "Dancing with Marjorie's
Ghost," and "October Chill."
Harcourt, 2001, 203 pp., o.p.; Magic Carpet, 2003, pap., 224 pp. (0-15-204912-6)
(BL 98:97; CCBB 55:39; HB 77:758; HBG 13:102; Kirkus 69:1133; SLJ Sep 2001 p. 234;
VOYA 24:374)

4-304 **VANDE VELDE, Vivian.** *A Coming Evil.* Gr. 5–9.
✫ Lizette, 13, living in German-occupied France during World War II, meets Gerard, the ghost of a knight murdered in 1314, who teaches her the importance of
helping her aunt hide Jewish and Gypsy children from the Nazis.
Houghton, 1998, 224 pp. (0-395-90012-3)
(BL 95:326; CCBB 52:36; HBG 10:83; Kirkus 66:1538; Kliatt Sep 1998 p. 14; SLJ Nov 1998
p. 131; VOYA 21:291)

4-305 **VANDE VELDE, Vivian.** *Ghost of a Hanged Man.* Gr. 4–7.
✫ Ben, 11, and his sister Anna battle a curse laid on their town by the ghost of
Jake Barnett, an outlaw hanged for murder.
Cavendish, 1998, 95 pp. (0-7614-5015-7); Marshall Cavendish, 2003, pap., 96
pp. (0-7614-5154-4)
(BL 95:591; CCBB 52:75; HB 74:742; HBG 10:76; Kirkus 66:1539; SLJ Oct 1998 p. 147)

4-306 **VANDE VELDE, Vivian.** *There's a Dead Person Following My Sister
✫ Around.* Gr. 4–7.
Ted uncovers his family's historic connection to the Underground Railroad
after experiencing eerie dreams about the ghosts haunting his little sister.

Harcourt, 1999, 143 pp. (0-15-202100-0); Penguin Putnam, 2001, pap., 160 pp. (0-14-131281-5)

(BL 96:124; CCBB 53:72; HBG 11:90; Kirkus 67:1507; SLJ Sep 1999 p. 228; VOYA 22:350)

4-307 *Victorian Ghost Stories: An Oxford Anthology.* **Selected by Michael Cox and R. A. Gilbert.** Gr. 10 up. (Orig. British pub. 1991.)
Thirty-five 19th-century British ghost stories by such authors as Rudyard Kipling, Charles Dickens, and Robert Louis Stevenson.
Oxford University Press, 1991, 497 pp. (0-19-214202-X)

(SLJ Mar 1992 p. 270; TLS Nov 22 1991 p. 8)

4-308 **VIVELO, Jackie.** *Chills in the Night: Tales That Will Haunt You.* Gr. 5–9.
Eight ghostly stories, including four published previously in *A Trick of the Light* (1987; see Chapter 3), plus "When Nothing's There at All," "The Haunted Schoolhouse," "A Ride on the Dumbwaiter," and "Ghost of Christmas Past."
DK, 1997, 123 pp. (0-7894-2463-0)

(BL 94:795; HBG 9:82; SLJ Jan 1998 p. 116)

VIVELO, Jackie. *A Trick of the Light: Stories to Read at Dusk.*
See Chapter 3, Fantasy Collections.

4-309 **WAGENER, Gerda.** *The Ghost in the Classroom.* Gr. 2–4. (Orig. Swiss pub. 1997.)
Only children can see Otto, the ghost in Tina's lunchbox, whose pranks disrupt her classroom and her home life.
Illus. by Uli Waas, North-South, 1997, 47 pp. (1-55858-799-3)

(BL 94:817; Kirkus 65:1651)

4-310 **WALLACE, Barbara Brooks.** *Peppermints in the Parlor.* **(Peppermints**
✫ **series, bk. 1).** Gr. 4–7.
Orphaned Emily Luccock discovers a terrifying secret after moving into her beloved aunt and uncle's San Francisco mansion, Sugar Hill Hall. In the sequel, *The Perils of Peppermints* (2003), Emily faces another frightening challenge at her new boarding school, Mrs. Spilking's Select Academy for Young Ladies.
Atheneum, 1980, 198 pp., o.p.; Aladdin, 1993, pap., 198 pp. (0-689-71680-X)

(BL 77:122; CCBB 34:142; HB 56:522; Kirkus 48:1519; SLJ Oct 1098 p. 152)

4-311 **WALLACE, Rich.** *Restless: A Ghost's Story.* Gr. 8–12.
✫ A ghost named Frank, whose high school athlete brother Herbie is trying to contact him, narrates this story about death and reincarnation.
Viking, 2003, 176 pp. (0-670-03605-6); Puffin, 2005, pap., 176 pp. (0-14-240309-1)

(BL 100:232; CCBB 57:79; Kirkus 71:1025; Kliatt Sep 2003 p. 14; SLJ Nov 2003 p. 150; VOYA 26:329, 27:15)

4-312 **WALLIN, Luke.** *The Slavery Ghosts.* Gr. 5–7.
Jake and Livy pass through a time gate into a world where Mrs. Ruffin, the ghost of a former plantation owner, holds the ghosts of her former slaves captive.
Bradbury, 1983, 121 pp., o.p.

(CCBB 37:20; SLJ Dec 1983 p. 70; Suth 3:439; VOYA 6:209)

WESLEY, Mary. *Haphazard House.*
See Chapter 10, Time Travel Fantasy.

4-313 WESTALL, Robert (Atkinson). *The Call and Other Stories.* Gr. 7–12.
★ (Orig. British pub. 1989.)
Six spooky stories including "The Badger," "The Red House Clock," "The Call," and "Woman and Home."
Viking, 1993, 120 pp. (0-670-82484-4)
(BL 89:802; CCBB 46:159; HB 69:468; HBG 4:313; Kirkus 61:69; SLJ Jan 1993 p. 134; VOYA 15:343)

4-314 WESTALL, Robert (Atkinson). *Christmas Spirit: Two Stories.* Gr. 4–7.
★ (Orig. pub. in England.)
In "Christmas Ghost," the first of two short stories set in Depression-era England, a young boy meets a ghost in a factory elevator who warns him that his father is in danger.
Illus. by John Lawrence, Farrar, 1991, 154 pp. (0-374-31260-5)
(BL 91:329; CCBB 48:69; HB 70:715; HBG 6:85; Kirkus 62:1422; SLJ Oct 1994 p. 44)

4-315 WESTALL, Robert (Atkinson). *Demons and Shadows: The Ghostly Best Stories of Robert Westall.* Gr. 7–12. (Orig. British pub. 1993.)
Eleven ghostly supernatural and horror stories, including "The Death of Wizards," "Graveyard Shift," and "A Walk on the Wild Side." The companion volume is *Shades of Darkness: More of the Ghostly Best Stories of Robert Westall* (1994).
Farrar, 1993, 288 pp. (0-374-31768-2)
(BL 90:332; HBG 5:92; SLJ Oct 1993 p. 158; VOYA 16:315)

4-316 WESTALL, Robert (Atkinson). *Ghost Abbey.* Gr. 5–9. (Orig. British pub.
★ 1988.)
The old abbey that Maggie's father is restoring exerts a ghostly and dangerous hold on her family and on Ms. MacFarlane, the owner.
Scholastic, 1989, 169 pp., o.p.
(BL 85:943; CCBB 42:161; HB 65:221, Kirkus 56:1817; SLJ Mar 1989 p. 202; Suth 4:434; VOYA 12:108)

4-317 WESTALL, Robert (Atkinson). *The Haunting of Chas McGill and Other*
★ *Stories.* Gr. 7–12. (Orig. British pub. 1983.)
A collection of eerie stories including "The Haunting of Chas McGill," in which the hero of Westall's realistic novel *The Machine Gunners* (1976; 1990) meets the ghost of a World War I army deserter just at the outbreak of World War II.
Greenwillow, 1983, 181 pp., o.p.
(BL 80:490; CCBB 37:120; HB 60:66; Kirkus 51:209; SLJ Jan 1984 p. 90; Suth 3:447; VOYA 7:98)

4-318 WESTALL, Robert (Atkinson). *In Camera and Other Stories.* Gr. 7–12.
★ (Orig. British pub. 1992.)
Five stories about supernatural occurrences that lurk behind daily life.
Scholastic, 1993, 152 pp., o.p.
(BL 89:2050; HB 69:468; HBG 4:313; Kirkus 61:236; SLJ Apr 1993 p. 144; VOYA 16:96)

4-319 **WESTALL, Robert (Atkinson).** *The Promise.* Gr. 6–10. (Orig. British pub.
✶ 1990.)
Fourteen-year-old Bob, in love with frail Valerie, promises to find her if she
ever gets lost, and the girl's ghost returns after her death to demand that he
keep his promise.
Scholastic, 1991, 176 pp., o.p.
(BL 87:1378; CCBB 44:207; HB 67:207; Kirkus 59:179; SLJ Mar 1991 p. 220; VOYA
14:104)

4-320 **WESTALL, Robert (Atkinson).** *The Scarecrows.* Gr. 6–9. (Orig. British
✶ pub. 1981.)
Angry and jealous about his mother's second marriage, 13-year-old Simon real-
izes that scarecrows wearing the clothes of three people once involved in a mur-
derous love triangle are slowly advancing across the field toward his new home.
Carnegie Medal, 1981; Boston Globe Horn Book Award Honor Book, 1982.
Greenwillow, 1981, 185 pp., o.p.
(CCBB 35:19; HB 57:546; Kirkus 49:1166; SLJ Aug 1981 p. 80; TLS 1981 p. 339)

4-321 **WESTALL, Robert (Atkinson).** *Shades of Darkness: More of the Ghostly
Best Stories of Robert Westall.* Gr. 7–12. (Orig. pub. in England.)
Eleven haunting tales, including "In Camera," "The Haunting of Chas McGill,"
and "The Call." This is a companion volume to *Demons and Shadows* (1993,
see above).
Farrar, 1994, 310 pp. (0-374-36758-2)
(BL 90:1527; HB 70:480; HBG 5:325; SLJ May 1994 p. 136; VOYA 17:162)

4-322 **WESTALL, Robert (Atkinson).** *The Watch House.* Gr. 7–9. (Orig. British
✶ pub. 1977.)
Ghosts from the past haunt a museum of shipwreck salvage and ensnare Anne
in their quest for vengeance.
Greenwillow, 1978, 218 pp., o.p.; Knopf, 1990, pap. (entitled *The Watch
Tower*), o.p.
(BL 74:1356; CCBB 31:187; HB 54:405; Kirkus 46:381; SLJ Apr 1978 p. 99, May 1978 p.
36; Suth 2:478; TLS 1977 p. 1408; VOYA 13:233)

4-323 *What Did Miss Darrington See? An Anthology of Feminist Supernatural
Fiction.* **Ed. by Jessica Amanda Salmonson.** Gr. 10 up.
Twenty-four ghostly stories written in the United States, England, and Latin
America between 1850 and 1988 by authors including Vita Sackville-West,
Mary E. Watkins Freeman, and Anne Sexton.
Feminist Pr., 1989, 263 pp., o.p.
(BL 86:38, 56; Kirkus 57:960)

4-324 **WHITNEY, Phyllis A(yame).** *The Island of Dark Woods.* Gr. 5–7.
While visiting their Aunt Serena on Staten Island, Laurie and Celia Kane see
the legendary phantom stagecoach said to stop at the house next door where a
young woman once died.
Illus. by Philip Wishnefsky, Westminster, 1951, 190 pp., o.p.; Westminster,
1967 (entitled *Mystery of the Strange Traveller*), 192 pp., o.p.
(Kirkus 35:1136; LJ 92:4271)

4-325 WIBBERLEY, Leonard (Patrick O'Connor). *The Quest of Excalibur.* Gr. 10 up.
King Arthur's ghost appears in 20th-century England to search for Excalibur, and manages to save Princess Pamela from abdicating to marry an American. Putnam, 1959, 190 pp., o.p.; Borgo Press, 1979, 190 pp., o.p.
(BL 56:120, 246; HB 36:59; Kirkus 27:612; LJ 84:3060)

4-326 WILDE, Nicholas. *Into the Dark.* Gr. 5–8. (Orig. British pub. 1987.)
✰ After Roly, a local boy, befriends blind 12-year-old Matthew during his holiday on the English coast, Matthew comes to understand that Roly is actually the ghost of a boy who lived a century earlier.
Scholastic, 1990, 201 pp. (0-5904-3424-1), 1992, pap. (0-5904-3423-3)
(BL 87:925; CCBB 44:74; HBG 2:76; Kirkus 58:1254; SLJ Nov 1990 p. 121; VOYA 13:292)

4-327 WILDE, Oscar (Fingal O'Flahertie Wills). *The Canterville Ghost.* Gr. 7 up. (Orig. British pub. 1906.)
Virginia's American family buys a home in England, and the resident ghost is outraged that they are not afraid of him. Scott Corbett's *The Discontented Ghost* (1978; see this chapter) is a related work.
Illus. by Lisbeth Zwerger, Picture Book Studio, 1986, 36 pp. (0-88708-027-8); Oxford University Press, 1988, o.p.; illus. by Lisbeth Zwerger, North-South, 1996, 44 pp. (1-55858-624-5), pap. (1-55858-611-3); illus. by Inga Moore, Candlewick, 1997, 128 pp. (0-7636-0132-2)
(BL 93:722; HBG 8:76, 9:60; SLJ Jan 1986 p. 85)

4-328 WILLIAMS (John), Ursula Moray. *Castle Merlin.* Gr. 4–6. (Orig. British
✰ pub. 1972.)
While vacationing at Castle Merlin, Susie and Bryan meet two medieval ghosts.
Nelson, 1972, 142 pp., o.p.
(BL 69:765; HB 48:471; Kirkus 40:1029, 1414; LJ 98:265; TLS 1972 p. 474)

WILLIAMS, Maiya. *The Golden Hour.*
See Chapter 10, Time Travel Fantasy.

4-329 WINDSOR, Patricia (Frances). *How a Weirdo and a Ghost Can Change Your Entire Life.* Gr. 4–6.
A Ouija board helps Martha and Teddy contact ghosts, who solve a number of neighborhood mysteries.
Illus. by Jacqueline Rogers, Dell, 1988, pap., 123 pp., o.p.
(Kirkus 54:1371; SLJ Nov 1986 p. 94)

WISEMAN, David. *Jeremy Visick.*
See Chapter 10, Time Travel Fantasy.

4-330 WOODRUFF, Elvira. *The Ghost of Lizard Light.* Gr. 4–6.
Nathaniel Witherspoon, the ghost of a boy who died 150 years ago, helps Jack Carlton adjust to his new hometown and his demanding father.
Illus. by Elaine Clayton, Knopf, 1999, 176 pp. (0-679-89281-8)
(CCBB 53:191; HBG 11:91; SLJ Jan 2000 p. 136)

Worlds Near and Far: Nine Stories of Science Fiction. **Ed. by Terry Carr.** See Chapter 3, Fantasy Collections.

4-331 WRIGHT, Betty Ren. *Christina's Ghost.* Gr. 4–6.
Christina's uncle refuses to believe that she has seen a ghost in a nearby haunted house until he meets the ghost himself.
Holiday, 1985, 105 pp. (0-8234-0581-8); Scholastic, 1987, pap. (0-590-42709-1)
(BL 82:815, 83:586; CCBB 39:120; SLJ Dec 1985 p. 96)

4-332 WRIGHT, Betty Ren. *Crandalls' Castle.* Gr. 5–7.
☆ After orphaned Sophia moves in with distant relatives, the Crandalls, she and her cousin Charli realize the potential danger in their Uncle Will's plan to convert a local haunted house into a bed and breakfast inn.
Holiday, 2003, 177 pp. (0-8234-1726-3)
(BL 99:1398; HBG 14:378; Kirkus 71:614; SLJ May 2003 p. 161)

WRIGHT, Betty Ren. *The Dollhouse Murders.*
See Chapter 11, Toy Fantasy.

4-333 WRIGHT, Betty Ren. *The Ghost Comes Calling.* Gr. 3–6.
☆ The ghost of an old man wronged by the town haunts Chad Weldon's log cabin. The sequels are *Too Many Secrets* (1997) and *A Ghost in the Family* (1998).
Scholastic, 1994, 128 pp. (0-590-47353-0), 1997, pap., 83 pp. (0-590-47354-9)
(BL 90:1083; CCBB 47:239; HB 70:594; HBG 5:305; SLJ Apr 1994 p. 132)

4-334 WRIGHT, Betty Ren. *The Ghost in Room 11.* Gr. 3–5.
☆ Matt reveals that he has seen a ghost in the school basement, but this further isolates him from his classmates.
Illus. by Jacqueline Rogers, Holiday, 1998, 112 pp. (0-8234-1318-7)
(BL 94:1136; CCBB 51:300; HBG 9:341; SLJ Mar 1998 p. 190)

4-335 WRIGHT, Betty Ren. *A Ghost in the House.* Gr. 4–8.
☆ Sarah discovers that her family's house is haunted by a vengeful ghost after Great-Aunt Margaret moves back into what was her childhood bedroom.
Scholastic, 1991, 160 pp. (0-5904-3606-6); Scholastic, 1995, pap. (0-590-43603-1)
(BL 88:523; CCBB 45:79; HB 67:202; HBG 3:75; Kirkus 59:1477; SLJ Nov 1991 p. 125; VOYA 14:39)

4-336 WRIGHT, Betty Ren. *The Ghost of Ernie P.* Gr. 4–7.
The ghost of a former class bully tries to exert power over Jeff to get revenge on a local witch.
Holiday, 1990, 130 pp. (0-8234-0835-3); Scholastic, 1992, pap. (0-5904-5073-5)
(BL 87:857; CCBB 44:133; HB 67:202; HBG 2:73; Kirkus 58:1537; SLJ Oct 1990 p. 122; VOYA 14:39)

4-337 WRIGHT, Betty Ren. *The Ghost of Popcorn Hill.* Gr. 2–5.
☆ Martin and Peter try to understand the connection between the ghostly man who visits their cabin at night and the mysterious sheepdog who romps on Popcorn Hill.

Illus. by Karen Ritz, Holiday, 1993, 81 pp., o.p.; Scholastic, 1994, pap. (0-590-47873-7)

(BL 89:1061; CCBB 46:333; HB 69:463; HBG 4:293; Kirkus 61:606; SLJ May 1993 p. 111)

4-338 **WRIGHT, Betty Ren.** *The Ghost Witch.* Gr. 3–5.
When Jenny realizes that her home is haunted by the ghostly witch of Willow-by Lane, she tries to find a different house for the ghost to haunt.
Illus. by Ellen Eagle, Holiday, 1993, 103 pp. (0-8234-1036-6)

(BL 90:931; CCBB 47:123; HBG 5:84; SLJ Dec 1993 p. 118)

4-339 **WRIGHT, Betty Ren.** *Ghosts Beneath Our Feet.* Gr. 4–6.
No one will believe Katie's hunch that warnings brought by a young woman's ghost portend a new tragedy in the abandoned iron mines below her uncle's Upper Peninsula Michigan town.
Holiday, 1984, 137 pp., o.p.

(BL 81:593; SLJ Apr 1985 p. 95)

4-340 **WRIGHT, Betty Ren.** *The Ghosts of Mercy Manor.* Gr. 4–7.
☆   Only Gwen's foster brother Jason believes that she has met the unhappy ghost of a young girl who disappeared near their house many years ago.
Scholastic, 1993, 172 pp. (0-590-43601-5); Scholastic, 1994, pap., 172 pp. (0-590-43602-3)

(BL 90:152; CCBB 47:27; HBG 5:84; Kirkus 61:944; SLJ Sep 1993 p. 236; VOYA 16:305)

4-341 **WRIGHT, Betty Ren.** *Haunted Summer.* Gr. 3–6.
☆   Nine-year-old Abby and her babysitter, Hannah, lay to rest a spiteful ghost who appears when an unusual music box arrives.
Scholastic, 1996, 99 pp. (0-590-47355-7)

(BL 92:1367; CCBB 49:283; HB 72:466; HBG 7:299; Kirkus 64:695; SLJ May 1996 p. 118)

4-342 **WRIGHT, Betty Ren.** *The Moonlight Man.* Gr. 6–9.
☆   Jenny, 15, and her younger sister Allie are determined to stay in their new house even though it is haunted.
Scholastic, 2000, 181 pp. (0-590-25237-2)

(BL 96:1103; CCBB 53:259; HBG 11:315; Kirkus 68:66; Kliatt Jan 2000, p. 12; SLJ Feb 2000 p. 128; VOYA 23:51)

4-343 **WRIGHT, Betty Ren.** *Out of the Dark.* Gr. 5–8.
☆   While staying in her grandmother's house, 12-year-old Jessie is haunted by frightening dreams of an angry woman.
Scholastic, 1995, 149 pp., o.p.

(BL 91:682; CCBB 48:219; HBG 6:306; Kirkus 63:235; SLJ Jan 1995 p. 110; VOYA 18:227)

4-344 **WRIGHT, Betty Ren.** *The Pike River Phantom.* Gr. 4–7.
The strange woman Charlie meets in an abandoned house near his grandparents' home is a ghost whose death had something to do with his grandmother and his cousin Rachel.
Holiday, 1988, 153 pp., o.p.

(BL 85:715; CCBB 42:132; Kirkus 56:1536; SLJ Oct 1988 p. 149; Suth 4:446)

4-345 WRIGHT, T. M. *Goodlow's Ghosts.* Gr. 10 up.
After a client unexpectedly kills him, Detective Sam Goodlow finds it hard to
believe that he has become a ghost.
Tor, 1993, 224 pp. (0-312-85466-8)
(BL 89:718, 722; Kirkus 60:1405; VOYA 16:107)

WRIGHTSON, (Alice) Patricia (Furlonger). *Balyet.*
See Chapter 6, High Fantasy: Myth or Legend Fantasy.

WRIGHTSON, (Alice) Patricia (Furlonger). *An Older Kind of Magic.*
See Chapter 9, Magic Adventure Fantasy.

4-346 WYSS, Thelma Hatch. *A Stranger Here.* Gr. 6–12.
☆   Jada Sinclair, 16, falls in love with Starr Freeman, the ghost of a World War II
pilot killed in action on the day Jada was born.
Harper, 1993, 132 pp. (0-06-021438-4); HarperTrophy, 1996, pap. (0-06-
447098-9)
(BL 89:1582; CCBB 46:361; HBG 4:313; Kirkus 61:236; SLJ May 1993 p. 130; VOYA
16:220)

YARBRO, Chelsea Quinn. *Monet's Ghost.*
See Chapter 7, High Fantasy: Travel to Other Worlds.

4-347 YEP, Laurence M(ichael). *The Ghost Fox.* Gr. 3–6.
☆   Drawn from a 17th-century Chinese story by Pu Sung-ling, this is the tale of a
boy named Little Lee, who must outwit a ghostly fox attempting to steal his
mother's soul and turn her into a stranger.
Illus. by Jean Mou-sien Tseng, Scholastic, 1994, 70 pp. (0-590-47204-6), 1997,
pap., 80 pp. (0-590-47205-4)
(BL 90:626; CCBB 47:240; HBG 5:345; Kirkus 61:1598; SLJ May 1994 p. 119)

4-348 YOLEN (Stemple), Jane (Hyatt). *Here There Be Ghosts.* Gr. 6–9.
Seven poems and 11 ghostly stories, including "The Moon Ribbon," "Prom
Ghost," and "Mrs. Ambroseworthy."
Harcourt, 1998, 120 pp. (0-15-201566-3)
(BL 95:485; SLJ Nov 1998 p. 132; VOYA 21:375, 22:16)

4-349 YOLEN (Stemple), Jane (Hyatt). *The Wizard Islands.* Gr. 4–7.
A collection of legends about islands, some of which involve ghosts and pirate
treasure.
Illus. by Robert M(ead) Quackenbush, Crowell, 1973, 115 pp., o.p.
(CCBB 27:167; HB 50:162; Kirkus 41:1368; LJ 99:1224)

**4-350 *Young Ghosts.* Ed. by Isaac Asimov, Martin H. Greenberg, and Charles
G. Waugh.** Gr. 6–9.
Twelve tales about the ghosts of children, written by Arthur Quiller-Couch,
M. R. James, and Ray Bradbury, among others.
Harper, 1985, 210 pp., o.p.
(BL 82:862, 874; SLJ Dec 1985 p. 96)

5

High Fantasy:
Alternate Worlds or Histories

High fantasy novels have been variously called epic fantasy, heroic fantasy, myth fantasy, other-world fantasy, and alternate world fantasy. In such works, the fate of the world hangs in the balance, while the forces of good and evil, or light and darkness, battle for control of humanity. For the purposes of this book, high fantasy novels have been divided into three chapters: Chapter 5, Alternate Worlds or Histories; Chapter 6, Myth and Legend; and Chapter 7, Travel to Other Worlds.

This chapter lists books about worlds other than our own. J. R. R. Tolkien suggested that these otherworlds be called "Secondary Worlds" and that the term "Primary World" be used for our own everyday world. It was his feeling that the only true fantasy stories are those involving a Secondary World. The stories listed in this chapter take place entirely in a Secondary World, or in an alternate version of the history of our own world. Tales of protagonists drawn from our own world into another are listed in Chapter 7, Travel to Other Worlds.

Although true science fiction stories have not been included in this book, "science-fantasy" tales, in which science is used to explain the existence of the Secondary World and magic is used thereafter, are included in this chapter.

5-1   **ABBEY, Lynn (pseud. of Marilyn Lorraine Abbey).** *The Black Flame.* Gr. 10 up.
Exiled warrior-priestess Rifkind rides her horse Turin across the swamps of the Felmargue to find the Black Flame, and becomes involved in a magical battle of the gods when she reaches the Well of Knowledge. This is the sequel to *Daughter of the Bright Moon* (1979, 1985), which won the John W. Campbell Award for best new science fiction writer of 1979.
Ace, 1980, 1985, pap., 376 pp., o.p.
(BL 77:29, 38; Kliatt 14:12; VOYA 3:40)

5-2   **ABBEY, Lynn (pseud. of Marilyn Lorraine Abbey).** *Jerlayne.* Gr. 10 up.
Jerlayne defies her mother, Elmeene, to marry Aulaudin the elf, only to discover that their life together is not quite what she'd had in mind.

DAW, 1999, pap., 519 pp. (0-88677-809-3)
(Kliatt July 1999 p. 20; VOYA 22:268)

5-3 **ADAMS, Hazard.** *The Truth About Dragons: An Anti-Romance.* Gr. 10 up.
Firedrake, an intellectual dragon living in California after an earthquake has severed the state from the rest of the United States, describes how mankind ruined the Earth.
Harcourt, 1971, 179 pp., o.p.
(BL 67:685, 741; Kirkus 39:15; LJ 96:653, 2938, 4160)

5-4 **ADAMS, Richard (George).** *Shardik.* Gr. 8 up. (Orig. British pub. 1974.)
In Ortelga, a giant bear found by a young hunter is proclaimed Lord Shardik, the sacred messenger of God.
Simon, 1975, 525 pp., o.p.
(BL 71:892, 905; Kirkus 43:251, 322; LJ 100:688)

5-5 **AIKEN, Joan (Delano).** *The Cockatrice Boys.* Gr. 7 up. (Orig. pub. in Eng-
☆ land.)
A small band of heroes, including cousins Dakin and Sauna, tries to overthrow the rule of the deadly monsters, or cockatrices, that have invaded England and taken over the country.
Tor, 1996, 224 pp. (0-312-86056-0)
(BL 93:69; Kirkus 64:1011; LJ Aug 1996 p. 120; SLJ Mar 1997 p. 214; VOYA 19:333, 20:10)

5-6 **AIKEN, Joan (Delano).** *The Kingdom and the Cave.* Gr. 4–6. (Orig. British pub. 1960.)
Prince Michael's cat is kidnapped after Michael uncovers the invasion plans of the people Down Under.
Illus. by Victor G. Ambrus, Doubleday, 1974, 160 pp., o.p.
(BL 70:871; HB 50:146; Kirkus 42:108; LJ 99:2258)

5-7 **AIKEN, Joan (Delano).** *The Whispering Mountain.* Gr. 5–8. (Orig. British
☆ pub. 1968.)
Orphaned Owen is falsely accused of stealing the legendary Golden Harp of Teirtu. Carnegie Medal Honour Book, 1968; Guardian Award for Children's Fiction, 1969.
Illus. by Frank Bozzo, Doubleday, 1969, 240 pp., o.p.; Starscape, 2002, pap., 304 pp. (0-765-34241-3)
(BL 66:563; CCBB 23:123; HB 46:39; Kirkus 37:1146; LJ 94:4610; Suth:5)

5-8 **AIKEN, Joan (Delano).** *The Wolves of Willoughby Chase.* **(The Wolves**
☆☆ **Chronicles, bk. 1).** Gr. 5–7. (Orig. British pub. 1962.)
In this first of ten action-filled spoofs of Victorian melodrama set in an England that never was, Bonnie and her cousin Sylvia run away from their sinister governess, are chased by wolves, and end up in an orphanage. With the help of a boy named Simon, they escape and thwart the plans of the evil Miss Slighcarp. In *Black Hearts in Battersea* (1964; Delacorte, 2000), orphaned Simon and his friends Dido and Justin are kidnapped and shipwrecked before they uncover the true facts of their births. In *Nightbirds on Nantucket* (1966; Delacorte, 2000), Dido is rescued from the sea, only to be put into the care of an

evil woman who is plotting against King James of England. In *The Cuckoo Tree* (1971; Delacorte, 2000), Dido foils a plot to put St. Paul's Cathedral on rollers and push it into the Thames to disrupt the royal coronation ceremony. In *The Stolen Lake* (1981; Delacorte, 2000), Dido is sent on a dangerous diplomatic mission to New Cambria in Roman South America, to help England's Queen Ginerva recover a stolen lake. In *Dido and Pa* (1986; Houghton, 2002), Dido and Simon are reunited in an attempt to stop Dido's wicked Pa from putting a Hanoverian pretender on England's throne. In *Is Underground* (1993, 1995), Dido's sister, Is, searches for her missing cousin Arun, and discovers that she and many other London children lured aboard a train to "Play-land" have ended up laboring in the undersea mines of Holdernesse. In *Cold Shoulder Road* (1996, 1997), Is and her cousin Arun tangle with dangerous smugglers as they search for Arun's missing mother and Is's missing older sister Penny. In *Dangerous Games* (1999, 2000), Dido travels to the island of Aratu in search of a nobleman whose knowledge of rare games may cheer the ailing King James, but she also uncovers a plot on the life of Aratu's king. In *Midwinter Nightingale* (2003), Dido returns to England and is kidnapped by the werewolf Baron Magnus, who is searching for her friend Simon and King Richard, both of whom have disappeared. *Cold Shoulder Road* won the 1995–1996 Anne Spencer Lindbergh Prize in Children's Literature.

Illus. by Pat Marriott, Doubleday, 1962, 1989, 168 pp., o.p.; illus. by Pat Marriott, Delacorte, 2000, 181 pp. (0-38-532790-0)

(Eakin:3; HBG 12:298; LJ 88:4076; TLS 1962 p. 901; VOYA 4:58)

5-9   ALAMA, Pauline J. *The Eye of Night.* Gr. 10 up.
Trenara's serving girl, Hwyn, has brought her mistress to Kelgarran Hall in order to steal the Eye of Night, a small stone containing a mysterious egg, and to take it on a perilous journey to Larioneth.
Bantam, 2002, pap., 451 pp. (0-553-58463-4)

(BL 98:1831; VOYA 25:290)

5-10   ALEXANDER, Lloyd (Chudley). *The Arkadians.* Gr. 5–9.
✮   After he uncovers a financial scandal at the castle, Lucian travels across Arkadia in search of a goddess, accompanied by a young woman named Joy-in-the-Dance and a poet transformed into a jackass.
Dutton, 1995, 272 pp. (0-525-45415-2); Puffin, 1997, pap., 272 pp. (0-14-038073-6)

(BL 91:1561; CCBB 48:375; HBG 6:293; Kirkus 63:630; SLJ May 1995 p. 104; VOYA 18:312, 19:86)

5-11   ALEXANDER, Lloyd (Chudley). *The Book of Three.* **(The Chronicles of**
✮   **Prydain, bk. 1).** Gr. 5–8.
In this first volume of the Chronicles of Prydain, a young pig keeper named Taran and a warrior named Gwydion set out to battle the Horned King. In *The Black Cauldron* (Holt, 1965; Holt, 1999), Taran and Prince Gwydion plan to destroy the Black Cauldron of the Lord of the Land of Death. *The Black Cauldron* was a 1966 John Newbery Medal Honor Book. In *The Castle of Llyr* (Holt, 1966; Holt, 1999), Taran and Prince Gwydion rescue the obstreperous Princess Eilonwy, who was kidnapped by the wicked Chief Steward. In *Taran Wanderer* (Holt, 1967; Holt, 1999), Taran has grown into a young man, journeying throughout Prydain in search of his true identity. In the final volume of

the series, *The High King* (Holt, 1968; pap., Holt, 1999), Taran plays a leading role in the final struggle of the people of Prydain against the Lord of the Land of Death. *The High King* won the John Newbery Medal in 1969 and was a finalist for the National Book Award the same year. *Coll and His White Pig* (1965; see below), *The Truthful Harp* (1967; see below), and *The Foundling and Other Tales of Prydain* (1973, 1999; see below) are also set in the land of Prydain.

Holt, 1964, 224 pp. o.p.; Holt, 1999, 190 pp. (0-8050-6132-0); Dell, 1999, pap., 224 pp. (0-440-40702-8)

(BL 61:344, 346, 80:95; CCBB 18:157; Eakin:4; HB 40:496; Kirkus 32:818; LJ 89:3465; TLS 1966 p. 1089)

5-12   ALEXANDER, Lloyd (Chudley). *Coll and His White Pig.* Gr. 2–4.
✫   The theft of his magical pig, Henwen, by Arawan, Lord of the Land of Death, drives Coll to attempt a dangerous rescue in this story set in the same world as the Chronicles of Prydain (1964–1968, 1999; see above).
Illus. by Evaline Ness, Holt, 1965, 26 pp., o.p.

(BL 62:407; CCBB 19:77; Eakin:4; HB 41:619; Kirkus 33:115; LJ 90:5506)

5-13   ALEXANDER, Lloyd (Chudley). *The Foundling and Other Tales of Pry-*
✫   *dain.* Gr. 4–7.
Six tales set in the land of Prydain before the birth of Taran, Assistant Pig Keeper, who is the main character of *The Book of Three* (see above) and its sequels.
Illus. by Margot Zemach, Holt, 1973, 87 pp., o.p.; Holt, 1999, 98 pp. (0-8050-6130-4)

(BL 70:594, 826; CCBB 27:122; HB 50:278; Kirkus 41:1308; LJ 98:3688, 3704; Suth 2:9)

5-14   ALEXANDER, Lloyd (Chudley). *Gypsy Rizka.* Gr. 5–8.
✫   Orphaned half-gypsy Rizka lives by her wits in her late mother's hometown, hoping that her father and his people will return for her.
Dutton, 1999, 176 pp. (0-525-46121-3); Penguin/Puffin, 2000, pap., 197 pp. (0-14-130980-6)

(BL 95:1327, 96:820; CCBB 52:27; HB 75:205; HBG 10:287; Kirkus 67:530; SLJ Mar 1999 p. 206)

5-15   ALEXANDER, Lloyd (Chudley). *The Iron Ring.* Gr. 5–9.
✫   After King Tamar loses his kindom in a dice game, an iron ring appears on his finger and he must make a dangerous journey to King Jaya's realm to keep his honor.
Dutton, 1997, 283 pp. (0-525-45597-3); Penguin, 1999, pap., 285 pp. (0-14-130348-4)

(BL 93:1572; CCBB 50:386; HB 73:447; HBG 8:295; Kirkus 65:716; SLJ May 1997 p. 128; VOYA 20:250, 363,, 21:11)

5-16   ALEXANDER, Lloyd (Chudley). *The Marvelous Misadventures of Sebas-*
✫   *tian: Grand Extravaganza, Including a Performance by the Entire Cast of the Gallimaufry Theatricus.* Gr. 4–6.
Caught in a revolution, Sebastian saves a cat from a witch, rescues a princess, and kills the regent by playing a magical violin. National Book Award, 1971.
Dutton, 1973, 204 pp. (0-525-34739-9); Dell, 1991, pap. (0-440-40549-1); Peter Smith, 2001 (0-84467-163-0)

(BL 67:266, 659; CCBB 24:85; Kirkus 38:949; LJ 95:4040, 4324; Suth:7)

5-17   **ALEXANDER, Lloyd (Chudley).** *The Rope Trick.* Gr. 4–7.

✷   Lidi, a talented young magician, searches for the legendary Ferramondo, who can teach her the celebrated rope trick and make her craft complete.

Dutton, 2002, 256 pp. (0-525-47020-4); Puffin, 2004, pap., 195 pp. (0-14-240119-6)

(BL 99:404; CBB 56:186; HB 78:745; HBG 14:74; Kirkus 70:1300; SLJ Sep 2002 p. 219; VOYA 25:393, 26:10)

5-18   **ALEXANDER, Lloyd (Chudley).** *The Truthful Harp.* Gr. 2–4.

✷   Whenever King Fflewddar tells a lie, one of his harp strings breaks, in this story set in the same world as the Chronicles of Prydain (1964–1968, 1999; see above).

Illus. by Evaline Ness, Holt, 1967, 32 pp., o.p.

(CCBB 21:89; HB 44:58; Kirkus 35:1268; LJ 92:4608; Suth:7)

5-19   **ALEXANDER, Lloyd (Chudley).** *Westmark.* (**Westmark Trilogy, bk. 1**).

✷✷   Gr. 5–10.

Theo and Mickle, an orphaned boy and a runaway girl, turn the tables on the king's evil minister, Cabbarus, when he tries to use them in a plot to gain the throne for himself. National Book Award for Children's Fiction, 1982. In *The Kestrel* (Dutton, 1982; Firebird, 2002), Theo becomes a bloodthirsty warrior known as the Kestrel, defending his love, Queen Mickle of Westmark. In *The Beggar Queen* (Dutton, 1984; Firebird, 2002), the government of Westmark is violently overthrown by ex-prime minister Cabbarus, forcing Mickle and Theo to engineer a bloody resistance movement.

Dutton, 1981, 184 pp., o.p.; Firebird/Penguin, 2002, pap., 237 pp. (0-14-131070-7)

(BL 77:1095, 80:351, 86:789; CCBB 34:185; HB 57:428; Kirkus 49:934; SLJ May 1981 pp. 23, 62; Suth 3:10; VOYA 4:41)

ALEXANDER, Lloyd (Chudley). *The Wizard in the Tree.*

See Chapter 12, Witchcraft and Sorcery Fantasy.

5-20   **ALLEN, Will.** *Swords for Hire: Two of the Most Unlikely Heroes You'll Ever Meet.* Gr. 5–12.

Sixteen-year-old Sam Hatcher and "sword-for-hire" Rigby Skeet rescue a young woman named Melinda, as well as King Olive and his kingdom, from the king's evil younger brother, King Boondar, in this fast-paced adventure story.

Illus. by David Michael Beck, CenterPunch, 2003, pap., 168 pp. (0-9724882-0-0)

(CCBB 56:389; Kliatt Sep 2003 p. 23; SLJ Aug 2003 p. 154; VOYA 26:145, 27:10)

5-21   *Alternative Histories: Eleven Stories of the World as It Might Have Been.* **Ed. by Charles G. Waugh and Martin H. Greenberg.** Gr. 10 up.

Eleven stories of historical speculation, including one about ex-slaves who form a nation called New Africa after the Civil War, and another about American colonists who fail to win their independence from the British.

Garland, 1986, 363 pp., o.p.

(BL 83:686, 704)

5-22   **ALTON, Andrea I.** *Demon of Undoing.* Gr. 10 up.

Although a deformed leg has kept Fenobar from becoming an Imkaira warrior,

he joins forces with a legendary human "demon" to defeat a rival clan.
Baen, 1988, pap., 308 pp., o.p.
(VOYA 11:292)

5-23 *Amazons!* **Ed. by Jessica Amanda Salmonson.** Gr. 10 up.
An anthology of stories on the theme of women warriors, written by a number
of fantasy writers including Andre Norton and C. J. Cherryh. Winner of the
World Fantasy Convention Award, Anthology/Collection Category, 1980.
Amazons II (1986) is a related work.
DAW, 1979, 1986, pap., 206 pp., o.p.
(BL 76:932, LJ 104:2488; VOYA 3:51)

5-24 **ANDERSON, Poul (William).** *The Merman's Children.* Gr. 10 up.
Two young merpeople of the dying faerie race who were driven from the
coasts of Denmark by the rise of Christianity fall in love and search together
for a new home.
Putnam, 1979, 258 pp., o.p.
(BL 76:216; Kirkus 47:823; Kliatt 15:11; LJ 104:1592; SLJ Nov 1979 p. 96)

5-25 **ANDERSON, Poul (William).** *A Midsummer Tempest.* Gr. 10 up.
In an alternate 17th-century England, faery King Oberon and Queen Titania
help King Charles I in his final battle against Cromwell and the Puritans by
giving the Royalists a magical wand and book to awaken the sleeping powers
of the land. Mythopoeic Fantasy Award, 1975. This is the sequel to *Three
Hearts and Three Lions* (1953, 1961, 1963, 1978) and *Operation Chaos*
(1971), and is followed by *Operation Luna* (1999).
Doubleday, 1974, 207 pp., o.p.
(BL 70:1080, 1098; Kirkus 42:74; LJ 99:1733)

ANDERSON, Poul (William). *The Time Patrol.*
See Chapter 10, Time Travel Fantasy.

5-26 **ANDERSON, Poul (William).** *War of the Gods.* Gr. 10 up.
Raised by a giantess after the death of his father, Danish Prince Hadding vows
to become a warrior, take back his kingdom, and take revenge on his father's
murderers.
Tor, 1997, 304 pp. (0-312-86315-2)
(BL 94:216; Kirkus 65:1165; LJ Sep 15, 1997 p. 106)

5-27 **ANDERSON, Poul (William), and ANDERSON, Karen.** *Gallicenae.* **(The
King of Ys series, bk. 2).** Gr. 10 up.
King Gratillonius of Ys, a mythical city-state in Britanny, across the Channel
from Roman Britain, must defend Ys from invading barbarians and from the
Roman Empire. This is the sequel to *Roman Mater* (1986), and is followed by
Dahut (1988) and *The Dog and the Wolf* (1988).
Baen, 1987, pap., 384 pp., o.p.
(VOYA 10:174)

5-28 **ANTHONY, Piers (pseud. of Piers A. D. Jacob).** *Blue Adept.* **(The
Apprentice Adept series, bk. 2).** Gr. 10 up.
Stile searches for an unknown enemy menacing him in both the magic world
of Phaze and the science-fictional world of Proton. While in Phaze he is helped

by a unicorn, kills a dragon, is given a magic flute, and gains the love of Lady Blue. This is the sequel to *Split Infinity* (1980, 1987) and is followed by *Juxtaposition* (1981, 1987), *Out of Phaze* (1987, 1988), *Robot Adept* (1988, 1989), *Unicorn Point* (1989, 1990), and *Phaze Doubt* (1990, 2005).
Ballantine, 1987, pap., 336 pp., o.p.
(Kirkus 49:390; Kliatt 16:17; LJ 106:1325)

5-29   **ANTHONY, Piers (pseud. of Piers A. D. Jacob).** *On a Pale Horse.* **(Incarnations of Immortality series, bk. 1).** Gr. 10 up.
When Zane's unsuccessful suicide attempt kills Death instead of himself, the young man finds that he must take over Death's job. The sequels are *Bearing an Hourglass* (1984), *With a Tangled Skein* (1985), *Wielding a Red Sword* (1986), *Being a Green Mother* (1987), *For Love of Evil* (1988), and *And Eternity* (1990).
Ballantine, 1983, 249 pp., o.p.
(BL 80:666, 676, 86:782, 903, 91:413; Kirkus 51:1020; VOYA 7:37)

5-30   **ANTHONY, Piers (pseud. of Piers A. D. Jacob).** *A Spell for Chameleon.*
★   **(Magic of Xanth series, bk. 1).** Gr. 10 up.
Exiled to Mundania from the magical land of Xanth for failing to demonstrate any magical talents, Bink and his friend Chameleon eventually discover that Bink's unique talent is that magic cannot harm him. British Fantasy Society Award, Best Novel, 1977. The sequels are *The Source of Magic* (1979), *Castle Roogna* (1979), *Centaur Aisle* (1981), *Ogre, Ogre* (1982), *Night Mare* (1982), *Dragon on a Pedestal* (1983), *Crewel Lye* (1984), *Golem in the Gears* (1986), *Vale of the Vole* (1987), *Heaven Scent* (1988), *Man from Mundania* (1989), *Isle of View* (1990), *Question Quest* (1991), *The Color of Her Panties* (1992), *Demons Don't Dream* (1993), *Harpy Thyme* (1994), *Geis of the Gargoyle* (1995, 1996), *Roc and a Hard Place* (1995, 1996), *Yon Ill Wind* (1996, 1997), *Faun and Games* (1997, 1998), *Zombie Lover* (1998, 1999), *Xone of Contention* (1999, 2000), *The Dastard* (2000, 2001), *Swell Foop* (2001, 2002), *Up in a Heaval* (2002, 2003), *Cube Route* (2003), and *Currant Events* (2004). *Xanth: The Quest for Magic* (Del Rey, 2002) comprises *A Spell for Chameleon*, *The Source of Magic*, and *Castle Roogna*.
Ballantine, 1977, 1987, pap., 352 pp., o.p.; Del Rey, 1997, pap. (0-345-41849-2)
(BL 86:903; Kliatt 12:12; LJ 102:2083)

5-31   **ANTHONY, Piers (pseud. of Piers A. D. Jacob), and LACKEY, Mercedes.** *If I Pay Thee Not in Gold.* Gr. 11 up.
The queen of Mazonia challenges her magically talented rival, Xylina, to undertake a dangerous quest in search of a powerful shard of crystal in this story for mature readers.
Baen, 1993, 416 pp. (0-671-72175-5)
(BL 89:1470, 1471; Kirkus 61:561; LJ June 15, 1993 p. 104; VOYA 16:305)

5-32   *An Armory of Swords.* **Ed. by Fred Saberhagen.** Gr. 6–12.
Eight stories by various authors, set in the same world as Saberhagen's Lost Swords series (see below), elaborating on the fates of 12 magical swords forged by the god Vulcan.
Tor, 1995, 317 pp., o.p.
(Kirkus 63:516; LJ Apr 15, 1995 p. 119; VOYA 18:312)

5-33   ASH, Sarah. *Lord of Snow and Shadows.* **(The Tears of Artamon, Vol. 1).** Gr. 10 up.
Raised by his mother, far away from his father's kingdom, Gavril inherits the throne of Aazhkendir after his father's murder and discovers dark secrets about his lineage. The sequel is *Prisoner of the Iron Tower* (2004).
Spectra/Bantam, 2003, 496 pp. (0-553-80334-4)
(BL 99:1967; Kirkus 71:783; LJ June 15, 2003 p. 104)

ASPRIN, Robert (Lynn). *Hit or Myth.*
See Chapter 12, Witchcraft and Sorcery Fantasy.

5-34   ASPRIN, Robert (Lynn). *Thieves' World.* **(Thieves' World saga, Vol. 1 [Orig. series title: Sanctuary Saga]).** Gr. 10 up.
The Thieves' World saga is a series of short-story collections and novels set in the crime-ridden city of Sanctuary, written by various authors but concerning the same characters. The stories in the first book were written by Marion Zimmer Bradley, Poul Anderson, Lynn Abbey, and Robert Asprin. The sequels are *Tales from the Vulgar Unicorn* (1980, 1985), *The Shadows of Sanctuary* (1981, 1985), *Season* (1982), *The Face of Chaos* (1983), *Wings of Omen* (1984), *The Dead of Winter* (1985), *Beyond Sanctuary* (by Janet Morris, 1985), *Beyond the Veil* (by Janet Morris, 1985), *Beyond Wizardwall* (by Janet Morris, 1986), *Soul of the City* (by Lynn Abbey, 1986), *Blood Ties* (1986), *Aftermath* (1987), *Shadowspawn* (by Andrew J. Offutt, 1987), *Dagger* (by David Drake, 1988), *Uneasy Alliances* (1988), *Stealer's Sky* (1989), *Turning Points* (2002), *Sanctuary: An Epic Novel of Thieves' World* (by Lynn Abbey, 2002), and *Enemies of Fortune* (2004). *Sanctuary* (Ace, 1984) contains books 1–3: *Tales from the Vulgar Unicorn*, and *Shadows of Sanctuary*. *Cross-Currents* (1984) contains books 4–6: *Storm Season, The Face of Chaos*, and *Wings of Omen*). *The Shattered Sphere* (1986) contains books 7–9: *The Dead of Winter, Soul of the City*, and *Blood Ties*). *The Price of Victory* (1987) contains books 10–12: *Aftermath, Uneasy Alliances*, and *Stealer's Sky*). *Thieves' World: First Blood* (2003) contains books 1 and 2.
Ace, 1979, 1984, 1990, 308 pp. (0-441-80591-4)
(BL 76:760)

5-35   ATWATER-RHODES, Amelia. *Hawksong.* Gr. 7–12.
Hoping to put an end to the centuries-long war between their families, shapeshifters Danica Shardae and Zane Cobriana brave prejudice and assassination attempts in their determination to marry each other. This is the first book in a planned series of four. The sequel is *Snakecharm* (2004).
Delacorte, 2003, 243 pp. (0-385-73071-3)
(HBG 15:106; Kirkus 71:856; SLJ Aug 2003 p. 154; VOYA 26:145, 27:10)

5-36   AUDLEY, Anselm. *Heresy.* **(Aquasilva trilogy, vol. 1).** Gr. 10 up. (Orig. British pub. 2001.)
Abducted by a secret group called the Heretics, Cathan develops his abilities as a mind mage, and realizes that his people have been enslaved by the Domain, warrior priests of Rantha. The sequels are *Inquisition* (2002) and *Crusade* (2004 in England).
Pocket, 2001, 416 pp. (0-7434-2738-6), 2002, pap. (0-7434-2739-4)
(BL 98:57; Kirkus 69:987; LJ Sep 15, 2001 p. 115)

5-37 **AVI (Avi Wortis).** *Bright Shadow.* Gr. 5–8.
Morwenna becomes enmeshed in the conflict between an evil king and his subjects after a dying wizard leaves her the kingdom's last five magic wishes.
Macmillan, 1985, 144 pp., o.p.
(CCBB 39:102; SLJ Dec 1985 p. 86; VOYA 9:37)

5-38 **B. B. (pseud. of D[enys] J[ames] Watkins-Pitchford).** *The Little Grey*
★ *Men.* Gr. 4–6. (Orig. British pub. 1942, entitled *The Little Grey Men: A Story for the Young in Heart.*)
Three gnomes search the length of Folly Brook for their lost brother, Cloudberry. Carnegie Medal winner, 1942. The sequel is *Down the Bright Stream* (British pub. 1948).
Illus. by the author, Scribner, 1949, 249 pp., o.p.; HarperCollins, 2004, entitled *The Little Grey Men: A Story for the Young in Heart*, 304 pp. (0-06-055448-7)
(BL 46:105; CCBB 2:8; HB 25:533; Kirkus 17:28; LJ 74:1541, 1919)

5-39 **BABBITT, Lucy Cullyford.** *The Oval Amulet.* Gr. 6–9.
Disguised as a boy, 17-year-old Paragrin escapes from a restrictive settlement with her only treasure, an oval amulet, determined to find the mysterious woman who gave it to her. The sequel is *Children of the Maker* (1988).
Harper, 1985, 244 pp., o.p.
(BL 81:1249, 1250; CCBB 38:180; SLJ Sep 1985 p. 141; VOYA 8:191)

5-40 **BABBITT, Lucy Cullyford.** *Where the Truth Lies.* Gr. 7–12.
Sanctuary-born atheist Kira, 17, is chosen to help Lillen and Eli, young representatives of the monotheistic Godsland and the polytheistic Tribes, to resolve their peoples' often violent conflicts over which religion is "true."
Orchard, 1993, 199 pp. (0-531-05473-X)
(BL 89:1424; CCBB 46:239; HBG 4:307; Kirkus 61:592; SLJ Mar 1993 p. 218; VOYA 16:98)

5-41 **BAKER, Kage.** *The Anvil of the World.* Gr. 11 up.
Posing as a caravan master while attempting to begin a new life, former assassin Smith uses his secret talents to protect his valuable cargo and the travelers in his care from attacks by demons and bandits.
Tor, 2003, 352 pp. (0-765-30818-5)
(BL 99:1967; Kirkus 71:838; LJ July 2003 p. 132)

5-42 **BAKKEN, Harald.** *The Fields and the Hills.* **(The Journey Once Begun series, bk. 1).** Gr. 5–9.
After orphaned 13-year-old Weyr runs away from his Tam village and joins a traveling band of Agari performers, his paranormal abilities become very useful.
Houghton, 1992, 228 pp. (0-395-59397-2)
(BL 89:595; CCBB 46:67; HBG 4:79; Kirkus 60:1057; SLJ Dec 1992 p. 108)

5-43 **BALL, Margaret.** *Changeweaver.* **(Flameweaver series, bk. 2).** Gr. 10 up.
Tamai Flameweaver uses magic to guide British explorer Charles Carrington into the forbidden Chin empire, where they become part of a revolutionary uprising against the corrupt Red Hat Buddhist monks who control the boy emperor. This is the sequel to *Flameweaver* (1991).
Baen, 1993, pap., 298 pp. (0-671-72173-9)
(Kliatt Sep 1993 p. 15; VOYA 16:222, 17:8)

5-44 **BARKER, M(uhammad) A(bd-Al-) R(ahman).** *The Man of Gold.* Gr. 10–12.

Harsan, a young priest of the god Thumis, becomes expert at deciphering the ancient language of Llayni, leading him to search for the legendary Man of Gold, said to be powerful enough to save the empire.

DAW, 1984, pap., 367 pp., o.p.

(LJ 109:1470; VOYA 7:335)

5-45 **BARNES, John.** *One for the Morning Glory.* Gr. 10 up.

Four new guardians—an alchemist, a witch, a maid, and a captain of the guard—arrive to raise Prince Amatus after he drinks the forbidden Wine of the Gods and loses his left side.

Tor, 1996, 320 pp. (0-312-86106-0)

(BL 92:1424, 1428; Kirkus 64:181; LJ Feb 15, 1996 p. 179)

5-46 **BARRETT, Neal.** *The Treachery of Kings.* Gr. 10 up.

In the midst of a war fueled by the plots of a sorcerer, Master Lizard-Maker Finn and his true love, Letitia Louise, arrive in a hot-air balloon to deliver a birthday gift from their king.

Bantam/Spectra, 2001, pap., 336 pp. (0-553-58196-1)

(BL 97:1991; VOYA 25:125)

5-47 **BARRON, T(homas) A.** *Tree Girl.* Gr. 3–6.

A shape-shifting bear cub befriends orphaned Rowanna, 9, and convinces her to explore the magical forest forbidden by her guardian.

Philomel, 2001, 128 pp. (0-399-23457-8); Ace, 2002, pap., 136 pp. (0-441-00994-8)

(BL 98:474; CCBB 55:51; HBG 13:70; Kirkus 69:934; SLJ Oct 2001 p. 148; VOYA 24:287)

5-48 **BARTHOLOMEW, Lois Thompson.** *The White Dove.* Gr. 6–8.

★ Imprisoned after her detested suitor sets himself up as king, Princess Tasha escapes and undertakes a dangerous mission inside the castle to aid the resistance.

Houghton, 2000, 208 pp. (0-618-00464-5)

(BL 96:1241; CCBB 53:306; HBG 11:299; Kirkus 68:626; Kliatt Mar 2000 p. 6; SLJ May 2000 p. 166; VOYA 23:110)

5-49 **BASE, Graeme.** *TruckDogs.* Gr. 4–8. (Orig. Australian pub. 2004, entitled *TruckDogs: A Novel in Four Bites.*)

In a village called Hubcap, in an alternate Australia where all of the inhabitants are vehicle/animal hybrids, the Mongrel gang of TruckDog kids is banished from town but returns to battle the bandit RottWheelers, who are out to steal the town's gasoline.

Abrams/Amulet, 2004, 192 pp. (0-8109-5031-6)

(BL 100:1058; Kirkus 72:218; SLJ Mar 2004 p. 203)

BASS, L. G. *Sign of the Qin.*

See Chapter 6, High Fantasy: Myth or Legend Fantasy.

5-50 **BATH, K. P.** *The Secret of Castle Cant.* Gr. 5–9.

★ Orphaned Lucy Wickwright, 11-year-old servant of the Baron's daughter, Pauline, becomes a spy for the Cause, in this humorous tale of mistaken identity.

Illus. by David Christiana, Little, 2004, 292 pp. (0-316-10848-0)
(BL 101:595; CCBB 58:7; Kirkus 72:860; SLJ Sep 2004 p. 198)

5-51   BAUDINO, Gael. *Strands of Starlight.* Gr. 7–12.
In an alternate 14th-century Europe terrorized by the Inquisition, a young healer named Miriam, fleeing accusations of witchcraft, is taken in by elves after she is almost killed by a man she once healed.
NAL, 1989, pap., 371 pp., o.p.
(Kliatt Apr 1990 p. 22; VOYA 13:36)

5-52   BAUER, Steven. *Satyrday: A Fable.* Gr. 10 up.
Enslaved by an evil great horned owl who has stolen the moon to bring down everlasting darkness, a raven named Deirdre escapes to help a satyr named Matthew, a boy named Derin, and Vera, a magic fox, rescue the moon and restore light to the world.
Illus. by Ron Miller, Berkley/Putnam, 1980, pap., 213 pp., o.p.
(Kirkus 548:1308; LJ 105:2591)

5-53   BAUM, L(yman) Frank. *The Enchanted Island of Yew: Whereon Prince Marvel Encountered the High Ki of Twi and Other Surprising People.* Gr. 3–5. (Orig. pub. Bobbs-Merrill, 1903.)
Prince Marvel of the Isle of Yew longs to be a mortal boy.
Books of Wonder, 1996, 178 pp., o.p.; illus. by George O'Connor, North Books, 2003, 150 pp. (1-58287-253-8); Wildside, 2001, pap., 140 pp. (1-58715-021-2)
(SLJ Aug 1996 p. 108)

BAXTER, Lorna. *The Eggchild.*
See Chapter 12, Witchcraft and Sorcery Fantasy.

5-54   BEAGLE, Peter S(oyer). *Giant Bones.* Gr. 10 up.
★   Six stories of giants, wizards, and magic, including "The Magician of Karakosk," "The Last Song of Sirit Byar," and "Lal and Soukyan," which features characters from the author's *The Innkeeper's Song* (1993; see below).
Penguin/Roc, 1997, pap., 288 pp. (0-451-45651-3)
(BL 93:1806, 94:732, 1607; Kirkus 65:992; VOYA 20:251, 21:11)

5-55   BEAGLE, Peter S(oyer). *The Innkeeper's Song.* Gr. 10 up.
Tikat refuses to accept the drowning death of his sweetheart, Lukassa, and vows to rescue her from the wizard beneath the riverbed. *Giant Bones* (Penguin, 1997) contains a story about the same characters.
NAL, 1993, 368 pp. (0-451-45288-7)
(BL 90:394, 395, 866; LJ Oct 15, 1993 p. 93)

5-56   BEAGLE, Peter S(oyer). *The Last Unicorn.* Gr. 10 up.
★   A magician and a very old but beautiful unicorn travel the world in search of others of her species.
Viking, 1968, 218 pp., o.p.; NAL, 1991, pap., 218 pp. (0-451-45052-3); Roc, 1994, pap., 224 pp. (0-451-45052-3)
(BL 64:824; Kirkus 36:19; LJ 93:2131)

5-57   BEAVERSON, Aiden. *The Hidden Arrow of Maether.* Gr. 5–9.
After Linn, 14, is beaten by her stepfather for refusing to marry a member of the violent Ranite sect, she runs away to the City of Trees, where she is taken in by the lysefolk.
Delacorte, 2000, 178 pp., o.p., 2002, pap., 193 pp. (0-440-41693-0)
(CCBB 54:214; HBG 12:69; Kirkus 68:1480; SLJ Dec 2000 p. 138)

5-58   BELL, Clare E. *The Jaguar Princess.* Gr. 10 up.
Mixcatl, apprentice scribe to the Aztec priests, discovers that she can transform herself into a jaguar and right ancient wrongs.
Tor, 1993, 448 pp., o.p.
(BL 90:417, 427; Kirkus 61:1034; VOYA 16:377, 17:10)

BELL, Clare E. *Ratha's Creature.*
See Chapter 2, Animal Fantasy.

5-59   BELL, Hilari. *Flame.* **(The Book of Sorahb trilogy, vol. 1).** Gr. 6–12.
★★   This action-filled story partially based on Persian legend is told from three young people's points of view: Soraya, hidden by her commander father to avoid becoming a sacrifice to ensure a Farsalan victory; Jiann, her illegitimate half-brother; and Kavi, a crippled peddler and spy for the attacking Hrum. The sequel is *Wheel* (2004).
Simon, 2003, 352 pp. (0-689-85413-7)
(BL 100:122; HB 79:607; HBG 15:106; Kirkus 71:1171; SLJ Nov 2003 p. 134; VOYA 26:321, 27:10)

BELL, Hilari. *The Goblin Wood.*
See Chapter 12, Witchcraft and Sorcery Fantasy.

5-60   BEMMANN, Hans. *The Stone and the Flute.* Gr. 10 up. (Orig. German pub. 1983.)
Two powerful talismans guide young Listener, son of the chieftain of Fraglund, on his quest to find his grandfather, the legendary Gentle Fluter, and the woman whose eye he sees in his magical stone.
Trans. by Anthea Bell, Viking, 1987, 855 pp., o.p.
(BL 83:946, 949; Kirkus 55:397; LJ May 15 1987 p. 101)

5-61   BENJAMIN, Curt. *The Prince of Shadow.* **(Seven Brothers series, bk. 1).** Gr. 11 up.
Lleshoi, 15, has forgotten the childhood trauma of his family members' murders and enslavement, but when the memories return, he leaves Pearl Island to find his lost brothers and reclaim the Kingdom of Kungol. The sequels are *The Prince of Dreams* (2002) and *Gates of Heaven* (2003).
DAW, 2001, 426 pp. (0-7564-0005-8), 2002, pap., 511 pp. (0-7564-0054-6)
(BL 98:200; VOYA 24:442)

5-62   BERBERICK, Nancy Verlan. *The Panther's Hoard.* Gr. 10 up.
While recovering from injuries sustained in the Witch Wars, dwarf Garroc Ghosts-Skald tells his foster granddaughter about her father's heroic quest to rescue the king's lost son.
Berkley/Ace, 1994, pap., 304 pp. (0-441-00009-6)
(BL 90:997, 1000; Kliatt May 1994 p. 14)

5-63 **BERG, Carol.** *Son of Avonar.* **(Bridge of D'Arnath series, bk. 1).** Gr. 10 up.

In self-imposed exile from the Four Realms to avoid persecution for sorcery, Seriana Marguerite of Comigor takes in a mute fugitive named D'Natheil who proves to be both mage and warrior, and whose fate is bound up with the Kingdom's war against magic. The sequels are *Guardians of the Keep* (2004), and *The Soul Weaver* (2005).

NAL/Roc, pap., 2004, 480 pp. (0-451-45962-8)

(BL 100:1047; Kliatt May 2004 p. 28)

5-64 **BERG, Carol.** *Song of the Beast.* Gr. 10 up.

Released from prison after 17 years, legendary bard Aidan MacAllister, cousin of Elyria's king, hides his identity to uncover the connection between his fascination with dragons and his sentence for treason.

NAL/Roc, 2003, pap., 480 pp. (0-451-45923-7)

(BL 99:1651; Kliatt July 2003 p. 28)

5-65 **BERTIN, Joanne.** *The Last DragonLord.* **(DragonLords series, bk. 1).** Gr.
 ★   10 up.

DragonLord Linden Rathan and sea captain Maurynna Erdon uncover a plot by a clandestine society, the Fellowship, to destroy the few remaining DragonLords in the world. The sequel is *Dragon and Phoenix* (1999, 2000).

Tor, 1998, 400 pp. (0-312-86429-9), 1999, pap., 500 pp. (0-812-54541-9)

(BL 95:312; Kirkus 66:1499; LJ Nov 15, 1998 p. 94; VOYA 22:12–18, 44)

5-66 **BETANCOURT, John Gregory.** *The Blind Archer.* Gr. 10 up.

Ker's rebellious attempts to test his magical talents result in his being sent on a quest to the world of the Faceless Demons.

Avon, 1988, pap., 233 pp. (0-380-75146-1)

(BL 84:1316, 1334; Kliatt Apr 1988 p. 18)

5-67 **BILLINGSLEY, Franny.** *The Folk Keeper.* Gr. 5–9.
 ★★   Disguised as a boy so that she can work as a Folk Keeper and placate the ravenous Folk who live beneath the foundling home, Corinna is summoned to become Folk Keeper at the Northern Isles estate on Cliffsend. Boston Globe Horn Book Award, 2000; Mythopoeic Fantasy Award for Children's Literature, 2000.

Simon, 1999, 162 pp. (0-689-82876-4); Aladdin, 2001, pap., 176 pp. (0-689-84461-1)

(BL 96:126, 1546; CCBB 53:43–44; HB 75:734, 77:43-47; HBG 11:74; Kirkus 67:1639; Kliatt Nov 1999 p. 9; SLJ Oct 1999 p. 144, Dec 1999 p. 39; VOYA 22:340)

5-68 **BILLINGSLEY, Franny.** *Well Wished.* Gr. 4–7.
 ★★   The foolish wish that 11-year-old Nuria makes at a wishing well transfers her mind and spirit into the body of her friend Catty, who is confined to a wheelchair. Anne Spencer Lindbergh Prize Honor Book, 1997–1998.

Atheneum, 1997, 170 pp. (0-689-81210-8); Aladdin, 2000, pap., 176 pp. (0-689-83255-9)

(BL 93:1694, 95:585; CCBB 50:274; HB 73:314; HBG 8:296; Kirkus 65:716; SLJ May 1997 p. 128, Dec 1997 p. 23)

BISHOP, Anne. *The Pillars of the World.*
See Chapter 12, Witchcraft and Sorcery Fantasy.

5-69   **BISSON, Terry.** *Fire on the Mountain.* Gr. 10 up.
An alternate history of the southern United States told from two points of view: that of Dr. Abraham, an ex-slave who witnessed John Brown's defeat of the Virginia militia at Harpers Ferry, thereby averting the Civil War and resulting in an independent socialist South known as Nova Africa; and that of his 20th-century granddaughter, Yasmin Odinga, whose astronaut husband has died on an African expedition to Mars.
Arbor, 1988, 192 pp., o.p.
(BL 84:1786, 1818; Kirkus 56:797)

5-70   **BLACKWOOD, Gary L.** *The Year of the Hangman.* Gr. 6–10.
★   Creighton Brown's mother ships him off to stay with his uncle, a colonial governor in an alternate 1777 America, where the rebellion has been put down and the rebel leaders have been exiled to Spanish New Orleans.
Dutton, 2002, 196 pp. (0-525-46921-4); Puffin, 2004, pap., 272 pp. (0-14-240078-5)
(BL 98:1945; CCBB 56:144; Kirkus 70:1216; Kliatt Sep 2002 p. 6; SLJ Sep 2002 p. 219; VOYA 25:269)

5-71   **BLAYLOCK, James P(aul).** *The Stone Giant.* (The Elfin Sequence, bk. 3). Gr. 10–12.
Theophile Escargot, exiled from Twombly Town for stealing his wife's pie, becomes a surprised hero in this humorous sequel to *The Elfin Ship* (Ballantine, 1982) and *The Disappearing Dwarf* (Ballantine, 1983).
Ace, 1989, pap., 264 pp., o.p.
(BL 85:1613; VOYA 12:369, 13:16)

5-72   **BODECKER, N(iels) M(ogens).** *Quimble Wood.* Gr. 2–4.
Four miniature people called Quimbles are forced to set up housekeeping in a forest.
Illus. by Branka Starr, Atheneum, 1981, 26 pp., o.p.
(BL 77:1296, Kirkus 49:431; SLJ Sep 1981 p. 104)

5-73   **BORCHARDT, Alice.** *The Silver Wolf.* (Silver Wolf trilogy, bk. 1). Gr. 10 up.
Regeane, a Roman teenager during Charlemagne's rise to power, can transform herself into a silver wolf and becomes a pawn in the struggle between her family and the barbarians. The sequels are *Night of the Wolf* (1999, 2000) and *The Wolf King* (2001).
Del Rey, 1998, 464 pp., o.p.; Ballantine, 1999, pap., 460 pp. (0-345-42361-5)
(Kirkus 66:753; LJ July 1998 p. 142; VOYA 21:364)

5-74   *Borderland, No. 1.* **Ed. by Terri Windling and Mark Arnold.** (Borderlands series, vol. 1). Gr. 7–12.
Four short stories written by Steven R. Boyett, Bellamy Bach, Charles de Lint, and Ellen Kushner, all set in the magical world of Borderland, which is surrounded by other warring worlds. The sequel is *Bordertown* (1986). Will Shetterly's *Elsewhere* (1991; see Chapter 7, High Fantasy: Travel to Other Worlds) and Emma Bull's *Finder* (Tor, 1994; see Chapter 7, High Fantasy: Travel to

Other Worlds) are also set in the world of Borderland. *Life on the Border*, ed. by Craig Shaw Gardner and Terry Windling (Tor, 1991), *Bordertown*, ed. by Terry Windling and Mark Alan Arnold (Doherty, 1996), and *The Essential Bordertown: A Traveller's Guide to the Edge of Faerie*, ed. by Terry Windling and Delia Sherman (Tor, 1998) are multi-author short story collections about Borderland.
NAL, 1986, pap., 252 pp., o.p.
(BL 82:1184; Kliatt 20:30; VOYA 9:233, 10:21)

5-75 **BRADLEY, Marion Zimmer.** *Hawkmistress!* **(Darkover series).** Gr. 10
☆ up.
Sixteen-year-old Romilly MacAran gives up her privileged life by refusing to marry the man her father has chosen and runs away to develop her unusual gift of mind control over hawks. This novel from the Darkover series (see *The Shattered Chain*, below) can stand on its own.
DAW, 1982, 1988, pap., 336 pp., o.p.
(BL 79:294; LJ 107:1722; VOYA 5:42)

5-76 **BRADLEY, Marion Zimmer.** *The Shattered Chain: A Darkover Novel.* **(Darkover series, bk. 1).** Gr. 10 up.
Lady Rohana of Ardais and a female band of Free Amazons arrive in the Dry Towns of Darkover, where all women are kept in chains, in order to free a royal captive and her slave-born daughter. The sequels are *Thendara House* (1983, 1988, DAW, 2002, pap.) and *City of Sorcery* (1984, DAW, 2002, pap.). *The Shattered Chain* has also been published in one volume with *Thendara House*, entitled *Oath of the Renunciates* (Doubleday, 1983). Bradley has written 26 novels set in the alternate world of Darkover. *Darkover Landfall* (1972) is the first in terms of internal chronology, but they need not be read in any specific order. The others in the series are *The Sword of Aldones* (Ace, 1962), *The Planet Savers* (Ace, 1962), *The Bloody Sun* (Ace, 1964, 1969), *Star of Danger* (Ace, 1965), *Winds of Darkover* (Ace, 1970), *The World Wreckers* (Ace, 1971), *The Spell Sword* (1974, 1988), *The Heritage of Hastur* (1975, 1988), *The Forbidden Tower* (1977, 1988), *Stormqueen* (1978, 1989), *Two to Conquer* (1980), *Sharra's Exile* (1981, 1988), *Sword of Chaos and Other Stories* (1982), *Hawkmistress!* (1982, 1988; see above), *Free Amazons of Darkover* (1985), *The Heirs of Hammerfell* (1990), *Leroni of Darkover* (1991), *Rediscovery: A Novel of Darkover* (1993), *Towers of Darkness* (1993), *Exile's Song* (1996, 1997), and *The Shadow Matrix* (1997, 1999). The following anthologies contain Darkover tales written by Bradley and by members of the Friends of Darkover: *The Keeper's Price and Other Stories* (1980), *The Other Side of the Mirror: And Other Darkover Stories* (DAW, 1987), *Red Sun of Darkover* (1987), *Four Moons of Darkover* (1988), *Spells of Wonder* (1989), *Domains of Darkover* (1990), *Renunciates of Darkover* (1991), *Marion Zimmer Bradley's Darkover* (1993), and *Snows of Darkover* (1994). *The Children of Hastur* (Doubleday, 1982) and *Heritage and Exile* (DAW, 2002, pap.) both contain *The Heritage of Hastur* and *Sharra's Exile*. The related Clingfire trilogy by Bradley and Deborah J. Ross includes *The Fall of Neskaya* (DAW, 2001), *Zandru's Forge* (2003), and *A Flame in Havi* (2004).
DAW, 1976, pap., 287 pp., o.p.
(BL 73:22; LJ 101:1227)

5-77   **BRADLEY, Marion Zimmer, MAY, Julian, and NORTON, Andre (pseud.**
☆   **of Alice Mary Norton).** *Black Trillium.* **(Trillium saga, bk. 1).** Gr. 10 up.
An evil sorcerer has taken over the Kingdom of Ruwenda and murdered the
king and queen, forcing the three princesses, each wearing a magic amulet, to
flee. Each of the three co-authors has written a story of one princess's quest to
defeat the sorcerer. The sequels are *Blood Trillium* (1992) written by Julian
May, *Golden Trillium* (1993) written by Norton, *Lady of the Trillium* (1995,
1996) written by Bradley, and *Sky Trillium* (1997) written by May.
Doubleday, 1990, 410 pp., o.p.; Bantam, 1991, pap. (0-553-29079-7)
(BL 86:1931, 1933, 87:967; Kirkus 58:842; LJ Aug 1990 p. 147; SLJ Nov 1990 p. 156;
VOYA 13:224, 14:9)

5-78   **BRADLEY, Marion Zimmer, NORTON, Andre (pseud. of Alice Mary**
Norton), and LACKEY, Mercedes. *Tiger Burning Bright.* Gr. 10 up.
Warrior princess Shelyra, her mother, Queen Lydana, and her priestess grand-
mother battle Emperor Balthasar and his evil sorcerer, Apolon, for control of
their goddess-worshiping city.
Morrow, 1995, 512 pp. (0-688-14360-1)
(BL 92:47, 51; Kirkus 63:989)

5-79   **BRADSHAW, Gillian (Marucha).** *The Dragon and the Thief.* Gr. 5–10.
☆   Seventeen-year-old Prahotep, attempting the trade of tomb-robbing, accidentally enters the cave of Hathor, the last dragon in ancient Thebes, and agrees to
help transport her treasure down the Nile to Nubia while she searches for others of her kind. In the sequel, *The Land of Gold* (1992), Prahotep and Hathor
rescue Kandaki, a Nubian princess, from death as a sacrifice to a terrifying
water dragon, and she joins their crew, intending to regain her stolen throne.
Greenwillow, 1991, 154 pp. (0-688-10575-0)
(BL 87:2039; CCBB 45:85; HBG 3:63; Kirkus 59:928; SLJ Oct 1991 p. 119)

5-80   **BRADSHAW, Gillian (Marucha).** *The Wolf Hunt.* Gr. 10 up.
Lady Marie Penthievre, abducted by Bretons from a convent in medieval
France, falls in love with Lord Tiarnan of Talensac in spite of the secret she
uncovers.
Tor/Forge, 2001, 384 pp. (0-312-87332-8)
(BL 97:2083; Kirkus 69:772; LJ Aug 2001 p. 158)

5-81   **BRAY, Patricia.** *Devlin's Luck.* Gr. 10 up.
Desperate for the means to support his late brother's family, widower Devlin
Stonehand volunteers to become the Chosen One, fated to die while battling
the enemies of the realm.
Bantam, 2002, pap., 480 pp. (0-553-58475-8)
(BL 98:1513; LJ May 15, 2002 p. 130; VOYA 25:199, 26:10)

5-82   **BRENNER, Mayer Alan.** *Spell of Apocalypse.* **(The Dance of the Gods**
series, bk. 4). Gr. 10 up.
Maximillian the Vaguely Disreputable, Favored-of-the-Gods, and Iskendarian
meet in Peridol to battle the powerful god Scapula. This final volume in the
series is preceded by *Catastrophe's Spell* (1989), *Spell of Intrigue* (1990), and
Spell of Fate (1992).

DAW, 1994, pap., 319 pp. (0-88677-602-3)
(Kliatt Sep 1994 p. 14; VOYA 17:153)

5-83   BRIGGS, Patricia. *Dragon Bones.* **(Dragon series, bk. 1).** Gr. 7 up.
Wardwick, 18, has long pretended to be mentally deficient as protection against his abusive father, Lord of Hurog Keep, but must now rescue his mute sister and use a magic ring to keep the mages from claiming the powerful dragon bones hidden beneath the keep. The sequel is *Dragon Blood* (2003).
Ace, 2002, pap., 295 pp. (0-441-00916-6)
(Kliatt May 2002 p. 23; VOYA 25:292)

5-84   BRITAIN, Kristen. *Green Rider.* **(Green Rider series, bk. 1).** Gr. 10 up.
A dying Green Rider gives Karigan G'ladheon a magic brooch and a vital message for King Zachary, but she must dodge rebels and renegades to find the king. The sequel is *First Rider's Call* (2003).
DAW, 1998, 504 pp. (0-88677-824-7), 2000, pap. (0-88677-858-1)
(Kirkus 66:1338; LJ Oct 15, 1998 p. 104; VOYA 21:364)

5-85   BRITTON, Susan McGee. *The Treekeepers.* Gr. 4–8.
Left on their own after their protectors Farwender and Soladin are captured by the evil Rendarren and his Searchers, a group of children led by orphaned Bird undertake a dangerous journey to plant the seed of the Tree That Speaks.
Dutton, 2003, 245 pp. (0-525-46944-3)
(BL 99:1465; CCBB 57:51; HBG 14:362; Kirkus 71:856; SLJ July 2003 p. 124)

BROOKS, Terry. *Magic Kingdom for Sale—Sold!*
See Chapter 8, Humorous Fantasy.

5-86   BROOKS, Terry. *The Sword of Shannara.* **(Shannara series, bk. 1).** Gr.
✷   10 up.
A band of elves, dwarfs, and trolls, reluctantly led by orphaned Shea, set off to find the legendary Sword of Shannara and defeat the forces of evil. The sequels are *The Elfstones of Shannara* (1982), *The Wishsong of Shannara* (1985), *The Scions of Shannara* (1990), *The Druid of Shannara* (1991), *The Elf Queen of Shannara* (1992), and *The Talismans of Shannara* (1993). The latter four are called the Heritage of Shannara series. *First King of Shannara* (1996) is a prequel. The Voyage of the Jerle Shannara is a sequel series containing *Ilse Witch* (2000), *Antrax Sky* (2001), and *Morgawr* (2002). The High Druid of Shannnara series begins with *Jarka Ruus: High Druid of Shannara* (2003). *Tanequil* (2004) is the second volume of the High Druid series. *The World of Shannara* (Ballantine, 2001, by Brooks and Teresa Patterson) is a companion volume to the series. *The Heritage of Shannara* (Del Rey, 2003) is composed of *The Scions of Shannara*, *The Druid of Shannara*, *The Elf Queen of Shannara*, and *The Talismans of Shannara*.
Illus. by the Brothers Hildebrandt, Random, 1977, 726 pp., o.p.; Del Rey, 1995, pap., 736 pp. (0-345-31425-5)
(BL 73:1147, 1155, 78:593, 86:904; Kirkus 45:108; LJ 102:946; SLJ Sep 1977 p. 152; VOYA 2:49)

5-87   BROWN, Mary. *Pigs Don't Fly.* Gr. 10 up.
A young woman named Summer takes to the road after her mother's death, wearing her unknown father's ring, which enables her to speak with animals.

Baen, 1994, 370 pp., o.p.

(BL 90:1184, 1188; Kliatt July 1994 p. 13; VOYA 17:219)

5-88   BROWN, Simon. *Inheritance.* **(Keys of Power trilogy, bk. 1).** Gr. 10 up.

After the dying Queen Usharna divides the four Keys of Power—the Scepter, the Sword, the Heart, and the Union—among her four children, Lynan, her youngest son, is wrongly accused of murdering the new king. The sequels are *Fire and Sword* (2004) and *Sovereign* (2004).

DAW, 2003, pap., 568 pp. (0-7564-0162-3)

(BL 100:217; VOYA 27:139)

5-89   BROWNE, N. M. *Basilisk.* Gr. 7–12. (Orig. British pub. 2004.)
☆   Rej, a catacomb-dweller, breaks the law and escapes from Below into the city of Lunnzia, where he is befriended by an Abover scribe named Donna who shares his dreams of flying dragons.

Bloomsbury, 2004, 350 pp. (1-58234-876-6)

(BL 100:1450; CCBB 57:457; Kirkus 72:391; SLJ June 2004 p. 135; VOYA 27:227)

5-90   BRUST, Steven K. (Zoltan). *The Paths of the Dead.* **(Viscont of Adri-**
☆   **lankha trilogy, bk. 1).** Gr. 10 up.

Zerika, heir to the Phoenix throne, returns to the ruined capital city of Dragaera, hoping to claim her right to become empress, in this tale set 2000 years after *The Phoenix Guards* (1991; see below). The sequel is *The Lord of Castle Black* (2003).

Tor, 2002, 432 pp. (0-312-86478-7), 2003, 448 pp. (0-8125-3417-4)

(BL 739; Kirkus 70:1510; LJ Dec 2002 p. 185; VOYA 26:146)

5-91   BRUST, Steven K. (Zoltan). *The Phoenix Guards.* Gr. 10 up.

Khaavren and his three Phoenix Guards companions—Lady Tazendra, Aerich, and Pel—serve the emperor while they engage in duels, fight battles, and search for adventure. This book takes place in an earlier period on Dragaera, the setting for Brust's Vlad Taltos series (1983–1988; see below). The sequels are *Five Hundred Years After* (1994), and the Viscount of Adrilankha trilogy, *The Paths of the Dead* (2002), *The Lord of Castle Black* (2003), and *Sethra Lavode* (2004).

Tor, 1991, 320 pp. (0-312-85157-X)

(BL 87:2108, 2110; Kirkus 59:1121; LJ Sep 15, 1991 p. 117; VOYA 15:40)

5-92   BRUST, Steven K. (Zoltan). *Taltos.* **(Vlad Taltos series, vol. 1).** Gr. 10 up.

The sorcerers of Dragaera keep its citizens in thrall, but Taltos has been able to practice his professions of detective, assassin, and witch in spite of them. The sequels are *Jhereg* (1983, 1987), *Yendi* (1984, 1987), *Tekla* (1987), *Phoenix* (1990), *Athyra* (1993) *Dragon* (Tor, 1998, 1999), *Orca* (1996), and *Issola* (2001). *Dragon* and *Orca* fall chronologically between *Jhereg* and *Yendi* (2001). The Viscount of Adrilankha trilogy is related: *The Paths of the Dead* (2002), *The Lord of Castle Black* (2003), and *Sethra Lavode* (2004). *The Book of Jhereg* (Ace, 1999, pap.) contains *Jhereg, Yendi,* and *Teckla. The Book of Taltos* (Ace, pap., 2002) contains *Taltos* and *Phoenix. The Phoenix Guards* (1991; see above) takes place in an earlier period on Dragaera.

Ace, 1988, pap., 181 pp., o.p.

(BL 84:1098; VOYA 11:137, 12:16)

5-93 **BUJOLD, Lois McMaster.** *The Curse of Chalion.* Gr. 10 up.
✷ Appointed tutor to Royesse Iselle, sister of the royal heir, a crippled former soldier named Cazaril becomes entangled in court intrigue and the royal family's fatal curse. Mythopoeic Fantasy Award for Adult Literature, 2002. The sequel is *Paladin of Souls* (2003).
HarperCollins, 2001, 448 pp. (0-380-97901-2); HarperTorch, 2002, pap., 512 pp. (0-380-81860-4)
(BL 97:1672; Kirkus 69:779; LJ July 2001 p. 131; SLJ Oct 2001 p. 194, Dec 2001 p. 50; VOYA 24:366)

5-94 **BUJOLD, Lois McMaster.** *The Spirit Ring.* Gr. 10 up.
In this fantasy set in an alternate Renaissance Italy, a sculptor's daughter battles a sorcerer for her father's soul after the sculptor agrees to animate the sorcerer's spirit ring.
Baen, 1992, 369 pp. (0-671-72142-9); Baen, 2000, pap., 369 pp. (0-671-57870-7)
(BL 89:37, 42; VOYA 16:36, 17:8)

5-95 **BUNCH, Chris.** *Storm of Wings.* **(Dragonmaster trilogy, bk. 1).** Gr. 10 up.
Hal Kailas, the sole survior of his Derain army unit after a bloody battle against the Roche, joins the dragon flyers seeking revenge for the deaths of his cavalry comrades. The sequels are *Knighthood of the Dragon* (2003) and *The Last Battle* (2004).
Orbit, 2002, pap., 410 pp. (1-84149-104-7)
(BL 99:70; VOYA 25:394)

5-96 **BUSH, Anne Kelleher.** *The Knight, the Harp, and the Maiden.* Gr. 10 up.
Lady Juilene becomes a traveling songsayer attempting to lift the curse of Lindos the evil magician after she fails to overthrow his rule.
Warner, 1999, pap., 328 pp. (0-446-60496-8)
(Kliatt Nov 1999 p, 24; VOYA 22:314, 23:10)

5-97 **BUTCHER, Jim.** *Furies of Calderon.* **(Codex Alera, bk. 1).** Gr. 10 up.
Tavi, a young man from the mountains of Alera, rescues Amara, a royal spy searching for traitorous Lords plotting to overthrow the First Lord.
Berkley/Ace, 2004, 448 pp. (0-441-01199-3)
(BL 101:318; LJ Sep 2004 p. 52)

5-98 **CALDECOTT, Moyra.** *The Tall Stones.* **(The Sacred Stones series, bk. 1).** Gr. 10 up.
Karne and his sister Kyra are trained by Maal, the old priest of their Bronze Age British village, in the powers and secrets held by the Circle of Stones, but their lives are threatened by an evil new priest. The sequels are *The Temple of the Sun* (1978) and *Shadow on the Stones* (1979).
Farrar, 1977, 234 pp., o.p.
(BL 74:1174; Kirkus 45:1057; LJ 103:383; SLJ May 1978 p. 89; TLS 1977 p. 864)

5-99 **CALHOUN, Dia.** *Aria of the Sea.* Gr. 6–10.
✷ Cerin the Gale, 13, attempts to forget her healing skills while trying to fulfill her late mother's dream of becoming a dancer in the Royal Ballet. Mythopoeic Fantasy Award for Children's Literature, 2001.

Winslow, 2000, 262 pp. (1-890817-25-2); Farrar, 2003, pap., 272 pp. (0-374-40454-2)

(CCBB 54:137; HBG 12:320; Kirkus 68:1352; Kliatt Nov 2000 p. 6; SLJ Sep 2000 p. 225; VOYA 23:272, 24:10)

5-100   CALHOUN, Dia. *Firegold.* Gr. 6–9.

✭   Blue-eyed Jonathon Bray, 13, feared by the brown-eyed valley folk, has headaches and visions that drive him to leave home and travel to the Red Mountains, home of the fearsome barbarian Dalriadas. *White Midnight* (2003; see below) is the prequel.

Illus. by Hervé Blondon, Winslow, 1999, 286 pp., o.p.; Farrar, 2003, pap., 368 pp. (1-374-42311-3)

(BL 95:1690, 96:618, 1546; CCBB 53:7; Kirkus 67:797; Kliatt May 1999 p. 9; SLJ June 1999 p. 126; VOYA 22:189, 23:10)

5-101   CALHOUN, Dia. *White Midnight.* Gr. 7–12.

After 15-year-old Rose's parents betroth her to Raymont Brae, the reputedly monstrous son of the master of Greengarden, Rose becomes pregnant and uncovers a family secret that will affect the future of the valley and of her unborn child. This is the prequel to *Firegold* (1999; see above).

Farrar, 2003, 304 pp. (0-374-38389-8)

(BL 100:231; CCBB 57:264; SLJ Mar 2003 p. 203; VOYA 26:410, 27:10)

CALLANDER, Don. *Aquamancer.*
See Chapter 12, Witchcraft and Sorcery Fantasy.

5-102   CARD, Orson Scott. *Hart's Hope.* Gr. 10 up.

Black sorcery practiced by young Princess Asineth of Burland, who had been forced into an unloving marriage to her country's conquerer, brings centuries of despair to the kingdom and its rulers.

Berkley, 1983, pap., 272 pp., o.p.; Tor, 1988, 1992, pap. (0-8125-2135-8)

(BL 79:1013; VOYA 6:212)

5-103   CARD, Orson Scott. *Seventh Son.* **(Tales of Alvin Maker, bk. 1).** Gr. 10

✭   up.

Something or someone is determined that young Alvin Miller, the seventh son of a seventh son, will never grow up to use his powerful magic in this novel set on the frontier of an alternate early 19th-century America. Mythopoeic Fantasy Award, 1988. The sequels are *Red Prophet* (1988, 2003), *Prentice Alvin* (1989, 2003), *Alvin Journeyman* (1995, 1996, 2003), *Heartfire: Tales of Alvin Maker* (1998, 1999, 2003), and *The Crystal City* (2003).

Tor, 1987, 241 pp. (0-312-93019-4), 1993, pap. (0-8125-3305-4); Tor, 2003, pap., 256 pp. (0-7653-4775-X)

(BL 8 3:1314, 84:838, 855, 1246, 86:904; Kirkus 55:895; LJ June 15, 1987 p. 89; SLJ Dec 1987 p. 109; VOYA 10:243, 11:13)

5-104   CARD, Orson Scott. *Songmaster.* Gr. 10 up.

Because 9-year-old Ansset's beautiful singing voice has captivated and tamed the formerly tyrannical emperor, Mikal the Terrible, the emperor's jealous advisers kidnap the boy and involve him in a plot to murder Mikal.

Dial, 1980, 320 pp., o.p.; Tor, 1987, 1992, 2002, pap., 348 pp. (0-312-87662-9)

(Kirkus 48:739; SLJ Oct 1980 p. 166; VOYA 3:31, 11:13)

5-105 **CARLYON, Richard.** *The Dark Lord of Pengersick.* Gr. 5–9.
After young Mabby steals the sorcerer Pengersick's magic ring, her friend Jago goes on a hazardous quest to learn the powers of enchantment so that he can fight the evil enchanter and restore the land of Kernow to the people.
Farrar, 1980, 176 pp., o.p.
(BL 77:39, 42; SLJ Aug 1980 p. 61)

5-106 **CARMODY, Isobelle.** *The Farseekers.* **(The Obernewtyn Chronicles, vol. 2).** Gr. 10 up. (Orig. Australian pub. 1990.)
After the Council exiles Elspeth Gordie and her fellow Misfits, they set up a society on Obernewtyn mountain for those with psychic powers. This is the sequel to *Obernewtyn* (1987, 1999) and is followed by *Ashling* (2001, 2003). *The Keeping* (2000) and *The Sending* (2004) are Australian sequels.
Tor, 2000, 304 pp. (0-312-86957-6)
(Kirkus 68:841; LJ July 2000 p. 147; VOYA 23:357;)

5-107 **CARTER, Lin.** *Mandricardo: New Adventures of Terra Magica.* **(Terra Magica series, bk. 3).** Gr. 7–12.
A knight and his amazon companion encounter magic, monsters, and wizards in the lands of Terra Magica. The preceding books in the series are *Kesrick* (1982) and *Dragonrouge* (1984), and the sequel is *Callipygia* (1988).
DAW, 1987, pap., 223 pp., o.p.
(Kliatt 21:20; VOYA 10:89,11:13)

5-108 **CARVER, Jeffrey A(llan).** *Dragon Rigger.* **(Star-Rigger series, bk. 3).** Gr. 10 up.
In this science-fantasy, Star-Rigger Jael LeBrae is called upon to help dragon friends by entering the Flux, an alternate reality, and battling evil forces threatening the Realm. This is the sequel to *Star Rigger's Way* (Doubleday, 1978) and *Dragons in the Stars* (Tor, 1992).
Tor, 1993, 475 pp. (0-312-85061-1)
(BL 89:1793, 1797; LJ June 15, 1993 p. 104; VOYA 16:306)

5-109 **CHANT, Joy (pseud. of Eileen Joyce Rutter).** *The Grey Mane of Morning.* **(Vandarei series, bk. 2).** Gr. 10 up. (Orig. British pub. 1977.)
In this story set in an earlier period of the history of Vandarei than *Red Moon and Black Mountain* (1970, 1976, see Chapter 7, High Fantasy: Travel to Other Worlds), the nomadic Alnei tribe of Khentor and the Golden People of the Walled Towns come into deadly conflict, and young Mor'anh emerges as an Alnei hero. *When Voiha Wakes* (1983) is set in the same world, and won the 1984 Mythopoeic Fantasy Award.
Illus. by Martin White, Unwin, 1977, 262 pp., o.p.
(BL 77:504; LJ 103:388)

5-110 **CHAPMAN, Vera.** *The Notorious Abbess.* **Ed. by Robert H. Boyer and Kenneth J. Zahorski.** Gr. 10 up. (Orig. pub in England.)
Twelfth-century abbess Hodierna travels by magic between England and the Holy Land, encountering a mermaid, a satyr, a werewolf, and the Devil himself.
Academy Chicago, 1997, 239 pp. (0-89733-387-X)
(BL 93:1805; Kirkus 65:1072; LJ Oct 15, 1997 p. 98)

5-111 CHASE, Carol. *Hawk's Flight.* Gr. 10 up.
Taverik the merchant and his fellow traveler, Marco, a woman in disguise, are chosen to help the forces of Zojikam battle evil in their own world and in the spirit world.
Baen, 1991, pap., 437 pp., o.p.
(Kliatt Sep 1991 p. 20; VOYA 14:237)

5-112 CHEN, Da. *Wandering Warrior.* Gr. 6–12.
✫ Orphaned Luka, raised as a wandering beggar fated to become the Chosen One who will free China from Mogo occupation, learns martial arts and survival skills in this fast-paced adventure.
Delacorte, 2003, 304 pp. (0-385-90089-9); Laurel Leaf, 2004, pap., 336 pp. (0-440-23771-8)
(BL 99:1064; CCBB 56:307; Kirkus 71:59; Kliatt Jan 3002 p. 6; SLJ Feb 2003 p. 140; VOYA 26:127)

5-113 CHERNENKO, Dan. *The Bastard King.* **(The Sceptre of Mercy series, bk. 1).** Gr. 10 up.
Boy King Lanius, son of a concubine, rules Avornis at the mercy of the noble regents until naval Captain Grus proclaims himself king and marries Lanius to his daughter. The sequel is *The Chernagor Pirates* (2004).
NAL/Roc, 2003, pap., 431 pp. (0-451-45914-8)
(BL 99:1152; Kliatt May 2003 p. 24; VOYA 26:322)

5-114 CHERRYH, C. J. (pseud. of Carolyn Janice Cherry). *Angel with the*
✫ *Sword.* Gr. 10 up.
Seventeen-year-old Altair Jones rescues an unconscious man named Mondragon from a canal, falls in love with him, and becomes determined to protect him from his powerful enemies in the city of Merovingen. The books in the Merovingen Nights series, edited by Cherryh, are set in the same world (see *Festival Moon*, below.
DAW, 1985, 293 pp., o.p.
(BL 81:1596, 1599; LJ Sep 15, 1985 p. 96; SLJ Nov 1985 p. 105)

5-115 CHERRYH, C. J. (pseud. of Carolyn Janice Cherry). *Exile's Gate.* **(The**
✫ **Quest of Morgaine, bk. 4).** Gr. 10 up.
In this fourth volume of the Morgaine series, white-haired Morgaine and her liegeman, Vanye, discover that Skarrin, the ruler of their world, is an exiled member of the ancient race to which Morgaine may belong. This is the sequel to *Gate of Ivrel* (1976), *The Well of Shiuan* (1978), and *The Fires of Azeroth* (1979). *Visible Light* (1986) contains one story set in Morgaine's world.
DAW, 1988, pap., 416 pp., o.p.
(BL 84:417, 418; Kliatt 22:18; LJ Dec 1, 1987 p. 131; VOYA 11:94, 12:14)

CHERRYH, C. J. (pseud. of Carolyn Janice Cherry). *Fortress in the Eye of Time.*
See Chapter 12, Witchcraft and Sorcery Fantasy.

5-116 CHERRYH, C. J. (pseud. of Carolyn Janice Cherry). *The Goblin Mirror.*
Gr. 10 up.
Left behind after his two older brothers travel beyond the mountains with the king's magician to battle the evil goblin queen, Prince Yuri decides to follow

them. The author's Rusalka trilogy—(see *Rusalka*, Chapter 12, Witchcraft and
Sorcery Fantasy)—is set in the same world.
Ballantine, 1992, 304 pp. (0-345-37278-6)
(BL 89:242, 247; Kirkus 60:953; LJ Sep 15 1992 p. 97; VOYA 16:100)

5-117   CHERRYH, C. J. (pseud. of Carolyn Janice Cherry). *Rider at the Gate.*
Gr. 10 up.
When a psychic nighthorse rider dies under mysterious circumstances, Danny
Fisher and his horse, Cloud, as well as Guil Stuart and Brionne set out to track
and destroy a rogue nighthorse. The sequel is *Cloud's Rider* (1996).
Warner, 1995, 437 pp. (0-446-51781-X), 1996, pap. (0-446-60345-7)
(BL 91:1933; Kirkus 63:819; Kliatt Jan 1997 p. 11)

**5-118   CHERRYH, C. J. (pseud. of Carolyn Janice Cherry), and ASIRE,
Nancy.** *Wizard Spawn.* **(The Sword of Knowledge series, vol. 2).** Gr. 7–12.
In this volume of a shared-world series about the beleaguered people of Sabis,
ruled by Ancar wizardry since their empire was conquered 500 years previous-
ly, Duran, an Ancarn wizard, leaves the royal court to work with the poor,
angering his Ancar neighbors by befriending some of the Sabirn. This is the
sequel to *A Dirge for Sabis* (1989), written by Cherryh and Leslie Fish, and is
followed by *Reap the Whirlwind* (1989), written by Cherryh and Mercedes
Lackey, and *The Sword of Knowledge* (2005), written by Cherryh, Lackey,
Fish and Nancy Asire.
Baen, 1989, pap., 275 pp., o.p.
(VOYA 13:37)

5-119   CHETWIN, Grace. *Child of the Air.* Gr. 5–8.
☆   Orphaned Myl and Brevan, 11 and 12, are forced into servitude after their
grandfather's death but are able to escape their harsh life after the discovery
that they can fly.
Illus. by the author, Macmillan, 1991, 256 pp. (0-02-718317-3)
(BL 87:1868; CCBB 44:234; HBG 2:275; Kirkus 59:469; SLJ June 1991 p. 100; VOYA
14:178)

5-120   CHETWIN, Grace. *The Chimes of Alyafaleyn.* Gr. 5–9.
☆   Caidy is furious that her talents with the magical "heynim," chimes controlling
weather and healing, have been suppressed by Tamborel, the master tuner.
Macmillan, 1993, 234 pp. (0-02-718222-3)
(BL 90:339; CCBB 47:117; HBG 5:85; Kirkus 61:1387; SLJ Nov 1993 p. 104; VOYA
16:378)

5-121   CHETWIN, Grace. *Gom on Windy Mountain: From Tales of Gom.* **(Tales
☆   of Gom quartet, vol. 1).** Gr. 6–8.
The strange runestone left him by his mother, Harga, leads fatherless young
Gom into mountain caves where he discovers the truth about his mother's disappearance on the day he was born. In the sequel, *The Riddle and the Rune:
From Tales of Gom in the Legends of Ulm* (1987), Gom travels across Ulm in
search of Harga, making both friends and enemies while he struggles to solve a
mysterious riddle. In *The Crystal Stair* (1988), Gom prepares for his seven-
year wizardry apprenticeship by undertaking a dangerous journey back to
Pen'langoth to find a mentor. In *The Starstone* (1989), Gom finishes his

apprenticeship with Folgen and is called to fight against the wicked Katak. *Gerrad's Quest* (Feral, 1998) is a related work.

Morrow, 1986, 224 pp., o.p.; Feral, 1999, pap., 195 pp. (1-930-09400-0)

(BL 82:1308; HB 62:743; SLJ May 1986 p. 89; VOYA 9:234)

5-122 CHRISTIAN, Deborah. *Kar Kalim.* Gr. 10 up.

Kar Kalim returns to Moontooth Tower to capture sorceress Inya, to whom he had once been apprenticed. *The Truthsayer's Apprentice* (1999; see below) is set in the same world.

Tor, 1997, 320 pp. (0-312-86341-1)

(Kirkus 65:841; LJ Aug 1997 p. 141; VOYA 20:323)

5-123 CHRISTIAN, Deborah. *The Truthsayer's Apprentice.* (The Loregiver series, vol. 1). Gr. 10 up.

Dalin of Nevi, apprentice to a murdered Truthsayer, decides to avenge his master's death and recover his magical robe of office. *Kar Kalim* (1997; see above) is set in the same world.

Tor, 1999, 384 pp., o.p., 2000, pap. (0-812-56547-9)

(Kirkus 67:1690; LJ Dec 1999 p. 192; VOYA 23:124)

5-124 CHRISTOPHER, John (pseud. of Christopher Samuel Youd). *A Dusk of Demons.* Gr. 5–8. (Orig. British pub. 1994.)

In a future world where people sacrifice others to the Dark One in order to save their own lives, Ben and Paddy search for their missing family.

Macmillan, 1994, 175 pp., o.p.

(BL 90:1803; CCBB 47:352; SLJ July 1994 p. 102)

5-125 CHRISTOPHER, John (pseud. of Christopher Samuel Youd). *The
★★ Prince in Waiting.* (The Winchester trilogy, vol. 1). Gr. 6–9. (Orig. British pub. 1970.)

After society is destroyed by earthquakes, Luke is rescued by a seer who involves the youth in a struggle for power over the medieval civilization that has arisen. In *Beyond the Burning Lands* (1971), Luke must battle his half-brother Peter for the throne of Winchester. In the final volume of this trilogy, *The Sword of the Spirits* (1972), Luke's battle accomplishments have made him a hero, but he has become a lonely man resigned to the fact that he must continue to fight more battles.

Macmillan, 1970, 182 pp., o.p.

(BL 67:306; CCBB 24:154; HB 47:54; Kirkus 38:1160; LJ 95:4051; Suth 2:72; TLS 1970 p. 1460)

5-126 CLAYTON, Jo. *A Bait of Dreams: A Five Summer Quest.* Gr. 10 up.

A jester, a dancer, and a young girl search out the source of the Ranga Eye jewels, deadly gems that drain the soul.

DAW, 1985, pap., 404 pp., o.p.

(Kliatt 19:24; LJ Feb 15, 1985 p. 182; VOYA 8:192)

5-127 CLAYTON, Jo. *Drum Warning.* (The Drums of Chaos trilogy, vol. 1). Gr. 10 up.

Every 700 years, the magically linked worlds of Glandair and Iomard touch, disrupting the inhabitants' lives until a hero is found to restore order. The sequels are *Drum Calls* (1997) and *Drum into Silence* (2002; by Clayton and

Kevin Andrew Murphy).
Tor, 1996, 384 pp. (0-312-86177-X)
(Kirkus 64:717; LJ July 1996 p. 170; VOYA 20:40)

5-128 CLAYTON, Jo. *The Magic Wars.* **(Wild Magic trilogy, bk. 3).** Gr. 10 up.
As Faan and her three companions travel in search of Faan's real mother, they
battle shape-shifters, ghosts, and gods. This is the sequel to *Wild Magic* (1991)
and *Wildfire* (1992).
DAW, 1993, pap., 367 pp. (0-88677-547-7)
(Kliatt May 1993 p. 13; VOYA 16:100)

5-129 CLAYTON, Jo. *Moongather.* **(Duel of Sorcery trilogy, bk. 1).** Gr. 10 up.
Serroi escapes from a wizard who tries to exploit her magic powers and
becomes a fugitive woman warrior. The sequels are *Moonscatter* (1983) and
Changer's Moon (1985). The Dancer trilogy, in which Serroi is also the hero-
ine, consists of *Dancer's Rise* (1993), *Serpent Waltz* (1994), and *Dance Down
the Stars* (1994).
DAW, 1982, pap., 240 pp., o.p.
(Kliatt Fall 1982 p. 18; LJ June 15, 1982 p. 1245)

5-130 CLAYTON, Jo. *Shadowspeer.* **(Shadith's Quest trilogy, bk. 1).** Gr. 10 up.
Vowing revenge for their imprisonment by Ginbiryol Seyirshi, Shadith, Kikun,
and Rohant—with the help of a roving Karintepe female street gang—set a
trap for the diabolical filmmaker whose "limited editions" destroy entire
worlds. This is the sequel to *Shadowplay* (1990) and is followed by *Shadowkill*
(1991).
DAW, 1990, pap., 342 pp., o.p.
(Kliatt Jan 1991 p. 20; VOYA 14:41)

5-131 COE, David B. *Children of Amarid.* **(The Lon Tobyn Chronicles, vol. 1).**
Gr. 7–12.
Jaryd joins the Children of Amarid, protectors of the people of Tobyn-Ser, to
expose the traitor responsible for brutal attacks by the mages' familiars. The
sequels are *The Outlanders* (1998, 1999) and *Eagle-Sage* (2000, 2001).
Tor, 1997, 383 pp. (0-312-85906-6), 1998, pap., 591 pp. (0-81255-254-7)
(Kirkus 65:422; LJ Apr 15, 1997 p. 123; VOYA 21:53)

5-132 COE, David B. *Rules of Ascension.* **(The Winds of the Forelands tetralo-
gy, vol. 1).** Gr. 10 up.
Attempting to avoid civil war in the Kingdom of Eibithar, a magically gifted
Qirsi seer and a young Eandi noble are ordered to search for the assassin of the
heir to a Forelands kingdom. The sequels are *Seeds of Betrayal* (2003, 2004)
and *Bonds of Vengeance* (2005).
Tor, 2002, 608 pp. (0-312-87807-9); Tor, 2003, pap., 672 pp. (0-8125-8984-X)
(BL 98:1098; Kirkus 70:227; LJ Mar 15, 2002 p. 111)

5-133 COLE, Adrian. *A Place Among the Fallen.* Gr. 10 up.
A young girl has a vision that comes true when Korbillian, a man with great
magical powers, arrives in Omara to save it from catastrophe.
Arbor House, 1987, 352 pp., o.p.; Avon, 1990, pap., 384 pp. (0-380-70556-7)
(BL 83:1655, 1672; VOYA 10:174)

5-134   **COLE, Allan.** *Wizard of the Winds.* **(Tales of the Timuras, vol. 1).** Gr. 10 up.
Two boyhood friends, warrior Iraj and potter Safar, share visions of becoming king and wizard, uniting the land of Esmir by overthrowing the demon rulers of Iraj's homeland. The sequels are *Wolves of the Gods* (1998) and *The Gods Awaken* (1999).
Ballantine/Del Rey, 1997, pap., 416 pp. (0-345-40176-X)
(BL 93:1668; Kirkus 65:508; Kliatt Nov 1997 p. 12)

5-135   **COLE, Allan, and BUNCH, Chris.** *The Far Kingdoms.* **(Amalric trilogy, vol. 1).** Gr. 11 up.
Amalric, son of a merchant, and Janos, a captain in the royal guard, search for the Far Kingdoms and battle an evil wizard threatening the future of their city, Orissa, in this story for mature readers. The sequels are *The Warrior's Tale* (1994) and *Kingdoms of the Night* (1995).
Ballantine, 1993, 409 pp. (0-345-38055-X)
(Kirkus 61:1034; VOYA 16:378)

5-136   **COLE, Allan, and BUNCH, Chris.** *The Warrior's Tale.* **(Anteros saga, vol. 1).** Gr. 10 up.
Captain Rali Emilie Antero and her all-women Maranon Guard track an evil sorcerer across the seas, beyond the end of the known world. The sequel is *The Warrior Returns* (1996; 1997, by Allan Cole). This series is related to *The Far Kingdoms* (1993; see above).
Del Rey, 1994, 438 pp., o.p., 1995, pap. (0-345-38734-1)
(Bl 91:405, 408; Kirkus 62:1174; VOYA 18:104)

5-137   **CONSTABLE, Kate.** *The Singer of All Songs.* **(Chanters of Tremaris trilogy, bk. 1).** Gr. 7–10. (Orig. Australian pub. 2002.)
Novice priestess Calwyn leaves her cloistered life to join a group of magic practitioners attempting to stop the sorcerer Samis from mastering all eight "chantments" in order to rule Temaris. The sequels are *The Waterless Sea* (2005) and *The Tenth Power* (2005).
Scholastic, 2004, 304 pp. (0-439-55478-0)
(BL 100:974; Kirkus 71:175; SLJ Apr 2004 p. 152; VOYA 27:11, 56)

5-138   **CONSTANTINE, Storm.** *Sea Dragon Heir.* **(The Chronicles of Magravandias, vol. 1).** Gr. 10 up.
Pharinet and Valraven, twin heirs to the Sea Dragon throne, subjugated for 200 years to the Lord of the Fire Drakes, make a desperate attempt to restore their kingdom. The sequels are *The Crown of Silence* (2001) and *The Way of Light* (2001).
Tor, 2000, 384 pp. (0-312-87306-9)
(Kirkus 68:24; Kliatt May 2001 p. 24; LJ Feb 15, 2000 p. 202)

5-139   **COOK, Dawn.** *First Truth.* **(Truth series, bk. 1).** Gr. 10 up.
Because she has inherited her missing father's magical talents, Alissa's mother convinces her to search for the Hold, where the Masters use magic to train the Keepers as storytellers. The sequels are *Hidden Truth* (2002) and *Forgotten Truth* (2003).

Berkely/Ace, 2002, pap., 336 pp. (0-441-00945-X)
(BL 98:1583; Kliatt Nov 2002 p. 23)

COOK, Glen. *Doomstalker.*
See Chapter 2, Animal Fantasy.

5-140 **COOK, Glen.** *Tower of Fear.* Gr. 10 up.
The city of Qushmarrah is under occupation by the Herodians and their conquering army of Dartars, but a group of revolutionaries plots to bring Nakar the sorcerer back to life and liberate the city.
Tor, 1989, 320 pp., o.p.
(BL 86:148, 163; Kirkus 57:1287; LJ Sep 15, 1989 p. 138)

COOK, Hugh. *The Wizards and the Warriors.*
See Chapter 12, Witchcraft and Sorcery Fantasy.

5-141 **COOKE, Catherine.** *Mask of the Wizard.* Gr. 7–12.
The First Priestess of the Three-Fold Goddess leads an army consisting of a young priestess, a guardsman, a renegade wizard, and the crown prince and princess across the Eleven Kingdoms to battle the evil Wizards of Akesh.
Tor, 1985, pap., 384 pp., o.p.
(VOYA 8:192)

5-142 **COOPER, Louise.** *The Master.* **(The Time Master trilogy, bk. 3).** Gr. 7–12.
The confrontation between the gods of Order and the gods of Chaos forces Tarod to decide which side he will follow. To understand this story, it would be helpful to have read the preceding volumes, *The Initiate* (1986) and *The Outcast* (1987).
Tor, 1987, pap., 285 pp., o.p.
(Kliatt Sep 1987 p. 24; VOYA 10:286)

5-143 **COOPER, Louise.** *Nemesis.* **(Indigo series, vol. 1).** Gr. 7–12.
To save the world, Princess Indigo must recapture the Seven Demons she accidentally released from the Tower of Regrets. The sequels are *Inferno* (1989), *Infanta* (1990), *Nocturne* (1990), *Troika* (1991), *Avatar* (1992), and *Revenant* (1993).
Tor, 1989, pap., 294 pp., o.p.
(Kliatt Sep 1989 p. 17, VOYA 12:287, 13:14)

5-144 **COOPER, Louise.** *The Sleep of Stone.* Gr. 7–12.
✶ A tragic story of unrequited love about Glysla, a winged shape-shifter, who tries to make Prince Anyr fall in love with her, first by assuming the shapes of various animals he befriends, and finally by kidnapping his betrothed, Sivorne, and imprisoning her in a "sleep of stone."
Illus. by John Collier, Macmillan, 1991, 138 pp. (0-689-31572-4); DAW, 1993, pap. (0-88677-555-8)
(BL 88:819; HBG 3:77; Kirkus 59:1531; SLJ Mar 1992 p. 256; VOYA 15:41)

5-145 **COSTIKYAN, Greg.** *By the Sword: Magic of the Plains.* **(Magic of the Plains series, vol. 1).** Gr. 10 up.
Plains warrior Nijon, banished from his tribe, travels to the city with his mon-

goose companion, Brother, where they fight their way to fortune.
Tor, 1993, 256 pp. (0-312-85489-7)
(BL 89:1678, 1682; Kirkus 61:492; VOYA 16:307)

5-146 COVILLE, Bruce. *The Dragon of Doom.* **(Moongobble and Me trilogy, bk. 1).** Gr. 2–4.
Young Edward accompanies Moongobble the magician on a quest to gather three golden acorns from the Dragon of Doom. The sequels are *The Weeping Werewolf* (2004) and *The Evil Elves* (2004).
Illus. by Katherine Coville, Simon, 2003, 69 pp. (0-689-85754-3); Aladdin, pap., 2005 (0-689-85757-8)
(CCBB 57:266; Kirkus 71:1448; SLJ Jan 2004 p. 96)

5-147 COVILLE, Bruce. *The Dragonslayers.* Gr. 4–6.
After her father offers her hand in marriage to the one who can slay Grizelda the witch's dragon, Princess Wilhelmina decides to kill the dragon herself.
Illus. by Katherine Coville, Simon, 1994, 128 pp. (0-671-89036-0), 1994, pap. (0-671-79832-4)
(BL 91:680; Kirkus 62:842; SLJ Feb 1995 p. 96)

5-148 COWPER, Richard (pseud. of John Middleton-Murray). *The Road to Corlay.* Gr. 10 up.
The death of a boy named Thomas, whose magical piping charmed beasts and men, leads to the formation of the cult of the White Bird in this haunting story set in a post-technological 30th century. The sequel is *A Dream of Kinship* (1981).
Pocket, 1979, 1986, pap., 239 pp., o.p.
(BL 76:435, 438; Kliatt 14:16)

5-149 COX, Palmer. *The Brownies: Their Book.* Gr. 3–5. (Stories written 1883–1887; orig. pub. 1887.)
Twenty-four stories in verse about tiny creatures who go ice-skating, take a balloon ride, go to school, and put on a circus. The sequels are *Another Brownie Book* (1890, 1941, 1967), *The Brownies at Home* (1891, 1938, 1968), *The Brownies Around the World* (1892, 1937), *The Brownies Through the Union* (1894), *The Brownies Abroad* (1898, 1934), *The Brownies' Latest Adventure* (1900), *The Brownies in the Philippines* (1903, 1939), *The Brownies' Many More Nights* (1912, 1939), and *The Brownies and Prince Florimel* (1918).
Illus. by the author, McGraw-Hill, 1967, 144 pp., o.p.; Dover, 1980, pap., o.p.; Buccaneer, 1995 (1-56849-662-1)
(HB 41:406; SLJ March 1981 p. 133)

5-150 CRADDOCK, Curtis. *Sparrow's Flight.* Gr. 10 up.
Companions Sparrow of Blackaker and the blind swordswoman Kisha resist the subjugation of their kingdom by the immortal Hezra-Thrall and his magical army.
Write Way, 2000, pap., 380 pp. (1-885173-85-7)
(BL 96:2015; LJ June 15, 2000 p. 121)

5-151 CROWLEY, John. *Aegypt.* **(Pierce Moffett series, vol. 1).** Gr. 10 up.
☆ Rosie Rasmussen and Pierce Moffett search out the netherworld of Aegypt

described in the writings of Fellowes Kraft, a world that exists beneath the surface of our own. The sequels are *Love and Sleep* (1994) and *Daemonomania* (2000, 2001).
Bantam, 1987, 390 pp., o.p.
(BL 83:809; Kirkus 55:240; LJ Mar 15, 1987 p. 92; VOYA 10:128; TLS Nov 20, 1987 p. 1294)

CULLUM, Janice A. *Lyskarion: The Song of the Wind.*
See Chapter 12, Witchcraft and Sorcery Fantasy.

5-152   CURRY, Jane Louise. *The Wolves of Aam.* Gr. 7–9.
An orphan named Runner and his friends Cat and Fith journey north through the Land of Tiddi to the mountain citadel of Ozel, in search of Runner's lost stone of power. The sequel is *Shadow Dancers* (1983).
Atheneum, 1981, 186 pp., o.p.
(BL 77:1084, 1097; HB 57:196; SLJ Apr 1981 p. 124; VOYA 4:63)

CUTTER, Leah R. *Paper Mage.*
See Chapter 12, Witchcraft and Sorcery Fantasy.

5-153   DALEY, Brian. *A Tapestry of Magics.* Gr. 10 up.
The heroic exploits of Crassmor, a reluctant young knight, include courting Lady Willow, whose tapestry controls the future of this alternate world.
Ballantine, 1983, pap., 304 pp., o.p.
(BL 79:1013, 1020; LJ 108:416)

5-154   DALKEY, Kara. *Ascension.* **(Water trilogy, bk. 1).** Gr. 6–9.
Sorely disappointed not to be chosen to compete for the honor of helping rule the city of Atlantis, mermyd Nia uncovers unexpected secrets about her undersea world. The sequels are *Reunion* (2002) and *Transformation* (2002).
Avon, 2002, pap., 240 pp. (0-06-440808-6)
(BL 98:934, 99:112; CCBB 55:276; Kirkus 69:1757; Kliatt May 2002 p. 24; SLJ Mar 2002 p. 230; VOYA 23:444)

5-155   DART-THORNTON, Cecilia. *The Ill-Made Mute.* **(The Bitterbynde, vol.**
✶   **I).** Gr. 10 up.
A mute girl named Imrhein escapes from servitude in Isse Tower with the help of a friendly traveler and learns hand speech to uncover the truth of her origins. The sequels are *The Lady of the Sorrows* (2002) and *The Battle of Evernight* (2003).
Warner, 2001, 437 pp. (0-446-52832-3), 2002, pap. (0-446-61080-1)
(BL 97:1539; Kirkus 69:299; LJ May 15, 2001 p. 167; VOYA 24:444, 25:13)

5-156   DAVID, Peter. *Sir Apropos of Nothing, The Woad to Wack and Wuin.* **(Sir Apropos of Nothing series, vol. 1).** Gr. 10 up.
Apropos decides to take revenge on the entire knightly class, including the king and queen, after his mother is murdered by a knight. The sequels are *The Woad to Wuin* (2002, 2003) and *Tong Lashing* (2003, 2005).
Pocket, 2001, 432 pp., o.p.; Pocket, 2002, pap., 672 pp. (0-7434-1234-6)
(BL 97:1855; Kirkus 69:780; LJ July 2001 p. 131)

DAWNAY, Romayne. *The Champions of Appledore.*
See Chapter 8, Humorous Fantasy.

5-157 **DEAN, Pamela.** *The Dubious Hills.* Gr. 10 up.

✶ After her parents' disappearance, Ary becomes responsible for her younger brother and sister, but begins to question the wisdom of an ancient spell cast over their region because she suspects her parents have become wolves. This book is set in the same world as the author's Secret Country trilogy, which includes *The Secret Country* (Ace, 1985; Firebird, 2003), *The Hidden Land* (Ace, 1986; Firebird, 2003), and *The Whim of the Dragon* (Ace, 1989; Firebird, 2003).

Tor, 1994, 320 pp. (0-312-85442-0), 1995, pap. (0-8125-2362-8)

(BL 90:1426; Kirkus 62:180; LJ Feb 15, 1994 p. 188; VOYA 17:155, 18:8)

5-158 **DE CAMP, L(yon) Sprague.** *The Honorable Barbarian.* Gr. 10 up.

Kerin, the younger brother of Jorian from the author's Reluctant King trilogy (*The Goblin Tower*, 1968, *The Clocks of Iraz*, 1971, and *The Unbeheaded King*, 1983) is sent to a country reminiscent of China to study clock mechanisms. In this humorous story, he rescues and marries a princess and battles sorcerers and demons.

Ballantine, 1989, 256 pp., o.p.

(BL 85:1783,1816; Kirkus 57:803; Kliatt Sep 1990 p. 20; LJ June 15, 1989 p. 83; VOYA 12:370)

5-159 **DE CAMP, L(yon) Sprague, and DE CAMP, Catherine Crook.** *The Incorporated Knight.* Gr. 10 up.

A bumbling knight named Sir Eudoric sets off on a series of adventures that prove him worthy of his title. *The Pixilated Peeress* (Ballantine, 1991; see below) is set in the same world.

Phantasia Press, 1987, 256 pp., o.p.

(BL 84:437, 466; LJ Oct 15, 1987 p. 95)

5-160 **DE CAMP, L(yon) Sprague, and DE CAMP, Catherine Crook.** *The Pixilated Peeress.* Gr. 10 up.

Sergeant Thorolf rescues fugitive Countess Yvette in a forest, only to see her transformed into an octopus by one inept sorcerer and taken prisoner by another. This story is set in the same world of Rhaetia as *The Incorporated Knight* (Phantasia, 1987; see above).

Ballantine, 1991, 208 pp., o.p., 1992, pap. (0-345-36733-2)

(BL 87:2108, 2110; Kirkus 59:764; VOYA 14:380, 15:10)

DE CHANCIE, John. *Castle Kidnapped.*

See Chapter 12, Witchcraft and Sorcery Fantasy.

DEITZ, Tom. *The Gryphon King.*

See Chapter 6, High Fantasy: Myth or Legend Fantasy.

5-161 **DEITZ, Tom.** *Springwar: A Tale of Eron.* **(The Chronicles of Eron, bk. 2).** Gr. 10 up.

In this complex story, Eddyn and Avall travel toward the royal citadel and find themselves under attack from the Ixtian army, led by Avall's sister, Merryn. The first book in the series is *Bloodwinter* (1999, 2000), and the sequels are *Summerblood* (2001, 2002) and *Warautumn* (2002).

Bantam, 2000, pap., 448 pp., o.p., 2001, pap., 576 pp. (0-553-57647-X)

(BL 96:2015; Kirkus 68:676; LJ July 2000 p. 147; VOYA 23:358)

5-162 **DEL VECCHIO, Gene.** *The Pearl of Anton.* Gr. 7–12. (Orig. British pub. 2004.)

Fifteen-year-old Jason Del, the last of the human race's Royal House, searches the world of Trinity for the Pearl of Anton, vitally important for his fated Final Contest against creatures of Evil.

Pelican, 2004, 256 pp. (1-58980-172-5)

(BL 100:1730; VOYA 27:312;)

5-163 **DELANY, Samuel R(ay) (Jr.).** *Tales of Nevèryön.* Gr. 10 up.

An adventure-filled tale of the life of Gorgik, a youth in the prehistoric empire of Nevèryön, who rises from mine slave to courtier to hero. The sequels are *Nevèryöna: Or, The Tale of Signs and Cities* (1983, 1994), *Flight from Nevèryön* (1985, 1994), and *The Bridge of Lost Desire* (1987), retitled *Return to Nevèryön* (1994).

Bantam, 1979, pap., 272 pp., o.p.

(BL 76:435; LJ 104:1593; VOYA 3:48)

5-164 **DE LARRABEITI, Michael.** *The Borribles.* **(Borrible trilogy, bk. 1).** Gr. 6–9. (Orig. British pub. 1975.)

After eight Borribles (violent street urchins who look like children) successfully raid a group of enemy creatures called Rumbles, they return home to find betrayal and disillusionment. *The Borribles Go for Broke* (Random, 1981, Ace, 1982) and *The Borribles: Across the Dark Metropolis* (Ace, 1988) are the sequels. *The Borrible Trilogy* (Pan Macmillan, 2003, 0-330-49085-0) contains all three volumes.

Macmillan, 1978, 239 pp., o.p.

(BL 74:1420, 1429; CCBB 31:174; Kirkus 46:182; SLJ May 1978 p. 76; Suth 2:120; TLS 1976 p. 1547)

5-165 **DE LINT, Charles.** *Dreams Underfoot: The Newford Collection.* Gr. 10 up.

☆ A collection of interconnected short stories set in the magical city of Newford, where Jilly, Geordie, and others meet ghosts, goblins, and mermaids. Many of De Lint's novels are set in Newford, Ontario, including *The Dreaming Place* (Macmillan, 1990; see Chapter 7, High Fantasy: Travel to Other Worlds), *Memory and Dream* (Tor, 1994), *Trader* (Tor, 1997), *Someplace to Be Flying* (Tor, 1998; see below), *Forests of the Heart* (2000), *The Onion Girl* (2001), and *Spirits in the Wires* (2003). A number of his short story collections are also set in Newford: *The Ivory and The Horn: A Newford Collection* (Tor, 1996, 1995), *Moonlight and Vines: A Newford Collection* (Tor, 1999; see below), and *Tapping the Dream Tree* (Tor, 2002). Some of the stories in *Waifs and Strays* (Viking, 2002; see below) are also set there.

Tor, 1993, 448 pp. (0-312-85205-3)

(BL 89:1301, 1308; Kirkus 61:189; LJ Mar 15, 1993 p. 111; SLJ Dec 1993 p. 149; VOYA 16:225)

5-166 **DE LINT, Charles.** *Into the Green.* Gr. 10 up.

The Lords of the Green, or Faerie, select young harper-witch Angharad to destroy a powerful puzzle box found in the desert.

Tor, 1993, 256 pp. (0-312-08087-5); Tor, 2001, pap., 256 pp. (0-765-30022-2)

(BL 90:258, 262; Kirkus 61:1105; LJ Oct 15, 1993 p. 93; VOYA 17:36)

5-167 **DE LINT, Charles.** *Moonlight and Vines: A Newford Collection.* Gr. 10 up. (Orig. pub. in Canada.)
Twenty-one magical stories and a poem set in Newford, Ontario, as are the tales in the author's *Dreams Underfoot* (see above), including "The Invisibles," "In the Quiet After Midnight," and "The Fields Beyond the Fields." World Fantasy Award, Best Collection, 2000.
Tor, 1999, 384 pp. (0-312-86518-X), 1999, pap., 461 pp. (0-812-56549-5)
(BL 95:655; Kirkus 66:1636; LJ Feb 15, 1999 p. 188)

5-168 **DE LINT, Charles.** *Someplace to Be Flying.* Gr. 10 up. (Orig. pub. in Cana-
☆ da.)
Photojournalist Lily Carson and gypsy cab driver Hank Walker investigate a community of shape-shifting First People living in the slums of Newford.
Tor, 1998, 384 pp. (0-312-85849-3), 1999, pap., 544 pp. (0-8125-5158-3)
(BL 94:785; Kirkus 65:1809; LJ Jan 1998 p. 148; VOYA 21:366, 22:13)

5-169 **DE LINT, Charles.** *Trader.* Gr. 10 up. (Orig. pub. in Canada.)
Stringed instrument craftsman Leonard Trader discovers that he and scoundrel Johnny Devlin have exchanged bodies and must learn to live each other's lives. This story is set in Newford, Ontario, the scene of many of the author's previous novels and story collections.
Tor, 1997, 352 pp. (0-312-85847-7)
(BL 93:826; Kirkus 64:1639; LJ Dec 1996 p. 152; VOYA 20:192, 21:12, 36)

5-170 **DE LINT, Charles.** *Waifs and Strays.* Gr. 7–12. (Orig. pub. in Canada.)
☆ Sixteen short stories with teenage protagonists, set in Bordertown, Newford, and Ottawa, mostly selected from the author's previously published work.
Viking, 2002, 416 pp. (0-670-03584-X)
(BL 99:312; CCBB 56:151; HBG 14:93; Kirkus 70:1221; SLJ Nov 2002 p. 160; VOYA 25:395, 26:11)

5-171 **DERESKE, Jo.** *Glom Gloom.* Gr. 5–7.
After Raymond's hated adversary, Gillus, is captured by the evil Weeuns, Raymond and his friends set out to free Gillus and to save their world.
Atheneum, 1985, 195 pp., o.p.
(BBL 82:335; SLJ Oct 1985 p. 171)

DICAMILLO, Kate. *The Tale of Despereaux: Being the Story of a Mouse, a Princess, Some Soup, and a Spool of Thread.*
See Chapter 2, Animal Fantasy.

5-172 **DICKINSON, John.** *The Cup of the World.* Gr. 9–12. (Orig. British pub.
☆ 2004.)
Sixteen-year-old Princess Phaedra insists on marrying the young knight who has long haunted her dreams, only to discover that his black magic powers portend disaster for her kingdom.
Illus. by Assheton Gorton, Random, 2004, 432 pp. (0-385-75034-X)
(BL 101:398; CCBB 58:118; Kirkus 72:863; Kliatt Sep 2004 p. 7; SLJ Sep 2004 p. 204)

5-173 **DICKINSON, Peter (pseud. of Malcolm de Brissac).** *The Blue Hawk.* Gr.
☆☆ 7–12. (Orig. British pub. 1976.)
In what could be ancient Egypt, a boy named Tron defies the high priests by

saving a sacrificial hawk, escapes inside the dead king's coffin, and joins the new king's fight to rule his own land. Carnegie Medal Commended Book, 1976; Guardian Award for Children's Fiction, 1977.

Little, Brown, 1976, 229 pp., o.p.

(BL 72:1584, 1595; HB 52:503; Kirkus 44:490, 549; LJ 101:1142; SLJ Nov 1976 p. 74; TLS 1976 p. 375)

5-174 **DICKINSON, Peter (pseud. of Malcolm de Brissac).** *The Devil's Chil-*
✯ *dren.* **(The Changes trilogy, bk. 1).** Gr. 6–9. (Orig. British pub. 1970.)
Nicky Gore becomes separated from her parents during the panic and confusion of The Changes, and is taken in by Sikhs suspected of witchcraft. Carnegie Medal Honour Book, 1970. *Heartsease* (1969; see below) and *The Weathermonger* (1968; see below) are set at a later period during The Changes in England.

Little, Brown, 1970, 187 pp., o.p.; Delacorte, 1986, 188 pp., o.p.

(BL 67:262, 267, 82:1604, 1611; CCBB 24:72; HB 46:616, 63:82; LJ 95:4347; Suth:102; TLS 1970 p. 417; VOYA 9:236)

5-175 **DICKINSON, Peter (pseud. of Malcolm de Brissac).** *Heartsease.* **(The**
✯ **Changes trilogy, bk. 2).** Gr. 6–9. (Orig. British pub. 1969.)
Four young people and a foreign "witch" with mechanical know-how escape from an England immersed in The Changes and flee to Ireland. *The Devil's Children* (1970; see above) is set in an earlier period during The Changes, and *The Weathermonger* (1968; see below) is set in England during a later period of The Changes.

Illus. by Nathan Goldstein, Little, Brown, 1969, 223 pp., o.p.; Delacorte, 1986, 235 pp. (0-385-29451-4); Dell, 1988, pap. (0-440-20096-2)

(HB 46:159; 63:82; Kirkus 37:1111; LJ 95:1638; TLS 1969 p. 687; VOYA 9:236)

5-176 **DICKINSON, Peter (pseud. of Malcolm de Brissac).** *The Ropemaker.* Gr.
✯✯ 6–12. (Orig. British pub. 2001.)
Realizing that something has gone wrong in their long-isolated valley, young Tilja and Tahl set out with her grandmother and his grandfather to search the empire for the sorcerer who can help them. John Newbery Medal Honor Book, 2002; Michael L. Printz Award Honor Book, 2002; Mythopoeic Fantasy Award for Children's Literature, 2002.

Delacorte, 2001, 376 pp. (0-385-72921-9); Dell, 2003, pap. (0-385-73063-2)

(BL 98:394, 1417; CCBB 55:169; HB 77:745; HBG 13:95; Kirkus 69:1547; SLJ Nov 2001 p. 154; VOYA 24:367, 25:13)

5-177 **DICKINSON, Peter (pseud. of Malcolm de Brissac).** *The Weathermon-*
✯ *ger.* **(The Changes trilogy, bk. 3).** Gr. 6–9. (Orig. British pub. 1968.)
Able to control the weather through magic, Geoffrey Tinker returns to an England that has somehow reverted to the Middle Ages. *The Devil's Children* (1970; see above) and *Heartsease* (1969; see above) are set in earlier periods during The Changes in England.

Little, Brown, 1969, 216 pp., o.p.; Delacorte, 1986, 190 pp., o.p.

(BL 65:1075; CCBB 22:156; HB 63:82; Kirkus 37:501; LJ 94:2499; Suth:103; VOYA 9:236)

5-178 **DICKSON, Gordon R(upert).** *The Dorsai Companion.* **(Childe Cycle, bk.
8).** Gr. 10 up.
Four short stories that fill in the gaps of Dickson's Dorsai series by explaining

events in Dorsai history. The other books in the series are *Necromancer* (1962, Tor, 1998; republished as *No Room for Men*, 1963), *Tactics of Mistake* (1971), *Soldier, Ask Not* (1967, 1980, 1998), *The Genetic General* (1960; expanded into *Dorsai!* 1976, 1980, 1993), *The Spirit of Dorsai* (1979, 1993; 2002, entitled *Dorsai Spirit*), *Lost Dorsai* (1980, 1993), *The Final Encyclopedia* (1984), and *The Final Encyclopedia: Volumes I and II* (1997). *Necromancer, Tactics of Mistake*, and *Dorsai!* were also published together as *Three to Dorsai!* (1976).
Ace, 1986, pap., 231 pp., o.p.
(VOYA 9:236)

5-179   DONALDSON, Stephen R(upert). *Daughter of Regals and Other Tales.* Gr. 10 up.
Eight short stories of fantasy, adventure, and horror.
Ballantine, 1985, pap., 304 pp., o.p.
(BL 80:1081, 1083; Kirkus 52:173; LJ 109:825; VOYA 7:205)

DOUGLAS, Carole Nelson. *Exiles of the Rynth.*
See Chapter 12, Witchcraft and Sorcery Fantasy.

5-180   DOUGLASS, Sara. *Beyond the Hanging Wall.* Gr. 10 up. (Orig. Australian
✶   pub. 1996.)
After apprentice healer Garth Baxtor, 14, discovers that Prince Maximillian, heir to the throne of Escator, is enslaved in a mine, he, a young marsh witch named Ravenna, and the abbot Vorstus attempt to rescue the prince.
Tor, 2003, 336 pp. (0-765-30449-X)
(BL 99:1877; Kirkus 71:838; LJ July 2003 p. 131; VOYA 26:501, 27:11)

5-181   DOUGLASS, Sara. *Threshold.* Gr. 10 up. (Orig. pub. in Australia.)
Master glassworkers Tirzah and her father are sold into slavery in the kingdom of Ashdod and assigned by the master mage, Boaz, to help build a huge glass pyramid called Threshold.
Tor, 2003, 448 pp. (0-312-87687-4)
(BL 100:74; Kirkus 71:944; LJ Aug 2003 p. 142)

5-182   DOUGLASS, Sara. *The Wayfarer Redemption.* **(Axis trilogy, bk. 1).** Gr. 10 up. (Orig. Australian pub. 1995, entitled *Battleaxe*.)
Lady Faraday runs away with her fiancé's outlawed half-brother, Axis, after she discovers that her people are endangered by the demonic Forbidden Ones. The sequels are *Enchanter* (1996, 2001), *Starman* (2002), *Sinner* (1997, 2000, 2004), *Crusader* (1997, 2000), and *Pilgrim* (2000).
Tor, 2000, 448 pp. (0-312-87717-X)
(BL 97:71; Kirkus 69:85)

5-183   DOWNER, Ann. *The Spellkey.* **(Spellkey trilogy, bk. 1).** Gr. 7 up.
✶   Two young people journey unwillingly to far-off Ninthstile together: Caitlin, exiled on suspicion of witchcraft because she has one blue eye and one green, and Badger, an illegitimate stable boy. Their journey is full of strange adventures that are inexplicably involved with a spellkey that "unlocks all doors." In the sequel, *The Glass Salamander* (1989), Caitlin searches the subterranean Otherworld for Myrrhlock the necromancer after her son (and Badger's) is

stolen in exchange for a goblin baby. In *The Books of the Keepers* (1993), Caitlin tries to find the four magical "Books of the Keepers," which are intertwined with the fate of their son Bram, kidnapped seven years earlier. *The Spellkey Trilogy* (Baen, 1995) contains all three books.
Atheneum, 1987, 208 pp., o.p.
(BL 84:384, 392, 86:904; HB 63:742; Kirkus 55:1068; SLJ Sep 1987 p. 194; VOYA 10:176)

5-184 DOYLE, Debra, and MacDONALD, James D. *Groogleman.* Gr. 6–9.
In this post-apocalyptic story, Dan enlists the help of a mysterious hunter named Joshua to rescue Leezie the Healer from the dangerous Grooglemen.
Yolen/Harcourt, 1996, 113 pp. (0-15-200235-9)
(CCBB 50:132; HBG 8:79; VOYA 20:116)

5-185 DOYLE, Debra, and MacDONALD, James D. *Knight's Wyrd.* Gr. 6–9.
✫ Newly knighted, young Will learns that his wyrd, or fate, will not include becoming Lord of Restonbury after his father's death, but will be to meet Death after experiencing adventures involving a sea hag, ghostly knights, a man-eating troll, and an immortal ogre. Mythopoeic Fantasy Award for Children's Literature, 1993.
Harcourt, 1992, 176 pp. (0-15-200764-4), 1997, pap. (0-15-201520-5)
(BL 89:589; CCBB 46:173; HB 69:89; HBG 4:80; Kirkus 60:1253; SLJ Nov 1992 p. 90; VOYA 16:102)

Dragon Tales. **Ed. by Isaac Asimov, Charles G. Waugh, and Martin Harry Greenberg.**
See Chapter 3, Fantasy Collections.

5-186 DRAKE, David. *The Sea Hag.* **(World of Crystal Walls series, vol. 1).** Gr. 10 up.
Promised at birth to the fearsome Sea Hag, 16-year-old Dennis runs away to become a hero and find true love in this science-fantasy.
Baen/Simon & Schuster, 1988, pap., 352 pp. (0-671-65424-1)
(BL 84:1894, 1914; VOYA 12:4)

5-187 DREYFUSS, Richard, and TURTLEDOVE, Harry. *The Two Georges: The Novel of an Alternate America.* Gr. 10 up.
After a right-wing militia group called the Sons of Liberty steals "The Two Georges," a painting that symbolizes the harmony between the British Crown and the American Colonies, Colonel Thomas Bushnell is assigned to get it back. The setting is an alternate 1996 America where the Revolution never happened.
Tor, 1996, 384 pp. (0-8125-4459-5)
(BL 92:899; Kirkus 64:31; LJ Mar 15, 1996 p. 98; VOYA 19:278)

DUANE, Diane (Elizabeth). *The Door into Fire.*
See Chapter 12, Witchcraft and Sorcery Fantasy.

DUANE, Diane (Elizabeth). *So You Want to Be a Wizard.*
See Chapter 12, Witchcraft and Sorcery Fantasy.

5-188 DUEY, Kathleen. *Moonsilver.* **(The Unicorn's Secret series, bk. 1).** Gr. 2–4.

Rescued as a toddler and raised by taciturn Old Simon, young Heart Avamir enlists the aid of Rosa, the village healer, when she finds an injured and starving white horse in the woods. The sequels are *The Silver Thread* (2001), *The Silver Bracelet* (2002), *The Mountains of the Moon* (2002), *The Sunset Gates* (2002), *True Heart* (2003), *Castle Avamir* (2003), and *The Journey Home* (2003).

Illus. by Omar Rayyan, Aladdin, 2001, pap., 80 pp. (0-689-84269-4)

(BL 98:856; CCBB 55:170; SLJ Dec 2001 p. 99)

5-189   **DUNCAN, Dave.** *The Cursed.* Gr. 10 up.

☆   A science-fantasy about innkeeper Gwin Solith, who attempts to restore the old empire with the magical help of the "cursed" after losing her own family to a plague of "star sickness."

Del Rey, 1995, 448 pp. (0-345-38951-4), 1996, pap. (0-345-38952-2)

(BL 91:1555, 1558; Kirkus 63:350; LJ Apr 15, 1995 p. 119; VOYA 18:313, 19:18)

5-190   **DUNCAN, Dave.** *The Cutting Edge.* **(Handful of Men tetralogy, vol. 1).** Gr. 10 up.

King Rap, once a kitchen boy with magic powers, becomes involved in a battle for the succession of the throne of the Impire, of which his small kingdom is a part. The sequels are *Upland Outlaws* (1993), *The Stricken Field* (1993), and *The Living God* (1994). Set 15 years later in the same world of Pandemia is the author's Man of His Word duology: *Magic Casement* (1990) and *Faery Lands Forlorn* (1991).

Ballantine, 1992, 400 pp. (0-345-37896-2), 1993, pap. (0-345-38167-X)

(BL 89:38, 42; Kirkus 60:886; LJ Aug 1992 p. 155)

5-191   **DUNCAN, Dave.** *The Gilded Chain: A Tale of the King's Blades.* **(The King's Blades series, bk. 1).** Gr. 10 up.

Sir Durandel has grown from a young troublemaker into a well-trained member of the King's Blades, swordsmen loyal to the monarch, but finds his loyalty tested by political intrigues at the royal court and at other courts. The sequels are *Lord of the Fire Lands* (1999, 2000) and *Sky of Swords* (2000, 2001). *The Jaguar Knights* (2004) is the fourth sequel. Duncan's King's Daggers series (see below) is set in the same world.

Avon, 1998, 352 pp. (0-380-97460-6); Eos, 1999, pap., 432 pp. (0-380-79126-9)

(BL 95:313; Kirkus 66:1161; LJ Oct 15, 1998 p. 103)

5-192   **DUNCAN, Dave.** *Paragon Lost: A Chronicle of the King's Blades.* **(The King's Daggers series, bk. 3).** Gr. 10 up.

Sir Beaumont, the finest swordsman of King Athelgar's Blades, is sent from Chivial to barbaric Skyrria to bring back Czar Igor's young sister-in-law to marry the king. This book is preceded by *Sir Stalwart* (1999) and *The Crooked House* (2000), and the sequel is *Impossible Odds* (2003). Duncan's King's Blades series (see above) is set in the same world.

Eos/HarperCollins, 2002, 368 pp. (0-380-97896-2); Eos, 2003, pap., 448 pp. (0-380-81835-3)

(BL 99:70; Kirkus 70:923; LJ Oct 15, 2002 p.98)

5-193   **DUNSANY, Lord (pseud. of Edward John Morton Drax Plunkett).** *The King of Elfland's Daughter.* Gr. 10 up. (Orig. British pub. 1924.)

In this classic fantasy tale, Prince Alveric of Erl crosses into Fairyland where, after many adventures, he wins the hand of Princess Lirazel; but their happiness is short-lived because the King of Elfland uses magic to bring his daughter back to him.

Putnam, 1924, 301 pp., o.p.; Del Rey, 1999, pap., 240 pp. (0-345-43191-X)

(BL 21:111; TLS 1924 pp. 402, 466)

5-194   EASTON, M. Coleman. *The Fisherman's Curse.* **(Glass Mistress series, bk. 2).** Gr. 10 up.

Kyala, the only girl ever apprenticed to a Master of Glass, maker of protective glass talismans, returns home to battle three gigantic monsters. This is the sequel to *Masters of Glass* (1985, 1987).

Warner, 1987, pap., 236 pp. (0-445-20332-3)

(BL 83:686; Kliatt 21:22)

5-195   EASTON, M. Coleman. *Spirits of Cavern and Hearth.* Gr. 10 up.

Yarkol Dolmi, an exiled Hakhan physician, and his Chirudak companions must battle subterranean spirits to save his people from destruction.

St. Martin's, 1988, 294 pp., o.p.

(Kirkus 56:1572; LJ Dec 1988 p. 138; VOYA 12:40)

5-196   EDDINGS, David (Carroll). *The Diamond Throne.* **(The Elenium Saga, vol. 1).** Gr. 10 up.

A warrior, a wizard, and a child search for a way to prevent the death of Queen Ehlana. The sequels are *The Ruby Knight* (1991) and *The Sapphire Rose* (1992). *Domes of Fire* (1993; see below) is the first book in the Tamuli trilogy, which is a related series. *The Rivan Codex: Ancient Texts of the Belgariad and the Malloreon* (1998) is a companion volume.

Ballantine, 1989, 464 pp. (0-345-35691-9), 1990, pap. (0-345-36769-3)

(BL 85:1218, 1219; Kirkus 57:508; LJ Apr 15, 1989 p. 102; VOYA 12:286)

5-197   EDDINGS, David (Carroll). *Domes of Fire.* **(Tamuli trilogy, bk. 1).** Gr. 10 up.

Prince Sparhawk, Queen Ehlana, and their daughter Danae travel to Tamul in hopes of foiling a coup against the Tamulian throne. The sequels are *The Shining Ones* (1993) and *The Hidden City* (1994, 1995). This trilogy continues the saga begun in the Elenium saga (1989–1992; see *The Diamond Throne*, above). *Belgarath the Sorcerer* (1995, 1996; written with Leigh Eddings) continues the story. *The Rivan Codex: Ancient Texts of the Belgariad and the Malloreon* (1998) is a companion volume.

Ballantine, 1993, 496 pp. (0-345-37321-9), 1993, pap. (0-345-38327-3)

(BL 89:379, 380; Kirkus 60:1389; LJ Dec 1992 p. 191; VOYA 16:102)

5-198   EDDINGS, David (Carroll). *Guardians of the West.* **(Malloreon series, bk. 1).** Gr. 10 up.

King Garion and his wife attempt to save their son from the evil sorcerer Zandramas in this first volume of a series that follows his Belgariad saga (see *Queen of Sorcery*, 1982, in Chapter 12, Witchcraft and Sorcery Fantasy). The sequels are *King of the Murgos* (1988), *Demon Lord of Karanda* (1988), *Sorceress of Darshiva* (1989), and *The Seeress of Kell* (1991). *Polgara the Sorceress* (1997) is a prequel to and retells the Malloreon and the Belgariad sagas

from the point of view of a 3,000-year-old sorceress. *The Rivan Codex: Ancient Texts of the Belgariad and the Malloreon* (1998) is a companion volume.
Ballantine, 1987, 460 pp. (0-345-33000-5), 1988, pap., 416 pp. (0-345-35266-1)
(BL 83:947, 86:904; Kirkus 55:259; LJ Apr 15, 1987 p. 102)

EDDINGS, David (Carroll). *Queen of Sorcery.*
See Chapter 12, Witchcraft and Sorcery Fantasy.

5-199   **EDDINGS, David (Carroll), and EDDINGS, Leigh.** *The Elder Gods.* **(The Dreamers Saga, bk. 1).** Gr. 10 up.
Dahlaine, Veltan, Zelana, and Aracia, gods who rule the four compass points of the Land of Dhrall, need human help to defeat the evil Vlagh who rules The Wasteland at the center of their kingdom. The sequel is *The Treasured One* (2005).
Warner/Aspect, 2003, 404 pp. (0-446-53221-5)
(BL 100:74; LJ Sep 15, 2003 p. 9)

5-200   **EDDINGS, David (Carroll), and EDDINGS, Leigh.** *The Redemption of Althalus.* Gr. 10 up. (Orig. British pub. 2000.)
Althalus is hired to steal a special book from the House at the End of the World, but he is unable to leave after finding the book until a talking cat teaches him to use the magic powers described inside.
Ballantine, 2000, 768 pp. (0-345-44077-3); Del Rey, 2001, pap., 792 pp. (0-345-44078-1)
(BL 97:390; Kirkus 68:1582; LJ Nov 15, 2000 p. 100)

5-201   **EDDISON, E(rik) R(ucker).** *The Worm Ouroboros; a Romance.* Gr. 10 up. (Orig. British pub. 1922.)
In this classic fantasy tale, the King of Demonland embarks on a heroic quest to find and free his greatest warrior, who has been enchanted by the King of Witchland. The books of the Zimiamvian trilogy are related: *The Menzian Gate* (British pub. 1958; Ballantine, 1969), *A Fish Dinner in Memison* (Dutton, 1941, 1942; Ballantine, 1968), and *Mistress of Mistresses* (Dutton, 1935; Ballantine, 1967, 1978).
Illus. by Keith Henderson, Boni, 1926, 445 pp., o.p.; illus. by Keith Henderson, Dutton, 1952, o.p.; Crown, 1962, 445 pp., o.p.; Wildside, 2004, pap. (0-80959-424-2)
(BL 23:38; TLS 1926 p. 676)

EDGERTON, Teresa. *Child of Saturn.*
See Chapter 12, Witchcraft and Sorcery Fantasy.

EDGERTON, Teresa. *Goblin Moon.*
See Chapter 12, Witchcraft and Sorcery Fantasy.

5-202   **EDGERTON, Teresa.** *The Grail and the Ring.* **(The Chronicles of Celydonn, bk. 2).** Gr. 10 up.
Newlyweds Gwenlliant and Tryffin search for the king's missing heir, who must do penance for his father's sin in order to lift a curse from the kingdom. This book was preceded by *The Castle of the Silver Wheel* (1993) and is followed by *The Moon and the Thorn* (1995).

Berkley/Ace, 1994, pap., 320 pp. (0-441-30057-6)

(BL 90:811; Kliatt May 1994 p. 16; VOYA 17:98)

5-203 **EGAN, Doris.** *The Gate of Ivory.* **(Ivory series, bk. 1).** Gr. 10 up.
★ A science-fantasy about Theodora, an anthropology student who becomes stranded on the magic-ruled planet of Ivory, where she works as a fortune-teller until a local sorcerer hires her to help him battle his enemies. The sequels are *Two-Bit Heroes* (1992) and *Guilt-Edged Ivory* (1992).
DAW, 1989, 320 pp., o.p.

(BL 85:1095, 1129; Kliatt Apr 1989 p. 24; LJ Feb 15, 1989 p. 179; VOYA 12:164, 13:12)

5-204 **EISENSTEIN, Phyllis.** *In the Red Lord's Reach.* Gr. 7–12.
Fifteen-year-old minstrel Alaric escapes the bloody tyranny of the Red Lord's castle by magically vanishing and reappearing in the North, where he joins a peaceful nomadic tribe. This is the sequel to *Born to Exile* (Arkham, 1978; NAL, 1989).
NAL, 1989, pap., 268 pp. (0-451-16073-8)

(LJ June 15, 1989 p. 83; VOYA 13:37)

5-205 **EISENSTEIN, Phyllis.** *Sorcerer's Son.* **(The Book of Elementals, vol. 1).** Gr. 10 up.
A gentle sorceress's son named Cray searches for the father he has never met, only to discover that his father is, in fact, the demon Gildrum. The sequels are *The Crystal Palace* (NAL, 1988) and *The City in Stone* (Meisha Merlin, 2004). Books 1 and 2 were republished in *The Book of Elementals, Vol. 1 and 2* (Meisha Merlin, 2003).
Ballantine, 1979, pap., 387 pp., o.p.; NAL, 1989, pap., 384 pp. (0-451-15683-8); entitled *The Book of Elementals, Vol. 1*, Meisha Merlin, 2003 (1-892065-94-0)

(BL 75:1482, 1485, 78:594; VOYA 2:53)

5-206 **ELDRIDGE, Roger.** *The Shadow of the Gloom-World.* Gr. 6–9. (Orig. British pub. 1977.)
Exiled from their subterranean worlds, Fernfeather and Harebell search for a better life above the ground.
Dutton, 1978, 191 pp., o.p.

(HB 54:401; SLJ May 1978 p. 76)

5-207 **ELGIN, (Patricia Anne) Suzette Haden.** *Twelve Fair Kingdoms.* **(The Ozark trilogy, bk. 1).** Gr. 10 up.
A 14-year-old girl sets out to rally the Twelve Kingdoms in hopes of defeating a magician threatening her world. The sequels are *The Grand Jubilee* (1981) and *And Then There'll Be Fireworks* (1981).
Doubleday, 1981, 183 pp., o.p.

(BL 77:1433, 1444, 78:594; Kirkus 49:390; LJ 106:1326)

5-208 **ELLIOTT, Kate.** *King's Dragon.* **(Crown of Stars saga, vol. 1).** Gr. 10 up.
Alain, an orphaned young prophet, and Liath, a lifelong fugitive, become entangled in the fate of their kingdom, Wendar, where a royal brother and sister are at war over the throne. The sequels are *Prince of Dogs* (1998, 1999),

The Burning Stone (1999, 2000), *Child of Flame* (2000, 2001), and *The Gathering Storm* (2003).
DAW, 1997, 532 pp. (0-88677-727-5), 1998, pap. (0-88677-771-2)
(BL 93:1008; Kirkus 64:1707; VOYA 20:116, 21:12)

5-209 **ELLIS, Sarah.** *The Several Lives of Orphan Jack.* Gr. 3–6. (Orig. Canadian
★ pub. 2003.)
Twelve-year-old Jack, raised at the Opportunities School for Orphans and
Foundlings, runs away and sets himself up in business as an "ideas peddler,"
selling "thoughts, concepts, plans, opinions, impressions, notions, and fancies."
Illus. by Bruno St.-Aubin, Groundwood, 2003, 88 pp. (0-88899-529-6)
(BL 100:668; CCBB 57:150; HB 79:742; HBG 15:78; Kirkus 71:1122; SLJ Dec 2003 p. 149)

5-210 *Elsewhere, Vol. 1.* **Ed. by Terri Windling and Mark Alan Arnold.** Gr. 10
up.
An anthology of fantasy tales about other worlds, by such authors as Ursula K.
Le Guin, Michael Moorcock, and Janny Wurts. World Fantasy Convention
Award, Best Anthology, 1982. The companion volumes are *Elsewhere, Vol. 2*
(1982) and *Elsewhere, Vol. 3* (1984).
Ace, 1981, pap., 366 pp., o.p.
(BL 78:634; SLJ Apr 1982 p. 88; VOYA 4:38)

5-211 **ENDE, Michael.** *Momo.* Gr. 10 up. (Orig. German pub. 1973; British title
★ *The Grey Gentlemen*, 1975.)
A girl named Momo who lives in a ruined amphitheater is beloved by the poor
people because she listens so carefully that everyone is able to think great
thoughts. When her friends' lives are threatened by the "men in grey," who
live off others' spare time, only Momo can save them from the plague of deadly tedium.
Trans. by J. Maxwell Brownjohn, Doubleday, 1985, 228 pp., o.p.
(BL 81:602; Kirkus 52:1168; Kliatt 20:57; LJ Jan 1985 p. 100; TLS July 11, 1975 p. 767;
VOYA 8:192)

5-212 **ENGH, M(ary) J(ane).** *The House in the Snow.* Gr. 4–6.
Cloaks of invisibility help Benjamin lead a rebellion against a gang of robbers
who enslave boys.
Illus. by Leslie W. Bowman, Orchard, 1987, 192 pp., o.p.; Scholastic, 1990,
pap., 144 pp. (0-590-42658-3)
(BL 84:476; CCBB 41:6; Kirkus 55:990; SLJ Sep 1987 p. 179)

5-213 **FALLON, Jennifer.** *Medalon.* **(Hythrun Chronicles, bk. 1).** Gr. 10 up.
(Orig. Australian pub. 2001.)
R'shiel, 18, and her Defender warrior half-brother Tarja escape the clutches of
their mother, First Sister of the Blade, and join a rebellion against the ruling
Sisterhood of Medalon. The sequel is *Treason Keep* (2004).
Tor, 2004, 400 pp. (0-765-30986-6)
(BL 100:1604; Kirkus 72:206; LJ Apr 15, 2004 p. 129)

5-214 *The Fantastic Imagination: An Anthology of High Fantasy.* **Ed. by Robert
H. Boyer and Kenneth J. Zahorski. (vol. 1).** Gr. 10 up.
Sixteen "high fantasy" short stories whose authors include George MacDonald,

C. S. Lewis, J. R. R. Tolkien, Lloyd Alexander, Peter S. Beagle, Ursula K. Le Guin, Lord Dunsany, John Buchan, Frank R. Stockton, and Sylvia Townsend Warner. *The Fantastic Imagination, Vol. 2* (1978) is a companion volume. Avon, 1977, pap., 325 pp., o.p.

(BL73:1338; Kliatt 11:9)

5-215 **FARLAND, David.** *The Sum of All Men.* **(The Runelords series, bk. 1).**
✭ Gr. 10 up.
Prince Gaborn Val Orden of Mystarria battles the forces of the nearly immortal Raj Ahren, who has laid siege to the palace of Princess Iome of Sylvarresta. The sequels are *Brotherhood of the Wolf* (1999, 2000), *Wizardborn* (2001, 2002), and *The Lair of Bones* (2003).
Tor, 1998, 480 pp. (0-312-86653-4); St. Martin's, 1999, pap., 624 pp. (0-8125-4162-6)

(BL 94:1601; Kirkus 66:785; LJ July 1998 p. 142; VOYA 21:442, 22:13)

5-216 **FARRELL, S. L.** *Holder of Lightning.* **(Cloudmages series, bk. 1).** Gr. 10 up.
Jenna Aoire, 17, discovers that she is destined to become the Holder of Lamh Shabhala, the strongest of the magical stones of power, and will gain the ability to channel its power. The sequels are *Mage of Clouds* (2004) and *Heir of Stone* (2005).
DAW, 2003, 448 pp. (0-7564-0130-5); DAW, 2004, pap., 624 pp. (0-7564-0152-6)

(BL 99:860; LJ Jan 2003 p. 165; VOYA 26:148, 27:11)

5-217 **FARRELL, Trace.** *The Ruins.* Gr. 10 up.
Tom works his way up from shoeshine boy to maitre d'hotel of The Ruins in this darkly magical tale set in a medieval-like post-Armageddon London.
NYU Press, 1998, 268 pp. (0-8147-2685-2)

(BL 94:1501; LJ May 1, 1998 p. 137, Oct 1, 1998 p. 54)

5-218 **FEIFFER, Jules.** *A Barrel of Laughs, A Vale of Tears.* Gr. 4–7.
With a good deal of help from Lady Sadie, shallow Prince Roger grows up during his journey through the Forever Forest, the Dastardly Divide, the Valley of Vengeance, and the Mountains of Malice.
Illus. by the author, HarperCollins, 1995, 180 pp. (0-06-205098-2)

(CCBB 49:189; HBG 7:61; Kirkus 63:1633; SLJ Jan 1996 p. 108)

5-219 **FEINTUCH, David.** *The Still.* **(Rodrigo of Caledon saga, vol. 1).** Gr. 10 up.
Young Prince Rodrigo of Caledon is forced to grow up quickly following the sudden death of his mother, the queen. The sequel is *The King* (2002, 2003).
Warner, 1997, pap., 688 pp. (0-446-67285-8), 1998, pap. (0-446-60551-4)

(BL 93:1805; Kirkus 65:684; Kliatt Sep 1997 pp. 18; VOYA 20:324, 21:12)

5-220 **FEIST, Raymond E.** *Krondor: The Betrayal.* **(Riftwar Legacy, vol. 1).** Gr. 10 up.
In this book set between the author's Riftwar (see below) and Serpentwar (see below) sagas, Squire James and his companions—a wizard, a renegade elf, an arch-magician, and another squire—face the invasion of Krondor by the dark elves and revolt from within by a group of powerful magicians. The sequels

are *Krondor: The Assassins* (1999, 2000) and *Krondor: Tear of the Gods* (2001). The author's Conclave of Shadows (see below) and Empire trilogy (see below) are related series.
Avon, 1998, 384 pp. (0-380-97715-X); Eos, 1999, pap., 432 pp. (0-380-79527-2)
(BL 95:313; Kirkus 66:1162; LJ Oct 15, 1998 p. 104)

5-221 FEIST, Raymond E. *Shadow of a Dark Queen*. (Serpentwar saga, vol. 1).
Gr. 10 up.
In a story set in the same universe as Feist's Riftwar Saga and Riftwar Legacy, Erik and Roo battle a clan of sorcerous serpents threatening Midkemia. The sequels are *Rise of a Merchant Prince* (1995), *Rage of a Demon King* (1997), and *Shards of a Broken Crown* (1998, 1999). The author's Conclave of Shadows (see below) and Empire trilogy (see below) are related series.
Morrow, 1994, 450 pp. (0-688-12408-9); Avon, 1995, pap. (0-380-72086-8)
(BL 90:1927, 1931; Kirkus 62:673)

5-222 FEIST, Raymond E. *Silverthorn*. (Riftwar saga, bk. 2). Gr. 10 up.
★ Prince Arutha and former bandit Jimmy the Hand set out on a perilous journey in search of the mythical silverthorn plant, needed to awaken the prince's betrothed from an enchanted slumber. This book is preceded by *Magician* (1982, 1984), and the sequels are *A Darkness at Sethanon* (1986), *Prince of the Blood* (1989, 1992), and *The King's Buccaneer* (1992). *Daughter of the Empire* (1987; see below), written by Feist and Janny Wurts, takes place in the same universe as this saga, as does *Shadow of a Dark Queen* (Morrow, 1994; see above), which is volume 1 of Feist's Serpentwar Saga. The paperback version of *Magician* was published in two volumes: *Magician: Apprentice* (1986, 1994) and *Magician: Master* (1986, 1994). Feist's Riftwar Legacy trilogy (see above) is set in time between the Riftwar and Serpentwar sagas (see above). The author's Conclave of Shadows (see below) and Empire trilogy (see below) are related series.
Doubleday, 1985, 1992, 360 pp. (0-385-19210-X); Bantam, 1986, pap., 336 pp. (0-553-25928-8)
(BL 81:1519, 86:905; Kirkus 53:450; LJ June 15, 1985 p. 74; VOYA 8:324)

5-223 FEIST, Raymond E. *Talon of the Silver Hawk*. (Conclave of Shadows, bk. 1). Gr. 10 up. (Orig. British pub. 2002.)
After he survives the massacre of his mountain-dwelling people, young Kieli takes the name Talon of the Silver Hawk, becomes a deadly swordsman while living with his enemies, and joins the Shadow Conclave, a secret society of sorcerers. This series is related to the author's Riftwar Legacy novels (see above), Serpentwar and Riftwar sagas (see above), and Empire trilogy (see above). The sequels are *King of Foxes* (2004) and *Exile's Return* (2005).
HarperCollins, 2003, 400 pp. (0-380-97708-7)
(BL 99:806; LJ Mar 15, 2003 p. 120)

5-224 FEIST, Raymond E., and WURTS, Janny. *Daughter of the Empire*. (Empire trilogy, vol. 1). Gr. 10 up.
Queen Mara of Acoma vows to avenge the deaths of her brother and father, even if it means killing her own husband. The sequels are *Servant of the Empire* (1990, 1992) and *Mistress of the Empire* (1992). These books are set in the same universe as Feist's Riftwar and Serpentwar sagas (see above) as well

as his Conclave of Shadows series (see above). The Riftwar Legacy trilogy is set in time between the Riftwar and Serpentwar sagas.

Doubleday, 1987, 394 pp., o.p.; Bantam, 1988, pap. (0-553-27211-X)

(BL 83:1564; Kirkus 55:755; LJ June 15, 1987 p. 88; VOYA 10:244, 287)

5-225 FERRIS, Jean. *Once Upon a Marigold.* Gr. 5–9.
☆ Raised in a cave by Ed, the troll who found him in the woods as a child, Christian, 17, falls in love with Princess Marigold, but winning her heart involves desperate measures.

Harcourt, 2002, 266 pp. (0-15-216791-9), 2004, pap., 288 pp. (0-15-205084-1)

(BL 99:226; CCBB 56:234; HB 78:571; HBG 14:79; Kirkus 70:1468; Kliatt Nov 2002 p. 8; SLJ Nov 2002 p. 164; VOYA 25:396, 26:11)

5-226 *Festival Moon.* **Ed. by C. J. Cherryh. (Merovingen Nights, no. 1).** Gr. 10 up.

A "shared world" anthology of stories by Cherryh, Lynn Abbey, Mercedes Lackey, and others, set in Merovin, the world of Cherryh's *Angel with the Sword* (1985; see above). The sequels are *Smuggler's Gold* (1988), *Divine Right* (1989), *Flood Tide* (1990), and *Endgame* (1991).

DAW, 1987, pap., 300 pp., o.p.

(BL 83:1180, 1198; LJ Mar 15, 1987 p. 93; VOYA 10:178)

5-227 FFORDE, Jasper. *The Eyre Affair.* **(Thursday Next series, bk. 1).** Gr. 10 up. (Orig. British pub. 2001.)

In an alternate Britain where time travel is common, detective Thursday Next pursues the dangerous forger Acheron Hades into the world of Charlotte Brontë's novel *Jane Eyre* to prevent him from changing the original manuscript. The sequels are *Thursday Next in Lost in a Good Book* (2003), *The Well of Lost Plots* (2004), and *Something Rotten* (2004).

Viking, 2002, 374 pp. (0-670-03064-3); Penguin, 2003, pap., 384 pp. (0-14-200180-5)

(Kirkus 69:1629; SLJ Oct 2002 p. 196, Dec 2002 p. 46; VOYA 25:339)

FIENBERG, Anna. *The Witch in the Lake.*
See Chapter 12, Witchcraft and Sorcery Fantasy.

5-228 FINCH, Sheila. *Infinity's Web.* Gr. 10 up.

Anastasia Valerie Stein is confronted with four different possible lives, due to a leak between parallel universes. In one she is a witch in a Nazi-ruled England, and in the others she is an unhappy housewife, a teacher, and an aging hippie.

Bantam, 1985, pap., 230 pp., o.p.

(BL 82:317; LJ Aug 1985 p. 120; VOYA 8:365)

5-229 FINDLAY, Jamieson. *The Blue Roan Child.* Gr. 5–8. (Orig. British pub.
☆ 2002.)

Orphaned young Syeira, who can communicate with winged horses, undertakes a journey to rescue two colts stolen from their mother, the wild mare Arwin, by Lord Ran.

Chicken House/Scholastic, 2004, 272 pp. (0-439-62752-4)

(BL 100:1726; CCBB 58:15; Kirkus 72:536; SLJ July 2004 p. 105; VOYA 27:313)

5-230   FISHER, Catherine. *The Oracle Betrayed.* Gr. 5–10. (Orig. British pub.
★   2003, entitled *The Oracle.*)
         The dying Archon, or god-on-earth, secretly informs young Mirany, one of the
         Nine who serve him, that she must find the boy meant to take his place and
         make sure that he becomes the new Archon. The sequel is *The Sphere of
         Secrets* (2005; British title *The Archon* [2004]).
         Greenwillow/HarperCollins, 2004, 352 pp. (0-06-057158-6)
         (BL 100:1059; CCBB 57:416; HB 80:181; Kirkus 72:132; SLJ Mar 2004 p. 210; VOYA
         27:58)

5-231   FISHER, Catherine. *Snow-Walker.* Gr. 6–10. (Orig. British pub. 1993,
★   1995, 1997.)
         A young woman named Jessa and Kari, the exiled son of the northern Snow-
         walker enchantress who has ensnared the land of the Jarlshold, attempt to use
         his inherited magic power to defeat his mother, Gudrun. This story was origi-
         nally published in England in three volumes: *The Snow-Walker's Son* (1993),
         The Empty Hand (1995), and *The Soul Thieves* (1997).
         Greenwillow/HarperCollins, 2004, 512 pp. (0-06-072475-7)
         (BL 101:106; CCBB 58:71; HB 80:581; Kirkus 72:684; SLJ Nov 2004 p. 143; VOYA
         27:313)

5-232   FISHER, Jude. *Sorcery Rising.* (Fool's Gold series, bk. 1). Gr. 10 up.
         When Eryan merchant's daughter Katla unwittingly breaks Istrian law by
         climbing the sacred mount, Sur's Castle, two Istrian elders vow to capture and
         burn her. The sequels are *Wild Magic* (2003) and *The Rose of the World* (2005).
         DAW, 2002, 528 pp. (0-7564-0083-X), 2003, pap., 528 pp. (0-7564-0110-0)
         (BL 98:1696; Kirkus 70:624; LJ July 2002 p. 127; VOYA 25:396, 26:11)

5-233   FISHER, Paul R. *The Ash Staff.* (Mole and Arien trilogy, bk. 1). Gr. 6–9.
         An irrepressible boy named Mole becomes the leader of a group of orphans
         fighting the evil powers of the enchanter Ammar. The sequels are *The Hawks
         of Fellheath* (1980) and *The Princess and the Thorn* (1981).
         Atheneum, 1979, 179 pp., o.p.
         (BL 76:448; CCBB 33:151; Kirkus 47:1067; SLJ Jan 1980 p. 68)

5-234   FISHER, Paul R. *Mont Cant Gold.* Gr. 7–10.
         Rhian Mont Cant struggles to win the approval of each of the seven guardian
         fates, to become High King of Rhewar.
         Atheneum, 1981, 251 pp., o.p.
         (BL 77:1191; SLJ Apr 1981 p. 126; VOYA 4:63)

5-235   FLEISCHMAN, (Albert) Sid(ney). *The Whipping Boy.* Gr. 4–6.
★★   Prince Brat decides to run away from home, taking his much-abused whipping
         boy, Jemmy, with him, but their roles are reversed when the boys are captured
         by the villains Cut-Water and Hold-Your-Nose-Billy. John Newbery Medal,
         1987.
         Illus. by Peter Sís, Greenwillow, 1986, 96 pp., LB (0-688-06216-4);
         HarperTrophy, 2003, pap., 306 pp. (0-06-052122-8)
         (BL 82:1018, 83:1135; CCBB 39:126; HB 62:325; Kirkus 54:715; SLJ May 1986 p. 90; Suth
         4:120)

5-236 **FLETCHER, Susan.** *Dragon's Milk.* **(The Dragon Chronicles, bk. 1).** Gr.
★★ 5–9.
Kaeldra becomes foster mother to three orphaned young dragons after she is
sent in search of dragon's milk to cure her younger sister's illness. The prequel
is *Flight of the Dragon Kyn* (1993; see below). In *Sign of the Dove* (1996,
1999), Kaeldra's foster sister, Lyf, helps Kaeldra's young son and some dragon
hatchlings elude pursuit by the queen's forces, who are killing dragons for
their hearts.
Macmillan, 1989, 242 pp. (0-689-31579-1), 1992, pap. (0-689-71623-0);
Simon, 1997, pap. (0-689-81515-8)
(BL 86:547; HB 66:69; HBG 1:81; Kirkus 57:1592; SLJ Nov 1989 p. 106; VOYA 12:288)

5-237 **FLETCHER, Susan.** *Flight of the Dragon Kyn.* **(The Dragon Chronicles,**
★ **bk. 2).** Gr. 5–10.
After the king tricks Kara into using her bird-calling powers to call down drag-
ons to be killed, she escapes and vows to protect the dragons. This is the pre-
quel to *Dragon's Milk* (1991; see above) and *Sign of the Dove* (1996, 1999).
Macmillan, 1993, 213 pp. (0-689-31880-4); Simon, 1997, pap. (0-689-81515-8)
(BL 90:931; CCBB 47:153; HB 70:73; HBG 5:86; Kirkus 61:1329; SLJ Nov 1993 p. 108;
VOYA 16:380)

5-238 **FLEWELLING, Lynn.** *The Bone Doll's Twin.* **(Tamir trilogy, bk. 1).** Gr.
9 up.
In order to save her life and allow her to become a warrior Queen, Princess
Tobin must be disguised as a boy and protected from evil wizards, her mother,
and her brother. The sequel is *Hidden Warrior* (2003).
Bantam/Spectra, 2001, pap., 544 pp. (0-553-57723-9)
(BL 98:305; VOYA 24:368, 25:13)

5-239 **FLINT, Eric.** *The Philosophical Strangler.* Gr. 10 up.
Professional assassin Greyboar and his dwarf sidekick Ignace take on a num-
ber of strangulation commissions, including that of the King of Sundjhab, in
this action adventure spoof. The prequel is *Forward the Mage* (2002, 2003).
Baen, 2001, pap., 342 pp. (0-671-31986-8)
(BL 97:1539; Kirkus 69:370; LJ May 15, 2001 p. 167; VOYA 24:289)

5-240 **FOON, Dennis.** *The Dirt Eaters.* **(The Longlight Legacy trilogy, bk. 1).**
Gr. 6–12. (Orig. pub. in Canada.)
Fifteen-year-old Roan and his younger sister Stowe, the only survivors of
Longlight's destruction, become separated when she is taken to the City and he
escapes into the wilderness from the Brothers, a band of warriors headed by a
man named Saint.
Annick, 2003, 320 pp. (1-55037-807-4), 2003, pap., 313 pp. (1-55037-806-6)
(CCBB 57:229; SLJ Jan 2004 p. 129; VOYA 26:502, 27:12)

5-241 **FORD, John M.** *The Dragon Waiting: A Masque of History.* Gr. 10 up.
A Welsh wizard recruits a band of Italian warriors to fight the spread of the
Byzantine Empire in England in this historical fantasy set in an alternate 15th-
century Europe ruled by magic. World Fantasy Award, 1983.
Timescape, 1983, 368 pp., o.p.; Avon, 1985, pap. (0-380-69887-0)
(BL 80:468; Kirkus 51:976; LJ 108:2174; SLJ Mar 1984 p. 178; VOYA 7:101)

5-242 FORWARD, Eve. *Animist.* Gr. 7–12.
As a recent graduate and slave of the College of Animism, Alex must find his Anim, the animal with which he will bond in order to use his magic talents.
Tor, 2000, 320 pp. (0-312-86891-X), 2001, pap., 376 pp. (0-81257-462-1)
(BL 96:1866; LJ June 15, 2000 p. 120; VOYA 23:274)

5-243 FORWARD, Eve. *Villains by Necessity.* Gr. 10 up.
Kaylana, the last surviving Druid mage in Chiaroscuro, realizes that it is up to her to restore the balance between good and evil in the world, aided by an assassin, a thief, a sorceress, a knight, and a centaur minstrel.
Tor, 1995, 480 pp. (0-312-85789-6)
(BL 91:1313, 1317; Kirkus 63:33; LJ Feb 15, 1995 p. 186)

5-244 FOSTER, Alan Dean. *Carnivores of Light and Darkness.* **(Journeys of the Catechist trilogy, vol. 1).** Gr. 10 up.
Dying nobleman Tarin Beckwith entreats Etjole Ehomba to rescue the Visioness Themarly of Laconda, who has been abducted by Hymneth the Possessed. The sequels are *Into the Thinking Kingdoms* (1999, 2000) and *A Triumph of Souls* (2000, 2001).
Warner, 1998, 344 pp. (0-446-52132-9), 1999, pap. (0-446-60697-9)
(Kirkus 66:537; LJ May 15, 1998 p. 118; VOYA 21:209)

5-245 FOSTER, Alan Dean. *Kingdoms of Light.* Gr. 7–12.
After the wizard Susnam Evyndd dies battling the Torumakk Horde, goblins drain all color from Gowdlands, leaving only the wizard's animals, transformed into human shape, to defeat the evil spell.
Warner, 2001, 372 pp. (0-446-52667-3), 2002, pap., 400 pp. (0-446-61061-5)
(Kirkus 68:1652; LJ Jan 2001 p. 163; VOYA 24:11, 51)

5-246 FRANCIS, Diana Pharoh. *Path of Fate.* Gr. 10 up.
Reluctantly drawn from life as a village healer to join the Blessed Lady's elite guard, Reisil and her bond mate, the goshawk Saljane, must find the kidnapped daughter of the Dure before civil war destroys their land. The sequel is *Path of Honor* (2004).
NAL/Roc, 2003, pap., 384 pp. (0-451-45950-4)
(BL 100:578; VOYA 27:141)

5-247 FRIEDMAN, C. S. *Black Sun Rising.* **(Cold Fire trilogy, vol. 1).** Gr. 10 up.
In the future world of Erna, where magic has been revived to deal with volcanic activity, a priest and a sorcerer join forces to battle evil. The sequels are *When True Night Falls* (1993) and *Crown of Shadows* (1995, 1996).
DAW, 1991, 496 pp., o.p., 1992, pap. (0-88677-527-2)
(BL 88:34, 39; LJ Nov 15 1991 p. 110)

5-248 FRIESNER, Esther M. *Druid's Blood.* Gr. 10 up.
A humorous tale set in an alternate England ruled by Celtic magic, where Queen Victoria's reign may be cut short by a treasonous conspiracy.
NAL, 1988, pap., 279 pp., o.p.
(BL 85:42; LJ June 15, 1988 p. 70)

FRIESNER, Esther M. *Majyk by Accident.*
See Chapter 12, Witchcraft and Sorcery Fantasy.

5-249 **FRIESNER, Esther M.** *Spells of Mortal Weaving.* **(The Twelve Kingdoms series, vol. 2).** Gr. 10 up.
Prince Alban finds his curse of unrequited love fulfilled when his quest for Lady Ursula takes him into the realm of the deadly Morgeld. This is the sequel to *Mustapha and His Wise Dog* (1985).
Avon, 1986, pap., 224 pp. (0-380-75001-5)
(BL 82:1360, 1388; LJ May 15, 1986 p. 81)

5-250 **FRIESNER, Esther M.** *Wishing Season.* Gr. 6–10.
★ After genie school star student Khalid forgets to limit a young merchant's wishes during his trial run in a lamp, they become stuck with each other.
Illus. by Frank Kelly Freas, Macmillan, 1993, 144 pp. (0-689-31574-0)
(BL 89:2049, 94:475; HBG 5:86; Kirkus 61:1389; SLJ Sep 1993 p. 229; VOYA 16:226, 17:9)

5-251 **FUNK, Bret M.** *Sword of Honor.* **(Boundary's Fall series, bk. 2).** Gr. 7 up. (Orig. pub. in England.)
Lorthas, the Darklord, imprisoned for a thousand years behind a magical boundary, plots his escape and enters the dreams of ex-slave Dahr and his orphaned companion, Jeran, as they attempt to warn the King of Madryn about the boundary's weakness. This is the sequel to *Path of Glory* (2001, 2002).
Tyrannosaurus, 2003, pap., 536 pp. (0-9718819-0-1)
(LJ Aug 2003 p. 142; SLJ Feb 2004 p. 147)

5-252 **FUNKE, Cornelia Caroline.** *Dragon Rider.* Gr. 4–7. (Orig. German pub.
★ 1997.)
Firedrake, a young silver dragon, is joined in his search for a legendary mountain haven by an orphaned boy named Ben, a cantankerous brownie, and Twigleg, a former spy for the evil Nettlebrand.
Illus. by the author, Scholastic, 2004, 528 pp. (0-439-45695-9)
(BL 100:1924; CCBB 58:72; HB 80:583; Kirkus 72:528; SLJ Oct 2004 p. 164; VOYA 27:314)

FURLONG, Monica (Navis). *Wise Child.*
See Chapter 12, Witchcraft and Sorcery Fantasy.

GARD, Joyce (pseud. of Joyce Reeves). *The Mermaid's Daughter.*
See Chapter 12, Witchcraft and Sorcery Fantasy.

GARDNER, Craig Shaw. *A Disagreement with Death.*
See Chapter 12, Witchcraft and Sorcery Fantasy.

5-253 **GARDNER, John (Champlin) (Jr.).** *In the Suicide Mountains.* Gr. 7 up.
A dwarf, a blacksmith's daughter, and a crown prince, all bent on suicide, meet in the mountains and find happiness together.
Illus. by Joe Servello, Knopf, 1977, 159 pp., o.p.
(BL 74:22, 32; CCBB 31:126; HB 54:194; Kirkus 45:868; LJ 102:1677; SLJ Dec 1977 p. 54)

GARNER, Alan. *The Well of the Wind.*
See Chapter 12, Witchcraft and Sorcery Fantasy.

5-254 **GARRETT, Randall.** *Lord Darcy Investigates.* **(Lord Darcy series, bk. 1).**
Gr. 10 up.

Four stories set in an alternate Anglo-French empire ruled by magic, where a detective named Lord Darcy solves mysteries. The sequels are *Murder and Magic* (Ace, 1979, 1982) and *Too Many Magicians* (Ace, 1967, 1983). Michael Jurland has written another sequel: *Ten Little Wizards* (Berkley/Ace, 1988).
Ace, 1981, 1983, 229 pp., o.p.
(BL 78:426, 435)

5-255   GARRISON, Peter. *The Changeling War*. (The Changeling Saga, vol. 1). Gr. 10 up.
Young people in two worlds escape their pursuers; Aubric, a warrior, flees into a network of tunnels beneath a castle, while on Earth two teenagers use their newfound magical powers to elude kidnapping gangsters. The sequels are *The Sorcerer's Gun* (1999) and *The Magic Dead* (2000).
Ace, 1999, pap., 352 pp. (0-441-00552-7)
(Kirkus 67:417; Kliatt July 1999 p. 22; LJ Apr 15, 1999 p. 149; VOYA 22:191)

5-256   GEMMELL, David. *Stormrider*. (Rigante saga, bk. 4). Gr. 7 up. (Orig. British pub. 2002.)
Gaise Macon takes the name of Stormrider to lead the Rigante people against the diabolical Winter Kay and his Knights of Sacrifice and Redeemers, who have killed the king and used his blood in a sacrifice. This book is preceded by *The Sword in the Storm* (1998, 2001), *Midnight Falcon* (1999, 2001), and *Ravenheart* (2001).
Del Rey, 2002, 400 pp. (0-345-44577-5)
(BL 98:776; Kirkus 70:79; SLJ Feb 2003 p. 172; VOYA 25:296)

5-257   GEMMELL, David. *White Wolf: A Novel of Druss the Legend*. (Drenai
✮ **Tales, vol. 10).** Gr. 10 up. (Orig. pub. in England.)
In this prequel to *Legend* (1984; Random, 1986; Del Rey, 1994), the first book in the series set in the violence-ridden world of the Drenai, repentant warrior Skilgannon takes up arms again and searches for a legendary temple in an attempt to resurrect his late wife. He meets Druss, the main character of the succeeding books, along the way. The other books in the series are *The King Beyond the Gate* (1985, 1990, 1995), *Quest for Lost Heroes* (1995), *Waylander* (1986, 1995), *In the Realm of the Wolf* (1992, 1998), *The First Chronicles of Druss the Legend* (1999), *The Legend of the Deathwalker* (1996, 1999), *Winter Warriors* (1997, 2000), *Hero in the Shadows* (2000), and *The Swords of Night and Day* (2004). *Drenai Tales* (Bantam, 2002) contains books 7–9.
Del Rey, 2003, 432 pp. (0-345-45831-1), 2004, pap., 480 pp. (0-345-45832-X)
(BL 99:1153; Kirkus 71:117; LJ Mar 15, 2003 p. 120; SLJ Sep 2003 p. 240)

5-258   GENTLE, Mary. *Rats and Gargoyles*. Gr. 10 up.
In this complex multicharacter story set in a magical Renaissance-like world, the human beings enslaved by human-sized Ratlords and devil-like Decan Overlords are preparing to revolt. The sequel is *The Architecture of Desire* (1993).
Viking, 1991, 414 pp. (0-451-45106-6); NAL, 1992, pap. (0-451-45173-2)
(BL 87:1627, 1630; Kirkus 59:291; LJ Mar 15, 1991 p. 119)

5-259   GILLIGAN, Elizabeth. *Magic's Silken Snare*. (Silken Magic, bk. 1). Gr. 10 up.
After her murdered sister's body is stolen, Luciana—sister-in-law of the Queen

of Tyrrhia, an alternate Renaissance Italy—braves dangerous court intrigues to unmask the murderers. The sequel is *The Silken Shroud* (2004).
DAW, 2003, pap., 556 pp. (0-7564-0127-5)
(BL 99:1454; Kliatt July 2003 p. 30)

GILLILAND, Alexis A(rnaldus). *Wizenbeak.*
See Chapter 12, Witchcraft and Sorcery Fantasy.

5-260 GILLULY, Sheila. *Greenbriar Queen.* Gr. 10 up.
After the king's death, his daughter comes out of hiding to battle her evil uncle for control of the kingdom.
NAL, 1988, 330 pp., o.p.
(BL 84:831, 855; Kliatt Apr 1988 p. 20; VOYA 11:192, 12:14)

5-261 GLASS, Isabel. *Daughter of Exile.* Gr. 10 up.
After her exiled father's assassination, teenage Lady Angarred Hashan travels to the royal court to demand justice, despite her family's poverty and her ignorance of the reason for her father's banishment.
Tor, 2004, 400 pp. (0-765-30745-6)
(BL 100:1277; Kirkus 72:113; VOYA 27:314)

5-262 GLOSS, Molly. *Outside the Gates.* Gr. 6–9.
☆   Exiled beyond the High Gates because of their magic abilities, a boy named Vren and a man called Rusche live peacefully until Rusche is kidnapped by the evil Spellbinder.
Atheneum, 1986, 120 pp., o.p.
(BL 83:270; CCBB 40:26; HB 68:209; Kirkus 54:1207; SLJ Mar 1987 p. 158; VOYA 10:38)

5-263 GOLDIN, Stephen. *Crystals of Air and Water.* (The Parsina Saga, vol. 3). Gr. 6–12.
Prince Ahmad and apprentice wizard Jaffar al-Sharif search a desert country far from their home for the three missing pieces of the Crystal of Oromasd, needed to save the world from domination by demons. This is the sequel to *Shrine of the Desert Mage* (1988) and *The Storyteller and the Jann* (1988).
Bantam, 1989, 292 pp. (0-553-27711-1)
(VOYA 12:1654, 13:12)

5-264 GOLDMAN, William W. *The Princess Bride: S. Morgenstern's Classic Tale of True Love and High Adventure.* Gr. 8 up.
In this parody of heroic fairy tales, Westley, the masked hero, tries to reclaim his beloved Buttercup from the evil Prince Humperdink of Florin, while Inigo Montoya, the great swordsman, continues his lifelong search for his father's murderer.
Harcourt, 1973, 320 pp., o.p.; Del Rey, 1990, pap., 416 pp. (0-345-34803-6); Ballantine, 1998, 399 pp. (0-345-43014-X)
(Kirkus 41:704; LJ 98:2570)

5-265 GOLDSTEIN, Lisa. *Summer King Winter Fool.* Gr. 10 up.
Vale and Taja search for the legitimate heir to the throne during an endless winter caused by the rule of pretenders and their sorcerous political intrigues.
Tor, 1994, 320 pp., o.p.
(BL 90:1668, 1671; Kirkus 62:349; LJ Apr 15, 1994 p. 117; VOYA 17:222)

5-266 **GOODKIND, Terry.** *Wizard's First Rule.* **(The Sword of Truth saga, vol.**
✭ **1). Gr. 11 up.**
Richard Cypher enlists the aid of wizards and dragons after he sets out to fight
evil with the Sword of Truth in this story for mature readers. The sequels are
Stone of Tears (1995, 1996), *Blood of the Fold* (1996), *Temple of the Winds*
(1997), *Soul of the Fire* (1999), *Faith of the Fallen* (2000), *The Pillars of Creation* (2001), and *Naked Empire* (2003).
Tor, 1994, 576 pp. (0-312-85705-5), 2003, pap., 836 pp. (0-765-34652-4)
(BL 91:28, 31; Kirkus 62:892; LJ Sep 15, 1994 p. 94; VOYA 17:347, 19:14)

5-267 **GOULART, Ron(ald Joseph).** *The Chameleon Corps and Other Shape
Changers.* **(The Chameleon Corps series, bk. 2). Gr. 10 up.**
Five of these 11 humorous science fiction and fantasy tales concern Ben Jol-
son, a shape-changing lieutenant in the Chameleon Corps. These stories are
preceded by *The Sword Swallower* (Doubleday, 1968), and the sequels are
Flux (DAW, 1974), *Spacehawk Inc.* (DAW, 1974), and *A Whiff of Madness*
(DAW, 1976).
Macmillan, 1972, 216 pp., o.p.
(BL 68:976, 998; Kirkus 40:283, 341; LJ 97:1742, 3472)

5-268 **GOULART, Ron(ald Joseph).** *The Prisoner of Blackwood Castle.* **Gr.
8–12.**
A humorous science-fantasy set in 1897, featuring detective Harry Challange,
a conjurer called the Great Lorenzo, and Princess Alicia of Orlandia, held prisoner by a vampire in Blackwood Castle.
Avon, 1984, pap., 174 pp., o.p.
(Kliatt 18:28; VOYA 7:266)

5-269 **GRAY, Margaret.** *The Ugly Princess and the Wise Fool.* **Gr. 3–6.**
Princess Rose is pressured into asking her fairy godmother to make her more
beautiful, according to tradition in the royal family, while her friend Jasper,
masquerading as a fool, tries to bring true wisdom to the Kingdom of Cous-
cous. *The Lovesick Salesman* (2004) is a prequel to this story.
Illus. by Randy Cecil, Holt, 2002, 167 pp. (0-8050-6847-3)
(BL 99:597; CCBB 56:158; HBG 14:81; SLJ Oct 2002 p. 111; VOYA 25:297)

5-270 **GREEN, Simon R.** *Blue Moon Rising.* **Gr. 7–12.**
The Darkwood, filled with demons, is creeping ever closer to King John's cas-
tle, destroying Forest Land as it comes, and it is up to the king's younger son,
Prince Rupert, and sword-wielding Princess Julia to save the kingdom.
NAL, 1991, pap., 476 pp. (0-451-45095-7)
(Kliatt Sep 1991 p. 23; VOYA 14:242)

5-271 **GREENO, Gayle.** *Finders-Seekers.* **(The Ghatti's Tale, bk. 1). Gr. 10 up.**
Doyce, a seeker, and her telepathic feline ghatti, Khar, are assigned to find the
murderers of her lover and his ghatti companion. The sequels are *Mind-Speak-
er's Call* (1994) and *Exiles' Return* (1995).
DAW, 1993, 496 pp. (0-88677-550-7)
(Kliatt July 1993 p. 16; LJ Apr 15, 1993 p. 130; VOYA 16:164, 17:10)

5-272 GREENWOOD, Ed. *The Kingless Land: A Tale of the Band of Four.* **(Tales of the Band of Four, bk. 1).** Gr. 10 up.
Lady Embra Silvertree, a shape-shifting healer, and two thieves search for the Dwaerindim stones in order to awaken the sleeping king and bring peace to their land. The sequels are *The Vacant Throne* (2001), *A Dragon's Ascension* (2002), and *The Dragon's Doom* (2003).
Tor, 2000, 304 pp. (0-312-86721-2)
(BL 96:1091; Kirkus 68:26; LJ Feb 15, 2000 p. 202)

5-273 GRIMSHAW, Nigel (Gilroy). *Bluntstone and the Wildkeepers.* Gr. 5–7.
(Orig. British pub. 1974.)
When the Wildkeepers are threatened by a builder named Bluntstone and his "yellow soil-eating monsters," the little people call on dark magic to save themselves. The sequel is *The Wildkeepers' Guest* (1978).
Faber, 1978, 152 pp., o.p.
(BL 75:1090; TLS 1974 p. 721)

5-274 GRIPE, Maria (Kristina). *In the Time of the Bells.* Gr. 5–9. (Orig. Swedish
★ pub. 1965.)
Young Prince Arvid's disregard for his royal duties bodes ill for the kingdom until the astrologers discover that his "whipping boy" is his brother and true heir to the throne.
Trans. by Sheila La Farge, illus. by Harald Gripe, Delacorte, 1976, 208 pp., o.p.
(BL 73:600, 606; CCBB 30:76; HB 53:51; Kirkus 44:982; SLJ Jan 1977 p. 92; TLS 1978 p. 767)

5-275 HALAM, Ann (pseud. of Gwyneth A. Jones). *The Daymaker.* Gr. 7–10.
★ (Orig. British pub. 1987.)
While studying magic at Covenant School, 10-year-old Zanne discovers a hidden cache of forgotten machines and searches for the legendary Daymaker, which can make machines run without magic. In the sequel, *Transformations* (1988), Zanne, now a Covener, is sent to investigate a community infected with black magic by a relic from a long-dead technological world.
Orchard, 1987, 173 pp., o.p.
(BL 84:466, 478; CCBB 41:28; HB 64:70; Kirkus 55:992; SLJ Oct 1987 p. 138; Suth 4:155; TLS 1987 p. 1205; VOYA 10:287)

HALE, F. J. *Ogre Castle.*
See Chapter 12, Witchcraft and Sorcery Fantasy.

HAMBLY, Barbara. *Dragonsbane.*
See Chapter 12, Witchcraft and Sorcery Fantasy.

5-276 HAMBLY, Barbara. *The Ladies of Mandrigyn.* **(The Unschooled Wizard trilogy, bk. 1).** Gr. 10 up.
The women of Mandrigyn trick Sun Wolf, a mercenary captain, into rescuing their men from the wizard who has conquered their city. The sequels are *The Witches of Wenshar* (1987) and *The Dark Hand of Magic* (1990). The first two titles were published together as *The Unschooled Wizard* (Doubleday, 1984–1987).
Ballantine, 1984, pap., 320 pp. (0-345-30919-7)
(BL 80:1378; LJ 109:599)

HAMBLY, Barbara. *The Rainbow Abyss.*
See Chapter 12, Witchcraft and Sorcery Fantasy.

HAMBLY, Barbara. *Sisters of the Raven.*
See Chapter 12, Witchcraft and Sorcery Fantasy.

HAMBLY, Barbara. *Stranger at the Wedding.*
See Chapter 12, Witchcraft and Sorcery Fantasy.

HAMBLY, Barbara. *The Time of the Dark.*
See Chapter 7, High Fantasy: Travel to Other Worlds.

5-277 **HANLEY, Victoria.** *The Seer and the Sword.* Gr. 6–10.
✶ Friends since childhood, Princess Torina and her freed slave Prince Landen
separately run away, each believing the other is dead. The sequel is *The Healer's Keep* (2002).
Holiday, 2000, 341 pp. (0-8234-1532-5); Dell Laurel Leaf, 2003, pap., 352 pp.
(0-440-22977-4)
(BL 97:808; CCBB 54:223; HBG 12:32; Kirkus 68:1681; Kliatt July 2003 p. 32; SLJ Mar
2001 p. 250)

5-278 **HAPTIE, Charlotte.** *Otto and the Flying Twins.* **(The First Book of the**
✶ **Karmidee).** Gr. 4–8. (Orig. British pub. 2002.)
Otto Hish has always thought his family members were "normal" citizens of
the City of Trees, but he discovers that magic blood runs in the family, and that
his own father is the king of the magical karmidees. The sequel is *Otto and the
Bird Charmers* (2004, 2005).
Holiday, 2004, 304 pp. (0-8234-1826-X)
(SLJ June 2004 p. 143)

HARDY, Lyndon. *Secret of the Sixth Magic.*
See Chapter 12, Witchcraft and Sorcery Fantasy.

5-279 **HARLAN, Thomas.** *The Shadow of Ararat.* **(Oath of Empire, bk. 1).** Gr.
10 up.
Dwyrin MacDonald, a young Irishman studying sorcery in Egypt, is caught up
in the 7th-century efforts of the eastern and western Roman emperors to conquer Persia. The sequels are *The Gate of Fire* (2000), *The Storm of Heaven*
(2001), and *The Dark Lord* (2002).
Tor, 1999, 512 pp. (0-312-86543-0)
(BL 95:1930; Kirkus 67:680; LJ Apr 15, 1999 p. 148)

5-280 **HARPER, Tara K.** *Wolfwalker.* **(Tales of the Wolves, bk. 1).** Gr. 7–12.
Healer and wolfwalker Dion, her wolf companion Gray Hishn, and her twin
brother, Rhom, join Aranur's band in an adventurous journey to rescue Aranur's sister and cousins from slave raiders. The sequels are *Shadow Leader*
(1991) and *Storm Runner* (1993).
Ballantine, 1990, pap., 310 pp. (0-345-36539-9)
(Kliatt Sep 1990 p. 21; LJ May 15, 1990 p. 99; VOYA 13:297, 14:13)

HARRIS, Deborah Turner. *The Burning Stone.*
See Chapter 12, Witchcraft and Sorcery Fantasy.

5-281 **HARRIS, Deborah Turner.** *Caledon of the Mists.* Gr. 10 up.
Trained as a sorceress, Princess Charlie must step in to lead the rebellion against the King of England after her brother is murdered. The sequel is *The Queen of Ashes* (1995).
Berkley/Ace, 1994, pap., 400 pp., o.p.
(BL 90:1781, 1787; Kliatt Sep 1994 p. 18, Sep 1995 p. 22; VOYA 17:156)

5-282 **HARRIS, Geraldine (Rachel).** *Prince of the Godborn.* **(Seven Citadels**
✭ **quartet, bk. 1).** Gr. 7–10. (Orig. British pub. 1982.)
Prince Kerish of Galkis is chosen to journey to the seven citadels of the sorcerers to find seven keys that will save his land from its enemies. *The Children of the Wind* (1983), *The Dead Kingdom* (1983), and *The Seventh Gate* (1984) complete the quartet.
Greenwillow, 1983, 186 pp., o.p.; Dell, 1987, pap. (0-440-95407-X)
(BL 79:770, 777, 86:905; CCBB 36:127; HB 59:312; Kirkus 50:1335; SLJ Nov 1983 p. 93; Suth 3:175; VOYA 6:215)

HARRIS, Rosemary (Jeanne). *The Moon in the Cloud.*
See Chapter 6, High Fantasy: Myth or Legend Fantasy.

5-283 **HARRISON, Harry.** *The Hammer and the Cross.* **(The Hammer and the Cross trilogy, bk. 1).** Gr. 10 up.
Shef, half Christian Norman and half pagan Norse, develops his own religion in an attempt to free an alternate 9th-century England from both sets of invaders. The sequels are *One King's Way* (1995, 1996) and *King and Emperor* (1996, 1997).
Tor, 1993, 480 pp. (0-312-85439-0)
(BL 90:132, 140; Kirkus 61:1035)

5-284 **HARRISON, M(ichael) John.** *The Pastel City.* **(Virconium series, bk. 1).** Gr. 10 up. (Orig. British pub. 1971.)
Poet and swordsman Cromis vows to help Queen Methret of Virconium in her battle against the Northern Barbarians who have released powerful ancient golems. The sequels are *A Storm of Wings* (1979), *The Floating Gods* (Pocket, 1983; British title *In Virconium*, 1982), and *Virconium Nights* (Ace, 1984).
Doubleday, 1972, 158 pp., o.p.
(BL 69:620, 644; Kirkus 40:1164; LJ 97:3932)

5-285 **HAYDON, Elizabeth.** *Rhapsody: Child of Blood.* **(The Rhapsody trilogy, vol. 1).** Gr. 10 up.
An assassin, a giant, and a young woman named Rhapsody travel to the center of the world, where a demon threatens the survival of the Great Tree, as well as the entire world, by waking the Primal Wyrm. The sequels are *Prophecy: Child of Earth* (2000, 2001) and *Destiny: Child of the Sky* (2001, 2002). Rhapsody is also the heroine of a second trilogy, the Symphony of Ages saga, which begins with *Requiem for the Sun* (2002) and continues with *Elegy for a Lost Star* (2004).
Doherty, 1999, 544 pp. (0-312-86752-2); Tor, 2000, pap., 656 pp. (0-8125-7081-2)
(BL 95:1986; Kirkus 67:1093; VOYA 22:414)

5-286 HAZEL, Paul. *Yearwood.* **(Finnbranch trilogy, bk. 1).** Gr. 10 up.
Finn, the bastard son of a Kell sorceress, sets out to find his birthright and discovers that his father was actually the High King. The sequels are *Undersea* (1982) and *Winter King* (1985). *The Wealdwife's Tale* (Avon, 1993) is also set in West Redding.
Little, Brown, 1980, 276 pp., o.p.
(HB 56:448; Kirkus 48:150; SLJ Apr 1980 p. 124; VOYA 3:28, 3:32, 4:48)

5-287 HEARN, Lian. *Across the Nightingale Floor.* **(Tales of the Otori trilogy,**
☆   **vol. 1).** Gr. 10 up. (Orig. pub. in England.)
Rescued by Lord Otori during the massacre of his village by Lord Iida, 16-year-old Takeo begins to wonder why Otori has taken such an interest in his developing magical abilities in this book set in an alternate feudal Japan. The sequels are *Grass for His Pillow* (2003) and *Brilliance of the Moon* (2004).
Riverhead, 2002, 304 pp. (1-57322-225-9), 2003, pap. (1-57322-332-8)
(BL 98:1885; Kirkus 70:828; Kliatt Sep 2003 p. 24; LJ Sep 15, 2002 p. 97; SLJ Nov 2002 p. 194, Dec 2002 p. 47; VOYA 26:236)

5-288 HEARNE, Betsy (Gould). *South Star.* Gr. 4–7.
After her parents' murders, Megan, a girl giant, flees the Screamer and follows the South Star across a vast plain and plateau toward a colony of giants. The sequel is *Home* (1979).
Illus. by Trina Schart Hyman, Atheneum, 1977, 84 pp., o.p.
(BL 74:375; CCBB 31:78; HB 53:662; Kirkus 45:990; SLJ Oct 1977 p. 112)

5-289 HELPRIN, Mark. *Winter's Tale.* Gr. 10 up.
Peter Lake escapes from a gang of murderous Manhattan thugs on the back of a flying milk wagon horse in this fast-moving Dickensian tale of romance, comedy, and adventure set in the "future" year 2000.
Harcourt, 1983, 608 pp. (0-15-197203-6); Pocket, 1990, pap., 704 pp. (0-671-72707-9)
(BL 79:1421; HB 60:229; Kirkus 51:717; LJ 108:1502)

5-290 HENRY, Maeve. *The Witch King.* Gr. 3–6. (Orig. British pub. 1987.)
Fifteen-year-old Robert dreams that he must go to the city that, according to prophecy, a Witch King will come from the sea to destroy.
Orchard, 1985, 126 pp., o.p.
(BL 84:1609; CCBB 41:206; Kirkus 56:363; SLJ June–July 1988 p. 104)

5-291 HIGHTMAN, Jason. *The Saint of Dragons.* Gr. 6–9.
Fearing that his son's life is in danger, Aldric St. George, the last Knight of the Order of Dragonhunters, removes Simon from his New England boarding school to help battle dragons threatening human existence in New York, Venice, Paris, Russia, China, and London.
HarperCollins/Eos, 2004, 304 pp. (0-06-054012-5)
(BL 100:1920; CCBB 58:77; Kirkus 72:866; Kliatt July 2004 p. 8; SLJ Sep 2004 p. 208)

5-292 HILL, Douglas (Arthur). *Blade of the Poisoner.* Gr. 6–10.
Three disciples of the good sorcerer Cyrl rescue 12-year-old Jarral from the malevolent Mephtik, who has cursed the boy with a deadly wound, and the four travel to find Cyrl and undo the curse. The sequel is *Master of Fiends* (1988).

Macmillan, 1987, 192 pp., o.p.; Bantam, 1989, pap., 224 pp. (0-553-27717-0)
(BL 84:466,480; Kirkus 55:1240; SLJ Oct 1987 p. 139; VOYA 10:178)

5-293 HIRSCH, Odo. *Bartlett and the Ice Voyage.* Gr.4–7. (Orig. Australian pub.
☆ 2001.)
Explorer Bartlett invents a way to bring the fabled melidrop fruit home for his
queen—inside an iceberg. The sequels are *Bartlett and the City of Flames*
(2003) and *Bartlett and the Forest of Plenty* (2004).
Illus. by Andrew McLean, Bloomsbury, 2003, 176 pp. (1-58234-797-2)
(BL 99:994; HBG 14:368; Kirkus 70:1694; SLJ Jan 2003 p. 138; VOYA 25:476)

5-294 HIRSCH, Odo. *Yoss.* Gr. 7–12. (Orig. Australian pub. 2001.)
In this allegorical tale, Yoss, 14, leaves his isolated village to explore the wider
world, where he is accused of theft, enslaved by a merchant, and eventually
manages to return home.
Delacorte, 2004, 304 pp. (0-385-90224-7)
(BL 101:232; CCBB 58:77; HB 80:585; Kirkus 72:867; SLJ Sep 2004 p. 208)

5-295 HITE, Sid. *Answer My Prayer.* Gr. 7–10.
☆ Lydia Swain and an angel named Ebol embark on a stormy sea voyage to per-
suade the King of Korasan to save the jeefwood forests of their land.
Holt, 1995, 182 pp. (0-8050-3406-4); Dell, 1997, pap. (0-440-22014-9)
(BL 91:1567; CCBB 49:16; HB 71:609; HBG 6:310; Kirkus 63:711; SLJ July 1995 p. 95;
VOYA 18:232)

5-296 HITE, Sid. *The Distance of Hope.* Gr. 6–9.
After Prince Yeshe begins to go blind, he goes on a dangerous journey to find
the White Bean Lama, hoping that his sight can be restored.
Holt, 1998, 198 pp. (0-8050-5054-X)
(BL 94:1236; HBG 9:331; Kirkus 66:581; Kliatt July 1998 p. 7; SLJ May 1998 p. 142;
VOYA 21:129)

HOBAN, Russell C(onwell). *The Mouse and His Child.*
See Chapter 1, Allegorical Fantasy and Literary Fairy Tales.

5-297 HOBB, Robin. *Assassin's Apprentice.* **(The Farseer saga, vol. 1).** Gr. 10
☆ up.
The existence of young Fitz, the king's illegimate son who was secretly raised
to serve as a royal assassin, comes to light when a struggle begins over the
royal succession. The sequels are *Royal Assassin* (1996, 1997) and *Assassin's
Quest* (1997, 1998). The author's Liveship Traders trilogy (see below) is set in
the same world, and The Tawny Man trilogy (see below) continues Fitz's
story. Hobb also writes as Megan Lindholm (see *Luck of the Wheels* in this
section).
Bantam, 1995, pap., 368 pp. (0-553-37445-1), 1996, pap., 464 pp. (0-553-
57339-X)
(BL 91:1381; Kirkus 63:275; Kliatt Sep 1995 p. 22; LJ Mar 15, 1995 p. 100)

5-298 HOBB, Robin. *Fool's Errand.* **(The Tawny Man trilogy, vol. 1).** Gr. 10 up.
Related to her Farseer trilogy (see above), Fitz, now in his mid-30s, is talked
into undertaking a new quest by his old friend the Fool, now called the Tawny
Man, after Prince Dutiful's romance-gone-wrong bodes ill for the future of the

kingdom. The sequels are *Golden Fool* (2003) and *Fool's Fate* (2004). The author's Liveship Traders trilogy (see below) is set in the same world. Hobb also writes as Megan Lindholm (see *Luck of the Wheels* in this section).
Bantam/Spectrum, 2002, 496 pp. (0-553-80148-1)
(BL 98:709; Kirkus 69:1461; VOYA 24:446)

5-299   HOBB, Robin. *Ship of Magic.* **(The Liveship Traders trilogy, vol. 1).** Gr. 10 up.
Driven off her family's sentient sailing ship, *Vivacia,* Althea Vestrit becomes a sailor and battles pirates in an attempt to reverse her family's fortunes. The sequels are *Mad Ship* (1999, 2000) and *Ship of Destiny* (2000, 2001). This series is set in the same world as the author's Farseer saga (see above) and Tawny Man trilogy (see above). Hobb also writes as Megan Lindholm (see *Luck of the Wheels* in this section).
Bantam, 1998, 704 pp. (0-553-10324-5)
(BL 94:1098, 1607; Kirkus 66:87; LJ Feb 15, 1998 p. 173; VOYA 21:283)

5-300   HODGELL, P(atricia) C(hristine). *God Stalk.* **(Dark of the Gods duology, vol. 1).** Gr. 10 up.
In flight after her home is destroyed, Jame, one of the last of the magical race of Kencyrs, finds refuge and new friends in Taitastigon, where she becomes involved in political, religious, and magical intrigues. The sequel is *Dark of the Moon* (1985). Both books have been republished in *Dark of the Gods* (Meisha Merlin, 2000).
Macmillan, 1982, 293 pp., o.p.
(BL 79:189, 198; LJ 107:1772)

5-301   HOFFMAN, Alice. *Green Angel.* Gr. 6–10.
✶   Named for her gardening talents, 15-year-old Green retreats into numbness and pain after her family is killed in the destruction of the city across the river from their home.
Scholastic, 2003, 128 pp. (0-439-44384-9), 2004, pap., 128 pp. (0-439-44385-7)
(BL 99:1462; CCBB 56:316; HB 79:211; HBG 14:368; Kirkus 71:61; Kliatt Jan 2003 p. 8; SLJ Mar 2003 p. 234; VOYA 26:51)

5-302   HOFFMAN, Lee. *Change Song.* Gr. 10 up.
Young Dorey joins forces with a Nightman named Ryik, whose job it is to control the elements with magic, in an attempt to save the world from destruction by uncontrollable natural forces.
Doubleday, 1972, 203 pp., o.p.
(BL 68:931, 940; Kirkus 40:15; LJ 97:217, 98:660)

HOFFMAN, Nina Kiriki. *A Red Heart of Memories.*
See Chapter 4, Ghost Fantasy.

5-303   HOOD, Daniel. *Scales of Justice.* **(Fanuilh series, vol. 4).** Gr. 10 up.
Liam Rhenford investigates the capital cases brought before the duke's court with the help of his dragon, Fanuilh, and a forbidden book called *Dominia Daemonologia,* until he, himself, is imprisoned in Deepenmoor dungeon. This book is preceded by *Fanuilh* (1994), *Wizard's Heir* (1995), and *Beggar's Banquet* (1997), and is followed by *King's Cure* (2000). *A Familiar Dragon* (Guild America, 1997) is a compilation of books 1–3.

Ace, 1998, pap., 304 pp. (0-441-00515-2)

(Kliatt May 1998 p. 21; LJ Mar 15, 1998 p. 99; VOYA 21:130)

5-304 **HOROWITZ, Anthony.** *The Devil and His Boy.* Gr. 5–9. (Orig. British pub.
✬ 1998.)
After the mysterious gentleman who brought Tom Falconer to London is murdered, Tom joins a group of players putting on the drama "The Devil and His Boy" in this story set in Elizabethan England.
Philomel, 2000, 192 pp. (0-399-23432-2); Puffin, 2001, pap., 182 pp. (0-698-11913-4)

(BL 96:922; CCBB 53:246; HBG 11:305; Kirkus 67:1885; Kliatt May 2000 p. 9; SLJ Apr 2000 p. 136; VOYA 23:35)

5-305 **HUFF, Tanya.** *Sing the Four Quarters.* **(Quarters series, bk. 1).** Gr. 10 up.
(Orig. pub. in Canada.)
Princess Annice must trade her royal privilege for permission to become a bard, a magical traveller with power over the kigh, spirits of earth, fire, water, and air. The sequels are *Fifth Quarter* (1995), *No Quarter* (1996), and *The Quartered Sea* (1999).
DAW, 1994, 410 pp. (0-88677-628-7)

(Kliatt May 1995 p. 14; VOYA 18:34)

5-306 **HUFF, Tanya.** *Summon the Keeper.* **(The Keeper's Chronicles, vol. 1).**
Gr. 7–12. (Orig. pub. in Canada.)
Claire Hanson and her talking cat, Austin, are summoned to the Elysian Fields Guesthouse where they discover a hidden Keeper, who remains asleep because of energy leaking through a hole in the fabric of the universe. The sequels are *The Second Summoning* (2001) and *Long Hot Summoning* (2003).
DAW, 1998, pap., 331 pp. (0-88677-784-4)

(LJ Apr 15, 1998 p. 119; VOYA 21:284, 22:13)

5-307 **HUGHART, Barry.** *Bridge of Birds: A Novel of an Ancient China That Never Was.* **(Master Li series, bk. 1).** Gr. 10 up.
Young Lu Yu and the great sage Lio Kao set off in search of a magic root to cure the mysterious illness suffered by the children of the village of Ku-Fu, and encounter ghosts and danger along the way. World Fantasy Award, 1984. The sequels are *The Story of the Stone* (1988) and *Eight Skilled Gentlemen* (1991).
St. Martin's, 1984, 256 pp., o.p.; Ballantine, 1985, pap., 278 pp. (0-345-32138-3)

(Kirkus 52:314; Kliatt Fall 1985 p. 22; LJ 109:997)

5-308 **HUGHES, Carol.** *Jack Black and the Ship of Thieves.* Gr. 5–8.
✬ Jack is captured by Captain Quixote and the gang of thieves who man the Hyperion after his father's airship, the *Bellerophon*, is lost.
Random, 2000, 240 pp. (0-375-90472-7), 2001, pap., 240 pp. (0-375-80473-0)

(BL 97:438; CCBB 54:22; HB 76:569; HBG 12:74; Kirkus 68:885; SLJ Sep 2000 p. 232; VOYA 24:133, 25:14)

5-309 **HUGHES, Matthew.** *Fools Errant: A Fantasy Picaresque.* Gr. 10 up.
Filidor Vesh, nephew of the ruler or Archon of old Earth, and his dwarf traveling companion encounter an evil wizard, fearsome beasts, and other challenges while traveling to a distant principality. The sequel is *Fool Me Twice* (2001).

Warner, 2001, pap., 304 pp. (0-446-60923-4)

(LJ Jan 2001 p. 163; VOYA 24:12, 53)

5-310 **HUGHES, Monica.** *Sandwriter.* Gr. 6–9. (Original Canadian pub. 1986.)
Spoiled Princess Antia matures during her visit to the desert kingdom of
Roshan, whose prince is rumored to be her future husband. The sequel is *The
Promise* (1992).
Henry Holt, 1988, 159 pp., o.p.

(BL 84:576, 1241, 1259; CCBB 41:138; Kirkus 56:55; SLJ Mar 1988 p. 214; VOYA 11:139)

HUGHES, Robert Don. *The Faithful Traitor.*
See Chapter 12, Witchcraft and Sorcery Fantasy.

5-311 *Imaginary Lands.* **Ed. by Robin McKinley.** Gr. 7 up.
✮ Nine tales about imaginary worlds, written by Peter Dickinson, P. C. Hodgell,
Patricia McKillip, Robin McKinley, Joan D. Vigne, Robert Westall, and Jane
Yolen. World Fantasy Convention Award, 1986. Robin McKinley's story "The
Stone Fey" was published in picture-book format by Harcourt, 1998.
Berkley, 1985, pap., o.p.; Greenwillow, 1986, 160pp., LB (0-688-05213-4)

(BL 82:609, 621, 628; CCBB 39:152; HB 62:459; Kirkus 54:870; SLJ May 1986 p. 106; TLS
1987 p. 857; VOYA 9:162)

5-312 **IRVINE, Ian.** *A Shadow on the Glass.* **(The View from the Mirror saga,
vol. 1).** Gr. 10 up.
Llian's final test before becoming a master chronicler is to retell the Tale of the
Forbidding, but when his version incorporates new knowledge, his future is
jeopardized. The sequels are *The Tower on the Rift* (2002), *Dark Is the Moon*
(2002), and *The Way Between the Worlds* (2002).
Warner, 2001, pap., 655 pp. (0-446-60984-6)

(LJ July 1, 2001 p. 131; VOYA 24:290)

IVES, David. *Monsieur Eek.*
See Chapter 8, Humorous Fantasy.

5-313 **JAMES, Betsy.** *Long Night Dance.* Gr. 7 up.
✮ Kat finds the rigid Upslope customs of her father's people too confining, but
not until the night she rescues a wounded Rigi man from across the sea does
she begin to declare her independence. In the sequel, *Dark Heart* (1992), Kat
has chosen to live among her dead mother's people, but fails the ritual ceremony that would allow her to join the Women's Circle.
Dutton, 1989, 170 pp. (0-525-44485-8); Simon Pulse, 2005, pap., 208 pp. (0-
689-85071-9)

(BL 85:1894, 1903; CCBB 42:277; HB 65:775; HBG 1:81; Kirkus 57:917; SLJ Aug 1989 p.
140; VOYA 12:226, 13:14)

5-314 **JANSSON, Tove (Marika).** *Finn Family Moomintroll.* **(Moomintroll
✮ series, bk. 1).** Gr. 4–6. (Orig. Finnish pub. 1949, orig. U.S. pub. Walck, 1951,
entitled *The Happy Moomins*, retitled *Finn Family Moomintroll*, 1958.)
Trouble comes to Moominvalley, home of the gnomelike Moomins, when
Moomintroll, Sniff, and Snufkin bring home a hobgoblin's hat. The sequels are
Moominsummer Madness (1961; Farrar, 1991), *Moominland Midwinter* (1962;
Farrar, 1992), *Tales from Moominvalley* (1964; Farrar, 1995), *The Exploits of*

Moominpappa (1966), *Moominpappa at Sea* (1967; Farrar, 1993), *A Comet in Moominland* (1959, 1968; Farrar, 1991), *Moominvalley in November* (1971, Farar, 2003), *Moominpappa's Memoirs* (Farrar, 1994), and *The Book About Moomin, Mymble and Little My* (Laughing Elephant, 1997; Nils Holgersson Award, Best Swedish Children's Book, 1953).
Trans. by Elizabeth Portch, illus. by the author, Walck, 1958, 1965, 170 pp., o.p.; Farrar, 1989, 174 pp., o.p.; Sunburst, 1990, pap., 176 pp. (0-374-42307-5)
(CCBB 5:74; HBG 1:81; LJ 77:653)

5-315 **JARVIS, Robin.** *Thorn Ogres of Hagwood.* **(The Hagwood trilogy, bk. 1).**
☆ Gr. 5–9. (Orig. British pub. 1999.)
Young Gamaliel Tumpin and his tribe of small, shape-shifting Werling folk are attacked by the terrible forces of the High Lady, who believes that Gamaliel can lead her to the golden casket containing her lost heart.
Silver Whistle/Harcourt, 2002, 256 pp. (0-15-216752-8); Magic Carpet, 2004, pap., 264 pp. (0-15-205122-8)
(BL 99:496, 1465; CCBB 56:161; HBG 14:83; Kirkus 70:1311; Kliatt Jan 2003 p. 8; SLJ Nov 2002 p. 169; VOYA 25:488, 26:12)

5-316 **JONES, Adrienne.** *The Hawks of Chelney.* Gr. 7–9.
☆ In this haunting tale, a lonely boy named Ski is persecuted by superstitious vil-lage elders because of his friendship with ospreys, "the Devil's servants."
Illus. by Stephen Gammell, Harper, 1978, 245 pp., o.p.
(BL 74:1108; CCBB 32:45; HB 54:283; Kirkus 46:640; SLJ Apr 1978 p. 94; VOYA 1:35)

5-317 **JONES, Dennis.** *The Stone and the Maiden.* **(The House of the Pandragore series, vol. 1).** Gr. 10 up.
Princess Mandine Dascaris and young warrior Key Mec Brander battle invad-ing barbarian Tathars led by an evil sorcerer, while looking for the mysterious Signata that can save their kingdom, the Ascendancy. The sequel is *The Mask and the Sorceress* (2001, 2002).
Avon, 1999, 432 pp. (0-380-97801-6); Eos, 2000, 432 pp. (0-380-80617-7)
(Kirkus 67:840; LJ July 1999 p. 143; SLJ Jan 2000 p. 156)

5-318 **JONES, Diana Wynne.** *Cart and Cwidder.* **(The Dalemark quartet, bk. 1).**
☆ Gr. 6–9. (Orig. British pub. 1975.)
Moril inherits an ancient cwidder, a lutelike instrument, whose mystical pow-ers save him and his family from the murderous Southern warriors. *Drowned Ammet* (1978; see below), *The Spellcoats* (1979; see below), and *The Crown of Dalemark* (1993, 1996, 2001; see *Drowned Ammet* below), which won the 1996 Mythopoeic Fantasy Award for Children's Literature, are also set in the land of Dalemark.
Atheneum, 1977, 193 pp., o.p.; Greenwillow, 1995, 214 pp. (0-688-13360-6); Greenwillow, 2001, 214 pp. (0-06-623745-9), 2001, pap. (0-06-447313-9)
(BL 73:1014; CCBB 30:161; HB 53:443; HBG 12:323; Kirkus 45:224; SLJ May 1977 p. 70; TLS 1975 p. 764; VOYA 13:229, 19:17)

5-319 **JONES, Diana Wynne.** *Castle in the Air.* Gr. 6–9. (Orig. British pub. 1990.)
☆ Abdulla the carpet merchant's daydreams about a princess, a genie, and a vil-lain become reality after he flies off on a shabby magic carpet. This story is

related to *Howl's Moving Castle* (1986, 2001; see Chapter 12, Witchcraft and Sorcery Fantasy).

Greenwillow, 1991, 208 pp. (0-688-09686-7); Greenwillow, 2001, 298 pp. (0-06-447345-7), HarperTrophy, 2001, pap. (0-06-447345-7)

(BL 87:1502, 88:873, 932; CCBB 44:143; HB 67:206; HBG 2:274; Kirkus 59:249; SLJ Apr 1991 p. 141)

JONES, Diana Wynne. *Charmed Life.*
See Chapter 10, Time Travel Fantasy.

JONES, Diana Wynne. *Dark Lord of Derkholm.*
See Chapter 12, Witchcraft and Sorcery Fantasy.

JONES, Diana Wynne. *Deep Secret.*
See Chapter 12, Witchcraft and Sorcery Fantasy.

5-320 **JONES, Diana Wynne. *Drowned Ammet.* (The Dalemark quartet, bk. 2).**
✶ Gr. 6–9. (Orig. British pub. 1977.)
Mitt's plot to revenge his father's death misfires and he escapes by ship to the Holy Islands. *Cart and Cwidder* (1977; see above) and *The Spellcoats* (1979; see below) are also set in the land of Dalemark. In the sequel, *The Crown of Dalemark* (1993, 1995, 2001), Mitt, having fled a murder charge in the South, is asked to assassinate Noreth, who plans to reunite Dalemark and become its queen. *The Crown of Dalemark* won the 1996 Mythopoeic Fantasy Award for Children's Literature.
Atheneum, 1978, 255 pp., o.p.; Greenwillow, 1995, 312 pp. (0-688-13361-4); Greenwillow, 2001, 312 pp. (0-06-029872-3), 2001, pap., 336 pp. (0-06-447314-7)
(BL 74:1255; CCBB 31:161; HB 54:403; HBG 12:323; Kirkus 46:177; SLJ Apr 1978 p. 85; TLS 1978 p. 377, VOYA 19:17)

5-321 **JONES, Diana Wynne. *The Homeward Bounders.* Gr. 6–9. (Orig. British**
✶ pub. 1981.)
When Jamie accidentally stumbles on the headquarters of "Their" war games, "They" discard him to the worlds on the Bounds, where he joins other Homeward Bounders in a battle to banish "Them."
Greenwillow, 1981, 224 pp. (0-688-00678-7); Greenwillow, 2002, 272 pp. (0-06-029886-3); Greenwillow, 2002, pap., 272 pp. (0-06-447353-8)
(BL:78:98, 108; CCBB 35:12; HB 57:542; HBG 13:392; Kirkus 49:1164; SLJ Sep 1981 p. 137; TLS 1981 pp. 339, 1361)

JONES, Diana Wynne. *The Magicians of Caprona.*
See Chapter 12, Witchcraft and Sorcery Fantasy.

JONES, Diana Wynne. *The Merlin Conspiracy.*
See Chapter 12, Witchcraft and Sorcery Fantasy.

JONES, Diana Wynne. *The Power of Three.*
See Chapter 6, High Fantasy: Myth or Legend Fantasy.

5-322 **JONES, Diana Wynne. *The Spellcoats.* (The Dalemark quartet, bk. 3).**
Gr. 6–10. (Orig. British pub. 1979.)

Tanaqui and her orphaned brother and sisters must flee their village because they look like the enemy Heathen. During their voyage, Tanaqui weaves their story into rugcoats, which prove to have magical powers. This story is set in the prehistory of Dalemark, the setting for *Cart and Cwidder* (1979; see above), *Drowned Ammet* (1978; see above), and *The Crown of Dalemark* (1993, 1995, 2001; see *Drowned Ammet* above), which won the 1996 Mythopoeic Fantasy Award for Children's Literature.

Atheneum, 1979, 249 pp., o.p.; Greenwillow, 1995, 280 pp. (0-688-13362-2); Greenwillow, 2001, 279 pp. (0-06-029873-1), 2001, pap. (0-06-447315-5)

(CCBB 33:111; HB 55:669; HBG 12:323; Kirkus 47:1072; SLJ Nov 1979 p. 89; VOYA 2:30, 19:17)

5-323   JONES, J(ulie) V(ictoria). *The Baker's Boy.* **(Book of Words trilogy, vol. 1).** Gr. 10 up. (Orig. British pub. 1995.)

Melliandra and Jack run away from Castle Harvell, Mellie to escape an unwanted marriage and orphaned baker's apprentice Jack to hide his new magical powers. The sequels are *A Man Betrayed* (1996) and *Master and Fool* (1996, 1997). The author's Sword of Shadows trilogy (see *A Fortress of Grey Ice*, below) is set in the same world.

Warner, 1995, 528 pp. (0-446-67097-9)

(Kirkus 63:676; Kliatt Sep 1995 p. 22; LJ May 15, 1995 p. 99; VOYA 18:172)

5-324   JONES, J(ulie) V(ictoria). *A Fortress of Grey Ice.* **(Sword of Shadows trilogy, bk. 2).** Gr. 10 up. (Orig. British pub. 2000.)

Lovers Raif Severance and Ash March are separated after she is kidnapped, and he must choose between attempting her rescue and completing his quest to find the Fortress of Black Ice. *A Cavern of Black Ice* (1999, 2000) is the first book of the trilogy, and *A Sword from Red Ice* (2004) is the sequel. This series is set in the same world as the author's Book of Words trilogy (see *The Baker's Boy*, above).

Warner, 2000, pap. (0-446-52476-X); Tor, 2003, pap., 672 pp. (0-765-30633-6)

(BL 99:1968; LJ Aug 2003 p. 142)

5-325   JONES, McClure. *Cast Down the Stars.* Gr. 7–10.

Glory and her friend Honor must repair a gap in the ancient serpent line to keep out barbarian invaders.

Holt, 1978, 186 pp., o.p.

(BL 75:178; CCBB 32:100; HB 55:68; SLJ Dec 1978 p. 53)

5-326   JONES, Terry. *The Lady and the Squire.* Gr. 5–7. (Orig. British pub. 2000.)

English friends Tom and Ann are joined by the aristocratic Emilia de Valois for a fast-paced series of adventures while traveling through war-torn medieval France. This book is the sequel to *The Knight and the Squire* (1997, 2000).

Illus. by Michael Foreman, Trafalgar Square, 2001, 304 pp. (1-86205-417-7)

(BL 97:1137; SLJ Mar 2001 p. 250)

5-327   JORDAN, Robert. *The Conan Chronicles.* **(Chronicles of Conan).** Gr. 7–12.

This compilation of three novels written by Jordan as sequels to Robert E. Howard's stories about Conan the Barbarian describes the magical adventures of a barbarian swordsman. The novels are *Conan the Invincible* (1982), *Conan the Defender* (1982), and *Conan the Unconquered* (1983). *The Further Chronicles of Conan* (1999) contains *Conan the Triumphant* (1983), *Conan the Magnificent* (1984), and *Conan the Victorious* (1984). Harry Turtledove has written a prequel about Conan's youth: *Conan of Venarium* (Tor, 2003).

Tor, 1995, 510 pp. (0-312-85929-5)

(Kirkus 63:596; Kliatt 18:22, 28; VOYA 18:384)

5-328 JORDAN, Robert. *The Eye of the World.* **(The Wheel of Time Saga, bk.**
✮ **1).** Gr. 10 up.

Rand, Matrim, and Perrin leave their farming village with an Aes Sedai, or witch, after it becomes clear that the Dark One has marked them for death. The sequels are *The Great Hunt* (1990), *The Dragon Reborn* (1991, 2002, pap.), *The Shadow Rising* (1992), *The Fires of Heaven* (1993), *Lord of Chaos* (1994), *A Crown of Swords* (1996, 1997), *The Path of Daggers* (1998), *Winter's Heart* (2000), and *Crossroads of Twilight* (2003). *A New Spring* (2004) is a prequel to the series.

Tor, 1990, 670 pp., o.p., 1990, pap. (0-8125-1181-6)

(BL 86:218, 220, 87:968, 1478; Kirkus 57:1791; LJ Feb 15, 1990 p. 215; VOYA 13:116, 14:10, 73)

5-329 JORDAN, Sherryl. *The Hunting of the Last Dragon.* Gr. 6–9. (Orig. New
✮ Zealand pub. 2002.)

Jin-wei, a young Chinese noblewoman, is rescued from a traveling carnival cage by Jude, an English peasant boy fated to kill the last dragon in 14th-century England.

HarperCollins, 2002, 128 pp. (0-06-028903-1); Eos, 2003, pap., 256 pp. (0-06-447231-0)

(BL 98:1416, 99:227; CCBB 56:23; HBG 13:392; Kirkus 70:735; Kliatt Sep 2003 p. 26; SLJ July 2002 p. 121; VOYA 25:202)

5-330 JORDAN, Sherryl. *Secret Sacrament.* Gr. 7–12. (Orig. New Zealand pub.
✮✮ 1996.)

Trained as a healer-priest at the Citadel, Gabriel falls in love with a Shinali woman named Ashila, but continues to be haunted by guilt about his childhood failure to save the life of a Shinali slave.

HarperCollins, 2001, 352 pp. (0-06-028905-8), 2003, pap., 512 pp. (0-06-447230-2)

(BL 97:1134, 98:225; CCBB 54:266; HBG 12:323; Kirkus 68:1683; SLJ Feb 2001 p. 118; VOYA 24:133, 25:14)

5-331 JORDAN, Sherryl. *Winter of Fire.* Gr. 7–12. (Orig. New Zealand pub.
✮ 1992.)

After Elsha rises from slave labor in the Quelled mines to become the powerful firelord, she speaks out against the dehumanizing Chosen's enslavement of the Quelled.

Scholastic, 1993, 336 pp. (0-590-45288-6)

(BL 90:1358; CCBB 46:214; HBG 4:309; Kirkus 61:62; SLJ Mar 1993 p. 221; VOYA 16:41)

5-332 JORDAN, Sherryl. *Wolf-Woman.* Gr. 6–10. (Orig. pub. in New Zealand, entitled *Tanith*, 1994.)

Adopted by Chief Ahern after being raised by wolves, Tanith must eventually choose between life with her wolf-hating clan or a return to the wolf pack.

Short List, Esther Glen Award, 1995.
Houghton, 1994, 168 pp. (0-395-70932-6); Dell, 1996, pap. (0-440-21969-8)
(BL 91:590, 1403; CCBB 48:131; HBG 6:88; SLJ Aug 1995 p. 38; VOYA 17:275)

5-333   **KAABERBOL, Lene.** *The Shamer's Daughter.* **(The Shamer Chronicles,**
★   **vol. 1).** Gr. 6–9. (Orig pub. in Denmark; orig. British pub. 2002.)
Eleven-year-old Dina is forced to use her despised inherited power to save her
imprisoned mother and an innocent boy accused of murder by forcing the true
villain to reveal his evil deeds. The sequels are *The Shamer's Signet* (2003,
2005) and *Shamer's War* (2005 in the UK).
Holt, 2004, 240 pp. (0-8050-7541-0)
(BL 100:1450; CCBB 57:377; HB 80:329; Kirkus 72:396; SLJ June 2004 p. 143; VOYA
27:42)

5-334   **KAY, Guy Gavriel.** *The Lions of Al-Rassan.* Gr. 10 up.
★   Ridrigo and Ammar, exiled warriors from opposing Jaddite and Asharite kingdoms, join forces, while a physician named Jehane bet Ishak falls in love with
both of them. This story follows *A Song for Arbonne* (1992; see below) and
both books are set several centuries later in the same world as the author's
Sarantine Mosaic series (1998–2004, see below).
HarperPrism, 1995, 528 pp. (0-06-105217-5), 1999, pap., 554 pp. (0-06-
105621-9)
(BL 81:1729; Kirkus 63:514; LJ June 15, 1995 p. 97; VOYA 18:234, 19:18)

5-335   **KAY, Guy Gavriel.** *Sailing to Sarantium.* **(The Sarantine Mosaic, bk. 1).**
Gr. 10 up.
Set several centuries earlier than *A Song for Arbonne* (1992; see below) and
The Lions of Al-Rassan (1995; see above), in a world similar to Byzantium,
Caius Crispin, a master mosaicist from Rhodius, travels to Sarantium to work
on the Great Temple after his family dies of the plague. The sequel is *Lord of
Emperors* (2000, 2001), and *The Last Light of the Sun* (2004) is set 300 years
later.
HarperPrism, 1998, 384 pp. (0-06-105117-9), 2000, pap., 546 pp. (0-06-
105990-0)
(BL 95:842; LJ Dec 1998 p. 161; VOYA 21:443, 22:14)

5-336   **KAY, Guy Gavriel.** *A Song for Arbonne.* Gr. 10 up. (Orig. Canadian pub.
1992.)
While the neighboring kingdoms of Arbonne (ruled by courtly love) and
Gorhaut (ruled by ambition) prepare for war, young Blaise flees Gorhaut and
allies himself with the powerful Arbonnian troubadour, Bertran. The sequel is
The Lions of Al-Rassan (1995; see above); both books are set several centuries
later that the author's Sarantine Mosaic (see above).
Crown, 1993, 513 pp. (0-517-59312-2); NAL, 1994, pap. (0-451-45332-8)
(BL 89:878, 886; Kirkus 60:1339)

5-337   **KELLEHER, Victor (pseud. of Michael Kitchener).** *Brother Night.* Gr.
★   6–9. (Orig. Australian pub. 1991.)
Rabon learns that Lal, the ugly swamp creature, is his twin brother, and that
both are destined to rule the land.

Illus. by Peter Clarke, Walker, 1991, 179 pp. (0-8027-8100-4)

(BL 87:1955; CCBB 44:241; HBG 2:275; SLJ May 1991 p. 111; VOYA 14:244, 15:9)

5-338 **KELLEHER, Victor (pseud. of Michael Kitchener).** *The Red King.* Gr.
☆ 6–9. (Orig. Australian pub. 1989.)

Timkin, a young acrobat and slave, joins an old thief named Petie, a huge bear named Bruno, and a monkey named Crystal in their efforts to dethrone the evil Red King.

Dial, 1990, 185 pp., o.p.; Oxford University Press, 1991, pap. (0-19-506976-5)

(BL 86:1540,1555; CCBB 43:269; HBG 1:256; Kirkus 58:650; SLJ July 1990 p. 89; VOYA 13:116, 14:12)

5-339 **KELLOGG, M(arjorie) Bradley.** *The Book of Earth.* **(The Dragon Quartet, vol. 1).** Gr. 7 up.

After an evil priest takes over her father's powers and orders the death of her friend Rainer, Erde runs away in search of a dragon named Earth, with whom she can magically communicate. The sequels are *The Book of Water* (1997) and *The Book of Fire* (2000).

DAW, 1995, 336 pp. (0-88677-574-4)

(Kliatt May 1995 p. 14; VOYA 18:8, 34)

5-340 **KENDALL, Carol (Seeger).** *The Firelings.* Gr. 7–9. (Orig. British pub. 1981.)

Marked by his fellow Firelings as a sacrifice to appease the volcano, a boy named Tackyobbie runs away and manages to fulfill an old prophecy. Mythopoeic Fantasy Award, 1983.

Atheneum, 1982, 252 pp., o.p.

(BL 78:1161; CCBB 35:151; HB 58:299; SLJ May 1982 p. 70; TLS 1981 p. 1065; VOYA 5:49)

5-341 **KENDALL, Carol (Seeger).** *The Gammage Cup.* Gr. 4–7. (British title *The*
☆☆ *Minnipins*, 1960.)

Four nonconformists banished to the mountains by their fellow Minnipins risk their lives to save the country when it is invaded by the Mushroom People. John Newbery Medal Honor Book, 1960. *The Whisper of Glocken* (1965; see below) takes place in the same land at a later time period.

Illus. by Erik Blegvad, Harcourt, 1959, o.p., 1990, pap., 283 pp. (0-15-230575-0); Harcourt, 2000, 284 pp. (0-15-202487-5); Harcourt, 2000, pap. (0-15-202493-X)

(BL 56:248; Eakin:187; HB 34:477; LJ 85:845)

5-342 **KENDALL, Carol (Seeger).** *The Whisper of Glocken.* Gr. 5–7.
☆ Five Minnipins become heroes in the course of adventures forced on them when flooding drives them from their homes. This story is set in the same world at a later time period than *The Gammage Cup* (1959; see above).

Illus. by Imero Gobbato, Harcourt, 1965, o.p., 1986, pap., 256 pp. (0-15-295699-9); Harcourt, 2000, 305 pp. (0-15-202511-1), Harcourt, 2000, pap. (0-15-202517-0)

(BL 62:331; CCBB 19:84; Eakin:187; HB 42:54; Kirkus 33:1042; LJ 90:5097)

5-343 **KENNEALY-MORRISON, Patricia.** *The Copper Crown: A Novel of the Keltiad.* **(Books of the Keltiad, vol. 1).** Gr. 10 up.

High Queen Aeron of Keltia proposes an alliance with Earth, precipitating a war with two hostile planetary systems, fought with magic as well as technology, in this blend of science fiction and fantasy. This book lists an alternative series title: Tales of Aeron. The sequels are *The Throne of Scone* (1986), *Blackmantle: A Triumph* (HarperPrism, 1997, 1998), and *The Deer's Cry* (HarperPrism, 1997, 1998, 1999). *The Silver Branch* (NAL, 1988) is a prequel. Kennealy-Morrison's Tales of Arthur series (see *The Hawk's Gray Feather* in Chapter 6, High Fantasy: Myth or Legend Fantasy) is set in the same world, but 1,500 years earlier.
Bluejay, 1984, o.p.; NAL, 1986, pap., 432 pp. (0-451-45050-7)
(Kirkus 52:936; LJ 109:2301; VOYA 8:364)

KENNEALY-MORRISON, Patricia. *The Hawk's Gray Feather: A Book of the Keltiad.*
See Chapter 6, High Fantasy: Myth or Legend Fantasy.

5-344   KERNER, Elizabeth. *Song in the Silence: The Tale of Lanen Kaelar.* Gr. 7–12.
Lanen Kaelar's dreams of dragons lead her to search for the True Dragons of the West, pursued by magical demons. The sequel is *The Lesser Kindred* (2001). The third book in the series is *Redeeming the Lost* (2004).
Tor, 1997, 384 pp. (0-312-85780-2), 1998, pap., 401 pp. (0-812-55044-7)
(BL 93:1008; Kirkus 64:1772; LJ Feb 15, 1997 p. 81; VOYA 20:118, 21:13, 21:37)

KERR, Katharine. *Daggerspell.*
See Chapter 12, Witchcraft and Sorcery Fantasy.

5-345   KERR, Katharine. *The Red Wyvern.* **(The Dragon Mage, vol. 1).** Gr. 10 ★ up.
Lilli puts her untrained magic abilities to use in the cause of Prince Mazyn, who is fighting a civil war to unite the land of Deverry. The sequels are *The Black Raven* (1999, 2000) and *The Fire Dragon* (2001). This book is set in the same world as the author's Deverry series (see *Daggerspell*, 1986, in Chapter 12, Witchcraft and Sorcery Fantasy) and her Westlands series (see below).
Bantam, 1997, 416 pp. (0-553-37290-4), 1998, pap. (0-553-57264-4)
(BL 94:312; Kirkus 65:1346; Kliatt Mar 1998 p. 19; LJ Nov 15, 1997 p. 79; VOYA 21:56)

5-346   KERR, Katharine. *A Time of Exile: A Novel of the Westlands.* **(Westlands series, vol. 1).** Gr. 10 up.
Half-elven Lord Rhodry grows to accept his elven heritage with the help of Wizard Aderyn and Master Wizard Nevyn. The sequels are *A Time of Omens* (1992), *Days of Blood and Fire* (1993), and *Days of Air and Darkness* (1994). Kerr's Deverry series is set in the same world (see *Daggerspell*, 1986, in Chapter 12, Witchcraft and Sorcery Fantasy), as is her Dragon Mage series (see above).
Doubleday, 1991, 416 pp., o.p.; Bantam, 1992, pap. (0-553-29813-5)
(BL 87:1282, 1283; Kirkus 59:510; LJ Mar 15, 1991 p. 119; VOYA 14:323)

KERR, Peg. *Emerald House Rising.*
See Chapter 12, Witchcraft and Sorcery Fantasy.

5-347 **KEYES, J. Gregory.** *The Briar King.* **(The Kingdoms of Thorn and Bone**
✮ **series, bk. 1).** Gr. 10 up.
The nightmare Briar King is waking, and the terrified inhabitants of Everon
turn to the king's youngest daughter, Princess Anne Dare, who enlists the aid
of the king's forester, Aspar White, priestly scholar Stephen Darige, queen's
guard Neil MeqVren, and swordsman Cazio da Chiovattio. The sequel is *The
Charnel Prince* (2004).
Del Rey, 2003, 560 pp. (0-345-44066-8), 2004, pap., 608 pp. (0-345-44070-6)
(BL 99:652; Kirkus 70:1578; LJ Jan 2003 p. 164; SLJ Aug 2003 p. 187; VOYA 26:12, 65)

5-348 **KEYES, J. Gregory.** *Newton's Cannon.* **(The Age of Unreason, vol. 1).**
✮ Gr. 10 up.
In an alternate Europe in 1715, an apprentice alchemist named Ben Franklin
makes discoveries that endanger his life and flees to the great alchemist Sir
Isaac Newton for protection. The sequels are *A Calculus of Angels* (1999),
Empire of Unreason (2000, 2001), and *The Shadows of God* (2001, 2002).
Ballantine, 1998, pap., 480 pp. (0-345-40605-2); Del Rey, 1999, pap., 384 pp.
(0-345-43378-5)
(BL 94:1601; Kirkus 66:537; Kliatt Sep 1998 p. 28; LJ May 15, 1998 p. 118, Jan 1999 p. 57;
VOYA 21:284)

KINDL, Patrice. *Goose Chase.*
See Chapter 8, Humorous Fantasy.

5-349 **KING, Stephen.** *The Eyes of the Dragon.* Gr. 9 up.
✮ .After old King Roland is mysteriously poisoned, his eldest son, Peter, is
imprisoned for the crime and Thomas, the younger son, assumes the throne
with the evil magician, Flagg, as his adviser.
Illus. by David Palladini, Viking, 1987, 336 pp. (0-670-81458-X); NAL, 1987,
pap. (0-451-16658-2)
(BL 83:370, 84:856; LJ Dec 1, 1986 p. 141; SLJ June–July 1987 p. 116; VOYA 10:121)

5-350 **KING, Stephen.** *The Gunslinger.* **(The Dark Tower saga, vol. 1).** Gr. 10
up.
A young gunslinger stalking a man in black befriends a boy with amnesia and
they travel together across a vast desert and into a long tunnel through the
mountains. The sequels are *The Drawing of the Three* (1989), *The Wastelands*
(1992), and *Wizard and Glass* (1997). *The Gunslinger* was originally serialized
in *The Magazine of Fantasy and Science Fiction* between 1978 and 1981 and
was published in a limited edition in 1982.
Illus. by Michael Whelan, NAL, 1988, pap., 224 pp. (0-451-16052-5)
(BL 84:1755, 1757; Kirkus 56:1019)

5-351 *Kingdoms of Sorcery.* **Ed. by Lin Carter.** Gr. 10 up.
Sixteen British and American tales of heroic fantasy, whose authors include J.
R. R. Tolkien and Richard Adams.
Doubleday, 1976, 218 pp., o.p.
(BL 72:1393; Kirkus 43:1308)

5-352 **KIRWAN-VOGEL, Anna.** *The Jewel of Life.* Gr. 5–8.
Apprenticed to old Master Crowe the apothecary, Duffy is thrilled to discover
that his new job involves magic as well as travel to other worlds in search of

the Philosopher's Stone, or Jewel of Life.
Illus. by David Wilgus, Harcourt, 1991, 128 pp. (0-15-200750-4)

(BL 87:1956; CCBB 44:241; HBG 2:269; Kirkus 59:605; SLJ June 1990 p. 110; VOYA 14:45)

5-353 KISLING, Lee. *The Fools' War.* Gr. 5–9.
★   Clemmy, 15, is asked to intercede with a blind miracle worker to convince God to make Lady Libby fall in love with King Fernholtz, and saves Mulberia from Turkish invaders.
Harper, 1992, 166 pp., LB (0-06-020837-6)

(BL 89:418; CCBB 46:181; HBG 4:72; Kirkus 60:1379; SLJ Oct 1992 p. 118)

5-354 KLASKY, Mindy L. *The Glasswright's Journeyman.* **(Glasswright's Saga, bk. 3).** Gr. 10 up.
King Hal of Morenia and his companion, glassmaker Rani Trader, travel to Liantine to broker an unwanted marriage in order to restore the fortunes of his people. This book is preceded by *The Glasswright's Apprentice* (2000) and *The Glasswright's Progress* (2001), and is followed by *The Glasswright's Test* (2003).
Roc, 2002, pap., 338 pp. (0-451-45884-2)

(BL 98:1696; VOYA 25:397)

5-355 KLASKY, Mindy L. *Season of Sacrifice.* Gr. 7–12.
Feeling unworthy of her responsibility as the Woodsinger, who must sing the history of her people to the Great Tree, guardian of their wisdom, Alana uses all of her powers to delve into the tree's magic to save two lost children.
NAL/Roc, 2002, pap., 352 pp. (0-451-45865-6)

5-356 KOLLER, Jackie French. *The Dragonling.* **(Dragon quartet, bk. 1).** Gr. 2–4.
Nine-year-old Derek befriends an orphaned dragonling after its mother is killed by village hunters and vows to help the baby dragon find his home in the valley of dragons. The sequels are *A Dragon in the Family* (1993), *Dragon Quest* (1997), and *Dragons and Kings* (1998).
Illus. by Judith Marshall, Little, Brown, 1990, 60 pp. (0-316-50148-4)

(BL 87:1059; HBG 2:67; Kirkus 58:1674; SLJ Feb 1991 p. 71)

5-357 KOLLER, Jackie French. *A Wizard Named Nell.* **(The Keepers trilogy, bk. 1).** Gr. 3–6.
Princess Arenelle of Eldearth finds a poor boy named Owen to take her place at the Academy of Witchcraft so that she can search her kingdom for a new apprentice Imperial Wizard. The sequels are *The Wizard's Apprentice* (2003) and *The Wizard's Scepter* (2004).
Simon/Aladdin, 2003, pap., 208 pp. (0-689-85591-5)

(BL 100:321; SLJ Nov 2003 p. 142)

5-358 KRITZER, Naomi. *Fires of the Faithful.* Gr. 10 up.
Studying the craft of music, and drawn to the beliefs of the Old Way, Eliana discovers that the Circle of ruling mages and the goddess-worshiping Fideli were responsible for the murders of her friends and family, who were Old Way followers.

Bantam, 2002, pap., 400 pp. (0-553-58517-7)

(BL 99:71; VOYA 25:488)

5-359 **KURTZ, Jane.** *The Feverbird's Claw.* Gr. 5–12.
Aristocratic temple handmaiden Moralin must use her forbidden warrior skills
to survive after she is kidnapped by the barbaric enemy Arkera.
Greenwillow, 2004, 304 pp. (0-06-000821-0)

(BL 100:1456; CCBB 57:379; Kirkus 72:443; SLJ May 2004 p. 151; VOYA 27:142)

5-360 **KURTZ, Katherine (Irene).** *The Bishop's Heir.* **(Histories of King Kel-**
★ **son, vol. 1).** Gr. 10 up.
King Kelson of Gwynedd must deal with a resurgence of the ancient conflict
between the human and Deryni races. The sequels are *The King's Justice*
(1985, 1995), *The Quest for Saint Camber* (1986), *King Kelson's Bride* (2000),
and *In the King's Service* (2003). The Chronicles of Deryni (see *The Deryni
Archives*, below) and the Heirs of Saint Camber trilogy (see *The Harrowing of
Gwynned*, below) are related series.
Ballantine, 1984, 1985, 1987, pap., 384 pp., o.p.

(BL 86:905; Kirkus 52:829; LJ 109:2162; SLJ Jan 1985 p. 92; VOYA 8:55, 364)

5-361 **KURTZ, Katherine (Irene).** *The Deryni Archives.* **(The Chronicles of**
★ **Deryni).** Gr. 10 up.
Nine stories about the magical Deryni, including "Lords of Sorandor," an
unpublished novella written in 1965, which served as the basis for *Deryni Rising* (1970). The series includes *Deryni Rising* (1970, 1976), *Deryni Checkmate*
(1972, 1976), *High Deryni* (1973, 1982), and *Deryni Magic* (1991). These
books are related to three other series: The Legends of Camber of Culdi, which
includes *Camber of Culdi* (1976), *Saint Camber* (1978), and *Camber the
Heretic* (1980); the Histories of King Kelson (see *The Bishop's Heir*, 1984,
above), and the Heirs of Saint Camber trilogy (see *The Harrowing of
Gwynned*, 1989, below). *Deryni Tales*, ed. by Kurtz (Ace, 2002), is a collection of short stories set in Deryni written by fans of the series.
Ballantine, 1986, pap., 325 pp., o.p.

(BL 82:1667, 1683; LJ Aug 1986 p. 174; SLJ Nov 1986 p. 116; VOYA 9:238)

5-362 **KURTZ, Katherine (Irene).** *The Harrowing of Gwynedd.* **(The Heirs of
Saint Camber trilogy, bk. 1).** Gr. 10 up.
In an earlier period of Gwynedd's history than the author's Histories of King
Kelson trilogy (see *The Bishop's Heir*, 1984, above), three young friends try to
save the outlawed race of Deryni, humans with magical powers, from extinction. The sequels are *King Javin's Year* (1992) and *The Bastard Prince* (1994,
1995). These books are related to two other series, the Chronicles of Deryni
(see *The Deryni Archives*, 1986, above), and the Legends of Camber of Caldi,
which includes *Camber of Caldi* (1976), *Saint Camber* (1978), and *Camber the
Heretic* (1980).
Ballantine, 1989, 400 pp. (0-345-33259-8), pap. (0-345-36314-0)

(BL 85:730, 731; Kirkus 56:1781; LJ Feb 15, 1989 p. 179; VOYA 12:166)

5-363 **KURTZ, Katherine (Irene), and HARRIS, Deborah Turner.** *The Temple
and the Stone.* **(Temple series, bk. 1).** Gr. 10 up.

In this prequel to the author's Adept series (see *The Adept* in Chapter 12, Witchcraft and Sorcery Fantasy), two Knights Templar, Arnault de Saint Clair and Torquil Lennox, return to Scotland from the Holy Land to battle ancient sorcery that opposes Scottish independence from England and threatens the survival of Christianity. The sequel is *The Temple and the Crown* (2001). The authors have also contributed short stories about the Knights Templar appearing in *Tales of the Knights Templar* (Warner, 1995), *On Crusade: More Tales of the Knights Templar* (1998; see Chapter 3, Fantasy Collections), and *Crusades of Fire: Mystical Tales of the Knights Templar* (2002).
Warner, 1998, 306 pp. (0-446-52260-0)
(BL 94:1798; Kirkus 66:854; LJ Aug 1998 p. 139; VOYA 21:444)

5-364   KUSHNER, Ellen, and SHERMAN, Delia. *The Fall of Kings.* Gr. 10 up.
✩   Theron Campion, of noble blood, and scholar Basil St. Cloud become involved in treasonous intrigues surrounding the restoration of the overthrown kings and their wizards. This is the sequel to Kushner's *Swordspoint: A Melodrama of Manners* (Arbor House, 1987), which is set 60 years earlier.
Bantam, 2002, pap., 496 pp. (0-553-38184-9), 2003, pap., 528 pp. (0-553-58594-0)
(BL 99:584; Kirkus 70:1271; LJ Nov 15, 2002 p. 195; SLJ May 2003 p. 180)

5-365   LACKEY, Mercedes. *Arrows of the Queen.* **(The Heralds of Valdemar trilogy, bk. 1).** Gr. 7 up.
Talia, a runaway Holdgirl, is chosen to become a trainee herald in the queen's elite guard and to care for young Princess Elspeth, heir to the throne. The sequels are *Arrow's Flight* (1987) and *Arrow's Fall* (1988). The author's Last Herald Mage series (see *Magic's Pawn*, below) and Mage Winds trilogy (see *Winds of Fate*, below) are set in the same world. The Mage War trilogy (see *The Black Gryphon*, below), written by Lackey and Larry Dixon, is set in Valdemar a thousand years earlier. *Storm Warning* (see below) starts the author's Mage Storms trilogy, also set in Valdemar, as is the Darian's Tale trilogy written by Lackey and Dixon (see *Owlflight*, below). *Brightly Burning* (2000, 2001) is also set in Valdemar, and *Take a Thief* (2001), *Exile's Honor* (2002, 2003), and *Exile's Valor* (2003) are prequels to this series. *Sword of Ice and Other Tales of Valdemar* (ed. by Lackey; DAW, 1997, 1999) and *Sun in Glory and Other Tales of Valdemar* (DAW, 2003) are anthologies of stories set in Valdemar. *The Valdemar Companion: A Guide to Mercedes Lackey's World of Valdemar* (DAW, 2001, by John Helfers and Denise Little) is an authorized guide to Valdemar.
DAW, 1987, 1991, 1996, pap., 320 pp. (0-88677-378-4)
(BL 86:905; VOYA 10:131)

5-366   LACKEY, Mercedes. *Bardic Voices: The Lark and the Wren.* **(Bardic Voices, bk. 1).** Gr. 10 up.
Rune, 14, dreams of joining the Bardic Guild and leaving home, where the villagers revile her illegitimacy. The sequels are *The Robin and the Kestrel* (1993, 1994), *The Eagle and the Nightingales* (1995, 1996), and *Four and Twenty Blackbirds* (1997, 1998). The first three books in this series were published together in *The Free Bards* (Baen, 1997, pap.). "Fiddler Fair," the short story that began this series, was published in the collection *Fiddler Fair* (Baen,

1998; see Chapter 3, Fantasy Collections). *A Cast of Corbies* (1994, 1995), written by the author and Josepha Sherman, is a related work.
Baen, 1992, pap., 488 pp., o.p.
(BL 89:1342; SLJ July 1992 p. 97; VOYA 15:44)

5-367 LACKEY, Mercedes. *By the Sword.* Gr. 10–12.
Kerowyn, granddaughter of a sorceress, chases bandits who used sorcery to kidnap her future sister-in-law. This story connects the author's Heralds of Valdemar trilogy (see *Arrows of the Queen*, above) with her Vows and Honor series (*Oathbound*, 1988; *Oathbreakers*, 1989; and *Oathblood* 1998) and is related to both her Last Herald Mage series (see *Magic's Pawn*, below) and her Mage Winds trilogy (see *Winds of Fate*, below), and to the Darian's Tale trilogy written by Lackey and Larry Dixon (see *Owlflight*, below).
DAW, 1991, pap., 492 pp., o.p.; DAW, 1994, pap., 352 p. (0-8867-7352-0)
(Kliatt Apr 1991 p. 20; VOYA 14:110)

LACKEY, Mercedes. *The Fairy Godmother.*
See Chapter 6, High Fantasy: Myth or Legend Fantasy.

5-368 LACKEY, Mercedes. *Joust.* **(Dragon Jousters series, bk. 1).** Gr. 10 up.
Rescued from servitude in occupied Alta, young Vetch becomes dragon-boy to Ari, one of the Tian Jousters, dragon-riders who patrol the skies. The sequels are *Alta* (2004) and *Sanctuary* (2005).
DAW, 2003, 448 pp. (0-7564-0122-4)
(BL 99:1286, 1458; VOYA 26:238, 27:13)

5-369 LACKEY, Mercedes. *Magic's Pawn.* **(The Last Herald Mage trilogy, bk.**
★ **1).** Gr. 11 up.
Vanyel, the last of Valdemar's Herald Mages, grows to accept his homosexuality but is grief stricken when his lover is killed in a blood feud in this fantasy for mature readers. The sequels are *Magic's Promise* (1990) and *Magic's Price* (1990). *Brightly Burning* (2000) is related to *Magic's Price*, as are the Darian's Tale trilogy by Lackey and Larry Dixon (see *Owlflight*, below). This series is set in the same world as the author's Heralds of Valdemar trilogy (see *Arrows of the Queen*, above) and her Mage Winds trilogy (see *Winds of Fate*, below). The Mage Wars trilogy (see *The Black Gryphon*, below) is set in Valdemar a thousand years earlier.
DAW, 1989, 1994, pap., 349 pp. (0-88677-352-0)
(BL 85:1783, 1817; Kliatt Sep 1989, p. 18; LJ June 15, 1989 p. 83; VOYA 13:14, 38)

LACKEY, Mercedes. *Oathblood.*
See Chapter 12, Witchcraft and Sorcery Fantasy.

5-370 LACKEY, Mercedes. *The River's Gift.* Gr. 10 up.
Fifteen-year-old Ariella uses her magical healing skills to gain the trust of Merod, a huge magical horse that helps her escape abduction by an unwanted suitor.
Penguin/Roc, 1999, 128 pp. (0-451-45759-5)
(BL 96:75; Kirkus 67:1180; VOYA 22:346, 23:12)

5-371 LACKEY, Mercedes. *The Serpent's Shadow.* Gr. 10 up.
Half-English, half-Indian physician Maya Witherspoon needs the help of Victorian British wizards to save London from destruction by the powers of the goddess Kali.
DAW, 2001, 352 pp. (0-88677-915-4)
(BL 97:1122; Kirkus 69:22; LJ Feb 15, 2001 p. 205; VOYA 24:291, 25:14)

5-372 LACKEY, Mercedes. *Storm Warning.* **(Mage Storms trilogy, bk. 1).** Gr. 10 up.
While their homelands, Valdemar and Karse, are battered by magically generated storms, Karal and An'Deshal travel to the Court of Valderon to form alliances against the powerful Eastern Empire. The sequels are *Storm Rising* (1995) and *Storm Breaking* (1996). This series is related to the author's Heralds of Valdemar trilogy (see *Arrows of the Queen*, above), Last Herald Mage trilogy (see *Magic's Pawn*, above), and Mage Winds trilogy (see *Winds of Fate*, below).
DAW, 1994, 448 pp. (0-88677-611-2), 1995, pap. (0-88677-661-9)
(BL 90:1725, 1726; Kirkus 62:741; LJ Aug 1994 p. 139; VOYA 17:224, 18:234)

5-373 **LACKEY, Mercedes.** *Winds of Fate.* **(The Mage Winds trilogy, vol. 1).**
✴ Gr. 10 up.
Darkwind, the Tayledras scout, meets Princess Elspeth while she searches for a mage who can save the realm of Valdemar from the wizardry of Ancar of Hardorn. The sequels are *Winds of Change* (1992) and *Winds of Fury* (1993). This trilogy follows the author's Heralds of Valdemar (see *Arrows of the Queen*, above) and Last Herald Mage (see *Magic's Pawn*, above) trilogies. *Storm Warning* (1994; see above), begins the author's Mage Storms trilogy, which is also set in Valdemar, as is the Darian's Tale trilogy written by Lackey and Larry Dixon (see *Owlflight*, below).
NAL, 1991, pap., 384 pp. (0-88677-489-6); DAW, 1992, pap. (0-88677-516-7)
(BL 87:2108, 2111; LJ Oct 15, 1991 p. 126; SLJ May 1992, p. 152; VOYA 14:384)

5-374 **LACKEY, Mercedes, and DIXON, Larry.** *The Black Gryphon.* **(The Mage Wars trilogy, bk. 1).** Gr. 10 up.
Archmage Urtho sends the Black Gryphon, Skandragon Rashke, on secret missions to battle the enemy Kiyamvir during the Mage Wars in this series set in Valdemar a thousand years earlier than the Heralds of Valdemar (see *Arrows of the Queen*, above) and the Last Herald Mage (see *Magic's Pawn*, above) trilogies. The sequels are *The White Gryphon* (1995, 1996) and *The Silver Gryphon* (1996, 1997).
NAL/DAW, 1994, 400 pp. (0-88677-577-9)
(BL 90:741, 743; Kirkus 61:1425; Kliatt May 1995 p. 16; LJ Dec 1993 p. 180; VOYA 17:37)

5-375 **LACKEY, Mercedes, and DIXON, Larry.** *Owlflight.* **(Darian's Tale trilogy).** Gr. 7–12.
In this story set in Valdemar after the Mage Storms trilogy (see *Storm Warning*, 1994, above), 13-year-old Darian escapes into the forest when his village is invaded and is rescued by the Hawkbrother Snowfire, who is attempting to re-establish the old lines of magic. The sequels are *Owlsight* (1998) and *Owlknight* (1999).

DAW, 1997, 304 pp. (0-88677-754-2), 1998, pap. (0-88677-804-2)

(BL 94:216; Kirkus 65:1168; LJ Oct 15, 1997 p. 98; VOYA 20:326)

LACKEY, Mercedes, and EMERSON, Ru. *Fortress of Frost and Fire.*
See Chapter 12, Witchcraft and Sorcery Fantasy.

5-376 **LACKEY, Mercedes, FLINT, Eric, and FREER, Dave.** *The Shadow of the Lion.* Gr. 10 up.
Posing as canal urchins in an alternate 16th-century Venice, half brothers Marco and Benito Valdosta, grandsons of the Duke of Ferrara, try to hide from the duke's mortal enemies, while the Grand Duke of Lithuania uses magic to battle the emperor of the holy Roman Empire. The sequel is *This Rough Magic* (2003).
Baen, 2002, 848 pp. (0-7434-3523-0), 2003, pap., 913 p. (0-7434-7147-4)

(BL 98:1219; Kirkus 70:149; VOYA 25:202)

LACKEY, Mercedes, and MALLORY, James. *The Outstretched Shadow.*
See Chapter 12, Witchcraft and Sorcery Fantasy.

5-377 **LA FEVERS, R. L.** *The Falconmaster.* Gr. 4–7.
Crippled 10-year-old Wat steals two baby falcons and runs away to the forest, where he is taken in by Griswold, the keeper of the forest, who teaches Wat about his own natural magic.
Dutton, 2003, 128 pp. (0-525-46993-1)

(BL 100:490; CCBB 57:156; HBG 15:97; Kirkus 71:1312; SLJ Jan 2004 p. 132)

5-378 **LAUMER, (John) Keith.** *The Shape Changer: A Science Fiction Novel.*
Gr. 10 up.
After examining a mysterious treasure, Lafayette O'Leary suddenly finds himself changing from shape to shape and traveling from world to world.
Putnam, 1972, 189 pp., o.p.

(BL 68:753, 766; LJ 97:790)

5-379 **LAWHEAD, Stephen R.** *In the Hall of the Dragon King.* **(The Dragon King trilogy, vol. 1).** Gr. 6–12.
An evil sorcerer has kidnapped Dragon King Eskevar in order to put Prince Jaspin on the throne, and it is up to young Quentin to warn the queen and rescue the king. The sequels are *The Warlords of Nin* (1983, 1989) and *The Sword and the Flame* (1984).
Crossway, 1982, 1982, 1989, pap., 351 pp., o.p.; Good News, 1990, pap. (0-89107-563-1); Avon, 1992, pap. (0-380-71629-1)

(Kirkus 50:651; SLJ Nov 1982 p. 101; VOYA 13:230)

5-380 **LAWHEAD, Stephen R.** *The Iron Lance.* **(The Celtic Crusades, vol. 1).**
Gr. 10 up.
Murdo follows his Crusader father and brothers from Scotland to the Holy Land in an attempt to reclaim their land from a nefarious neighboring lord. The sequels are *The Black Rood* (Eos, 2000) and *The Mystic Rose* (Eos, 2001).
HarperPrism, 1998, 448 pp. (0-06-105032-6)

(BL 95:655; Kirkus 66:1422; LJ Dec 1998 p. 162, Feb 1, 1999 p. 74)

5-381 LAWRENCE, Ann (Margaret). *The Half Brothers.* Gr. 5–8.

☆ All three of Duchess Ambra's cousins want to marry her, but only one is willing to let her be herself.

Walck, 1973, 172 pp., o.p.

(BL 70:341; CCBB 27:97; HB 50:51; LJ 99:891; Suth 2:274; TLS 1973 p. 685)

5-382 LAWRENCE, Louise (pseud. of Elizabeth Rhoda Holden). *The Warriors of Taan.* Gr. 7–11. (Orig. British pub. 1986.)

After their world has been overrun by the Otherworlders, Elana, destined to become the Reverend Mother of the Sisterhood of Taan, and Khian, heir to the throne, meet by chance and fall in love.

Harper, 1988, 249 pp., o.p.

(BL 84:993, 1001; HB 64:789; Kirkus 56:56; SLJ Feb 1988 p. 84; VOYA 10:289)

5-383 LAWRENCE, Michael. *The Poppy Kettle Papers.* Gr. 5–8. (Orig. Australian pub. 1999.)

Astute, Andante, Don Avante, Aloof, and Arnica, five miniature survivors of a tidal wave, set out across the Pacific Ocean in a clay teapot, searching for a safer home.

Illus. by Robert Ingpen, Pavilion, 2000, 128 pp. (1-86205-282-4)

(Kirkus 68:121; SLJ Mar 2000 p. 240)

5-384 LEE, John. *The Unicorn Quest.* **(The Unicorn Saga, bk. 1).** Gr. 7–12.

Jarrod and Marianna are sent in search of a unicorn needed to save their world from an enemy invasion. The sequels are *The Unicorn Dilemma: A Saga of War and Magic* (1988, 1992), *The Unicorn Solution* (1991), *The Unicorn Peace* (1993), and *The Unicorn War* (1995).

Tor, 1986, 381 pp., o.p.

(Kliatt Spring 1986 p. 22; VOYA 9:163)

5-385 LEE, Tanith. *Anackire.* **(The Wars of Vis trilogy, bk. 2).** Gr. 10 up. (Orig. pub. in England.)

Young Prince Kesarh's ambitions for power over the land of Karmiss are complicated by his daughter, whose mother is an incarnation of the goddess Anackire, and by the appearance of a long-lost hero's son. This is the sequel to *The Storm Lord* (1978, 1986) and is followed by *The White Serpent* (1988).

DAW, 1983, pap., 414 pp., o.p.

(BL 80:469; VOYA 7:38)

5-386 LEE, Tanith. *Black Unicorn.* **(Unicorn trilogy, bk. 1).** Gr. 7 up. (Orig.

☆ British pub. 1991.)

Tanaquil has always been able to mend anything, in spite of her sorceress mother's disappointment in her inability to perform magic, so when her catlike peeve finds some strange golden bones, Tanaquel reconstructs them into a unicorn. The sequels are *Gold Unicorn* (1994) and *Red Unicorn* (1997; pap. 2003).

Del Rey, 1988, pap. (0-345-33528-7); Macmillan, 1991, 144 pp. (0-689-31575-9)

(BL 88:428; CCBB 45:67; HB 68:746; HBG 3:79; Kirkus 59:1288; SLJ Nov 1991 p. 134; VOYA 14:324, 15:9)

**5-387 LEE, Tanith. *Companions on the Road: Two Novellas.* Gr. 10 up. (Orig.
pub. in Britain separately as *Companions on the Road*, 1975, and *The Winter
Players*, 1976.)**
In the first of these novellas, "Companions on the Road," two soldiers and a
"snatch purse" set off with the fabled cup of Avillis, but are pursued by three
mysterious "undead": the evil Lord of Avillis, his son, and his daughter. In
"The Winter Players," a wicked priest-lord uses a young man named Cyrdin
and a 17-year-old priestess named Oaive as pawns in his attempt to gain power
over a magical relic.
St. Martin's, 1977, 256 pp., o.p.
(Kirkus 45:1014; TLS 1976 p. 1242)

5-388 LEE, Tanith. *Cyrion.* Gr. 10 up. (Orig. British pub. 1982.)
Seven short stories and a novella about a wanderer named Cyrion who uses
logic to outwit sorcery.
DAW, 1982, pap., 304 pp. o.p.
(BL 79:483; LJ 107:1772; VOYA 6:45)

**5-389 LEE, Tanith. *Dark Castle, White Horse.* Gr. 10 up. (Orig. British pub. sepa-
rately as *The Castle of Dark*, 1978, and *Prince on a White Horse*, 1982.)**
In the first novella, "The Castle of Dark," a young harper must fight a fearsome creature to rescue a maiden; and in "Prince on a White Horse," a prince
is puzzled by the angry maidens he meets and the useless battles he has fought.
DAW, 1986, pap., 302 pp., o.p.
(Kliatt 20:26; LJ Apr 15, 1986 p. 98; TLS July 23, 1982 p. 794; VOYA 9:164)

5-390 LEE, Tanith. *The Dragon Hoard.* Gr. 4–6. (Orig. British pub. 1986.)
The witch Maligna's angry gift to Prince Jasleth—that he become a raven for
one hour every day—comes in handy when he joins a quest for the Dragon
Hoard treasure.
Illus. by Graham Oakley, Farrar, 1971, 162 pp., o.p.
(HB 48:49; Kirkus 39:1120; TLS 1971 p. 1511)

5-391 LEE, Tanith. *East of Midnight.* Gr. 10 up. (Orig. British pub. 1977.)
Dekteon, a young slave, escapes through a Vortex Gate into a parallel world
where he is tricked into exchanging lives with Zaister, the doomed Sun King-
consort of the ruling Daughter of Night.
St. Martin's, 1978, 175 pp., o.p.
(Kirkus 46:334; TLS 1977 p. 1246)

5-392 LEE, Tanith. *A Heroine of the World.* Gr. 10 up. (Orig. British pub. 1989.)
Fourteen-year-old noblewoman Ara must escape from captivity by her coun-
try's invaders before she can fulfill a prophecy predicting her great powers.
DAW, 1989, pap., 448 pp., o.p.
(BL 85:1949, 1969; LJ Aug 1989 p. 167; VOYA 12:372)

5-393 LEE, Tanith. *Mortal Suns.* Gr. 10 up. (Orig. pub. in England.)
Rescued from the Temple of Death, infant Callistra, born without feet, is raised
at the Court of the Great Sun as a Princess of Akhemony and is chosen to be
the consort of the next King.

Overlook, 2003, 336 pp. (1-58567-207-6)
(BL 100:75; Kirkus 71:783; LJ July 2003 p. 133)

5-394 LEE, Tanith. *Piratica: Being a Daring Tale of a Singular Girl's Adventure Upon the High Seas.* Gr. 6 up. (Orig. British pub. 2004.)
Artemesia, 16, runs away to London from her boarding school, to find her pirate queen mother's former crew and convince them to set sail once again.
Dutton, 2004, 320 pp. (0-525-47324-6)
(BL 101:323; CCBB 58:132; Kirkus 72:869; VOYA 27:316)

5-395 LEE, Tanith. *Sung in Shadow.* Gr. 10 up. (Orig. pub. in England.)
This love story about Romulan and Iuletta is a retelling of "Romeo and Juliet," set in a magical alternate Renaissance Italy.
DAW, 1983, pap., 349 pp., o.p.
(BL 79:1448; LJ 108:1019; VOYA 6:283)

5-396 LEE, Tanith. *Wolf Tower* **(The Claidi Journals series, bk. 1).** Gr. 6–9.
★ (British title: Law of the Wolf Tower, 1998.)
Sixteen-year-old slave Claidi rescues Nemian, a hot-air balloonist captured by soldiers, and runs away with him into the dreaded Waste, where they are taken in by a gypsy-like band. The sequels are *Wolf Star* (2001; British title *Wolf Star Rise*, 2000), *Wolf Queen* (2002; British title *Queen of the Wolves*, 2001), and *Wolf Wing* (2002, 2003).
Dutton, 2002, 240 pp. (0-525-46394-1); Firebird, 2001, pap., 240 pp. (0-14-230030-6)
(BL 96:1543; CCBB 53:409; HBG 11:318; Kirkus 68:635; Kliatt Nov 2000 p. 7; SLJ June 2000 p. 148; VOYA 23:197, 24:12)

***Legends: Stories by the Masters of Modern Fantasy.* Ed. by Robert Silverberg.**
See Chapter 3, Fantasy Collections.

5-397 LE GUIN, Ursula K(roeber). *Gifts.* Gr. 7–12.
★ After young Orrec develops the extrasensory gift of "Unmaking," he chooses to wear a blindfold to protect his family and friends from the effect of his powers.
Harcourt, 2004, 288 pp. (0-15-205123-6)
(BL 100:1924; CCBB 58:86; HB 80:589; Kirkus 72:744; SLJ Sep 2004 p. 210)

5-398 LE GUIN, Ursula K(roeber). *A Wizard of Earthsea.* **(The Earthsea Cycle,**
★★ **vol. 1).** Gr. 6 up.
In this first volume of the Earthsea quintet, young Ged, studying the art of wizardry, accidentally conjures up a terrifying creature that threatens the existence of the entire world of Earthsea. Boston Globe Horn Book Award, 1969. In *The Tombs of Atuan* (Atheneum, 1971, 1985; Aladdin, 2001, pap.), Ged, now a wizard, invades the forbidden undertomb and labyrinth of Atuan, forcing Tenar to choose between remaining as High Priestess to the Dark Ones or escaping from Atuan. *The Tombs of Atuan* was a John Newbery Medal Honor Book, 1972, a National Book Award finalist, 1972, and a Phoenix Award Honor Book, 1991. In *The Farthest Shore* (Atheneum, 1972, 1985; Aladdin, 2001, pap.), Ged, now Archmage of Roke, and Prince Arren of Enlad make an arduous journey into the Shadow Kingdom of the dead to confront an evil mage who has upset the balance between life and death. *The Farthest Shore* won the

National Book Award, 1973. In *Tehanu: The Last Book of Earthsea* (1990, 1991, Aladdin, 2001, pap.), Tenar, now a middle-aged widow, takes on the tasks of healing an abused child named Therru, and Ged, who lost his magical powers in a battle to save the world. Nebula Award, Best Novel, 1991. In *The Other Wind* (2001), Orm Irian, Tehanu, Ged, Tenar, the sorcerer Alter, and King Lebannen work together to mend the earth, right ancient wrongs, and bring peace to Earthsea. *The Other Wind* won the 2002 World Fantasy Award for Best Novel. *Tales from Earthsea* (2001) contains five stories set in Earthsea, before and after the time of the original trilogy, including "Dragonfly," the story of the dragon Orm Irian.

Illus. by Ruth Robbins, Parnassus, 1968, o.p.; Atheneum, 1991, 208 pp. (0-689-31720-4); Spectra, 2004, pap., 192 pp. (0-55338-304-3)

(BL 65:546, 901, 80:95; CCBB 22:144; HB 45:59; LJ 94:2073, 2104, 4582; TLS 1973 p. 379, 1977 p. 863)

5-399 **LEITH, Valery.** *The Company of Glass.* **(The Everien Tales, bk. 1).** Gr. 10
★   up.

Exiled Quintar, now called Tarquin the Free, returns to Everien to lead the clans against the invading Pharicians, and discovers that his best friend's daughter, Istar, plans to undertake the quest that destroyed her father. The sequels are *The Riddled Night* (2000, 2001) and *The Way of the Rose* (2001, 2002).

Bantam, 1999, pap., 432 pp., o.p., 2000, pap., 544 pp. (0-553-57899-5)

(BL 95:1681; Kirkus 67:761; Kliatt Nov 1999 p. 27; LJ June 15, 1999 p. 112; VOYA 22:414)

5-400 **LEVIN, Betty (Lowenthal).** *The Banished.* Gr. 5–7.
★

In exchange for ending her banished people's exile, Siri is forced to make a dangerous sea journey with a fearsome Furfolk girl to deliver an ice bear to the king. This is a prequel to *The Ice Bear* (1986; see below).

Greenwillow, 1999, 152 pp. (0-688-16602-4)

(BL 95:2058; HB 75:742; HBG 11:82; Kirkus 67:1055; SLJ Oct 1999 p. 154)

5-401 **LEVIN, Betty (Lowenthal).** *The Ice Bear.* Gr. 6–8.
★

After the evil Lord Uris orders the deaths of the absent king's great white bear and her keeper, young Wat, a baker's assistant, helps the keeper's daughter, Kaila, escape with the last bear cub. *The Banished* (1999; see above) is a prequel to this story.

Greenwillow, 1986, 192 pp., o.p.

(BL 83:580; CCBB 40:91; HB 63:56; Kirkus 54:1207; SLJ Oct 1986 p. 192; TLS 1987 p. 804; VOYA 9:220)

5-402 **LEVINE, Gail Carson.** *The Two Princesses of Bamarre.* Gr. 4–8.
★

Captured by the dragon Vollys, Princess Addie is determined to find the secret cure for her older sister's mortal illness, the Gray Death.

HarperCollins, 2001, 256 pp. (0-06-029316-0); HarperTrophy, 2004, pap., 293 pp. (0-06-057580-8)

(BL 97:1558; CCBB 55:65; HB 77:330; HBG 12:310; Kirkus 69:333; Kliatt May 2001 p. 12; SLJ May 2001 p. 155; VOYA 24:134, 24:408, 25:14)

5-403 **LEVY, Robert.** *Clan of the Shape-Changers.* Gr. 6–9.

Green-eyed Susan keeps her shape-changing abilities a secret from the dangerous shaman Ometerer, until she is forced to reveal her powers to save the lives

of two orphaned children. *The Misfit Apprentice* (1995) is set in the same world.
Houghton, 1994, 192 pp. (0-395-66612-0)
(BL 90:1436, 94:475; HBG 5:321; Kirkus 62:398; SLJ May 1994 p. 128; VOYA 17:99)

5-404 *Liavek.* **Ed. by Will Shetterly and Emma Bull.** Gr. 10 up.
Eleven tales set in the trading city of Liavek at the mouth of the Cat River.
Each story was written by a different author, among them Gene Wolfe and
Jane Yolen. *Liavek: The Players of Luck* (1986), *Liavek: Wizard's Row* (1987),
and *Liavek: Spells of Binding* (1988) are companion works.
Berkley, 1985, pap., 288 pp., o.p.
(BL 81:1637, 1657; VOYA 8:325)

LINDGREN, Astrid. *The Brothers Lionheart.*
See Chapter 7, High Fantasy: Travel to Other Worlds.

5-405 **LINDGREN, Astrid.** *Ronia, the Robber's Daughter.* Gr. 4–6. (Orig.
☆ Swedish pub. 1981.)
Ronia and Birk, offspring of two rival robber chieftains, fall in love and run off
together into the goblin- and harpy-infested forest. Mildred L. Batchelder
Award, 1984.
Viking, 1983, 176 pp., o.p.
(BL 79:1095, 86:790; HB 59:304; Kirkus 51:459; SLJ Aug 1983 p. 67)

5-406 **LINDHOLM, Megan.** *Luck of the Wheels.* **(Ki series, bk. 4).** Gr. 10 up.
Ki and Vandien take on the challenge of transporting an unlikable youth with
telepathic powers to a distant city where they become involved in a rebel plot
to seize the throne. This is the sequel to *Harpy's Flight* (1983), *The
Windsingers* (1984), and *The Limbreth Gate* (1984). Lindholm also writes as
Robin Hobb (see *Assassin's Apprentice, Fool's Errand,* and *Ship of Magic* in
this section).
Ace, 1989, pap., 256 pp., o.p.
(BL 86:726, 736)

5-407 **LINDSKOLD, Jane M.** *Through Wolf's Eyes.* **(Firekeeper saga, bk. 1).**
Gr. 10 up.
Raised by wolves since infancy, Firemaker returns to human society to discov-
er that she is the only living heir to King Tedric and needs her wolvish
instincts to navigate through this new world. The sequels are *Wolf's Head,
Wolf's Heart* (2002), and *The Dragon of Despair* (2003).
Tor, 2001, 608 pp. (0-312-87427-8), 2002, pap. (0-8125-7548-2)
(BL 97:1856; Kirkus 69:905; LJ Aug 2001 p. 171; VOYA 24:370, 25:14)

5-408 **LISLE, Holly.** *Diplomacy of Wolves.* **(The Secret Texts trilogy, bk. 1).** Gr.
10 up.
Pursued by demons, diplomat Kait Galweigh flees her home after uncovering a
magical plot against her family. *Vincalis the Agitator* (2002, 2003) is a prequel. The sequels are *Vengeance of Dragons* (1999, 2000) and *Courage of Falcons* (2000, 2001).

Warner, 1998, pap., 352 pp. (0-446-67395-1), 1999, pap., 416 pp. (0-446-60746-0)

(BL 95:313; LJ Oct 15, 1998 p. 103; VOYA 21:369, 22:14)

5-409 **LISLE, Janet Taylor.** *The Lampfish of Twill.* Gr. 5–7.
★ The fishcatchers of Twill believe all their problems are caused by huge lamp-fish, which they hunt and occasionally kill, but when old Zeke and young Eric are pulled down by the underwhirl into the lampfishes' undersea world, they discover the truth about the creatures.
Illus. by Wendy Anderson Halperin, Orchard, 1991, 161 pp. LB (0-531-05963-4); Scholastic, 1995, pap. (0-590-46040-4)

(CCBB 45:43; HB 68:72; HBG 3:69; Kirkus 59:1288; SLJ Sep 1991 p. 256)

5-410 **LOGSTON, Anne.** *Exile.* Gr. 7 up.
Neve, apprentice Guardian of the Crystal Keep, undertakes a dangerous journey to find the original elven Guardians who will determine whether her magic skills are great enough to take over from her father.
Ace, 1999, pap., 272 pp. (0-441-00669-8)

(Kliatt Jan 2000 p. 23; VOYA 22:348)

5-411 **LOGSTON, Anne.** *Shadow.* **(Shadow series, bk. 1).** Gr. 7–12.
Shadow, a professional elven thief, becomes enmeshed in the power struggle between the Council of Churches and the Guild of Thieves when she steals an unusual bracelet from a young nobleman. The sequels are *Shadow Hunt* (1992), *Shadow Dance* (1992), *Greendaughter* (1993), *Dagger's Edge* (1994), *Dagger's Point* (1995), and *Wild Blood* (1995).
Ace, 1991, pap., 185 pp. (0-441-75989-0)

(Kliatt Jan 1992 p. 18; VOYA 15:111)

5-412 **LONGMAN, Harold S.** *Andron and the Magician.* Gr. 4–6.
The Magician of the Far Places teaches Andron, son of a poor fisherman, that he must use his own inner resources to find his fortune.
Illus. by Richard Cuffari, Seabury, 1971, 143 pp., o.p.

(Kirkus 39:1071; LJ 97:1607)

5-413 **LONGYEAR, Barry B(rookes).** *The God Box.* Gr. 10 up.
The gift of a magical many-drawered box that grants Korvas whatever he needs—but not whatever he wants—propels the former flying-carpet merchant on a perilous journey to fulfill a prophecy.
NAL, 1989, pap., 235 pp., o.p.

(BL 85:1435, 1456; LJ Apr 15, 1989 p. 102)

5-414 **LOVETT, Margaret (Rose).** *The Great and Terrible Quest.* Gr. 5–7. (Orig.
★★ British pub. 1967.)
A runaway boy and a wounded knight join forces to search for the true heir to the throne.
Holt, 1967, 187 pp., o.p.; Varsitybooks, 2001, pap. (1-88784-032-X)

(BL 64:546; CCBB 21:30; HB 43:597; Kirkus 35:879; LJ 92:4614; TLS 1967 p. 451)

5-415 **LOWRY, Lois.** *Gathering Blue.* Gr. 6–9.
★★ In this book set in the same future world as the author's *The Giver* (1993; see below) and *Messenger* (2004; see below), orphaned Kira's embroidery talent

leads the Council of Guardians to award her the job of repairing the Singer's robe, on which the history of their world is recorded.

Houghton, 2000, 224 pp. (0-618-05581-9); Dell, 2002, pap., 240 pp. (0-440-22949-9)

(BL 96:1896, 97:863; CCBB 54:111; HB 76:573; Kirkus 68:887; SLJ Aug 2000 p. 186; VOYA 23:276, 24:12)

5-416   LOWRY, Lois. *The Giver.* **Gr. 6–9.**

☆☆   In a future world devoted to sameness, Jonas, 12, is chosen to be the next Receiver, the one to whom the elderly Giver imparts the memories of their world and of Elsewhere, the world beyond their borders. Boston Globe Horn Book Award Honor Book, 1993; John Newbery Medal, 1994. *Gathering Blue* (2000; see above) and *Messenger* (2004; see below) are companion volumes set in the same world.

Houghton, 1993, 208 pp. (0-395-64566-2); Dell, 2002, pap., 179 pp. (0-440-23768-8)

(BL 89:1506, 90:868, 1336, 1355, 1358; CCBB 46:257; HB 69:458, 717; HBG 4:310; Kirkus 61:301; SLJ May 1993 p. 124, Dec 1993 p. 26; VOYA 16:167, 17:10, 17:72)

5-417   LOWRY, Lois. *Messenger.* **Gr. 6–10.**

☆   Teenage Matty must leave the Village and his beloved blind caregiver, Seer, to rescue his friend Kira before the villagers complete a wall to keep newcomers out. The author's *The Giver* (1993; see above) and *Gathering Blue* (2000; see above) are companion volumes set in the same future world.

Houghton, 2004, 176 pp. (0-618-40441-4)

(BL 100:1056; CCBB 57:427; HB 80:332; Kirkus 72:333; SLJ Apr 2004 p. 156; VOYA 27:144)

5-418   LUCAS, George, and CLAREMONT, Chris. *Shadow Moon.* **(Chronicles of the Shadow War, bk. 1). Gr. 10 up.**

As she nears her 13th birthday, Princess Elora is ready to take over her kingdom, but her sorcerer godfather, Willow Ufgood, discovers a plot to turn her into a puppet ruler. The sequels are *Shadow Dawn* (1997, 1998; written by Chris Claremont) and *Shadow Star* (1999; by Chris Claremont) in this series based on events begun in Lucas's film *Willow*.

Bantam, 1995, 454 pp., o.p., 1996, pap., 464 pp. (0-553-57285-7)

(BL 92:211; VOYA 18:384)

5-419   LUENN, Nancy. *Goldclimbers.* **Gr. 6–9.**

Fifteen-year-old apprentice goldsmith Aracco, who secretly longs for the adventurous life of the gold climbers who scale the mountainous cliffs above his village, decides, after his best friend's death in a climbing accident, to climb the mountains alone in search of the legendary golden city of Terenger.

Macmillan, 1991, 184 pp. (0-689-31585-6)

(BL 87:1869; CCBB 44:169; HBG 2:276; Kirkus 59:473; SLJ June 1991 p. 127; VOYA 14:111, 15:10)

5-420   LUKEMAN, Tim. *Witchwood.* **Gr. 10 up.**

Hoping to escape her life in the workhouse, orphaned Fiona attempts to revive the magic fading from the land of Therrilyn.

Pocket, 1984, 192 pp., o.p.

(BL 80:944, 965; Kirkus 51:1150; LJ 108:2346)

5-421 LYNN, Elizabeth A. *Dragon's Winter.* Gr. 10 up.
Karadur Atani lays siege to his twin brother's stronghold after the talisman that
would have allowed his transformation into a dragon is stolen and his brother
is enslaved by the spirit of an evil sorcerer. The sequel is *Dragon's Treasure*
(2004).
Berkley/Ace, 1998, 352 pp. (0-441-00502-0); Ace, 1999, pap., 341 pp. (0-441-
00611-6)
(BL 94:1307; LJ Apr 15, 1998 p. 118; VOYA 21:211)

**5-422 LYNN, Elizabeth A. *Watchtower.* (The Chronicles of Tornor, bk. 1). Gr.
10 up.**
Princess Sorren, disguised as a messenger, helps her brother Errel and his chief
warrior, Ryke, escape from imprisonment by the southern invaders who have
captured their castle, and they travel to Vanima, a Utopian mountain community where they learn the skills they need to defeat their enemies. World Fantasy
Convention Award, Best Novel, 1980. The sequels are *The Dancers of Arun*
(1979; Ace, 2000, pap.) and *The Northern Girl* (1980; Ace, 2000, pap.).
Ace, 1979, 1986, pap., 240 pp., o.p.; Ace, 2000, pap., 245 pp. (0-441-00687-6)
(BL 75:1203, 1212; Kirkus 46:1346; SLJ Apr 1979 p. 75)

5-423 LYON, Steve. *The Gift Moves.* Gr. 6–9.
After Path Down the Mountain is sent to apprentice with master weaver Heron,
she begins to question who she is and what her society's values are.
Houghton, 2004, 240 pp. (0-618-39128-2)
(Kirkus 72:397; SLJ June 2004 p. 148; VOYA 27:144)

5-424 MacAVOY, R(oberta) A(nn). *Lens of the World.* (Nazhuret Saga, vol. 1).
☆   **Gr. 11 up.**
Orphaned and undersized Nazhuret grows up in a military school, learns the
trade of lens making, and eventually becomes a warrior who will save the
king's life in this story for mature readers. The sequels are *King of the Dead*
(1991) and *The Belly of the Wolf* (1994).
Morrow, 1990, 288 pp., o.p.; Avon, 1991, pap. (0-380-71016-1)
(BL86:1666, 1668; Kirkus 58:696; LJ May 15, 1990 p. 98; SLJ Dec 1990 p. 135)

5-425 McCAFFREY, Anne (Inez). *Crystal Singer.* (Crystal trilogy, bk. 1). Gr.
☆   **10 up. (Orig. British pub. 1982.)**
Killashandra Ree uses her musical talent to become one of the most successful
crystal miners on the planet of Ballybran. The sequels are *Killashandra* (1985)
and *Crystal Line* (1992).
Ballantine, 1982, 1985, pap., 320 pp., o.p.; Sagebrush, 1985, rebound (0-6139-
2199-2)
(BL 78:1394; LJ 107:1487; SLJ Nov 1982 p. 106; VOYA 5:45)

**5-426 McCAFFREY, Anne (Inez). *Dragonflight.* (The Dragonriders of Pern,
vol. 1). Gr. 10 up. (Orig. British pub. 1968.)**
In this first volume of McCaffrey's series set on the dragon-filled planet of
Pern, a young woman named Lessa joins the riders of the great winged dragons
as they battle the deadly threads that periodically fall from the sky. The prequel
is *Dragonsdawn* (1988). The sequels are *Dragonquest* (orig. British pub. 1971;
Ballantine, 1979, 1981, pap.), *The White Dragon* (orig. British pub. 1978; Bal-

lantine, 1979, 1980, pap.; Ultramarine, 1981), *Moreta: Dragon Lady of Pern* (Ballantine, 1983, 1984, pap.), *Nerilka's Story: A Pern Adventure* (Ballantine, 1986), *The Renegades of Pern* (1989), *All the Weyrs of Pern* (1991, 1992), *The Dolphins of Pern* (1994, 1996), *Dragonseye* (1997), *The Masterharper of Pern* (1998), *The Skies of Pern* (2001), and *Dragon's Kin* (2003, by Anne and Todd McCaffrey). Todd McCaffrey has written another sequel entitled *Dragonsblood* (2004). McCaffrey wrote three Pern novels for young adult readers: *Dragonsong* (1976; see below), *Dragonsinger* (1977), and *Dragondrums* (1979). *The Chronicles of Pern: First Fall* (1993) is a short story collection about the history of Pern, and *A Gift of Dragons* (2002) is another collection of stories set in Pern. The story collection *The Girl Who Heard Dragons* (Tor, 1994, 1995) contains one Pern novella. *The White Dragon* won the 1979 Gandalf Award (for Book-Length Fantasy). *Dragonriders of Pern* (Del Rey, 1988) contains the first three volumes in this series.
Walker, 1969, 309 pp., o.p.; Del Rey, 2002, pap., 320 pp. (0-3454-5633-5); Del Rey, 2005, pap., 320 pp. (0-3454-8426-6)
(TLS 1969 p. 1215)

**5-427 McCAFFREY, Anne (Inez). *Dragonsong*. (The Harper-Hall trilogy, vol.
★★   1). Gr. 5–10.**
Menolly, angered by her people's refusal to let a "mere woman" become a Harper, runs away to make her home with a family of fire dragons. In *Dragonsinger* (1977, 1978, 2003), Menolly struggles through her first year of Harper training and continues to care for her brood of fire lizards. In *Dragondrums* (1979, 1980, 2003), Piemer, a friend of Menolly, is trained as a drummer and sent on a mysterious journey by the Masterharper of Pern. All three books were collected in *The Harper Hall of Pern* (Doubleday, 1979). McCaffrey's related Dragonriders of Pern series, written for adults, begins with *Dragonflight* (see above).
Macmillan, 1976, 204 pp., o.p.; Aladdin, 2003, pap., 208 pp. (0-689-86008-0)
(BL 72:1253, 1266, 80:353; CCBB 29:177; HB 52:406; Kirkus 44:391; SLJ Apr 1976 p. 91; Suth 2:294)

5-428 McCAFFREY, Anne (Inez). *No One Noticed the Cat*. Gr. 6–12.
Prince Jamas of Esphania's intelligent cat, Niffy, helps him to outwit the Queen of Mauritia, who poisons anyone who interferes with her ambitions.
Roc, 1996, 128 pp., o.p.; Wildside, 2004, pap., 144 pp. (0-8095-0088-4)
(Kirkus 64:1110; VOYA 20:11, 44)

5-429 McCAFFREY, Laura Williams. *Alia Walking*. Gr. 5–9.
Longing to become a warrior woman, or Keenten, 12-year-old Alia and her friend Kay capture two enemy Beechians who reveal a dangerous secret about the leaders of Alia's village.
Clarion, 2003, 224 pp. (0-618-19461-4)
(BL 99:1199; HBG 14:371; Kirkus 71:392; SLJ June 2003 p. 146; VOYA 26:326)

5-430 MACE, Elisabeth. *Out There*. Gr. 7–10. (Orig. British pub. 1975, entitled *Ransome Revisited*.)
An unnamed man undertakes a fearsome journey to escape his unhappy life and to find the legendary Colony. *The Travelling Man* (1976) is the British sequel.

Greenwillow, 1978, 181 pp., o.p.
(BL 74:807; CCBB 31:145; Kirkus 46:111; SLJ Mar 1978 p. 138)

McGARRY, Terry. *Illumination.*
See Chapter 12, Witchcraft and Sorcery Fantasy.

McGOWEN, Tom (Thomas E.). *The Magician's Apprentice.*
See Chapter 12, Witchcraft and Sorcery Fantasy.

5-431 McINTYRE, Vonda N. *The Moon and the Sun.* Gr. 10 up.
Twenty-year-old Marie-Joseph, younger sister of a Jesuit scientist at the court
of Louis XIV of France, discovers that the sea lady captured by her brother is
not a monster.
Pocket, 1997, 416 pp. (0-671-56765-9)
(BL 93:1806; Kirkus 65:991)

5-432 McKENZIE, Ellen Kindt. *A Bowl of Mischief.* Gr. 5–8.
After the death of his wise adopted father, the fakir Phufadia, mischievous
young Ranjii travels to the kingdom of Superus, whose people are starving
while the selfish king gorges himself.
Henry Holt, 1992, 134 pp. (0-8050-2090-X)
(BL 89:598; HBG 4:73; Kirkus 60:1446; SLJ Nov 1992 p. 95)

5-433 McKENZIE, Ellen Kindt. *The Golden Band of Eddris.* Gr. 5–8.
Elyden and her brother, Keld, lure the witch Eddris away from Adnor to the
mountains, where they attempt to overcome her evil powers.
Hold, 1998, 293 pp. (0-8050-4389-6)
(BL 94:1000; HBG 9:334; Kirkus 66:58; SLJ Mar 1998 p. 216; VOYA 21:56)

5-434 McKENZIE, Ellen Kindt. *Taash and the Jesters.* Gr. 5–7.
An orphan named Taash and two court jesters attempt to foil the Duke of
Xon's plot to take over the kingdom. The sequel is *Kashka* (1987).
Holt, 1968, 233 pp., o.p., 1992, 245 pp. (0-8050-2381-X)
(BL 65:451, 901; HBG 4:83; Kirkus 36:1048)

5-435 McKIERNAN, Dennis L. *Dragondoom.* **(Mithgar saga, bk. 6).** Gr. 10 up.
A story in two parts about the dragon-slaying quests of twins Elgo and Elwyn,
warrior prince and princess of Jord, and their mortal enemy, the dwarf lord
Thork. This book is set in Mithgar, the same world as the author's Iron Tower
trilogy: *The Dark Tide* (1984), *Shadows of Doom* (1984), and *The Darkest Day*
(1984). His Silver Call duology, *Trek to KaggenCor* (1986; see below) and *The
Brega Path* (1986), is set several hundred years later. Other books set in Mith-
gar include *Dragondoom* (1990, 2002), *The Eye of the Hunter* (1992), *The
Voyage of the Fox Rider* (1993), *The Dragonstone* (1996), *Into the Forge*
(1997), *Into the Fire* (1998), *Silver Wolf, Black Falcon* (2000, 2001), *Tales of
Mithgar* (Penguin, 1994), and *Red Slippers: More Tales of Mithgar* (Roc,
2004).
Bantam, 1990, 485 pp., o.p.; Roc, 2002, pap., 528 pp. (0-451-45881-8)
(LJ Feb 15, 1990 p. 215; VOYA 13:118)

5-436 McKIERNAN, Dennis L. *Into the Fire.* **(Hel's Crucible duology, bk. 2).**
Gr. 10 up.

Having delivered a mysteriously powerful coin to King Agron, Tipperton and Beau must fight alongside the king's army in the Great War of the Ban against the Black Mage Modru. This is the sequel to *Into the Forge* (1997, 1998) and is set in the same world as the author's Mithgar Saga (see *Dragondoom*, above), the Iron Tower trilogy (*The Dark Tide*, 1984, *Shadows of Doom*, 1984, and *The Darkest Day*, 1984), and the Silver Call duology (see *Trek to Kraggen-Cor*, below).
Pengin/Roc, 1998, 480 pp. (0-451-45701-3); Roc, 1999, pap., 531 pp. (0-451-45732-3)
(BL 95:73; LJ Sep 15, 1998 p. 116; VOYA 21:285)

5-437 McKIERNAN, Dennis L. *Trek to Kraggen-Cor.* **(Silver Call duology, bk. 1). Gr. 6–12.**
Peregrin Fairhill and Cotton Buckleburr, two Warrow wee-folk, join a band of dwarves and the human Lord Kian to battle the evil spawn and regain the dwarf homeland. The sequel is *The Brega Path* (1986). This duology is set several hundred years later in the same world of Mithgar as the author's Iron Tower trilogy: *The Dark Tide* (1984), *Shadows of Doom* (1984), and *The Darkest Day* (1984), as well as *Dragondoom* (1990; see above). *Tales of Mithgar* (Penguin, 1994) and *Red Slippers: More Tales of Mithgar* (2004) are collections of stories set in Mithgar, as are *The Eye of the Hunter* (1992), *The Voyage of the Fox Rider* (1993), *The Dragonstone* (1996, 1997), *Silver Wolf, Black Falcon* (2000, 2001), and the Hel's Crucible duology (see *Into the Fire*, above), which follow *Tales of Mithgar* chronologically. *Trek to Kraggen-Cor* and *The Brega Path* were published together as *The Silver Call* (Roc, 2001, pap. [0-45145-861-3]).
Doubleday, 1986, 188 pp., o.p.
(Kirkus 54:429; Kliatt Sep 1987, p. 29; LJ May 15, 1986 p. 81; VOYA 9:239)

5-438 McKILLIP, Patricia A(nne). *Alphabet of Thorn.* **Gr. 10 up.**
Young Nepenthe, a scribe and translator in the royal library of Raine, secretly helps the newly crowned queen uncover the mysteries hidden in an ancient book written in a forgotten language of thorns.
Berkley/Ace, 2004, 320 pp. (0-441-01130-6)
(BL 100:840; LJ Jan 2004 p. 167; VOYA 27:232)

5-439 McKILLIP, Patricia A(nne). *The Book of Atrix Wolfe.* **Gr. 10 up.**
Horrified at the massacre caused by his murderous Hunter, the mage Atrix Wolfe transforms himself into a wolf and hides for 20 years until he is called back when the the Queen of the Woods abducts Prince Talis of Pelucir.
Berkley/Ace, 1995, 256 pp. (0-441-00211-0); Ace, 1995, pap. (0-441-00361-3)
(BL 91:1933, 1936; Kirkus 63:676)

5-440 McKILLIP, Patricia A(nne). *The Changeling Sea.* **Gr. 7 up.**
✫ Periwinkle curses the sea after her father's drowning, only to become enmeshed in an evil sea queen's curse on two princes switched at birth.
Macmillan, 1988, 139 pp., o.p.; Penguin, 2003, pap., 144 pp. (0-14-131262-9)
(BL 85:151, 162; CCBB 42:15; HB 64:790; Kirkus 56:1153; SLJ Nov 1988 p. 127; VOYA 11:247, 12:13)

5-441   McKILLIP, Patricia A(nne). *The Cygnet and the Firebird.* Gr. 10 up.
Sorceress Nyx Ro and her cousin Meguet, guardian of the Cygnet, must protect
Ro Holding from a powerful dragon-born mage. This book is related to *The
Sorceress and the Cygnet* (1991; see below).
Ace, 1993, 240 pp. (0-441-12628-6); Ace, 1995, pap. (0-441-00237-4)
(BL 90:132, 140; Kirkus 61:898; SLJ May 1994 p. 143; VOYA 16:311)

5-442   McKILLIP, Patricia A(nne). *The Forgotten Beasts of Eld.* Gr. 6–9.
⋆⋆ Sybel, a sorceress, lovingly raises an abandoned baby named Tam only to dis-
cover that his real father is the greatest enemy of the man she loves. World
Fantasy Award, Best Novel, 1975.
Atheneum, 1974, 217 pp., o.p.; Magic Carpet, 1996, pap., 352 pp. (0-15-
200869-1)
(BL 71:173, 767; CCBB 28:82; Kirkus 42:743; LJ 99:2748)

5-443   McKILLIP, Patricia A(nne). *In the Forests of Serre.* Gr. 10 up.
Inconsolable following the deaths of his young wife and unborn child, and
angry about his father's plans to select a new bride, Prince Ronan of Serre follows a firebird into the forest, where he unknowingly meets Sidonie, his reluctant bride-to-be, and a young wizard named Gyre.
Berkley/Ace, 2003, 304 pp. (0-441-01011-3)
(BL 99:1652; LJ May 15, 2003 p. 131; VOYA 26:414, 27:13)

5-444   McKILLIP, Patricia A(nne). *Moon-Flash.* Gr. 7–10.
⋆⋆ Kyreol and her friend Terje set off in a boat to explore the world outside the
boundaries of Riverworld, and in doing so make some astonishing discoveries
about the fate of Kyreol's mother and the true nature of their world. The sequel
is *The Moon and the Face* (1985).
Atheneum, 1984, 150 pp., o.p.; Puffin, 2005, pap., 304 pp. (0-14-240301-6)
(BL 81:636, 642; CCBB 38:10; HB 60:763; SLJ Dec 1984 p. 92; Suth 3:287; VOYA 8:56)

5-445   McKILLIP, Patricia A(nne). *Ombria in Shadow.* Gr. 10 up.
An enchantress, a bastard prince, and the former mistress of the late Prince of
Ombria unite in an effort to keep the boy Kyel—the heir to the throne—alive
while in the care of Ombria's power-hungry regent, Domina Pearl. World Fan-
tasy Award, Best Novel, 2003.
Ace, 2002, 298 pp. (0-441-00895-X), 2003, pap., 287 pp. (0-441-01020-2)
(LJ Jan 2002 p. 158; VOYA 25:130)

5-446   McKILLIP, Patricia A(nne). *The Riddle-Master of Hed.* **(The Star-Bear-**
⋆ **er trilogy, vol. 1).** Gr. 6–9.
Morgan, the peace-loving ruler of Hed, is driven to uncover the meaning of the
three stars on his forehead. In *Heir of Sea and Fire* (1977), Raederle, Morgan's
love, uses her magical powers to search for Morgan, who is inexplicably missing. In the final volume of this trilogy, *Harpist in the Wind* (1979), Morgan
and Raederle battle numerous enemies during his struggle to become heir to
the throne of the High One. All three books were collected in *Riddle of the
Stars* (Science Fiction Book Club, 1979) and in *Riddle Master: The Complete
Trilogy* (Ace, 1999, pap.).

Atheneum, 1976, 240 pp., o.p.; Ace, 1999, pap., entitled *Riddle Master*, 578 pp. (0-441-00596-9)

(BL 73:468, 475; CCBB 30:109; HB 52:625; Kirkus 44:1044; Kliatt 12:13; SLJ Oct 1976 p. 119)

5-447 **McKILLIP, Patricia A(nne).** *Song for the Basilisk.* Gr. 10 up.
☆ Rook's nightmares about the childhood massacre of his family compel him to return to the city of his birth and right the wrongs done to him.
Berkley, 1998, 320 pp. (0-441-00447-4); Ace, 1999, pap., 306 pp. (0-441-00678-7)

(BL 94:1978; Kirkus 66:1074; LJ Sep 15, 1998 p. 116; VOYA 21:445, 22:14)

5-448 **McKILLIP, Patricia A(nne).** *The Sorceress and the Cygnet.* Gr. 10 up.
☆ Corleu crosses a forbidden threshold between the real world and legend in search of the mythical Cygnet, needed to rescue his people, the Wayfolk, who have become lost between worlds. *The Cygnet and the Firebird* (1993; see above) is a related story.
Ace, 1991, 231 pp. (0-441-77564-0), 1992, pap. (0-441-77567-5)

(BL 87:1458, 1461; Kirkus 59:444; Kliatt Apr 1992, p. 16; LJ May 15, 1991 p. 111; SLJ Oct 1991 p. 160; VOYA 14:112)

5-449 **McKILLIP, Patricia A(nne).** *The Throme of the Erril of Sherill.* Gr. 4–6.
Before he will permit his daughter to wed Cnite Caerles, King Magnus orders the young man to bring him the Throme, an ancient magical document.
Illus. by Julia Noonan, Atheneum, 1973, 68 pp., o.p.

(CCBB 27:82; Kirkus 41:686; LJ 98:2654)

5-450 **McKINLEY, (Jennifer Carolyn) Robin (Turrell).** *The Blue Sword.*
☆☆ **(Damar series, bk. 1).** Gr. 6–12.
Harry Crewe is kidnapped by Corlath, King of the Damarians, and reluctantly realizes that they possess the same mysterious powers. John Newbery Medal Honor Book, 1983. The prequel is *The Hero and the Crown* (1984; see below). *Deerskin* (1993; see Chapter 6, High Fantasy: Myth or Legend Fantasy) is a story for mature readers set at a later time in Damar, and *A Knot in the Grain and Other Stories* (1994; see below) contains four stories set in the world of Damar. *The Stone Fey* (Harcourt, 1988) is a picture-book version of a story set in Damar, originally published in *Imaginary Lands* (Greenwillow, 1985; see this section), and "A Pool in the Desert" is another short story set in Damar, published in *Water: Tales of the Elemental Spirits* by McKinley and her husband, Peter Dickinson (Putnam, 2002; see below).
Greenwillow, 1982, 288 pp. (0-688-00938-7); Puffin, 2000, pap., 288 pp. (0-14-130975-X)

(BL 79:198, 247, 671, 980, 80:353, 86:785, 905; CCBB 36:112; HB 58:660, 59:330; SLJ Jan 1983 p. 86; Suth 3:287; VOYA 6:46)

McKINLEY, (Jennifer Carolyn) Robin (Turrell). *Deerskin.*
See Chapter 6, High Fantasy: Myth or Legend Fantasy.

5-451 **McKINLEY, (Jennifer Carolyn) Robin (Turrell).** *The Hero and the*
☆☆ *Crown.* **(Damar series, bk. 2).** Gr. 6–12.
Princess Aerin of Damar becomes a legendary dragonslayer, fulfilling her destiny as savior of her kingdom, in this prequel to *The Blue Sword* (1982; see above) and *Deerskin* (1993; see Chapter 6, High Fantasy: Myth or Legend

Fantasy). John Newbery Medal, 1985. *A Knot in the Grain and Other Stories* (1994; see below) contains four stories set in the world of Damar. *The Stone Fey* (Harcourt, 1988) is a picture-book version of a story set in Damar, originally published in *Imaginary Lands* (Greenwillow, 1985), and "A Pool in the Desert" is another short story set in Damar, published in *Water: Tales of the Elemental Spirits* by McKinley and her husband, Peter Dickinson (see below). Greenwillow, 1984, 256 pp., LB (0-688-02593-5); Ace, 1998, pap. (0-441-00499-7); Puffin, 2000, pap., 240 pp. (0-14-130981-4)

(BL 81:211, 250, 86:905; CCBB 38:30; HB 61:59; SLJ Oct 1984 p. 169; Suth 3:287; TLS 1985 p. 958; VOYA 7:388)

5-452 **McKINLEY, (Jennifer Carolyn) Robin (Turrell).** *A Knot in the Grain* ✮ *and Other Stories.* Gr. 7–12.

Four of these five love stories—"The Healer," "The Stagman," "Touk's House," and "Buttercups"—are set in the same world of Damar as the author's *The Blue Sword* (1982; see above) and *The Hero and the Crown* (1984; see above).

Greenwillow, 1994, 192 pp. (0-688-09201-2); HarperTrophy, 1995, pap. (0-06-440604-0)

(BL 90:2039; CCBB 47:327; HB 70:458; HBG 5:322; Kirkus 62:778; SLJ May 1994 p. 128; VOYA 17:225)

5-453 **McKINLEY, (Jennifer Carolyn) Robin (Turrell).** *The Stone Fey.* Gr. 6–10.

Maddy, a shepherdess betrothed to a young farmer, forgets everything about her real life while spending long days in the hills enchanted by a Stone Fey. This story was originally published in *Imaginary Lands* (Greenwillow, 1985; see above) and is set in Damar, as are the author's *The Blue Sword* (1982; see above) and *The Hero and the Crown* (1984; see above).

Illus. by John Clapp, Harcourt, 1998, 52 pp. (0-15-200017-8)

(BL 95:484; CCBB 52:22; HBG 10:305; SLJ Jan 1999 p. 130)

5-454 **McKINLEY, (Jennifer Carolyn) Robin (Turrell).** *Sunshine.* Gr. 10 up.

After Sunshine Seddon is abducted by a gang of vampires, she uses her magic abilities to escape, along with an imprisoned vampire named Constantine, to whom she is inexplicably drawn. Mythopoeic Fantasy Award for Adult Literature, 2004.

Berkley, 2003, 400 pp. (0-425-19178-8)

(BL 100:399; Kirkus 71:1039; VOYA 26:416, 27:13)

5-455 **McKINLEY, (Jennifer Carolyn) Robin (Turrell), and DICKINSON,** ✮✮ **Peter.** *Water: Tales of the Elemental Spirits.* Gr. 7–12.

Six short stories written by husband and wife Dickinson and McKinley, including "Mermaid Song," "Sea Serpent," and "Kraken" by Dickinson and "The Sea-King's Son," "Water Horse," and "A Pool in the Desert" by McKinley. The last story is set in Damar, as are the author's *The Blue Sword* (1982; see above) and *The Hero and the Crown* (1984; see above).

Putnam, 2002, 272 pp. (0-399-23796-8); Ace, 2003, pap., 266 pp. (0-441-01056-3)

(BL 98:1416; CCBB 55:410; HB 78:466; HBG 13:393; Kirkus 70:808; Kliatt July 2003 p. 33; SLJ June 2002 p. 142; VOYA 25:130)

5-456 McMULLAN, Kate. *New Kid at School.* **(Dragon Slayers' Academy series, bk. 1).** Gr. 3–6.

On his very first dragon-killing assignment from the Dragon Slayers' Academy, young Wiglaf, failed by his cowardly magic sword, discovers that knock-knock jokes are the dragon's secret weakness. The sequels are *Revenge of the Dragon Lady* (1997, 2003), *Class Trip to the Cave of Doom* (1998, 2003), *A Wedding for Wiglaf* (1998, 2003), *Knight for a Day* (1999, 2003), *Sir Lancelot, Where Are You?* (1999, 2003), *Wheel of Misfortune* (1999, 2003), *Countdown to the Year 1000* (1999, 2003), *97 Ways to Train a Dragon* (2003), *Help! It's Parents' Day at DSA* (2004), *Danger! Wizards at Work* (2004), *The Ghost of Sir Herbert Dungeonstone* (2004), *Beware! It's Friday the 13th!* (2005), and *Pig Latin—Not Just for Pigs!* (2005). *Crime in Camelot* (Macmillan, 2000) is a related story.

Illus. by Bill Basso, Putnam, pap., 1997, 96 pp. (0-448-41592-5); Grosset, pap., 2003, 112 pp. (0-448-43108-4)

(BL 94:637; HBG 9:76; Kirkus 65:1460; SLJ May 1998 p. 120)

5-457 McMULLEN, Sean. *Voyage of the Shadowmoon.* **(Moonworlds Saga, bk.**
★ **1).** Gr. 10 up. (Orig. Australian pub. 2002.)

Only the crew of the *Shadowmoon*, a small drab schooner, know that it is actually a spy ship manned by a priestess, a vampire, a eunuch, and others bent on finding an ancient weapon called Silverdeath. The sequel is *Glass Dragons* (2004).

Tor, 2002, 496 pp. (0-312-87740-4), 2004, pap. (0-7653-0609-3)

(BL 99:652; Kirkus 70:1578:LJ Dec 2002 p. 184; VOYA 26:151)

5-458 *Magic in Ithkar.* **Ed. by Andre Norton and Robert Adams.** Gr. 10 up.
★ Thirteen "shared world" tales set in the magical kingdom of Ithkar, each written by a different author, among them Andre Norton and C. J. Cherryh. *Magic in Ithkar 2* (1985), *Magic in Ithkar 3* (1986), and *Magic in Ithkar 4* (1987) are companion works.

Tor, 1988, pap., 320 pp., o.p.

(BL 81:1436, 1448; Kliatt 19:24; SLJ Aug 1985 p. 88; VOYA 8:268)

MAGUIRE, Gregory. *Wicked: The Life and Times of the Wicked Witch of the West.*
See Chapter 12, Witchcraft and Sorcery Fantasy.

MARCELLAS, Diana. *Mother Ocean, Daughter Sea.*
See Chapter 12, Witchcraft and Sorcery Fantasy.

5-459 MARCO, John. *The Eyes of God.* Gr. 10 up.

King Akeela and his closest friend, Lukien, the Bronze Knight of Liiria, fall in love with the same woman—Akeela's new bride, whose marriage has sealed the peace between their long-warring cities. The sequel is *The Devil's Armor* (2004).

DAW, 2001, 789 pp., o.p., 2003, pap., 779 pp. (0-7564-0096-1)

(LJ Jan 2002 p. 159; VOYA 25:128, 26:13)

5-460 **MARCO, John.** *The Jackal of Nar.* **(Tyrants and Kings, vol. 1).** Gr. 7–12.
☆ A complex story of war, rebellion, treachery, and magic, in which warrior Prince Richius Vantran follows the emperor's orders to put down a popular uprising in the magical kindgom of Lucel-Lor, only to find that his father and wife have been murdered on orders from the emperor's spymaster. The sequels are *The Grand Design* (2000, 2001) and *The Saints and the Sword* (2001).
Bantam, 1999, pap., 784 pp. (0-553-37984-4), 2000, pap., 754 pp. (0-553-57887-1)
(Kirkus 67:111; Kliatt July 1999 p. 23; LJ Feb 15, 1999 p. 187; VOYA 22:192, 23:12)

5-461 **MARK, Jan (pseud. of Janet Marjorie Brisland).** *Aquarius.* Gr. 7–10.
☆ (Orig. British pub. 1982.)
Because Viner's water-divining skills have made him an outcast in his rain-soaked land, he runs away in search of someone who can bring dryness and sunshine to his world.
Atheneum, 1984, 223 pp., o.p.
(CCBB 37:209; HB 60:598; SLJ Apr 1985 p. 98; Suth 3:295; TLS 1982 p. 791)

5-462 **MARK, Jan (pseud. of Janet Marjorie Brisland).** *Divide and Rule.* Gr. 8
☆ up. (Orig. British pub. 1979.)
Hanno spends a frightening year in the power of the temple priests, only to learn that he will be sacrificed if he does not join them.
Crowell, 1980, 264 pp., o.p.
(BL 76:1522; CCBB 33:196; HB 56:415; Kirkus 48:516; SLJ Aug 1980 p. 77; TLS 1979 p. 122)

5-463 **MARKS, Laurie J.** *Fire Logic.* **(Elemental Logic, bk. 1).** Gr. 10 up.
After the witch who governs Shaftal dies without an heir, the country is over-run by Sainite warriors, leaving the fate of its peaceful mountain people in the hands of young Zanja, a homeless emissary, her mentor, and a half-blood giant. The sequel is *Earth Logic* (2004).
Tor, 2002, 336 pp. (0-312-87887-7)
(BL 98:1699; Kirkus 70:461; LJ May 15, 2002 p. 129; VOYA 25:298, 26:13)

5-464 **MARTIN, George R. R.** *A Game of Thrones.* **(A Song of Ice and Fire saga, vol. 1).** Gr. 10 up.
Ned Stark discovers that King Robert's "son" is actually the child of the queen and her brother, but before he can tell the king, his friend is murdered by the queen's family and Ned is imprisoned. The sequels are *A Clash of Kings* (1999, 2000), *A Storm of Swords* (2000), and *A Feast for Crows* (2003).
Bantam, 1996, 672 pp. (0-553-10354-7), 1997, pap. (0-553-57340-3)
(BL 92:1889, 1891; Kirkus 64:936)

5-465 **MARTIN, Graham Dunstan.** *Giftwish.* Gr. 5–8. (Orig. British pub. 1978.)
Ewan is tricked into going to the Castle Midnight to fight the wicked Necro-mancer in order to fulfill an ancient prophecy. The sequel is *Catchfire* (1982), in which Ewan, newly crowned King of Feydom, and Catchfire, the witch girl, struggle to break the enchantment wrought by the wizard Hoodwill.
Houghton, 1981, 202 pp., o.p.
(BL 77:1191, 1197; HB 57:197; SLJ Apr 1981 p. 129)

5-466 **MAY, Julian.** *Conqueror's Moon.* **(Boreal Moon trilogy, bk. 1).** Gr. 10 up.

Deveron Austrey, former spy for Prince Conrig Wincantor, describes Conrig's plan to unite all four kingdoms of High Blenholme under his rule, with the aid of the sorcerer/princess of Moss.
Ace, 2003, 400 pp. (0-441-01132-2)
(BL 100:655; VOYA 27:144)

5-467 MAYHAR, Ardath. *Lords of the Triple Moons.* Gr. 7–9.
Sixteen-year-old Johab, one of the last of the Old Lords of Rehannoth, uses his mental powers to escape from prison and to free his land from the evil ones who murdered his family.
Atheneum, 1983, 141 pp., o.p.
(BL 79:1059, 1096; SLJ Sep 1983 p. 137; VOYA 6:148)

5-468 MAYHAR, Ardath. *Makra Choria.* Gr. 7–9.
Choria uses her inherited powers to dethrone her older sister, who gained the throne of Makraitis by having their father killed.
Atheneum, 1987, 193 pp., o.p.
(HB 58:347; Kirkus 55:58; SLJ Apr 1987 p. 112; VOYA 10:92)

5-469 MAYHAR, Ardath. *Runes of the Lyre.* Gr. 7–12.
A science-fantasy about Yinri, a runaway girl who discovers the secret gateway into the Kingdom of Hasyih where she meets both her real and her foster fathers, becomes "The Queen Who Was to Come," and gathers her forces to battle the evil Hasyisi.
Atheneum, 1982, 214 pp., o.p.
(HB 58:520; SLJ Sep 1982 p. 141; VOYA 5:45)

5-470 MAYHAR, Ardath. *The Saga of Grittel Sundotha.* Gr. 7–10.
Seven-foot-tall Grittel wanders the land of Garetha using her magical powers to rescue the helpless as she searches for her true destiny.
Atheneum, 1985, 204 pp., o.p.
(BL 81:1051, 1060; SLJ Aug 1985 p. 79)

5-471 MAYHAR, Ardath. *Soul-Singer of Tyrnos.* Gr. 6–9.
Trained as a Soul-Singer to keep goodness and justice in the souls of the people, Yeleeve is chosen to fight the evil that is corrupting the land of Tyrnos. *Runes of the Lyre* (1982) is a related work.
Atheneum, 1981, 195 pp., o.p.
(BL 78:98, 110; CCBB 35:91; SLJ Feb 1982 p. 90)

5-472 MAYNE, William (James Carter). *Antar and the Eagles.* Gr. 5–8. (Orig.
★★   British pub. 1989.)
In this suspenseful story, a boy named Antar is stolen by eagles, who teach him to communicate and to fly so that he can rescue a golden egg containing the future Great Eagle.
Delacorte, 1990, 166 pp., o.p.; Walker, 1999, pap. (0-7445-7228-2)
(BL 86:1803; CCBB 43:169; HB 66:457; HBG 1:254; Kirkus 58:267; SLJ June 1990 p. 124; Suth 4:247; VOYA 13:365, 14:9)

5-473 MICHAELS, Melisa C. *Far Harbor.* Gr. 7–12.
Having run away from her abusive Terran foster family, Ugly finds a shard of crystal at an abandoned shrine that shows her visions of Hawke, a young

prince searching for the partner he needs to save his people from their Terran masters.

Tor, 1989, pap., 248 pp., o.p.

(Kliatt Sep 1989 p. 20; VOYA 12:290, 13:12)

5-474   MICKLEM, Sarah. *Firethorn.* Gr. 10 up.

After Firethorn runs away from her village to spend a year alone in the forest, she agrees to accompany Sir Galan to his war camp as his mistress, and must use her healing arts to shape both of their fates. This is the first book of an upcoming trilogy.

Scribner, 2004, 400 pp. (0-7432-4794-9); Spectra, 2005, pap., 400 pp. (0-553-38340-X)

(BL 100:1713; Kirkus 72:206; LJ June 1, 2004, p. 128)

5-475   MIRRLEES, Hope. *Lud-in-the-Mist.* Gr. 10 up. (Orig. British pub. 1926.)

Master Chanticleer, the mayor of the seaport town of Mist, sets out to discover the identity of the smuggler bringing fairy fruits over the border from Fairy-land into the sober land of Dorimare.

Knopf, 1927, o.p.; Ballantine, 1970, 1977, pap., 273 pp., o.p.; Wildside, 2002, 288 pp. (1-58715-963-5), 2002, pap., 288 pp. (1-58715-962-7)

(BL 23:384; TLS Jan 13, 1927 p. 26)

5-476   MODESITT, L(eland) E(xton), Jr. *Legacies.* **(Corean Chronicles, bk. 1).**
✮   Gr. 10 up.

Alucius must keep his magical Talent a secret while growing up, but after he joins the militia and is captured and enslaved by the enemy army, his magical abilities come in handy. The sequels are *Darknesses* (2003) and *Scepters* (2004).

Tor, 2002, 560 pp. (0-765-30561-5), 2003, pap., 608 pp. (0-765-34513-7)

(BL 99:395; Kirkus 70:1272; LJ Nov 15, 2002 p. 105; VOYA 26:66)

5-477   MODESITT, L(eland) E(xton), Jr. *The Magic of Recluce.* **(Saga of the Recluce series, bk. 1).** Gr. 10 up.

Lerris is bored by his woodworking apprenticeship and life in general on the orderly island of Recluce, so he undertakes a "dangergeld" or quest that leads to his participation in the battle between the forces of order and chaos. The sequels are *Towers of the Sunset* (1992), *The Magic Engineer* (1994), *The Order War* (1995, 1996), *The Death of Chaos* (1995), *Fall of Angels* (1996), *The Chaos Balance* (1997), *The White Order* (1998), *The Colors of Chaos* (1999, 2000), and *Wellspring of Chaos* (2003). The Cyador saga (see *Magi'i of Cyador*, below) is a related series.

Tor, 1991, 448 pp., o.p.

(BL 87:1698, 1702; Kirkus 59:510; LJ Apr 15, 1991 p. 129; SLJ Sep 1991 p. 294; VOYA 14:247)

5-478   MODESITT, L(eland) E(xton), Jr. *Magi'i of Cyador.* **(Cyador Saga, bk.**
✮   **1).** Gr. 10 up.

Too independent to suit the High Magi'i, magus-in-training Lorn is sent to fight barbarians on the frontier of Cyador in this story related to the author's Recluce saga (see *The Magic of Recluce*, above). The sequel is *Scion of Cyador* (2000, 2001).

Tor, 2000, 544 pp. (0-312-87226-7), 2001, pap., 544 pp. (0-8125-7948-8)

(BL 96:1440; Kirkus 68:344; LJ Apr 15, 2000 p. 126; VOYA 23:198, 24:13)

5-479 MOON, Elizabeth. *Surrender None: The Legacy of Gird.* Gr. 10 up.
Gird, a peace-loving farmer's son, leads a peasant uprising against the tyrannical overlords. This is the prequel to *The Deed of Paksenarrion* (1992; 2003),
which was originally published separately as *Sheepfarmer's Daughter* (1988),
Divided Allegiance (1988), and *Oath of Gold* (1989). The Deed of Paksenarrion trilogy tells the story of a sheepfarmer's daughter named Paksenarrion
who becomes a soldier, protected by her holy St. Gird medallion, and is eventually transformed into a Paladin, or warrior chosen by the gods.
Baen, 1990, 530 pp., o.p., 1996, pap., 864 pp. (0-671-87747-X)

(BL 86:1960, 1971; Kliatt Sep 1990, p. 22; VOYA 13:300)

5-480 MOORCOCK, Michael (John). *The Dragon in the Sword.* **(The Eternal
Champion saga, bk. 3).** Gr. 10 up.
Erehose sets sail to search for his lost love, Ermizhad, and meets Count Von
Bek, a refugee from the Third Reich. This is the sequel to *The Eternal Champi-
on: A Fantastic Romance* (Dell, 1970, 1978, 1987) and *Phoenix in Obsidian*
(Mayflower, 1970; retitled *The Silver Warrior*, Dell, 1973, 1985). *The
Dreamthief's Daughter: A Tale of the Albino* (2001; see below) and *The
Skrayling Tree: A Tale of the Albino* (2003, 2004) are related stories.
Ace, 1986, 298 pp., o.p.

(BL 83:34, 52; Kirkus 54:1072; LJ Sep 15, 1986 p. 102; VOYA 9:292, 11:12)

5-481 MOORCOCK, Michael (John). *The Dreamthief's Daughter: A Tale of the
Albino.* **(Tales of the Albino).** Gr. 10 up.
Count Ulric von Bek discovers that Emperor Elric of Melnibone is actually he
himself in another time period. This story links Moorcock's Eternal Champion
series (see *The Dragon in the Sword*, above) and Elric saga (see *The Fortress of
the Pearl*, below). The sequels are *The Skrayling Tree: The Albino in America*
(2003, 2004) and *The White Wolf's Son: The Albino in the Middle March* (2005).
Warner, 2001, 343 pp., o.p., 2002, pap., 460 pp. (0-446-61120-4)

(BL 97:1361; Kirkus 69:223; LJ Apr 15, 2001 p. 137)

5-482 MOORCOCK, Michael (John). *The Fortress of the Pearl.* **(The Elric
saga, vol. 8).** Gr. 10 up.
Elric, the albino sorcerer and heir to the kingdom of Melnibone, is tricked into
helping an evil lord of Quarzhasaat search for the Pearl at the Heart of the
World. The sequel is *The Revenge of the Rose* (1991). The preceding volumes
in the saga are *Elric of Melnibone* (1972, 1986, 1992; abridged as *The Dream-
ing Jewels*, 1972), *The Sailor on the Seas of Fate* (1976, 1987, 1989); *The
Weird of the White Wolf* (1977, 1983, 1989), *The Vanishing Tower* (1970,
1977, 1983; also titled *The Sleeping Sorceress*, 1971), *The Bane of the Black
Pearl* (1977, 1984), *Stormbringer* (1965; rev. ed. 1977, 1984), and *Elric at the
End of Time* (1985, 1986). Two related titles are *The Stealer of Souls and
Other Stories* (1965) and *Elric, the Return to Melnibone* (1973). The author's
Tales of the Albino series (see *The Dreamthief's Daughter: A Tale of the Albi-
no*, above) is related.
Ace, 1989, 240 pp., o.p.

(BL 86:148; Kirkus 57:1206; LJ Sep 15, 1989 p. 138; VOYA 12:373, 13:12)

5-483 **MOORCOCK, Michael (John).** *The Ice Schooner: A Tale.* Gr. 10 up.
(Orig. British and U.S. pub. 1969.)
An ice schooner captain, living at the end of a future ice age, makes an ill-fated
pilgrimage to the sacred city of New York.
Berkley, 1969, pap., 208 pp., o.p.; Harper, 1977, 192 pp., o.p.
(BL 73:1485, 1490; Kirkus 45:509; LJ 102:1868)

5-484 **MORLAND, Alanna.** *Leopard Lord.* Gr. 10 up.
Varian, the new Baron of Leopard's Gard, tries to avoid following the dictates
of the dark god's curse on his family by refusing to sacrifice his young wife.
Shackle and Sword (1999) takes place in the same world.
Ace, 1999, 260 pp. (0-441-00606-X)
(Kliatt May 1999 p. 27; VOYA 22:193, 23:12)

5-485 **MORRIS, William.** *The Well at the World's End.* Gr. 10 up. (Orig. British
and U.S. pub. 1896.)
A boy named Ralph grows to manhood while undertaking an adventure-filled
quest to find the well at the world's end. According to Tymn, Zahorski, and
Boyer in *Fantasy Literature: A Core Collection and Reference Guide* (Bowker, 1979), Morris could be called the father of modern high fantasy, and this
work is his most significant. His work influenced many others, including Lord
Dunsany, J. R. R. Tolkien, and C. S. Lewis. Robert D. San Souci has adapted
this story into a book for younger readers entitled *The Well at the End of the
World* (Seastar, 2004).
Longman, 1903, 1913, 496 pp., o.p.; Ballantine, 1970, 1978, o.p.; Wildside,
2000, 332 pp. (1-58715-088-3)
(HB 3:20–22)

MORRISSEY, Dean, and KRENSKY, Stephen (Alan). *The Moon Robber.*
See Chapter 7, High Fantasy: Travel to Other Worlds.

5-486 **MURPHY, Shirley Rousseau.** *Nightpool.* **(Dragonbards trilogy, bk. 1).**
✫ Gr. 7–10.
Young Prince Tebriel, badly injured by his father's murderer, is nursed by a
colony of intelligent otters until he is strong enough to seek out the legendary
singing dragon and avenge his father's death. In *The Ivory Lyre* (1987; 1988),
Tebriel and his telepathic dragon, Seastrider, join the resistance against the evil
ones bent on taking over their world. In *The Dragonbards* (1988; 1989, pap.)
Teb and the other dragonbards challenge the dark lord Quazelzeg and his army
of the unliving.
Harper, 1985, 250 pp., o.p.
(BL 82:53,67, 86:905; CCBB 39:33; SLJ Dec 1985 p. 104; VOYA 8:326)

5-487 **MURPHY, Shirley Rousseau.** *The Ring of Fire.* **(The Children of Ynell
series).** Gr. 7–9.
Zephy and Thorn search for a lost jade runestone that will protect them from
the tyrants of Kubal. *The Wolf Bell* (1979) is set in a previous time, and the
sequels are *The Castle of Hape* (1980), *Caves of Fire and Ice* (1980), and *The
Joining of the Stone* (1981).

Atheneum, 1977, 232 pp., o.p.
(BL 74:368, 378; Kirkus 45:791; SLJ Oct 1977 p. 116; VOYA 3:46)

5-488 MYERS, Walter Dean. *Shadow of the Red Moon.* Gr. 5–9.
Three Okalian children, immune to the Plague, are sent out of Crystal City to search for the Ancient Land in this science-fantasy.
Illus. by Christopher Myers, Scholastic, 1995, 183 pp. (0-590-45895-7)
(BL 92:548; CCBB 49:135; HBG 7:66; Kirkus 63:1568; SLJ Dec 1995 p. 106; VOYA 19:42)

5-489 MYRA, Harold (Lawrence). *The Shining Face.* Gr. 12 up.
Despite a prophecy foretelling the coming of a blind princess who will free her people, Mela resists her fate. This is a sequel to *Children in the Night* (1991), and the final book in the trilogy is *Morning Child* (1994).
Zondervan, 1993, 256 pp. (0-310-58771-9)
(BL 89:852; VOYA 16:312, 17:19)

5-490 NEASON, Rebecca. *The Thirteenth Scroll.* Gr. 10 up.
Blind healer Lysandra and two companions set out to find Selia, an unknown child destined to rule Aghamore, and to protect her from others scheming to win the throne for themselves. The sequel is *The Truest Power* (2002).
Warner, 2001, pap., 432 pp. (0-446-60953-6)
(BL 97:1672; VOYA 24:215)

5-491 NEWMAN, Robert (Howard). *The Shattered Stone.* Gr. 6–8.
In fulfillment of an ancient prophecy, two children without memories search for part of a stone inscription that will bring peace to their land.
Illus. by John Gretzer, Atheneum, 1975, 231 pp., o.p.
(BL 72:305; HB 51:465; Kirkus 43:1186; SLJ Nov 1975 p. 81)

NICHOLS, (Joanna) Ruth. *The Left-Handed Spirit.*
See Chapter 12, Witchcraft and Sorcery Fantasy.

5-492 NICHOLSON, William. *The Wind Singer: An Adventure.* **(The Wind on Fire trilogy, bk. 1).** Gr. 5–8. (Orig. British pub. 2000.)
Kestrel and her twin brother Bowman attempt to escape the rigid rules and caste system of their world by searching for the voice of the Wind Singer, a silent sculpture in the middle of Amaranth. Nestlé Smarties Prize, Gold Award, 2000. The sequels are *Slaves of the Mastery* (2001; 2003), in which Kestrel vows to rescue her enslaved people after the twins are separated when the city of Amaranth is attacked and destroyed, and *Firesong* (2002; 2003).
Illus. by Peter Sís, Hyperion, 2000, 358 pp. (0-7868-2494-8), 2003, pap., 384 pp. (0-7868-1799-2); Hyperion, pap., 2004, 496 pp. (0-7868-1826-3)
(BL 97:438; HBG 12:325; SLJ Dec 2000 p. 146; VOYA 24:13, 54)

5-493 NILES, Douglas. *A Breach in the Watershed.* **(The Watershed trilogy, vol. 1).** Gr. 10 up.
A small band of humans and magical creatures stand together to save their world from the evil Dassadek, who has pierced the Watershed mountains that separate the human, faerie, and demon lands. The sequels are *Darkenheight* (1996, 1997) and *War of Three Waters* (1997, 1998).
Ace, 1995, 448 pp. (0-441-00208-0), 1996, pap., 447 pp. (0-441-00349-4)
(LJ Aug 1995 p. 122; Kirkus 63:745; Kliatt Nov 1995 p. 18; VOYA 18:386, 19:17, 20:120)

5-494 **NIVEN, Larry.** *The Magic Goes Away.* **(Magic trilogy, vol. 1).** Gr. 10 up.
A quest to replenish the earth's source of magic is undertaken by four magicians and a Greek swordsman. The sequels are *Magic May Return* (1983) and *More Magic* (1984).
Illus. by Esteban Maroto, Ace, 1978, 1985, pap., 213 pp., o.p.
(BL 75:856, 861; SLJ Mar 1979 p. 153)

5-495 **NIVEN, Larry, and POURNELLE, Jerry.** *The Burning City.* Gr. 10 up.
Whandal returns to his childhood home in the Burning City to contend with old enemies and the fire god Yangin-Atep, aided by a water elemental created by the last mage of Atlantis.
Pocket, 2000, 544 pp. (0-671-03660-2), 2001, pap. (0-671-03661-0)
(BL 96:1091; Kirkus 68:217; LJ Mar 15, 2000 p. 131)

NIX, Garth. *Sabriel.*
See Chapter 12, Witchcraft and Sorcery Fantasy.

5-496 **NORTON, Andre (pseud. of Alice Mary Norton).** *The Crystal Gryphon.*
☆ **(Kerovan and Joisan books, vol. 1).** Gr. 7–10.
Kerovan and his wife, Joisan, fight foreign invaders and the Dark Powers to regain the throne of Ulm. *The Jargoon Pard* (1974; see below) is a companion volume, and *Gryphon in Glory* (1981) and *Gryphon's Eyrie* (1985, 1989) are the sequels. These books are related to Norton's Witch World series (see Chapter 7, High Fantasy: Travel to Other Worlds) and to her Witch World: The Turning trilogy (see *Storms of Victory*, below).
Atheneum, 1972, o.p.
(BL 69:192, 204; Kirkus 40:948; LJ 97:4080; TLS 1973 p. 1114)

5-497 **NORTON, Andre (pseud. of Alice Mary Norton).** *The Jargoon Pard.* Gr.
7–9.
Kethan's magical powers save him from being used as a pawn in the power struggle for the throne of the House of Car Do Prawn. This is a companion volume to *The Crystal Gryphon* (1972; see above) and is related to Norton's Witch World series (see Chapter 7, High Fantasy: Travel to Other Worlds) and to her Witch World: The Turning trilogy (see *Storms of Victory*, below).
Atheneum, 1974, 194 pp., o.p.
(BL 71:46; HB 51:153; LJ 99:2748; TLS 1975 p. 1052)

5-498 **NORTON, Andre (pseud. of Alice Mary Norton).** *The Mark of the Cat.*
☆ Gr. 10 up.
After he is left alone in the desert wilderness to complete his "solo," Hynkkel and the fierce desert sandcats become blood brothers and he follows his fate toward the emperor's palace. The sequel, *Year of the Rat*, was first published in *Mark of the Cat/Year of the Rat* (Meisha Merlin, 2002).
Ace, 1992, 248 pp. (0-441-52020-0)
(BL 88:1316; LJ Apr 15, 1992 p. 125; SLJ Feb 1993 p. 126; VOYA 15:178, 16:10)

5-499 **NORTON, Andre (pseud. of Alice Mary Norton).** *The Monster's Legacy.*
Gr. 7 up.
Apprentice embroiderer Sarita escapes murderous invaders with the earl's infant son and hides in mountains rumored to be the home of a monster.

Illus. by Jody A. Lee, Simon, 1966, 151 pp. (0-689-80731-7)
(BL 92:1356; HBG 7:304; SLJ June 1996 p. 154; VOYA 19:171)

NORTON, Andre (pseud. of Alice Mary Norton). *Quag Keep.*
See Chapter 6, High Fantasy: Myth or Legend Fantasy.

5-500 NORTON, Andre (pseud. of Alice Mary Norton). *Scent of Magic.* Gr. 10 up.
In a dukedom where many odors carry magical properties, scullery maid Willadine's acute sense of smell portends magical powers and she is brought to the ducal court.
Avon, 1998, 368 pp. (0-380-97687-0)
(BL 94:1979; Kirkus 66:1004; LJ Sep 15, 1998 p. 116)

5-501 NORTON, Andre (pseud. of Alice Mary Norton). *Wind in the Stone.* Gr. 10 up.
Raised secretly in the forest, young Falice, a rare Wind-senser, battles her twin brother, Fogar, raised by a ruthless mage, in order to free the valley from tyranny.
Avon, 1999, 288 pp. (0-380-97602-1)
(BL 96:424; Kirkus 67:1452; LJ Nov 15, 1999 p. 102)

NORTON, Andre (pseud. of Alice Mary Norton). *Witch World.*
See Chapter 7, High Fantasy: Travel to Other Worlds.

5-502 NORTON, Andre (pseud. of Alice Mary Norton), and GRIFFIN, P(auline) M. *Storms of Victory.* **(Witch World: The Turning trilogy, bk. 1).** Gr. 10 up.
Two novellas set in Witch World after the Turning, a huge magical war. In "Port of Dead Ships," a woman faces an evil sea creature; in "Sea Keep," another woman struggles to protect her dale. The sequels are *Flight of Vengeance* (1992) by Norton, Griffin, and Mary Schaub and *On Wings of Magic* (1994) by Norton, Sacha Miller, and Patricia Matthews. This trilogy is related to Norton's Witch World series (see *Witch World*, Chapter 7, High Fantasy: Travel to Other Worlds).
Tor, 1991, 1994, pap., 432 pp., o.p.
(BL 87:1180; Kirkus 59:219; VOYA 14:182)

NORTON, Andre (pseud. of Alice Mary Norton), and LACKEY, Mercedes. *The Elvenbane: An Epic High Fantasy of the Halfblood Chronicles.*
See Chapter 12, Witchcraft and Sorcery Fantasy.

5-503 NORTON, Andre (pseud. of Alice Mary Norton), and MILLER, Sasha. *To the King a Daughter.* **(Cycle of Oak, Yew, Ash, and Rowan, bk. 1).** Gr. 6–10.
Raised by Zazar, one of the Fates, after her mother dies in childbirth, Ashen grows into her magic powers while the land of Rendel is ruled by the power-hungry Queen Ysa. The sequels are *Knight or Knave* (2001) and *A Crown Disowned* (2002).
Tor, 1999, 320 pp. (0-312-87336-0); 2001, pap., 314 pp. (0-8125-7757-4)
(Kirkus 68:1985; LJ Sep 15, 2000 p. 119; VOYA 23:435)

5-504 ODOM, Mel. *The Rover.* Gr. 10 up.

✶ Young halfling librarian Wick Lamplighter is kidnapped by pirate dwarfs, battles Boneblights, becomes enslaved by goblinkin, and is rescued by thieves, pursued by assassins, and attacked by dragons in this action-packed and humorous adventure. The sequel is *The Destruction of the Books* (2005), set nearly a century later.

Tor, 2001, 416 pp. (0-312-87882-6); Forge, 2002, pap., 512 pp. (0-7653-4194-8)

(BL 97:1992; Kirkus 69:837; LJ Aug 2001 p. 171; SLJ Jan 2002 p. 171; VOYA 24:373, 25:15)

5-505 O'LEARY, Patrick. *The Gift.* Gr. 10 up.

✶ The wizards' cure for King Simon's deafness makes him telepathic until an orphaned boy named Tim uses magic to heal the king and the two confront their common enemies, the Night Usher and his rook, Tomen.

Tor, 1997, 288 pp. (0-312-86402-7), 1998, pap., 287 pp. (0-312-86403-5)

(BL 94:312, 732; Kirkus 65:1165; LJ Oct 15, 1997 p. 97; VOYA 21:132)

On Crusade: More Tales of the Knights Templar. **Ed. by Katherine Kurtz.**
See Chapter 3, Fantasy Collections.

5-506 OPPEL, Kenneth. *Airborn.* Gr. 6–10. (Orig. Canadian pub. 2004.)

✶ Attacked by pirates, the airship carrying cabin boy Matt Cruse and passenger Kate de Vries crashes onto a desert island, where, before their capture and imprisonment, they come upon the mysterious Cloud Cats. Canadian Governor General's Literary Award for Children's Literature, 2004.

Eos/HarperCollins, 2004, 368 pp. (0-06-053181-9)

(BL 100:1720; CCBB 57:477; HB 80:459; Kirkus 72:496; SLJ July 2004 p. 110; VOYA 27:145)

ORR, A. *The World in Amber.*
See Chapter 12, Witchcraft and Sorcery Fantasy.

PALMER, David R. *Threshold.*
See Chapter 8, Humorous Fantasy.

5-507 PAOLINI, Christopher. *Eragon.* **(Inheritance trilogy, bk. 1).** Gr. 7–12.

✶ (Orig. self-published, 2002.)

When the iridescent blue stone he finds hatches into a dragon, Eragon's life as a dragon rider begins and he seeks to avenge the death of his uncle and the destruction of his home. The sequel is *Eldest* (2005).

Knopf, 2003, 509 pp. (0-375-92668-2); Paolini, 2002, pap., 472 pp. (0-966621-33-6)

(BL 99:1981; CCBB 57:163; HBG 15:113; Kirkus 71:967; Kliatt Sep 2003 p. 10; SLJ Sep 2003 p. 218; VOYA 26:240, 27:14)

5-508 PATON WALSH, Jill (Gillian Bliss). *Torch.* Gr. 6–10. (Orig. British pub.

✶ 1987.)

Cal and Dio make a deathbed promise to the old Guardian to care for his magical torch and to search for the "games" for which he had been guarding it in this story set in what could be Greece in a future time.

Farrar, 1988, 176 pp., o.p.

(BL 84:1420, 1439; CCBB 41:191; Kirkus 56:371; SLJ May 1988 p. 111; TLS 1989 p. 648; VOYA 11:139)

5-509 **PATTISON, Darcy.** *The Wayfinder.* Gr. 5–8.
★ Apprentice Wayfinder Winchal Eldras, 11, is chosen by the prince of the Heartland to make a dangerous journey through the Great Rift to search for the Well of Life, accompanied by royal gazehound Lady Kala.
Greenwillow, 2000, 200 pp. (0-06-029157-5)
(BL 97:821; CCBB 54:192; HBG 12:77; SLJ Jan 2001 p. 134; VOYA 24:54)

5-510 **PAXSON, Diana L.** *Lady of Light.* **(The First Book of Westria).** Gr. 10 up.
King Jehan of Westria searches for a wife who will be able to use the jewels of the four natural elements to better the kingdom. The sequels are *Lady of Darkness* (1983), *Silverhair the Warrior* (1986), *The Earthstone* (1987), *The Sea Star* (1988), *Wind Crystal* (1990), and *The Jewel of Fire* (1992).
Pocket, 1982, pap., 261 pp., o.p.
(Kliatt 17:16; LJ 107:2355)

5-511 **PIERCE, Meredith Ann.** *Birth of the Firebringer.* **(Firebringer trilogy, vol. 1).** Gr. 7–10.
The son of the prince of unicorns discovers that he is Firebringer, destined to save his race from their enemies, the gryphons. The sequels are *Dark Moon* (1992, 2003) and *The Son of Summer Stars* (1996, 2003).
Macmillan, 1985, 234 pp., o.p.; Firebird/Penguin, 2003, pap., 202 pp. (0-14-250053-4)
(BL 82:861, 870; CCBB 39:94; Kirkus 53:1090; SLJ Jan 1986 p. 70)

5-512 **PIERCE, Meredith Ann.** *The Darkangel.* **(The Darkangel trilogy, vol. 1).**
★ Gr. 6–10.
Even though she is falling in love with him, Aeriel must slay the beautiful but horrifying Darkangel vampire. I.R.A. Children's Book Award, 1983. In *A Gathering of Gargoyles* (1984, 1985, 1998), Aeriel makes a hazardous journey to gather five gargoyles in preparation for a final battle with the White Witch who enslaved her lover. In *The Pearl of the Soul of the World* (1990, 1998), Aeriel attempts to destroy the White Witch by bringing her a pearl containing all the Ancientlady's knowledge of the world.
Little, Brown, 1982, 223 pp., o.p.; Harcourt, 1998, pap., 204 pp. (0-15-201768-2)
(BL 78:1236, 1260, 80:353, 86:785, 905, 91:415; CCBB 35:213; HB 58:416; Kirkus 50:376; SLJ Mar 1982 p. 160; VOYA 5:40)

5-513 **PIERCE, Meredith Ann.** *Treasure at the Heart of the Tanglewood.* Gr.
★ 7–10.
Brown Hannah, a young healer who has lost her memory, escapes a wizard's imprisonment in Tanglewood after her would-be rescuer is transformed from a knight into a fox.
Viking, 2001, 256 pp. (0-670-89247-5); Firebird, 2003, pap. (0-14-250013-5)
(BL 97:1557, 98:1417; CCBB 54:419; HB 77:460; HBG 12:314; Kirkus 69:504; Kliatt Mar 2001 p. 14; SLJ June 2001 p. 153; VOYA 24:135, 25:15)

5-514 **PIERCE, Meredith Ann.** *The Woman Who Loved Reindeer.* Gr. 7–12.
★ A young girl named Caribou and the magical reindeer she raised lead her tribe

on a dangerous journey to a new home.

Little, Brown, 1985, 242 pp., o.p.; Tor, 1989, pap. (0-8125-0305-8); Harcourt, 2000, pap., 256 pp. (0-15-201799-2)

(BL 82:330, 340; CCBB 39:75; HB 62:208; Kirkus 53:992; SLJ Dec 1985 p. 104; VOYA 9:41, 13:138)

5-515   PIERCE, Tamora. *Alanna: The First Adventure.* **(Song of the Lioness,**
☆   **bk. 1).** Gr. 6–10.

Alanna and her twin brother, Alan, secretly change places as they are sent away from home for training. She is determined to ignore her magical powers and become a knight; he wants to become a sorcerer, not a knight. In *In the Hand of the Goddess* (1984; 1990, pap.; Random, 1997, pap.; Simon, 2002), Alanna has reached the level of squire to Prince Jonathan when she becomes suspicious that a sorcerer, Duke Roger, is plotting against the royal family. In *The Woman Who Rides Like a Man* (1986; 1990, pap.; 1997, pap.; Atheneum, 2003), Alanna, now a knight, proves her prowess as a warrior by aiding a tribe of desert raiders who declare her their shaman. *Lioness Rampant* (1988; 1990, pap.; 1997, pap.; Atheneum, 2003) completes the series. The author's Immortals series (see *Wild Magic: The Immortals*, below) and her Protector of the Small series (see *First Test*, below) are set in the same world. *Trickster's Choice* (2003; see below) is the first book in the Daughter of the Lioness series, about Alanna's daughter, Alianne.

Macmillan, 1983, 252 pp., o.p.; Random, 1997, pap. (0-679-80114-6); Simon, 2002, 240 pp. (0-689-85323-8)

(BL 78:1236, 1260, 80:353; CCBB 35:213; HB 58:416; HBG 14:86; Kirkus 50:376; SLJ Mar 1982 p. 160; VOYA 5:40)

5-516   PIERCE, Tamora. *First Test.* **(Protector of the Small series, bk. 1).** Gr.
☆   5–8.

Keladry, 10, has a difficult probationary knighthood training year because neither the trainer, Lord Wyldon, nor the other pages want to have a girl in the program. In the sequel, *Page* (2000, 2001), Keladry uses her wits and fighting skills to protect others being bullied during her next three years as a page and repels an attack by bandits. In *Squire* (2001, 2003), 14-year-old Keladry is chosen as squire for Lord Raoul, commander of the King's Own Guard, and adopts a fledgling griffin. In *Lady Knight* (2002, 2003), Keladry has completed eight grueling years of training and is called into service to search for an evil mage who is using chidren to create murderous weapons. This series is related to the author's three other series set in the Kingdom of Tortall—Song of the Lioness quartet (see *Alanna: The First Adventure*, above), the Immortals series (see *Wild Magic: The Immortals*, below), and Daughter of the Lioness (see *Trickster's Choice*, below).

Random, 1999, 224 pp. (0-679-98914-5), 1999, pap. (0-679-88917-5)

(BL 95:1832, 96:1546; CCBB 52:398; HBG 10:298; SLJ July 1999 p. 99; VOYA 23:127)

PIERCE, Tamora. *Magic Steps.*
See Chapter 12, Witchcraft and Sorcery Fantasy.

PIERCE, Tamora. *Sandry's Book.*
See Chapter 12, Witchcraft and Sorcery Fantasy.

5-517 **PIERCE, Tamora.** *Trickster's Choice.* **(Daughter of the Lioness series,**
✶ **bk. 1).** Gr. 6–12.
Alanna's daughter Alianne, or Aly, 16, lives out the dream her parents disapproved of by becoming a spy after her capture by slave traders in the Copper Isles. In the sequel, *Trickster's Queen* (2004), 17-year-old Aly has become the leader of a network of raka rebels and uses her magic to protect two sisters, Dove and Sarai Balitang, fated to rule the post-rebellion Copper Isles. This series follows Pierce's Song of the Lioness series (see *Alanna: The First Adventure*, above), and is set in the same world as the Immortals series (see *Wild Magic: The Immortals*, below) and Protector of the Small series (see *First Test*, above).
Random, 2003, 446 pp. (0-375-91466-8)
(BL 100:6660; CCBB 57:120; HB 80:90; HBG 15:100; Kirkus 71:1129; Kliatt Nov 2003 p. 8; SLJ Dec 2003 p. 158; VOYA 26:326, 27:14)

5-518 **PIERCE, Tamora.** *Wild Magic: The Immortals.* **(The Immortals, bk. 1).**
✶ Gr. 6–10.
Shy assistant horsemistress Daine begins to accept her gift of wild magic and learns from the Wizard Numain (trapped in the form of a hawk) how valuable her powers will be to the kingdom's future. In *Wolf-Speaker* (1994; 1997; 2003), Daine, 14, is called back from her mage training by a pack of wolves to help prevent the overthrow of the king. In *The Emperor Mage* (1995; 1997, 2003), Daine's ability to communicate with and heal animals leads her to join a delegation sent to make peace with an enemy emperor. *The Realms of the Gods* (1996; 1997, 2003) is the final book of the series. These books are related to the author's Song of the Lioness quartet (see *Alanna: The First Adventure*, above), her Daughter of the Lioness series (see *Trickster's Choice*, above), and her Protector of the Small series (see *First Test*, above).
Macmillan, 1992, 208 pp. (0-689-31761-1); Random, 1997, pap., 299 pp. (0-679-88288-X); Atheneum, 2003, 299 pp. (0-689-85611-3)
(BL 89:419; CCBB 46:188; HB 69:93; HBG 4:83; Kirkus 60:1314; SLJ Nov 1992 p. 98; VOYA 15:356, 16:16)

5-519 **PINI, Wendy, and PINI, Richard.** *ElfQuest: The Novel, Journey to Sorrow's End.* **(ElfQuest Saga, bk. 1).** Gr. 6–12.
The wolf-riding Elf tribe, driven from their home by humans, crosses a desert in search of a new home. This novel was originally published in comic-book format. The sequels are *ElfQuest, Book 2* (1983), *ElfQuest, Book 3* (1984), and *ElfQuest, Book 4* (1985). The Blood of Ten Chiefs books are shared-world anthologies dealing with the history of the ElfQuest characters, written by well-known fantasy authors including C. J. Cherryh, Piers Anthony, Nancy Garden, and Diana Paxson. They are *The Blood of Ten Chiefs*, (Tor, 1986), *Wolfsong* (Tor, 1988), *Winds of Change* (Tor, 1989), *Against the Wind* (Tor, 1990), and *The Quest Begins* (Ace, 1996). *ElfQuest: Bedtime Stories* by Wendi Lee and Terry Beatty (Warp, 1994) is a collection of related stories written for children in grades 4 to 6, and *That Way Lies Camelot* (HarperPrism, 1996) contains three stories set in the world of the Blood of Ten Chiefs series.
Berkley, 1984 (0-425-07009-3), 1985, pap. (0-425-08458-2)
(BL 79:602, 606; VOYA 6:46)

5-520   **POWERS, Tim.** *The Stress of Her Regard.* Gr. 10 up.
☆   Doctor Michael Crawford entreats the poets Shelley, Byron, and Keats to help get rid of the evil spirits that killed his wife and are haunting his life. Mythopoeic Fantasy Award, 1990.
Ace, 1989, 392 pp., o.p., 1991, pap. (0-441-79097-6)
(BL 86:42; VOYA 12:373, 13:16)

5-521   **PRATCHETT, Terry.** *The Amazing Maurice and His Educated Rodents.*
☆   **(Discworld series).** Gr. 6–9. (Orig. British pub. 2001.)
Scam artists Maurice the cat and six intelligent rats con the inhabitants of town after town into paying Maurice to pipe out rat infestations until Maurice and his friends are forced to work with humans to defeat a truly evil adversary. Carnegie Medal, 2001. This is the author's first Discworld novel for younger readers.
HarperCollins, 2001, 256 pp. (0-06-001233-1), 2001, pap. (0-06-001234-X)
(BL 98:842, 1417; CCBB 55:217; HB 78:217; HBG 13:380; Kirkus 69:1490; Kliatt Nov 2001 p. 10; SLJ Dec 2001 p. 142; VOYA 24:450, 25:15)

5-522   **PRATCHETT, Terry.** *The Color of Magic.* **(Discworld series, vol. 2).** Gr. 10 up. (Orig. British pub. 1983, entitled *The Colour of Magic.*)
Kin Arad and two nonhuman companions travel to a flat earth where they meet dragons and robots and embark on a series of madcap adventures. The first book in the series is *Strata* (1981, 1991), and the sequels are *Wyrd Sisters* (1980, 1988), *The Light Fantastic* (1986, 2000), *Equal Rites* (1987, 2000), *Mort* (1987, 2001), *Sourcery* (1989, 2001), *Pyramids* (1989, 2001), *Guards! Guards!* (1989), *Eric* (1990, 1992, 1995, 2002), *Moving Pictures* (1990, 1992), *Reaper Man* (1991), *Witches Abroad* (1991, 1993), *Small Gods* (1992, 1994); *Lords and Ladies* (1992, 1994, 1995), *Men at Arms* (1993, 1996), *Soul Music* (1994, 1995), *Interesting Times* (1994, 1997), *Maskerade* (1995, 1997), *Hogfather* (1996, 2000), *Feet of Clay* (1996), *Jingo* (1997, 1998), *Carpe Jugulum* (1998, 2000), *The Last Continent* (1998), *The Truth* (2000, 2001), *The Fifth Elephant* (2000, 2001), *Thief of Time* (2001), *The Last Hero* (2001), *Night Watch* (2002), *The Monstrous Regiment* (2003), and *Going Postal* (2004). Pratchett has also written two Discworld novels for younger readers, *The Amazing Maurice and His Enchanted Rodents* (2001; see above) and *The Wee Free Men* (2003; see below).
St. Martin's, 1983, 210 pp., o.p.; Harper, 2000, pap., 210 pp. (0-06-102071-0)
(Kirkus 51:913; LJ 108:1975)

5-523   **PRATCHETT, Terry.** *Truckers.* **(The Bromeliad trilogy, bk. 1).** Gr. 5–9.
☆   (Orig. British pub. 1989.)
The secure world of the miniature people or "nomes" whose lives have flourished beneath the floorboards of the Arnold Brothers Department Store seems fated for extinction when they learn of the imminent demolition of their home, until Masklin shows them a way to escape. In *Diggers* (1991, 2004), the nomes have fled to a deserted rural quarry, but life in the country proves difficult, especially after human beings return. In *Wings* (1991, 2004), the nomes stow away on the Concorde from England to Florida and attempt to use a communications satellite to summon a ship to take them away from Earth. *The Bromeliad Trilogy: Truckers, Diggers, and Wings* (2003) contains all three books.
Delacorte, 1990, 246 pp., o.p.; HarperTrophy, 2004, pap., 288 pp. (0-06-

009496-6)

(BL 86:1432, 1457; HB 66:202, 80:158; HBG 1:254, 15:101; Kirkus 58:49; VOYA 13:366, 14:13)

5-524   PRATCHETT, Terry. *The Wee Free Men.* **(Discworld series).** Gr. 6–10.
✭   (Orig British pub. 2003.)
Tiffany Aching follows the Elf Queen who kidnapped her brother into Fairy-land, accompanied by a formerly human toad and a fierce band of six-inch-tall Wee Free Men. This is the author's second Discworld novel for younger read-ers. In the sequel, *A Hat Full of Sky: The Continuing Adventures of Tiffany Aching and the Wee Free Men* (2004), Tiffany, now apprenticed to a mountain witch named Miss Level, needs the help of the Wee Free Men to battle a hiver, a supernatural parasite bent on taking over her magic and her mind.
HarperCollins, 2003, 275 pp. (0-06-001237-4); HarperTrophy, 2004, pap., 375 pp. (0-06-001238-2)
(BL 99:1465; CCBB 56:458; HB 79:355, 80:11; HBG 14:387; Kirkus 71:610, 1404; Kliatt May 2003 p. 13; SLJ May 2003 p. 158; VOYA 26:240)

5-525   PRATT, (Murray) Fletcher. *The Well of the Unicorn.* Gr. 10 up.
Airar Alvarson leads the rebels of the Iron Ring in their battle against the Vulking invaders of Dalarna.
Sloane, 1948, 338 pp., o.p.; Ballantine/Del Rey, 1981, pap., o.p.
(Kirkus 15:628; LJ 72:1685)

5-526   PREISS, Byron (Cary), and REAVES, Michael. *Dragonworld.* Gr. 10 up.
Falsely accused of being a spy for the murderous neighboring kingdom of Sim-balla, Amsel of Fandora travels to the land of the Dragons to discover who is killing both kingdoms' children.
Bantam, 1979, 1983 (rev. ed.), pap., 560 pp., o.p.
(BL 76:544, 550, 78:594; SLJ Jan 1980 p. 82)

5-527   PULLMAN, Philip. *The Firework-Maker's Daughter.* Gr. 4–7. (Orig.
✭   British pub. 1995.)
Aided by a white elephant and his keeper, Lila battles pirates, a tiger, and Raz-vani the Fire-Fiend on her journey to find the magical royal sulphur that will show she is a true fireworks artist like her father.
Illus. by S. Saelig Gallagher, Scholastic, 1999, 112 pp. (0-590-18719-8), 2001, pap. (0-349-22420-9)
(BL 96:260, 822, 1546; CCBB 53:181; HBG 11:86; Kirkus 67:1651; SLJ Nov 1999 p. 163; VOYA 22:338)

5-528   PULLMAN, Philip. *The Golden Compass.* **(His Dark Materials trilogy,**
✭✭   **bk. 1).** Gr. 7 up. (Orig. British pub. 1995, entitled *Northern Lights.*)
Lyra Belacqua runs away from her guardian, Mrs. Coulter, after she discovers the woman's connection to the child-stealing Gobblers, and flees to the North where her uncle, Lord Asriel, is held prisoner by armored bears. Carnegie Medal, 1995; British Children's Book of the Year Award, 1996; Guardian Children's Fiction Prize, 1996; YALSA Top Ten Best Books for Young Adults, 1997. In *The Subtle Knife* (1997, 2001), Will Parry escapes through a window from our world into another world, where he meets Lyra and her demon, Pantalaimon, and the two young people travel from world to world searching for the mysterious Dust and Will's missing father. In *The Amber*

Spyglass (2000, 2003), the concluding volume of Pullman's complex allegory of the Fall of Adam and Eve, Lyra and Will are reunited for the final battle between evil, represented by the Church, and good, represented by Dust and the human ability to choose and experience love. British Children's Book of the Year, 2000; Carnegie Medal Highly Commended Book, 2000; Whitbread Book of the Year, and Children's Book of the Year, 2001. In *Lyra's Oxford* (2003), an episode set two years later, the birds of Oxford protect Lyra from a witch's murderous plot. *The Book of Dust* is a planned prequel to the trilogy. Knopf, 1996, 397 pp. (0-679-87924-2); Dell, 2001, pap., 399 pp. (0-440-41832-1)

(BL 92:1179, 93:1294, 1305, 94:475; CCBB 49:277; HB 72:464; HBG 7:296; Kirkus 64:379; LJ Feb 15, 1996 p. 176; SLJ Apr 1996 p. 158; VOYA 20:84, 21:133)

5-529 RANDALL, David. *Clovermead: In the Shadow of the Bear.* **(In the Shad-**
✮ **ow of the Bear series, bk. 1).** Gr. 6–9.
After the bear's tooth she finds and wears around her neck binds Clovermead to a violent cult of bear worshipers, she and her innkeeper father must flee their home, and set out to undo the consequences of a crime he committed long ago.
McElderry, 2004, 304 pp. (0-689-86639-9)

(BL 100:1834; CCBB 57:434; Kirkus 72:580; SLJ July 2004 p. 112; VOYA 27:233)

5-530 RAWN, Melanie. *Dragon Prince.* **(Dragon Prince trilogy, vol. 1).** Gr. 10 up.
Peace seems almost within grasp because of the approaching arranged marriage between Sioned of Goddess Keep and Prince Rohan of Stronghold, but political intrigue touches off another war. The sequels are *The Star Scroll* (1989) and *Sunrunner's Fire* (1990). This trilogy is followed by the Dragon Star trilogy (1990–1993; see below).
DAW, 1988, pap., 574 pp., o.p.

(LJ Nov 15, 1988 p. 88; VOYA 12:186)

5-531 RAWN, Melanie. *The Ruins of Ambrai.* **(Exiles trilogy, vol. 1).** Gr. 10 up.
Three motherless sisters raised apart discover that their magical powers are key to the survival of the world of Lenfell and its Mage Guardians. The sequels are *The Mageborn Traitor* (1997, 1998) and *The Captal's Tower* (2004).
DAW, 1994, 688 pp. (0-88677-619-8), 1996, pap. (0-88677-668-6)

(VOYA 17:351; LJ Oct 15, 1994 p. 90)

5-532 RAWN, Melanie. *Stronghold.* **(Dragon Star trilogy, bk. 1).** Gr. 10 up.
Crown Prince Pol and his cousin Lord Andry of Goddess Keep strongly disagree over the use of ancient magic to fight a seemingly invincible invasion force that has arrived on their shores, in this story that will be best understood by readers of the author's Dragon Prince trilogy (see *Dragon Prince*, above). The sequels are *The Dragon Token* (1992) and *Skybowl* (1993).
DAW, 1990, 487 pp., o.p.

(Kirkus 58:1431; LJ Nov 15, 1990 p. 95; VOYA 14:47)

5-533 RAWN, Melanie, ROBERSON, Jennifer, and ELLIOTT, Kate. *The Golden Key.* Gr. 10 up.
In this volume containing three connected novels written by three authors, Sario Grijalva uses his magical powers to imprison his beautiful cousin inside

a painting, causing centuries of feuding between the royal families of Tira Virte.

DAW, 1996, 784 pp. (0-88677-691-0), 1997, pap. (0-88677-746-1)

(BL 93:69; Kirkus 64:1108; VOYA 19:340, 20:10)

5-534 RAY, Mary (Eva Pedder). *The Golden Bees.* Gr. 7–9. (Orig. British pub. 1984.)

Young Kenofer journeys across the oceans and mountains of ancient Greece to retrieve a princess's lost golden earring. This is the sequel to *Song of Thunder* (1978).

Faber, 1984, 152 pp., o.p.

(CCBB 37:211; HB 60:477; SLJ Aug 1984 p. 86)

5-535 REEVES, James (pseud. of John Morris Reeves). *The Cold Flame.* Gr. 5–7.

A soldier uses a witch's unquenchable blue flame to win himself a kingdom and a princess.

Illus. by Charles Keeping, Meredith, 1967, 137 pp., o.p.

(HB 45:419; LJ 94:1799; TLS 1967 p. 1142)

5-536 REICHERT, Mickey Zucker. *Beyond Ragnarok.* **(The Renshai Chronicles, vol. 1).** Gr. 10 up.

A band of young people—including a princess, the Royal Bard's son, a female warrior, an apprentice knight, and a thief—search for the only living heir to the throne of Bearn in this continuation of the author's Renshai trilogy (1992–1993; see below) set 300 years later. The sequels are *Prince of Demons* (1996, 1997) and *The Children of Wrath* (1998, 1999).

DAW, 1995, 676 pp. (0-88677-658-9), 1996, pap., 744 pp. (0-88677-701-1)

(Kliatt Nov 1996 p. 16; VOYA 20:120)

5-537 REICHERT, Mickey Zucker. *Flightless Falcon.* Gr. 10 up.

Upon release from prison for stealing food, Tamison discovers that his family has disappeared and sets off with a fortune-teller and a prison guard to find them.

DAW, 2000, 336 pp. (0-88677-900-6), 2001, pap., 307 pp. (0-7564-0000-7)

(BL 96:1866; Kirkus 68:758; LJ June 15, 2000 p. 121; VOYA 23:364)

5-538 REICHERT, Mickey Zucker. *The Last of the Renshai.* **(Renshai trilogy, vol. 1).** Gr. 10 up.

Rache, the lone survivor of a fearless warrior race, works training gladiators until he reluctantly agrees to join forces with the wizards to prevent a great war ordained by the gods. The sequels are *The Western Wizard* (1992) and *Child of Thunder* (1993). The Renshai Chronicles continue the saga (see *Beyond Ragnarok*, above).

DAW, 1992, 1996, pap., 640 pp. (0-88677-503-5)

(BL 88:684, 686; Kliatt Apr 1992, p. 16; LJ Dec 1991 p. 203; VOYA 15:114)

5-539 REICHERT, Mickey Zucker, and WINGERT, Jennifer. *Spirit Fox.* Gr. 10 up.

Kiarda was born without the spirit-link to an orphaned fox her father killed, but as she matures she realizes that she can transform herself into a fox, an ability

reviled by the armed invaders of the Marchlands.
DAW, 1998, 368 pp. (0-88677-806-9); 2000, pap., 446 pp. (0-88677-807-7)
(Kirkus 66:1499; LJ Dec 1998 p. 162; VOYA 22:125, 23:13)

5-540   REIMANN, Katya. *Prince of Fire and Ashes.* **(The Tielmaran Chronicles, vol. 3).** Gr. 10 up.
Witch Gaultry Blas tries to save young assassin Tullier from becoming a sacrificial victim dedicated to Prince Benet's coronation as King of Tielmark. The preceding books in this series are *Wind from a Foreign Sky* (1996) and *A Tremor in the Bitter Earth* (1998).
Tor, 2002, 480 pp. (0-312-86009-9)
(Kirkus 70:777; VOYA 25:401)

5-541   RESNICK, Laura. *In Legend Born.* Gr. 10 up.
A sorcerer, two warriors, an immortal, and an aristocrat become resistance fighters in Sileria, opposing the tyranny of the Valdani overlords. *The White Dragon* (2003) and *The Destroyer Goddess* (2003) are sequels and the first two books of the author's In Fire Forged series.
Tor, 1998, 464 pp. (0-312-89055-9), 2000, pap., 724 pp. (0-812-55547-3)
(BL 94:1979; Kirkus 66:937; LJ July 1998 p. 142; VOYA 21:446)

5-542   REYNOLDS, Alfred. *Kiteman of Karanga.* Gr. 6–9.
Having used his Kitewing glider to escape from Karanga after being banished for cowardice, Karl discovers enemy forces plotting to invade his country.
Knopf, 1985, 217 pp., o.p.; Bantam, 1987, pap. (entitled *Kiteman*), 208 pp., o.p.
(BL 82:217; Kliatt Jan 1987 p. 18; SLJ Nov 1985 p. 90)

5-543   REYNOLDS, Susan Lynn. *Strandia.* Gr. 7 up. (Orig. Canadian pub. 1991.)
Rejected by her people after she pretends to lack the telepathic "talent" of dolphin-calling in order to avoid an unwanted marriage, Sand is taken in by the Midislanders on Strandia.
Farrar, 1991, 277 pp. (0-374-37274-8)
(CCBB 45:20; HBG 3:80; Kirkus 59:933; SLJ Sep 1991 p. 284; VOYA 14:325)

5-544   ROBERSON, Jennifer. *A Pride of Princes.* **(Chronicles of the Cheysuli, bk. 5).** Gr. 10 up.
The Cheysuli Princes Brennan, Hart, and Corin—shape-shifting warriors who become animals at will—must fulfill a prophecy and battle evil sorcery before they can rule their kingdoms in Homana. The other books in the series are *Shapeshifters* (1984), *The Song of Homana* (1985), *Legacy of the Sword* (1986), *Track of the White Wolf* (1987), *Daughters of Lion* (1989), *Flight of the Raven* (1990), and *Tapestry of Lions* (1992). *The Lion Throne* (DAW, 2001, pap.) contains *Flight of the Raven* and *A Tapestry of Lions*.
DAW, 1988, pap., 453 pp., o.p.
(Kliatt Apr 1988 p. 24, Apr 1989 p. 26; VOYA 11:196, 12:15, 167)

5-545   ROBERSON, Jennifer. *Sword-Breaker.* **(Tiger and Del series, bk. 4).** Gr. 7–12.
Sword-dancers Tiger and Del search for the sorcerer Shaka Obre who can exorcise the spirit of his evil brother from one of their swords. Preceding vol-

umes are *Sword Dancer* (1986), *Sword-Singer* (1988), and *Sword-Maker* (1989), and the sequels are *Sword-Born* (1998, 1999) and *Sword-Sworn* (2002).
DAW, 1991, 460 pp., o.p.
(Kliatt Sep 1991 p. 28; VOYA 14:325, 15:11)

5-546 ROBERTS, Katherine. *Song Quest.* **(The Echorium sequence, bk. 1).** Gr. 5–8. (Orig. British pub. 1999.)
Two young Singers, Rialle and Kherron, must use the five ancient Songs of Power to save the merlees (merpeople) from slaughter by Frazhin, who plans to rule the world using the black Khiz crystal. In the sequel, *Crystal Mask* (2002), set 20 years later, Frazhin has regained his powers, causing Rialle's son, Renn, and Shaiala, a wild girl raised by centaurs, to set out on a voyage to thwart his evil plans. *Dark Quetzal* (2003) is the third book in the series.
Element Children's, 2000, 236 pp. (1-902618-94-7); Scholastic, 2002, pap., 272 pp. (0-439-33892-1)
(CCBB 55:416; HBG 11:97; SLJ Feb 2000 p. 125; VOYA 25:53)

5-547 ROBERTS, Keith (John Kingston). *Pavane.* Gr. 10 up.
In an alternate Britain in which Queen Elizabeth I was assassinated, the Spanish Armada triumphed, and the nonindustrial world is ruled by the Pope, a revolution of the oppressed is brewing.
Doubleday, 1968, 288 pp., o.p.
(Kirkus 36:930; LJ 93:4580, 94:1347)

5-548 RODDA, Emily. *Rowan of Rin.* **(Rowan of Rin series, bk. 1).** Gr. 3–6.
★ (Orig. Australian pub. 1993.)
Young herder Rowan is chosen to accompany a group of Rin villagers journeying to find the dragon that controls their water source, because only Rowan can reveal the clues on the magical map of their journey. Children's Book Council of Australia Book of the Year for Young Readers Award, 1994. In the sequel, *Rowan and the Travelers* (1994, 2001), the arrival of a nomadic tribe, the Travelers, coincides with the townsfolk of Rin falling into a deep sleep, and only Rowan and half-Traveler Allun are left awake to fight the mysterious enemy threatening Rin. In *Rowan and the Keeper of the Crystal* (1996, 2002), Rowan must assume his mother's ancestral task of choosing the new Keeper of the Crystal after she is poisoned and falls into a coma. In *Rowan and the Zebak* (1999, 2002), Rowan and three companions must rescue his younger sister, Annad, after she is kidnapped by a winged, fanged grach and taken to the land of the Zebak. The fourth sequel is *Rowan and the Ice-Creepers* (2003), and *Rowan of the Bukshah* was published in Australia in 2003.
Greenwillow, 2001, 151 pp. (0-06-029708-5); HarperTrophy, 2002, pap., 160 pp. (0-06-441019-6)
(BL 97:1682; CCBB 54:385; HB 77:461; HBG 12:314; SLJ June 2001 p. 154)

ROHAN, Michael Scott. *The Anvil of Ice.*
See Chapter 12, Witchcraft and Sorcery Fantasy.

5-549 ROSENBERG, Joel. *D'Shai.* Gr. 10 up.
When Kami, a clumsy young acrobat, ignores the laws of D'Shai by falling in

love with a nobleman's daughter, he is punished with an accusation of murder. The sequel is *Hour of the Octopus* (1994).
Ace, 1991, pap., 327 pp. (0-441-15751-3)
(BL 87:1115, 1120; Kliatt Apr 1991 p. 21; VOYA 14:47)

RUCKER, Rudy. *The Hollow Earth: The Narrative of Mason Algiers Reynolds of Virginia.*
See Chapter 7, High Fantasy: Travel to Other Worlds.

5-550   RUPP, Rebecca. *The Waterstone.* Gr. 5–9.
✶   Young Tad and Birdie of the miniature Fisher tribe discover that an evil nixie has caused the Great Drying that is endangering all life in their world, and that Tad is destined to save the Tribes.
Candlewick, 2002, 275 pp. (0-7636-0726-6); Candlewick, 2005, pap., 288 pp. (0-7636-2294-X)
(CCBB 56:76; HBG 16:374; Kirkus 70:962; SLJ Nov 2002 p. 174; VOYA 25:491, 26:13)

5-551   RUSCH, Kristine Kathryn. *The Black Queen.* **(The Black Throne series, bk. 1).** Gr. 10 up.
A mysterious portent compels Gift, former king and brother of Arianna, the Black Queen, their uncle Bridge, and their cousin Lyndred to visit Arianna on the Blue Isle, where they must battle the spirit of an evil sorcerer. The sequel is *The Black King* (2000). This series is set in the same world as the author's The Fey series (*The Sacrifice*, 1995; *Changeling*, 1996; *The Rival*, 1997; *The Resistance*, 1998; and *Victory*, 1998).
Bantam, 1999, pap., 480 pp. (0-553-58115-5); HarperTorch, 2002, pap. (0-380-79227-3)
(Kliatt Nov 1999 p. 28; LJ July 1999 p. 143; VOYA 23:50)

5-552   RUSCH, Kristine Kathryn. *The White Mists of Power.* Gr. 7–12.
Before Byron, abandoned as a child, can prove his claim to be the long-lost Prince Adric, his father the king is assassinated and only the mysterious and magical Cache Enos is left to identify him. World Fantasy Award, 1992.
NAL, 1991, 1994, pap., 304 pp. (0-451-45120-1)
(LJ Nov 15, 1991 p. 111; VOYA 15:46, 16:16)

5-553   RUSHDIE, Salman. *Haroun and the Sea of Stories.* Gr. 10 up. (Orig. British pub. 1990.)
Storyteller Rashid Khalifa loses his tale-spinning powers after his wife runs away with another man, so he and his son Haroun travel into the Twilight Strip in an attempt to regain his abilities, only to find that a war is raging over the damming of the polluted Stream of Stories. Mythopoeic Fantasy Award for Children's Literature, 1992.
Viking, 1991, 210 pp. (0-670-83804-7); 1991, pap. (0-14-015737-9)
(BL 87:203; Kliatt Jan 1992 p. 12; LJ Nov 1, 1990 p. 127, Sep 15, 1990 p. 67; TLS Sep 28, 1990 p. 1036, Dec 15, 1991 p. 13)

RUSSELL, Sean. *The Compass of the Soul.*
See Chapter 12, Witchcraft and Sorcery Fantasy.

5-554   RUSSELL, Sean. *The Initiate Brother.* Gr. 7–12.
Set in an alternate ancient Japan, this is the story of Shuyun, the mysterious

and powerful spiritual adviser to the emperor's most feared and hated enemy, Lord Shonto, told from many points of view, including that of the Black Tiger, the emperor's martial arts expert, and Lady Nishima, Lord Shonto's adopted daughter.
DAW, 1991, pap., 480 pp., o.p.
(Kliatt Sep 1991 p. 28; VOYA 14:249)

5-555 RUSSELL, Sean. *The One Kingdom.* (The Swan's War series, bk. 1). Gr. 10 up.
Three young men from the north—Tam, Fynnol, and Baore—set out for adventure but become embroiled in the violent century-long clan war for the vacant throne of Ayr. The sequel is *The Isle of Battle* (2003).
HarperCollins/Eos, 2001, 463 pp. (0-380-97489-4)
(Kirkus 68:1727; LJ Feb 15, 2001 p. 204; SLJ Aug 2001 p. 211; VOYA 24:294)

5-556 RYDILL, Jessica. *Children of the Shaman.* Gr. 10 up.
A complex tale about shaman Yuda Vasileyvich, who tries to reconnect with his estranged daughter, Annat, and son, Malchik, while investigating the murder of Isabel, his former lover.
NAL, 2003, pap., 368 pp. (0-451-45911-3)
(BL 99:979, 1458; Kliatt July 2003 p. 34; VOYA 26:240)

5-557 SABERHAGEN, Fred. *Empire of the East.* Gr. 10 up.
After the wizard's troops murder the boy's parents and kidnap his sister, 16-year-old Rolf is recruited by a rebel band to battle Ominor, the wizard Emperor of the East.
Ace, 1979, 1983, pap., 558 pp., o.p.; Baen, 1990, pap., 576 pp., o.p.
(Kliatt 14:18; SLJ Mar 1980 p. 147)

5-558 SABERHAGEN, Fred. *The First Book of Lost Swords: Woundhealer's Story.* (The Lost Swords series, bk. 1). Gr. 10 up.
Prince Mark of Tasavalta seeks the magical sword, Woundhealer, to cure his blind and epileptic son. The sequels are *The Second Book of Lost Swords: Sightblinder's Story* (1987), *The Third Book of Lost Swords: Stonecutter's Story* (1988), *The Fourth Book of Lost Swords: Farslayer's Story* (1989), *The Fifth Book of Lost Swords: Coinspinner's Story* (1989), *The Sixth Book of Lost Swords: Mindsword's Story* (1990), *The Seventh Book of Lost Swords: Wayfinder's Story* (1992), and *The Last Book of Lost Swords: Shieldbreaker's Story* (1994). This is a companion series to Saberhagen's Book of Swords trilogy (see *The Second Book of Swords*, below). *An Armory of Swords* (1995) is an anthology of stories set in the same world. The author's Books of the Gods series (*The Face of Apollo*, 1998; *Ariadne's Web*, 2000; *The Arms of Hercules*, 2000; and *God of the Golden Fleece*, 2001) are prequels to the Lost Swords series.
Tor, 1986, 1991, pap. 281 pp. (0-8125-2058-0)
(BL 82:1667, 1683, 86:905; Kirkus 54:1330; LJ Oct 15, 1986 p. 114; VOYA 9:293, 10:22)

5-559 SABERHAGEN, Fred. *The Second Book of Swords.* (Book of Swords trilogy, vol. 2). Gr. 10 up.
Mark manages to enter the treasure trove of the Blue Temple in search of the 12 swords of power needed to aid Sir Andrew in his battle against magical

foes. This is the sequel to *The First Book of Swords* (1983), and is followed by *The Third Book of Swords* (1984). The author's Lost Swords series (see *The First Book of Lost Swords*, above) is a companion series. *The Complete Book of Swords* (Science Fiction Book Club, 1985), and *The First Swords* (Tor, 1999, pap., 0-312-86916-9) contain all three volumes.
Tor, 1983, 1991, pap., 313 pp., o.p.
(BL 80:667, 677; Kliatt Winter 1984 p. 24)

SABIN, E. Rose. *A School for Sorcery.*
See Chapter 12, Witchcraft and Sorcery Fantasy.

5-560 SALSITZ, R(hodi) A. V(ilott). *The Unicorn Dancer.* Gr. 10 up.
Lady Alorie, last of the House of Sergius, must find and dance for the unicorns, the guardians of her world, to revenge the murders of her father and grandfather. The sequel is *Daughter of Destiny* (1988).
NAL, 1986, pap., 256 pp., o.p.
(Kliatt 20:28; LJ Dec 1986 p. 142; VOYA 9:293, 10:24, 40)

5-561 SALSITZ, R(hodi) A. V(ilott). *Where Dragons Lie.* **(Dragons trilogy, bk. 1).** Gr. 10 up.
Soldier's son Dar and Princess Sharlin join a wizard and a dwarf on an adventure-filled trek across deserts to find the place where dragons go to die. The sequels are *Where Dragons Rule* (1987) and *Night of Dragons* (1990).
NAL, 1985, pap., 255 pp., o.p.
(Kliatt Spring 1986 p. 25; VOYA 9:90)

5-562 SALVATORE, R. A. *The Demon Awakes.* **(The Demon Wars trilogy, bk. 1).** Gr. 10 up.
Orphaned Elbryan Wyndon and Pony Ault become guardians of magical gemstones that help them and the elves battle a demon, goblins, giants, and dwarves attempting to conquer the world. The sequels are *The Demon Spirit* (1998) and *The Demon Apostle* (1999). This trilogy is followed by *Mortalis* (2000), and the Second Demon Wars Saga: *Ascendance* (2001), *Transcendence* (2002), and *Immortalis* (2003). *Highwayman* (2004) begins a related series set in Corona.
Del Rey, 1997, 528 pp., o.p.; Ballantine, 1998, pap. (0-345-42162-0)
(BL 93:1483; Kirkus 65:423; LJ Apr 15, 1997 p. 124; VOYA 20:396)

5-563 SALVATORE, R. A. *The Sword of Bedwyr.* **(The Crimson Shadow series, bk. 1).** Gr. 7 up.
After the populace of Eriador is enslaved by evil overlords, a young nobleman named Luthien Bedwyr becomes an outlaw who leaves behind the crimson mark of his shadow. The sequels are *Luthien's Gamble* (1996) and *The Dragon King* (1996).
Warner, 1995, 247 pp. (0-446-51726-7), 1996, pap. (0-446-60272-8)
(BL 91:901, 904; Kliatt May 1996 p. 19; LJ Dec 1994 p. 139; VOYA 18:9, 39)

5-564 SALVATORE, R. A. *The Thousand Orcs.* **(The Hunter's Blades trilogy, vol. 1).** Gr. 10 up.
Dark elf Drizzt Do'Urden falls in love with a human woman, Catti-brie, the daughter of his friend Bruenor Battlehammer, causing Drizzt to be drawn into

the dwarf and human battle against mountain giants and orcs. The sequels are *The Lone Drow* (2003) and *The Two Swords* (2004). Both books are set in the Forgotten Realms universe of the "Dungeons and Dragons"-themed fantasy fiction novels written by Salvatore and Ed Greenwood, Richard Awlin, and Troy Denning: the Avatar trilogy by Awlinson (1989), the Dark Elf trilogy by Salvatore (1989–1991), the Shadow of the Avatar trilogy by Greenwood (1995), the Paths of Darkness series by Salvatore (1999–2002), the Return of the Archwizards trilogy by Denning (2001–2002), *Legacy of the Drow* by Salvatore (2001), the Icewind Dale trilogy by Salvatore (2001), and the Cleric Quintet by Salvatore (2002).
Wizards of the Coast, 2002, 352 pp. (0-7869-2804-2)
(BL 99:309; LJ Nov 15, 2002 p. 105; SLJ Feb 2003 p. 173)

5-565 SCARBOROUGH, Elizabeth Ann. *Bronwyn's Bane.* **(The Aragonia series, vol. 3).** Gr. 10 up.
Cursed at birth with an inability to tell the truth, amazonian Princess Bronwyn is sent away to her cousin Carol's for the duration of a war, whereupon the two young women attempt to lift Bronwyn's curse and end the war on their own. This book is preceded by *Song of Sorcery* (1982) and *The Unicorn Creed* (1983) and is followed by *The Christening Quest* (1985).
Bantam, 1983, pap., 352 pp., o.p.
(BL 80:847; LJ 108:2346; SLJ Apr 1984 p. 130)

5-566 SCOTT, Melissa, and BARNETT, Lisa A. *Point of Hopes.* **(Astreiant series, bk. 1).** Gr. 10 up.
Children have been disappearing from the city of Astreiant, in a world where magic and astrology are real, and pointsman Nico Rath is assigned to find them. The sequel is *Point of Dreams* (2001).
Tor, 1995, 384 pp. (0-312-85844-2); Doherty, 1997, pap., o.p.
(BL 92:458, 461; Kirkus 63:1387; LJ Oct 15, 1995 p. 91)

SEDGWICK, Marcus. *The Book of Dead Days.*
See Chapter 12, Witchcraft and Sorcery Fantasy.

5-567 SEDGWICK, Marcus. *The Dark Horse.* Gr. 5–9. (Orig. British pub. 2002.)
✭ When their village is attacked by Dark Horse warriors from the north, 16-year-old Sigurd, Lawspeaker of his Nordic people, the Storm, is betrayed by his adopted younger sister, Mouse.
Random, 2003, 160 pp. (0-385-73054-3); Laurel Leaf, 2004, pap., 224 pp. (0-440-41908-5)
(BL 99:995; CCBB 56:421; HB 79:217; HBG 14:388; Kirkus 70:1773; Kliatt Jan 2003 p. 11; SLJ Mar 2003 p. 237; VOYA 26:68)

SHERMAN, Josepha. *Child of Faerie, Child of Earth.*
See Chapter 6, High Fantasy: Myth or Legend Fantasy.

5-568 SHERMAN, Josepha. *Gleaming Bright.* Gr. 5–9.
Princess Finola hopes to save her kingdom, but she must first battle a wizard to find a magical box called Gleaming Bright.
Walker, 1994, 176 pp. (0-8027-8296-5)
(BL 90:1253; CCBB 47:302; HBG 5:324; SLJ May 1994 p. 135; VOYA 17:100)

5-569 SHERMAN, Josepha. *The Shining Falcon.* Gr. 10 up.
While his sorcerer cousin plots a takeover of his kingdom, a wounded prince who has taken the form of a falcon is nursed back to health by a banished noblewoman who does not suspect his true identity. *The Horse of Flame* (1990) is set in the same world.
Avon, 1989, pap., 342 pp., o.p.
(BL 86:528, 541; LJ Nov 15, 1989 p. 108)

5-570 SHERMAN, Josepha. *Windleaf.* Gr. 6–9.
✮ Count Thierry, 18, must recover three faerie objects lost in the mortal world to win his true love, Glinfinial, the half-human daughter of the faerie lord.
Walker, 1993, 128 pp., o.p.
(BL 90:519; Kirkus 61:1529; SLJ Dec 1993 p. 138; VOYA 16:385, 17:8)

5-571 SHINN, Sharon. *Archangel.* **(Samaria series, bk. 1).** Gr. 7–12.
Would-be Archangel Gabriel's new wife, a slave named Rachel, refuses to settle into angelic freedom until the lot of her Edori people is improved in this science-fantasy. The sequels are *Jovah's Angel* (1997, 1998), *The Alleluia Files* (1998, 1999), *Angelica* (2003), and *Angel-Seeker* (2004).
Ace, 1996, pap., 448 pp. (0-441-00330-3); 1997, pap. (0-441-00432-6)
(BL 92:1492, 1494, 93:763; Kirkus 64:412)

5-572 SHINN, Sharon. *The Safe-Keeper's Secret.* Gr. 7–12.
✮ Raised from infancy by Damiana, the Safe-Keeper to whom he was given on the day she gave birth to Fiona, Reed grows up in a nurturing community, but he is haunted by the secret of his heritage.
Viking, 2004, 240 pp. (0-670-05910-2)
(BL 100:1452; CCBB 57:437; Kirkus 72:448; Kliatt May 2004 p. 13; SLJ June 2004 p. 150; VOYA 27:147)

5-573 SHINN, Sharon. *Summers at Castle Auburn.* Gr. 10 up.
Corie, 17, realizes that her dazzling cousin Bryan, heir to the throne, is arrogant and selfish, and that it is up to her to save the beloved magical aliora from enslavement.
Berkley/Ace, 2001, pap., 355 pp. (0-441-00803-8)
(BL 97:1544; Kliatt July 2001 p. 27; VOYA 24:216, 25:16)

5-574 SHWARTZ, Susan. *Silk Roads and Shadows.* Gr. 10 up. (Orig. British pub. 1988.)
Alexandria, sister of the emperor of Byzantium, undertakes a desperate journey to the Empire of Chin to steal silkworms that could save Byzantium's vitally important silk industry.
Tor, 1990, pap., 337 pp., o.p.
(Kliatt Sep 1990, p. 24; VOYA 13:258)

5-575 SILVERBERG, Robert. *The Gate of Worlds.* Gr. 7–10.
✮ If the Great Plague had killed three quarters of the European population during the Middle Ages, perhaps North America today would be ruled by the Aztecs, South America by the Incas, and Europe by the Turks. It is in such a version of the 20th century that Dan Beauchamp sets sail from Turkish England to Aztec North America. *Beyond the Gate of Worlds* (Tor, 1991, 1993) is a related collection of stories by Silverberg and other authors.

Holt, 1967, 2000, 244 pp. (0-03-063770-8)
(BL 64:250; CCBB 21:18; Kirkus 35:609; LJ 92:3204; TLS 1978 p. 1396)

5-576 SILVERBERG, Robert. *Kingdoms of the Wall.* Gr. 10 up.
Young Poilar is chosen to lead 40 pilgrims on a dangeous sacred quest over a huge wall near their village.
Bantam, 1993 (c. 1992), 320 pp., o.p.
(BL 89:795, 800; LJ Feb 15, 1993 p. 196; VOYA 16:170)

5-577 SILVERBERG, Robert. *Lord Valentine's Castle.* **(The Majipoor Cycle,**
✫   **bk. 1).** Gr. 10 up.
Young Lord Valentine, ruler of Majipoor, wanders his land as an amnesiac juggler until he realizes that his mind and personality have been transferred to someone else's body, and that an imposter is ruling his kingdom. The sequels are *The Majipoor Chronicles* (Arbor, 1982), *Valentine Pontifex* (Arbor, 1983), and *The Mountains of Majipoor* (1995). The Prestimion trilogy (see *Sorcerers of Majipoor,* below) is also part of the Majipoor cycle.
Harper, 1980, o.p.; Eos, 1995, pap., 528 pp. (0-06-105487-9)
(BL 76:1110, 77:622, 1148, 78:594; Kirkus 48:247; Kliatt 15:23; LJ 105:1008; SLJ Sep 1980 p. 93; TLS 1980 p. 1265; VOYA 3:53)

5-578 SILVERBERG, Robert. *Sorcerers of Majipoor.* **(The Prestimion Trilogy,**
vol. 1). Gr. 10 up.
To the consternation of Lord Confalume, the ruling coronal of Majipoor, an oracle calls Prince Prestimion, more versed in hunting than in courtly duties, to become the new coronal. This prequel to the author's Majipoor Cycle (see *Lord Valentine's Castle,* above) takes place a thousand years before the time of Lord Valentine. The sequels are *Lord Prestimion* (1999) and *The King of Dreams* (2001).
HarperPrism, 1997, 480 pp. (0-06-105254-X); Eos, 1998, pap., 624 pp. (0-06-105780-0)
(BL 93:1620; Kirkus 65:842; LJ June 15, 1997 p. 101; VOYA 21:14, 60)

5-579 SIMAK, Clifford D(onald). *Enchanted Pilgrimage.* Gr. 10 up.
✫   Mark and his traveling companions are set upon by witches, trolls, and other fearful creatures during their journey through the wildlands in search of "the old ones."
Putnam, 1975, 230 pp., o.p.
(BL 71:863; 72:1038; Kirkus 43:203; LJ 100:783; SLJ May 1975 p.75)

5-580 SIMAK, Clifford D(onald). *Where the Evil Dwells.* Gr. 10 up.
In an alternate Roman Middle Ages, a nobleman's son named Harcourt, the Abbot Guy, the maiden Yolanda, and the gruff thousand-year-old Knurly Man set off on a quest for the soul of a legendary saint.
Ballantine, 1983, pap., 256 pp., o.p.
(BL 79:484, 490; Kirkus 50:956; VOYA 5:46)

5-581 SMITH, Sherwood. *Crown Duel.* **(The Crown and Court Duet, bk. 1).** Gr.
✫   7–10.
Meliara and Bran promised their dying father to protect their lands and to keep the ancient covenant with the Hill People, but to fulfill their promise they must challenge King Galdran and his army. In the sequel, *Court Duel* (1998, 2002),

Countess Meliara rebels against life at court while exchanging letters with a mysterious suitor. The author's short story "Beauty," published in the anthology *Firebirds* (Firebird, 2003), centers on Meliara's children.
Harcourt, 1997, 214 pp. (0-15-201608-2); Firebird/Penguin, 2001, pap., 471 pp. (0-14-230151-5)

(BL 93:1430, 94:475; CCBB 50:414; HBG 8:316; Kirkus 65:650; SLJ Aug 1997 p. 158; VOYA 20:121, 21:14)

5-582   SMITH, Sherwood. *Wren to the Rescue.* **(Wren series, bk. 1).** Gr. 5–9.
✫   Wren's best friend, Tess, reveals that she is actually a princess hiding in their orphanage from the evil Wizard Andreus. When Tess is abducted, Wren sets out to rescue her. In *Wren's Quest* (1993), Wren leaves magician school to search for her true parents, accompanied by Connor, while Princess Tess is kidnapped in a plot against the royal family. In *Wren's War* (1995), Princess Teressa's parents are murdered, but she decides to take the reins of power away from her enemies. *Wren's War* was a 1995–1996 Anne Spencer Lindbergh Prize Honor Book. A fourth book in the series, *Wren Journeymage*, is forthcoming.
Harcourt, 1990, 216 pp. (0-15-200975-2); Dell, 1993, pap. (0-440-40773-7); Dutton, 2004, pap., 216 pp. (0-14-240160-9)

(BL 87:857; HB 67:202; HBG 2:72; Kirkus 58:1092; SLJ Nov 1990 p. 140; VOYA 13:302, 14:13)

5-583   SMITH, Stephanie A. *Snow-Eyes.* Gr. 6–9.
Amarra, or Snow-Eyes, is taken from her family to become a "servitor" of the Lake Mother, where she learns occult skills from the other women servitors. The sequel is *The Boy Who Was Thrown Away* (1987).
Atheneum, 1985, 184 pp., o.p.

(CCBB 39:37; SLJ Oct 1985 p. 187; VOYA 9:42)

5-584   SNICKET, Lemony (Daniel Handler). *The Bad Beginning.* **(A Series of**
✫   **Unfortunate Events, vol. 1).** Gr. 4–7.
The Baudelaire children—Violet, Klaus, and baby Sunny—suffer misfortune after misfortune, beginning with their parents' deaths and followed by their new life with a distant cousin, the evil Count Olaf, in this mock-gothic satire. The sequels are *The Reptile Room* (1999, 2000), *The Wide Window* (2000, 2001), *The Miserable Mill* (2000, 2001), *The Austere Academy* (2000, 2001), *The Ersatz Elevator* (2001, 2002), *The Vile Village* (2001, 2002), *The Hostile Hospital* (2001, 2002), *The Carnivorous Carnival* (2002, 2003), *The Slippery Slope* (2003), and *The Grim Grotto* (2004). *The Ominous Omnibus* (2005) contains volumes 1–3.
Illus. by Brett Helquist, HarperCollins, 1999, 176 pp. (0-06-028312-2); Scholastic, 2000, pap. (0-06-028312-2)

(BL 96:707; CCBB 53:32; HBG 11:88; Kirkus 67:1139; LJ Nov 1, 2001 p. 160; SLJ Nov 1999 p. 165)

5-585   SNYDER, Zilpha Keatley. *Below the Root.* **(Green-Sky trilogy, vol. 1).**
✫   Gr. 5–8.
Raamo D'Ok's curiosity about the dreaded land beneath his treetop world of Green-Sky leads him to rescue a girl named Terra and uncover the secret of the world below. In *And All Between* (1976, 1985), Terra escapes from the under-

world of Erd to Green-Sky, where she is rescued by Raamo and Neric, who plan to free all of the Erdlings. In *Until the Celebration* (1977, 1985), the Kindar and the Erdlings are finally about to be united, but plans for the celebration are disrupted by dissidents within each tribe and by the disappearance of Pomma and Terra.

Illus. by Alton Raible, Atheneum, 1975, 231 pp., o.p.; Dell, 1992, pap., 244 pp. (0-440-21266-9)

(BL 71:764; CCBB 28:186; Kirkus 43:239; SLJ Sep 1975 p. 112; Suth 2:424)

5-586   SNYDER, Zilpha Keatley. *Song of the Gargoyle.* Gr. 5–9.

☆   A boy named Tymmon and a doglike gargoyle travel the country together, entertaining in villages and towns while they search for Tymmon's kidnapped father.

Delacorte, 1991, 232 pp. (0-385-30301-7); Dell, 1994, pap. (0-440-40898-9)

(BL 87:1127; CCBB 44:177; HBG 2:278; Kirkus 59:323; SLJ Feb 1991 p. 8; VOYA 14:358)

5-587   SNYDER, Zilpha Keatley. *Squeak Saves the Day and Other Tooley Tales.* Gr. 3–6.

The Tiddlers are miniature people who avoid human STOMPERS, in these seven stories about Nipper and Trinket Tooley and their parents.

Illus. by Leslie Morrill, Delacorte, 1988, 192 pp., o.p.; Dell, 1992, pap. (0-440-40585-8)

(CCBB 41:189; Kirkus 51:625; SLJ Aug 1988 p. 98)

5-588   *Spells of Wonder.* Ed. by Marion Zimmer Bradley. Gr. 10 up.

Sixteen tales about strong heroines who use magic to battle the dangers they find in their alternate worlds. This is a companion volume to the *Sword and Sorceress* books (see title entry below).

DAW, 1989, pap., 288 pp., o.p.

(BL 86:149, 165; LJ Sep 15, 1989 p. 139; VOYA 12:375)

5-589   SPRINGER, Nancy. *Chains of Gold.* Gr. 10 up.

☆   Arlen, destined to be sacrificed as the Summer King to bring fertility to the fields of Catena, falls in love with his "bride," Cerilla, refuses to go through with the annual ritual, and flees with her.

Arbor House, 1986, 230 pp., o.p.

(BL 82:1667; Kirkus 54:1074; LJ Aug 1986 p. 174; VOYA 9:241, 10:21)

5-590   SPRINGER, Nancy. *Madbond.* (The Sea King trilogy, bk. 1). Gr. 10 up.

Two young men, Dannoc and Rad Korridun, become blood brothers and set out to find their parents, the kings of the Seal Kindred and the Red Hart tribes, in order to fight the evil that has come to their land. The sequels are *Mindbond* (1987) and *Godbond* (1988).

Tor, 1987, pap., 214 pp., o.p.

(BL 84:31, 55; Kliatt 21:29; VOYA 10:180)

5-591   SPRINGER, Nancy. *The Sable Moon.* (The Chronicles of Isle, bk. 3). Gr. 10 up.

Crown Prince Trevyn completes a quest during which he is enslaved and freed, studies to become a sorcerer, visits the land of elves, and returns home to save his kingdom. This book is preceded by *The White Hart* (1979) and *The Silver*

Sun (1980, 1983, revised from *The Book of Suns*, 1977). It is followed by *The Black Beast* (1982, 1986) and *The Golden Swan* (1983). The latter two books were published together as *The Book of Vale* (1985).
Pocket, 1981, 1986, pap., 264 pp., o.p.
(BL 77:1188; VOYA 4:64)

5-592 SPRINGER, Nancy. *Wings of Flame.* Gr. 10 up.
The orphan girl Seda saves Prince Kyrem of Devan after he is attacked by an evil wizard.
Tor, 1985, 1986, pap., 256 pp., o.p.
(BL 81:1297, 1327; Kirkus 53:117; LJ Mar 15, 1985 p. 75)

5-593 STACKPOLE, Michael A. *Fortress Draconis.* **(The DragonCrown War Cycle, bk. 1).** Gr. 10 up.
Rebel warriors Crow and Resolute recognize that Will, a 15-year-old thief, is the hero destined to thwart sorceress Chytrine's plans to become empress of the world. *The Dark Glory War* (2000) is the prequel, and the sequels are *When Dragons Rage* (2002) and *The Grand Crusade* (2003).
Bantam Spectra, 2001, pap., 528 pp. (0-553-37919-4)
(BL 98:560; Kirkus 69:1397; VOYA 25:54)

5-594 STACKPOLE, Michael A. *Once a Hero.* Gr. 10 up.
The enchanted sword, Cleaveheart Elfward, is wielded against the empire of the Reithrese by two heroes, a human named Neal and an elf named Genevera, in two interconnected stories that take place 500 years apart.
Bantam, 1994, pap., 512 pp. (0-553-56112-X)
(BL 90:1333, 1338; Kliatt Sep 1994 p. 22)

5-595 STASHEFF, Christopher. *The Shaman.* **(The Star Stone series, vol. 1).** Gr. 10 up.
Human warrior Chearne and half-elf trickster Lucoyo are aided by the godlike Lomallin in their struggle against Ulahane the Red, leader of the Elder Race giants who have enslaved the world. The sequel is *The Sage* (1996, 1997).
Ballantine, 1995, 368 pp., o.p.
(BL 92:48, 51; Kirkus 63:905; LJ Sep 15, 1995 p. 97)

5-596 STEARNS, Pamela (Fujimoto). *The Fool and the Dancing Bear.* Gr. 5–7.
Only a dancing bear can revive King Rolf's kingdom after its enchantment by a queen who is jealous of the king's love for her younger sister.
Illus. by Ann Strugnell, Little, Brown, 1979, 167 pp., o.p.
(BL 75:1581; CCBB 33:57; HB 55:416; Kirkus 47:742; SLJ Sep 1979 p. 148; Suth 3:408)

5-597 STEELE, Mary Q(uintard Govan). *Journey Outside.* Gr. 5–8.
☆ Dilar escapes the subterranean life of the Raft People and finds his way up to an unfamiliar sunlit world. John Newbery Medal Honor Book, 1970.
Illus. by Rocco Negri, Viking, 1969, 143 pp., o.p.
(BL 65:1276; CCBB 23:119; HB 45:309; Kirkus 37:506; LJ 94:3227; TLS 1970 p. 1264)

5-598 STEELE, Mary Q(uintard Govan). *The True Men.* Gr. 5–7.
Driven from his home with the True Men because his skin has begun to glow in the dark, Ree is taken in by two weavers.

Greenwillow, 1976, 144 pp., o.p.

(CCBB 30:82; HB 53:55; Kirkus 44:1045; SLJ Jan 1977 p. 97)

5-599 STEUSSY, Marti. *Forest of the Night.* Gr. 10 up.

A young woman named Hashti ventures alone into the wilds of New Lebanon seeking the highly intelligent feathered tigers said to roam this world.

Ballantine, 1987, pap., 265 pp., o.p.

(BL 83:1564, 159; LJ May 15, 1987 p. 101; VOYA 11:12)

5-600 STEVENSON, Laura C(aroline). *The Island and the Ring.* Gr. 7–12.

☆ Princess Tania escapes from her beloved father's burning castle with a sapphire ring that is the source of her enemy's power, which she vows to use to save her people and destroy him.

Houghton, 1991, 304 pp. (0-395-56401-8)

(BL 88:690; CCBB 45:50; HBG 3:73; Kirkus 59:1409; SLJ Sep 1991 p. 284; VOYA 14:327)

5-601 STEVERMER, Caroline. *A College of Magics.* Gr. 10 up.

Faris Nallaneen, 17, longs to complete her degree in magic, but is called home to Galazon by way of Paris, encountering assassins and sorcery along the way. The sequel is *A Scholar of Magics* (2004). These stories are set a century later in the same world as Stevermer's and Patricia Wrede's *Sorcery and Cecelia* (1988, 2003; see Wrede below), and Wrede's *Mairelon the Magician* (1991, 1992; see below).

Tor, 1994, 384 pp. (0-312-85689-X); Starscape, 2002, pap., 468 pp. (0-765-34245-6)

(BL 90:1185, 1188; Kirkus 62:104; VOYA 17:160)

5-602 STEVERMER, Caroline. *When the King Comes Home.* Gr. 9 up.

☆ Apprenticed to an artist in the city of Aravis, Hail Rosmer finds a 200-year-old medal depicting the late King Julian and becomes obsessed with a prophecy that all dreams will be made real when the king returns.

Tor, 2000, 240 pp. (0-312-87214-3), 2001, pap., 236 pp. (0-8125-8981-5)

(BL 97:625; Kirkus 68:1394; LJ Nov 15, 2000 p. 101; VOYA 24:14, 57)

5-603 STEWART, Paul, and RIDDELL, Chris. *Beyond the Deepwoods.* **(The**

☆ **Edge Chronicles, bk. 1).** Gr. 5–7. (Orig. British pub. 1998.)

Orphaned Twig leaves his woodtroll foster parents' home to search for his birth father, the captain of a sky pirate ship. The sequels are *Stormchaser* (1999, 2004), *Midnight over Sanctaphrax* (2000, 2004), *The Curse of the Gloam-glozer* (2005), and *The Last of the Sky Pirates* (2005).

Illus. by Chris Riddell, Knopf, 2004, 280 pp. (0-385-75069-2)

(BL 100:1844; CCBB 58:40; Kirkus 72:635; SLJ Sep 2004. 218; VOYA 27:147)

5-604 STEWART, Sean. *Clouds End.* Gr. 10 up.

Brook and the other Clouds End islanders are forced to unleash the magical and deadly Mist to keep the Forest People from conquering their islands.

Berkley/Ace, 1996, 384 pp. (0-441-00347-8); Ace, 1998, pap. (0-441-00525-X)

(BL 92:1889, 1891; Kirkus 64:792; LJ Aug 1996 p. 120)

5-605 STEWART, Sean. *Galveston.* Gr. 10 up.

☆ Ever since a tidal wave of magic wiped out modern technology during Mardi Gras in 2004, the world has been ruled by magic, and the dying ruler's daugh-

ter, Sloane, must bargain for her mother's life with the demon god of Mardi
Gras, Lord Momus.
Berkley, 2000, 464 pp. (0-441-00686-8); Ace, 2001, pap., 454 pp. (0-441-
00800-3)
(BL 96:1335; Kirkus 68:27; LJ Feb 15, 2000 p. 202; VOYA 23:200)

5-606 STIRLING, S. M., and MEIER, Shirley. *The Cage.* Gr. 10 up.
Sold into slavery by Habiku, the man who ruined her trading business, Megan
and her warrior companion Shkai'ra return seeking vengeance.
Baen, 1989, 1991, pap., 402 pp. (0-671-72047-3)
(BL 85:1950; VOYA 13:40)

5-607 STODDARD, James. *The High House.* Gr. 10 up.
Carter Anderson attempts to undo the damage of a childhood misdeed, losing
his father's keys to the High House with its many entrances to other worlds, a
loss that has allowed anarchists to threaten the balance of the universe. The
sequel is *The False House* (2000).
Warner, 1998, pap., 336 pp. (0-446-60679-0)
(Kliatt Mar 1999 p. 26; VOYA 21:448)

5-608 STRAUSS, Victoria. *The Burning Land.* Gr. 10 up.
Axane, a young sorceress living in the secluded Refuge of Arsace, fears the
coming of Gyalo, a Shaper or sorcerer who may threaten the peace of the
recently liberated land.
HarperCollins/Eos, 2004, 496 pp. (0-380-97891-1)
(BL 100:840; LJ Jan 2004 p. 168; VOYA 27:147)

STROUD, Jonathan. *The Amulet of Samarkand.*
See Chapter 12, Witchcraft and Sorcery Fantasy.

5-609 SUCHARITKUL, Somtow. *Utopia Hunters: Chronicles of the High
Inquest.* **(The Inquestor trilogy, bk. 3).** Gr. 10 up.
Young Jenjen, a light-weaver who has been unwillingly appointed to the clan
of Dark-weavers, listens to an ancient Rememberer's tales of the Dispersal of
Man and overcomes her fear of Darkness. This is the sequel to *Light on the
Sound* (Pocket, 1982) and *The Throne of Madness* (Pocket, 1983).
Bantam, 1984, pap., 255 pp., o.p.
(LJ 109:2301; VOYA 8:140)

5-610 SWOPE, Sam. *Jack and the Seven Deadly Giants.* Gr. 2–4.
✭   Foundling Jack sets off on the back of a cow to save his village from the seven
terrible giants threatening the land.
Illus. by Carll Cneut, Farrar, 2004, 100 pp. (0-374-33670-9)
(BL 100:1622; CCBB 57:486; HB 80:336; SLJ May 2004 p. 125)

5-611 *Sword and Sorceress: An Anthology of Heroic Fantasy.* **Ed. by Marion
Zimmer Bradley. (Sword and Sorceress series, vol. I).** Gr. 10 up.
Fifteen tales of magical and warlike women by authors including Diana Paxson and Phyllis Ann Karr. *Spells of Wonder* (1989; see entry above) is a companion volume. The other books in this series are *Sword and Sorceress II*
(1985), *Sword and Sorceress III* (1986), *Sword and Sorceress IV* (1987),
Sword and Sorceress V (1988), *Sword and Sorceress VI* (1990), *Sword and*

Sorceress VII (1990), *Sword and Sorceress VIII* (1991), *Sword and Sorceress IX* (1992), *Sword and Sorceress X* (1993), *Sword and Sorceress XI* (1994), *Sword and Sorceress XII* (1995), *Sword and Sorceress XIII* (1996), *Sword and Sorceress XIV* (1997), *Sword and Sorceress XV* (1998), *Sword and Sorceress XVI* (1999), *Sword and Sorceress XVII* (2000), *Sword and Sorceress XVIII* (2001), *Sword and Sorceress XIX* (2002), *Sword and Sorceress XX* (2003), and *Sword and Sorceress XXI* (2004).
DAW, 1986, pap., 256 pp., o.p.
(BL 80:1601, 1610; Kliatt 18:24; LJ 109:998)

5-612 **TARR, Judith.** *Alamut.* **(The Hounds of God cycle, bk. 4).** Gr. 10 up.
✫ Prince Aidan of Rhiyana attempts to avenge the murder of his nephew, Gereint, in medieval Jerusalem, but falls in love with the assassin, the immortal Morgiana. The sequel, *The Dagger and the Cross: A Novel of the Crusades* (1991), completes a five-book cycle that began with the Hounds of God Cycle (see *The Isle of Glass*, below).
Doubleday, 1989, 480 pp., o.p.
(BL 86:895, 902; Kirkus 57:1568; LJ Dec 1989 p. 176; VOYA 13:120, 14:9)

TARR, Judith. *Devil's Bargain.*
See Chapter 12, Witchcraft and Sorcery Fantasy.

5-613 **TARR, Judith.** *The Hall of the Mountain King.* **(Avaryan Rising, vol. 1).** Gr. 10 up.
Prince Mirain's claim to the throne of Ianon is disputed by his treacherous mortal relatives in this first volume of the Avaryan Rising series. In the sequel, *The Lady of Han-Gilen* (1987), warrior princess Elian rejects her royal suitors and runs away disguised as a boy to search for her childhood love, Mirain, son of the Sun God. In *A Fall of Princes* (1988; 1989, pap.), Elian and Mirain's son, 21-year-old Prince Sarevan of Avaryan, and his hated enemy, 15-year-old Prince Hirel of Asanion, meet by chance, grow into a close friendship, and vow to end the conflict between their kingdoms. The first three books in this series were published together in *Avaryan Rising* (Orb, 1997). The sequels are *Arrows of the Sun* (1993, 1995), *Spear of Heaven* (1994), *Roc and a Hard Place* (1995), and *Tides of Darkness* (2002). The second set of three books can be found in *Avaryan Resplendent* (Orb, 2003).
Bluejay, 1986, 288 pp., o.p.
(BL 83:192, 220; Kirkus 54:1332; VOYA 9:293, 11:12)

5-614 **TARR, Judith.** *The Isle of Glass.* **(The Hounds of God Cycle, vol. 1).** Gr. ✫ 10 up.
Brother Alfred, torn between his pursuits of healing and scholarship and the secret knowledge of his elven blood, abandons his life at St. Ruan's Abbey after a seriously wounded ambassador of elven King Gwydion places the fate of three fueding kingdoms in his hands. In the sequel, *The Golden Horn* (1985), Alfred and his elven companion Thea travel to Constantinople during the Fourth Crusade, but Thea disappears when the crusaders sack the city. In *The Hounds of God* (1986), the elven kingdom of Rhiyana is attacked by the Hounds of God, who kill the king's son and kidnap Thea and her newborn twins. *Alamut* (1989; see above), and *The Dagger and the Cross* (1991) are related works that complete the cycle. The first three books in the cycle are

also called the Hounds and the Falcon trilogy and were published together as
The Hound and the Falcon (Doubleday, 1986; Orb, pap., 1993).
Bluejay, 1985, 288 pp., o.p.; Tor, 1986, pap., 288 pp. (0-8125-5600-3)
(BL 81:824, 838; Kirkus 52:1172; Kliatt 20:30; LJ Feb 15, 1985 p. 182; VOYA 8:141, 194, 365)

5-615   **TARR, Judith.** *Lady of Horses.* **(Epona series, bk. 1).** Gr. 10 up.
Sparrow hides her gifts of divination and power over horses until she and her
sister-in-law Keen are forced to flee, taking the king's stallion with them. *The
Shepard Kings* (Forge, 1999, 2001), *The White Mare's Daughter* (Forge,
2001), and *Daughter of Lir* (Forge, 2003) are related stories.
Tor, 2000, 400 pp. (0-312-86114-1); Forge, 2002, pap., 416 pp. (0-312-87572-X)
(BL 96:1862; Kirkus 68:594)

5-616   **TARR, Judith.** *Pride of Kings.* Gr. 10 up.
While Richard Lionheart is away on the Crusades, a young man named Arslan
uses magic to help the king's brother John gain power in a magical pagan
world separated from England by a "shield of mist and magic." The sequels are
Devil's Bargain (2002) and *House of War* (2003).
NAL/Roc, 2001, pap., 464 pp. (0-451-45847-8)
(BL 97:2102; Kirkus 69:988; LJ Sep 15, 2001 p. 115; VOYA 24:451)

5-617   **TARR, Judith.** *Throne of Isis.* Gr. 10 up.
Queen Cleopatra's priestess, Dione, becomes involved in the power struggle
between the Queen's Roman lover, Anthony, and Julius Caesar's heir, Octa-
vian. Set in the same ancient Egyptian world as the author's *The Lord of the
Two Lands* (1993; see Chapter 6, High Fantasy: Myth or Legend Fantasy).
Tor, 1994, 384 pp. (0-312-85363-7); 1995, pap. (0-812-52079-3)
(BL 90:1516, 1523; Kirkus 62:173; LJ Apr 1, 1994 p. 134; VOYA 17:150)

5-618   **TAYLOR, Cora.** *On Wings of a Dragon.* Gr. 6 up. (Orig. Canadian pub.
2001.)
The stories of two young women intersect near the climax of this tale: Kour'el,
a winged being captured by a dragon, and Maighdlin, a palace slave and granddaughter of the imprisoned king's huntsman.
Fitzhenry, 2001, 251 pp. (1-55041-674-X), 2003, pap. (1-55041-782-7)
(SLJ Dec 2001 p. 147; VOYA 25:205, 26:14)

5-619   **TAYLOR, L. A.** *Cat's Paw.* Gr. 10 up.
☆   Government investigator Miranda uses magic to search for her husband, the
lightkeeper of Gwynnhead, who has mysteriously disappeared.
Ace, 1995, pap., 224 pp. (0-441-00181-5)
(BL 91:1314, 1317; Kliatt May 1995 p. 19; LJ Mar 15, 1995 p. 101; SLJ June 1995 p. 146;
VOYA 18:111)

5-620   **TEPPER, Sheri S.** *Jinian Footseer.* **(Jinian trilogy).** Gr. 10 up.
Young Jinian seeks out "sevens" of wizardly women in order to unleash her
own magical powers and save the beings from the elder times. The sequels are
Dervish Daughter (1986) and *Jinian Star-Eye* (1986). This trilogy is related to
the author's Mavin Manyshaped trilogy (see *The Song of Mavin Manyshaped*,
below) and her True Game trilogy: *Kings Blood Four* (1983), *Necromancer
Nine* (1983),and *Wizard's Eleven* (1984).

Tor, 1985, pap., 284 pp., o.p.

(BL 82:380, 398, 86:906; Kliatt 20:22; VOYA 8:366, 397)

5-621 TEPPER, Sheri S. *Northshore.* **(The Awakeners, vol. 1).** Gr. 10 up.

Pamra, a young woman escaping from life in a priesthood that enslaves the bodies of "awakened" dead, is rescued by Thrasne, a boatman who hides her from creatures bent on killing her. The sequel is *Southshore* (1987; 1988, pap.). The two books were published together as *The Awakeners: Northshore and Southshore*, St. Martin's, 1994 (0-312-89022-2).

Tor, 1988, 256 pp., o.p.

(BL 83:530; Kirkus 55:267; LJ Feb 15, 1987 p. 164; VOYA 10:93, 11:13)

5-622 TEPPER, Sheri S. *Singer from the Sea.* Gr. 10 up.

☆ In this science-fantasy, Genevieve is brought to the royal court of Haven, realizes how many young noblemen's wives have died, and begins to remember her late mother's secret childhood teachings, which contradict the rigid social order and roles for women.

Avon Eos, 1999, 400 pp. (0-380-97480-0); Eos, 2000, pap., 544 pp. (0-380-79199-4)

(BL 95:1389; Kirkus 67:259; LJ Apr 15, 1999 p. 148; SLJ Oct 1999 p. 179)

5-623 TEPPER, Sheri S. *The Song of Mavin Manyshaped.* **(Mavin Manyshaped trilogy, bk. 1).** Gr. 10 up.

Mavin Manyshaped flees Danderbat Keep with her brother Mertin and calls upon her shape-shifting talents to save a plague-stricken city. The sequels are *The Flight of Mavin Manyshaped* (1985) and *The Search of Mavin Manyshaped* (1985). There are two companion trilogies—the Jinian trilogy (see *Jinian Footseer*, above) and the True Game trilogy: *Kings Blood Four* (1983), *Necromancer Nine* (1983), and *Wizard's Eleven* (1984).

Ace, 1985, pap., 183 pp., o.p.

(BL 81:1297, 1327, 86:906; VOYA 8:195)

5-624 THOMPSON, Kate. *The Beguilers.* Gr. 6–9.

☆ Rilka sets out to capture a beguiler, a dangerous ghostlike creature, with the help of elder Hemmy and a blind mountain porter named Marik.

Dutton, 2001, 183 pp. (0-525-46806-4); Firebird, 2003, pap., 192 pp. (0-14-250139-5)

(CCBB 55:222; HB 78:85; HBG 13:102; Kirkus 69:1369; Kliatt Sep 2001 p. 14; SLJ Oct 2001 p. 173; VOYA 24:374, 25:16)

5-625 THOMSON, Amy. *Storyteller.* Gr. 10 up.

After an orphaned street urchin named Samad is adopted by Teller, the oldest living Keeper of the Thalassa's history and customs, he becomes a guide for her and her telepathic fish, Abeha.

Berkley/Ace, 2003, pap., 384 pp. (0-441-01094-6)

(BL 100:589; LJ Nov 15, 2003 p. 101; VOYA 27:234)

TOLKIEN, J(ohn) R(onald) R(euel). *Farmer Giles of Ham.*

See Chapter 1, Allegorical Fantasy and Literary Fairy Tales.

5-626   TOLKIEN, J(ohn) R(onald) R(euel). *The Fellowship of the Ring.* (Lord
★★   **of the Rings trilogy, vol. 1).** Gr. 8 up. (Orig. British and U.S. pub. 1954.)
In this first volume of the trilogy set in Middle-Earth, following *The Hobbit*
(1938; see below), Frodo Baggins inherits a magic ring from his uncle Bilbo
and begins a journey to protect it from the evil powers who seek it. In *The Two
Towers* (orig. British pub. 1954; U.S. 1955; Houghton, 1967; 2005, pap.),
Frodo and Sam take the ring to the borders of the Dark Kingdom while the
members of the Company of the Ring battle the wizard Saruman and his goblin
army. In *The Return of the King* (orig. British and U.S. pub. 1955; Houghton,
1967; 2005, pap.), Frodo and Sam bring the ring to Mount Doom where it is
destroyed to help the forces of good win their struggle against the Dark Lord.
The Adventures of Tom Bombadil and Other Verses from "The Red Book"
(1962, 1963, 1991) is a related work. Tolkien's son, Christopher Tolkien, has
edited seven volumes of previously unpublished legends about the history of
Middle-Earth: *The Silmarillion* (1979; 1978 Gandalf Award [for Book-Length
Fantasy]), *Unfinished Tales of Numenor and Middle-Earth* (1980, 1982;
Mythopoeic Fantasy Award, 1981), *The Book of Lost Tales* (1983, 1984,
1986), *The Book of Lost Tales, Volume 2* (1984), *The Lays of the Beleriad*
(1985), *The Shaping of Middle-Earth: The Quenta, the Ambrakanta, and the
Annals* (1986), and *The Treason of Isengard* (1989).
Houghton, 1967, 1992, 440 pp. (0-395-64738-X), 1988, pap. (0-395-27223-8);
Ballantine, 1986, pap. (0-345-33970-3), 1999, pap., 432 pp. (0-618-00222-7),
2005, pap. (0-618-57494-8)
(BL 51:204; HB 31:104, 43:491; Kirkus 22:598; TLS 1954 p. 541)

5-627   TOLKIEN, J(ohn) R(onald) R(euel). *The Hobbit; Or, There and Back
★★   Again.* Gr. 5 up. (Orig. British pub. 1937; orig. U.S. pub. Houghton, 1938.)
A wizard tricks a peace-loving Hobbit named Bilbo Baggins into going on a
hazardous quest to recover stolen dwarf treasure from the dragon Smaug.
Bilbo's Last Song (1990) is a picture-book version of one of Bilbo's poems,
describing his preparations for leaving home. The Lord of the Rings trilogy
(see above) continues the saga of Middle-Earth.
Houghton, 1966 (rev. ed.), 317 pp. (0-395-07122-4); illus. by Michael (R.)
Hague, Houghton, 1984 (collector's ed.), 320 pp. (0-395-36290-3); Houghton,
2001, 333 pp. (0-168-16221-6), pap. (0-168-15052-X), 2002, pap., 320 pp. (0-
618-26030-7)
(BL 34:304, 80:52, 528; CCBB 38:96; HB 14:92, 94, 174; LJ 63:385, 819; SLJ Dec 1984 p.
86; TLS 1937 p. 714)

TOLKIEN, J(ohn) R(onald) R(euel). *Smith of Wootton Major.*
See Chapter 1, Allegorical Fantasy and Literary Fairy Tales.

5-628   TOWER, S. D. (pseud.). *The Assassins of Tamurin.* Gr. 10 up. (Orig. Cana-
dian pub. 2002.)
Trained as a spy after her childhood adoption by the Despotana of Tamurin,
Lale works her way into the confidence of the enemy Sun King, Terem Rathai,
and realizes nearly too late that she loves him.
HarperCollins, 2003, 464 pp. (0-380-97803-2)
(BL 99:862; Kirkus 70:1579; LJ Jan 2003 p. 165; VOYA 26:153, 27:15)

5-629 **TOWNSEND, John Rowe.** *The Fortunate Isles.* Gr. 7–10. (Orig. British
★ pub. 1989.)
Eleni and her friend Andreas run away to Gold Island after he convinces her
that her unusual blue eyes and dark hair mean that she is the Messenger, bound
by prophecy to seek out the Living God.
Harper, 1989, 248 pp., o.p.
(BL 86:446, 465; CCBB 43:98; HB 66:211; HBG 1:77; Kirkus 57:1410; SLJ Oct 1989 p.
138; Suth 4:414; VOYA 12:292, 13:12)

5-630 **TURNBULL, Ann (Christine).** *The Wolf King.* Gr. 5–7. (Orig. British pub.
1975.)
Grayla and Coll search the wolf-infested forest for their father and brother,
aided by the Dark People and the magical Elder Folk.
Seabury, 1976, 141 pp., o.p.
(BL 72:1339; Kirkus 44:473; SLJ Sep 1976 p. 126; TLS 1975 p. 1450)

5-631 **TURNER, Megan Whalen.** *The Thief.* Gr. 5 up.
★★ In exchange for freedom from the King of Eddis's prison, a young thief named
Gen agrees to steal a legendary jewel hidden in a distant temple. John Newbery
Medal Honor Book, 1996. In the sequel, *The Queen of Attolia* (2000), war
escalates between the kingdoms of Attolia and Eddis after Gen, the royal thief,
is released from an Attolian prison minus his right hand.
Greenwillow, 1996, 224 pp. (0-688-14627-9); Puffin, 1998, pap., 219 pp. (0-
14-038834-6)
(BL 93:863, 1296, 1305, 94:475; CCBB 50:117; HB 72:747; HBG 8:85; Kirkus 64:905; SLJ
Oct 1996 p. 150; VOYA 20:114)

5-632 **TURTLEDOVE, Harry.** *Into the Darkness.* **(Darkness saga, bk. 1).** Gr. 10
up.
In this alternate version of World War II, dragons serve as airpower, magic
wands replace rifles, leviathan-riders battle at sea, and behemoth rhinoceroses
take the place of tanks. The sequels are *Darkness Descending* (2000), *Through
the Darkness* (2001), *Rulers of Darkness* (2002), *Jaws of Darkness* (2003), and
Out of the Darkness (2004).
Tor, 1999, 544 pp. (0-312-86895-2); 2000, pap., 684 pp. (0-8125-7472-9)
(BL 95:1104, 1678; Kirkus 67:338)

5-633 **TURTLEDOVE, Harry.** *Sentry Peak.* Gr. 10 up.
The North has seceded from the South in order to keep its serfs in this alternate
version of the U.S. Civil War. The sequels are *Marching Through Peachtree*
(2001) and *Advance and Retreat* (2002).
Baen, 2000, 416 pp. (0-671-57887-1); Simon, 2001, pap., 506 pp. (0-671-
31846-2)
(BL 97:71; Kirkus 68:1148; LJ Sep 15, 2000 p. 118; VOYA 24:57)

5-634 **VANCE, Jack (pseud. of John Holbrook Vance).** *Cugel's Saga.* **(The
Dying Earth Saga, bk. 3).** Gr. 10 up.
Cugel the Clever travels across half a world seeking vengeance against the sor-
cerer Iucounu. This book is preceded by *The Dying Earth* (Lancer, 1950; Pock-
et, 1982), *The Eyes of the Overworld* (Ace, 1966, 1980), and *A Quest for
Simbils* (written by Michael Shea, DAW, 1974). It is followed by *Rhialto the*

Marvellous (1984). All four books have been published in *Tales of the Dying Earth*, St. Martin's, 2000, 752 pp. (0-3128-7456-1).
Simon, 1983, 334 pp., o.p.
(BL 80:185; Kirkus 51:979; LJ 108:2173; VOYA 7:102)

5-635 VANCE, Jack (pseud. of John Holbrook Vance). *Suldrun's Garden.* **(Lyonesse trilogy, bk. 1).** Gr. 10 up.
Imprisoned by her father for refusing to help him gain control of the Elder Isles, Princess Suldren manages to find a lover and escape. The sequels are *The Green Pearl* (1985, 1986) and *Madouc* (Underwood-Miller, 1989; Ace, 1990, pap.).
Underwood-Miller, 1983, o.p.
(BL 79:1263, 1269, 86:906; Kirkus 51:213; VOYA 6:218)

5-636 VANDE VELDE, Vivian. *Dragon's Bait.* Gr. 6–10.
✫ Left as dragon's bait by fellow villagers who want to take over her late father's shop, 15-year-old Alys is amazed to discover that the huge dragon can transform himself into a young man who agrees to take revenge on her former neighbors.
Harcourt, 1992, 144 pp. (0-15-200726-1); Dell, 1997, pap. (0-440-21982-5); Harcourt, 2003, pap., 208 pp. (0-15-216663-7)
(BL 89:139; CCBB 46:126; HB 69:213; HBG 4:84; Kirkus 60:994; SLJ Sep 1992 p. 261; VOYA 16:48)

VANDE VELDE, Vivian. *Magic Can Be Murder.*
See Chapter 12, Witchcraft and Sorcery Fantasy.

5-637 VANDE VELDE, Vivian. *Never Trust a Dead Man.* Gr. 6–10.
✫ Falsely accused of murdering Farold, his rival for the heart of Anora, a witch rescues 17-year-old Selwin from sure death in the burial caves.
Harcourt, 1999, 192 pp. (0-15-201899-9); Dell, 2001, pap., 194 pp. (0-440-22828-X)
(BL 95:1402; CCBB 52:297; HB 75:339; HBG 10:300; Kirkus 67:458; Kliatt July 1999 p. 13; SLJ May 1999 p. 131, Dec 1999 p. 44; VOYA 22:196, 23:14)

5-638 VAN SCYOC, Sydney J(oyce). *Bluesong.* **(The Darkchild trilogy, vol. 2).** Gr. 10 up.
In this second volume of the science-fantasy trilogy that began with *Darkchild* (1982, 1985) and is followed by *Starsilk* (1984), Darkchild's son, Danior, and niece, Keva, search for her father among a tribe of desert dwellers. All three books have been published in one volume entitled *Daughters of the Sunstone* (Science Fiction Book Club, 1985, o.p.).
Berkley, 1983, 1985, pap., 261 pp., o.p.
(BL 79:1450, 1458; Kirkus 51:272; VOYA 6:218)

5-639 VAN SCYOC, Sydney J(oyce). *Drowntide.* Gr. 10 up.
Prince Keiris enters a world beneath the sea to search for his long-lost twin sister.
Berkley, 1987, pap., 220 pp., o.p.
(BL 83:1412, 1436; VOYA 10:181)

5-640   **VOIGT, Cynthia.** *Elske.* **(The Kingdom series, bk. 4).** Gr. 8–12.
★   Having escaped death in her Volkaric homeland, Elske, 12, becomes handmaiden to Beriel, an exiled noblewoman, who convinces Elske to join her in an
attempt to win back her throne. This story is set in the same world as the
author's *Jackaroo* (1985; see below), *On Fortune's Wheel* (1990; see below),
and *Wings of a Falcon* (1993; see below).
Simon, 1999, 245 pp. (0-689-82472-6); Simon Pulse, 2003, pap., 312 pp. (0-
689-86438-8)
(BL 96:125; CCBB 53:152; HB 76:85; HBG 11:98; Kirkus 67:1653; SLJ Oct 1999 p. 160;
VOYA 22:274, 23:14)

5-641   **VOIGT, Cynthia.** *Jackaroo.* **(The Kingdom series, bk. 1).** Gr. 6–10.
★   Independent-minded Gwyn, the innkeeper's daughter, takes on the role of the
legendary Jackaroo, a masked rider who inspires hope in the poor and
oppressed. *On Fortune's Wheel* (1990; see below) takes place at a later time in
the same world, and *The Wings of a Falcon* (Scholastic, 1993; see below) and
Elske (1999; see above) are also set in this world.
Macmillan, 1985, 291 pp. (0-689-31123-0); Simon Pulse, 2003, pap., 385 pp.
(0-689-86435-3)
(BL 82:126; CCBB 39:19; SLJ Dec 1985 p. 96; Suth 4:423)

5-642   **VOIGT, Cynthia.** *On Fortune's Wheel.* **(The Kingdom series, bk. 2).** Gr.
★★   6–12.
Birle, the granddaughter of Gwyn in *Jackaroo* (1985; see above), falls in love
with a young runaway earl and travels downriver to the sea with him, encountering adventure, shipwreck, capture by pirates, slavery, and freedom. *The
Wings of a Falcon* (Scholastic, 1993; see below) and *Elske* (1999; see above)
are also set in this world.
Macmillan, 1990, 276 pp. (0-689-31636-4); Aladdin, 1999, pap. (0-689-82957-4)
(BL 86:1156; HB 66:341; HBG 1:254; Kirkus 58:187; Kliatt Sep 1991 p. 18; SLJ Mar 1990
p. 240; VOYA 13:40, 14:12)

5-643   **VOIGT, Cynthia.** *The Wings of a Falcon.* **(The Kingdom series, bk. 3).**
★   Gr. 7–12.
After Oriel and Griff escape from slavery on the Damall's Island, they travel to
the kingdom to compete for the hand of Princess Merlis. This story is set in the
same world as *Jackaroo* (1985; see above), *On Fortune's Wheel* (1990; see
above), and *Elske* (1999; see above).
Scholastic, 1993, 480 pp. (0-590-46712-3); Point Signature, 1995, pap. (0-590-
46713-1)
(CCBB 47:25; HB 70:207; HBG 5:91; Kirkus 61:1009; SLJ Oct 1993 p. 156; VOYA 16:314,
17:9)

5-644   **VOLSKY, Paula.** *The Gates of Twilight.* Gr. 10 up.
★   Renille and Jathondi must open the gate between two worlds to stop the priests
of a bloodthirsty cult from murdering a young woman in this story set in an
alternate 19th-century colonial India called Aveshq.
Bantam, 1996, pap., 352 pp. (0-553-37394-3); Bantam Spectra, 1997, pap.,
389 pp. (0-553-57269-5)
(BL 92:920, 923, 93:764; Kirkus 64:32; Kliatt May 1996 p. 19, May 1997 p. 16; LJ Mar 15,
1996 p. 98; VOYA 19:173)

5-645 **VOLSKY, Paula.** *The Grand Ellipse.* Gr. 10 up.

✮ Luzelle Devaire, Girays V'Alisante, and Over-Commander Karsler Stornzof compete in the Grand Ellipse, a terrifying fast-paced race through many lands, during which contestants face dangerous tribesmen, ghosts, captivity, and mayhem.

Bantam/Spectra, 2000, 560 pp., o.p.; Bantam, 2001, pap., 659 pp. (0-553-58012-4)

(BL 97:71; Kirkus 68:1241; LJ Sep 15, 2000 p. 118; VOYA 24:58)

5-646 **VOLSKY, Paula.** *The Luck of Relian Kru.* Gr. 10 up.

Relian Kru's lifelong bad luck is compounded when he is kidnapped by a sorcerer who wants to use Relian's special powers for his own ends.

Ace, 1987, pap., 304 pp., o.p.

(BL 83:1412, 1437)

5-647 **VOLSKY, Paula.** *The Wolf of Winter.* Gr. 10 up.

✮ When Varis, younger brother of Rhazaulle's ruler, uses necromancy to gain the throne, his niece, Shalindra, is sent into exile to escape a sentence of death.

Bantam, 1993, pap., 368 pp., o.p.; Bantam, 1995, pap. (0-553-56879-5)

(BL 90:505, 509; Kirkus 61:1233; LJ Nov 15, 1993 p. 103; VOYA 17:102)

5-648 **VORNHOLT, John.** *The Troll King.* **(The Troll trilogy, bk. 1).** Gr. 5–8.

A young troll named Rollo finds himself at the center of his people's revolt against the ogres and sorcerers who have kept them enslaved for generations. The sequels are *The Troll Queen* (2003) and *The Troll Treasure* (2003).

Simon, 2002, pap., 240 pp. (0-7434-2412-3)

(BL 98:1965; CCBB 56:129; Kliatt Nov 2002 p. 28; SLJ Aug 2002 p. 198; VOYA 25:299)

WAECHTER, Friedrich, and EILERT, Bernd. *The Crown Snatchers.*
See Chapter 1, Allegorical Fantasy and Literary Fairy Tales.

5-649 **WALTON, Jo.** *Tooth and Claw.* Gr. 10 up.

After the death of their father, Bon Agornin, five dragon siblings must deal with his deathbed confession while they vie for power within the family. World Fantasy Award, Best Novel, 2004.

Tor, 2003, 256 pp. (0-765-30264-0)

(BL 100:589; Kirkus 71:1160; LJ Oct 15, 2003 p. 102)

WANGERIN, Walter, Jr. *The Book of the Dun Cow.*
See Chapter 1, Allegorical Fantasy and Literary Fairy Tales.

5-650 **WARBURG, Sandol Stoddard (pseud. of Sandol Stoddard).** *On the Way Home.* Gr. 6–9.

Alexi, his friend Bear, and Alexi's double, Twain, rescue a fair maiden, kill an ice-worm monster, and escape from the Monkey King.

Illus. by Daniel Stolpe, Houghton, 1973, 137 pp. o.p.

(BL 70:546; Kirkus 41:1202, 1351; LJ 99:578)

5-651 **WARNER, Sylvia Townsend.** *Kingdoms of Elfin.* Gr. 10 up.

✮ A collection of haunting, interconnected tales about the winged inhabitants of ancient Elfin kingdoms beneath various European hillsides.

Viking, 1976, 222 pp., o.p.; Penguin, 1977, pap., o.p.

(Kirkus 44:1179, 1112; LJ 102:220; TLS 1977 p. 25)

5-652 WATERS, Elisabeth. *Changing Fate.* Gr. 7–12.
Shape-changer Acila runs her father's estate until he is killed, whereupon she flees, in wolf-form, from Lord Ranulf to avoid marrying him and losing her inheritance.
DAW, 1994, 240 pp. (0-88677-608-2)

(Kliatt July 1994 p. 18; VOYA 17:41)

5-653 WATSON, Ian. *Queenmagic, Kingmagic.* Gr. 10 up.
The game is ending in a land where life is chess played with human pieces, and two young pawn-squires from opposing kingdoms who have fallen in love realize they must escape to another world if they want to stay together.
St. Martin's, 1988, 205 pp., o.p.

(BL 84:908, 926; Kirkus 57:26; LJ Feb 15, 1988 p. 181; VOYA 11:98)

WATT-EVANS, Lawrence (pseud. of Richard Watt Evans). *Crosstime Traffic.*
See Chapter 3, Fantasy Collections.

5-654 WATT-EVANS, Lawrence (pseud. of Richard Watt Evans). *Dragon Weather.* **(Obsidian Chronicles, bk. 1).** Gr. 10 up.
Young Arlian becomes a "dragonheart" after he survives the destruction of his village by dragons, but he is sold into slavery by the evil Lord Dragon. The sequels are *The Dragon Society* (2001, 2003) and *Dragon Venom* (2003, 2004).
Tor, 1999, 480 pp. (0-312-86978-9); 2000, pap., 553 pp. (0-812-58955-6)

(Kirkus 67:1355; Kliatt May 2001 p. 29; VOYA 23:14, 51)

5-655 WATT-EVANS, Lawrence (pseud. of Richard Watt Evans). *The Misenchanted Sword.* **(Legends of Ethshar series, vol. 1).** Gr. 10 up.
Caught behind enemy lines, Ethshar army scout Valder is cursed by a wizard, causing his sword to remain unsheathed until it has killed someone. The sequels are *With a Single Spell* (1987, 1989, 1993), *The Unwilling Warlord* (1989), *The Blood of a Dragon* (1991), *The Spell of the Black Dagger* (1993), *Taking Flight* (1993), *Night of Madness* (2000, 2002), and *Ithanalin's Restoration* (2002).
Ballantine, 1985, pap., 292 pp., o.p.; Wildside, 2000, pap., 226 pp. (1-58715-282-7)

(BL 82:468; Kliatt Jan 1986 p. 22)

5-656 WATT-EVANS, Lawrence (pseud. of Richard Watt Evans). *Touched by the Gods.* Gr. 10 up.
Malledd is reluctant to follow the destiny predicted by a sorcerer at his birth, but he is forced to take up arms when the empire is threatened by the attack of an army of the undead.
Tor, 1997, 384 pp. (0-312-86060-9), 1998, pap., 536 pp. (0-8125-4595-8)

(BL 94:457; Kirkus 65:1345; LJ Nov 15, 1997 p. 79; VOYA 21:136)

5-657 WATT-EVANS, Lawrence (pseud. of Richard Watt Evans), and FRIESNER, Esther M. *Split Heirs.* Gr. 9 up.
A humorous tale set in the Kingdom of Hydrangea whose triplet heirs must be

kept apart to protect their mother's life.
Tor, 1993, 320 pp. (0-312-85320-3)
(BL 89:1950, 1953; VOYA 16:314, 17:8)

5-658   WEBER, David. *The War God's Own.* Gr. 10 up.
Bahzell Bahnakson and Brandark, hradani giants, lead their companions on a quest to unite their people with the war god Tomanak against the dark god Shama. This is the sequel to *Oath of Swords* (1995).
Baen, 1998, 400 pp. (0-671-87873-5); 1999, pap., 382 pp. (0-671-57792-1)
(BL 94:16808; Kirkus 66:374; LJ Apr 15, 1998 p. 118; VOYA 21:374)

5-659   WEIS, Margaret. *Mistress of Dragons.* **(The Dragonvarld Trilogy, bk. 1).** Gr. 10 up.
Draconas, a dragon in human form, recruits young King Edward of Ramsgate to accompany him on a mission to overthrow the evil Mistress of Dragons, and the high priestess Melisande chooses to escape with them. The sequel is *The Dragon's Son* (2004).
Tor, 1993, 400 pp. (0-765-30468-6); Tor, 2004, pap., 352 pp. (0-765-34390-8)
(BL 99:1459; Kirkus 71:650; VOYA 26:242, 27:15)

5-660   WEIS, Margaret. *The Prophet of Akhian.* **(Rose of the Prophet trilogy, vol. 3).** Gr. 10 up.
Four companions who have restored life to two gods on the Isle of Galos must rally the nomadic tribes to rescue the women and children held captive by the Priests of Kich. This is the sequel to *The Will of the Wanderer* (1989) and *The Paladin of the Night* (1989).
Bantam, 1989, 390 pp., o.p.
(VOYA 12:376)

5-661   WEIS, Margaret, and HICKMAN, Tracy. *Dragon Wing.* **(The Death Gate cycle, vol. 1).** Gr. 10 up.
Hugh the Hand is recruited to kill the prince of the Volkaran Isles, an assignment that he feels is unjust, while the dwarves plot insurrection deep beneath the earth. The sequels are *Elvin Star* (1990), *Fire Sea* (1991), *Serpent Mage* (1992), *The Hand of Chaos* (1993), *Into the Labyrinth* (1993), and *The Seventh Gate* (1994).
Bantam, 1990, 448 pp., o.p.
(BL 86:619, 621; Kirkus 57:1713; LJ Dec 1989 p. 177; VOYA 13:120, 398)

5-662   WEIS, Margaret, and HICKMAN, Tracy. *The DragonLance Chronicles.* **(Chronicles trilogy, bk. 1).** Gr. 7–12.
Tanis—half human, half elf—leads his band through numerous battles and adventures related to the fantasy game Dungeons and Dragons. This collection contains three books originally published separately: *Dragons of Autumn Twilight* (1984), *Dragons of Winter Night* (1985), and *Dragons of Spring Dawning* (1985). *Dragons of the Summer Flame* (1995, 2002) is the fourth book in the series. It is followed by the Legends trilogy (see *DragonLance Legends*, below). The Tales trilogy anthologies are *The Magic of Krynn* (1987), *Kender, Gully Dwarves, and Gnomes* (1987), and *Love and War* (1987). The Tales II trilogy anthologies are *The Reign of Istar* (1992), *The Cataclysm* (1992), and *The War of the Lance* (1992); *The Second Generation* (1994) is also a DragonLance

anthology. *Temple of the Dragonslayer* by Tim Waggoner (Wizards of the Coast, pap., 2004) is the first volume of Dragonlance: The New Adventures series. More than 30 fantasy gaming tie-in sequels to the DragonLance novels have been written by Mark Anthony, Tonya R. Carter, Tina Daniell, Jeff Grubb, Richard A. Knaak, Mary Kurchoff, Douglas Niles, Dan Parkinson, Ellen Porath, Ellen Dodge Severson, Barbara and Scott Siegal, Kevin Stein, Paul B. Thompson, Nancy Varian, Michael Williams, Teri Williams, and Steve Winter. TSR, 1988, 1,032 pp., o.p.; Wizards of the Coast, 2001, 1,232 pp. (0-7869-2681-3)
(VOYA 12:46)

5-663   WEIS, Margaret, and HICKMAN, Tracy. *DragonLance Legends.* **(Legends trilogy, bk. 1).** Gr. 7–12.
These stories involve characters from the fantasy game Dungeons and Dragons, particularly the ingenious Kender thief, Tasslehoff Burrfoot, and the twins, Caramon the warrior and Raistlin the wizard. This collection is the sequel to *The DragonLance Chronicles* (TSR, 1988; see above) and contains *Time of the Twins* (1986), *Test of the Twins* (1986), and *War of the Twins* (1986), originally issued separately.
TSR, 1988, 905 pp., o.p.
(VOYA 12:118, 13:12)

5-664   WEIS, Margaret, and HICKMAN, Tracy. *Forging the Darksword.* **(Darksword saga, vol. 1).** Gr. 10 up.
Earth's witches have fled to Merilon, where they are no longer persecuted for practicing magic, but Joram, born without magical powers, decides to join a secret society that practices science. The sequels are *Doom of the Darksword* (1988), *Triumph of the Darksword* (1988, 1997), and *Legacy of the Darksword* (1997, 1998).
Bantam, 1988, pap., 391 pp., o.p.
(BL 84:831, 855; LJ Dec 1987 p. 130; VOYA 11:141)

5-665   WEIS, Margaret, and HICKMAN, Tracy. *Well of Darkness.* **(The Sovereign Stone trilogy, bk. 1).** Gr. 10 up.
Prince Dagnarus convinces Gareth, his whipping boy and friend, to learn void magic in order to help him take King Tamaris's throne away from Dagnarus's older half brother, Prince Helms. The sequels are *Guardians of the Lost* (2001) and *Journey into the Void* (2003).
HarperCollins/Eos, 2000, 464 pp. (0-06-105180-2); HarperTorch, 2001, pap., 592 pp. (0-06-102057-5)
(BL 97:222; Kirkus 68:1068; LJ Sep 15, 2000 p. 118; VOYA 24:58)

5-666   WELLS, Angus. *Exiles Children.* **(Exiles Saga, bk. 1).** Gr. 10 up.
The fates of two groups of people in different worlds are linked: a young thief, a tavern girl, and a gentleman, who become friends after each is convicted of a crime under unjust laws, and the people of Kel-Ta-Witko whose protective magic is being destroyed by the invading Breakers. *Exiles Challenge* (1996) concludes the series.
Bantam, 1995, 1996, pap., 592 pp., o.p.; Spectra, 1996, pap., 592 pp. (0-553299-03-4)
(BL 92:689, 693; Kliatt May 1996 p. 20)

5-667 **WELLS, Angus.** *Lords of the Sky.* Gr. 7–12.
Dhar storyteller Daviot and a blind sorceress named Ruyan discover that dragons are the true Skylords who can bring peace to their warring world.
Bantam, 1994, pap., 578 pp., o.p.
(Kliatt Mar 1995 p. 20; LJ Sep 15, 1994 p. 94; VOYA 18:39)

5-668 **WELLS, Angus.** *Yesterday's Kings.* Gr. 10 up.
After a young forester named Cullyn is accused of treason and heresy by an evil Kandarian priest for aiding Lofantyl, a Durrym man in love with the Kandarian Border Lord's daughter, he flees across the river that separates the two warring peoples.
Bantam, 2001, pap., 328 pp. (0-553-57796-4)
(Kliatt July 2001 p. 28; VOYA 24:218, 25:16)

5-669 **WELLS, Martha.** *City of Bones.* Gr. 10 up.
✮   A young relic trader of low status named Khat, and Elen, a high-ranking assistant Warder, become unlikely allies on a dangerous quest to understand ancient relics that hold the secrets to the origin of their world.
Tor, 1995, 384 pp. (0-312-85686-5); 1996, pap. (0-8125-6708-0)
(BL 91:1737, 1741; Kirkus 63:434; LJ May 15, 1995 p. 99, Feb 15, 1996 p. 200; VOYA 18:388)

WELLS, Martha. *The Death of the Necromancer.*
See Chapter 12, Witchcraft and Sorcery Fantasy.

5-670 **WEST, Michelle.** *Hunter's Oath.* Gr. 10 up.
Orphaned Stephen is chosen to be the Huntbrother and companion of Gilliam of Elseth, and possibly to die for him during the Sacred Hunt. *Hunter's Death* (1996) concludes the duology.
DAW, 1995, pap., 1,427 pp. (0-88677-681-3)
(Kliatt Jan 1996 p. 18; VOYA 18:318)

5-671 **WESTALL, Robert (Atkinson).** *The Cats of Seroster.* Gr. 7–12. (Orig.
✮   British pub. 1984.)
Gentle Cam is possessed by his magic dagger, which, with the help of some large, power-wielding cats, turns him into the Seroster, a legendary hero destined to lead his people against their enemies.
Greenwillow, 1984, 349 pp., o.p.; Macmillan, 1995, new ed., 288 pp. (0-330-29239-0)
(BL 81:362, 86:907; CCBB 38:75; HB 61:188; Kirkus 52:108; SLJ Jan 1985 p. 88; TLS 1984 p. 1375; VOYA 8:58)

5-672 **WHEELER, Deborah.** *Northlight.* Gr. 10 up.
Ranger Kardith sets out to find her missing friend, Avi, along with Avi's younger brother Terris, after the city of Laurea is engulfed in chaos following the assassination of its beloved leader.
DAW, 1995, 251 pp. (0-88677-639-2)
(Kliatt May 1995 p. 19; VOYA 18:111)

5-673 **WILDER, Cherry (pseud. of Cherry Barbara Lockett Grimm).** *A Princess*
✮   *of the Chameln.* **(The Rulers of Hylor series, vol. 1).** Gr. 8–12.
After Princess Aidris Am Firn's parents are assassinated, she flees to Athion

where she becomes a cavalry soldier living under a false name until she can return to Chameln as Queen. In *Yorath the Wolf* (1984), young Yorath has been brought up in secret by the court magician because, as heir to the throne of Hylor, he is under a decree of death. In *The Summer's King* (1986), vain young King Sham Am Zor is tricked by the sorcerer Rosmer into undergoing a deadly ordeal of trickery and magic. The final book in the series is *The Wanderer* (2004), begun by Wilder and completed by Katya Reimann.
Atheneum, 1984, 272 pp., o.p.
(BL 80:1111; HB 60:479; SLJ May 1984 p. 95; VOYA 7:269)

5-674 WILLETT, John (William Mills). *The Singer in the Stone.* Gr. 5–7.
Angelina is the only one who cares enough to help Rubythroat, the last of the Dreamers, bring back storytelling, song, and dance to the world of the Plain People.
Houghton, 1981, 86 pp., o.p.
(BL 77:1342, 1348; CCBB 35:19; Kirkus 49:636; SLJ Sep 1981 p. 132)

5-675 WILLEY, Elizabeth. *A Sorcerer and a Gentleman.* Gr. 10 up.
When the feud between Emperor Avril of Landuc and his brother, Prospero, the sorcerer of Argylle, threatens to become war, Prospero's daughter, Freia, flies away on her pet gryphon, and a young sorcerer named Dewar searches for a previously unknown source of magic in this story related to Shakespeare's *The Tempest*. The sequel is *The Price of Blood and Honor* (1996, 1997), and these stories are related to the author's *The Well-Favored Man: The Tale of the Sorcerer's Nephew* (1993; see below).
Tor, 1995, 448 pp. (0-312-85783-7); 1996, pap. (0-8125-5047-1)
(BL 91:1933, 1936, 92:739; Kirkus 63:820; VOYA 18:388)

5-676 WILLEY, Elizabeth. *The Well-Favored Man: The Tale of the Sorcerer's Nephew.* Gr. 10 up.
Young sorcerer-prince Gwydion has inherited the throne after the mysterious disappearances of his father and uncle, and is kept busy defending the kingdom from dragons, monsters, diplomatic intrigue, and a woman who may be his long-lost sister. *A Sorcerer and a Gentleman* (1995; see above) and its sequel, *The Price of Blood and Honor* (1996, 1997) are related books.
Tor, 1993, 448 pp. (0-312-85590-7)
(BL 90:422, 428; Kirkus 61:1036; LJ Sep 15, 1993 p. 109; VOYA 17:41)

5-677 WILLIAMS, Jay. *The Time of the Kraken.* Gr. 7–10.
☆   In this science-fantasy, two warring tribes unite in the face of the coming of monstrous beasts called Kraken, while Thorgeir, his bride, and his blood brother set out for the legendary Temple of Arveid in search of help against the destructive beasts.
Macmillan, 1977, 168 pp., o.p.
(BL 74:609; CCBB 31:120; SLJ Sep 1977 p. 150; TLS 1978 p. 377)

5-678 WILLIAMS, Tad. *Caliban's Hour.* Gr. 10 up.
In this sequel to Shakespeare's *The Tempest*, Caliban seeks revenge on his abusive former master and mistress, Prospero and Miranda, by holding Miranda captive and threatening her death.

HarperCollins, 1994, 208 pp. (0-06-105204-3); Harper, 1995, pap. (0-06-105413-5)

(BL 91:804, 808; LJ Nov 15, 1994 p. 89)

5-679 WILLIAMS, Tad. *The Dragonbone Chair.* **(Memory, Sorrow and Thorn trilogy, bk. 1).** Gr. 10 up.
In thrall to the black magician Pyrates, King Elias of Osten Ard decides to destroy his brother, Josua, and a kitchen helper named Simon rises to become a hero after he joins Josua's forces. The sequels are *Stone of Farewell* (1990) and *To Green Angel Tower* (1993).
DAW, 1988, 672 pp., o.p.; 1989, pap. (0-88677-384-9)

(BL 84:906, 1866, 1868; Kirkus 56:1199; LJ Sep 15, 1988 p. 95; SLJ Apr 1989 p. 128; VOYA 11:296, 12:14)

5-680 WILLIAMS, Tad, and HOFFMAN, Nina Kiriki. *Child of an Ancient City.* Gr. 6–12.
The surviving travelers of a caravan pillaged by bandits must tell stories around the campfire all night long to keep away a bloodthirsty vampyr.
Illus. by Greg Hildebrandt, Macmillan, 1992, 137 pp. (0-689-31577-5)

(BL 89:662; HBG 4:85; SLJ Jan 1993 p. 134; VOYA 16:48, 17:8)

5-681 WILSON, Diane Lee. *I Rode a Horse of Milk White Jade.* Gr. 6–10.
✭ Oyuna tells her granddaughter the story of her life in 1339 Mongolia, including her journey on a talking horse to the court of Kublai Khan, where she delivers a mysterous package in hopes of bringing good luck to her clan.
Orchard, 1998, 232 pp. (0-531-30024-2); HarperTrophy, 1999, pap., 304 pp. (0-06-440773-X)

(BL 94:1313; CCBB 51:378; HBG 9:348; Kirkus 66:410; Kliatt Mar 1998 p. 6; SLJ June 1998 p. 154; VOYA 21:215)

5-682 WOLFE, Gene (Rodman). *The Shadow of the Torturer.* **(The Book of the New Sun, vol. 1).** Gr. 10 up.
In this first volume of a tetralogy that combines fantasy and science fiction, Severian, an exiled apprentice of the Torturer's Guild, travels across a future earth immersed in winter due to its dying sun. As he travels toward his new appointment, his mysterious sword involves him in a duel with poisonous weapons, and he is given a strange jewel. World Fantasy Convention Award, 1981. The sequels are *The Claw of the Conciliator* (1981), *The Sword of the Lictor* (1981, 1982; British Fantasy Society Best Novel Award, 1982), *The Citadel of the Autarch* (Ultramarine, 1983), and *The Urth of the New Sun* (1987). *Nightside of the Long Sun* (Tor, 1993) is also set in the Whorl, and is the first volume of the Book of the Long Sun science fiction series, which includes *Lake of the Long Sun* (1994), *Calde of the Long Sun* (1994), *Exodus from the Long Sun* (1996), and *Epiphany of the Long Sun* (2000). The Book of the Short Sun trilogy is a related science fiction series and includes *On Blue's Waters* (1999), *In Green's Jungles* (2000, 2001), and *Return to the Whorl* (2001).
Simon, 1980, 304 pp., o.p.

(BL 76:1594; Kirkus 48:400; LJ 105:1192; SLJ Sep 1980 p. 93)

5-683 **WOLFE, Gene (Rodman).** *Soldier of the Mist.* Gr. 10 up.
✫ A head injury causes Latro, a young Greek soldier in 479 B.C., to lose his
memory and wander the land, meeting gods, goddesses, and other supernatural
beings. *Soldier of Arete* (1989) completes the duology, and *Latro in the Mist*
(Orb, 2003) contains both books.
Tor, 1987, 352 pp., o.p.
(BL 82:1475, 86:906; Kirkus 54:1324; LJ Nov 15, 1986 p. 112; VOYA 9:294, 10:23)

5-684 **WOOD, Mackay.** *Wolf's Cub.* Gr. 10 up.
Newlywed Prince Herric unexpectedly takes over the throne of Athagar and
discovers that he has many enemies.
Write Way, 1998, pap., 400 pp. (1-885173-30-X)
(BL 95:574; LJ Nov 15, 1998 p. 94)

5-685 **WOODING, Chris.** *The Haunting of Alaizabel Cray.* Gr. 8–12. (Orig.
✫ British pub. 2001.)
Thaniel Fox, 17, a wych-hunter attempting to protect Victorian London from a
plague of wych-kyn, rescues a young woman named Alaizabel, who has
escaped from a violent cult called the Fraternity. Nestlé Smarties Book Prize
Silver Medal, 2001.
Orchard, 2004, 304 pp. (0-439-54656-7); Orchard, 2005, pap., 292 pp. (0-439-
59851-6)
(BL 100:1925; CCBB 58:46; HB 80:718; Kirkus 72:815; SLJ Aug 2004 p. 132; VOYA
27:321.)

5-686 **WREDE, Patricia C(ollins).** *Caught in Crystal.* Gr. 7–12.
Once a member of the Sisterhood of Stars and now a widowed innkeeper and
mother of two, Kayl is called back into service to fight the evil influence of the
Magicseekers by destroying a magic crystal hidden within the Twisted Tower.
Ace, 1987, 293 pp., o.p.
(VOYA 10:133)

5-687 **WREDE, Patricia C(ollins).** *Dealing with Dragons.* **(Enchanted Forest**
✫ **Chronicles, bk. 1).** Gr. 6–9.
Princess Cimorene vows that she would rather be eaten by a dragon than act
like a "proper" princess and marry a dull prince, so she volunteers to be cap-
tured by the powerful dragon Kazul. In *Searching for Dragons* (1991, 2002),
Cimorene and young King Morwen set off on a flying carpet in search of
Kazul, who has disappeared. In *Calling on Dragons* (1993, 2003), Queen
Cimorene sets out to retrieve King Mendanbar's stolen magic sword, accompa-
nied by a witch, a magician, and the dragon king, Kazul. In the concluding volume, *Talking to Dragons* (1985; rev. ed., 1993, 2003), set 16 years later,
Cimorene's son, Daystar, faces wizards and monsters when he tries to rescue
his father, King Mendanbar. The entire series was published in *The Enchanted
Forest Chronicles* boxed set, Harcourt, 2003 (0-15-205052-3). Wrede's *Book
of Enchantments* (1996; see Chapter 3, Fantasy Collections) contains some stories about the same characters.
Harcourt, 1990, 192 pp. (0-15-222900-0); Harcourt, 2002, pap., 240 pp. (0-15-
204566-X)
(BL 87:331, 969, 91:416; HBG 2:86; Kirkus 58:1094; SLJ Dec 1990 pp. 25, 112; VOYA
13:370, 14:10)

5-688   WREDE, Patricia C(ollins). *The Harp of Imach Thyssel.* **(Lyra series, bk. 2).** Gr. 10 up.
The legendary harp found by Emereck, a young minstrel, must be guarded from sorcerers who seek it and must never be played. This is the sequel to *Shadow Magic* (1982) and is set in the same world as *Daughter of Witches* (1983) and *The Raven Ring* (1994).
Ace, 1985, pap., 234 pp., o.p.
(BL 81:1374, 1390, 86:907)

5-689   WREDE, Patricia C(ollins). *Mairelon the Magician.* Gr. 10 up.
✶   Sixteen-year-old Kim, a proficient pickpocket disguised as a boy in an alternate Regency London, travels across England with a magician who is trying to clear his name. In *The Magician's Ward* (1997, 1998, 2002), Kim has been taken on as Lord Richard Merrill (formerly Mairelon the Magician)'s ward, and tries to use her magical abilities to solve a burglary at her guardian's home, while being transformed into a lady. These books are set in the same world as Wrede's and Caroline Stevermer's *Sorcery and Cecilia* (1988, 2003; see below), and Stevermer's *A College of Magics* (1994; see above).
Tor, 1991, 288 pp. (0-312-85041-7); Starscape, 2002, pap., 312 pp. (0-765-34232-4)
(BL 87:1783, 1788, 88:872; Kirkus 59:572; LJ May 15, 1991 p. 111; SLJ Feb 1992, p. 122; VOYA 14:327)

5-690   WREDE, Patricia C(ollins). *The Seven Towers.* Gr. 10 up.
Jermain flees the Sevairn court and takes over command of the armies of the wizard King Carachel, in an attempt to preserve the Seven Kingdoms and destroy their monstrous enemy.
Ace, 1984, pap., 264 pp., o.p.
(BL 80:1154, 1161; VOYA 7:148)

5-691   WREDE, Patricia C(ollins), and STEVERMER, Caroline. *Sorcery and Cecilia; Or, The Enchanted Chocolate Pot: Being the Correspondence of Two Young Ladies of Quality Regarding Various Magical Scandals in London and the Country.* Gr. 6–10. (Alternate title *Sorcery and Cecilia, Or, The Enchanted Chocolate Pot: Being the Correspondence of Two Young Ladies of Quality Regarding Various Magical Scandals in London and the Country.*)
Two cousins in an alternate Regency England exchange letters about their gentlemen friends and magical exploits in this humorous spoof of a Regency romance. In the sequel, *The Grand Tour: Being a Revelation of Matters of High Confidentiality and Greatest Importance, Including Extracts from the Intimate Diary of a Noblewoman and the Sworn Testimony of a Lady of Quality* (2004), Cecy, James, Kate, and Thomas, honeymooning on the Continent, attempt to thwart a wizardly plot to crown a new Emperor of Europe. Wrede's *Mairelon the Magician* (1991; see above) and Stevermer's *A College of Magics* (1994; see above) are set in the same world.
Ace, 1988, pap., 197 pp., o.p.; Harcourt, 2003, 320 pp. (0-15-204615-1); Harcourt, pap., 2004 (0-15-205300-X)
(BL 84:1575, 1598; CCBB 56:466; HB 79:572; HBG 14:389; Kirkus 71:613; VOYA 11:248, 12:16, 26:154)

5-692   WURTS, Janny. *Curse of the Mistwraith.* **(The Wars of Light and Shadow, vol. 1).** Gr. 10 up.
Only the combined powers of Arithon and Lysaer, two brothers raised as enemies, can lift the 500-year-old curse of the Mistwraith that darkens the land of Athera. The sequels are *Ships of Merior* (1995), *Warhost of Vastmark* (1995, 1996), and the sub-cycle Alliance of Light: *Fugitive Prince* (1997, 1998), *Grand Conspiracy* (1999, 2000), and *Peril's Gate* (2002; see below).
Roc, 1994, 688 pp. (0-451-45306-9); Penguin, 1993, pap., 611 pp. (0-451-45306-9)
(BL 90:997, 1000; Kirkus 61:1494; Kliatt Mar 1995 p. 20)

5-693   WURTS, Janny. *The Master of White Storm.* Gr. 10 up.
Korendir, a mysterious soldier-for-hire, leads a galley slave revolt after a life spent battling wizards and rescuing princesses.
NAL, 1992, pap., 413 pp. (0-451-45167-8)
(BL 88:1344, 1348; LJ Mar 15, 1992 p. 129)

5-694   WURTS, Janny. *Peril's Gate.* **(Alliance of Light series, vol. 3).** Gr. 10 up.
Wounded Arithon, Master of Shadow, must aid the sorcerers of the Fellowship of Seven in their struggle to hold onto the magic that keeps the world of Athera in balance. The preceding volumes in this series are *Fugitive Prince* (1997, 1998) and *Grand Conspiracy* (1999). This series is a sub-cycle of the Wars of Light and Shadow series: *Curse of the Mistwraith* (1993, 1994; see above), *Ships of Merior* (1995), and *Warhost of Vastmark* (1995, 1996).
HarperCollins, 2002, 736 pp. (0-06-105220-5); Eos, 2003, pap., 960 pp. (0-06-105467-4)
(BL 98:710; Kirkus 69:1462; VOYA 25:493)

5-695   WURTS, Janny. *Sorcerer's Legacy.* Gr. 10 up.
A sorcerer who appears in the pregnant Queen Eleinne's dungeon after the murder of her husband convinces the queen to travel to the world of Pendaire and save the life of Prince Darion by marrying him and bearing him a child.
Bantam, 1989, pap., 246 pp. (0-553-27846-0)
(VOYA 12:229, 13:15)

WURTS, Janny. *Stormwarden.*
See Chapter 12, Witchcraft and Sorcery Fantasy.

5-696   YEP, Laurence M(ichael). *Dragon of the Lost Sea.* **(Dragon Quartet, bk.**
✭   **1).** Gr. 5–8.
Shimmer, banished princess of the Dragon Clan, joins forces with a 13-year-old boy named Thorn to win back the Lost Sea of the dragons from the enchantress Civit. In *Dragon Steel* (1985), Shimmer and Thorn escape imprisonment in her undersea kingdom and fight numerous battles to restore the kingdom of the Inland Sea to the dragon clan. In *Dragon Cauldron* (1991), Shimmer and Thorn continue their quest for the magic cauldron that will bring back the sea. In *Dragon War* (1992), Shimmer, Monkey, and Indigo attempt to rescue Thorn from the Boneless King's palace, where his soul has been imprisoned in the powerful cauldron.
Harper, 1982, 224 pp., o.p.; HarperTrophy, 1994, pap., 224 pp. (0-06-440227-4)
(BL 79:250, 978; CCBB 36:59; Kirkus 50:1107; SLJ Nov 1982 p. 93; Suth 3:464; VOYA 5:47)

YOLEN (Stemple), Jane (Hyatt). *Boots and the Seven Leaguers: A Rock-and-Troll Novel.*
See Chapter 8, Humorous Fantasy.

5-697 **YOLEN (Stemple), Jane (Hyatt).** *Dragon's Blood.* **(Pit Dragons trilogy,**
✫ **bk. 1).** Gr. 7–10.
Jakkin steals and trains a young dragon to earn the money to buy his freedom. In *Heart's Blood* (1984, 1996, 2004), Jakkin oversees the hatching of his beloved Dragon's first clutch, is drawn into a terrorist plot, and is forced to flee with Akki, the daughter of his former master. In *A Sending of Dragons* (1987, 1989, 1997, 2004), Jakkin and Akki enter a subterranean labyrinth populated by a primitive race that practices sacrificial rituals.
Delacorte, 1982, 256 pp., o.p.; Dell, 1984, pap. (0-440-91802-2); Harcourt, 2004, pap. (0-15-205126-0)
(BL 78:1236, 1262, 86:906; CCBB 35:220; HB 58:418; SLJ Sep 1982 p. 146; Suth 3:466; VOYA 5:51)

YOLEN (Stemple), Jane (Hyatt). *Here There Be Dragons.*
See Chapter 3, Fantasy Collections.

5-698 **YOLEN (Stemple), Jane (Hyatt).** *The Magic Three of Solatia.* Gr. 5–7.
✫ A wisewoman named Sianna and her son, Lann, use three magic buttons to keep out of danger's way and to rescue an enchanted bird-girl from a wizard-king.
Illus. by Julia Noonan, Crowell, 1974, 172 pp., o.p.
(BL 71:574; CCBB 28:172; Kirkus 42:1207; SLJ Jan 1975 p. 51; Suth 2:490)

5-699 **YOLEN (Stemple), Jane (Hyatt).** *Sister Light, Sister Dark.* **(The Great Alta saga, bk. 1).** Gr. 10 up.
Raised in a mountainous community of women warriors who worship the white goddess, Alta, orphaned Jenna discovers that she is vitally important to the future of this warrior tribe. The first sequel is *White Jenna* (1989), and the two books were published together in *The Books of Great Alta* (Tor, 1997, pap, 0-312-86258X). The second sequel is *The One-Armed Queen* (Tor, 1998, pap.).
Tor, 1988, 252 pp., o.p.; 1989, pap. (0-8125-0249-3); Tor, 2003, 156 pp. (0-15-204913-4)
(BL 85:220, 259; Kirkus 56:1367; SLJ Dec 1988 p. 132; VOYA 12:16, 48)

YOLEN (Stemple), Jane (Hyatt). *Wizard's Hall.*
See Chapter 12, Witchcraft and Sorcery Fantasy.

ZAMBRENO, Mary Frances. *A Plague of Sorcerers.*
See Chapter 12, Witchcraft and Sorcery Fantasy.

ZELAZNY, Roger (Joseph Christopher). *Jack of Shadows.*
See Chapter 12, Witchcraft and Sorcery Fantasy.

ZELAZNY, Roger (Joseph Christopher). *Madwand.*
See Chapter 12, Witchcraft and Sorcery Fantasy.

5-700 **ZELAZNY, Roger (Joseph Christopher).** *Nine Princes in Amber.* **(Amber series, bk. 1).** Gr. 10 up.
Although he has lost all memory of his life in the land of Amber, Corwin slowly begins to recover his special powers and to fight for his princely birthright. The sequels are *The Guns of Avalon* (1972, 1974), *The Sign of the Unicorn* (1975, 1976), *The Hand of Oberon* (1976, 1977), *The Courts of Chaos* (1978, 1979), *Trumps of Doom* (1985), *Blood of Amber* (1986), *Sign of Chaos* (1987), *Knight of Shadows* (1989), and *Prince of Chaos* (1991, 1992). *Roger Zelazny's Visual Guide to Castle Amber* (Avon, 1988) is an illustrated guide to the Amber lore written by Zelazny and Neil Randall.
Doubleday, 1970, o.p.; Gregg Press, 1979 (repr. of 1970 ed.), 188 pp., o.p.; Harper, 1995, pap. (0-380-01430-0)
(BL 67:84, 142, 86:906; Kirkus 38:484; LJ 95:2513)

5-701 **ZELAZNY, Roger (Joseph Christopher), and LINDSKOLD, Jane M.** *Lord Demon.* Gr. 10 up.
Lord Demon Kai Wren, a master glass-blower, is determined to find and punish the demon who murdered his valuable human servant, Oliver O'Keefe.
Avon, 1999, 288 pp. (0-380-97333-2); Eos, 2000, pap., 336 pp. (0-380-77023-7)
(BL 95:2038; Kirkus 67:842; LJ July 1999 p. 142)

5-702 **ZETTNER, Pat.** *The Shadow Warrior.* Gr. 7 up.
☆ Llyndreth accepts the aid of Angborn the giant and the goblin Zorn when she sets out to find her brother, missing since he left to fight the Shadow Warriors.
Macmillan, 1990, 220 pp., o.p.; Random, 1994 (0-517-13720-8)
(BL 86:1892, 1903; HB 66:341; HBG 1:254; Kirkus 58:189; SLJ May 1990 p. 129; VOYA 13:122, 14:12)

5-703 **ZICREE, Marc Scott, and HAMBLY, Barbara.** *Magic Time.* **(Magic Time series, bk. 1).** Gr. 10 up.
In a future world, Cal Griffin tries to save his sister, who was transformed into a mythical creature when the Source opened, enabling magic to work and causing modern technology to fail. The sequels are *Angelfire* (2002) and *Ghostlands* (2004).
HarperCollins/Eos, 2001, 384 pp. (0-06-105068-7)
(BL 98:388; Kirkus 69:1331; VOYA 25:403, 26:14)

5-704 **ZIMNIK, Reiner.** *The Bear and the People.* Gr. 4–7. (Orig. German pub.
☆ 1956.)
Dearman and his talking bear, Brown One, entertain throughout the countryside until jealous villagers attack them.
Trans. by Nina Ignatowicz, illus. by the author, Harper, 1971, 78 pp., o.p.
(BL 68:670; Kirkus 39:436; LJ 96:2367, 4160; TLS 1972 p. 1328)

6

High Fantasy:
Myth or Legend Fantasy

High fantasy novels have been variously called epic fantasy, heroic fantasy, myth fantasy, other-world fantasy, and alternate world fantasy. In such works, the fate of the world hangs in the balance, while the forces of good and evil, or light and darkness, battle for control of humanity. For the purposes of this book, high fantasy novels have been divided into three chapters: Chapter 5, Alternate Worlds or Histories; Chapter 6, Myth and Legend; and Chapter 7, Travel to Other Worlds.

This chapter lists books that are retellings of myth or legend, as well as stories in which contemporary protagonists are drawn into the mythic struggle of good versus evil. Many of these works are retellings or expansions of the Arthurian legends, of Andersen and Grimm fairy tales, and of Celtic or Norse mythology.

6-1 **ABBEY, Lynn (pseud. of Marilyn Lorraine Abbey).** *Unicorn and Dragon.*
☆ Gr. 10 up.
The conflict between Alison, the last of the Druidic Saxon priestesses, and her foster-sister, Wildecent, a Norman sorceress, embodies the theme of an old culture reluctantly giving way before a new one, in this novel set in 11th-century Saxon England.
Avon, 1987, pap., 240 pp. (0-380-75567-X)
(Kliatt 21:19, LJ Feb 15, 1987 p. 165; SLJ June–July 1987 p. 115)

6-2 **AIKEN, Joan (Delano).** *Winterthing: A Play for Children.* Gr. 6–8. (Orig. British pub. 1972.)
Upon their arrival on mysterious Winter Island, four children and their peculiar old aunt take in a foundling baby, and as the years go by, they realize that only the baby is aging.
Illus. by Arvis Stewart, Holt, 1972, 79 pp., o.p.
(BL 69:490; CCBB 26:85; HB 49:149; Kirkus 40:1314; LJ 97:4075; TLS 1973 p. 681)

6-3   **ALCOCK, Vivien (Dolores).** *Singer to the Sea God.* Gr. 6–10. (Orig. British
✫   pub. 1992.)
Slave singer Phaidon escapes by ship after the legendary hero Perseus uses
Medusa's bloody head to turn the king and his courtiers to stone.
Delacorte, 1993, 208 pp., o.p.; Dell, 1995, pap. (0-440-41003-7); Peter Smith,
1997 (0-8446-6887-7)
(BL 89:1578; CCBB 46:168; HB 69:463; HBG 4:307; Kirkus 60:1567; SLJ Mar 1993 p. 196;
VOYA 16:33)

6-4   **ALCOCK, Vivien (Dolores).** *The Stonewalkers.* Gr. 5–8.
✫   Lightning strikes the old metal bracelet Poppy has placed on the arm of a gar-
den statue, and the statue comes to life, with frightening consequences.
Delacorte, 1983, 192 pp., o.p.; Houghton, 1998, pap. (0-395-81652-1)
(BL 79:962; CCBB 36:181; HB 59:299; Kirkus 51:120; SLJ May 1983 pp. 31, 68; Suth 3:9;
TLS 1981 p. 1354; VOYA 6:144)

ALEXANDER, Lloyd (Chudley). *The Book of Three.*
See Chapter 5, High Fantasy: Alternate Worlds or Histories.

6-5   **ALLEN, Judy.** *The Lord of the Dance.* Gr. 6–8. (Orig. British pub. 1976.)
In the rubble of a collapsed building, Mike meets the Sun King and the Earth
Queen.
Dutton, 1977, 124 pp., o.p.
(CCBB 31:25; HB 53:536; Kirkus 45:580; SLJ Sep 1977 p. 139; TLS 1976 p. 1544)

6-6   **ALLENDE, Isobel.** *City of the Beasts.* Gr. 6–12.
Alex, accompanying his journalist grandmother on a research trip into the
Brazilian Amazon jungle, becomes involved in the struggle of the Stone Age
Indian "People of the Mist" to survive exploitation by adventurers and entre-
preneurs. The sequel is *Kingdom of the Golden Dragon* (2004).
Trans. by Margaret Sayers Peden, HarperCollins, 2002, 416 pp. (0-06-050917-
1), 2004, pap. (0-06-053503-2)
(BL 99:590, 592; CCBB 56:225; HB 79:65; HBG 14:91; Kirkus 70:1462; SLJ Nov 2002 p.
154; VOYA 25:484, 26:10)

6-7   **ALMOND, David.** *Skellig.* Gr. 5–8. (Orig. British pub. 1998.)
✫✫   Burdened with worry about his baby sister's illness, Michael finds a ragged,
dusty man named Skellig living in his new home's rundown garage, and then
he and his friend Mina discover that Skellig is growing wings. Carnegie Medal
winner, 1998; Whitbread Children's Book Award, 1998; Michael L. Printz
Honor Book, 2000.
Delacorte, 1999, 183 pp. (0-385-32653-X); Random, 2001, pap., 192 pp. (0-
440-22908-1)
(BL 95:974, 1691, 96:821; CCBB 52:231; HB 75:326; HBG 10:287; Kirkus 67:1794; Kliatt
Jan 1999 p. 6; SLJ Feb 1999 p. 104)

6-8   **ALTOM, Laura Marie.** *Kissing Frogs.* Gr. 11 up.
Biologist Lucy Gordon, humiliated after her mistaken identification of a new
breed of frogs, kisses an unusual frog that is immediately transformed into a
naked man who says he's an enchanted prince.
Love Spell, 2004, pap., 368 pp. (0-505-52568-2)
(BL 100:652; LJ Nov 15, 2003 p. 55)

6-9   **ALTON, Steve.** *The Malifex.* Gr. 5–10.
After he accidentally summons Amergin, an aged disciple of Merlin, into the
21st century, Sam enlists the mage's help in battling the Malifex, an ancient
spirit bent on polluting Britain.
Carolrhoda, 2002, 182 pp. (0-8225-0959-8)
(BL 99:122; HBG 16:378; Kirkus 70:126; SLJ Nov 2002 p. 154; VOYA 25:290)

6-10   **ANDERSON, Poul (William).** *Mother of Kings.* Gr. 10 up.
In this retelling of tales from the 10th-century Icelandic sagas, Gunnhild,
daughter of a Norse lord, marries Eirik Blood-ax, son of the Finnish High
King, and helps him and their sons rule their chaotic kingdom.
Tor, 2001, 384 pp. (0-312-87448-0)
(BL 98:57; Kirkus 69:1252; LJ Oct 15, 2001 p. 112; VOYA 24:365)

**Atlantis. Ed. by Isaac Asimov, Martin H. Greenberg, and Charles G.
Waugh.**
See Chapter 3, Fantasy Collections.

6-11   **ATTANASIO, A(lfred) A(ngelo).** *The Eagle and the Sword.* Gr. 10 up.
In this version of King Arthur's story, Arthur is a ruthless warrior and adopted
Saxon son of Celtic chief Kyner. This is the sequel to *The Dragon and the Uni-
corn* (1996, 1997) and is followed by *The Wolf and the Crown* (1998).
HarperPrism, 1997, 352 pp. (0-06-109298-3)
(Kirkus 65:595; LJ June 15, 1997 p. 101; VOYA 20:322)

6-12   **ATTANASIO, A(lfred) A(ngelo).** *Kingdom of the Grail.* Gr. 10 up.
A dying Welsh baroness on a 12th-century crusade to the Holy Land recruits a
young Jewish girl to impersonate her, rule Wales, and take revenge on her ene-
mies, in this story involving the legend of the Holy Grail.
Harper, 1992, 512 pp. (0-06-017965-1), 1992, pap., (0-06-109979-1)
(BL 88:1086, 1095; Kirkus 60:3; LJ Feb 15, 1992 p. 200; SLJ July 1992 p. 96)

6-13   **BABBITT, Natalie (Zane Moore).** *Tuck Everlasting.* Gr. 4–7.
★★   After a sinister stranger uncovers the Tuck family secret, their discovery of the
fountain of youth, it is left to a little girl named Winnie Foster to save her
friends from the stranger's evil plan. Phoenix Award Honor Book, 1995.
Farrar, 1975, 139 pp. (0-374-37848-7), 2000, pap., 171 pp. (0-374-48012-5)
(BL 72:510, 80:95; HB 52:47; Kirkus 43:1181; SLJ Dec 1975 p. 50; Suth 2:22)

BAEHR, Patricia. *The Search for Happily-Ever-After.*
See Chapter 7, High Fantasy: Travel to Other Worlds.

6-14   **BAKER, E. D.** *The Frog Princess.* Gr. 5–8. (Orig. British pub. 2002.)
Hiding in a swamp to avoid an arranged marriage, Princess Esmeralda kisses a
talking frog and is herself transformed into a frog. In the sequel, *Dragon's
Breath* (2003), Princess Emma and her friend Prince Eadric try to save their
land from an invading king, but must first convince Princess Emma's fearsome
grandmother to break a spell she cast on their friend Hagwood, transforming
him into an otter. The sequel is *Once Upon a Curse* (2004).
Bloomsbury, 2002, 220 pp. (1-58234-799-9)
(BL 99:597; CCBB 56:226; Kirkus 70:1526; SLJ Jan 2003 p. 133; VOYA 25:394)

6-15   **BAKER, (Robert) Michael (Graham).** *The Mountain and the Summer*
✶   *Stars: An Old Tale Newly Ended.* Gr. 4–6. (Orig. British pub. 1968.)
Owen Morgan, son of a Welsh farmer and a fairy, enters the land under Black
Mountain to search for his mother.
Illus. by Erika Weihs, Harcourt, 1969, 124 pp., o.p.
(BL 65:1122; CCBB 23:21; HB 45:303; Kirkus 37:303; LJ 94:1178; TLS 1968 p. 1113)

6-16   **BANKS, Lynne Reid.** *Melusine: A Mystery.* Gr. 7–12. (Orig. British pub.
✶   1988.)
Roger discovers, to his horror, that the owner of the decaying French chateau
where his family is vacationing is sexually abusing his daughter, Melusine,
who is named for a legendary creature who was both woman and snake.
Harper, 1989, 248 pp., o.p., 1991, pap. (0-06-447054-7)
(BL 86:273, 343; CCBB 43:1; HB 65:626; HBG 1:76; Kirkus 57:1071; SLJ Nov 1989 p. 124;
TLS 1988 p. 1322; VOYA 12:340)

6-17   **BARRON, T(homas) A.** *The Great Tree of Avalon: Child of the Dark*
Prophecy. **(The Great Tree of Avalon trilogy, bk. 1).** Gr. 6–12.
Two 17-year-old boys raised together, orphaned eagle-keeper Scree and
wilderness guide Tamwyn, must discover which is the true heir of Merlin, and
which is the Dark Child, fated to destroy Avalon.
Philomel, 2004, 432 pp. (0-399-23763-1)
(BL 101:122; Kirkus 72:910; Kliatt Sep 2004 p. 4; SLJ Oct 2004 p. 154;)

6-18   **BARRON, T(homas) A.** *The Lost Years of Merlin.* **(The Lost Years of**
✶   **Merlin series, vol. 1).** Gr. 5–10.
In this first volume of a series about Merlin's youth, an orphaned boy who has
lost his memory is taken in by a healer who names him Emrys; as the boy
grows up, he discovers his powers of magic and second sight. In *The Seven*
Songs of Merlin (1997, 2000), young Emrys must make the dangerous Long
Journey to the Otherworld to bring back the Elixir of Dagda and save the life
of his newfound mother. In *The Fires of Merlin* (1998, 2002), Valdearg, the
last emperor of the dragons, mistakenly blames young Merlin for the slaughter
of his dragon hatchlings and threatens the land of Fincayra. In *The Mirror of*
Merlin (1999, 2001), Merlin enters the Haunted Marsh to search for his stolen
sword, and the witch Nimue infects him with a deadly illness. In *The Wings of*
Merlin (2000, 2002), Merlin must convince the warring inhabitants of Fincayra
to unite against the forces of Rhita Gawr, warlord of the spirit world.
Putnam/Philomel, 1996, 321 pp. (0-399-23018-1); Ace, 2002, pap., 284 pp. (0-
441-00930-1)
(BL 93:118, 1288, 94:475; HBG 8:62; Kirkus 64:1044; SLJ Sep 1996 p. 201; VOYA 19:216)

6-19   **BASS, L. G.** *Sign of the Qin.* **(Outlaw of Moonshadow Marsh, bk. 1).** Gr.
6–10.
Prince Zong is raised by Monkey after his mother, Silver Lotus, is sentenced to
death and flees into exile, while Yanu, god of Death, sends monsters and
demons to prepare the empire for his invasion, in this complex adventure story
related to Chinese mythology.
Hyperion, 2004, 224 pp. (0-7868-1918-9)
(BL 100:1451; CCBB 57:363; HB 80:446; Kirkus 72:324; SLJ Apr 2004 p. 148; VOYA
27:139)

6-20   **BEAGLE, Peter S(oyer).** *The Folk of the Air.* Gr. 10 up.
Itinerant lutenist Joe Farrell, staying with old friends in California, becomes involved in acting out fantasy role-playing games, but things turn nasty when a young witch unleashes an evil, destructive power. Mythopoeic Fantasy Award, 1987.
Ballantine, 1987, 336 pp., o.p., 1988, pap., 330 pp., o.p.
(BL 83:370; Kirkus 54:1738)

BEAR, Greg(ory Dale). *The Infinity Concerto.*
See Chapter 7, High Fantasy: Travel to Other Worlds.

6-21   **BENCHLEY, Nathaniel (Goddard).** *Demo and the Dolphin.* Gr. 3–4.
Demo travels on a talking dolphin into the legendary past, where he meets Odysseus and other figures from Greek mythology.
Illus. by Stephen Gammell, Harper, 1981, 88 pp., o.p.
(Kirkus 49:1344; HB 57:663; SLJ Jan 1982 p. 72)

6-22   **BENÉT, Stephen Vincent.** *The Devil and Daniel Webster.* Gr. 9 up.
☆   Daniel Webster battles the devil for the soul of a poor New Hampshire farmer in this version of the Faust legend.
Illus. by Harold Denison, Farrar, 1937, 61 pp., o.p.; Penguin, 2000, pap., 482 pp., entitled *The Devil and Daniel Webster and Other Writings* (0-14-043740-1)
(BL 34:107; TLS 1938 p. 91)

6-23   **BERGER, Thomas (Louis).** *Arthur Rex: A Legendary Novel.* Gr. 10 up.
☆   In this often humorous contemporary reworking of Thomas Malory's legend of Camelot, Arthur invents knightly conduct because of his guilt over Excalibur's invincibility, Guinevere is a liberated woman, and Launcelot is an anguished failure.
Delacorte, 1978, 499 pp., o.p.; Dell, 1979, pap., 512 pp., o.p.
(BL 75:275; Kirkus 46:701; LJ 103:2260)

6-24   **BERRY, James R.** *The Magicians of Erianne.* Gr. 6–10.
Having lost all memory of his past life, Ronan is asked by the Master Mage of the dragons to travel from Erianne to King Arthur's England to find Arthur's stolen sword.
Harper, 1988, 256 pp., o.p.
(BL 84:1730, 1733; Kirkus 56:1056; SLJ Sep 1988 p. 105; VOYA 11:94, 12:15)

6-25   **BERRY, Liz.** *The China Garden.* Gr. 7–12. (Orig. British pub. 1994.)
☆   The summer before she leaves home for university, Clare discovers a secret surrounding an ancient maze and seven Moon Gates in the abandoned China Garden on Ravensmere estate.
Farrar, 1996, 285 pp., o.p.; Harper Tempest, 1999, pap., 288 pp. (0-380-73228-9)
(BL 92:1252, 93:1288; CCBB 49:257; HBG 7:300; SLJ May 1996 p. 132; VOYA 19:93)

6-26   **BISSON, Terry.** *Talking Man.* Gr. 10 up.
According to this contemporary extrapolation of the Book of Genesis, God (Talking Man) was so pleased with his creation of our world that he decided to stay here, marry a mortal woman, and have a daughter named Crystal, who rides to his rescue in a '62 Chrysler when her father disappears.

Arbor House, 1986, 185 pp., o.p.

(BL 83:191, 217, 83:777, 86:906; Kirkus 54:1325; LJ Oct 15, 1986 p. 114; VOYA 9:290, 11:14)

6-27 **BLACK, Holly.** *Tithe: A Modern Faerie Tale.* Gr. 9–12.

✴ Kaye, 16, having returned to her childhood home with her alcoholic rock musician mother, seeks out the faeries who befriended her as a child and discovers that she is to become a human sacrifice in the battle between the Seelie and the Unseelie courts of Faery.

Simon, 2002, 320 pp. (0-689-84924-9), 2004, pap., 326 pp. (0-689-86704-2)

(BL 99:1064, 1290; CCBB 56; 188; HBG 14:91; Kirkus 70:1303; SLJ Oct 2002 p. 158; VOYA 25:292)

6-28 **BLAYLOCK, James P(aul).** *The Paper Grail.* Gr. 10 up.

While young museum curator Howard Barton searches for a valuable and magical ancient Japanese sketch whose mysterious owner has disappeared, Howard discovers that a witch is also looking for this Hokusai drawing.

Ace, 1991, 384 pp. (0-441-65126-7), 1992, pap. (0-441-65127-5)

(BL 87:1698, 1700; Kirkus 59:570; LJ Apr 15, 1991 p. 129)

6-29 **BLOCK, Francesca Lia.** *The Rose and the Beast: Fairy Tales Retold.* Gr.

✴ 9 up.

Nine mature retellings of classic fairy tales, including "Wolf" ("Little Red Riding Hood"), "Beast" ("Beauty and the Beast"), "Glass" ("Cinderella"), and "Snow" ("Snow White").

HarperCollins, 2000, 240 pp. (0-06-028130-8), 2001, pap., (0-06-440745-4)

(BL 96:2131, 97:692; CCBB 54:97; HBG 12:82; Kirkus 68:1480; SLJ Sep 2000 p. 225; VOYA 23:431)

6-30 **BODGER, Joan (Mercer).** *The Forest Family.* Gr. 4–8. (Orig. pub. in Canada.)

Many familiar folktales are woven into this story of Bernardo the woodcutter, his wife, Sylvania, and their daughters, Rosy and Daisy, whose peaceful lives are forever changed after Bernardo goes off to war.

Illus. by Mark Lang, Tundra, 1999, 100 pp. (0-88776-485-1)

(BH 76:71; HBG 11:74; SLJ Jan 2000 p. 128)

BOND, Nancy (Barbara). *A String in the Harp.*

See Chapter 10, Time Travel Fantasy.

6-31 **BORCHARDT, Alice.** *The Dragon Queen.* **(Tales of Guinevere, bk. 1).** Gr. 10 up. (Orig. British pub. 2001.)

Young Guinevere, raised by wolves, discovers that she has an affinity for dragons, and her loyalty is torn between archdruid Merlin and the sorcerers who honor the old ways. The sequels are *The Raven Warrior* (2003) and *Winter King* (2005).

Ballantine, 2001, 473 pp. (0-345-44399-3); Del Rey, 2003, pap. (0-345-44400-0)

(SLJ Feb 2002 p. 154; VOYA 25:12, 48)

6-32 **BOWERS, Gwendolyn.** *The Lost Dragon of Wessex.* Gr. 5–8. (Orig. British pub. 1957.)

Merlin's prophecy of peace in Britain is fulfilled when a 13-year-old boy named Wulf brings a dragon ring, the lost treasure of King Arthur, to King Alfred's court.

Illus. by Charles Geer, Walck, 1957, 188 pp., o.p.

(BL 53:505; HB 33:223; Kirkus 25:276; LJ 82:2188)

6-33   **BRADLEY, Marion Zimmer.** *The Firebrand.* Gr. 10 up. (Orig. British pub. 1987.)

In this retelling of the legendary fall of Troy, King Priam's daughter, Kassandra, is cursed by the god Apollo, who decrees that her prophetic visions will be regarded as the ravings of a madwoman.

Simon, 1987, 590 pp., o.p.; Pocket, 1991, pap., 624 pp. (0-671-74406-2)

(BL 84:90, 92; Kirkus 55:1177; LJ Oct 15, 1987 p. 90)

6-34   **BRADLEY, Marion Zimmer.** *The Forest House.* Gr. 10 up. (Orig. British
✮   pub. 1993.)

The last remaining Druid priestesses in Roman Britain try to preserve their ancient rituals while keeping peace between the two peoples. In the sequel, *Lady of Avalon* (1997), High Priestess Caillean and her foster son, Gawen, are called to the defense of Avalon in three different centuries. These books are prequels to Bradley's *The Mists of Avalon* (1982; see below), as is Bradley's *Priestess of Avalon* (2001; see below).

Viking, 1994, 476 pp. (0-670-84454-3); NAL, 1995, pap., 416 pp. (0-451-45424-3)

(BL 90:875, 876; Kirkus 62:81; LJ Mar 15, 1994 p. 104; SLJ Oct 1994 p. 158)

6-35   **BRADLEY, Marion Zimmer.** *The Mists of Avalon.* **(Avalon series, bk. 1).**
✮   Gr. 10 up. (Orig. British pub. 1982.)

Morgaine, Viviane, and Guinevere—King Arthur's sister, aunt, and wife, respectively—alternately tell the story of Arthur's rise to the throne, his betrayal, and his death. The prequels are *The Forest House* (1994; see above), *Lady of Avalon* (1997), and *Priestess of Avalon* (2000, 2001). Diana L. Paxson has written a prequel to *The Mists of Avalon*, entitled *Marion Zimmer Bradley's Ancestors of Avalon* (Viking, 2004).

Knopf, 1982, 892 pp., o.p.; Ballantine, 1985, pap., 396 pp. (0-345-33385-3); Del Rey, 2000, 912 pp. (0-345-44118-4)

(BL 79:409, 410, 86:906; Kirkus 50:1200; LJ 107:2351)

6-36   **BRADLEY, Marion Zimmer.** *Night's Daughter.* Gr. 10 up. (Orig. British pub. 1985.)

A reinterpretation of Mozart's opera tale "The Magic Flute," in which Prince Tamion and Princess Pamina face ordeals of earth, air, water, and fire as they try to unravel the conflict between the Queen of the Night and Sarastro, in order to rule their world in peace.

Ballantine, 1985, pap., 249 pp., o.p.

(BL 81:1159, 1177; Kliatt 19:24; VOYA 8:366)

6-37   **BRADLEY, Marion Zimmer.** *Priestess of Avalon.* Gr. 10 up. (Orig. British pub. 2000.)

In this prequel to *The Mists of Avalon* (1982; see above), Princess Eilan, or Helena of Avalon, elopes with the Roman general Constantius and bears his son Constantine, only to be dropped from favor when he becomes Caesar. Viking, 2001, 394 pp. (0-670-91023-6); Roc, 2002, pap. (0-451-45862-1)

(BL 97:1510; Kirkus 69:456; LJ June 15, 2001 p. 106; VOYA 24:443)

6-38   **BRADSHAW, Gillian (Marucha).** *Beyond the North Wind.* Gr. 5–9.
☆   Aristeas, a young poet given magical powers by Apollo, is captured by gigantic one-eyed monsters and befriended by telepathic griffins who help him to escape.
Greenwillow, 1993, 192 pp. (0-688-11357-5)

(BL 89:1312; HBG 4:307; Kirkus 61:297; SLJ Apr 1993 p. 117; VOYA 16:223, 17:8)

6-39   **BRADSHAW, Gillian (Marucha).** *Hawk of May.* **(King Arthur trilogy,**
☆   **bk. 1).** Gr. 10 up.
Young Gwalchmai, the son of evil Queen Morgawse, struggles for acceptance at King Arthur's court after Arthur rejects his offer of allegiance. The sequels are *Kingdom of Summer* (1981; NAL, 1982, pap.) and *In Winter's Shadow* (1982).
Simon, 1980, 313 pp., o.p.; Spectra, 1992, pap. (0-553-29922-0)

(BL 76:1656, 1669, 77:1148, 86:904; Kirkus 48:378; LJ 105:1008; SLJ Aug 1980 p. 81)

6-40   **BRENNAN, J. H.** *Shiva: An Adventure of the Ice Age.* **(Shiva trilogy, bk. 1).** Gr. 5–8.
To her clan's horror, Shiva, an orphaned 12-year-old Cro-Magnon girl, befriends a young Neanderthal boy named Doban, and their friendship helps defuse the hatred between the two peoples after Shiva finds her tribal totem, a magical saber-toothed tiger skull. The sequels are *Shiva Accused* (1991) and *Shiva's Challenge* (1992).
Harper, 1990, 184 pp., o.p., 1992, pap. (0-06-440392-0)

(BL 87:855; HBG 2:77; Kirkus 58:1453; SLJ Dec 1990 p. 100)

6-41   **BRIGGS, K(atharine) M(ary).** *Hobberdy Dick.* Gr. 6–8. (Orig. British pub.
☆   1955.)
A hobgoblin named Hobberdy Dick uses his magic to help the children of the manor.
Greenwillow, 1977, 239 pp., o.p.

(BL 73:1417; CCBB 31:7; HB 53:311; Kirkus 45:166; SLJ May 1977 p. 59)

6-42   **BRIGGS, K(atharine) M(ary).** *Kate Crackernuts.* Gr. 6–9. (Orig. British
☆   pub. 1963; rev. ed. 1979.)
Jealousy of her new stepdaughter, Katherine, drives Kate Maxwell's mother to bewitch the girl, and the two Kates run away together, in this retelling of the folktale of the same name.
Greenwillow, 1980, 224 pp., o.p.

(BL 76:1360; HB 56:304; Kirkus 48:369; SLJ May 1980 p. 73; VOYA 3:26)

6-43   **BRINDEL, June Rachuy.** *Ariadne.* Gr. 10 up.
Two narrators—Ariadne, the young high priestess of Crete, and Daedalus, the Greek refugee physician at the Cretan court—tell this exciting tale of Ariadne's love for Theseus of Athens and of the end of matriarchal rule in the Western world.

St. Martin's, 1980, 246 pp., o.p.

(Kirkus 48:1094; LJ 105:2229; SLJ Jan 1981 p. 74)

BROOKE, William J. *A Telling of the Tales: Five Stories.*
See Chapter 3, Fantasy Collections.

6-44 **BRUCHAC, Joseph.** *Dawn Land.* **(Dawn Land trilogy, vol. 1).** Gr. 10 up.
☆ In this tale set 10,000 years ago, Abenaki warrior Young Hunter is chosen by
the elders of The Dawn Land to go on a mystical journey to the land of The
People of the Long Lodges, the Iroquois, in order to prevent the destruction of
their world. The sequels are *Long River* (1995) and *The Waters Between: A
Novel of the Dawn Land* (1998).
Illus. by Murv Jacob, Fulcrum, 1993, 318 pp. (1-55591-134-X), 1995, pap.,
336 pp. (1-55591-215-X)

(BL 90:1357; Kirkus 61:316; LJ May 1, 1993 p. 114, Oct 1, 1993 p. 48; SLJ Aug 1993 p.
205)

6-45 **BRUST, Steven K. (Zoltan).** *Brokedown Palace.* Gr. 10 up.
A miraculous tree grows in Fenario, a land ruled by four brothers, in this tale
adapted from Hungarian folklore.
Ace, 1986, pap., 270 pp., o.p.

(BL 82:851; VOYA 9:86)

6-46 **BRYHER, Winifred (pseud. of Annie Winifred Ellerman).** *A Visa for*
☆ *Avalon.* Gr. 8–10.
Six people whose world is engulfed in revolution escape to the legendary
island of Avalon.
Harcourt, 1965, 119 pp., o.p.; Paris Press, 2004, pap., 192 pp. (1-930464-07-X)

(BL 61:980; CCBB 18:143; Kirkus 33:198; LJ 90:1929)

6-47 **BUCHAN, John.** *The Watcher by the Threshold and Other Tales.* Gr. 10
up. (Orig. British pub. 1902.)
Three of the five stories in this collection are fantasies: "The Far Islands,"
"The Watcher by the Threshold," and "The Outgoing of the Tide." "The Far
Islands" is about a young man's tragic involvement with the Celtic legend of
the Isle of the Apple-Trees.
Doran, 1918, 319 pp., o.p.; Nelson, 1922, 264 pp., o.p.; Cannongate, 1998, 348
pp., entitled *The Watcher by the Threshold: Shorter Scottish Fiction*; House of
Stratus, 2001, pap., 206 pp. (1-842327-95-X)

(BL 15:265)

BUFFIE, Margaret. *The Watcher.*
See Chapter 7, High Fantasy: Travel to Other Worlds.

6-48 **BULL, Emma.** *War for the Oaks.* Gr. 10 up.
Rock guitarist Eddi McCandry is drawn into a war between two Fairy Courts
in this fantasy set in contemporary Minneapolis. *Elvendude* by Mark Shepherd
(Baen, 1994) is a related work.
Ace, 1989, pap., 309 pp., o.p.

(BL 84:112, 132, 1246; 86:906; VOYA 10:286)

6-49 **BURNFORD, Sheila (Philip [née Every] Cochrane).** *Mr. Noah and the Second Flood.* Gr. 5 up. (Orig. Canadian pub. 1973.)
After Mr. Noah rebuilds the ark to escape a pollution-caused flood, he is shocked to discover how many animals have become extinct.
Illus. by Michael Foreman, Washington Square, 1974, pap., 64 pp., o.p.
(CCBB 27:59; Kirkus 41:753; LJ 98:3474; TLS 1973 p. 386)

6-50 **CADNUM, Michael.** *In a Dark Wood.* Gr. 7–12.
☆ A retelling of the Robin Hood legend, from the point of view of Lord Geoffrey, the Sheriff of Nottingham. The companion volume, *Forbidden Forest: The Story of Little John and Robin Hood* (2002), retells the stories of John Little's meeting with Robin Hood and of Robin's romance with Margaret Lea.
Orchard, 1998, 246 pp. (0-531-30071-4); Penguin, 1999, pap., 256 pp. (0-14-130638-6)
(BL 94:1124; CCBB 51:354; HB 74:219; HBG 9:343; Kirkus 66:55; SLJ Apr 1998 p. 128; VOYA 21:206)

6-51 *Camelot: A Collection of Original Arthurian Stories.* **Ed. by Jane (Hyatt)**
☆ **Yolen (Stemple).** Gr. 4–6.
Ten stories and a song about King Arthur's life, written by Terry Pratchett, Anne McCaffrey, Nancy Springer, Diana Paxson, and others.
Illus. by Winslow Pels, Philomel/Putnam, 1995, 198 pp. (0-399-22540-4)
(BL 92:931; HB 72:202; HBG 7:135; SLJ Jan 1996 p. 127)

6-52 *The Camelot Chronicles: Heroic Adventures from the Time of King Arthur.* **Ed. by Mike Ashley.** Gr. 10 up. (Orig. British pub. 1992.)
A collection of 18 Arthurian stories and novellas written by Jane Yolen, Vera Chapman, Howard Pyle, Phyllis Ann Karr, and others. *The Merlin Chronicles* (1995; see title entry below) and *The Pendragon Chronicles* (1989, 1990; see title entry below) are companion volumes, as are *The Chronicles of the Holy Grail* (1986) and *The Chronicles of the Round Table* (1997).
Carroll, 1992, 432 pp. (0-88184-912-X)
(LJ Sept. 1, 1992; VOYA 176:36, 17:10)

6-53 *Camelot Fantastic.* **Ed. by Lawrence Schimel and Martin H. Greenberg.** Gr. 6–12.
Seven original Arthurian stories, including "The Sword of the North" by Rosemary Edghill, "The Raven's Quest" by Lawrence Schimel, and "The Feasting of the Hungry Man" by Ian McDowell.
DAW, 1998, pap., 288 pp. (0-88677-790-9)
(Kliatt Nov 1998 p. 20; VOYA 21:365)

CAMERON, Eleanor (Frances Butler). *Time and Mr. Bass: A Mushroom Planet Book.*
See Chapter 10, Time Travel Fantasy.

6-54 **CANNING, Victor.** *The Crimson Chalice.* Gr. 10 up.
This retelling of the Arthurian epic concentrates on the Celtic chieftain Arturo's battles against the Saxon invaders of Roman Britain.
Morrow, 1978, 540 pp., o.p.
(BL 74:1717, 1726; Kirkus 46:649; LJ 103:1529)

CARD, Orson Scott. *Enchantment: A Classic Fantasy with a Modern Twist.*
See Chapter 7, High Fantasy: Travel to Other Worlds.

6-55   **CARSON, Anne.** *Autobiography of Red: A Novel in Verse.* Gr. 10 up.
A contemporary retelling, in verse, of the Greek legend of Geryon, the winged monster slain by Herakles.
Knopf, 1998, 160 pp. (0-375-40133-4)
(BL 94:1294, 95:317, 781; LJ May 15, 1998 p. 88; TLS Dec 4, 1998 p. 10)

6-56   **CAVANAGH, Helen.** *Panther Glade.* Gr. 4–8.
Stranded overnight on a Florida island, Bill is forced to confront his fears of the Everglades and ancient Indian spirits.
Simon, 1993, 148 pp., o.p.
(BL 89:1808; CCBB 46:278; HBG 4:295; Kirkus 61:717; SLJ June 1993 p. 104; VOYA 16:214)

CHABON, Michael. *Summerland.*
See Chapter 7, High Fantasy: Travel to Other Worlds.

6-57   **CHAMBERLIN, Ann.** *The Merlin of St. Giles' Well.* **(The Joan of Arc Tapestries, vol. 1).** Gr. 10 up.
Yann, the adopted son of Guy de Rais, is educated in Merlin's magical Old Religion and has visions of Joan of Arc's future salvation of France. The sequel is *The Merlin of the Oak Wood* (2001, 2003).
Tor, 1999, 320 pp. (0-312-86551-1), 2001, pap., 320 pp. (0-312-87591-6)
(BL 96:75, 1532; Kirkus 67:1180; VOYA 22:412)

6-58   **CHAN, Gillian.** *The Carved Box.* Gr. 6–8. (Orig. Canadian pub. 2001.)
The dog adopted by orphaned Callum after he is sent from Scotland to live with cousins in Canada comes with a sealed box and understands human speech.
Kids Can, 2001, 232 pp. (1-55074-895-5)
(BL 98:312; Kirkus 69:1208; SLJ Oct 2001 p. 152; VOYA 25:49)

6-59   **CHANT, Joy (pseud. of Eileen Joyce Rutter).** *The High Kings: Arthur's Celtic Ancestors.* Gr. 10 up.
Retellings of tales about the Celtic heroes who ruled the British Isles before Arthur came to power.
Illus. by George Sharp; Bantam, 1983, 1985, pap., 244 pp., o.p.
(Kliatt 20:19; LJ Nov. 15, 1983, p. 2164)

CHANT, Joy (pseud. of Eileen Joyce Rutter). *Red Moon and Black Mountain: The End of the House of Kendreth.*
See Chapter 7, High Fantasy: Travel to Other Worlds.

6-60   **CHAPMAN, Vera.** *The Enchantresses.* Gr. 10 up. (Orig. British pub. 1998.)
Arthur's three half-sisters, Morgause, Vivian, and Morgan, are taught the sorcerous arts by Merlin, who marries Vivian and hides young Arthur from his sisters' evil intentions in this prequel to the author's "The Three Damosels trilogy" (1975–1978; see below).

Gollancz, 1999, 224 pp. (0-575-06524-9)

(BL 95:1388; Kirkus 67:336; LJ Apr 15, 1999 p. 148)

6-61   CHAPMAN, Vera. *The Green Knight.* (The Three Damosels trilogy, bk. 2). Gr. 10 up. (Orig. British pub. 1975.)
This retelling of "Sir Gawain and the Green Knight" is from the perspective of 15-year-old Vivian, niece of the sorceress Morgan Le Fay, and 18-year-old Gawain, whose knightly chastity is reluctantly tested by Vivian, at her aunt's insistence. The first book in this series, *The King's Damosel* (1976, 1978), describes the adventures of Lady Lynett, who is forced into an unwanted marriage and then becomes King Arthur's damosel, or royal messenger to his Knights. In the final book, *King Arthur's Daughter* (1976, 1978), Lady Lynett comes to the aid of Ursulet, Arthur and Guinevere's daughter and proclaimed heir to the throne, who is forced into hiding after Arthur's defeat and the breaking up of the Round Table. *The Enchantresses* (Gollancz, 1999; see above) is a prequel.
Avon, 1978, pap., 173 pp., o.p.

(Kliatt 12:5)

6-62   CHERRYH, C. J. (pseud. of Carolyn Janice Cherry). *The Dreamstone.* (Arafel's Saga, bk. 1). Gr. 10 up. (Revised and expanded from the novella "Ealdwood," 1981.)
Arafel, the last of the guardian spirits of Ealdwood, narrates this haunting tale of the last stand of faerie and magic against humanity and iron. The sequel is *The Tree of Swords and Jewels* (1983, pap., 1991). Both novels have been reissued with a new ending in *Dreaming Tree* (DAW, 1997; 0-88677-782-8).
DAW, 1983, 1987, pap., 192 pp., o.p.

(BL 79:1075, 1084; LJ 108:603; VOYA 6:148)

CHERRYH, C. J. (pseud. of Carolyn Janice Cherry). *Rusalka.*
See Chapter 12, Witchcraft and Sorcery Fantasy.

6-63   CHRISTIAN, Catherine. *The Pendragon.* Gr. 10 up.
Bedivere, Arthur's boyhood friend and lifelong companion, narrates this story of Artus's life from age 12 through his initiation rites with Celidon the Merlin, his tragic love for Vivian (Ygern), his betrayal, and his death.
Warner, 1978, 607 pp., o.p.

(Kirkus 46:1260; LJ 104:126)

6-64   CLARKE, Pauline (pseud. of Pauline [Clarke] Hunter Blair). *The Two Faces of Silenus.* Gr. 5–7. (Orig. British pub. 1992.)
Drusilla and Rufus's wish at an Italian fountain brings the ancient god Silenus to life.
Coward, 1972, 160 pp., o.p.

(CCBB 26:73; HB 48:594; Kirkus 40:1244; TLS 1972 p. 1325)

6-65   COATSWORTH, Elizabeth (Jane). *The Enchanted: An Incredible Tale.*
☆   **Gr. 7–9.**
David Ross does not believe in Indian legends about the animals of the Enchanted Forest assuming human form, so he does not hesitate to buy an abandoned farm on the very edge of the woods.

Pantheon, 1951, 157 pp., o.p.; illus. by Mary Frank, Pantheon, 1968, 151 pp., o.p.; Blackberry, 1992, pap., 156 pp., o.p.

(BL 47:381; HB 27:316; Kirkus 19:233, 36:343; LJ 76:1236, 93:2119)

6-66   **COATSWORTH, Elizabeth (Jane).** *Marra's World.* Gr. 3–5.

☆   Marra does not understand her grandmother's hatred of her or her father's dis-interest until she discovers that her mother was a selkie, or seal-woman, who went back to live in the sea.

Pantheon, 1951, 157 pp., o.p.; illus. by Krystyna Turska, Greenwillow, 1975, 83 pp., o.p.

(BL 72:448; CCBB 29:107; HB 52:48; Kirkus 43:1129; SLJ Apr 1976 p. 70; Suth 2:90)

6-67   **COATSWORTH, Elizabeth (Jane).** *Silky: An Incredible Tale.* Gr. 7–10.

Silky, a young girl with strange powers, appears one day and helps Cephas Hewes control his temper and end his shiftless ways.

Illus. by John Carroll, Pantheon, 1953, 144 pp., o.p.

(HB 29:229; LJ 78:1164; TLS 1953 p. 813)

6-68   **COCHRAN, Molly, and MURPHY, Warren.** *The Forever King.* **(Arthur**

☆   **Blessing trilogy, bk. 1).** Gr. 10 up.

In this contemporary version of the Arthurian legend, King Arthur has been reincarnated as a 10-year-old boy named Arthur Blessing, who joins forces with Merlin and the reincarnated Sir Galahad to fight terrorists and a psychotic killer. The sequels are *The Broken Sword* (Tor, 1997) and *The Third Magic* (2003).

Tor, 1992, 368 pp. (0-312-85227-4)

(BL 88:1925, 1929; Kirkus 60:625; LJ June 15, 1992 p. 100; SLJ Dec 1992 pp. 24, 146; VOYA 15:291, 16:10)

6-69   **COHEN, Barbara.** *Roses.* Gr. 7–10.

The relationships of talented high school senior Isabel with a middle-aged florist and her would-be boyfriend, Rob, help her to overcome a fear of close-ness with anyone but her father, in this modern version of "Beauty and the Beast."

Lothrop, 1984, 224 pp., o.p.

(BL 80:963; CCBB 37:163; SLJ Aug 1984 p. 82)

6-70   **COHEN, Barbara.** *Unicorns in the Rain.* Gr. 7–9.

☆   Nikki falls in love with a young man whose family has been told by God to build an ark to save themselves and their animals (including two unicorns) from a disastrous flood.

Atheneum, 1980, 164 pp., o.p.; Macmillan, 1988 (repr.), pap., 176 pp. (0-02-042210-5); Peter Smith, 1992 (0-8446-6484-7)

(BL 77:1148; CCBB 34:29; SLJ Sep 1980 p. 80; VOYA 3:31)

6-71   **COLLINS, Meghan.** *The Willow Maiden.* Gr. 1–4.

A young man deeply in love with a Willow Maiden learns that he must let her go back to her willow tree every Spring or their love will not survive.

Illus. by Laszlo Gal, Dial, 1985, 40 pp., o.p.

(BL 82:625; SLJ Jan 1986 p. 55)

6-72   **CONEY, Michael Greatrex.** *The Celestial Steam Locomotive.* **(Song of the**
☆   **Earth series, vol. 1).** Gr. 10 up.
In this science-fantasy set in the far future, three humans—Manuel, Zozula, and the Girl-with-No-Name—are chosen by the god Starquin to become the Triad who will change the course of history by going on a quest to find the True Humans aboard the Celestial Steam Locomotive. The sequels are *Gods of the Greatway* (1984), *Fang, the Gnome* (NAL, 1988), and *King of the Scepter'd Isle* (NAL 1989).
Houghton, 1983, 302 pp., o.p.
(Kirkus 51:790; LJ Sep 15, 1983 p. 1811; SLJ Dec 1983 p. 89; VOYA 7:205)

6-73   **COOLIDGE, Olivia E(nsor).** *The King of Men.* Gr. 7 up.
☆   This retelling of Greek legends follows the life of King Agamemnon from his childhood to his marriage to Clytemnestra, alternating with scenes of the gods quarreling on Mount Olympus and affecting the fates of the mortals.
Illus. by Ellen Raskin, Houghton, 1966, 230 pp., o.p.
(BL 63:37; CCBB 20:106; HB 42:438; Kirkus 34:311; LJ 91:3264)

6-74   **COONEY, Caroline B.** *Goddess of Yesterday.* Gr. 7–12.
☆☆   Anaxandra, 12, the only survivor of an attack on King Nicander of Siphnos' household, pretends to be Princess Callisto when she is rescued by King Menelaus of Sparta, whose jealous wife, Helen, will soon begin a love affair with Prince Paris of Troy.
Delacorte, 2002, 192 pp. (0-385-72945-6); Dell, 2003, pap., 272 pp. (0-440-22930-8)
(BL 98:1704; CCBB 55:397; HBG 13:389; Kirkus 70:730; SLJ June 2002 p. 134; VOYA 25:200)

6-75   **COONTZ, Otto.** *Isle of the Shape-Shifters.* Gr. 5–8.
Theo's summer on Nantucket Island takes on frightening proportions when she discovers that the descendants of local Indian tribes plan to use her in their ancient shape-shifting rites, to regain the island for themselves.
Houghton, 1983, 209 pp., o.p.
(BL 80:856; CCBB 37:124; SLJ Mar 1984 p. 157)

6-76   **COOPER (Grant), Susan (Mary).** *Over Sea, Under Stone.* **(The Dark Is**
☆☆   **Rising sequence, vol. 1).** Gr. 5–8. (Orig. British pub. 1965.)
Simon, Jane, and Barney Drew set out to find King Arthur's grail, touching off a great struggle between good and evil forces, the Light and the Dark. In *The Dark Is Rising* (Atheneum, 1973; Macmillan, 1986, pap.; 1999), a boy named Will Stanton travels into the past in search of six magic signs needed by the forces of the Light to hold back the forces of Darkness. Boston Globe Horn Book Award, 1973; Carnegie Medal Commended Book, 1973; John Newbery Medal Honor Book, 1974. In *Greenwitch* (Atheneum, 1974; Macmillan, 1986, pap.; 1999), it falls to Jane, Simon, and Barney to retrieve from the sea creature, Greenwitch, a manuscript needed to interpret the inscription on King Arthur's grail. In *The Grey King* (Atheneum, 1975; Macmillan, 1986, pap.; 2000), Will and an albino boy named Bran Davies search for the golden harp needed to waken King Arthur's knights for the final battle against the Dark. Carnegie Medal Commended Book, 1975; John Newbery Medal, 1976; Tir na n-Og Award, 1976. In the final volume of this series, *Silver on the Tree*

(Atheneum, 1977; Macmillan, 1986, pap.; 2000), all five children are summoned to a Welsh mountainside where Will and Bran search for the crystal sword, Eiras, while the Drews meet King Arthur and prepare for the ultimate battle against the forces of Darkness. Tir na n-Og Award, 1978.
Illus. by Margery Gill, Harcourt, 1966, 252 pp. (0-15-259034-X), 1989, pap., 256 pp. (0-02-042785-9); Aladdin, 2000, pap., 196 pp. (0-689-84035-7)
(BL 63:118; TLS 1965 p. 513)

6-77   **COOPER (Grant), Susan (Mary).** *Tam Lin.* Gr. 1–6.
✶   Margaret, daughter of the king, falls in love with Tam Lin and saves him from the elfin queen in this retelling of the Scottish ballad.
Illus. by Warwick Hutton, Macmillan, 1991, 32 pp. (0-689-50505-1)
(BL 87:1191; HB 67:340; HBG 2:289; Kirkus 59:43; SLJ May 1991 p. 88)

6-78   **CORNWELL, Bernard.** *The Winter King: A Novel of Arthur.* **(The Warlord Chronicles, vol. 1).** Gr. 10 up.
In this version of the King Arthur saga, Arthur is a warlord pledged to protect his infant nephew Mordred, heir to the Kingdom of Britain. The sequels are *Enemy of God* (1997) and *Excalibur* (1998).
St. Martin's 1996, 448 pp. (0-312-14447-4)
(BL 92:1421, 1428; Kirkus 64:312; LJ May 15, 1996 p. 83)

COVILLE, Bruce. *Juliet Dove, Queen of Love.*
See Chapter 9, Magic Adventure Fantasy.

6-79   **CREW, Gary.** *Strange Objects.* Gr. 8–12. (Orig. Australian pub. 1990.)
Alternately told through the notebook entries of 16-year-old Stephen and various anthropological publications, this is a fantasy-mystery about the strange events following Stephen's discovery of a mummified hand and a 300-year-old journal written by murderers. Children's Book Council of Australia Book of the Year Award, 1991.
Simon, 1993, 224 pp., o.p.
(BL 89:1812; CCBB 47:7; HBG 4:308; Kirkus 61:658; SLJ May 1993 p. 124; VOYA 16:162, 17:19)

6-80   **CROMPTON, Anne Eliot.** *Merlin's Harp.* Gr. 10 up. (Orig. British pub.
✶   1995.)
Merlin convinces Niviene, daughter of the Lady of the Lake, that she must leave the forest of the Fey in order to help King Arthur, with whom she falls in love.
Fine, 1995, 224 pp. (1-55611-463-X); NAL, 1997, pap., 304 pp. (0-451-45583-5)
(BL 92:388, 392; Kirkus 63:1297; LJ Sep 15, 1995 p. 97; SLJ Dec 1995 p. 144)

CROSS, Gillian (Clare Arnold). *The Dark Behind the Curtain.*
See Chapter 4, Ghost Fantasy.

6-81   **CROSSLEY-HOLLAND, Kevin.** *The Seeing Stone.* **(Arthur Trilogy, vol.**
✶✶   **1).** Gr. 5–10. (Orig. British pub. 2000, entitled *Arthur: The Seeing Stone.*)
Arthur, 13, longs to become a squire rather than a "schoolman," and he is fascinated by visions of another Arthur within the polished obsidian stone his friend Merlin has given him. Nestlé Smarties Prize, Bronze Award, 2000;

Guardian Children's Fiction Award, 2001; Tir na n-Og Award, 2001. In the sequel, *At the Crossing Places* (2001, 2002), Arthur discovers the identity of his real father, and vows to find his mother too, while training to be Lord Stephen's squire on a crusade to the Holy Land. In *King of the Middle March* (2003, 2004), the final book in the trilogy, young Arthur witnesses the violence of the Crusades first hand, while watching the dissolution of King Arthur's Camelot in his magical stone.

Levine/Scholastic, 2001, 368 pp. (0-439-26326-3); Levine, 2002, pap. (0-439-43524-2)

(BL 98:315, 1417; HB 77:743; HBG 13:96; Kirkus 69:1421; Kliatt Sep 2001 p. 6; SLJ Oct 2001 p. 152; VOYA 24:367)

6-82   CURLEY, Daniel. *Ann's Spring.* Gr. 4–6.
Spring reverts to winter when neighborhood boys lock Mother Nature's children in an old truck and prevent them from supervising the changing of the seasons.
Illus. by Donna Diamond, Crowell, 1977, 48 pp., o.p.
(CCBB 31:12; Kirkus 45:46; SLJ Jan 1977 p. 90)

6-83   CURLEY, Daniel. *Billy Beg and the Bull.* Gr. 3–5.
Billy Beg flees his wicked stepmother and, with his friend the bull, sets out on an adventure-filled journey from Ireland to China, in this retelling of tales from Irish folklore.
Illus. by Frank Bozzo, Crowell, 1978, 127 pp., o.p.
(BL 74:1677; HB 54:289; Kirkus 46:243; SLJ May 1978 p. 65)

6-84   CURRY, Ann. *The Book of Brendan.* Gr. 5–7. (Orig. British pub. 1989.)
Two children and some magical beasts that have come to life from an illuminated manuscript thwart an evil sorcerer's plot to take over King Arthur's kingdom.
Holiday, 1990, 170 pp., o.p.
(BL 86:1445; CCBB 43:156; HBG 1:256; SLJ May 1990 p. 103; VOYA 13:226)

6-85   CURRY, Jane Louise. *Beneath the Hill.* Gr. 5–8.
✶   When strip mining threatens the mountain home of the Fair Folk, Miggle, Dub, and Stevie help them return to their ancestral land. This is the sequel to *The Change Child* (1969).
Illus. by Imero Gobbato, Harcourt, 1967, 255 pp., o.p.
(BL 63:1146; CCBB 21:25; HB 43:461; LJ 92:2020; Kirkus 35:61; TLS 1968 p. 1113)

CURRY, Jane Louise. *The Daybreakers.*
See Chapter 10, Time Travel Fantasy.

6-86   CURRY, Jane Louise. *The Sleepers.* Gr. 5–8.
✶   Four young English people meet Myrdain the Sorcerer, who asks their help in foiling a plot to murder King Arthur and his knights in their sleep.
Illus. by Gareth Floyd, Harcourt, 1968, 255 pp., o.p.
(BL 65:61; HB 44:427; Kirkus 36:459; TLS 1969 p. 351)

CURRY, Jane Louise. *The Watchers.*
See Chapter 10, Time Travel Fantasy.

CUTT, W(illiam) Towrie. *Seven for the Sea.*
See Chapter 10, Time Travel Fantasy.

6-87 **DALKEY, Kara.** *Goa.* **(Blood of the Goddess trilogy, vol. 1).** Gr. 10 up.
Thomas Chinnery, a 16th-century English apothecary, travels to the Por-
tuguese Indian colony of Goa, where he meets an alchemist who owns a pow-
der that can bring the dead to life. The sequels are *Bijapur* (1997) and
Bhagavati (1998).
Tor, 1996, 256 pp. (0-312-86000-5), 1997, pap., 224 pp. (0-8125-4942-2)
(BL 92:1888, 1891; Kirkus 64:791; VOYA 20:115)

6-88 **DALKEY, Kara.** *Little Sister.* Gr. 7–10.
☆ In this story set in 12th-century Japan, 13-year-old Mitsuko, along with a
shape-shifting tengu and other creatures from Japanese folklore, must rescue
Mitsuko's eldest sister after the murder of her betrothed. In the sequel, *The
Heavenward Path* (1998), Mitsuko, now 16, tries to escape an arranged marriage by flying off on the wings of Goranu, but must battle the gods of two
ancient Japanese religions.
Harcourt, 1996, 200 pp. (0-15-201392-X); Puffin, 1998, pap., 200 pp. (0-14-
038631-9)
(BL 93:340; CCBB 50:132; HBG 8:64; Kirkus 64:1149; SLJ Dec 1996 p. 120; VOYA
20:334)

6-89 **DALKEY, Kara.** *The Nightingale.* Gr. 6 up.
In this novelized version of the Hans Christian Andersen story (see Chapter 1,
Allegorical Fantasy and Literary Fairy Tales), the nightingale is a beautiful
flute player in love with the Emperor in 10th-century Japan.
Ace, 1988, 221 pp., o.p.
(BL 84:1786; VOYA 11:192, 12:15)

DART-THORNTON, Cecilia. *The Ill-Made Mute.*
See Chapter 5, High Fantasy: Alternate Worlds or Histories.

6-90 **DAVID, Peter.** *Knight Life.* Gr. 7–12.
In this humorous version of the King Arthur saga, Arthur and Merlin have
returned to life in the 21st century because they are greatly needed, and Arthur
campaigns to become mayor of New York, but his "totally honest" campaign
attracts the attention of both Merlin and his enemy, Morgan Le Fey. The
sequel is *One Knight Only* (2003).
Ace, 1987, 193 pp., o.p.; Berkley/Ace, 2002, 352 pp. (0-441-00936-0)
(BL 98:1695; LJ June 15, 2002 p. 100; VOYA 10:176, 25:293)

6-91 **DEAN, Pamela.** *Juniper, Gentian, and Rosemary.* Gr. 10 up.
☆ Gentian, 13, and her two sisters live busy, contented lives until a mysterious
young man draws them into a strange science project and changes everything,
in this story based on an old folk ballad.
Tor, 1998, 352 pp. (0-312-86004-8), 1999, pap. (0-312-85970-8)
(BL 94:1600; Kirkus 66:700; LJ June 15, 1998 p. 110; SLJ Dec 1998 p. 146; VOYA 21:336)

6-92 **DEAN, Pamela.** *Tam Lin.* Gr. 10 up.
☆ In this updated version of the 16th-century Scottish ballad set on a 20th-centu-
ry Minnesota college campus, Janet Carter, an English literature major, discov-

ers that she must defy the Faerie Queen to rescue her own true love.
Tor, 1991, 288 pp. (0-312-85137-5)
(BL 87:1627, 1630; Kirkus 59:365; LJ Mar 15, 1991 p. 119; VOYA 14:238)

6-93 **DEITZ, Tom.** *The Gryphon King.* Gr. 10 up.
Two medieval English artifacts, a sword and a manuscript, arrive at the University of Georgia and entangle faculty and students in a deadly magical battle between two mythical worlds.
Avon, 1989, pap., 406 pp., o.p.
(BL 85:1873, 1894, 86:906; LJ May 15, 1989 p. 92)

DEITZ, Tom. *Windmaster's Bane.*
See Chapter 7, High Fantasy: Travel to Other Worlds.

DE LINT, Charles. *The Dreaming Place.*
See Chapter 7, High Fantasy: Travel to Other Worlds.

6-94 **DE LINT, Charles.** *Forests of the Heart.* Gr. 10 up. (Orig. pub. in Canada.)
☆ The Gentry, dangerous Irish elemental spirits who are homeless in the New World ruled by local spirits called manitou, offer Musgrave Wood immortality if she will help them defeat the manitou and the Native American witches defending them.
Tor, 2000, 400 pp. (0-312-86519-8), 2001, pap., 384 pp. (0-312-87568-1)
(BL 96:1655; Kirkus 68:518; Kliatt Nov 2001 p. 20; LJ May 15, 2000 p. 128; VOYA 24:11, 50)

6-95 **DE LINT, Charles.** *Jack the Giant-Killer.* Gr. 10 up. (Orig. Canadian pub. 1987.)
A young Canadian named Jacky Rowan finds herself caught up in a Scottish fairy tale in which she becomes Jack the Giant-Killer. Canadian Science Fiction and Fantasy Award, 1988. In the sequel, *Drink Down the Moon* (1990), Jacky is kidnapped by a wizard who has stolen the fairy power of the moon.
Ace, 1987, 202 pp., o.p.; *Jack of Kinrowan* Tor, 1999, pap., 412 pp. (0-312-86959-2) contains *Jack, the Giant Killer* and *Drink Down the Moon*
(BL 84:752, 775, 86:906; Kirkus 55:1425; VOYA 11:38)

6-96 **DE LINT, Charles.** *Moonheart.* Gr. 10 up. (Orig. pub. in Canada.)
Sara Kendell is caught up in an ancient battle between good and evil after she finds four mysterious objects and meets Kieran Foy, apprentice to an ancient Welsh mage. The sequel is *Spiritwalk* (Tor, 1992).
Ace, 1984, pap., 496 pp., o.p.
(BL 81:558, 582; VOYA 7:335)

DE LINT, Charles. *Someplace to Be Flying.*
See Chapter 5, High Fantasy: Alternate Worlds or Histories.

DEXTER, Catherine. *The Oracle Doll.*
See Chapter 11, Toy Fantasy.

6-97 **DICKINSON, Peter (pseud. of Malcolm de Brissac).** *Merlin Dreams.* Gr.
☆ 6–12. (Orig. British pub. 1988.)
While Merlin sleeps through his enchantment, his nine dreams become the sto-

ries in this book—dreams of dragons, unicorns, damsels, and knights. Kate Greenaway Medal Highly Commended Book, 1988.

Illus. by Alan Lee, Delacorte, 1988, 167 pp., o.p.

(BL 85:934, 938; CCBB 42:96; HB 65:210; Kirkus 56:1525; SLJ Dec 1988 p. 120; TLS 1988 p. 1323; VOYA 11:293)

6-98 **DIXON, Marjorie (Mack).** *The Forbidden Island.* Gr. 5–7. (Orig. British
☆ pub. 1960.)

Libby makes a forbidden visit to the Irish Island of Thunder and finds it to be inhabited by an ancient race of people who live by violent, age-old laws.

Illus. by Richard Kennedy, Criterion, 1960, 201 pp., o.p.

(HB 36:515; Kirkus 28:760; LJ 86:4223; TLS May 20, 1960 p. iv)

6-99 **DOHERTY, Berlie.** *Daughter of the Sea.* Gr. 6–8. (Orig. British pub. 1996.)
☆ Fisherman Munroe and his wife, Jannet, adore the selkie infant they find, name her Gioga, and refuse to give her back when her real father comes to claim her.

Illus. by Sian Bailey, DK, 1997, 114 pp. (0-7894-2469-X); Dell, 2000, pap., 115 pp. (0-440-22794-1)

(BL 94:319; CCBB 51:122; HB 73:679; HBG 9:85; Kirkus 65:1386; SLJ Sep 1997 p. 213; VOYA 21:12, 54)

6-100 **DOHERTY, Berlie.** *The Famous Adventures of Jack.* Gr. 3–5. (Orig.
☆ British pub. 2000.)

Many of the well-known Jack stories are interwoven in this tale of a girl named Jill who listens to old Mother Greenwood's stories about Jack while searching for him.

Illus. by Sonja Lamut, Greenwillow, 2001, 128 pp. (0-06-623619-3)

(BL 98:318; CCBB 55:54; HB 77:760)

6-101 **DOKEY, Cameron.** *The Storyteller's Daughter.* Gr. 6–10.

A novelized retelling of the Arabian Nights story of Shaharazad, in which a blind 17-year-old girl and Maju, a blind storyteller, work together to create stories that will win the king's heart and save Shaharazad's life.

Simon, 2002, pap., 221 pp. (0-7434-2220-1)

(Kliatt Nov 2002 p. 18; SLJ Dec 2002 p. 136; VOYA 26:36)

DONNEHOWER, Bruce. *Miko, Little Hunter of the North.*

See Chapter 1, Allegorical Fantasy and Literary Fairy Tales.

6-102 **DONOGHUE, Emma.** *Kissing the Witch: Old Tales in New Skins.* Gr. 9
☆ up. (Orig. British pub. 1997.)

Thirteen familiar folktales, including "Cinderella," "Rumpelstiltskin," and "Beauty and the Beast," retold from a feminist lesbian perspective.

HarperCollins, 1997, 228 pp. (0-06-027575-8); HarperTrophy, 1999, pap., 240 pp. (0-06-440772-1)

(BL 93:1684; CCBB 50:280; HBG 9:85; Kirkus 65:221; SLJ June 1997 p. 117; TLS June 27, 1997 p. 23; VOYA 20:192, 21:12)

DRAKE, David. *Lord of the Isles.*

See Chapter 7, High Fantasy: Travel to Other Worlds.

DUNKLE, Clare B. *The Hollow Kingdom.*
See Chapter 7, High Fantasy: Travel to Other Worlds.

6-103   **DUNLOP, Eileen (Rhona).** *Clementina.* Gr. 6–10. (Orig. British pub. 1985.)
☆   Spending a month visiting a friend at a Scottish estate, Daisy finds herself caught up in frightening events surrounding 20th-century Clementina and her ties to a young woman who was involved in the death of a young man in 1746. Holiday, 1987, 156 pp., o.p.

(BL 83:1286, 1687; CCBB 40:186; HB 63:466; Kirkus 55:635; SLJ May 1987 p. 109; Suth 4:104; VOYA 10:119)

6-104   **EICKHOFF, Randy Lee.** *The Destruction of the Inn.* **(The Ulster Cycle, vol. 4).** Gr. 10 up.
An adventure-filled translation of the famous Irish epic about Connaire, High King of Ireland, whose great-grandmother was a fairy. The preceding volumes are *The Raid* (1997), *The Feast* (1999), and *The Sorrows* (2000); the sequels are *He Stands Alone* (2002) and *The Red Branch Tales* (2003).
Tor/Forge, 2001, 288 pp. (0-312-87026-4)

(BL 97:1353; Kirkus 69:143)

6-105   **ESTEY, Dale.** *A Lost Tale.* Gr. 10 up. (Orig. British pub. 1980.)
Brigid falls in love with a wounded German soldier and enlists the aid of druids and a unicorn to protect him from the British authorities.
St. Martin's, 1980, 208 pp., o.p.

(BL 76:1490, 1520, 77:621, 78:594, 86:906; Kirkus 48:305; LJ 105:1000; SLJ Dec 1980 p. 78)

6-106   *Excalibur.* **Ed. by Richard Gilliam, Martin H. Greenberg, and Edward E. Kramer.** Gr. 10 up.
Thirty stories and poems narrated by King Arthur's sword, written by Esther Friesner, Jane Yolen, Marion Zimmer Bradley, Diana L. Paxson, Judith Tarr, Mercedes Lackey, and others.
Warner, 1995, pap., 470 pp. (0-446-67084-7)

(Kliatt Sep 1995 p. 21; VOYA 18:231)

Faerie Tales. **Ed. by Martin H. Greenberg and Russell Davis.**
See Chapter 3, Fantasy Collections.

6-107   **FARJEON, Eleanor.** *The Glass Slipper.* Gr. 5–7. (Orig. British pub. 1946
☆   and 1955.)
A humorous retelling of the "Cinderella" story.
Illus. by Ernest H. Shepard, Viking, 1956, 187 pp., o.p.; Harper, 1986, 213 pp., o.p.; HarperCollins, 1995, 224 pp. (0-06-440561-3)

(BL 52:282, 83:350; HB 32:120, 63:84; Kirkus 24:43; LJ 81:1309)

6-108   **FARJEON, Eleanor.** *The Silver Curlew.* Gr. 3–6. (Orig. British pub. 1953.)
☆   A young queen must give up her child unless she can guess the Spindle-Imp's name, in this novel-length version of "Rumpelstiltskin."
Illus. by Ernest H. Shepard, Viking, 1954, 162 pp., o.p.; Oxford University Press, 1969, o.p.

(BL 50:345; CCBB 8:29; HB 30:174; Kirkus 22:114; LJ 79:1064)

6-109 **FARMER (Mockridge), Penelope.** *A Castle of Bone.* Gr. 5–8. (Orig. British
✮ pub. 1972.)
Hugh panics when his friend Penn enters a magic cupboard and is changed into
a baby.
Atheneum, 1972, 151 pp., o.p.
(BL 69:572; CCBB 26:153; HB 49:52; Kirkus 40:1201; LJ 98:652; TLS 1972 p. 802)

6-110 **FARMER (Mockridge), Penelope.** *Eve: Her Story.* Gr. 10 up. (Orig. British
pub. 1986.)
A retelling of the biblical creation story from Eve's point of view, that of an
intelligent woman determined to learn all she can about her world.
Mercury, 1988, 188 pp., o.p.
(BL 84:604, 625; Kirkus 55:1594; LJ Dec 1987 p. 127)

6-111 **FARMER (Mockridge), Penelope.** *Year King.* Gr. 10 up. (Orig. British pub.
1977.)
Jealous of his twin brother's academic and social successes, Lan, 18, finds that
he can enter Lew's body and share his life, but these transformations make him
feel even more inadequate and resentful of his twin.
Atheneum, 1977, 232 pp., o.p.
(CCBB 31:125; HB 54:76; Kirkus 45:1205; SLJ Jan 1978 p. 94; TLS 1977 p. 1246)

6-112 **FARMER, Nancy.** *The Sea of Trolls.* Gr. 5–9.
✮ Kidnapped by Viking berserkers, Saxon Jack, 11, saves himself and his
younger sister, Lucy, by revealing his Bardic powers, and then uses his magic
against a shape-shifting troll queen.
Atheneum/Jackson, 2004, 480 pp. (0-689-86744-1); Simon, 2005, 480 pp. (0-
689-86096-X)
(BL 101:475; CCBB 58:119; HB 80:706; Kirkus 72:913; Kliatt Sep 2004 p. 8; SLJ Oct 2004
p. 163; VOYA 27:313)

6-113 **FINNEY, Charles G(randison).** *The Circus of Dr. Lao.* Gr. 10 up.
The mysterious Dr. Lao brings his magical menagerie of mythical beasts and
legendary figures to a small Arizona town.
Illus. by Boris Artzybasheff, Viking, 1935, 154 pp., o.p.; Lightyear, 1993, LB
(0-89968-402-5); University of Nebraska Press, 2002, pap., 154 pp. (0-
803269-07-2)
(Kliatt 11:9)

FISK, Pauline. *Midnight Blue.*
See Chapter 7, High Fantasy: Travel to Other Worlds.

6-114 **FISK, Pauline.** *The Secret of Sabrina Fludde.* Gr. 5–8. (Orig. British pub.
2001, entitled *Sabrina Fludde.*)
A young girl who has lost her memory emerges from the river in the Welsh
village of Pengwern, chooses the name Abren, and is claimed by a stranger
insisting she is the girl's mother, in this first volume of a planned trilogy.
Bloomsbury, 2002, 256 pp. (1-58234-754-9); Bloomsbury, 2002, pap., 256 pp.
(0-7475-5935-X)
(BL 99:114; SLJ July 2002 p. 119)

6-115 **FLEET, Robert C.** *Last Mountain.* Gr. 10 up.

Nancy (Annunciata), a girl from the Los Angeles barrios, becomes the Lady Fair of the last of the unicorns in this complex story connecting the Aztecs, the Conquistadors, and modern-day gang warfare.
Ace, 1994, pap., 304 pp. (0-441-00062-2)
(Kliatt Nov 19094 p. 18; LJ June 15, 1994 p. 99; VOYA 17:155)

6-116   FLETCHER, Susan. *Shadow Spinner.* **Gr. 5–9.**
★   A novelized version of the "Arabian Nights" story of Shaharazad, whose story-telling skills save her life and mesmerize the sultan for 1,001 nights, told through the eyes of a servant girl named Marjan, smuggled out of the palace to find new tales from an old storyteller.
Illus. by Alex Leon, Atheneum, 1998, 219 pp. (0-689-81852-1); Aladdin,1999, pap. (0-689-83051-3)
(BL 94:1746; CCBB 51:394; HB 74:488; HBG 9:329; Kirkus 66:657; SLJ June 1998 p. 145, Dec 1998 p. 24; VOYA 22:36)

6-117   FLIEGER, Verlyn. *Pig Tale.* **Gr. 7–12.**
An abandoned baby girl is named Mokie, or Little Pig-girl, and raised as an outcast by the villagers of Little Wicken, until she runs away with one of the piglets into the forest, where she is taken in by gypsies.
Hyperion, 2002, 336 pp. (0-7868-0792-X)
(BL 99:590; CCBB 56:198; HBG 14:94; Kirkus 70:1468; SLJ Dec 2002 p. 137; VOYA 25:486)

6-118   FLINT, Kenneth C. *Cromm.* **Gr. 10 up.**
Colin McMahon discovers that he is the reincarnation of a 4th-century Celtic warrior who once fought an ancient god named Cromm, revived in the 20th century by a secret cult.
Doubleday, 1990, 387 pp., o.p.; Bantam, 1991, pap. (0-553-28851-2)
(BL 86:1267, 1276; Kirkus 58:69; LJ Feb 15, 1990 p. 215)

6-119   FLINT, Kenneth C. *The Dark Druid.* **(Finn MacCumhal trilogy, bk. 3). Gr. 10 up.**
The Dark Druid is angered when legendary Irish hero Finn MacCumhal rescues a young woman from an evil enchantment. This is the sequel to *Challenge of the Clans* (1986) and *The Storm Shield* (1987).
Bantam, 1987, pap., 326 pp., o.p.
(LJ Aug 1987 p. 147; VOYA 10:287)

6-120   FLINT, Kenneth C. *The Riders of the Sidhe.* **(The Sidhe trilogy, vol. 1). Gr. 10 up.**
Lugh of the Long Arm and his companions—Aine, the sea-god's sister, and Gilla, the jester—battle the Formorian invaders of ancient Ireland in this retelling of a Celtic legend. The sequels are *Champion of the Sidhe* (1984) and *Master of the Sidhe* (1984).
Bantam, 1984, pap., 272 pp., o.p.
(LJ 109:1253; VOYA 7:206)

6-121   FLYNN, Casey. *Most Ancient Song.* **(The Gods of Ireland series, bk. 1). Gr. 7–12.**
In a reworking of Ireland's Celtic myths of gods and heroes, this is the story of the peaceful Nemedians who are forced to take up arms to defend themselves

from the evil Fomor after crossing the sea to find a new home on a beautiful green island. The sequel is *The Enchanted Isles* (1991).
Bantam, 1991, pap., 261 pp. (0-553-28832-6)
(Kliatt Apr 1991 p. 18; VOYA 14:179)

6-122 FORREST, Elizabeth. *Phoenix Fire.* Gr. 7 up.
Chinese archaeologists excavating the grave of Ch'in Dynasty Emperor Huang unwittingly wake two long-buried mythical creatures, the Phoenix and a huge and terrible Demon, who clash at the edge of the La Brea Tar Pits in contemporary Los Angeles.
DAW, 1992, pap., 364 pp. (0-88677-515-9)
(LJ Mar 15, 1992 p. 129; VOYA 15:173)

6-123 FRIEDMAN, Michael Jan. *The Seekers and the Sword.* **(Norse trilogy, bk. 2).** Gr. 10 up.
In this retelling of Norse mythology, Vidar, one of the immortal but not invulnerable race of the Aesir, must find the lost Sword of Frey to restore peace to Alfheim. This is the sequel to *The Hammer and the Horn* (1985) and is followed by *The Glove of Maiden's Hair* (1987).
Warner, 1985, pap., 263 pp., o.p.
(BL 82:733; LJ Dec 1985 p. 129)

FRIESNER, Esther M. *Gnome Man's Land.*
See Chapter 7, High Fantasy: Travel to Other Worlds.

FRIESNER, Esther M. *The Sherwood Game.*
See Chapter 8, Humorous Fantasy.

6-124 FRIESNER, Esther M. *Yesterday We Saw Mermaids.* Gr. 10 up.
As three other ships leave Spain to search for the Indies in 1492, a fourth ship, once a tiny brass model, sets sail with an unusual mixture of passengers: two officials of the Inquisition, a gypsy, a sorceress, and a pregnant Jewish virgin.
Tor, 1992, 157 pp. (0-312-85352-1)
(SLJ June 1993 p. 142; VOYA 15:348)

6-125 FRY, Rosalie K(ingsmill). *The Secret of the Ron Mor Skerry.* Gr. 4–6.
☆ (Orig. British pub. 1957, entitled *Child of the Western Isles.*)
Fiona McConville searches the Western Isles for her little brother, Jamie, whose mysterious disappearance is connected to local legends about the selkies of Ron Mor Skerry.
Illus. by the author, Dutton, 1959, 95 pp., o.p.; Hyperion, 1995, pap., 89 pp. (entitled *The Secret of Roan Inish*) (0-7868-1063-7)
(BL 55:513; HB 35:214; Kirkus 27:39; LJ 84:1696)

6-126 FURLONG, Monica (Navis). *Robin's Country.* Gr. 4–7. (Orig. British pub. 1994.)
A mute servant boy runs away from his life of abuse and joins Robin Hood's band in Sherwood Forest.
Knopf, 1995, 140 pp. (0-679-84332-9)
(BL 91:1497; CCBB 48:343; HBG 6:297; SLJ Apr 1995 p. 132)

GAIMAN, Neil. *Neverwhere.*
See Chapter 7, High Fantasy: Travel to Other Worlds.

6-127 **GALLOWAY, Priscilla.** *Snake Charmer.* Gr. 7–10. (Orig. pub. in Canada.)
☆ Something is not quite right at the Greek island sleep disorder clinic visited by
Canadian Dusa and her mother in a desperate attempt to cure the girl's night-
mares of writhing snakes, in this story related to the myth of Medusa.
Delacorte, 1998, 231 pp. (0-385-32264-X); Dell, 2000, pap. (0-440-22017-3)
(BL 94:1746; CCBB 51:32; HBG 9:344; Kirkus 66:737; Kliatt May 1998 p. 6; SLJ July 1998
p. 95)

6-128 **GALLOWAY, Priscilla.** *Truly Grim Tales.* Gr. 7 up. (Orig. pub. in Canada.)
☆ Eight dark retellings of familiar folktales, including "Cinderella," "Snow
White," and "Rapunzel."
Delacorte, 1995, 132 pp. (0-385-32200-3); Dell, 1998, pap. (0-440-22728-3)
(BL 92:152, 1278,, 1294; CCBB 49:158; HB 72:78; HBG 7:72; Kirkus 63:856; Kliatt Nov
1995 p. 22; SLJ Sep 1995 p. 218)

6-129 **GARD, Joyce (pseud. of Joyce Reeves).** *Talargain.* Gr. 6–8. (Orig. British
☆ pub. 1964.)
A 7th-century orphan, fascinated by the seals near his Fame Island home,
appears in modern England and describes his life and attempts to aid King
Aldfrith in uniting the British tribes.
Holt, 1965, 251 pp., o.p.
(BL 61:1029; CCBB 19:8; Eakin:134; HB 41:175; Kirkus 33:243; LJ 90:1558)

6-130 **GARDEN, Nancy.** *Fours Crossing.* **(Fours Crossing trilogy, bk. 1).** Gr.
6–8.
Melissa and her friend Jed are kidnapped by a hermit who has kept spring from
coming to their New Hampshire town, Fours Crossing. *Watersmeet* (1983) and
The Door Between (1987) are the sequels in this trilogy involving Celtic
mythology.
Farrar, 1981, 199 pp., o.p.
(BL 77:1252; CCBB 34:170; HB 57:431; SLJ May 1981 p. 72)

6-131 **GARDNER, Craig Shaw.** *The Other Sinbad.* **(Arabian Nights trilogy, bk.
1).** Gr. 7 up.
Sinbad the Porter undertakes the eighth voyage of his namesake, Sinbad the
Sailor, and is haunted by the creatures his namesake encountered on his first
seven adventures. The sequels to this humorous story are *A Bad Day for Ali
Baba* (1992) and *The Last Arabian Night* (1993).
Ace, 1991, pap., 248 pp. (0-441-76720-6)
(Kliatt Apr 1992, p. 14; VOYA 14:382, 15:10)

6-132 **GARDNER, John (Champlin) (Jr.).** *Grendel.* Gr. 10 up.
☆ This version of the Anglo-Saxon legend of Beowulf is told from the point of
view of Grendel, the marauding monster whom Beowulf sets out to destroy.
Illus. by Emil Antonucci, Knopf, 1971, o.p.; Vintage, 1989, pap., 192 pp. (0-
679-72311-0)
(BL 68:353; Kirkus 39:762; LJ 96:2670, 97:1180; TLS 1972 p. 793)

6-133   GARFIELD, Leon. *The Wedding Ghost.* Gr. 7 up. (Orig. British pub. 1985.)
✫   Jack and Jill open a strange wedding gift, a mysterious map that leads Jack through foggy London into a demonic forest where a dust-covered Sleeping Beauty lies in a golden mansion.
Illus. by Charles Keeping, Oxford University Press, 1987, 66 pp., o.p.; Oxford University Press, 1999, pap., 64 pp. (0-19-272395-2)
(BL 83:1275; CCBB 40:144; HB 63:611; Kirkus 55:637; SLJ June–July 1987 p. 106; Suth 4:130; TLS 1985 p. 350)

6-134   GARFIELD, Leon, and BLISHEN, Edward. *The God Beneath the Sea.*
✫   Gr. 8 up. (Orig. British pub. 1970.)
This story poetically weaves together the legends of Greek mythology, including those about Prometheus, Pandora, and Persephone. Carnegie Medal, 1970; Kate Greenaway Medal, Honors List, 1970.
Illus. by Zevi Blum, Pantheon, 1971, 212 pp., o.p.
(BL 68:144, 150; CCBB 25:56; HB 47:477; LJ 96:2137; TLS 1970 p. 1254)

6-135   GARFIELD, Leon, and BLISHEN, Edward. *The Golden Shadows: A*
✫   *Recreation of Greek Legends.* Gr. 7 up. (Orig. British pub. 1973.)
An old bard travels through ancient Greece collecting stories, which are woven into this powerful version of the myths surrounding the life of Heracles.
Illus. by Charles Keeping, Pantheon, 1973, 159 pp., o.p.
(BL 70:592; CCBB 27:78; HB 50:45; Kirkus 41:1370, LJ 99:1226; TLS 1973 p. 675)

GARNER, Alan. *Elidor.*
See Chapter 7, High Fantasy: Travel to Other Worlds.

6-136   GARNER, Alan. *The Owl Service.* Gr. 6–9. (Orig. British pub. 1967.)
✫✫   A curse on the set of owl-decorated china that Gwyn, Alison, and Roger found in the attic turns the two boys against each other and threatens Alison's life. Carnegie Medal, 1967; Guardian Award for Children's Fiction, 1968.
Walck, 1968, 202 pp., o.p.; Philomel, 1979, 156 pp., o.p.; Harcourt, 1999, pap., 219 pp. (0-15-201798-4)
(BL 65:310, 900; CCBB 22:58; HB 44:563; Kirkus 36:1058; LJ 93:3980; Suth:143; TLS 1967 p. 1134, 1969 p. 1384)

6-137   GARNER, Alan. *The Weirdstone of Brisingamen.* (Tales of Alderley, vol.
✫   1). Gr. 5–8. (Orig. British pub. 1960.)
The stone on Susan's bracelet is the key to power over 140 knights who lie in an enchanted sleep within a nearby mountain. After this weirdstone is stolen, two dwarfs help Susan and her brother, Colin, make a torturous journey to recover it and return it to its rightful owner. In the sequel, *The Moon of Gomrath* (orig. British pub. 1963; U.S. 1967, 1981, 1998), Susan's bracelet brings the witch Morrigan and her evil moon spirits into the 20th century to battle the good dwarfs and elves.
Walck, 1961, 253 pp., o.p.; Philomel, 1979, 224 pp., o.p.; Harcourt, 1998, pap. (0-15-201796-8)
(BL 76:718; CCBB 15:29; HB 46:45; Kirkus 37:940; LJ 95:786; SLJ May 1980 p. 90)

6-138   GARNETT, David. *Two by Two: A Story of Survival.* Gr. 8 up. (Orig. British pub. 1963.)
Two girls disguise themselves as monkeys and stow away on Noah's ark in

order to survive the flood.
Atheneum, 1964, 143 pp., o.p.
(BL 60:489; LJ 89:653; TLS 1963 p. 781)

6-139 GEAR, W. Michael, and GEAR, Kathleen O'Neal. *People of the Fire.* **(The First North Americans, bk. 2).** Gr. 10 up.
In this fantasy saga based on Native American folklore and mysticism, young Little Dancer, destined to become a powerful dreamer, is the Red Hand people's only hope against the machinations of the brutal chief draining the power from the sacred Wolf Bundle. This is the sequel to *People of the Wolf* (1990) and is followed by *People of the Earth* (1992), *People of the River* (1992), *People of the Sea* (1994), *People of the Lakes* (1995), *People of the Lightning* (1996), *People of the Silence* (1997), *People of the Mist* (1998), *People of the Masks* (1998), *People of the Owl: A Novel of Prehistoric North America* (2003, 2004), and *People of the Raven* (2004).
Tor, 1991, pap., 467 pp., o.p.
(BL 87:1011, 1049; VOYA 14:95)

6-140 GELLIS, Roberta. *Bull God.* Gr. 10 up.
Ariadne's parents dedicate her to the god Dionysus, but she goes against the god's wishes to raise her monstrous half-brother, the Minotaur, in this retelling of the Greek myth.
Baen, 2000, pap., 480 pp. (0-671-57868-5)
(Kliatt Nov 2000 p. 18; VOYA 23:274, 24:11)

6-141 GEMMELL, David. *Lion of Macedon.* Gr. 10 up. (Orig. British pub. 1990.)
Parmenion, a half-Spartan, half-Macedonian warrior in pre-Alexandrian Greece, rises to become second in command to Philip of Macedonia. The sequel is *Dark Prince* (1993).
Ballantine, 1992, pap., 560 pp. (0-345-37911-X)
(LJ Sep 15, 1992 p. 97; Kliatt Mar 1993 p. 16)

6-142 GIBLIN, James Cross. *The Dwarf, the Giant, and the Unicorn: A Tale of King Arthur.* Gr. 2–5.
The giant son of a dwarf helps King Arthur after he and his knights are shipwrecked on an island.
Illus. by Claire Ewart, Clarion, 1996, 48 pp. (0-395-60520-2)
(BL 93:666; HBG 8:101; Kirkus 64:1465; SLJ Oct 1996 p. 113)

6-143 GODWIN, Parke. *Beloved Exile.* **(The Camelot trilogy, bk. 2).** Gr. 10 up.
King Arthur's widow, Queen Guenevere, narrates this story of her expulsion from Camelot after her husband's death, her enslavement, and her dream of returning to her homeland. This is the sequel to *Firelord* (Doubleday, 1980, 1994). In *The Last Rainbow* (1985, 1995), Patrick, an injured priest, falls in love with the Faerie queen, who wants him to save her people.
Bantam, 1984, pap., 422 pp. (0-553-24924-X); Avon, 1995, pap. (0-380-70995-3)
(BL 80:1273, 1274; Kirkus 52:367; LJ 109:1253; SLJ Nov 1984 p. 145)

6-144 GODWIN, Parke. *Sherwood.* **(Robin Hood duology, bk. 1).** Gr. 10 up.
A retelling of the Robin Hood legend set a hundred years earlier than usual,

during the Norman Conquest of Britain in 1066, with Robin as an Anglo-Saxon leader resisting William the Conquerer, and the Sheriff of Nottingham as a sympathetic young Norman knight. The sequel is *Robin and the King* (1993).
Morrow, 1991, 384 pp. (0-688-05264-9)
(BL 87:1842, 1843; Kirkus 59:748; LJ July 1991 p. 134)

6-145 GODWIN, Parke. *The Tower of Beowulf.* Gr. 10 up.
Beowulf matures from foolish young warrior to mythic hero after he battles the monstrous Grendel and his giant mother, Sigyn, slays a dragon, and becomes King of the Geats, in this novelized version of the Norse epic.
Morrow, 1995, 256 pp. (0-688-12738-X); Avon, 1996, pap. (0-380-72165-1)
(BL 92:39, 51; Kirkus 63:904; LJ Aug 1995 p. 122; SLJ Feb 1996 p. 131)

6-146 GOLDSTEIN, Lisa. *The Alchemist's Door.* Gr. 10 up.
After his assistant unleashes a demon, 16th-century English specialist in the occult Dr. John Dee flees to Prague, seeking the aid of Rabbi Judah Leow to create a golem that will protect the world against dark spirits.
Tor, 2002, 256 pp. (0-765-30150-4), 2003, pap., 288 pp. (0-765-30151-2)
(BL 98:1698; Kirkus 70:624; Kliatt July 2003 p. 32; LJ Aug 2002 p. 151; VOYA 26:150, 27:12)

6-147 GOLDSTEIN, Lisa. *Strange Devices of the Sun and Moon.* Gr. 10 up.
Widowed bookseller Alice Wood discovers that the exiled fairy folk have returned to Elizabethan London and that her missing son, Arthur, is to become their King.
Tor, 1993, 304 pp. (0-312-85460-9)
(BL 89:1041, 1045; Kirkus 60:1471; LJ Dec 1992 p. 191; VOYA 16:164)

6-148 GORDON, John (William). *The Giant Under the Snow: A Story of Suspense.* Gr. 5–7. (Orig. British pub. 1968.)
An ancient brooch gives Jonquil, Bill, and Arthur the ability to fly in order to protect the Seal of Power from the huge Green Man.
Illus. by Rocco Negri, Harper, 1970, 200 pp., o.p.
(BL 67:492; Kies:68; Kirkus 38:1037; LJ 95:4374)

6-149 GORDON, John (William). *The House on the Brink: A Story of Suspense.* Gr. 8 up. (Orig. British pub. 1970.)
At "the house on the brink," Dick and Helen are drawn into a strange game involving divining for water and the lost treasure of King John.
Harper, 1971, 217 pp., o.p.
(HB 47:489; Kirkus 39:683; LJ 96:4199; TLS 1970 p. 1251)

6-150 GOROG, Judith. *Winning Scheherazad.* Gr. 5–9.
In this sequel to the "Arabian Nights" tale about the girl who saves her own life by telling her captor 1,001 stories, Scheherazad, now Storyteller of the Kingdom, tries to escape from an unwanted suitor by running away to the desert.
Macmillan, 1991, 112 pp. (0-689-31648-8)
(BL 87:1193; CCBB 44:218; HBG 2:290; Kirkus 59:392; SLJ Apr 1991 p. 118; VOYA 14:170)

6-151 **GREELEY, Andrew M(oran).** *The Magic Cup: An Irish Legend.* Gr. 10 up.

King Cormac of Ireland falls in love with the slave girl Brigid while searching for the Holy Grail.

McGraw-Hill, 1979, 246 pp., o.p.

(BL 76:540, 548; Kirkus 47:1081; Kliatt 19:10; LJ 104:2118)

6-152 *The Green Man: Tales from the Mythic Forest.* **Ed. by Ellen Datlow and**
☆ **Terri Windling.** Gr. 7–12.

Fifteen short stories and three poems about mythical beings, written by Gregory Maguire, Patricia McKillip, Charles de Lint, Tanith Lee, and others. World Fantasy Award, Best Anthology, 2003. *The Faery Reel: Tales from the Twilight Realm* (2004; see Chapter 3, Fantasy Collections) is a companion volume.

Illus. by Charles Vess, Viking, 2002, 368 pp. (0-670-03526-2); Puffin, 2004, pap., 400 pp. (0-14-240029-7)

(BL 98:1412, 99:1296; CCBB 55:277; HBG 13:454; Kirkus 70:651; SLJ July 2002 p. 118; VOYA 25:126, 26:11)

6-153 **GREEN, Roger J(ames).** *The Fear of Samuel Walton.* **(The Stone Cycle, vol. 1).** Gr. 10 up. (Orig. British pub. 1984.)

Having found an old book that reveals that a Stone on the hill above the Walton farm grows powerful every thousand years and takes human lives on Midsummer Day, Samuel fears that he will be unable to protect his family from the coming evil. The sequels are *The Lengthening Shadow* (1986), *The Devil Finds Work* (1987), and *They Watched Him Die* (1988).

Illus. by David Parkins, Oxford University Press, 1984, 235 pp., o.p.

(BL 81:982; HB 61:315; SLJ May 1985 p. 101; TLS Feb 22, 1985 p. 101)

6-154 **GREENE, Jacqueline Dembar.** *The Leveller.* Gr. 6–8.

Tom Cook is a young man who steals from the rich to help the poor despite the fact that his mother gave his soul to the Devil to save him from childhood death, in this version of the Faust legend.

Walker, 1984, 128 pp., o.p.

(BL 80:1549; CCBB 37:146; HB 60:474; SLJ Apr 1984 p. 114)

6-155 **GRUNDY, Stephan.** *Attila's Treasure.* Gr. 10 up.

The unlikely friendship of captive Burgundian Prince Hagan with fellow hostage Frankish Prince Walhari leads Hagan to help Walhari flee with Hildegune, betrothed of Attila, king of the Huns. This story is related to the author's *Rhinegold* (1994).

Bantam, 1996, pap., 549 pp. (0-553-37774-4)

(BL 92:1881; Kirkus 64:919; Kliatt Nov 1996 p. 8)

6-156 **GUARD, David.** *Deirdre: A Celtic Legend.* Gr. 10 up.

A druidic prophecy that Deirdre's beauty would bring death and destruction to the land of Ulster causes the king to imprison her, but she falls in love with a young knight and flees the country, bringing about war and their deaths.

Celestial Arts, 1981 (c1977), 118 pp., o.p.; Tricycle, 1993 (repr. 1977 ed.), 120 pp., o.p.

(BL 74:375; SLJ Nov 1977 p. 79)

6-157 **GUY, Rosa (Cuthbert).** *My Love, My Love, or the Peasant Girl.* Gr. 9 up.

✯ This touching story about the ill-fated love of a Caribbean peasant girl for a rich young man she rescued from a car crash is based on Hans Christian Andersen's "The Little Mermaid" (see Chapter 1, Allegorical Fantasy and Literary Fairy Tales).

Holt, 1985, pap., 119 pp., o.p.; Coffee House Pr., 2002, pap., 168 pp. (1-56689-131-0)

(BL 82:108, 124; Kirkus 53:891; LJ Oct 15, 1985 p. 101; SLJ Jan 1986 p. 84; VOYA 9:30)

6-158 **HADDIX, Margaret Peterson.** *Just Ella.* Gr. 6–10.

✯ Ella, 15, discovers that life after the ball includes a prince who is no longer charming and a repressive life at the castle, until friendship with tutor Jed Reston convinces her to find true happiness for herself in this novelized adaptation of "Cinderella."

Simon, 1999, 185 pp. (0-689-82186-7); Aladdin, 2001, pap., 240 pp. (0-689-83128-5)

(BL 96:123; CCBB 53:93; HBG 11:94; Kirkus 67:1311; Kliatt Sep 1999 p. 8; SLJ Sep 1999 p. 225; VOYA 22:346)

6-159 **HALDEMAN, Linda (Wilson).** *Esbae: A Winter's Tale.* Gr. 10 up.

In order to pass his college finals, a lazy young man makes a bargain with the demon Asmodeas, involving the sacrifice of a coed who had come under the protection of the exiled sprite Esbae.

Avon, 1981, 1984, pap., 224 pp., o.p.

(BL 78:537, 545, 594; Kliatt 16:21; VOYA 5:39)

6-160 **HALDEMAN, Linda (Wilson).** *The Lastborn of Elvinwood.* Gr. 10 up.

Ian James is captured by fairies in a local forest, is reduced to fairy size, and becomes a reluctant participant in their plot to exchange a fairy for a female human child.

Doubleday, 1978, 237 pp., o.p.

(BL 75:860, 78:594; Kirkus 46:962, 1077; TLS 1981 p. 1375)

6-161 **HALE, Shannon.** *The Goose Girl.* Gr. 6–10. (Orig. British pub. 2003.)

✯✯ Betrayed by her guards and lady-in-waiting on her journey to marry the prince of a neighboring kingdom, Princess Anidori-Kiladra escapes and becomes a goose girl, in this novelization of the Grimm brothers' fairy tale, the first volume of a planned trilogy. In *Enna Burning* (2004), the Princess's 16-year-old friend Enna learns to speak the language of fire, endangering herself and everyone she loves.

Bloomsbury, 2003, 388 pp. (1-58234-843-X), 2005, pap., 400 pp. (1-58234-990-8)

(BL 99:1971; CCBB 57:106; HBG 15:93; Kirkus 71:910; Kliatt July 2003 p. 12; SLJ Aug 2003 p. 160; VOYA 26:325, 27:12)

6-162 **HAMILL, Pete.** *Forever.* Gr. 12 up.

Cormac O'Connor, seeking to avenge his parents' murders, follows the Earl of Warren from Ireland to 18th-century New York City, where he is given the gift of eternal life, in this novel for mature readers based on Celtic mythology.

Little, Brown, 2001, 624 pp. (0-316-34111-8); Back Bay, 2003, pap. (0-316-73569-8)

(BL 99:707; Kirkus 70:1789;)

HAMILTON (Adoff), Virginia (Esther). *The All Jahdu Storybook.*
See Chapter 8, Humorous Fantasy.

6-163 **HAMILTON (Adoff), Virginia (Esther).** *The Magical Adventures of Pret-*
★ *ty Pearl.* Gr. 7–10.
Young Pretty Pearl is transformed from a god-child into a human as she helps relieve the suffering of the black slaves in the pre-Civil War South.
Harper, 1983, 320 pp., LB, o.p., 1986, pap. (0-06-440178-2); HarperTrophy, 1998, pap. (0-06-440178-2)

(BL 79:1020, 1034; CCBB 36:167; HB 59:312; Kirkus 51:380; SLJ Apr 1983 p. 123, May 1983 p. 32; Suth 3:172; VOYA 6:215)

6-164 **HAMLETT, Christina.** *The Enchanter.* Gr. 10 up.
Merlin travels to 20th-century Washington, D.C., to find his true love, Catherine, now a newspaper reporter, and to ask her help in retrieving Excalibur.
Evans, 1990, 220 pp., o.p.

(BL 87:26, 36; LJ Aug 1990 p. 141)

HAMLEY, Dennis. *Pageants of Despair.*
See Chapter 10, Time Travel Fantasy.

HANTMAN, Clea. *Heaven Sent.*
See Chapter 8, Humorous Fantasy.

6-165 **HARRIS, Rosemary (Jeanne).** *The Moon in the Cloud.* **(The Nile trilogy,**
★★ **bk. 1).** Gr. 6–8. (Orig. British pub. 1968.)
In this, the first volume of a trilogy, Reuben agrees to go to Egypt in search of a pair of lions and a royal cat in order to pay for his family's passage on Noah's Ark. Carnegie Medal, 1968. In *The Shadow on the Sun* (1970), the young king of Egypt disguises himself to court the chamberlain's daughter, Meri-Mekhmet, who is kidnapped, and he sends his friend Reuben to rescue her. In *The Bright and Morning Star* (1972), Reuben and Thamar arrive in Egypt to find a cure for their son's illness, and become enmeshed in a power struggle between the advisers to the prince and princess.
Macmillan, 1968, 182 pp., o.p.; Peter Smith, 1989, o.p.

(BL 66:982; CCBB 23:159; HB 46:167, 64:236; Kirkus 38:7; LJ 95:1911, 1953, 4325; Suth:169)

6-166 **HARRIS, Rosemary (Jeanne).** *The Seal-Singing.* Gr. 7–10. (Orig. British
★ pub. 1971.)
Miranda's eerie resemblance to an infamous Scottish ancestor portends her own supernatural power over the seals.
Macmillan, 1971, 245 pp., o.p.

(BL 68:364; CCBB 25:57; HB 48:57; Kirkus 39:954; LJ 96:4190; Suth:169; TLS 1971 p. 1318)

HARRISON, Mette Ivie. *Mira, Mirror.*
See Chapter 12, Witchcraft and Sorcery Fantasy.

6-167   **HASTINGS, Selina.** *Sir Gawain and the Green Knight.* Gr. 3 up. (Orig.
✭   British pub. 1981.)
This is a retelling of the Arthurian tale of young Gawain's testing by the Green
Knight. *Sir Gawain and the Loathly Lady* (1985, 1987), a companion volume,
won the Kate Greenaway Medal for its illustrations by Juan Wijngaard, 1985.
Illus. by Juan Wijngaard, Lothrop, 1981, 32 pp. (0-688-00592-6)
(BL 78:44; CCBB 39:47; HB 57:673; Kirkus 49:1298; SLJ Oct 1981 p. 142; Suth 4:66; TLS
1981 p. 1360)

6-168   **HELPRIN, Mark.** *Swan Lake.* (Swan Lake trilogy, bk. 1). Gr. 6 up.
✭   An elderly royal tutor tells the Prince's daughter the tragic love story of Prince
Siegfried and the swan maiden Odette in this beautifully illustrated noveliza-
tion of the ballet. In *A City in Winter* (1996; World Fantasy Award, Best
Novella, 1997), the 10-year-old princess, raised in secret after her parents'
murders, hides in the palace kitchens posing as a "yam curler" as she tries to
rally rebel forces to overthrow the usurper who has claimed her throne. In *The
Veil of Snows* (1997), the protagonist, now a young queen, worries about the
disappearance of her husband and the possible return of the usurper.
Illus. by Chris Van Allsburg, Houghton, 1989, 80 pp. (0-395-49858-9), 1992,
pap. (0-395-64647-2)
(BL 86:274, 349; CCBB 43:85; HB 66:63; HBG 1:72; Kirkus 57:1530; SLJ Dec 1989 p 125;
VOYA 12:356)

6-169   **HERMAN, John.** *Labyrinth.* Gr. 7 up.
✭   In two parallel stories that eventually merge, 14-year-old Gregory uses violence to cope with his father's suicide, while Gregor is chosen to represent his
nation as a sacrifice to the Minotaur living at the heart of a labyrinth.
Philomel, 2001, 188 pp. (0-399-23571-X)
(CCBB 55:59; HB 77:451; HBG 12:322; Kirkus 69:66; Kliatt May 2001 p. 11; SLJ Aug 2001
p. 183; VOYA 24:133)

HICKMAN, Janet. *Ravine.*
See Chapter 7, High Fantasy: Travel to Other Worlds.

6-170   **HIEATT, Constance B(artlett).** *The Knight of the Cart.* Gr. 5–7.
✭   Sir Lancelot rescues Queen Guinevere from the evil Sir Malagant, in this
Arthurian retelling from medieval sources. *Sir Gawain and the Green Knight*
(1967), *The Knight of the Lion* (1968), *The Joy of the Court* (1971), *The Sword
and the Grail* (1972), *The Castle of the Ladies* (1973), and *The Minstrel Knight*
(1974) are companion volumes.
Illus. by John Gretzer, Crowell, 1969, 85 pp., o.p.
(BL 66:516; CCBB 23:129; HB 45:671; Kirkus 37:1067; LJ 95:242)

6-171   **HIGHWATER, Jamake.** *Rama: A Legend.* Gr. 6–9.
Prince Rama and his younger brother Lakshmana challenge the evil ruler,
Ravana, after Prince Rama's goddess-wife, Sita, is kidnapped, in this fictional
retelling of the Hindu epic called "The Ramayana."
Holt, 1994, 185 pp. (0-8050-3052-2)
(BL 91:590; HBG 6:88; Kirkus Dec 15, 1984 p. 1565; SLJ Dec 1994 p. 135; VOYA 17:348)

6-172   **HILL, Pamela Smith.** *The Last Grail Keeper.* Gr. 6–9.
Visiting an archaeological dig on Glastonbury Tor, Felicity, 16, is amazed to

discover that she can see into the world of Arthurian England and uncovers a connection to the Holy Grail.

Holiday, 2001, 227 pp. (0-8234-1574-0)

(BL 98:565; CCBB 55:208; HBG 13:97; Kirkus 69:1484; SLJ Dec 2001 p. 134; VOYA 25:128, 26:12)

6-173   HODGES, Margaret, adapt. *The Kitchen Knight: A Tale of King Arthur.*
★   Gr. 3–5.

Sir Gareth spends a year scrubbing pots in King Arthur's kitchen and then helps Lady Linesse rescue her sister from the Red Knight.

Illus. by Trina Schart Hyman, Holiday, 1990, 52 pp. (0-8234-0787-X), 1993, pap. (0-8234-1063-3)

(BL 87:660, 970; CCBB 44:62; HB 67:77; HBG 2:101; Kirkus 58:1324; SLJ Jan 1991 p. 101; Suth 4:18; TLS July 12, 1991 p. 21)

6-174   HOLDSTOCK, Robert (P.) (pseud. of Robert Faulcon). *Celtika.* **(The Merlin Codex, bk. 1).** Gr. 10 up. (Orig. British pub. 2001.)

Centuries before King Arthur's birth, mage Merlin helps Jason search for his children, who may not have been murdered by their sorcerer mother, Medea, after all, in this revision of the Greek myth. The sequel is *The Iron Grail* (Simon, 2002; Tor, 2004).

Tor, 2003, 368 pp. (0-765-30692-1), 2004, pap. (0-7653-4904-3)

(BL 99:1286; Kirkus 71:276; LJ Mar 15, 2003 p. 120; VOYA 26:150)

6-175   HOLDSTOCK, Robert (P.) (pseud. of Robert Faulcon). *Mythago Wood.*
★   **(Ryhope Woods series, bk. 1.).** Gr. 10 up. (Orig. British pub. 1984.)

Upon his return from battle in World War II, Steven Huxley and his brother Christian are inexorably drawn into a horrifying world within the forest near their home, a world where mythical creatures actually exist. World Fantasy Convention Award, Best Novel, 1985. The sequels are *Lavondyss* (Morrow, 1989), *The Hollowing* (Penguin, 1994), *Ancient Echoes* (1996), and *Gate of Ivory, Gate of Horn* (1997, 2001).

HarperCollins, 1985, 252 pp., o.p.; Orb, 2003, pap., 336 pp. (0-765-30729-4)

(BL 82:468, 482; Kirkus 53:1048; LJ Nov 15, 1985 p. 112; TLS 1985 p. 284; VOYA 9:40)

6-176   HOLLAND, Cecelia. *The Angel and the Sword.* Gr. 10 up.

Disguised as a knight named Roderick, Princess Ragny flees to France from her small Spanish kingdom after her mother's death, and the King of France insists that his daughter must marry this fearless warrior.

Tor, 2000, 304 pp. (0-312-86890-1)

(BL 97:786; Kirkus 68:1507; LJ Nov 1, 2000 p. 134)

6-177   HOLLICK, Helen. *The Kingmaking.* **(Pendragon's Banner trilogy, bk. 1).** Gr. 10 up. (Orig. British pub. 1994.)

The youth and young manhood of the future King Arthur are described in this first novel of a trilogy. The sequels are *Pendragon's Banner* (1995, 1996) and *Shadow of the King* (1996, 1997).

Heinemann, 1995, 608 pp. (0-312-13533-5)

(BL 93:385, 392; Kirkus 63:1211; LJ Nov 15, 1995 p. 103)

6-178   HOLT, Tom. *Who's Afraid of Beowulf?* Gr. 10 up. (Orig. British pub. 1988.)

By removing a brooch from a Viking ship found at a Scottish archaeological dig, Hildy Frederiksen awakens a Norse king, his wizard, and his warriors, who need her help to fight their ancient enemy, an evil sorcerer.
St. Martin's, 1989, 208 pp., o.p.; Ace, 1991, pap. (0-441-88591-8)
(BL 85:835, 861; Kirkus 56:1781; VOYA 12:116, 13:16)

6-179   HOOVER, H(elen) M(ary). *The Dawn Palace: The Story of Medea.* Gr. 7–12.
A retelling of the Greek legend of Jason and Medea, portraying Medea as a beautiful, intelligent woman betrayed by her love for handsome, arrogant Jason, who takes her away from her home in Colchis to a life in Greece where she is despised and feared.
Dutton, 1988, 244 pp., o.p.
(BL 84:1667, 1676; CCBB 41:207; Kirkus 56:539; SLJ Sep 1988 p. 198; VOYA 11:238)

6-180   HOWE, John. *The Knight with the Lion: The Story of Yvain.* Gr. 4–6.
A retelling of Chretien de Troyes' 12th-century story of King Arthur's knight, Yvain, who defeats the Black Knight, battles a dragon, rescues a white lion, and wins the love of a queen.
Illus. by John Howe, Little, Brown, 1996, 32 pp. (0-316-37583-7)
(CCBB 50:209; HBG 8:102; SLJ Sep 1996 p. 217)

6-181   HUDDY, Delia. *Time Piper.* Gr. 6–9. (Orig. British pub. 1976.)
✫   While assisting a young scientist in building a time machine, Luke falls in love with a mysterious girl called Hare who is somehow connected to the missing children of 12th-century Hamelin.
Greenwillow, 1979, 237 pp., o.p.
(CCBB 33:29; HB 55:309; Kirkus 47:580; SLJ Mar 1979 p. 140; TLS Dec 10, 1976 p. 1547)

6-182   HUFF, Tanya. *Gate of Darkness, Circle of Light.* Gr. 10 up.
Although almost no one on Earth believes in magic, Rebecca and Roland realize they must find an Adept of Light to prevent an Adept of Darkness's Midsummer's Night sacrifice from loosing Darkness across the world. The sequel is *The Fire's Stone* (1990). *Of Darkness, Light, and Fire* (DAW, pap., 2002) contains both books.
DAW, 1989, pap., 272 pp., o.p.
(BL 86:528, 540; LJ Nov 15, 1989 p. 108; VOYA 13:38, 14:11)

6-183   HUNTER, Mollie (pseud. of Maureen Mollie Hunter McVeigh McIl-
✫   **wraith).** *A Stranger Came Ashore.* Gr. 6–8. (Orig. British pub. 1975.)
No one but Robbie suspects that the handsome stranger who wishes to marry his sister might be the Great Selkie, a legendary seal-man who carries young girls off to the bottom of the sea. Boston Globe Horn Book Award Honor Book for Fiction, 1976.
Harper, 1975, 192 pp., o.p.
(BL 72:303, 80:95; CCBB 29:79; HB 51:592; Kirkus 43:1067; SLJ Dec 1975 p. 31; Suth 2:233; TLS 1975 p. 1053)

HUNTER, Mollie (pseud. of Maureen Mollie Hunter McVeigh McIl-wraith). *The Walking Stones: A Story of Suspense.*
See Chapter 12, Witchcraft and Sorcery Fantasy.

6-184   IHIMAERA, Witi. *The Whale Rider.* Gr. 7–12. (Written in New Zealand, 1987; orig. pub. 1992.)
Rawiri, a young Maori man, narrates this story about the way his little niece, Kahu, rejected by her grandfather as the next tribal leader, re-creates their ancestor's mythical whale ride.
Harcourt, 2003, 152 pp. (0-15-205017-5), 2003, pap. (0-15-205017-5)
(BL 99:1881; HBG 15:95; Kirkus 71:678; Kliatt Nov 2003 p. 15; LJ Sep 2003 p. 214; VOYA 26:311)

INGRAM, Tom (Thomas Henry). *The Night Rider.*
See Chapter 10, Time Travel Fantasy.

6-185   IPCAR, Dahlov (Zorach). *The Queen of Spells.* Gr. 6–9.
✶   In this retelling of the ballad of Tam Lin, Janet is able to enter the Green World to save her lover, Tom, but only on Halloween night.
Viking, 1973, 128 pp., o.p.
(BL 70:51; CCBB 27:45; Kirkus 41:396; LJ 98:2665)

6-186   IRVING, Washington. *The Legend of Sleepy Hollow.* Gr. 4 up. (Alternate
✶   title *The Headless Horseman*; orig. U.S. pub. in *The Sketch-Book of Geoffrey Crayon, Gent.*, 1819; as a separate tale, 1849.)
Ichabod Crane, a superstitious schoolmaster courting a wealthy farmer's beautiful daughter, is frightened off by his rival Brom Bones, masquerading as the legendary headless horseman.
Illus. by Arthur Rackham, McKay, 1928, 102 pp., o.p.; illus. by Leonard Everett Fisher, Watts, 1966, 58 pp., o.p.; retold by Robert D. San Souci, illus. by Daniel San Souci, Doubleday, 1986, 32 pp., o.p.; illus. by Barry Moser, Harcourt, 1986 (entitled *Two Tales: Rip Van Winkle and The Legend of Sleepy Hollow*), o.p.; adapt. by Diane Wolkstein, illus. by R. W. Alley, Morrow, 1987, 32 pp., o.p.; illus. by Arthur Rackham, Morrow. 1990, 112 pp. (0-688-05276-2); illus. by Gary Kelley, Stewart, 1990, 64 pp. (1-55670-046-6); illus. by Michael Garland, Boyds Mills, 1992, 62 pp., o.p.; adapt. and illus. by Will Moses, Philomel, 1995, 48 pp. (0-399-22687-7); adapt. and illus. by Emma Harding, Holt. 1995, 32 pp. (entitled *The Headless Horseman*) (0-8050-3584-2); illus. by Russ Flint, Ideal, 1996, 64 pp. (0-8249-4160-8); illus. by Gary Kelley, Creative, 2002 (orig. pub. Stewart, 1990), 64 pp. (1-56846-145-3); Wildside, 2004, 108 pp. (0-809594-08-0)
(BL 25:174, 83:623, 641, 87:1125, 89:513, 92:316, 624, 96:358; Bookshelf 1929 p. 21; HB 67:224, 72:193; HBG 2:72, 75, 4:71, 7:56, 14:68; Kirkus 63:1112; LJ 91:2210; Mahony 2:260; SLJ Nov 1992 p. 94, Oct 1995 p. 134, Nov 1995 p. 102)

6-187   IRVING, Washington. *Rip Van Winkle.* Gr. 4–7. (Orig. pub. in *The Sketch-
✶   Book of Geoffrey Crayon, Gent.*, 1819; as a separate tale in 183?.)
After a drinking bout with some strange little men, Rip Van Winkle falls asleep for 20 years.
Illus. by Arthur Rackham, Doubleday, 1905, 57 pp., o.p.; illus. by Maria Louise Kirk, Stokes, 1908, 39 pp., o.p.; illus. by Charles Robinson, Stokes, 1915, 63 pp., o.p.; illus. by N. C. Wyeth, McKay, 1921, 86 pp., o.p.; illus. by Arthur Rackham, Harper, 1967, 64 pp., o.p.; retold by Catherine Storr, illus. by Peter Wingham, Raintree, 1984 (0-8172-2108-5); adapt. by Morrell Gipson, illus. by Daniel San Souci, Doubleday, 1984, 1987, pap., o.p.; illus. by Barry

Moser, Harcourt, 1986 (entitled *Two Tales: Rip Van Winkle and The Legend of Sleepy Hollow*), o.p.; illus. by N. C. Wyeth, Morrow, 1987, 110 pp. (0-688-07459-6); adapt. and illus. by Thomas Locker, Dial, 1988, LB (0-8037-0521-2); retold and illus. by John Howe, Little, Brown, 1988, 32 pp. (0-316-37578-0), pap. (0-316-37584-5); illus. by Arthur Rackham, Dial, 1992, 124 pp. (0-8037-1264-2); illus. by Gary Kelley, Creative, 1993, 62 pp. LB (0-88682-631-4); adapt. and illus. by Rich Meyerowitz, Rabbit Ears, 1995 (0-689-80193-9); adapt. and illus. by Will Moses, Putnam/Philomel, 1999, 48 pp. (0-399-23152-8); illus. by Arthur Rackham, Sea Star/North-South, 2000, 109 pp. (1-58717-039-6); Black Dome Pr., 2003, 110 pp. (1-88378-940-0)

(BL 18:65, 63:586, 81:589, 791, 84:64, 85:408, 96:530; CCBB 38:150, 53:134; HBG 4:71, 5:77, 11:67, 12:308; Kirkus 56:1241; LJ 47:869, 92:350; Mahony 2:260; SLJ Mar 1985 p. 154, Nov 1987 p. 92, Dec 1993 p. 112, Dec 1995 p. 104, Oct 1999 p. 121)

6-188 **ISH-KISHOR, Sulamith.** *The Master of Miracle: A New Novel of the*
✭ *Golem.* Gr. 5–8.
A huge clay being created by the Rabbi of Prague to protect the Jews from anti-Semitic attacks goes on a rampage when its creator tries to destroy it.
Illus. by Arnold Lobel, Harper, 1971, 108 pp., o.p.
(BL 68:394, 669; HB 47:611; Kirkus 39:1120; LJ 96:3902)

6-189 **JAMES, Cary.** *King and Raven.* Gr. 10 up.
The peasant boy Micah becomes a servant at Camelot, plotting to avenge his sister's death at the hands of drunken knights, but is forced to flee to France and becomes a knight himself.
Tor, 1995, 384 pp. (0-312-85870-1)
(Kirkus 63:904; LJ Sep 15, 1995 p. 97; VOYA 18:384)

6-190 **JAMES, J. Alison.** *Runa.* Gr. 6–9.
American 13-year-old Runa is drawn into an ancient family curse while visiting her Swedish grandfather.
Macmillan, 1993, 138 pp. (0-689-31708-5)
(BL 89:1958; CCBB 47:12; HBG 4:299; Kirkus 61:662; SLJ July 1993 p. 101; VOYA 16:228)

6-191 **JENNINGS, Patrick.** *The Wolving Time.* Gr. 6–9.
✭ Young Laszlo fails to keep his parents' abilities to shape-change into wolves a secret from a girl named Muno, but she decides to keep their secret from the other 16th-century French villagers.
Scholastic, 2003, 208 pp. (0-439-39555-0), 2005, pap., 208 pp. (0-439-39556-9)
(BL 100:231; CCBB 57:235; HBG 15:110; Kirkus 71:1225; SLJ Jan 2004 p. 130; VOYA 26:413, 27:12)

6-192 **JOHNSON, Dorothy M(arie).** *Witch Princess.* Gr. 6–9.
The enchanter Medea creates the illusion of evil occurrences to escape from Corinth with her sons and to save her father's land from the Argonauts, in this retelling of a Greek legend.
Illus. by Carolyn Gather, Houghton, 1967, 192 pp., o.p.
(BL 64:681, 700; Kirkus 35:1145; LJ 92:3850)

6-193 **JOHNSTON, Norma.** *Pride of Lions: The Story of the House of Atreus.* Gr. 8–12.

A powerful retelling of the tragic story of King Agamemnon and Queen Clytemnestra—the father who sacrifices his daughter, Iphigenia, to aid the cause of the Trojan War, and the mother whose revenge on her husband curses the lives of their other children, Electra and Orestes.

Atheneum, 1979, 156 pp., o.p.; Vivisphere, 2002, 200 pp. (1-892323-73-7)

(BL 76:110; HB 56:180; SLJ Nov 1979 p. 88)

6-194 JOHNSTON, Norma. *Strangers Dark and Gold.* Gr. 7–12.
✷   A poetic retelling of the tragic Greek myth of Jason and Medea, the story of a young sailor questing for the Golden Fleece who wins the love of the virgin priestess of Hecate, the princess of Colchis.

Atheneum, 1975, 240 pp., o.p.

(BL 71:1070, 1075; CCBB 29:12; Kirkus 43:245; SLJ Apr 1975 p. 66)

6-195 JONES, Courtway. *In the Shadow of the Oak King.* **(Dragon's Heirs trilogy, bk. 1).** Gr. 10 up.

In this retelling of Arthurian lore, Arthur's older half-brother, Pelleas, helps Myrddin to raise Arthur from childhood until his marriage to Guinevere. The sequels are *Witch of the North* (1992) and *A Prince in Camelot* (1995).

Pocket, 1991, 320 pp., o.p.

(Kirkus 59:687; LJ Aug 1991 p. 150; SLJ Apr 1992 p. 163)

6-196 JONES, Diana Wynne. *Eight Days of Luke.* Gr. 7–9. (Orig. British pub.
✷   1975.)

The miserable life of orphaned David changes dramatically after he recites a curse, releasing a fire-loving boy named Luke from an other-world prison.

Greenwillow, 1988, 150 pp. (0-688-08006-5), 2003, 240 pp. (0-06-623741-6), pap., 240 pp. (0-06-447357-0)

(BL 85:320; CCBB 42:11; HB 64:789; Kirkus 56:1061; SLJ Sep, 1988 p. 184; Suth 4:206; TLS 1975 p. 365; VOYA 11:295)

JONES, Diana Wynne. *Fire and Hemlock.*
See Chapter 12, Witchcraft and Sorcery Fantasy.

6-197 JONES, Diana Wynne. *Hexwood.* Gr. 7–12. (Orig. British pub. 1993.)
✷   In this science-fantasy, Ann discovers that the Reigners, five people who control the universe, have managed to change the course of time on Hexwood Farm and have brought Arthur and Merlin back to life.

Greenwillow, 1994, 204 pp. (0-688-12488-7); HarperTrophy, 2002, pap., 464 pp. (0-06-447355-4); Greenwillow, 2002, 464 pp. (0-06-029888-X)

(BL 90:1803; CCBB 47:290; HBG 5:320, 14:96; Kirkus 62:305; SLJ Mar 1994 p. 236; VOYA 17:223)

6-198 JONES, Diana Wynne. *The Power of Three.* Gr. 6–9. (Orig. British pub. 1976.)

An ancient curse is revived and entangles three psychic children, a race of giants, and a group of shape-shifting Dorig in a struggle for water. Commended Book, Guardian Award for Children's Fiction, 1977.

Greenwillow, 1977, 250 pp., o.p.; Greenwillow, 2003, 328 pp. (0-06-623743-2)

(BL 74:298; HBG 15:110; Kirkus 45:790; SLJ Nov 1977 p. 58; TLS 1976 p. 383)

JUKES, Mavis. *Cinderella 2000.*
See Chapter 8, Humorous Fantasy.

6-199 KARR, Phyllis Ann. *The Idylls of the Queen.* Gr. 10 up.
After one of the knights of Arthur's Round Table dies of poisoning, Sir Kay
must conduct an investigation to clear Queen Guinevere, suspected of the mur-
der.
Ace, 1982, pap., 352 pp., o.p.
(BL 79:92, 105; VOYA 5:38)

6-200 KATZ, Welwyn Wilton. *False Face.* Gr. 6–9. (Orig. Canadian pub. 1987.)
Two Iroquois false-face masks exude an evil power that exacerbates the ten-
sions between 13-year-old Laney and her divorced mother and threaten
Laney's life.
Macmillan, 1988, 200 pp. (0-689-50456-X)
(BL 85:399, 410; Kirkus 56:1151; SLJ Nov 1988 p. 126, VOYA 11:286)

KATZ, Welwyn Wilton. *The Third Magic.*
See Chapter 7, High Fantasy: Travel to Other Worlds.

6-201 KEANEY, Brian. *No Need for Heroes.* Gr. 5–8. (Orig. British pub. 1989.)
Princess Ariadne of Crete rejects both her mad father, King Minos, and the
new male cult of the Bull, in favor of the goddess cult of the Great Mother and
her own independence, in this retelling of the Greek myth of the Minotaur.
Oxford University Press, 1989, 114 pp., o.p.
(CCBB 42:253; Kirkus 57:838; SLJ July 1989, p. 91; VOYA 12:166)

6-202 KENNEALY-MORRISON, Patricia. *The Hawk's Gray Feather: A Book
of the Keltiad.* **(The Tales of Arthur, vol. 1).** Gr. 10 up.
The bard Taliesin, foster brother of Arthur, heir to the throne of Keltia, narrates
this story of Arthur's rebellion against Edeyrn, the tyrannical Death-Druid who
overthrew the Royal House of Don and has ruled Keltia through sorcery and
bloodshed for the past 200 years. The sequels are *The Oak Above the Kings*
(HarperPrism, 1994) and *The Hedge of Mist* (1996). This series is set 1,500
years earlier in the same world as Kennealy-Morrison's Books of the Keltiad
series: see *The Copper Crown* (1984; Chapter 5, High Fantasy: Alternate
Worlds or Histories).
NAL, 1990, 400 pp. (0-451-45053-1); Roc, 1991, pap., 400 pp. (0-451-45005-1)
(Kliatt Apr 1991 p. 20; LJ Mar 15, 1990 p. 116; VOYA 13:229, 14:142)

6-203 KESEY, Ken. *The Sea Lion: A Story of the Sea Cliff People.* Gr. 3–6.
☆   Only orphaned, physically handicapped Eemook recognizes the true identity of
the evil sea spirit who appears among his Pacific Northwest coastal people,
and it is up to him to save his tribe from destruction.
Illus. by Neil Waldman, Viking, 1991, 48 pp. (0-670-83916-7); Puffin, 1995,
pap. (0-14-054950-1)
(BL 88:328; CCBB 45:95; HBG 3:67; Kirkus 59:1161; SLJ Nov 1991 p. 101)

6-204 KEYES, J. Gregory. *The Waterborn.* (Chosen of the Changeling saga, bk.
✫ 1). Gr. 10 up.
Perkar's nightmares of the emperor's daughter calling to him compel him to
travel from the lands ruled by the Forest Lord to the city of Nhol, ruled by the
River God. The sequel is *The Blackgod* (1997, 1998).
Ballantine, 1996, 448 pp. (0-345-40393-2), 1997, pap., 384 pp. (0-345-39670-7)
(BL 92:1324; Kirkus 64:568; LJ June 15, 1996 p. 96; VOYA 20:252)

6-205 KINDL, Patrice. *Lost in the Labyrinth.* Gr. 6–10.
✫ The arrival of Theseus, prince of Athens, among the annual shipment of
Athenian slaves sent to guard their half-human, half-bull brother, the Minotaur,
has a profound impact on the lives of 14-year-old Princess Xenodice and her
older sister, Ariadne, in this story based on Greek myth.
Houghton, 2002, 194 pp. (0-618-16684-X)
(BL 99:484; CCBB 56:114; HB 78:760; HBG 14:83; Kirkus 70:1134; Kliatt Sep 2002 p. 10;
SLJ Nov 2002 p. 170; VOYA 25:488)

6-206 KING, Bernard. *Starkadder.* Gr. 10 up.
The legendary Norse warrior Starkadder has been cursed with immortality by
the Fates and will be allowed to die only after committing three terrible betray-
als. The sequel is *Vargr-Moon* (1988).
St. Martin's, 1987, 244 pp., o.p.
(Kirkus 55:1355; LJ Oct 15, 1987 p. 95; VOYA 10:288)

6-207 KING-SMITH, Dick. *Hogsel and Gruntel and Other Animal Stories.* Gr.
2–4. (Orig. British pub. 1996.)
Fifteen fractured fairy tales with porcine main characters, including "The
Princess and the Pig," "Little Red Riding Pig," and "Goldipig and the Three
Bears."
Illus. by Michael Terry, Orchard, 1999, 128 pp. (0-531-30208-3)
(BL 96:528; HBG 11:67; SLJ Oct 1999 p. 117)

KING-SMITH, Dick. *The Water Horse.*
See Chapter 9, Magic Adventure Fantasy.

KIPLING, (Joseph) Rudyard. *Kipling's Fantasy.*
See Chapter 3, Fantasy Collections.

6-208 *Knight Fantastic.* **Ed. by Martin H. Greenberg and John Helfers.** Gr.
7–12.
Fifteen tales about legendary knights, written by Andre Norton, Esther Fries-
ner, Josepha Sherman, Jane Yolen, and others.
DAW, 2002, pap., 320 pp. (0-7564-0052-X)
(BL 98:1219; LJ Mar 15, 2002 p. 112; VOYA 25:398)

6-209 KUSHNER, Ellen. *Thomas the Rhymer.* Gr. 10 up.
✫ After the Queen of Elfland captures wandering minstrel Thomas the Rhymer,
she enslaves him for seven years and then casts him out, cursed with a tongue
that can speak only the truth, in this novelization of the English folktale.
Mythopoeic Fantasy Award, 1991; World Fantasy Convention Award, Best
Novel, 1991.

Morrow, 1990, 224 pp., o.p.; Tor, 1991, pap. (0-8125-1445-9); Spectra, 2004, pap., 304 pp. (0-55358-697-1)
(BL 86:1420, 1430; Kirkus 58:211; LJ Mar 15, 1990 p. 116)

6-210   LACKEY, Mercedes. *The Black Swan.* **Gr. 10 up.**
✮   In this novelized adaptation of the ballet "Swan Lake," the evil sorcerer Von Rothbart is forced into a bargain with Odette, the princess he enchanted into a swan, while his daughter, the sorceress Odile, grows into her own powers.
DAW, 1999, 376 pp. (0-88677-833-6), 2000, pap., 402 pp. (0-88677-890-5)
(BL 95:1681; Kirkus 67:496; LJ May 15, 1999 p. 131; SLJ Jan 2000 p. 158; VOYA 22:346)

6-211   LACKEY, Mercedes. *The Fairy Godmother.* **Gr. 11 up.**
Elena becomes an apprentice to her own Fairy Godmother after her "traditional" Cinderella-like life doesn't work out, and she ends up transforming other legendary lives in the Five Hundred Kingdoms.
Harlequin, 2004, 432 pp. (0-373-80202-1); Luna, 2004, pap., 496 pp. (0-373-80245-5)
(BL 100:837, 101:222; LJ Feb 15, 2004 p. 112)

6-212   LACKEY, Mercedes. *Firebird.* **Gr. 10 up.**
In this novelization of the Russian folktale, Prince Ilya falls in love with the Firebird, an enchanted maiden with dazzling powers.
Tor, 1996, 352 pp. (0-312-85812-4), 1997, pap. (0-812-55074-9)
(BL 93:826; Kirkus 64:1570; SLJ May 1997 p. 164; VOYA 20:118)

6-213   LACKEY, Mercedes. *The Gates of Sleep.* **(Elemental Masters series, bk. 1). Gr. 10 up.**
Future water master Marina Roeswood is cursed to die at age 18 by her estranged Aunt Arachne, in this novelized version of "Sleeping Beauty."
DAW, 2002, 389 pp. (0-7564-0060-0), 2003, pap., 448 pp. (0-7564-0101-1)
(BL 98:1389; Kliatt May 2003 p. 26; SLJ Sep 2002 p. 256)

LACKEY, Mercedes, and EDGHILL, Rosemary. *Beyond World's End.*
See Chapter 12, Witchcraft and Sorcery Fantasy.

6-214   LACKEY, Mercedes, and GELLIS, Roberta. *This Scepter'd Isle.* **(The Scepter'd Isle series, bk. 1). Gr. 10 up.**
Elves cause confusion at England's Tudor court after speculation grows that Henry VIII may name his illegitimate son, Harry Fitzroy, as his heir, and the elvish courts attempt to control "the red-haired babe." The sequel is *Ill Met by Moonlight* (2005).
Baen, 2004, 496 pp. (0-7434-7156-3), 2005, pap., 672 pp. (0-7434-9889-5)
(BL 100:1048; LJ Feb 15, 2004 p. 167)

LA MOTTE FOUQUÉ, Baron Friedrich Heinrich Karl de. *Undine.*
See Chapter 1, Allegorical Fantasy and Literary Fairy Tales.

6-215   LANGRISH, Katherine. *Troll Fell.* **(Troll series, bk. 1). Gr. 5–7. (Orig.**
✮   **pub. in England.)**
After his father's funeral, orphaned Peer Ulfsson is taken into servitude by his previously unknown twin step-uncles, Baldur and Grim, who live beneath the trolls' mountain, treat him cruelly, and plan to sell human children to the Troll

King. The sequel is *Troll Mill* (2005 in the UK).
HarperCollins, 2004, 272 pp. (0-06-058305-3); Eos, 2005, pap., 304 pp. (0-06-058306-1)
(BL 100:1457; CCBB 58:25; Kirkus 72:538; SLJ July 2004 p. 106; VOYA 27:143)

6-216   LAWHEAD, Stephen R. *The Silver Hand*. (Song of Albion series, bk. 2).
Gr. 10 up. (Orig. British pub. 1992.)
Llew of the Silver Hand vows revenge against the false High King who cut off
Llew's hand and blinded the royal bard, in this reworking of Celtic lore. This is
the sequel to *The Paradise War* (1991; Avon, 1993, pap.) and is followed by
The Endless Knot (1994, c1993).
Lion, 1992, 400 pp. (0-7459-2230-9), 1993, pap. (0-7459-2245-7); Zondervan,
1998, pap., 400 pp. (0-3102-1822-5); Lion, 2002, pap., 416 pp. (0-7459-2510-3)
(BL 88:1749, 1752; Kirkus 60:54)

6-217   LAWHEAD, Stephen R. *Taliesin*. (Pendragon Cycle, bk. 1). Gr. 10 up.
(Orig. pub. in England.)
A retelling of an Arthurian legend about the bard Taliesin and his love for
Charis, the princess of Atlantis. The sequels are *Merlin* (1988, 1990), *Arthur*
(1989, 1990), *Pendragon* (1994), *Grail* (1997), and *Avalon: The Return of
King Arthur* (2000).
Good News, 1987, pap., 452 pp., o.p.; Zondervan, 1996, pap., 539 pp. (0-310-20505-0)
(BL 84:31, 54; Kirkus 55:965; LJ Aug 187 p. 146)

**6-218   LAWRENCE, Louise (pseud. of Elizabeth Rhoda Holden). *The Earth
Witch*.** Gr. 7–12.
The belligerent old woman to whom young Owen is drawn becomes increas-
ingly younger as Spring approaches, but after he falls in love with her, he is
devastated when she leaves him.
Harper, 1981, 214 pp., o.p.
(BL 77:1296; CCBB 35:33; HB 57:310; Kirkus 49:745; SLJ May 1981 p. 74; VOYA 4:30)

6-219   LAWRENCE, Louise (pseud. of Elizabeth Rhoda Holden). *Star Lord*. Gr.
✮   8–10.
A young Star Lord crashes into the Welsh mountains and is hidden from the
British Security by Rhys Williams and his family.
Harper, 1978, 176 pp., o.p.
(BL 75:369; CCBB 32:65; HB 55:525; Kirkus 46:1310; SLJ Oct 1978 p. 156; Suth 2:274;
VOYA 1:33)

LAWSON, John S(hults). *The Spring Rider*.
See Chapter 10, Time Travel Fantasy.

6-220   LEE, Tanith. *Red as Blood; or Tales from the Sisters Grimmer*. Gr. 10 up.
✮   (Orig. British pub. 1982.)
A collection of well-known fairy tales such as "Snow White," "Cinderella,"
and "The Pied Piper of Hamelin," reworked with strange and original twists.
DAW, 1983, 1986, pap., 208 pp., o.p.
(BL 79:715, 719; LJ 108:147; VOYA 7:206)

LEE, Tanith. *Sung in Shadow.*
See Chapter 5, High Fantasy: Alternate Worlds or Histories.

6-221 LEE, Tanith. *Tamastara; or the Indian Nights.* Gr. 10 up. (Orig. British pub. 1983.)
Seven supernatural tales drawn from the Hindu tradition and set in India, including "Foreign Skins," "Tamastara," and "Oh, Shining Star."
DAW, 1984, pap., 174 pp., o.p.
(BL 80:1294, 1339; LJ 109:826; VOYA 7:206)

LE GUIN, Ursula K(roeber). *A Wizard of Earthsea.*
See Chapter 5, High Fantasy: Alternate Worlds or Histories.

L'ENGLE, Madeleine. *Many Waters.*
See Chapter 10, Time Travel Fantasy.

6-222 LEVIN, Betty (Lowenthal). *Landfall.* Gr. 7–10.
During a visit to the Scottish island of Kelda, New Hampshire-born Liddy becomes convinced that she has spoken with a selkie and uncovers a terrible crime perpetrated against the seals.
Atheneum, 1979, 216 pp., o.p.
(CCBB 33:98; HB 55:669; Kirkus 47:1005; SLJ Nov 1979 p. 89)

LEVIN, Meyer. *The Spell of Time: A Tale of Love in Jerusalem.*
See Chapter 1, Allegorical Fantasy and Literary Fairy Tales.

6-223 LEVINE, Gail Carson. *Ella Enchanted.* Gr. 5–8.
★★ Cursed at birth with the gift of obedience, Ella must do whatever anyone, even ogres and wicked stepsisters, tells her to, in this novel-length retelling of "Cinderella." John Newbery Medal Honor Book, 1998.
HarperCollins, 1997, 232 pp. (0-06-027510-3), 2004, pap., 288 pp. (0-06-055886-5)
(BL 93:1423, 94:734, 1618,, 95:565; CCBB 50:327; HB 73:325; HBG 8:304; Kirkus 65:225; SLJ Apr 1997 p. 138, Dec 1997 p. 26; VOYA 20:194, 365, 21:38, 40)

6-224 LEVINE, Gail Carson. *The Fairy's Mistake.* **(The Princess Tales, bk. 1).**
★ Gr. 3–6.
Neither the reward that fairy Ethelinda had prepared for the good sister nor the punishment for the nasty one work out the way she had planned, in this version of the French folktale "Toads and Diamonds." Five companion tales set in the kingdom of Biddle are *The Princess Test* (1999; based on Andersen's "The Princess and the Pea"), *Princess Sonora and the Long Sleep* (1999; based on Perrault's "Sleeping Beauty), *Cinderellis and the Glass Hill* (2000; based on Perrault's "Cinderella"), *For Biddle's Sake* (2002; based on Lang's "Puddocky"), and *The Fairy's Return* (2002; based on Grimm's "The Golden Goose"). *The Princess Tales, Volume 1* (2003) contains the first three stories, and *The Princess Tales, Volume 2* (2004) contains the other three.
Illus. by Mark Elliot, HarperCollins, 1999, 87 pp. (0-06-028061-1)
(BL 95:1531; CCBB 52:320; HB 75:332; HBG 10:296; Kirkus 67:631; SLJ May 1999 p. 92)

6-225 LICKISS, Rebecca. *Never After.* Gr. 7 up.
Seeking adventure, Princess Vevila and her cousin, Prince Althelstan, decide

to use magic to awaken three princes sleeping in an enchanted castle.
Berkley/Ace, 2002, pap., 261 pp. (0-441-00907-7)
(BL 98:1696; Kliatt Nov 2002 p. 24; VOYA 25:398)

6-226 LILLINGTON, Kenneth (James). *Selkie.* Gr. 7–9. (Orig. British pub.
1985.)
Saved from drowning by a selkie, or seal-woman, Cathy is determined to find
her new friend's magical skin and return it, in spite of the villagers' hatred and
superstition.
Faber, 1985, 145 pp., o.p.
(BL 81:1179, 1196; SLJ May 1985 p. 111; TLS Feb 1985 p. 214; VOYA 8:325)

6-227 LIVELY, Penelope (Margaret Low). *Astercote.* Gr. 6–8. (Orig. British pub.
1970.)
Mair and Peter Jenkins attempt to recover a missing medieval chalice said to
have kept the Black Plague away from their town.
Dutton, 1971, 154 pp., o.p.
(HB 47:172; TLS 1970 p. 421)

6-228 LIVELY, Penelope (Margaret Low). *The Whispering Knights.* Gr. 4–7.
⋆ (Orig. British pub. 1971.)
William, Martha, and Susie inadvertently bring the sorcerer Morgan Le Fay to
life.
Illus. by Gareth Floyd, Dutton, 1976, 160 pp., o.p.; Egmont, 1995, pap., o.p.
(BL 72:1467; CCBB 30:13; HB 52:499; Kirkus 44:593; SLJ Sep 1976 p. 121; Suth 2:289;
TLS 1971 p. 774)

6-229 LIVELY, Penelope (Margaret Low). *The Wild Hunt of the Ghost Hounds.*
⋆ Gr. 5–8. (Orig. British pub. 1971, entitled *The Wild Hunt of Hagworthy.*)
Lucy uses magic to save her friend Kester from the ghostly horned riders who
threaten his life while he takes part in an ancient stag-hunting dance.
Dutton, 1972, 141 pp., o.p.; Egmont, 1989, o.p., 1992, pap. (0-7497-0786-0),
entitled *The Wild Hunt of Hagworthy*
(BL 68:1004; CCBB 26:28; HB 48:376; Kirkus 40:402; LJ 97:2964)

6-230 LLYWELYN, Morgan. *Bard: The Odyssey of the Irish.* Gr. 10 up. (Orig.
pub. in England.)
Amergin, a visionary Celtic bard, inspires his warrior clan, the Gaels, to cross
the ocean from the Iberian peninsula to Ierne (Ireland), where they conquer the
gentle inhabitants by force in this retelling of 4th-century Irish history.
Houghton, 1984, 463 pp., o.p.
(BL 81:3, 5; Kirkus 52:706; LJ 109:1863; SLJ Sep 1985 p. 154)

6-231 LLYWELYN, Morgan. *Druids.* Gr. 10 up. (Orig. British pub. 1991.)
Fifteen-year-old Ainvar, protégé of the chief druid of the Order of the Wise,
leads his Celtic Carnute tribe against Caesar's Roman legions as they are
attempting to conquer Gaul.
Morrow, 1991, 448 pp. (0-688-08819-8)
(BL 87:692, 693; Kirkus 58:1631; LJ Jan 1991 p. 154; SLJ July 1991 p. 97)

6-232 LLYWELYN, Morgan. *Finn MacCool.* Gr. 10 up. (Orig. British pub. 1994,
entitled *Finn MacCool, the Legendary Hero of Old Ireland.*)

Legendary hero Finn MacCool and his band become the first Irish army to serve the High King, Cormac MacAirt, in this novelized retelling of Celtic myth.

Tor/Forge, 1994, 432 pp. (0-312-85476-5); Tor, 2002, 400 pp. (0-312-87737-4)

(BL 90:979; Kirkus 62:90; LJ Mar 15, 1994 p. 101; SLJ Dec 1994 p. 144)

LLYWELYN, Morgan. *The Horse Goddess.*
See Chapter 12, Witchcraft and Sorcery Fantasy.

6-233 LLYWELYN, Morgan. *The Isles of the Blest.* Gr. 10 up. (Orig. British pub. 1989.)
Connla, the Irish warrior, soon regrets his bargain with the fairy woman who transported him to the Isles of the Blest, where he finds eternal peace.
Ace, 1989, pap., 176 pp., o.p.

(BL 85:1614, 1638; VOYA 12:290, 13:13)

6-234 LLYWELYN, Morgan. *Lion of Ireland: The Legend of Brian Boru.* Gr. 10 up. (Orig. pub. in England.)
A spellbinding retelling of the rise of Brian Boru, warrior and king of 10th-century Ireland.
Houghton, 1979, 522 pp., o.p.

(BL 76:757, 765; Kirkus 47:1451; LJ 105:225)

6-235 LLYWELYN, Morgan. *Red Branch.* Gr. 10 up. (Orig. pub. in England.)
Young Setanta grows up to join the king's Red Branch warrior band and becomes the legendary warrior Cuchulain, a hero in the Irish feud with the Kingdom of Connaught.
Morrow, 1989, 600 pp., o.p.; Ivy, 1990, pap. (0-8041-0591-X)

(BL 85:818, 819; Kirkus 57:79)

6-236 LOCKLEY, Ronald Mathias. *The Seal-Woman.* Gr. 8 up. (Orig. British pub. 1974.)
Convinced that she is a seal-princess, an Irish girl named Shian lives alone in the wild, awaiting the coming of her seal-prince.
Bradbury, 1975, 178 pp., o.p.

(BL 72:228, 1038; Kirkus 43:869; SLJ Nov 1975 p. 96; TLS 1974 p. 1405)

6-237 LOGAN, Carolyn F. *The Power of the Rellard.* Gr. 5–7. (Orig. Australian
✮ pub. 1986.)
After recovering from an illness that has left her with a withered arm, Lucy discovers that she has been endowed with an ancient magical power that endangers her life and those of her older brother and sister.
Angus and Robertson, 1987, o.p.; Macmillan, 1988, 278 pp., o.p.

(BL 83:1749, 84:1183; Kirkus 56:281; SLJ Nov 1987 p. 105; VOYA 11:88)

6-238 LYNN, Tracy. *Snow.* Gr. 7–10.
In this tale, based loosely on "Snow White," teenage Jessica escapes her father and jealous stepmother's home in Wales and runs away to London, where she is taken in by a group who call themselves "the lonely ones."
Simon, 2003, pap., 259 pp. (0-689-85556-7)

(CCBB 56:369; Kliatt July 2003 p. 33; SLJ Aug 2003 p. 163; VOYA 26:238)

6-239 LYONS, Mary E. *Knockabeg: A Famine Tale.* Gr. 4–7.
In an attempt to protect the people of Knockabeg, the Faeries agree to battle the evil Nuckelavees, who are spreading the potato blight in this tale set during the 19th-century Irish potato famine.
Houghton, 2001, 128 pp. (0-618-09283-8)
(BL 98:571; CCBB 55:26; HBG 13:88; Kirkus 69:1127; SLJ Sep 2001 p. 226; VOYA 24:292, 25:15)

6-240 MacAVOY, R(oberta) A(nn). *Tea with the Black Dragon.* **(Black Dragon**
☆ **duology, bk. 1).** Gr. 10 up. (Orig. British pub. 1983.)
Searching for her missing daughter, Martha Macnamara seeks the help of Mayland Long, an Asian gentleman who claims to have the magical powers of a 1,000-year-old Imperial Chinese black dragon. The sequel is *Twisting the Rope* (1986).
Bantam, 1984, pap., 192 pp., o.p.
(BL 79:1448, 1458, 86:907; LJ 108:1018; VOYA 6:216)

6-241 McCAFFREY, Anne (Inez). *Black Horses for the King.* Gr. –10.
☆ Young Galwyn helps King Artos, later known as King Arthur, to bring Libyan horses to England for his knights and learns how to care for and heal the large beasts.
Harcourt, 1996, 240 pp. (0-15-227322-0); Del Rey, 2004, pap., 179 pp. (0-345-46863-5)
(BL 92:1698; CCBB 49:306; HB 72:467; HBG 7:303; Kirkus 64:534; SLJ June 1996 p. 153; VOYA 19:272)

6-242 McCAUGHREAN, Geraldine (Jones). *The Stones Are Hatching.* Gr. 6–9.
☆ (Orig. British pub. 1999.)
Young witch Alexia, shell-shocked soldier Mad Sweeney, and an ancient creature named Obby Orse recognize young Phelim as "Jack o'Green," and carry the unwilling boy off on a quest to save England and the world from the awakening Stoor Worm and its hatchlings.
HarperCollins, 2000, 231 pp. (0-06-028766-7), 2002, pap., 243 pp. (0-06-447218-3)
(CCBB 53:366; HB 76:462; HBG 11:308; Kirkus 68:717; SLJ June 2000 p. 150; VOYA 23:277)

6-243 McDONALD, Ian. *King of Morning, Queen of Day.* Gr. 10 up.
In three separate stories, each about a different generation of young Irish women, Emily, Jessica, and Enye are tempted to use their elfin magic. One of the women was abused as a child.
Bantam, 1991, pap., 400 pp. (0-553-29049-5)
(BL 87:1937; LJ Jan 15, 1991 p. 109; VOYA 14:324)

6-244 McKENZIE, Nancy A. *Grail Prince: A Novel of Galahad, Son of Lancelot.* Gr. 10 up. (Orig. British pub. 2002.)
After the deaths of Arthur and many of his knights, Sir Lancelot's estranged son, Galahad, gives up the woman he loves to fulfill Arthur's request that he find the Holy Grail. This is the sequel to *Queen of Camelot* (2002; orig. pub. as *The Child Queen*, 1994, and *The High Queen*, 1995). *Prince of Dreams* (2004; see below) is a companion volume.

Del Rey/Ballantine, 2003 (0-7394-3178-1), 2003, pap., 528 pp. (0-345-45648-3)
(BL 99:646; LJ Nov 15, 2002 p. 102; VOYA 26:151, 27:13)

6-245 McKENZIE, Nancy A. *Prince of Dreams: A Tale of Tristan and Essylte.*
Gr. 10 up. (Orig. British pub. 2003.)
Widowed High King Markion, ruling Britain a generation after Arthur's death,
sends his nephew, Tristan of Lyonesse, to bring back the future queen, Essylte
of Wales, in this tragic love story. This is a companion to *Grail Prince* (2003;
see above), *The Child Queen* (1994), and *The High Queen* (1995).
Del Rey, 2004, pap., 432 pp. (0-345-45650-5)
(BL 100:655; VOYA 27:144)

6-246 McKIERNAN, Dennis L. *Once Upon a Winter's Night.* Gr. 10 up.
Stolen from her family's farm by a great white bear who takes her to Faery,
Camille falls in love with the Prince of Summerland, but loses him when her
curiosity activates a curse on the royal family.
Penguin/Roc, 2001, 413 pp. (0-451-45840-0); Roc, 2002, pap., 413 pp. (0-451-
45854-0)
(BL 97:1739; VOYA 24:372)

6-247 McKILLIP, Patricia A(nne). *The Tower at Stony Wood.* Gr. 10 up.
Cyan Dag, knight to the King of Yves, leaves the royal wedding after a myste-
rious bard tells him to rescue the king's true queen, imprisoned in a tower, in
this variation on the Arthurian tale of "The Lady of Shalott."
Berkley/Ace, 2000, 294 pp. (0-441-00733-3)
(BL 96:1534; Kirkus 68:431; VOYA 23:277, 24:13)

6-248 McKINLEY, (Jennifer Carolyn) Robin (Turrell). *Beauty: A Retelling of*
☆☆ *the Story of Beauty and the Beast.* Gr. 5–9.
A beautiful girl marries a Beast and grows to love him in this novel-length version of the old French tale written by Madame le Prince de Beaumont. Phoenix
Award Honor Book, 1998. McKinley has also written another version of this
story for slightly older readers, entitled *Rose Daughter* (Greenwillow, 1997,
1998; see below).
Harper, 1978, 245 pp., LB (0-06-024149-7), 1993, pap., 256 pp. (0-06-440477-3)
(BL 75:222; 80:96, 353, 91:415; CCBB 32:67; HB 55:201, 59:71; Kirkus 46:1307; SLJ Nov
1978 p. 65; Suth 2:301; TLS 1983 p. 1312; VOYA 1:40)

6-249 McKINLEY, (Jennifer Carolyn) Robin (Turrell). *Deerskin.* **(Damar**
☆ **series, bk. 3).** Gr. 11 up.
Princess Lissar escapes into the mountains with her beloved fleethound, Ash,
after being beaten and raped by her royal father in this dark retelling of Perrault's fairy tale "Donkeyskin" for mature readers. This story is set at a later
time in the world of *The Blue Sword* (1982; see Chapter 5, High Fantasy:
Alternate Worlds or Histories) and *The Hero and the Crown* (1984; see Chapter 5, High Fantasy: Alternate Worlds or Histories).
Ace, 1993, 320 pp. (0-441-14226-5); Ace, 2005, pap., 384 pp. (0-441-01239-6)
(BL 89:1416, 1420; CCBB 47:16; Kirkus 61:494; LJ Apr 15, 1993 p. 130; SLJ Sep 1993 p.
261; VOYA 16:168, 17:8)

6-250 McKINLEY, (Jennifer Carolyn) Robin (Turrell). *The Outlaws of Sher-*
☆ *wood.* Gr. 7–12.

In this version of the Robin Hood story, Robin's accidental killing of the sheriff's man and his escape into the forest lead to his taking charge of the native Saxons' rebellion against the Norman invaders of Britain.

Greenwillow, 1988, 282 pp. (0-688-07178-3); Ace, 1989, pap. (0-441-64451-1)

(BL 85:703; HB 65:218; Kirkus 56:1530; SLJ Jan 1989 p. 94; VOYA 12:44)

6-251 **McKINLEY, (Jennifer Carolyn) Robin (Turrell).** *Rose Daughter.* Gr.
✮✮ 7–12.

Beauty's recurrent nightmares of a monster waiting at the end of a long dark corridor come to life when she goes to live in a Beast's castle, in this novelization of "Beauty and the Beast." McKinley has also written another version of this story for readers in grades 5 to 9, entitled *Beauty* (Harper, 1978, 1993; see above).

Greenwillow, 1997, 275 pp. (0-688-15439-5); Ace, 1998, pap., 292 pp. (0-441-00583-7)

(BL 93:1898, 94:475, 733, 1618; CCBB 51:58; HB 73:574; HBG 9:88; Kirkus 65:877; SLJ Sep 1997 p. 219; VOYA 20:366, 394, 21:13, 38)

6-252 **McKINLEY, (Jennifer Carolyn) Robin (Turrell).** *Spindle's End.* Gr. 7 up.
✮✮ In this expanded retelling of "Sleeping Beauty," baby Rosie is rescued and raised by an orphaned 16-year-old fairy named Katriona, who gives Rosie the ability to speak with animals. Anne Spencer Lindbergh Prize Honor Book, 1999–2000.

Putnam, 2000, 432 pp. (0-399-23466-7); Firebird/Penguin, 2002, pap., 422 pp. (0-698-11950-9)

(BL 96:1543, 97:693, 1561; CCBB 53:288; HB 76:317; HBG 11:318; Kirkus 68:303; SLJ June 2000 p. 150; VOYA 23:12, 49)

McKINNEY, Meagan. *The Ground She Walks Upon.*
See Chapter 12, Witchcraft and Sorcery Fantasy.

6-253 **McLAREN, Clemence.** *Aphrodite's Blessings: Love Stories from the*
✮ *Greek Myths.* Gr. 7–12.

Three women from Greek mythology—Atalanta, Andromeda, and Psyche—tell their stories of heartbreak, love, and marriage. The author has written two other novelized versions of Greek mythology from a female point of view: *Inside the Walls of Troy* (1996; see below) and *Waiting for Odysseus* (2000; see below).

Atheneum, 2001, 208 pp. (0-689-84377-1)

(BL 98:1145; CCBB 55:288; HBG 13:393; Kirkus 69:1688; SLJ Jan 2002 p. 137; VOYA 25:45)

6-254 **McLAREN, Clemence.** *Inside the Walls of Troy: A Novel of the Women Who Lived in the Trojan War.* Gr. 7–10.

The story of the Trojan War as seen through the eyes of two women: Helen, brought to Troy by her lover, Prince Paris, and Paris's sister, Cassandra, whose premonitions of disaster are ignored by her compatriots. The author has written two other novels of Greek mythology from a female point of view: *Aphrodite's Blessings* (2002; see above) and *Waiting for Odysseus* (2000, 2004; see below).

Atheneum, 1996, 199 pp. (0-689-31820-0); Dell, 1998, pap., 199 pp. (0-440-22749-6)

(CCBB 50:106; HBG 8:82; Kirkus 64:1238; SLJ Oct 1996 p. 148; VOYA 19:338)

6-255 McLAREN, Clemence. *Waiting for Odysseus.* Gr. 7–10.

A retelling of "The Odyssey" from the points of view of four women: Penelope, Circe, Athena, and Eurycleia. The author has written two other novels of Greek mythology from a female point of view: *Inside the Walls of Troy* (1996; see above) and *Aphrodite's Blessings* (2002; see above).

Illus. by Robert Goldstrom, Atheneum, 2000, 149 pp. (0-689-82875-6); Simon, 2004, pap. (0-689-86705-0)

(BL 96:1236; CCBB 53:215; Kirkus 68:61:VOYA 22:240, 23:48)

6-256 MacLEISH, Roderick. *Prince Ombra.* Gr. 10 up.

Eight-year-old Bentley Ellicott finds a secret stone used by famous heroes throughout history in their battles against Prince Ombra and realizes that it is his turn to fight the evil Prince of Darkness.

Cogdon, 1982, 305 pp., o.p.

(Kirkus 50:1069; LJ 107:2191)

6-257 McMULLAN, Kate. *Have a Hot Time, Hades!* **(Myth-o-Mania series, bk. 1). Gr. 4–7.**

Hades, ruler of the Underworld, tells the "true" stories behind the Greek myths in this first book in a humorous series. The sequels are *Phone Home, Persephone!* (2002), *Say Cheese, Medusa!* (2002), *Nice Shot, Cupid* (2002), *Stop that Bull, Theseus!* (2003), *Keep a Lid on It, Pandora* (2003), *Get to Work, Hercules* (2003), and *Go for the Gold, Atalanta* (2003).

Illus. by David La Fleur, Hyperion, 2002, 160 pp. (0-7868-0857-8), 2002, pap. (0-7868-1664-3)

(BL 99:497; CCBB 56:166; HBG 14:84; Kirkus 70:885)

6-258 McNAUGHTON, Janet. *An Earthly Knight.* Gr. 7–10. (Orig. Canadian pub. 2003.)

After 16-year-old Jenny falls in love with an enchanted young lord named Tam Lin, she helps him to break the spell, in this tale set in medieval Scotland.

HarperCollins, 2003, 272 pp. (0-06-008993-8); HarperTrophy, 2005, pap., 352 pp. (0-06-008994-6)

(BL 100:1053; CCBB 57:382; Kirkus 72:136; SLJ Mar 2004 p. 216; VOYA 27:317)

6-259 MAGUIRE, Gregory. *Confessions of an Ugly Stepsister.* Gr. 10 up.
✫ A retelling of "Cinderella" set in 17th-century Holland and narrated by Iris, the bright but not beautiful stepsister of the tulip-merchant's daughter, Cinderling.

Illus. by Bill Sanderson, HarperCollins, 1999, 272 pp. (0-06-039282-7); Regan, 2000, pap., 372 pp. (0-06-098752-9)

(BL 96:232; Kirkus 67:1335; LJ Sep 1, 1999 p. 234; SLJ Apr 2000 p. 160)

MAGUIRE, Gregory. *Leaping Beauty: And Other Animal Fairy Tales.*
See Chapter 8, Humorous Fantasy.

6-260 MAGUIRE, Gregory. *Mirror Mirror.* Gr. 10 up.

Jealous of the beauty of her young stepdaughter, Lucrezia Borgia orders the child's murder and continues her pursuit after Bianca's rescue, in this retelling of "Snow White" set in Renaissance Italy.

Regan, 2003, 304 pp. (0-06-039384-X)

(BL 100:57; Kirkus 71:1147; SLJ Mar 2004 p. 249)

6-261 **MAHFOUZ, Naguib.** *Arabian Nights and Days.* Gr. 10 up. (Orig. Egyptian
★   pub. 1979.)
A modern re-creation of and sequel to "The Thousand and One Nights,"
including stories of moral dilemmas, compromise, transformations, cruelty,
and corruption.
Trans. by Denys Johnson-Davies, Doubleday, 1995, 304 pp. (0-385-46888-1);
Anchor, 1995, pap., 240 pp. (0-385-46901-2)
(BL 91:372; Kirkus 62:1434; LJ Nov 15, 1994 p. 87; TLS Mar 10, 1995 p. 23)

6-262 **MAJOR, Kevin (Gerald).** *Blood Red Ochre.* Gr. 7–9. (Orig. Canadian pub.
1989.)
In alternating chapters set in two different periods, Dauoodaset, the last mem-
ber of a Canadian Indian tribe, and David, a 15-year-old contemporary Canadi-
an, tell their stories. The link between their lives is Nancy, a new girl in
David's class, who is transformed into Sanawdithit, the lost love of
Dauoodaset, after she and David canoe out to Red Ochre Island. Young Adult
Canadian Book Award Runner Up, 1989.
Delacorte, 1989, 147 pp. (0-385-29794-7); Dell, 1990, pap. (0-440-20730-4)
(BL 87:178; CCBB 42:200; HB 65:659; Kirkus 57:297; SLJ Apr 1989 p. 119; VOYA 12:104)

6-263 **MALLORY, James.** *Merlin: Part 1, The Old Magic.* **(Merlin trilogy, bk.
1).** Gr. 10 up.
Queen Mab creates the half-mortal, half-fairy baby who will become the wiz-
ard Merlin, gives him to a loving foster mother to raise, and brings him to the
Hollow Hills for training in magic. The sequels are *The King's Wizard* (1999)
and *The End of Magic* (2000).
Warner, 1999, pap., 273 pp. (0-446-60766-5)
(LJ Aug 1999 p. 148; VOYA 22:272, 23:12)

6-264 **MALONE, Patricia.** *The Legend of Lady Ilena.* Gr. 6–10.
After her parents' deaths, 15-year-old Ilena, an outsider in the Druid village,
goes to the fortress of Dun Alyn to become a warrior and discovers her unexpected destiny, in this story related to the Arthurian myths.
Delacorte, 2002, 232 pp. (0-385-90030-9); Laurel Leaf, 2003, pap., 240 pp. (0-
440-22909-X)
(BL 98:842; CCBB 55:287; HBG 13:393; Kirkus 69:1760; SLJ Jan 2002 p. 137; VOYA
25:488, 26:13)

6-265 **MALORY, Sir Thomas.** *Le Morte D'Arthur.* Gr. 6 up. (Written in 1485;
★★   orig. British pub. 1634, orig. U.S. pub. Macmillan, 1879.)
This medieval masterpiece, which combined the many legends about the reign
of King Arthur and the quest for the Holy Grail, is the primary source used for
contemporary retellings of the Arthurian legends. Numerous adaptations of
Malory's tales have been published over the years, with various titles.

The following are arranged alphabetically by title:

*The Acts of Arthur and His Noble Knights from the Winchester Manuscripts of
Thomas Malory and Other Sources.* Retold by John (Ernst) Steinbeck. Farrar,
1976, 1993, 363 pp., o.p.

Arthur, High King of Britain, adapt. by Michael Morpurgo, illus. by Michael
Foreman, Harcourt, 1995, 138 pp. (0-15-200080-1)

Arthur Pendragon of Britain. Ed. by John W. Donaldson, illus. by Andrew Wyeth, Putnam, 1943, 542 pp., o.p.

The Book of King Arthur and His Noble Knights. Adapt. by Nancy MacLeod, illus. by Henry C. Pitz, Lippincott, 1949, 325 pp., o.p.

*The Boy's King Arthur: Sir Thomas Malory's History of King Arthur and His Knights of the Round Table. Retold by Sidney Lanier, illus. by N. C. Wyeth, Scribner, 1917, 1952, 321 pp., o.p.; Knopf, 1989, c.1917, 321 pp., o.p.

King Arthur and His Knights. Illus. by Mead Schaeffer and John Rea Neill, Rand, 1924, 1936, o.p.; retold by Mary MacLeod, illus. by Howard Pyle, Parents, 1966 (c.1964), 324 pp., o.p.; ed. by Eugene Vinaver, Oxford University Press, 1975, pap. (0-19-501905-9)

King Arthur and His Knights of the Round Table. Adapt. by Roger Lancelyn Green, illus. by Aubrey Beardsley, Knopf, 1953, 1993, o.p.; adapt. by Roger Lancelyn Green, illus. by Lotte Reiniger, Puffin, 1994, 2003, pap., 330 pp. (0-14-250100-X).

King Arthur and the Legends of Camelot. Adapt. by Molly Perham, illus. by Julek Heller, Viking, 1993, 176 pp. (0-670-84990-1)

King Arthur and the Round Table. Adapt. and illus. by Hudson Talbott, Morrow, 1995, 48 pp. (0-688-11340-0)

King Arthur: The Sword in the Stone. Adapt. and illus. by Hudson Talbott, Morrow, 1991, 56 pp., LB (0-688-09404-X)

The Legend of King Arthur. Adapt. by Robin Lister, illus. by Alan Baker, Doubleday, 1990 (orig. British pub. 1988), 96 pp., o.p.

Merlin and the Making of the King. Illus. by Trina Schart Hyman, Holiday, 2004, 40 pp. (0-8234-1647-X).

Of Swords and Sorcerers: The Adventures of King Arthur and His Knights. Ed. by Margaret Hodges and Margery Evernden, illus. by David Frampton, Macmillan, 1993, 112 pp. (0-684-19437-6)

The Romance of King Arthur and His Knights of the Round Table. Ed. by Alfred W. Pollard, illus. by Arthur Rackham, Macmillan, 1917, 1927, 517 pp., o.p.

Stories of King Arthur. Adapt. by U. Waldo Cutler, illus. by Elinore Blaisdell, Crowell, 1941, o.p.

Stories of King Arthur and His Knights. Retold by Barbara Leonie Picard, illus. by Roy Morgan, Walck, 1955, 291 pp., o.p.

The Story of Idylls of the King. Adapt. by Lord Alfred Tennyson and Inez N(ellie) (Canfield) McFee, illus. by Maria L. Kirk, Stokes, 1912, 394 pp., o.p.

*The Story of King Arthur and His Knights. Adapt. by Howard Pyle, Macmillan, 1903, 1933, 1984, 320 pp. (0-684-14814-5); NAL, 1986, pap. (0-451-52488-8); Peter Smith, 1990 (0-8446-2766-6); Scribner, 1993, o.p. [see Pyle entry, below].

Tales of King Arthur. Ed. and abridged by Michael Senior, Schocken, 1981, c 1980, 321 pp., o.p.; Macmillan, 1900, 1986, pap., 768 pp. (0-02-022560-1);

Dutton, 1908, 1941, o.p.; ed. by Ernest Rhys, Dent, 1972 (2 vols.), o.p.; ed. by R. M. Lumiansky, Scribner, 1982, o.p.

See also HIEATT, Constance, B(artlett). *The Knight of the Cart* (Crowell, 1969; above); HODGES, Margaret. *The Kitchen Knight: A Tale of King Arthur* (Holiday, 1990; above); MORPURGO, Michael. *Arthur, High King of Britain* (Harcourt, 1995; below); PHILIP, Neil. *The Tale of Sir Gawain* (Putnam, 1987; below); SAN SOUCI, Robert D. *Young Merlin* (Doubleday, 1990; below); SCHILLER, Barbara. *The Kitchen Knight* (Holt, 1965; below); SCHILLER, Barbara. *The Wandering Knight* (Dutton, 1971; below); SERAILLIER, Ian (Lucien). *The Challenge of the Green Knight* (Walck, 1976; below); STEWART, Mary. *The Crystal Cave* (Morrow, 1970; below); SUTCLIFF, Rosemary. *The Sword and Circle: King Arthur and the Knights of the Round Table* (Dutton, 1981; below); and WHITE, T. H. *The Once and Future King* (Putnam, 1958; below)

(BL 9:215, 14:142, 39:460, 46:18, 58:646, 73:294, 78:694, 79:654, 80:1392, 86:1990, 88:528, 89:1963, 101:241; CCBB 44:12, 45:75, 47:12, 20, 48:317; HB 25:544, 53:561, 60:359; HBG 1:277, 3:93; Kirkus 30:82, 44:1025, 58:800, 59:1094, 61:598, 939, 72:742; Kliatt Fall 1986 p. 28; LJ 66:798, 101:2178, 107:459, 108:208; SLJ Apr 1977 p. 84, Oct 1990 p. 136, Sep 1991 p. 273, Aug 1993 p. 174, Sep 2004 p. 188; TLS 1917 p. 613, 1967 p. 1126, 1977 p. 536; VOYA 3:55)

6-266 **MARILLIER, Juliet.** *Daughter of the Forest.* **(Sevenwaters trilogy, vol.**
★★ **1).** Gr. 10 up. (Orig. pub. in New Zealand.)
After their new stepmother transforms her six brothers into swans, Sorcha, bewitched into silence and taken across the sea to Britain, spends three years spinning yarn from blistering starwort, weaving it into cloth, and making six magical shirts to break the spell, in this novel based on the Grimm fairy tale, "The Six Swans," and the Andersen fairy tale, "The Wild Swans." In *Son of the Shadows* (2001, 2002), Liadan, Sorcha's younger daughter, falls in love with a mysterious tattooed outlaw whose arrival coincides with the rise of evil that threatens Sevenwaters, their peaceful Irish home. In *Child of the Prophecy* (2002, 2003), Fainne, daughter of Sorcha's older daughter, Niamh, and Ciaran, the former Druidic sorcerer, returns to Sevenwaters and is tricked by her sorcerous grandmother, Lady Oonagh, into using her magic to destroy her family's peaceful existence.
Tor, 2000, 384 pp. (0-312-84879-X), 2001, pap., 411 pp. (0-312-87530-4)
(BL 96:1534, 97:860; Kirkus 68:431; LJ May 15, 2000 p. 129; VOYA 23:362, 24:12)

6-267 **MARILLIER, Juliet.** *Wolfskin.* Gr. 10 up. (Orig. New Zealand pub. 2002.)
After 15-year-old Eyvind becomes a fearless Viking Wolfskin warrior, the gods take him to the Islands of Orkney, where he battles the resident Picts and falls in love with a young priestess. *Foxmask* (2004) is set 18 years later.
Tor, 2003, 496 pp. (0-765-30672-7)
(BL 99:1652; Kirkus 71:714; LJ May 15, 2003 p. 131)

6-268 **MARSTON, Elsa.** *The Ugly Goddess.* Gr. 5–8.
A statue of goddess Taweret, protector of women, comes to life to help the Pharaoh's daughter, 14-year-old Princess Mertet, and Hector, the young Greek soldier who loves her, in this tale set during the Persian conquest of Egypt in 525 B.C.

Cricket, 2001, 218 pp. (0-8126-2667-2)
(BL 99:891; HBG 14:85; SLJ Dec 2002 p. 144)

6-269 **MARTIN, Rafe.** *The World Before This One: A Novel Told in Legend.* Gr.
★ 5–8.
Orphaned Crow finds a boulder that tells him the great legends of the Seneca
people, stories of the Long Ago Time.
Illus. by Calvin Nicholls, Scholastic, 2002, 208 pp. (0-590-37976-3)
(HBG 14:85; Kirkus 70:1534; Kliatt Nov 2002 p. 12; SLJ Dec 2002 p. 165; VOYA 25:490)

6-270 **MAYER, Marianna.** *Noble-Hearted Kate: A Celtic Tale.* Gr. 4–6.
In this adaptation and expansion of the Scottish fairy tales "Kate Crackernuts"
and "Tam Lin," Kate frees her stepsister Meghan from a witch's spell and res-
cues a prince from the fairy realm.
Illus. by Winslow Pels, Bantam, 1990, 64 pp., o.p.
(BL 87:1194; CCBB 44:171; HBG 2:75)

6-271 **MAYER, Marianna.** *The Sorcerer's Apprentice; A Greek Fable.* Gr. 3–5.
Apprentice enchanter Alex casts a spell of his own while Bleise, the sorcerer,
is away, but has no idea how to cancel it when things get out of hand.
Illus. by David Wiesner, Bantam, 1989, 64 pp., o.p.
(BL 86:1093; HBG 1:82; Kirkus 57:1751; SLJ May 1990 p. 107)

6-272 **MAYNE, William (James Carter).** *Earthfasts.* Gr. 6–8. (Orig. British pub.
★★ 1966.)
A curious cold-flamed candle, powerful enough to reverse time, endangers the
lives of David and Keith when it brings King Arthur and his knights back to
life.
Dutton, 1967, 154 pp., o.p.
(BL 68:1050; CCBB 20:172; HB 43:343; Kirkus 35:508; LJ 92:1750; Suth 274; TLS 1966 p.
1080)

MAZER, Anne. *A Sliver of Glass and Other Uncommon Tales.*
See Chapter 3, Fantasy Collections.

6-273 **MEANY, Dee Morrison.** *Iseult: Dreams That Are Done.* Gr. 10 up.
A retelling of the tragic love story of Tristan and Iseult.
Ace, 1985, pap., 229 pp., o.p.
(BL 82:195, 216; VOYA 9:41)

6-274 **MENDEZ, Phil.** *The Black Snowman.* Gr. K–4.
When a magic Kente, or African shawl, brings Jacob and Pee Wee Miller's
snowman to life, the snowman tells the boys about ancestral African heroes
before helping Jacob save his younger brother's life.
Illus. by Carole Byard, Scholastic, 1989, 48 pp., o.p.
(BL 86:352; CCBB 43:65; HBG 1:67; Kirkus 57:1478; SLJ Sep 1989 p. 230)

6-275 **MENOTTI, Gian Carlo.** *Amahl and the Night Visitors.* Gr. 1–5. (Orig. Ital-
★ ian pub. 1938.)
A narrative version of the Menotti opera about the physically handicapped
shepherd boy who leads the Three Kings to the Christ Child's manger and
leaves his own special gift.

Adapt. by Frances Frost, illus. by Roger Duvoisin, McGraw-Hill, 1952, 1962, 86 pp., o.p.; illus. by Michele Lemieux, HarperCollins, 1986, 64 pp., LB (0-688-05426-9)

(BL 49:112, 83:274, 1138; CCBB 6:40, 40:54; HB 28:310, 402, 61:762, 62:725–727; Kirkus 20:550; LJ 77:1747, 2184; SLJ Oct 1986 p. 113)

6-276 *Merlin.* **Ed. by Martin H. Greenberg.** Gr. 7–12.
Twenty contemporary tales about the Arthurian wizard Merlin, written by Esther M. Friesner, Jane Yolen, and Diana L. Paxson, among others.
DAW, 1999, pap., 308 pp. (0-88677-841-7)
(Kliatt Nov 1999 p. 25; VOYA 22:415, 23:12)

6-277 *The Merlin Chronicles.* **Ed. by Mike Ashley.** Gr. 10 up. (Orig. pub. in England.)
Seventy-two stories about the Arthurian wizard Merlin, written by Jane Yolen, Charles de Lint, Tanith Lee, and others. *The Camelot Chronicles* (1994; see title entry above) and *The Pendragon Chronicles* (1989, 1990; see title entry below) are related volumes, as are *The Chronicles of the Holy Grail* (1996) and *The Chronicles of the Round Table* (1997).
Caroll & Graf, 1995, pap., 448 pp. (0-7867-0275-3)
(Kliatt Jan 1996 p. 12; LJ Nov 15, 1995 p. 103; VOYA 19:108)

6-278 **MILES, Rosalind.** *Guenevere, Queen of the Summer Country.* **(The Guenevere novels, vol. 1).** Gr. 10 up. (Orig. British pub. 1998.)
In this feminist version of the Arthurian tales, Guenevere, queen of the matriarchal society of Camelot, marries Arthur, a warrior king, to unite Britain, and they must battle her uncle Malgaunt, the wizard Merlin, and his half-sister, Morgan, all bent on destroying them. The sequels are *Knight of the Sacred Lake* (2000, 2001) and *Child of the Holy Grail* (2001, 2002).
Crown, 1999, 432 pp. (0-609-60362-0)
(BL 95:726; LJ Jan 1999 p. 156)

6-279 **MILES, Rosalind.** *Isolde, Queen of the Western Isle.* **(Tristan and Isolde trilogy, bk. 1).** Gr. 10 up.
Having fallen in love while Isolde nursed Tristan back to health after a battle wound, Tristan, nephew of the King of Cornwall, is ordered to bring Isolde, Princess of the Western Isle, to Cornwall to marry King Mark. The sequels are *The Maid of the White Hands* (2003) and *The Lady of the Sea* (2004).
Crown, 2002, 368 pp. (0-609-60960-2); Three Rivers, 2003, pap., 368 pp. (1-400047-86-2)
(BL 98:1822; Kirkus 70:692; LJ July 2002 p. 121)

6-280 **MINOT, Stephen.** *Surviving the Flood.* Gr. 10 up.
Noah's youngest son, Ham, decides to set the official record straight, in this humorous report about what really happened aboard Noah's ark.
Atheneum, 1981, 320 pp., o.p.; Second Chance, 1987 (repr. of 1981 ed.), 306 pp., o.p.
(BL 78:178, 188; Kirkus 49:895; LJ 106:2049)

6-281 **MITCHELL, Stephen.** *The Frog Prince: A Parable of Love and Transformation.* Gr. 10 up.
In this humorous expansion of "The Frog Prince" story set in Renaissance

France, a princess makes a bargain with a talking frog because she senses that he is an enchanted prince, and she is falling in love with him.
Crown/Harmony, 1999, 176 pp., o.p.
(BL 96:8; Kirkus 67:1443)

6-282 MOORE, John. *Slay and Rescue.* Gr. 11 up.
A bawdy parody of novelized fairy tales about 17-year-old Prince Charming whose raging hormones lead him to court Cinderella, Sleeping Beauty, and Snow White, while slaying dragons, battling evil sorcerers, and rescuing princesses.
Baen, 1993, pap., 226 pp. (0-671-72152-6)
(Kliatt May 1993 p. 18; VOYA 16:168)

6-283 MORPURGO, Michael. *Arthur, High King of Britain.* Gr. 4–7. (Orig.
☆ British pub. 1994.)
Saved from drowning by an old man who tells the boy the story of his life, the contemporary 12-year-old boy realizes that his rescuer is King Arthur Pendragon. *Sir Gawain and the Green Knight* (Candlewick, 2004) is the companion volume.
Illus. by Michael Foreman, Harcourt, 1995, 137 pp. (0-15-200080-1); Egmont, 1996, pap., 143 pp., o.p.
(BL 91:1947; CCBB 48:317; HBG 6:301; SLJ July 1995 p. 89)

6-284 MORPURGO, Michael. *King of the Cloud Forests.* Gr. 6–9. (Orig. British
☆ pub. 1987.)
Fourteen-year-old Ashley Anderson escapes the Japanese invasion of China during World War II, attempting to cross the Himalayas on foot; he is rescued by a band of yeti, or abominable snowmen, who believe he is a god. Carnegie Medal Commended Book, 1987.
Viking, 1988, 146 pp., o.p.; Puffin, 1991, pap. (0-14-032586-7)
(BL 84:1820, 1840, 85:879; CCBB 41:234; HB 64:634; Kirkus 56:764; SLJ Sep 1988 p. 200; Suth 4:296; TLS 1988 p. 200)

6-285 MORPURGO, Michael. *Robin of Sherwood.* Gr. 4–8. (Orig. British pub.
☆ 1966.)
A contemporary boy finds a human skeleton within the roots of a massive oak uprooted by a storm, and begins to dream of Robin Hood's adventures in that very forest.
Illus. by Michael Foreman, Harcourt, 1996, 113 pp. (0-15-201315-6)
(BL 93:350, 1308; CCBB 50:181; HBG 8:104; Kirkus 64:1155; SLJ Feb 1997 p. 121; VOYA 20:330)

6-286 MORRESSY, John. *The Juggler.* Gr. 7–12.
☆ Longing to become the greatest juggler in the world, Beran sells his soul to the devil in exchange for dazzling prowess.
Holt, 1996, 261 pp., o.p.; HarperTrophy, 1998, pap., 361 pp. (0-06-447174-8)
(BL 92:1586; CCBB 49:272; HBG 7:303; Kirkus 64:451; SLJ June 1996 p. 153; VOYA 19:170)

6-287 MORRIS, Gerald. *The Ballad of Sir Dinadan.* **(The Denizens of Camelot**
☆ **series, bk. 5).** Gr. 5–9.

Eighteen-year-old Sir Dinadan, younger brother of Sir Tristram, and his companion, the Moorish knight Palimides, travel through Britain in search of wrongs to right. Morris has written five other books set in Camelot: *Parsifal's Page* (2001; see below), *The Savage Damsel and the Dwarf* (2000; see below), *The Squire's Tale* (1998, 2000; see below), *The Squire, His Knight and His Lady* (1999, 2000), and *The Princess, the Crone, and the Dung-Cart Knight* (2004; see below).

Houghton, 2003, 256 pp. (0-618-19099-6), 2005, pap., 245 pp. (0-618-54894-7)

(BL 99:1589; CCBB 56:324; HB 79:353; HBG 14:372; Kirkus 71:237; Kliatt Mar 2003 p. 14; SLJ Apr 2001 p. 166; VOYA 26:152)

6-288   MORRIS, Gerald. *Parsifal's Page*. (The Denizens of Camelot series, bk.
☆   **4). Gr. 5–10.**

The adventures of King Arthur's knight Sir Parsifal, told through the eyes of Piers, his 11-year-old page. Morris has written five other books set in Camelot: *The Ballad of Sir Dinadan* (2003; see above), *The Savage Damsel and the Dwarf* (2000; see below), *The Squire's Tale* (1998, 2000; see below), *The Squire, His Knight and His Lady* (1999, 2000), and *The Princess, the Crone, and the Dung-Cart Knight* (2004; see below).

Houghton, 2001, 240 pp. (0-618-05509-6), 2004, pap., 240 pp. (0-618-43237-X)

(BL 97:1558; CCBB 54:311; HB 77:333; HBG 12:312; Kirkus 69:186; SLJ Apr 2001 p. 146; VOYA 24:134)

6-289   MORRIS, Gerald. *The Princess, the Crone, and the Dung-Cart Knight*.
☆   **(The Denizens of Camelot series, bk. 6). Gr. 6–9.**

Grieving over the deaths of her mother and guardian, burned as witches, Sarah, 13, travels to Camelot to report the kidnapping of Queen Guinevere and Sir Kai and joins the knights who vow to rescue them, in this adaptation of Chretien de Troyes' *The Knight of the Cart*. Morris has written five other books set in Camelot: *The Ballad of Sir Dinadan* (2003; see above), *The Savage Damsel and the Dwarf* (2000; see below), *The Squire's Tale* (1998, 2000; see below), *The Squire, His Knight and His Lady* (1999, 2000), and *Parsifal's Page* (2001; see above).

Houghton, 2004, 320 pp. (0-618-37823-5)

(BL 100:1450; CCBB 57:288; HB 80:335; Kirkus 71:182; SLJ May 2004 p. 154; VOYA 27:145)

6-290   MORRIS, Gerald. *The Savage Damsel and the Dwarf*. (The Denizens of
☆   **Camelot series, bk. 3). Gr. 6–9.**

Lady Lynet, 16, travels to Camelot with a dwarf and a kitchen knave to ask for King Arthur's aid in stopping the Red Knight from slaughtering the suitors of her older sister, Lyonesse. Morris has written five other books set in Camelot: *The Ballad of Sir Dinadan* (2003; see above), *Parsifal's Page* (2000; see above), *The Squire's Tale* (1998, 2000; see below), *The Squire, His Knight and His Lady* (1999, 2000), and *The Princess, the Crone, and the Dung-Cart Knight* (2004; see above).

Houghton, 2000, 213 pp. (0-395-97126-8), 2004, pap., 224 pp. (0-618-19681-1)

(BL 96:1244, 1544; CCBB 53:326; HB 76:317; HBG 11:309; Kirkus 68:482; SLJ May 2000 p. 174; VOYA 23:127, 24:13)

6-291   **MORRIS, Gerald.** *The Squire's Tale.* **(The Denizens of Camelot series,**
  ✶   **bk. 1).** Gr. 6–9.
      Orphaned 14-year-old Terence survives the dangers of life as squire to Sir
      Gawain and uncovers the secret of his own family history. In the sequel, *The*
      Squire, His Knight and His Lady (1999, 2001), Sir Gawain accepts the chal-
      lenge of the mysterious Green Knight, and Terence accompanies him on a
      potentially tragic quest. Morris has written four other books set in Camelot:
      The Ballad of Sir Dinadan (2003; see above), *Parsifal's Page* (2000; see
      above), *The Savage Damsel and the Dwarf* (2000; see above), and *The*
      Princess, the Crone, and the Dung-Cart Knight (2004; see above).
      Houghton, 1998, 212 pp. (0-395-86959-5); Laurel Leaf, 2000, pap., 212 pp. (0-
      440-22823-9)
      (BL 94:1436, 96:1544; CCBB 51:385; HB 74:492; HBG 9:334; Kirkus 66:342; SLJ July
      1998 p. 97; VOYA 21:212)

6-292   **MORRIS, Kenneth.** *The Book of the Three Dragons.* **Ed. by R. Reginald**
      and Douglas Melville. Gr. 10 up. (Orig. British pub. 1930.)
      In this retelling of the fourth branch of the Welsh *Mabinogion*, the immortal
      hero Manawyddan embarks on numerous adventures as he seeks to recover
      two treasures stolen from the gods: a magical breastplate and the divine harp of
      Alawn. This is the sequel to *The Fates of the Princes of Dyfed* (1913, 1914,
      1978, 1980), which retells the first three branches of the *Mabinogion*.
      Ed. by R. Reginald and Douglas Melville, illus. by Ferdinand Huszti Horvath,
      Longman, 1930, 206 pp., o.p.; Cold Spring Press, 2004, pap., 312 pp. (1-
      59360-027-5)
      (BL 27:266)

6-293   **MULLIN, Caryl Cude.** *A Riddle of Roses.* Gr. 4–7. (Orig. Canadian pub.
      2000.)
      Meryl longs to become a bard and sets out for Avalon after she is expelled
      from the hall for reading Taliesin's collection of songs and adventures.
      Second Story, 2000, pap., 180 pp. (1-896764-28-2)
      (BL 97:1138; VOYA 24:53)

6-294   **MURPHY, Pat (pseud. of E[mmet] Jefferson Murphy).** *The Falling*
   ✶   *Woman: A Fantasy.* Gr. 10 up.
      While excavating an ancient Mayan city, archaeologist Elizabeth Butler con-
      jures up the ghost of a Mayan priestess who offers to bring the Mayan gods
      back to life if Elizabeth will sacrifice the life of her estranged daughter. Nebula
      Award, Best Novel, 1988.
      Tor, 1986, 288 pp., o.p.
      (BL 83:34, 52; Kirkus 54:1319; LJ Oct 15, 1986 p. 114; VOYA 10:40)

      MURPHY, Shirley Rousseau, and SUGGS, Welch. *Medallion of the*
      Black Hound.
      See Chapter 7, High Fantasy: Travel to Other Worlds.

6-295   **MUSSET, Paul-Edmé de.** *Mr. Wind and Madam Rain.* Gr. 3–5. (Orig. pub.
      in France; orig. U.S. pub. Harper, 1864.)
      A collection of magical adventures retold from the folklore of Brittany.
      Trans. by Emily Makepeace, illus. by Charles Bennett, Putnam, 1905, o.p.;

Harper, 1908, 126 pp., o.p.
(BL 1:23, 5:64; Mahony 1:23)

MYERS, John Myers. *Silverlock.*
See Chapter 7, High Fantasy: Travel to Other Worlds.

6-296 MYERS, Walter Dean. *The Legend of Tarik.* Gr. 7–9.
Armed with a magic sword and the Crystal of Truth, Tarik seeks revenge
against the murderous El Muerte in this saga set in medieval North Africa.
Viking, 1981, 185 pp., o.p.
(BL 77:1444, 1449; HB 57:434; SLJ May 1981 p. 76; VOYA Oct 1981 p. 36)

6-297 NAPOLI, Donna Jo. *Beast.* Gr. 8 up.
✫ Prince Orasmyn of Persia, cursed and transformed into a lion who can be
restored only by the love of a woman, travels to France and restores the rose
gardens of a haunted castle in this retelling of "Beauty and the Beast."
Atheneum, 2000, 272 pp. (0-689-83589-2); Simon, 2002, pap., 272 pp. (0-689-
83590-6); Simon Pulse, 2004, pap., 260 pp. (0-689-87005-1)
(BL 97:233, 1561; CCBB 54:76; HB 76:577; HBG 12:86; Kirkus 68:1548; SLJ Oct 2000 p.
168, Dec 2000 p. 54; VOYA 23:278, 24:13, 409)

6-298 NAPOLI, Donna Jo. *Bound.* Gr. 6 up.
✫ After her father's death, Xing Xing tries to help her step-sister, ill due to her
newly bound feet, and attends a festival wearing her late mother's silk gown
and gold slippers, in this reworking of the traditional Chinese "Cinderella"
story.
Simon/Atheneum, 2004, 192 pp. (0-689-86175-3)
(BL 101:652; Kirkus 72:1046; Kliatt Nov 2004 p. 10; SLJ Nov 2004 p. 150)

6-299 NAPOLI, Donna Jo. *Breath.* Gr. 7–10.
✫ After nearly everyone in Hameln in 1284 becomes ill from a grain-poisoning
fungus, the townspeople blame a boy named Salz and the town's rats, so Salz
finds a piper with musical powers who promises to free Hameln of rats. Gold-
en Kite Fiction Honor Award, 2003.
Atheneum, 2003, 272 pp. (0-689-86174-5); Simon Pulse, 2005, pap., 240 pp.
(0-689-86177-X)
(BL 100:232; CCBB 57:72; HB 80:85; HBG 15:112; Kirkus 71:1274; Kliatt Nov 2003 p. 8;
SLJ Nov 3002 p. 143; VOYA 26:416)

6-300 NAPOLI, Donna Jo. *Crazy Jack.* Gr. 7–10.
✫✫ Desperate to find his missing father, lost after climbing a cliff in search of a
pot of gold, Jack, 16, climbs a magic bean stalk and enters a giant's home, in
this novelized version of "Jack and the Beanstalk."
Delacorte, 1999, 134 pp. (0-385-32627-0); Dell, 2001, pap., 134 pp. (0-440-
22788-7)
(BL 96:355; CCBB 53:144; HB 76:80; HBG 11:96; Kirkus 67:1504; Kliatt Sep 1999 p. 12;
SLJ Nov 1999 p. 160; VOYA 22:348, 23:12)

6-301 NAPOLI, Donna Jo. *The Great God Pan.* Gr. 7–10.
✫ After the nature god Pan falls in love with Iphigenia, daughter of Helen of
Troy, his previously uncomplicated, pleasure-filled life is no longer enough for
him, in this reworking of Greek myths.

Random, 2003, 149 pp. (0-385-90120-8); Laurel Leaf, 2005, 160 pp. (0-440-22925-1)

(BL 99:1464; CCBB 56:456; HBG 15:113; Kirkus 71:681; Kliatt July 2003 p. 15; SLJ June 2003 p. 147; VOYA 26:416, 27:14)

NAPOLI, Donna Jo. *The Magic Circle.*
See Chapter 12, Witchcraft and Sorcery Fantasy.

NAPOLI, Donna Jo. *The Prince of the Pond: Otherwise Known as De Fawg Pin.*
See Chapter 8, Humorous Fantasy.

6-302   NAPOLI, Donna Jo. *Sirena.* Gr. 7–12.
✫   The mermaid Sirena flees to the island of Lemnos after the deaths of her sister and some shipwrecked sailors and rescues and falls in love with the Trojan warrior Philoctetes, in this novelized version of tales from the Trojan War.
Scholastic, 1998, 224 pp. (0-590-38388-4), 2000, pap., 224 pp. (0-590-38389-2)
(BL 95:221; CCBB 52:140; HBG 10:81; Kirkus 66:1386; Kliatt Sep 15, 1998 p.8; SLJ Oct 1998 p. 143; VOYA 21:369, 22:14)

6-303   NAPOLI, Donna Jo. *Zel.* Gr. 7–12.
✫✫   Thirteen-year-old Zel's loving mother uses black magic to lock her child in a tower rather than let her marry a young nobleman, in this novel-length retelling of "Rapunzel."
Dutton, 1996, 224 pp. (0-525-45612-0); Puffin, 1998, pap., 240 pp. (0-14-130116-3)
(BL 93:118; CCBB 49:381; HB 72:603; HBG 8:82; Kirkus 64:691; SLJ Sep 1996 p. 227, Dec 1996 p. 31; VOYA 20:13, 44)

6-304   NAPOLI, Donna Jo, and TCHEN, Richard. *Spinners.* Gr. 8–12.
✫   In this novelized version of "Rumpelstiltskin," a mysterious spinner rescues 15-year-old Saskia from the king's dungeon because he knows she is his own daughter, born to his lost love, the miller's late wife.
Dutton, 1999, 197 pp. (0-525-46065-9); Puffin, 2001, pap., 208 pp. (0-14-131110-X)
(BL 96:124; CCBB 53:25; HBG 11:96; Kirkus 67:887; Kliatt Nov 1999 p. 12; SLJ Sep 1999 p. 229; VOYA 22:348, 23:13)

6-305   NATHAN, Robert (Gruntal). *The Elixir.* Gr. 10 up.
An American historian and the mysterious girl he meets at Stonehenge travel back and forth through time, reliving the Arthurian legend of Merlin and Nimue.
Knopf, 1971, 177 pp., o.p.
(BL 68:183; Kirkus 39:608; LJ 96:2544, 3915, 4161)

6-306   NEWMAN, Robert (Howard). *Merlin's Mistake.* Gr. 5–8.
Tertius's knowledge of the future hampers Merlin's attempts to free himself from the bonds of Nimue. The sequel is *The Testing of Tertius* (1973, 1985).
Illus. by Richard Lebenson, Atheneum, 1970, 237 pp., o.p.; Volo/Hyperion, 2002, pap. (0-7868-1546-9)
(BL 66:1162; HB 46:298, 60:223, 63:491, 78:429; Kirkus 38:174; LJ 95:2309; TLS 1971 p. 390)

NEWMAN, Robert (Howard). *The Shattered Stone.*
See Chapter 5, High Fantasy: Alternate Worlds or Histories.

6-307 **NEWMAN, Sharan.** *Guinevere.* **(Guinevere trilogy, bk. 1).** Gr. 10 up.
✶ (Orig. British pub. 1980.)
This is the story of Queen Guinevere's childhood love for a unicorn. The
sequels are *The Chessboard Queen* (1983) and *Guinevere Evermore* (1985,
1986, 1998).
St. Martin's, 1981, 257 pp., o.p., 1984, pap., 296 pp. (0-312-35321-9); Tor,
1996, pap. (0-312-86233-4)
(BL 77:796, 806; Kirkus 48:1482; Kliatt 18:29; LJ 106:815; SLJ Apr 1981 p. 146)

NIMMO, Jenny. *The Snow Spider.*
See Chapter 9, Magic Adventure Fantasy.

6-308 **NIMMO, Jenny.** *Ultramarine.* Gr. 5–8. (Orig. British pub. 1990.)
Arion, a mysterious new friend who rescues sea creatures, helps two lonely
children, Ned and Nell, unravel the secret of their heritage and their connection
to the sea. The sequel is *Rainbow and Mr. Zed* (1994).
Dutton, 1992, 192 pp. (0-525-44869-1)
(BL 88:1593; CCBB 45:301; HBG 3:276; Kirkus 60:327; SLJ May 1992 p. 116; VOYA
15:113)

NODELMAN, Perry. *The Same Place But Different.*
See Chapter 7, High Fantasy: Travel to Other Worlds.

6-309 **NORMAN, Roger.** *Albion's Dream: A Novel of Terror.* Gr. 6–10. (Orig.
✶ British pub. 1990.)
English boarding-school student Edward discovers that whatever happens on
the board of an old game called Albion's Dream also happens in real life.
Delacorte, 1992, 209 pp., o.p.
(BL 89:48; CCBB 46:84; HB 68:724; HBG 4:75; Kirkus 60:923; SLJ Oct 1992 p. 120;
VOYA 15:241)

NORTON, Andre (pseud. of Alice Mary Norton). *Here Abide Monsters.*
See Chapter 7, High Fantasy: Travel to Other Worlds.

6-310 **NORTON, Andre (pseud. of Alice Mary Norton).** *Huon of the Horn.* Gr.
6–9.
An exciting retelling of the legend of the Duke of Bordeaux from the Charle-
magne saga.
Illus. by Joe Krush, Harcourt, 1951, 208 pp., o.p.
(Kirkus 19:632; LJ 76:2126)

6-311 **NORTON, Andre (pseud. of Alice Mary Norton).** *Quag Keep.* Gr. 7–10.
✶ With identical bracelets locked to their wrists, seven strangers journey to the
lair of the powerful being who has enslaved them.
Atheneum, 1978, 224 pp., o.p.
(BL 74:1176; HB 54:285; SLJ Mar 1978 p. 139; VOYA 1:42, 2:58)

NORTON, Andre (pseud. of Alice Mary Norton). *Steel Magic.*
See Chapter 7, High Fantasy: Travel to Other Worlds.

6-312 **NORTON, Andre, and SHWARTZ, Susan.** *Imperial Lady: A Fantasy of Han.* Gr. 10 up.
Exiled from the Chinese emperor's court to the barbaric land of the Hsiung-nu, Silver Snow uses her wits and magic skills to protect herself and her husband from the tribal shaman.
Tor, 1980, 320 pp., o.p., 1990, pap. (0-8125-0722-3)
(BL 85:1950, 1969; Kirkus 57:959; Kliatt Sep 1990 p. 22; LJ Aug 1989 p. 117; VOYA 13:119)

6-313 **NYE, Robert.** *Beowulf; a New Telling.* Gr. 5–8.
A modernized version of the Anglo-Saxon epic about Beowulf's conquest of the monsters Grendel, She, and the Firedrake.
Illus. by Alan E. Cober, Hill, 1968, 116 pp., o.p.; Laurel Leaf, 1982, pap., 112 pp. (0-440-90560-5)
(BL 65:839; HB 45:49)

6-314 **OGIWARA, Noriko.** *Dragon Sword and Wind Child.* Gr. 7–12. (Orig.
✫ Japanese pub. 1988.)
Orphaned 15-year-old Saya thinks she will become a handmaiden in the palace of Prince Tsukishiro, one of the immortal children of the God of Light, but she discovers that she is dedicated to his enemy, the Goddess of Darkness, in this complex novel based on Japanese mythology.
Trans. by Cathy Hirano, Farrar, 1993, 329 pp. (0-374-30466-1)
(BL 89:2050; CCBB 46:355; HBG 4:311; Kirkus 61:666; SLJ Sep 1993 p. 252; VOYA 16:169)

6-315 **OPPENHEIM, Shulamith (Levey).** *The Selchie's Seed.* Gr. 4–6.
✫ Marian had never suspected that her ancestors were seal people until the night she was drawn to a white whale in the ocean near her island home.
Illus. by Diane Goode, Bradbury, 1975, 83 pp., o.p.
(BL 72:580; CCBB 29:129; Kirkus 43:1287; SLJ Jan 1976 p. 49; Suth 2:345)

6-316 **ORGEL, Doris.** *Ariadne, Awake!* Gr. 5–9.
✫ Daughter of the cruel King Minos of Crete, Princess Ariadne falls in love with Theseus, an Athenian to be sacrificed to the monstrous Minotaur, and helps him to escape, in this novelized retelling of the Greek myth.
Illus. by Barry Moser, Viking, 1994, 74 pp. (0-670-85158-2)
(BL 90:1599; CCBB 37:330; HB 70:589; HBG 5:343; Kirkus 61:561; SLJ June 1994 p. 152)

6-317 **ORGEL, Doris.** *The Princess and the God.* Gr. 7–10.
✫ Jealous of Princess Psyche's beauty, the goddess Venus sends her son Cupid to punish the princess, but they fall in love, in this version of the Greek myth.
Orchard, 1996, 128 pp. (0-531-08866-9); Dell, 1997, pap. (0-440-22691-0)
(BL 92:926; CCBB 49:199; HBG 7:304; Kirkus 64:140; SLJ Apr 1996 p. 157)

6-318 **ORGEL, Doris.** *We Goddesses: Athena, Aphrodite, Hera.* Gr. 6–9.
Three interrelated first-person accounts of the lives of Greek goddesses: Athena, goddess of wisdom; Aphrodite, goddess of love; and Hera, queen of the gods.
Illus. by Marilee Heyer, DK, 1999, 112 pp. (0-7894-2586-6)
(BL 96:429; CCBB 53:102; HBG 11:96; Kirkus 67:1649; SLJ Oct 1999 p. 156)

6-319 **ORLOCK, Carol (Ellen).** *The Goddess Letters: The Demeter-Persephone Myth Retold.* Gr. 10 up.
After her daughter's abduction by Hades, Demeter exchanges a series of letters with Persephone chronicling the decline of goddess worship on Earth, in an unusual feminist retelling of Greek myth.
St. Martin's, 1987, 220 pp., o.p.
(Kirkus 55:415; SLJ Feb 1988 p. 95)

6-320 *Orphans of the Night.* **Ed. by Josepha Sherman.** Gr. 6–10.
Eleven tales about teenagers and mythical creatures, written by Lawrence Watt-Evans, Pamela F. Service, Esther M. Friesner, Jane Yolen, and others.
Walker, 1995, 162 pp. (0-8027-8368-6)
(Bl 91:1753; HBG 6:375; Kirkus 63:716; SLJ June 1995 p. 132; VOYA 18:317)

6-321 **OSBORNE, Mary Pope.** *Favorite Medieval Tales.* Gr. 3–7.
☆ Nine retellings of Arthurian and other medieval stories, including "Robin Hood" and "The Song of Roland."
Illus. by Troy Howell, Scholastic, 1998, 86 pp. (0-590-60042-7); Hyperion, 2002, pap., 86 pp. (0-439-14134-6)
(BL 94:1515; HBG 9:366; Kirkus 66:664; SLJ Aug 1998 p. 182)

6-322 **OSBORNE, Mary Pope.** *Haunted Waters.* Gr. 7–10.
☆ In this dark version of the 19th-century German fairy tale *Undine* by Baron Friedrich de La Motte Fouqué (see Chapter 1, Allegorical Fantasy and Literary Fairy Tales), Lord Huldbrand of Ringstetten is trapped by a flood on a demon-haunted peninsula, where he falls in love with a beautiful girl named Undine.
Candlewick, 1994, 152 pp. (1-56402-119-X), 1996, pap., 160 pp. (1-56402-588-8)
(BL 91:492; HB 70:761; HBG 6:90; Kirkus 62:1137; SLJ Dec 1994 p. 111; VOYA 17:350)

6-323 **O'SHEA, (Catherine) Pat(ricia Shiels).** *The Hounds of the Morrigan.* Gr.
☆ 6–9. (Orig. British pub. 1985.)
The ancient book Pidge finds brings the evil Queen Morrigan and her two witchlike assistants to his door, threatening the future of the world.
Holiday, 1986, 469 pp., o.p.; HarperTrophy, 1999, pap., 688 pp. (0-06-447205-1)
(BL 82:1144; CCBB 39:215; HB 62:451; Kirkus 54:870; SLJ Mar 1986 p. 169, Feb 1987 p. 34, Apr 1987 p. 48; Suth 4:308; TLS Nov 1985 p. 1358; VOYA 10:22)

6-324 *Out of Avalon: An Anthology of the Old Magic and New Myths.* **Ed. by Jennifer Roberson.** Gr. 6 up.
Fifteen Arthurian tales written by Katherine Kerr, Marion Zimmer Bradley, Diana L. Paxson, Judith Tarr, and others.
Roc, 2001, pap., 336 pp. (0-451-45831-1)
(Kliatt July 2001 p. 27; VOYA 24:292, 25:15)

6-325 **PARK, (Rosina) Ruth (Lucia).** *My Sister Sif.* Gr. 6–9. (Orig. Australian pub. 1986.)
Fourteen-year-old Riko and her sister Sif run away from their school in Sydney and return to their island home, where their mother and brother live beneath the sea.
Viking, 1991, 180 pp. (0-670-83924-8)

(BL 87:1560; CCBB 44:201; HBG 2:278; Kirkus 59:675; SLJ May 1991 p. 94; TLS Sep 4, 1987 p. 964; VOYA 14:100)

6-326   PASSEY, Helen K. *Speak to the Rain.* Gr. 6–10.
Grief over their mother's death draws Janna's younger sister into a spirit world connected with a Northwest Indian totem pole near an isolated lake.
Macmillan, 1989, 160 pp., o.p.
(BL 86:736, 746; HBG 1:83; Kirkus 57:1595; SLJ Sep 1989 p. 256; VOYA 12:280)

6-327   PATERSON, Katherine, reteller. *Parzival: The Quest of the Grail Knight.*
✰   Gr. 5–9.
In this retelling of the Arthurian legend of the Holy Grail, Parzival becomes a knight and leaves Arthur's court, and his adventures culminate in a visit to the Angler, or Fisher King, where he is doomed to a life of dishonor.
Lodestar, 1998, 128 pp. (0-525-67579-5); Puffin, 2000, pap., 144 pp. (0-14-130573-8)
(BL 94:1123, 96:1544; CCBB 51:334; HBG 9:366; Kirkus 66:60; Kliatt Mar 1998 p. 5; SLJ Feb 1998 p. 109; VOYA 21:132)

6-328   PATTOU, Edith. *East.* Gr. 6–10.
✰   After a white bear convinces the father of 14-year-old Rose to let her live in his distant castle, Rose must make a dangerous journey to rescue the bear from the Troll Queen, in this novel-length version of the Norwegian folktale "East of the Sun and West of the Moon." YALSA Top Ten Best Books for Young Adults, 2004.
Harcourt, 2003, 498 pp. (0-15-204563-5); Magic Carpet, 2005, pap., 516 pp. (0-15-205221-6)
(BL 1000:123; CCBB 57:73; HBG 15:113; Kirkus 71:1180; Kliatt Sep 2003 p. 10; SLJ Dec 2003 p. 158; VOYA 26:416)

6-329   PATTOU, Edith. *Hero's Song: The First Song of Eirren.* Gr. 6–10.
Young Colun is joined in his search for his missing sister, Nessa, by the bard Talisen, a master archer, and one of the Fair Folk. In *Fire Arrow: The Second Song of Eirren* (1998, 1999), master archer Brie inherits a magic fire arrow that leads her to seek revenge on her father's murderers.
Harcourt, 1991, 320 pp. (0-15-233807-1); Harcourt, 1998, pap., 333 pp. (0-152-01636-8)
(BL 88:429; CCBB 45:102; HBG 3:71; Kirkus 59:1406; SLJ Jan 1992 p. 137; VOYA 14:385)

6-330   PAXSON, Diana L. *The Book of the Spear.* **(The Hallowed Isle series, part 2).** Gr. 10 up.
Oesc, a Saxon warrior, opposes Arthur with a magic spear in this second volume of a four-part Arthurian saga. This book is preceded by *The Book of the Sword* (1999), and the sequels are *The Book of the Cauldron* (2000) and *The Book of the Stone* (2000).
Avon, 1999, pap., 200 pp. (0-380-80546-4)
(Kliatt Sep 1999 p. 28; SLJ Aug 1999 p. 188)

6-331   PAXSON, Diana L. *The Serpent's Tooth.* Gr. 10 up.
King Lear's youngest daughter tells the story of the king's marriages to three captive queens, the birth of his three daughters, and his betrayal by the older two, in this retelling of the King Lear legend set in Iron Age Britain.

Morrow, 1991, 394 pp. (0-688-08339-0)

(BL 87:2034, 2037; Kirkus 59:628)

6-332   PAXSON, Diana L. *The Wolf and the Raven*. (Wodan's Children trilogy,
☆   **vol. 1). Gr. 10 up.**

This story sets the scene for the tragic love affair between Brunahild, a 5th-century Hun princess studying sorcery, and Sigfrid, a royal youth apprenticed to a smith, in this retelling of the Germanic mythological saga. The sequels are *The Dragons of the Rhine* (1995) and *The Lord of Horses* (1996).

Morrow, 1993, 320 pp., o.p.; Avon, 1994, pap., 352 pp. (0-380-76526-8)

(BL 89:1298, 1308; Kirkus 61:89; LJ Mar 19, 1993 p. 111; SLJ Sep 1993 p. 263)

6-333   PAXSON, Diana L., and MARTINE-BARNES, Adrienne. *Master of*
***Earth and Water*. (Finn MacCool trilogy, vol. 1). Gr. 10 up.**

Fionn mac Cumhal (Finn MacCool), raised in the forest by a sorcerer and a warrior, discovers his magical powers and royal blood in this first volume of a trilogy based on Celtic mythology. The sequels are *The Shield Between the Worlds* (1994) and *Sword of Fire and Shadow* (1995).

Morrow, 1993, 416 pp. (0-688-12505-0)

(BL 89:1410, 1420; Kirkus 61:266; LJ Apr 15, 1993 p. 130)

PEARCE, (Ann) Philippa. *The Squirrel Wife*.
See Chapter 1, Allegorical Fantasy and Literary Fairy Tales.

6-334   PECK, Sylvia. *Seal Child*. Gr. 4–6.
☆   Molly's vacation friend, Meara, living on an island off the coast of Maine, has a sadness about her that Molly cannot understand until the day Meara saves Molly from drowning.

Illus. by Robert Andrew Parker, Morrow, 1989, 208 pp. (0-688-08682-9); Bantam, 1991, pap. (0-553-15868-6)

(BL 86:188; CCBB 43:91; HB 66:65; HBG 1:81; Kirkus 57:1479; SLJ Nov 1989 p. 112; Suth 4:321)

6-335   *The Pendragon Chronicles: Heroic Fantasy from the Time of King Arthur*.
☆   **Ed. by Mike Ashley. Gr. 10 up. (Orig. British pub. 1989.)**

A collection of Arthurian stories whose authors include Jane Yolen, Andre Norton, and John Steinbeck. *The Camelot Chronicles* (1992; see title entry above), *The Merlin Chronicles* (1995; see title entry above), *The Chronicles of the Holy Grail* (1996), and *The Chronicles of the Round Table* (1997) are companion volumes.

Bedrick, 1990, 417 pp. (0-87226-335-5), 1991, pap. (0-87226-228-6)

(BL 86:1688, 1694; Kliatt Sep 1991 p. 19; LJ Apr 15, 1990 p. 127; SLJ Aug 1990 p. 174; VOYA 13:232, 14:12)

6-336   PHILIP, Neil. *The Tale of Sir Gawain*. Gr. 6–10.

Elderly and wounded, Sir Gawain tells his young squire old tales of the Round Table: stories of magic, love, adventure, and betrayal.

Illus. by Charles Keeping, Putnam, 1987, 112 pp., o.p.

(BL 84:774 787; CCBB 41:73; HB 64:78; TLS 1987 p. 1261)

6-337   PHILLIPS, Ann. *The Oak King and the Ash Queen*. Gr. 6–8. (Orig. British
pub. 1984.)

Twelve-year-old English twins Dan and Daisy are reluctantly drawn into the battle between the Oak King and the Ash Queen, living trees fighting to preserve the natural balance of the forest.

Oxford University Press, 1985, 171 pp., o.p.

(BL 82:68; HB 61:458; SLJ Nov 1985 p. 100; VOYA 8:269)

6-338 **The Phoenix Tree: An Anthology of Myth Fantasy. Ed. by Robert H. Boyer and Kenneth J. Zahorski.** Gr. 10 up.

Sixteen short story retellings of myths, whose authors include Lord Dunsany, Richard Adams, Evangeline Walton, and Vera Chapman.

Avon, 1980, pap., 279 pp., o.p.

(BL 77:309, 322; Kliatt 15:20)

PIERCE, Meredith Ann. *Waters Luminous and Deep: Shorter Fictions.*
See Chapter 3, Fantasy Collections.

6-339 **PLUM-UCCI, Carol. *The She.*** Gr. 8–12.
✰ Orphaned 17-year-old Evan Barrett revisits his old seaside home to uncover the truth about his parents' deaths and about a legendary sea monster called The She, said to eat ships.

Harcourt, 2003, 288 pp. (0-15-216819-2)

(BL 100:239; CCBB 57:121; Kirkus 71:1180; Kliatt Sep 2003 p. 10; SLJ Oct 2003 p. 174; VOYA 26:405)

6-340 **POLLAND, Madeleine A(ngela Cahill). *Deirdre.*** Gr. 7–9.
Even though the old king keeps his daughter Deirdre imprisoned in a castle, she is unable to evade her tragic fate.

Illus. by Seon Morrison, Doubleday, 1967, 166 pp., o.p.

(BL 63:1050; CCBB 21:16; HB 43:465; Kirkus 35:424; TLS 1967 p. 1133)

POOLE, Josephine. *The Visitor: A Story of Suspense.*
See Chapter 12, Witchcraft and Sorcery Fantasy.

PRATCHETT, Terry. *The Amazing Maurice and His Educated Rodents.*
See Chapter 5, High Fantasy: Alternate Worlds or Histories.

6-341 **PRICE, Susan. *The Devil's Piper.*** Gr. 6–9. (Orig. British pub. 1973.)
✰ In this novel written by a 16-year-old girl, the parents of four children spirited off by a sly luchorpan ask the Devil for help in finding them.

Greenwillow, 1976, 216 pp., o.p.

(BL 72:981; HB 52:292; Kirkus 44:392; SLJ Apr 1976 p. 92; TLS 1973 p. 1429)

PRICE, Susan. *Ghost Dance: The Czar's Black Angel.*
See Chapter 12, Witchcraft and Sorcery Fantasy.

PRICE, Susan. *The Ghost Drum.*
See Chapter 12, Witchcraft and Sorcery Fantasy.

PRICE, Susan. *Ghost Song.*
See Chapter 12, Witchcraft and Sorcery Fantasy.

PRUE, Sally. *Cold Tom.*
See Chapter 9, Magic Adventure Fantasy.

6-342 **PULLMAN, Philip.** *I Was a Rat!* Gr. 4–7. (Orig. British pub. 1999.)
✶ The child adopted by elderly Bob and Joan insists that he was once a rat, but no one connects the boy to the fairy tale marriage of Prince Richard and Lady Aurelia, once known as Cinderella.
Illus. by Kevin Hawkes, Knopf, 2000, 192 pp. (0-375-90176-0); Dell, 2002, pap., 165 pp. (0-440-41661-2)
(BL 96:1023; CCBB 53:220; HB 76:82; HBG 11:310; Kirkus 67:1962; SLJ Mar 2000 p. 241, Dec 2000 p. 55; VOYA 22:241)

6-343 **PURTILL, Richard.** *Enchantment at Delphi.* Gr. 7–9.
Visiting Greece to further her studies of Greek mythology, Alice Grant is transported into ancient times by a strange mist and becomes involved in the struggle by the gods Apollo, Athena, and Dionysius to protect the Delphic oracle from the Dark Powers.
Harcourt, 1986, 149 pp., o.p.
(CCBB 40:74; Kirkus 54:1375; SLJ Nov 1986 p. 107)

6-344 **PYLE, Howard.** *The Merry Adventures of Robin Hood of Great Renown in Nottinghamshire.* Gr. 5 up. (Orig. pub. Scribner, 1883, 1911, 1931.)
Outlawed Robin Hood and his band, including Little John, Will Scarlett, and Friar Tuck, rob the wealthy to aid the poor and are pursued by the Sheriff of Nottingham.
Illus. by the author, Scribner, 1946, 1954, 212 pp., o.p.; Abdo, 2002, 238 pp. (1-57765-694-6); Chronicle, 2002, 173 pp. (0-8118-3399-2); illus. by Scott McKowen, Sterling, 2004, 344 pp. (1-4027-1456-4)
(BL 43:140; LJ 72:84 and 79)

6-345 **PYLE, Howard.** *The Story of King Arthur and His Knights.* Gr. 5–12.
✶✶ (Orig. pub. 1903.)
This is the first of a classic four-volume retelling of the Arthurian legends. The three companion volumes are *The Story of the Champions of the Round Table* (1905, 1968, 1984, 2004), *The Story of Sir Launcelot and His Companions* (1907, 1985, 1991), and *The Story of the Grail and the Passing of Arthur* (1910, 1985, 1992).
Illus. by the author, Scribner, 1903, 1933, 312 pp., o.p.; illus. by the author, Macmillan, 1984 (repr. of 1903 ed.), 320 pp. (0-684-14814-5); Signet, 1986, pap. (0-451-52488-8); Peter Smith, 1990 (0-8446-2766-6); Abdo, 2002, 238 pp. (1-57765-691-1), entitled *King Arthur and the Knights of the Round Table*
(BL 80:1392, 1401; HB 60:359; Kliatt 20:28)

6-346 **RAYNER, William.** *Stag Boy.* Gr. 7–10. (Orig. British pub. 1972.)
✶ Whenever Jim Hooper wears an ancient stag-horn helmet, he is transformed into a huge black stag.
Harcourt, 1973, 160 pp., o.p.
(BL 69:902, 909; HB 49:387; Kirkus 4:259; LJ 98:1692; TLS 1972 p. 1318)

6-347 **REAVES, Michael.** *Street Magic.* Gr. 10 up.
Danny Thayer, a 16-year-old runaway living on the San Francisco streets, discovers he is a fairy changeling after he meets the scatterlings, who are runaways from Faerie.

Tor, 1991, 320 pp. (0-312-85125-1)

(BL 87:2034, 2037; Kirkus 59:640; LJ June 15, 1991 p. 109; SLJ Apr 1991 p. 164)

6-348 REEVES, James (pseud. of John Morris Reeves). *Maildun the Voyager.*
Gr. 4–6. (Orig. British pub. 1971.)
A retelling of an Irish legend about a young man who sails beyond the Western
Isles to avenge his father's murder.
Illus. by Rocco Negri, Walck, 1972, 104 pp., o.p.

(HB 48:464; Kirkus 40:1104; LJ 97:4074)

6-349 RENAULT, Mary (pseud. of Mary Challans). *The King Must Die.* Gr. 10
☆   up.
Seventeen-year-old King Theseus joins a group of young people conscripted to
become bull dancers on the island of Crete, where he becomes renowned at the
dangerous sport and manages to overthrow the Cretan Kingdom. The sequel is
The Bull from the Sea (1962).
Pantheon, 1958, 1980 (0-394-43195-2); Vintage, 1988, pap., 352 pp. (0-394-
75104-3); Arrow, 2004, pap., 384 pp. (0-09-946352-0)

(BL 54:574, 587; Kirkus 26:341; LJ 83:2053; TLS 1958 p. 528)

6-350 RICE, Robert. *The Last Pendragon.* Gr. 10 up.
Eleven years after King Arthur's death, Bedwyr, the last of his knights, travels
through Britain giving aid to the tribes who are battling the Saxons and completing Arthur's final request to find his sword, Caliburn, and cast it into the lake.
Walker, 1991, 209 pp. (0-8027-1180-4)

(Kirkus 59:1428; SLJ May 1992 p. 152)

6-351 RICHARDSON, Bill. *After Hamelin.* Gr. 5–8.
Penelope's deafness leaves her immune to the Pied Piper's spell, and her gift
of Deep Dreaming allows her to rescue Hamelin's lost children from the
enchanter.
Annick, 2000, 227 pp. (1-55037-629-2); Firefly, 2001, pap., 227 pp. (1-55037-
628-4)

(BL 97:1139; Kirkus 68:1550; SLJ Apr 2001 p. 148; VOYA 24:14, 56)

RINALDI, Ann. *Millicent's Gift.*
See Chapter 9, Magic Adventure Fantasy.

6-352 RIORDAN, James. *King Arthur.* Gr. 5–7. (Orig. British pub. 1998.)
This version of the Arthurian legend focuses mainly on the beginning and end
of Arthur's life.
Illus. by Victor G. Ambrus, Oxford University Press, 1998, 96 pp. (0-19-
274176-4)

(BL 965:330; VOYA 21:368)

6-353 ROBBINS, Ruth. *Taliesin and King Arthur.* Gr. 3–5.
☆   When the young poet Taliesin tells the magical story of his birth at the Grand
Contest of Poets, King Arthur proclaims him the greatest bard of all.
Illus. by the author, Parnassus, 1970, 31 pp., o.p.

(BL 67:452; CCBB 24:98; HB 47:166; Kirkus 38:1288; LJ 96:1119)

6-354 **ROBERSON, Jennifer.** *Lady of the Forest.* **(Sherwood Forest series, bk. 1).** Gr. 10 up.
A romantic adventure based on the legend of Robin Hood, set in 13th-century England. The sequel is *Lady of Sherwood* (1999, 2000).
Zebra, 1992, 608 pp. (0-8217-3919-0)
(BL 88:1899, 1900; Kirkus 60:876; LJ Aug 1992 p. 152)

ROBERTS, Nora. *Key of Light.*
See Chapter 9, Magic Adventure Fantasy.

6-355 **ROGASKY, Barbara,** adapt. *The Golem: A Version.* Gr. 4–8.
✰ A novel-length retelling of the 16th-century Jewish legend about the giant man created by Rabbi Loew to protect the Jews of Prague from anti-Semitic persecution.
Illus. by Trina Schart Hyman, Holiday, 1996, 96 pp. (0-8234-0964-3)
(BL 93:335; CCBB 50:27; HBG 8:74; Kirkus 64:1407; SLJ Oct 1996 p. 126)

6-356 **ROOT, Phyllis.** *The Listening Silence.* Gr. 4–7.
Orphaned 13-year-old Kiri, raised by Mali the village healer, goes into the wilderness on a vision quest to understand her ability to send her spirit into other people and animals.
Harper, 1992, 106 pp. LB (0-06-025093-3)
(BL 88:1380; CCBB 45:191; HBG 3:269; Kirkus 60:616; SLJ June 1992 p. 125)

ROSENBERG, Joel. *The Fire Duke.*
See Chapter 7, High Fantasy: Travel to Other Worlds.

RUSH, Alison. *The Last of Danu's Children.*
See Chapter 7, High Fantasy: Travel to Other Worlds.

6-357 **RUSSELL, Barbara Timberlake.** *The Taker's Stone.* Gr. 6–10.
Teenage Fischer is bullied into stealing some of the magical stones hidden from Belial by Keeper Solomon, setting in motion a confrontation between the forces of good and evil at the exact center of the United States in 1811.
DK/Kroupa, 1999, 231 pp. (0-7894-2568-8)
(BL 96:515, 1546; CCBB 53:105; HBG 11:97; Kirkus 67:1651; SLJ Dec 1999 p. 140; VOYA 22:273)

6-358 **SABERHAGEN, Fred.** *Dancing Bears.* Gr. 10 up.
American big-game hunter John Sherwood's visit to tsarist Russia pits him against a legendary shape-changing, man-eating bear.
Tor, 1996, 352 pp. (0-312-85798-5)
(BL 92:799, 802; LJ Dec 1995 p. 163)

6-359 **SABERHAGEN, Fred.** *The Face of Apollo: The First Book of the Gods.* **(Book of the Gods, vol. 1).** Gr. 10 up.
A fierce battle between Apollo and Hades results in the sun god entering 15-year-old Jeremy Redthorn's body, improving his love life and giving him power over his enemies. The sequels are *Ariadne's Web* (2000), *The Arms of Hercules* (2000), *God of the Golden Fleece* (2001), and *Gods of Fire and Thunder* (2002). This series is a prequel to the author's Lost Swords series (see

The First Book of Lost Swords: Woundhealer's Story in Chapter 5, High Fantasy: Alternate Worlds or Histories).
Tor, 1998, pap., 384 pp. (0-312-86623-2), 1999, pap. (0-812-57189-4)
(BL 94:1307; Kirkus 66:161; LJ Jan 1998 p. 149; VOYA 21:447)

6-360 SABUDA, Robert, adapt. *Arthur and the Sword.* Gr. 1–4.
The story of King Arthur's life, from pulling Excalibur from the anvil to becoming king of England, illustrated with stained-glass-like images.
Illus. by the adaptor, Atheneum, 1995, 32 pp. (0-689-31987-8)
(BL 92:478; HBG 7:94; Kirkus 63:1500)

6-361 SALSITZ, R(hodi) A. V(ilott). *The Twilight Gate.* Gr. 6–10.
While their mother undergoes chemotherapy, George, 15, Leigh, 13, and Mindy, 5, spend the summer with their mother's ex-husband and accidentally unleash magical forces of good and evil. This author also writes as R. A. V. Salsitz.
Illus. by Alan M. Clark, Walker, 1993, 181 pp. (0-8027-8213-2)
(BL 89:1506; CCBB 46:357; HBG 4:312; Kirkus 61:379; SLJ May 1993 p. 108; VOYA 16:104, 170)

6-362 SAMPSON, Fay. *Pangur Ban: The White Cat.* **(The Pangur Ban Celtic Fantasies series, bk. 2).** Gr. 5–8. (Orig. British pub. 1989.)
The shape-shifting white cat Pangur Ban must rescue his friends—Niall, the artist monk bewitched by mermaids, and Princess Finnglas of Wales, captured by a terrifying sea monster—in this story adapted from Celtic myth and the 9th-century Welsh poem, "Pangur Ban." *Shape-Shifter: The Naming of Pangur Ban* (1989, 2003) is the first book in the series, followed by *Finnglas of the Horses* (1989, 2003), *Finnglas and the Stones of Choosing* (1989, 2003), and *The Serpent of Senargad* (British pub. 1989).
Lion, 2003 (0-6138-7257-6), pap., 154 pp. (0-7459-4762-X)
(BL 99:1662; SLJ Nov 2003 p. 146)

6-363 SAN SOUCI, Robert D. *Young Merlin.* Gr. 2–5.
This is the story of Merlin's childhood and youth, culminating in his creation of Stonehenge and his vision of Arthur's future greatness. Companion volumes include *Young Guinevere* (1993), *Young Lancelot* (1996), and *Young Arthur* (1997).
Illus. by Daniel R. Home, Doubleday, 1990, 32 pp. (0-385-24800-8)
(BL 86:1990; HBG 1:276; Kirkus 58:880; SLJ Sep 1990 p. 220)

6-364 SARGENT, Sarah. *Lure of the Dark.* Gr. 7–10.
The empty home life of 14-year-old Ginny, with an alcoholic mother and an indifferent father, leaves her vulnerable to the dark power of Loki, the Norse god in wolf form, who tempts her toward suicide.
Four Winds, 1984, 118 pp., o.p.
(BL 80:1551; CCBB 37:191; SLJ Aug 1984 p. 86; VOYA 7:332)

6-365 SARGENT, Sarah. *Watermusic.* Gr. 6–9.
A haunting story in which Laura's flute-playing brings a huge white bat and a female ogre to life, whose battle symbolizes the struggle between love and intellect.

Clarion, 1986, 120 pp., o.p.

(BL 82:1087; CCBB 39:195; SLJ May 1986 p. 109)

6-366   SATHRE, Vivian. *Slender Ella and Her Fairy Hogfather.* Gr. 1–4.
☆   All of the characters in this version of "Cinderella" are pigs, including the fairy hogfather who helps Slender Ella go to the hoedown and marry the wealthy rancher.
Illus. by Sally Anne Lambert, Delacorte, 1999, 48 pp. (0-385-32516-9); Dell, 1999, pap. (0-440-41397-4)

(BL 95:1338; CCBB 52:294; HBG 10:284; Kirkus 68:71; SLJ June 1999 p. 107)

6-367   SCARBOROUGH, Elizabeth Ann. *The Healer's War: A Fantasy Novel of Vietnam.* Gr. 11 up.
Army nurse Kitty McCully is given an amulet by an old Vietnamese mystic that enables her to see people's auras, understand their true motives, and heal them, in this novel for mature readers set during the Vietnam War. Nebula Award, Best Novel, 1990.
Doubleday, 1988, 303 pp., o.p.

(BL 85:450, 471; Kirkus 56:1366; VOYA 12:118, 13:72)

6-368   SCHILLER, Barbara, adapt. *Erec and Enid.* Gr. 3–5.
☆   A retelling based on Arthurian legend from the French of Chretien de Troyes, in which Erec, a knight of Arthur's court, battles a cruel knight who mistreated Guinevere's attendants and wins the hand of Enid.
Trans. by the adapter, illus. by Ati Forberg, Dutton, 1970, 48 pp., o.p.

(BL 67:423; CCBB 24:144; HB 46:612; Kirkus 38:1158; LJ 95:4326, 4355)

6-369   SCHILLER, Barbara, adapt. *The Kitchen Knight.* Gr. 3–4.
☆   King Arthur's nephew, Gareth, proves himself worthy of becoming a knight by laboring for a year as a palace kitchen boy, in this story adapted from Sir Thomas Malory's *Le Morte d'Arthur*. *The Wandering Knight* (Dutton, 1971; see below) is a companion volume that retells the story of young Lancelot.
Illus. by Nonny Hogrogian, Holt, 1965, 64 pp., o.p.

(HB 41:277; Kirkus 33:374; LJ 90:3122)

6-370   SCHILLER, Barbara, adapt. *The Wandering Knight.* Gr. 4–6.
Sir Lancelot du Lac battles and bests many knights in his search for adventure, in this story adapted from Sir Thomas Malory's *Le Morte d'Arthur*. *The Kitchen Knight* (Holt, 1965; see above) is a companion volume.
Illus. by Herschel Levit, Dutton, 1971, 55 pp., o.p.

(CCBB 25:163; Kirkus 39:880; LJ 96:3470)

6-371   SCHMIDT, Gary D. *Straw into Gold.* Gr. 5–9.
☆   Furious that young Tousle has tried to halt the execution of rebel prisoners, the King declares that he will spare their lives only if Tousle and the blind rebel, Innis, solve a riddle, in this sequel to the story "Rumpelstiltskin."
Clarion, 2001, 172 pp. (0-618-05601-7)

(BL 97:2108; CCBB 55:35; HBG 12:326; SLJ Aug 2001 p. 188; VOYA 24:451, 25:16)

6-372   SCHREIBER, Ellen. *Teenage Mermaid.* Gr. 5–8.
In this humorous tale, surfer Spencer is rescued from drowning by a mermaid named Waterlilly, and the two 15-year-olds fall in love.

HarperCollins, 2003, 160 pp. (0-06-008205-4)

(BL 99:1881; CCBB 57:34; HBG 14:375; SLJ Aug 2003 p. 166; VOYA 26:242;)

6-373 SEREDY, Kate. *The White Stag.* Gr. 5–8.
The white stag and the red eagle help guide Hunor, Magyar, Bendeguz, Attila, and their people to found the land of Hungary. John Newbery Medal, 1938.
Illus. by the author, Viking, 1937, 94 pp., o.p.

(BL 34:197; HB 13:366, 378; LJ 62:807, 63:34, 691)

6-374 SERRAILLIER, Ian (Lucien). *The Challenge of the Green Knight.* Gr.
★ 6–9. (Orig. British pub. 1966.)
Gawain of Camelot is tested by a huge green knight who allows Gawain to behead him, then picks up his head and vows to return in 12 months to strike an exchange blow.
Illus. by Victor G. Ambrus, Walck, 1976, 56 pp., o.p.

(BL 64:275, 329; CCBB 21:84; HB 43:466; Kirkus 35:653; LJ 92:3204; TLS 1966 p. 1078)

6-375 SERVICE, Pamela F. *Weirdos of the Universe, Unite!* Gr. 5–7.
★ Researching a school essay on mythology, Mandy and Owen accidentally bring to life the mythical figures Baba Yaga, Coyote, the Horned King, Siegfried, and Lung Nu the Chinese Dragon Princess, all of whom enlist Mandy and Owen's aid in saving the earth from alien invaders.
Macmillan, 1992, 160 pp. (0-689-31746-8); Fawcett, 1993, pap. (0-449-70429-7)

(BL 88:1603; CCBB 45:278; HBG 3:270; Kirkus 60:260; SLJ June 1992 p. 125; VOYA 15:179)

SERVICE, Pamela F. *When the Night Wind Howls.*
See Chapter 12, Witchcraft and Sorcery Fantasy.

6-376 SERVICE, Pamela F. *Winter of Magic's Return.* Gr. 5–8.
★ Welly and Heather befriend a young man who has lost his memory and become embroiled in a struggle to awaken King Arthur and save Britain from evil. In *Tomorrow's Magic* (1987, 1988), a youthful Merlin and King Arthur appear from the past and join Heather and Welly in an attempt to use magic to unite Britain.
Atheneum, 1985, 192 pp., o.p.

(BL 82:269; CCBB 39:56; HB 61:742; Kliatt 21:25; SLJ Dec 1985 p. 94)

6-377 SEYMOUR, Miranda (pseud. of Miranda Sinclair). *Medea.* Gr. 10 up.
Three narrators—Jason, Aegeus, and Medea—tell this dramatic story of the king's daughter who agrees to become the priestess of Hecate, goddess of death, in exchange for promised political power; falls in love with Jason; and finally loses any chance for love or for power.
St. Martin's, 1982, 248 pp., o.p.

(Kirkus 50:299; LJ 107:1013; SLJ Dec 1982 p. 88)

6-378 SHANNON, Mark. *Gawain and the Green Knight.* Gr. K–4.
Gawain, the youngest of King Arthur's knights, challenges the monstrous Green Knight in this retelling of the Celtic tale.
Illus. by David Shannon, Putnam, 1994, 30 pp. (0-399-22446-7)

(BL 90:1832; HBG 6:110; Kirkus 62:1281)

6-379 SHERMAN, Josepha. *Child of Faerie, Child of Earth.* Gr. 6–10.
Mistreated by her father, the Count d'Aulnoy, and his toadlike new wife, Graciosa is tempted to return the love of Percinet, half-mortal son of the Queen of Faerie, and flee with him to the Faerie realm, in this adaptation of one of Madame d'Aulnoy's French fairy tales.
Illus. by Rick Farley, Walker, 1992, 176 pp. (0-8027-8112-8)
(BL 88:1107; HBG 3:277; Kirkus 60:398; SLJ May 1992 p. 134; VOYA 15:47)

6-380 SHERMAN, Josepha. *King's Son, Magic's Son.* Gr. 10 up.
The newly crowned king meets Aidan, his magician half-brother, for the first time, after Aidan's dying mother makes him promise to aid his brother, in this folkloric version of the tale of two brothers who fall in love with the same princess.
Baen, 1994, pap., 323 pp. (0-671-87602-3)
(BL 90:1781, 1787; Kliatt Sep 1994 p. 22)

6-381 *Sherwood: Original Stories from the World of Robin Hood.* **Ed. by Jane**
★ **(Hyatt) Yolen (Stemple).** Gr. 5–9.
Eight short stories related to the Robin Hood legend, written by Nancy Springer, Mary Frances Zambreno, Jane Yolen, and others.
Illus. by Dennis Nolan, Philomel, 2000, 134 pp. (0-399-23182-X); Puffin, 2002, pap., 134 pp. (0-698-11953-3)
(CCBB 54:42; HBG 11:386; Kirkus 68:806; SLJ Aug 2000 p. 192; VOYA 23:128, 24:14)

6-382 SHWARTZ, Susan. *The Grail of Hearts.* Gr. 10 up.
In this version of the Arthurian tale of Parsival, set in 1st-century Jerusalem, a woman named Kundry is condemned to wander the earth until the guardian of the Holy Grail, a wise fool named Parsifal, saves her and protects the Grail from an evil sorcerer.
Tor, 1992, 308 pp. (0-312-85176-6), 1993, pap. (0-8125-5409-4)
(BL 88:916, 923; Kirkus 59:1503; LJ Dec 1991 p. 202; VOYA 15:243)

6-383 SILVERBERG, Robert. *Gilgamesh the King.* Gr. 10 up.
★ Young Gilgamesh grows to manhood, is crowned king, and must eventually face his own mortality in this powerful retelling of the 5,000-year-old Sumerian epic.
Arbor House, 1984, 290 pp., o.p.
(BL 81:3, 5; Kirkus 52:874; LJ 109:1980)

SILVERMAN, Maida. *The Magic Well.*
See Chapter 1, Allegorical Fantasy and Literary Fairy Tales.

6-384 SINGER, Isaac Bashevis. *The Golem.* Gr. 5–7.
★ A clay giant named Joseph is brought to life to protect the endangered Jews of Prague.
Illus. by Uri Shulevitz, Farrar, 1982, 96 pp., o.p.; illus. by Uri Shulevitz, Farrar, 1996, 96 pp. (0-374-42746-1)
(BL 79:504, 980; CCBB 36:97; HB 59:48, 331; Kirkus 50:1237; SLJ Dec 1982 p. 68; Suth 3:394; TLS 1983 p. 776)

SINGER, Marilyn. *The Circus Lunicus.*
See Chapter 9, Magic Adventure Fantasy.

6-385 **SKURZYNSKI, Gloria (Joan).** *What Happened in Hamelin.* Gr. 5–7.
✮ A charismatic stranger with a silvery flute lures the rats and then the children out of the village of Hamelin, in this retelling of the legend as seen through the eyes of Geist, an orphaned baker's apprentice.
Four Winds, 1979, 177 pp., o.p.; Random, 1993, pap., 192 pp. (0-679-83645-4)
(BL 76:669; CCBB 33:119; HB 56:57; Kirkus 47:1376; SLJ Jan 1980 p. 75)

6-386 **SLOAN, Carolyn.** *The Sea Child.* Gr. 5–7. (Orig. British pub. 1987.)
Jessie's father knows that her mother, Mara, will soon call 10-year-old Jessie to her from their isolated seaside home, so he tries to introduce his daughter, who swims like a mermaid and does not feel the cold, to other mainland children in hopes of keeping her with him.
Holiday, 1988, 128 pp., o.p.
(BL 85:942; CCBB 42:84; HB 65:75; Kirkus 56:1328; SLJ Oct 1988 p. 148; Suth 4:385)

6-387 **SMITH, Doris Buchanan.** *Voyages.* Gr. 5–8. (Orig. British pub. 1989.)
✮ Twelve-year-old Janessa retreats from the terrifying memories of her abduction and injuries during a robbery by traveling on an origami boat from her hospital bed to Asgard, home of the Norse gods.
Viking, 1980, 176 pp., o.p., 1991, pap. (0-14-032224-8)
(BL 86:558; CCBB 43:148; HB 66:203; HBG 1:81; Kirkus 57:1332; SLJ Nov 1989 p. 114)

SMITH, L(isa) J. *Night of the Solstice.*
See Chapter 7, High Fantasy: Travel to Other Worlds.

6-388 **SNEVE, Virginia Driving Hawk.** *The Trickster and the Troll.* Gr. 3–6.
Two legendary characters, a giant Norwegian troll and Iktomi, the Lakota trickster, become friends because both of their peoples are abandoning belief in folk heroes.
University of Nebraska, 1997, 110 pp. (0-8032-4261-1)
(BL 93:236; LJ July 1997 p. 92; SLJ Dec 1997 p. 146)

6-389 *Snow White, Blood Red.* **Ed. by Ellen Datlow and Terri Windling.** Gr. 11 up.
Dark, often violent versions of familiar tales, and reworkings of folktale themes, written by Patricia McKillip, Jane Yolen, Tanith Lee, Charles de Lint, Esther Friesner, and others. The editors have compiled five companion volumes: *Black Thorn, White Rose* (1994, 2001), *Ruby Slippers, Golden Tears* (1995), *Black Swan, White Raven* (1997, 1998), *Silver Birch, Blood Moon* (1999), and *Black Heart, Ivory Bones* (2000). The editors have also compiled two collections of retold tales for readers in grades 6–10: *A Wolf at the Door, and Other Retold Fairy Tales* (Simon, 2000; see title entry below) and *Swan Sister: Fairy Tales Retold* (Simon, 2003; see below).
Morrow, 1993, 432 pp. (0-688-10913-6); Eos, 1995, pap., 432 pp., o.p.
(BL 89:879; Kirkus 60:1711)

6-390 **SNYDER, Midori.** *The Flight of Michael McBride.* Gr. 10 up.
Michael confronts vengeful Irish fairies who have followed him from Boston to the 1870s western frontier to punish him for his mother's marriage to a human.

Tor, 1994, 320 pp. (0-312-85410-2)
(LJ Oct 15, 1994 p. 90; VOYA 18:110)

SNYDER, Zilpha Keatley. *The Truth About Stone Hollow.*
See Chapter 4, Ghost Fantasy.

6-391 **SPINNER, Stephanie.** *Quiver.* Gr. 7–10.
★ A novelized version of the Greek myth of Atalanta who, raised by a she-bear after abandonment by her royal father, becomes a great runner and swears to marry only the man who can best her in a foot race.
Knopf, 2002, 176 pp. (0-375-81489-2); Laurel Leaf, 2005, pap., 192 pp. (0-440-23819-6)
(BL 99:870; CCBB 56:251; HB 79:85; HBG 13:99; Kirkus 70:1321; SLJ Oct 2002 p. 172; VOYA 25:402, 26:14)

SPRINGER, Nancy. *The Friendship Song.*
See Chapter 7, High Fantasy: Travel to Other Worlds.

6-392 **SPRINGER, Nancy.** *I Am Mordred: A Tale from Camelot.* Gr. 7–10.
★★ Mordred, son of King Arthur and his half-sister, Morgause, desperately tries to evade his fate as his father's murderer, embarking on a dangerous quest to seek advice from Merlin. *I Am Morgan Le Fay: A Tale from Camelot* (2001, 2002; see below) is a companion volume.
Philomel, 1998, 184 pp., o.p.; Firebird/Penguin, 2002, pap., 185 pp. (0-698-11841-3)
(BL 94:1439, 1618, 95:782,, 96:1545; CCBB 51:375; HB 74:219; HBG 9:339; Kirkus 66:62; Kliatt Sep 1998 p. 12; SLJ May 1998 p. 149; VOYA 21:61)

6-393 **SPRINGER, Nancy.** *I Am Morgan Le Fay: A Tale from Camelot.* Gr.
★ 6–10.
Arthur's half-sister, Morgan, bitterly retells the story of her life, from the murder of her father by Arthur's father when she was 6 to her jealous vow to destroy the king. *I Am Mordred: A Tale from Camelot* (1998, 2002; see above) is a companion volume.
Philomel, 2001, 224 pp. (0-399-23451-9); Firebird/Penguin, 2002, pap., 227 pp. (0-698-11974-6)
(BL 97:1046; CCBB 54:315; HB 77:96; HBG 12:326; Kirkus 69:50; Kliatt May 2001 p. 14; SLJ Mar 2001 p. 256; VOYA 23:436, 24:14)

6-394 **SPRINGER, Nancy.** *Rowan Hood: Outlaw Girl of Sherwood Forest.*
★ **(Rowan Hood trilogy, bk. 1).** Gr. 4–8.
Rosemary, 13, disguises herself as a boy named Rowan to search for her unknown father, the outlaw Robin Hood, after the murder of her healer mother. In *Lion Claw* (2002), gentle Lionel, Rowan's friend, stands up to his tyrannical father, Lord Lionclaw, and attempts to rescue Rowan after her capture by hunters. In *Outlaw Princess of Sherwood* (2003), runaway Princess Ettie has spent a year hiding in Sherwood Forest to avoid an arranged marriage, when her father, King Solon, tries to trap her by imprisoning the queen within a gilded cage. In *Wild Boy: A Tale of Rowan Hood* (2004), Rook, the young "wild boy" of Sherwood Forest, wavers between pity and a thirst for vengeance after he finds the Sheriff of Nottingham's son, Tod, caught in a trap. The series concludes with *Rowan Hood Returns: The Final Chapters* (2005).

Philomel, 2001, 170 pp. (0-399-23368-7); Penguin/Putnam, 2002, pap. (0-698-11972-X)

(BL 97:1561, 98:1417; CCBB 55:36; HBG 12:316; Kirkus 69:506; Kliatt May 2001 p. 14; SLJ July 2001 p. 114; VOYA 24:136)

STEINBECK, John (Ernst), reteller. *The Acts of King Arthur and His Noble Knights from the Winchester Manuscripts of Thomas Malory and Other Sources.*
See Malory, Sir Thomas. *Le Morte d'Arthur*, above.

6-395 **STEPHENS, James.** *Deirdre.* Gr. 8 up. (Orig. British and U.S. pub. Macmil-
☆ lan, 1923.)
King Conachur raises Deirdre in exile to evade a fateful prophecy, but his jealousy of Deirdre's love for another man brings about the very tragedy he had sought to avoid, in this retelling of an Irish legend.
Illus. by Nonny Hogrogian, Macmillan, 1970, 202 pp., o.p.; Arden, 1978 (repr. of 1924 ed.), o.p.
(BL 20:103; HB 46:395; Kirkus 38:331; LJ 95:1957; TLS 1923 p. 618)

STEPHENS, James. *In the Land of Youth.*
See Chapter 7, High Fantasy: Travel to Other Worlds.

6-396 **STEWART, Mary (Florence Elinor).** *The Crystal Cave.* **(Merlin trilogy,**
☆☆ **vol. 1).** Gr. 10 up. (Orig. British pub. 1970.)
In this first volume of Stewart's Arthurian trilogy, young Merlin has a difficult childhood at the court of the King of Wales, where he is trained in magic by a learned wizard and eventually becomes involved in efforts to unite all of Britain. Mythopoeic Fantasy Award, 1971. In *The Hollow Hills* (Morrow, 1973; Fawcett, 1984; Eos, 2003), Merlin brings up young Arthur and helps him search for the magical sword, Caliburn. Mythopoeic Fantasy Award, 1974. *The Last Enchantment* (Morrow, 1979; Fawcett, 1984; Eos, 2003) deals with Arthur's reign and Merlin's death. *Mary Stewart's Merlin Trilogy* (Morrow, 1980, 919 pp. [0-688-00347-8]) contains all three books. *The Wicked Day* (orig. British pub. 1983; Morrow, 1984; Eos, 2003) is a related work in which Arthur's illegitimate son, Mordred, brings about the prophesied "wicked day," after he is left in charge of the kingdom while Arthur battles the Romans in Brittany.
Morrow, 1970, 521 pp., o.p.; Fawcett, 1989, pap., 384 pp. (0-449-20644-0); Eos, 2003, pap., 512 pp. (0-06-054825-8)
(BL 67:287, 305, 655; HB 46:503; Kirkus 38:528; LJ 95:2830, 3082, 4328)

6-397 **STORR, Catherine (Cole).** *Thursday.* Gr. 7–10. (Orig. British pub. 1971.)
Bee Earnshaw believes that it was Thursday Townsend's involvement with the fairy folk, and not a nervous breakdown, that made Thursday so lonely and withdrawn.
Harper, 1972, 274 pp., o.p.
(BL 69:295, 303; HB 49:148; Kirkus 40:730; LJ 97:3465)

6-398 **SUTCLIFF, Rosemary.** *Black Ships Before Troy: The Story of the Iliad.*
☆ Gr. 5–9. (Orig. British pub. 1993.)
The war between the Greeks and the Trojans begins with Aphrodite's role in Helen's flight from Greece with her Trojan lover, Paris, and ends with the

bloody siege of Troy. The story continues with *The Wanderings of Odysseus: The Story of the Odyssey* (1996).

Illus. by Alan Lee, Delacorte, 1993, 128 pp. (0-385-31069-2)

(BL 90:439, 1357; CCBB 47:169; HBG 5:110; Kirkus 61:1337; Kliatt Sep 1996 p. 3; SLJ Jan 1994 p. 130, June 1994 p. 52)

6-399 **SUTCLIFF, Rosemary.** *The Sword and the Circle: King Arthur and the* ☆☆ *Knights of the Round Table.* **(Arthur trilogy, bk. 1).** Gr. 6–10. (Orig. British pub. 1981.)

Thirteen Arthurian stories retold mainly from Sir Thomas Malory's *Le Morte d'Arthur* (see Malory, above), involving King Arthur, Merlin, Sir Lancelot, and Morgan La Fay. Sutcliff's trilogy of Arthurian retellings continues with *The Light Beyond the Forest: The Quest for the Holy Grail* (orig. British pub. 1979; U.S. 1980, 1994), which retells the adventures of Gawain, Bors, Percival, Lancelot, and Galahad as they search for the Holy Grail. In *The Road to Camlann: The Death of King Arthur* (orig. British pub. 1981; U.S. 1982, 1994), Mordred, Arthur's illegitimate son, undermines the relationship of Arthur, Guenevere, and Lancelot, to bring about the tragic end of the company of the Round Table. Boston Globe Horn Book Award Honor Book in Fiction, 1983.

Dutton, 1981, 261 pp., o.p.; Puffin, 1994, pap. (0-14-037149-4)

(BL 78:644, 655, 86:906; CCBB 35:96; HB 58:59; Kirkus 50:141; SLJ Jan 1981 p. 90; Suth 3:416; TLS 1981 p. 341)

6-400 **SUTCLIFF, Rosemary.** *Sword at Sunset.* Gr. 10 up. (Orig. British pub. ☆ 1963.)

Artos the Bear leads his people to thrust back the barbarian invaders of Britain in this version of the Arthurian legend.

Coward, 1963, 495 pp., o.p.; Tor, 1987, pap., o.p.

(BL 59:814, 822; HB 39:634; LJ 88:2786, 2930; TLS 1963 p. 473)

6-401 **SUTCLIFF, Rosemary.** *Tristan and Iseult.* Gr. 5–9. (Orig. British pub. ☆ 1971.)

A poetic retelling of the legendary love story of Tristan and Iseult. Carnegie Medal Highly Commended Book, 1971; Boston Globe Horn Book Award, 1972.

Dutton, 1971, 150 pp., o.p.; Farrar, 1991, pap., o.p.

(BL 68:431, 435, 670; CCBB 25:129; HB 47:620; Kirkus 39:1015; TLS 1971 p. 764)

6-402 *Swan Sister: Fairy Tales Retold.* **Ed. by Ellen Datlow and Terri Windling.** ☆ Gr. 6–9.

Thirteen original stories related to traditional folk- and fairy tales, written by Bruce Coville, Midori Snyder, Nina Kiriki Hoffman, Jane Yolen, and others. This is a companion volume to *A Wolf at the Door: And Other Retold Fairy Tales* (2000; see title entry below). The editors have also compiled six volumes of dark retellings for older readers in grades 10 up: *Snow White, Blood Red* (1993, 1995; see title entry above), *Black Thorn, White Rose* (1994, 2001), *Ruby Slippers, Golden Tears* (1995), *Black Swan, White Raven* (1997, 1998), *Silver Birch, Blood Moon* (1999), and *Black Heart, Ivory Bones* (2000).

Simon, 2003, 176 pp. (0-689-84613-4); Aladdin, 2005, pap., 176 pp. (0-689-87837-0)

(BL 100:232; CCBB 57:97; Kirkus 71:1121; SLJ Dec 2003 p. 148)

SWOPE, Sam. *Jack and the Seven Deadly Giants.*
See Chapter 5, High Fantasy: Alternate Worlds or Histories.

6-403 **SYNGE, (Phyllis) Ursula.** *Land of Heroes: A Retelling of the Kalevala.* Gr.
✮ 6 up. (Orig. British pub. 1977, entitled *Kalevala*.)
Three magician-heroes—Vainamoinen the singer, Ilmarinen the smith, and
Lemminkainen the rogue—vie for the hand of the beautiful daughter of the
sorcerer, Mistress Louhi, in this retelling of Finnish folklore.
Atheneum, 1978, 222 pp., o.p.
(BL 74:1342, 1355; CCBB 32:55; HB 54:289; SLJ Sep 1978 p. 150; TLS 1977 p. 1410)

6-404 **SYNGE, (Phyllis) Ursula.** *Swan's Wing.* Gr. 7 up. (Orig. British pub. 1981.)
In this extension of Hans Christian Andersen's story *The Wild Swans* (see
Chapter 1, Allegorical Fantasy and Literary Fairy Tales), Lothar, the self-cen-
tered 11th Prince who retained a swan's wing instead of one arm, Gerda, the
goose-girl who loves him, and Matthew, a tormented sculptor in love with
Gerda, travel the land in search of a cure for Lothar's affliction.
Bodley Head, 1984, 155 pp., o.p.
(BL 81:436, 451; SLJ Mar 1985 p. 183; VOYA 8:366)

6-405 **SYNGE, (Phyllis) Ursula.** *Weland, Smith of the Gods.* Gr. 5–8. (Orig.
British pub. 1972.)
Physically handicapped Weland and his brothers ignore their mother's warn-
ings and leave home to find the Valkyries in this retelling of Norse myth from
the Icelandic poetic Edda.
Illus. by Charles Keeping, Phillips, 1973, 94 pp. (0-87599-200-5)
(BL 70:335, 343; LJ 99:577; TLS 1972 p. 1322)

6-406 **TALBOTT, Hudson, adapt.** *King Arthur: The Sword in the Stone.* **(Tales
of King Arthur, bk. 1).** Gr. 2–5.
A shortened version of King Arthur's life from birth to coronation, centered
around the tournament where he pulls the sword from a stone to help his broth-
er, Kay. The companion volumes are *King Arthur and the Round Table* (1995),
Excalibur (1996), and *Lancelot* (1999).
Illus. by the adapter, Morrow, 1991, 56 pp. (0-688-09404-X)
(Kirkus 59:1094; SLJ Sep 1991 p. 273)

6-407 **TARR, Judith.** *Kingdom of the Grail.* Gr. 10 up.
✮ Roland, a shape-changing knight at Charlemagne's court, vows to free Merlin
from imprisonment in an enchanted forest, in this reworking of the medieval
epic poem "The Song of Roland."
Penguin/Roc, 2000, pap., 464 pp. (0-451-45797-8); Roc, 2004, pap., 497 pp.
(0-451-46004-9).
(BL 96:2126; Kirkus 68:993; Kliatt Mar 2001 p. 27; LJ Aug 2000 p. 167; VOYA 23:436,
24:15)

6-408 **TARR, Judith.** *Lord of the Two Lands.* Gr. 10 up.
When Alexander the Great sets out to conquer the world, Meriamon, priestess
daughter of the Pharaoh of Egypt, becomes his trusted adviser.
Tor, 1993, 320 pp. (0-312-85362-9)
(BL 89:1036, 1045; Kirkus 60:1533; VOYA 16:171, 17:10)

6-409 **TEMPEST, John.** *Vision of the Hunter.* Gr. 10 up.
Banished from his adopted tribe in a time of food scarcity, Finn develops a plan to domesticate the vital reindeer herds and liberate his people from their harsh new leaders.
Harper, 1989, 288 pp., o.p.; Pocket, 1991, pap. (0-671-69409-X)
(BL 85:1250, 1276, 86:995; Kirkus 57:16; LJ Mar 15, 1989 p. 88)

6-410 **TENNY, Dixie.** *Call the Darkness Down.* Gr. 7–12.
American-born Morfa Owen researches her Welsh heritage and uncovers her family's ties to ancient Druidic powers, almost costing her her life.
Atheneum, 1984, 185 pp., o.p.
(BL 80:1111, 1122; CCBB 37:175; Kirkus 52:J23; SLJ May 1984 p. 104; VOYA 7:198)

6-411 **TEPPER, Sheri S.** *Beauty: A Novel.* Gr. 10 up.
☆ The diary, written in 1347, of a half-mortal, half-fairy 15-year-old girl named Beauty describes the magical and frightening course of her life, in this retelling of the fairy tale "Sleeping Beauty."
Doubleday, 1991, 432 pp. (0-385-41939-2); Bantam, 1992, pap. (0-553-29527-6)
(BL 87:2012, 88:872; Kirkus 59:701; LJ Aug 1991 p. 150; SLJ Feb 1992 p. 121; VOYA 14:327)

6-412 **THOMAS, Gwyn, and CROSSLEY-HOLLAND, Kevin, adapt.** *Tales from the Mabinogion.* Gr. 5–9. (Orig. British pub. 1984.)
These medieval Welsh heroic fantasy tales form the basis of the works of many well-known authors of contemporary fantasy, including Alan Garner, Lloyd Alexander, and Susan Cooper.
Trans. by the adapters, illus. by Margaret Jones, Overlook, 1985, 88 pp., o.p.; Overlook, 2005, 96 pp. (1-58567-556-3).
(BL 81:1123; CCBB 38:190)

6-413 **THOMSON, Sarah L.** *The Dragon's Son.* Gr. 7–12.
☆ This story of Arthur's life is told from three points of view: that of Nimue, in love with the bard Myrddin; of Morgan, Arthur's half-sister; and of Medraud, Arthur's vengeful son.
Orchard, 2001, 181 pp. (0-531-30333-0)
(BL 97:1675; CCBB 54:425; HBG 12:326; Kirkus 69:508; Kliatt May 2001 p. 15; SLJ July 2001 p. 114; VOYA 24:136, 25:16)

6-414 **TOLSTOY, Nikolai.** *The Coming of the King: The First Book of Merlin.*
☆ **(Merlin trilogy, bk. 1).** Gr. 10 up. (Orig. British pub. 1987.)
Merlin the sorcerer tells King Ceneu of Prydein the story of his life and the history of the ancient land of Prydein.
Bantam, 1989, 640 pp., o.p.
(BL 85:1250; Kirkus 57:249; Kliatt Sep 1990 p. 24; LJ Apr 1, 1989 p. 115; VOYA 12:292, 13:12)

6-415 **TOMLINSON, Theresa.** *The Forestwife.* **(Forestwife Saga, bk. 1).** Gr.
☆ 6–10.
Fifteen-year-old Marian runs away from home to avoid an unappealing marriage and joins the forest folk. In the sequel, *Child of the May* (1998, 2000), Magda, apprentice to forestwife Marian, joins Robert (Robin Hood) in his attempt to rescue Lady Matilda and her daughter Isabel from the Sheriff of

Nottingham. The final sequel is *The Path of the She Wolf* (2000).
Orchard, 1995, 170 pp. (0-531-09450-2); Dell, 1997, pap., 170 pp. (0-440-41350-8)

(BL 91:741, 1241, 1289; CCBB 48:252; HBG 6:305; Kirkus 63:397; SLJ Mar 1995 p. 225; VOYA 18:100)

6-416 TREGARTHEN, Enys (pseud. of Nellie Sloggett). *The White Ring.* Gr.
✮ 4–6.

In this retelling of a Cornish legend, the King and Queen of Fairyland take on the forms of an old man and a little girl, respectively, until they are able to return to their own world.
Adapt. by Elizabeth Yates, illus. by Nora S(picer) Unwin, Harcourt, 1949, 65 pp., o.p.

(BL 45:286; CCBB 2:6; HB 25:210; Kirkus 17:150; LJ 74:557)

6-417 TUNNELL, Michael O. *Wishing Moon.* Gr. 6–10.
✮ In this sequel to "Aladdin," a spoiled princess throws an old lamp at a girl named Aminah, who is determined to use her three monthly wishes to help those in need, to the disdain of the jinni.
Dutton, 2004, 272 pp. (0-525-47193-6)

(BL 100:1921; CCBB 57:487; Kirkus 72:499; Kliatt May 2004 p. 14; SLJ July 2004 p. 113; VOYA 27:148)

6-418 TURTLEDOVE, Harry. *Between the Rivers.* Gr. 10 up.
In a world resembling ancient Mesopotamia, Kimash, ruler of Gibil, a young merchant named Sharur, and a foreign thief named Habbazu join forces to steal a powerful talisman that can prevent the gods from interfering in human affairs.
Tor, 1998, 384 pp. (0-312-86202-4)

(BL 94:786; Kirkus 66:28; LJ Jan 1998 p. 149; VOYA 21:448)

TWAIN, Mark (pseud. of Samuel Clemens). *A Connecticut Yankee in King Arthur's Court.*
See Chapter 10, Time Travel Fantasy.

6-419 VALENCAK, Hannelore. *When Half-Gods Go.* Gr. 8–12. (Orig. Austrian pub. 1974.)
Tired of her lover Andreas's contemptuous treatment during an archaeological tour of Greece, Barbara strikes out on her own and is befriended by a young Greek named Alexander, who might be the god Hermes come to life.
Trans. by Patricia Crampton, Morrow, 1976, 192 pp., o.p.

(BL 73:316, 327; CCBB 30:84; HB 52:630; Kirkus 44:910; SLJ Oct 1976 p. 121)

VAN ALLSBURG, Chris. *The Stranger.*
See Chapter 1, Allegorical Fantasy and Literary Fairy Tales.

6-420 VANDE VELDE, Vivian. *The Rumpelstiltskin Problem.* Gr. 4–8.
Six new and humorous variations on the "Rumpelstiltskin" story, explaining why a king would believe that a poor girl could spin straw into gold and other inconsistencies.
Houghton, 2000, 116 pp. (0-618-05523-1); Scholastic, 2002, pap., 116 pp. (0-439-30529-2)

(CCBB 54:239; HBG 12:80; Kirkus 68:1435; SLJ Nov 2000 p. 177; VOYA 23:365)

6-421 VANDE VELDE, Vivian. *Tales from the Brothers Grimm and the Sisters*
✮   *Weird.* Gr. 4–8.
Ten humorous stories and three poems presenting alternative versions of famil-
iar fairy tales, including "Hansel and Gretel," "Red Riding Hood," and
"Rumpelstiltskin."
Harcourt, 1995, 128 pp. (0-15-200220-0); Dell, 1997, pap., 128 pp. (0-440-
41300-1)
(CCBB 49:73; HB 72:201; HBG 7:70; Kirkus 63:1118; SLJ Jan 1996 p. 126)

6-422 VIGUIE, Debbie. *Scarlet Moon.* Gr. 7–12.
Assisting her blacksmith father while her brother fights in the Crusades, Ruth
meets a young nobleman whose green eyes remind her of the wolf who
attacked her as a child, in this reworking of "Little Red Riding Hood."
Simon Pulse, pap., 2004, 176 pp. (0-689-86716-6)
(Kirkus 72:278; Kliatt Sep 2004 p. 33; VOYA 27:234)

Visions of Wonder: An Anthology of Christian Fantasy. **Ed. by Robert H.**
Boyer and Kenneth J. Zahorski.
See Chapter 3, Fantasy Collections.

6-423 VOEGELI, Max. *The Wonderful Lamp.* Gr. 5–7. (Orig. German pub. 1952.)
In legendary Baghdad, Ali the beggar boy searches for Aladdin's magic lamp
and ends up aboard the ship of Sinbad the sailor. The sequel is *The Prince of*
Hindustan (1961).
Trans. by E. M. Prince, illus. by Felix Hoffmann, Oxford University Press,
1955, 228 pp., o.p.
(BL 51:455; CCBB 9:13; HB 31:260; Kirkus 23:358)

6-424 VOIGT, Cynthia. *Orfe.* Gr. 9–12.
A dark contemporary version of the myth of Orpheus and Eurydice, in which
Orfe, lead singer in a heavy metal band, falls in love with Yuri, a recovering
addict, who succumbs to his addiction on their wedding day.
Atheneum, 1992, 120 pp. (0-689-31771-9); Scholastic, 1994, pap. (0-590-
47442-1)
(CCBB 46:92; HB 68:731; HBG 4:84; Kirkus 60:1385; SLJ Dec 1992 p. 133; VOYA 15:288)

6-425 WALKER, Kenneth Macfarlane, and BOUMPHREY, Geoffrey. *The Log*
of the Ark. Gr. 5–7. (Orig. British pub. 1923, entitled *The Log of the Arc*,
1923; orig. U.S. pub. Dutton, 1926, entitled *What Happened in the Arc?*)
A humorous retelling of the story of Noah.
Pantheon, 1960, 214 pp., o.p.
(BL 23:139, 57:33; HB 36:217)

6-426 WALKER, Mary Alexander. *The Scathach and Maeve's Daughters.* Gr.
6–9.
A shape-shifter and warrior from Celtic folklore, the Scathach uses her supernatural powers to aid four related women named Maeve: in 8th-century Scotland, 12th-century England, 17th-century Canada, and New York City in the
year 2000. The story is marred by its stereotypical depiction of Canadian Iroquois people.

Macmillan, 1990, 119 pp., o.p.

(BL 87:328; HBG 2:86; Kirkus 58:1537; SLJ Dec 1990 p. 125; VOYA 13:304)

6-427 WALTON, Evangeline (pseud. of Evangeline Ensley). *The Prince of Annwn.* **(The Mabinogion tetralogy, bk. 1).** Gr. 10 up.

In this retelling of the first branch of the Welsh *Mabinogion*, Prince Pwyll of Dyfed, Wales, battles Havgan, a ruler in the Kingdom of Death, and then travels into the Bright World in search of a bride, Rhiannon of the Birds. The sequels are *The Children of Llyr* (1971, 1978, 1992), *The Song of Rhiannon* (1972, 1978, 1992; Mythopoeic Fantasy Award, 1973), and *The Virgin and the Swine* (Willett, 1936; repr. as *The Island of the Mighty*, 1970, 1979, 1993). Random, 1971, 179 pp., o.p.; Collier, 1992, pap., 179 pp. (0-02-026471-2)

(VOYA 2:48)

6-428 WALTON, Jo. *The King's Peace.* **(Tir Tanagiri series, bk. 1).** Gr. 10 up.

✮ In this variation on the Arthurian tales, female warrior Sulien apGwein supports King Urdo's attempts to restore peace to Tir Tanagiri. The sequels are *The King's Name* (2001) and *The Prize in the Game* (2002). Tor, 2000, 416 pp. (0-312-87229-1), 2001, pap., 530 pp. (0-7653-4327-4)

(BL 97:327; Kirkus 68:1241; LJ Oct 15, 2000, p. 108; VOYA 24:15, 58)

WANGERIN, Walter, Jr. *The Book of the Dun Cow.*

See Chapter 1, Allegorical Fantasy and Literary Fairy Tales.

6-429 WANGERIN, Walter, Jr. *The Crying for a Vision.* Gr. 7–12.

✮ In this novelized version of a Lakota myth, outcast orphan Moves Walking, or Waskin Mani, hears the voices of ghosts and animals and is the only one who can save the tribes from starvation. Simon, 1994, 279 pp. (0-671-79911-8); Simon Pulse, pap. (0-689-80650-7)

(BL 91:747; CCBB 48:179; HBG 6:92; Kirkus 62:1546; SLJ Jan 1995 p. 138; VOYA 18:28)

6-430 WATSON, Elsa. *Maid Marian.* Gr. 10 up.

Hoping to avoid a second arranged, loveless marriage, and to thwart the plans of Queen Eleanor of Aquitaine, 17-year-old Marian Fitzwater enters Sherwood Forest seeking help from the outlaw Robin Hood. Crown, 2004, 304 pp. (1-4000-5041-3); Three Rivers, 2005, pap., 320 pp. (1-4000-8-76-5)

(BL 100:1039; Kirkus 72:60; LJ Apr 2004 p. 125;)

6-431 WEIN, Elizabeth E. *The Winter Prince.* Gr. 6–12.

✮✮ Medraut, High King Artos's eldest, but illegitimate son, describes his love for and rivalry with his half-brother, Lleu, a relationship complicated by the sorcery of Medraut's mother, Morgause, who is also Artos's sister. In *A Coalition of Lions* (2003), Goewin, daughter of High King Artos, must flee Britain after her family is killed, finding refuge in the court of Aksum, where she uses her power to protect her young nephew Telemakos. In *The Sunbird* (2004), Telemakos, half-Ethiopian son of Medraut, attempts to spy for the emperor on the salt smugglers of the Aksumite Empire, but is captured and enslaved in the salt mines. Macmillan, 1993, 202 pp. (0-689-31747-6); Firebird, 2003, pap. (0-14-250014-3)

(BL 90:615; HB 70:208; HBG 5:91; Kirkus 61:1153; SLJ Oct 1993 p. 158; VOYA 16:314)

6-432 WELLMAN, Manly Wade. *Cahena.* Gr. 10 up.
A retelling of the story of the Cahena, a legendary warrior-priestess in 8th-century North Africa who fought to her death against the Moslem conquest.
Doubleday, 1986, 182 pp., o.p.
(BL 83:625, 642; LJ Dec 1986 p. 141)

6-433 WELLMAN, Manly Wade. *The Old Gods Waken.* **(Silver John series, bk.**
★   **3). Gr. 10 up.**
Only John, a wandering minstrel with a silver-stringed guitar, realizes the danger posed to his Appalachian home by the sinister revival of a druidic cult. This book is preceded by *Who Fears the Devil?* (1963) and *Worse Things Waiting* (1973). The sequels are *After Dark* (1980, 1984), *The Lost and the Lurking* (1981, 1984), *The Hanging Stones* (1982, 1984), *The Voice of the Mountain* (1984), and *The Valley So Low* (1987). *John the Balladeer* (Baen, 1988) is a collection of related short stories. In 1984, Manly Wade Wellman was given a British Fantasy Society Special Award.
Doubleday, 1979, 186 pp., o.p.
(BL 76:758; Kirkus 47:1292; LJ 104:2666)

WESTALL, Robert (Atkinson). *The Devil on the Road.*
See Chapter 10, Time Travel Fantasy.

6-434 WHITE, T(erence) H(anbury). *The Once and Future King.* Gr. 10 up.
★★   (Orig. British pub. 1958.)
A revised omnibus edition of White's retelling of Arthurian legends. The first three sections of this book were originally published separately: *The Sword in the Stone* (1939; see below), *The Witch in the Wood* (1939; here called "The Queen of Air and Darkness"), *The Ill-Made Knight* (1940), and the previously unpublished section, "The Candle in the Wind." *The Book of Merlyn*, written in 1941, was originally intended as the fifth and final book of the saga (University of Texas Pr., 1977; Berkley, 1978, 1988, pap.).
Putnam, 1958, 677 pp. (0-399-10597-2); Ace, 1996, pap. (0-441-00383-4)
(BL 55:48; Kirkus 26:429; LJ 83:2184; TLS 1958 p. 224)

6-435 WHITE, T(erence) H(anbury). *The Sword in the Stone.* **(Camelot series,**
★   **bk. 1). Gr. 5–8.** (Orig. British pub. 1938.)
Merlyn the sorcerer teaches young King Arthur about magic and history. This story and its sequel, *The Witch in the Wood* (1939), were revised to become the first two parts of *The Once and Future King* (1958; see above).
Illus. by the author, Putnam, 1939, 312 pp., o.p.; illus. by Dennis Nolan, 1993, 256 pp., o.p.; Dell, 1999, pap. (0-440-98445-9)
(BL 35:191; HBG 5:83; Kirkus 61:1082; TLS 1938 p. 571)

6-436 WHYTE, Jack. *The Skystone.* **(Camulod Chronicles, vol. 1). Gr. 10 up.**
(Orig. Canadian pub. 1992.)
This version of the Arthurian legend is set in Roman Britain, 365 A.D., where Gaius Publius Varrus, a retired centurion and ironsmith, discovers mysterious ore-bearing stones linked to the arrival of King Arthur. The sequels are *The Singing Sword* (1996, 2002), *The Eagle's Brood* (1997, 1998), *The Saxon Shore* (1998, 1999), *The Fort at River's Bend* (1999, 2000), *The Sorcerer: Metamorphosis* (1999, 2000), and *Uther* (2001).

Doherty, 1996, 498 pp. (0-8125-5138-9); Tor, 2002, pap., 352 pp. (0-7653-0372-8)

(Kirkus 63:1729; Kliatt Mar 1997 p. 14; LJ Dec 1995 p. 163)

WIBBERLEY, Leonard (Patrick O'Connor). *The Quest of Excalibur.*
See Chapter 4, Ghost Fantasy.

6-437 WIESEL, Elie(zer). *The Golem; the Story of a Legend.* Gr. 10 up.
☆ An old gravedigger in 16th-century Prague tells this story of Yossel, the huge
clay figure created by Rabbi Yehuda Loew to protect the Jews from persecution.
Trans. by Anne Borchardt, illus. by Mark Podwal, Summit, 1983, 105 pp., o.p.
(BL 80:847, 853; LJ 109:510)

6-438 WIGNELL, Edel. *Escape by Deluge.* Gr. 5–8. (Orig. Australian pub. 1989.)
☆ Water-loving Shelley discovers that only a huge rainstorm and flood can free
the mythical bunyip trapped for decades in the underground pipes beneath their
apartment building.
Holiday, 1990, 142 pp., o.p.
(BL 86:2096; HB 66:337; HBG 1:255; Kirkus 58:657; SLJ May 1990 p. 114; VOYA 13:233, 14:10)

WILDE, Oscar (Fingal O'Flahertie Wills). *The Picture of Dorian Gray.*
See Chapter 1, Allegorical Fantasy and Literary Fairy Tales.

6-439 WILHELM, Kate (Katie Gertrude). *Cambio Bay.* Gr. 10 up.
The suspenseful story of six guests whose lives become intertwined with legends about the Native American family who once lived on the site of Miss
Luisa's huge Victorian guesthouse overlooking Cambio Bay, California.
St. Martin's, 1990, 294 pp., o.p.
(BL 86:1122, 1124; Kirkus 58:230; LJ Mar 15, 1990 p. 116)

6-440 WILLARD, Nancy (Margaret). *Beauty and the Beast.* Gr. 2–6.
☆ Beauty's family moves to the woods after her father, a wealthy New York City
merchant, goes bankrupt in this retelling of the French fairy tale set in the
United States in 1900.
Illus. by Barry Moser, Harcourt, 1992, 69 pp. (0-15-206052-9)
(BL 89:504; CCBB 46:80; HB 68:734; HBG 4:99; Kirkus 60:1318; SLJ Oct 1992 p. 123, Dec 1992 p. 23)

WILLIAMS, Thomas (Alonzo). *Tsuga's Children.*
See Chapter 7, High Fantasy: Travel to Other Worlds.

6-441 WILSON, David Henry. *The Coachman Rat.* Gr. 10 up. (Orig. German pub.
☆ 1985.)
Robert the rat's wish to become human is granted when a fairy godmother
transforms him into a coachman to chauffeur Amadea to the ball, but trouble
begins when the spell ends at midnight in this "Cinderella" story told from an
unusual point of view.
Carroll & Graf, 1989, 171 pp., o.p.; Baen, 1990, pap., 218 pp., o.p.
(BL 86:38, 56, 907, 995; Kirkus 57:1120; LJ Oct 15 1989 p. 105; VOYA 12:376, 13:12)

6-442 *A Wolf at the Door, and Other Retold Fairy Tales.* **Ed. by Ellen Datlow**
✮   **and Terri Windling.** Gr. 6–10.
Dark retellings of 13 classic tales written by Jane Yolen, Gregory Maguire, Tanith Lee, Patricia McKillip, and others. *Swan Sister: Fairy Tales Retold* (2003; see title entry above) is a companion volume. The editors have also compiled six volumes of dark retellings for readers in grades 10 up: *Snow White, Blood Red* (1993, 1995; see title entry above), *Black Thorn, White Rose* (1994, 2001), *Ruby Slippers, Golden Tears* (1995), *Black Swan, White Raven* (1997, 1998), *Silver Birch, Blood Moon* (1999), and *Black Heart, Ivory Bones* (2000).
Simon, 2000, 192 pp. (0-689-82138-7); Simon Pulse, 2001, pap. (0-689-82139-5)
(BL 97:73; CCBB 53:396; Kirkus 68:794; SLJ Aug 2000 p. 180; VOYA 23:129)

6-443 **WOLF, Christa.** *Medea: A Modern Retelling.* Gr. 10 up. (Orig. pub. in Germany.)
In this novelized version of the Greek legend, Medea is a courageous healer whose strengths antagonize her father and her hero-husband, Jason.
Trans. by John Cullen, Doubleday, 1998, 192 pp. (0-385-49060-7)
(BL 94:1430; Kirkus 66:364; LJ Apr 15, 1998 p. 117; TLS Apr 17, 1998 p. 22)

6-444 **WOLF, Joan.** *The Road to Avalon.* Gr. 10 up.
Arthur's love for his childhood friend and aunt, Morgan, threatens his marriage to Gwenhyfar and the future of his reign.
NAL, 1988, 368 pp., o.p.
(Kirkus 56:858; LJ Oct 15, 1988 p. 105; VOYA 13:138)

6-445 **WOLFE, Gene (Rodman).** *Castleview.* Gr. 10 up.
✮   The mysterious medieval castle for which Castleview, Illinois, was named turns out to be the property of King Arthur's nemesis, Morgan Le Fay.
Tor, 1990, 400 pp., o.p.; Orb, 1997, pap. (0-312-86304-7)
(BL 86:866, 869; Kirkus 58:230; Kliatt Apr 1991 p. 60; LJ Mar 15, 1990 p. 116)

6-446 **WOOLLEY, Persia.** *Child of the Northern Spring.* **(Guinevere trilogy, bk. 1).** Gr. 10 up.
This Arthurian legend is retold through the eyes of young Gwen, soon to become Queen Guinevere. The sequels are *Queen of the Summer Stars* (1990) and *Guinevere: The Legend in Autumn* (1991).
Poseidon, 1987, 418 pp., o.p.; Pocket, pap., 1994 (9-994-93378-7)
(BL 83:1410, 1437, 84:1250; Kirkus 55:422; LJ June 1, 1987 p. 131)

6-447 **WREDE, Patricia C(ollins).** *Snow White and Rose Red.* Gr. 10 up.
In this novelization of the Grimm fairy tale set in Elizabethan England on the edge of the Faerie Kingdom, the bear befriended by the two sisters is the enchanted son of Queen Elizabeth.
Tor, 1989, 224 pp., o.p.
(BL 85:1511, 1540, 86:907, 995; Kirkus 57:510; VOYA 12:294)

6-448 **WRIGGINS, Sally.** *The White Monkey King: A Chinese Fable.* Gr. 4–6.
In ancient China, a monkey prankster with magical powers meets his match when he challenges the Buddha.

Illus. by Ronni Solbert, Pantheon, 1977, 113 pp., o.p.

(CCBB 31:104; HB 53:529; Kirkus 45:487; SLJ Mar 1978 p. 135; Suth 2:487)

6-449 **WRIGHTSON, (Alice) Patricia (Furlonger).** *Balyet.* Gr. 6–9. (Orig. Aus-
☆ tralian pub. 1989.)
Rebellious 14-year-old Jo ignores the frantic warnings of her Granny Willet to
stay away from Balyet, a dangerous wild aboriginal spirit who was banished
from her tribe a thousand years earlier.
Macmillan, 1989, 144 pp., o.p.

(BL 85:1370, 1393; CCBB 42:161; HB 56:493; Kirkus 57:632; SLJ Apr 1989 p. 120; Suth
4:446; VOYA 12:119, 13:11)

6-450 **WRIGHTSON, (Alice) Patricia (Furlonger).** *The Ice Is Coming.* **(Wirrun**
☆☆ **trilogy, bk. 1).** Gr. 6–9. (Orig. Australian pub. 1976.)
Wirrun, a young Aborigine, discovers that the ancient ice people, or Ninya, are
on the march, forming ice all over the land, and realizes that it is up to him to
find the most ancient Nargun, or rock monster, to stop them. Australian Children's Book of the Year Award, 1978; Guardian Award Commended Book,
1978. In *The Dark Bright Water* (1978, 1979), Wirrun uses magic to fight an
enemy deep within the earth. In *Journey Behind the Wind* (1981), the evil Wulgaru, master of a mysterious death-bringing thing, causes Wirrun's water-spirit
wife to disappear, and Wirrun must confront Wulgaru to save the land. All
three books are combined in *The Song of Wirrun* (Arrow/Random, 1987; 0-
7126-1150-9).
Atheneum, 1977, 222 pp., o.p.

(BL 74:559; CCBB 31:104; HB 54:57; Kirkus 45:996; SLJ Nov 1977 p. 65; Suth 2:487)

WRIGHTSON, (Alice) Patricia (Furlonger). *Moon Dark.*
See Chapter 2, Animal Fantasy.

6-451 **WRIGHTSON, (Alice) Patricia (Furlonger).** *The Nargun and the Stars.*
☆ Gr. 5–8. (Orig. Australian pub. 1973.)
The lives of Simon Brent and his elderly cousins are threatened by the Nargun,
a rocklike monster from the past. Australian Children's Book of the Year
Award, 1974.
Atheneum, 1974, 1986, 184 pp., o.p.

(BL 70:1108, 71:768; 83:415; CCBB 28:72; HB 50:382, 63:84; Kirkus 42:302; LJ 99:2300;
Suth 2:488; TLS 1973 p. 1434; VOYA 9:292)

YEP, Laurence M(ichael). *Dragon of the Lost Sea.*
See Chapter 5, High Fantasy: Alternate Worlds or Histories.

YEP, Laurence M(ichael). *The Tiger's Apprentice.*
See Chapter 9, Magic Adventure Fantasy.

6-452 **YOLEN (Stemple), Jane (Hyatt).** *Briar Rose.* Gr. 10 up.
After the death of the beloved grandmother who told her versions of "Sleeping
Beauty" throughout her childhood, Becca discovers the truth about her family's connection to the Holocaust. Mythopoeic Fantasy Award for Adult Literature, 1993.

Tor, 1992, 192 pp. (0-312-85135-9), 1993, pap. (0-8125-5862-6); Starscape, 2002, pap. (0-765-34230-8)

(BL 89:125, 133; Kirkus 60:888; LJ Sep 15, 1992 p. 97; SLJ Apr 1993 p. 150)

6-453 YOLEN (Stemple), Jane (Hyatt). *The Dragon's Boy.* Gr. 5–7.
⋆   Artos, a young kennel boy, learns wisdom from an old dragon hidden in a secret cave, in this retelling of the lore about King Arthur's boyhood. Yolen has written many other books about King Arthur, including *Sword of the Rightful King* (2003; see below).
Harper, 1990, 120 pp. LB (0-06-026790-9)

(BL 87:165; CCBB 44:134; HB 67:72; HBG 2:73; Kirkus 58:1175; SLJ Oct 1990 p. 122)

6-454 YOLEN (Stemple), Jane (Hyatt). *Greyling: A Picture Story from the*
⋆   *Islands of Shetland.* Gr. 2–4.
A selchie, or seal-boy, raised by a fisherman and his wife, reverts to his seal form to save his foster father's life.
Illus. by William Stobbs, Philomel, 1968, 29 pp., o.p.; illus. by David Ray, Putnam, 1991, 40 pp. (0-399-22262-6)

(BL 87:1975; CCBB 22:151; HB 45:44; Kirkus 59:733; LJ 94:2096; SLJ Aug 1991 p. 158; Suth:342; TLS 1969 p. 695)

6-455 YOLEN (Stemple), Jane (Hyatt). *Merlin and the Dragons.* Gr. 3–5.
Unable to sleep, young King Arthur visits Merlin, who tells him a story from his own youth about Arthur's father, Uther Pendragon, and his defeat of King Vortigern.
Illus. by Li Ming, Dutton, 1995, 40 pp. (0-525-65214-0)

(BL 92:164; HBG 7:51; SLJ Mar 1996 p. 198)

6-456 YOLEN (Stemple), Jane (Hyatt). *Merlin's Booke.* Gr. 7–12.
Ten stories and poems about the Arthurian wizard, Merlin, beginning with a ballad prophesying his birth and ending with an epitaph in which an archaeological team proclaims to a group of skeptical journalists the finding of Merlin's body. Yolen has written many other books about Merlin, including *Merlin and the Dragons* (1995; see above) and the Young Merlin Trilogy (see *Passager*, 1996, below).
Illus. by Thomas Canty, SteelDragon, 1986, 178 pp., o.p.; Ace, 1986, pap. (0-441-52552-0)

(LJ Feb 1, 1987 p. 80; VOYA 9:242)

6-457 YOLEN (Stemple), Jane (Hyatt). *Passager.* **(The Young Merlin trilogy,**
⋆   **bk. 1).** Gr. 4–8.
Master Robin takes in an 8-year-old abandoned boy named Merlin. In the sequel, *Hobby* (1996, 1998), 12-year-old Merlin is captured by a rogue named Fowler, who forces the boy to perform in his traveling magic show. In *Merlin* (1997, 1998), Merlin is taken in by wild folk who want to use his prophetic powers, but he escapes with the help of a child named Cub, who will grow up to become King Arthur. *The Young Merlin Trilogy* (Harcourt, 2004) contains all three books. The trilogy won the 1998 Mythopoeic Fantasy Award for Children's Literature. Yolen has written many other books about Merlin, including *Merlin and the Dragons* (1995; see above) and *Merlin's Booke* (1986; see above).

Harcourt, 1996, 76 pp. (0-15-200391-6); Apple, 1998, pap. (0-590-37073-1)
(BL 92:1508; HB 72:466; HBG 7:299; SLJ May 1996 p. 118)

6-458 YOLEN (Stemple), Jane (Hyatt). *The Sea Man.* Gr. 3–5.
The lieutenant in charge of a 1663 sailing ship rescues a merman trapped in a net, but both are threatened by the superstitious crew.
Illus. by Christopher Denise, Philomel, 1998, 41 pp. (0-399-22939-6)
(BL 95:496; HBG 9:324; SLJ Oct 1998 p. 119)

6-459 YOLEN (Stemple), Jane (Hyatt). *Sword of the Rightful King: A Novel of*
★★ ***King Arthur.* Gr. 6–9.**
A young boy named Gawen, who becomes Merlin's assistant at Camelot, is actually a girl named Guinevere, disguised in order to seek revenge on Arthur's nephew, Sir Gawaine. Yolen has written many other books about King Arthur, including *The Dragon's Boy* (1990; see above).
Harcourt, 2003, 368 pp. (0-15-202527-8); Harcourt, 2004, pap., 376 pp. (0-15-202533-2)
(BL 99:1464; CCBB 57:41; HB 79:359; HBG 14:389; Kirkus 71:686; Kliatt May 2003 p. 15; SLJ July 2003 p. 135; VOYA 26:154)

6-460 YOLEN (Stemple), Jane (Hyatt). *Tam Lin: An Old Ballad.* Gr. 3–7.
★   Jennet MacKenzie rescues her true love, Tam Lin, from fairy bondage in this retelling of the Scottish ballad.
Illus. by Charles Mikolaycak, Harcourt, 1990, 32 pp. (0-15-284261-6)
(BL 87:158; HB 67:78; HBG 2:101; Kirkus 58:1255; SLJ Jan 1991 p. 109)

6-461 YOLEN (Stemple), Jane (Hyatt). *The Wild Hunt.* Gr. 6–9.
Two boys, Jerold and Gerund, become pawns in a deadly match between Lady Summer and her husband, the Horned King Winter.
Illus. by Francisco Mora, Harcourt, 1995, 160 pp. (0-15-200211-1)
(BL 91:1755; CCBB 49:35; HBG 6:307; Kirkus 63:718; SLJ June 1995 p. 134; VOYA 18:319)

6-462 YOLEN (Stemple), Jane (Hyatt), and HARRIS, Robert J. *Odysseus in*
★   ***the Serpent Maze.* (Young Heroes series, bk. 1). Gr. 4–7.**
Thirteen-year-old Odysseus, captured by pirates, joins young prisoners Penelope and Helen to fight the beasts in Daedelus' maze on the island of Crete. In *Hippolyta and the Curse of the Amazons* (2002), 13-year-old Hippolyta defies Amazon law by taking her doomed newborn brother to his father, the King of Troy. In *Atalanta and the Arcadian Beast* (2003), 12-year-old Atalanta and the bear cub she raised join the village hunters and the king's forces to search for the terrible beast that killed her father. The fourth book in the series is *Jason and the Gorgon's Blood* (2004).
HarperCollins, 2001, 256 pp. (0-06-028735-7); HarperTrophy, 2002, pap. (0-06-440847-7)
(BL 97:1561; CCBB 54:357; HBG 12:319; Kirkus 68:1768; SLJ July 2001 p. 116)

YOUMANS, Marly. *The Curse of the Raven Mocker.*
See Chapter 7, High Fantasy: Travel to Other Worlds.

6-463 **YOUNG, Robert F.** *The Vizier's Second Daughter.* Gr. 7–12.
Sent into the past to kidnap Scheherazade for duplication by a supplier of wax museum figures, Bill Billings grabs her younger sister, Dunyzad, by mistake, and must fight Ali Baba in order to escape.
DAW, 1985, pap., 203 pp., o.p.
(Kliatt 19:30; VOYA 8:196)

ZELAZNY, Roger (Joseph Christopher), and SHECKLEY, Robert. *If at Faust You Don't Succeed.*
See Chapter 10, Time Travel Fantasy.

ZETTEL, Sarah. *A Sorcerer's Treason: A Novel of Isavalta.*
See Chapter 7, High Fantasy: Travel to Other Worlds.

ZETTEL, Sarah. *The Usurper's Crown.*
See Chapter 7, High Fantasy: Travel to Other Worlds.

7

High Fantasy:
Travel to Other Worlds

High fantasy novels have been variously called epic fantasy, heroic fantasy, myth fantasy, other-world fantasy, and alternate world fantasy. In such works, the fate of the world hangs in the balance, while the forces of good and evil, or light and darkness, battle for control of humanity. For the purposes of this book, high fantasy novels have been divided into three chapters: Chapter 5, Alternate Worlds or Histories; Chapter 6, Myth and Legend; and Chapter 7, Travel to Other Worlds.

This chapter lists books involving travel between our world and another. J. R. R. Tolkien suggested that such other-worlds be called "Secondary Worlds" and that the term "Primary World" be used for our own everyday world. It was his feeling that the only true fantasy stories are those involving a Secondary World. Stories that take place entirely in a Secondary World are listed in Chapter 5.

7-1 **AAMODT, Donald.** *A Name to Conjure With.* Gr. 10 up.
Sandy MacGregor is reluctantly transported to the world of Zarathandra, where he becomes involved in a battle between a god and a goddess.
Avon, 1989, pap., 272 pp. (0-380-75137-2)
(BL 85:1949, 1967; LJ June 15, 1989 p. 84; VOYA 12:218)

7-2 **ABBEY, Lynn (pseud. of Marilyn Lorraine Abbey).** *Behind Time.* **(Time series, bk. 1).** Gr. 10 up.
Emma Merrigan uses her inherited magic abilities to enter Hell, in order to rescue her long-lost mother. This is the sequel to *Out of Time* (2000), and is followed by *Talking Time* (2004) and *Down Time* (2005).
Berkley/Ace, 2001, pap., 304 pp. (0-441-00831-3)
(BL 97:1855; Kliatt Sep 2001 p. 20; VOYA 24:365)

ABELL, Kathleen. *King Orville and the Bullfrogs.*
See Chapter 1, Allegorical Fantasy and Literary Fairy Tales.

7-3 **ADAIR, Gilbert.** *Alice Through the Needle's Eye: The Further Adven-*
★ *tures of Lewis Carroll's "Alice."* Gr. 4–7. (Orig. British pub. 1984, entitled
Alice Through the Needle's Eye: A Third Adventure for Lewis Carroll's Alice.)
In this contemporary sequel to Lewis Carroll's *Alice's Adventures in Wonderland* (see below) and *Through the Looking Glass*, Alice slips through the eye
of her needle and sets off on adventures with a Country Mouse, Jack and Jill,
and the Red and White Queens.
Illus. by Jenny Thorne, Dutton, 1985, 184 pp., o.p.
(BL 81:1188; Kirkus 53:1; LJ Apr 15, 1985 p. 84; TLS Jan 4, 1985 p. 18)

ADLER, David A. *Jeffrey's Ghost and the Leftover Baseball Team.*
See Chapter 4, Ghost Fantasy.

AIKEN, Joan (Delano). *Winterthing: A Play for Children.*
See Chapter 6, High Fantasy: Myth or Legend Fantasy.

7-4 **ALEXANDER, Lloyd (Chudley).** *The First Two Lives of Lukas-Kasha.*
★★ Gr. 5–8.
Lukas volunteers to participate in a magic act and unexpectedly ends up in the
land of Abadan, where he is made king despite the objection of the Grand
Vizier. National Book Award Finalist, Children's Book Category, 1979.
Dutton, 1978, 224 pp., o.p.; Puffin, 1998, pap., 224 pp. (0-14-130057-4)
(BL 75:42; CCBB 32:57; HB 55:513; Kirkus 46:878; SLJ Oct 1978 p. 141; Suth 2:8)

7-5 **ALEXANDER, Lloyd (Chudley).** *The Illyrian Adventure.* **(Vesper Holly**
★ **Adventure series, bk. 1).** Gr. 5–9.
In this adventure-filled romp set in the 1870s, young Vesper Holly travels to
the kingdom of Illyria to continue her late father's research on Illyria's leg-
endary magical warriors. In *The El Dorado Adventure* (1987; 2000), Vesper
goes to the Central American country of El Dorado, where she is in constant
danger from numerous villains as she attempts to save the homelands of the
Chirica Indians. *The Drackenberg Adventure* (1988; 2001), *The Jedera Adven-
ture* (1989; 2001), and *The Philadelphia Adventure* (1990; 2002) continue
Vesper's exploits.
Dutton, 1986, 160 pp., o.p.; Puffin, 2000, pap., 132 pp. (0-14-130313-1)
(BL 82:1134, 1137, 83:794, 1136; CCBB 39:142; HB 62:447; Kirkus 54:543; Kliatt 21:19;
SLJ May 1986 p. 99; VOYA 9:232, 10:22)

ALLEN, Judy. *The Lord of the Dance.*
See Chapter 6, High Fantasy: Myth or Legend Fantasy.

ANDERSEN, Hans Christian. *The Snow Queen.*
See Chapter 1, Allegorical Fantasy and Literary Fairy Tales.

7-6 **ANDERSON, Kevin J., and BETANCOURT, John Gregory.** *Born of*
Elven Blood. Gr. 6–8.
Hit on the head during a mugging, Maria wakes up in the land of Faery, where
she is rescued by Cyn and his sister Deirdre, elves under attack from enemy
trogs.
Illus. by John Howe, Atheneum, 1995, 138 pp., o.p.
(HBG 6:307; SLJ June 1995 p. 128)

7-7   **ANTHONY, Mark.** *Beyond the Pale.* **(The Last Rune saga, vol. 1).** Gr. 7–12.

Bar owner Travis Wilder and emergency room physician Grace Beckett fall from Colorado into the world of Eldh, where they are able to work rune magic against the forces of the Pale King. The sequels are *The Keep of Fire* (1999, 2000), *The Dark Remains* (2001), *Blood of Mystery* (2002), and *The Gates of Winter* (2003).

Bantam, 1998, pap., 576 pp. (0-553-37955-0)

(Kirkus 66:1338; LJ Nov 15, 1998, p. 94; VOYA 22:44)

7-8   **ANTHONY, Piers (pseud. of Piers A. D. Jacob).** *Virtual Mode.* **(Mode**
★   **series, bk. 1).** Gr. 10 up.

Darius, King of Hlanter, brings 14-year-old Colene home with him after he falls in love with the suicidal girl during a visit to our world. The sequels are *Fractal Mode* (1992), *Chaos Mode* (1993, 1995), and *DoOon Mode* (2001, 2003).

Putnam, 1991, 323 pp. (0-399-13661-4); Ace, 1991, pap. (0-441-86503-8)

(BL 87:890, 891; Kirkus 58:1715; Kliatt Apr 1992 p. 12; LJ Feb 15, 1991 p. 224; SLJ Nov 1991 p. 115; VOYA 15:38)

7-9   **ANTHONY, Piers (pseud. of Piers A. D. Jacob), and FARMER, Philip Jose.** *The Caterpillar's Question.* Gr. 10 up.

When an art student named Jack drives Tappy, a nearly catatonic girl, across country to a clinic, they find themselves in another world, where Tappy is transformed into a powerful spirit.

Ace, 1992, 272 pp. (0-441-09488-0)

(BL 89:37, 42; LJ Sep 15, 1992 p. 97; SLJ Apr 1993 p. 149; VOYA 15:289)

7-10   **ANTHONY, Piers (pseud. of Piers A. D. Jacob), and KORNWISE, Robert Ian.** *Through the Ice.* Gr. 6–12.

Set upon by punkers who try to drown him under the ice, Seth awakens in another world where he and his three companions attempt to defeat Nefarious, an enchanter bent on destroying the world; this story was begun by Kornwise before his death and completed by Anthony.

Illus. by Daniel R. Home, Underwood-Miller, 1989, 199 pp., o.p.

(HB 66:67; HBG 1:82; Kirkus 57:1367; VOYA 12:369)

7-11   **ASKOUNIS, Christina.** *The Dream of the Stone.* Gr. 7–12.

A mysterious stone sent by her missing brother helps 15-year-old Sarah and her new friend, Angel, escape from villainous CIPHER agents into another world.

Farrar, 1993, 304 pp. (0-374-31877-8)

(BL 89:1806; CCBB 46:307; HBG 4:307; Kirkus 61:656; SLJ June 1993 p. 126; VOYA 16:160)

7-12   **BAEHR, Patricia.** *The Search for Happily-Ever-After.* Gr. 3–5.

Ketti enters fairy tale land, hoping to learn the secret of happiness from Cinderella, Briar Rose, and other well-known characters.

BridgeWater, 1995, 142 pp., o.p.

(BL 92:1019; SLJ Nov 1995 p. 96)

BAKER, (Robert) Michael (Graham). *The Mountain and the Summer Stars: An Old Tale Newly Ended.*
See Chapter 6, High Fantasy: Myth or Legend Fantasy.

7-13 **BALL, Brian.** *The Quest for Queenie.* Gr. 2–5.
Harry pulls the magical sword Sigismund out of a pile of trash and travels to Mandragora to rescue his dog, Queenie, who was kidnapped by the Bad Wizard.
Illus. by Lisa Thiesing, Little, Brown, 1991, 88 pp. (0-316-07961-8)
(BL 87:1965; HBG 2 :257; Kirkus 59:668; SLJ June 1991 p. 100)

7-14 **BALL, Margaret.** *No Earthly Sunne.* Gr. 10 up. (Orig. pub. in England.)
Four hundred years after his kidnapping and abduction to the land of Faerie, Christopher Arundel is rescued by a 20th-century musician named Ellen, who has been troubled by nightmares of the past.
Baen, 1994, pap., 352 pp. (0-671-87633-3)
(BL 91:740, 743; Kliatt Mar 1995 p. 14; VOYA 18:101)

7-15 **BALL, Margaret.** *The Shadow Gate.* Gr. 10 up. (Orig. pub. in England.)
An illustration in a rare fantasy novel draws a young woman into Elfland, where she is proclaimed its long-lost queen.
Baen, 1991, pap., 352 pp., o.p.
(BL 87:910, 917, 88:872; SLJ Sep 1991 p. 297, Oct 1991 p. 172; VOYA 14:105)

7-16 **BARKER, Clive.** *Abarat.* **(The Books of Abarat quartet, bk. 1).** Gr. 7–12.
★ When Candy Quackenbush dives into the sea that has mysteriously appeared near her Minnesota home, she surfaces on an island in the archipelago of Abarat and becomes embroiled in a power struggle between the Lord of Midnight and the architect of Commexo City. The sequel is *Days of Magic, Nights of War* (2004).
Illus. by the author, HarperCollins, 2002, 432 pp. (0-06-051084-6); HarperTrophy, 2003, pap., 432 pp. (0-06-440733-0)
(BL 99:120, 592; CCBB 56:265; HBG 16:378; Kirkus 70:1303; Kliatt Nov 2002 p. 6; SLJ Oct 2002 p. 154; VOYA 25:291)

7-17 **BARKER, Clive.** *The Thief of Always: A Fable.* Gr. 10 up.
Bored at home, 10-year-old Harvey follows a con man named Rictus to Mr. Hood's Holiday House at the edge of a strange black lake filled with huge, sad-eyed fish, a place where children can do anything they want.
Harper, 1992, 240 pp. (0-06-017724-1); HarperCollins, 2002, pap., 224 pp. (0-06-440994-5)
(BL 89:379; Kirkus 60:1144; VOYA 16:34)

7-18 **BARLOW, Jennifer.** *Hamlet Dreams.* Gr. 10 up.
After Zac becomes trapped in dreams allowing him to enter another world, leaving him comatose, his girlfriend, Cecile, decides to hospitalize him.
Aardwolf, 2002, pap., 219 pp. (0-9706225-1-1)
(BL 98:824; LJ Jan 2002 p. 159)

7-19 **BARRIE, Sir J(ames) M(atthew).** *Peter Pan.* Gr. 4 up. (Orig. British pub. as
✮ a play entitled *Peter Pan; or, The Boy Who Wouldn't Grow Up*, 1904; U.S.
pub. 1905. The novel, entitled *Peter and Wendy*, was published in 1911.)
Peter Pan teaches three children to fly to Never Never Land, but a jealous fairy
betrays them to Captain Hook's pirate band. *Peter Pan in Kensington Gardens*
(abridged from *The Little White Bird*, 1892; orig. British pub. in this format,
1906; U.S. pub. Scribner, 1906, 1937, o.p.; see Chapter 1, Allegorical Fantasy
and Literary Fairy Tales.) is a related work that describes Peter's infant adventures with the birds and fairies of Kensington Gardens. Barrie also wrote a
sequel play entitled *When Wendy Grew Up: An Afterthought* (Nelson, 1957).
Karen Wallace has written a dark prequel to Peter Pan for young adults, entitled *Wendy* (Simon, 2004; see Chapter 9, Magic Adventure Fantasy), and Laurie Fox has written an adult sequel about Wendy's descendants entitled *The
Lost Girls* (Simon, 2004; 0-7432-1790-X). Dave Barry and Ridley Pearson
have written a prequel to *Peter Pan*, entitled *Peter and the Starcatchers* (2004;
see Chapter 9, Magic Adventure Fantasy).
Illus. by F(rancis) D(onkin) Bedford, Scribner, 1911 (entitled *Peter and
Wendy*), 353 pp., o.p.; illus. by Mabel Lucie Attwell, Scribner, 1921 (entitled
Peter Pan and Wendy), 185 pp., o.p.; illus. by Nora S(picer) Unwin, Scribner,
1950, 242 pp., o.p.; illus. by Trina Schart Hyman, Macmillan, 1980, 184 pp.
(0-684-16611-9); ed. by Josette Frank, illus. by Diane Goode, Random, 1983,
1987, 65 pp. (0-394-89226-7); illus. by Michael (R.) Hague, Holt, 1987, 159
pp. (0-8050-0276-6); NAL, 1987, pap. (0-451-52088-2); illus. by Jan Omerod,
Viking, 1987, 204 pp., o.p.; illus. by Scott Gustafson, Viking, 1991, 192 pp.
(0-670-84180-3); illus. by Greg Becker, Antique, 1998, 144 pp. (1-85149-702-
1); illus. by Scott Gustafson, Viking, 1998, 192 pp. (0-670-84180-3); entitled
Peter Pan: A Classic Illustrated Edition; illus. compiled by Cooper Edens,
Chronicle, 2000, 173 pp. (0-8118-2297-4); illus. by Trina Schart Hyman,
Atheneum, 2001 (reissue of Scribner, 1980 ed.), 200 pp. (0-689-83078-5);
illus. by Michael (R.) Hague, Holt, 2003 (reissue of 1987 ed.) (0-8050-7245-
4); illus. by Charles Vess, Tor, 2003, 224 pp. (0-7653-0809-6)
(BL 8:171, 47:18, 77:807, 79:1140, 84:700, 858, 97:537; Bookshelf 1923–1924 p. 15; CCBB
3:66, 6:12, 11:66, 34:125, 36:162; HB 26:387, 56:661; HBG 10:288, 13:81, 15:87; Kirkus
59:1466; Mahony 1:35; SLJ Dec 1980 p. 57, Aug 1983 p. 48, Jan 1992 p. 108, Dec 2000 p.
138; Suth 3:40; TLS 1981 p. 1363)

7-20 **BARTHOLOMEW, Barbara.** *The Time Keeper.* **(The Timeways trilogy,
bk. 1).** Gr. 6–10. (British title *The Timekeeper*.)
Jeanette and her brother Neil are transported into a world with two moons
where they are befriended by a boy named Jesse and his unicorn. The sequels
are *Child of Tomorrow* (1985) and *When Dreamers Cease to Dream* (1985).
Signet, 1985, pap., 191 pp., o.p.
(Kliatt 19:20; SLJ Dec 1985 p. 97; VOYA 8:323)

7-21 **BAUM, L(yman) Frank.** *Sky Island: Being the Further Adventures of
Trot and Cap'n Bill After Their Visits to the Sea Fairies.* Gr. 4–6. (Orig.
pub. Reilly, 1912, 1970.)
A magic umbrella takes Button Bright, Trot, and Cap'n Bill from California to
Sky Island, a city in the air, where they meet the Rainbow's Daughter, Poly-
chrome. This is the sequel to *The Sea Fairies* (1911, 1969).

Illus. by John R. Neill, Books of Wonder, 1995, 288 pp. (0-929605-02-0);
Dover, 2002, pap., 300 pp. (0-486-42360-3)
(LJ 95:1936; SLJ Jan 1996 p. 68)

7-22 **BAUM, L(yman) Frank.** *The Wizard of Oz.* Gr. 3–6. (Orig. title *The Won-*
★ *derful Wizard of Oz*, 1900.)
A cyclone blows Dorothy from Kansas to the Land of Oz, where the price of
her trip home is the death of the Wicked Witch of the West. There are 54 Oz
sequels written for children, and two more have been written for young adult
and adult readers. Baum wrote the first 14: *The Land of Oz* (retitled *The Mar-*
vellous Land of Oz) (1904, 1987, 1996, 2001), *Ozma of Oz* (1907; Morrow,
1989, 2001), *Dorothy and the Wizard in Oz* (1908; Morrow, 1990), *The Road*
to Oz (1909; Morrow, 1991), *The Emerald City of Oz* (1910; Morrow, 1993),
The Patchwork Girl of Oz (1913, 1995), *Tik-Tok of Oz* (1914, 1996), *The*
Scarecrow of Oz (1915, 1997), *Rinki-tink of Oz* (1916), *The Lost Princess of*
Oz (1917, 1998), *The Tin Woodman of Oz* (1918, 1999), *The Magic of Oz*
(1919, 1999), *Glinda of Oz* (1920, 2002), and *The Visitors from Oz* (Reilly,
1960, 1998). Baum also wrote *Little Wizard Stories of Oz* (1913; Morrow,
1994). The series was continued by Ruth Plumly Thompson, Frank Joslyn
Baum, John Rea Neill, Jack Snow, Rachel R. Cosgrove, Eloise Jarvis
McGraw, and Lauren McGraw Wagner. Thompson wrote *The Royal Book of*
Oz (1921, 1985,1997), *Kabumpo in Oz* (1922, 1985), *The Cowardly Lion of Oz*
(1923, 1985), *Grampa in Oz* (1924, 1985), *The Lost King of Oz* (1925, 1985),
The Hungry Tiger of Oz (1926, 1985), *The Gnome King of Oz* (1927, 1985),
The Giant Horse of Oz (1928, 1985), *Jack Pumpkinhead of Oz* (1929, 1985),
The Yellow Knight of Oz (1930, 1985), *Pirates in Oz* (1931, 1985), *The Purple*
Prince of Oz (1932, 1985), *Ojo in Oz* (1933, 1986), *Speedy in Oz* (1934, 1986),
The Wishing Horse of Oz (1935, 1986), *Captain Salt in Oz* (1936, 1996),
Handy Mandy in Oz (1937, 1996), *The Silver Princess in Oz* (1938, 1996),
Ozoplaning with the Wizard of Oz (1939, 1996), *Yankee in Oz* (Oz Club,
1972), and *The Enchanted Island of Oz* (Oz Club, 1976). Frank Joslyn Baum
wrote *The Laughing Dragon of Oz* (Whitman, 1934). Neill wrote *The Wonder*
City of Oz (1940, 1996), *The Scalawagons of Oz* (1941; Morrow, 1991), and
Lucky Bucky in Oz (1942; Morrow, 1992). Snow wrote *The Magical Mimics in*
Oz (1946, 1997), *The Shaggy Man of Oz* (1949, 1991), and *Who's Who in Oz*
(1954, 1988). Cosgrove wrote *The Hidden Valley of Oz* (1951), and McGraw
and Wagner coauthored *Merry-Go-Round in Oz* (1963; Morrow, 1990, 1996)
and *The Forbidden Fountain of Oz* (Reilly, 1980). Other additions to the series
include *A Barnstormer in Oz* by Philip Jose Farmer (Berkley, 1982, 1983),
Ozma and the Wayward Wand by Polly Berends (Random, 1985), *Dorothy and*
the Seven-Leaf Clover by Dorothy F. Haas (Random, 1985), *Mister Tinker in*
Oz by James Howe (Random, 1985), *Dorothy and the Magic Belt* by Susan
Saunders (Random, 1985), *Return to Oz* by Joan D. Vinge (Ballantine, 1985),
Dorothy of Oz by Roger S. Baum (Morrow, 1989), *How the Wizard Came to*
Oz (Books of Wonder, 1991, 1993) by Donald Abbott, *The Giant Garden of*
Oz (1993, 1995) by Eric Shanower, and *Paradox in Oz* by Edward Einhorn
(Hungry Tiger, 2000). Martin Gardner has written a sequel for young adults
and adults called *Visitors from Oz: The Wild Adventures of Dorothy, the Scare-*
crow, and the Tin Woodman in the United States (St. Martin's, 1998). Gregory
Maguire has written a prequel for young adults and adults called *Wicked: The*

Life and Times of the Wicked Witch of the West (HarperCollins, 1995; see Chapter 12, Witchcraft and Sorcery Fantasy).

Illus. by Evelyn Copelman, adapted from the illus. of W. W. Denslow, Putnam, 1956, deluxe ed., 206 pp. (0-448-06026-4); illus. by Michael (R.) Hague, Holt, 1982, 219 pp. (0-8050-0221-9); Puffin, 1983, pap. (0-14-035001-2); adapt. by Deborah Hautzig, illus. by Joseph A. Smith, Random, 1984, 56 pp., LB (0-394-95331-2); illus. by Barry Moser, University of California/Pennyroyal, 1986, 268 pp., o.p.; illus. by W. W. Denslow, Morrow, 1987 (entitled *The Wonderful Wizard of Oz*), 316 pp. (0-688-06944-4); illus. by Charles Santore, Outlet, 1991, 96 pp., LB (0-517-06655-6); illus. by Lisbeth Zwerger, North-South, 1996, 103 pp. (1-55858-638-5); illus. by Michael (R.) Hague, Holt, 2000 (entitled *The Wizard of Oz*), 220 pp. (0-8050-6430-3); illus. by W. W. Denslow, HarperCollins, 2000 (entitled *The Wonderful Wizard of Oz*), 267 pp. (0-06-029323-3); HarperTrophy, 2001, pap.

(BL 79:673, 82:1661, 1682, 84:470, 93:430; CCBB 4:10, 36:21; HB 63:82; HBG 8:62; SLJ Oct 1982 p. 148, Dec 1991 p. 78, Nov 1996 p. 103; Suth 3:43; TLS 1982 p. 1308)

7-23 BEAGLE, Peter S(oyer). *The Unicorn Sonata.* Gr. 10 up.

A 13-year-old girl named Joey Rivera follows the sound of ethereal music into the land of Shei'rah, where she meets the Eldest, a race of unicorns who are going blind.

Illus. by Robert Rodriquez, Turner, 1996, 160 pp., o.p.

(BL 92:1853; Kirkus 64:1011; LJ Sep 15, 1996 p. 100)

7-24 BEAR, Greg(ory Dale). *The Infinity Concerto.* **(Songs of Earth and Power sequence, bk. 1).** Gr. 10 up.

An old house is the gateway to another world entered by 16-year-old Michael Perrin, who meets the powerful Sidhe of Celtic legend. The sequel is *The Serpent Mage* (1986). *Songs of Earth and Power* (Tor, 1996, 0-81253603-7) contains expanded versions of both books.

Berkley, 1984, pap., 352 pp., o.p.

(BL 81:557, 582, 86:904; VOYA 8:54, 365)

7-25 BEATON-JONES, Cynon. *The Adventures of So Hi.* Gr. 4–6. (Orig. British pub. 1951.)

The wind carries a Chinese boy named So Hi and his kite across the sea, where he meets a lovable dragon and embarks on a series of adventures. The sequel is *So Hi and the White Horse* (1952, 1957).

Illus. by John Ward, Vanguard, 1956, 178 pp., o.p.

(BL 53:228; CCBB 10:1 14; HB 32:445; LJ 82:224)

7-26 BENSON, E(dward) F(rederic). *David Blaize and the Blue Door.* Gr. 4–6. (Orig. British pub. 1918.)

Six-year-old David locks the shining blue door behind him and escapes into a topsy-turvy nonsense world. *David Blaize* (1916) and *David Blaize of Kings* (1924; British title: *David of Kings*) are related stories but are not fantasies.

Illus. by H(enry) J(ustice) Ford, Doubleday, 1919, 217 pp., o.p.

(BL 16:100; HB 3:17–23; LJ 45:980; Mahony 1:38; TLS 1918 p. 642)

7-27 BERGENGREN, Ralph Wilhelm. *David the Dreamer: His Book of Dreams.* Gr. 2–4.

David and his dog, Fido, share many strange adventures in Dreamland.
Illus. by Tom Freud, Atlantic Monthly, 1922, 67 pp., o.p.
(BL 19:90; Bookshelf 1923–1924 p. 7; HB 3:18, 21)

7-28   BERTON, Pierre. *The Secret World of Og.* Gr. 3–5. (Orig. Canadian pub. 1961.)
Five children are imprisoned in the subterranean world of Og, whose small green inhabitants learned to speak from comic books.
Illus. by William Winter, Little, Brown, 1962, 146 pp., o.p.
(BL 58:688; HB 38:176; Kirkus 30:181; LJ 87:2020)

BIANCO, Pamela. *Little Houses Far Away.*
See Chapter 11, Toy Fantasy.

BLACK, Holly. *Tithe: A Modern Faerie Tale.*
See Chapter 6, High Fantasy: Myth or Legend Fantasy.

7-29   BLACKWOOD, Gary L. *Beyond the Door.* Gr. 5–9.
Scott and his friend Tully go through a doorway in the library stacks into the pastoral world of Gale'tin, where an evil wizard wants them to bring him modern technology to increase his power.
Macmillan, 1991, 144 pp., o.p.
(BL 87:1 125; CCBB 44:159; HBG 2:270; Kirkus 59:171; SLJ Mar 1991 p. 192; VOYA 14:105)

7-30   BLAYLOCK, James P(aul). *Land of Dreams.* Gr. 10 up.
During Solstice, when visits to strange lands become possible, Skeezix and Jack find a boat-sized shoe on a California beach and travel to the "land of dreams."
Morrow, 1987, 272 pp. (0-87795-898-X)
(Kirkus 55:895; LJ Aug 1987 p. 146; VOYA 10:242)

7-31   BOMANS, Godfried (Jan Arnold). *Eric in the Land of the Insects.* Gr. 4–7. (Orig. Dutch pub. 1947.)
To avoid taking an exam, Eric enters an insect world by stepping into a painting.
Trans. by Regina Louise Kornblith, illus. by Mark Richardson, Houghton, 1994, 197 pp. (0-395-65231-6)
(BL 90:1347; CCBB47:313; HBG 5:307; Kirkus 62:299; SLJ Mar 1994 p. 222)

BOSTON, L(ucy) M(aria Wood). *The Castle of Yew.*
See Chapter 9, Magic Adventure Fantasy.

7-32   BOSTON, L(ucy) M(aria Wood). *The Guardians of the House.* Gr. 4–6.
★   (Orig. British pub. 1974.)
A collection of peculiar masks and carved heads in an old mansion lures Tom Morgan to a jungle temple, a submerged Roman villa, and an Indian cave.
Illus. by Peter Boston, Atheneum, 1975, 52 pp., o.p.
(CCBB 29:3; HB 51:265; Kirkus 43:121; SLJ May 1975 p. 52; TLS 1974 p. 1373)

BOSTON, L(ucy) M(aria Wood). *The Sea Egg.*
See Chapter 9, Magic Adventure Fantasy.

7-33 **BOWEN, William A(lvin).** *Merrimeg.* Gr. 3–5.
On her way to do some errands, a little girl named Merrimeg finds herself in strange places, meeting chimney imps, starlight fairies, appleseed elves, and gnomes.
Illus. by Emma L(illian) Brock, Macmillan, 1923, 1938, 166 pp., o.p.
(BL 20:143; Bookshelf 1923–1924 Suppl. p. 1; Mahony 2:132)

7-34 **BOYER, Elizabeth H.** *The Troll's Grindstone.* **(The Wizard's War trilogy, bk. 1).** Gr. 10 up.
A man named Leif, kidnapped by elves to impersonate the enemy of the sorcerer Sorkvir, saves himself by stealing a magic sword. The sequels are *The Curse of Slagfid* (1989) and *The Dragon's Carbuncle* (1990).
Ballantine, 1986, pap., 342 pp., o.p.
(BL 82:1587, 1604; VOYA 10:35)

7-35 **BRADLEY, Marion Zimmer.** *The House Between the Worlds.* Gr. 10 up.
Cameron Fenton enters the faerie world while conducting an ESP experiment, and stays to help battle an evil threat to the world.
Doubleday, 1980, 244 pp., o.p.
(BL 76:1409, 78:593; Kirkus 48:397; LJ 105:1192)

7-36 **BRADLEY, Marion Zimmer, and LISLE, Holly.** *Glenraven.* **(Glenraven series, bk. 1).** Gr. 10 up.
Friends Jayjay and Sophie vacation in Glenraven, a magical medieval country located between France and Italy, unaware that the Machnan people have called them there for a reason. The sequel is *In the Rift* (1998, 1999).
Baen, 1996, 394 pp. (0-671-87738-0), 1997, pap., 394 pp. (0-671-87799-2);
Baen, 2002, pap., 416 pp. (0-671-87799-2)
(Kliatt Nov 1997 p. 12; LJ Aug 1996 p. 120)

7-37 **BRAY, Libba.** *A Great and Terrible Beauty.* Gr. 8–12.
✮ After her mother's sudden death in India in 1895, Gemma Doyle is sent to England to attend Spence Academy, where she uses her forbidden magic powers to enter The Realms and speak with her mother's spirit, while her classmates attempt to use her magic for more dangerous purposes.
Delacorte, 2003, 416 pp. (0-385-90161-5), 2005, pap., 432 pp. (0-385-73231-7)
(BL 100:606; CCBB 57:366; Kirkus 71:1358; SLJ Feb 2004 p. 45; VOYA 27:54)

7-38 **BRENNAN, Herbie.** *Faerie Wars.* Gr. 6–10. (Orig. pub. in England, 2003.)
✮ Sent through a defective portal from his world into contemporary England, Prince Pyrgus Malvae needs the help of teenage Henry Atherton and former armed robber Mr. Fogarty to evade those threatening him and to return to his own world. The sequel is *The Purple Emperor* (2004).
Bloomsbury, 2003, 370 pp. (1-58234-810-3), 2003, pap., 384 pp. (1-58234-943-6)
(BL 99:1464; CCBB 56:352; HBG 14:379; Kirkus 71:746; SLJ July 2003 p. 123; VOYA 26:146)

7-39 **BRIN, David.** *The Practice Effect.* Gr. 10 up.
Dennis Nuel, a young physicist, is transported to a magical alternate world, where he discovers that he is a wizard.

Bantam, 1984, 1985, pap., 288 pp., o.p.
(BL 80:1377, 1391; LJ 109:600; VOYA 8:54)

7-40   BRITTAIN, Bill. *The Mystery of the Several Sevens.* Gr. 3–5.
Fifth-grade substitute teacher Mr. Merlin transports two of his favorite students to another world in order to find the seven dwarfs' missing diamonds.
Illus. by James Warhola, HarperCollins, 1994, 96 pp. (0-06-024459-3)
(BL 91:600; HBG 6:73; SLJ Dec 1994 p. 104)

BROCKMEIER, Kevin. *City of Names.*
See Chapter 9, Magic Adventure Fantasy.

7-41   BROWNE, N. M. *Warriors of Alavna.* Gr. 6–12. (Orig. British pub. 2000.)
Fifteen-year-old classmates Dan and Ursula are summoned by a sorcerer into a world resembling Roman Britain, where they become warriors fighting with the Combrogi against the invading Ravens. The sequel is *Warriors of Camlann* (2003).
Bloomsbury, 2002, 320 pp. (1-58234-775-1), 2004, pap., 312 pp. (1-58234-916-9)
(CCBB 56:40; Kirkus 70:1305; SLJ Jan 2003 p. 133; VOYA 25:485)

BRYHER, Winifred. *A Visa for Avalon.*
See Chapter 6, High Fantasy: Myth or Legend Fantasy.

7-42   BUFFIE, Margaret. *The Watcher.* **(The Watcher's Quest trilogy, bk. 1).**
Gr. 6–9. (Orig. Canadian pub. 2000.)
Emma, 16, discovers that she is a changeling, a watcher who must protect her fragile younger sister from other-worldly supernatural forces. In *The Seeker* (2002, 2003), Emma hopes to assuage her mother's grief for her lost child by rescuing her true sister from Argadnel, ruled by her changeling sister, Summer. The third book in the series is *The Finder* (2004).
Kids Can, 2000, 264 pp. (1-55074-829-7), 2002, pap., 260 pp. (1-55074-831-9)
(BL 97:537; HBG 12:82; Kirkus 68:1191; SLJ Oct 2000 p. 155; VOYA 23:431)

7-43   BULL, Emma. *Finder: A Novel of the Borderlands.* **(Borderlands series,**
✮   **vol. 6).** Gr. 10 up.
Bordertown police officer Sunny Rico offers to keep Orient's criminal past a secret if he will use his Finder sixth sense to help her solve a murder case involving a deadly drug rumored to transform humans into elves, and he leads her into the Elflands, a world of magic and crime. The first three volumes in this series are multi-author anthologies (see *Borderland* (1986) in Chapter 5, High Fantasy: Alternate Worlds or Histories), and the fourth and fifth volumes, *Elsewhere* (1991) and *Nevernever* (1993), were written by Will Shetterly (see below, this chapter).
Tor, 1994, 317 pp. (0-312-85418-8), 2003, pap., 317 pp. (0-7653-4777-6)
(BL 90:1064, 1067, 91:1399; Kirkus 61:1555; Kliatt Sep 1995 p. 18; LJ Feb 15, 1994 p. 188; SLJ June 1995 p. 143; VOYA 17:96, 18:8)

BURTON, Philip. *The Green Isle.*
See Chapter 1, Allegorical Fantasy and Literary Fairy Tales.

7-44   **CARD, Orson Scott.** *Enchantment: A Classic Fantasy with a Modern*
✭   *Twist.* Gr. 10 up.
American graduate student Ivan is drawn back to his childhood home in the
Ukraine, where a mysterious creature in a circular pit pulls him into an ancient
Slavic world.
Ballantine/Del Rey, 1999, 400 pp. (0-345-41687-2); Del Rey, 2000, pap., 432
pp. (0-345-41688-0)
(BL 95:1103; Kirkus 67:257; Kliatt Sep 1999 p. 54; SLJ Dec 1999 p. 163; VOYA 22:269,
23:10)

7-45   **CARLSEN, Ruth Christoffer.** *Ride a Wild Horse.* Gr. 4–6.
Julie pretends to be suffering from memory loss while she searches for an
escape hatch back into her own world.
Illus. by Beth Krush and Joe Krush, Houghton, 1970, 164 pp., o.p.
(BL 67:338; Kirkus 38:1145; LJ 96:264)

7-46   **CARPENTER, Christopher.** *The Twilight Realm.* Gr. 7–12.
Five teenagers engaged in a fantasy role-playing game are suddenly pulled into
the world of Xhandarre, where they become warriors and enchanters fighting
an evil sorcerer plotting to enter our world.
Putnam, 1986, 237 pp., o.p.
(BL 82:1387, 1392; Kirkus 54:549; SLJ Aug 1986 p. 99; VOYA 9:160)

7-47   **CARROLL, Lewis (pseud. of Charles Ludwidge Dodgson).** *Alice's*
✭✭   *Adventures in Wonderland.* Gr. 5–8. (Orig. British pub. 1865; written in
1863, entitled *Alice's Adventures Underground.*)
Alice follows a white rabbit into a curious world, where she meets the Mad
Hatter and the Queen of Hearts. Barry Moser's illustrations for the 1982 edi-
tion were awarded the American Book Award for Pictorial Design, 1983.
Anthony Browne's illustrations for the 1988 edition were Highly Commended
by the Kate Greenaway Medal, 1989. In Carroll's *Through the Looking Glass
and What Alice Found There* (written 1870; orig. U.S. pub. 1899; Morrow,
1993), Alice steps through a mirror into a backward world. Charles Edward
Carryl wrote a related story called *Davy and the Goblin, or What Followed
Reading "Alice's Adventures in Wonderland"* (Houghton, 1909, 1920; see this
section). *Alice Through the Needle's Eye* is a contemporary sequel written by
Gilbert Adair (Dutton, 1985; see this section). *Alitji in Dreamland: An Aborig-
inal Version of Lewis Carroll's "Alice in Wonderland,"* adapted by Nancy
Sheppard (Tricycle, 1992; see this section), is an Australian version. *Fantastic
Alice: New Stories from Wonderland*, ed. by Margaret Weis (Ace, 1995, 1999),
is a collection of related stories for older readers.
Illus. by John Tenniel, Macmillan, 1888, 1898, 1902, 192 pp., o.p.; illus. by
Arthur Rackham, Heinemann/Doubleday, 1907, 1933, 161 pp., o.p.; illus. by
Willy Pogany, Dutton, 1929, 192 pp., o.p.; illus. by Leonard Weisgard, Harper,
1949, 159 pp. (entitled *Alice's Adventures in Wonderland; and Through the
Looking Glass*); illus. by Arthur Rackham, Watts, 1966, 161 pp., o.p.; illus. by
Tove Jansson, Delacorte, 1977, 120 pp., o.p.; illus. by Barry Moser, University
of California Press, 1982, 146 pp., o.p; illus. by Barry Moser, Harcourt, 1991,
145 pp. (0-15-104230-6), pap. (0-15-604426-9); illus. by Michelle Wriggins,
Knopf, 1983, 143 pp., o.p.; illus. by Justin Todd, Outlet, 1984 (0-517-55591-
3); illus. by Michael (R.) Hague, Holt, 1985, 122 pp. (0-8050-0212-X); illus.

by John Tenniel, Bantam, 1985, 256 pp. (0-553-21173-0); Scholastic, 1988, pap. (0-590-42035-6); Holt, 1986 (entitled *Alice's Adventures Under Ground*, facsimile ed.), 112 pp., o.p.; illus. by Anthony Browne, Knopf, 1988, 118 pp., o.p.; illus. by Peter Weevers, Putam, 1989, 126 pp., o.p.; illus. by Markéta Prachatická, Wellington, 1989 (Orig. Czech pub. 1982), 165 pp. (entitled *Alice's Adventures in Wonderland and Through the Looking Glass*), o.p.; comp. by Cooper Edens, with illus. from more than 25 classic editions, Bantam, 1989, 208 pp. (entitled *Alice's Adventures in Wonderland: The Ultimate Illustrated Edition*), o.p.; Knopf, 1992 (entitled *Alice's Adventures in Wonderland and Through the Looking Glass*), 336 pp. (0-679-41795-8); illus. by John Tenniel, Morrow, 1992, 208 pp. (0-688-11087-8); adapt. and illus. by Tony Ross, Macmillan, 1994, 93 pp. (0-689-31864-2); illus. by Abelardo Morell, Dutton, 1998, 115 pp. (0-525-46094-2); illus. by Helen Oxenbury, Candlewick, 1999, 207 pp. (0-7636-0804-1); illus. by Lisbeth Zwerger, North-South, 1999, 103 pp. (0-7358-1166-0); illus. selected by Cooper Edens, Chronicle, 2000, 140 pp. (0-8118-2274-5); illus. by John Tenniel, Aladdin, 2000, pap., 176 pp. (0-689-83375-X); illus. by DeLoss McGraw, Harper-Collins, 2001, 181 pp. (0-06-029498-1); illus. by Arthur Rackham, North-South, 2002, 172 pp. (1-58717-152-X); illus. by Iassen Ghiuselev, Simply Read/Words, 2004, 116 pp. (1-894965-00-0); illus. by Michael Foreman, Sterling, 2004, 176 pp. (1-4027-1652-4)

(BL 4:119, 51:210, 63:189, 79:76, 80:678, 81:646, 1552, 82:682, 85:480, 1188, 86:544, 1086, 1158, 87:1172, 95:1412, 96:922, 97:537, 100:968; Bookshelf 1932 p. 8; CCBB 3:11, 5:21, 36, 9:66, 38:162, 43:106, 53:125; HB 1:34; HB 5:48, 42:76, 326, 49:284, 56:80, 59:73, 59:732, 61:74, 62:344, 65:208, 68:604, 76:72; HBG 1:82, 3:261, 5:307, 10:289, 11:75, 13:82, 369; Kirkus 56:1401, 57:1823; LJ 91:5258; Mahony 2:276; SLJ Jan 1984 p. 73, Aug 1985 p. 62, Nov 1985 p. 82, Nov 1988 p. 110, Jan 1990 p. 98, May 1990 p. 102, Aug 1992 p. 99, Oct 1999 p. 110, Jan 2000 p. 93, Nov 2000 p. 150, June 2004 p. 104, Nov 2004 p. 92; Suth 4:61; TLS 1972 p. 1525, 1985 p. 18)

7-48 **CARRYL, Charles Edward.** *The Admiral's Caravan.* Gr. 4–6. (Orig. pub. in *St. Nicholas* magazine, 1891–1892.)
A little girl visits a land inhabited by the animals from Noah's ark.
Illus. by Reginald B. Birch, Houghton, 1909, 1920, 140 pp., o.p.
(Bookshelf 1928 p. 11; HB 3:21; Mahony 2:276)

7-49 **CARRYL, Charles Edward.** *Davy and the Goblin, or What Followed Reading "Alice's Adventures in Wonderland."* Gr. 3–5. (Reprint of 1885 ed.; orig. pub. in *St. Nicholas* magazine, 1884, 1885.)
After reading *Alice in Wonderland* (see Carroll, above), Davy sets off on a voyage with a goblin.
Illus. by E. B. Bensell and H(erman) I(lfeld) Bacharach, Houghton, 1909, 1920, 198 pp., o.p.; University Microfilms, 1967, 160 pp., o.p.
(BL 25:173; Bookshelf 1932 p. 8; HB 3:18, 21, 7:115; Mahony 2:276)

7-50 **CHABON, Michael.** *Summerland.* Gr. 5 up.
☆ Reluctant baseball player Ethan Feld and his teammate, Jennifer T. Rideout travel through several parallel worlds to rescue Ethan's inventor father, kidnapped by the legendary Coyote. Mythopoeic Fantasy Award for Children's Literature, 2003.
Hyperion, 2002, 512 pp. (0-7868-0877-2), 2004, pap., 512 pp. (0-7868-1615-5)

(BL 98:1884, 99:592; CCBB 56:193; HB 78:751; HBG 14:76; Kirkus 70:1395; LJ Sep 1, 2002 p. 49; SLJ Nov2002 p. 41, Dec 2002 p. 41; TLS Nov 15, 2002 p. 23; VOYA 24:198)

7-51   **CHANT, Joy (pseud. of Eileen Joyce Rutter).** *Red Moon and Black*
★★   *Mountain: The End of the House of Kendreth.* **(Vandarei series, bk. 1).**
Gr. 6–10. (Orig. British pub. 1970.)
A prophecy calls three children into Vandarei, the Starlit Land: Nick and Pene-
lope to the Black Mountain lair of the sorcerer Fendarl, and Oliver to join a
warrior band battling the Black Lord. Mythopoeic Fantasy Award, 1972. *The
Grey Mane of Morning* (1977, see Chapter 5, High Fantasy: Alternate Worlds
or Histories) and *When Voiha Wakes* (1983; Mythopoeic Fantasy Award,
1984) are set in the same world.
Dutton, 1971, 227 pp., o.p.
(BL 72:1584, 1594; CCBB 30:22; Kirkus 44:600; SLJ Sep 1976 p. 130; TLS 1970 p. 1449)

7-52   **CHARNAS, Suzy McKee.** *The Kingdom of Kevin Malone.* Gr. 7 up.
Amy chases neighborhood bully Kevin Malone through Central Park into the
magical world of Fayre Farre, where they become princess and prince and are
menaced by the White One. Mythopoeic Fantasy Award for Children's Literature, 1994.
Harcourt, 1993, 224 pp., o.p.; Magic Carpet, 1997, pap. (0-15-201191-9)
(BL 89:1808; HBG 4:308; Kirkus 61:594; SLJ Jan 1994 p. 132; VOYA 16:162)

7-53   **CHASE, Mary (Coyle).** *Loretta Mason Potts.* Gr. 4–6.
★   Bewitched for seven years, Loretta refuses to live with her real family and
draws her brother, Colin, into the enchantment with her.
Illus. by Harold Berson, Lippincott, 1958, 221 pp., o.p.; Peter Smith, 1989 (0-
8446-6428-6)
(BL 55:189; Kirkus 26:711; LJ 84:248)

7-54   **CHETWIN, Grace.** *Out of the Dark World.* Gr. 5–8.
Nightmares filled with cries for help convince Meg that she must enter the
Dark World to rescue a young cousin whose spirit has been taken over by the
forces of evil.
Lothrop, 1985, 160 pp., o.p.
(CCBB 39:105; SLJ Jan 1986 p. 64)

7-55   **CHEW, Ruth (Silver).** *Do-It-Yourself Magic.* Gr. 3–5.
A magic double-headed hammer, which enables Rachel and Scott to make
objects larger or smaller, helps them prevent a burglary and takes them inside a
medieval castle.
Illus. by the author, Hastings, 1988, 127 pp., o.p.
(BL 84:932; CCBB 41:113; Kirkus 55:1731; SLJ Mar 1988 p. 188)

7-56   **CHRISTOPHER, John (pseud. of Christopher Samuel Youd).** *Fireball.*
★   **(Fireball trilogy, bk. 1).** Gr. 5–8. (Orig. British pub. 1981.)
British Simon and his American cousin Brad are sent into the parallel world of
20th-century Roman Britain, where they take part in a Christian revolution
against the Romans and escape on a ship bound for the New World. In *New
Found Land* (1983), Brad, Simon, and their Roman friends, Bos and Curtius,
make a dangerous journey across the North American continent, battling
Algonquins and Vikings, and arrive at an Aztec settlement on the Pacific

Coast. In *Dragon Dance* (1986), Simon and Brad are kidnapped by slavers and taken to China, where they learn the secret of the fireball that began their adventures.

Elsevier/Dutton, 1981, 148 pp., o.p.

(BL 77:1083, 1097; CCBB 35:7; HB 57:307; SLJ Apr 1981 p. 122; Suth 3:85; TLS 1981 p. 1069; VOYA 4:38)

7-57   CLEMENTS, Bruce. *Two Against the Tide.* Gr. 5–7.
Tom and Sharon are kidnapped and taken to an island where the inhabitants have found the secret of everlasting youth.

Farrar, 1967, 199 pp., o.p., 1987, pap., 224 pp., o.p.

(BL 64:542; HB 43:587; Kirkus 35:966, 1444; SLJ 93:289)

7-58   COATSWORTH, Elizabeth (Jane). *Knock at the Door.* Gr. 3–5.
A half-fairy, half-mortal boy named Stephen helps his mortal father escape from imprisonment in Fairyland to the Outer World.

Illus. by F(rancis) D(onkin) Bedford, Macmillan, 1931, 73 pp., o.p.

(BL 28:155; HB 7:311; LJ 57:865; Mahony 3:202)

7-59   COLFER, Eoin. *The Wish List.* Gr. 6–10. (Orig. Irish pub. 2000.)
In this science-fantasy set in Ireland, orphaned teenage Meg is sent back to Earth from the hereafter by Saint Peter and Beelzebub to help the old neighbor she had tried to rob to right the mistakes he made in his life.

Hyperion/Miramax, 2003, 252 pp. (0-7868-1863-8); Scholastic, 2004, pap., 252 pp. (0-439-44336-9)

(CCBB 57:146; HBG 15:107; Kirkus 71:1221; SLJ Dec 2003 p. 148; VOYA 26:410)

7-60   COLLINS, Suzanne. *Gregor the Overlander.* **(The Underland Chronicles, ☆   vol. II).** Gr. 4–7.
Gregor, 11, and his younger sister, Boots, enter the nightmarish Underland after falling down an air duct in their New York City apartment building and discover that their missing father is being held prisoner there. In the sequel, *Gregor and the Prophecy of Bane* (2004), Gregor returns to the Underland to rescue Boots, kidnapped by giant rats who plan to lure Gregory back and destroy him in order to conquer the Underland. *Gregor and the Curse of the Warmbloods* (2005) is the third book in the series.

Scholastic, 2003, 320 pp. (0-435-43536-6)

(BL 100:608; CCBB 57:185; HB 79:609; HBG 15:89; Kirkus 71:1014, 1402; SLJ Nov 2003 p. 134; VOYA 26:322, 27:11)

COOMBS, Patricia. *The Lost Playground.*
See Chapter 11, Toy Fantasy.

7-61   COOPER (Grant), Susan (Mary). *Green Boy.* Gr. 4–7.
Brothers Trey and Lou cross between the tides from their Bahamian island, threatened by developers, to a polluted future world where young Lou is welcomed by Underground revolutionaries as the savior Green Man.

McElderry, 2002, 208 pp. (0-689-84751-3); Aladdin, 2003, pap., 208 pp. (0-689-84760-2)

(BL 98:1136; CCBB 55:315; HB 78:326; HBG 13:370; Kirkus 70:102; SLJ Feb 2002 p. 130)

7-62   COOPER (Grant), Susan (Mary). *Seaward.* Gr. 6–9.

✶   West and Cally become traveling companions after being wrenched into an unnamed world, where their treacherous journey takes them ever seaward in search of parents they fear are dead.
Macmillan, 1983, 180 pp., o.p.
(BL 80:158, 168, 169; CCBB 37:65; HB 60:59; Kirkus 51:202; SLJ Oct 1983 p. 157; Suth 3:100; TLS 1983 p. 1317; VOYA 7:37)

7-63   COOPER, Paul Fenimore. *Tal: His Marvelous Adventures with Noom-Zor-Noom.* Gr. 4–6.
Tal's journey to the kingdom of Troom ends with the discovery that he is the king's long-lost son.
Illus. by Ruth Reeves, Ungar, 1929, 305 pp., o.p.; Purple House, 2001, 305 pp. (1-930900-08-2)
(BL 26:285; HB 5:45, 49, 14:143, 34:124; Mahony 3:203; Moore 51:427; TLS 1930 p. 979)

7-64   CORBETT, Scott. *The Mysterious Zetabet.* Gr. 1–3.
Zachary Zwicker finds Zyxland to be the perfect place for him, because the names of all the important places and things begin with Z.
Illus. by Jon McIntosh, Little, Brown, 1979, 48 pp., o.p.
(CCBB 33:4; Kirkus 47:576; SLJ Sep 1979 p. 107)

7-65   COVILLE, Bruce. *The Dark Abyss.* **(The Dungeon series, vol. 2).** Gr. 10 up.
When Clive Folliot leaves England in 1868 to search the African jungle for his missing twin brother, Neville, he and his companions never expect to find themselves in a multilayered world called The Dungeon. The idea for this series was developed by Philip Jose Farmer. The first book is *The Black Tower* by Richard A. Lupoff (1988), and the sequels are *Valley of Thunder* by Charles de Lint (1989), *The Lake of Fire* by Robin W. Bailey (1989), *The Hidden City* by Charles de Lint (1990), and *Final Battle* by Richard A. Lupoff (1990).
Illus. by Robert Gould, Bantam, 1989, pap., 311 pp., o.p.
(VOYA 12:221)

7-66   COVILLE, Bruce. *Into the Land of the Unicorns.* **(The Unicorn Chronicles, vol. 1).** Gr. 4–6.
Hoping to avoid capture by her enemies, Cara "leaps" into the land of the unicorns, where she is befriended by a powerful dragon and the Unicorn Queen. In the sequel, *Song of the Wanderer* (1999, 2001), Cara tries to evade pursuit by the Hunters in order to rescue her grandmother and bring her back to Luster.
Scholastic, 1994, 159 pp. (0-590-45955-4), 1999, pap. (0-439-10838-1)
(BL 91:325, 94:475; HBG 6:74; SLJ Oct 1994 p. 120; VOYA 17:285:)

7-67   CROSS, John Kier. *The Other Side of Green Hills.* Gr. 5–7. (Orig. British pub. 1946, entitled *The Owl and the Pussycat*.)
Five children exploring a world on the other side of their old house meet the Moon Folk and an evil sorcerer.
Illus. by Robin Jacques, Coward, 1947, 190 pp., o.p.
(CCBB 1:2; HB 23:443; LJ 72:1473)

7-68   CROWNFIELD, Gertrude. *The Little Tailor of the Winding Way.* Gr. 3–5.

Jorin the tailor enters a land of happiness.
Illus. by Willy Pogány, Macmillan, 1917, 132 pp., o.p.
(BL 14:230; Mahony 2:163)

7-69   CUSHMAN, Carolyn. *Witch and Wombat.* Gr. 10 up.
Bentwood the troll disguises Grimmworld as a virtual reality game in order to
attract tourists whose belief in magic will boost the supply of magical energy
supporting his world.
Warner, 1994, pap., 316 pp., o.p.
(LJ Apr 15, 1994 p. 117; VOYA 17:154)

DAHL, Roald. *James and the Giant Peach: A Children's Story.*
See Chapter 9, Magic Adventure Fantasy.

7-70   DAHL, Roald. *The Minpins.* Gr. K–4. (Orig. British pub. 1991.)
✶   When Billy goes exploring in the Forest of Sin, he meets the Minpins, tiny
people who live high in the trees and are terrified of the Terrible Bloodsucking
Toothplucking Stone Chuckling Spittler.
Illus. by Patrick Benson, Viking, 1991, 48 pp. (0-670-84168-4)
(BL 88:447; CCBB 45:61; HB 68:64; HBG 3:57; Kirkus 59:1285; SLJ Nov 1991 p. 92; TLS
Nov 22, 1991 p. 23)

7-71   DALTON, Annie. *Out of the Ordinary.* Gr. 6–10. (Orig. British pub. 1988.)
✶   Molly's ability to see and hear things that others cannot qualifies her to care
for Floris, a mute child from another world whose enemies are trying to find
him.
Harper, 1990, 256 pp., o.p.
(BL 87:436; CCBB 44:113; HBG 2:85; Kirkus 58:1083; SLJ Oct 1990 p. 140; VOYA
13:295, 14:12)

7-72   DAVIDSON, Lionel. *Under Plum Lake.* Gr. 7 up. (Orig. British pub. 1980.)
A 12-year-old boy exploring a smugglers' cave on the Cornwall coast enters
the netherworld of Egon, an advanced civilization.
Knopf, 1980, 136 pp., o.p.
(Kirkus 48:1097; LJ 105:2236; TLS 1980 p. 1325; VOYA 4:54)

7-73   DE HAVEN, Tom. *The Orphan's Tent.* Gr. 7–12.
Alice and her brother, Ike, follow teenage drifter and would-be rock star Del
into a dangerous world called the Garden of Eden, hoping to save Del from a
cult that kidnaps orphans.
Illus. by Christopher H. Bing, Atheneum, 1996, 188 pp. (0-689-31967-3)
(HBG 8:78; Kirkus 64:1150; SLJ Oct 1996 p. 144; VOYA 19:268)

7-74   DE HAVEN, Tom. *Walker of Worlds.* (Chronicles of the King's Tramp,
✶   **vol. 1).** Gr. 11 up.
Pursued by sorcerers and monsters from another world, Jack comes to Earth
and tries to expose a drug company's research scandal, in this violent story for
mature readers. The sequels are *The End-of-Everything Man* (1991) and *The
Last Human* (1992).
Doubleday, 1990, 341 pp. (0-385-26430-5)
(BL 86:2076; Kirkus 58:748; LJ May 15, 1990 p. 99; VOYA 13:228, 14:13)

7-75 **DEITZ, Tom.** *Windmaster's Bane.* **(David Sullivan series, bk. 1).** Gr. 10 up.
David Sullivan enters the fairy kingdom through a crack in the world and becomes enmeshed in a power struggle between the Sidhe of Celtic myth and the Windmaster. The sequels are *Fireshaper's Doom* (1987), *Darkthunder's Way* (1989), *Sunshaker's War* (1990), *Stoneskin's Revenge* (1991), *Dreamseeker's Road* (1995), *Ghostcountry's Wrath* (1995), *Landslayer's Law* (1997), and *Warstalker's Track* (1999).
Avon, 1986, pap., 279 pp., o.p.
(BL 83:475, 502, 86:904)

7-76 **DE LINT, Charles.** *The Dreaming Place.* Gr. 7 up. (Orig. Canadian pub.
✮ 1990.)
Nina and Ashley, 16-year-old cousins, alternately narrate this tale in which Nina is kidnapped by a manitou, or Native American earth spirit, and Ash enters the spirit world to offer herself in her cousin's place. Many of De Lint's other novels are also set in Newford, Ontario, including *Dreams Underfoot* (Tor, 1993; see Chapter 5, High Fantasy: Alternate Worlds or Histories), *Memory and Dream* (1994), *Trader* (Tor, 1997), *Someplace to be Flying* (Tor, 1998; see Chapter 5, High Fantasy: Alternate Worlds or Histories), *Forests of the Heart* (2000), and *The Onion Girl* (2001), as well as a number of short story collections: *The Ivory and The Horn: A Newford Collection* (Tor, 1996, c1995), *Moonlight and Vines: A Newford Collection* (Tor, 1999; see Chapter 5, High Fantasy: Alternate Worlds or Histories), *Tapping the Dream Tree* (Tor, 2002), and some of the stories in *Waifs and Strays* (Viking, 2002; see Chapter 5, High Fantasy: Alternate Worlds or Histories).
Illus. by Brian Froud, Macmillan, 1990, 138 pp. (0-689-31571-6); Warner, 1992, pap. (0-446-36287-5)
(BL 87:734; CCBB 44:114; HBG 2:89; Kirkus 58:1454; SLJ Feb 1991, p. 93; VOYA 13:362, 14:10)

DE LINT, Charles. *Moonheart.*
See Chapter 6, High Fantasy: Myth or Legend Fantasy.

7-77 **DE LINT, Charles.** *Yarrow: An Autumn Tale.* Gr. 10 up. (Orig. pub. in Canada.)
Canadian fantasy author Caitlin Midhir discovers that the only way to escape from the vampire who is feasting on her dreams is to enter an alternate world populated by gnomes and elves.
Ace, 1986, pap., 244 pp., o.p.
(BL 83:625, 641; VOYA 9:291)

7-78 **DELL, Joan.** *The Missing Boy.* Gr. 4–6.
A young cockney girl named Deborah puts on a pair of magical 3-D glasses and is transported into a five-dimensional world where she helps a young boy to see again.
Illus. by Sheila Greenwald, Putnam, 1958, 192 pp., o.p.
(HB 35:130; Kirkus 26:819; LJ 84:249)

DE REGNIERS, Beatrice Schenk (Freedman). *Penny.*
See Chapter 1, Allegorical Fantasy and Literary Fairy Tales.

7-79 **DICKINSON, Peter (pseud. of Malcolm de Brissac).** *A Box of Nothing.*
✶ Gr. 4–8. (Orig. British pub. 1985.)
A magical box filled with ancient nothing takes James to a future world dump
patrolled by a vicious organization of rats and where he is befriended by a
creature called the Burra.
Illus. by Ian Newsham, Delacorte, 1988, 110 pp., o.p.
(CCBB 41:153; HB 54:630; Kirkus 56:691; SLJ June–July 1988, p. 103; TLS 1985 p. 347)

7-80 **DICKSON, Gordon R(upert).** *The Dragon and the George.* **(Dragon**
✶ **Knight series, bk. 1).** Gr. 10 up. (Orig. pub. in England.)
Jim Eckert finds himself transplanted into the body of a dragon in an alternate
world where his fiancée is being held captive. British Fantasy Society Award,
Best Novel, 1976. This story was based in part on Dickson's novelette "St.
Dragon and the George" published in *The Magazine of Fantasy and Science
Fiction* (Sept. 1957). The story was also published in *Dragon Tales*, ed. by
Isaac Asimov (Fawcett, 1982; see Chapter 3, Fantasy Collections). The sequels
are *The Dragon Knight* (Tor, 1990), *The Dragon on the Border* (1992), *Drag-
on at War* (1992), *The Dragon, the Earl, and the Troll* (1994; pap., 1996), *The
Dragon and the Djinn* (1996, 1998), *The Dragon and the Gnarly King* (1997),
The Dragon in Lionesse (1998), and *The Dragon and the Fair Maid of Kent*
(2000).
Ballantine, 1976, 1987, pap., 279 pp., o.p.
(BL 73:994, 1001, 78:594; Kliatt 11:10; VOYA 1:54)

7-81 **DONALDSON, Stephen R(upert).** *Lord Foul's Bane.* **(The Chronicles of**
✶ **Thomas Covenant, the Unbeliever, vol. 1).** Gr. 10 up. (Orig. pub. in England.)
In this first volume of a complex and powerful fantasy trilogy, Thomas
Covenant, a successful author shunned by family and friends because he has
leprosy, is struck by a car and awakens in The Land, where he reluctantly
agrees to help the Lords of Revelstone recover the Staff of Law, needed to
thwart Lord Foul's destructive plans. The sequels are *The Illearth War* (1977,
1978) and *The Power That Preserves* (1977, 1979). The three have been published in a three-volume boxed set entitled *The Chronicles of Thomas
Covenant* (Ballantine, 1982). British Fantasy Society Best Novel Award, 1978.
This trilogy is succeeded by a second trilogy called The Second Chronicles of
Thomas Covenant: *The Wounded Land* (1981), *The One Tree* (1983), and
White Gold Wielder (1983). *The Runes of the Earth* (Putnam, 2004) is the first
book of The Last Chronicles of Thomas Covenant.
Holt, 1977, 369 pp., o.p.; Ballantine, 1987, pap., o.p.; Del Rey, 1997, 496 pp.
(0-345-41843-3)
(BL 74:600, 606, 78:594, 86:904; Kirkus 45:865; LJ 102:2184)

7-82 **DONALDSON, Stephen R(upert).** *The Mirror of Her Dreams.* **(Mor-
dant's Need duology, bk. 1).** Gr. 10 up. (Orig. British pub. 1986.)
Gerarden, a bumbling young sorcerer, is sent into our world to search for a
champion to save the Kingdom of Mordant, and he stumbles across Terisa
Morgan, who makes the impulsive decision to return with him to Mordant. The
sequel is *A Man Rides Through* (1987).
Ballantine, 1986, 535 pp., o.p.; Del Rey, 2003, pap., 656 pp. (0-345-45985-7)
(BL 82:1633, 1636, 83:761; Kirkus 54:1326; LJ Nov 15, 1986 p. 112)

7-83 **DOUGLAS, Carole Nelson.** *Cup of Clay.* **(Taliswoman duology, vol. 1).** Gr. 10 up.
Alison Carver, a Minnesota journalist, is transported to the land of Veil, where she is given the task of guarding a magical cup that safeguards the existence of her new world. The sequel is *Seed upon the Wind* (1992).
Tor, 1991, 352 pp. (0-312-85146-4), 1992, pap. (0-8125-1248-0)
(BL 88:34, 38; Kirkus 59:975; LJ Sep 15, 1991 p. 116; VOYA 14:380)

DOUGLAS, Carole Nelson. *Exiles of the Rynth.*
See Chapter 12, Witchcraft and Sorcery Fantasy.

7-84 **DRAGT, Tonke.** *The Towers of February: A Diary by an Anonymous (for the Time Being) Author with Added Punctuation and Footnotes.* Gr. 5–9. (Orig. pub. in the Netherlands.)
In this science-fantasy, Tim convinces his scientist friend, Mr. Avla, to take him along on a travel experiment to a coexisting world. Once there, however, Tim realizes that he has lost his memory and his name.
Trans. by Maryka Rudnik, Morrow, 1975, 251 pp., o.p.
(BL 72:572, 577; CCBB 29:109; HB 52:163; Kirkus 43:1192; SLJ Jan 1976 p. 45)

7-85 **DRAKE, David.** *Lord of the Isles.* **(Lord of the Isles saga, bk. 1).** Gr. 10 up.
The fall of the first Kingdom of the Isles sends the sorcerer Tenoctris a thousand years into the future to find a young man named Garrick, destined to revive the ancient realm. The sequels are *Queen of Demons* (1998, 1999), *Servant of the Dragon* (1999, 2000), *Mistress of the Catacombs* (2001, 2002), *Goddess of the Ice Realm* (2003), and *Master of the Cauldron* (2004).
Tor, 1997, 448 pp. (0-312-85396-3), 1998, pap., 625 pp. (0-8125-2240-0)
(BL 93:1886; Kirkus 65:841; LJ Sep 15, 1997 p. 106; VOYA 20:392)

DUANE, Diane (Elizabeth). *The Book of Night with Moon.*
See Chapter 12, Witchcraft and Sorcery Fantasy.

DUANE, Diane (Elizabeth). *So You Want to Be a Wizard.*
See Chapter 12, Witchcraft and Sorcery Fantasy.

7-86 **DUGGAN, Maurice (Noel).** *Falter Tom and the Water Boy.* Gr. 3–5. (Orig. pub. in New Zealand, 1958.)
A sea-boy invites an old sailor named Falter Tom to come and live in the realm of the sea kings. Esther Glen Award, 1959.
Illus. by Kenneth Rowell, Phillips, 1959, 61 pp., o.p.
(CCBB 13:112; HB 36:128; LJ 84:3925; TLS 1975 p. 365)

7-87 **DUNKLE, Clare B.** *The Hollow Kingdom.* **(The Hollow Kingdom trilogy,**
✮ **bk. 1).** Gr. 6–10.
Abducted by Marak, the Goblin King, orphaned Kate is taken into the goblin's underground world and forcibly married to him, in this variation on the "Beauty and the Beast" theme. The sequels are *Close Kin* (2004) and *In the Coils of the Snake* (2005). Mythopoeic Fantasy Award for Children's Literature, 2004.
Holt, 2003, 230 pp. (0-8050-7390-6)
(BL 100:608; CCBB 57:227; HBG 15:108; Kirkus 71:1223; SLJ Dec 2003 p. 149; VOYA 27:58)

7-88 **DURRELL, Gerald (Malcolm).** *The Talking Parcel.* Gr. 4–6. (Orig. British pub. 1974.)
A parrot, a spider, and a toad enlist the help of three children to save Mythologia after fire-breathing Cockatrices steal the books of magic.
Illus. by Pamela Johnson, Lippincott, 1975, 191 pp., o.p.
(BL 71:1127; HB 51:268; Kirkus 43:453; SLJ May 1975 p. 54; TLS 1974 p. 1380)

7-89 **EAGER, Edward (McMaken).** *Knight's Castle.* Gr. 4–6.
★ Roger, Ann, Jack, and Eliza find their way into a medieval world where they become knights and battle giants. In the sequel, *Time Garden* (1958; Harcourt, 1999), they return to the past, and in *Half Magic* (1954, 1999; see Chapter 9, Magic Adventure Fantasy) and *Magic by the Lake* (1957, 1999), their parents have magic adventures as children.
Illus. by N(iels) M(ogens) Bodecker, Harcourt, 1956, 183 pp., 1985, 1989, pap., o.p.; Harcourt, 1999 (0-15-202074-8); 1999, pap. (0-15-202073-X)
(BL 52:281; HB 32:120; HBG 10:290; Kirkus 23:859; LJ 81:766)

7-90 **ECKERT, Allan W.** *The Dark Green Tunnel.* **(Mesmerian Annals, bk. 1).** Gr. 5–7.
The dark-green tunnel near their cousin William's Everglades home ends at a turnstile through which William and twins Lara and Barbaby enter Mesmeria, a kingdom enslaved by its evil king. The sequel is *The Wand: The Return to Mesmeria* (1985).
Illus. by David Wiesner, Little, Brown, 1984, 256 pp., o.p.
(BL 80:1114; CCBB 37:185; SLJ Aug 1984, p. 72)

7-91 **EMERSON, Ru.** *Night Threads: The Calling of the Three.* **(Night Threads series, vol. 1).** Gr. 10 up.
Threads of magic pull three Californians, Jennifer, a young attorney, her older sister, Robyn, and Robyn's teenage son, into a medieval world to help an exiled nobleman regain his throne. The sequels are *The Two in Hiding* (1991), *One Land, One Duke* (1992), *The Craft of Light* (1993), *The Art of the Sword* (1994), and *The Science of Power* (1995).
Ace, 1990, 256 pp., o.p.
(BL 87:421, 430; Kliatt Jan 1991 p. 20; LJ Sep 15, 1990 p. 104; VOYA 14:42)

7-92 **ENDE, Michael.** *The Neverending Story.* Gr. 5 up. (Orig. German pub.
★ 1979.)
A boy named Bastian becomes so engrossed in reading a book about young Atreyu's quest to find a cure for the ailing Empress of Fantasiana that he enters the book himself, saves Fantasiana, and sets off on his own adventures.
Trans. by Ralph Mannheim, illus. by Roswitha Quadflieg, Doubleday, 1983, 396 pp., o.p.; Puffin, 1996, pap., 444 pp. (0-14-038633-5); Dutton, 1997, 396 pp. (0-525-45758-5)
(BL 80:488, 496; HB 60:228; HBG 9:70; Kirkus 51:844; TLS 1983 p. 1317)

FARMER (Mockridge), Penelope. *A Castle of Bone.*
See Chapter 6, High Fantasy: Myth or Legend Fantasy.

7-93 **FARMER (Mockridge), Penelope.** *William and Mary: A Story.* Gr. 5–7.
✷ (Orig. British pub. 1974.)
Mary and William find that a rare shell has the power to carry them into an
aquarium, back to the fall of Atlantis, and to a world beneath the sea.
Atheneum, 1974, 160 pp., o.p.
(BL 71:168; CCBB 28:93; HB 50:690; Kirkus 42:1160; LJ 99:3052; Suth 2:141; TLS 1974 p.
1380)

7-94 **FARTHING, Alison.** *The Mystical Beast.* Gr. 4–6. (Orig. British pub. 1976.)
Sara and Henry enter the Other Side after meeting Lavinia, daughter of the
Hereditary Keeper of the Mystical Beast, and organize a hectic search for the
Beast, to avert a terrible occurrence.
Illus. by Anne Mieke, Hastings, 1978, 123 pp., o.p.
(CCBB 32:42; SLJ Oct 1978 p. 144; TLS 1976 p. 882)

FEYDY, Anne (Lindbergh Sapieyevski). *Osprey Island.*
See Chapter 9, Magic Adventure Fantasy.

7-95 **FIELD, Rachel (Lyman).** *Eliza and the Elves.* Gr. 2–4.
Tales and rhymes about elfin life and the possibility of stumbling into their
green land.
Illus. by Elizabeth MacKinstry, Macmillan, 1926, 1946, 96 pp., o.p.
(BL 23:136; HB 2:42; Mahony 2:279; Moore:130)

FIELD, Rachel (Lyman). *The Magic Pawnshop; a New's Year Eve Fantasy.*
See Chapter 9, Magic Adventure Fantasy.

7-96 **FISCHER, Marjorie.** *Red Feather.* Gr. 3–5.
When the Queen of Fairyland needs a new mortal child to be her maid, she
commands that a fairy child be exchanged for baby Rosemary, but the two
babies look identical and no one can tell them apart.
Illus. by Davine, Modern Age, 1937, 151 pp., o.p.; illus. by Davine, Messner,
1950, 149 pp., o.p.
(BL 34:112; CCBB 3:68; LJ 75:1756, 2085)

7-97 **FISK, Pauline.** *Midnight Blue.* Gr. 6–9. (Orig. British pub. 1990.)
✷✷ Bonnie escapes life with her hateful grandmother and ineffectual mother by
stowing away on a hot air balloon to an alternate version of her own unhappy
world. Nestlé Smarties Grand Prix for Children's Books, 1990.
Lion, 1990, 217 pp., o.p., 1992, pap. (0-7459-1925-1); Chariot Victor, 1992,
pap., 217 pp. (0-7459-1848-4); Bloomsbury, 2003, 217 pp. (1-58234-829-4)
(BL 87:1464, 100:325; HBG 1:255, 15:91; Kirkus 71:123; SLJ Nov 2003 p. 138; VOYA
26:412, 27:11)

7-98 **FLECKER, (Herman) James Elroy.** *The King of Alsander.* Gr. 6 up. (Orig.
British pub. 1914.)
In this tale written by an English poet, Norman Price walks out of a grocer's
shop one day and steps into the legendary white city of Alsander.
Putnam, 1914, o.p.; Knopf, 1926, 286 pp., o.p.
(HB 3:18–22)

7-99 **FRANCE, Anatole (pseud. of Jacques Anatole François Thibault).** *Bee, the Princess of the Dwarfs.* Gr. 5–7. (Orig. French pub. 1882; orig. U.S. title *Honey-Bee*, 1911, 1924.)
After she is spirited away by nixies, Honey-Bee is crowned princess of the dwarfs, but she longs for her home and her playmate, George.
Trans. by Peter Wright, illus. by Charles Robinson, Dutton, 1912, 127 pp., o.p.
(BL 9:40; Mahony 1:25)

7-100 **FREEMAN, Martha.** *The Spy Wore Shades.* Gr. 4–6.
Eleven-year-old Dougie Minners meets Varloo, a spy from the Hekkian world, and discovers that a secret underground civilization exists in the caves near his home.
HarperCollins, 2001, 235 pp. (0-06-029270-9)
(BL 98:318; Kirkus 69:658; SLJ Aug 2001 p. 178)

7-101 **FRIESNER, Esther M.** *Gnome Man's Land.* **(Tim Desmond trilogy, bk. 1).** Gr. 10 up.
After ancient mythical creatures escape from the Faerie world into ours through a leak in a Brooklyn delicatessen, high school student Tim Desmond finds himself under the "protection" of a banshee. The sequels are *Harpy High* (1991) and *Unicorn U* (1992).
Ace, 1991, pap., 235 pp., o.p.
(BL 87:805, 817; VOYA 14:42)

7-102 **FRY, Rosalie K(ingsmill).** *The Mountain Door.* Gr. 4–6. (Orig. British pub. 1960.)
Fenella returns to the fairies who once exchanged her for a human baby, and meets Nell, the girl whose place she took.
Illus. by the author, Dutton, 1961, 128 pp., o.p.
(BL 57:612; HB 37:269; Kirkus 29:163; LJ 86:1983; TLS Nov 25, 1960 p. x)

7-103 **GAIMAN, Neil.** *Coraline.* Gr. 5–8. (Orig. British pub. 2002.)
☆ Coraline discovers that the empty flat next door to her family's apartment is a strange alternate world where her "other parents" have black button eyes and urge her to stay forever. Hugo Award, Best Novella, 2003.
Illus. by Dave McKean, HarperCollins, 2002, 176 pp. (0-06-623744-0), 2003, pap. (0-380-80734-3)
(BL 98:1948, 99:592; CCBB 56:106; HB 78:755; HBG 14:79; Kirkus 70:881; SLJ Aug 2002 p. 184, Dec 2002 p. 42; VOYA 25:296, 26:11)

7-104 **GAIMAN, Neil.** *Neverwhere.* Gr. 10 up. (Orig. British pub. 1996.)
Richard Mayhew follows a girl called Door into an underground alternative "London Below," where they try to determine why her family was murdered.
Avon, 1997, 352 pp. (0-380-97363-4), 1998, pap., 388 pp. (0-380-78901-9)
(BL 94:732; Kirkus 65:822; LJ June 15, 1997 p. 97)

7-105 **GAIMAN, Neil.** *Stardust.* Gr. 10 up. (Orig. British pub. 1998.)
Half-fairy Tristran Thorn has promised to bring a fallen star back over the wall from Faerie to England, but a witch and the sons of the Lord of Stormhold want the star themselves. Mythopoeic Fantasy Award for Adult Literature, 1999.
Avon, 1998, 256 pp. (0-380-97728-1), 2000, pap., 336 pp. (0-380-80455-7)

(BL 95:451, 1678, 96:819; Kirkus 66:1551; LJ Jan 1999 p. 148; SLJ Feb 1999 p. 142; VOYA 22:270, 23:11)

7-106 GALL, Alice (Crew), and CREW, Fleming. *The Royal Mimkin.* Gr. 3–5.
Binney and Mr. Tidd board a flying boat to another world.
Illus. by Camille Masline, Oxford University Press, 1934, 128 pp., o.p.
(BL 31:99; Bookshelf 1934–1935 p. 5; HB 10:298; LJ 60:213; Mahony 3:205)

7-107 GARDNER, Craig Shaw. *Dragon Sleeping.* **(The Dragon Circle trilogy, bk. 1).** Gr. 10 up.
A summer hurricane hurls the residents of Chestnut Circle from their suburban 1967 lives into a world ruled by warring wizards and a sleeping dragon. The sequels are *Dragon Walking* (1995) and *Dragon Burning* (1996, 1997).
Ace, 1994, 368 pp., o.p.
(LJ May 15, 1994 p. 103; VOYA 17:156)

GARFIELD, Leon. *The Wedding Ghost.*
See Chapter 6, High Fantasy: Myth or Legend Fantasy.

7-108 **GARNER, Alan.** *Elidor.* Gr. 6–8. (Orig. British pub. 1965.)
☆ Roland, Helen, Nicholas, and David unexpectedly stumble into the medieval kingdom of Elidor, where they promise to protect four treasures from the evil beings that follow them back into 20th-century England. Carnegie Medal Commended Book, 1965.
Walck, 1967, 186 pp., o.p.; Philomel, 1979, 148 pp., o.p.; Dell, 1993, pap. (0-440-40763-X); Harcourt, 1999, pap., 192 pp. (0-15-201797-6)
(BL 63:1099; HB 43:462; Kirkus 35:269; LJ 92:2449; TLS 1965 p. 1131)

7-109 GEE, Maurice (Gough). *The Halfmen of O.* Gr. 5–8. (Orig. pub. in New Zealand, 1982.)
Susan and her cousin Nick are chosen to set things right in the Land of O, a country in turmoil ever since the invasion of the murderous Halfmen.
Oxford University Press, 1983, 204 pp., o.p.
(BL 79:1400; SLJ Sep 1983 p. 134; TLS 1982 p. 1302)

7-110 GEE, Maurice (Gough). *The World Around the Corner.* Gr. 3–6. (Orig. pub. in New Zealand, 1981.)
An old woman tells Caroline that she must keep her magical antique spectacles away from the evil Mr. Grimble.
Illus. by Gary Hebley, Oxford University Press, 1984, 72 pp., o.p.
(CCBB 38:25; SLJ Oct 1981 p. 141, Apr 1985 p. 87)

7-111 GENTLE, Mary. *A Hawk in Silver.* Gr. 7–9. (Orig. British pub. 1978.)
A strange silver coin takes 15-year-olds Holly and Chris out of their tension-filled lives at an English school ruled by an abusive gang of girls, and draws them into a magical world where a unicorn helps them stop a bitter war between the hill dwellers and the sea people.
Lothrop, 1985, 240 pp., o.p.
(BL 81:1050, 1058; CCBB 38:125; SLJ May 1985 p. 100; TLS 1978 p. 376; VOYA 8:138)

7-112 GIDEON, Melanie. *The Map That Breathed.* Gr. 5–9.
Nora Sweetkale, 12, steps through a portal made by her new friend, Billy

Nolan, into Sansaera, an island world endangered by the Provisioner, who sucks the souls out of young children.

Holt, 2003, 256 pp. (0-8050-7142-3)

(BL 100:609; CCBB 57:230; HBG 15:92; Kirkus 71:1224; SLJ Dec 2003 p. 152; VOYA 26:503)

7-113 **GILMAN (Butters), Dorothy.** *The Maze in the Heart of the Castle.* Gr. 6–10.

The sudden deaths of his beloved parents compel 16-year-old Colin to undertake a perilous journey through a maze, deep within the castle atop Rheembeck Mountain.

Doubleday, 1983, 230 pp., o.p.; Fawcett, 1991, pap. (0-449-70398-3)

(BL 79:1138, 1143; CCBB 36:16; SLJ Dec 1983 p. 66; VOYA 6:214)

7-114 **GOLDS, Cassandra.** *Michael and the Secret War.* Gr. 6–9. (Orig. Australian pub. 1985.)

When the Secret War between Good and Evil seeps into our world through Michael's cracked mirror, he and his sister, Sarah Jane, are enlisted to aid the forces of Good.

Macmillan, 1989, 184 pp., o.p.

(HBG 1:83; Kirkus 57:1326; SLJ Oct 1989 p. 133; VOYA 12:289, 13:14)

7-115 **GOLDSTEIN, Lisa.** *Dark Cities Underground.* Gr. 10 up.

Journalist Ruth Berry and her estranged adult son Jerry find themselves wandering through the dangerous underground world she created and wrote about when he was a child.

Tor, 1999, 256 pp. (0-312-86828-6), 2000, pap. (0-312-86827-8)

(BL 95:1678; Kirkus 67:579; LJ June 15, 1999 p. 112)

7-116 **GORDON, John (William).** *The Edge of the World.* Gr. 7–9. (Orig. British
✷   pub. 1983.)

Tension and horror predominate as Tekker and Kit slip back and forth between the fens near their home and a bewitched land at the edge of the world, where they attempt to rescue a woman imprisoned by Ma Grist.

Atheneum, 1983, 186 pp., o.p.

(HB 59:581; Kirkus 51:175; SLJ Jan 1984 p. 75; TLS 1983 p. 1047; VOYA 6:343)

GOUDGE, Elizabeth (de Beauchamp). *The Valley of Song.*
See Chapter 1, Allegorical Fantasy and Literary Fairy Tales.

7-117 **GOULD, Joan.** *Otherborn.* Gr. 6–9.

Shipwrecked on a tropical island called the Land of Light, Mark and Allegra discover the inhabitants' secret: the young people are the tribal elders and the old people are the newborn children.

Coward, 1980, 160 pp., o.p.

(CCBB 34:53; HB 57:190; SLJ Sep 1980 p. 71; Suth 3:157)

7-118 **GRAY, Nicholas Stuart.** *Grimbold's Other World.* Gr. 5–7. (Orig. British pub. 1963.)

A goatherd named Muffler gets into trouble when he returns to a world of darkness shown him by Grimbold the cat.

Illus. by Charles Keeping, Meredith, 1968, 184 pp., o.p.
(BL 64:1185; Kirkus 36:114; TLS 1963 p. 427)

7-119 **GREAVES, Margaret.** *The Dagger and the Bird: A Story of Suspense.* Gr.
☆   4–7. (Orig. British pub. 1971.)
When Bridget and Luke discover that their brother, Simon, is a fairy
changeling, they journey to the Kingdom of the Good People to find their real
brother.
Illus. by Laszlo Kubinyi, Harper, 1975, 144 pp., o.p.
(BL 71:618; HB 51:147; Kirkus 43:374; SLJ May 1975 p. 70)

7-120 **GREEN, Simon R.** *Drinking Midnight Wine.* Gr. 10 up. (Orig. British pub.
2001.)
Bookstore clerk Toby Dexter follows a beautiful woman named Gayle through
a disappearing door into the magical world of Mysterie, where they enlist the
aid of Jimmy Thunder, God for Hire, to help make sense of the conflict that
has engulfed the realm.
NAL/Roc, 2002, pap., 304 pp. (0-451-45867-2); NAL, 2003, pap. (0-451-
45935-0)
(BL 98:930; LJ Feb 15, 2002 p. 181)

7-121 **GREGORIAN, Joyce Ballou.** *The Broken Citadel.* **(Sibby Barron trilogy,
bk. 1).** Gr. 7–9.
A shaft of sunlight in an abandoned house takes Sibby into the lands of
Tredana and Treclere, where she joins Prince Leron in his fight against Queen
Simirimia. The sequels are *Castledown* (1977) and *The Great Wheel* (Tor,
1987).
Illus. by the author, Atheneum, 1975, 373 pp., o.p.
(BL 72:235; HB 52:154; Kirkus 43:782; SLJ Nov 1975 p. 90)

7-122 **GRIFFIN, Peni R(ae).** *The Maze.* Gr. 4–6.
Caroline's stepbrother Hector chases her into a painting of a mountainside
maze, where they battle a minotaur and outwit a sphinx.
McElderry, 1994, 120 pp. (0-689-50624-4)
(CCBB 48:166; HBG 6:77; SLJ Jan 1995 p. 108)

GRIFFIN, Peni R(ae). *Otto from Otherwhere.*
See Chapter 9, Magic Adventure Fantasy.

7-123 **GRIPE, Maria (Kristina).** *The Land Beyond.* Gr. 5–8. (Orig. Swedish pub.
1967.)
An explorer, a young king, and a princess travel to a world not found on any
map.
Trans. by Sheila La Farge, illus. by Harald Gripe, Delacorte, 1974, 214 pp.,
o.p.
(HB 51:152; Kirkus 42:949; LJ 99:3045; TLS 1975 p. 1457)

7-124 **GUNN, Neil Miller.** *The Green Isle of the Great Deep.* Gr. 10 up. (Orig.
British pub. 1944.)
Old Hector and his grandson, Art, fall through a Scottish pond onto the Green
Isle, where the old man is imprisoned and the boy is hunted down for interro-

gation by the Questioner. This is the sequel to *Young Art and Old Hector* (1991; orig. British pub. 1942).
Walker, 1995, 256 pp., o.p.
(BL 91:1479; Kirkus 64:332; LJ May 15, 1995 p. 94)

7-125 GURNEY, James. *Dinotopia: A Land Apart from Time.* Gr. 4 up.
Shipwrecked on an uncharted island, Boston biologist Arthur Denison and his son, Will, discover Dinotopia, a land where dinosaurs and humans live together in a harmonious society. The sequels written by Gurney are *Dinotopia: Lost City* (1992), *Dinotopia: Firestorm* (1997), *Dinotopia: Dream Ship* (1999), and *Dinotopia: The World Beneath* (1999). Other authors have also written sequels: *Dinotopia: Windchaser* (1995, by Scott Ciencin), *Dinotopia: Hatchling* (1995, by Midori Snyder), *Dinotopia: Lost* (1998, 2002, by Alan Dean Foster), *Dinotopia: The Maze* (1998, by Inc. Second Age), *The Hand of Dinotopia* (1999, by Alan Dean Foster), *Dinotopia: Thunder Falls* (1999, by Scott Ciencin), *Dinotopia: Sky Dance* (2002, by Scott Ciencin), *Dinotopia: Chomper* (2002, by Don Glut), and *Dinotopia: Return to Lost City* (2002, by Scott Ciencin).
Illus. by the author, Turner, 1992, 159 pp., o.p.; HarperCollins, 1998, 168 pp. (0-06-028003-4)
(BL 89:329; Kirkus 60:921; SLJ Dec 1992 p. 110)

HACKETT, Walter Anthony. *The Swans of Ballycastle.*
See Chapter 1, Allegorical Fantasy and Literary Fairy Tales.

7-126 HAMBLY, Barbara. *The Silent Tower.* **(Windrose Chronicles, bk. 1).** Gr. 10 up.
Kidnapped and taken into an alternate world where magic works, Joanna, a young computer programmer, becomes embroiled in the intrigues of the Empire of Perryth. The sequels are *Search the Seven Hills* (1987), *The Silicon Mage* (1988), and *Dog Wizard* (1993). *Stranger at the Wedding* (1994; see Chapter 12, Witchcraft and Sorcery Fantasy) is set in the same world.
Ballantine, 1988, pap., 369 pp., o.p.
(BL 83:550, 571, 86:905; LJ Dec 1986 p. 142)

7-127 HARDING, Lee. *Misplaced Persons.* Gr. 7–9. (Orig. pub. in *Science Fantasy* magazine, 1961; orig. Australian pub. 1979, entitled *Displaced Person.*)
Graeme is horrified to discover that he has become invisible in his own world and has slipped into a dim gray parallel world.
Harper, 1979, 149 pp., o.p.
(CCBB 32:174; Kirkus 47:580)

7-128 HARRIS, Anne. *Inventing Memory.* Gr. 10 up.
The lives of Wendy Chrenko, a graduate student in anthropology, and Shula, an ancient Sumerian slave and priestess of the goddess Inanna, become intertwined after Wendy tries a dangerous experiment in an attempt to prove the existence of a matriarchal Sumerian society.
Tor, 2004, 336 pp. (0-312-86539-2)
(BL 100:1146; Kirkus 72:18)

HENRY, Jan. *Tiger's Chance.*
See Chapter 9, Magic Adventure Fantasy.

7-129   HICKMAN, Janet. *Ravine.* Gr. 4–7.
A misty ravine divides the world of "wizard's boy" Ulf, forced to serve in the king's household, from the present-day world of Jeremy, whose dog crosses the ravine to Ulf, in this story based on the German hero saga of "Gudrun the Fair."
Greenwillow, 2002, 215 pp. (0-06-029367-5)
(BL 98:1846; CCBB 56:19; HB 78:331; HBG 13:374; SLJ Oct 2002 p. 164)

7-130   HILGARTNER, Beth. *Colors in the Dreamweaver's Loom.* Gr. 6–10.
✯   Zan Scarsdale becomes lost in the woods after her father's death and ends up in another world, where she becomes a warrior hero of the gentle Orathi tribe. In the sequel, *The Feast of the Trickster* (1991), five of Zan's Orathi companions are sent to our world to search for Zan after the Trickster pulls her back through the void and erases her memories.
Houghton, 1989, 256 pp., o.p.
(BL 86:53, 772, 906, 994.; HB 65:775; HBG 1:81; Kirkus 57:1403; SLJ Oct 1989 p. 119; VOYA 12:224)

7-131   HILL, David. *Time Out.* Gr. 6–9.
Comatose and near death after a cross-country race training accident, Kit slips into a parallel world where he is a champion runner who has nightmares about another life and is inspired by his new running partner, Alrika.
Cricket, 2001, 117 pp. (0-8126-2899-3)
(CCBB 55:104; HBG 13:97; SLJ Oct 2001 p. 160)

HILL, Elizabeth Starr. *Ever-After Island.*
See Chapter 9, Magic Adventure Fantasy.

7-132   HILTON, James. *Lost Horizon.* Gr. 8 up. (Orig. British pub. 1933.)
✯   Four survivors of a plane crash in Tibet find their way to the lamasery of Shangri-La, an oasis of eternal youth, but they long to return home.
Morrow, 1933, 1936, 281 pp., o.p.; Pocket, 1991, pap., 231 pp. (0-671-66427-1); Morrow, 1996, 272 pp. (0-688-14656-2); Perennial, 2004, pap., 256 pp. (0-06-059452-7)
(BL 30:79; TLS 1933 p. 648)

7-133   HOBAN, Russell C(onwell). *The Trokeville Way.* Gr. 7–10. (Orig. British pub. 1996.)
After hitting his head during a beating by a bully, Nick Hartly descends into the world of a painting called "The Trokeville Way," in this complex story filled with wordplay and poetry.
Knopf, 1996, 118 pp. (0-679-88560-9)
(BL 93:588; CCBB 50:209; HBG 8:80; Kirkus 64:1533; SLJ Dec 1996 p. 136; TLS Mar 29, 1996 p. 24)

7-134   HOFFMAN, Mary. *Stravaganza: City of Masks.* (Stravaganza series, bk.
✯   1). Gr. 6 up. (Orig. British pub. 2002.)
Each night, Lucien, an English boy undergoing cancer treatment, enters an alternate 16th-century Venice called Belleza, where he becomes Luciano,

apprentice to a powerful magician, and member of a time-traveling brotherhood. In the sequel, *Stravaganza: City of Stars* (2003), horse-loving Georgia Grady escapes from her abusive stepbrother to Remora, where she becomes the jockey Giorgio Gredi to compete in the annual Stellalata horse race. The third book in the series is *Stravaganza: City of Flowers* (2005).
Bloomsbury, 2002, 256 pp. (1-58234-791-3); Bloomsbury, 2004, pap., 352 pp. (1-58234-917-7)
(BL 99:407; CCBB 56:238; Kirkus 70:1392; SLJ Nov 2002 p. 168; VOYA 25:396)

HOFFMANN, E(rnst) T(heodor) A(madeus). *The Nutcracker.*
See Chapter 11, Toy Fantasy.

7-135 HOWARD, Joan (pseud. of Patricia Gordon). *The Oldest Secret.* Gr. 6–8.
Clues in an ancient book lead Hugh to an island populated by legendary beings.
Illus. by Garry MacKenzie, Viking, 1953, 128 pp., o.p.
(BL 50:84; CCBB 7:62; HB 29:362; Kirkus 21:429)

HOWARD, Joan (pseud. of Patricia Gordon). *The Thirteenth Is Magic.*
See Chapter 9, Magic Adventure Fantasy.

7-136 HOWE, James. *Babes in Toyland.* Gr. 3–5.
In this story based on the libretto of Victor Herbert's 1903 operetta by the same name, Jane and Alan survive a shipwreck, arranged by their greedy Uncle Barnaby, and escape to Toyland, where they meet Mother Goose characters and are reunited with their true loves.
Illus. by Allen Atkinson, Harcourt, 1986, 96 pp., o.p.
(BL 83:352; Kirkus 54:1370; SLJ Oct 1986 p. 112)

7-137 HOYT, Sarah A. *Ill Met by Moonlight.* Gr. 10 up.
✫ Young Will Shakespeare enters the world of Fairie after his wife, Nan, and their infant daughter are stolen by Prince Quicksilver of Elvenland, who wants to make Nan his queen. The sequels are *All Night Awake* (2002) and *Any Man So Daring* (2003).
Berkley/Ace, 2001, 278 pp. (0-441-00860-7); Ace, 2002, pap., 304 pp. (0-441-00983-2)
(BL 98:305; Kirkus 69:1330; Kliatt Jan 2003 p. 20; LJ Oct 15, 2001 p. 112; VOYA 24:447)

7-138 HUDSON, W(illiam) H(enry). *Green Mansions: A Romance of the Tropical Forest.* Gr. 10 up. (Orig. British pub. 1893.)
The romance between a magical girl of the forest and an Amazon jungle adventurer ends tragically after he introduces her to the outside world and her paradise is destroyed.
Putnam, 1904, o.p.; illus. by E. McKnight Kauffer, Knopf, 1916, 1943, 350 pp., o.p.; illus. by Keith Henderson, World, 1931, o.p.; illus. by E. McKnight Kauffer, Random, 1944, 303 pp., o.p.; Oxford University Press, 1998, pap., 209 pp. (0-19-283288-3); Classic Books, 2001, pap. (0-7426-8540-3); Indy-Publish.com, 2002, 208 pp. (1-4043-0460-6), pap. (1-4043-0461-4)
(BL 12:482, 22:428, 27:417, 41:304, 46:201)

7-139 HUNTER, Mollie (pseud. of Maureen Mollie Hunter McVeigh McIl-
✫ **wraith).** *The Haunted Mountain: A Story of Suspense.* Gr. 4–7. (Orig.

British pub. 1972.)

A stubborn Highlander named MacAllister, enslaved by the fairy folk for refusing to pay a tithe, is rescued by his dog and his son.

Illus. by Laszlo Kubinyi, Harper, 1972, 144 pp., o.p.

(BL 68:909; CCBB 26:9; HB 48:269; Kirkus 40:401; LJ 97:1928; Suth:203; TLS 1972 p. 1323)

7-140   HUTCHINS, Hazel (J.). *The Prince of Tarn.* Gr. 4–6. (Orig. pub. in Canada.)

The Prince of Tarn, a character from a book written by Fred's late mother, arrives at 11-year-old Fred's home and demands help to return to his kingdom.

Illus. by Ruth Ohi, Annick, 1997, 143 pp. (1-55037-439-7)

(BL 94:1011; SLJ Feb 1998 p. 109)

7-141   IBBOTSON, Eva. *The Secret of Platform 13.* Gr. 4–7. (Orig. British pub. ☆   1994.)

A wizard, an ogre, a fay and a hag leave their magical island to search for a kidnapped baby prince brought to London through a gateway hidden beneath Platform 13 of an abandoned railway station.

Illus. by Sue Porter, Dutton, 1998, 231 pp. (0-525-45929-4); Puffin, 1999, pap. (0-14-130286-0)

(BL 94:1011; HBG 9:332; Kirkus 66:57; SLJ Mar 1998 p. 214, Dec 1998 p. 25)

7-142   INGELOW, Jean. *Mopsa the Fairy.* Gr. 4–6. (Orig. British and U.S. pub. 1869.)

A boy named Jack crawls into the hollow of an old thorn tree and finds himself in Fairyland.

Illus. by Dora Curtis and Diana Stanley, Dutton, 1964, 142 pp., o.p.;

Kessinger, 2004, pap., 120 pp. (1-41913-510-4)

(BL 60:882; Bookshelf 1923–1924, p. 15; HB 3:48, 40:377; LJ 26:67; Mahony 2:281)

7-143   IPCAR, Dahlov (Zorach). *A Dark Horn Blowing.* Gr. 7–10.

Nora is unwillingly drawn into an unknown world to care for the infant son of a dying queen.

Viking, 1978, 228 pp., o.p.

(BL 74:1610; Kirkus 46:510; SLJ Nov 1978 p. 82; VOYA 1:42, 3:55)

IPCAR, Dahlov (Zorach). *The Queen of Spells.*

See Chapter 6, High Fantasy: Myth or Legend Fantasy.

7-144   JAMES, Mary (pseud. of Maryjane Meaker; a.k.a. M. E. Kerr). *The Shuteyes.* Gr. 4–7.

Chester Dumbello's wish to escape his small Mississippi town is granted when a one-eyed parrot takes him to Alert, where he is imprisoned in the Tower of Loathing.

Scholastic, 1993, 176 pp. (0-590-45069-7)

(HBG 4:299; Kirkus 61:62; SLJ Apr 1993 p. 120)

7-145   JONES, Adrienne. *The Mural Master.* Gr. 5–7.

Four children follow Til Pleeryn, the mural master, through one of his murals into the land of Pawthania, on a mission to free the captive king.

Illus. by David White, Houghton, 1974, 249 pp., o.p.
(CCBB 28:44; HB 50:283; LJ 99:2271)

7-146 **JONES, Diana Wynne.** *Dogsbody.* Gr. 6–8. (Orig. British pub. 1976.)
★ Visiting Earth in search of a sacred object that fell from the sky, Sirius, the Dog Star, takes on a dog's form and befriends a lonely human girl. Carnegie Medal Commended Book, 1975.
Greenwillow, 1977, 1988, 256 pp., o.p.; Greenwillow, 2001, 261 pp. (0-06-029880-4); HarperTrophy, 2001, pap. (0-06-441038-2),
(BL 73:1414, 1421; CCBB 30:176; HB 53:319; Kirkus 45:95; SLJ May 1977 p. 62; TLS 1976 p. 383; VOYA 2:57, 11:294, 12:13)

7-147 **JONES, Diana Wynne.** *The Lives of Christopher Chant.* **(Chrestomanci**
★★ **series, bk. 1).** Gr. 5–9. (Orig. British pub. 1988.)
After Christopher discovers that his dreams are so realistic that he can actually visit other worlds and bring things back from them, he must decide whether his beloved uncle's encouragement of these expeditions is altruistic or part of a frightening illegal scheme. Carnegie Medal Commended Book, 1988. This book is a prequel to *Charmed Life* (1978; see Chapter 10, Time Travel Fantasy), *The Magicians of Caprona* (1980; see Chapter 12, Witchcraft and Sorcery Fantasy), and *Witch Week* (1982; see Chapter 12, Witchcraft and Sorcery Fantasy). *Mixed Magics: Four Tales of Chrestomanci* (2000, 2001; see Chapter 12, Witchcraft and Sorcery Fantasy) is a related work. The four Chrestomanci novels have been reissued as *The Chronicles of Chrestomanci* (Greenwillow, 2001). Vol. 1 (0-06-447268-X) contains *Charmed Life* and *The Lives of Christopher Chant.* Vol. 2 (0-064-47269-8) contains *Witch Week* and *The Magicians of Caprona.*
Greenwillow, 1988, 230 pp. (0-688-07806-0); Greenwillow, 2001, 261 pp. (0-06-029877-4), pap. (0-688-16365-3)
(BL 84:1523, 1529, 85:879; CCBB 41:140; HB 64:208; HBG 12:308; Kirkus 51:619; SLJ May 1988 p. 98; Suth 4:207; TLS 1989 p. 378; VOYA 11:96, 12:14)

7-148 **JONES, Diana Wynne.** *A Tale of Time City.* Gr. 6 up. (Orig. British pub.
★ 1987.)
When 11-year-old Vivian Smith is kidnapped by time travelers who mistake her for the Time Lady, she plunges from 1939 London to Time City, where she helps her kidnappers thwart a wicked plot to alter history.
Greenwillow, 1987, 288 pp., o.p.; Greenwillow, 2002, pap., 336 pp. (0-06-447351-1)
(BL 84:569; CCBB 41:31; HB 64:71; Kirkus 55:1158; SLJ Sep 1987 p. 196; TLS 1987 p. 1283; VOYA 10:288, 11:14)

JONES, Terry. *Nicobobinus.*
See Chapter 8, Humorous Fantasy.

7-149 **JUSTER, Norton.** *The Phantom Tollbooth.* Gr. 5–7.
★ Finding a boy-sized car and tollbooth in his bedroom, Milo drives off to rescue the lost princesses, Rhyme and Reason, aided by the Spelling Bee and a watchdog named Tock.
Illus. by Jules Feiffer, Knopf, 1961, 1972, 255 pp. (0-394-81500-9), 1993, pap. (0-394-82037-1); illus. by Jules Feiffer, Random, 1996, 256 pp. (0-394-81500-9)
(CCBB 15:112; HBG 8:69; LJ 87:332; TLS 1962 p. 892)

7-150   KATZ, Welwyn Wilton. *The Third Magic.* Gr. 7–10. (Orig. Canadian pub. 1988.)

In this complex Arthurian fantasy, Morgan, a 20th-century Canadian teenager, is transported to the Celtic kingdom of Nwm, where she becomes Morgan Le Fay, twin sister of Arddu, or Arthur. Governor General's Literary Award for Children's Literature, 1988; Runner-Up, Canadian Library Association Best Book of the Year for Children, 1989.

Macmillan, 1989, 208 pp., o.p.; Groundwood, 2000, pap., 218 pp. (0-88899-385-4)

(BL 85:1274, 1300; CCBB 42:150; Kirkus 57:294; SLJ May 1989 p. 126; VOYA 12:116)

7-151   KAY, Elizabeth. *The Divide.* Gr. 5–9. (Orig. British pub. 2003.)

Felix, 13, passes out while traveling in Costa Rica, awakens in a magical world where humans are thought to be mythical beings, and is captured, along with his new elfin friend Betony, by the evil Snakeweed. The sequel is *Back to the Divide* (2004).

Chicken House/Scholastic, 2003, 320 pp. (0-439-45696-7)

(BL 99:1762; CCBB 57:154; HBG 15:96; Kirkus 71:860; Kliatt Nov 2003 p. 6; SLJ Sep 2003 p. 215; VOYA 26:237)

7-152   KAY, Guy Gavriel. *The Summer Tree.* **(Fionavar Tapestry trilogy, bk. 1).** Gr. 10 up. (Orig. Canadian pub. 1984.)

Five Canadian college students are summoned into the alternate world of Fionavar, where they are destined to play legendary roles in the coming war against the Dark, just as the evil Unraveller escapes its 1,000-year imprisonment. The sequels are *The Wandering Fire* (1986, Roc, 2001, pap.; Canadian Science Fiction and Fantasy Award, 1987) and *The Darkest Road* (1986; Roc, 2001, pap.).

Arbor House, 1985, 324 pp., o.p.; NAL, 1992, pap., 400 pp. (0-451-45138-4); Onyx, 2001, pap., 400 pp. (0-451-45822-2)

(BL 82:4, 86:905, 88:1092, 1095; Kirkus 53:984; LJ Oct 15, 1985 p. 104)

7-153   KAYE, Marvin. *The Incredible Umbrella.* Gr. 10 up.

A magic umbrella transports a young Pennsylvania college professor into a number of alternate literary worlds, including the London of Charles Dickens and Sir Arthur Conan Doyle, the Cornwall of Gilbert and Sullivan, and the worlds of the Arabian Nights, Frankenstein, and Flatland. The sequel is *The Amorous Umbrella* (1981).

Doubleday, 1979, 218 pp., o.p.

(BL 75:853, 860; LJ 104:213)

7-154   KENEALLY, Thomas (Michael). *Ned Kelly and the City of the Bees.* Gr. 5–7. (Orig. British pub. 1978.)

Miniaturized by a kindly bee named Apis, Ned Kelly spends the summer recuperating from appendicitis, inside a bee hive.

Illus. by Stephen Ryan, Godine, 1981, 120 pp., o.p.

(HB 57:535; Kirkus 49:1160; SLJ Nov 1981 p. 93; TLS 1978 p. 1396)

7-155   KENNEDY, X. J. (pseud. of Joseph Charles Kennedy). *The Owlstone*
☆   *Crown.* Gr. 4–6.

Twins Timothy and Verity Tibb enter the world of Owlstonia in search of their lost grandparents and, with the help of talking animal friends, manage to over-

throw the villainous dictator. The sequel is *The Eagle as Wide as the World* (1997).
Illus. by Michele Chessare, Atheneum, 1983, 210 pp., o.p.; Front Street, 2005, pap. (1-93242-535-7)
(BL 80:992; Kirkus 51:192; SLJ Jan 1984 p. 78)

7-156 **KEY, Alexander (Hill).** *The Forgotten Door.* Gr. 5–7.
☆ When he falls from another world into a remote mountain town, Jon's mind-reading ability generates fear and greed in the villagers who find him.
Westminster, 1965, 126 pp., o.p.
(CCBB 18:151; HB 41:392; Kirkus 33:117; LJ 90:972; TLS 1966 p. 449)

7-157 **KING, Stephen, and STRAUB, Peter (Francis).** *The Talisman.* Gr. 10 up.
As 12-year-old Jack Sawyer travels cross-country from California, searching for a magic stone to save his mother's life, he visits the Territories, an alternate-past world where another woman's life is in danger.
Viking, 1984, 644 pp. (0-670-69199-2); Berkley, 1985, pap., 784 pp. (0-425-10533-4)
(BL 81:686, 708; Kirkus 52:771; LJ 109:2080; SLJ Jan 1985 p. 92; VOYA 8:49)

KINGSLEY, Charles. *The Water Babies: A Fairy Tale for a Land Baby.*
See Chapter 1, Allegorical Fantasy and Literary Fairy Tales.

7-158 **KROPP, Lloyd.** *The Drift.* Gr. 10 up.
Becalmed in the Sargasso Sea, Peter Sutherland discovers an unknown ship-dwelling community called The Drift, whose inhabitants welcome him lovingly and urge him to stay.
Doubleday, 1969, 240 pp., o.p.
(BL 65:997, 1069; LJ 94:1162; TLS 1969 p. 910)

7-159 **KRÜSS, James (Jacob Heinrich).** *The Happy Islands Behind the Winds.*
Gr. 3–6. (Orig. German pub. 1959.)
Captain Madirankowitsch and his crew discover an island paradise governed by talking animals. The sequel is *Return to the Happy Islands* (1967).
Trans. by Edelgard Brühl, illus. by Eberhart Binder-Strassfurt, Atheneum, 1966, 153 pp., o.p.
(Kirkus 34:1097; LJ 91:5750)

KUSHNER, Ellen. *Thomas the Rhymer.*
See Chapter 6, High Fantasy: Myth or Legend Fantasy.

7-160 **KUTTNER, Henry.** *The Startling Worlds of Henry Kuttner.* Gr. 10 up.
Three novellas about people who travel to alternate worlds: "The Portal in the Picture," "Valley of the Flame" (orig. pub. Ace, 1964), and "The Dark World."
Warner, 1987, pap., 368 pp., o.p.
(BL 83:550, 571; VOYA 10:130)

7-161 **LACKEY, Mercedes, and LISLE, Holly.** *When the Bough Breaks.* Gr. 11 up.
A tale for mature readers about Lianne, a teacher who falls in love with a humanlike elf named Maclyn, and Amanda, an unhappy little girl whose fate is tied to the survival of the world of Faerie. Related books in the SERRAted

Edge series are *Born to Run* (1992; see Chapter 12, Witchcraft and Sorcery Fantasy), *Wheels of Fire* (1992), and *Chrome Circle* (1994). *The Chrome Borne* (1999) contains *Born to Run* and *Chrome Circle*. *The Otherworld* (2000) contains *Wheels of Fire* and *When the Bough Breaks*.
Baen, 1993, pap., 279 pp. (0-671-72154-2)
(Kliatt May 1993 p. 16; VOYA 16:166)

7-162 LAMPMAN, Evelyn Sibley. *The City Under the Back Steps.* Gr. 4–6.
After they insult the Queen ant, Craig and Jill dwindle to insect size and are put to work inside the ant colony.
Illus. by Honoré Valintcourt, Doubleday, 1960, 210 pp., o.p.
(HB 36:510; Kirkus 28:816; LJ 85:4567)

LANGTON, Jane (Gillson). *The Diamond in the Window.*
See Chapter 9, Magic Adventure Fantasy.

LAWRENCE, Louise (pseud. of Elizabeth Rhoda Holden). *Star Lord.*
See Chapter 6, High Fantasy: Myth or Legend Fantasy.

7-163 LAWRENCE, Michael. *A Crack in the Line.* **(The Withern Rise trilogy,**
☆ **part 1).** Gr. 8–12. (Orig. British pub. 2003.)
Still grieving on the second anniversary of his mother's death, Alaric is transported into an alternate world where the mother of his "twin," Naia, is still alive. The sequel is *Small Eternities* (2004).
Greenwillow, 2004, 336 pp. (0-06-072478-1); HarperTempest, 2005, pap., 384 pp. (0-06-072479-X)
(BL 100:1731; CCBB 58:85; Kirkus 72:689; SLJ Aug 2004 p. 124; VOYA 27:316;)

7-164 LE GUIN, Ursula K(roeber). *The Beginning Place.* Gr. 8 up. (British title
☆ *The Threshold*, 1980.)
Irene resents Hugh's intrusion into the otherworld she has found, but the two unhappy young people are drawn together on their quest to destroy a terrible beast.
Harper, 1980, 183 pp. (0-06-012573-X), 1990, 1991, pap. (0-06-100148-1);
Tor, 2005, pap., 240 pp. (0-7653-4625-7)
(BL 76:756, 77:621, 1148, 86:907; CCBB 34:14; HB 56:333; Kirkus 47:1393, 1437; LJ 105:227; SLJ Apr 1980 p. 132; Suth 3:259; TLS Dec 12, 1980 p. 1408; VOYA 3:38)

7-165 LEVY, Robert. *Escape from Exile.* Gr. 6–8.
Struck by lightning, 13-year-old Daniel awakens in a strange world where he can communicate with animals, a skill that makes him a valuable asset to both sides in the ongoing civil war.
Houghton, 1993, 176 pp., o.p.
(BL 89:1314; HBG 4:301; SLJ May 1993 p. 106; VOYA 16:166)

7-166 LEWIS, C(live) S(taples). *The Lion, the Witch, and the Wardrobe.* **(The**
☆☆ **Chronicles of Narnia, bk. 1).** Gr. 4–7. (Orig. British pub. 1950.)
After the White Witch casts a spell over the land of Narnia, ensnaring Edmund and drawing Susan, Peter, and Lucy into Narnia too, they join the great lion Aslan's struggle to break the witch's enchantment. Lewis believed that the Narnia series ought to be read in the following order: first, *The Magician's Nephew* (1955, 1970, 2003), in which young Digory and Polly borrow the

magic rings of Digory's sorcerer-uncle and are transported to Narnia, just as Aslan is singing it into existence. Many years later, four children exploring the house of the now-elderly Digory stumble through a magic wardrobe into Narnia, in *The Lion, the Witch, and the Wardrobe* (1951, 1983, 2003). In *The Horse and His Boy* (1954; Carnegie Medal Commended Book, 1954; 2000, pap.), two children and their talking horses flee into Narnia: Shasta to escape imprisonment and Aravis to avoid an unwanted marriage. In *Prince Caspian: The Return to Narnia* (1951; 2000, pap.), Lucy, Edmund, Susan, and Peter help Aslan save Prince Caspian from his murderous uncle and restore him to the throne of Narnia. In *The Voyage of the Dawn Treader* (1952; 2000, pap.), Edmund, Lucy, their cousin Eustace, and Prince Caspian sail to World's End aboard the *Dawn Treader*, in search of seven missing noblemen. In *The Silver Chair* (1953; 2000, pap.), Aslan sends Eustace and Jill on a quest to free King Caspian's missing son, Prince Rilian, from an enchantment and bring him back to Narnia. In the final volume of the series, *The Last Battle* (1956; 2000, pap.), Aslan calls on all creatures who believe in and love Narnia to return for the final battle against the forces of evil. *The Last Battle* won the Carnegie Medal, 1956. All seven books have been published together in *The Complete Chronicles of Narnia*; illus. by Pauline Baynes, HarperCollins, 1998, 526 pp. (0-06-028137-5), and HarperCollins, 2001, pap., 768 pp. (0-06-623850-1). The first two chapters of *The Lion, the Witch, and the Wardrobe* have been published by HarperCollins in picture-book versions illustrated by Deborah Maze: *Edmund and the White Witch* (1997) and *Lucy Steps Through the Wardrobe* (1997). *The Wood Between the Worlds* (1999) is a chapter from *The Magician's Nephew*. Other books in this HarperCollins World of Narnia picture-book series include *Aslan* (1998), *Aslan's Triumph* (1998), and *Aslan on the Move* (2000).
Illus. by Pauline Baynes, Macmillan, 1951, 1988, 154 pp. (0-02-758120-9); illus. by Michael (R.) Hague, Macmillan, 1983, 183 pp. (0-02-758200-0); HarperCollins, 1997, 175 pp. (0-06-027724-6); HarperTrophy, 2002, pap. (0-06-447104-7); HarperCollins, 2003, special edition book and CD, illus. in full color by Pauline Baynes, 110 pp. (0-06-055649-8)
(BL 47:208, 80:96, 683; CCBB 4:35; HB 27:54; HBG 9:75, 10:69; Kirkus 18:514; LJ 75:1756; SLJ Jan 1984 p. 79)

7-167   LICKISS, Rebecca. *Eccentric Circles.* Gr. 10 up.
Piper Dickerson discovers that her late grandmother's cottage garden is the doorway to Faerie, and suspects that elves, wizards, and dwarves might have caused her grandmother's death.
Berkley/Ace, 2001, pap., 218 pp. (0-441-00828-3)
(BL 97:1856; Kliatt Sep 2001 p. 26; VOYA 24:335, 370)

7-168   LILLINGTON, Kenneth (James). *Jonah's Mirror.* Gr. 6 up. (Orig. British pub. 1988.)
Jonah Sprockett invents a mirror that sends him into a world of knights, wizards, and damsels in distress, and then he begins to wonder whether he really wants to spend the rest of his life there.
Faber, 1988, 148 pp., o.p.
(SLJ Oct 1988 p. 162; TLS 1988 p. 369)

7-169   LINDBERGH, Anne Spencer. *Bailey's Window.* Gr. 4–6.
Anna, Carl, and their friend Ingrid are astonished to be able to step through a

picture drawn by Anna's obnoxious cousin, Bailey, and have magical adventures at a carnival, in a forest, and in the past.
Illus. by Kinuko Craft, Harcourt, 1984, 115 pp., o.p.
(BL 80:1250; CCBB 37:208; SLJ May 1984 p. 82)

7-170 LINDGREN, Astrid. *The Brothers Lionheart.* Gr. 6–8. (Orig. Swedish pub. 1973.)
Two brothers, Jonathan and Karl, are reunited after death in a land called Nangiyala, where they fight a vicious tyrant and his dragon to liberate the other inhabitants.
Trans. by Joan Tate; illus. by J. K. Lambert, Viking, 1975, 183 pp., o.p.; Purple House, 2004, 231 pp. (1-93090-024-4)
(HB 51:594; Kirkus 43:777; SLJ Oct 1975 p. 100)

7-171 LINDGREN, Astrid. *Mio, My Son.* Gr. 4–6. (Orig. pub. in Sweden.)
After a genie carries Mio away from his unhappy foster home, he is adopted by the King of Faraway Land.
Trans. by Marianne Turner, illus. by Don Wikland, Viking, 1956, 179 pp., o.p.; Purple House, 2003, 179 pp. (1-930900-23-6)
(BL 53:304; Kirkus 24:868; LJ 82:588)

7-172 LINKLATER, Eric (Robert Russell). *The Pirates in the Deep Green Sea.* Gr. 5–7. (Orig. British pub. 1949.)
Two boys journey beneath the sea to enlist the aid of Davy Jones in their battle with pirates.
Illus. by William Reeves, Macmillan, 1949, 398 pp., o.p.; Jane Nissen, 2000 (1-90325-206-7)
(BL 46:52; HB 25:411; Kirkus 17:324; LJ 74:1105, 1542; TLS July 15, 1949 p. iii)

LITTLE, Jane. *Sneaker Hill.*
See Chapter 12, Witchcraft and Sorcery Fantasy.

LOFTING, Hugh. *The Story of Doctor Dolittle.*
See Chapter 8, Humorous Fantasy.

7-173 *Lost Worlds, Unknown Horizons: Nine Stories of Science Fiction.* **Ed. by**
✫ **Robert Silverberg.** Gr. 10 up.
Nine stories of adventure in other worlds, whose authors include Jack Finney, Edgar Allan Poe, H. G. Wells, and Robert Silverberg.
Nelson, 1978, 192 pp., o.p.
(BL 75:745; Kirkus 46:976, 1077; SLJ Apr 1979 p. 72; VOYA 2:48)

LOVEJOY, Jack. *The Rebel Witch.*
See Chapter 12, Witchcraft and Sorcery Fantasy.

7-174 LYON, George Ella. *Gina. Jamie. Father. Bear.* Gr. 6–9.
✫ Gina's secret appointments with a psychic after her mother's departure result in dreamlike visits to an enchanted wood, where she meets a boy named Jamie who is also trying to reclaim his family.
Atheneum, 2002, 144 pp. (0-689-84370-4)
(BL 99:754; CCBB 56:165; HB 78:576; Kirkus 70:1228; SLJ Aug 2002 p. 194; VOYA 25:298, 26:13)

7-175 McCUTCHEN, H. L. *LightLand.* Gr. 5–8.
Best friends Lottie and Lewis, both 11, are transported from their small Iowa town to LightLand, ruled by the NightKing, who steals people's memories to control their destinies.
Orchard, 2002, 230 pp. (0-439-39565-8); Scholastic, 2004, pap., 230 pp. (0-439-39566-6)
(CCBB 56:244; HBG 13:96; Kirkus 70:1612; SLJ Nov 2002 p. 172; VOYA 25:400, 26:13)

MacDONALD, George. *At the Back of the North Wind.*
See Chapter 1, Allegorical Fantasy and Literary Fairy Tales.

MacDONALD, George. *The Golden Key.*
See Chapter 1, Allegorical Fantasy and Literary Fairy Tales.

7-176 MACE, Elisabeth. *Under Siege.* Gr. 7–10. (Orig. British pub. 1988.)
Sixteen-year-old Morris becomes a giant in his uncle's room-sized, computerized fantasy game, complete with castle, and discovers that he can communicate with two of the tiny people.
Orchard, 1990, 224 pp., o.p.
(BL 86:1970, 1993; HBG 1:256; Kirkus 58:501; SLJ Apr 1990 p. 144; VOYA 13:107)

McGOWEN, Tom (Thomas E.). *Odyssey from River Bend.*
See Chapter 2, Animal Fantasy.

7-177 McGOWEN, Tom (Thomas E.). *The Shadow of Fomor.* Gr. 4–7.
On a visit to Ireland, Rick and his cousin Moira suddenly find themselves in the Great Forest of the Middle Kingdom, battling to save the Old Magic.
Dutton, 1990, 128 pp., o.p.
(BL 86:1634; HBG 1:255; SLJ May 1990 p. 107; VOYA 13:39)

7-178 McGRAW, Eloise Jarvis. *The Moorchild.* Gr. 4–7.
★★ Half-fairy, half-human Saaski grows up twice, first with the fairy folk and a second time in a human village, where she is taunted for being different. John Newbery Medal Honor Book, 1996; Boston Globe Horn Book Honor Book, 1996; Golden Kite Award, 1996.
McElderry, 1996, 241 pp. (0-689-80654-X); Aladdin, 1998, pap., 241 pp. (0-689-82033-X)
(BL 92:1178, 93:1302,, 94:475; CCBB 49:345; HB 72:598; HBG 7:294; Kirkus 64:376; SLJ Apr 1996 p. 136; VOYA 19:108)

7-179 McHARGUE, Georgess. *Elidor and the Golden Ball.* Gr. 3–4.
Elidor breaks the Faeries' trust when he steals a magic ball to prove to his mother that he really had lived with them.
Illus. by Emanuel Schoengut, Dodd, 1973, 61 pp., o.p.
(BL 70:388; Kirkus 41:1036; LJ 99:201)

7-180 MacINTYRE, F. Gwynplaine. *The Woman Between the Worlds.* Gr. 10 up.
A plea for help from an invisible woman abducted from another world transforms the life of a Victorian tattoo artist.
Dell, 1994, pap., 240 pp., o.p.
(BL 90:1064, 1068; Kirkus 62:24; Kliatt May 1994 p. 18; LJ Feb 15, 1994 p. 188)

7-181 **McKENZIE, Ellen Kindt.** *Drujienna's Harp.* Gr. 5–8.
A San Francisco curio shop is the entrance to the terror-ridden land of T'Pahl, where Tha and Duncan attempt to topple a tyrant from power.
Dutton, 1971, 305 pp., o.p.
(BL 67:908; CCBB 25:12; HB 47:614; Kirkus 39:434; LJ 96:1814)

McKIERNAN, Dennis L. *Once Upon a Winter's Night.*
See Chapter 6, High Fantasy: Myth or Legend Fantasy.

7-182 **McKILLIP, Patricia A(nne).** *Something Rich and Strange.* **(A Tale of Brian Froud's Faerielands, vol. 2).** Gr. 10 up.
Two strangers compel Megan and Jonah to leave their Pacific Northwest home and enter an underwater world because Megan's artwork and Jonah's fossil research both focus on the sea. The first book in this series is *The Wild Wood* by Charles De Lint (1994).
Illus. by Brian Froud, Bantam, 1994, 224 pp., o.p.; iBooks, 2004, pap., 208 pp. (0-7434-9820-8)
(BL 91:245, 314; VOYA 18:9, 37)

7-183 **McKILLIP, Patricia A(nne).** *Winter Rose.* Gr. 10 up.
☆ A handsome stranger named Corbett touches the lives of two sisters, Laurel and Rois, forcing Rois to cross the border into Faerie to rescue Corbett from a wintry prison and to save her sister's life.
Berkley, 1996, 272 pp. (0-441-00334-6); Ace, 2002, pap., 272 pp. (0-441-00934-4)
(BL 92:1812, 1815; Kirkus 64:718; LJ July 1996 p. 170; VOYA 19:338, 20:13)

7-184 **McNEILL (ALEXANDER), Janet.** *Tom's Tower.* Gr. 5–7. (Orig. British pub. 1965.)
Tom is unexpectedly summoned into an unfamiliar world, where he must protect the king's treasure from two corrupt courtiers.
Illus. by Mary Russon, Little, Brown, 1967, 182 pp., o.p.
(HB 43:464; Kirkus 35:132; TLS 1965 p. 513)

7-185 **McNISH, Cliff.** *The Doomspell: A Battle Between Good and Evil.* Gr. 5–8. (Orig. British pub. 2001.)
Pulled through their cellar wall into the world of Ithrea, Rachel and Eric find that they have the magical powers needed to battle Dragwena the witch.
Illus. by Geoff Taylor, Penguin Putnam, 2002, 214 pp. (0-8037-2710-0)
(BL 98:1418; CCBB 56:70; HBG 13:378; Kirkus 70:737; SLJ June 2002 p. 142)

7-186 **MAGUIRE, Gregory.** *The Daughter of the Moon.* Gr. 5–7.
Unhappy living with her stepmother in Chicago, Erikka is drawn into a watercolor painting of Canaan Lake, New York.
Farrar, 1980, 257 pp., o.p.
(CCBB 33:219; HB 56:299; Kirkus 48:585; SLJ May 1980 p. 69)

7-187 **MAHY, Margaret (May).** *Dangerous Spaces.* Gr. 5–8. (Orig. New Zealand
☆ pub. 1991.)
Anxious to escape from her cousin Flora's chaotic home after the deaths of her parents, Anthea, 11, is drawn into the dream world of Viridian, where the ghost of her great-uncle begs her to accompany him on the "journey beyond."

Viking, 1991, 160 pp. (0-670-83734-2); Puffin, 1993, pap. (0-14-036362-9)

(BL 87:1799; CCBB 44:222; HB 67:330; HBG 2:262; Kirkus 59:319; SLJ Apr 1991 p. 121; TLS July 12, 1991, p. 20; VOYA 14:111, 15:9)

MASEFIELD, John (Edward). *The Midnight Folk: A Novel.*
See Chapter 9, Magic Adventure Fantasy.

7-188 MATAS, Carol, and NODELMAN, Perry. *Of Two Minds.* Gr. 5–9. (Orig. Canadian pub. 1994.)
Lenora tries to avoid marrying Coren by jumping into an unknown fantasy land where her magical powers are useless. The sequels are *More Minds* (1996), *Out of Their Minds* (1998), and *A Meeting of the Minds* (1999).
Simon, 1995, 200 pp. (0-689-80138-6); Point Fantasy, 1998, pap., 200 pp. (0-590-39468-1)

(HBG 7:65; Kirkus 63:1354; SLJ Oct 1995 p. 136, Dec 1995 p. 22; VOYA 19:23, 40, 88)

7-189 MAYNE, William (James Carter). *All the King's Men.* Gr. 5 up. (Orig.
★ British pub. 1982.)
Three unusual stories, including one fantasy, "Boy to Island," about two people captured by fairies in the west of Scotland.
Delacorte, 1988, 192 pp., o.p.

(CCBB 41:142; HB 64:633; Kirkus 56:203; SLJ Apr 1988 p. 103; TLS 1982 p. 788; VOYA 11:96)

MEDDAUGH, Susan. *Lulu's Hat.*
See Chapter 9, Magic Adventure Fantasy.

7-190 MERRITT, A(braham P.). *The Ship of Ishtar.* Gr. 10 up. (Orig. pub. 1924.)
An ancient Babylonian stone sends John Kenton from New York City into an alternate world aboard the magical ship of Ishtar, where he falls in love with the Princess Sharane and helps her to battle the Ruler of the Dead.
Illus. by Virgil Finlay, Borden, 1924, 1949, 1990, 309 pp., o.p.; Macmillan, 1991, pap., 304 pp. (0-02-022871-6)

(TLS 1926 p. 397)

7-191 MIESEL, Sandra. *Shaman.* Gr. 10 up.
Two shamans, human and otter, summon professor Ria Legarde into their alternate world to develop her magic powers, in this expanded and revised version of *Dreamrider* (Ace, 1982).
Baen, 1989, pap., 320 pp., o.p.

(BL 79:190, 199, 86:42, 54; VOYA 5:39)

7-192 MODESITT, L(eland) E(xton), Jr. *The Soprano Sorceress.* **(The Spellsong Cycle, vol. 1).** Gr. 9 up.
Mourning the death of her eldest daughter, music teacher Anna finds herself in a world where her musical abilities make her a sorcerer and songs are magical spells. The sequels are *The Spellsong War* (1998), *Darksong Rising* (1999), *The Shadow Sorceress* (2001), and *Shadowsinger* (2002).
Tor, 1997, 512 pp. (0-312-86022-6), 1998, pap., 672 pp. (0-8124-4559-1)

(BL 93:929; Kirkus 64:1773; VOYA 20:253)

7-193 **MOLESWORTH, Mary Louisa (Stewart).** *The Cuckoo Clock.* Gr. 4–6.
(Orig. British pub. 1877.)
The cuckoo in Griselda's new home takes her through its clock into a magical
land. The sequel is *A Christmas Child* (1880).
Illus. by Ernest H. Shepard, Dutton, 1954, 165 pp., o.p.; Dent, 1974 (repr. of
1954 ed.), o.p.; Garland, 1976 (bound with *The Tapestry Room*), o.p.; illus. by
Ernest Shepard, Peter Smith, 1980, 208 pp., o.p.; Jane Nissen, 2002 (1-
903252-14-8); Kessinger, 2004, pap., 12 pp. (1-41915-839-2)
(BL 18:95, 22:77, 27:216, 36:118, 51:48; Bookshelf 1932 p. 2; HB 1[Jun 1925]:32, 2[Nov
1925]:29, 3[May 1927]:17–22, 30:324, 344; 38:66; Mahony 2:291)

7-194 **MOLLOY, Michael.** *The House on Falling Star Hill.* Gr. 4–8. (Orig.
British pub. 2004.)
After a stranger named Hunter arrives in his grandparents' quiet English vil-
lage, Tim discovers a portal into a magical world called Tallis, whose citizens
are caught in a war between the ruling duke and the deposed king.
Chicken House/Scholastic, 2004, 384 pp. (0-439-57740-3)
(BL 100:1456; CCBB 57:342; Kirkus 72:274; SLJ Apr 2004 p. 158; VOYA 27: 232)

7-195 **MONACO, Richard.** *Journey to the Flame.* Gr. 10 up.
British and German forces set out to discover the secrets of the lost city of Kôr,
while World War I begins in Europe. This is a contemporary sequel to Sir
H(enry) Rider Haggard's *She* (1886, 1911, 1961, 1976), *Ayesha, the Return of
She* (1905, 1912), *She and Allan* (1920, 1931), and *Wisdom's Daughter* (1923).
Bantam, 1985, pap., 203 pp., o.p.
(LJ Nov 15, 1985, p. 112)

7-196 **MOON, Sheila (Elizabeth).** *Knee-Deep in Thunder.* Gr. 6–9.
✯ A blue-green stone takes Maris to the Great Land, where she and her animal
companions capture savage beasts that were terrifying the people. Maris
returns to the Great Land in *Hunt Down the Prize* (1971).
Illus. by Peter Parnall, Atheneum, 1967, 307 pp., o.p.; Guild for Psychological
Studies, 1986, pap., 307 pp. (0-917479-08-4)
(BL 64:503; CCBB 21:98; HB 43:589; Kirkus 35:968; LJ 92:3853; Suth:285)

7-197 **MORRISSEY, Dean, and KRENSKY, Stephen (Alan).** *The Moon Rob-
ber.* **(Magic Door series, bk. 1).** Gr. 3–5.
Michael, Sarah, and Joey enter a world called Great Kettles, where they help
Captain Luna, the man in the moon, to return the moon to its orbit and thwart
the giant who stole it. The sequels are *The Winter King* (2002, 2003), and
Monsters on the Radio (2004). Morrissey has illustrated two picture books
about the realm: *Great Kettles: Ship of Dreams* (Abrams, 1994) and *The Great
Kettles: A Tale of Time* (Abrams, 1997).
Illus. by Dean Morrissey, HarperCollins, 2001, 64 pp. (0-06-028582-6);
HarperTrophy, 2001, pap. (0-06-442113-9)
(BL 97:1559; HBG 12:293; SLJ Sep 2001 p. 200)

7-198 **MUNDY, Talbot (pseud. of William Lancaster Gribbon).** *OM, The Secret
of Abhor Valley.* **(The Jingrim/Ramsden series, bk. 6).** Gr. 10 up. (Orig.
British pub. 1924.)
A young English adventurer in India during the 1920s sets out to find a piece

of jade with supernatural powers and the hidden valley inhabited by a holy lama who can reveal the secrets of the universe. The 23 books in this series, published between 1916 and 1939, are all somewhat related, although they have different main characters. In order of publication they are *King of the Khybers* (1916; aka *King of the Kyber Rifles*), *The Winds of the World* (1916), *Him Singh's Tale* (1918), *Guns of the Gods* (1921), *The Caves of Terror* (1924), *The Nine Unknown* (1924), *Ramsden* (1926; aka *The Devil's Guard*), *The Woman Ayisha* (1930), *The Hundred Days* (1930), *Jingrim* (1931; aka *Jingrim Sahib*, 1953), *The Lost Trooper* (1931), *C. I. D.* (1932), *Jungle Jest* (1932), *The Lion of Petra* (1932), *The King in Check* (1933; aka *Affair in Araby*, 1953), *The Gunga Sahib* (1933), *The Mystery of Khufu's Tomb* (1933), *Jingrim and Allah's Peace* (1933), *The Red Flame of Erinpura* (1934), *The Seventeen Thieves of El-Kalil* (1935), *The Thunder Dragon Gate* (1937), and *Old Ugly Face* (1939).

Crown, 1924, 392 pp., o.p.; Amereon, repr. of 1924 ed., n.d. (0-89190-490-5); Wildside, 2002, 296 pp. (1-59224-931-0), pap. (1-59224-955-8); Kessinger, 2004, pap., 396 pp. (0-7661-9348-9)

(BL 21:234; TLS 1925 p. 57)

7-199   MURPHY, Shirley Rousseau. *The Catswold Portal.* Gr. 10 up.
Queen Siddonie transforms Melissa, rightful heir to the throne of the Netherworld, into a calico cat left to die along a U.S. highway in 1957, but Melissa is taken in by an artist named Branden West.
Penguin, 1992, 416 pp. (0-451-45146-5)

(BL 88:1509, 1516, 89:842; Kirkus 60:147; LJ Mar 15, 1992 p. 129; SLJ Aug 1992 p. 189, Dec 1992 p. 24)

7-200   MURPHY, Shirley Rousseau, and SUGGS, Welch. *Medallion of the Black Hound.* Gr. 5–8.
A magic medallion transports David to the land of Meryn, where he joins a band of warriors battling the evil Balcher, who is attempting to take control of both worlds.
Harper, 1989, 182 pp., o.p.

(BL 86:462; HBG 1:84; SLJ Oct 1989 p. 120)

7-201   MYERS, John Myers. *Silverlock.* Gr. 10 up.
A young man shipwrecked in a land called the Commonwealth finds it to be populated by characters from classical literature, including Beowulf, Robin Hood, and Don Quixote. The sequel is *The Moon's Fire-Eating Daughter* (Donning, 1981).
Lippincott, 1949, 314 pp., o.p.; *Silverlock and the Silverlock Companion*, NESFA, 2004, 511 pp. (1-886778-52-3); Ace, 2005, pap., 384 pp. (0-441-01247-7)

(BL 46:48, 100:1277; Kirkus 17:310; LJ 74:1095)

NASTICK, Sharon. *Mr. Radagast Makes an Unexpected Journey.*
See Chapter 8, Humorous Fantasy.

NATHAN, Robert (Gruntal). *The Snowflake and the Starfish.*
See Chapter 12, Witchcraft and Sorcery Fantasy.

7-202 NAYLOR, Phyllis Reynolds. *Sang Spell.* Gr. 6–10.
✶ Rescued by the inhabitants of a remote Appalachian village and cared for after a mugging, Josh begins to understand that he might never be able to escape from these descendants of fugitive Melungeon settlers.
Simon, 1998, 176 pp. (0-689-82007-0); Simon Pulse, 2000, pap., 224 pp. (0-689-82006-2)
(BL 95:228, 1691; HB 74:736; HBG 10:81; Kirkus 66:1387; Kliatt Jan 1999 p. 8; SLJ Oct 1998 p. 143; VOYA 21:446, 22:15)

7-203 NESBIT (Bland), E(dith). *The Magic City.* Gr. 5–7. (Orig. British pub. 1910.)
Awakening in the middle of the night, Philip finds himself in a city made of books, blocks, and toys.
Illus. by H(arold) R. Millar, Coward, 1958, 333 pp., o.p.; Gregg, 1981, 333 pp., o.p.; Books of Wonder, 1996, 256 pp. (0-929605-62-4); Sea Star/North-South, 2000, 212 pp. (1-58717-024-8)
(BL 57:32; HB 36:309; HBG 12:313; LJ 85:3224)

NESBIT (Bland), E(dith). *Wet Magic.*
See Chapter 9, Magic Adventure Fantasy.

7-204 NICHOLS, (Joanna) Ruth. *The Marrow of the World.* Gr. 5–7. (Orig. Canadian pub. 1972.)
Summoned into another world by her dying half-sister, Linda is ordered to bring back the essence of life, in exchange for her freedom. Canadian Library Association Best Book of the Year for Children, 1973.
Illus. by Trina Schart Hyman, Atheneum, 1972, 168 pp., o.p.
(BL 69:717; Kirkus 40:1191; LJ 98:262)

7-205 NICHOLS, (Joanna) Ruth. *A Walk Out of the World.* Gr. 5–7. (Orig. Canadian pub. 1969.)
✶ Judith and her brother Tobit follow a strange light into a world once ruled by their ancestors, where they mastermind a plot to overthrow the hated King Hagerrak.
Illus. by Trina Schart Hyman, Harcourt, 1969, 192 pp., o.p.
(BL 65:1178; CCBB 22:180; HB 45:412; Kirkus 37:304; LJ 94:2677)

7-206 NIX, Garth. *Mister Monday.* **(The Keys to the Kingdom series, bk. 1).** Gr. 5–9. (Orig. Australian pub. 2003.)
Seventh-grader Arthur Penhaligon outwits a supernatural being named Mister Monday by surviving a near-fatal asthma attack and using the mysterious key he was given to enter Mr. Monday's world. The sequels are *Grim Tuesday* (2004) and *Drowned Wednesday* (2005).
Scholastic, 2003, pap., 361 pp. (0-439-55123-4); Scholastic, 2005, pap., 368 pp. (0-439-70369-7)
(CCBB 57:200; SLJ Dec 2003 p. 158; VOYA 26:506, 27:14)

7-207 NODELMAN, Perry. *The Same Place but Different.* Gr. 5–9. (Orig. Canadian pub. 1994.)
✶ John Nesbit must enter the land of the Strangers to rescue his baby sister, Andrea, traded for a changeling by evil fairies bent on taking over the world. In the sequel, *A Completely Different Place* (1997), John awakens from a

nightmare to find himself back in the Strangers' land, shrunken to miniature size, where he must keep his friend Cheryl from being transformed into a Stranger.

Simon, 1995, 181 pp. (0-671-88415-8); Simon, 1995, pap., 192 pp. (0-671-89839-6)

(BL 92:304; CCBB 48:393; HB 71:601; HBG 6:312; Kirkus 63:784; SLJ May 1995 p. 109; VOYA 18:174)

7-208   NORTH, Joan. *The Light Maze*. Gr. 6–9.
✶   Kit Elting uses a medieval ornament called a Lightstone to enter the light maze and set Tom Nancarrow free.

Farrar, 1971, 185 pp., o.p.

(BL 68:392; CCBB 26:12; HB 48:156; Kirkus 39:1132; LJ 96:4192; Suth:297; TLS 1972 p. 1329)

7-209   NORTON, Andre (pseud. of Alice Mary Norton). *Here Abide Monsters*. Gr. 7–9.
Nick and Linda stumble into legendary Avalon, where they become fugitives hunted by dangerous demons and mythical beasts.

Atheneum, 1974, 215 pp., o.p.

(BL 70:485; Kirkus 41:760; LJ 98:3708)

7-210   NORTON, Andre (pseud. of Alice Mary Norton). *Knave of Dreams*. Gr. 7 up.
After crossing into a parallel world called Ulad, Ramsey Kimble becomes Kaskar, doomed son of the late emperor.

Viking, 1975, 252 pp., o.p.

(BL 72:294; Kirkus 43:856; SLJ Nov 1975 p. 94; TLS 1976 p. 1242)

7-211   NORTON, Andre (pseud. of Alice Mary Norton). *Operation Time Search*. Gr. 7–10.
Ray Osborne is caught up in the conflict between the peoples of Atlantis and Mu after he steps from 1980s' America through a time-space opening into an alternate world.

Harcourt, 1967, 224 pp., o.p.

(BL 64:442; HB 43:760; Kirkus 35:747; LJ 92:3202)

7-212   NORTON, Andre (pseud. of Alice Mary Norton). *Steel Magic*. Gr. 5–7.
✶   Eric, Sara, and Greg Lowry enter Avalon through a miniature castle and search for Arthur's sword and Merlin's ring in order to save the land from evil.

Illus. by Robin Jacques, World, 1965, 155 pp., o.p.; Starscape, 2005, pap., 128 pp. (0-7653-5297-4)

(CCBB 19:151; HB 41:629; LJ 90:5519; TLS 1967 p. 451)

7-213   NORTON, Andre (pseud. of Alice Mary Norton). *Witch World*. (Witch
✶   **World series, vol. 1; Simon Tregarth sequence, bk. 1). Gr. 8 up.**
Simon Tregarth escapes from his post-World War II pursuers through a dimension portal into Estcarp, where the Witches use magic to battle their enemies. This book and the first five sequels listed here are called the Simon Tregarth sequence: *Web of the Witch World* (Ace, 1964; Gregg, 1977), *Three Against the Witch World* (Ace, 1965, pap.; Gregg, 1977), *Warlock of the Witch World* (Ace, 1967, pap.; Gregg, 1977), *Sorceress of the Witch World* (Ace, 1968,

pap.; Gregg, 1977), and *Spell of the Witch World* (DAW, 1972, pap.; Gregg, 1977). The following are related books: *Year of the Unicorn* (Ace, 1965, pap.; Gregg, 1977), *The Crystal Gryphon* (Atheneum, 1972; Tor, 1985; see Chapter 5, High Fantasy: Alternate Worlds or Histories); *The Jargoon Pard* (Atheneum, 1974; Fawcett, 1978, pap.; Ballantine, 1986, pap.; see Chapter 5, High Fantasy: Alternate Worlds or Histories), *Trey of Swords* (Grosset, 1977; Ace, 1983, pap.), *Zarsthor's Bane* (Ace, 1978), *Horn Crown* (DAW, 1981, 1985, pap.), *Gryphon in Glory* (Atheneum, 1981; Ballantine, 1983, pap.), *'Ware Hawk* (Atheneum, 1983; Ballantine, 1984, pap.), *Gryphon's Eyrie* (Tor, 1984; 1985, 1989, pap.) by Norton and A(nn) C(arol) Crispin, *Lore of the Witch World* (DAW, 1987), and *The Gate of the Cat* (Ace, 1987). *Tales of the Witch World* (St. Martin's, 1987), *Tales of the Witch World, 2* (St. Martin's, 1988), *Four from the Witch World* (Tor, 1989), *Tales of the Witch World, 3* (Tor, 1990), and *Songsmith* (Tor, 1992) are anthologies of short stories by authors other than Norton. Witch World: The Turning series includes *Storms of Victory* (Tor, 1991; see Chapter 5, High Fantasy: Alternate Worlds or Histories), *Flight of Vengeance* (Tor, 1992), and *On the Wings of Magic* (1994). *The Key of the Keplian* (1995) by Norton and Lyn McConchie, *The Warding of Witch World* (1996, 1998) by Norton, and *Ciara's Song* (1998) by Norton and McConchie continue the series.
Ace, 1963, 1988, pap., 222 pp., o.p.
(SLJ 1977 p. 153)

7-214 NORTON, Andre (pseud. of Alice Mary Norton). *Wraiths of Time.* Gr. 7–12.
Radiation from a curious artifact thrusts Tallahassee Mitford into the Nubian kingdom of Meroë, where she takes on the memories and powers of Princess Ashake to battle evil forces from another world.
Atheneum, 1976, 210 pp., o.p.; Tor, 1992, pap., 256 pp. (0-8125-4752-7)
(BL 73:138, 180; CCBB 30:96; Kirkus 44:740; SLJ Oct 1976 p. 120; Suth 2:338)

7-215 NORTON, Mary (Pearson). *Are All the Giants Dead?* Gr. 4–6.
James goes on a guided tour of fairy tale land, where he battles a giant to save Princess Dulcibel from an ill-fated marriage to a frog.
Illus. by Brian Froud, Harcourt, 1975, 123 pp., o.p., 1978, pap. (0-15-607888-0)
(BL 72:627; CCBB 29:129; HB 51:465; Kirkus 43:1131; SLJ Sep 1975 p. 107; TLS 1975 p. 1053)

7-216 O'BRIEN, Robert C. (pseud. of Robert Leslie Conly). *The Silver Crown.* Gr. 5–8.
Ellen's bejeweled crown saves her from death by fire but endangers her life because of its potential for overthrowing the terrible Hieronymus Machine.
Illus. by Dale Payson, Atheneum, 1968, 247 pp., o.p.; Atheneum, 2001, 322 pp. (0-689-84106-X); Scholastic, 2001, pap. (0-689-84111-6)
(HB 44:174; HBG 13:90; LJ 93:1802; TLS 1973 p. 1115)

7-217 O'DONOHOE, Nick. *The Magic and the Healing.* **(Crossroads trilogy,**
☆ **bk. 1).** Gr. 8–12.
A group of veterinary students are taken on a field trip to the magical world of Crossroads, where healers use magic to treat their mythological patients. The

sequels are *Under the Healing Sign* (1995) and *The Healing of Crossroads* (1996).
Ace, 1994, pap., 336 pp. (0-441-00053-3)
(BL 91:1403; Kliatt Sep 1994 p. 20; LJ May 15, 1994 p. 103; SLJ Aug 1995 p. 38; VOYA 17:158)

7-218 O'HANLON (Meek), Jacklyn. *The Door.* Gr. 5–8.
Rachel steps through The Door into a frightening world populated by the captives of Burt Pelf.
Dial, 1978, 76 pp., o.p.
(CCBB 32:49; Kirkus 46:498; SLJ Apr 1978 p. 87)

7-219 OSTERWEIL, Adam. *The Amulet of Komondor.* Gr. 5–7.
Their favorite fantasy game, DragonSteel, sends Joe and Katie into the world of Komondor, whose inhabitants look like Japanese cartoon characters.
Illus. by Peter Thorpe, Front Street, 2003, 184 pp. (1-886910-81-2)
(BL 100:611; HBG 15:100; Kirkus 71:1180; SLJ Dec 2003 p. 158)

7-220 PALMER, Mary. *The Dolmop of Dorkling.* Gr. 3–5.
On Dorkling Island, Stafford trains the watermelon-armed navy and is proclaimed king.
Illus. by Fen Lasell, Houghton, 1967, 155 pp., o.p.
(BL 64:335; CCBB 21:31; Kirkus 35:652; LJ 92:2454)

PATON WALSH, Jill (Gillian Bliss). *Matthew and the Sea Singer.*
See Chapter 1, Allegorical Fantasy and Literary Fairy Tales.

PATTEN, Brian. *Mr. Moon's Last Case.*
See Chapter 9, Magic Adventure Fantasy.

PAYNE, Joan Balfour (Dicks). *Magnificent Milo.*
See Chapter 9, Magic Adventure Fantasy.

7-221 PIKE, Christopher. *Alosha.* **(Alosha trilogy, bk. 1).** Gr. 6–9.
Thirteen-year-old Alison Warner and her friends, exploring in the California mountains, enter a magical world where she may become Alosha, Queen of the fairies, if she can pass seven tests.
Tor, 2004, 304 pp. (0-765-31098-8)
(CCBB 58:34; Kliatt July 2004 p. 12; LJ July 2004 p. 76; SLJ Oct 2004 p. 176; VOYA 27:318)

PINKWATER, D(aniel) Manus. *Lizard Music.*
See Chapter 8, Humorous Fantasy.

7-222 POPE, Elizabeth Marie. *The Perilous Gard.* Gr. 6–9.
★★ The centuries-old spell surrounding the castle of Perilous Gard envelops Kate Sutton when she is enslaved by the Fairy Folk. John Newbery Medal Honor Book, 1975.
Illus. by Richard Cuffari, Houghton, 1974, 272 pp. (0-395-18512-2); Puffin, 1991, pap. (0-14-034912-X); illus. by Richard Cuffari, Houghton, 2001, 320 pp. (0-618-16967-9) and pap. (0-618-15073-0)
(BL 70:1201; HB 50:287; Kirkus 42:433; LJ 99:1484)

7-223 **POSTMA, Lidia.** *The Stolen Mirror.* Gr. 1–4. (Orig. pub. in the Netherlands.)
A magical bicycle takes Michael into a world of wizards, fairies, and a dragon.
Illus. by the author, McGraw-Hill, 1976, 26 pp., o.p.
(BL 72:1468; CCBB 30:29; Kirkus 44:532; SLJ Feb 1977 p. 58)

PRATCHETT, Terry. *The Wee Free Men.*
See Chapter 5, High Fantasy: Alternate Worlds or Histories.

7-224 **PRUE, Sally.** *Cold Tom.* Gr. 5–8. (Orig. British pub. 2002.)
★   Condemned to death by his elfin tribe, Tom runs away and hides among the
human "demons," helped by a girl named Anna who shows him the "horror" of
human affection. Nestlé Smarties Prize, Silver Award, 2002.
Scholastic, 2003, 192 pp. (0-439-48268-2); Oxford University Press, 2002,
pap., 144 pp. (0-19-271887-8); Scholastic, pap., 2004, 187 pp. (0-439-48269-0)
(BL 100:241; CCBB 57:122; HB 79:466; HBG 14:373; Kirkus 71:863; Kliatt May 2003 p.13;
SLJ Sep 2003 p. 219; VOYA 26:326)

PYLE, Howard. *The Garden Behind the Moon: A Real Story of the Moon
Angel.*
See Chapter 1, Allegorical Fantasy and Literary Fairy Tales.

PYLE, Howard. *Twilight Land.*
See Chapter 1, Allegorical Fantasy and Literary Fairy Tales.

7-225 **REEVES, James (pseud. of John Morris Reeves).** *The Strange Light.* Gr.
4–6. (Orig. British pub. 1964.)
Christina finds her way into a land whose occupants are characters in as yet
unwritten books.
Illus. by J. C. Kocsis, Rand, 1966, 152 pp., o.p.
(BL 63:491; CCBB 20:97; Kirkus 34:689; LJ 91:5237; TLS 1964 p. 602)

7-226 **REGAN, Dian Curtis.** *Princess Nevermore.* Gr. 5–8.
Just before her sixteenth birthday, Princess Quinella of Mandria finds herself
in the world she had always longingly watched through a wishing pool.
Scholastic, 1995, 224 pp., o.p.
(CCBB 49:103; HBG 7:68; Kirkus 1356; SLJ Sep 1995 p. 202; VOYA 18:317)

7-227 **REICHERT, Mickey Zucker.** *The Beasts of Barakhai.* **(The Books of
Barakhai, vol. 1).** Gr. 8 up.
A biology student named Ben is lured into the world of Barakhai by a shape-
shifting laboratory rat who plans to help other involuntary shape-shifters wrest
power from their rulers. The sequel is *The Lost Dragons of Barakhai* (2002,
2003).
DAW, 2001, 336 pp. (0-7564-0013-9), 2002, pap., 347 pp. (0-7564-0040-6)
(BL 97:1992; LJ Aug 1001 p. 171; VOYA 24:373)

7-228 **RHYS, Mimpsey.** *Mr. Hermit Crab: A Tale for Children by a Child.* Gr.
4–6.
In this story written by a 14-year-old girl, Lucia and Louisa, both 10, enter a
world of danger and enchantment.

Illus. by Helen Sewell, Macmillan, 1929, 190 pp., o.p.

(BL 26:208; HB 5:52–53; Mahony 3:413; Moore:30, 427)

7-229 RILEY, Louise. *Train for Tiger Lily.* Gr. 4–6. (Orig. Canadian pub. 1954.)
A magical train takes five children to Tiger Lily, where wishes are granted by
a Master of Magic. Canadian Library Association Best Book of the Year for
Children, 1956. The sequel is *A Spell at Scoggin's Crossing* (1960).
Illus. by Christine Price, Viking, 1954, 186 pp., o.p.

(BL 51:117; Kirkus 22:485; LJ 79:916, 80:192)

7-230 ROBERTS, Katherine. *Spellfall.* Gr. 5–8. (Orig. British pub. 2000.)
Natalie, 12, finds a magical spell in a supermarket parking lot and is captured
by an evil Spellmage named Hawk, who understands that she has inherited
great powers of sorcery from her late mother, an Earthhaven Spellmage.
Chicken House/Scholastic, 2001, 250 pp. (0-439-29653-6); Chicken House,
2004, pap., 240 pp. (1-90343-417-3)

(BL 98:574; CCBB 55:217; HBG 13:91; Kirkus 69:1300; SLJ Oct 2001 p. 168; VOYA
24:373, 25:16)

7-231 RODDA, Emily. *The Charm Bracelet.* **(The Fairy Realm series, bk. 1).**
Gr. 1–4. (Orig. pub. in Australia.)
Her grandmother's charm bracelet brings Jessie into a world of mythical crea-
tures who need her grandmother, heir to the throne, to renew the spell that
keeps this world safe. The sequels are *The Flower Fairies* (2003), *The Third
Wish* (2003), *The Last Fairy-Apple Tree* (2003), *The Magic Key* (2004), *The
Unicorn* (2004), and *The Star Cloak* (2005).
Illus. by Raoul Vitale, HarperCollins, 2003, 128 pp. (0-06-009584-9)

(BL 99:892; CCBB 56:286; HBG 14:358; Kirkus 71:65; SLJ Aug 2003 p. 140)

7-232 RODDA, Emily. *Finders Keepers.* Gr. 4–7. (Orig. Australian pub. 1990.)
✮   Computer game-loving Patrick is pulled through his television screen into
another world, where he becomes a contestant on the quiz show "Finders
Keepers" and searches for lost objects belonging to the three Seekers. Children's Book Council of Australia Book of the Year Award for Younger Readers, 1991. The sequel is *The Timekeeper* (1993).
Illus. by Noela Young, Greenwillow, 1991, 184 pp., o.p.

(BL 88:625; CCBB 45:104; HBG 3:72; Kirkus 59:1349; SLJ Aug 1991 p. 168)

7-233 ROSENBERG, Joel. *The Fire Duke.* **(Keepers of the Hidden Ways trilogy, bk. 1).** Gr. 10 up.
Ian discovers that the father of his college friend Torrie is a fugitive from the
land of Faerie, after Torrie's mother and their friend Maggie are abducted by
werewolves and taken to Tir Na Nog. The sequels are *The Silver Stone* (1996)
and *The Crimson Sky* (1998).
ArvoNova Morrow, 1995, 368 pp. (0-688-14153-6)

(BL 91:1555; Kirkus 63:433; VOYA 18:236)

7-234 ROSENBERG, Joel. *The Sleeping Dragon.* **(Guardians of the Flame
Saga, vol. 1).** Gr. 10 up.
Seven college students playing a fantasy role-playing game discover that they
have crossed into another world where their survival depends on finding the
Gate Between Worlds. The sequels are *The Sword and the Chain* (1984, 1993),

The Silver Crown (1985), *The Heir Apparent* (1987), *Guardians of the Flame: The Warriors* (1985), *Guardians of the Flame: The Heroes* (1989), *The Warrior Lives* (1988, 1990), *The Road to Ehvenor* (1991, 1992), *The Road Home* (1995), *Not Exactly the Three Musketeers* (1999, 2000), *Not Quite Scaramouche* (2001), *Not Really the Prisoner of Zenda* (2003), and *To Home and Ehvenor* (2004). *Guardians of the Flame* (Baen, 2003) is an omnibus edition of the first three volumes in the series.

NAL, 1983, pap., 253 pp., o.p.; Dutton, 1986, o.p.; Roc, 1993, pap. (0-451-45350-6)

(Kliatt Winter 1984 p. 24; LJ 108:1976; VOYA 7:102)

ROWLING, J[oanne] K[athleen]. *Harry Potter and the Sorcerer's Stone.*
See Chapter 12, Witchcraft and Sorcery Fantasy.

7-235 RUBIN, Amy Kateman. *Children of the Seventh Prophecy.* Gr. 5–7.
Alice and Bernard are recruited by Klig, a troll prince-child, to help outwit the evil Unking who is plotting to take control of both human and troll worlds.
Warne, 1981, 178 pp.,o.p.
(BL 77:1449; CCBB 35:56; Kirkus 49:801; SLJ Sep 1981 p. 129; VOYA 4:44)

7-236 RUBINSTEIN, Gillian. *Under the Cat's Eye: A Tale of Morph and Mystery.* Gr. 5–8. (Orig. Australian pub. 1997.)
Jai and his parents have no idea that Drake, headmaster of Nexhath boarding school, is stealing the souls of the students and faculty, in this science-fantasy.
Simon, 1998, 208 pp. (0-689-81800-9)
(BL 94:2008; CCBB 52:111; HB 74:741; HBG 10:74; Kirkus 66:1292; SLJ Oct 1998 p. 146; VOYA 21:288)

7-237 RUCKER, Rudy. *The Hollow Earth: The Narrative of Mason Algiers Reynolds of Virginia.* Gr. 11 up.
Fifteen-year-old Mason, his slave companion, Atha, and Edgar Allan Poe travel from the pre-Civil War South to the center of the earth and back again, in this science-fantasy suggested for mature readers.
Morrow, 1990, 288 pp., o.p.
(BL 87:32, 38; Kirkus 58:972; LJ Aug 1990 p. 147)

7-238 RUFFELL, Ann. *Pyramid Power.* Gr. 6–9.
The mail-order pyramid with magical powers transports Martin into a dream world, where he learns to cope with a potential stepfather he dislikes.
Watts, 1981, 159 pp., o.p.
(CCBB 35:36; SLJ Feb 1983 p. 82; TLS 1982 p. 345)

7-239 RUSH, Alison. *The Last of Danu's Children.* Gr. 7–10.
Matt and Kate enter the Otherworld, battle the forces of evil who have bewitched Kate's sister Anna, and call forth the Lord of Light to help save their world.
Houghton, 1982, 240 pp., o.p.
(BL 79:364, 373; CCBB 36:96; Kliatt 18:22; SLJ Jan 1983 p. 87)

7-240 SABERHAGEN, Fred. *Pyramids.* Gr. 10 up.
Tom Scheffler is transported to an alternate ancient Egypt whose gods are living beings. The sequel is *After the Fact* (1987).

Baen, 1987, pap., 311 pp., o.p.
(BL 83:550, 571; VOYA 10:93)

SAINT-EXUPÉRY, Antoine (Jean-Baptiste-Marie-Roger) de. *The Little Prince.*
See Chapter 1, Allegorical Fantasy and Literary Fairy Tales.

7-241   **SALVATORE, R. A.** *The Woods Out Back.* **(Spearwielder's Tale, vol. 1).**
✶   Gr. 10 up.
Gary Leger, bored with his job in a plastics factory, takes a walk in the woods and awakens in another world, where he becomes a warrior helping the Land of Faerie battle an evil witch. The sequels are *The Dragon's Dagger* (1994) and *Dragonslayer's Return* (1995). All three books are contained in *Spearwielder's Tale* (Ace, 2004; 0-441-01194-2).
Ace, 1993, pap., 290 pp., o.p.; Ace, 1996, pap. (0-441-90872-1)
(BL 90:422, 428; Kliatt Mar 1994 p. 20; LJ Oct 15, 1993 p. 93; VOYA 16:385)

7-242   **SCOTT, Evelyn.** *Witch Perkins: A Story of the Kentucky Hills.* Gr. 6–8.
A sinister witch disguised as a white cat takes Ella into a frightening dream world.
Illus. by Vera Clare, Holt, 1929, 322 pp., o.p.
(HB Nov 1929, pp. 30-33; Mahony 3:404; Moore:93)

7-243   **SHELLEY, Rick.** *Son of the Hero.* **(Varayan Memoir trilogy, bk. 1).** Gr. 7–12.
Home from college on vacation, Gil Tyner finds a secret basement room that leads into the kingdom of Varay, where he must take up his dead father's quest to defeat the enemies besieging the kingdom. The sequels are *The Hero of Varay* (1991) and *The Hero King* (1994).
Viking, 1990, 256 pp., o.p.
(Kliatt Jan 1991 p. 24; VOYA 13:367)

7-244   **SHEPPARD, Nancy, adapt.** *Alitji in Dreamland: An Aboriginal Version of Lewis Carroll's "Alice in Wonderland."* Gr. 4 up. (Orig. Australian pub. 1975.)
A bilingual Pitjantjatjara and English version of *Alice in Wonderland* (see Carroll, above), in which Alitji follows a white kangaroo into Dreamland.
Illus. by Donna Leslie, Tricycle, 1992, 105 pp. (0-89815-478-2)
(CCBB 46:190; HBG 4:102; SLJ Feb 1993 p. 95)

7-245   **SHERMAN, Josepha.** *The Shattered Oath.* Gr. 7–12.
Exiled from the Sidhe world to medieval Ireland, Prince Ardagh Lithanial passes himself off as a visitor from Cathay.
Baen, 1995, pap., 396 pp. (0-671-87672-4)
(Kliatt Mov. 1995 p. 20; VOYA 18:317)

7-246   **SHERMAN, Josepha.** *Strange and Ancient Name.* Gr. 10 up.
Half-human, half-Faerie Prince Hauberin is forced to make a dangerous journey into the human world to discover the secret of his human heritage.
Baen, 1993, pap., 386 pp. (0-671-72151-8)
(Kliatt May 1993 p. 19; VOYA 16:104)

7-247   SHETTERLY, Will. *Elsewhere.* **(Borderlands series, vol. 4).** Gr. 8–12.

✶   In Bordertown, on the boundary between the real world and Faerie, Ron searches for his brother, Tony, and finds gangs of runaway elves, humans, and "halfies" living violent lives in abandoned buildings. This book is set in the Bordertown/Borderlands world of Terri Winding's anthology written for adults, *Borderland* (NAL, 1986, Tor, 1992; see Chapter 5, High Fantasy: Alternate Worlds or Histories). In the sequel, *Nevernever* (1993, Harcourt, pap., 2004), set several months later, Wolfboy, formerly called Ron, is unable to protect young Florida, the missing heir of Faerie, who is kidnapped by the River Rats. *Finder: A Novel of the Borderlands* by Emma Bull (Tor, 1994; see above) is also set in Bordertown. This series also includes a number of multi-author short story collections: *Life on the Border* (ed. by Craig Shaw Gardner and Terry Windling; Tor, 1991), *Bordertown* (ed. by Terry Windling and Mark Alan Arnold; Doherty, 1996), and *The Essential Bordertown: A Traveller's Guide to the Edge of Faerie* (ed. by Terry Windling and Delia Sherman; Tor, 1998).

Harcourt, 1991, 224 pp. (0-15-200731-8); Tor, 1992, pap. (0-8125-2003-3); Harcourt, 2004, pap., 282 pp. (0-15-205209-7)

(BL 88:430; CCBB 45:74; HBG 3:80; Kirkus 59:1409; SLJ Nov 1991, p. 134; VOYA 14:326)

7-248   SHUSTERMAN, Neal. *Downsiders.* Gr. 6–10.

✶   When Talon ventures out of his Downside world beneath the New York City subway system and into the forbidden world above, he meets a Topside girl named Lindsay and breaks the rules by bringing her back with him into the tunnels.

Simon, 1999, 246 pp. (0-689-80375-3); Simon Pulse, 2001, pap., 256 pp. (0-689-83969-3)

(CCBB 53:31; HBG 10:299; Kirkus 67:889; Kliatt May 1999 p. 13; SLJ July 1999 p. 100; VOYA 22:196, 23:13)

SILVERMAN, Maida. *The Magic Well.*
See Chapter 1, Allegorical Fantasy and Literary Fairy Tales.

SIMAK, Clifford D(onald). *Enchanted Pilgrimage.*
See Chapter 1, Allegorical Fantasy and Literary Fairy Tales.

7-249   SINGER, Marilyn. *Charmed.* Gr. 5–8.
Twelve-year-old Miranda and her invisible cat friend, Bastable, battle the evil Charmer, who has used mind control and drugs to conquer other worlds.
Macmillan, 1990, 224 pp., o.p.
(BL 87:922; HBG 2:80; Kirkus 58:1536; SLJ Dec 1990 p. 111; VOYA 13:302, 14:10)

7-250   SINGER, Marilyn. *Horsemaster.* Gr. 6–9.
After dreaming of flight on a winged horse, Jessica is thrust into another world to become the protector of an ancient tapestry needed by the next Horsemaster to rule the war-torn land.
Atheneum, 1985, 179 pp., o.p.
(BL 81:1390, 1406; SLJ Sep 1985 p. 149; VOYA 8:194)

SLEATOR, William (Warner III). *Among the Dolls.*
See Chapter 11, Toy Fantasy.

SMITH, Doris Buchanan. *Voyages.*
See Chapter 6, High Fantasy: Myth or Legend Fantasy.

7-251 SMITH, L(isa) J. *Night of the Solstice.* Gr. 5–8.
Claudia, Alys, Charles, and Janie travel into the Wildworld to free the sorcerer
Morgana and battle an evil magician bent on enslaving our world. The sequel
is *Heart of Valor* (1990).
Macmillan, 1987, 231 pp. (0-02-785840-5); Harper, 1993, pap. (0-06-106172-7)
(CCBB 41:125; HB 64:212; Kirkus 55:1397; SLJ Jan 1988 p. 76; VOYA 10:292)

SNYDER, Zilpha Keatley. *The Unseen.*
See Chapter 9, Magic Adventure Fantasy.

SOBOL, Donald J. *"My Name Is Amelia."*
See Chapter 10, Time Travel Fantasy.

7-252 SPRINGER, Nancy. *The Friendship Song.* Gr. 5–7.
Sixth-grade friends Harper and Rawnie both love the rock group Neon Shadow, so when Nico, the lead singer, collapses during a performance, the girls
enter a spirit world of dead musicians and attempt to bring him back to life, in
this story with parallels to the Orpheus legend.
Macmillan, 1992, 114 pp. (0-689-31727-1)
(BL 88:941; Kirkus 60:120; HBG 3:270; Kirkus 60:120; SLJ Apr 1992 p. 125)

7-253 SPRINGER, Nancy. *Red Wizard.* Gr. 5–8.
Unhappy at home, Ryan runs away to the hut of a bumbling wizard in another
world, inadvertently bringing with him a red crayon talisman that might help
him get home.
Macmillan, 1990, 138 pp., o.p.
(HBG 1:255; Kirkus 58:270; SLJ July 1990 p. 79; VOYA 13:40)

7-254 STASHEFF, Christopher. *Her Majesty's Wizard.* **(A Wizard in Rhyme
series, bk. 1).** Gr. 10 up.
Reading a runic verse plunges Matt into the land of Merovence, where he helps
Princess Alisande to regain her throne. The sequels are *The Oathbound Wizard*
(1993, Del Rey, pap., 2004), *The Witch Doctor* (1994), *The Secular Wizard*
(1994, 1995), *My Son the Wizard* (1997, 1998), *The Haunted Wizard* (2000),
The Crusading Wizard (2000), *The Feline Wizard* (2000), and *A Wizard in a
Feud* (2001).
Ballantine, 1986, 1993, pap., 342 pp., o.p.
(BL 83:192, 220; LJ Oct 15, 1986 p. 114)

7-255 STEARNS, Pamela (Fujimoto). *Into the Painted Bear Lair.* Gr. 4–6.
A visit to a toy store takes Gregory into a fairy tale kingdom, where a hungry
bear and a knight help him rescue a princess from a dragon and awaken an
enchanted prince.
Illus. by Ann Strugnell, Houghton, 1976, 153 pp., o.p.
(BL 73:670; CCBB 30:133; HB 53:164; Kirkus 44:1170; SLJ Dec 1976 p. 56)

7-256 **STEPHENS, James.** *In the Land of Youth.* Gr. 5–7. (Orig. pub. in Ireland.)
In the first of two tales retold from Irish folklore, Nera enters the Land of
Faerie on All Hallows' Eve. In the second tale, Etain, the beautiful wife of
Midir, is abducted and returned.
Macmillan, 1924, 304 pp., o.p.
(BL 21:199)

STEWART, Mary (Florence Elinor). *Ludo and the Star Horse.*
See Chapter 1, Allegorical Fantasy and Literary Fairy Tales.

STORR, Catherine (Cole). *Thursday.*
See Chapter 6, High Fantasy: Myth or Legend Fantasy.

7-257 **STRAUSS, Victoria.** *Worldstone.* Gr. 7–12.
Alexina Taylor, orphaned and unhappy in her exile from New York City, dis-
covers that she has psychic powers when a thief from another world links his
mind with hers, enabling his escape into our world.
Macmillan, 1985, 324 pp., o.p.
(BL 82:398, 415; CCBB 39:159; SLJ Jan 1986 p. 75)

7-258 **SWAHN, Sven.** *The Island Through the Gate.* Gr. 6–8. (Orig. pub. in Swe-
den.)
Stranded on the isolated island of Oberair, Michael is prevented from leaving
by the superstitious islanders and their leader, Gourven the sorcerer.
Trans. by Patricia Crampton, Macmillan, 1974, 183 pp., o.p.
(BL 70:1059; HB 50:154; Kirkus 42:187; LJ 99:2279)

7-259 **SWIFT, Jonathan.** *Gulliver's Travels into Several Remote Nations of the*
★   *World.* Gr. 5 up. (Orig. British pub. 1726.)
In these editions adapted for young people, Gulliver is shipwrecked on Lil-
liput, an island of miniature people, and then travels to Brobdingnag, Land of
Giants. A contemporary sequel is *Castaways in Lilliput* by Henry Winterfeld
(Harcourt, 1960; see this section).
Illus. by Arthur Rackham, Dutton, 1957, 210 pp., o.p.; adapt. by Padraic
Colum, illus. by Willy Pogány, Macmillan, 1962, 260 pp., o.p.; ed. by Ronald
Storer, Oxford University Press, 1972, pap. (0-19-421764-7); illus. by David
Small, Morrow, 1983, 94 pp., o.p.; adapt. by James Riordan, illus. by Victor G.
Ambrus, Oxford University Press, 1992, 96 pp. (0-19-279897-9); adapt. by
Ann Keay Beneduce, illus. by Gennady Spirin, Philomel, 1993, 32 pp. (entitled
Gulliver's Adventures in Lilliput) (0-399-22021-6); adapt. by Margaret
Hodges, Holiday, 1995, 32 pp. (entitled *Gulliver in Lilliput*) (0-8234-1147-8)
(BL 44:118, 45:145, 80:817, 89:599, 90:71, 91:1500; Bookshelf 1932 p. 23; CCBB 2:6, 3:19,
48:361; HB 1[Nov 1924]:8, 39:604, 71:450; HBG 4:77, 5:70, 6:267; Kirkus 60:1316,
61:1338, 64:384; Mahony 2:297; SLJ Jan 1984 p. 82, Oct 1993 p. 132, June 1995 p. 114)

TARN, (Sir) W(illiam) W(oodthorpe). *The Treasure of the Isle of Mist: A*
Tale of the Isle of Skye.
See Chapter 9, Magic Adventure Fantasy.

7-260 **TEPPER, Sheri S.** *Marianne, the Magus, and the Manticore.* Gr. 10 up.

Marianne, an American college student from the tiny principality of Alphen-licht, finds herself in an alternate world battling a magus, or sorcerer, and a deadly manticore.
Ace, 1985, pap., 185 pp., o.p.
(BL 82:662, 677; VOYA 9:91)

7-261 **THESMAN, Jean.** *Between.* Gr. 6–9.
☆ Charlotte, 14, is drawn to a forbidden forest while visiting Puget Sound in 1941 and discovers Darkworld, home to mythical creatures awaiting the return of their lost leader.
Viking, 2002, 224 pp. (0-670-03561-0)
(BL 98:1709; CCBB 55:343; HBG 13:384; Kirkus 70:500; Kliatt May 2002 p. 14; SLJ May 2002 p. 162)

7-262 **THOMPSON, Julian F(rancis).** *Gypsyworld.* Gr. 7–12.
Five teenagers bought or kidnapped by the king and queen of Gypsyworld are taken into this parallel world to convince the inhabitants to help Earth solve its environmental problems.
Henry Holt, 1992, 227 pp. (0-8050-1907-3); Puffin, 1993, pap. (0-14-036531-1)
(BL 89:49; CCBB 46:24; HBG 4:84; Kirkus 60:994; SLJ Sep 1992 p. 280; VOYA 16:96)

TOLKIEN, J(ohn) R(onald) R(euel). *Smith of Wootton Major.*
See Chapter 1, Allegorical Fantasy and Literary Fairy Tales.

TOWNE, Mary. *Goldenrod.*
See Chapter 9, Magic Adventure Fantasy.

7-263 **TOWNLEY, Roderick.** *The Great Good Thing.* Gr. 4–7.
☆ Princess Sophie leaves the world of the book she lives in to visit the world of the reader, a girl named Claire, and must return to Claire's world many years later so that the book's characters can survive. The sequel is *Into the Labyrinth* (2002).
Simon, 2001, 232 pp. (0-689-84324-0); Aladdin, 2002, pap., 240 pp. (0-689-85328-9)
(BL 97:1398; CCBB 55:37; HBG 12:317; Kirkus 69:593; Kliatt May 2001 p. 15; SLJ July 2001 p. 114)

TREGARTHEN, Enys. *The White Ring.*
See Chapter 6, High Fantasy: Myth or Legend Fantasy.

7-264 **TROTT, Susan.** *The Sea Serpent of Horse.* Gr. 4–6.
A young girl must choose between staying forever in an undersea world or returning to her unhappy life on land.
Illus. by Irene Burns, Little, Brown, 1973, 117 pp., o.p.
(BL 70:546; Kirkus 41:1045, 1358; LJ 99:577)

7-265 **TURNER, Nancy Byrd.** *Zodiac Town: The Rhymes of Amos and Ann.* Gr. 3–5.
A rhyming story about two children who travel to Zodiac Town.
Illus. by Winifred Bromhall, Little, Brown, 1921, 131 pp., o.p.
(BL 18:93; LJ 47:869)

URE, Jean. *The Wizard in the Woods.*
See Chapter 12, Witchcraft and Sorcery Fantasy.

7-266 **VANDE VELDE, Vivian.** *Heir Apparent.* Gr. 6–9.
✭ In this science-fantasy, 14-year-old Giannine Bellisario is trapped inside a computer-generated fantasy kingdom, where her life is truly endangered. Anne Spencer Lindbergh Prize, 2001–2002.
Harcourt, 2002, 256 pp. (0-15-204560-0); Magic Carpet, 2004, pap., 336 pp. (0-15-205125-2)
(BL 99:982; CCBB 56:177; HB 78:764; HBG 14:89; Kirkus 70:1403; SLJ Oct 2002 p. 174; VOYA 25:403, 26:14)

7-267 **VENOKUR, Ross.** *The Cookie Company.* Gr. 4–7.
An unusual fortune cookie sends Alex Grindlay, 13, into another world, where he is pursued by an evil game-show host who is trying to kill him.
Delacorte, 2000, 181 pp. (0-385-32680-7)
(BL 96:930; CCBB 53:226; HBG 11:314; Kirkus 67:1892; SLJ Feb 2000 p. 126)

7-268 **WALKER, Gwen.** *The Golden Stile.* Gr. 4–6.
Climbing the Golden Stile leading to the moon, Noel meets a little man who grants his wishes for adventure.
Illus. by C(yril) Walter Hodges, Day, 1958, 188 pp., o.p.
(HB 34:479; Kirkus 26:606; LJ 83:3304)

WELLS, Martha. *The Wizard Hunters.*
See Chapter 12, Witchcraft and Sorcery Fantasy.

7-269 **WERBER, Bernard.** *Empire of the Ants.* Gr. 7–12. (Orig. French pub. 1991.)
Ignoring their late uncle Edmond's warning not to enter the cellar of the Paris house they have inherited, the Wells family discovers an ant empire where a heroic ant and her companions battle other insects and animals while looking for a secret weapon.
Trans. by Margaret Rocques, Bantam, 1998, 256 pp., o.p.
(BL 94:779; Kirkus 66:21; LJ Feb 1, 1998 p. 114; VOYA 21:214)

7-270 **WERSBA, Barbara.** *The Land of Forgotten Beasts.* Gr. 3–5.
Scientifically minded Andrew is magically transported to a land of mythical beasts who are doomed because people no longer believe in them.
Illus. by Margot Tomes, Atheneum, 1964, 88 pp., o.p.
(HB 40:499; Kirkus 32:651; LJ 89:3477; TLS 1965 p. 1130)

7-271 **WHEELER, Thomas.** *Loose Chippings.* Gr. 7–10. (Orig. pub. in England.)
Stranded after his car breaks down in the village of Loose Chippings, Bob Vickery finds the town to be full of secrets.
Phillips, 1969, 190 pp., o.p.
(BL 66:50; Kirkus 37:247; LJ 94:1802)

7-272 **WHEELER, Thomas.** *Lost Threshold: A Novel.* Gr. 8–10. (Orig. pub. in England.)
His father's disappearance brings James MacGregor into another world, where he leads an uprising against the tyrants in power and finds a wife.

Phillips, 1968, 189 pp., o.p.
(BL 65:167; Kirkus 36:467; LJ 93:3328)

7-273 WHITE, Eliza Orne. *The Enchanted Mountain.* Gr. 3–5.
Four children are taken to an enchanted mountain, where they learn to be polite and industrious.
Illus. by E. Pollak Ottendorff, Houghton, 1911, 107 pp., o.p.
(BL 8:183; HB 3:17–22)

7-274 WICKENDEN, Dan. *The Amazing Vacation.* Gr. 5–7.
☆ Cousin Emmeline sends Ricky and Joanna through a magic window to search for her lost turquoise gemstone.
Illus. by Erik Blegvad, Harcourt, 1956, 216 pp., o.p.
(BL 53:230; HB 32:352; Kirkus 24:475; LJ 82:230)

7-275 WILLARD, Nancy (Margaret). *Sailing to Cythera, and Other Anatole Stories.* **(Anatole trilogy, bk. 1).** Gr. 3–5.
Three stories about a boy named Anatole and his journeys to magical lands, including one tale in which he enters the wallpaper of his bedroom to meet the Blimlim. The sequels are *The Island of the Grass King: The Further Adventures of Anatole* (1979) and *Uncle Terrible: More Adventures of Anatole* (1982).
Illus. by (Michael) David McPhail, Harcourt, 1974, 72 pp., o.p.
(BL 71:573; Kirkus 43:19; LJ 99:2281)

7-276 WILLIAMS, Jay. *The Hero from Otherwhere.* Gr. 5–7.
Jesse and Rich, sent to the principal's office for fighting, end up instead in the kingdom of Gwyliath, charged with finding a magic rope to shackle the fiendish wolf, Fenris.
Walck, 1972, 175 pp., o.p.
(BL 69:407; CCBB 26:99; Kirkus 40:1193; LJ 98:1399)

7-277 WILLIAMS, Tad. *The War of the Flowers.* Gr. 10 up.
The dark tale of a struggling rock musician named Theo Vilmos, who finds his way into the land of Faerie, where he is hunted by the ruling families and caught up in a revolution.
DAW, 2003, 656 pp. (0-7564-0135-6); DAW, 2004, pap., 832 pp. (0-7564-0181-X)
(BL 99:1428; LJ May 15, 2003 p. 130;)

7-278 WILLIAMS, Thomas (Alonzo). *Tsuga's Children.* Gr. 10 up.
☆ Arn and Jen are two young children who find their way into a mythical valley beyond a waterfall, where they are taken in by Tsuga, leader of a peace-loving tribe.
Random, 1977, 239 pp., o.p.
(BL 73:1327; Kirkus 45:245; LJ 102:1046; SLJ Oct 1977 p. 130)

7-279 WILLIS, Paul J. *No Clock in the Forest.* Gr. 7–12.
Grace and Lance, two runaway campers on Queen's Mountain, are rescued from a bog by Lady Lira and imprisoned in the caverns below the mountains of the Three Queens.

Good News, 1991, pap., 219 pp. (0-89107-599-2)
(LJ Nov 1, 1991 p. 66; VOYA 14:250)

7-280 WILSON, Robert Charles. *Gypsies*. Gr. 10 up.
Karen has always repressed her childhood memories of creating doors into
other worlds with her brother and sister, until she discovers that her teenage
son, Michael, has similar powers and is haunted by the same Gray Man of her
own nightmares.
Doubleday, 1989, 240 pp., o.p.; Bantam, 1990, pap., 311 pp. (0-553-28304-9)
(BL 85:837, 863, 86:907, 995; Kirkus 56:1646; VOYA 12:293, 13:258)

7-281 WINDLING, Terri. *The Wood Wife*. Gr. 10 up.
✫   Maggie Black leaves her unhappy marriage behind after inheriting the Arizona
desert home of another poet, Davis Cooper, whose late wife's haunting paint-
ings of supernatural creatures are connected to his mysterious death.
Tor, 1996, 320 pp. (0-312-85988-0), 1997, pap., 304 pp. (0-8125-4929-5)
(Kirkus 64:1196; LJ Oct 15, 1996 p.93; SLJ July 1997 p. 117; VOYA 19:341, 20:13)

7-282 WINTERFELD, Henry. *Castaways in Lilliput*. Gr. 5–7. (Orig. German pub.
1958.)
Two hundred and fifty years after Gulliver's visit, the Lilliputians are again
alarmed by the appearance of giants, three human children whose raft accidentally drifted to Lilliput, in this modern sequel to *Gulliver's Travels* by Jonathan
Swift (1726; see above).
Trans. by Kyrill Schabert, illus. by William M. Hutchinson, Harcourt, 1960,
188 pp., o.p., 1990, pap., 220 pp. (0-15-214822-1); trans. by Kyrill Schabert,
illus. by William M. Hutchinson, Harcourt, 2002 (0-15-216298-4), 2002, pap.
(0-15-216286-0)
(BL 56:577; Eakin:355; HB 36:292; HBG 14:90; LJ 85:2484)

7-283 WINTHROP (Mahony), Elizabeth. *The Castle in the Attic*. Gr. 4–6.
✫   Angry that his lifelong baby-sitter is leaving him, 10-year-old William uses a
magic token to shrink them both small enough to enter the world inside an
elaborate toy castle. In the sequel, *The Battle for the Castle* (1993, 1994),
William, now 12, and his friend Jason, are given a magic coin that takes them
and their bicycles back in time to the Middle Ages.
Illus. by Trina Schart Hyman, Holiday, 1985, 192 pp. (0-8234-0579-6); Yearling, 2000, pap., 192 pp. (0-3758-0677-6)
(BL 82:761; CCBB 39:40; HB 62:204; SLJ Feb 1986 p. 91; VOYA 9:37)

7-284 WOLFE, Gene (Rodman). *The Knight*. (Wizard Knight duology, bk. 1).
Gr. 10 up.
After a teenaged boy enters the magical world of Mythgarthr, he is trans-
formed into a knight named Able, searching for the dragon who holds a special
sword. The sequel is *The Wizard* (2004).
Tor, 2004, 432 pp. (0-765-30989-0), 2005, pap. (0-765-31348-0)
(BL 100:735; LJ Dec 2003 p. 173)

7-285 WOLFE, Gene (Rodman). *There Are Doors*. Gr. 10 up.
A man named Green follows a former lover named Lara into a goddess-worshiping world where he is imprisoned in a mental hospital.

Tor, 1988, 313 pp., o.p., 2001, pap., 320 pp. (0-312-87230-5)
(BL 85:99; Kirkus 65:1438; LJ Nov 15, 1988 p.87; VOYA 12:48)

7-286 WOOD, Marcia. *The Secret Life of Hilary Thorne.* Gr. 4–6.
Hilary Thorne has the ability to enter the worlds of her favorite books and make friends with the characters, but her family's move to a new town forces her to pay more attention to the real world.
Macmillan, 1988, 128 pp., o.p.
(BL 84:1932; Kirkus 56:1412; SLJ Oct 1988 p. 149)

7-287 YARBRO, Chelsea Quinn. *Monet's Ghost.* Gr. 6–9.
Fifteen-year-old Geena Howe thinks herself into one of Monet's waterlily paintings, but arrives in a haunted castle and realizes that she might never find the way home.
Illus. by Pat Morrissey, Atheneum, 1997, 151 pp. (0-689-80732-5)
(BL 93:1687, 94:475, 1618; HBG 8:311; Kirkus 65:960; SLJ June 1997 p. 129; VOYA 20:197)

7-288 YOUMANS, Marly. *The Curse of the Raven Mocker.* Gr. 6–8.
Young Adanta leaves her family's cottage in the Blue Ridge Mountains and enters the land of the Hidden People to search for her missing parents and a legendary healing lake, in this story based on Cherokee legends.
Farrar, 2003, 288 pp. (0-374-31667-8)
(BL 100:125; HBG 15:105; Kirkus 71:1133; SLJ Dec 2003 p. 162; VOYA 27:149)

7-289 YOUNG, Ella. *The Unicorn with Silver Shoes.* Gr. 5–7.
Ballor's Son and Flame of Joy escape to the Land of the Ever Young.
Illus. by Robert Lawson, McKay, 1932, 213 pp., o.p.
(BL 29:80, Bookshelf 1933 p. 6; CCBB 11:104; HB 34:124; LJ 58:43; Mahony 3:213; TLS 1932 p. 893)

YOUNG, Robert F. *The Vizier's Second Daughter.*
See Chapter 6, High Fantasy: Myth or Legend Fantasy.

7-290 ZETTEL, Sarah. *A Sorcerer's Treason: A Novel of Isavalta.* **(Isavalta tril-**
★ **ogy, bk. 1).** Gr. 8 up.
Lighthouse keeper Bridget Lederle follows a stranger she rescued from drowning into the magic world of Isavalta, where she becomes a sorcerer trying to keep the heir to the throne alive. The prequel is *The Usurper's Crown* (2003; see below), and the sequel is *The Firebird's Vengeance* (2004).
Tor, 2002, 528 pp. (0-312-87441-3), 2003, pap., 512 pp. (0-7653-4374-6)
(BL 98:1313; Kirkus 70:533; LJ Apr 15, 2002 p. 127; VOYA 25:205, 26:141)

7-291 ZETTEL, Sarah. *The Usurper's Crown: A Novel of Isavalta.* **(Isavalta**
★ **trilogy, bk. 2).** Gr. 7 up.
In this prequel to *A Sorcerer's Treason* (2002; see above), set a generation earlier, young sorcerer Empress Medeoan of Isavalta is betrayed by her beloved new husband, who declares war on the neighboring Hung Tse, forcing them to release their Firebird. The sequel is *The Firebird's Vengeance* (2004).
Tor, 2003, 528 pp. (0-312-87442-1)
(BL 99:1153; Kirkus 71:353; LJ Mar 15, 2003 p. 120; VOYA 26:154, 27:15)

8

Humorous Fantasy

Listed here are a variety of humorous and exaggerated tales, including fast-paced comic plots, tales of people with bizarre pets, tall tales, and amusing stories of inanimate objects that come to life.

ADAIR, Gilbert. *Alice Through the Needle's Eye: The Further Adventures of Lewis Carroll's "Alice."*
See Chapter 7, High Fantasy: Travel to Other Worlds.

8-1 **AHLBERG, Allan.** *The Better Brown Stories.* Gr. 3–6. (Orig. British pub.
★ 1995.)
When the Brown family rebels against the novel in which they are characters, the author tries to write new chapters for each of them, with hilarious results.
Illus. by Fritz Wegner, Viking, 1996, 97 pp. (0-670-85894-3), 1998, pap., 112 pp. (0-14-037369-1)
(BL 92:832; CCBB 49:182; HB 72:590; HBG 7:289; Kirkus 63:1766; SLJ Feb 1995 p. 100)

8-2 **AHLBERG, Allan.** *The Clothes Horse and Other Stories.* Gr. 1–4. (Orig. British pub. 1987.)
Six short, humorous stories about people who take everyday expressions literally, including "The Jack Pot," in which a giant collects boys named Jack and keeps them in a pot.
Illus. by Janet Ahlberg, Viking, 1988, 32 pp., o.p.; Puffin, 1992, pap., 32 pp. (0-14-032907-2)
(Kirkus 56:119; SLJ Apr 1988 p. 77)

8-3 **AHLBERG, Allan.** *The Giant Baby.* Gr. 2–5. (Orig. British pub. 1994.)
After a giant baby is left on their doorstep, Alice and her parents foil a kidnapper and outwit social services and a mad scientist to keep him safe.
Illus. by Fritz Wegner, Viking, 1995, 156 pp. (0-670-84864-6); Viking Penguin, 1999, 176 pp. (0-14-036380-7)
(HBG 6:293; SLJ July 1995 p. 76)

8-4   **AHLBERG, Allan.** *The Man Who Wore All His Clothes.* **(The Gaskitts series, bk. 1).** Gr. 2–4. (Orig. British pub. 2001.)
Gus and Gloria Gaskitt and their parents capture a bank robber while their cat, Horace, watches it all on TV. The sequels are *The Woman Who Won Things* (2002) and *The Cat Who Got Carried Away* (2003).
Illus. by Katharine McEwan, Candlewick, 2001, 80 pp. (0-7636-1432-7); Walker, 2002, pap. (0-7445-8995-9)
(HBG 13:70; Kirkus 69:1352; SLJ Oct 2001 p. 62)

AHLBERG, Allan. *Ten in a Bed.*
See Chapter 9, Magic Adventure Fantasy.

8-5   **AHLBERG, Janet.** *Jeremiah in the Dark Woods.* Gr. 2–4. (Orig. British pub. 1977.)
Who stole Jeremiah Obadiah Jackenory Jones's auntie's tarts: three hungry bears, a wolf with a craving for grandmas, a Mad Hatter, a crocodile with a clock in his stomach, or a girl named Goldilocks?
Illus. by Allan Ahlberg, Viking, 1978, 47 pp. o.p.
(BL 74:1426; Kirkus 46:237; SLJ May 1978 p. 49)

8-6   **AIKEN, Joan (Delano).** *Arabel's Raven.* Gr. 4–7. (Orig. British pub. 1972, entitled *Tales of Arabel's Raven.*)
Life in the Jones's house just isn't the same after Mr. Jones brings home a raven named Mortimer, who enjoys eating stairs and sleeping in the refrigerator. The sequels are *Arabel and Mortimer* (1981), *Mortimer's Cross* (1984), and *Mortimer Says Nothing* (1987).
Illus. by Quentin Blake, Doubleday, 1974, 118 pp., o.p.
(CCBB 28:1; HB 50:278; Kirkus 42:478; LJ 99:2258)

8-7   **AIKEN, Joan (Delano).** *Armitage, Armitage, Fly Away Home.* Gr. 4–7.
☆   (Orig. British pub. 1965.)
Harriet and Mark's parents are proud of their unusual children's incredible adventures.
Illus. by Betty Fraser, Doubleday, 1968, 214 pp., o.p.
(BL 65:183; CCBB 22:1; HB 44:558; Kirkus 36:603; LJ 93:3296)

AIKEN, Joan (Delano). *The Faithless Lollybird.*
See Chapter 3, Fantasy Collections.

AIKEN, Joan (Delano). *A Foot in the Grave.*
See Chapter 4, Ghost Fantasy.

AIKEN, Joan (Delano). *The Kingdom and the Cave.*
See Chapter 5, High Fantasy: Alternate Worlds or Histories.

8-8   **AIKEN, Joan (Delano).** *Up the Chimney Down and Other Stories.* Gr. 5–8.
☆   (Orig. British pub. 1984.)
Eleven eerie and humorous tales, including "The Missing Heir," "The Midnight Rose," and "The Happiest Sheep in London."
Harper, 1985, 248 pp., o.p.
(BL 82:807; CCBB 39:121; HB 62:205; Kirkus 53:1139; SLJ Dec 1985 p. 85; TLS May 1984 p. 558; VOYA 8:323)

AIKEN, Joan (Delano). *The Whispering Mountain.*
See Chapter 5, High Fantasy: Alternate Worlds or Histories.

AIKEN, Joan (Delano). *The Wolves of Willoughby Chase.*
See Chapter 5, High Fantasy: Alternate Worlds or Histories.

ALEXANDER, Lloyd (Chudley). *The Cat Who Wished to Be a Man.*
See Chapter 2, Animal Fantasy.

ALEXANDER, Lloyd (Chudley). *Gypsy Rizka.*
See Chapter 5, High Fantasy: Alternate Worlds or Histories.

ALEXANDER, Lloyd (Chudley). *The Illyrian Adventure.*
See Chapter 7, High Fantasy: Travel to Other Worlds.

ALLEN, Will. *Swords for Hire: Two of the Most Unlikely Heroes You'll Ever Meet.*
See Chapter 5, High Fantasy: Alternate Worlds or Histories.

ALTOM, Laura Marie. *Kissing Frogs.*
See Chapter 6, High Fantasy: Myth or Legend Fantasy.

AMATO, Mary. *The Word Eater.*
See Chapter 9, Magic Adventure Fantasy.

ANDERSON, Mary. *F*T*C* Superstar.*
See Chapter 2, Animal Fantasy.

ANDERSON, Mildred Napier. *A Gift for Merimond.*
See Chapter 1, Allegorical Fantasy and Literary Fairy Tales.

ANDREWS, Allen. *The Pig Plantagenet.*
See Chapter 2, Animal Fantasy.

8-9 **ANDREWS, Frank (Emerson).** *The Upside-Down Town.* Gr. 3–5.
Anne and Rickie visit a town where everything is done backward.
Illus. by Louis Slobodkin, Little, Brown, 1958, 60 pp., o.p.
(BL 54:449; CCBB 11:106; Kirkus 26:34; LJ 83:1282)

ANGELL, Judie. *The Weird Disappearance of Jordan Hall.*
See Chapter 9, Magic Adventure Fantasy.

ANNETT (Pipitone Scott), Cora. *When the Porcupine Moved In.*
See Chapter 2, Animal Fantasy.

ANTHONY, Piers (pseud. of Piers A. D. Jacob). *A Spell for Chameleon.*
See Chapter 5, High Fantasy: Alternate Worlds or Histories.

ANTHONY, Piers (pseud. of Piers A. D. Jacob), and LACKEY, Mercedes. *If I Pay Thee Not in Gold.*
See Chapter 5, High Fantasy: Alternate Worlds or Histories.

8-10 **ARDAGH, Philip.** *The Fall of Fergal: Or, Not So Dingly in the Dell.*
(Unlikely Exploits trilogy, bk. 1). Gr. 5–7. (Orig. British pub. 2002.)

A fast-paced humorous tale about the five red-headed McNally siblings, including Fergal and Le Fay, who are staying at the Dell Hotel while Le Fay competes as a finalist in a national typing competition. The sequels are *Heir of Mystery: The Second Unlikely Exploit* (2003, 2004) and *The Rise of the House of McNally* (2004).

Illus. by David Roberts, Holt, 2004, 144 pp. (0-8050-7476-7)

(CCBB 57:406; Kirkus 72:437; SLJ July 2004 p. 98)

8-11   ARDAGH, Philip. *A House Called Awful End.* **(The Eddie Dickens trilogy, bk. 1).** Gr. 5–7. (Orig. British pub. 2000, entitled *Awful End.*)

Eddie, age 11, is sent on a series of outrageous adventures with his odd Uncle Jack and Mad Aunt Maude after his parents contract a disease that leaves them "crinkly around the edges." The sequels are *Dreadful Acts* (2003) and *Terrible Times* (2003).

Illus. by David Roberts, Holt, 2002, 144 pp. (0-8050-6828-7); Scholastic, 2003, pap., 128 pp. (0-439-53759-2)

(BL 99:600; CCBB 56:141; HBG 14:74; Kirkus 70:1026; SLJ Sep 2002 p. 219; VOYA 25:291)

ASIMOV, Isaac. *Azazel.*

See Chapter 9, Magic Adventure Fantasy.

ASPRIN, Robert (Lynn). *Hit or Myth.*

See Chapter 12, Witchcraft and Sorcery Fantasy.

8-12   ATWATER, Richard (Tupper), and ATWATER, Florence (Hasseltine
✶   **Carroll).** *Mr. Popper's Penguins.* Gr. 3–5.

A paperhanger named Mr. Popper is given a penguin as a gift, and quite soon, his problems multiply into 12 penguins. John Newbery Medal Honor Book, 1939.

Illus. by Robert Lawson, Little, Brown, 1938, 138 pp. (0-316-05842-4), 1992, pap., 151 pp. (0-316-05843-2); Dell, 1992, pap., 144 pp. (0-440-21370-3)

(BL 35:86; HB 14:370; LJ 63:818)

8-13   AUCH, Mary Jane. *I Was a Third Grade Science Fair Project.* Gr. 2–4.

Brian, Josh, and Dougie's science fair project backfires when, after hypnotizing Artful the dog to think he's a cat, Artful begins to speak, and Josh becomes a cat. The sequels are *I Was a Third Grade Spy* (2001) and *I Was a Third Grade Bodyguard* (2003).

Illus. by Herm Auch, Holiday, 1998, pap., 96 pp., o.p.; Dell, 1999, pap., 96 pp. (0-440-41606-X)

(BL 94:1243; HBG 9:315; Kirkus 66:334; SLJ May 1998 p. 106)

8-14   AVI (Avi Wortis). *Emily Upham's Revenge: Or, How Deadwood Dick*
✶   *Saved the Banker's Niece: A Massachusetts Adventure.* Gr. 4–6.

Emily and her friend Seth need money to get back home to Boston, but their plans to rob a bank go awry in this suspenseful spoof of a Victorian melodrama.

Illus. by Paul O. Zelinsky, Pantheon, 1978, 172 pp., o.p.; Morrow, 1992, 172 pp. (0-688-11898-4), pap. (0-688-11899-2)

(BL 74:1098; CCBB 31:170; HBG 4:63; Kirkus 46:304; SLJ Mar 1978 p. 24)

8-15   **BABBITT, Natalie (Zane Moore).** *The Devil's Storybook.* Gr. 4–6.
★★   Ten humorous tales about Satan's battles with humans. National Book Award Finalist, Children's Fiction Category, 1975. *The Devil's Other Storybook* (1987, 1989) is a companion volume.
Illus. by the author, Farrar, 1974, 102 pp., o.p.
(BL 71:37, 765; CCBB 28:58; HB 50:134; Kirkus 42:679; Suth 2:22; TLS 1976 p. 882)

8-16   **BABBITT, Natalie (Zane Moore).** *Goody Hall.* Gr. 4–6.
★   The mystery surrounding the death of young Willet Goody's father is solved after a seance visitation by Shakespeare and a nighttime visit to Mr. Goody's tomb.
Illus. by the author, Farrar, 1971, 1991, 176 pp., o.p.
(BL 67:954; CCBB 25:21; HB 47:380; Kirkus 39:431; LJ 96:1780, 1820; SLJ Aug 1992 p. 99; Suth:23)

BABCOCK (Thompson), Betty (Elizabeth S.). *The Expandable Pig.*
See Chapter 9, Magic Adventure Fantasy.

BAKER, Betty (Lou). *Save Sirrushany! (Also Agotha, Princess Gwyn and All the Fearsome Beasts).*
See Chapter 1, Allegorical Fantasy and Literary Fairy Tales.

BAKER, E. D. *The Frog Princess.*
See Chapter 6, High Fantasy: Myth or Legend Fantasy.

BAKER, Kage. *The Anvil of the World.*
See Chapter 5, High Fantasy: Alternate Worlds or Histories.

BAKER, Margaret Joyce. *Fifteen Tales for Lively Children.*
See Chapter 3, Fantasy Collections.

BAKER, Margaret Joyce. *Porterhouse Major.*
See Chapter 9, Magic Adventure Fantasy.

BALL, Brian. *The Quest for Queenie.*
See Chapter 7, High Fantasy: Travel to Other Worlds.

BALL, Duncan. *Selby: The Secret Adventures of a Talking Dog.*
See Chapter 2, Animal Fantasy.

BANKS, Lynne Reid. *Harry the Poisonous Centipede: A Story to Make You Squirm.*
See Chapter 2, Animal Fantasy.

BARNES, John. *One for the Morning Glory.*
See Chapter 5, High Fantasy: Alternate Worlds or Histories.

BATH, K. P. *The Secret of Castle Cant.*
See Chapter 5, High Fantasy: Alternate Worlds or Histories.

8-17   **BAUER, Joan.** *Thwonk.* Gr. 7–10.
★   A. J. has second thoughts after her wish comes true when Cupid "thwonks" handsome Peter, and he falls in love with her.

Delacorte, 1995, 213 pp. (0-385-32092-2); Puffin, 2001, pap., 215 pp. (0-698-11914-2)

(BL 91:814, 92:1276; CCBB 48:157; HBG 6:307, 13:95; Kirkus 63:220; SLJ Jan 1995 p. 134; VOYA 17:335)

BAUER, Steven. *A Cat of a Different Color.*
See Chapter 2, Animal Fantasy.

BEAGLE, Peter S(oyer). *A Fine and Private Place, A Novel.*
See Chapter 4, Ghost Fantasy.

8-18 **BEEKS, Graydon.** *Hosea Globe and the Fantastical Peg-Legged Chu.* Gr. 4–6.
Hosea and his talking dog are ordered to bring a scientist capable of controlling cyclones and typhoons to their secret island home.
Illus. by Carol Nicklaus, Atheneum, 1974, 170 pp., o.p.

(BL 71:813; Kirkus 43:305; SLJ Oct 1975 p. 94)

8-19 **BELL, Norman (Edward).** *The Weightless Mother.* Gr. 4–6.
After Mrs. Flipping accidentally swallows weightlessness pills, she floats out of the house and off into the sky.
Illus. by W. T. Mars, Follett, 1967, 144 pp., o.p.

(BL 64:384; HB 43:459; Kirkus 35:339; LJ 92:2647)

8-20 **BENDICK, Jeanne.** *The Blonk from Beneath the Sea.* Gr. 3–5.
Peter and his uncle, Professor Pokeberry, discover a prehistoric sea creature (half-fish, half-seal), nickname it the Blonk, and put it on display at the oceanarium.
Illus. by the author, Watts, 1958, 55 pp., o.p.

(CCBB 11:90; HB 34:265; Kirkus 26:133; LJ 83:1940)

8-21 **BENNETT, John.** *The Pigtail of Ah Lee Ben Loo, with Seventeen Other Laughable Tales.* Gr. 3–5.
This collection of humorous stories and poems was a John Newbery Medal Honor Book, 1929.
Illus. by the author, Longmans, 1928, 298 pp., o.p.

(BL 25:126; HB 4[Nov 1928]:82; Mahony 2:273; Moore:47, 430)

BERGER, Thomas (Louis). *Arthur Rex: A Legendary Novel.*
See Chapter 6, High Fantasy: Myth or Legend Fantasy.

BEST, (Oswald) Herbert. *Desmond's First Case.*
See Chapter 2, Animal Fantasy.

BETHANCOURT, T(homas) Ernesto (pseud. of Tom Paisley). *The Dog Days of Arthur Cane.*
See Chapter 9, Magic Adventure Fantasy.

BLACKWOOD, Algernon (Henry). *The Adventures of Dudley and Gilderoy.*
See Chapter 2, Animal Fantasy.

BLAYLOCK, James P(aul). *The Stone Giant.*
See Chapter 5, High Fantasy: Alternate Worlds or Histories.

8-22 **BLUNT, Wilfrid (Jasper Walter).** *Omar; a Fantasy for Animal Lovers.* Gr. 10 up.
Omar, the rare talking bander-snatch, is given to Rose Bavistock for her 50th birthday.
Illus. by John Verney, Doubleday, 1968, 192 pp., o.p.
(BL 65:866, 875; Kirkus 36:836; SLJ Dec 15, 1968 p. 4740)

BODE, N. E. (pseud. of Julianna Baggott). *The Anybodies.*
See Chapter 9, Magic Adventure Fantasy.

8-23 **BODECKER, N(iels) M(ogens).** *Carrot Holes and Frisbee Trees.* Gr. 3–5.
The Plumtree family's love of gardening produces carrots big enough to "grow" postholes, bringing them unexpected business opportunities.
Illus. by Nina Winters, Macmillan, 1983, 48 pp., o.p.
(BL 80:404; HB 60:49; SLJ Jan 1984 p. 72)

BOMANS, Godfried (Jan Arnold). *Eric in the Land of the Insects.*
See Chapter 7, High Fantasy: Travel to Other Worlds.

BOND, (Thomas) Michael. *A Bear Called Paddington.*
See Chapter 2, Animal Fantasy.

BOND, (Thomas) Michael. *Here Comes Thursday.*
See Chapter 2, Animal Fantasy.

BOND, (Thomas) Michael. *Tales of Olga Da Polga.*
See Chapter 2, Animal Fantasy.

BOSWORTH, Beth. *Tunneling.*
See Chapter 10, Time Travel Fantasy.

BOUCHER, Anthony (pseud. of William Anthony Parker White). *The Compleat Werewolf.*
See Chapter 3, Fantasy Collections.

BOURLIAGUET, Léonce. *The Giant Who Drank from His Shoe and Other Stories.*
See Chapter 3, Fantasy Collections.

BOURLIAGUET, Léonce. *A Sword to Slice Through Mountains and Other Stories.*
See Chapter 3, Fantasy Collections.

BOWEN, Vernon. *The Wonderful Adventures of Ting Ling.*
See Chapter 1, Allegorical Fantasy and Literary Fairy Tales.

8-24 **BRELIS, Nancy (Burns).** *The Mummy Market.* Gr. 5–7.
★ The Martin children visit the Mummy Market to select a new mother.
Illus. by Ben Shecter, Harper, 1966, 145 pp., o.p.
(CCBB 20:38; HB 42:707; Kirkus 34:757; LJ 91:5222; Suth:50)

BRENNAN, Herbie. *Emily and the Werewolf.*
See Chapter 12, Witchcraft and Sorcery Fantasy.

8-25 **BRENNAN, Herbie.** *Fairy Nuff: A Tale of Bluebell Wood.* **(Tales of Bluebell Wood, bk. 1).** Gr. 3–5. (Orig. British pub. 2001.)
Fairy Nuff's misadventures with a barrel of gunpowder and a candle cause Widow Buhiss to send her groundskeeper to get rid of him, permanently. The sequel is *Nuff Said: Another Tale of Bluebell Wood* (2002).
Illus. by Ross Collins, Bloomsbury, 2002, 128 pp. (1-58234-770-0)
(BL 98:1955; Kirkus 70:801; SLJ Aug 2002 p. 147)

BRIGGS, Anita. *Hobart.*
See Chapter 2, Animal Fantasy.

8-26 **BRIGHT, Robert.** *Richard Brown and the Dragon.* Gr. 2–4.
✭ Richard Brown uses a fire extinguisher to battle a dragon and win the hand of Princess Rosalie, in this story retold from an anecdote by Samuel Clemens.
Illus. by the author, Doubleday, 1952, 2000, 81 pp. (0-385-07467-0)
(BL 49:18; CCBB 6:13; HB 28:319; Kirkus 20:498; LJ 77:1661)

8-27 **BRINK, Carol Ryrie.** *Andy Buckram's Tin Men.* Gr. 5–7.
A bolt of lightning brings Andy's tin-can robots to life in time to help him rescue two children from a flood.
Illus. by W. T. Mars, Viking, 1966, 192 pp., o.p.
(BL 62:774; CCBB 19:143; Kirkus 34:245; LJ 91:3255)

8-28 **BRINK, Carol Ryrie.** *Baby Island.* Gr. 3–5.
Two little girls and two babies are shipwrecked on a desert island off the coast of Australia.
Illus. by Helen Sewell, Macmillan, 1937, 1954, 172 pp., o.p.; Aladdin, 1993, pap., 160 pp., o.p.
(BL 34:196; HB 13:284; LJ 62:811, 881)

BRISSON, Pat. *Hot Fudge Hero.*
See Chapter 9, Magic Adventure Fantasy.

8-29 **BRITTAIN, Bill.** *All the Money in the World.* Gr. 3–6.
A group of friends who find all the money in the world deposited in their backyard are sought out by the army, by kidnappers, and by the president of the United States.
Illus. by Charles Robinson, Harper, 1979, 160 pp., o.p.; Aladdin, 1993, pap., 160 pp. (0-689-71751-2)
(CCBB 32:170; Kirkus 47:328; SLJ Mar 1979 p. 135)

BRITTAIN, Bill. *The Fantastic Freshman.*
See Chapter 9, Magic Adventure Fantasy.

8-30 **BRÖGER, Achim.** *Bruno.* Gr. 4–6. (Orig. German pub. 1973.)
Amazing things keep happening to Bruno: a dinosaur comes for dinner, snowmen and statues talk to him, and he meets 42 doubles of himself. The sequel is *Bruno Takes a Trip* (1978).

Trans. by Hilda Van Stockum, illus. by Ronald (Norbert) Himler, Morrow, 1975, 160 pp., o.p.

(BL 72:622; Kirkus 43:1128; SLJ Nov 1975 p. 71)

8-31   **BRÖGER, Achim.** *Little Harry.* Gr. 3–5. (Orig. German pub. 1979.)
Seventeen tales from Little Harry's imagination, in which he meets a vacuum cleaner-witch and a human alarm clock, and he learns to fly.
Trans. by Elizabeth Crawford, illus. by Judy Morgan, Morrow, 1979, 189 pp., o.p.

(BL 75:1153; Kirkus 47:451; SLJ May 1979 p. 50)

8-32   **BROOKS, Terry.** *Magic Kingdom for Sale—Sold!* **(The Magic Kingdom**
✮   **of Landover series, bk. 1).** Gr. 10 up.
The magic kingdom bought by Ben Holliday for a million dollars turns out to be possessed by a demon prince who has defeated all previous human rulers. The sequels are *The Black Unicorn* (1987), *Wizard at Large* (1988), *The Tangle Box* (1994, 1995), and *Witches' Brew* (1995).
Ballantine, 1986, 324 pp., o.p.

(BL 82:913, 83:1117, 86:904; Kirkus 54:254; LJ Apr 15, 1986 p. 97)

BROOKS, Walter Rollin. *Freddy Goes to Florida.*
See Chapter 2, Animal Fantasy.

8-33   **BROWN, Jeff.** *Flat Stanley.* **(Stanley Lambchop series, bk. 1).** Gr. 2–4.
✮   Stanley Lambchop, squashed flat as a pancake after a huge bulletin board falls on him, is lowered through sidewalk gratings, mailed to California, and disguised as a framed painting to capture art thieves. The sequels are *A Lamp for the Lambchops* (1983; which was republished in 1996 and 2003 as *Stanley and the Magic Lamp*), *Invisible Stanley* (1996, 1999, 2001), *Stanley, Flat Again!* (2003), *Stanley in Space* (2003), and *Stanley's Christmas Adventure* (2003).
Illus. by Tomi Ungerer, Harper, 1964, 64 pp., LB (0-06-020681-0); HarperTrophy, 2003, pap., 80 pp. (0-06-009791-4)

(BL 60:875; HB 40:274; LJ 89:1850; TLS 1968 p. 583)

8-34   **BUCHWALD, Art.** *The Bollo Caper: A Fable for All Ages.* Gr. 4–6.
Having escaped a fur coat fate, Bollo the leopard romps through a zoo, a swamp, a park, the White House, and the U.S. Senate in this satirical spoof on ecology and politics.
Illus. by Julie Brinckloe, Doubleday, 1973, 56 pp., o.p.

(BL 70:998; CCBB 27:172; Kirkus 42:422; LJ 99:1471)

BUCHWALD, Emilie. *Floramel and Esteban.*
See Chapter 2, Animal Fantasy.

BUFFIE, Margaret. *The Warnings.*
See Chapter 9, Magic Adventure Fantasy.

BURMAN, Ben Lucien. *High Water at Catfish Bend.*
See Chapter 2, Animal Fantasy.

8-35 **BURN, Doris.** *The Tale of Lazy Lizard Canyon.* Gr. 2–4.
The long-standing feud between the Hokums and the Burleys is settled by the marriage of Lafe Hokum and Mattie Mae Burley.
Illus. by the author, Putnam, 1977, 48 pp., o.p.
(BL 73:1495; Kirkus 45:425; SLJ Sep 1977 p. 103)

BUTTERS, Dorothy G(ilman). *Papa Dolphin's Table.*
See Chapter 2, Animal Fantasy.

8-36 **BUTTERWORTH, Oliver.** *The Enormous Egg.* Gr. 4–6.
✫ Nate Twitchell's new pet hatches from a leatherlike egg and turns out to be a baby triceratops. In *The Narrow Passage* (1973), Nate and Nicol meet a prehistoric man.
Illus. by Louis Darling, Little, Brown, 1956, 187 pp., o.p., 1993, pap., 188 pp. (0-316-11920-2)
(BL 52:298; CCBB 9:91; Eakin:56; HB 32:187; Kirkus 24:45; LJ 81:1042)

8-37 **BUTTERWORTH, Oliver.** *The Trouble with Jenny's Ear.* Gr. 4–6.
✫ After Jenny discovers that one of her ears is sensitive enough to hear other people's thoughts, her brothers concoct an ingenious money-making scheme.
Illus. by Julian de Miskey, Little, Brown, 1960, 275 pp., o.p., 1993, pap. (0-316-11922-9)
(BL 56:546; CCBB 13:143; Eakin:56; HB 36:215; Kirkus 28:184; LJ 85:2034)

BUZZATI, Dino. *The Bears' Famous Invasion of Sicily.*
See Chapter 2, Animal Fantasy.

8-38 **BYNG, Georgia.** *Molly Moon's Incredible Book of Hypnotism.* **(Molly Moon series, bk. 1).** Gr. 4–6. (Orig. British pub. 2002.)
Molly Moon escapes from Hardwick House orphanage using hypnotism to win a local talent show, and then makes herself into a child star by hypnotizing the entire city of New York. The sequels are *Molly Moon Stops the World* (2004), *Molly Moon's Hypnotic Holiday* (England, 2004), and *Molly Moon's Hypnotic Time Travel Adventure* (2005).
HarperCollins, 2003, 371 pp. (0-06-051406-X); HarperTrophy, 2004, pap., 400 pp. (0-06-051409-4)
(CCBB 57:7; HBG 14:363; Kirkus 71:605; SLJ June 2003 p. 137)

8-39 **CALLEN, Larry (Lawrence Willard, Jr.).** *Pinch.* Gr. 5–8.
✫ Pinch Grimball trains his pet pig, Homer, to be the best bird-hunting pig in Four Corners, Louisiana.
Illus. by Marvin Friedman, Little, Brown, 1976, 179 pp., o.p.
(BL 72:1260, 73:1425; CCBB 30:5; HB 52:394; Kirkus 44:134; SLJ Apr 1976 p. 70, May 1976 p. 34)

CANFIELD, Dorothy (pseud. of Dorothea Frances [Canfield] Fisher). *Made-to-Order Stories.*
See Chapter 3, Fantasy Collections.

ČAPEK, Karel. *Nine Fairy Tales and One More Thrown In for Good Measure.*
See Chapter 3, Fantasy Collections.

8-40   CAREY, Valerie Soho. *The Devil and Mother Crump.* Gr. 2–4.
Old Mother Crump is so mean that she defeats both the Devil and Death.
Illus. by Arnold Lobel, Harper, 1987, 39 pp., o.p.
(BL 84:257; HB 64:50; Kirkus 55:1316; SLJ Nov 1987 p. 87)

8-41   CARKEET, David. *I Been There Before.* Gr. 10 up.
After Halley's comet brings Mark Twain back to life in 1985, the literary world
begins to doubt that he was the true author of his famous works.
Harper, 1985, 384 pp., o.p.
(BL 82:307, 327; Kirkus 53:801; SLJ Sep 1986 p. 152)

8-42   CARLSEN, Ruth Christoffer. *Henrietta Goes West.* Gr. 4–6.
The Nelson family travels westward in their automobile, Henrietta.
Illus. by Wallace Tripp, Houghton, 1966, 185 pp., o.p.
(CCBB 19:175; Kirkus 34:475; LJ 91:3256)

CARLSEN, Ruth Christoffer. *Mr. Pudgins.*
See Chapter 9, Magic Adventure Fantasy.

CARLSEN, Ruth Christoffer. *Sam Bottleby.*
See Chapter 9, Magic Adventure Fantasy.

8-43   CARLSON, Natalie Savage. *Alphonse, That Bearded One.* Gr. 3–5.
✮   Trained to take a clever woodsman's place as a soldier, Alphonse the bear caus-
es chaos in the French Canadian army.
Illus. by Nicolas Mordvinoff, Harcourt, 1954, 78 pp., o.p.
(BL 50:325; CCBB 7:70; Eakin:59; HB 30:174; Kirkus 22:197; LJ 79:783)

CARLSON, Natalie Savage. *Evangeline, Pigeon of Paris.*
See Chapter 2, Animal Fantasy.

8-44   CARLSON, Natalie Savage. *Hortense, the Cow for a Queen.* Gr. 4–6.
A French cow named Hortense is kidnapped by pirates and shipwrecked on the
coast of Africa.
Illus. by Nicolas Mordvinoff, Harcourt, 1957, 95 pp., o.p.
(BL 53:458; CCBB 11:92; HB 33:208, 298; Kirkus 25:274; LJ 82:1684)

CARTER, Lin. *Mandricardo.*
See Chapter 5, High Fantasy: Alternate Worlds or Histories.

CASSERLEY, Anne Thomasine. *Barney the Donkey.*
See Chapter 2, Animal Fantasy.

CATLING, Patrick Skene. *The Chocolate Touch.*
See Chapter 9, Magic Adventure Fantasy.

CAUFIELD, Don, and CAUFIELD, Joan. *The Incredible Detectives.*
See Chapter 2, Animal Fantasy.

8-45   CHARLES, Prince of Wales. *The Old Man of Lochnagar.* Gr. K–4. (Written, 1969; orig. British pub. 1980.)

Six humorous episodes about a very old Scotsman's adventures, which include meeting a merman, being carried off by an eagle, and drinking a shrinking formula.

Illus. by Hugh Casson, Farrar, 1980, 46 pp., o.p.

(BL 77:807; CCBB 34:147; Kirkus 49:209; SLJ Feb 1981 p. 55)

8-46 **CHASE, Mary (Coyle).** *Harvey, a Play.* Gr. 6 up. (Orig. pub. 1944, entitled *Harvey, a Comedy in Three Acts.*)

Elwood Down has an invisible rabbit friend named Harvey in this humorous story adapted from Chase's 1943 play, *The White Rabbit.*

Illus. by R. O. Blechman, Oxford University Press, 1953, 89 pp., o.p.

(BL 49:234; LJ 8:525)

CHASE, Mary (Coyle). *Mrs. McThing: A Play.*

See Chapter 12, Witchcraft and Sorcery Fantasy.

CHOCOLATE, Debbie. *Pigs Can Fly! The Adventures of Harriet Pig and Friends.*

See Chapter 2, Animal Fantasy.

CHRISMAN, Arthur Bowie. *Shen of the Sea: Chinese Stories for Children.*

See Chapter 3, Fantasy Collections.

8-47 **CHRISTIAN, Mary Blount.** *Sebastian (Super Sleuth) and the Crummy Yummies Caper.* **(Sebastian [Super Sleuth] series, bk. 1).** Gr. 3–4.

Sebastian the dog detective uncovers a dognapping plot, saves Chummy the Wonder Dog, and captures a would-be thief, although his master manages to take all the credit. The sequels are *Sebastian (Super Sleuth) and the Hair of the Dog Mystery* (1982), *Sebastian (Super Sleuth) and the Bone to Pick Mystery* (1983), *Sebastian (Super Sleuth) and the Case of the Santa Claus Caper* (1984), *Sebastian (Super Sleuth) and the Secret of the Skewered Skier* (1984), *Sebastian (Super Sleuth) and the Clumsy Cowboy* (1985), *Sebastian (Super Sleuth) and the Purloined Sirloin* (1986), *Sebastian (Super Sleuth) and the Stars-in-His-Eyes Mystery* (1987, 1990), *Sebastian (Super Sleuth) and the Egyptian Connection* (1988), *Sebastian (Super Sleuth) and the Time Capsule Caper* (1989), *Sebastian (Super Sleuth) and the Baffling Bigfoot* (1990), *Sebastian (Super Sleuth) and the Mystery Patient* (1991), *Sebastian (Super Sleuth) and the Impossible Crime* (1992), *Sebastian (Super Sleuth) and the Copycat Crime* (1993), and *Sebastian (Super Sleuth) and the Flying Elephant* (1994).

Illus. by Lisa McCue, Macmillan, 1983, 64 pp., o.p.

(BL 79:1272; Kirkus 51:375; SLJ May 1983 p. 91)

CHRISTOPHER, Matt(hew F.). *The Dog That Stole Football Plays.*

See Chapter 9, Magic Adventure Fantasy.

CLARK, Douglas W. *Alchemy Unlimited.*

See Chapter 12, Witchcraft and Sorcery Fantasy.

CLEARY, Beverly (Bunn). *The Mouse and the Motorcycle.*

See Chapter 2, Animal Fantasy.

CLIFFORD, Eth. *Flatfoot Fox and the Case of the Missing Eye.*
See Chapter 2, Animal Fantasy.

COBALT, Martin (pseud. of William Mayne). *Pool of Swallows.*
See Chapter 4, Ghost Fantasy.

8-48 **CONFORD, Ellen.** *Diary of a Monster's Son.* Gr. 2–4.
Young Bradley describes life with a monster for a father.
Illus. by Tom Newsom, Little, Brown, 1999, 76 pp. (0-316-15245-5)
(BL 95:1946; CCBB 52:347; HBG 10:277; SLJ July 1999 p. 68)

CONFORD, Ellen. *The Frog Princess of Pelham.*
See Chapter 9, Magic Adventure Fantasy.

COONTZ, Otto. *Hornswoggle Magic.*
See Chapter 9, Magic Adventure Fantasy.

COOPER (Grant), Susan (Mary). *The Boggart.*
See Chapter 9, Magic Adventure Fantasy.

COOPER (Grant), Susan (Mary). *Jethro and the Jumbie.*
See Chapter 9, Magic Adventure Fantasy.

8-49 **CORBALIS, Judy.** *The Ice Cream Heroes.* Gr. 4–7.
When Oscar and Henrietta travel to the Himalayas to bring an ice pick to
Oscar's mountain-climbing mother, they are imprisoned by a villain bent on
stealing all the ice cream in the world.
Illus. by David Parkins, Little, Brown, 1989, 160 pp., o.p.
(HB 66:61; HBG 1:82; Kirkus 57:1745)

CORBETT, Scott. *The Discontented Ghost.*
See Chapter 4, Ghost Fantasy.

8-50 **CORBETT, Scott.** *Ever Ride a Dinosaur?* Gr. 4–6.
Bronson the talking brontosaurus visits his old friends at the Museum of Natur-
al History.
Illus. by Mircea Vasiliu, Holt, 1969, 128 pp., o.p.
(CCBB 23:41; HB 45:409; Kirkus 37:558; LJ 94:2111; Suth:91)

CORBETT, Scott. *The Great Custard Pie Panic.*
See Chapter 12, Witchcraft and Sorcery Fantasy.

CORBETT, Scott. *The Lemonade Trick.*
See Chapter 9, Magic Adventure Fantasy.

8-51 **COREN, Alan.** *Arthur the Kid.* **(Arthur series, bk. 1).** Gr. 3–5. (Orig.
★ British pub. 1977.)
Ten-year-old Arthur's career as leader of a gang of bank-robbing gunslingers
takes an about-face when they save the bank from another gang. The sequels
are *Buffalo Arthur* (1978), *The Lone Arthur* (1978), *Railroad Arthur* (1978),
Klondike Arthur (1979), *Arthur's Last Stand* (1979), *Arthur and the Great
Detective* (1980), *Arthur and the Purple Panic* (1984), *Arthur versus the Rest*
(1985), and *Arthur and the Bellybutton Diamond* (Britain, 1981).

Illus. by John Astrop, Little, Brown, 1978, 74 pp., o.p. .
(BL 74:1616; CCBB 32:26; Kirkus 46:594; SLJ Sep 1978 p. 133; Suth 2:103)

COSTIKYAN, Greg. *By the Sword: Magic of the Plains.*
See Chapter 5, High Fantasy: Alternate Worlds or Histories.

COUNSEL, June. *A Dragon in Class 4.*
See Chapter 9, Magic Adventure Fantasy.

COVILLE, Bruce. *The Dragon of Doom.*
See Chapter 5, High Fantasy: Alternate Worlds or Histories.

COVILLE, Bruce. *The Dragonslayers.*
See Chapter 5, High Fantasy: Alternate Worlds or Histories.

COVILLE, Bruce. *Jennifer Murdley's Toad.*
See Chapter 9, Magic Adventure Fantasy.

COVILLE, Bruce. *Jeremy Thatcher, Dragon Hatcher.*
See Chapter 9, Magic Adventure Fantasy.

COVILLE, Bruce. *Juliet Dove, Queen of Love.*
See Chapter 9, Magic Adventure Fantasy.

COVILLE, Bruce. *The Skull of Truth.*
See Chapter 9, Magic Adventure Fantasy.

8-52   **COWELL, Cressida.** *How to Train Your Dragon: By Hiccup Horrendous Haddock III: Translated from an Old Norse Legend.* Gr. 4–7. (Orig. British pub. 2003.)
Son of a Viking warrior chief, Hiccup is just not the heroic type, and after he is swallowed by a huge dragon, he escapes through the monster's nose. *Hiccup the Seasick Viking* (2000) is a related story for young readers.
Illus. by the author, Little, Brown, 2004, pap., 224 pp. (0-316-73737-2)
(BL 100:1453; Kirkus 72:392; SLJ July 2004 p. 69)

CRAIG, Amanda. *Love in Idleness.*
See Chapter 9, Magic Adventure Fantasy.

CREECH, Sharon. *Pleasing the Ghost.*
See Chapter 4, Ghost Fantasy.

CRESSWELL (Rowe), Helen. *Almost Goodbye.*
See Chapter 9, Magic Adventure Fantasy.

CRESSWELL (Rowe), Helen. *The Bongleweed.*
See Chapter 9, Magic Adventure Fantasy.

8-53   **CRESSWELL (Rowe), Helen.** *The Piemakers.* Gr. 4–6. (Orig. British pub.
✯   1967.)
A family of bakers, competing against their cousins for the king's prize, concocts a meat pie big enough to serve 2,000 people. Carnegie Medal Commended Book, 1967.

Illus. by W. T. Mars, Lippincott, 1967, 142 pp., o.p.; illus. by Judith Gwyn Brown, Macmillan, 1980, 117 pp., o.p.; Oxford University Press, 1999, pap., 136 pp. (0-19-271809-6)

(BL 64:1041, 77:404; HB 56:662, 57:215; Kirkus 36:261; LJ 93:2536; SLJ Sep 1980 p. 68; TLS 1967 p. 445)

CRESSWELL (Rowe), Helen. *Time Out.*
See Chapter 10, Time Travel Fantasy.

8-54   CRETAN, Gladys. *Joey's Head.* Gr. 1–4.
Angry with his little brother for messing up his baseball cards, Mike mixes up a magic brew, wishes that Joey would disappear, and is astonished to find that only Joey's head has vanished.
Illus. by Blanche Sims, Simon & Schuster, 1991, 48 pp. (0-671-73201-3), 1993, pap. (0-671-86699-0)

(BL 87:2155; HBG 3:57; SLJ Dec 1991 p. 84)

CUSHMAN, Carolyn. *Witch and Wombat.*
See Chapter 7, High Fantasy: Travel to Other Worlds.

8-55   CUYLER, Margery. *Weird Wolf.* Gr. 2–5.
Nine-year-old Harry Walpole is desperate to cure a condition he inherited from his grandfather; every time there's a full moon, he turns into a werewolf.
Illus. by Dirk Zimmer, Henry Holt, 1989, 72 pp., o.p.

(BL 86:743; CCBB 43:107; HBG 1:84; Kirkus 57:1602; SLJ Apr 1990 p. 116)

8-56   DAHL, Roald. *The BFG.* Gr. 4–6. (Orig. British pub. 1982.)
Kidnapped by the BFG (Big Friendly Giant) and taken to Giant Country, orphaned Sophie and her vegetarian giant friend are horrified to find that the other giants eat "human beans," and they ask the Queen of England to put a stop to it.
Illus. by Quentin Blake, Farrar, 1982, 221 pp., o.p.; Knopf, 1993 (0-679-42813-5); Puffin, 2001, pap., 208 pp. (0-14-131137-1)

(BL 79:608, 685; CCBB 36:86; HB 59:165; Kirkus 50:1153; SLJ Dec 1982 p. 43; TLS 1982 p. 1303)

DAHL, Roald. *Charlie and the Chocolate Factory.*
See Chapter 9, Magic Adventure Fantasy.

8-57   DAHL, Roald. *Esio Trot.* Gr. 2–5. (Orig. British pub. 1990.)
Mr. Hoppy keeps substituting ever-larger tortoises for Mrs. Silver's pet Alfie, hoping to convince her to marry him. Nestlé Smarties Prize for Children's Books, Ages 6–8, 1990.
Illus. by Quentin Blake, Viking, 1990, 64 pp. (0-670-83451-3); Puffin, 1992, pap. (0-14-036099-9)

(BL 87:442; CCBB 44:82; HBG 2:66; Kirkus 58:1393; SLJ Nov 1990, p. 113; Suth 4:90; TLS 1990 p. 509)

DAHL, Roald. *Fantastic Mr. Fox.*
See Chapter 2, Animal Fantasy.

DAHL, Roald. *George's Marvelous Medicine.*
See Chapter 9, Magic Adventure Fantasy.

DAHL, Roald. *The Magic Finger.*
See Chapter 9, Magic Adventure Fantasy.

8-58　**DAHL, Roald.** *Matilda.* Gr. 3–7. (Orig. British pub. 1988.)
☆☆　Brilliant first-grader Matilda triumphs over her book-hating parents and Miss Trunchbull, the odious school principal.
Illus. by Quentin Blake, Viking, 1988, 240 pp. (0-670-82439-9); Puffin, 1998, pap., 240 pp. (0-14-130106-6)
(CCBB 42:30; HB 65:68; Kirkus 56:1237; SLJ Oct 1988 p. 143; Suth 4:90; TLS 1988 p. 573)

8-59　**DAHL, Roald.** *The Twits.* Gr. 3–6. (Orig. British pub. 1980.)
The terrible Twit family keeps the Muggle-Wump monkeys in a cage until the local birds free them and take revenge on the Twits.
Illus. by Quentin Blake, Knopf, 1981, 76 pp., o.p.; Puffin, 1991, pap. (0-14-034640-6); Knopf, 2002, 87 pp. (0-375-92242-3)
(CCBB 34:149; HBG 3:64, 14:77; Kirkus 49:356; SLJ May 1981 p. 63; TLS Nov 21, 1980 p. 1330)

8-60　**DAHL, Roald.** *The Vicar of Nibbleswicke.* Gr. 4–6. (Orig. British pub. 1991.)
The shy vicar's parishioners are shocked by his colorful language, caused by "Back-to-Front Dyslexia," in this story written to benefit the British Dyslexia Institute.
Illus. by Quentin Blake, Viking, 1992, 24 pp. (0-670-84384-9); Puffin, 2004, pap., 48 pp. (0-14-034891-3)
(BL 88:939; HBG 3:254; Kirkus 60:51; SLJ May 1992 p. 112)

DAHL, Roald. *The Witches.*
See Chapter 12, Witchcraft and Sorcery Fantasy.

8-61　**DAHL, Tessa.** *School Can Wait.* Gr. 3–5. (Orig. British pub. 1990.)
Jack and his parents head for the North Pole after they find Blitzen, one of Father Christmas's reindeer, lost in their backyard.
Illus. by Korky Paul, Viking, 1991, 64 pp. (0-670-84170-6); Puffin, 1992, pap., 64 pp. (0-14-034336-9)
(BL 88:940; HBG 3:64; Kirkus 59:1341; SLJ Jan 1992 p. 108)

DANA, Barbara. *Zucchini.*
See Chapter 2, Animal Fantasy.

DAVID, Lawrence. *Horace Splattly: The Cupcaked Crusader.*
See Chapter 9, Magic Adventure Fantasy.

DAVID, Peter. *Knight Life.*
See Chapter 6, High Fantasy: Myth or Legend Fantasy.

DAVID, Peter. *Sir Apropos of Nothing, the Woad to Wack and Wuin.*
See Chapter 5, High Fantasy: Alternate Worlds or Histories.

DAVIES, Andrew (Wynford). *Conrad's War.*
See Chapter 10, Time Travel Fantasy.

8-62   DAVIES, Andrew (Wynford). *Marmalade and Rufus.* Gr. 3–5. (Orig. British pub. 1979.)
Marmalade Atkins, the worst-behaved girl in the world, joins forces with an ornery talking donkey named Rufus to wreak havoc at the El Poco Nightclub, the Midnight Steeplechase, and a Christmas pageant. The British sequels are *Marmalade Atkins' Dreadful Deeds* (1982), *Marmalade Atkins in Space* (1982), *Educating Marmalade* (1983), *Danger—Marmalade at Work* (1984), and *Marmalade Atkins Hits the Big Time* (1984).
Illus. by Bert Dodson, Crown, 1983, 84 pp., o.p.
(BL 80:82; CCBB 37:46; HB 59:572; Kirkus 51:659; SLJ Sep 1983 p. 121)

8-63   DAVIES, Valentine. *It Happens Every Spring.* Gr. 7 up.
A secret formula developed by a college professor enables him to pitch St. Louis to a World Series victory.
Farrar, 1949, 224 pp., o.p.
(BL 45:359; Kirkus 17:238; LJ 74:955, 1031)

DAVIES, Valentine. *The Miracle on 34th Street.*
See Chapter 1, Allegorical Fantasy and Literary Fairy Tales.

8-64   DAWNAY, Romayne. *The Champions of Appledore.* Gr. 3–5.
Iona the mouse and her companions, three humans and a dragon named Grunwinkle, try to rid the land of Appledore of vicious wolves.
Illus. by the author, Four Winds, 1994, 144 pp. (0-02-789355-3)
(HBG 5:308; Kirkus 62:627; SLJ Aug 1994 p. 154)

DE CAMP, L(yon) Sprague. *The Honorable Barbarian.*
See Chapter 5, High Fantasy: Alternate Worlds or Histories.

DE CAMP, L(yon) Sprague, and DE CAMP, Catherine Crook. *The Incorporated Knight.*
See Chapter 5, High Fantasy: Alternate Worlds or Histories.

DE CAMP, L(yon) Sprague, and DE CAMP, Catherine Crook. *The Pixilated Peeress.*
See Chapter 5, High Fantasy: Alternate Worlds or Histories.

DELANEY, M(ichael) C(lark). *Birdbrain Amos.*
See Chapter 2, Animal Fantasy.

8-65   DELANEY, M(ichael) C(lark). *Henry's Special Delivery.* Gr. 3–6.
Armed with a knapsack full of junk food and a live, talking panda, ordered with two proof-of-purchase seals from his favorite cereal, Henry is determined to win the heart of Heather, his secret love.
Illus. by Lisa McCue, Dutton, 1984, 138 pp., o.p.
(BL 80:1547; CCBB 37:202; SLJ Oct 1984 p. 156)

DEVITA, James. *Blue.*
See Chapter 9, Magic Adventure Fantasy.

8-66   DEWEESE, (Thomas Eugene) Gene. *The Adventures of a Two-Minute Werewolf.* Gr. 5–7.

One incredible day, 14-year-old Walt Cribbens discovers that he has turned into a werewolf.

Illus. by Ronald Fritz, Doubleday, 1983, 132 pp., o.p.

(BL 79:1274; SLJ May 1983 p. 91)

8-67   **DICKINSON, Peter (pseud. of Malcolm de Brissac).** *Chuck and Danielle.*
✮   Gr. 4–6. (Orig. British pub. 1996.)

Danielle's dog, Chuck, is frightened of everything, but she manages to foil a purse-snatcher and help her mistress find out about the father she never knew.

Illus. by Kees de Kiefte, Delacorte, 1996, 115 pp. (0-385-32188-0); Dell, 1996, pap., 118 pp. (0-440-41087-8)

(BL 92:1178, 93:765; CCBB 49:189; HB 72:593; HBG 7:291; Kirkus 63:1701; SLJ Feb 1996 p. 100)

DICKINSON, Peter (pseud. of Malcolm de Brissac). *The Iron Lion.*
See Chapter 1, Allegorical Fantasy and Literary Fairy Tales.

DICKINSON, Peter (pseud. of Malcolm de Brissac). *Time and the Clock Mice, Etcetera.*
See Chapter 2, Animal Fantasy.

DILLON, Barbara. *A Mom by Magic.*
See Chapter 9, Magic Adventure Fantasy.

DILLON, Barbara. *Mrs. Tooey and the Terrible Toxic Tar.*
See Chapter 12, Witchcraft and Sorcery Fantasy.

DILLON, Barbara. *My Stepfather Shrank!*
See Chapter 9, Magic Adventure Fantasy.

DILLON, Barbara. *What's Happened to Harry?*
See Chapter 12, Witchcraft and Sorcery Fantasy.

8-68   **DOLBIER, Maurice (Wyman).** *A Lion in the Woods.* Gr. 4–6.

A newspaper reporter makes up a story about a lion at large in Forest Park.

Illus. by Robert Henneberger, Little, Brown, 1955, 115 pp., o.p.

(BL 51:301; CCBB 8:77; HB 31:111; LJ 80:999)

8-69   **DOYLE, Roddy.** *The Giggler Treatment.* Gr. 2–5. (Orig. pub. in Ireland.)

The color-changing, elf-like Gigglers target Mr. Mack to step in dog "poo" because he sent his sons to bed without supper the previous night. The sequel is *Rover Saves Christmas* (2001).

Illus. by Brian Ajhar, Scholastic, 2000, 112 pp. (0-439-16299-8), 2001, pap., 112 pp. (0-439-16300-5)

(HBG 12:60; Kirkus 68:1355; SLJ Nov 2000 p. 119)

DREYFUSS, Richard, and TURTLEDOVE, Harry. *The Two Georges: The Novel of an Alternate America.*
See Chapter 5, High Fantasy: Alternate Worlds or Histories.

DRURY, Roger W(olcott). *The Champion of Merrimack County.*
See Chapter 2, Animal Fantasy.

8-70 **DRURY, Roger W(olcott).** *The Finches' Fabulous Furnace.* Gr. 4–6.
☆ The Finch family tries to keep the volcano in their basement a secret, while safeguarding their town.
Illus. by Erik Blegvad, Little, Brown, 1971, 149 pp., o.p.
(BL 67:907; CCBB 25:4; HB 47:382; LJ 97:1169; Suth:108)

8-71 **DU BOIS, William (Sherman) Pène.** *The Alligator Case.* Gr. 3–5.
☆ A case involving a circus alligator and three suspicious strangers is solved by a boy detective, even before the crime is committed. *The Horse in the Camel Suit* (1967) is the sequel.
Illus. by the author, Harper, 1965, 63 pp., o.p.
(BL 62:330; CCBB 19:31; Eakin:103; HB 41:497; Kirkus 33:827; LJ 90:3788)

8-72 **DU BOIS, William (Sherman) Pène.** *Call Me Bandicoot.* Gr. 3–5.
A young con artist named Ermine Bandicoot is responsible for the color of New York Harbor's tobacco-brown water.
Illus. by the author, Harper, 1970, 63 pp., o.p.
(CCBB 24:105; Kirkus 38:1095; LJ 95:4326, 4354; Suth:109)

8-73 **DU BOIS, William (Sherman) Pène.** *The Flying Locomotive.* Gr. 1–4.
A fairy godmother gives a special wish to a Swiss locomotive.
Illus. by the author, Viking, 1941, 48 pp., o.p.
(HB 17:356, 381; LJ 66:878)

8-74 **DU BOIS, William (Sherman) Pène.** *The Forbidden Forest.* Gr. 3–5.
☆ Lady Adelaide the kangaroo, Buckingham the bulldog, and Spider Max the champion boxer are hailed as heroes for stopping World War I.
Illus. by the author, Harper, 1978, 56 pp., o.p.
(BL 75:215; CCBB 32:78; HB 55:515; Kirkus 46:946; SLJ Sep 1978 p. 122; Suth 2:130; TLS 1978 p. 1397)

8-75 **DU BOIS, William (Sherman) Pène.** *The Giant.* Gr. 4–6.
☆ A gigantic 8-year-old boy named El Muchacho, whose toys are live, wild animals and real trains and trucks, makes a visit to Paris.
Illus. by the author, Viking, 1954, 124 pp., o.p.
(BL 51:114; CCBB 8:98; Eakin:103; HB 30:434; Kirkus 22:529; LJ 80:190; Suth:212)

8-76 **DU BOIS, William (Sherman) Pène.** *The Great Geppy.* Gr. 4–6.
A red and white striped horse detective called the Great Geppy is hired to investigate problems at the Bolt Bros. Circus.
Illus. by the author, Viking, 1940, 1946, 92 pp., o.p.
(BL 36:368; HB 16:166, 175, 60:223; LJ 65:502, 847)

8-77 **DU BOIS, William (Sherman) Pène.** *Lazy Tommy Pumpkinhead.* Gr. 2–4.
☆ Tommy is so lazy that he begins each day by sliding from his automatic bed into an automatic bath, to be automatically dressed and fed, until the day the electricity fails.
Illus. by the author, Harper, 1966, 32 pp., o.p.
(CCBB 20:87; HB 43:61; Kirkus 34:1095; LJ 91:6190)

8-78 **DU BOIS, William (Sherman) Pène.** *Otto and the Magic Potatoes.* **(Otto**
✶ **series, bk. 4).** Gr. 2–4.
In this sequel to *Otto at Sea* (1936, 1958, 1964), *Otto in Texas* (1959), and *Otto in Africa* (1961), Otto, a lovable giant-sized dog, is kidnapped by Baron Backgammon, who is trying to grow gigantic potatoes and roses.
Illus. by the author, Viking, 1970, 48 pp., o.p.
(BL 66:1406; CCBB 24:57; Kirkus 38:238; LJ 95:1940)

8-79 **DU BOIS, William (Sherman) Pène.** *Peter Graves.* Gr. 5–7.
Peter uses a retired inventor's antigravity alloy to try such feats as tightrope walking upside down and performing the Indian rope trick.
Illus. by the author, Viking, 1950, 168 pp., o.p.
(BL 47:140; CCBB 4:19; HB 26:375; Kirkus 18:518)

8-80 **DU BOIS, William (Sherman) Pène.** *The Squirrel Hotel.* Gr. 3–6.
✶ A retired toy dealer and bee-orchestra conductor describes his hotel for squirrels, which is equipped with all the modern conveniences.
Illus. by the author, Viking, 1952, 48 pp., o.p.; Gregg, 1980, o.p.
(BL 48:269; HB 28:106; Kirkus 20:71; LJ 77:727)

8-81 **DU BOIS, William (Sherman) Pène.** *The Three Policemen, or Young Bottsford of Farbe Island.* Gr. 4–6.
The mystery of the stolen fishing nets on the fabulous island of Farbe is solved by three policemen, with the help of young Bottsford.
Illus. by the author, Viking, 1938, 1960, 95 pp., o.p.
(BL 57:190; HB 14:365, 375, 36:485; LJ 63:818, 978)

8-82 **DU BOIS, William (Sherman) Pène.** *The Twenty-One Balloons.* Gr. 5–7.
✶ Professor William Waterman Sherman is tired of teaching arithmetic, so he sails off in a balloon to see the world and lands on the volcanic island of Krakatoa. John Newbery Medal, 1948.
Illus. by the author, Viking, 1947, 180 pp. (0-670-73441-1); Puffin, 1986, pap., 184 pp. (0-14-032097-0)
(BL 43:296; HB 23:214; LJ 72:819)

DUFFEY, Betsy. *A Boy in the Doghouse.*
See Chapter 2, Animal Fantasy.

DUGGAN, Alice. *Violet's Finest Hour.*
See Chapter 2, Animal Fantasy.

DUTTON, Sandra. *The Magic of Myrna C. Waxweather.*
See Chapter 9, Magic Adventure Fantasy.

DYER, Heather. *The Fish in Room 11.*
See Chapter 9, Magic Adventure Fantasy.

EASTON, Patricia Harrison. *Davey's Blue-Eyed Frog.*
See Chapter 9, Magic Adventure Fantasy.

EBERHARDT, Thom. *Rat Boys: A Dating Experiment.*
See Chapter 9, Magic Adventure Fantasy.

8-83   EDMONDS, Walter D(umaux). *Uncle Ben's Whale.* Gr. 3–5.
A canal skipper named Uncle Ben harpoons a whale and sets up a museum inside it.
Illus. by William Gropper, Dodd, 1931, 1955, 90 pp., o.p.
(BL 52:60; Kirkus 23:646; LJ 80:2641)

EDMONDSON, Madeline. *Anna Witch.*
See Chapter 12, Witchcraft and Sorcery Fantasy.

8-84   EGNER, Thorbjørn. *The Singing Town.* Gr. 1–4. (Orig. Norwegian pub. 1955.)
In this musical comedy, three robbers and a pet lion frighten the villagers of Kardemomma. Awarded first prize by the Norwegian Ministry of Church and Education, 1955.
Trans. by Evelyn Ramsden and Leila Berg, illus. by the author, Macmillan, 1959, 105 pp., o.p.
(HB 35:387; LJ 84:3630; TLS Dec 4, 1959 p. iv)

ELISH, Dan. *Jason and the Baseball Bear.*
See Chapter 2, Animal Fantasy.

8-85   ELISH, Dan. *The Worldwide Dessert Contest.* Gr. 4–6.
John Appleteller and his culinary team long to wrest the gold medal in the worldwide dessert contest away from sly Sylvester Sweet, the self-proclaimed king of dessert.
Illus. by John Steven Gurney, Orchard, 1988, 224 pp., o.p.
(BL 84:1735; Kirkus 56:760; SLJ May 1988 p. 96)

ELLIS, Sarah. *The Several Lives of Orphan Jack.*
See Chapter 5, High Fantasy: Alternate Worlds or Histories.

EMSHWILLER, Carol. *Carmen Dog.*
See Chapter 2, Animal Fantasy.

8-86   ENDE, Michael. *The Night of Wishes, or The Satanarcheolidealcohellish Notion Potion.* Gr. 7–9. (Orig. German pub. 1989.)
A tomcat and a raven, secret agents from the High Council of Animals, have been assigned to stop Shadow Sorcery Minister Beelzebub Preposteror and his Aunt Tyrannia Vampirella's wicked plans to make 10 species of animals extinct, kill 10,000 trees, and bring a new plague into the world before New Year's Day.
Trans. by Heike Schwarzbauer and Rick Takvorian, Farrar, 1992, 244 pp. (0-374-19594-3)
(BL 88:2004; CCBB 46:174; HBG 4:67; Kirkus 60:847; SLJ Aug 1992 p. 154; VOYA 15:291)

ERWIN, Betty K. *Aggie, Maggie and Tish.*
See Chapter 9, Magic Adventure Fantasy.

ERWIN, John. *Mrs. Fox.*
See Chapter 2, Animal Fantasy.

8-87 **EUSTIS, Helen.** *Mr. Death and the Redheaded Woman.* Gr. 5 up. (Orig. pub. in the *Saturday Evening Post*, 1950.)
Redheaded Maud Applegate sets out to convince Mr. Death to restore the life of her own true love, Billy-Be-Damn Bangtry.
Illus. by Reinhard Michl, Green Tiger Press, 1983, pap., 32 pp., o.p.
(BL 80:170; HB 60:50; SLJ Jan 1984 p. 84)

8-88 **EVANS, Douglas.** *The Elevator Family.* Gr. 3–6.
The Wilson family moves into "Otis," a San Francisco hotel elevator, and spends their vacation solving the problems of staff and other guests.
Delacorte, 2000, 87 pp. (0-385-32723-4); Random, 2001, pap. (0-440-41650-7)
(BL 96:1667; CCBB 53:398; HBG 11:303; Kirkus 68:713)

8-89 **EVANS, Douglas.** *Math Rashes: And Other Classroom Tales.* Gr. 2–4.
Nine quirky stories tell about third graders whose problems are solved by a gnome, by rampaging playground equipment, and by a mealworm named Bob.
Illus. by Larry DiFiori, Front Street, 2000, 112 pp. (1-886910-66-9)
(BL 97:819; HBG 12:60; SLJ Nov 2000 p. 119)

8-90 **EVARTS, Hal G.** *Jay-Jay and the Peking Monster.* Gr. 6–9.
Aunt Hattie's experiments on ancient human bones bring a boy named Zurria to life and involve Jay-Jay with the Marines, gangsters, and a Chinese attaché.
Scribner, 1978, 185 pp., o.p.
(BL 74:1492; HB 54:401; Kirkus 46:500; SLJ May 1978 p. 86)

8-91 **EZO (pseud.).** *My Son-in-Law, the Hippopotamus.* Gr. 4–6. (Orig. pub. in France.)
Madame Hournarette's wild tales about her son-in-law, Baldomer the hippo, inspire two Parisian children to search for him in Africa.
Trans. by Hugh Shelley, illus. by Quentin Blake, Abelard-Schuman, 1962, 160 pp., o.p.
(HB 38:602; LJ 87:3201)

FARJEON, Eleanor. *The Glass Slipper.*
See Chapter 6, High Fantasy: Myth or Legend Fantasy.

8-92 **FARJEON, Eleanor.** *Gypsy and Ginger.* Gr. 3–5. (Orig. pub. in England.)
Gypsy and Ginger live in a weather house and emerge to explore London according to the weather.
Dutton, 1920, 164 pp., o.p.
(BL 17:353)

FAST, Howard (Melvin). *A Touch of Infinity: Thirteen New Stories of Fantasy and Science Fiction.*
See Chapter 3, Fantasy Collections.

FEAGLES, Anita MacRae. *Casey, the Utterly Impossible Horse.*
See Chapter 2, Animal Fantasy.

FEIFFER, Jules. *A Barrel of Laughs, a Vale of Tears.*
See Chapter 5, High Fantasy: Alternate Worlds or Histories.

FERRIS, Jean. *Once Upon a Marigold.*
See Chapter 5, High Fantasy: Alternate Worlds or Histories.

FIENBERG, Anna. *Ariel, Zed and the Secret of Life.*
See Chapter 9, Magic Adventure Fantasy.

8-93   **FIENBERG, Anna.** *Horrendo's Curse.* Gr. 4–6. (Orig. Australian pub. 2002.)
After he and his 12-year-old classmates are dragooned by pirates, Horrendo's good manners and gourmet cooking skills win over their captors.
Illus. by Kim Gamble, Annick/Firefly, 2002, 160 pp. (1-55037-773-6); Annick, 2002, pap. (1-55037-772-8)
(BL 99:664; HBG 16:366; Kirkus 70:1127; SLJ Feb 2003 p. 141)

FIENBERG, Anna. *The Magnificent Nose (and Other Marvels).*
See Chapter 9, Magic Adventure Fantasy.

8-94   **FIENBERG, Anna.** *Wiggy and Boa.* Gr. 3–7. (Orig. Australian pub. 1988.)
✰   Boa and her friend, Wiggy, struggle to save her sea captain uncle from savage pirates she magically summoned from an island prison. Australian Children's Book of the Year Award, Runner-up, 1988. The Australian sequel is *Pirate Trouble for Wiggy and Boa* (1997).
Illus. by Ann James, Houghton, 1990, 112 pp., o.p.
(CCBB 43:158; HB 66:454; HBG 1:254; Kirkus 58:575; SLJ May 1990 p. 104)

FINE, Anne. *The Chicken Gave It to Me.*
See Chapter 2, Animal Fantasy.

FINNEY, Jack (pseud. of Walter Branden Finney). *Marion's Wall: A Novel.*
See Chapter 4, Ghost Fantasy.

FINNEY, Patricia. *I, Jack.*
See Chapter 2, Animal Fantasy.

FISHER, Leonard Everett. *Noonan: A Novel About Baseball, ESP, and Time Warps.*
See Chapter 10, Time Travel Fantasy.

8-95   **FLEISCHMAN, (Albert) Sid(ney).** *By the Great Horn Spoon.* Gr. 4–6.
✰   Jack Flagg runs away from his Boston home to make his fortune in the California gold fields, accompanied by Praiseworthy, his butler.
Illus. by Eric Von Schmidt, Little, Brown, 1963, 1988, 193 pp., o.p., pap. (0-316-28612-5)
(BL 60:207; CCBB 17:110; HB 39:598; LJ 88:3348)

FLEISCHMAN, (Albert) Sid(ney). *A Carnival of Animals.*
See Chapter 2, Animal Fantasy.

8-96   **FLEISCHMAN, (Albert) Sid(ney).** *Chancy and the Grand Rascal.* Gr. 4–6.
✰   Chancy, orphaned and searching for his long-lost sister, Indiana, meets a tall-tale-telling uncle and a sly villain named Colonel Plugg.

Illus. by Eric Von Schmidt, Little, Brown, 1966, 1989, 190 pp., o.p., pap. (0-316-26012-6); Greenwillow, 1977, 192 pp. (0-688-14923-5); pap. (0-688-14924-3)

(BL 63:119; CCBB 20:41; HB 42:569; HBG 8:299; Kirkus 34:625; LJ 91:5226; Suth:126; TLS 1967 p. 1145)

FLEISCHMAN, (Albert) Sid(ney). *The Ghost in the Noonday Sun.*
See Chapter 4, Ghost Fantasy.

8-97   **FLEISCHMAN, (Albert) Sid(ney).** *The Ghost on Saturday Night.* Gr. 3–5.
☆   Opie becomes a town hero when he exposes Dr. Pepper's traveling ghost-raising show as a front for bank robberies. An adaptation of this story was published in *Faces in the Dark: A Book of Scary Stories* (ed. by Chris Powling; Kingfisher, 1994).
Illus. by Eric Von Schmidt, Little, Brown, 1974, 64 pp. (0-316-28583-8); illus. by Laura Cornell, Greenwillow, 1977, 64 pp. (0-688-14919-7); pap. (0-688-14920-0)

(BL 70:1252; CCBB 28:61; HB 50:379; Kirkus 42:535; LJ 99:2267; Suth 2:148; TLS 1975 p. 770)

FLEISCHMAN, (Albert) Sid(ney). *The Hey Hey Man.*
See Chapter 1, Allegorical Fantasy and Literary Fairy Tales.

8-98   **FLEISCHMAN, (Albert) Sid(ney).** *Humbug Mountain.* Gr. 4–6.
☆   Grandpa Flint's "property" in the boomtown of Sunshine, Dakota, turns out to be an abandoned riverboat in a ghost town, but the family makes the best of things by joining the gold rush. Boston Globe Horn Book Award, 1979; National Book Award Finalist, Children's Fiction Category, 1979.
Illus. by Eric Von Schmidt, Little, Brown, 1978, 149 pp., o.p.; Yearling, 1998, pap., 144 pp. (0-440-41403-2)

(BL 75:477, 80:95; CCBB 32:113; HB 55:640; Kirkus 46:1071; SLJ Sep 1978 p. 136; Suth 2:149)

8-99   **FLEISCHMAN, (Albert) Sid(ney).** *Jim Bridger's Alarm Clock, and Other*
☆   *Tall Tales.* Gr. 2–4.
Three tall tales concern an army scout and mountain man named Jim Bridger, including one in which he uses the echo of fireworks to outwit bank robbers.
Illus. by Eric Von Schmidt, Dutton, 1978, 56 pp., o.p.

(BL 75:808; HB 55:191; Kirkus 42:124; SLJ Apr 1979 p. 55)

8-100   **FLEISCHMAN, (Albert) Sid(ney).** *Jingo Django.* Gr. 4–6.
☆   Orphaned Jingo Hawks and his benefactor, Mr. Peacock-Hemlock-Jones, travel from Boston to Mexico trying their hands at horse trading, river piloting, portrait painting, and treasure hunting.
Illus. by Eric Von Schmidt, Little, Brown, 1971, 172 pp., o.p.

(BL 67:954, 68:669; HB 47:383, 63:439; Kirkus 39:432; LJ 96:2916; TLS 1971 p. 1509)

8-101   **FLEISCHMAN, (Albert) Sid(ney).** *McBroom Tells the Truth.* Gr. 3–5.
☆   (British title *McBroom's Wonderful One Acre Farm.*)
Farmer McBroom's crops grow so fast that his 11 children can ride on the pumpkins and use the cornstalks for pogo sticks. The sequels, all published by Little, Brown, are *McBroom and the Big Wind* (1967; rev. ed. 1982), *McB-*

room's Ear (1969), *McBroom's Ghost* (1971; rev. ed. 1981), *McBroom's Zoo* (1972; rev. ed. 1982), *McBroom the Rainmaker* (1973; Golden Kite Award Honor Book, 1973; rev. ed. 1982), *McBroom Tells a Lie* (1976; British title: *Here Comes McBroom!*), *McBroom and the Beanstalk* (1978), *McBroom and the Great Race* (1980), and *McBroom's Almanac* (1984). *McBroom's Wonderful One-Acre Farm: Three Tall Tales* (Greenwillow, 1992) contains "McBroom Tells the Truth," "McBroom and the Big Wind," and "McBroom's Ear." *Here Comes McBroom! Three More Tall Tales* (Greenwillow, 1992) contains "McBroom in the Rain," "McBroom's Ghost," and "McBroom's Zoo."

Illus. by Walter Lorraine, Grosset, 1966, 48 pp., o.p.; Little, Brown, 1981 (repr. of 1966 ed.) (0-316-28550-1)

(BL 62:662; CCBB 19:129; HB 42:193; HBG 4:56; Kirkus 33:1187; LJ 91:424; SLJ Aug 1992 p. 99; Suth1:27)

8-102 **FLEISCHMAN, (Albert) Sid(ney).** *Me and the Man on the Moon-Eyed*
✶ *Horse.* Gr. 3–5.
The circus train's visit to Furnace Flats is almost ruined by a desperado named Step-and-a-half Jackson, but young Clint saves the day.
Illus. by Eric Von Schmidt, Little, Brown, 1977, 57 pp., o.p.
(BL 73:1652; HB 53:553; Kirkus 45:46; SLJ May 1977 p. 61)

FLEISCHMAN, (Albert) Sid(ney). *The Midnight Horse.*
See Chapter 4, Ghost Fantasy.

8-103 **FLEISCHMAN, (Albert) Sid(ney).** *Mr. Mysterious and Company.* Gr. 4–6.
✶ Mr. Mysterious and his magician family travel across the country in a covered wagon, entertaining people with wonderful feats of magic.
Illus. by Eric Von Schmidt, Little, Brown, 1962, 151 pp., o.p.; Greenwillow, 1977, 160 pp. (0-688-14921-9); HarperTrophy, 1997, 160 pp., pap. (0-688-14922-7)
(BL 58:728; HB 38:279; HBG 8:299; LJ 87:1318)

8-104 **FLEISCHMAN, Paul (Taylor).** *Finzel the Farsighted.* Gr. 2–4.
✶ Although Finzel the fortune teller can barely see, his predictions enable him to outwit his greedy brother, Osip.
Illus. by Marcia Sewall, Dutton, 1983, 48 pp., o.p.
(BL 80:484; CCBB 37:86; Kirkus 51:147; SLJ Dec 1983 p. 65; Suth 3:134)

FLEISCHMAN, Paul (Taylor). *Graven Images: Three Stories.*
See Chapter 4, Ghost Fantasy.

8-105 **FLEMING, Ian (Lancaster).** *Chitty-Chitty Bang Bang: The Magical Car.*
✶ Gr. 4–6. (Orig. British pub. 1964.)
The Pott family's rattletrap auto can both fly and float, and it takes them across the English Channel to the underground hideout of England's worst gangster.
Illus. by John Burningham, Random, 1964, 111 pp., o.p.; illus. by Brian Selznick, Random, 2003 (0-375-92591-0), 2006, pap., 160 pp. (0-375-83283-1)
(BL 61:435; CCBB 18:73, 22:77; HB 41:167, 80:158; HBG 15:78; LJ 89:4646)

FLINT, Eric. *The Philosophical Strangler.*
See Chapter 5, High Fantasy: Alternate Worlds or Histories.

FLORA, James (Royer). *Grandpa's Ghost Stories.*
See Chapter 4, Ghost Fantasy.

FLORA, James (Royer). *Wanda and the Bumbly Wizard.*
See Chapter 12, Witchcraft and Sorcery Fantasy.

FOOTE, Timothy (Gilson). *The Great Ringtail Garbage Caper.*
See Chapter 2, Animal Fantasy.

8-106 **FORESTER, C(ecil) S(cott).** *Poo-Poo and the Dragons.* Gr. 3–5.
Harold "Poo-Poo" Brown brings home a dragon named Horatio.
Illus. by Robert Lawson, Little, Brown, 1942, 142 pp., o.p.
(HB 18:332; LJ 67:682; TLS 1942 p. 573)

FORWARD, Eve. *Villains by Necessity.*
See Chapter 5, High Fantasy: Alternate Worlds or Histories.

FORWARD, Toby. *Pie Magic.*
See Chapter 9, Magic Adventure Fantasy.

FORWARD, Toby. *Traveling Backwards.*
See Chapter 9, Magic Adventure Fantasy.

8-107 **FOSTER, John T(homas).** *Marco and the Tiger.* Gr. 4–6.
✶ Marco concocts wild schemes to protect the aging Bengal tiger he met while delivering newspapers.
Illus. by Lorence Bjorklund, Dodd, 1967, 128 pp., o.p.
(BL 64:273; HB 43:462; Kirkus 35:57; LJ 92:2020)

8-108 **FRANK, Lucy.** *The Annoyance Bureau.* Gr. 5–8.
✶ Lucas, age 12, becomes assistant to an irritable Santa named Izzy Gribits at the Annoyance Bureau, a New York agency charged with removing or disabling life's small annoyances.
Jackson/Atheneum, 2002, 176 pp. (0-689-84903-6)
(BL 99:491; CCBB 56:154; Kirkus 70:1389; Kliatt Nov 2002 p. 9; SLJ Oct 2002 p. 59)

FRESCHET, Bernice (Louise Speck). *Bernard of Scotland Yard.*
See Chapter 2, Animal Fantasy.

FRESCHET, Gina. *Winnie and Ernst.*
See Chapter 2, Animal Fantasy.

8-109 **FRIESNER, Esther M.** *Elf Defense.* Gr. 10 up.
A small Connecticut town is overrun with faerie creatures after the human wife of the king of American elves announces that she wants a divorce.
NAL, 1988, pap., 224 pp., o.p.
(BL 84:1223, 1241, 86:906; LJ Feb 15, 1988 p. 180)

FRIESNER, Esther M. *Gnome Man's Land.*
See Chapter 7, High Fantasy: Travel to Other Worlds.

FRIESNER, Esther M. *Majyk by Accident.*
See Chapter 12, Witchcraft and Sorcery Fantasy.

8-110 **FRIESNER, Esther M. *The Sherwood Game.*** Gr. 10 up.
A virtual reality game based on the Robin Hood legends veers out of control when Robin leads his merry men out of the game and into the real world.
Baen, 1995, pap., 384 pp. (0-671-87641-4)
(BL 91:1064, 1067; Kliatt July 1995 p. 14; VOYA 18:170)

FRIESNER, Esther M. *Wishing Season.*
See Chapter 5, High Fantasy: Alternate Worlds or Histories.

FROMAN, Elizabeth Hull. *Eba, the Absent-Minded Witch.*
See Chapter 12, Witchcraft and Sorcery Fantasy.

***Fun Phantoms: Tales of Ghostly Entertainment.* Ed. by Seon Manley and Gogo Lewis.**
See Chapter 4, Ghost Fantasy.

8-111 **FYLEMAN, Rose (Amy). *The Strange Adventures of Captain Marwhopple.*** Gr. 3–5. (Orig. British pub. 1931.)
Uncle Billiwinks tells humorous stories of Captain Marwhopple's adventures.
Illus. by Gertrude Lindsay, Doubleday, 1932, 166 pp., o.p.
(LJ 57:864; TLS 1931 p. 957)

FYLEMAN, Rose (Amy). *Tea Time Tales.*
See Chapter 3, Fantasy Collections.

GAGE, Wilson (pseud. of Mary Q[uintard] Govan Steele). *The Ghost of Five Owl Farm.*
See Chapter 4, Ghost Fantasy.

8-112 **GANNETT (Kahn), Ruth Stiles. *The Wonderful House-Boat-Train.*** Gr. 2–4.
A retired railroad engineer and his grandchildren move to a house in the country that looks like a train and floats like a boat.
Illus. by Fritz Eichenberg, Random, 1949, 64 pp., o.p.
(BL 46:161; HB 26:37; Kirkus 17:653; LJ 75:112)

GARDNER, Craig Shaw. *A Disagreement with Death.*
See Chapter 12, Witchcraft and Sorcery Fantasy.

GARDNER, Craig Shaw. *The Other Sinbad.*
See Chapter 6, High Fantasy: Myth or Legend Fantasy.

GARNETT, David. *Two by Two: A Story of Survival.*
See Chapter 6, High Fantasy: Myth or Legend Fantasy.

8-113 **GATHORNE-HARDY, Jonathan. *Operation Peeg.*** Gr. 4–6. (Orig. British
☆ pub. 1968, entitled *Jane's Adventures on the Island of Peeg.*)
After a rocket explosion sets the island of Peeg adrift in the Atlantic Ocean, two little girls and a housekeeper are caught up in a power struggle between two long-lost World War II soldiers and an evil billionaire. The sequels are *The Airship Ladyship Adventure* (1977) and *Jane's Adventures in and out of the Book* (Overlook, 1981).
Illus. by Glo Coalson, Lippincott, 1974, 192 pp., o.p.
(CCBB 28:77; HB 51:147; Kirkus 42:1060, 43:6; LJ 99:2740; TLS 1968 p. 1377)

GERAS, Adèle. *The Cats of Cuckoo Square: Two Stories.*
See Chapter 2, Animal Fantasy.

8-114 **GERAS, Adèle.** *The Fabulous Fantoras: Book One: Family Files.* **(The Fabulous Fantoras series, bk. 1).** Gr. 4–6. (Orig. pub. in England.)
Ozzy, the Fantoras' cat, narrates the adventures of his human family, each of whom has a different magical ability. The sequel is *Book Two: Family Photographs* (1999).
Avon, 1998, 144 pp. (0-380-97547-5)
(BL 95:490; HBG 10:66; SLJ Jan 1999 p. 127)

GIBSON, Katharine. *Cinders.*
See Chapter 1, Allegorical Fantasy and Literary Fairy Tales.

8-115 **GIFALDI, David.** *Gregory, Maw and the Mean One.* Gr. 4–6.
Twelve-year-old Gregory, raised by a crow, avoids a disastrous encounter with awful Norbert Meaney by offering to take Norbert back through time to find his missing heart.
Illus. by Andrew Glass, Houghton, 1992, 136 pp. (0-395-60821-X)
(HBG 4:68; Kirkus 60:1060; SLJ Nov 1992, p. 91)

GILLILAND, Alexis A(rnaldus). *Wizenbeak.*
See Chapter 12, Witchcraft and Sorcery Fantasy.

GILMORE, Kate. *Enter Three Witches.*
See Chapter 12, Witchcraft and Sorcery Fantasy.

GLEITZMAN, Morris. *Toad Rage.*
See Chapter 2, Animal Fantasy.

GLIORI, Debi. *Pure Dead Magic.*
See Chapter 12, Witchcraft and Sorcery Fantasy.

8-116 **GOGOL, Nikolai.** *The Nose.* Gr. 3 up. (Orig. Russian pub. as a short story.)
Kovaliov searches St. Petersburg for his missing nose, only to be told that it has become an "independent individual."
Illus. by Gennady Spirin, Godine, 1993, 28 pp. (0-87923-963-8)
(BL 89:1814; HBG 4:285; SLJ Aug 1993 p. 163)

GOLDMAN, William W. *The Princess Bride: S. Morgenstern's Classic Tale of True Love and High Adventure.*
See Chapter 5, High Fantasy: Alternate Worlds or Histories.

GORMLEY, Beatrice. *Best Friend Insurance.*
See Chapter 9, Magic Adventure Fantasy.

GORMLEY, Beatrice. *Fifth Grade Magic.*
See Chapter 9, Magic Adventure Fantasy.

GORMLEY, Beatrice. *Paul's Volcano.*
See Chapter 9, Magic Adventure Fantasy.

GOULART, Ron(ald Joseph). *The Chameleon Corps and Other Shape Changers.*
See Chapter 5, High Fantasy: Alternate Worlds or Histories.

GOULART, Ron(ald Joseph). *The Prisoner of Blackwood Castle.*
See Chapter 5, High Fantasy: Alternate Worlds or Histories.

GRANT, Vicki. *The Puppet Wrangler.*
See Chapter 9, Magic Adventure Fantasy.

GRAVES, Robert. *The Big Green Book.*
See Chapter 9, Magic Adventure Fantasy.

GRAY, Margaret. *The Ugly Princess and the Wise Fool.*
See Chapter 5, High Fantasy: Alternate Worlds or Histories.

GRAY, Nicholas Stuart. *The Apple Stone.*
See Chapter 9, Magic Adventure Fantasy.

GRAY, Nicholas Stuart. *A Wind from Nowhere.*
See Chapter 3, Fantasy Collections.

GREEN, Phyllis. *Eating Ice Cream with a Werewolf.*
See Chapter 9, Magic Adventure Fantasy.

8-117 **GREENBURG, Dan.** *A Ghost Named Wanda.* **(The Zack Files, bk. 1).** Gr. 2–5.
Ten-year-old Zack tries to get rid of the 8-year-old poltergeist haunting his apartment, in the first of his weird and wacky adventures. The sequels are *Great-Grandpa's in the Litter Box* (1996), *Through the Medicine Cabinet* (1996), *Zap! I'm a Mind Reader* (1996), *The Volcano Goddess Will See You Now* (1997), *Bozo the Clone* (1997), *Dr. Jekyll, Orthodontist* (1997), *I'm Out of My Body, Please Leave a Message* (1997), *My Son the Time Traveler* (1997), *Never Trust a Cat Who Wears Earrings* (1997), *Now You See Me—Now You Don't* (1998), *Elvis the Turnip—and Me* (1998), *The Misfortune Cookie* (1998), *Hang a Left at Venus* (1999), *Evil Queen Tut and the Great Ant Pyramids* (1999), *Yikes! Grandma's a Teenager* (1999), *How I Fixed the Year 1000 Problem* (1999), *How I Went from Bad to Verse* (2000), *The Boy Who Cried Bigfoot* (2000), *Don't Count on Dracula* (2000), *This Body's Not Big Enough for Both of Us* (2000), *Greenish Eggs and Dinosaurs* (2001), *My Grandma, Major League Slugger* (2001), *Trapped in the Museum of Unnatural History* (2002), *Me and My Mummy* (2002), *My Teacher Ate My Homework* (2002), *Tell a Lie and Your Butt Will Grow* (2002), *Just Add Water . . . and Scream!* (2003), and *It's Itchcraft* (2003).
Illus. by Jack E. Davis, Putnam/Grosset, 1996, 59 pp. (0-448-41290-X); Grossett, 1996, pap., 59 pp. (0-448-41261-6)
(HBG 8:291; SLJ Feb 1997 p. 81)

8-118 **GREENBURG, Dan.** *Young Santa.* Gr. 4–7.
Young Santa spends an ordinary childhood in Sioux City, Iowa, until his father is transferred to the North Pole, where Santa gets a job talking to children in a department store.

Illus. by Warren Miller, Viking, 1991, 89 pp. (0-670-83905-1)
(BL 88:313; Kirkus 59:930; SLJ Oct 1991, p. 30)

GREER, Gerry, and RUDDICK, Bob. *Max and Me and the Time Machine.*
See Chapter 10, Time Travel Fantasy.

GRIFFITH, Helen V(irginia). *Emily and the Enchanted Frog.*
See Chapter 9, Magic Adventure Fantasy.

8-119 GRIGGS, Terry. *Cat's Eye Corner.* Gr. 5–7. (Orig. Canadian pub. 2001.)
Olivier spends the summer at his grandfather's unusual mansion, Cat's Eye Corner, undertaking a magical scavenger hunt created by his step-grandmother, Sylvia de Whosit of Whatsit.
Raincoast, 2003, pap., 168 pp. (1-55192-350-5)
(BL 99:1761; SLJ Aug 2003 p. 159)

GROSSER, Morton. *The Snake Horn.*
See Chapter 10, Time Travel Fantasy.

GUTMAN, Dan. *Qwerty Stevens, Stuck in Time with Benjamin Franklin.*
See Chapter 10, Time Travel Fantasy.

HAHN, Harriet. *James, the Connoisseur Cat.*
See Chapter 2, Animal Fantasy.

HALE, Bruce. *The Chameleon Wore Chartreuse: From the Tattered Casebook of Chet Gecko, Private Eye.*
See Chapter 2, Animal Fantasy.

HALE, F. J. *Ogre Castle.*
See Chapter 12, Witchcraft and Sorcery Fantasy.

8-120 HALE, Lucretia P(eabody). *The Complete Peterkin Papers.* Gr. 5–8.
✫ (British titles *The Peterkin Papers* and *The Last of the Peterkins*; orig. pub. 1880.)
The Peterkin family's problems are solved by the common sense of the Lady from Philadelphia. *The Lady Who Put Salt in Her Coffee* (Harcourt, 1989) is an illustrated version of the first of the Peterkin stories, adapted by Amy Schwartz for children in grades 3 to 5.
Illus. by the author, Houghton, 1960, 1974, 302 pp., o.p.; IndyPublish.com, 2002 (entitled *The Peterkin Papers*), 152 pp. (1-404-32416-X); Kessinger, 2004, pap., 136 pp. (entitled *The Peterkin Papers*), (1-419-17709-5)
(BL 57:190; Bookshelf 1932 p. 12; HB 1:4–7, 1:44; Kirkus 28:905; LJ 50:803, 85:4567)

8-121 HALL, Lynn. *Dagmar Schultz and the Angel Edna.* **(Dagmar Schultz**
✫ **series, bk. 3).** Gr. 5–8.
Thirteen-year-old Dagmar's guardian angel, the late Aunt Edna, disapproves of Dagmar's resolve to find a boyfriend, until Aunt Edna falls in love herself. This is the sequel to *The Secret Life of Dagmar Schultz* (1988; not a fantasy) and *Dagmar Schultz and the Powers of Darkness* (1989). It is followed by *Dagmar Schultz and the Green-Eyed Monster* (1991).

Macmillan, 1989, 86 pp. (0-6841-9097-4), 1992, pap. (0-689-71615-X)
(BL 86:457; HB 65:770; HBG 1:70; Kirkus 57:1245; SLJ Sep 1989 p. 250; VOYA 12:276)

8-122 HAMILTON (Adoff), Virginia (Esther). *The All Jahdu Storybook.* Gr. 3–6.
Fifteen stories tell about the magical shape-shifting trickster Jahdu; 11 of them were previously published in *Jahdu* (Greenwillow, 1980), *The Time-Ago Tales of Jahdu* (1969), and *Time-Ago Lost: More Tales of Jahdu* (1973).
Illus. by Barry Moser, Harcourt, 1991, 108 pp. (0-15-239498-2)
(BL 88:697; CCBB 45:127; HBG 3:66; Kirkus 59:1402; SLJ Jan 1992 p. 109)

8-123 HAMILTON, Richard. *Violet and the Mean and Rotten Pirates.* Gr. 3–5. (Orig. British pub. 2003.)
Eight-year-old Violet joins a pirate band that decides to form a floating pirate circus.
Illus. by Sam Hearn, Bloomsbury, 2003, pap., 126 pp. (1-58234-848-0)
(BL 99:1890; Kirkus 71:804; SLJ Dec 2003 p. 114)

8-124 HANTMAN, Clea. *Heaven Sent.* **(Goddesses series, bk. 1).** Gr. 6–10.
Sent to Earth as punishment for resisting their father Zeus's plans to marry Thalia to Apollo, teenage goddesses Thalia, Era, and Polly adore their new life as attractive high school coeds. The sequels are *Three Girls and a God* (2002), *Muses on the Move* (2002), and *Love or Fate* (2002).
Avon, 2002, pap., 192 pp. (0-06-440875-2)
(BL 98:1010; CCBB 55:241; Kliatt May 2002 p. 26; SLJ Mar 2002 p. 230; VOYA 24:446)

HARVEY, Dean. *The Secret Elephant of Harlan Kooter.*
See Chapter 9, Magic Adventure Fantasy.

8-125 HARVEY, Jayne. *Great-Uncle Dracula.* Gr. 2–4.
New in school after her family's move to Transylvania to live with her Great-Uncle Dracula, Emily discovers that her classmates are all werewolves, ghosts, witches, or vampires. The sequel is *Great-Uncle Dracula and the Dirty Rat* (1993).
Illus. by Abby Carter, Random, 1992, 79 pp., o.p.
(CCBB 46:113; HBG 4:57; SLJ Sep 1992 p. 204)

8-126 HASELEY, Dennis. *Doctor Gravity.* Gr. 7 up.
The 207 townspeople of Avebury, Ohio, find themselves 4.2 miles up in the air after Dr. Gravity sells them his Formula Number 2 to cure the heaviness of gravity.
Farrar, 1992, 322 pp. (0-374-31842-5)
(CCBB 46:147; HB 69:211; HBG 4:81; Kirkus 60:1376; SLJ Dec 1992 p. 133; VOYA 15:292, 16:10)

HASS, E. A. *Incognito Mosquito, Private Insective.*
See Chapter 2, Animal Fantasy.

8-127 HAUFF, Wilhelm. *A Monkey's Uncle.* Gr. 4–6. (Orig. pub. in Germany.)
A newcomer decides to introduce an orangutan as his nephew.
Retold by Doris Orgel, illus. by Mitchell Miller, Farrar, 1969, 74 pp., o.p.
(Kirkus 37:1109; LJ 95:241)

HAYES, Geoffrey. *The Alligator and His Uncle Tooth: A Novel of the Sea.*
See Chapter 2, Animal Fantasy.

HAYES, Sheila. *Zoe's Gift.*
See Chapter 4, Ghost Fantasy.

HAYNES, Betsy. *The Ghost of the Gravestone Hearth.*
See Chapter 4, Ghost Fantasy.

8-128   HEIDE, Florence Parry. *The Shrinking of Treehorn.* **(Treehorn trilogy,**
★   **bk. 1).** Gr. 2–4.
No one believes that Treehorn is growing smaller and smaller every day. The
sequels are *Treehorn's Treasure* (1981) and *Treehorn's Wish* (1984). *The
Adventures of Treehorn* (Holiday, 1982; Dell, 1983, pap.) includes all three
tales.
Illus. by Edward Gorey, Holiday, 1971, 64 pp., o.p.
(BL 68:564, 669; CCBB 25:156; HB 48:45; Kirkus 39:1118; LJ 97:763, 1884)

HEIDENREICH, Elke. *Nero Corleone: A Cat's Story.*
See Chapter 2, Animal Fantasy.

HELPRIN, Mark. *Winter's Tale.*
See Chapter 5, High Fantasy: Alternate Worlds or Histories.

HENDRY, Diana. *A Camel Called April.*
See Chapter 9, Magic Adventure Fantasy.

HEWETT, Anita. *The Bull Beneath the Walnut Tree and Other Stories.*
See Chapter 3, Fantasy Collections.

HIGHTMAN, Jason. *The Saint of Dragons.*
See Chapter 5, High Fantasy: Alternate Worlds or Histories.

HILDICK, E(dmund) W(allace). *The Case of the Dragon in Distress: A
McGurk Fantasy.*
See Chapter 10, Time Travel Fantasy.

8-129   HILDICK, E(dmund) W(allace). *The Dragon That Lived Under Manhat-
tan.* Gr. 3–4.
Jimmy tries to convince the mayor of New York to allow a shy vegetarian drag-
on to live beneath the city.
Illus. by Harold Berson, Crown, 1970, 62 pp., o.p.
(BL 67:420; Kirkus 38:1143; LJ 95:4337)

HIRSCH, Odo. *Bartlett and the Ice Voyage.*
See Chapter 5, High Fantasy: Alternate Worlds or Histories.

8-130   HISER, Constance. *Night of the Werepoodle.* Gr. 2–4.
Not only does Jonathan have trouble with a bully at his new school, but when a
neighbor's dog bites him, Jonathan turns into a werepoodle.
Illus. by Cynthia Fisher, Holiday, 1994, 122 pp., o.p.
(BL 90:1820; HBG 5:311; SLJ June 1994 p. 130)

HISER, Constance. *No Bean Sprouts, Please!*
See Chapter 9, Magic Adventure Fantasy.

HITE, Sid. *Dither Farm.*
See Chapter 9, Magic Adventure Fantasy.

HOBAN, Russell C(onwell). *Dinner at Alberta's.*
See Chapter 2, Animal Fantasy.

8-131 **HOBAN, Russell C(onwell).** *How Tom Beat Captain Najork and His Hired*
☆ *Sportsmen.* Gr. 3–5. (Orig. British pub. 1974.)
Tom's Aunt Fidget Wonkham-Strong hires Captain Najork to teach Tom a lesson about foolish behavior, but even that doesn't stop him. Whitbread Literary Award, Children's Books Category, 1974. The sequel is *A Near Thing for Captain Najork* (1976).
Illus. by Quentin Blake, Atheneum, 1974, 32 pp., o.p.
(BL 71:766; CCBB 28:78; HB 51:138; Kirkus 42:1299, 43:2; LJ 99:2733; Suth 2:216; TLS 1974 p. 718)

HOBAN, Russell C(onwell). *Jim Hedgehog and the Lonesome Tower.*
See Chapter 2, Animal Fantasy.

HOBAN, Russell C(onwell). *Trouble on Thunder Mountain.*
See Chapter 2, Animal Fantasy.

8-132 **HOBAN, Russell C(onwell).** *The Twenty-Elephant Restaurant.* Gr. K–4.
A wobbly table, strengthened enough for an elephant to dance on, inspires an old man to build a restaurant featuring 20 dancing elephants.
Illus. by Emily Arnold McCully, Atheneum, 1978, 37 pp., o.p.
(BL 74:1494; CCBB 32:10; Kirkus 46:299; SLJ May 1978 p. 56)

8-133 **HODGES, C(yril) Walter.** *Sky High: The Story of a House That Flew.* Gr. 3–5. (Orig. pub. in England, entitled *The Flying House.*)
Uncle Ben's latest invention, super-inflating gas, causes Nicky and Linda's house to float off into the sky.
Illus. by the author, Coward, 1947, 112 pp., o.p.
(BL 44:189; HB 23:436; LJ 72:1543)

HOFFMANN, Eleanor. *The Four Friends.*
See Chapter 2, Animal Fantasy.

HOLM, Jennifer L., and HAMEL, Jonathan. *The Postman Always Brings Mice.*
See Chapter 2, Animal Fantasy.

8-134 **HOLMAN (Valen), Felice.** *The Blackmail Machine.* Gr. 4–6.
☆ A flying treehouse enables Murk and Arabella to "blackmail" the government into preserving wildlife and bringing peace to the world.
Illus. by Victoria de Larrea, Macmillan, 1968, 182 pp., o.p.
(BL 64:995; CCBB 21:129; HB 44:173; Kirkus 35:1472; LJ 93:870; TLS 1968 p. 1112)

8-135 HOLMAN (Valen), Felice. *The Escape of the Giant Hogstalk.* Gr. 3–6.
A national emergency is declared after a gigantic plant in the Royal Botanic Gardens grows out of control.
Illus. by Ben Shecter, Scribner, 1974, 96 pp., o.p.
(CCBB 28:28; HB 50:283; Kirkus 42:363; LJ 99:2270; Suth 2:223)

8-136 HOLMAN (Valen), Felice. *The Future of Hooper Toote.* Gr. 5–7.
Hooper Toote can walk on air.
Illus. by Gahan Wilson, Scribner, 1972, 138 pp., o.p.
(BL 69:529; CCBB 25:171; Kirkus 40:259; LJ 97:2951; Suth:193)

HOLMAN (Valen), Felice. *The Witch on the Corner.*
See Chapter 12, Witchcraft and Sorcery Fantasy.

8-137 HOOKS, William H(arris). *Mean Jake and the Devils.* Gr. 3–5.
✫ Mean old Jake manages to outwit three generations of devils in these three tales told to a boy by his grandmother.
Illus. by Dirk Zimmer, Dial, 1981, 64 pp., o.p.
(BL 78:756; CCBB 35:172; HB 58:164; Kirkus 50:202; SLJ Jan 1982 p. 77)

HOREJS, Vít. *Pig and Bear.*
See Chapter 2, Animal Fantasy.

8-138 HORNE, Richard Henry. *The Good-Natured Bear: A Story for Children of All Ages.* Gr. 4–6. (Orig. British pub. 1846; U.S. 1854.)
A good-natured uncle, disguised as a bear, tells the Littlepump children moralistic and humorous tales about his wandering life.
Illus. by Lisl Hummel, Macmillan, 1927, 159 pp., o.p.
(BL 24:168; HB 3:44; LJ 53:484, 1033; Mahony 2:147)

8-139 HORNIK, Laurie Miller. *Zoo School.* Gr. 3–5.
Ursula, Drake, and their friends love their new Zoo School, where the animals and the zookeepers are the teachers, so they try to save the school after the Inspectors decide to close it.
Illus. by Debbie Tilley, Clarion, 2004, 144 pp. (0-618-34204-4)
(BL 100:1726; Kirkus 72:492; SLJ June 2004 p. 110)

8-140 HORVATH, Polly. *The Pepins and Their Problems.* Gr. 4–7.
✫ The Pepin family must constantly ask their "dear readers" for solutions to their problems, including toads in their shoes, becoming stranded on their roof, a family cow who gives lemonade instead of milk, and a neighbor who has fallen in love with a barber pole.
Illus. by Marylin Hafner, Farrar, 2004, 192 pp. (0-374-35817-6)
(BL 100:1934; CCBB 58:79; HB 80:586; Kirkus 72:687; SLJ Aug 2004 p. 124;)

HORWITZ, Elinor Lander. *The Strange Story of the Frog Who Became a Prince.*
See Chapter 12, Witchcraft and Sorcery Fantasy.

HOWE, Deborah, and HOWE, James. *Bunnicula: A Rabbit Tale of Mystery.*
See Chapter 2, Animal Fantasy.

HUGHART, Barry. *Bridge of Birds: A Novel of an Ancient China That Never Was.*
See Chapter 5, High Fantasy: Alternate Worlds or Histories.

HUGHES, Carol. *Jack Black and the Ship of Thieves.*
See Chapter 5, High Fantasy: Alternate Worlds or Histories.

HUGHES, Dean. *Nutty's Ghost.*
See Chapter 4, Ghost Fantasy.

HUGHES, Frieda. *Getting Rid of Aunt Edna.*
See Chapter 12, Witchcraft and Sorcery Fantasy.

HUGHES, Richard (Arthur Warren). *Don't Blame Me!*
See Chapter 3, Fantasy Collections.

HUGHES, Ted (Edward James). *Tales of the Early World.*
See Chapter 3, Fantasy Collections.

8-141 **HUNTER, Mollie (pseud. of Maureen Mollie Hunter McVeigh McIl-**
☆ **wraith).** *The Smartest Man in Ireland.* Gr. 4–6. (Orig. British pub. 1963, entitled *Patrick Kentigen Keenan.*)
Patrick's boastful claim that he's the smartest man in Ireland tempts the fairy folk to test him.
Illus. by Charles Keeping, Funk, 1965, 95 pp., o.p.; Magic Carpet, 1996, pap., 128 pp. (0-15-200993-0)
(BL 62:487; HB 41:629; Kirkus 33:821; TLS 1963 p. 427)

HUNTER, Mollie (pseud. of Maureen Mollie Hunter McVeigh McIlwraith). *Thomas and the Warlock.*
See Chapter 12, Witchcraft and Sorcery Fantasy.

8-142 **HUNTER, Norman (George Lorimer).** *The Incredible Adventures of Professor Branestawm.* Gr. 5–7. (Orig. British pub. 1933.)
Professor Branestawm's zany inventions include a clock that strikes thirteen and a time machine. The sequels are *The Best of Branestawm* (1981), *Professor Branestawm's Building Bust-Up* (1982), *Professor Branestawm's Mouse War* (1982), *The Peculiar Triumph of Professor Branestawm* (British), *Professor Branestawm up the Pole* (British), *Professor Branestawm's Great Revolution* (British), and *Professor Branestawm's Treasure Hunt* (British).
Illus. by W. Heath Robinson, Bodley Head, 1979, 203 pp., o.p.
(BL 76:558; SLJ Aug 1980 p. 64; TLS 1970 p. 1458)

HUTCHINS, Hazel (J.). *The Three and Many Wishes of Jason Reid.*
See Chapter 9, Magic Adventure Fantasy.

8-143 **HUTCHINS, Pat (Goundry).** *Follow That Bus!* Gr. 2–4.
☆ After their teacher and their schoolbus are hijacked by robbers, Miss Beaver's second-grade class rescues her and captures the bandits. The sequel is *The Mona Lisa Mystery* (1981).
Illus. by Laurence Hutchins, Greenwillow, 1977, 102 pp., o.p.; Knopf, 1988 (repr. of 1977 ed.), pap., 112 pp. (0-394-80792-8)

(BL 73:1498; CCBB 31:48; HB 53:442; Kirkus 45:351; SLJ Apr 1977 p. 55; TLS 1977 p. 1412)

8-144 **HUTCHINS, Pat (Goundry).** *The House That Sailed Away.* Gr. 4–6.
✮ A house that floats out to sea, a battle with pirates, a landing on a cannibal island, and the discovery of buried treasure are just some of the adventures in store for Morgan and his family.
Illus. by Laurence Hutchins, Greenwillow, 1975, 150 pp. (0-688-84013-2)
(BL 72:303; CCBB 29:64; HB 51:593; Kirkus 43:777; SLJ Sep 1975 p. 84; TLS 1976 p. 882)

IBBOTSON, Eva. *Dial-a-Ghost.*
See Chapter 4, Ghost Fantasy.

IBBOTSON, Eva. *The Great Ghost Rescue.*
See Chapter 4, Ghost Fantasy.

IBBOTSON, Eva. *The Haunting of Granite Falls.*
See Chapter 4, Ghost Fantasy.

IBBOTSON, Eva. *Island of the Aunts.*
See Chapter 9, Magic Adventure Fantasy.

IBBOTSON, Eva. *Not Just a Witch.*
See Chapter 12, Witchcraft and Sorcery Fantasy.

IBBOTSON, Eva. *The Secret of Platform 13.*
See Chapter 7, High Fantasy: Travel to Other Worlds.

IBBOTSON, Eva. *Which Witch?*
See Chapter 12, Witchcraft and Sorcery Fantasy.

8-145 **IRVING, Washington.** *Knickerbocker's History of New York.* Gr. 8 up.
(Orig. pub. 1812, entitled *A History of New York, from the Beginning of the World to the End of the Dutch Dynasty.*)
This is a shortened version of Irving's comic history of New York City.
Ed. by Anne Carroll Moore, illus. by James Daugherty, Doubleday, 1928, 1940, 427 pp., o.p.; Firebird, 2002, pap., 280 pp. (Vol 1: 1-56554-945-7; Vol. 2: 1-56554-946-5)
(BL 12:302, 25:174, 56:359, 450; HB 4:77; Moore:138, 431)

8-146 **IVES, David.** *Monsieur Eek.* Gr. 5–7.
Emmaline, age 13, and her friend Flurp defend a "French foreigner" monkey accused of theft by Mayor Overbite and Shmink the Bailiff of MacOongafoondsen.
HarperCollins, 2001, 192 pp. (0-06-029529-5)
(BL 97:1883; Kirkus 69:586; SLJ June 2001 p. 150; VOYA 24:133)

JACQUES, Brian. *The Ribbajack and Other Curious Yarns.*
See Chapter 3, Fantasy Collections.

JACQUES, Brian. *Seven Strange and Ghostly Tales.*
See Chapter 4, Ghost Fantasy.

JAMES, Mary (pseud. of Maryjane Meaker; a.k.a. M. E. Kerr). *Shoebag.*
See Chapter 2, Animal Fantasy.

JAMES, Mary (pseud. of Maryjane Meaker; a.k.a. M. E. Kerr). *The Shuteyes.*
See Chapter 7, High Fantasy: Travel to Other Worlds.

8-147 **JANEWAY, Elizabeth (Hall).** *Ivanov Seven.* Gr. 5–8.
✶   Stepan's curiosity and independence cause problems after he joins the czar's army.
Illus. by Eros Keith, Harper, 1967, 176 pp., o.p.
(BL 64:502; HB 43:750; Kirkus 35:1145; LJ 92:4261)

JARRELL, Randall. *The Gingerbread Rabbit.*
See Chapter 1, Allegorical Fantasy and Literary Fairy Tales.

JENNINGS, Paul. *Unreal! Eight Surprising Stories.*
See Chapter 3, Fantasy Collections.

8-148 **JETER, K. W.** *Infernal Devices: A Mad Victorian Fantasy.* Gr. 10 up.
✶   A witty, adventure-filled romp about the owner of a clock repair shop in Victorian London who becomes involved with a mechanical man, a pair of con men, a gentleman bent on blowing up the world, and the peculiar fishlike inhabitants of Wetwick.
St. Martin's, 1987, 282 pp., o.p.
(BL 83:1253, 1275; Kirkus 55:261; LJ Apr 15, 1987 p. 103; VOYA 10:130)

JOCELYN, Marthe. *The Invisible Day.*
See Chapter 9, Magic Adventure Fantasy.

8-149 **JOHNSTON, Tony.** *The Mummy's Mother.* Gr. 3–6.
After his mother is stolen by grave robbers and sold to a museum, a 4,000-year-old mummy called Ramose leaves his tomb, boards a talking camel, follows his mother's mummy to New York aboard a cruise ship, and attempts to rescue her.
Blue Sky/Scholastic, 2003, 160 pp. (0-439-32462-9)
(BL 100:497; CCBB 57:195; HBG 15:81; Kirkus 71:1225; SLJ Oct 2003 p. 168)

JONES, Diana Wynne. *Archer's Goon.*
See Chapter 12, Witchcraft and Sorcery Fantasy.

JONES, Diana Wynne. *Castle in the Air.*
See Chapter 5, High Fantasy: Alternate Worlds or Histories.

JONES, Diana Wynne. *Dark Lord of Derkholm.*
See Chapter 12, Witchcraft and Sorcery Fantasy.

JONES, Diana Wynne. *Hexwood.*
See Chapter 6, High Fantasy: Myth or Legend Fantasy.

JONES, Diana Wynne. *Howl's Moving Castle.*
See Chapter 12, Witchcraft and Sorcery Fantasy.

JONES, Diana Wynne. *The Ogre Downstairs.*
See Chapter 9, Magic Adventure Fantasy.

JONES, Diana Wynne. *Stopping for a Spell: Three Fantasies.*
See Chapter 9, Magic Adventure Fantasy.

JONES, Diana Wynne. *A Tale of Time City.*
See Chapter 7, High Fantasy: Travel to Other Worlds.

JONES, Diana Wynne. *Wild Robert.*
See Chapter 9, Magic Adventure Fantasy.

JONES, Miranda. *Make a Wish!*
See Chapter 9, Magic Adventure Fantasy.

8-150 JONES, Terry. *Fairy Tales.* Gr. 3–5. (Orig. British pub. 1981.)
An oversized book containing 30 short, humorous tales for reading aloud.
Illus. by Michael Foreman, Schocken, 1983, 127 pp., o.p.; Puffin, 1986, 1993,
pap., 160 pp. (0-14-032262-0)
(CCBB 36:169; Suth 3:222; TLS 1981 p. 1360)

8-151 JONES, Terry. *Fantastic Stories.* Gr. 3–6. (Orig. British pub. 1993.)
Twenty-one humorous tales, including "The Improving Mirror," "The Slow
Ogre," and "The Flying King."
Illus. by Michael Foreman, Viking, 1993, 128 pp. (0-670-84899-9); Chivers
(large type ed.), 1993, 128 pp. (0-7451-1908-5)
(BL 89:2070; CCBB 46:284; HBG 4:299; SLJ Jan 1994 p. 114)

JONES, Terry. *The Lady and the Squire.*
See Chapter 5, High Fantasy: Alternate Worlds or Histories.

8-152 JONES, Terry. *Nicobobinus.* Gr. 5–7. (Orig. British pub. 1985.)
Nicobobinus and his friend Rosie make a madcap journey to the Land of Drag-
ons seeking a cure for Nicobobinus's enchanted golden foot.
Illus. by Michael Foreman, Bedrick, 1986, 176 pp., o.p.
(BL 82:1613; SLJ Aug 1986 p. 94; TLS 1986 p. 174)

8-153 JONSSON, Runer. *Viki Viking.* Gr. 4–6. (British title: *Vike the Viking*; orig.
Swedish pub. 1963.)
Chief Halvar's son Viki hates fighting but still manages to rescue his father's
troops.
Trans. by Birgit Rogers and Patricia Lowe, illus. by Ewert Karlsson, World,
1968, 143 pp., o.p.
(BL 64:1094; CCBB 21:129; HB 44:324; Kirkus 35:1473; LJ 93:2114; TLS 1969 p. 689)

8-154 JUKES, Mavis. *Cinderella 2000.* Gr. 6–9.
Ashley's fairy godmother intervenes after the 14-year-old's stepmother Phyllis
insists that Ashley babysit for her bratty twin stepsisters on New Year's Eve.
Delacorte, 1999, pap., 199 pp. (0-385-32711-0)
(BL 96:352; HBG 11:81; Kliatt Sep 1999 p. 10; SLJ Nov 1999 p. 160; VOYA 22:335)

JUSTER, Norton. *The Phantom Tollbooth.*
See Chapter 7, High Fantasy: Travel to Other Worlds.

KARR, Kathleen. *Gideon and the Mummy Professor.*
See Chapter 9, Magic Adventure Fantasy.

8-155 **KÄSTNER, Erich.** *The Little Man.* **(The Little Man trilogy, bk. 1).** Gr.
★ 4–6. (Orig. Swiss pub. 1963.)
Two-inch-tall Maxie Pichelsteiner gains fame by becoming Professor Hokus
Von Pokus's invisible right-hand man. Mildred L. Batchelder Award, 1968.
The sequels are *The Little Man and the Big Thief* (1970) and *The Little Man
and the Little Miss* (Britain, 1969).
Trans. by James Kirkup, illus. by Rick Schreiter, Knopf, 1966, 183 pp., o.p.
(BL 63:728; CCBB 20:124; Kirkus 34:1101; LJ 91:6192; Suth:220; TLS 1966 p. 1077)

KAUFMAN, Charles. *The Frog and the Beanpole.*
See Chapter 2, Animal Fantasy.

KAYE, Marvin. *The Incredible Umbrella.*
See Chapter 7, High Fantasy: Travel to Other Worlds.

8-156 **KEELE, Luqman, and PINKWATER, D(aniel) Manus.** *Java Jack.* Gr.
4–8.
While Jack is traveling from Missouri to Indonesia in search of his missing parents, he is kidnapped, pilots an airplane, acquires a magic needle, fights a gang
of pirates, and travels out of the universe.
Harper, 1980, 152 pp., o.p.
(HB 56:297; Kirkus 48:584; SLJ May 1980 p. 68)

KEMP, Gene. *Jason Bodger and the Priory Ghost.*
See Chapter 4, Ghost Fantasy.

8-157 **KENNEDY, William, and KENNEDY, Brendan.** *Charlie Malarkey and
the Belly-Button Machine.* Gr. 2–4.
Charlie Malarkey and Iggy Gowalowicz wake up to discover that their belly
buttons have been stolen by a salesman named Ben Bubie and his mysterious
machine. The sequel is *Charlie Malarkey and the Singing Moose* (1994).
William Kennedy is a Pulitzer Prize-winning author, and Brendan Kennedy is
his son.
Illus. by Glen Baxter, Little, Brown, 1986, 40 pp., o.p.
(Kirkus 54:1728; SLJ Dec 1986 p. 90)

KENNEMORE, Tim. *Circle of Doom.*
See Chapter 9, Magic Adventure Fantasy.

KESEY, Ken. *Little Tricker the Squirrel Meets Big Double the Bear.*
See Chapter 2, Animal Fantasy.

8-158 **KINDL, Patrice.** *Goose Chase.* Gr. 6–9.
★ In this fairy tale spoof, Goose Girl, rewarded by a grateful old woman with diamond tears and gold dust in her hair, is rescued from a locked tower by her
magical geese after she refuses to marry a dull prince and a greedy king.
Houghton, 2001, 224 pp. (0-618-03377-7); Puffin, 2002, pap., 224 pp. (0-14-
230208-2)

(BL 97:155, 98:1417; CCBB 54:306; HB 77:454; HBG 12:309; Kirkus 69:250; Kliatt Mar 2001 p. 10; SLJ Apr 2001 p. 144; VOYA 24:134, 25:14)

KINDL, Patrice. *Owl in Love.*
See Chapter 12, Witchcraft and Sorcery Fantasy.

8-159 **KINDL, Patrice.** *The Woman in the Wall.* Gr. 5–10.
✮ Anna's shyness makes her nearly invisible, enabling her to hide for so many years that even her family has nearly forgotten she exists.
Houghton, 1997, 185 pp. (0-395-83014-1); Puffin, 1998, pap., 192 pp. (0-14-130124-4)
(BL 93:1236; CCBB 50:251; HB 73:458; HBG 8:314; Kirkus 65:382; SLJ Apr 1997 p. 138, Jan 1998 p. 40; VOYA 20:186, 21:37)

KING, (David) Clive. *The Town That Went South.*
See Chapter 2, Animal Fantasy.

KING-SMITH, Dick. *Ace: The Very Important Pig.*
See Chapter 2, Animal Fantasy.

KING-SMITH, Dick. *Animal Stories.*
See Chapter 2, Animal Fantasy.

KING-SMITH, Dick. *The Cuckoo Child.*
See Chapter 2, Animal Fantasy.

KING-SMITH, Dick. *The Fox-Busters.*
See Chapter 2, Animal Fantasy.

KING-SMITH, Dick. *Funny Frank.*
See Chapter 2, Animal Fantasy.

8-160 **KING-SMITH, Dick.** *George Speaks.* Gr. 2–5. (Orig. British pub. 1988.)
Laura, fed up with all the attention paid to her baby brother George, discovers that he can speak and is tired of being treated like a baby.
Illus. by Judy Brown, Millbrook, 2002, 96 pp. (0-7613-2519-0)
(BL 98:1014; CCBB 55:369; HBG 13:359; Kirkus 70:415; SLJ Mar 2002 p. 190)

8-161 **KING-SMITH, Dick.** *Harry's Mad.* Gr. 3–6. (Orig. British pub. 1986.)
✮ Just after Harry discovers that Madison, the parrot he inherited from a great-uncle, can talk like a human, Mad is stolen by a burglar.
Illus. by Jill Bennet, Crown, 1988, 123 pp., o.p.; Yearling, 1997, pap., 128 pp. (0-679-88688-5)
(BL 83:1680, 84:1274; CCBB 40:171; HB 63:463; Kirkus 55:221; SLJ May 1987 p. 101, Dec 1987 p. 37; Suth 4:218; TLS Nov 1986 p. 1347)

KING-SMITH, Dick. *Hogsel and Gruntel and Other Animal Stories.*
See Chapter 6, High Fantasy: Myth or Legend Fantasy.

KING-SMITH, Dick. *The Jenius.*
See Chapter 2, Animal Fantasy.

KING-SMITH, Dick. *Martin's Mice.*
See Chapter 2, Animal Fantasy.

8-162 KING-SMITH, Dick. *Mr. Potter's Pet.* Gr. 2–4. (Orig. British pub. 1976.)
✯ Mr. Potter's new pet, a mynah bird named Everest, both speaks and understands human speech.
Illus. by Mark Teague, Hyperion, 1996, 64 pp. (0-7868-0174-3); Disney, 1997, pap., 128 pp. (0-7868-1206-0)
(BL 92:1366; CCBB 49:231; HBG 7:294; Kirkus 64:532; SLJ Apr 1996 p. 112)

8-163 KING-SMITH, Dick. *Pretty Polly.* Gr. 3–5. (Orig. British pub. 1992.)
✯ Abigail names her chicken Polly and teaches her to talk because she cannot afford to buy a parrot at a pet shop.
Illus. by Marshall Peck, Crown, 1992, 120 pp., o.p.
(BL 89:327; CCBB 46:45; HB 69:85; HBG 4:71; Kirkus 60:921; SLJ Sep 1992 p. 254)

KING-SMITH, Dick. *The Swoose.*
See Chapter 2, Animal Fantasy.

KING-SMITH, Dick. *Titus Rules!*
See Chapter 2, Animal Fantasy.

KIRK, Daniel. *Rex Tabby: Cat Detective.*
See Chapter 2, Animal Fantasy.

KISLING, Lee. *The Fools' War.*
See Chapter 5, High Fantasy: Alternate Worlds or Histories.

8-164 KLEIN, Robin. *Thing.* Gr. 1–4. (Orig. British pub. 1982.)
Emily's pet rock hatches into a baby stegosaurus that grows to the size of a small rhinoceros and prevents a robbery in their landlady's apartment. The sequel is *Thingnapped!* (1984, 1985).
Illus. by Alison Lester, Oxford University Press, 1983, 32 pp., o.p.
(BL 79:1402; CCBB 37:52; SLJ Mar 1984 p. 146)

8-165 KOENIG, Richard. *The Seven Special Cats.* Gr. 3–5.
Mrs. Thwickle predicts havoc and chaos in New York City if an old building housing seven cats is demolished.
Illus. by Peggy Bacon, World, 1961, 57 pp., o.p.
(BL 58:36; HB 37:156; LJ 86:1690)

KONIGSBURG, E(laine) L(obl). *Up from Jericho Tel.*
See Chapter 9, Magic Adventure Fantasy.

KORELITZ, Jean Hanff. *Interference Powder.*
See Chapter 9, Magic Adventure Fantasy.

8-166 KOTZWINKLE, William. *Trouble in Bugland: A Collection of Inspector*
✯ *Mantis Mysteries.* Gr. 7 up.
Five short mystery tales star Inspector Mantis and his grasshopper sidekick, characters modeled on Sir Arthur Conan Doyle's Sherlock Holmes and Dr. Watson.
Illus. by Joe Servello, Godine, 1983, 152 pp., o.p.; Godine, 1996, pap., 190 pp. (1-56792-070-5)
(BL 80:469, 490, 498; HB 60:196; Kirkus 51:1022; SLJ Feb 1984 p. 74)

KOVACS, Deborah. *Brewster's Courage.*
See Chapter 2, Animal Fantasy.

KRAAN, Hanna. *Tales of the Wicked Witch.*
See Chapter 12, Witchcraft and Sorcery Fantasy.

KRENSKY, Stephen (Alan). *Castles in the Air and Other Tales.*
See Chapter 3, Fantasy Collections.

KRÜSS, James (Jacob Heinrich). *The Happy Islands Behind the Winds.*
See Chapter 7, High Fantasy: Travel to Other Worlds.

KURTZ, Katherine (Irene). *St. Patrick's Gargoyle.*
See Chapter 9, Magic Adventure Fantasy.

LABATT, Mary. *Strange Neighbors.*
See Chapter 2, Animal Fantasy.

LAMPMAN, Evelyn Sibley. *Captain Apple's Ghost.*
See Chapter 4, Ghost Fantasy.

8-167 **LAMPMAN, Evelyn Sibley.** *The Shy Stegosaurus of Cricket Creek.* Gr. 5–7.
Joey, Joan, and a shy dinosaur named George capture a thief. The sequel is *The Shy Stegosaurus of Indian Springs* (1962).
Illus. by Hubert Buel, Doubleday, 1955, 218 pp., o.p.; Purple House, 2001, 219 pp. (1-930900-09-0)
(BL 52:150; HB 31:377; LJ 80:2386)

LAUBER, Patricia (Grace). *Purrfectly Purrfect.*
See Chapter 2, Animal Fantasy.

LAUMER, (John) Keith. *The Shape Changer: A Science Fiction Novel.*
See Chapter 5, High Fantasy: Alternate Worlds or Histories.

8-168 **LAWRENCE, Michael.** *The Poltergoose: A Jiggy McCue Story.* **(Jiggy McCue stories, bk. 1).** Gr. 4–7. (Orig. British pub. 1999.)
Jiggy McCue finds it difficult to convince his parents that their new home is haunted by the ghost of a goose named Hetty, whose grave was disturbed when their subdivision was built. The sequels are *Toilet of Doom* (2001, 2002), *The Killer Underpants* (2002, 2003), *Maggot Pie* (2002), and *The Snottle* (2003).
Dutton, 2002, 132 pp. (0-525-46839-0)
(BL 98:858; HBG:13:376; Kirkus 69:1760; SLJ Mar 2002 p. 232)

LAWSON, Robert. *Ben and Me: A New and Astonishing Life of Benjamin Franklin as Written by His Good Mouse, Amos: Lately Discovered.*
See Chapter 2, Animal Fantasy.

LAWSON, Robert. *Captain Kidd's Cat: Being the True and Dolorous Chronicle of Wm. Kidd, Gentleman and Merchant of New York; Late Captain of the Adventure Galley; Of the Vicissitudes Attending His Unfortunate Cruise in Eastern Waters, of His Unjust Trial and Execution,*

as Narrated by His Faithful Cat, McDermot, Who Ought to Know.
See Chapter 2, Animal Fantasy.

LAWSON, Robert. *The Fabulous Flight.*
See Chapter 9, Magic Adventure Fantasy.

LAWSON, Robert. *I Discover Columbus: A True Chronicle of the Great Admiral and His Finding of the New World, Narrated by the Venerable Parrot Aurelio, Who Shared in the Glorious Venture.*
See Chapter 2, Animal Fantasy.

8-169 LAWSON, Robert. *McWhinney's Jaunt.* Gr. 3–5.
Professor McWhinney flies off to Hollywood on his z-gas-powered bicycle.
Illus. by the author, Little, Brown, 1951, 77 pp., o.p.
(BL 48:16; CCBB 5:6; Kirkus 19:294; LJ 76:1341)

LAWSON, Robert. *Mr. Revere and I: Being an Account of Certain Episodes in the Career of Paul Revere, Esq., as Recently Revealed by His Horse, Scheherazade, Late Pride of His Royal Majesty's 14th Regiment of Foot.*
See Chapter 2, Animal Fantasy.

LAWSON, Robert. *Mr. Twigg's Mistake.*
See Chapter 2, Animal Fantasy.

8-170 LAWSON, Robert. *Mr. Wilmer.* Gr. 4–6.
Fame and fortune come to timid Mr. Wilmer after he realizes that he can communicate with animals.
Illus. by the author, Little, Brown, 1945, 218 pp., o.p.
(BL 41:287; Kirkus 13:92; LJ 70:534)

8-171 LAWSON, Robert. *Smeller Martin.* Gr. 4–6.
✭   Davy Martin's extraordinary sense of smell helps the police solve a crime and makes Davy a celebrity at school.
Illus. by the author, Viking, 1950, 157 pp., o.p.
(BL 47:104; CCBB 4:5; HB 26:474; Kirkus 18:470; LJ 75:2084)

8-172 LAZARUS, Keo Felker. *The Shark in the Window.* Gr. 4–6.
Shelly's new pet shark can swim through the air.
Illus. by Laurel Schindelman, Morrow, 1972, 159 pp., o.p.
(BL 69:357; CCBB 26:45; Kirkus 40:940; LJ 97:3806; Suth:241)

8-173 LEE, Robert C. *The Iron Arm of Michael Glenn.* Gr. 5–8.
After Mike's pitching arm is accidentally exposed to Professor Von Heiner's experiment, he leaps from Little League baseball to pitching for the San Francisco Giants. The sequel is *The Day It Rained Forever* (1968).
Illus. by Al Fiorentino, Little, Brown, 1965, 153 pp., o.p.
(Kirkus 33:752; LJ 90:4636)

LEE, Tanith. *Princess Hynchatti and Some Other Surprises.*
See Chapter 3, Fantasy Collections.

8-174 LEESON, Robert (Arthur). *Genie on the Loose.* **(Genie trilogy, bk. 2).** Gr. 6–8. (Orig. British pub. 1984.)
Keeping wily Abdul the genie in check proves to be more difficult than Alec Bowden expected. This is the sequel to *The Third Class Genie* (1975; Harper-Collins, 1983), and it is followed by *The Last Genie* (1993).
HarperCollins, 1984, 144 pp. (0-00-672294-6)
(BL 81:524; SLJ Jan 1985 p. 87)

8-175 LE GRAND (pseud. of Le Grand Henderson). *How Baseball Began in Brooklyn.* Gr. 3–5.
It seems that baseball was accidentally invented in New Amsterdam by ten Dutch colonial boys and a Native American.
Illus. by the author, Abingdon, 1958, 58 pp., o.p.
(BL 54:540; CCBB 11:97; Eakin:205; HB 34:108; LJ 83:1604)

8-176 LE GRAND (pseud. of Le Grand Henderson). *How Space Rockets Began.* Gr. 3–5.
Windwagon Smith invents a steam wagon that can fly to the moon.
Illus. by the author, Abingdon, 1960, 64 pp., o.p.
(HB 36:289; Kirkus 28:89; LJ 85:2040)

8-177 LE GRAND (pseud. of Le Grand Henderson). *Matilda.* Gr. 4–6.
A goat named Matilda becomes a student at Columbia University.
Illus. by the author, Abingdon, 1956, 63 pp., o.p.
(BL 53:52; Eakin:205; Kirkus 24:353; LJ 81:2041)

LE GUIN, Ursula K(roeber). *Solomon Leviathan's Nine Hundred and Thirty-First Trip Around the World.*
See Chapter 2, Animal Fantasy.

LEROE, Ellen. *Leap Frog Friday.*
See Chapter 9, Magic Adventure Fantasy.

LEROY, Gen. *Taxi Cat and Huey.*
See Chapter 2, Animal Fantasy.

LEVERICH, Kathleen. *Brigid the Bad.*
See Chapter 9, Magic Adventure Fantasy.

LE VERT, John. *The Flight of the Cassowary.*
See Chapter 1, Allegorical Fantasy and Literary Fairy Tales.

LEVINE, Gail Carson. *The Fairy's Mistake.*
See Chapter 6, High Fantasy: Myth or Legend Fantasy.

8-178 LEVITIN, Sonia (Wolff). *Jason and the Money Tree.* Gr. 4–6.
After the 10-dollar bill Jason's grandfather gave him sprouts into a money tree, he has difficulty accounting for his sudden wealth.
Illus. by Pat Porter, Harcourt, 1974, 121 pp., o.p.
(BL 70:1057; CCBB 27:180; Kirkus 42:300; LJ 99:2274)

LEVOY, Myron. *The Magic Hat of Mortimer Wintergreen.*
See Chapter 12, Witchcraft and Sorcery Fantasy.

LEVY, Elizabeth. *A Hare-Raising Tail.*
See Chapter 2, Animal Fantasy.

LICKISS, Rebecca. *Never After.*
See Chapter 6, High Fantasy: Myth or Legend Fantasy.

LILLINGTON, Kenneth (James). *An Ash-Blond Witch.*
See Chapter 12, Witchcraft and Sorcery Fantasy.

LILLINGTON, Kenneth (James). *Jonah's Mirror.*
See Chapter 7, High Fantasy: Travel to Other Worlds.

LINDBERGH, Anne Spencer. *Nick of Time.*
See Chapter 10, Time Travel Fantasy.

LINDENBAUM, Pija. *Else-Marie and Her Seven Little Daddies.*
See Chapter 9, Magic Adventure Fantasy.

8-179 LINDGREN, Astrid. *Pippi Longstocking.* **(Pippi Longstocking series, bk.**
✫   **1).** Gr. 4–6. (Orig. Swedish pub. 1945.)
Life is never dull for Annika and Tommy after the strongest child in the world
moves in next door, with her pet monkey and her horse. The sequels are *Pippi
Goes on Board* (1957; British title *Pippi Goes Abroad*), *Pippi in the South Seas*
(1959), and *Pippi on the Run* (1976). *The Adventures of Pippi Longstocking*,
illus. by Michael Chesworth, Viking, 1997, 290 pp. (0-670-87612-7), combines
the three original Pippi books into one volume. *Pippi Longstocking's After-
Christmas Party* (1996) is a picture-book sequel. The Pippi Longstocking Storybook series introduces chapters from the original books: *Pippi Goes to
School* (1998); *Pippi Goes to the Circus* (1999), *Pippi's Extraordinary Ordinary Day* (1999), and *Pippi to the Rescue* (2000).
Trans. by Florence Lamborn, illus. by Louis Glanzman, Viking, 1950, 158 pp.
(0-670-55745-5); Puffin, 1997, pap. (0-14-030957-8)
(BL 47:208; CCBB 4:21; HB 26:376; HBG 9:75; Kirkus 18:515; LJ 75:1754)

8-180 LINDSAY, Norman (Alfred William). *The Magic Pudding: Being the
Adventures of Bunyip Bluegum and His Friends Bill Barnacle and Sam
Sawnoff.* Gr. 3–5. (Orig. Australian pub. 1918.)
A koala, a sailor, and a penguin find a magic pudding.
Illus. by the author, Farrar, 1936, 159 pp., o.p.; HarperCollins, 1998 (0-207-
18355-4); New York Review of Books, 2004, 172 pp. (1-590-17101-2)
(HB 80:488–489; LJ 61:809, 62:38; TLS 1936 p. 974)

LINKLATER, Eric (Robert Russell). *The Pirates in the Deep Green Sea.*
See Chapter 7, High Fantasy: Travel to Other Worlds.

8-181 LISLE, Janet Taylor. *The Dancing Cats of Applesap.* Gr. 4–6.
Ten-year-old Melba vows to save the drugstore home of Miss Toonie's fabu-
lous dancing cats.
Illus. by Joelle Shefts, Bradbury, 1984, 169 pp., o.p.; Macmillan, 1993, pap.,
176 pp. (0-689-71687-7)
(BL 80:1550; CCBB 37:208; SLJ Oct 1984 p. 159)

LISLE, Janet Taylor. *The Great Dimpole Oak.*
See Chapter 1, Allegorical Fantasy and Literary Fairy Tales.

8-182 **LIVELY, Penelope (Margaret Low).** *Uninvited Ghosts and Other Stories.*
⭐ Gr. 4–6. (Orig. British pub. 1984.)
Eight hilarious tales are told about ghosts, a dragon, and a Martian who invade ordinary family life.
Illus. by John Lawrence, Dutton, 1985, 119 pp., o.p.
(BL 81:1459; CCBB 38:189; HB 61:450; Kirkus 53:34; SLJ Aug 1985 p. 68; Suth 4:251; TLS 1984 p. 1381)

LOBE, Mira. *The Grandma in the Apple Tree.*
See Chapter 9, Magic Adventure Fantasy.

LOCKE, Angela. *Mr. Mullett Owns a Cloud.*
See Chapter 9, Magic Adventure Fantasy.

8-183 **LOFTING, Hugh.** *The Story of Doctor Dolittle.* **(Doctor Dolittle series, bk.**
⭐ **1).** Gr. 3–6.
When a great plague strikes the animals of Africa, Doctor Dolittle, the best animal doctor in the world, travels to Africa to save them. Lofting's depiction of black Africans has been criticized as racist, and the Delacorte revised editions have changed or eliminated the prejudicial passages. The sequels are *The Voyages of Doctor Dolittle* (1922; John Newbery Medal, 1923; rev. ed., 1988; HarperCollins, 2002), *Doctor Dolittle's Post Office* (1923, 2000), *Doctor Dolittle's Circus* (1924; Delacorte, 1988; Lippincott, 2000), *Doctor Dolittle and the Green Canary* (1924, 1950, 1989), *Doctor Dolittle's Zoo* (1925; Lippincott, 1975), *Doctor Dolittle's Caravan* (1926), *Doctor Dolittle's Garden* (1927, Random, 1966), *Doctor Dolittle in the Moon* (1928; Lippincott, 2000), *Gub-Gub's Book: An Encyclopedia of Food* (1932; Simon, 1992), *Doctor Dolittle's Return* (1933; Lippincott, 2000), *Doctor Dolittle and the Secret Lake* (1948, 1977), and *Doctor Dolittle's Puddleby Adventures* (1952, 2000). *Doctor Dolittle: A Treasury* (Random, 1992) is a collection of tales.
Illus. by the author, Lippincott, 1920, 172 pp., o.p.; Delacorte, 1988 (rev. ed.), o.p.; illus. by Michael (R.) Hague, Morrow, 1997, 159 pp. (0-688-14001-7); Kessinger, 2004, pap., 80 pp. (1-41918-383-4); Dover, 2005, pap., 96 pp. (0-4864-3883-X)
(BL 19:193, 84:1838; Bookshelf 1932 p. 8; HB 24:341; HBG 9:75; Mahony 2:284; Moore:426)

LORD, Beman. *The Perfect Pitch.*
See Chapter 9, Magic Adventure Fantasy.

LURIE, Morris. *The Twenty-Seventh Annual African Hippopotamus Race.*
See Chapter 2, Animal Fantasy.

McBRATNEY, Sam. *The Ghosts of Hungryhouse Lane.*
See Chapter 4, Ghost Fantasy.

8-184 **MacDONALD, Betty (Campbell Bard).** *Mrs. Piggle-Wiggle.* **(Mrs. Piggle-Wiggle series, bk. 1).** Gr. 2–5.

Mrs. Piggle-Wiggle has magical cures for all children's ailments, including the won't-pick-up-toys cure, the answer-backer cure, and the selfishness cure. The sequels are *Mrs. Piggle-Wiggle's Farm* (1954), *Hello, Mrs. Piggle-Wiggle* (1957), and *Mrs. Piggle-Wiggle's Magic* (1957). HarperCollins has also published four picture-book versions of Mrs. Piggle-Wiggle Adventures.

Lippincott, 1947, illus. by Richard Bennett, 118 pp., o.p.; illus. by Hilary Knight, Harper, 1957 (rev. ed.), 118 pp., o.p.; HarperCollins, 1975, 118 pp. (0-397-31712-3), 1985, pap. (0-06-440148-0)

(BL 43:260; HB 23:213; Kirkus 15:127; LJ 72:590, 739)

McHUGH, Elizabet. *Beethoven's Cat.*
See Chapter 2, Animal Fantasy.

8-185 McINERNY, Ralph M. *Quick as a Dodo.* Gr. 6 up.
Dormer, a literate dodo who hatches from a strange Easter egg, decides to free a caged rabbit and escape from his owner's home.
Illus. by Pam Butterworth, Juniper, 1977, 116 pp., o.p.; Vanguard, 1978, 116 pp., o.p.
(BL 75:27, 39; LJ 103:973)

MacKELLAR, William. *Alfie and Me and the Ghost of Peter Stuyvesant.*
See Chapter 4, Ghost Fantasy.

McMULLAN, Kate. *New Kid at School.*
See Chapter 5, High Fantasy: Alternate Worlds or Histories.

MACOUREK, Miloš. *Max and Sally and the Phenomenal Phone.*
See Chapter 9, Magic Adventure Fantasy.

8-186 MAGUIRE, Gregory. *Leaping Beauty: And Other Animal Fairy Tales.* Gr. 4–7.
Eight animal parodies of well-known fairy tales, including "Goldifox and the Three Chickens" and "Leaping Beauty."
Illus. by Chris L. Demarest, HarperCollins, 2004, 208 pp. (0-06-056418-0)
(BL 100:1726; Kirkus 72:632; SLJ Aug 2004 p. 126;)

8-187 MAGUIRE, Gregory. *Seven Spiders Spinning.* **(The Hamlet Chronicles, bk. 1).** Gr. 5–7.
Seven tarantulas from the ancient past invade a classroom in Hamlet, Vermont, just before Halloween, and each spider goes on a heroic quest. The sequels are *Six Haunted Hairdos* (1997), *Five Alien Elves* (1998), *Four Stupid Cupids* (2000), *Three Rotten Eggs* (2002), *A Couple of April Fools* (2004), and *One Final Firecracker* (2005).
Illus. by Dirk Zimmer, Clarion, 1994, 132 pp. (0-395-68965-1); HarperTrophy, 1995, pap., 144 pp. (0-06-440595-8)
(BL 91:136, 1411; CCBB 48:57; HBG 6:80; Kirkus 62:989; VOYA 18:24)

8-188 MAHY, Margaret (May). *The Birthday Burglar and A Very Wicked Head-*
✫ *mistress.* Gr. 2–6. (Orig. New Zealand pub. 1984.)
In the first of two wacky tales, young Bassington decides to steal other people's birthdays; in the second, evil Miss Taffeta opens a boarding school for wealthy children and, to save money, pretends to be all of the teachers.

Illus. by Margaret Chamberlain, Godine, 1988, 137 pp. (0-87923-720-1); Morrow, 1993, pap. (0-688-12470-4)

(BL 85:580; CCBB 42:47; Kirkus 56:1244; SLJ Dec 1989 p. 109; TLS 1984 p. 1458)

8-189 **MAHY, Margaret (May).** *The Blood-and-Thunder Adventure on Hurri-*
✫ *cane Peak.* Gr. 4–6. (Orig. New Zealand pub. 1989.)
Huxley and Zaza Hammond are new students at the Unexpected School atop Hurricane Peak, run by a magician named Mr. Warlock, whose true love, Belladonna Doppler, is pursued by the nefarious Sir Quincey Judd-Sprockett. *The Pirates' Mixed-Up Voyage: Dark Doings in the Thousand Islands* (Dial, 1993; see below) is also set in Hookywalker.
Illus. by Wendy Smith, Macmillan, 1989, 144 pp., o.p.; Dell, 1991, pap. (0-440-40422-3)

(BL 86:460; CCBB 43:38; HB 65:772; HBG 1:81; Kirkus 57:1162; SLJ Oct 1989 p. 120; TLS 1989 p. 37)

8-190 **MAHY, Margaret (May).** *Bubble Trouble and Other Poems and Stories.*
✫ Gr. 3–6. (Orig. New Zealand pub. 1991.)
Two silly stories and three funny poems include "The Gargling Gorilla" and "Bubble Trouble."
Illus. by the author, Macmillan, 1992, 80 pp. (0-689-50557-4)

(BL 89:664; CCBB 46:80; HBG 4:59; Kirkus 60:1258; SLJ Oct 1992 p. 118)

8-191 **MAHY, Margaret (May).** *The Chewing-Gum Rescue and Other Stories.*
Gr. 3–5. (Orig. New Zealand pub. 1982.)
Eleven whimsical short stories include "The Devil and the Corner Grocer" and "The World's Highest Tray Cloth."
Illus. by Jan Ormerod, Overlook, 1991, 141 pp., o.p.

(HBG 3:267; Kirkus 59:1595; SLJ Feb 1992 p. 87)

MAHY, Margaret (May). *The Door in the Air and Other Stories.*
See Chapter 9, Magic Adventure Fantasy.

8-192 **MAHY, Margaret (May).** *The Great Piratical Rumbustification, and The*
✫ *Librarian and the Robbers.* Gr. 3–6. (Orig. New Zealand pub. 1978.)
Two humorous stories are told about a pirate babysitter and a beautiful librarian who rescues herself from kidnappers.
Illus. by Quentin Blake, Godine, 1986, 64 pp. (0-87923-629-9); Morrow, 1993, pap. (0-688-12469-0)

(CCBB 40:92; Kirkus 54:1584; SLJ Mar 1987 p. 163; Suth 4:262; TLS 1978 p. 1398)

MAHY, Margaret (May). *The Horribly Haunted School.*
See Chapter 4, Ghost Fantasy.

8-193 **MAHY, Margaret (May).** *Nonstop Nonsense.* Gr. 4–7. (Orig. New Zealand
✫ pub. 1977.)
Humorous stories and nonsense verse concern book ghosts, a poetic cat, a word witch, and a green-toothed, good-hearted monster.
Illus. by Quentin Blake, Macmillan, 1989, 120 pp., o.p.

(BL 85:1551; CCBB 42:257; HB 56:496; SLJ May 1989 p. 110)

8-194 **MAHY, Margaret (May).** *The Pirates' Mixed-Up Voyage: Dark Doings in*
✳ *the Thousand Islands.* Gr. 4–6. (Orig. New Zealand pub. 1983.)
Lionel Wafer and his Ye Olde Pirate Shippe Tea Shoppe staff decide to become
real pirates bent on stealing a huge diamond doorknob owned by a legendary
millionaire. This story, like *The Blood-and-Thunder Adventure on Hurricane
Peak* (McElderry, 1989; see above), is set in Hookywalker.
Illus. by Margaret Chamberlain, Dial, 1993, 180 pp. (0-8037-1350-9)
(BL 89:908; HB 69:334; HBG 4:301; Kirkus 61:461; SLJ Apr 1993 p. 124)

8-195 **MAHY, Margaret (May).** *Raging Robots and Unruly Uncles.* Gr. 4–6.
✳ (Orig. New Zealand pub. 1981.)
Prudence detests Lilly Rose Blossom, the blond, blue-eyed robot gift from her
seven virtuous cousins, and she sends them a crime-minded robot named
Nadger in return.
Illus. by Peter Stevenson, Overlook, 1993, 94 pp., o.p.
(BL 89:1230; HBG 4:301; Kirkus 61:65; SLJ Mar 1993 p. 214; TLS Nov 20, 1981 p. 1357)

8-196 **MAHY, Margaret (May).** *Tick Tock Tales: Twelve Stories to Read Around
the Clock.* Gr. K–5. (Orig. New Zealand pub. 1993.)
Twelve witty tales concern magical transformations, pirates, orphans, and
learning to fly.
Illus. by Wendy Smith, McElderry, 1994, 92 pp., o.p.
(HBG 5:303; Kirkus 62:230; SLJ Apr 1994 p. 110)

8-197 **MAHY, Margaret (May).** *Tingleberries, Tuckertubs and Telephones: A
✳ Tale of Love and Ice-Cream.* Gr. 3–5. (Orig. New Zealand pub. 1995.)
Shy, young Saracen Hobday manages to outwit a gang of pirates led by the
notorious Grudge-Gallows.
Illus. by Robert Staermose, Viking, 1996, 96 pp. (0-670-86331-9)
(BL 92:835; CCBB 49:236; HB 72:336; HBG 7:294; SLJ Feb 1996 p. 102)

8-198 **MANES, Stephen.** *Chicken Trek: The Third Strange Thing That Hap-
pened to Oscar Noodleman.* **(Oscar Noodleman trilogy, bk. 3).** Gr. 4–6.
Oscar and his cousin, Dr. Prechtwinkle, attempt to win a prize offered by the
Bagful O' Chicken Company, using a Picklemobile that can travel to any spot
on Earth in a matter of seconds. This is the sequel to two humorous science fic-
tion tales: *That Game from Outer Space* (1983) and *The Oscar J. Noodleman
Television Network* (1984).
Illus. by Ron Barrett, Dutton, 1987, 128 pp., o.p.
(BL 83:1750; CCBB 41:13; Kirkus 55:860; SLJ Aug 1987 p. 86)

MANES, Stephen. *Monstra vs. Irving.*
See Chapter 9, Magic Adventure Fantasy.

8-199 **MANES, Stephen.** *Some of the Adventures of Rhode Island Red.* Gr. 3–6.
Folk-hero Rhode Island Red is an egg-sized boy who was raised by chickens.
He can outsmart foxes, and he aims to marry the mayor's daughter.
Illus. by William Joyce, Harper, 1990, 117 pp. LB (0-397-32348-4), 1993, pap.
(0-06-440358-0)
(BL 86:1994; CCBB 43:272; HBG 1:255; SLJ July 1990 p. 77)

8-200 **MANNING, Rosemary (Joy).** *Dragon in Danger.* **(Dragon series, bk. 2).** Gr. 4–6. (Orig. British pub. 1959.)
The first dragon to appear in 500 years, R. Dragon is offered a starring role in the town's annual pageant. The sequel to *Green Smoke* (1957), it is followed by *The Dragon's Quest* (1962), *Dragon in Summer* (British), and *Dragon in the Harbour* (Penguin, 1980).
Illus. by Constance Marshall, Doubleday, 1960, 169 pp., o.p.
(Kirkus 28:775; LJ 85:4569; TLS May 29, 1959 p. xiii)

MARICONDA, Barbara. *Witch Way to the Beach.*
See Chapter 12, Witchcraft and Sorcery Fantasy.

MARSHALL, James (Edward). *Rats on the Roof and Other Stories.*
See Chapter 2, Animal Fantasy.

MARSHALL, James (Edward). *A Summer in the South.*
See Chapter 2, Animal Fantasy.

MARSHALL, James (Edward). *Taking Care of Carruthers.*
See Chapter 2, Animal Fantasy.

8-201 **MARTIN, Ann M(atthews).** *Ma and Pa Dracula.* Gr. 3–6.
After Jonathan Primave discovers that his parents are vampires, he demands to be allowed to stay awake during the day and go to school like other children.
Illus. by Dirk Zimmer, Holiday, 1989, 112 pp., o.p.
(BL 86:672; CCBB 43:142; HBG 1:84; Kirkus 57:1330; SLJ Sep 1989 p. 256)

MAZER, Anne. *The Accidental Witch.*
See Chapter 12, Witchcraft and Sorcery Fantasy.

MAZER, Harry. *The Dog in the Freezer: Three Novellas.*
See Chapter 2, Animal Fantasy.

MEACHAM, Margaret. *A Mid-Semester Night's Dream.*
See Chapter 9, Magic Adventure Fantasy.

8-202 **MELENDEZ, Francisco.** *The Mermaid and the Major: Or, The True Story of the Invention of the Submarine.* Gr. 4 up. (Orig. Spanish pub. 1987.)
Major Monday falls in love with a mermaid and invents a submarine to follow her into the depths of the sea. Awarded Spain's Ministry of Culture National Prize for Illustration, 1987.
Illus. by the author, adapt. by Robert Morton, trans. by William Dyckes, Abrams, 1991, 64 pp. (0-8109-3619-4)
(HBG 3:70; Kirkus 59:1231; SLJ Jan 1992 p. 114)

8-203 **MENDOZA, George.** *Gwot! Horribly Funny Hairticklers.* Gr. 3–5.
Three ghastly tales tell about a huge, black snake that grows bigger each time its head is chopped off, an old woman who eats a hairy toe, and the hunt for the horrible Gumberoo.
Illus. by Steven Kellogg, Harper, 1967, 41 pp., o.p.
(Kirkus 35:1048; LJ 92:4615)

8-204   MERRILL, Jean (Fairbanks). *The Pushcart War.* Gr. 5–7.
☆   Traffic congestion in New York City brings on a war between the truck drivers
        and the pushcart owners.
        Illus. by Ronni Solbert, Harper, 1964, 1992, 222 pp., LB (0-06-020822-8);
        Tempo, 2000, pap. (0-448-07453-2)
        (BL 61:219, 80:96; Eakin:223; HB 40:378; LJ 89:2828)

8-205   MERRILL, Jean (Fairbanks). *The Toothpaste Millionaire.* Gr. 4–5.
        Eleven-year-old Lucas starts his own toothpaste factory to compete with the
        higher-priced name-brand toothpastes.
        Houghton, 1974, 96 pp. (0-395-18511-4), 1993, pap. (0-395-66954-5)
        (BL 70:1254; CCBB 28:49; HB 50:137; Kirkus 42:480; Suth 2:316)

MILLER, Judi. *Ghost in My Soup.*
See Chapter 4, Ghost Fantasy.

MILNE, A(lan) A(lexander). *Prince Rabbit and the Princess Who Could
Not Laugh.*
See Chapter 1, Allegorical Fantasy and Literary Fairy Tales.

MILNE, A(lan) A(lexander). *Winnie-the-Pooh.*
See Chapter 11, Toy Fantasy.

MINOT, Stephen. *Surviving the Flood.*
See Chapter 6, High Fantasy: Myth or Legend Fantasy.

MITCHARD, Jacquelyn. *Starring Prima! The Mouse of the Ballet Jolie.*
See Chapter 2, Animal Fantasy.

MITCHELL, Stephen. *The Frog Prince: A Parable of Love and Transformation.*
See Chapter 6, High Fantasy: Myth or Legend Fantasy.

MONSELL, Mary Elise. *Crackle Creek.*
See Chapter 2, Animal Fantasy.

MONSELL, Mary Elise. *The Mysterious Cases of Mr. Pin.*
See Chapter 2, Animal Fantasy.

MOORE, John. *Slay and Rescue.*
See Chapter 6, High Fantasy: Myth or Legend Fantasy.

MOORE, Margaret Eileen. *Willie Without.*
See Chapter 2, Animal Fantasy.

8-206   MORGENSTERN, Susie. *Princesses Are People, Too: Two Modern Fairy
        Tales.* Gr. 2–5. (Orig. pub. in France.)
        Two whimsical tales about princesses: "Even Princesses Have to Go to School"
        and "Someday My Prince Will Scratch."
        Trans. by Bill May, illus. by Serge Bloch, Viking, 2002, 62 pp. (0-670-03567-
        X); Puffin, 2004, pap., 52 pp. (0-14-240040-8)
        (BL 98:1527; CCBB 55:334; HBG 13:362; Kirkus 70:662; SLJ May 2002 p. 124)

MORRESSY, John. *A Voice for Princess.*
See Chapter 12, Witchcraft and Sorcery Fantasy.

MORRIS, Gerald. *The Savage Damsel and the Dwarf.*
See Chapter 6, High Fantasy: Myth or Legend Fantasy.

MORRISON, Dorothy Nafus. *Vanishing Act.*
See Chapter 9, Magic Adventure Fantasy.

8-207 MÜNCHAUSEN, Karl. *The Adventures of Baron Münchausen.* Gr. 3–6.
(Orig. German pub. 1781–1783; U.S. pub. 1813.)
These tales, originally printed anonymously in Germany, 1781–1783, are sometimes attributed to Karl Friedrich Hieronymus, Baron Von Münchausen. They
were translated into English and edited by Rudolf Erich Raspé in 1786. They
were first published in the U.S. (1813) entitled *Gulliver Redivivus; or the Curious and Entertaining Travels and Adventures by Sea and by Land of the
Renowned Baron Munchausen; Including a Tour to the United States of America in the Year 1803; and the First Chapters of a Second Tour in 1816.* In *The
Baron Rides Out: The Adventures of Baron Munchausen* (Putnam, 1985, 1986),
the fabulous Baron Münchausen travels to a Ceylonese jungle where he meets a
gigantic alligator, a huge lion, and an enormous giant called Peter the Great.
Two companion volumes, both edited by Adrian Mitchell, are *The Baron on the
Island of Cheese: More Adventures of Baron Munchausen* (1986) and *The
Baron All at Sea: More Adventures of Baron Munchausen* (1987).
Illus. by W. Heath Robinson, Dutton, 1903, 256 pp. (entitled *The Surprising
Travels and Adventures of Baron Münchausen*), o.p.; retold by John Martin
(pseud. of Morgan Shepard), illus. by Gordon Ross, Houghton, 1921, 185 pp.
(entitled *The Children's Münchausen*), o.p.; illus. by Gustave Doré, Pantheon,
1944, 213 pp., o.p.; retold by Erich Kästner, trans. by Richard Wilson and Clara
Wilson, illus. by Walter Trier, Messner, 1951, 1957 (entitled *Baron Mün-
chausen, His Wonderful Travels and Adventures*), 68 pp., o.p.; illus. by Fritz
Kredel, Heritage, 1952 (entitled *The Singular Adventures of Baron Mün-
chausen*), 175 pp., o.p.; retold by Angelita von Münchhausen, illus. by Harry
Carter, Devin-Adair, 1960 (entitled *The Real Münchhausen: Authentic Tales of
the Fabulous Baron of Bodenwerder*), 224 pp., o.p.; ed. and illus. by Brian
Robb, Deutsch, 1979 (orig. British pub. 1947; entitled *12 Adventures of the
Celebrated Baron Münchausen*), 105 pp., o.p.; ed. by Adrian Mitchell, illus. by
Patrick Benson, Putnam, 1986 (orig. British pub. 1985, entitled *The Baron
Rides Out: A Baron Münchausen Tall Tale*), 28 pp., o.p.; adapt. by Peter Nickl,
trans. by Elizabeth B. Taylor, illus. by Binette Schroeder, North-South, 1992
(orig. Swiss pub. in this ed., 1977) (entitled *The Wonderful Travels and Adventures of Baron Münchausen*), 56 pp. (1-55858-134-0); adapt. by Rudolph Erich
Raspe, Wildside, 2001 (entitled *The Surprising Adventures of Baron Munchausen*), 220 pp. (1-58715-569-9)
(BL 18:162, 25:87, 41:157; Bookshelf 1924–1925 p. 15, 1932 p. 23; HB 55:536; Kirkus
12:483, 54:1451; LJ 69:1006, 86:575, 96:3470; SLJ Feb 1980 p. 60, May 1986 p. 82, Jan 1987
p. 76; TLS 1985 pp. 355, 1435)

8-208 MURPHY, Jill. *Jeffrey Strangeways.* Gr. 3–6. (Orig. British pub. 1991.)
✮ Clumsy Jeffrey longs to become a knight, so he tells his mother that Sir Walter
of Winterwood has offered him a job, and he sets off to seek his dream.

Illus. by the author, Candlewick, 1992, 140 pp. (1-56402-018-5)

(BL 88:1840; CCBB 46:20; HBG 3:268; Kirkus 60:673; SLJ May 1992 p. 114)

MURPHY, Jill. *The Worst Witch.*
See Chapter 12, Witchcraft and Sorcery Fantasy.

8-209 MYERS, Walter Dean. *The Black Pearl and the Ghost; or, One Mystery After Another.* Gr. 2–4.
Two humorous mystery stories: one involves a stolen pearl, the other a haunted manor house.
Illus. by Robert M(ead) Quackenbush, Viking, 1980, 40 pp., o.p.

(BL 76:1297; CCBB 33:180; HB 56:301; Kirkus 48:514; SLJ May 1980 p. 85)

MYERS, Walter Dean. *Three Swords for Grenada.*
See Chapter 2, Animal Fantasy.

8-210 NAPOLI, Donna Jo. *The Prince of the Pond: Otherwise Known as De*
☆ *Fawg Pin.* **(The Frog Prince series, bk. 1).** Gr. 3–6.
A female frog is mystified by the unfroglike behavior of a male she finds one day, tangled in a pile of human clothing, in this humorous version of "The Frog Prince." In *Jimmy, the Pickpocket of the Palace* (1995), Pin's son, Jimmy the frog, endures a difficult transformation to become a boy. The third book in the series is *Gracie, the Pixie of the Puddle* (2004).
Illus. by Judith Byron Schachner, Dutton, 1992, 151 pp., o.p.

(BL 89:909; CCBB 46:153; Kirkus 60:1259; SLJ Oct 1992 p. 118)

8-211 NASH, Mary (Hughes). *While Mrs. Coverlet Was Away.* Gr. 4–6.
☆ After both their father and housekeeper are called out of town, Molly, Malcolm, and Todd manage on their own. The sequels are *Mrs. Coverlet's Magicians* (1961; 2001) and *Mrs. Coverlet's Detectives* (1965).
Illus. by Garrett Price, Little, Brown, 1958, 133 pp., o.p.; Volo/Hyperion, 2002 (0-7868-1695-3)

(BL 55:137; CCBB 12:52; Eakin:243; HB 34:386, 78:429–430; Kirkus 26:380; LJ 83:2502)

8-212 NASTICK, Sharon. *Mr. Radagast Makes an Unexpected Journey.* Gr. 4–7.
A seventh-grade class is amazed to find that their experiment in "immaterialism" has made their teacher, Mr. Radagast, disappear.
Illus. by Judy Glasser, Crowell, 1981, 85 pp., o.p.

(BL 77:1346; Kirkus 49:504; SLJ May 1981 p. 67)

NAYLOR, Phyllis Reynolds. *Bernie and the Bessledorf Ghost.*
See Chapter 4, Ghost Fantasy.

NAYLOR, Phyllis Reynolds. *The Grand Escape.*
See Chapter 2, Animal Fantasy.

NESBIT (Bland), E(dith). *The Last of the Dragons.*
See Chapter 1, Allegorical Fantasy and Literary Fairy Tales.

NIXON, Joan Lowery. *Gus and Gertie and the Missing Pearl.*
See Chapter 2, Animal Fantasy.

NIXON, Joan Lowery. *Magnolia's Mixed-Up Magic.*
See Chapter 2, Animal Fantasy.

8-213 **NÖSTLINGER, Christine.** *Konrad.* Gr. 4–6. (Orig. Austrian pub. 1975;
✰✰ British pub. 1976, entitled *Conrad: The Hilarious Adventures of a Factory-Made Child.*)
After Konrad, a canned, mail-order child, is allowed to move in with Mrs. Bartolotti, his perfect behavior disturbs his new mother and angers his classmates. Mildred L. Batchelder Award, 1978.
Trans. by Anthea Bell, illus. by Carol Nicklaus, Watts, 1977, 135 pp., o.p.
(BL 74:482; CCBB 31:98; HB 53:665; SLJ Nov 1977 p. 60; Suth 2:339; TLS 1977 p. 348)

8-214 **OAKLEY, Graham.** *Henry's Quest.* Gr. 5 up.
✰ In a future post-technology England, the king sends a shepherd named Henry on a quest for the magical substance "gasoline," in order to win the hand of Princess Isolde.
Illus. by the author, Atheneum, 1986, 32 pp., o.p.
(BL 83:893, 902; CCBB 40:133; Kirkus 54:1374; SLJ Dec 1986 p. 107; TLS 1986 p. 1345)

OLSON, Helen Kronberg. *The Strange Thing That Happened to Oliver Wendell Iscovitch.*
See Chapter 9, Magic Adventure Fantasy.

ORMONDROYD, Edward. *David and the Phoenix.*
See Chapter 9, Magic Adventure Fantasy.

OSBORNE, Mary Pope. *Dinosaurs Before Dark.*
See Chapter 10, Time Travel Fantasy.

OSTERWEIL, Adam. *The Amulet of Komondor.*
See Chapter 7, High Fantasy: Travel to Other Worlds.

OSTERWEIL, Adam. *The Comic Book Kid.*
See Chapter 10, Time Travel Fantasy.

PAGET, (Reverend) F(rancis) (pseud. of William Churne of Stafford-shire). *The Hope of the Katzekopfs; or, the Sorrow of Selfishness: A Fairy Tale.*
See Chapter 1, Allegorical Fantasy and Literary Fairy Tales.

8-215 **PALMER, David R.** *Threshold.* Gr. 10 up.
✰ Peter Cory is recruited as the savior of the universe by a beautiful witch who looks like Tinkerbell without wings, in this spoof of heroic fantasy. Two sequels have been planned but not published as of early 2005.
Bantam, 1985, pap., 274 pp., o.p.
(BL 82:468, 482; Kliatt 20:24; LJ Dec 1985 p. 130; VOYA 9:89)

PALMER, Mary. *The Dolmop of Dorkling.*
See Chapter 7, High Fantasy: Travel to Other Worlds.

PALMER, Robin (Riggs). *Wise House.*
See Chapter 2, Animal Fantasy.

PARKER, (James) Edgar (Jr.). *The Dream of the Dormouse.*
See Chapter 2, Animal Fantasy.

PARKER, (James) Edgar (Jr.). *The Question of a Dragon.*
See Chapter 2, Animal Fantasy.

8-216 PARKER, (James) Edgar (Jr.). *Rogue's Gallery.* Gr. 4–6.
This crime story spoof stars master criminal Hoimie-the-stoat, Reynolds the
policefox, and Matou, a tomcat gone straight.
Illus. by the author, Pantheon, 1969, 63 pp., o.p.
(CCBB 23:104; Kirkus 37:1113)

8-217 PARKER, Nancy Winslow. *The Spotted Dog: The Strange Tale of a
Witch's Revenge.* Gr. 2–4.
A witch turns the Cruikshank-Jones's baby Eileen into a dog, but the family
does not seem to mind; they enjoy winning ribbons at dog shows.
Illus. by the author, Dodd, 1980, 46 pp., o.p.
(BL 77:407; Kirkus 48:1395; SLJ Dec 1980 p. 54)

8-218 PARRISH, Anne. *The Story of Appleby Capple.* Gr. 3–5.
★ A boy has alphabetical adventures while searching for a rare zebra moth. John
Newbery Medal Honor Book, 1951.
Illus. by the author, Harper, 1950, 184 pp., o.p.
(BL 47:225; CCBB 4:22; HB 26:457, 467, 27:20; Kirkus 18:512; LJ 75:1745, 76:338)

PASCAL, Francine. *Hangin' Out with Cici.*
See Chapter 10, Time Travel Fantasy.

PEABODY, Paul. *Blackberry Hollow.*
See Chapter 2, Animal Fantasy.

PECK, Richard (Wayne). *The Ghost Belonged to Me: A Novel.*
See Chapter 4, Ghost Fantasy.

8-219 PENNYPACKER, Sara. *Dumbstruck.* Gr. 4–7. (Orig. British pub. 1994.)
Ivy and her friend Will escape from the Wretched Dear Darlings Blessed
Haven Orphanage, run by cruel Armilda and Borage Clott, to search for Ivy's
missing parents, and they decide to return and free the other orphans.
Illus. by Mary Jane Auch, Holiday, 1994, 149 pp. (0-8234-1123-0)
(CCBB 47:369; HBG 5:314; Kirkus 61:562; SLJ May 1994 p. 118)

PENNYPACKER, Sara. *Stuart's Cape.*
See Chapter 9, Magic Adventure Fantasy.

8-220 PETRIE, Stuart. *The Voyage of Barracks.* Gr. 4–6. (Orig. British pub.
1967.)
An English family ties their house to a hot-air balloon and soars off around the
world.
Illus. by the author, Meredith, 1968, 120 pp., o.p.
(BL 65:754; Kirkus 36:643; LJ 93:3308; TLS 1967 p. 1133)

PFEFFER, Susan Beth. *Sara Kate, Superkid.*
See Chapter 9, Magic Adventure Fantasy.

8-221 PILKEY, Dav. *The Adventures of Captain Underpants: An Epic Novel.*
⭑ **(Captain Underpants series, bk. 1).** Gr. 2–4.
After fourth-graders Harold and George hypnotize the principal into thinking he is a superhero named Captain Underpants, he escapes and begins hunting down bad guys in his underwear. The sequels are *Captain Underpants and the Attack of the Talking Toilets* (1999), *Captain Underpants and the Invasion of the Incredibly Naughty Cafeteria Ladies from Outer Space* (1999), *Captain Underpants and the Perilous Plot of Professor Poopypants* (2000), *Captain Underpants and the Wrath of the Wicked Wedgie Woman* (2001), *Captain Underpants and the Big Bad Battle of the Bionic Booger Boy, part 1: Night of the Nasty Nostril Nuggets* (2003), and *Captain Underpants and the Big Bad Battle of the Bionic Booger Boy, part 2: Revenge of the Ridiculous Robo-Boogers* (2003).
Illus. by the author, Blue Sky, 1997, 128 pp. (0-590-84627-2); Scholastic, 1997, pap., 117 pp. (0-590-84628-0)
(BL 93:1819; HBG 9:79; Kirkus 65:878; SLJ Dec 1997 p. 99)

PINKWATER, D(aniel) Manus. *Blue Moose.*
See Chapter 2, Animal Fantasy.

8-222 PINKWATER, D(aniel) Manus. *The Frankenbagel Monster.* Gr. 2–5.
⭑ Harold Frankenbagel creates Bagelnuculus in his quest to become the greatest bagel maker in history, but he must stop the monster bagel after it goes mad and heads off toward a lox warehouse.
Illus. by the author, Dutton, 1986, 24 pp., o.p.
(BL 83:356; HB 62:742; Kirkus 54:1584; SLJ Oct 1986 p. 165)

8-223 PINKWATER, D(aniel) Manus. *The Hoboken Chicken Emergency.* Gr. 3–5.
⭑ Arthur Bobowicz's adoption of a 266-pound chicken meets with opposition from his parents, the mayor, and the townspeople. In the sequel, *Looking for Bobowicz: A Hoboken Chicken Story* (2004), Henrietta, the 266-pound hen, helps Ivan and his friends, Bruno and Loretta, solve the thefts of Ivan's bike and their Classic Comics collection.
Illus. by the author, Prentice-Hall, 1977, 1984, 83 pp., o.p.; illus. by Jill Pinkwater, Atheneum, 1999, 109 pp. (0-689-83060-2); Aladdin, 1999, pap. (0-689-82889-6)
(BL 73:1268; CCBB 30:163; HB 53:316, 61:755; HBG 11:80; Kirkus 45:166; SLJ Sep 1977 p. 134)

8-224 PINKWATER, D(aniel) Manus. *Jolly Roger: A Dog of Hoboken.* Gr. 3–5.
Jolly Roger (half husky, half chow chow) is befriended by The Kid and becomes the leader of the Hoboken dock dogs.
Illus. by the author, Lothrop, 1984, 64 pp., o.p.
(BL 82:69; HB 61:559; Kirkus 53:35; SLJ Sep 1985 p. 138)

8-225 PINKWATER, D(aniel) Manus. *The Last Guru.* Gr. 5–7.
After 12-year-old Harold Blatz invests his racetrack winnings in a hamburger chain and becomes a billionaire, the Blatz family tries to escape their newfound fame by moving to a castle in the Bavarian Alps, and then to a village in India.
Illus. by the author, Dodd, 1978, 115 pp., o.p.
(BL 75:548; CCBB 32:124; Kirkus 46:1189; SLJ Nov 1978 p. 66)

8-226 PINKWATER, D(aniel) Manus. *Lizard Music.* Gr. 4–6.
✳ Victor cannot understand why lizards and the Chicken Man turn up wherever he goes, until he is taken to an invisible, lizard-run island.
Illus. by the author, Dodd, 1976, 157 pp., o.p.; Yearling, 1996, pap., 144 pp. (0-440-41319-2)
(BL 73:41, 80:96; CCBB 30:112; HB 53:161; Kirkus 44:846; SLJ Oct 1976 p. 110)

PINKWATER, D(aniel) Manus. *The Magic Pretzel.*
See Chapter 9, Magic Adventure Fantasy.

8-227 PINKWATER, D(aniel) Manus. *The Muffin Fiend.* Gr. 3–5.
Inspector Charles LeChat tracks down an extraterrestrial muffin thief who needs thousands of muffins to fuel a rocket for his trip home.
Illus. by the author, Lothrop, 1986, 48 pp., o.p.
(CCBB 39:156; HB 62:324, Kirkus 54:475; SLJ Aug 1986 p. 97)

8-228 PINKWATER, D(aniel) Manus. *The Worms of Kukumlima.* Gr. 5–8.
Ronald Donald Almandotter, his grandfather, Seumas Finneganstein, and Sir Charles Pelicanstein go on a safari into wildest Kukumlima to capture a huge, intelligent worm. This story is also included in Pinkwater's *Four Fantastic Novels* (Aladdin, 2000, pap., 619 pp. [0-689-83488-8]).
Illus. by the author, Elsevier-Dutton, 1981, 152 pp., o.p.
(BL 77:1034; CCBB 35:35; Kirkus 49:571; SLJ May 1981 p. 68; VOYA 5:41)

8-229 PINKWATER, D(aniel) Manus. *Yobgorgle: Mystery Monster of Lake Ontario.* Gr. 5–7.
Only a corned beef sandwich will remove the curse on the captain of the "Flying Piggie" submarine. This story is also included in Pinkwater's *Four Fantastic Novels* (Aladdin, 2000, pap., 619 pp. [0-689-83488-8[).
Illus. by the author, Houghton, 1979, 138 pp., o.p.
(BL 76:126; Kirkus 47:1068; SLJ Nov 1979 p. 80)

POCHOCKI, Ethel. *The Attic Mice.*
See Chapter 2, Animal Fantasy.

8-230 POMERANTZ, Charlotte. *Detective Poufy's First Case: Or the Missing Battery-Operated Pepper Grinder.* Gr. 3–5.
A lonely dragon named Dragobert turns out to be the robber who broke into Rosie Maloon's house and left all the electrical gadgets running.
Illus. by Mary Norman, Addison-Wesley, 1976, 64 pp., o.p.
(BL 73:476; Kirkus 44:796; SLJ Dec 1976 p. 65)

POMERANTZ, Charlotte. *The Downtown Fairy Godmother.*
See Chapter 9, Magic Adventure Fantasy.

8-231 POPHAM, Hugh. *The Fabulous Voyage of the Pegasus.* Gr. 4–6.
Lee-O! sets sail on the Pegasus in search of a narwhal and the sea god, Poseidon.
Illus. by Graham Oakley, Phillips, 1959, 150 pp., o.p.
(HB 35:301; Kirkus 27:176; LJ 84:1700)

PRATCHETT, Terry. *The Amazing Maurice and His Educated Rodents.*
See Chapter 5, High Fantasy: Alternate Worlds or Histories.

PRATCHETT, Terry. *The Color of Magic.*
See Chapter 5, High Fantasy: Alternate Worlds or Histories.

PRATCHETT, Terry. *The Wee Free Men.*
See Chapter 5, High Fantasy: Alternate Worlds or Histories.

8-232 PREUSSLER, Otfried. *The Robber Hotzenplotz.* **(The Robber Hotzenplotz trilogy, bk. 1).** Gr. 5–7. (Orig. pub. in Germany.)
Kasperl and Seppel are trapped in the hideout of a notorious bandit, Hotzenplotz. The sequels are *Further Adventures of the Robber Hotzenplotz* (1971) and *The Final Adventures of the Robber Hotzenplotz* (Britain, 1974).
Trans. by Anthea Bell, illus. by F. J. Tripp, Abelard-Schuman, 1965, 126 pp., o.p.
(Kirkus 33:107; LJ 90:2409; TLS 1964 p. 1081)

8-233 PREUSSLER, Otfried. *The Wise Men of Schilda.* Gr. 4–6. (Orig. pub. in Germany.)
The foolish inhabitants of Schilda try to prove their cleverness to the rest of the world.
Trans. by Anthea Bell, illus. by F. J. Tripp, Abelard-Schuman, 1963, 185 pp., o.p.
(BL 60:44; CCBB 17:128; HB 39:286; LJ 88:2553)

8-234 PULLMAN, Philip. *Count Karlstein.* Gr. 5–8. (Orig. British pub. 1982.)
☆ After 14-year-old servant Hildi Kelmar uncovers Count Karlstein's plot to sacrifice his nieces to the Demon Huntsman, she joins forces with Lucy, Charlotte, and a con artist to thwart his plans.
Illus. by Diane Bryan, Knopf, 1998, 243 pp. (0-679-89255-9), 2000, pap., 256 pp. (0-679-89255-9)
(BL94:1991; CCBB 52:71; HB 74:613; HBG 10:73; Kirkus 66:971; SLJ Sep 1998 p. 208)

PULLMAN, Philip. *The Firework-Maker's Daughter.*
See Chapter 5, High Fantasy: Alternate Worlds or Histories.

PULLMAN, Philip. *I Was a Rat!*
See Chapter 6, High Fantasy: Myth or Legend Fantasy.

8-235 PULLMAN, Philip. *Spring-Heeled Jack.* Gr. 3–7. (Orig. British pub. 1989.)
☆ Rose, Lily, and Ned escape from an orphanage in Victorian England, only to be captured by Mack the Knife's gang, and saved by the hero Spring-Heeled Jack.
Illus. by David Mostyn, Knopf, 1991, 112 pp., o.p., pap. (0-679-81057-9); Knopf, 2002 (0-375-91601-6)
(CCBB 45:46; HB 78:431; HBG 3:72, 13:380; Kirkus 59:793; SLJ Dec 1991 p. 117)

QUACKENBUSH, Robert M(ead). *Express Train to Trouble: A Miss Mallard Mystery.*
See Chapter 2, Animal Fantasy.

8-236 RASKIN, Ellen. *Figgs and Phantoms.* Gr. 5–7.
☆ Mona Lisa Newton does not appreciate her kooky relatives—including her tap-dancing mother, twin brothers Romulus and Remus, contortionist Truman Figg, and cousin Fido Figg—until her beloved uncle dies. John Newbery Medal Honor Book, 1975.

Illus. by the author, Dutton, 1974, 1977, 160 pp., o.p.; Peter Smith, 2001 (0-8446-7153-3)

(BL 71:46; CCBB 28:98; HB 50:138; Kirkus 42:425; LJ 99:1451, 1475, 3247; Suth 2:374)

8-237 **RASKIN, Ellen.** *The Mysterious Disappearance of Leon (I Mean Noel).* Gr.
✶ 5–7.
Married at ages 5 and 7 to solve their parents' business problems, Caroline (Little Dumpling) and Leon (Noel) Carillon do not see each other again for 14 clue-filled, puzzle-filled, and secret code-filled years.
Illus. by the author, Dutton, 1971, 1977, 149 pp., o.p.; Puffin, 1989, pap. (0-14-032945-5)

(BL 68:394, 670; CCBB 25:79; HB 48:51; Kirkus 39:1122; LJ 96:4160; Suth:323)

8-238 **RASKIN, Ellen.** *The Tattooed Potato and Other Clues.* Gr. 5–7.
✶ Dickory Dock's detective work leads her to the blackmailers of a brilliant artist and the murderer of her parents.
Dutton, 1975, 170 pp., o.p.

(BL 71:967; CCBB 29:52; HB 51:271; Kirkus 43:457; SLJ Apr 1975 p. 69, Dec 1975 p. 32; Suth 2:374; TLS 1976 p. 1548)

RAYNER, Mary (Yoma, née Grigson). *Mrs. Pig Gets Cross; and Other Stories.*
See Chapter 2, Animal Fantasy.

RAZZI, Jim (James), and RAZZI, Mary. *The Search for King Pup's Tomb.*
See Chapter 2, Animal Fantasy.

REGAN, Dian Curtis. *Monster of the Month Club.*
See Chapter 9, Magic Adventure Fantasy.

REICHE, Dietlof. *I, Freddy.*
See Chapter 2, Animal Fantasy.

8-239 **REIT, Seymour.** *Benvenuto.* Gr. 3–5.
Paolo brings home a baby dragon from summer camp.
Illus. by Will Winslow, Addison-Wesley, 1974, 126 pp., o.p.

(BL 70:878; Kirkus 42:301; LJ 99:2276)

8-240 *Ribbiting Tales: Original Stories About Frogs.* **Ed. by Nancy Springer.** Gr.
3–6.
These eight humorous tales about frogs are written by Bruce Coville, Jane Yolen, Janet Taylor Lisle, and others.
Illus. by Tony DiTerlizzi, Philomel, 2000, 128 pp., o.p.; Puffin, 2002, 117 pp. (0-698-11952-5)

(BL 97:541; Kirkus 68:1433; SLJ Jan 2001 p. 108; VOYA 23:278)

RICHEMONT, Enid. *The Magic Skateboard.*
See Chapter 9, Magic Adventure Fantasy.

8-241 **RICHLER, Mordecai.** *Jacob Two-Two Meets the Hooded Fang.* Gr. 3–5.
(Orig. Canadian pub. 1975.)

Jacob is teased for his habit of saying everything twice, but he proves to be courageous after his capture by the Slimers and their chief, the Hooded Fang. Winner, Canadian Library Association Best Book of the Year for Children, 1976. The sequels are *Jacob Two-Two and the Dinosaur* (1987) and *Jacob Two-Two's First Spy Case* (1997).

Illus. by Fritz Wegner, Knopf, 1975, 87 pp., o.p.; Bantam, 1987, pap. (0-317-64199-9)

(CCBB 28:184; Kirkus 43:568; SLJ Sep 1975 p. 90; TLS 1976 p. 376)

8-242 RIDLEY, Philip. *Krindlekrax; or, How Ruskin Splinter Battled a Horrible Monster and Saved His Entire Neighborhood.* Gr. 3–6. (Orig. British pub. 1991.)

Nine-year-old Ruskin, afraid of the local bully, has dreams of becoming a hero, dreams that come true after he climbs down into the dark sewer and tames Krindlekrax, the dragon who lives in the depths. Nestlé Smarties Prize for Children's Books, 1991.

Illus. by Gary Hovland, Knopf, 1992, 144 pp., o.p.; Faber, 2002, pap., 96 pp. (0-5712-1543-2)

(BL 88:1280; HBG 3:269; Kirkus 60:471; SLJ Mar 1992 p. 241)

8-243 RINKOFF, Barbara (Jean). *Elbert, the Mind Reader.* Gr. 4–6.

Elbert's new filling enables him to tune in on other people's thoughts, a talent he uses to impress the football coach so that he can join the team.

Illus. by Paul Galdone, Lothrop, 1967, 112 pp., o.p.

(BL 64:594; CCBB 21:65; Kirkus 35:809; LJ 92:3855)

8-244 RIOS, Tere (Teresa). *The Fifteenth Pelican.* Gr. 4–6.

On the windy island of San Juan, Sister Bertrille's large, white headpiece enables her to fly like a pelican.

Illus. by Arthur King, Doubleday, 1965, 118 pp., o.p.

(Kirkus 33:782; LJ 90:4076)

ROBERTS, Willo Davis. *The Magic Book.*
See Chapter 9, Magic Adventure Fantasy.

RODDA, Emily. *The Pigs Are Flying!*
See Chapter 9, Magic Adventure Fantasy.

8-245 RODGERS (Guettel), Mary. *Freaky Friday.* **(Freaky Friday trilogy, bk.**
★★ **1).** Gr. 5–7.

One morning, Annabel Adams awakens to discover that she has traded bodies with her mother. In *A Billion for Boris* (1974, 1976, pap. 1999, entitled *ESP TV*), a television set that broadcasts tomorrow's programs gives Annabel the urge to do good deeds, but inspires her friend Boris to make a fortune at the racetrack. In *Summer Switch* (1982, pap. 1999), Annabel's brother, Ben, inadvertently trades bodies with his father while Ben is at summer camp and his father is on a business trip to Hollywood.

Harper, 1972, 155 pp., LB (0-06-025049-6); HarperCollins, 1999, pap. (0-06-440046-8), 2003, pap. (0-06-057010-5)

(BL 68:910, 80:96; CCBB 26:15; HB 48:378; Kirkus 40:267; LJ 97:1608)

ROGERS, Mark E. *The Adventures of Samurai Cat.*
See Chapter 2, Animal Fantasy.

8-246 ROUNDS, David. *Cannonball River Tales.* Gr. 3–6.
These five tall-tale episodes about North Dakotan Tom Terry include one about finding a dragon's silver treasure.
Illus. by Alix Berenzy, Sierra, 1992, 104 pp. (0-87156-577-3)
(BL 89:909; Kirkus 60:1447; SLJ Dec 1992 p. 113)

8-247 ROUNDS, Glen (Harold). *The Day the Circus Came to Lone Tree.* Gr. 3–4.
☆ The townspeople of Lone Tree are treated to some unwelcome entertainment when a circus lion and his trainer stampede all of the town's livestock. The sequels are *Mr. Yowder and the Lion Roar Capsules* (1976), *Mr. Yowder and the Steamboat* (1977), *Mr. Yowder and the Giant Bull Snake* (1978), *Mr. Yowder and the Train Robbers* (1981), and *Mr. Yowder and the Windwagon* (1983). Three of the sequels have been published in a single volume entitled *Mr. Yowder, the Peripatetic Sign Painter* (1980).
Illus. by the author, Holiday, 1973, 39 pp., o.p.
(BL 70:545; CCBB 27:85; HB 52:393; Kirkus 41:1155; LJ 99:203; Suth 2:387)

RUFF, Matt. *Fool on the Hill.*
See Chapter 9, Magic Adventure Fantasy.

RUSHDIE, Salman. *Haroun and the Sea of Stories.*
See Chapter 5, High Fantasy: Alternate Worlds or Histories.

SABERHAGEN, Fred. *Empire of the East.*
See Chapter 5, High Fantasy: Alternate Worlds or Histories.

8-248 SACHAR, Louis. *Wayside School Is Falling Down.* Gr. 3–6.
Thirty wacky episodes about the children in Mrs. Jewels's classroom on the top floor of the 30-story-high Wayside School. This is the sequel to *Sideways Stories from Wayside School* (Follett, 1978; Knopf, 1990), and it is followed by *Wayside School Gets a Little Stranger* (1995). *Sideways Arithmetic from Wayside School* (Scholastic, 1989) is a related nonfiction work.
Illus. by Joel Schick, Lothrop, 1989, 192 pp. (0-688-07868-8), o.p.; HarperTrophy, 1998, pap., 160 pp. (0-380-73150-9)
(BL 85:1553; Kirkus 57:127; SLJ May 1989 p. 111)

8-249 SANDBURG, Carl (August). *Rootabaga Stories.* Gr. 4 up. (Orig. pub.
☆ 1922.)
This collection of 49 humorous tales was written by the well-known American poet. David Small has illustrated a version of one story, entitled *The Huckabuck Family and How They Raised Popcorn in Nebraska and Quit and Came Back* (Farrar, 1999, 0-374-33511-7). *Rootabaga Pigeons* (1923, 1974) and *Potato Face* (1930) are companion volumes. An omnibus volume was published in 1936. *More Rootabagas* contains ten previously unpublished tales (Knopf, 1993; illus. by Michael Hague, Harcourt, 1989, 1990, pap., entitled *Rootabaga Stories: Part Two*; Harcourt, 2003; 2003, pap., entitled *More Rootabaga Stories*).
Illus. by Maud Petersham and Miska Petersham, Harcourt, 1951, 218 pp., o.p.; illus. by Michael (R.) Hague, Harcourt, 1988 (entitled *Rootabaga Stories: Part*

One), 192 pp. (0-15-269061-1), 1990, pap., o.p.; Harcourt, 1989, pap.; Harcourt, 2003 (0-15-204709-3), pap. (0-15-204714-X)
(BL 19:92, 85:580; HB 27:129; Moore:426; SLJ Feb 1989 p. 82)

SANVOISIN, Eric. *The Ink Drinker.*
See Chapter 9, Magic Adventure Fantasy.

SATHRE, Vivian. *Slender Ella and Her Fairy Hogfather.*
See Chapter 6, High Fantasy: Myth or Legend Fantasy.

8-250 SAUNDERS, George. *The Very Persistent Gappers of Frip.* Gr. 6–12.
Every day the children of Frip must remove the shrieking gappers from the goats they adore and cast them back into the sea.
Illus. by Lane Smith, Villard, 2000, 96 pp. (0-375-50383-8)
(SLJ Jan 2001 p. 160; VOYA 23:435, 24:14)

SCARBOROUGH, Elizabeth Ann. *Bronwyn's Bane.*
See Chapter 5, High Fantasy: Alternate Worlds or Histories.

SCARBOROUGH, Elizabeth Ann. *The Godmother.*
See Chapter 9, Magic Adventure Fantasy.

8-251 SCARBOROUGH, Elizabeth Ann. *The Harem of Aman Akbar; or The Djinn Decanted.* Gr. 10 up.
A nobleman turned into an ass while searching for a fourth wife is forced to rely on his other three wives and his mother to rescue him.
Bantam, 1984, pap., 215 pp., o.p.
(BL 81:561, 583; LJ 109:1775)

SCHAEFFER, Susan Fromberg. *The Autobiography of Foudini M. Cat.*
See Chapter 2, Animal Fantasy.

SCHEFFLER, Ursel. *Rinaldo, The Sly Fox.*
See Chapter 2, Animal Fantasy.

SCHREIBER, Ellen. *Teenage Mermaid.*
See Chapter 6, High Fantasy: Myth or Legend Fantasy.

SCHWED, Antonia Holding. *Noah and Me: A Novel.*
See Chapter 2, Animal Fantasy.

8-252 SCIESZKA, Jon. *The Frog Prince, Continued.* Gr. 1–4.
✫ The former frog and the princess whose kiss transformed him into a prince are not happily married, so the prince decides to find someone who can change him back.
Illus. by Steve Johnson, Viking, 1991, 32 pp. (0-670-83421-1); Puffin, 1994, pap., 32 pp. (0-14-054285-X)
(BL 87:1880, 88:1367, 1369; CCBB 44:225; HB 67:451; HBG 2:230; Kirkus 59:732; SLJ May 1991 p. 83)

SCIESZKA, Jon. *Knights of the Kitchen Table.*
See Chapter 10, Time Travel Fantasy.

8-253 SCIESZKA, Jon. *The Stinky Cheese Man and Other Fairly Stupid Tales.*
✸ Gr. 2–8.
These raucous retellings of familiar fairy tales include "The Gingerbread Boy" transformed into "The Stinky Cheese Man," "The Ugly Duckling" who grows up to be an ugly duck, and "Little Red Running Shorts" who outruns the wolf. Caldecott Medal Honor Book, 1993.
Illus. by Lane Smith, Viking, 1992, 56 pp. (0-670-84487-X); Viking, 2002, pap., 32 pp. (0-670-03569-6)
(BL 89:56, 844; CCBB 46:33, 53; HB 68:720; HBG 4:62; Kirkus 60:1193; SLJ Sep 1992, p. 210, Dec 1992 p. 23)

8-254 SCIESZKA, Jon. *The True Story of the 3 Little Pigs: By A. Wolf.* Gr. K–4.
✸ Mr. A. Wolf has been terribly misunderstood; he was only trying to borrow some sugar to make a cake for his dear old granny when his cold caused those huge sneezes that accidentally blew down the pigs' houses. Now he is in jail and he wants everyone to know that he was framed.
Illus. by Lane Smith, Viking, 1989, 32 pp. (0-670-82759-2); Puffin, 1996, pap., 32 pp. (0-14-054451-8)
(BL 86:74; CCBB 43:19; HB 66:58; HBG 1:46; Kirkus 57:1167; SLJ Oct 1989 p. 108, Mar 1990 p. 153)

8-255 SEABROOKE, Brenda. *The Vampire in My Bathtub.* Gr. 4–7.
When he opens an old trunk, Jeff meets Eugene, a "good" French vampire who was locked away for a hundred years by his evil cousin `Vennard as punishment for loving the beautiful vampire Carlotta.
Holiday, 1999, 150 pp. (0-8234-1505-8)
(BL 96:927; HB 76:84; HBG 11:87; SLJ Dec 1999 p. 140)

SEEMAN, Elizabeth (Brickel). *The Talking Dog and the Barking Man.*
See Chapter 2, Animal Fantasy.

SEIDLER, Tor. *Mean Margaret.*
See Chapter 2, Animal Fantasy.

SEIDLER, Tor. *The Wainscott Weasel.*
See Chapter 2, Animal Fantasy.

SELDEN (Thompson), George. *The Cricket in Times Square.*
See Chapter 2, Animal Fantasy.

SELDEN (Thompson), George. *The Genie of Sutton Place.*
See Chapter 9, Magic Adventure Fantasy.

SELDEN (Thompson), George. *Irma and Jerry.*
See Chapter 2, Animal Fantasy.

SENDAK, Maurice (Bernard). *Higglety Pigglety Pop! Or, There Must Be More to Life.*
See Chapter 2, Animal Fantasy.

SEUSS, Dr. (pseud. of Theodor Seuss Geisel). *The 500 Hats of Bartholomew Cubbins.*
See Chapter 1, Allegorical Fantasy and Literary Fairy Tales.

Shape Shifters: Fantasy and Science Fiction Tales About Humans Who Can Change Their Shapes. **Ed. by Jane (Hyatt) Yolen (Semple).**
See Chapter 3, Fantasy Collections.

8-256 SHEARER, Alex. *Professor Sniff and the Lost Spring Breezes.* Gr. 3–5.
The souvenir hurricane Professor Sniff brings back from Florida consumes all the wind in Calendar Hill, turns into Typhoon Trevor, and wreaks havoc on the countryside.
Illus. by Tony Kenyon, Orchard, 1998, 112 pp. (0-531-30079-X)
(BL 94:1322; HBG 9:338; SLJ Apr 1998 p. 110)

8-257 SHEARER, Alex. *The Summer Sisters and the Dance Disaster.* Gr. 3–5.
The three Summer children follow the instructions in a book they find in the attic and create all kinds of weather to sell to the public.
Illus. by Tony Kenyon, Orchard, 1998, 104 pp. (0-531-33080-X)
(BL 94:1446; HBG 9:338; Kirkus 66:409; SLJ May 1998 p. 126)

SHEEHAN, Carolyn, and SHEEHAN, Edmond. *Magnifi-Cat.*
See Chapter 2, Animal Fantasy.

SHIPTON, Paul. *Bug Muldoon: The Garden of Fear.*
See Chapter 2, Animal Fantasy.

SHREEVE, Elizabeth. *Hector Springs Loose.*
See Chapter 2, Animal Fantasy.

SHUSTERMAN, Neal. *The Eyes of Kid Midas.*
See Chapter 9, Magic Adventure Fantasy.

8-258 SILVERSTEIN, Shel(by). *Uncle Shelby's Story of Lafcadio, the Lion Who Shot Back.* Gr. 3–5.
Lafcadio the lion teaches himself to shoot a hunting rifle and becomes a famous circus star.
Illus. by the author, Harper, 1963, 112 pp., LB (0-06-025675-3)
(CCBB 17:85; LJ 88:4858)

SIMAK, Clifford D(onald). *The Goblin Reservation.*
See Chapter 10, Time Travel Fantasy.

8-259 SIMONT, Marc. *The Contest at Paca.* Gr. 3–5.
☆ The feuding soldiers and university students of Paca challenge each other to a stew-eating contest.
Illus. by the author, Harper, 1959, 60 pp., o.p.
(BL 55:634; HB 35:301; Kirkus 27:300; LJ 84:2084; TLS Nov 25, 1960 p. iv)

SIMONT, Marc. *Mimi.*
See Chapter 2, Animal Fantasy.

8-260 SINCIC, Alan. *Edward Is Only a Fish.* Gr. 2–4.
Edward escapes from his goldfish bowl when Mr. Billingsley leaves the bathwater running and the house fills with water.
Illus. by R. W. Alley, Holt, 1994, 56 pp. (0-8050-3491-9)
(BL 91:930; Kirkus 62:1577; SLJ Feb 1995 p. 100)

SINGER, Isaac Bashevis. *Naftali the Storyteller and His Horse, Sus, and Other Stories.*
See Chapter 3, Fantasy Collections.

SINGER, Isaac Bashevis. *Stories for Children.*
See Chapter 3, Fantasy Collections.

SINGER, Isaac Bashevis. *Zlateh the Goat and Other Stories.*
See Chapter 3, Fantasy Collections.

SINGER, Marilyn. *The Circus Lunicus.*
See Chapter 9, Magic Adventure Fantasy.

SINGER, Marilyn. *The Fido Frame-Up.*
See Chapter 2, Animal Fantasy.

8-261 SLOTE, Alfred. *My Robot Buddy.* Gr. 2–4.
Jack is mistaken for his robot by a gang of robotnappers, but the robot rescues him.
Illus. by Joel Schick, Harper, 1975, 1991, 80 pp., o.p.
(BL 72:460; CCBB 29:102; Kirkus 43:999; SLJ Oct 1975 p. 92)

8-262 *Smart Dragons, Foolish Elves.* **Ed. by Alan Dean Foster and Martin H. Greenberg.** Gr. 10 up.
These 19 contemporary, humorous, fantasy stories were written by Robert Silverberg, Roger Zelazny, Esther M. Friesner, and others.
Ace, 1991, 352 pp. (0-441-18481-2)
(BL 87:1458, 1461; VOYA 14:113)

SNICKET, Lemony (Daniel Handler). *The Bad Beginning.*
See Chapter 5, High Fantasy: Alternate Worlds or Histories.

SNYDER, Zilpha Keatley. *Black and Blue Magic.*
See Chapter 9, Magic Adventure Fantasy.

8-263 SOMMER-BODENBURG, Angela. *My Friend the Vampire.* **(Vampire series, bk. 1).** Gr. 3–5. (Orig. German pub. 1982.)
Nine-year-old Tony makes friends with Rudolf, the young vampire he finds on his window sill, but worries about keeping his parents and his new friend's family apart. The sequels are *The Vampire Moves In* (1984), *The Vampire Takes a Trip* (1985), *The Vampire on the Farm* (1989, 1990), and *The Vampire in Love* (1991).
Illus. by Amelie Glienke, Dial, 1984, 160 pp., LB (0-8037-0046-6)
(CCBB 38:56; HB 60:333; SLJ Aug 1984 p. 78)

SONENKLAR, Carol. *Bug Boy.*
See Chapter 9, Magic Adventure Fantasy.

SPEARING, Judith (Mary Harlow). *The Ghosts Who Went to School.*
See Chapter 4, Ghost Fantasy.

8-264 SPENCER, William Browning. *Zod Wallop.* Gr. 10 up.

☆ When fellow patients escape from the psychiatric institute, children's book author Harry Gainsborough begins to think that the dark fantasy he wrote has come to life.

Illus. by Bill Koeb, St. Martin's, 1995, 288 pp. (0-312-13629-3); White Wolf, 1997, pap., 310 pp. (1-56504-870-9)

(BL 92:386, 392; Kirkus 63:1377; LJ Oct 15, 1995 p. 91; VOYA 18:388)

8-265 SPINNER, Stephanie, and WEISS, Ellen. *Gerbilitis.* **(Weebie Zone series, bk. 1).** Gr. 2–4.

Garth is suddenly able to understand animal speech after his third-grade-class gerbil, Weebie, bites him. The sequels are *Sing, Elvis, Sing!* (1996), *Born to Be Wild* (1997), *Bright Lights, Little Gerbil* (1997), *The Bird Is the Word* (1997), and *We're Off to See the Lizard* (1998).

Illus. by Steve Björkman, HarperCollins, 1996, pap., 75 pp., o.p.

(BL 93:862; SLJ Nov 1996 p. 110)

8-266 SPURR, Elizabeth. *Mrs. Minetta's Car Pool.* Gr. 1–3.

Trips to school in Mrs. Minetta's car pool turn into fantastic adventures whenever the children fly off into the sky in her red convertible.

Illus. by Blanche Sims, Macmillan, 1985, 32 pp., o.p.

(BL 81:1463; CCBB 38:195; SLJ Sep 1985 p. 126)

STAHL, Ben(jamin). *Blackbeard's Ghost.*
See Chapter 4, Ghost Fantasy.

STASHEFF, Christopher. *Her Majesty's Wizard.*
See Chapter 7, High Fantasy: Travel to Other Worlds.

8-267 STEELE, William O(wen). *Andy Jackson's Water Well.* Gr. 4–6.

☆ Andy Jackson and Chief Ticklepitcher are traveling to East Tennessee to fetch a water well for drought-stricken Nashville, but Andy cannot control his temper.

Illus. by Michael Ramos, Harcourt, 1959, 80 pp., o.p.

(BL 55:426; Eakin:307; HB 35:214; Kirkus 27:224; LJ 84:1700)

8-268 STEELE, William O(wen). *Daniel Boone's Echo.* Gr. 3–5.

Daniel Boone helps Aaron Adamsale overcome his fear of the Sling-Tailed Galootis and the One-Horned Sumpple.

Illus. by Nicolas Mordvinoff, Harcourt, 1957, 79 pp., o.p.

(BL 54:146; HB 33:490; Kirkus 25:771; LJ 82:2976)

8-269 STEELE, William O(wen). *Davy Crockett's Earthquake.* Gr. 3–5.

☆ Davy Crockett meets up with a comet while out shooting bears in Tennessee.

Illus. by Nicolas Mordvinoff, Harcourt, 1956, 64 pp., o.p.

(BL 52:346; Eakin:308; HB 32:188; Kirkus 24:242; LJ 81:2045)

8-270 STEELE, William O(wen). *The No-Name Man of the Mountain.* Gr. 4–6.

☆ A young man outwits his trick-playing older brothers.

Illus. by Jack E. Davis, Harcourt, 1964, 79 pp., o.p.

(BL 61:805; CCBB 18:110; Eakin:308; HB 41:58; Kirkus 32:894; LJ 89:4642)

STEFANEC-OGREN, Cathy. *Sly, P.I.: The Case of the Missing Shoes.*
See Chapter 2, Animal Fantasy.

STERMAN, Betsy, and STERMAN, Samuel. *Backyard Dragon.*
See Chapter 9, Magic Adventure Fantasy.

STEVENSON, James. *Here Comes Herb's Hurricane!*
See Chapter 2, Animal Fantasy.

STEVENSON, James. *Oliver, Clarence, and Violet.*
See Chapter 2, Animal Fantasy.

STEVENSON, James. *The Supreme Souvenir Factory.*
See Chapter 2, Animal Fantasy.

STEWART, Jennifer J. *If That Breathes Fire, We're Toast!*
See Chapter 10, Time Travel Fantasy.

8-271 **STOCKTON, Frank (Francis) R(ichard).** *The Casting Away of Mrs. Lecks and Mrs. Aleshine.* Gr. 7 up. (Orig. pub. 1886; bound with its sequel, *The Dusantes*, 1888.)
The humorous adventures of two New England widows are related. The sequel is *The Dusantes*, 1888.
Illus. by George Richards, Appleton-Century, 1933, 290 pp., o.p.
(BL 30:23; Bookshelf 1933 p. 9; HB 9:155; LJ 58:804; Mahony 3:484)

STOLZ, Mary (Slattery). *Casebook of a Private (Cat's) Eye.*
See Chapter 2, Animal Fantasy.

STOLZ, Mary (Slattery). *Deputy Shep.*
See Chapter 2, Animal Fantasy.

STOLZ, Mary (Slattery). *Quentin Corn.*
See Chapter 2, Animal Fantasy.

STOLZ, Mary (Slattery). *Tales at the Mousehole.*
See Chapter 2, Animal Fantasy.

8-272 **STORR, Catherine (Cole).** *Clever Polly and the Stupid Wolf.* Gr. 3–5. (Orig. British pub. 1955; U.S. 1970, entitled *The Adventures of Polly and the Wolf.*)
In spite of the wolf's attempts to disguise himself as a fox and as Father Christmas, he never manages to capture Polly. The British sequels are *Polly and the Wolf Again* (1970) and *Tales of Polly and the Hungry Wolf* (1980).
Illus. by Marjorie-Ann Watts, Faber, 1979, 95 pp., o.p; Chivers (large-type ed.), 1992, 117 pp. (0-7451-1623-X)
(LJ 95:3054; SLJ Jan 1980 p. 62)

STRAUSS, Linda Leopold. *A Fairy Called Hilary.*
See Chapter 9, Magic Adventure Fantasy.

STRUGATSKII, Arkadii Natanovich, and **STRUGATSKII, Boris Natanovich.** *Monday Begins on Saturday.*
See Chapter 12, Witchcraft and Sorcery Fantasy.

8-273　**SWAYNE, Samuel,** and **SWAYNE, Zoa.** *Great Grandfather in the Honey*
☆　*Tree.* Gr. 1–4.
With one round of ammunition and a net, Great-Grandfather captures a bear, a fish, 24 geese, a partridge, a deer, 12 turkeys, and a barrel of wild honey.
Illus. by the authors, Viking, 1949, 54 pp., o.p.
(BL 46:86; CCBB 3:10; HB 25:411; Kirkus 17:465; LJ 74:1531, 75:51)

SWOPE, Sam. *Jack and the Seven Deadly Giants.*
See Chapter 5, High Fantasy: Alternate Worlds or Histories.

8-274　**TANNEN, Mary.** *Huntley Nutley and the Missing Link.* Gr. 4–6.
Huntley decides that the apelike creature he has found is an Australopithecus, or "missing link" between apes and humans, and discovers that the creature loves television and video games.
Illus. by Rob Sauber, Knopf, 1983, 121 pp., o.p.
(BL 79:1405; CCBB 36:219; Kirkus 51:525; SLJ Sep 1983 p. 128)

TAYLOR, L. A. *Cat's Paw.*
See Chapter 5, High Fantasy: Alternate Worlds or Histories.

8-275　**THOMPSON, Julian F(rancis).** *Hard Time.* Gr. 8 up.
In this satirical tale, a leprechaun inhabiting the body of ninth-grader Annie's Life Skills class doll encourages her to submit a controversial story to her high school's literary magazine, resulting in her banishment to a disciplinary wilderness school.
Atheneum, 2003, 256 pp. (0-689-85424-2)
(BL 100:746; Kirkus 71:1277; SLJ Jan 2004 p. 137; VOYA 26:419)

8-276　**THOMPSON, Julian F(rancis).** *Herb Seasoning.* Gr. 9–12.
Herbie Hertzman visits the Castles in the Air counseling agency after high school graduation, where he whirls a giant wheel of fortune and is transported into numerous zany situations as he investigates his possible destinies.
Scholastic, 1990, 272 pp., o.p., 1991, pap. (0-590-43024-6)
(BL 86:1792, 1794; CCBB 43:149; HBG 1:258; Kirkus 58:271; SLJ Mar 1990 p. 240; VOYA 13:111)

THURBER, James (Grover). *The Wonderful O.*
See Chapter 1, Allegorical Fantasy and Literary Fairy Tales.

TITUS, Eve. *Basil of Baker Street.*
See Chapter 2, Animal Fantasy.

8-277　**TODD, Barbara Euphan (pseud. of Barbara Euphan [Todd] Bower).**
Worzel Gummidge, the Scarecrow of Scatterbrook Farm. **(Worzel Gummidge series, bk. 1).** Gr. 3–6. (Orig. British titles: *Worzel Gummidge*, 1936, and *Worzel Gummidge Again*, 1937.)
Worzell Gummidge is a scarecrow who comes alive. The British sequels are *More About Worzel Gummidge* (1938), *Worzel Gummidge and Saucy Nancy*

(1947), *Worzel Gummidge Takes a Holiday* (1949), *Earthy Mangold and Worzel Gummidge* (1949), *Worzel Gummidge and the Railway Scarecrows* (1955), *Worzel Gummidge at the Circus* (1956), and *Worzel Gummidge and the Treasure Ship* (1958).
Illus. by Ursula Koering, Putnam, 1947, 200 pp., o.p.
(Kirkus 15:190; LJ 72:595)

TODD, Ruthven. *Space Cat.*
See Chapter 2, Animal Fantasy.

TOLLE, Jean Bashor. *The Great Pete Penney.*
See Chapter 9, Magic Adventure Fantasy.

TRAVERS, P(amela) L(yndon). *Mary Poppins.*
See Chapter 9, Magic Adventure Fantasy.

TUNNELL, Michael O. *Wishing Moon.*
See Chapter 6, High Fantasy: Myth or Legend Fantasy.

UPENSKY, Eduard. *Uncle Fedya, His Dog, and His Cat.*
See Chapter 9, Magic Adventure Fantasy.

VAN ALLSBURG, Chris. *The Sweetest Fig.*
See Chapter 1, Allegorical Fantasy and Literary Fairy Tales.

VANDE VELDE, Vivian. *The Rumpelstiltskin Problem.*
See Chapter 6, High Fantasy: Myth or Legend Fantasy.

8-278 VANDE VELDE, Vivian. *Smart Dog.* Gr. 4–6.
A talking dog named Sherlock escapes from an experimental laboratory and is taken in by a girl named Amy, who hides him from her parents, her teacher, and the local university.
Harcourt, 1998, 146 pp. (0-15-201847-6); Yearling, 2000, pap., 160 pp. (0-440-41610-8)
(BL 95:121; CCBB 52:114; HB 74:743; HBG 10:76; Kirkus 66:1294; SLJ Nov 1998 p. 131)

VANDE VELDE, Vivian. *Tales from the Brothers Grimm and the Sisters Weird.*
See Chapter 6, High Fantasy: Myth or Legend Fantasy.

VANDE VELDE, Vivian. *Witch's Wishes.*
See Chapter 9, Magic Adventure Fantasy.

VANDE VELDE, Vivian. *Wizard at Work: A Novel in Stories.*
See Chapter 12, Witchcraft and Sorcery Fantasy.

VAN LEEUWEN, Jean. *The Great Christmas Kidnapping Caper.*
See Chapter 2, Animal Fantasy.

8-279 VAN STOCKUM, Hilda (Gerarda). *Kersti and Saint Nicholas.* Gr. 2–5.
Naughty Kersti convinces St. Nicholas to leave gifts for the bad children instead of the good ones.

Illus. by the author, Viking, 1940, 72 pp., o.p.
(BL 37:328; HB 16:435; LJ 65:849, 928)

8-280 VASILIU, Mircea. *Hark, the Little Angel.* Gr. 2–4.
A mischievous little angel spends a few days on Earth disguised as a little boy.
Illus. by the author, Day, 1965, 48 pp., o.p.
(CCBB 19:71; Kirkus 33:979; LJ 90:4530)

8-281 VAUGHAN, Agnes Carr. *Lucian Goes A-Voyaging.* Gr. 3–5.
These tall tales, in a similar vein to Baron Münchausen's tales (see this chapter), are adapted from the Greek of Lucian.
Illus. by Harrie Wood, Knopf, 1930, 139 pp., o.p.
(BL 27:68; HB 6:127–130, 146, 7:117; LJ 55:465; Mahony 3:213; TLS 1930 p. 717)

VENOKUR, Ross. *The Amazing Frecktacle.*
See Chapter 9, Magic Adventure Fantasy.

VENOKUR, Ross. *The Cookie Company.*
See Chapter 7, High Fantasy: Travel to Other Worlds.

WABER, Bernard. *Dear Hildegarde.*
See Chapter 2, Animal Fantasy.

WABER, Bernard. *Mice on My Mind.*
See Chapter 2, Animal Fantasy.

WAECHTER, Friedrich, and EILERT, Bernd. *The Crown Snatchers.*
See Chapter 1, Allegorical Fantasy and Literary Fairy Tales.

WAGENER, Gerda. *The Ghost in the Classroom.*
See Chapter 4, Ghost Fantasy.

WALKER, Kenneth Macfarlane, and BOUMPHREY, Geoffrey. *The Log of the Ark.*
See Chapter 6, High Fantasy: Myth or Legend Fantasy.

WALLACE, Barbara Brooks. *Miss Switch to the Rescue.*
See Chapter 12, Witchcraft and Sorcery Fantasy.

Wandering Stars: An Anthology of Jewish Fantasy and Science Fiction.
Ed. by Jack Dann.
See Chapter 3, Fantasy Collections.

WATKINS, Will. *Sid Seal, Houseman.*
See Chapter 2, Animal Fantasy.

WATT-EVANS, Lawrence (pseud. of Richard Watt Evans). *Crosstime Traffic.*
See Chapter 3, Fantasy Collections.

WATT-EVANS, Lawrence (pseud. of Richard Watt Evans), and FRIES-NER, Esther M. *Split Heirs.*
See Chapter 5, High Fantasy: Alternate Worlds or Histories.

WEALES, Gerald (Clifford). *Miss Grimsbee Is a Witch.*
See Chapter 12, Witchcraft and Sorcery Fantasy.

8-282 **WEAVER, Jack.** *Mr. O'Hara.* Gr. 4–6.
Mr. O'Hara entertains the customers in his general store with tall tales about his life in Ireland.
Illus. by the author, Viking, 1953, 160 pp., o.p.
(CCBB 7:34; HB 29:221; Kirkus 21:115; LJ 78:705)

8-283 **WEISS, Ellen, and FRIEDMAN, Mel.** *The Adventures of Ratman.* Gr. 2–5.
Eight-year-old Tod dons his new rat costume and is instantaneously transformed into the comic book-style superhero Ratman, who rescues neighbors from danger before his powers disappear.
Illus. by Dirk Zimmer, Random, 1990, 64 pp., o.p.
(BL 86:2183; CCBB 44:18; HBG 2:68)

8-284 **WERSBA, Barbara.** *The Brave Balloon of Benjamin Buckley.* Gr. 2–4.
✶ Benjamin and his cat stow away aboard a hot-air balloon.
Illus. by Margot Jones, Atheneum, 1963, 66 pp., o.p.
(BL 60:632; CCBB 17:102; HB 39:500; LJ 88:122)

WHITCHER, Susan. *Real Mummies Don't Bleed: Friendly Tales for October Nights.*
See Chapter 3, Fantasy Collections.

WHITE, Anne Hitchcock. *Junket.*
See Chapter 2, Animal Fantasy.

WHITE, Anne Hitchcock. *The Story of Serapina.*
See Chapter 2, Animal Fantasy.

WHITE, E(lwyn) B(rooks). *Stuart Little.*
See Chapter 2, Animal Fantasy.

WHITE, E(lwyn) B(rooks). *The Trumpet of the Swan.*
See Chapter 2, Animal Fantasy.

8-285 **WHYBROW, Ian.** *Little Wolf's Book of Badness.* **(Little Wolf series, bk.**
✶ **1).** Gr. 3–5.
Little Wolf's family sends him to Cunning College for badness lessons from the nastiest wolf of all, Uncle Bigbad, but Little Wolf has other ideas. The sequels are *Little Wolf's Diary of Daring Deeds* (2000), *Little Wolf's Haunted Hall for Small Horrors* (2000), *Little Wolf's Postbag* (2000), *Dear Little Wolf* (2000, 2002), *Little Wolf, Forest Detective* (2001), *Little Wolf's Big Book of Badness and Daring Deeds* (2001), *Little Wolf's Handy Book of Poems* (2002), *Little Wolf, Pack Leader* (2002), *Little Wolf's Big Book of Spooks and Clues* (2002), *Little Wolf: Terror of the Shivery Sea* (2004), and *Badness for Beginners* (2005).
Illus. by Tony Ross, Carolrhoda, 1999, 130 pp. (1-57505-410-8), 2001, pap., 132 pp. (1-57505-550-3)
(HB 76:86; HBG 11:90; Kirkus 67:1585; SLJ Nov 1999 p. 132)

8-286 WIBBERLEY, Leonard (Patrick O'Connor). *McGillicuddy McGotham.*
Gr. 4–6.
Timothy Patrick Fegus Kevin Sean Desmond McGillicuddy is the first lep-
rechaun diplomat posted to America.
Illus. by Aldren A. Watson, Little, Brown, 1956, 111 pp., o.p.
(BL 52:312; Kirkus 24:55; LJ 81:833)

8-287 WIBBERLEY, Leonard (Patrick O'Connor). *The Mouse That Roared.*
☆ **(The Grand Fenwick series, bk. 2).** Gr. 7 up.
Attempting to revive its national economy, the tiny duchy of Grand Fenwick
declares war on the United States, hoping for a quick defeat and large war repa-
rations, but its 23 longbowmen not only win the war, they capture the top secret
Q-Bomb! The prequel is *Beware of the Mouse* (1958), and the sequels are *The
Mouse on the Moon* (1962), *The Mouse on Wall Street* (1969), and *The Mouse
That Saved the West* (Morrow, 1981).
Little, Brown, 1955, 279 pp., o.p.; Scholastic, 1998, pap. (0-590-03438-3);
Four Walls, 2003, pap., 280 pp. (1-568-58249-8)
(BL 51:190, 83:1593; Kirkus 22:788; LJ 79:1506)

WIBBERLEY, Leonard (Patrick O'Connor). *The Quest of Excalibur.*
See Chapter 4, Ghost Fantasy.

8-288 WIEMER, Rudolf Otto. *The Good Robber, Willibald.* Gr. 2–4. (Orig. Ger-
man pub. 1965.)
Willibald the robber steps out of Manni's storybook, ready for trouble.
Trans. by Barbara Kowall Gollob, illus. by Marie Marcks, Atheneum, 1968, 65
pp., o.p.
(CCBB 21:167; Kirkus 36:181; TLS 1969 p. 699)

WILKINS (Freeman), Mary E(leanor). *The Pumpkin Giant.*
See Chapter 1, Allegorical Fantasy and Literary Fairy Tales.

WILLARD, Barbara. *Spell Me a Witch.*
See Chapter 12, Witchcraft and Sorcery Fantasy.

WILLARD, Nancy (Margaret). *The Marzipan Moon.*
See Chapter 1, Allegorical Fantasy and Literary Fairy Tales.

WILLEY, Elizabeth. *The Well-Favored Man: The Tale of the Sorcerer's
Nephew.*
See Chapter 5, High Fantasy: Alternate Worlds or Histories.

WILLIAMS, Jay. *The Practical Princess and Other Liberating Fairy
Tales.*
See Chapter 3, Fantasy Collections.

8-289 WILLIAMS (John), Ursula Moray. *The Cruise of the Happy-Go-Gay.* Gr.
☆ 3–5. (Orig. British pub. 1967.)
Aunt Hegarty and her five nieces sail off in search of buried treasure.
Illus. by Gunvor Edwards, Meredith, 1968, 151 pp., o.p.
(BL 64:1046; CCBB 22:87; HB 44:424; Kirkus 35:1474; LJ 93:298; Suth:424)

WILLIAMS (John), Ursula Moray. *The Nine Lives of Island Mackenzie.*
See Chapter 2, Animal Fantasy.

8-290 **WILLIAMS (John), Ursula Moray.** *Tiger Nanny.* Gr. 4–6. (Orig. British
pub. 1964, entitled *Johnnie Tiger-Skin.*)
A tiger cub becomes the perfect nanny for the Harper children,
Illus. by Gunvor Edwards, Nelson, 1974, 128 pp., o.p.
(CCBB 28:140; HB 51:151; Kirkus 42:805; SLJ Jan 1975 p. 42)

WILLIS, Connie. *To Say Nothing of the Dog; or, How We Found the
Bishop's Bird Stump at Last.*
See Chapter 10, Time Travel Fantasy.

WILSON, A. N. *Hazel the Guinea Pig.*
See Chapter 2, Animal Fantasy.

WILSON, Gahan. *Harry, the Fat Bear Spy.*
See Chapter 2, Animal Fantasy.

WINDSOR, Patricia (Frances). *How a Weirdo and a Ghost Can Change
Your Entire Life.*
See Chapter 4, Ghost Fantasy.

WINTHROP (Mahony), Elizabeth. *The Red-Hot Rattoons.*
See Chapter 2, Animal Fantasy.

8-291 *With Cap and Bells: Humorous Stories to Tell and to Read Aloud.* **Ed. by
Mary Gould Davis.** Gr. 4–6.
This collection includes humorous tales by Carl Sandburg, Frank R. Stockton,
Mary Eleanor Wilkins, and others.
Illus. by Richard Bennett, Harcourt, 1937, 246 pp., o.p.
(BL 34:12; HB 13:286; LJ 62:782)

8-292 **WOOD, James Playsted.** *An Elephant in the Family.* Gr. 2–4.
Three children and their parents adopt a talking elephant. The sequels are *The
Elephant in the Barn* (Harper, 1961), *The Elephant on Ice* (Seabury, 1965), and
The Elephant Tells (Reilly, 1968).
Illus. by Kurt Werth, Nelson, 1957, 64 pp., o.p.
(CCBB 11:32; HB 33:223; LJ 82:1803)

8-293 **WORK, Rhoda O.** *Mr. Dawson Had a Farm.* Gr. 1–4.
✫ A lazy farmer gets himself into humorous predicaments. The sequels are *Mr.
Dawson Had an Elephant* (1959) and *Mr. Dawson Had a Lamb* (1963).
Illus. by Dorothy Maas, Bobbs-Merrill, 1951, 131 pp., o.p.
(BL 47:386; CCBB 4:47; HB 27:247; LJ 76:880)

WREDE, Patricia C(ollins). *Book of Enchantments.*
See Chapter 3, Fantasy Collections.

WREDE, Patricia C(ollins). *Dealing with Dragons.*
See Chapter 5, High Fantasy: Alternate Worlds or Histories.

WREDE, Patricia C(ollins). *Mairelon the Magician.*
See Chapter 5, High Fantasy: Alternate Worlds or Histories.

WREDE, Patricia C(ollins), and STEVERMER, Caroline. *Sorcery and Cecilia.*
See Chapter 5, High Fantasy: Alternate Worlds or Histories.

WRIGHT, Betty Ren. *The Ghost of Ernie P.*
See Chapter 4, Ghost Fantasy.

WRIGHT, T. M. *Goodlow's Ghosts.*
See Chapter 4, Ghost Fantasy.

WRIGHTSON, (Alice) Patricia (Furlonger). *An Older Kind of Magic.*
See Chapter 9, Magic Adventure Fantasy.

WYSS, Thelma Hatch. *A Stranger Here.*
See Chapter 4, Ghost Fantasy.

YEP, Laurence M(ichael). *The Curse of the Squirrel.*
See Chapter 2, Animal Fantasy.

YEP, Laurence M(ichael). *The Imp That Ate My Homework.*
See Chapter 9, Magic Adventure Fantasy.

YOLEN (Stemple), Jane (Hyatt). *The Acorn Quest.*
See Chapter 2, Animal Fantasy.

8-294 **YOLEN (Stemple), Jane (Hyatt).** *Boots and the Seven Leaguers: A Rock-*
☆ *and-Troll Novel.* Gr. 6–8.
After trolls Gog and Pooka are hired as roadies for their favorite rock group, Boots and the Seven Leaguers, they discover that Gog's little brother has been kidnapped.
Harcourt, 2000, 192 pp. (0-15-202557-X), 2003, pap., 159 pp. (0-15-202563-4)
(BL 97:526; Kliatt Sep 2003 p. 29; SLJ Oct 2000 p. 175; VOYA 23:365, 24:15)

8-295 **YOLEN (Stemple), Jane (Hyatt).** *The Giants' Farm.* Gr. 1–4.
Five humorous stories are told about the giants who run Fe-Fi-Fo-Farm: Grizzle, Stout, Grab, Grub, and Dab. The sequel is *The Giants Go Camping* (1979).
Illus. by Tomie de Paola, Houghton, 1977, 48 pp., o.p.
(BL 74:382; Kirkus 45:849; SLJ Dec 1977 p. 57)

YOLEN (Stemple), Jane (Hyatt). *Hobo Toad and the Motorcycle Gang.*
See Chapter 2, Animal Fantasy.

YOLEN (Stemple), Jane (Hyatt). *Piggins.*
See Chapter 2, Animal Fantasy.

8-296 **YOLEN (Stemple), Jane (Hyatt).** *Sleeping Ugly.* Gr. 1–3.
☆ A beautiful but nasty princess named Miserella gets her comeuppance when Prince Charming's kisses awaken homely but virtuous Plain Jane and he forgets all about sleeping Miserella.

Illus. by Diane Stanley, Putnam, 1981, 64 pp., o.p.; Putnam, 1997, pap., 64 pp. (0-698-11560-0)
(BL 78:656; CCBB 35:99; Kirkus 49:1158; SLJ Dec 1981 p. 75; Suth 3:467)

YOLEN (Stemple), Jane (Hyatt). *Wizard's Hall.*
See Chapter 12, Witchcraft and Sorcery Fantasy.

8-297 **YORK, Carol Beach.** *Pudmuddles.* Gr. 2–4.
The Pudmuddle family does everything backward, including bathing fully clothed and eating breakfast at night and dinner in the morning.
Harper, 1993, 44 pp. (0-06-020436-2)
(BL 89:1435; HBG 4:292; Kirkus 61:606; SLJ May 1993 p. 92)

YOUNG, Robert F. *The Vizier's Second Daughter.*
See Chapter 6, High Fantasy: Myth or Legend Fantasy.

ZELAZNY, Roger (Joseph Christopher), and SHECKLEY, Robert. *If at Faust You Don't Succeed.*
See Chapter 10, Time Travel Fantasy.

ZEMACH, Harve(y Fischtrom). *The Tricks of Master Dabble.*
See Chapter 1, Allegorical Fantasy and Literary Fairy Tales.

9

Magic Adventure Fantasy

The majority of the books in this chapter are about ordinary people who gain magical powers or come in contact with magical objects, creatures, or events. A lighthearted tone usually prevails in this type of fantasy. Most tales involving extrasensory perception (ESP) or the occult have been excluded from this guide.

9-1   **ADLER, C(arole) S(chwerdtfeger).** *Eddie's Blue-Winged Dragon.* Gr. 4–7.
Eddie's angry longing for revenge against the school bully who taunts him because he has cerebral palsy brings a glass dragon to life to fight Eddie's battle with fire.
Putnam, 1988, 144 pp., o.p.
(BL 85:704; Kirkus 56:1399; SLJ Jan 1989, p. 72; Suth 4:2)

9-2   **AHLBERG, Allan.** *Ten in a Bed.* Gr. 3–6. (Orig. British pub. 1983.)
★   Every night, Dinah Price finds her bed occupied by a new fairy-tale character, none of whom will let her go to sleep.
Illus. by André Amstutz, Viking, 1989, 95 pp. (0-670-82042-3); Puffin, 1991, pap. (0-14-032531-X)
(BL 86:446; CCBB 43:25; HBG 1:82; Kirkus 57:1153; Suth 4:4)

AHLBERG, Janet. *Jeremiah in the Dark Woods.*
See Chapter 8, Humorous Fantasy.

AIKEN, Joan (Delano). *The Faithless Lollybird.*
See Chapter 3, Fantasy Collections.

AIKEN, Joan (Delano). *Smoke from Cromwell's Time and Other Stories.*
See Chapter 3, Fantasy Collections.

AIKEN, Joan (Delano). *Up the Chimney Down and Other Stories.*
See Chapter 8, Humorous Fantasy.

9-3 **ALCOCK, Vivien (Dolores).** *The Monster Garden.* Gr. 5–9. (Orig. British
★ pub. 1988.)
When the experimental cell-matter she stole from her father's laboratory grows
into a monster, Frankie tries to hide it from her family. Carnegie Medal Commended Book, 1988.
Delacorte, 1988, 144 pp., o.p.; Houghton, 2000, pap., 176 pp. (0-618-00337-1)
(BL 85:263; CCBB 42:24; HB 64:781; Kirkus 56:1235; SLJ Oct 1988 p. 138; Suth 4:6; TLS
1988 p. 433; VOYA 11:292, 12:15)

ALCOCK, Vivien (Dolores). *The Stonewalkers.*
See Chapter 6, High Fantasy: Myth or Legend Fantasy.

ALLEN, Judy. *The Spring on the Mountain.*
See Chapter 1, Allegorical Fantasy and Literary Fairy Tales.

ALMOND, David. *Skellig.*
See Chapter 6, High Fantasy: Myth or Legend Fantasy.

ALTON, Steve. *The Malifex.*
See Chapter 6, High Fantasy: Myth or Legend Fantasy.

9-4 **AMATO, Mary.** *The Word Eater.* Gr. 4–6.
Sixth-grader Lerner Chanse discovers that whenever a paper-eating worm
named Flip eats a word from a book, the object disappears in real life.
Illus. by Christopher Ryniak, Holiday, 2000, 151 pp. (0-8234-1468-X)
(BL 97:437; CCBB 54:5; HBG 12:68; Kirkus 68:790; SLJ Oct 2000 p. 155)

9-5 **ANCKARSVÄRD, Karin (Inez Maria).** *Bonifacius the Green.* Gr. 3–5.
(Orig. Swedish pub. 1952.)
Bonifacius the dragon helps children to gain self-confidence.
Trans. by C. M. Anckarsvärd and K. H. Beales, illus. by Ingrid Rossell,
Abelard-Schuman, 1961, 95 pp., o.p.
(HB 38:314; Kirkus 30:7; LJ 87:1314; TLS Dec 4, 1961 p. vii)

9-6 **ANDERSON, Janet S.** *Going Through the Gate.* Gr. 4–7.
★ The five sixth-graders graduating from Miss Clough's one-room school know
that something special always happens at the "going through the gate" ceremony, but none can imagine how their lives will change.
Dutton, 1997, 133 pp. (0-525-45836-0); Puffin, 2000, pap., 144 pp. (0-14-
130698-X)
(BL 94:1010; CCBB 51:191; HBG 9:66; Kirkus 65:1106; SLJ Nov 1997 p. 114)

9-7 **ANDERSON, Joy.** *Juma and the Magic Jinn.* Gr. 2–4.
★ Hoping to solve his problems at school, Juma calls up his family's magic jinn,
who grants his wishes in unexpected ways.
Illus. by Charles Mikolaycak, Lothrop, 1986, 32 pp., LB (0-688-05444-7)
(BL 83:266; HB 62:729; Kirkus 54:1123; SLJ Dec 1986 p. 78)

9-8 **ANDERSON, M. T.** *The Game of Sunken Places.* Gr. 5–9.
An enchanted board game at his eccentric Uncle Max's Vermont house draws
Gregory and his friend Brian into a dangerous adventure battling trolls and
ogres and discovering secret underground cities.

Scholastic, 2004, 272 pp. (0-439-41660-4), 2005, pap. (0-439-41661-2)

(BL 100:1452; CCBB 58:5; Kirkus 72:575; SLJ Sep 2004 p. 198; VOYA 27:139)

ANDREWS, Frank (Emerson). *The Upside-Down Town.*
See Chapter 8, Humorous Fantasy.

9-9 **ANGELL, Judie.** *The Weird Disappearance of Jordan Hall.* Gr. 5–8.
Hired as an assistant in his girlfriend's father's magic shop, Jordan Hall follows a black cat into the "disappearing box" and becomes invisible.
Watts, 1987, 121 pp., o.p.

(BL 84:52, 57; HB 64:61; SLJ Nov 1987 p. 102)

9-10 **ANSA, Tina McElroy.** *Baby of the Family.* Gr. 10 up.
Lena, born with a caul—or membrane—over her face, has the ability to predict the future in this story about a loving African American family in rural Georgia.
Harcourt, 1989, 263 pp., o.p.

(BL 86:524, 539, 994; Kirkus 57:1265; SLJ June 1990 p. 144)

ARDAGH, Philip. *A House Called Awful End.*
See Chapter 8, Humorous Fantasy.

9-11 **ARNOLD, Tim.** *The Winter Mittens.* Gr. 2–4.
Addie's magic mittens make it snow whenever she wears them; when she can't take them off on Christmas Day, a blizzard threatens to bury the town.
Illus. by the author, Macmillan, 1988, 32 pp., o.p.

(BL 85:704; HB 64:761; Kirkus 56:1463; SLJ Jan 1989 p. 58)

9-12 **ASIMOV, Isaac.** *Azazel.* Gr. 10 up.
A tiny demon named Azazel grants George a number of wishes in these short stories.
Doubleday, 1988, 216 pp., o.p.

(BL 85:367; Kirkus 56:1364; LJ Nov 15, 1988 p. 88; VOYA 12:39, 13:138)

ASKOUNIS, Christina. *The Dream of the Stone.*
See Chapter 7, High Fantasy: Travel to Other Worlds.

9-13 **AUGARDE, Steve.** *The Various.* **(The Various series, bk. 1).** Gr. 5–8.
(Orig. British pub. 2003.)
Twelve-year-old Midge becomes the focus of the anger of the knee-high Various at human encroachment on their English forest refuge. Nestlé Smarties Book Prize, Bronze Award, 2003. The British sequel is *Celandine* (2005).
Random, 2004, 448 pp. (0-385-75037-4)

(BL 100:750; CCBB 57:361; Kirkus 71:1357; SLJ Mar 2004 p. 203; VOYA 27:312)

AVI (Avi Wortis). *Tom, Babette, and Simon: Three Tales of Transformation.*
See Chapter 1, Allegorical Fantasy and Literary Fairy Tales.

BABBITT, Natalie (Zane Moore). *Tuck Everlasting.*
See Chapter 6, High Fantasy: Myth or Legend Fantasy.

9-14 BABCOCK (Thompson), Betty (Elizabeth S.). *The Expandable Pig.* Gr. 3–5.
Pig suddenly expands like a balloon and takes Gary and his three dogs on a trip to England.
Illus. by the author, Scribner, 1949, 114 pp., o.p.
(CCBB 2:1; HB 25:410, 436; Kirkus 17:323; LJ 74:1541, 1760)

BACON, Martha (Sherman). *The Third Road.*
See Chapter 10, Time Travel Fantasy.

BACON, Peggy. *The Ghost of Opalina, or Nine Lives.*
See Chapter 4, Ghost Fantasy.

9-15 BACON, Peggy. *The Magic Touch.* Gr. 3–4.
Recipes from a witch's cookbook transform Ben, Esther, and Ted into animals.
Illus. by the author, Little, Brown, 1968, 112 pp., o.p.
(BL 63:183; HB 44:556; Kirkus 36:690; LJ 94:292)

BAEHR, Patricia. *The Search for Happily-Ever-After.*
See Chapter 7, High Fantasy: Travel to Other Worlds.

9-16 BAKER, Margaret. *Patsy and the Leprechauns.* Gr. 2–4. (Orig. British pub. 1932.)
Patsy decides that the quickest way to make money is to steal a leprechaun's gold.
Illus. by Mary Baker, Duffield, 1933, 109 pp., o.p.
(BL 29:208; Bookshelf 1933 p. 6; LJ 58:710; Mahony 3:103; TLS 1932 p. 894)

9-17 BAKER, Margaret. *Pollie Who Did as She Was Told.* Gr. 3–4.
Pollie accidentally washes out all of the magic potion-containing bottles when she tidies up the Wise Woman's house.
Illus. by Mary Baker, Dodd, 1934, 100 pp., o.p.
(LJ 60:304; Mahony 3:104; TLS 1934 p. 838)

9-18 BAKER, Margaret. *The Water Elf and the Miller's Child.* Gr. 2–4.
A mischievous young water elf plays tricks on the frogs, cranes, and fish living at the mill pond.
Illus. by Mary Baker, Duffield, 1928, 84 pp., o.p.
(BL 25:126; HB 4[Nov 1928]:76; Mahony 2:131)

BAKER, Margaret Joyce. *Homer the Tortoise.*
See Chapter 2, Animal Fantasy.

9-19 BAKER, Margaret Joyce. *The Magic Sea Shell.* Gr. 3–5. (Orig. British pub. 1959.)
Three children find a magic sea shell and meet a wish-granting mermaid.
Illus. by Susan Elson, Holt, 1960, 122 pp., o.p.
(Kirkus 28:6, LJ 85:2033; TLS Dec 4, 1959 p. xxii)

9-20 BAKER, Margaret Joyce. *Porterhouse Major.* Gr. 4–6. (Orig. British pub. 1967.)

Rory uses her mother's magic books to create a gigantic cat named Porterhouse.

Illus. by Shirley Hughes, Prentice-Hall, 1967, 116 pp., o.p.

(CCBB 21:105, 121; Suth:26; TLS 1967 p. 451)

9-21 **BAKER, Olaf.** *Bengey and the Beast.* Gr. 5–7.
Bengey uses magic to destroy the horrible Gunderbust.
Illus. by Victor J. Dowling, Dodd, 1947, 243 pp., o.p.
(BL 43:260; HB 23:212; LJ 72:466, 597)

9-22 **BALL, Duncan.** *Emily Eyefinger.* (**Emily Eyefinger series, bk. 1**). Gr. 2–4.
Emily was born with an extra eye on the end of her left index finger, which comes in handy against a school bully and a bank robber. The sequels are *Emily Eyefinger, Secret Agent* (1993) and *Emily Eyefinger and the Lost Treasure* (1994).
Illus. by George Ulrich, Simon & Schuster, 1992, 82 pp. (0-671-74618-9)
(BL 88:1599; HBG 3:253; SLJ July 1992, p. 56)

9-23 **BANKS, Lynne Reid.** *The Fairy Rebel.* Gr. 5–6. (Orig. British pub. 1985.)
The queen of the fairies is angered when Tiki uses her fairy powers to help a human couple, Jan and Charles, have a baby.
Illus. by William Geldart, Doubleday, 1988, 125 pp., o.p.; Delacorte, 2003, 119 pp. (0-385-90116-X); Yearling, 2004, pap., 128 pp. (0-440-41925-5)
(BL 85:642; HBG 15:87; Kirkus 56:1319; SLJ Oct 1988 p. 143)

9-24 **BANKS, Lynne Reid.** *The Indian in the Cupboard.* (**The Indian in the**
☆ **Cupboard series, bk. 1**). Gr. 4–7. (Orig. British pub. 1980.)
An old wall cupboard turns Patrick and Omri's toy cowboy and Indian into miniature people named Boone and Little Bear, who immediately begin to fight. In *The Return of the Indian* (1986), Omri and Patrick reinstitute the magic after Little Bear is gravely wounded in the French and Indian Wars. In *The Secret of the Indian* (1989, 1990), Patrick uses the key to the magic cupboard to travel back in time to the Old West, but accidentally brings back a tornado to present-day England. In *The Mystery of the Cupboard* (1993), Omri uncovers the connection between the cupboard's magical origins and his family's tragic history. In *The Key to the Indian* (1998), Omri and his father make a dangerous trip back through time to help Little Bear's 18th-century Iroquois family. The first book in this series has been criticized for its stereotypical representation of the Native American characters.
Illus. by Brock Cole, Doubleday, 1981, 1985, 181 pp. (0-385-17051-3); Avon, 1982, pap. (0-380-60012-9); HarperCollins, 1991 (0-00-330247-4); HarperTrophy, 1995, pap., 208 pp. (0-380-72568-4)
(CCBB 35:22; HB 57:662; SLJ Dec 1981 p. 59; TLS 1980 p. 1326)

9-25 **BANKS, Lynne Reid.** *Maura's Angel.* Gr. 4–7. (Orig. British pub. 1977.)
Maura helps her mother care for their Belfast family while Da is away fighting with the IRA, and when a fallen angel named Angela joins their household, Maura takes on the task of teaching her how to be human.
Avon, 1998, 150 pp. (0-380-97590-4)
(HBG 9:325; Kirkus 66:734; SLJ Aug 1998 p. 160)

BARRIE, Sir J(ames) M(atthew). *Peter Pan.*
See Chapter 7, High Fantasy: Travel to Other Worlds.

9-26 BARRY, Dave, and PEARSON, Ridley. *Peter and the Starcatchers.* Gr. 5–8.
In this prequel to J. M. Barrie's *Peter Pan* (1904; 1911; see Chapter 7, High Fantasy: Travel to Other Worlds), a group of orphaned boys and their leader, Peter, battle Black Stache the pirate for a mysterious substance that allows people to fly, while a young Starcatcher named Molly Aster tries to protect the precious "starstuff."
Hyperion, 2004, 442 pp. (0-7868-5445-6)
(BL 101:121; CCBB 58:113; HB 80:578; Kirkus 72:737; SLJ Oct 2004 p. 154;)

BARZINI, Luigi (Giorgio, Jr.). *The Little Match Man.*
See Chapter 11, Toy Fantasy.

BATTLES, Edith. *The Witch in Room 6.*
See Chapter 12, Witchcraft and Sorcery Fantasy.

BAUER, Joan. *Thwonk.*
See Chapter 8, Humorous Fantasy.

9-27 BAUER, Marion Dane. *Touch the Moon.* Gr. 4–6.
★   Jennifer's tiny china horse turns into Moonseeker, a talking palomino stallion who teaches her how to ride as she teaches him courage.
Illus. by Alix Berenzy, Houghton, 1987, 96 pp., o.p.
(BL 84:144; CCBB 41:2; HB 63:608; Kirkus 55:1388; SLJ Nov 1987 p. 102)

BAUM, L(yman) Frank. *Sky Island: Being the Further Adventrues of Trot and Cap'n Bill After Their Visits to the Sea Fairies.*
See Chapter 7, High Fantasy: Travel to Other Worlds.

BEACHCROFT, Nina. *Well Met by Witchlight.*
See Chapter 12, Witchcraft and Sorcery Fantasy.

9-28 BEACHCROFT, Nina. *The Wishing People.* Gr. 4–6. (Orig. British pub. 1980.)
Released from a spell that imprisoned them inside a barometer, Tom and Mrs. Tom grant ten wishes to Martha and her friend Jonathan.
Dutton, 1982, 181 pp., o.p.
(BL 78:954; Kirkus 50:553; SLJ Apr 1982 p. 65)

BEAGLE, Peter S(oyer). *A Dance for Emilia.*
See Chapter 4, Ghost Fantasy.

BEATON-JONES, Cynon. *The Adventures of So Hi.*
See Chapter 7, High Fantasy: Travel to Other Worlds.

9-29 BECKER, Eve. *Thirteen Means Magic.* **(Abracadabra series, bk. 1).** Gr. 5–7.
On her 13th birthday, Dawn discovers that if she arches her left eyebrow, she can cause magical events to occur. The sequels are *The Love Potion* (1989),

The Magic Mix-Up (1989), *The Sneezing Spell* (1989), *Too Much Magic* (1990), and *The Popularity Potion* (1990).
Bantam, 1989, pap., 144 pp., o.p.
(BL 86:839; SLJ Nov 1989 p. 125)

9-30   BECKHORN, Susan Williams. *The Kingfisher's Gift.* Gr. 5–7.
When Franny Morrow goes to live with her grandmother after her father's death, she is accompanied by two fairies and a water sprite searching for a long-lost treasure.
Philomel, 2002, 182 pp. (0-399-23712-7)
(BL 98:1418; HBG 13:367; Kirkus 70:562; SLJ July 2002 p. 113)

BEDARD, Michael. *A Darker Magic.*
See Chapter 12, Witchcraft and Sorcery Fantasy.

9-31   BELDEN, Wilianne Schneider. *Frankie!* Gr. 4–6.
All of the O'Rileys have magical powers, but Frankie also happens to be a griffin.
Illus. by Stewart Daniels, Harcourt, 1987, 163 pp., o.p.
(SLJ Dec 1987 p. 83; VOYA 11:36)

9-32   BELL, Hilari. *Songs of Power.* Gr. 5–8.
In this science-fantasy, Annis, trained in magic by her Inuit grandmother, is the only one who understands that the problems on her scientist parents' undersea station are being caused by magic.
Hyperion, 2000, 224 pp. (0-7868-2487-5)
(CCBB 53:270; HBG 11:300; Kirkus 68:710; Kliatt May 2000 p. 5; SLJ May 2000 p. 166)

9-33   BELL, Thelma Harrington. *Take It Easy.* Gr. 5–7.
An invisible genie comes forth each time 13-year-old Margie rubs her brass elephant.
Illus. by Corydon Bell, Viking, 1953, 172 pp., o.p.
(Kirkus 21:428; LJ 78:2042)

BELLAIRS, John. *The Curse of the Blue Figurine.*
See Chapter 12, Witchcraft and Sorcery Fantasy.

9-34   BELLAIRS, John. *The Dark Secret of Weatherend.* **(Anthony Munday**
★   **series, bk. 2).** Gr. 5–8.
Anthony suspects that the exceptionally harsh Minnesota winter has been caused by J. K. Borkman, a dead millionaire who once plotted to destroy the world. This is the sequel to *The Treasure of Alpheus Winterborn* (1978, 1997) and is followed by *The Lamp from the Warlock's Tomb* (1988, 1999) and *The Mansion in the Mist* (1992, 1995).
Dial, 1984, 182 pp. (0-8037-0072-5); Bantam, 1986, pap. (0-553-15375-7); Puffin, 1997, pap., 182 pp. (0-14-038006-X)
(BL 80:1186; HB 60:326; Kirkus 52:J36; SLJ May 1984 p. 103; VOYA 8:46)

BELLAIRS, John. *The House with the Clock in Its Walls.*
See Chapter 4, Ghost Fantasy.

9-35　**BENCHLEY, Nathaniel (Goddard).** *The Magic Sled.* **(British title:** *The Magic Sledge***).** Gr. 3–5.
No snow for his new sled? Fred finds that magic can make more snow than he ever dreamed of.
Illus. by Mel Furukawa, Harper, 1972, 44 pp., o.p.
(BL 68:1002; CCBB 25:134; Kirkus 40:68; LJ 97:1593)

BENDICK, Jeanne. *The Goodknight Ghost.*
See Chapter 4, Ghost Fantasy.

9-36　**BENNETT, Rodney.** *Eagle Boy.* Gr. 6–9. (Orig. British pub. 1986.)
Abandoned by his parents, who feared that the other villagers would blame the lame and mute boy for their crop failures, Stephan is raised by a golden eagle who teaches him to fly.
Deutsch, 1989, 163 pp., o.p.
(SLJ Aug 1989 p. 138; VOYA 12:211)

BENSON, E(dward) F(rederic). *David Blaize and the Blue Door.*
See Chapter 7, High Fantasy: Travel to Other Worlds.

BERESFORD, Elizabeth. *Invisible Magic.*
See Chapter 10, Time Travel Fantasy.

BERESFORD, Elizabeth. *Travelling Magic.*
See Chapter 10, Time Travel Fantasy.

9-37　**BERGENGREN, Ralph Wilhelm.** *Susan and the Butterbees.* Gr. 4–6.
Fairy Maud grants Susan's wish for 47 Butterbee uncles to appear whenever she needs entertainment or help.
Illus. by Anne Vaughan, Longmans, 1947, 175 pp., o.p.
(HB 23:212; Kirkus 15:163; LJ 72:643)

BERTON, Pierre. *The Secret World of Og.*
See Chapter 7, High Fantasy: Travel to Other Worlds.

9-38　**BETHANCOURT, T(homas) Ernesto (pseud. of Tom Paisley).** *The Dog Days of Arthur Cane.* Gr. 6–9.
Arthur is transformed into a stray mutt by a classmate he has ridiculed.
Holiday, 1976, 160 pp., o.p.
(HB 53:157; Kirkus 44:848; SLJ Jan 1977 p. 99; TLS 1978 p. 1082)

9-39　**BIANCO, Margery (Winifred) Williams.** *The Hurdy-Gurdy Man.* Gr. 2–4.
The magical music of the hurdy-gurdy man changes the lives of the prim inhabitants of an overly tidy town.
Illus. by Robert Lawson, Oxford University Press, 1933, 55 pp., o.p.; Gregg, 1980, 56 pp., o.p.
(BL 30:184; HB 9:204; LJ 58:897)

BILLINGSLEY, Franny. *Well Wished.*
See Chapter 5, High Fantasy: Alternate Worlds or Histories.

9-40　**BINNS, Archie (Fred).** *The Radio Imp.* Gr. 4–7.

Jim Tompkins's secondhand Irish radio reports on the future as well as the past. The sequel is *Secret of the Sleeping River* (1952).
Illus. by Rafaello Busoni, Winston, 1950, 216 pp., o.p.
(BL 46:266; CCBB 3:49; HB 26:193; Kirkus 18:69; LJ 75:706)

BLACK, Holly. *Tithe: A Modern Faerie Tale.*
See Chapter 6, High Fantasy: Myth or Legend Fantasy.

9-41 **BLOCK, Francesca Lia.** *I Was a Teenage Fairy.* Gr. 8–12.
✮ Mab, a red-haired finger-sized fairy, convinces unhappy 16-year-old model Barbie Marks to take control of her life away from her manipulative mother and abusive photographer.
Cotler/HarperCollins, 1998, 160 pp. (0-06-027747-5); HarperCollins, 2000, pap., 186 pp. (0-06-440862-0)
(BL 95:412; CCBB 52:7; HB 74:725; HBG 10:77; Kirkus 66:1282; SLJ Dec 1998 p. 118; VOYA 21:280, 22:12)

9-42 **BODE, N. E. (pseud. of Julianna Baggott).** *The Anybodies.* Gr. 5–8.
Spending the summer with her birth father after discovering that she and Howard Bone were switched at birth, Fern Drudger discovers that her father is an "Anybody," or shape-shifter, searching for a magical book called "The Art of Being Anybody" before his enemy can find it.
Illus. by Peter Ferguson, HarperCollins, 2004, (0-06-055736-2)
(BL 100:1841; Kirkus 72:487; SLJ July 2004 p. 98)

BOMANS, Godfried (Jan Arnold). *Eric in the Land of the Insects.*
See Chapter 7, High Fantasy: Travel to Other Worlds.

9-43 **BONHAM, Frank.** *The Friends of the Loony Lake Monster.* Gr. 4–6.
A baby dinosaur hatches from an orange egg and adopts Gussie as its mother.
Dutton, 1972, 135 pp., o.p.
(BL 69:711; CCBB 26:71; Kirkus 40:1097; LJ 97:3803)

9-44 **BOSTON, L(ucy) M(aria Wood).** *The Castle of Yew.* Gr. 3–5. (Orig. British
✮ pub. 1965.)
Two boys peer into a castle-shaped yew bush and find that they have shrunken to a few inches in height and are now inside the castle.
Illus. by Margery Gill, Harcourt, 1965, 58 pp., o.p.
(BL 62:327; CCBB 19:42; HB 42:192; Kirkus 33:903; LJ 90:4609; TLS 1965 p. 513)

BOSTON, L(ucy) M(aria Wood). *The Children of Green Knowe.*
See Chapter 4, Ghost Fantasy.

9-45 **BOSTON, L(ucy) M(aria Wood).** *The Fossil Snake.* Gr. 4–6. (Orig. British pub. 1975.)
The fossilized prehistoric snake that Rob hid under his radiator comes to life and begins to grow.
Illus. by Peter Boston, Atheneum, 1976, 53 pp., o.p.
(BL 72:1259; HB 52:287; Kirkus 44:199; SLJ May 1976 p. 56; TLS 1975 p. 1060)

BOSTON, L(ucy) M(aria Wood). *The Guardians of the House.*
See Chapter 7, High Fantasy: Travel to Other Worlds.

9-46 **BOSTON, L(ucy) M(aria Wood).** *Nothing Said.* Gr. 3–5. (Orig. British pub.
✫   1971.)
Libby meets a small, weeping dryad and promises to find her a new tree to
replace the one felled by a storm.
Illus. by Peter Boston, Harcourt, 1971, 64 pp., o.p.
(BL 67:746; CCBB 25:2; HB 47:286; LJ 96:2128; TLS 1971 p. 1317)

9-47 **BOSTON, L(ucy) M(aria Wood).** *The River at Green Knowe.* Gr. 5–7.
✫   (Orig. British pub. 1959.)
While canoeing on the river near Green Knowe, Ping, Oskar, and Ida meet a
hermit, a giant, and winged horses. Ping's adventures continue in *An Enemy at
Green Knowe* (1964, 2002) and in a moving realistic story called *A Stranger at
Green Knowe* (1961, 2002). *The Children of Green Knowe* (1954, 2002; see
Chapter 3, Ghost Fantasy), *The Treasure of Green Knowe* (1958, 2002), and
The Stones of Green Knowe (1976, 2002; see Chapter 10, Time Travel Fantasy)
are related stories.
Illus. by Peter Boston, Harcourt, 1959, o.p., 1966, pap., 153 pp., o.p.; Harcourt,
2002 (0-15-202613-4); 2002, pap. (0-15-202607-X)
(CCBB 13:27; HB 78:427; Kirkus 27:701; LJ 84:3318; TLS Dec 4, 1959 p. xvii)

9-48 **BOSTON, L(ucy) M(aria Wood).** *The Sea Egg.* Gr. 4–5. (Orig. British pub.
✫   1967.)
Toby and Joe find a green, egg-shaped stone that hatches into a sea boy.
Illus. by Peter Boston, Harcourt, 1967, 94 pp., o.p.
(BL 63:1045; CCBB 21:1; HB 43:460; Kirkus 35:498; LJ 92:2647; Suth:47; TLS 1967 p.
1133)

BOWEN, William A(lvin). *Merrimeg.*
See Chapter 7, High Fantasy: Travel to Other Worlds.

9-49 **BOWEN, William A(lvin).** *The Old Tobacco Shop: A True Account of
What Befell a Little Boy in Search of Adventure.* Gr. 5–7.
Tales told by the old tobacco shop owner involve Freddie in thrilling pirate
adventures. John Newbery Medal Honor Book, 1922.
Macmillan, 1921, 236 pp., o.p.
(BL 18:159; Bookshelf 1923–1924 p. 8; LJ 47:869; Mahony 1:39; Moore:426)

BRADBURY, Ray (Douglas). *The Halloween Tree.*
See Chapter 10, Time Travel Fantasy.

9-50 **BRAND, Christianna (pseud. of Mary [Christianna Milne] Lewis).** *Nurse
Matilda.* Gr. 2–5.
It takes only one stamp of Nurse Matilda's big black stick to straighten out the
Browns' naughty children. The sequels are *Nurse Matilda Goes to Town* (1967)
and *Nurse Matilda Goes to Hospital* (1975).
Illus. by Edward Ardizzone, Dutton, 1964, 127 pp., o.p.; Gregg, 1980, 128 pp.,
o.p.
(BL 61:436; HB 40:497; Kirkus 32:732; LJ 89:3468; TLS 1964 p. 589)

BRENNAN, Herbie. *Faerie Wars.*
See Chapter 7, High Fantasy: Travel to Other Worlds.

9-51 **BRENNER, Barbara (Johnes).** *The Flying Patchwork Quilt.* Gr. 2–4.
Determined to fly, 5-year-old Ellen tries paper wings, balloons, and an umbrella before she succeeds with a magical patchwork quilt.
Illus. by Fred Brenner, Young Scott, 1965, 42 pp., o.p.
(CCBB 20:4; Kirkus 33:749; LJ 90:3778)

9-52 **BRIGGS, Raymond.** *The Man.* Gr. 3–5. (Orig. British pub. 1992.)
The tiny man who appears in John's bedroom one morning becomes a demanding resident who refuses to be treated like a toy.
Illus. by the author, Random, 1995, 64 pp., o.p.
(BL 92:931; CCBB 499:185; HB 72:315)

9-53 **BRISSON, Pat.** *Hot Fudge Hero.* Gr. 2–4.
☆ Second-grader Bertie has three adventures, including one in which his fairy godfather helps him learn to play the saxophone.
Illus. by Diana Cain Bluthenthal, Holt, 1997, 72 pp. (0-8050-4551-1); Scholastic, 1998, pap. (0-590-03094-9)
(BL 93:1333; CCBB 50:351; HB 73:450; HBG 8:288; Kirkus 65:550; SLJ July 1997 p. 60)

9-54 **BRITTAIN, Bill.** *The Fantastic Freshman.* Gr. 5–9.
Stanley Muffet's daydreams of football stardom, becoming student council president, and dating the head cheerleader all come suddenly true, but his magical good luck creates a few problems.
Harper, 1988, 154 pp., o.p.
(BL 85:67, 72; Kirkus 56:1056; SLJ Sept 1988 p. 182; VOYA 11:235)

BRITTAIN, Bill. *The Mystery of the Several Sevens.*
See Chapter 7, High Fantasy: Travel to Other Worlds.

9-55 **BRITTAIN, Bill.** *Wings.* Gr. 6–7.
Everyone is shocked when 12-year-old Ian grows wings, especially his father, who fears they will put a damper on his own political career.
Harper, 1991, 135 pp. LB (0-06-020649-7)
(BL 88:519; CCBB 45:57; HBG 3:63; Kirkus 59:1007; SLJ Oct 1991 p. 119; VOYA 14:320)

9-56 **BROCK, Betty.** *No Flying in the House.* Gr. 3–5.
Annabel, a half-mortal, half-fairy child, is tempted by a wicked fairy to misuse her magic powers.
Illus. by Wallace Tripp, Harper, 1970, 139 pp., o.p.
(BL 66:1340; CCBB 24:38; Kirkus 38:450; LJ 95:2531; Suth:52)

BROCK, Betty. *The Shades.*
See Chapter 4, Ghost Fantasy.

9-57 **BROCKMEIER, Kevin.** *City of Names.* Gr. 5–7.
Howie's fifth-grade classroom book order includes "The Secret Guide to North Melwood," containing instructions for magical transportation around his hometown and into a parallel universe.
Viking, 2002, 144 pp. (0-670-03565-3)
(BL 98:1720; CCBB 55:312; HBG 43:368; Kirkus 70:649; SLJ July 2002 p. 113)

9-58 **BROOKE, William J.** *A Brush with Magic.* Gr. 4–7.
✭ Liang, found as a baby clutching a paintbrush, discovers that the pictures he
paints come to life in this story based on a Chinese folktale.
Illus. by Michael Koelsh, Harper, 1993, 137 pp. (0-06-022973-X)
(BL 90:827; CCBB 47:148; HBG 5:73; Kirkus 61:1458; SLJ Jan 1994 p. 112; VOYA 17:7,
34)

9-59 **BROOKS, Terry.** *Running with the Demon.* **(The Word and the Void trilogy, bk. 1).** Gr. 10 up.
One hot Fourth of July weekend, 14-year-old Nest Freemark is told that she
must use the magic she inherited from her grandmother to save the U.S. from
worldwide war. The sequels are *A Knight of the Word* (1998) and *Angel Fire
East* (1999).
Ballantine/Del Rey, 1997, 432 pp. (0-345-37962-4); Del Rey, 1998, pap., 448
pp. (0-345-42258-9)
(BL 93:1773; Kirkus 65:1072; LJ Sep 15, 1997 p. 105; VOYA 21:11, 52)

9-60 **BROWN, Palmer.** *Beyond the Pawpaw Trees: The Story of Anna Lavinia.*
Gr. 4–6.
Anna Lavinia has a number of strange adventures during a trip to her aunt's
house, culminating in the discovery of her long-lost father. In a sequel, *The Sil-
ver Nutmeg* (1956), Anna Lavinia discovers another world on the other side of
the dew pond near her house.
Illus. by the author, Harper, 1954, 121 pp., o.p.
(CCBB 8:66; HB 30:343; Kirkus 22:385; LJ 79:2254)

9-61 **BROWNE, Frances.** *Granny's Wonderful Chair and Its Tales of Fairy*
✭ *Times.* Gr. 4–6. (Orig. British pub. 1856; repr. 1887, retitled *The Story of the
Lost Fairy Book*; orig. U.S. pub. 1892.)
Snowflower's magical chair tells wondrous stories and helps her find the king's
long-lost brother.
Illus. by Clara E. Atwood, Heath, 1900, 1930 (entitled *The Wonderful Chair
and the Tales It Told*), 192 pp., o.p.; illus. by Katherine Pyle, Dutton, 1916,
1925, 1933, 211 pp., o.p.; illus. by Emma L. Brock, Macmillan, 1924 (entitled
Granny's Wonderful Chair), 184 pp., o.p.; illus. by D(enys) J(ames) Watkins-
Pitchford, Dutton, 1963, 150 pp., o.p.; Dutton, 2000 (0-525-30912-8)
(BL 21:74, 59:859; Bookshelf 1928 p. 10; HB 1[June 1925]:30, 39:402; LJ 26:67, 50:803;
Mahony 2:274)

9-62 **BRUÈRE, Martha (Bensley).** *Sparky-for-Short.* Gr. 3–4.
An electric spark released from the radio is really a radio photograph of a lost
boy.
Illus. by the author, Coward, 1930, 85 pp., o.p.
(LJ 55:995; Mahony 3:132; Moore 131, 431)

9-63 **BUCHAN, John.** *The Magic Walking-Stick.* Gr. 5–7. (Orig. Canadian pub.
1932.)
Bill's magic walking stick takes him to the South Pacific and to darkest Africa,
where it helps him restore a prince to his throne.
Illus. by Arthur E. Becher, Houghton, 1932, 215 pp., o.p.
(Bookshelf 1933:11; LJ 58:806; TLS 1932 pp. 840, 867)

BUFFETT, Jimmy, and BUFFETT, Savannah Jane. *Trouble Dolls.*
See Chapter 11, Toy Fantasy.

9-64 **BUFFIE, Margaret.** *The Warnings.* Gr. 7 up. (Orig. Canadian pub. 1989,
★ entitled *The Guardian Circle*.)
Fifteen-year-old Rachel and her new friend Will discover that her Aunt Irene
and the elderly Fossils who live with her aunt have special magical powers, and
need Rachel's help to keep an ancient spirit from seizing their stone of power.
Scholastic, 1991, 256 pp. (0-5904-3665-1)
(BL 87:1464; CCBB 44:160; HBG 2:275; Kirkus 59:105; SLJ Apr 1991 p. 141; VOYA 14:93)

BULLETT, Gerald W(illiam). *The Happy Mariners.*
See Chapter 10, Time Travel Fantasy.

9-65 **BURGESS, Melvin.** *The Earth Giant.* Gr. 4–7. (Orig. British pub. 1996.)
Amy and her brother Peter try to protect the giant creature she found living
beneath the roots of a fallen tree.
Putnam, 1997, 154 pp. (0-399-23187-0)
(BL 94:328; CCBB 51:196; HBG 9:68; Kirkus 65:1529; SLJ Oct 1997 p. 128)

9-66 **BURGESS, Thornton W(aldo).** *Tommy and the Wishing-Stone.* Gr. 4–6.
Tommy finds a Wishing-Stone in the meadow that can transform him into any
wild animal. The sequels are *Tommy's Change of Heart* (Little, 1921) and
Tommy's Wishes Come True (Little, 1921).
Illus. by Harrison Cady, Century, 1915, 290 pp., o.p.
(BL 12:294; Mahony 1:24)

9-67 **BURNETT (Townsend), Frances (Elizabeth) Hodgson.** *Racketty-Packetty
House, as Told by Queen Crosspatch.* Gr. 3–5. (Orig. British and U.S. pub.
1906.)
When Cynthia replaces her tumbledown doll house with an elegant new one,
Queen Crosspatch of the fairies steps in to save the old discarded dolls. This is
the sequel to *Queen Silverbell* (Century, 1906) and is followed by *Spring
Cleaning, as Told by Queen Crosspatch* (1908).
Illus. by Harold Berson, Scribner, 1961 (entitled *Racketty Packetty House and
Other Stories*), 190 pp., o.p.; illus. by Harrison Caddy, Dodd, 1961, 111 pp.,
o.p.; illus. by Holly Johnson, Lippincott, 1975, 60 pp., o.p.; Dover, 2002, pap.,
128 pp. (0-486-41860-X)
(BL 2:249, 58:111, 203, 72:362; HB 37:549; Kirkus 43:1065; LJ 95:1192; Mahony 1:40;
Mahony 2:127; SLJ Nov 1975 p. 42; TLS 1968 p. 589)

BUTTERWORTH, Oliver. *The Enormous Egg.*
See Chapter 8, Humorous Fantasy.

9-68 **BYARS, Betsy (Cromer).** *The Winged Colt of Casa Mia.* Gr. 5–7.
The colt Charles is given when he comes to live on his Uncle Coot's ranch
turns out to have wings!
Illus. by Richard Cuffari, Viking, 1973, 128 pp., o.p.
(CCBB 27:107; HB 50:47; LJ 98:3448; Suth 2:71)

9-69 **CALHOUN, Mary (pseud. of Mary Huiskamp Wilkins).** *Magic in the Alley.* Gr. 4–6.
Cleery buys a box of magic items in an alley junk shop.
Illus. by Wendy Watson, Atheneum, 1970, 167 pp., o.p.
(BL 67:55; HB 46:295; Kirkus 38:242; LJ 95:1939)

9-70 **CALHOUN, Mary (pseud. of Mary Huiskamp Wilkins).** *Ownself.* Gr. 4–6.
Laurabelle summons up a joyful fairy who convinces the girl to defy her stern father.
Harper, 1975, 160 pp., o.p.
(CCBB 29:59; HB 51:265; Kirkus 43:371; SLJ Apr 1975 p. 50)

9-71 **CAMERON, Eleanor (Frances Butler).** *The Terrible Churnadryne.* Gr.
★ 4–6.
Few people believe the stories of a tremendous beast seen near Redwood Cove, so Tom and Jennifer decide to track it down themselves.
Illus. by Beth Krush and Joe Krush, Little, Brown, 1959, 125 pp., o.p.
(BL 56:247; Eakin:58; HB 35:481; Kirkus 27:701; LJ 84:3629)

9-72 **CARLSEN, Ruth Christoffer.** *Mr. Pudgins.* Gr. 3–6.
Whenever Mr. Pudgins baby-sits for John's family, the faucets run with soda pop and the bathtubs fly.
Illus. by Margaret Bradfield, Houghton, 1951, 163 pp., o.p.
(BL 47:240; CCBB 4:26; HB 27:1; LJ 76:415)

9-73 **CARLSEN, Ruth Christoffer.** *Sam Bottleby.* Gr. 4–6.
A fairy godfather cares for Trygve and Solveig after they are stranded at the airport.
Illus. by Wallace Tripp, Houghton, 1968, 151 pp., o.p.
(Kirkus 36:1282; LJ 94:1324)

CARROLL, Lewis (pseud. of Charles Ludwidge Dodgson). *Alice's Adventures in Wonderland.*
See Chapter 7, High Fantasy: Travel to Other Worlds.

CASSEDY, Sylvia. *Behind the Attic Wall.*
See Chapter 4, Ghost Fantasy.

9-74 **CATLING, Patrick Skene.** *The Chocolate Touch.* Gr. 3–5.
John Midas transforms everyone, even his mother, into chocolate statues because of his insatiable craving for chocolate. The sequel is *John Midas in the Dreamtime* (1986).
Illus. by Mildred Coughlin McNutt, Morrow, 1952, 95 pp., o.p.; illus. by Margot Apple, HarperCollins, 1979, 126 pp. (revision of 1952 ed.), LB (0-688-32187-9); Yearling, 1996, pap., 96 pp. (0-440-41289-7), 1998, pap., 87 pp. (0-440-22796-8)
(BL 49:18, 75:1579; Kirkus 20:369; SLJ Sep 1979 p. 131)

CHARLES, Prince of Wales. *The Old Man of Lochnagar.*
See Chapter 8, Humorous Fantasy.

CHARNAS, Suzy McKee. *The Bronze King.*
See Chapter 12, Witchcraft and Sorcery Fantasy.

CHARNAS, Suzy McKee. *The Kingdom of Kevin Malone.*
See Chapter 7, High Fantasy: Travel to Other Worlds.

CHASE, Mary (Coyle). *Loretta Mason Potts.*
See Chapter 7, High Fantasy: Travel to Other Worlds.

CHESNUTT, Charles Waddell. *Conjure Tales.*
See Chapter 3, Fantasy Collections.

CHETWIN, Grace. *Out of the Dark World.*
See Chapter 7, High Fantasy: Travel to Other Worlds.

CHEW, Ruth (Silver). *Do-It-Yourself Magic.*
See Chapter 7, High Fantasy: Travel to Other Worlds.

9-75 **CHEW, Ruth (Silver).** *Mostly Magic.* Gr. 3–4.
Emily and her younger brother Dick are given a miniature ladder that can take them anywhere and a pencil that causes anything it writes to happen.
Illus. by the author, Holiday, 1982, 126 pp., o.p.
(BL 78:1521; SLJ Dec 1982 p. 64)

CHEW, Ruth (Silver). *No Such Thing as a Witch.*
See Chapter 12, Witchcraft and Sorcery Fantasy.

CHEW, Ruth (Silver). *The Would-Be Witch.*
See Chapter 12, Witchcraft and Sorcery Fantasy.

9-76 **CHRISTOPHER, Matt(hew F.).** *The Dog That Stole Football Plays.* Gr. 2–4.
Mike can communicate with his Airedale, Harry, who advises him on football plays after listening to the opposing team's coaches. The sequels are *The Dog That Called the Signals* (1982), *The Dog That Pitched a No-Hitter* (1988), *The Dog That Stole Home* (1993, 1996), and *The Dog That Called the Pitch* (1998).
Illus. by Bill Ogden, Little, Brown, 1980, 1993, 48 pp. (0-316-14082-1); Little, Brown, 1997, pap., 48 pp. (0-316-13423-6)
(CCBB 34:4; Kirkus 48:909; SLJ May 1980 p. 84)

9-77 **CHRISTOPHER, Matt(hew F.).** *The Kid Who Only Hit Homers.* Gr. 3–5.
Syl's dream of winning the Best Athlete Ever trophy comes true, all because of his mysterious baseball coach, George Baruth. The sequel is *Return of the Home Run Kid* (1992).
Illus. by Harvey Kidder, Little, Brown, 1972, 151 pp., o.p., 1986, pap. (0-316-13987-4); Little, Brown, 2005, pap., 144 pp. (0-316-73773-0)
(Kirkus 40:34; LJ May 15, 1972 p. 1929)

9-78 **CHRISTOPHER, Matt(hew F.).** *Skateboard Tough.* Gr. 4–6.
The glorious skateboard Brett unearths enables him to perform incredibly difficult tricks, until he discovers that the skateboard's previous owner was killed while riding it.

Illus. by Paul Casale, Little, Brown, 1991, 162 pp. (0-316-14247-6), 1994, pap., 168 pp. (0-316-14241-7)
(BL 87:1797; CCBB 44:212; HBG 2:268; Kirkus 59:728; SLJ June 1991 p. 74)

9-79 CLAPP, Patricia. *King of the Doll House.* Gr. 3–4.
Tiny King Borra Borra and his family of 12 move into Ellie's dollhouse for the summer.
Illus. by Judith Gwyn Brown, Lothrop, 1974, 94 pp., o.p.
(CCBB 28:74; Kirkus 42:680; LJ 99:2738)

CLARKE, Judith. *Teddy B. Zoot.*
See Chapter 11, Toy Fantasy.

CLARKE, Pauline (pseud. of Pauline [Clarke] Hunter Blair). *The Return of the Twelves.*
See Chapter 11, Toy Fantasy.

CLARKE, Pauline (pseud. of Pauline [Clarke] Hunter Blair). *The Two Faces of Silenus.*
See Chapter 6, High Fantasy: Myth or Legend Fantasy.

COATES, Anna. *Dog Magic.*
See Chapter 2, Animal Fantasy.

COATSWORTH, Elizabeth (Jane). *Pure Magic.*
See Chapter 1, Allegorical Fantasy and Literary Fairy Tales.

9-80 COATSWORTH, Elizabeth (Jane). *Troll Weather.* Gr. 2–4.
Selma sees the trolls' golden castles on the mountainside above her Norwegian village.
Illus. by Ursula Arndt, Macmillan, 1967, 41 pp., o.p.
(BL 63:944; HB 43:198; Kirkus 35:3; LJ 92:1309)

9-81 COBLENTZ, Catherine Cate. *The Blue Cat of Castle Town.* Gr. 4–6.
A blue cat steps out of a carpet and wanders through the town of Castleton.
John Newbery Medal Honor Book, 1950.
Illus. by Janice Holland, McKay, 1949, 123 pp., o.p.; Countryman, 1983, pap., 124 pp., o.p.
(BL 46:15; CCBB 2:1; HB 25:412; LJ 74:1105)

9-82 COLFER, Eoin. *Artemis Fowl.* **(Artemis Fowl series, bk. 1).** Gr. 5–8.
✫ (Orig. pub. in Ireland.)
Artemis Fowl, age 12, concocts an elaborate plan to recoup his Irish criminal family's fortune by kidnapping elven police officer Holly Short and holding her for ransom in exchange for a ton of fairy gold. British Children's Book of the Year, 2001. In *Artemis Fowl, the Arctic Incident* (2002) Artemis, now 13, joins forces with Holly and the LEP to rescue his father from the Russian Mafiya and to track down a dangerous gang of smugglers. British Children's Book of the Year, 2002. In *Artemis Fowl: The Eternity Code* (2003), Artemis and Captain Holly attempt to bring Artemis's murdered bodyguard back to life and to retrieve a fairy technology supercomputer from double-crossing Jon Spiro. *Artemis Fowl: The Opal Deception* (2005) is the fourth book in the series. Two

companion books are *The Artemis Fowl Files* (2004) and *Artemis Fowl: The Seventh Dwarf* (2004; British).
Hyperion, 2001, 288 pp. (0-7868-0801-2); Miramax, 2002, pap., 304 pp. (0-7868-1707-0)
(BL 97:1554; CCBB 54:406; HB 77:449; HBG 12:301; Kirkus 69:496; LJ June 15, 2001 p. 102, Nov 1, 2001 p. 160; VOYA 24:211)

COLLODI, Carlo. *The Adventures of Pinocchio.*
See Chapter 11, Toy Fantasy.

9-83   CONFORD, Ellen. *The Frog Princess of Pelham.* Gr. 4–7.
Kissed by the most popular boy in school, wealthy Chander turns into a frog and decides to appear on a TV talk show to find a solution to her problem.
Little, Brown, 1997, 106 pp. (0-316-15246-3)
(BL 93:1241; CCBB 50:390; Kirkus 65:638; SLJ June 1997 p. 114)

9-84   CONFORD, Ellen. *Genie with the Light Blue Hair.* Gr. 6–9.
☆   A cigar-smoking genie named Arthur appears after 15-year-old Jean lights her seemingly useless birthday present lamp; but her wishes never turn out as planned.
Bantam, 1989, 160 pp., o.p.
(BL 85:1000; CCBB 42:145; HB 65:215; Kirkus 57:47; SLJ Feb 1989 p. 100; VOYA 12:26)

9-85   COONTZ, Otto. *Hornswoggle Magic.* Gr. 3–5.
Jenny the shopping-bag lady uses magical coins, or hornswoggles, to jam the new vending machine and save Mr. Wiseman's newsstand from going out of business.
Illus. by the author, Little, Brown, 1981, 88 pp., o.p.
(BL 78:705; SLJ Feb 1982 p. 73)

9-86   COOPER (Grant), Susan (Mary). *The Boggart.* Gr. 4–7.
☆   After Emily accidentally releases a mischievous Boggart from an ancient Scottish desk, he makes himself at home in modern-day Toronto, causing problems for the Volnik family. In *The Boggart and the Monster* (1997), the Boggart stows away in Jessup and Emily's camping gear on their visit to Loch Ness, where he tries to make contact with his monster cousin.
Macmillan, 1993, 196 pp., o.p.; Aladdin, 1995 (0-689-80173-4)
(BL 89:908, 90:869; CCBB 46:208; HB 69:330; HBG 4:296; Kirkus 60:1570; SLJ Jan 1993 p. 96)

9-87   COOPER (Grant), Susan (Mary). *Jethro and the Jumbie.* Gr. 2–4.
☆   Furious with his older brother for breaking a promise to take him fishing, 8-year-old Jethro marches off into the bush and has a series of magical adventures.
Illus. by Ashley Bryan, Atheneum, 1979, 28 pp., o.p.
(BL 76:610; CCBB 33:91; HB 56:51; Kirkus 48:120; SLJ Feb 1980 p. 44)

COOPER (Grant), Susan (Mary). *Over Sea, Under Stone.*
See Chapter 6, High Fantasy: Myth or Legend Fantasy.

9-88   COOPER, Helen. *Sandmare.* Gr. 2–4. (Orig. British pub. 2002.)
The horse Polly and her father draw on the beach wants to be free, and is helped to escape from the sand.

Illus. by Ted Dewan, Farrar, 2003, 72 pp. (0-374-36406-0)

(BL 99:1591; CCBB 56:309; HBG 14:353; Kirkus 71:141; SLJ July 2003 p. 89)

CORBETT, Scott. *Ever Ride a Dinosaur?*
See Chapter 8, Humorous Fantasy.

CORBETT, Scott. *The Great Custard Pie Panic.*
See Chapter 12, Witchcraft and Sorcery Fantasy.

9-89 **CORBETT, Scott.** *The Lemonade Trick.* **(The Trick series, bk. 1).** Gr. 4–6.
✭ Kirby's new chemistry set can change a person's character, but the fun ends when it changes his friend Bumps into a bully. The sequels are *The Mailbox Trick* (1961), *The Disappearing Dog Trick* (1963), *The Limerick Trick* (1964), *The Turnabout Trick* (1967), *The Hairy Horror Trick* (1969), *The Hateful Plateful Trick* (1971), *The Home Run Trick* (1973), and *The Black Mask Trick* (1976).
Illus. by Paul Galdone, Little, Brown, 1960, 103 pp., o.p.

(BL 56:633; CCBB 13:128; HB 36:128; Kirkus 28:90; LJ 85:2035)

9-90 **CORBETT, Sue.** *12 Again.* Gr. 5–9.
This story is told alternately from the perspectives of 12-year-old Patrick and his mother, Bernadette, who has been transformed into a 12-year-old called Detta and is the new girl in Patrick's school.
Dutton, 2002, 160 pp. (0-525-46899-4)

(BL 99:122; CCBB 56:54; HBG 14:77; Kirkus 70:878; SLJ July 2002 p. 118; VOYA 25:200)

9-91 **CORDER, Zizou (pseud. of Louisa Young and Isabel Adomakoh Young).**
✭ *Lionboy.* **(The Lionboy trilogy, bk. 1).** Gr. 4–8. (Orig. British pub. 2003.)
After Charlie Ashanti's parents are kidnapped, he escapes from London aboard a Floating Circus bound for Paris, aided by his ability to speak with stray city cats and the caged circus lions. In the sequel, *Lionboy: The Chase* (2004), Charlie, King Boris of Bulgaria, and a pride of former circus lions search Venice for Charlie's missing parents, only to find that they've been imprisoned by the Corporacy in Vence, France.
Dial, 2004, 288 pp. (0-8037-2982-0); Puffin, 2004, pap., 275 pp. (0-14-240226-5)

(BL 100:852; CCBB 57:322; Kirkus 71:1358; SLJ Jan 2004 p. 128; VOYA 26:500)

9-92 **CORLETT, William.** *The Steps up the Chimney.* **(The Magician's House Quartet, bk. 1).** Gr. 5–8. (Orig. British pub. 1990.)
William Constant and his younger sisters Mary and Alice discover a secret staircase inside the chimney of their Uncle Jack's house in Wales and meet Stephen Tyler, a magician from the past who warns them of danger. The sequels are *The Door in the Tree* (1991, 2000), *The Bridge in the Clouds* (1992, 2001), and *The Tunnel Behind the Waterfall* (1991, 2001).
Pocket/Archway, 2000, pap., 272 pp. (0-7434-1001-7)

(SLJ May 2002 p. 148; YOYA 23:342)

9-93 **COUNSEL, June.** *A Dragon in Class 4.* Gr. 3–5. (Orig. British pub. 1984.)
An omniscient and vain young dragon named Scales adopts Sam as his boy and secretly helps him and his classmates with their school assignments.
Illus. by Jill Bennett, Faber, 1984, 102 pp., o.p.

(CCBB 38:21; SLJ Dec 1984 p. 79)

9-94 **COVILLE, Bruce.** *Jennifer Murdley's Toad.* **(Magic Shop books, vol. 3).**
⋆ Gr. 3–6.
After her worst fifth-grade enemy turns into a toad, Jennifer realizes that the
talking toad she bought at Mr. Elives's magic shop transforms anyone who
kisses it. *The Monster's Ring* (1982, 2002; see below), *Jeremy Thatcher, Drag-
on Hatcher* (1991; see below), *The Skull of Truth* (1997; see below), and *Juliet
Dove, Queen of Love* (2003; see below) involve the same magic shop.
Illus. by Gary A. Lippincott, Harcourt, 1992, 160 pp. (0-15-200745-8); Pocket,
1993, pap. (0-671-79401-9)
(BL 88:1357; CCBB 45:292; HBG 3:262; Kirkus 60:462; SLJ Sept 1992 p. 250)

9-95 **COVILLE, Bruce.** *Jeremy Thatcher, Dragon Hatcher.* **(Magic Shop**
⋆ **books, vol. 2).** Gr. 5–7.
The small marbled ball Jeremy buys at Mr. Elives's magic shop turns out to be
a dragon egg that hatches into a scaly red dragon named Tiamat, invisible
except to Jeremy and one friend. *The Monster's Ring* (1982, 2002; see below),
Jennifer Murdley's Toad (1992; see above), *The Skull of Truth* (1997; see
below), and *Juliet Dove, Queen of Love* (2003; see below) involve the same
magic shop.
Illus. by Gary A. Lippincott, Harcourt, 1991, 160 pp. (0-15-200748-2); Pocket,
1992, pap. (0-671-74782-7)
(BL 87:1798; HBG 2:265; Kirkus 59:246; SLJ May 1991 p. 91; VOYA 14:106)

9-96 **COVILLE, Bruce.** *Juliet Dove, Queen of Love.* **(Magic Shop Books, vol.**
5). Gr. 4–7.
Shy middle-school student Juliet is stunned to discover that the amulet she was
given at Mr. Elives's magic shop is attracting boys by the dozens because
Cupid, god of love, is trapped inside. This book is related to *The Monster's
Ring* (1982, 2002; see below), *Jeremy Thatcher, Dragon Hatcher* (1991, 1992;
see above), *Jennifer Murdley's Toad* (1992, 1993; see above), and *The Skull of
Truth* (1997; see below).
Harcourt, 2003, 180 pp. (0-15-204561-9); Magic Carpet, 2005, pap., 208 pp.
(0-15-205217-8)
(BL 100:854; HBG 15:89; SLJ Dec 2003 p. 148)

9-97 **COVILLE, Bruce.** *The Monster's Ring.* **(Magic Shop books, vol. 1).** Gr.
4–6.
At Elives's Magic Supply Store, Russell finds a ring that can turn him into a
monster—but can he turn himself back? *Jeremy Thatcher, Dragon Hatcher*
(1991; see above), *Jennifer Murdley's Toad* (1992, see above), *The Skull of
Truth* (1997; see below), and *Juliet Dove, Queen of Love* (2003; see above) also
involve Mr. Elives's magic shop.
Illus. by Katherine Coville, Pantheon, 1982, 87 pp., o.p.; Harcourt, 2002, 128
pp. (0-15-204618-6), 2003, pap. (0-689-85692-X)
(BL 79:498; HBG 14:77; SLJ Feb 1983 p. 75)

9-98 **COVILLE, Bruce.** *The Skull of Truth.* **(Magic Shop books, vol. 4).** Gr.
⋆ 4–7.
After 12-year-old Charlie steals the skull of Hamlet's jester, "poor Yorick,"
from a magic shop, he discovers that he can no longer tell lies. This book is
related to *The Monster's Ring* (1982, 2002; see above), *Jeremy Thatcher, Drag-

on Hatcher (1991, 1992; see above), *Jennifer Murdley's Toad* (1992, 1993; see above), and *Juliet Dove, Queen of Love* (2003; see above).
Harcourt, 1997, 181 pp. (0-15-275457-1); Pocket, 1999, pap., 208 pp. (0-671-02343-8)
(BL 94:328; HBG 9:69; SLJ Oct 1997 p. 131, Dec 1997 p. 24, April 1998 p. 39)

9-99   CRAIG, Amanda. *Love in Idleness.* Gr. 10 up. (Orig. British pub. 2003.)
Polly, Theo, Tania and Robbie Noble, an English family renting a Tuscan villa called Casa Luna, have invited six more adults and a third child to vacation with them, but unexpected events begin occurring after the children meet fairies living in the garden in this story based on "A Midsummer Night's Dream."
Doubleday, 2003, 352 pp. (0-385-50776-3); Anchor, 2004, pap., 352 pp. (1-40003-107-9)
(Kirkus 71:768; LJ June 15, 2003 p. 99; SLJ Oct 2003 p. 207; TLS Aug 8, 2003 p. 18)

9-100   CREEDON, Catherine. *Blue Wolf.* Gr. 5–9.
✮
Spending the summer at his Aunt Louise's Washington state mountain cabin, Jamie, 14, begins to understand that he comes from a family of shape-shifters who can transform themselves into wolves.
HarperCollins, 2003, 192 pp. (0-06-050869-8); HarperTrophy, 2005, pap., 192 pp. (0-06-050870-1)
(BL 100:607; Kirkus 71:1222; SLJ Oct 2003 p. 162; VOYA 27:140)

9-101   CRESSWELL (Rowe), Helen. *Almost Goodbye.* Gr. 2–4. (Orig. British pub. 1990.)
Gumball Gumford is granted his wish for invisibility when he and Susie Potts find a genie in a magic lamp while collecting "white elephants" for their school sale.
Illus. by Judy Brown, Dutton, 1992, 62 pp. (0-525-44858-6)
(CCBB 46:8; HBG 3:253; SLJ Sept 1992 p. 202)

9-102   CRESSWELL (Rowe), Helen. *The Beachcombers.* Gr. 5–8. (Orig. British
✮   pub. 1972.)
On holiday at the coast, Ned is caught in a feud between the beachcombing Pickerings and the scavenging Dallakers, distant cousins searching for their lost family treasure.
Macmillan, 1972, 133 pp., o.p.
(BL 69:646; CCBB 26:74; HB 49:52; TLS 1972 p. 1312)

9-103   CRESSWELL (Rowe), Helen. *The Bongleweed.* Gr. 5–7. (Orig. British pub.
✮   1973.)
The magic seeds that Becky plants change neatly manicured Pew Gardens into a jungle of bongleweed. Carnegie Medal Commended Book, 1973.
Macmillan, 1973, 138 pp., o.p.; Oxford University Press, 2003, pap., 184 pp. (0-19-275344-4)
(BL 70:540; CCBB 27:174; Kirkus 41:1159; LJ 98:3143; Suth 2:109; TLS 1973 p. 1428)

9-104   CRESSWELL (Rowe), Helen. *The Secret World of Polly Flint.* Gr. 5–7.
✮   (Orig. British pub. 1982.)
Banished to live with her Aunt Em during her father's recuperation from a mine accident, fanciful Polly Flint senses the magic surrounding an ancient

maypole and becomes involved with Time Gypsies who have "slipped the net of time" between Polly's world and the centuries-old village of Grimstone, which disappeared from that very site. Runner-up, Whitbread Literary Award, Children's Book Category, 1982.

Illus. by Shirley Felts, Macmillan, 1984, 176 pp., o.p., 1991, pap. (0-689-71532-3)

(BL 80:1624; CCBB 37:183; HB 60:465:Kirkus 52:J38; SLJ Aug 1984 p. 70; Suth 3:107)

9-105 CRESSWELL (Rowe), Helen. *The White Sea Horse.* Gr. 3–5. (Orig. British pub. 1964.)

Six donkeys mysteriously disappear after the mayor of Piskerton takes away the tiny white horse Molly's fisherman father drew up in his net.

Illus. by Robin Jacques, Lippincott, 1964, 64 pp., o.p.

(Kirkus 33:904; LJ 90:5511; TLS 1964 p. 605)

CRETAN, Gladys. *Joey's Head.*
See Chapter 8, Humorous Fantasy.

CREW, Gary. *Strange Objects.*
See Chapter 6, High Fantasy: Myth or Legend Fantasy.

9-106 CROSS, Gillian (Clare Arnold) (pseud. of Claire Arnold). *The Dark Ground.* **(The Dark Ground Trilogy, bk. 1).** Gr. 5–8. (Orig. British pub. 2004.)

Robert has no idea that he has been miniaturized when he finds himself naked and alone, battling monstrous jungle creatures. The British sequel is *The Black Room* (2005).

Dutton, 2004, 256 pp. (0-525-47350-5); Oxford University Press, 2005, pap., 224 pp. (0-19-275381-9)

(BL 101:106; HB 80:587; Kirkus 72:739; SLJ Sep 2004 p. 202;)

9-107 CROSS, Gillian (Clare Arnold) (pseud. of Claire Arnold). *Pictures in the*
★ *Dark.* Gr. 6–10. (Orig. British pub. 1996.)

Charlie slowly realizes that his classmate's younger brother Peter is able to escape his unhappy home life by transforming himself into an otter.

Holiday, 1996, 197 pp. (0-8234-1267-9); Puffin, 1998, pap. (0-14-038958-X)

(BL 93:858; CCBB 50:161–162; HB 73:54; HBG 8:78; Kirkus 64:1530)

9-108 CROSS, Gillian (Clare Arnold) (pseud. of Claire Arnold). *Twin and Super-Twin.* Gr. 4–6. (Orig. British pub. 1990.)

Cornered by a neighborhood gang, twins Ben and David discover that if Ben concentrates hard enough he can transform David's right arm into amazing things, including a hissing snake.

Illus. by Maureen Bradley, Holiday, 1990, 176 pp., o.p.

(BL 87:521; CCBB 44:113; HBG 2:74; Kirkus 58:1248; SLJ Jan 1991 p. 88)

CROSS, John Kier. *The Other Side of Green Hills.*
See Chapter 7, High Fantasy: Travel to Other Worlds.

CROTHERS, Samuel McChord. *Miss Muffet's Christmas Party.*
See Chapter 1, Allegorical Fantasy and Literary Fairy Tales.

CURLEY, Daniel. *Ann's Spring.*
See Chapter 6, High Fantasy: Myth or Legend Fantasy.

CURRY, Jane Louise. *Beneath the Hill.*
See Chapter 6, High Fantasy: Myth or Legend Fantasy.

9-109 CURRY, Jane Louise. *The Egyptian Box.* Gr. 4–7.
Tee initially loves having Shabti, an ancient Egyptian servant she and her brother accidentally brought to life, available to do her chores and homework, but then Shabti begins taking over Tee's life at school.
Simon, 2002, 192 pp. (0-689-84273-2)
(BL 98:1722; CCBB 55:31; HBG 13:370; Kirkus 70:253; SLJ Mar 2002 p. 226)

9-110 CURRY, Jane Louise. *Mindy's Mysterious Miniature.* **(pap. title:** *The*
☆   *Mysterious Shrinking House***; British title:** *The Housenapper***).** Gr. 3–5.
Mindy and her neighbor, Mrs. Bright, are captured and shrunk to miniature size by Mr. Putt's miniaturizing machine. The "reducer" strikes again in *The Lost Farm* (1974), when Pete McCubbin and his family's entire farm are miniaturized by the unscrupulous Professor Lilliput.
Illus. by Charles Robinson, Harcourt, 1970, 157 pp., o.p.
(BL 67:340; CCBB 24:104; HB 46:616; Kirkus 38:1146; LJ 95:4374; Suth:96; TLS 1971 p. 774)

CUYLER, Margery. *Weird Wolf.*
See Chapter 8, Humorous Fantasy.

9-111 DAHL, Roald. *Charlie and the Chocolate Factory.* Gr. 3–6. (Orig. British pub. 1964.)
Charlie Bucket is one of five lucky children who win a tour of Wonka's wonderful chocolate factory. The sequel is *Charlie and the Great Glass Elevator* (1972, 1991, 2002). Dahl's depiction of Wonka's helpers as mischievous, music-loving, chocolate-colored pygmies has been judged derogatory toward African Americans.
Illus. by Joseph Schindelman, Knopf, 1964, 161 pp., o.p.; Puffin, 1998, pap., 154 pp. (0-14-130115-5); Knopf, 2002 (0-375-91525-7)
(CCBB 18:115; HB 78:428–429; HBG 3:64; Kirkus 32:1009; LJ 89:5004; TLS 1978 p. 1398)

9-112 DAHL, Roald. *George's Marvelous Medicine.* Gr. 3–5. (Orig. British pub. 1981.)
Eight-year-old George mixes up a batch of "medicine" that causes his grouchy grandmother to grow so tall that she bursts through the roof.
Illus. by Quentin Blake, Knopf, 1982, 1990, 89 pp., o.p.; Puffin, 1991, pap. (0-14-034641-4); Knopf, 2002, 101 pp. (0-375-92206-7)
(CCBB 35:166; HBG 3:57, 14:77; SLJ Apr 1982 p. 57; TLS 1981 p. 839)

9-113 DAHL, Roald. *James and the Giant Peach: A Children's Story.* Gr. 3–5. (Orig. British pub. 1961.)
A magic potion enables James to escape from his cruel aunts and travel across the ocean in a huge peach, with human-sized insects as traveling companions. Richard R. George turned this story into a play entitled *Roald Dahl's James and the Giant Peach: A Play* (Penguin, 1983, pap.; Sagebrush, 2003).

Illus. by Nancy Ekholm Burkert, Knopf, 1961, 118 pp., LB (0-394-91282-9); illus. by Lane Smith, Knopf, 1996, 126 pp. (0-679-88090-9); Puffin, 2001, pap., 146 pp. (0-14-130467-7); Knopf, 2002, 154 pp. (0-375-91424-2)
(CCBB 15:57; HBG 14:77; Kirkus 29:727; LJ 86:4036)

9-114 **DAHL, Roald.** *The Magic Finger.* Gr. 2–4. (Orig. British pub. 1966.)
★ Zak puts the Magic Finger on her teacher and her duck-hunting neighbors, changing the former into a cat and the latter into bird-sized people hunted by huge ducks.
Illus. by William (Sherman) Pène du Bois, Harper, 1966, 46 pp., LB (0-06-021382-5); Viking, 1996, 62 pp. (0-670-85252-X); Puffin, 1998, pap., 64 pp. (0-14-130229-1); Puffin, 2004, pap., 64 pp. (0-14-131129-0)
(BL 63:264; Kirkus 34:830; LJ 91:5224)

9-115 **DAHL, Tessa.** *Gwenda and the Animals.* Gr. 2–5. (Original British pub. 1989.)
Gwenda takes revenge on an uncle who teases the zoo animals after she finds she can understand their speech.
Illus. by Anthony Carnabuci, Viking, 1990, 48 pp., o.p.
(BL 87:1059; HBG 2:67; Kirkus 58:1248; SLJ Dec 1990 p. 75)

9-116 **DALKEY, Kara.** *Steel Rose.* Gr. 7–12.
Pittsburgh performance artist T. J. Kaminski tries working a magic spell to make audiences love her work, but instead draws immortal admirers from the land of Faerie.
Roc, 1997, 320 pp. (0-451-45639-4)
(Kliatt Mar 1998 p. 18; VOYA 21:53)

DALTON, Annie. *Out of the Ordinary.*
See Chapter 7, High Fantasy: Travel to Other Worlds.

DANK, Gloria Rand. *The Forest of App.*
See Chapter 1, Allegorical Fantasy and Literary Fairy Tales.

9-117 **DAVID, Lawrence.** *Horace Splattly: The Cupcaked Crusader.* **(Horace Splattly: The Cupcaked Crusader series, bk. 1).** Gr. 2–4.
Ten-year-old Horace eats his sister's experimental cupcakes and is transformed into a superhero. The sequels are *Horace Splattly: When Second Graders Attack* (2000), *The Terror of the Pink Dodo Balloons* (2003), *To Catch a Clownosaurus* (2003), and *The Most Evil, Friendly Villain Ever* (2004).
Illus. by Barry Gott, Dutton, 2001, 144 pp. (0-525-46763-7); Puffin, 2002, pap., 137 pp. (0-14-230021-7)
(HBG 13:72; Kirkus 70:565; SLJ Oct 2001 p. 113)

DAVIES, Valentine. *The Miracle on 34th Street.*
See Chapter 1, Allegorical Fantasy and Literary Fairy Tales.

DAWSON, Carley. *Mr. Wicker's Window.*
See Chapter 10, Time Travel Fantasy.

9-118 DAWSON, Mary. *Tecwyn, the Last of the Welsh Dragons.* Gr. 4–5.
Megan and Hugh Moran adopt a baby dragon hatched from an egg found at the bottom of a Welsh lake.
Illus. by Ingrid Fetz, Parents, 1967, 72 pp., o.p.
(HB 43:461; LJ 92:2648)

9-119 DAWSON, Mitchell. *The Magic Firecrackers.* Gr. 4–6.
✯ Uncle Dick brings the Carsons some 600-year-old wish-granting Chinese firecrackers.
Illus. by Kurt Wiese, Viking, 1949, 192 pp., o.p.
(BL 46:144; CCBB 3:14; HB 26:36; Kirkus 17:510)

9-120 DEAN, Jan. *Finders.* Gr. 7–10. (Orig. British pub. 1993.)
✯ Sixteen-year-old Helen realizes that she has inherited her grandfather's gift and has become a "finder," one who can locate missing people and who learns secrets by touching.
McElderry, 1995, 176 pp. (0-689-50612-0)
(BL 91:1561, 1750; CCBB 48:303; HB 71:608; HBG 6:309; Kirkus 63:709; SLJ July 1995 p. 95; VOYA 18:216)

DEFELICE, Cynthia. *The Strange Night Writing of Jessamine Colter.*
See Chapter 1, Allegorical Fantasy and Literary Fairy Tales.

DE HAVEN, Tom. *The Orphan's Tent.*
See Chapter 7, High Fantasy: Travel to Other Worlds.

9-121 DE LA MARE, Walter (John). *Crossings: A Fairy Play.* Gr. 4–6. (Orig. British pub. 1921.)
Four children spend their winter holiday at an old English country house inhabited by fairies.
Illus. by Dorothy P. Lathrop, Knopf, 1923, 170 pp., o.p.; Classic Books, 2000 (0-7426-3051-X)
(BL 20:221; Mahony 2:383)

DE LA MARE, Walter (John). *The Magic Jacket.*
See Chapter 3, Fantasy Collections.

DE LINT, Charles. *A Circle of Cats.*
See Chapter 2, Animal Fantasy.

DE LINT, Charles. *The Little Country.*
See Chapter 12, Witchcraft and Sorcery Fantasy.

9-122 DERBY, Sally. *Jacob and the Stranger.* Gr. 1–4.
✯ Lazy Jacob discovers that the strange plant he's caring for has begun blossoming with miniature tigers, panthers, cougars, lions, and wildcats, filling his house with magical cats.
Illus. by Leonid Gore, Ticknor, 1994, 32 pp., o.p.
(BL 91:40; HB 70:583; HBG 6:65; Kirkus 62:843; SLJ Sep 1994 p. 182)

9-123 DE REGNIERS, Beatrice Schenk (Freedman). *The Boy, the Rat, and the Butterfly.* Gr. 2–4.

After he finds a jar of wish-granting bubble solution, Peter can stop worrying about his butterfly friend's short lifespan.
Illus. by Haig Shekerjian and Regina Shekerjian, Atheneum, 1971, 40 pp., o.p.
(CCBB 25:104; HB 47:475; Kirkus 39:805)

9-124 DERMAN, Martha. *Tales from Academy Street.* Gr. 5–7.
Eight stories, set in the houses along Academy Street during one school year, involve talking sneakers, a gardener who may be a mallard duck, and some ghostly spiders who take over a computer.
Scholastic, 1991, 103 pp. (0-5904-3703-8), 1992, pap. (0-590-43704-6)
(CCBB 45:7; HBG 3:65; Kirkus 59:930; SLJ Aug 1991 p. 164; VOYA 14:238)

9-125 DEVITA, James. *Blue.* Gr. 5–9.
A boy named Morgan is mysteriously transformed into a blue marlin after he is hospitalized with a strange illness.
HarperCollins., 2001, 282 pp. (0-06-029546-5)
(BL 97:1557; CCBB 54:334; HBG 12:302; SLJ May 2001 p. 149; VOYA 24:211)

DEXTER, Catherine. *A Is for Apple, W Is for Witch.*
See Chapter 12, Witchcraft and Sorcery Fantasy.

DEXTER, Catherine. *The Gilded Cat.*
See Chapter 4, Ghost Fantasy.

DEXTER, Catherine. *The Oracle Doll.*
See Chapter 11, Toy Fantasy.

DICKINSON, Peter (pseud. of Malcolm de Brissac). *A Box of Nothing.*
See Chapter 7, High Fantasy: Travel to Other Worlds.

9-126 DICKINSON, Peter (pseud. of Malcolm de Brissac). *Inside Grandad.* Gr. 3–7. (Orig. British pub. 2004.)
✭ After 11-year-old Gavin's beloved Grandad suffers a debilitating stroke, a selkie enables them to communicate mind-to-mind.
Random, 2004, 128 pp. (0-385-74641-5); Yearling, 2005, pap., 128 pp. (0-5534-8782-5)
(BL 100:854; CCBB 57:269; HB 80:80; Kirkus 71:1449; SLJ Jan 2004 p. 129)

9-127 DILLON, Barbara. *The Good-Guy Cake.* Gr. 2–4.
A "good-guy" cake baked in a magic oven turns Marvin into a suspiciously polite and helpful little boy.
Illus. by Alan Tiegreen, Morrow, 1980, 64 pp., o.p.
(BL 77:458; CCBB 34:91; Kirkus 48:1163; SLJ Mar 1981 p. 130)

9-128 DILLON, Barbara. *A Mom by Magic.* Gr. 4–6.
Jessica's request at a department store wishing-well transforms mannequin Amalie Evans into Jessica's mom until Christmas Day.
Illus. by Jeffrey Lindberg, Harper, 1990, 144 pp., o.p.
(BL 87:742; CCBB 44:27; HBG 2:77; SLJ Sept 1990 p. 224)

DILLON, Barbara. *Mrs. Tooey and the Terrible Toxic Tar.*
See Chapter 12, Witchcraft and Sorcery Fantasy.

9-129 DILLON, Barbara. *My Stepfather Shrank!* Gr. 3–6.
When her new stepfather eats some "weight-reduction" candy and shrinks to four and one-half inches in height, it is up to 9-year-old Mallory to reverse the magic before her mother comes home.
Illus. by Paul Casale, Harper, 1992, 128 pp. LB (0-06-021581-X); 1994, pap., 128 pp. (0-06-440459-5)
(BL 89:596; CCBB 46:109; HBG 4:66; Kirkus 60:1374; SLJ Sept 1992 p. 250)

DILLON, Barbara. *What's Happened to Harry?*
See Chapter 12, Witchcraft and Sorcery Fantasy.

9-130 DITERLIZZI, Tony, and BLACK, Holly. *The Field Guide.* **(The Spider-**
✴   **wick Chronicles, bk. 1).** Gr. 3–6.
In the old house their mother has inherited, Mallory, Simon, and Jared Grace discover a secret room and a field guide to fairies, but their destruction of a boggart's home causes the creature to play nasty tricks in revenge. The sequels are *The Seeing Stone* (2003), *Lucinda's Secret* (2003), *The Ironwood Tree* (2004), and *The Wrath of Mulgarath* (2004).
Illus. by Tony DiTerlizzi, 2003, 107 pp. (0-689-85936-8)
(CCBB 56:442; HBG 14:365; Kirkus 71:604; SLJ July 2003 p. 95; VOYA 26:234)

9-131 DIVAKARUNI, Chitra Banerjee. *The Conch Bearer.* Gr. 5–8.
✴   Fatherless Anand and orphaned Nisha travel through India searching for a magical conch shell stolen from the brotherhood of the elderly healer Abhaydatta.
Roaring Brook, 2003, 272 pp. (0-7613-2793-2); Aladdin, 2005, pap., 227 pp. (0-689-87242-9)
(BL 100:236; HB 80:81; HBG 15:90; Kirkus 71:1071; SLJ Dec 2003 p. 149; VOYA 26:501)

DIXON, Marjorie (Mack). *The Forbidden Island.*
See Chapter 6, High Fantasy: Myth or Legend Fantasy.

DIXON, Rachel. *The Witch's Ring.*
See Chapter 12, Witchcraft and Sorcery Fantasy.

DOLBIER, Maurice (Wyman). *The Half-Pint Jinni, and Other Stones.*
See Chapter 3, Fantasy Collections.

9-132 DOLBIER, Maurice (Wyman). *The Magic Shop.* Gr. 3–5.
✴   Dick and Denise buy their father a magic wand as a birthday gift.
Illus. by Fritz Eichenberg, Random, 1946, 74 pp., o.p.
(BL 43:19; HB 22:350, 456; Kirkus 14:324; LJ 71:1054)

DOWNER, Ann. *Hatching Magic.*
See Chapter 10, Time Travel Fantasy.

9-133 *Dragons and Dreams: A Collection of New Fantasy and Science Fiction*
✴   ***Stories.*** **Ed. by Jane (Hyatt) Yolen (Stemple), Martin H. Greenberg, and Charles G. Waugh.** Gr. 5–9.
Ten imaginative tales by Patricia McKillip, Jane Yolen, Diana Wynne Jones, Diane Duane, Patricia MacLachlan, Zilpha Keatley Snyder, and others.
Harper, 1986, 180 pp., o.p.
(BL 82:1219; CCBB 39:200; HB 62:459; SLJ May 1986 p. 99; VOYA 9:87, 10:21)

9-134 DRAKE, Emily. *The Magickers.* **(Magickers, bk. 1).** Gr. 5–7.
Ravenwyng, the "creativity and leadership" camp in the Grand Tetons where Jason, 11, is a first-time camper, turns out to offer training in "magick." The sequels are *The Curse of Arkady* (2002), *Dragon Guard* (2003), and *The Gate of Bones* (2004).
DAW, 2001, 344 pp. (0-88677-935-9)
(BL 97:2006, 98:1416; SLJ Dec 2001 p. 133; VOYA 24:288, 25:13)

DRUON, Maurice (Samuel Roger Charles). *Tistou of the Green Thumbs.*
See Chapter 1, Allegorical Fantasy and Literary Fairy Tales.

DUANE, Diane (Elizabeth). *So You Want to Be a Wizard.*
See Chapter 12, Witchcraft and Sorcery Fantasy.

9-135 DUNLOP, Eileen (Rhona). *The House on Mayferry Street.* Gr. 7–10. (Orig. British pub. 1976, entitled *A Flute in Mayferry Street.*)
Mysterious flute music and the search for hidden treasure bring excitement into the lives of Colin and his invalid sister Marion.
Illus. by Phillida Gili, Holt, 1977, 204 pp., o.p.
(BL 74:611; CCBB 31:91; HB 54:54; Kirkus 45:990; SLJ Dec 1977 p. 62)

9-136 DURGIN, Doranna. *Seer's Blood.* Gr. 7–12.
Only Blaine Kendricks heeds Dacey Childers's warning about the return of the murderous Annekteh, and she feels compelled to join the young seer in a struggle to save the mountain people of Shadow Hollers.
Baen, 2000, pap., 345 pp. (0-671-57877-4)
(Kliatt Nov 2000 p. 18; VOYA 23:358)

9-137 DURRELL, Gerald (Malcolm). *The Fantastic Flying Journey.* Gr. 3–6. (Orig. British pub. 1987.)
When their scientist Great-Uncle Lancelot takes twins Conrad and Ivan and their sister Emma on a hot-air balloon trip around the world, he gives them the magical ability to communicate with any animal.
Illus. by Graham Percy, Simon & Schuster, 1989, 152 pp., o.p.
(BL 85:1973; HBG 1:83; Kirkus 57:915; SLJ July 1989 p. 82)

9-138 DUTTON, Sandra. *The Magic of Myrna C. Waxweather.* Gr. 3–5.
Ten-year-old Bertha Zuchelli's fairy godmother appears with three magical items—a fan, a boa, and a black satin camisole—to help overcome Bertha's reputation as teacher's pet.
Illus. by Matthew Clark, Macmillan, 1987, 96 pp., o.p.
(BL 83:1745; CCBB 40:186; Kirkus 55:372; SLJ Apr 1987 p. 93)

9-139 DYER, Heather. *The Fish in Room 11.* Gr. 3–5.
After Toby accidentally endangers the Flots, his merfolk friends, he decides to hide them in the attic of The Grand, the seaside hotel where he's lived since he was abandoned as a baby.
Illus. by Peter Bailey, Chicken House/Scholastic, 2004, 158 pp. (0-439-57975-9); Scholastic, 2005, pap., 160 pp. (0-439-57976-7)
(BL 100:1726; CCBB 57:414; Kirkus 72:441; SLJ June 2004 p. 106;)

9-140 EAGER, Edward (McMaken). *Half Magic.* Gr. 3–6.

★★ Jane, Mark, Katharine, and Martha find a coin that grants half of every wish they make. The sequel is *Magic by the Lake* (1957; Harcourt, 1999), and two related books describe the magical adventures of their children, *Knight's Castle* (1956; Harcourt, 1999; see Chapter 7, High Fantasy: Travel to Other Worlds) and *Time Garden* (1958; Harcourt, 1999).

Illus. by N(iels) M(ogens) Bodecker, Harcourt, 1954, 217 pp. (0-15-233078-X); illus. by N. M. Bodecker, Harcourt, 1999, 192 pp. (0-15-202069-1), 1999, pap. (0-15-202068-3); illus. by N. M. Bodecker, Harcourt, 2004 (0-15-205302-6)

(BL 50:363; CCBB 7:86; HB 30:174; HBG 10:290; Kirkus 22:232; LJ 79:784; TLS Nov 19, 1954 p. vii)

EAGER, Edward (McMaken). *Knight's Castle.*
See Chapter 7, High Fantasy: Travel to Other Worlds.

9-141 EAGER, Edward (McMaken). *Magic or Not?* Gr. 4–6.

★ Did the wishes of Laura, James, Lydia, and Kip come true because of magic or was it only coincidence? The sequel is *The Well-Wishers* (1960; Harcourt, 1999, pap.).

Illus. by N(iels) M(ogens) Bodecker, Harcourt, 1959, 190 p., o.p.; Harcourt, 1999, pap., 199 pp. (0-15-202080-2)

(BL 55:424; CCBB 12:131; HB 35:213; HBG 11:77; Kirkus 26:906; LJ 84:1332; TLS Dec 4, 1959 p. xiv)

9-142 EAGER, Edward (McMaken). *Seven-Day Magic.* Gr. 4–6.

★ The main characters in Susan's library book turn out to be Susan herself and the friends who share her seven magic adventures.

Illus. by N(iels) M(ogens) Bodecker, Harcourt, 1962, 156 pp., o.p; Harcourt, 1999, pap., 191 pp. (0-15-202078-0)

(CCBB 16:78; HB 38:602; HBG 11:77; LJ 88:863; TLS 1963 p. 427)

9-143 EASTON, Patricia Harrison. *Davey's Blue-Eyed Frog.* Gr. 2–5.

★ Davey keeps putting off kissing the bossy talking frog he caught, even though she told him that she's actually Princess Amelia, enchanted by a wizard.

Illus. by Mike Wohnoutka, Clarion, 2003, 104 pp. (0-618-18185-7)

(BL 99:1197; CCBB 56:397; HBG 14:354; Kirkus 71:606; SlJ July 2003 p. 95)

9-144 EBERHARDT, Thom. *Rat Boys: A Dating Experiment.* Gr. 5–9.

After bragging about their dates for the Spring Fling, 14-year-olds Marci and Summer use a magic ring to turn two pet rats into boys; but nothing goes as planned.

Hyperion, 2001, 160 pp. (0-7868-0696-6)

(BL 98:466; Kirkus 69:1422; SLJ Nov 2001 p. 154; VOYA 24:368)

ECKERT, Allan W. *The Dark Green Tunnel.*
See Chapter 7, High Fantasy: Travel to Other Worlds.

9-145 EDGHILL, Rosemary. *The Sword of Maiden's Tears.* Gr. 10 up.

When elven lord Rohannan Melior is mugged on a New York street, the magical Sword of Maiden's Tears is stolen, and Ruth Marlowe and her friends are drawn into a perilous quest to find it.

DAW, 1994, 284 pp. (0-88677-622-8)
(Kliatt Jan 1995 p. 14; LJ Nov 15, 1994 p. 90; VOYA 17:286, 18:9)

EDWARDS, Dorothy (Brown). *The Witches and the Grinnygog.*
See Chapter 12, Witchcraft and Sorcery Fantasy.

9-146 **EHRLICH, Amy.** *Lucy's Winter Tale.* Gr. K–4.
A juggler from a traveling carnival awakens Lucy and convinces her to help
him find his lost sweetheart, a high-wire artist.
Illus. by Troy Howell, Dial, 1992, 32 pp. LB (0-8037-0661-8)
(BL 88:1942; CCBB 46:144; Kirkus 60:1060; SLJ Sept 1992 p. 202)

9-147 **ELIOT, Ethel (Augusta) Cook.** *Buttercup Days.* Gr. 4–6.
Fairy Tim appears from Fairyland to spend the summer with the parsonage
children.
Illus. by Julia Daniels, Doubleday, 1924, 188 pp., o.p.
(BL 21:30; Bookshelf 1924–1925 Suppl. p. 1; Mahony 2:135; HB 1[Oct 1924]:4)

ELISH, Dan. *Jason and the Baseball Bear.*
See Chapter 2, Animal Fantasy.

9-148 **ELKIN, Benjamin.** *Al and the Magic Lamp.* Gr. 2–4.
Every time Al tries to wish on Aladdin's magic lamp, something goes wrong.
Illus. by William Wiesner, Harper, 1963, 31 pp., o.p.
(BL 60:207; CCBB 16:125; HB 39:280; LJ 88:2550)

ENDE, Michael. *The Neverending Story.*
See Chapter 7, High Fantasy: Travel to Other Worlds.

9-149 **ENRIGHT, Elizabeth (Wright).** *Zeee.* Gr. 2–4.
✸   Pandora Smith gives a temperamental fairy a safe new home in her dollhouse.
Illus. by Irene Haas, Harcourt, 1965, 46 pp., o.p.; illus. by Susan Gaber, Har-
court, 1993, 48 pp. (0-15-299958-2)
(BL 89:1830; CCBB 18:127; HB 41:276; HGB 4:285; Kirkus 33:309, 61:454; LJ 90:2883;
SLJ June 1993 p. 73)

9-150 **ERWIN, Betty K.** *Aggie, Maggie and Tish.* Gr. 3–5.
Three elderly sisters bring magic into the lives of the four Eliot children. The
sequel is *Where's Aggie?* (1967).
Illus. by Paul Kennedy, Little, Brown, 1965, 154 pp., o.p.
(BL 62:330; HB 41:628; Kirkus 33:626; LJ 90:4615)

ESTERN, Anne Graham. *The Picolinis and the Haunted House.*
See Chapter 11, Toy Fantasy.

ESTES, Eleanor (Ruth Rosenfeld). *The Witch Family.*
See Chapter 12, Witchcraft and Sorcery Fantasy.

9-151 **EVANS, Douglas.** *The Classroom at the End of the Hall.* Gr. 3–5.
Eleven stories about life in a third-grade classroom where magic abounds.
Illus. by Lawrence Di Fiori, Front Street, 1996, 132 pp., o.p.
(BL 92:1900; CCBB 50:10; HGB 8:65; Kirkus 64:978; SLJ Oct,. 1996 p. 120)

9-152 EWING, Juliana (Horatia Gatty). *The Brownies.* Gr. 4–6. (Orig. British pub. 1865; U.S., 1901, in *The Brownies and Other Tales*.)
Lazy children become helpful Brownies in this story that gave rise to the Brownie Scout name.
Illus. by Katherine Milhous, Scribner, 1946, 50 pp., o.p.; illus. by Ernest H. Shepard, Dutton, 1954, o.p.
(BL 43:140; Kirkus 14:523; LJ 72:83)

9-153 FARALLA, Dana. *The Singing Cupboard.* Gr. 3–5. (Orig. British pub. 1962.)
A magical mouse takes Nils and Ulla on a journey from Denmark to England.
Illus. by Edward Ardizzone, Lippincott, 1963, 94 pp., o.p.
(BL 60:630; HB 40:174; LJ 88:4852; TLS 1962 p. 900)

9-154 FARALLA, Dana. *The Wonderful Flying-Go-Round.* Gr. 4–6. (Orig. pub.
✫ in England.)
Mr. and Mrs. Florabella drift across the town dump in a red balloon and decide to create a playground complete with a Flying-Go-Round.
Illus. by Harold Berson, World, 1965, 94 pp., o.p.
(BL 62:528; CCBB 20:24; HB 42:52; Kirkus 33:905; LJ 90:5076)

FARBER, Norma (Holzman). *Six Impossible Things Before Breakfast.*
See Chapter 3, Fantasy Collections.

9-155 FARJEON, Eleanor. *Elsie Piddock Skips in Her Sleep.* Gr. 3–5. (Orig.
✫ British pub. 1937.)
Seven-year-old Elsie's rope-skipping abilities so impress the fairies that they teach her their magic skills, and a hundred years later she puts those skills to work against a greedy developer. This story, originally published in Farjeon's collection, *Martin Pippin in the Daisy Field* (1937, 1963), was also republished in a larger format with new illustrations by Voake (Candlewick, 2000).
Illus. by Charlotte Voake, Candlewick, 1997, 64 pp. (0-7636-0133-0); Candlewick, 2000 (0-7636-0790-8)
(BL 97:547; HBG 9:60:Kirkus 65:1456; SLJ Oct 2000 p. 122)

9-156 FARJEON, Eleanor. *Kaleidoscope.* Gr. 4–6. (Orig. British pub. 1928; U.S. 1929.)
A collection of stories about a boy named Anthony who lives near a magical millpond where he searches for secrets.
Illus. by Edward Ardizzone, Walck, 1963, 157 pp., o.p.; Goodchild, 1986, 152 pp., o.p.
(LJ 88:4083)

9-157 FARJEON, Eleanor. *Mr. Garden.* Gr. 3–5. (Orig. British pub. in this format 1965.)
A tiny man works wonders in Harry and Angela's garden.
Illus. by Jane Paton, Walck, 1966, 39 pp., o.p.
(CCBB 20:139; HB 42:429; LJ 91:4312; TLS 1966 p. 448)

9-158 FARMER (Mockridge), Penelope. *The Magic Stone.* Gr. 5–7. (Orig. British pub. 1964.)

Obsession with a magic stone blinds Caroline and Alice to the growing rivalry between their younger brothers' gangs.

Illus. by John Kaufmann, Harcourt, 1964, 223 pp., o.p.

(CCBB 18:53; HB 41:52; Kirkus 32:898; LJ 89:4646; TLS 1965 p. 513)

9-159 **FARMER (Mockridge), Penelope.** *The Summer Birds.* Gr. 4–7. (Orig.
★★   British pub. 1962.)
A strange boy spends the summer teaching Charlotte, Emma, and their friends to fly, but the magic ends when they learn his true identity. Carnegie Medal Commended Book, 1962. The sequels are *Charlotte Sometimes* (1969, see Chapter 10, Time Travel Fantasy) and *Emma in Winter* (1966).

Illus. by James J. Spanfeller, Harcourt, 1962, 155 pp., o.p.

(BL 58:728; CCBB 15:124; HB 38:176; Kirkus 30:58; LJ 87:2032; TLS 1985 p. 348)

FARMER (Mockridge), Penelope. *William and Mary: A Story.*
See Chapter 7, High Fantasy: Travel to Other Worlds.

FARTHING, Alison. *The Mystical Beast.*
See Chapter 7, High Fantasy: Travel to Other Worlds.

9-160 **FAULKNER, William (Cuthbert).** *The Wishing Tree.* Gr. 4 up. (Written 1927.)
A strange red-headed boy leads a birthday-girl and her friends on a magical hunt for the wishing tree in this story by the Nobel Prize-winning author.

Illus. by Don Bolognese, Random, 1967, 81 pp., o.p.; Garland, 1990 (0-685-33244-6)

(BL 63:1132; LJ 92:1176; TLS Nov 1967 p. 1133)

9-161 **FAUST, Minister.** *The Coyote Kings of the Space Age Bachelor Pad.* Gr. 11 up. (Orig. pub. in Canada.)
"The Coyote Kings," graduate student/dishwasher Hamza and his roommate, inventor/video store clerk Yehat, uncover a plot by former friends and drug dealers to take over the world, using the magic of an ancient Egyptian artifact called a zodiascope.

Del Rey, pap., 2004, 544 pp. (0-345-46635-7)

(BL 100:1712; LJ Apr 15, 2004 p. 128)

9-162 **FEYDY, Anne (Lindbergh Sapieyevski).** *Osprey Island.* Gr. 4–6.
Through magic, Lizzie, Charles, and Amy enter identical paintings of their houses and meet on an island called Carmar-Ogali-Retne.

Illus. by Maggie Smith, Houghton, 1974, 164 pp., o.p.

(CCBB 28:128; HB 51:146; Kirkus 42:1201; LJ 98:3045)

9-163 **FIELD, Rachel (Lyman).** *The Magic Pawnshop: A New Year's Eve Fantasy.* Gr. 3–5.
While tending Minerva MacLoon's shop on New Year's Eve, Prinda Bassett uses magic to spark a romance between Rose Martha and Christopher Marlowe Green.

Illus. by Elizabeth MacKinstry, Dutton, 1927, 125 pp., o.p.

(BL 24:125; HB 3[Nov 1927]:47; LJ 53:484)

9-164 **FIENBERG, Anna.** *Ariel, Zed and the Secret of Life.* Gr. 4–7. (Orig. Australian pub. 1992.)
In a world where book characters come to life, Ariel and Zed, children of writers, are forced to spend their school holiday on an island populated by rebellious fictional characters.
Allen, 1994, pap., 184 pp. (1-86373-276-4)
(BL 90:1947; SLJ June 1994 p. 126)

FIENBERG, Anna. *Horrendo's Curse.*
See Chapter 8, Humorous Fantasy.

9-165 **FIENBERG, Anna.** *The Magnificent Nose (and Other Marvels).* Gr. 2–4. (Orig. Australian pub. 1991.)
A golden spider called Aristan gives the children in these five whimsical stories advice about discovering their special talents and putting them to good use.
Illus. by Kim Gamble, Little, Brown, 1992, 48 pp. (0-316-28195-6)
(BL 89:438; HB 68:582; Kirkus 60:920; SLJ Jan 1993 p. 74)

FIENBERG, Anna. *Wiggy and Boa.*
See Chapter 8, Humorous Fantasy.

9-166 **FINE, Anne.** *Bad Dreams.* Gr. 4–6. (Orig. British pub. 2000.)
✮ Melanie discovers that her new friend Imogene wears a magical necklace enabling her to predict the future, and Mel becomes determined to free Imogene from its powers.
Delacorte, 2000, 134 pp. (0-385-32757-9); Dell Yearling, 2001, pap., 144 pp. (0-440-41690-6)
(BL 96:1667; CCBB 53:356; HBG 11:303; Kirkus 68:796; SLJ June 2000 p. 144)

FINNEY, Charles G(randison). *The Circus of Dr. Lao.*
See Chapter 6, High Fantasy: Myth or Legend Fantasy.

9-167 **FITCH, Marina.** *The Seventh Heart.* Gr. 7–12.
After Gillian's housemate Melanie disappears during a San Francisco earthquake, Gillian is approached by mysterious "spirit-helpers" of Earth and Wind, who ask for her help in saving the world.
Ace, 1997, pap., 310 pp. (0-441-00451-2)
(Kliatt Nov 1997 p. 14; VOYA 20:324, 21:12)

FLEISCHMAN, (Albert) Sid(ney). *The Hey Hey Man.*
See Chapter 1, Allegorical Fantasy and Literary Fairy Tales.

9-168 **FORBUS, Ina B(ell).** *The Magic Pin.* Gr. 4–6.
Neelie, the seventh granddaughter of a seventh granddaughter, inherits a brooch enabling her to speak to animals.
Illus. by Corydon Bell, Viking, 1956, 138 pp., o.p.
(CCBB 10:135; Kirkus 24:435; LJ 81:2726)

9-169 **FORWARD, Toby.** *Pie Magic.* Gr. 3–5. (Orig. British pub. 1995.)
Teased about his weight, Bertie tries a "guaranteed" magic weight-loss potion that leaves him floating on the ceiling.

Illus. by Laura Cornell, Tambourine/Morrow, 1996, 110 pp. (0-688-14511-6)
(HB 72:595; HBG 8:66)

9-170 **FORWARD, Toby.** *Traveling Backward.* Gr. 4–6. (Orig. British pub. 1992,
★ entitled *Travelling Backwards.*)
Saddened by her grandfather's imminent death, Fanny offers him a magic
potion that makes him become younger each day.
Illus. by Laura Cornell, Tambourine/Morrow, 1994, 128 pp. (0-688-13076-3);
Puffin, 1996, pap. (0-14-037875-8)
(BL 91:40:CCBB 48:44; HBG 6:76; Kirkus 62:983; SLJ Aug 1994 p. 154)

9-171 **FOSBURGH, Liza.** *Bella Arabella.* Gr. 3–5.
Lonely Arabella's wish to become a cat is granted by her talking feline Miran-
da, but Arabella finds that life as a cat is not quite what she imagined.
Illus. by Catherine Stock, Macmillan, 1985, 102 pp., o.p.
(BL 82:756; CCBB 39:127; SLJ Mar 1986 p. 162)

FOSTER, Elizabeth. *Gigi: The Story of a Merry-Go-Round Horse.*
See Chapter 11, Toy Fantasy.

FRANCHI, Anna. *The Little Lead Soldier.*
See Chapter 11, Toy Fantasy.

FRANK, Lucy. *The Annoyance Bureau.*
See Chapter 8, Humorous Fantasy.

9-172 **FRAZIER, Neta Lohnes.** *The Magic Ring.* Gr. 4–6.
Fairy child gives sensible Rebecca Osborn a magic ring and three wishes.
Illus. by Kathleen Voute, Longmans, 1959, 149 pp., o.p.
(BL 56:247; HB 35:382; Kirkus 27:402; LJ 84:3926)

9-173 **FRITZ, Jean (Guttery).** *Magic to Burn.* Gr. 4–6.
On a ship bound for America, Stephen and Ann meet a stowaway boggart
named Blaze.
Illus. by Beth Krush and Joe Krush, Coward, 1964, 255 pp., o.p.
(BL 61:711; CCBB 18:74; LJ 89:3470)

9-174 **FROST, Frances.** *Then Came Timothy.* Gr. 4–6.
Kathy and her grandparents have an eventful three-day visit with an Irish lep-
rechaun.
Illus. by Richard Bennett, Whittlesey, 1950, 155 pp., o.p.
(BL 47:47; HB 26:375; Kirkus 18:418; LJ 75:1834)

FRY, Rosalie K(ingsmill). *The Mountain Door.*
See Chapter 7, High Fantasy: Travel to Other Worlds.

9-175 **FRY, Rosalie K(ingsmill).** *Mungo.* Gr. 3–5.
Richie's summer adventures with a sea monster take him to an uncharted isle
inhabited by a shipwrecked sailor.
Illus. by Velma Ilsley, Farrar, 1972, 123 pp., o.p.
(BL 68:1004; HB 48:370; Kirkus 40:324)

9-176 FUNKE, Cornelia Caroline. *Inkheart.* Gr. 5–9. (Orig. pub. in Germany.)
✫ Since her mother's disappearance years ago, Meggie has adopted a peaceful, bookish life that becomes complicated and dangerous after the arrival of a mysterious stranger named Dustfinger; she discovers that fictional characters can come to life, including the monstrous Capricorn who wants to enslave her father.
Trans. by Anthea Bell, Chicken House/Scholastic, 2003, 544 pp. (0-439-53164-0); Scholastic, 2004, pap. (0-439-53165-9)
(BL 99:115; CCBB 57:272; HB 80:81; HBG 15:92; Kirkus 71:1174, 1402; SLJ Oct 2003 p. 164; VOYA 26:412, 27:12)

9-177 FUNKE, Cornelia Caroline. *The Thief Lord.* Gr. 6–9. (Orig. German pub.
✫ 2000.)
After their mother's death, Prosper, 12, and Boniface, 5, run away from Hamburg to Venice, where they are taken in by a "family" of children living in an abandoned movie theatre, led by Scipio, the Thief Lord. Mildred L. Batchelder Award, 2003.
Trans. by Oliver Latsch, Chicken House/Scholastic, 2002, 352 pp. (0-439-40437-1); Scholastic, 2003, pap., 376 pp. (0-439-42089-X)
(BL 99:401, 1308; CCBB 56:106; HB 78:754; HBG 14:79; Kirkus 70:1128; Kliatt Sep 2002 p. 8; SLJ Oct 2002 p. 163, Dec 2002 p. 42; VOYA 26:49)

9-178 FYLEMAN, Rose (Amy). *A Princess Came to Our Town.* Gr. 4–6. (Orig. pub. in England.)
Fairy princess Finestra grows tired of living in a fairy castle and makes a sudden appearance in the local marketplace.
Illus. by Erick Berry, Doubleday, 1928, 158 pp., o.p.
(BL 16:316; Mahoney 2:279)

9-179 GAGE, Wilson (pseud. of Mary Q[uintard] Govan Steele). *Miss Osborne-*
✫ *the-Mop.* Gr. 4–6.
Jody's magic brings a dust mop to life, but she soon regrets her actions.
Illus. by Paul Galdone, Philomel, 1963, 156 pp., o.p.
(BL 59:747; CCBB 16:110; Eakin:133; HB 39:382; LJ 88:2143)

GALL, Alice (Crew), and CREW, Fleming. *The Royal Mimkin.*
See Chapter 7, High Fantasy: Travel to Other Worlds.

9-180 GALLICO, Paul (William). *The House That Wouldn't Go Away.* Gr. 5–7.
Visions of the Victorian mansion that once stood on the site of their apartment building enable Miranda and her brothers to delve into the lives of their neighbors.
Delacorte, 1980, 234 pp., o.p.
(BL 76:1290; CCBB 32:189; HB 56:406; SLJ Aug 1980 p. 64)

9-181 GANDOLFI, Silvana. *Aldabra: Or, the Tortoise Who Loved Shakespeare.*
Gr. 5–9. (Orig. pub. in Italy.)
Elisa, 10, determined to protect her eccentric Venetian grandmother, Nonna Eia, from those threatening her with institutionalization, discovers that the women of their family can transform themselves into other creatures in order to trick death.

Trans. by Lynne Sharon Schwartz, Levine/Scholastic, 2004, 160 pp. (0-439-49741-8)

(BL 100:1360; CCBB 57:464; Kirkus 72:269; SLJ Aug 2004 p.122; VOYA 27:228)

9-182 GANNETT (Kahn), Ruth Stiles. *My Father's Dragon.* Gr. 3–5.

✶ When a stray alley cat tells him about a captive baby dragon, Elmer Elevator decides to run away and rescue it. John Newbery Medal Honor Book, 1949. The sequels are *Elmer and the Dragon* (1950, 1987) and *The Dragons of Blueland* (1951, 1987). All three tales are collected in *Three Tales of My Father's Dragon*, Random, 1998, 242 pp. (0679-88911-6).

Illus. by Ruth Chrisman Gannett, Random, 1948, 1986, 88 pp., LB (0-394-91438-4); Knopf, 1987, pap., 96 pp. (0-394-89048-5)

(BL 44:320, 83:708; CCBB 1:2; HB 26:266, 63:82; HBG 9:329; Kirkus 16:194; LJ 73:604, 824)

GARDEN, Nancy. *Fours Crossing.*
See Chapter 6, High Fantasy: Myth or Legend Fantasy.

GEE, Maurice (Gough). *The World Around the Corner.*
See Chapter 7, High Fantasy: Travel to Other Worlds.

GENTLE, Mary. *A Hawk in Silver.*
See Chapter 7, High Fantasy: Travel to Other Worlds.

GERAS, Adèle. *The Fabulous Fantoras: Book One: Family Files.*
See Chapter 8, Humorous Fantasy.

9-183 GERSTEIN, Mordicai. *Fox Eyes.* Gr. 3–5.
Sharpnose the fox longs to be a human, to play the violin like young Martin, and to eat Aunt Zavella's chickens, and one day he trades bodies with Martin and his wishes come true.

Illus. by the author, Golden, 2001, 94 pp., o.p.; Golden, 2005, pap., 80 pp. (0-307-26509-9)

(CCBB 55:14; HBG 12:290; Kirkus 69:801; SLJ Nov 2001 p. 123)

GLIORI, Debi. *Pure Dead Magic.*
See Chapter 12, Witchcraft and Sorcery Fantasy.

GODDEN (Dixon), (Margaret) Rumer. *Fu-Dog.*
See Chapter 11, Toy Fantasy.

9-184 GOLD, Carolyn J. *Dragonfly Secret.* Gr. 4–6.
When Nathan and Jessie's Gramps finds a tiny wounded fairy and begins nursing it back to health, the family decides to keep the fairy a secret from the social worker evaluating Gramps for a nursing home.

Illus. by Karen A. Jerome, Atheneum, 1997, 133 pp. (0-689-31938-X)

(BL 93:1817; HBG 8:300; Kirkus 65:720; SLJ July 1997 p. 68)

GOLDS, Cassandra. *Michael and the Secret War.*
See Chapter 7, High Fantasy: Travel to Other Worlds.

9-185 GOLDSTEIN, Lisa. *Walking the Labyrinth.* Gr. 10 up.
Molly Travers uncovers a magical family legacy, plus a generations-old feud between the American and English branches of her family.
Tor, 1996, 256 pp. (0-312-86175-3), 1998, pap. (0-312-85968-6)
(BL 92:1682, 1686; Kirkus 64:494; LJ May 15, 1996 p. 86)

9-186 GORDON, Amy. *Midnight Magic.* Gr. 2–4.
Life with Jake and Sam's weekend babysitter, Uncle Harry, is full of fairy-tale surprises.
Illus. by Judy Clifford, Bridgewater, 1995, 64 pp., o.p.
(HBG 7:54; SLJ Dec 1995 p. 80)

GORDON, John (William). *The Giant Under the Snow: A Story of Suspense.*
See Chapter 6, High Fantasy: Myth or Legend Fantasy.

9-187 GORMLEY, Beatrice. *Best Friend Insurance.* Gr. 4–6.
Maureen's purchase of "best friend insurance" from mysterious Mr. Costue results in her mother's transformation into a girl named Kitty who expects Maureen to run the household.
Illus. by Emily Arnold McCully, Dutton, 1983, 147 pp., o.p.
(BL 80:813; CCBB 37:87; SLJ Feb 1984 p. 70)

9-188 GORMLEY, Beatrice. *Fifth Grade Magic.* Gr. 4–6.
A delinquent apprentice fairy godmother named Errora does a bungled job of granting fifth-grader Gretchen's wish to be the lead in the class play. The sequel is *More Fifth Grade Magic* (1989, 1990).
Illus. by Emily Arnold McCully, Dutton, 1982, 131 pp., o.p.
(BL 79:564; HB 58:516; SLJ Oct 1982 p. 152)

9-189 GORMLEY, Beatrice. *Mail-Order Wings.* Gr. 4–6.
Andrea finds she can actually fly using her Wonda-Wings Kit, but she becomes frightened when the wings won't come off. The sequel is *The Ghastly Glasses* (1985).
Illus. by Emily Arnold McCully, Elsevier-Dutton, 1981, 164 pp., o.p.; Avon, 1984, pap., 164 pp. (0-380-67421-1)
(BL 78:235; CCBB 35:107; SLJ Dec 1981 p. 63; Suth 3:157)

9-190 GORMLEY, Beatrice. *Paul's Volcano.* Gr. 4–7.
Paul and Adam's science project, a papier-mâché volcano, begins to grow during the night and they fear that they've summoned up an ancient volcano god.
Illus. by Cat Bowen Smith, Houghton, 1987, 144 pp., o.p.
(BL 83:1445; Kirkus 55:552; SLJ Mar 1987 p. 158)

GOROG, Judith. *In a Creepy, Creepy Place, and Other Scary Stories.*
See Chapter 3, Fantasy Collections.

GOROG, Judith. *On Meeting Witches at Wells.*
See Chapter 4, Ghost Fantasy.

9-191 GOUDGE, Elizabeth (de Beauchamp). *Linnets and Valerians.* Gr. 5–7.
★   (Orig. pub. in England.)
After Mrs. Valerian takes in the runaway Linnet children, they decide to repay
her kindness by searching for her long-lost son; in the process, they encounter a
witch, giants, and magic cats.
Illus. by Ian Ribbons, Coward, 1946, 290 pp., o.p.; Gregg, 1981, 290 pp., o.p.;
Dell, 1992, pap. (0-440-40590-4); Penguin/Putnam, 2001, pap. (0-14-230026-8)
(BL 61:578; CCBB 18:74; Eakin:145; HB 40:615, 78:432; TLS 1964 p. 1077)

9-192 GOUDGE, Elizabeth (de Beauchamp). *The Little White Horse.* Gr. 5–8.
★   (Orig. British pub. 1946.)
Magical creatures help Maria Merryweather fight the evil Black Men of the for-
est. Carnegie Medal, 1946.
Illus. by C(yril) Walter Hodges, Coward, 1947, 280 pp., o.p.; Gregg, 1980, 280
pp., o.p.; Dell, 1992, pap., 272 pp. (0-440-40734-6); Penguin/Putnam, 2001,
pap. (0-14-230027-6)
(BL 43:349; HB 23:212, 78:432; Kirkus 15:167; LJ 72:738)

9-193 GOUDGE, Elizabeth (de Beauchamp). *Smoky-House.* Gr. 5–8. (Orig.
British pub. 1940.)
Fairies help the Trequddick children save their father from betrayal as a smug-
gler.
Illus. by Richard Floethe, Coward, 1940, 286 pp., o.p.
(BL 37:94; HB 16:343, 430; LJ 65:849, 878; TLS 1940p. 634)

9-194 GRAHAM, Harriet. *A Boy and His Bear.* Gr. 4–7. (Orig. British pub. 1995.)
Dickon and the bear cub with whom he can communicate are forced to flee
from Elizabethan England to France, where they join a traveling circus.
McElderry, 1996, 196 pp. (0-689-80943-3)
(CCBB 50:206; HBG 8:79; Kirkus 64:1322; SLJ Nov 1996 p. 104, Dec 1996 p. 29)

9-195 GRANT, Vicki. *The Puppet Wrangler.* Gr. 5–7. (Orig. Canadian pub. 2004.)
Visiting her Toronto children's television producer aunt, Telly, 12, meets Bit-
sie, a manipulative talking puppet who involves Telly in a series of incredible
escapades.
Orca, 2004, pap., 174 pp. (1-55143-304-4)
(CCBB 57:466; SLJ Aug 2004 p. 122)

9-196 GRAVES, Robert. *The Big Green Book.* Gr. 2–3.
Jack uses spells from a big green magic book to fool his overprotective aunt
and uncle into letting him have more freedom.
Illus. by Maurice (Bernard) Sendak, Crowell-Collier, 1962, 1968, 61 pp., o.p.;
Macmillan, 1985, o.p.
(BL 81:1333; HB 61:437)

9-197 GRAY, Genevieve S(tuck). *The Seven Wishes of Joanna Peabody.* Gr. 3–5.
Joanna is granted seven wishes by Aunt Thelma, a Special Spirit who appears
on the Peabody's TV screen.
Illus. by Elton Fax, Lothrop, 1972, 61 pp., o.p.
(BL 69:493; CCBB 26:154; Kirkus 40:939; LJ 97:3806)

9-198 **GRAY, Luli.** *Falcon's Egg.* Gr. 4–7.

✶ The unusual scarlet egg that 11-year-old Falcon finds in New York's Central Park hatches into a dragon. The sequel is *Falcon and the Charles Street Witch* (2002).

Houghton, 1995, 133 pp., o.p.; Dell, 1997, pap., 133 pp. (0-395-71128-0)

(BL 92:162; CCBB 489:55; HB 72:336; HBG 7:61; Kirkus 63:945; SLJ Sep 1995 p. 199, Dec 1995 p. 21; VOYA 18:382)

9-199 **GRAY, Nicholas Stuart.** *The Apple Stone.* Gr. 5–7. (Orig. British pub. 1965.)

A golden Apple Stone brings a stuffed bird, a model rocket, a leopard-skin rug, and a stone gargoyle to life.

Illus. by Charles Keeping, Hawthorn, 1969, 230 pp., o.p.

(BL 66:408; CCBB 23:128; Kirkus 37:777; LJ 94:4582, 4606; TLS 1965 p. 1131)

9-200 **GREEN, Phyllis.** *Eating Ice Cream with a Werewolf.* Gr. 4–6.

The chicken that turns up in Nancy's bed is only one of many strange things that happen when Brad and Nancy's wacky babysitter decides to try out her new hobby, witchcraft,

Illus. by Patti Stern, Harper, 1983, 121 pp., o.p.

(BL 79:1465; CCBB 36:189; HB 59:302)

9-201 **GREEN, Susan.** *Self-Portrait with Wings.* Gr. 5–7.

When the wings Jennifer drew on her self-portrait appear in real life, she is able to do a fabulous "Jennifer Jump" on ice skates.

Little, Brown, 1989, 206 pp., o.p.

(BL 85:1649; CCBB 42:275; HB 65:620; Kirkus 57:762; SLJ May 1989 p. 109)

GRIFFIN, Adele. *Witch Twins.*
See Chapter 12, Witchcraft and Sorcery Fantasy.

9-202 **GRIFFIN, Peni R(ae).** *Hobkin.* Gr. 5–8.

Running away from their stepfather's abuse, Liza and Kay Franklin take over an abandoned farmhouse where Liza does the household chores with the help of Hobkin, a brownie who traveled to West Texas from England with the farm's former owner.

Macmillan, 1992, 202 pp. (0-689-50539-6); Puffin, 1993, pap. (0-14-036356-4)

(BL 88:1378; CCBB 45:261; HBG 3:263; Kirkus 60:537; SLJ June 1992 p. 136; VOYA 15:94)

9-203 **GRIFFIN, Peni R(ae).** *Margo's House.* Gr. 3–6.

When Margo's Dad is hospitalized with a heart attack, Margo is transformed into Sis, one of the dolls in the house he was building for her.

McElderry, 1996, 122 pp. (0-689-80944-1)

(BL 93:130; CCBB 50:97; HBG 8:67; Kirkus 64:1322; SLJ Oct 1996 p. 122)

GRIFFIN, Peni R(ae). *The Maze.*
See Chapter 7, High Fantasy: Travel to Other Worlds.

9-204 GRIFFIN, Peni R(ae). *Otto from Otherwhere.* Gr. 4–6.
A science-fantasy about Paula and Peter, who find an odd-looking alien with a beautiful singing voice, name him Otto, try to pass him off as their cousin, and help him find his way home.
Macmillan, 1990, 192 pp., o.p.
(BL 86:1702; CCBB 43:264; HBG 1:258; Kirkus 58:499; SLJ Aug 1990 p. 146)

GRIFFITH, Helen V(irginia). *Caitlin's Holiday.*
See Chapter 11, Toy Fantasy.

9-205 GRIFFITH, Helen V(irginia). *Emily and the Enchanted Frog.* Gr. 1–3.
☆ In these three stories, Emily meets an unwilling frog prince, a wish-granting elf, and a hermit crab that thinks it's a mermaid.
Illus. by Susan Condie Lamb, Greenwillow, 1989, 32 pp., o.p.
(BL 86:180; CCBB 43:33; HBG 1:49; Kirkus 57:989; SLJ Sept 1989 p. 226)

GRIGGS, Terry. *Cat's Eye Corner.*
See Chapter 8, Humorous Fantasy.

GROSSER, Morton. *The Snake Horn.*
See Chapter 10, Time Travel Fantasy.

9-206 GRUMBLE, Rosemary. *Jonothon and Large.* Gr. 2–4. (Orig. British pub. 1965.)
The sea-serpent that Jonothon raised returns to save him and his father from a hurricane at sea.
Illus. by the author, Bobbs-Merrill, 1966, 88 pp., o.p.
(Kirkus 38:340; LJ 92:2014; TLS 1965 p. 1131)

9-207 GUILLOT, René. *Nicolette and the Mill.* Gr. 2–4. (Orig. pub. in France.)
An emerald fairy ring enables Nicolette to understand the language of animals.
Trans. by Gwen Marsh, illus. by Charles Mozley, Abelard-Schuman, 1960, 79 pp., o.p.
(Kirkus 28:949; LJ 86:373; TLS May 20, 1960 p. vii)

GURNEY, James. *Dinotopia: A Land Apart from Time.*
See Chapter 7, High Fantasy: Travel to Other Worlds.

GUTMAN, Dan. *Honus and Me: A Baseball Card Adventure.*
See Chapter 10, Time Travel Fantasy.

HAAS, Dorothy F. (Dee Francis). *The Bears Up Stairs.*
See Chapter 2, Animal Fantasy.

9-208 HABER, Melissa Glenn. *The Heroic Adventures of Hercules Amsterdam.* Gr. 4–7.
Ten year-old Hercules Amsterdam, 3 inches tall, finds a hidden city inside a mousehole, discovers that he can speak mouse-squeak, and attempts to save the mice from an imminent rat attack.
Dutton, 2003, 224 pp. (0-525-47119-7); Puffin, 2004, pap., 218 pp. (0-14-240216-8)
(CCBB 57:105; Kirkus 71:804; HBG 14:367; SLJ June 2003 p. 142; VOYA 26:324)

HACKETT, Walter Anthony. *The Swans of Ballycastle.*
See Chapter 1, Allegorical Fantasy and Literary Fairy Tales.

9-209 HAENEL, Wolfram. *The Extraordinary Adventures of an Ordinary Hat.*
Gr. 2–4. (Orig. pub. in Switzerland.)
A black bowler hat sets off on the adventurous life it dreamed of during many
years on a hat shop shelf.
Trans. by J. Alison James, illus. by Christa Unzer-Fischer, North-South, 1994,
61 pp., o.p.; North-South, 1995, pap. (1-55858-410-2)
(BL 90:1947; HBG 5:274; SLJ July 1994 p. 77)

9-210 HAENEL, Wolfram. *Lila's Little Dinosaur.* Gr. 2–4. (Orig. pub. in Switzerland.)
Lila adopts a baby dinosaur that follows her home from New York's Museum
of Natural History.
Trans. by J. Alison James, illus. by Alex de Wolf, North-South, 1994, 64 pp.
(1-55858-310-6)
(BL 91:820; HBG 6:66; Kirkus 62:1530)

HALAM, Ann. *The Daymaker.*
See Chapter 5, High Fantasy: Alternate Worlds or Histories.

HAMILTON (Adoff), Virginia (Esther). *The All Jadhu Storybook.*
See Chapter 8, Humorous Fantasy.

9-211 HAMLEY, Dennis. *Blood Line.* Gr. 9–12. (Orig. British pub. 1989.)
A strange television saga unfolds in television-obsessed Rory's home, causing
the high school loner to become haunted by questions about his family's past.
Deutsch, 1990, pap., 160 pp, o.p.
(BL 87:46; SLJ Sept 1990 p. 250)

9-212 HANLEY, Eve. *The Enchanted Toby Jug.* Gr. 3–5. (Orig. British pub. 1964.)
A Toby jug comes to life and tells stories to four children.
Illus. by Nora S(picer) Unwin, Washburn, 1965, 134 pp., o.p.
(Kirkus 33:6; LJ 90:960; TLS 1964 p. 602)

9-213 HANSEN, Ron. *The Shadowmaker.* Gr. 3–6.
✶ Drizzle, the poorest child in town, manages to outwit the Shadowmaker, a mys-
terious man who sells shadows of people's secret dreams.
Illus. by Margot Tomes, Harper, 1987, 80 pp., LB (0-06-022203-4)
(BL 83:1446; CCBB 40:125; HB 63:605; Kirkus 55:719; SLJ Aug 1987 p. 83)

HARRIS, Rosemary (Jeanne). *Sea Magic and Other Stories of
Enchantment.*
See Chapter 3, Fantasy Collections.

9-214 HARVEY, Dean. *The Secret Elephant of Harlan Kooter.* Gr. 3–5.
Harlan's problems with bullies and his solo paper route are solved after he
finds Hannibal the talking elephant hiding in his garage.
Illus. by Mark Richardson, Houghton, 1992, 130 pp. (0-395-62523-8)
(CCBB 46:113; HB 68:724; HBG 4:69; Kirkus 60:1187; SLJ Nov 1992 p. 91)

HASELEY, Dennis. *Doctor Gravity.*
See Chapter 8, Humorous Fantasy.

9-215 HASELEY, Dennis. *Trick of the Eye.* Gr. 7–10.
Thirteen-year-old Richard tries to remember what happened in his past that enables him to hear and understand the voices of figures inside famous paintings, voices that tell him he has forgotten something important.
Dial, 2004, 208 pp. (0-8037-2856-5)
(BL 100:1919; CCBB 57:467; Kirkus 72:270; SLJ April 2004 p. 155; VOYA 27:58)

HAUFF, Wilhelm. *The Adventures of Little Mouk.*
See Chapter 1, Allegorical Fantasy and Literary Fairy Tales.

HAWKINS, Laura. *Figment, Your Dog, Speaking.*
See Chapter 2, Animal Fantasy.

HAWTHORNE, Julian. *Rumpty-Dudget's Tower: A Fairy Tale.*
See Chapter 1, Allegorical Fantasy and Literary Fairy Tales.

9-216 HEAL (Berrien), Edith. *What Happened to Jenny.* Gr. 3–5.
Neighborhood dogs take Jenny on a tour of the city although she is supposed to be in bed recovering from the measles.
Illus. by Abbi Giventer, Atheneum, 1962, 62 pp., o.p.
(HB 39:53, 76; Kirkus 30:559)

9-217 HEARNE, Betsy (Gould). *Wishes, Kisses, and Pigs.* Gr. 4–6.
✶ Did Louise Tolliver's wish on an evening star cause the odd things happening in Tolliver's Hollow, starting with the disappearance of her father and brother and the mysterious appearance of a white pig and a large hoot owl?
Simon, 2001, 133 pp. (0-689-84122-1); Aladdin, 2003, pap., 144 pp. (0-689-86347-0)
(BL 97:1278; CCBB 54:373; HB 77:326; HBG 12:306; SLJ April 2002 p. 140)

9-218 HENDRICH, Paula (Griffith). *Who Says So?* Gr. 4–6.
Lucinda conjures up an apparition and decides to use it as her science project at the county fair.
Illus. by Trina Schart Hyman, Lothrop, 1972, 160 pp., o.p.
(CCBB 26:56; Kirkus 40:259; LJ 98:644)

9-219 HENDRY, Diana. *A Camel Called April.* Gr. 2–3. (Orig. British pub. 1990.)
When the animals from Harry's dreams begin appearing in the park next door, he tries to dream them away, but one camel refuses to leave.
Illus. by Thor Wickstrom, Lothrop, 1991, 48 pp. (0-688-10193-3)
(HBG 2:255; SLJ Aug 1991 p. 150)

9-220 HENDRY, Diana. *Harvey Angell.* **(Harvey Angell trilogy).** Gr. 4–7. (Orig.
✶ British pub. 1991.)
When Harvey Angell rents the attic room in Henry's Aunt Agatha's rooming house, music and magic transform the other residents and family secrets are revealed. Whitbread Children's Book Award, 1991. The sequels are *Harvey Angell and the Ghost Child* (1997, 2002) and *Harvey Angell Beats Time* (2000, 2002).

Pocket/Minstrel, 2001, pap., 160 pp. (0-7434-2828-5)

(BL 98:858; SLJ Dec 2001 p. 134; VOYA 25:13, 51)

9-221 HENEGHAN, James. *Flood.* Gr. 5–8.

★ Saved by the Sheehogue, or Little People, from drowning in the flood that killed his mother and stepfather, 11-year-old Andy runs away from his Aunt Mona's home to live with his charming but drunken father, who tells him tales of the Sheehogue.

Farrar, 2002, 192 pp. (0-374-35057-4); Groundwood, 2002, pap., 192 pp. (0-88899-466-4)

(BL 98:1258; CCBB 55:281; HB 78:461; HBG 13:392; Kirkus 70:181; SLJ April 2002 p. 150)

9-222 HENRY, Jan. *Tiger's Chance.* Gr. 3–5.

★ A tiger rug with magic whiskers takes Jennifer and her cat Midnight to his jungle home.

Illus. by Hilary Knight, Harcourt, 1957, 138 pp., o.p.

(BL 53:460; CCBB 10:130; Eakin:156; HB 33:222; Kirkus 25:218; LJ 82:2190)

HENRY, Maeve. *A Gift for a Gift: A Ghost Story.*
See Chapter 4, Ghost Fantasy.

9-223 HESS, Fjeril. *The Magic Switch.* Gr. 2–4.

Marenka's magic birch switch enables her to talk to animals, trees, and flowers.

Illus. by Neva Kanaga Brown, Macmillan, 1929, 74 pp., o.p.

(BL 26:166; HB 5:46, 49; Mahony 3:173)

9-224 HESSE, Karen. *A Time of Angels.* Gr. 6–9.

★ Hannah is haunted by visions of an angel while suffering through the influenza epidemic that kills her aunt and threatens her sisters in 1918.

Hyperion, 1995, 250 pp. (0-7868-0087-9); Disney, 1997, pap., 256 pp. (0-7868-1209-5)

(BL 92:618; CCBB 49:161; HBG 7:62; Kirkus 63:1429; SLJ Dec 1995 p. 131)

9-225 HILL, Douglas (Arthur). *Penelope's Pendant.* Gr. 4–6. (Orig. British pub. 1990.)

The tarnished pendant Perry finds on the beach proves to have magic powers when she is threatened by a gang of older boys.

Doubleday, 1991, 112 pp., o.p.

(BL 87:1493; HBG 2:270; Kirkus 59:107; SLJ Mar 1991 p. 193)

9-226 HILL, Elizabeth Starr. *Ever-After Island.* Gr. 4–6.

Ryan and Sara search the Cavern of the Winds for the magic jewel needed to break the spell that binds their father.

Dutton, 1977, 160 pp., o.p.

(BL 73:1497; CCBB 31:34; Kirkus 45:575; SLJ Sept 1977 p. 130)

9-227 HILLER, Catherine. *Abracatabby.* Gr. 2–4.

Although Adam's black kitten, Abracatabby, can do magic and grant wishes, the cat doesn't want anyone else to know his secret.

Illus. by Victoria de Larrea, Coward, 1981, 62 pp., o.p.

(BL 77:1350; Kirkus 49:799; SLJ Nov 1981 p. 77)

HISER, Constance. *The Missing Doll.*
See Chapter 11, Toy Fantasy.

9-228 HISER, Constance. *No Bean Sprouts, Please!* Gr. 2–4.
The lunch box James's Uncle Wesley sends for his ninth birthday turns his
health-food lunches into delicious cheeseburgers and fries.
Illus. by Carolyn Ewing, Holiday, 1989, 57 pp. (0-8234-0760-8); Pocket, 1991,
pap. (0-671-72325-1)
(BL 86:743; HBG 1:75; Kirkus 57:1826; SLJ Nov 1989 p. 83)

9-229 HITE, Sid. *Dither Farm.* Gr. 6–10.
☆ The Dither family's quiet life on the farm is transformed when their world-trav-
eling Great-Aunt Emma leaves orphaned 11-year-old Warren and a magic carpet in their care. In the sequel, *Those Darn Dithers* (1996), the eccentric Dither
family has an eventful summer: Archibald helps his friend Carl deal with a
ghost, Holly joins an equestrian Wild West show, Emmet tries to create a
vaudeville show, and Great-Aunt Emma invents an astral projection device.
Henry Holt, 1992, 216 pp. (0-8050-1871-9); Laurel Leaf, 1996, pap. (0-440-
21944-2)
(BL 88:1676; HBG 3:274; Kirkus 60:719; SLJ May 1992 p. 133; VOYA 16:90)

9-230 HOBBS, Will. *Kokopelli's Flute.* Gr. 5–8.
☆ Playing the small Anasazi flute he finds after frightening off some New Mexico
grave robbers, Tepary Jones is transformed into a pack rat.
Illus. by Susan Saelig-Gallagher and Michelle Barnes Mikaelsen,
Simon/Atheneum, 1995, 148 pp. (0-689-31974-6); HarperTrophy, 1997, pap.,
176 pp. (0-380-72818-4)
(BL 92:304; HBG 7:63; SLJ Oct 1995 p. 134; VOYA 18:372)

9-231 HOFFMAN, Alice. *Aquamarine.* Gr. 5–7.
Best friends and neighbors Hailey and Claire, facing permanent separation at
summer's end, find a mermaid named Aquamarine stranded near the ocean's
edge. This story has been republished in *Alice Hoffman's Water Tales, Two
Novels: Aquamarine and Indigo* (2003).
Scholastic, 2001, 112 pp. (0-439-09863-7), 2002, pap. (0-439-09864-5)
(BL 97:1278, 98:1278; CCBB 54:224; Kirkus 69:259; Kliatt Mar 2001 p. 10; SLJ Mar 2001 p.
250)

9-232 HOFFMAN, Alice. *Indigo.* Gr. 5–8.
Three outsider friends, orphaned 13-year-old Martha Glimmer, and web-fin-
gered brothers Trevor and Eli McGill, run away from landlocked Oak Grove
and are caught in a flash flood. This story has been republished in *Alice Hoff-
man's Water Tales, Two Novels: Aquamarine and Indigo* (2003).
Scholastic, 2002, 84 pp. (0-439-25635-6), 2003, pap. (0-439-25636-4)
(BL 98:1961; CCBB 55:367; HBG 13:374; Kliatt May 2002 p. 10; SLJ Aug 2002 p. 188;
VOYA 25:202)

9-233 HOFFMAN, Mary. *The Four-Legged Ghosts.* Gr. 2–5. (Orig. British pub.
☆ 1992, entitled *The Ghost Menagerie.*)
Alex and Carrie's pet mouse, Cedric, can magically summon the ghosts of all
the pets who ever lived in the Brodie's house.

Illus. by Laura L. Seeley, Dial, 1993, 96 pp. (0-8037-1466-1); Puffin, 1995, pap., 96 pp. (0-14-037601-1)

(BL 90:60; CCBB 47:156; HBG 5:66; Kirkus 61:1002; SLJ Aug 1993 p. 164)

9-234 HOFFMAN, Nina Kiriki. *A Fistful of Sky.* Gr. 10 up.
Gypsum LaZelle, a disappointed 18-year-old late-bloomer from a magically endowed family, falls ill and awakens with the disturbing ability to draw personalities out of inanimate objects.
Berkley/Ace, 2002, 368 pp. (0-441-00975-1); Ace, 2004, pap., 368 pp. (0-441-01177-2)

(BL 99:308; VOYA 26:64)

9-235 HOFFMANN, Eleanor. *Mischief in Fez.* Gr. 4–6.
Mousa's new stepmother brings evil Djinns to disrupt the household, but a desert fox flies the boy over the mountains to find a magical solution to his problems.
Illus. by Fritz Eichenberg, Holiday, 1943, 109 pp., o.p.

(BL 39:373; HB 19:170; LJ 68:433, 825)

HOFFMANN, E(rnst) T(heodor) A(madeus). *The Nutcracker.*
See Chapter 11, Toy Fantasy.

9-236 HOLCH, Greg. *The Things with Wings.* Gr. 5–8.
☆   When Newton's friend Vanessa tastes the fruit of a strange tree in a mysterious garden, she is transformed into a huge caterpillar and then into an emerald rainbow butterfly.
Scholastic, 1998, 229 pp. (0-590-93501-1); Apple, 1999, pap., 240 pp. (0-590-93502-X)

(BL 94:2005; HB 74:488; HBG 9:331; Kirkus 66:659; SLJ May 1998 p. 142; VOYA 21.:129)

HOLT, Tom. *Who's Afraid of Beowulf?*
See Chapter 6, High Fantasy: Myth or Legend Fantasy.

9-237 HOPP, Zinken. *The Magic Chalk.* Gr. 3–5. (Orig. Norwegian pub. 1948.)
John uses a witch's magic chalk to draw a boy who comes to life.
Trans. by Suzanne Bergensdahl, illus. by Malvin Neset, McKay, 1959, 127 pp., o.p.

(Kirkus 27:492; LJ 85:844; TLS Nov 25, 1960 p. x)

9-238 HORSEMAN, Elaine. *Hubble's Bubble.* Gr. 5–7. (Orig. British pub. 1964.)
Sarah and Marie must keep their experiments with black magic spells secret from three unexpected visitors.
Norton, 1964, 220 pp., o.p.

(LJ 89:4196; TLJ 1964 p. 602)

HOUGH, (Helen) Charlotte (Woodyatt). *Red Biddy and Other Stories.*
See Chapter 3, Fantasy Collections.

HOUSMAN, Laurence. *The Rat-Catcher's Daughter: A Collection of Stories.*
See Chapter 3, Fantasy Collections.

9-239 **HOWARD, Alice (Woodbury).** *Sokar and the Crocodile: A Fairy Story of Egypt.* Gr. 3–5.
A young Egyptian boy named Sokar finds himself inside a fairy story, searching for a magic lotus bud.
Illus. by Coleman Kubinyi, Macmillan, 1928, 1948, 58 pp., o.p.
(BL 25:170; HB 4[Nov 1928]:79, 4[Aug 1928]:19, 7:115; Mahony 2:424)

HOWARD, Joan (pseud. of Patricia Gordon). *The Oldest Secret.*
See Chapter 7, High Fantasy: Travel to Other Worlds.

9-240 **HOWARD, Joan (pseud. of Patricia Gordon).** *The Thirteenth Is Magic.*
Gr. 4–6.
A black cat takes Ronnie and Gillian up to the magical 13th floor of their apartment building. The sequel is *The Summer Is Magic* (1952).
Illus. by Adrienne Adams, Lothrop, 1950, 170 pp., o.p.
(BL 47:224; CCBB 4:20; HB 27:31; Kirkus 18:725; LJ 76:338)

HOYLAND, John. *The Ivy Garland.*
See Chapter 4, Ghost Fantasy.

HUFF, Tanya. *Gate of Darkness, Circle of Light.*
See Chapter 6, High Fantasy: Myth or Legend Fantasy.

9-241 **HUGHES, Carol.** *Toots and the Upside-Down House.* Gr. 3–5. (Orig. British pub. 1996.)
When Toots is captured by the fairies who protect her house, she becomes entangled in a war between the fairies and enemy goblins and sprites. The sequels are *Toots Underground* (2001), *Toots Upside Down Again* (1998 in England), and *Toots Underwater!* (1999 in England).
Illus. by J. Garrett Sheldrew, John Stevenson, and Anthony Stacchi, Random, 1997, 141 pp. (0-679-98653-7); Random, 2000, pap., 144 pp. (0-679-88654-0)
(BL 94:125; HBG 8:302; SLJ Oct 1997 p. 98)

9-242 **HUGHES, Dean.** *Theo Zephyr.* Gr. 5–7.
Sixth-grader Brad's imaginary hero, Theo Zephyr, comes to life and exacts revenge on the school bully.
Macmillan, 1987, 128 pp., o.p.
(CCBB 40:210; Kirkus 55:1071; SLJ Oct 1987 p. 126; VOYA 10:201)

9-243 **HUGHES, Shirley.** *Enchantment in the Garden.* Gr. 1–4. (Orig. British pub. 1996.)
Lonely Valerie brings to life the garden statue of Cherubino, a sea god's son, and he becomes her best friend.
Illus. by the author, Lothrop/Morrow, 1997, 64 pp. (0-688-14597-3)
(BL 93:1575; CCBB 50:399; HB 73:192; HBG 8:291; Kirkus 65:558; SLJ May 1997 p. 100)

9-244 **HUNT, Marigold.** *Hester and the Gnomes.* Gr. 2–5.
Hester discovers that a group of gnomes have set up housekeeping in a hollow tree on her father's farm.
Illus. by Jean Chariot, Whittlesey, 1955, 124 pp., o.p.
(HB 31:376; Kirkus 23:417; LJ 80:2645)

9-245 HUNTER, Mollie (pseud. of Maureen Mollie Hunter McVeigh McIl-wraith). *The Ferlie.* Gr. 4–6. (Orig. British pub. 1968.)
Hob the herd boy enters into a battle of wits with a ferlie over some stolen cattle.
Illus. by Joseph Cellini, Funk, 1968, 128 pp., o.p.
(BL 65:498; CCBB 22:95; HB 45:55)

9-246 HUNTER, Mollie (pseud. of Maureen Mollie Hunter McVeigh McIl-
✭ **wraith).** *The Mermaid Summer.* Gr. 4–7. (Orig. British pub. 1988.)
In order to bring home their banished grandfather, Anna and Jon try to tame the mermaid who has power over their Scottish fishing village.
Harper, 1988, 128 pp., o.p.
(BL 84:1676, 85:879; CCBB 41:180; HB 65:70; Kirkus 54:828; SLJ June–July 1988 p. 105; Suth 4:195)

9-247 HUNTER, Mollie (pseud. of Maureen Mollie Hunter McVeigh McIl-
✭ **wraith).** *The Wicked One: A Story of Suspense.* Gr. 5–8. (Orig. British pub. 1977.)
Scotsman Colin Grant moves his family to America to avoid the devilish tricks of the Grollican, only to find that the demon has followed them.
Harper, 1977, 128 pp., o.p.
(BL 73:1339, 1352; CCBB 30:160; HB 53:442; Kirkus 45:426; SLJ May 1977 pp. 36, 62; Suth 2:234)

9-248 HURLBUTT, Isabelle B. *Little Heiskell.* Gr. 3–4.
Little Heiskell, a soldier-shaped weathervane, descends from the markethouse roof to bring Christmas cheer to the children of Hagerstown.
Illus. by Alida Conover, Dutton, 1928, 59 pp., o.p.
(BL 25:127; Bookshelf 1929 p. 12; HB 4[Nov 1928]:80; Mahony 2:716)

9-249 HUTCHINS, Hazel (J.). *Anastasia Morningstar.* Gr. 3–5. (Orig. Canadian pub. 1984, entitled *Anastasia Morningstar and the Crystal Butterfly*.)
Sarah hopes to use Anastasia Morningstar's magical talents as a science project, after she watches her neighbor turn an annoying boy into a frog.
Illus. by Julie Tennent, Viking, 1989, 88 pp., o.p.; Puffin, 1992, pap. (0-14-034343-1)
(BL 86:2090; HBG 1:256; SLJ Aug 1990 p. 148)

HUTCHINS, Hazel (J.). *The Prince of Tarn.*
See Chapter 7, High Fantasy: Travel to Other Worlds.

9-250 HUTCHINS, Hazel (J.). *The Three and Many Wishes of Jason Reid.* Gr.
✭ 2–5. (Orig. Canadian pub. 1983.)
Jason convinces leprechaun-like Quicksilver to grant him a wish that won't just make him a better baseball player, but will make a difference in the world.
Illus. by Julie Tennent, Viking, 1988, 89 pp., o.p.; Puffin, 1990, pap. (0-14-032178-0)
(BL 84:1926; CCBB 41:208; Kirkus 56:279; SLJ May 1989 p. 97; Suth 4:197)

9-251 IBBOTSON, Eva. *Island of the Aunts.* Gr. 5–8. (Orig. British pub. 1999.)
✭ Three elderly sisters kidnap three English children to help them care for the mermaids, selkies, and other magical creatures on their island home.

Illus. by Kevin Hawkes, Dutton, 2000, 281 pp. (0-525-46484-0); Penguin Puntam, 2001, pap. (0-14-230049-7)

(BL 97:706; CCBB 54:225; Kirkus 68:1424; HBG 12:74; SLJ Nov 2000 p. 156, Dec 2000 p. 54)

INGELOW, Jean. *Mopsa the Fairy.*
See Chapter 7, High Fantasy: Travel to Other Worlds.

IRVING, Washington. *Rip Van Winkle.*
See Chapter 6, High Fantasy: Myth or Legend Fantasy.

9-252   **JAMES, M(ontague) R(hodes).** *The Five Jars.* Gr. 7 up. (Orig. British pub. 1922.)
The magical contents of five jars discovered by an Englishman reveal the fairy world all around him.
Illus. by Gilbert James, Longman, 1922, 172 pp., o.p.; Arno, 1976 (repr. of 1922 ed.), 172 pp., o.p.
(BL 19:224; HB 3[May 1927]:22)

JAMES, Mary. *Shoebag.*
See Chapter 2, Animal Fantasy.

JAMES, Mary. *The Shuteyes.*
See Chapter 7, High Fantasy: Travel to Other Worlds.

JANE, Pamela. *Noelle of the Nutcracker.*
See Chapter 11, Toy Fantasy.

9-253   **JARRELL, Randall.** *Fly by Night.* Gr. 3–4.
☆   A young boy floats out into the night, sees into dreams, listens to animals talking, and visits an owl's nest to hear a bedtime poem-story.
Illus. by Maurice (Bernard) Sendak, Farrar, 1969, 1976, 1985, 40 pp., o.p.
(BL 73:474; CCBB 30:92; HB 53:52, 62:616; Kirkus 44:1137; SLJ Nov 1976 p. 59; Suth 2:241)

JENNINGS, Paul. *Unreal! Eight Surprising Stories.*
See Chapter 3, Fantasy Collections.

9-254   **JENNINGS, Richard W.** *Orwell's Luck.* Gr. 5–7.
☆   The injured rabbit the 12-year-old narrator rescues and names Orwell sends her coded messages within the daily newspaper horoscope.
Houghton, 2000, 146 pp. (0-618-03628-8)
(BL 97:435, 1561; CCBB 54:107; HBG 12:74; Kirkus 68:886; SLJ Oct 2000 p. 161; VOYA 23:266)

9-255   **JOCELYN, Marthe.** *The Invisible Day.* **(The Invisible trilogy, bk. 1).** Gr. 3–5.
Using a magical makeup kit that makes her invisible, Billie evades her overly protective mother and sets out to explore New York City. The sequels are *The Invisible Harry* (1998) and *The Invisible Enemy* (2002).
Illus. by Abby Carter, Dutton, 1997, 134 pp. (0-525-45908-1)
(BL 94:813; HBG 9:332; SLJ March 1998 p. 180)

9-256 JOHANSEN, Hannah. *Dinosaur with an Attitude.* Gr. 3–6. (Orig. Swiss pub. 1993.)
Zawinul's magical name causes one of his Easter eggs to hatch into a small talking dinosaur called a compsognathus. Austrian Children's Book Prize, 1993.
RDR/Wetlands, 1994, 144 pp., o.p.
(BL 90:2044; SLJ Aug 1994 p. 156)

9-257 JOHNSON, Elizabeth. *Break a Magic Circle.* Gr. 3–5.
An invisible boy asks Tilly to help break the magical spell on him.
Illus. by Trina Schart Hyman, Little, Brown, 1971, 70 pp., o.p.
(BL 68:109; CCBB 25:27; HB 47:482; Kirkus 39:676)

9-258 JOHNSON, Elizabeth. *No Magic, Thank You.* Gr. 3–4.
Gordon and Debbie's belief in magic helps them win a contest against the Unlucks, increasing the good luck in the world.
Illus. by Garrett Price, Little, Brown, 1964, 55 pp., o.p.
(CCBB 18:119; HB 40:499; Kirkus 32:550)

9-259 JOHNSON, Elizabeth. *Stuck with Luck.* Gr. 3–5.
✮ Tom wishes for a dog but gets a powerless leprechaun instead.
Illus. by Trina Schart Hyman, Little, Brown, 1967, 88 pp., o.p.
(BL 64:198; HB 43:589; Kirkus 35:740; LJ 92:3187)

JONES, Adrienne. *The Mural Master.*
See Chapter 7, High Fantasy: Travel to Other Worlds.

9-260 JONES, David Lee. *Unicorn Highway.* Gr. 6–12.
Thaddy Williams discovers that his neighbor, Mr. Tucker, is growing wheat for a unicorn and Thaddy decides that all his dreams would come true if he could only ride the unicorn.
Avon, 1992, pap., 339 pp., o.p.
(Kliatt Sept 1992 p. 22; VOYA 15:44, 16:16)

JONES, Diana Wynne. *Aunt Maria.*
See Chapter 12, Witchcraft and Sorcery Fantasy.

JONES, Diana Wynne. *Eight Days of Luke.*
See Chapter 6, High Fantasy: Myth or Legend Fantasy.

JONES, Diana Wynne. *The Lives of Christopher Chant.*
See Chapter 7, High Fantasy: Travel to Other Worlds.

9-261 JONES, Diana Wynne. *The Ogre Downstairs.* Gr. 5–8. (Orig. British pub.
✮✮ 1974.)
Amazing things happen when Johnny and Malcolm use the chemistry sets given to them by their new stepfather, "The Ogre."
Dutton, 1975, 191 pp., o.p.; Greenwillow, 1990, 182 pp. (0-688-09195-4); Greenwillow, 2002, 224 pp. (0-06-029583-9); HarperTrophy, 2002, pap., 224 pp. (0-06-447350-3)
(BL 71:1075; CCBB 28:179; HB 51:464, 66:480; HBG 1:254; Kirkus 43:453; SLJ Sept 1975 p. 105; Suth 2:246; VOYA 13:116)

9-262 JONES, Diana Wynne. *Stopping for a Spell: Three Fantasies.* Gr. 3–6.
✫ (Orig. pub. separately in England as *Chair Person*, 1989, *The Four Grannies*, 1980, and *The Fearsome Friend*, 1975.)
Three fantasy novellas about a boy who magically transforms four grannies into one, an unwelcome visitor driven away by furniture he has insulted, and an old armchair that comes to life as an obnoxious person.
Illus. by Joseph A. Smith, Greenwillow, 1993, 148 pp. (0-688-11367-2); illus. by Mark Zug, Greenwillow, 2004, 144 pp. (0-06-056205-6); HarperTrophy, 2004, pap., 144 pp. (0-06-056206-4)
(CCBB 46:348; HBG 4:299; Kirkus 61:663; SLJ July 1993 p. 85)

JONES, Diana Wynne. *Warlock at the Wheel and Other Stories.*
See Chapter 12, Witchcraft and Sorcery Fantasy.

9-263 JONES, Diana Wynne. *Wild Robert.* Gr. 3–6. (Orig. British pub. 1989.)
Boredom drives Heather to wish for the wizard Wild Robert's return to Castlemaine, but the mischievous 350-year-old sorcerer causes unanticipated difficulties.
Illus. by Mark Zug, Greenwillow/HarperCollins, 2003, 112 pp. (0-06-055531-9)
(BL 100:237; HBG 15:81; Kirkus 71:1074; SLJ Oct 2003 p. 128;)

9-264 JONES, Elizabeth Orton. *Twig.* Gr. 3–5.
A little girl named Twig finds a fairy living in a tomato can.
Illus. by the author, Macmillan, 1942, 152 pp., o.p.; Purple, 2002, 152 pp. (1-930900-05-8)
(BL 39:256; HB 19:102; LJ 67:884, 68:173)

9-265 JONES, Miranda. *Make a Wish!* **(Little Genie series, bk. 1).** Gr. 2–4.
(Orig. pub. in England.)
The tiny genie who appears when Ali rubs her flea market lava lamp grants Ali's wishes, but something goes wrong each time. The sequels are *Double Trouble* (2004), *A Puff of Pink* (2004), and *Castle Magic* (2004).
Illus. by David Calver, Delacorte, 2004, 128 pp. (0-385-90168-2)
(BL 100:857, 1619; CCBB 57:281; Kirkus 72:38; SLJ Feb 2004 p. 115)

JUKES, Mavis. *Cinderella 2000.*
See Chapter 8, Humorous Fantasy.

JUSTER, Norton. *The Phantom Tollbooth.*
See Chapter 7, High Fantasy: Travel to Other Worlds.

9-266 KARR, Kathleen. *Gideon and the Mummy Professor.* Gr. 5–8.
✫ Twelve-year-old Gideon's con-artist father tries to sell a valuable scarab found in the wrappings of their ancient Egyptian mummy, and the pair are pursued by other thieves and a voodoo queen, in this fast-moving tale set in 1885 New Orleans.
Farrar, 1993, 137 pp. (0-374-32563-4)
(BL 89:1958; CCBB 47:12; HB 69:599; HBG 4:300; Kirkus 61:663; SLJ June 1993 p. 107)

KATZ, Welwyn Wilton. *The Third Magic.*
See Chapter 7, High Fantasy: Travel to Other Worlds.

9-267 **KATZ, Welwyn Wilton.** *Whalesinger.* Gr. 7–10.

★ Shy Marty, spending the summer as an au pair on the California coast, discovers that she can communicate telepathically with a gray whale swimming offshore, in this complicated story involving environmental research, sunken treasure, and suspense.
Macmillan, 1990, 212 pp. (0-689-50511-6); Dell, 1993, pap. (0-440-21419-X)
(BL 87:1125; CCBB 44:144; HBG 2:266; Kirkus 59:47; SLJ May 1991 p. 111; VOYA 14:31)

KAYE, Marvin. *The Incredible Umbrella.*
See Chapter 7, High Fantasy: Travel to Other Worlds.

KEELE, Luqman, and PINKWATER, D(aniel) Manus. *Java Jack.*
See Chapter 8, Humorous Fantasy.

9-268 **KEEP, Linda Lowery.** *Mission Down Under.* **(Hannah and the Angels series, bk. 1).** Gr. 4–6.
Hannah's guardian angels send her to Australia to help her friend Ian track down poachers of endangered animals. The sequels are *Searching for Lulu* (1998), *Mexican Treasure Hunt* (1998), *Notes from the Blue Mountains* (1998), *Saving Uncle Sean* (1999), *Mardi Gras Mix-Up* (1999), *Trouble on Ice* (1999), *Last Chance in France* (2000), *Missing Piece in Greece* (2000), and *Panda-Monium in China* (2001).
Random, 1998, pap., 127 pp. (0-679-89081-5)
(BL 94:1881; SLJ Nov 1998 p. 122)

KEMP, Gene. *Mr. Magus Is Waiting for You.*
See Chapter 12, Witchcraft and Sorcery Fantasy.

KENNEDY, (Jerome) Richard. *Amy's Eyes.*
See Chapter 11, Toy Fantasy.

9-269 **KENNEDY, (Jerome) Richard.** *Crazy in Love.* Gr. 3–5.
Kindness to an old woman gains Diana a husband who worries that Diana is a "crazy wife" because she talks to a donkey.
Illus. by Marcia Sewall, Elsevier, 1980, 57 pp., o.p.
(BL 77:625; HB 57:51; Kirkus 49:7; SLJ Jan 1981 p. 62)

KENNEDY, William, and KENNEDY, Brendan. *Charlie Malarkey and the Belly-Button Machine.*
See Chapter 8, Humorous Fantasy.

9-270 **KENNEMORE, Tim.** *Circle of Doom.* Gr. 3–6. (Orig. British pub. 2001.)
★ Thirteen-year-old Lizzie Sharp decides to become a witch, mixing magic potions and setting spells with the help of her younger brother Max and skeptical 10-year-old Dan.
Illus. by Tim Archbold, Farrar, 2003, 208 pp. (0-374-31284-2)
(BL 99:1594; HB 80:11; HBG 15:96; Kirkus 71:768, 1403; SLJ May 2003 p. 156)

9-271 **KESSLER, Liz.** *The Tail of Emily Windsnap.* Gr. 5–7. (Orig. British pub. 2003.)

In her seventh-grade swim class, Emily discovers that when she is immersed in water she is transformed into a mermaid; her subsequent undersea explorations unlock her mother's long-forgotten secret.
Illus. by Sarah Gibb, Candlewick, 2004, 224 pp. (0-7636-2483-7)
(BL 100:1599; CCBB 57:378; SLJ June 2004 p. 144; VOYA 27:142)

KINDL, Patrice. *Owl in Love.*
See Chapter 12, Witchcraft and Sorcery Fantasy.

9-272 **KING-SMITH, Dick.** *Billy the Bird.* Gr. 3–5. (Orig. British pub. 2000.)
Mary Bird discovers that her younger brother knows how to fly on nights with a full moon.
Illus. by Susie Jenkin Pearce, Hyperion, 2001, 128 pp. (0-7868-0586-2)
(BL 97:2006; HBG 12:309; Kirkus 69:587; SLJ June 2001 p. 121)

KING-SMITH, Dick. *George Speaks.*
See Chapter 8, Humorous Fantasy.

9-273 **KING-SMITH, Dick.** *Harriet's Hare.* Gr. 2–4. (Orig. British pub. 1994.)
✮ The magical adventures of 8-year-old Harriet and a hare named Wiz, who spend the summer together on her father's farm in England.
Illus. by Roger Roth, Crown, 1995, 128 pp. (0-517-59830-2); Random, 1997, pap., 104 pp. (0-679-88551-X)
(BL 91:1499; CCBB 48:351; HBG 6:300; Kirkus 63:471)

KING-SMITH, Dick. *Harry's Mad.*
See Chapter 8, Humorous Fantasy.

KING-SMITH, Dick. *Lady Daisy.*
See Chapter 11, Toy Fantasy.

9-274 **KING-SMITH, Dick.** *Paddy's Pot of Gold.* Gr. 2–5. (Orig. British pub.
✮ 1990.)
Eight-year-old Brigid meets Paddy, a tiny 174-year-old leprechaun who lives on her father's farm.
Illus. by David Perkins, Crown, 1992, 114 pp., o.p.
(BL 88:1379; CCBB 45:266; HBG 3:265; Kirkus 60:325; SLJ May 1992 p. 90)

9-275 **KING-SMITH, Dick.** *The Queen's Nose.* Gr. 3–6. (Orig. British pub. 1983.)
✮ An unusual coin grants Harmony Parker seven wishes.
Illus. by Jill Bennett, Harper, 1985, 111 pp., o.p.
(BL 82:262; CCBB 38:209; HB 61:555; SLJ Aug 1985 p. 66)

KING-SMITH, Dick. *The Toby Man.*
See Chapter 2, Animal Fantasy.

9-276 **KING-SMITH, Dick.** *The Water Horse.* Gr. 3–5. (Orig. British pub. 1990.)
✮ Kirstie's grandpa recognizes the creature that hatches from an egg she found on the beach as a Water Horse, the legendary Scottish sea monster that is part turtle, part horse, part frog, and part alligator.

Illus. by David Parkins, Crown, 1998, 108 pp. (0-517-80027-6); Random, 2000, pap., 128 pp. (0-375-80352-1)

(BL 95:230; HB 74:733; HBG 10:68; Kirkus 66:1286; SLJ Oct 1998 p. 102)

9-277 KOFF, Richard M(yram). *Christopher.* Gr. 5–8.
The mysterious "Headmaster" shows Christopher how to use his supernatural powers to read minds, change his size, and make himself invisible.
Illus. by Barbara Reinertson, Celestial Arts, 1981, 128 pp., o.p.
(CCBB 35:110; SLJ Feb 1982 p. 78; VOYA 4:34)

9-278 KOLLER, Jackie French. *If I Had One Wish . . . .* Gr. 5–7.
Alec's wish that his little brother had never been born comes true, with disastrous results for their family.
Little, Brown, 1991, 161 pp. (0-316-50150-6)
(BL 88:506; CCBB 45:96; HBG 3:68; Kirkus 59:1471; SLJ Nov 1991 p. 120)

9-279 KONIGSBURG, E(laine) L(obl). *Up from Jericho Tel.* Gr. 5–9.
☆   Jeanmarie and Malcolm are summoned into ghostly Tallulah's underground boudoir, where they become invisible in order to recover Tallulah's missing Regina Stone necklace.
Macmillan, 1986, 192 pp. (0-689-31194-X); Aladdin, 1998, pap., 192 pp. (0-689-82332-0)
(BL 82:1304, 1312, 1313, 83:794, 1136; CCBB 39:131; HB 62:327; Kirkus 54:209; SLJ May 1986 p. 93, Apr 1987 p. 48; Suth 4:224; VOYA 9:219)

KOOIKER, Leonie. *The Magic Stone.*
See Chapter 12, Witchcraft and Sorcery Fantasy.

9-280 KORELITZ, Jean Hanff. *Interference Powder.* Gr. 4–6.
Fifth-grader Nina's plan to soften the blow of a low test score—by painting her mother a picture of herself with a perfect score—backfires when the interference powder she sprinkles on the picture gives her the highest grade in the class, and causes her to sing whenever she tries to speak.
Marshall Cavendish, 2003, 144 pp. (0-7614-5139-0)
(BL 100:412; HBG 15:96; Kirkus 71:1273; SLJ Dec 2003 p. 153)

9-281 KORSCHUNOW, Irina. *Adam Draws Himself a Dragon.* Gr. 1–4. (Orig.
☆   German pub. 1978; British pub. 1982, entitled *Johnny's Dragon.*)
Adam's imaginary dragon friend gives him the confidence to do better at school, to make friends, and to lose some excess weight.
Trans. by James Skofield, illus. by Mary Rahn, Harper, 1986, 57 pp., o.p.
(BL 82:1312; CCBB 40:11; HB 62:587; Kirkus 54:638; SLJ Sept 1986 p. 123)

9-282 KORSCHUNOW, Irina. *Small Fur.* Gr. K–4. (Orig. German pub. 1984.)
Lonely after his best friend moves away from the forest, a furry, human-faced creature named Small Fur passes through a magic green gate and meets an elf who teaches him to fly. The sequel is *Small Fur Is Getting Bigger* (1986, 1990).
Trans. by James Skofield, illus. by Reinhard Michl, Harper, 1988, 72 pp., o.p.
(BL 85:321; CCBB 41:209; Kirkus 54:829; SLJ Nov 1988 p. 90)

9-283 KRENSKY, Stephen (Alan). *The Dragon Circle.* Gr. 4–6.
The Wynd children are kidnapped by five dragons who plan to use the children's magic powers to search for treasure. The sequels are *The Witching Hour* (1981, 1990) and *A Ghostly Business* (1984, 1990).
Illus. by A. Delaney, Atheneum, 1977, 116 pp., o.p.
(BL 74:477; CCBB 31:97; Kirkus 45:728; SLJ Oct 1977 p. 115)

9-284 KURTZ, Katherine (Irene). *St. Patrick's Gargoyle.* Gr. 10 up.
Paddy, a former avenging angel and now a gargoyle on Dublin's St. Patrick's Cathedral, is determined to punish church vandals, and tries to keep a major demon bound beneath Clontarf Castle.
Berkley/Ace, 2001, 240 pp. (0-441-00725-2); Ace, 2002, pap., 291 pp. (0-441-00905-0)
(BL 97:1042; Kirkus 69:22; LJ Feb 15, 2001 p. 205; VOYA 24:335)

9-285 KURZWEIL, Allen. *Leon and the Spitting Image.* Gr. 4–6.
✫ Leon's required fourth-grade sewing project—an image of his teacher, Miss Hagmeyer ("The Hag")—gives him power over her and helps him defeat the class bully, Henry Lumpkin. The sequel is *Leon and the Champion Chip* (2005).
Illus. by Bret Bertholf, Greenwillow, 2003, 304 pp. (0-06-053931-3); HarperTrophy, 2005, pap., 320 pp. (0-06-053932-1)
(BL 100:412; CCBB 57:155; HB 80:83; HBG 15:97; Kirkus 71:1019; SLJ Nov 2003 p. 142., VOYA 26:504, 27:12)

9-286 KUSHNER, Donn. *A Book Dragon.* Gr. 6–10. (Orig. Canadian pub. 1987.)
✫ A 600-year-old dragon emerges in present-day Canada to protect his treasure, a medieval illuminated book, from an unscrupulous land developer threatening to demolish the store where the book is hidden.
Henry Holt, 1988, 197 pp., o.p.
(BL 84:1820, 1837; HB 64:627; Kirkus 56:659; SLJ June–July 1988 p. 118)

LACKEY, Mercedes, and DIXON, Larry. *Born to Run.*
See Chapter 12, Witchcraft and Sorcery Fantasy.

9-287 LAFAYE, Alexandria. *Dad in Spirit.* Gr. 4–6.
Ebon Jones and his family are overjoyed when the spirit of his comatose father appears, until Ebon realizes that reuniting his Dad's body and soul is the only way to save his father's life.
Simon, 2001, 176 pp. (0-689-81514-X)
(BL 97:2006; CCBB 54:412; HBG 12:310; Kirkus 69:588; SLJ June 2001 p. 152)

9-288 LAGERLÖF, Selma (Ottiliana Lovisa). *The Wonderful Adventures of*
✫ *Nils.* Gr. 5–7. (Orig. Swedish pub. 1906–1907; U.S. 1908.)
An elf turns a boy named Nils into a Thumbling, smaller than the animals he once mistreated. *The Further Adventures of Nils* (1907) is included in this edition.
Doubleday, 1925, 430 pp., o.p.; trans. by Velma Swanston Howard, illus. by H. Baumhauer, Pantheon, 1947, 539 pp., o.p.; Dover, 1995, pap., 256 pp. (0-486-28611-8); Wildside, 2003, pap., 284 pp. (0-61379-961-5)
(BL 4:22, 22:171, 44:118; Bookshelf 1932 p. 8; CCBB 1:4; HB 1[June 1925]:30, 7:118, 23:451; LJ 72:1544; Mahony 2:283)

LAMPMAN, Evelyn Sibley. *The Shy Stegosaurus of Cricket Creek.*
See Chapter 8, Humorous Fantasy.

9-289 LANCASTER, Clay. *Periwinkle Steamboat.* Gr. 2–4.
Nothing ever happens on Pennypacker Square, until the night a flying ferry-boat takes Timmy and his friends to the other side of the world.
Illus. by the author, Viking, 1961, 54 pp., o.p.
(HB 37:261; LJ 86:1984)

9-290 LANGTON, Jane (Gillson). *The Diamond in the Window.* **(The Hall Fam-**
✮ **ily Chronicles, bk. 1.).** Gr. 5–7.
The mysterious disappearances of two children and an Indian prince intrigue Eleanor and Eddie, who search for the key to the mystery, the Star of India Diamond. In *The Swing in the Summerhouse* (1967, 2001) Eleanor and Eddie go on magic adventures by swinging out through each of the summerhouse's six sides. In *The Astonishing Stereoscope* (1971, 2001), an optical toy sends Eleanor into the past. Their cousin Georgie has her own adventures in *The Fledgling* (1980, 2002; see below).
Illus. by Erik Blegvad, Harper, 1962, 256 pp., o.p.
(CCBB 16:30; HB 38:481, 78:427–428; LJ 87:3895)

9-291 LANGTON, Jane (Gillson). *The Fledgling.* Gr. 5–7.
✮✮ Georgie's parents fear for her safety when an old Canada goose teaches the little girl to fly. John Newbery Medal Honor Book, 1981; Phoenix Award Honor Book, 2000. *The Fragile Flag* (1984) is a realistic sequel, and *The Time Bike* (2000, 2002) is a fantasy sequel. Georgie's cousins, Eleanor and Eddie, have their own magic adventures in *The Diamond in the Window* (1962, 2001; see above), *The Swing in the Summerhouse* (1967, 2001), and *The Astonishing Stereoscope* (1971, 2001).
Harper, 1980, 192 pp., LB (0-06-023679-5); HarperCollins, 2002 (0-06-023679-5); HarperTrophy, 2002, pap., 192 pp. (0-06-440121-9)
(BL 76:1365, 80:95; CCBB 33:218; HB 56:408, 78:427–428; Kirkus 48:513; SLJ Sept 1980 p. 73)

LANIER, Sterling E(dmund). *The War for the Lot: A Tale of Fantasy and Terror.*
See Chapter 2, Animal Fantasy.

9-292 LATHROP, Dorothy P(ulis). *The Colt from Moon Mountain.* Gr. 3–5.
Cynthy befriends an elusive snow-white colt who runs wild on Moon Mountain.
Illus. by the author, Macmillan, 1941, 1956, 62 pp., o.p.
(BL 38:162; HB 17:460; LJ 66:879, 67:42)

9-293 LATHROP, Dorothy P(ulis). *The Dog in the Tapestry Garden.* Gr. 2–4.
The dog in the tapestry on Maria's wall comes to life.
Illus. by the author, Macmillan, 1962, 40 pp., o.p.
(CCBB 16:83; HB 38:481; LJ 87:3203)

9-294 LATHROP, Dorothy P(ulis). *The Little White Goat.* Gr. 1–4.
On May Day Eve, a magical goat leads Debby and Pats into the forest, where they play with the forest creatures.

Illus. by the author, Macmillan, 1933, 58 pp., o.p.

(BL 30:185; HB 9:206; LJ 59:321; Mahony 3:80)

9-295 LATHROP, Dorothy P(ulis). *The Lost Merry-Go-Round.* Gr. 3–5.
Children have magic adventures while riding merry-go-round animals through Flitter-mouse Wood at night.
Illus. by the author, Macmillan, 1934, 104 pp., o.p.

(BL 31:177; Bookshelf 1934–1935 p. 6; HB 10:360; Mahony 3:107)

9-296 LAWRENCE, Ann (Margaret). *Tom Ass: Or, the Second Gift.* Gr. 4–6.
(Orig. British pub. 1972.)
Two elfin gifts bring fortune and adventure to Tom and his wife, Jennifer.
Illus. by Mila Lazarevich, Walck, 1973, 132 pp., o.p.

(BL 70:173; CCBB 27:46; HB 49:378; Kirkus 41:600)

LAWRENCE, Michael. *The Poltergoose: A Jiggy McCue Story.*
See Chapter 8, Humorous Fantasy.

9-297 LAWSON, Amy. *Star Baby.* Gr. 3–5.
☆ Allie's ninth birthday wish for a baby brother comes true when a Star Baby falls from the sky into her father's arms.
Illus. by Margot Apple, Harcourt, 1992, 72 pp., o.p.

(BL 88:1762; CCBB 45:268; HBG 3:266; Kirkus 60:467; SLJ May 1992, p 114)

9-298 LAWSON, Julie. *Goldstone.* **(Goldstone trilogy, bk. 1).** Gr. 5–7. (Orig. Canadian pub. 1997.)
The goldstone pendant she inherits after her mother's death in an avalanche gives 12-year-old Karin frightening dreams involving the future of her father's railroad crew and another avalanche. The sequels are *Turns on a Dime* (1999) and *The Ghost of Avalanche Mountain* (2000).
Stoddart, 1998, pap., 176 pp. (0-7737-5891-7)

(BL 94:1882; SLJ May 1998 p. 146)

9-299 LAWSON, Robert. *The Fabulous Flight.* Gr. 4–6.
Seven-year-old Peter Peabody Pepperell III shrinks to 4 inches in height and flies off on a seagull's back.
Illus. by the author, Little, Brown, 1949, 152 pp., o.p.

(BL 46:37; CCBB 2:5; HB 25:410, 61:77; Kirkus 17:394; LJ 74:1542, 1682)

LE GUIN, Ursula K(roeber). *Catwings.*
See Chapter 2, Animal Fantasy.

9-300 LEROE, Ellen. *Leap Frog Friday.* Gr. 2–4.
After an argument with his older brother, Ollie uses the magic rocks he got for his birthday to turn Danny into a frog.
Illus. by Dee de Rosa, Dutton, 1992, 64 pp. (0-525-67370-9)

(BL 89:60; Kirkus 60:1311; SLJ Nov 1992 p. 72)

9-301 LEVERICH, Kathleen. *Brigid the Bad.* **(Brigid trilogy, bk. 2).** Gr. 2–4.
Brigid asks her 9-year-old fairy godmother, Maribel, to cast a spell that will make her friends and family obey her. This is the sequel to *Brigid Bewitched* (1994) and is followed by *Brigid Beware!* (1995).

Illus. by Dan Andreasen, Random, 1995, 72 pp. (0-679-97340-0)
(BL 92:705; SLJ Mar 1996 p. 177)

9-302 LEVINE, Gail Carson. *The Wish.* Gr. 4–8.
Wilma's wish for popularity is granted after she helps an old woman on the subway, but only at school, and only until her graduation, three weeks away.
HarperCollins, 2000, 208 pp. (0-06-027901-X); HarperTrophy, 2001, pap., 197 pp. (0-06-447361-9)
(BL 96:1462; CCBB 53:324; HBG 11:307; Kirkus 68:635; SLJ May 2000 p. 173)

LEVINSON, Marilyn. *Rufus and Magic Run Amok.*
See Chapter 12, Witchcraft and Sorcery Fantasy.

LEWIS, C(live) S(taples). *The Lion, the Witch, and the Wardrobe.*
See Chapter 7, High Fantasy: Travel to Other Worlds.

LEWIS, Hilda (Winifred). *The Ship That Flew.*
See Chapter 10, Time Travel Fantasy.

LINDBERGH, Anne Spencer. *Bailey's Window.*
See Chapter 7, High Fantasy: Travel to Other Worlds.

LINDBERGH, Anne Spencer. *The Hunky-Dory Dairy.*
See Chapter 10, Time Travel Fantasy.

LINDBERGH, Anne Spencer. *The Shadow on the Dial.*
See Chapter 10, Time Travel Fantasy.

9-303 LINDBERGH, Anne Spencer. *Travel Far, Pay No Fare.* Gr. 5–8.
☆ Owen and his cousin Parsley use a magic bookmark from the library's summer reading club to travel into their favorite books and bring back whatever they can carry, until they find out that Owen's divorced mom is planning to marry Parsley's widowed dad.
Harper, 1992, 192 pp. LB (0-06-021776-6)
(BL 89:513; CCBB 46:78; HBG 4:72; Kirkus 60:1380; SLJ Dec 1992 p. 113; VOYA 16:26)

9-304 LINDE, Gunnel (Geijerstam). *The White Stone.* Gr. 4–6. (Orig. Swedish pub. 1964.)
Fia and Hampus are transformed into fearless Fideli and Prince Perilous. Nils Holgersson Award for best Swedish children's book, 1965.
Trans. by Richard Winston and Clara Winston, illus. by Imero Gobbato, Harcourt, 1966, 185 pp., o.p.
(BL 63:734; CCBB 20:156; HB 42:717; Kirkus 34:1053; LJ 91:5232)

9-305 LINDENBAUM, Pija. *Else-Marie and Her Seven Little Daddies.* Gr. K–3.
☆ (Orig. Swedish pub. 1991.)
Else-Marie is embarrassed that her seven tiny daddies must pick her up after school on the day her mother works late, but no one seems to notice anything out of the ordinary.
Adapt. by Gabrielle Charbonnet, illus. by the author, Henry Holt, 1991, 32 pp. (0-8050-1752-6)
(BL 88:952; CCBB 45:161; HBG 3:39; Kirkus 59:1535; SLJ Mar 1992 p. 216)

9-306 LINDGREN, Astrid. *Karlsson-on-the-Roof.* Gr. 3–5. (Orig. Swedish pub. 1955; British pub. 1958.)

No one believes Eric's story that a small, mischievous flying man is living on his roof. *Karlson Flies Again* (1977), *Erik and Karlson on the Roof* (1958, 1975), and *The World's Best Karlson* (1980) are the British sequels.

Trans. by Marianne Turner, illus. by Jan Pyk, Viking, 1971,128 pp., o.p.

(CCBB 26:28; Kirkus 39:1156; LJ 97:1168; TLS 1975 p. 373)

LINDGREN, Astrid. *Mio, My Son.*

See Chapter 7, High Fantasy: Travel to Other Worlds.

9-307 LINKLATER, Eric (Robert Russell). *The Wind on the Moon.* Gr. 5–7.

A magical wind from the moon turns two girls into kangaroos and helps them rescue their father. Carnegie Medal, 1944.

Illus. by Nicolas Bentley, Macmillan, 1944, 323 pp., o.p.; New York Review of Books, 2004 (1-59017-100-4)

(BL 41:140; HB 21:112, 80:488–489; Kirkus 12:458; TLS 1944 p. 574)

9-308 LISLE, Janet Taylor. *The Gold Dust Letters.* **(Investigators of the**
☆   **Unkown, bk. 1).** Gr. 3–5.

Angela, Georgina, and Poco call themselves Investigators of the Unknown and attempt to find the origin of the gold dust spilling from letters they receive from the fairy Pilaria. The sequels are *Looking for Juliette* (1994), *A Message from the Match Girl* (1995), and *Angela's Aliens* (1996).

Orchard/Jackson, 1994, 116 pp., o.p.; HarperTrophy, 1996, pap., 128 pp. (0-380-72516-9)

(BL 90:1007; CCBB 47:366; HBG 5:313; Kirkus 62:399; SLJ April 1994 p. 128)

9-309 LISLE, Janet Taylor. *The Lost Flower Children.* Gr. 3–6.
☆   Motherless Olivia and Nellie, 9 and 4, search for magical teacups in their Great-Aunt Minty's garden in order to break the fairy spell that has transformed the flower children.

Illus. by Satomi Ichikawa, Philomel, 1999, 112 pp. (0-399-23393-8); Puffin, 2001, pap., 128 pp. (0-698-11880-4)

(BL 95:1690; CCBB 52:112; HB 75:333; HBG 10:296; Kirkus 67:632; SLJ June 1999 p. 100, Dec 1999 p. 42)

9-310 LISLE, Rebecca. *Copper.* Gr. 4–7. (Orig. British pub. 2002.)

Orphaned 10-year-old Copper Beech must flee London for the Marble Mountains, where she and her talking teddy bear are taken in by Wood Clan relations who live in an enchanted tree house, and she tries to find her missing parents.

Putnam, 2004, 208 pp. (0-399-24211-2)

(BL 100:1060; CCBB 57:336; Kirkus 72:85; SLJ Jan 2004 p. 132)

9-311 LOBE, Mira. *The Grandma in the Apple Tree.* Gr. 2–4. (Orig. Austrian pub.
☆   1965.)

Andi's imaginary grandma takes him on tiger hunts and voyages to pirate-infested seas.

Trans. by Doris Orgel, illus. by Judith Gwyn Brown, McGraw-Hill, 1970, 95 pp., o.p.

(BL 67:703; CCBB 24:126; HB 47:163; LJ 96:1109)

9-312 LOCKE, Angela. *Mr. Mullett Owns a Cloud.* Gr. 3–5. (Orig. British pub. 1982.)
A shepherd named Mr. Mullett is given a gift of a small cloud named Napoleon, but the cloud proves to be quite vain and impulsive.
Illus. by Ian Newsham, Chatto, 1983, 128 pp., o.p.
(HB 60:196; SLJ Feb 1984 p. 75)

9-313 LOFTING, Hugh. *The Twilight of Magic.* Gr. 5–7.
Anne and Giles learn about magic from Agnes the wise woman, who is believed to be a witch.
Illus. by Lois Lenski, Stokes, 1930, 303 pp., o.p.; Harper, 1967 (reprint of 1930 ed.), 303 pp., o.p.; illus. by Tatsuro Kiuchi, Simon, 1993, pap., 246 pp. (0-671-78358-0)
(BL 27:367; HBG 5:79; Kirkus 35:60; LJ 56:278; VOYA 16:383)

LOGAN, Carolyn F. *The Power of the Rellard.*
See Chapter 6, High Fantasy: Myth or Legend Fantasy.

9-314 LORD, Beman. *The Perfect Pitch.* Gr. 2–4.
Mr. Watts, the new local wish-granter, has trouble granting Tommy's wish to become a super-star baseball pitcher.
Illus. by Harold Berson, Walck, 1965, 55 pp., o.p.; Gregg, 1981, 55 pp., o.p.
(CCBB 19:85; Kirkus 33:823; LJ 90:4636, 4637)

LORING, Selden M(elville). *Mighty Magic: An Almost-True Story of Pirates and Indians.*
See Chapter 10, Time Travel Fantasy.

LOVEJOY, Jack. *The Rebel Witch.*
See Chapter 12, Witchcraft and Sorcery Fantasy.

9-315 LUENN, Nancy. *Unicorn Crossing.* Gr. 3–5.
Jenny longs to see a unicorn while staying at Unicorn Crossing, but only her family's elderly hostess, Mrs. Donovan, takes her wish seriously.
Illus. by Peter E. Hanson, Macmillan, 1987, 64 pp., o.p.
(BL 84:67; CCBB 41:12; Kirkus 55:1395; SLJ Oct 1987 p. 126)

9-316 LYNCH, Patricia (Nora). *The Turf-Cutter's Donkey: An Irish Story of Mystery and Adventure.* Gr. 4–6. (Orig. British pub. 1934.)
Eileen, Seamus, and Long Ears the Donkey meet a leprechaun and travel through ancient Ireland. The sequels are *The Turf-Cutter's Donkey Goes Visiting* (1936) and *The Turf-Cutter's Donkey Kicks Up His Heels* (1939).
Illus. by Jack B. Yeats, Button, 1935, 245 pp., o.p.
(BL 32:22; Bookshelf 1935 p. 3; HB 11:295; LJ 61:115; Mahony 3:207)

LYON, George Ella. *Gina. Jamie. Father. Bear.*
See Chapter 7, High Fantasy: Travel to Other Worlds.

9-317 MacALPINE, Margaret H(esketh Murray). *The Black Gull of Corie Lachan.* Gr. 4–6. (Orig. British pub. 1964.)
Searching for their missing father, rumored to have been abducted by the wee folk, Morag and Rory are followed by a strange black gull.

Illus. by James Armstrong, Prentice-Hall, 1965, 105 pp., o.p.
(CCBB 19:102; Kirkus 33:627; LJ 91:427; TLS 1964 p. 602)

9-318 **McCAUGHREAN, Geraldine (Jones).** *A Pack of Lies.* Gr. 6–10. (Orig.
★ British pub. 1988.)
Business in their used-furniture store improves dramatically after a strange
young man moves into Ailsa and her widowed mother's house and charms
potential customers with elaborate stories about the objects they are consider-
ing. Carnegie Medal, 1988; Guardian Award for Children's Fiction, 1989.
Oxford University Press, 1989, 168 pp. (0-19-271612-3); Oxford University
Press, 2002, pap., 176 pp. (0-19-275203-0)
(BL 85:1718; CCBB 42:232; Kirkus 57:839; SLJ May 1989 p. 126; TLS 1988 p. 1322)

McCAUGHREAN, Geraldine (Jones). *The Stones Are Hatching.*
See Chapter 6, High Fantasy: Myth or Legend Fantasy.

McCUTCHEN, H. L. *LightLand.*
See Chapter 7, High Fantasy: Travel to Other Worlds.

MacDONALD, Betty (Campbell Bard). *Mrs. Piggle-Wiggle.*
See Chapter 8, Humorous Fantasy.

9-319 **MacDONALD, Greville.** *Billy Barnicoat: A Fairy Romance for Young and
Old.* Gr. 5–8. (Orig. British pub. 1922.)
In this story written by George MacDonald's son, a boy cast up by the sea onto
the Cornish coast searches for his inheritance while battling smugglers, storms,
and a witch. The sequel is *Count Billy* (1928).
Illus. by F(rancis) D(onkin) Bedford, Dutton, 1923, 230 pp., o.p.
(BL 20:146; Bookshelf 1932 p. 8; Mahony 2:290; Moore:426)

MACE, Elisabeth. *Under Siege.*
See Chapter 7, High Fantasy: Travel to Other Worlds.

9-320 **McEWAN, Ian.** *The Daydreamer.* Gr. 4–7. (Orig. British pub. 1994.)
★ Are Peter's peculiar adventures, such as swapping bodies with a cat, a baby,
and a grownup, only taking place inside his head?
Illus. by Anthony Browne, HarperCollins, 1994, 192 pp. (0-06-024426-7);
Anchor, 2000, pap., 160 pp. (0-385-49805-5)
(BL 91:43; CCBB 48:56; HBG 6:80; Kirkus 62:1133; SLJ Oct 1994 p. 126; TLS Sep 30, 1994
p. 25; VOYA 18:36)

9-321 **McGRAW, Eloise Jarvis.** *Joel and the Great Merlini.* Gr. 3–5.
The Great Merlini teaches Joel how to perform real magic.
Illus. by Jim Arnosky, Pantheon, 1979, 59 pp., o.p.
(CCBB 33:156; SLJ Feb 1980 p. 58)

MacHALE, D. J. *Pendragon: The Never War.*
See Chapter 10, Time Travel Fantasy.

9-322 **McHARGUE, Georgess.** *Beastie.* Gr. 4–7.
★ Mary, Theo, and Scott discover that the "beastie" their scientist parents are
stalking in a Scottish loch may die because of their expedition.

Delacorte, 1992, 192 pp., o.p.

(BL 88:1029; CCBB 45:216; HBG 3:267; Kirkus 60:540; SLJ July 1992 p. 74)

9-323 McHARGUE, Georgess. *Stoneflight.* Gr. 5–7.

✭ Jane's home life is unbearable until she discovers the joys of night flight on the back of a stone griffin come to life.

Illus. by Arvis Stewart, Viking, 1975, 222 pp., o.p.

(BL 71:762; CCBB 29:50; HB 51:268; Kirkus 43:239; SLJ Mar 1975 p. 98)

McKAY, Hilary. *The Amber Cat.*
See Chapter 4, Ghost Fantasy.

9-324 McKAY, Hilary. *Saffy's Angel.* Gr. 4–7. (Orig. British pub. 2001.)

✭✭ After Saffron discovers that the people she thought were her parents and siblings are actually her aunt, uncle, and cousins, she runs away to Sienna, Italy, where she and her birth mother once lived. Boston Globe Horn Book Honor Book, 2002; Whitbread Children's Book of the Year, 2002. The sequel, *Indigo's Star* (2004), is not a fantasy.

McElderry, 2002, 160 pp. (0-689-84933-8); Aladdin, 2003, pap., 160 pp. (0-689-84934-6)

(BL 98:1594; CCBB 55:332; HB 78:466, 79:16, 38; HBG 13:377; Kirkus 70:661; SLJ May 2002 p. 156, Dec 2002 p. 44)

McKEAN, Thomas. *The Secret of the Seven Willows.*
See Chapter 10, Time Travel Fantasy.

9-325 MacKELLAR, William. *The Smallest Monster in the World.* Gr. 3–5.
A kelpie introduces Wullie Watson to Maggie the sea monster.

Illus. by Ursula Koering, McKay, 1969, 113 pp., o.p.

(BL 66:621; HB 46:36; Kirkus 37:1064; LJ 95:1628)

9-326 McKELVEY, Douglas Kaine. *The Angel Knew Papa and the Dog.* Gr. 3–6.
An angel saves 7-year-old Evangeline after her father is swept away from their log cabin in a flash flood.

Putnam/Philomel, 1996, 89 pp. (0-399-23042-4)

(BL 93:242; CCBB 50:22; HBG 8:71; Kirkus 64:1155)

MacLEISH, Roderick. *Prince Ombra.*
See Chapter 6, High Fantasy: Myth or Legend Fantasy.

MacLEOD, Charlotte (Matilda Hughes). *The Curse of the Giant Hogweed.*
See Chapter 10, Time Travel Fantasy.

9-327 McLERRAN, Alice. *Dragonfly.* Gr. 4–6.
The baby dragon that hatches from a strange egg Jason found becomes a family pet, until it outgrows their garage.

Absey, 2000 (1-888842-15-6), pap., 142 pp. (1-888842-22-9)

(CCBB 54:30; Kirkus 68:1044; SLJ Jan 2001 p. 132)

McMULLAN, Kate. *Under the Mummy's Spell.*
See Chapter 4, Ghost Fantasy.

9-328 **McNEILL (ALEXANDER), Janet.** *A Monster Too Many.* Gr. 3–5.
Sam and Joe prevent their sea monster's incarceration in a zoo by returning it to the sea.
Illus. by Ingrid Fetz, Little, Brown, 1972, 60 pp., o.p.
(BL 68:1004; Kirkus 40:136; LJ 97:2232)

McNEILL, Janet. *Tom's Tower.*
See Chapter 7, High Fantasy: Travel to Other Worlds.

9-329 **MACOUREK, Miloš.** *Max and Sally and the Phenomenal Phone.* Gr. 2–4.
(Orig. Czech pub. 1980.)
A magical telephone changes the lives of third-graders Max Blair and Sally Chase, whose adventures include transforming a neighbor's dog into a boy.
Trans. by Dagmar Herrmann, illus. by Adolf Born, Wellington, 1989, 84 pp., o.p.
(BL 86:745; CCBB 43:142; SLJ Feb 1990 p. 76)

MAETERLINCK, Maurice. *The Children's Blue Bird.*
See Chapter 1, Allegorical Fantasy and Literary Fairy Tales.

Magicats! **Ed. by Jack Dann and Gardner Dozois.**
See Chapter 2, Animal Fantasy.

MAGUIRE, Gregory. *The Daughter of the Moon.*
See Chapter 7, High Fantasy: Travel to Other Worlds.

MAGUIRE, Gregory. *Lightning Time.*
See Chapter 10, Time Travel Fantasy.

MAHY, Margaret (May). *Alchemy.*
See Chapter 12, Witchcraft and Sorcery Fantasy.

MAHY, Margaret (May). *The Blood-and-Thunder Adventure on Hurricane Peak.*
See Chapter 8, Humorous Fantasy.

9-330 **MAHY, Margaret (May).** *The Door in the Air and Other Stories.* Gr. 6–10.
☆ (Orig. New Zealand pub. 1988.)
Nine humorous magical stories about princes, witchcraft, and magic in the contemporary world.
Illus. by Diana Catchpole, Delacorte, 1991, 112 pp. (0-385-30252-5); Dell, 1993, pap. (0-440-40774-5)
(BL 87:1125; CCBB 44:170; HB 67:201; HBG 2:263; Kirkus 59:474; SLJ Apr 1991 p. 121; VOYA 14:246, 15:9)

9-331 **MAHY, Margaret (May).** *The Girl with the Green Ear: Stories About*
☆ *Magic in Nature.* Gr. 5–6. (Orig. New Zealand pub. in four collections: 1972, 1973, 1975, 1986.)
Nine magical stories with ecological themes, originally published in New Zealand in *The First Margaret Mahy Storybook* (1972), *The Second Margaret Mahy Storybook* (1973), *The Third Margaret Mahy Storybook* (1975), and *The Downhill Crocodile Whizz and Other Stories* (1986).
Illus. by Shirley Hughes, Knopf, 1992, 102 pp., o.p.
(BL 88:1280; CCBB 45:270; HBG 3:267; Kirkus 60:468; SLJ July 1992 p. 61)

MAHY, Margaret (May). *The Haunting.*
See Chapter 12, Witchcraft and Sorcery Fantasy.

9-332 **MAHY, Margaret (May).** *A Tall Story and Other Tales.* Gr. 2–5. (Orig. New Zealand pub. in three collections: 1972, 1973, 1975; orig. British pub. 1991.)
Eleven short stories about magical happenings in everyday life, involving ghosts, witches, and monsters; originally published in New Zealand in *The First Margaret Mahy Story Book* (1972), *The Second Margaret Mahy Story-book* (1973), and *The Third Margaret Mahy Storybook* (1975).
Illus. by Jan Nesbitt, Macmillan, 1992, 88 pp., o.p.
(BL 88:1029; HBG 3:267; Kirkus 60:117; SLJ Mar 1992 p. 238)

MAJOR, Kevin (Gerald). *Blood Red Ochre.*
See Chapter 6, High Fantasy: Myth or Legend Fantasy.

9-333 **MANES, Stephen.** *An Almost Perfect Game.* Gr. 4–7.
Whatever Jake writes on his scorecard seems to come true during the local minor league baseball team's pennant race.
Scholastic, 1995, 163 pp. (0-590-44432-8)
(BL 91:1771; SLJ June 1995 p. 112; VOYA 18:161)

MANES, Stephen. *Chicken Trek: The Third Strange Thing That Happened to Oscar Noodleman.*
See Chapter 8, Humorous Fantasy.

9-334 **MANES, Stephen.** *Monstra vs. Irving.* Gr. 2–4.
When Irving's little sister Claire drinks the Monster-Ade formula he ordered from a magazine, she is transformed into Monstra, with fangs, claws, a horn, and bat wings.
Illus. by Michael Sours, Henry Holt, 1989, 74 pp. (0-8050-0836-5), 1991, pap. (0-8050-1642-2)
(BL 86:1006; CCBB 43:115; HBG 1:84; Kirkus 57:1681; SLJ Jan 1990 p. 106)

9-335 **MARIA, Consort of Ferdinand, King of Rumania.** *The Magic Doll of Rumania; a Wonder Story in Which East and West Do Meet; Written for American Children.* Gr. 4–6.
An American girl named Nancy travels throughout Rumania with her magic doll.
Illus. by Maud and Miska Petersham, Stokes, 1929, 319 pp., o.p.
(Bookshelf, 1925–1926, p. 1; Mahony 3:54)

MARTIN, Rafe. *The World Before This One: A Novel Told in Legend.*
See Chapter 6, High Fantasy: Myth or Legend Fantasy.

9-336 **MASEFIELD, John (Edward).** *The Midnight Folk: A Novel.* Gr. 5–7.
✫ (Orig. British pub. 1927.)
Five animals help Kay solve the mystery of his great-grandfather's stolen treasure. In the sequel, *The Box of Delights: Or, When the Wolves Were Running* (1935), Kay battles evil forces to save the magical Box of Delights.
Illus. by Rowland Hilder, Macmillan, 1932, 282 pp., o.p.

(BL 24:264, 287, 28:396, 401; Bookshelf 1932 p. 24; LJ 53:856; Moore:332, 427; TLS 1927 p. 906)

9-337 MASON, Arthur. *The Wee Men of Ballywooden.* Gr. 4–7.
☆   Times were hard for Danny Fay and the others until the Wee Men returned to their Irish village. The sequel is *From the Horn of the Moon* (1931).
Illus. by Robert Lawson, Doubleday, 1930, 266 pp., o.p.; Viking, 1952, 214 pp., o.p.
(BL 27:167; CCBB 6:34; HB 6:331, 7:121, 29:62; LJ 56:452, 77:1747; Mahony 3:207; Moore:435)

9-338 MAXWELL, William (Keepers). *The Heavenly Tenants.* Gr. 3–5.
☆   The constellations descend from the sky to care for the Marvells' farm.
Illus. by Ilonka Karasz, Harper, 1946, 56 pp., o.p.; Parabola, 1992, 60 pp. (0-930407-25-3)
(BL 43:90, 277; HB 22:455; Kirkus 14:455; LJ 71:1412, 1720; SLJ Aug 1992 p. 99)

9-339 MAYNE, William (James Carter). *The Blue Boat.* Gr. 4–6. (Orig. British
☆   pub. 1957.)
Christopher and Hugh meet a goblin and a giant while exploring a magical lake. Carnegie Medal Commended Book, 1957.
Illus. by Geraldine Spence, Dutton, 1960, 173 pp., o.p.
(BL 56:609; CCBB 14:178; Kirkus 28:49; LJ 85:2479)

9-340 MAYNE, William (James Carter). *The Glass Ball.* Gr. 3–5. (Orig. British
☆   pub. 1961.)
Max and Niko follow a magical rolling glass ball.
Illus. by Janet Duchesne, Dutton, 1962, 2000, 63 pp., o.p.
(BL 58:796; Eakin:228; HB 38:374; LJ 87:2026)

9-341 MAYNE, William (James Carter). *A Grass Rope.* Gr. 4–6. (Orig. British
☆   pub. 1957.)
Four children weave a special rope to capture a unicorn. Carnegie Medal, 1957.
Illus. by Lynton Lamb, Dutton, 1962, 166 pp., o.p.
(Eakin:224; HB 38:600; LJ 87:4622)

9-342 MAYNE, William (James Carter). *The Green Book of Hob Stories.* **(Hob
☆   series, bk. 1).** Gr. 2–3. (Orig. British pub. 1984.)
Five tales about an invisible 2-foot-tall man who magically resolves household problems. Hob's adventures continue in *The Blue Book of Hob Stories* (1984), *The Yellow Book of Hob Stories* (1984), and *The Red Book of Hob Stories* (1984), which have been republished in *The Book of Hob Stories* (Candlewick, 1997). In *Hob and the Goblins* (1994), Hob and his family move to the country, where he must protect them from other magical creatures. In *Hob and the Peddler* (1997), a peddler sells Hob to a nice family, then hides a stolen sea serpent's egg in the pond behind their house.
Illus. by Patrick Benson, Putnam, 1984, 25 pp., o.p.
(BL 80:1550; CCBB 38:32; HB 60:468; HBG 9:63; SLJ Oct 1984 p. 160, Nov 1997 p. 94; Suth 3:298; TLS Mar 3, 1984 p. 338)

MAZER, Harry. *The Dog in the Freezer: Three Novellas.*
See Chapter 2, Animal Fantasy.

9-343 MEACHAM, Margaret. *A Mid-Semester Night's Dream.* Gr. 5–7.
Seventh-grade Morgan's fairy godmother, Greta Fleetwing, turns out to be a well-intentioned but inept student fairy godmother, whose magic love spells often go awry.
Holiday, 2004, 154 pp. (0-8234-1815-4)
(BL 100:1728; CCBB 57:382; Kirkus 72:333: SLJ Aug 2004 p. 126)

9-344 MEDDAUGH, Susan. *Lulu's Hat.* Gr. 3–5.
Orphaned Lulu follows a dog into a magical top hat and finds herself in "Deep Magic space," where she is transformed into a magician and learns what happened to her birth parents.
Illus. by the author, Houghton, 2002, 74 pp. (0-618-15277-6)
(BL 98:1527; CCBB 55:333; HBG 13:361; SLJ May 2002 p. 123)

9-345 MEIGS, Cornelia (Lynde). *The Wonderful Locomotive.* Gr. 3–5.
A little boy named Peter takes old engine number 44 for its last exciting cross-country run.
Illus. by Berta Hader and Elmer Hader, Macmillan, 1928, 104 pp., o.p.
(BL 25:171; Bookshelf 1932 p. 8; HB 4[Aug 1928]:13, 32–33, 76, 7:115, 20:347–349; Mahony 2:141)

MELLECKER, Judith. *Randolph's Dream.*
See Chapter 1, Allegorical Fantasy and Literary Fairy Tales.

MENDEZ, Phil. *The Black Snowman.*
See Chapter 6, High Fantasy: Myth or Legend Fantasy.

MILES, (Mary) Patricia. *The Gods in Winter.*
See Chapter 1, Allegorical Fantasy and Literary Fairy Tales.

MOERI, Louise. *Star Mother's Youngest Child.*
See Chapter 1, Allegorical Fantasy and Literary Fairy Tales.

MOLESWORTH, Mary Louisa (Stewart). *The Cuckoo Clock.*
See Chapter 7, High Fantasy: Travel to Other Worlds.

9-346 MOLESWORTH, Mary Louisa (Stewart). *The Tapestry Room: A Child's Romance.* Gr. 4–6. (Orig. British and U.S. pubs. 1879.)
A family of French children living in an old chateau have wonderful dreams and adventures.
Illus. by Walter Crane, Random, 1961, 217 pp., o.p.; Garland, 1976 (bound with *The Cuckoo Clock*, 1877, 1954), 502 pp., o.p.
(HB 38:66; Mahony 2:291)

9-347 MONATH, Elizabeth. *Topper and the Giant.* Gr. 3–5.
Mat and his dog, Topper, are given a magic charm by a giant they rescue from an avalanche.
Illus. by the author, Viking, 1960, 60 pp., o.p.
(HB 36:216; Kirkus 28:144; LJ 85:2029)

9-348 MOON, Grace Purdie, and MOON, Carl. *Lost Indian Magic: A Mystery Story of the Red Man as He Lived Before the White Men Came.* Gr. 5–7.

A brave young Indian boy must recover his tribe's magic jewel, a turquoise elephant stolen long ago.
Illus. by Carl Moon, Stokes, 1918, 301 pp., o.p.
(BL 15:1512; Mahony 2:538)

9-349 MOORE, Anne Carroll. *Nicholas: A Manhattan Christmas Story.* Gr. 4–6.
An 8-inch-tall Dutch boy arrives in New York City on Christmas Eve, determined to see everything of interest, past and present. John Newbery Medal Honor Book, 1925. The sequel is *Nicholas and the Golden Goose* (1932).
Illus. by Jay Van Everen, Putnam, 1924, 331 pp., o.p.
(BL 21:158; Bookshelf 1927 p. 10; HB 1[Nov 1924]:13; LJ 50:803; Mahony 2:717)

MORGAN, Clay. *The Boy Who Spoke Dog.*
See Chapter 2, Animal Fantasy.

9-350 MORGAN, Helen (Gertrude Louise Axford). *Satchkin Patchkin.* Gr. 2–4.
(Orig. British pub. 1966.)
Satchkin Patchkin is a small green man who lives in an apple tree. *Mother Farthing's Luck* (1971) is the British sequel.
Illus. by Shirley Hughes, M. Smith, 1970, 64 pp., o.p.
(CCBB 24:63; LJ 95:4340; TLS 1966 p. 1092)

MORGAN, Robin. *The Mer-Child: A Legend for Children and Other Adults.*
See Chapter 1, Allegorical Fantasy and Literary Fairy Tales.

MORPURGO, Michael. *Arthur, High King of Britain.*
See Chapter 6, High Fantasy: Myth or Legend Fantasy.

MORPURGO, Michael. *Robin of Sherwood.*
See Chapter 6, High Fantasy: Myth or Legend Fantasy.

9-351 MORPURGO, Michael. *The Sandman and the Turtles.* Gr. 3–6. (Orig. British pub. 1991.)
The Sandman crafted by cousins Michael and Polly at the beach comes to life, just as it did in their Welsh grandfather's stories.
Putnam/Philomel, 1994, 79 pp. (0-399-22672-9)
(BL 91:44; HBG 6:81; Kirkus 62:1539)

9-352 MORRISON, Dorothy Nafus. *Vanishing Act.* Gr. 5–8.
Joanna performs magic tricks at her school's talent show and impresses everyone in the audience, including some crooks, when she uses a device called a transmuter to make herself invisible.
Macmillan, 1989, 202 pp., o.p.
(BL 86:188; HBG 1:72; Kirkus 57:1248; SLJ Nov 1989 p. 112)

MULLARKEY, Lisa Geurdes. *The Witch's Portraits.*
See Chapter 12, Witchcraft and Sorcery Fantasy.

9-353 MULOCK, Diana (pseud. of Dinah Craik). *The Adventures of a Brownie as Told to My Child.* Gr. 3–5. (Orig. British pub. 1872.)
Six tales in which only children can see the brownie work his mischief.

Illus. by Mary Seaman, Macmillan, 1952, 122 pp., o.p.; Amereon, 1976 (bound with *The Little Lame Prince*, 1874, 1948) (0-84881-109-7)

(BL 15:153, 20:224; HB 28:422; LJ 50:803; Mahony 1:36)

9-354 MURPHY, Catherine Frey. *Songs in the Silence.* Gr. 4–7.
Rescued at sea by Melae, a pilot whale with whom she can communicate, a girl named Hallie rescues another injured whale named Globe while her family is preoccupied with her badly burned younger brother.
Macmillan, 1994, 192 pp. (0-02-767730-3)

(BL 90:1534; CCBB 47:296; HBGF 5:314; Kirkus 62:635; SLJ June 1994 p. 133)

9-355 MURPHY, Pat. *Wild Angel.* Gr. 10 up.
Three-year-old Sarah is raised by wolves after her parents' murders during the California Gold Rush, but her life is threatened after the murderer hears stories about a beautiful wild girl.
Tor, 2000, 288 pp. (0-312-86626-7); Tor, 2001, pap., 352 pp. (0-8125-9042-2)

(BL 96:1866; Kirkus 68:840; LJ July 2000 p. 147)

9-356 MURPHY, Rita. *Harmony.* Gr. 6–9.
✶ Having fallen from the sky as an infant star, Harmony, who is now 15 and able to move objects without touching them and to hear the thoughts of others, longs to protect the Tennessee white pine forest where she and her adoptive parents live.
Delacorte, 2002, 128 pp. (0-385-72938-3); Laurel Leaf, 2004, pap., 160 pp. (0-440-22923-5)

(BL 99:222; HB 79:81; HBG 14:86; Kirkus 70:1316; Kliatt Nov 2002 p. 14; SLJ Oct 2002 p. 169; VOYA 25:400)

9-357 MURPHY, Rita. *Night Flying.* Gr. 6–10.
✶ Like her mother, aunts, and grandmother, Georgia Hansen can fly, but her grandmother enforces strict rules of behavior until rebellious Aunt Carmen arrives and reveals family secrets.
Delacorte, 2000, 144 pp. (0-385-32748-X); Dell, 2002, pap., 131 pp. (0-440-22837-9)

(BL 97:809; CCBB 54:190; HB 76:577; HBG 12:85; Kirkus 68:1044; Kliatt Nov 2000 p. 8; SLJ Nov 2000 p. 160; VOYA 23:277)

NABB, Magdalen. *The Enchanted Horse.*
See Chapter 11, Toy Fantasy.

NASTICK, Sharon. *Mr. Radagast Makes an Unexpected Journey.*
See Chapter 8, Humorous Fantasy.

NESBIT (Bland), E(dith). *The Complete Book of Dragons.*
See Chapter 3, Fantasy Collections.

9-358 NESBIT (Bland), E(dith). *The Deliverers of Their Country.* Gr. 3–5. (Orig.
✶ British pub. in *Strand Magazine*, 1899; U.S. pub. in *The Book of Dragons*, 1901, 1973; this ed. orig. pub. in Austria, 1985.)
Harry and Effie awaken a marble statue of St. George to ask his advice on fighting the plague of dragons infesting England.

Illus. by Lisbeth Zwerger, Picture Book Studio, 1985, 32 pp. (0-88708-005-7); North-South, illus. by Lisbeth Zwerger, 1996, 25 pp. (1-55858-623-7)

(BL 82:759; CCBB 39:93; HB 62:195; SLJ Apr 1986 p. 91; TLS July 1986 p. 789)

9-359 **NESBIT (Bland), E(dith).** *The Enchanted Castle.* Gr. 5–7. (Orig. British
☆   pub. 1907.)
A magical ring transports Gerald, Jimmy, and Cathy to a garden of stone monsters surrounding a castle.
Illus. by H(arold) R. Millar, Coward, 1933, o.p.; illus. by Cecil Leslie, Dutton, 1964, o.p.; illus. by Paul O. Zelinsky, Morrow, 1992, 304 pp. (0-688-05435-8); Puffin, 2004, pap., 304 pp. (0-14-036743-8)

(BL 30:24, 60, 89:738; Bookshelf 1933 p. 9; HB 8:153, 214, 69:232; HBG 4:75; Kirkus 32:293, 60:1263; LJ 58:1052; Mahony 3:208)

9-360 **NESBIT (Bland), E(dith).** *Five Children and It.* **(The Five Children trilo-**
☆   **gy, bk. 1).** Gr. 5–7. (Orig. British pub. 1902.)
Anthea, Jane, Robert, Cyril, and the Baby uncover a Psammead, or Sand Fairy, who reluctantly agrees to grant their wishes. In *The Phoenix and the Carpet* (1904, 1949, 1960, 1987; Puffin, pap., 1996; Wildside, 2002) a magic carpet carrying a phoenix egg takes the children on magical journeys to Persia. In *The Story of the Amulet* (see Chapter 10, Time Travel Fantasy), which was the first time-travel fantasy ever written for children, the Sand Fairy helps the children travel to ancient Egypt, Babylon, and Rome. All three books were published in one volume entitled *The Five Children; Containing Five Children and It; The Phoenix and the Carpet; The Story of the Amulet* (Coward, 1930).
Illus. by J. S. Goodall, Looking Glass, 1905, 1948, 1959, 255 pp., o.p.; illus. by H(arold) R. Millar, Coward, 1949, 1963, 223 pp., o.p.; ed. by Sandra Kemp, Oxford University Press, 1994, pap. (0-19-283163-1); Puffin, 1996, pap., 256 pp. (0-14-036735-7); illus. by Paul O. Zelinsky, Books of Wonder, 1999, 246 pp. (0-688-13545-5); Wildside, 2002, 192 pp. (1-59224-942-6); Penguin, 2004, pap., 207 pp. (0-14-303915-6)

(BL 27:215; HB 6:332, 25:297, 579; HBG 11:84; LJ 74:618; Mahony 2:291)

NESBIT (Bland), E(dith). *The House of Arden.*
See Chapter 10, Time Travel Fantasy.

NESBIT (Bland), E(dith). *The Magic City.*
See Chapter 7, High Fantasy: Travel to Other Worlds.

9-361 **NESBIT (Bland), E(dith).** *The Magic World.* Gr. 5–7. (Orig. British pub.
1912.)
Twelve fantasy tales including "The Cat-hood of Maurice," "Accidental Magic," and "The Magician's Heart."
Illus. by H(arold) R. Millar and Spencer Pryse, Coward, 1960, 280 pp., o.p.; Puffin, 1996, pap., 256 pp. (0-14-036765-9)

(BL 57:32; HB 36:309; LJ 85:3224; TLS 1981 p. 348)

9-362 **NESBIT (Bland), E(dith).** *Wet Magic.* Gr. 5–7. (Orig. British pub. 1913.)
Four children rescue a mermaid and are taken on an undersea adventure.

Illus. by H(arold) R. Millar, Coward, 1938, 1960, 244 pp., o.p.; Books of Wonder, 1996, 256 pp. (0-929605-63-2); North-South, 2001, Illus. by H(arold) R. Millar, 182 pp. (1-58717-054-X)

(BL 57:32; HB 13:378, 36:309; HBG 12:313; LJ 62:881, 63:691, 85:3224)

9-363 NESBIT (Bland), E(dith). *The Wonderful Garden; or the Three C's.* Gr. 5–7. (Orig. British pub. 1911.)

Carolyn, Charlotte, and Charles find an old book of magic and a magical garden.

Illus. by H(arold) R. Millar, Coward, 1960, o.p.; Elsevier, 2000, o.p.

(BL 32:80, 57:32; Bookshelf 1935 p. 2; HB 11:296, 36:309, 61:196; LJ 60:830, 85:3224; Mahony 3:209)

9-364 NIMMO, Jenny. *Griffin's Castle.* Gr. 5–7. (Orig. British pub. 1994.)

Eleven-year-old Dinah makes the exciting discovery that she can bring wild animal stone carvings to life, but she doesn't anticipate that they may turn against her.

Orchard, 1997, 198 pp. (0-531-30006-4)

(CCBB 50:291; HBG 8:306; Kirkus 65:560; SLJ June 1997 p. 124; VOYA 20:188)

NIMMO, Jenny. *Midnight for Charlie Bone.*

See Chapter 12, Witchcraft and Sorcery Fantasy.

9-365 NIMMO, Jenny. *The Snow Spider.* **(Gwyn Griffiths trilogy, bk. 1).** Gr.
✩ 4–7. (Orig. British pub. 1986.)

On his 10th birthday, Gwyn's grandmother gives him five magic gifts to help solve the mystery of his sister's disappearance in the Welsh mountains. Nestlé Smarties Grand Prix for Children's Books, 1986. Tir na n-Og Award, 1987. In the sequel, *Orchard of the Crescent Moon* (1989; British title: *Emlyn's Moon*, 1987), Gwyn's magic and the friendship of a little girl named Nia save Gwyn's cousin Emlyn from the evil creatures that took Gwyn's sister away. The third book in the trilogy is *The Chestnut Soldier* (1991).

Dutton, 1987, 144 pp., o.p.

(BL 83:1751; CCBB 40:216; HB 63:613; Kirkus 55:861; SLJ Aug 1987 p. 87; Suth 4:304)

NIX, Garth. *Mister Monday.*

See Chapter 7, High Fantasy: Travel to Other Worlds.

9-366 NIXON, Joan Lowery. *The Gift.* Gr. 4–6.

Brian's Irish grandfather enchants him with tales of pookas, fairies, and leprechauns, and he resolves to bring a real leprechaun home with him.

Illus. by Andrew Glass, Macmillan, 1983, 96 pp., o.p.

(BL 79:1036; CCBB 36:214; Kirkus 51:524; SLJ May 1983 p. 74)

NIXON, Joan Lowery. *Magnolia's Mixed-Up Magic.*

See Chapter 2, Animal Fantasy.

NORMAN, Roger. *Albion's Dream: A Novel of Terror.*

See Chapter 6, High Fantasy: Myth or Legend Fantasy.

9-367 NORTH, Joan. *The Cloud Forest.* Gr. 5–8.

The Annerlie Ring causes Andrew to have disturbing dreams of the Cloud Forest.

Farrar, 1966, 180 pp. o.p.

(BL 63:326; CCBB 20:96; HB 42:564; Suth:297; TLS 1965 p. 1133)

9-368 NORTON, Andre (pseud. of Alice Mary Norton). *Fur Magic.* Gr. 5–7.
Corey is afraid of everything on his foster uncle's ranch until the Changer, part-coyote and part-man, turns him into a beaver named Yellow Shell.
Illus. by John Kaufmann, World, 1968, 174 pp., o.p.

(HB 45:172; Kirkus 36:1164; LJ 94:877; TLS 1969 p. 689)

NORTON, Andre (pseud. of Alice Mary Norton). *Lavender Green Magic.*
See Chapter 10, Time Travel Fantasy.

9-369 NORTON, Andre (pseud. of Alice Mary Norton), and MILLER, Phyllis.
Seven Spells to Sunday. Gr. 5–7.
Gifts and spells found in a purple and silver mailbox in a vacant lot bring hope into the lives of foster children Monnie and Bim.
Atheneum, 1979, 144 pp., o.p.

(BL 75:1219; Kirkus 47:741; SLJ Mar 1979 p. 143)

9-370 NORTON, Mary (Pearson). *Bedknob and Broomstick.* Gr. 4–6. (Orig.
★★   British pub. 1943 and 1946.)
In this two-part story, a witch gives Paul, Carey, and Charles a magical bed-knob, enabling their bed to fly through time. This book was originally published in two volumes in England as *The Magic Bedknob or; How to Become a Witch in Ten Easy Lessons* in 1943 and *Bonfires and Broomsticks*, in 1946.
Illus. by Erik Blegvad, Harcourt, 1957, 189 pp., o.p.; Harcourt, 2000, illus. by Erik Blegvad, 229 pp. (0-15-202450-6); pap. (0-15-202456-5)

(BL 54:177; CCBB 11:98; HB 33:489; HBG 12:313; Kirkus 25:638; LJ 69:355, 82:3248; TLS Nov 15, 1957 p. iii)

9-371 NORTON, Mary (Pearson). *The Borrowers.* **(The Borrowers series, bk.**
★★   **1).** Gr. 4–7. (Orig. British pub. 1952.)
Pod, Homily, and Arrietty Clock, a family of tiny people who live by "borrow-ing" from humans, must flee for their lives after Arrietty makes friends with a human boy. Carnegie Medal, 1952. In *The Borrowers Afield* (1955; 2003), the Clocks live precariously outdoors in an old boot, until they are rescued from the winter snows by Arrietty's friend, the game-keeper's son. In *The Borrowers Afloat* (1959; 2003), a young Borrower named Spiller guides the family on an exciting trip through the drains to the river, where they settle in a tea kettle, only to be washed away by a flood. Carnegie Medal Commended Book, 1959. In *The Borrowers Aloft* (1961; 2003), the Clocks' safe, happy life in a minia-ture railway village is interrupted when they are kidnapped by greedy Mr. and Mrs. Platter. In *Poor Stainless* (1971; republished in *The Borrowers Aloft: Plus the Short Tale of Poor Stainless*, 2003), Homily tells Arrietty about Stainless, a young Borrower who spent a glorious week in a candy store, while his worried family searched for him. In *The Borrowers Avenged* (1982; 2003), the Clocks move into a rectory and rid themselves forever of the money-hungry Platters and their plot to put the Borrowers on display. The first four books were published together as *The Borrowers Omnibus* (Dent, 1966).
Illus. by Beth Krush and Joe Krush, Harcourt, 1953, 180 pp. (0-15-209987-5); illus. by Michael (R.) Hague, Harcourt, 1991, 177 pp. (0-15-209991-3); illus.

by Diana Stanley, Harcourt, 2003 (0-15-204928-2); Odyssey, 2003, pap., 192 pp. (0-15-204737-9)

(BL 50:4, 40, 80:96; CCBB 7:25; Eakin:249; HB 29:456, 80:158; HBG 3:70; Kirkus 21:483; LJ 78:1699)

ODGERS, Sally Farrell. *Drummond: The Search for Sarah.*
See Chapter 11, Toy Fantasy.

9-372 **O'FAOLÁIN, Eileen (Gould).** *The Little Black Hen; An Irish Fairy Story.* Gr. 4–6. (Orig. pub. in Ireland.)
Garret and Julie lift a spell laid on a changeling hen by Cliona, the fairy queen. Garret has other magic adventures in *King of the Cats* (Morrow, 1942), *Miss Pennyfeather and the Pooka* (Random, 1946), and *Miss Pennyfeather in the Springtime* (pub. in Ireland, 1946).
Illus. by Aldren A. Watson, Random, 1940, 135 pp., o.p.
(BL 37:20; HB 16:339, 342; LJ 65:715, 848; TLS 1940 p. 633)

OGILVY, Ian. *Measle and the Wrathmonk.*
See Chapter 12, Witchcraft and Sorcery Fantasy.

9-373 **OLSON, Helen Kronberg.** *The Strange Thing That Happened to Oliver Wendell Iscovitch.* Gr. 1–4.
Oliver Wendell's fat cheeks enable him to hold his breath and float through the air.
Illus. by Betsy Lewin, Dodd, 1983, 62 pp., o.p.
(BL 79:1221; CCBB 37:14; SLJ Sept 1938 p. 110; Suth 3:328)

OPPENHEIM, Shulamith (Levey). *The Selchie's Seed.*
See Chapter 6, High Fantasy: Myth or Legend Fantasy.

9-374 **ORMONDROYD, Edward.** *David and the Phoenix.* Gr. 4–6.
★ David meets the Phoenix on a mountain ledge and helps him outwit a scientist bent on capturing the mythical creature.
Illus. by Joan Raysor, Follett, 1957, 173 pp., o.p.
(BL 54:113; CCBB 11:38; HB 33:401; Kirkus 25:583; LJ 82:3249)

ORMONDROYD, Edward. *Time at the Top.*
See Chapter 10, Time Travel Fantasy.

OSBORNE, Mary Pope. *Dinosaurs Before Dark.*
See Chapter 10, Time Travel Fantasy.

OSTERWEIL, Adam. *The Comic Book Kid.*
See Chapter 10, Time Travel Fantasy.

9-375 **OUIDA (pseud. of [Marie] Louise de la Ramée).** *The Nürnberg Stove.* Gr. 4–6. (Orig. British pub. 1882, in *Stories for Children;* U.S. pub. in *The Nürnberg Stove and Other Stories*, 1901, 1928.)
A boy named August hides inside his family's porcelain stove and goes on a journey when the stove is sold.
Illus. by Maria Louise Kirk, Lippincott, 1905, 1916, o.p.; illus. by Frank Boyd, Macmillan, 1928, 1952, 122 pp., o.p.; Kessinger, 2004, pap., 52 pp. (1-41917-578-5)
(BL 12:392, 21:160, 25:253, 49:209; HB 4[Aug 1928]:9, 28:421; Mahony 2:296)

9-376 PALMER, Mary. *The Teaspoon Tree.* Gr. 3–5.
A girl named Andulasia searches for the magical Teaspoon Tree.
Illus. by Carlota Dodge, Houghton, 1963, 114 pp., o.p.
(CCBB 16:115; HB 39:174; LJ 88:1769)

9-377 PARKER, Richard. *M for Mischief.* Gr. 3–5. (Orig. British pub. 1965.)
Andrew and Milly find an old-fashioned stove with a magical dial that cooks
foods that bring on invisibility and transformation into animals.
Illus. by Charles Geer, Hawthorn, 1966, 90 pp., o.p.
(HB 42:307; Kirkus 34:57; LJ 91:2697; TLS 1965 p. 513)

PARKER, Richard. *The Old Powder Line.*
See Chapter 10, Time Travel Fantasy.

9-378 PARKER, Richard. *Spell Seven.* Gr. 3–5. (Orig. British pub. 1971.)
Carolyn gives her brother Norman a magic wand.
Illus. by Trevor Ridley, Nelson, 1971, 127 pp., o.p.
(HB 47:385; LJ 96:2920; TLS 1971 p. 774)

9-379 PARRISH, Anne, and PARRISH, Dillwyn. *Knee-High to a Grasshopper.*
Gr. 4–6.
Little Man "ungrows" to the size of a meadow mouse.
Illus. by the authors, Macmillan, 1923, 209 pp., o.p.
(BL 20:107; Bookshelf 1923–1924 Suppl. p. 2; HB 7:61–67; LJ 50:803; Mahony 2:291)

PASCAL, Francine. *Hangin' Out with Cici.*
See Chapter 10, Time Travel Fantasy.

PATON WALSH, Jill (Gillian Bliss). *Matthew and the Sea Singer.*
See Chapter 1, Allegorical Fantasy and Literary Fairy Tales.

9-380 PATTEN, Brian. *Mr. Moon's Last Case.* Gr. 5–8. (Orig. British pub. 1975.)
A leprechaun called Nameon, who accidentally entered the human world and is
desperately trying to get home, is pursued by a detective named Mr. Moon and
aided by the members of the Secret Society for the Protection of Leprechauns.
Illus. by Mary Moore, Scribner, 1976, 158 pp., o.p.
(BL 73:410; CCBB 30:111; HB 52:626; Kirkus 44:974; SLJ Feb 1977 p. 67)

9-381 PAYNE, Joan Balfour (Dicks). *The Leprechaun of Bayou Luce.* Gr. 3–5.
☆ Josh helps a leprechaun win back the gold that was stolen by pirate ghosts.
Illus. by the author, Hastings, 1957, 60 pp., o.p.
(BL 54:208; CCBB 11:39; HB 33:489; Kirkus 25:689; LJ 83:240)

9-382 PAYNE, Joan Balfour (Dicks). *Magnificent Milo.* Gr. 3–5.
After a young centaur named Milo accidentally falls from his mountain home,
he joins a traveling circus in an attempt to find his way home again.
Illus. by the author, Hastings, 1958, 64 pp., o.p.
(BL 55:137; HB 34:478; Kirkus 26:605; LJ 84:253)

9-383 PEARCE, (Ann) Philippa. *A Dog So Small.* Gr. 4–6. (Orig. British pub.
1962.)
A powerful imaginary chihuahua comes to life whenever Ben closes his eyes.

Illus. by Antony Maitland, Lippincott, 1963, 142 pp., o.p.

(BL 59:946; CCBB 16:131; HB 39:284, 60:499; LJ 88:2149; TLS 1962 p. 397)

9-384 PEARCE, (Ann) Philippa. *Lion at School: And Other Stories.* Gr. 3–5.
✯ (Orig. British pub. 1985.)
Nine tales, including "The Lion at School," "The Executioner," and "The Crooked Little Finger."
Illus. by Caroline Sharpe, Greenwillow, 1986, 122 pp., o.p.

(BL 82:1616; CCBB 39:177; Kirkus 54:716; SLJ Sept 1986 p. 138; Suth 4:320)

9-385 PEARCE, (Ann) Philippa. *The Little Gentleman.* Gr. 3–6. (Orig. pub. in
✯ England.)
After Mr. Franklin asks a young girl named Bet to read aloud in his garden, she meets a talking mole named Little Gentleman.
Illus. by Tom Pohrt, Greenwillow/HarperCollins, 2004, 208 pp. (0-06-073161-3)

(BL 100:1937; CCBB 58:180; HB 80:594; Kirkus 72:692; SLJ Sep 2004 p. 177;)

9-386 PEARCE, (Ann) Philippa. *Mrs. Cockle's Cat.* Gr. 2–4. (Orig. British pub.
✯ 1961.)
The wind sweeps a balloon-seller named Mrs. Cockle off in search of her lost cat.
Illus. by Antony Maitland, Lippincott, 1962, 32 pp., o.p.

(BL 58:694; CCBB 15:130; HB 38:172; LJ 87:2026; TLS Dec 1, 1961 p. xiv)

PEARCE, (Ann) Philippa. *Tom's Midnight Garden.*
See Chapter 10, Time Travel Fantasy.

PEARSON, Kit. *Awake and Dreaming.*
See Chapter 4, Ghost Fantasy.

PEASE, (Clarence) Howard. *The Gypsy Caravan.*
See Chapter 10, Time Travel Fantasy.

PENDERGRAFT, Patricia. *The Legend of Daisy Flowerdew.*
See Chapter 1, Allegorical Fantasy and Literary Fairy Tales.

9-387 PENNYPACKER, Sara. *Stuart's Cape.* Gr. 2–4.
Stuart has an adventure whenever he wears his superhero cape, including the day he eats too much angel food cake and begins to fly. The sequel is *Stuart Goes to School* (2003).
Illus. by Martin Matje, Scholastic, 2002, 64 pp. (0-439-30180-7); Scholastic, 2004, pap., 64 pp. (0-439-30181-5)

(BL 99:125; Kirkus 70:961; SLJ Nov 2002 p. 133)

PFEFFER, Susan Beth. *Rewind to Yesterday.*
See Chapter 10, Time Travel Fantasy.

9-388 PFEFFER, Susan Beth. *Sara Kate, Superkid.* Gr. 2–4.
Eight-year-old Sara Kate's inherited magical powers work on Tuesdays, Thursdays, and some Saturdays, but her powers begin to wear off when she tries to

use them in a basketball free throw contest. The sequel is *Sara Kate Saves the World* (1995).
Illus. by Suzanne Hutchins, Holt, 1994, 58 pp. (0-8050-3147-2)
(BL 91:682; CCBB 48:174; HBG 6:69; SLJ Dec 1994 p. 79)

9-389 **PFEFFER, Susan Beth.** *The Trouble with Wishes.* Gr. 2–4.
★ Katie finds a magic lamp on her way home from school, but her three wishes cause unexpected problems.
Illus. by Jennifer Plecas, Holt, 1996, 71 pp. (0-8050-3826-4)
(BL 92:1507; CCBB 49:349; HBG 7:287; SLJ June 1996 p. 107)

PHILLIPS, Ann. *The Oak King and the Ash Queen.*
See Chapter 6, High Fantasy: Myth or Legend Fantasy.

PIKE, Christopher. *Alosha.*
See Chapter 7, High Fantasy: Travel to Other Worlds.

PIKE, Christopher. *Sati.*
See Chapter 1, Allegorical Fantasy and Literary Fairy Tales.

9-390 **PINKWATER, D(aniel) Manus.** *Magic Camera.* Gr. 2–3.
Charles's antique camera can make real things disappear and imaginary things become real.
Illus. by the author, Dodd, 1974, 35 pp., o.p.
(BL 70:878; Kirkus 42:53)

9-391 **PINKWATER, D(aniel) Manus.** *The Magic Pretzel.* **(The Werewolf Club series, bk. 1).** Gr. 2–4.
Fourth-grader Norman Gnormal joins a school club for student werewolves, even though he isn't really a shape-shifter like the others. The sequels are *The Lunchroom of Doom* (2000), *The Werewolf Club Meets Dorkula* (2001), *The Werewolf Club Meets the Hound of the Basketballs* (2001), and *The Werewolf Club Meets Oliver Twit* (2002).
Illus. by Jill Pinkwater, Simon, 2000, 78 pp. (0-689-83800-X)
(BL 95:2030; CCBB 54:35; HBG 12:66; SLJ Nov 2000 p. 129)

PINKWATER, D(aniel) Manus. *Wingman.*
See Chapter 10, Time Travel Fantasy.

9-392 **POLESE, Carolyn.** *Something About a Mermaid.* Gr. 2–4.
The mermaid Janie finds at the beach does not adjust well to life in an apartment.
Illus. by Gail Owens, Dutton, 1978, 27 pp., o.p.
(BL 75:867; Kirkus 47:66; SLJ Mar 1979 p. 129)

9-393 **POMERANTZ, Charlotte.** *The Downtown Fairy Godmother.* Gr. 3–5.
Olivia's fairy godmother is an amateur who needs a lot of practice to perfect her wish-granting abilities.
Illus. by Susanna Natti, Addison-Wesley, 1978, 45 pp., o.p.
(CCBB 32:70; Kirkus 46:1190; SLJ Nov 1978 p. 67)

PORTE, Barbara Ann. *Jesse's Ghost and Other Stories.*
See Chapter 3, Fantasy Collections.

POSTMA, Lidia. *The Stolen Mirror.*
See Chapter 7, High Fantasy: Travel to Other Worlds.

9-394 POSTMA, Lidia. *The Witch's Garden.* Gr. 1–3. (Orig. pub. in the Netherlands.)
Seven children exploring the garden of a tumbledown house meet elves and see circus ghosts dancing in a magic tree.
Illus. by the author, McGraw-Hill, 1979, 23 pp., o.p.
(CCBB 33:54; SLJ Sept 1979 p. 119; Suth 3:352)

9-395 POTTER, Miriam (S.) Clark. *Sally Gabble and the Fairies.* Gr. 3–5.
Old Sally Gabble makes friends with the fairies after she catches a particularly troublesome one in a trap.
Illus. by Helen Sewell, Macmillan, 1929, 87 pp., o.p.
(BL 26:237; HB 5:49; Mahony 3:109)

9-396 PROYSEN, Alf. *Little Old Mrs. Pepperpot and Other Stories.* Gr. 3–5. (Orig. Swedish pub. 1957; British pub. 1959.)
Twelve stories, mostly about a woman who can shrink to the size of a pepper shaker. The sequels are *Mrs. Pepperpot Again* (1961; republished as *Mrs. Pepperpot and the Moose*, Farrar, 1991), *Mrs. Pepperpot to the Rescue* (1964, 1988), *Mrs. Pepperpot in the Magic Wood* (Pantheon, 1968; Viking, 1988), *Mrs. Pepperpot's Outing* (Pantheon, 1971), *Mrs. Pepperpot's Busy Day* (Random, 1980, 1989), *Mrs. Pepperpot's Christmas* (Random, 1987), *Mrs. Pepperpot and the Hidden Treasure* (Random, 1987), *Mrs. Pepperpot Minds the Baby* (Random, 1987), *Mrs. Pepperpot's Year* (1988, Viking, 1999), and *Mrs. Pepperpot Goes Berry Picking* (Farrar, 1990). All of the stories have been collected in *Mrs. Pepperpot Stories* (Random, 2000).
Trans. by Marianne Helwig, illus. by Bjorn Berg, Astor House, 1960, 1999, 95 pp., o.p.
(HB 36:216; Kirkus 28:235; LJ 85:2042; SLJ Feb 1992 p. 77; TLS May 29, 1959 p. xiii)

PRUE, Sally. *Cold Tom.*
See Chapter 7, High Fantasy: Travel to Other Worlds.

9-397 PULLMAN, Philip. *Clockwork.* Gr. 4–7. (Orig. British pub. 1997, entitled
★ *Clockwork, or All Wound Up.*)
When Fritz tells the guests at a German inn a frightening story about a king with a clockwork heart, a madman, and a mechanical knight animated by black magic, the story's characters come to life. Carnegie Medal Commended Book, 1996; Nestlé Smarties Silver Award, 1997.
Illus. by Leonid Gore, Scholastic, 1998, 128 pp. (0-590-12999-6), 1999, pap. (0-590-12998-8)
(BL 95:229, 1691; CCBB 52:143; HB 74:740; HBG 10:73; Kirkus 66:1536; Kliatt Sep 1998 p. 10; SLJ Oct 1998 p. 145, Dec 1998 p. 26; VOYA 21:370, 22:15)

PULLMAN, Philip. *Spring-Heeled Jack.*
See Chapter 8, Humorous Fantasy.

PYLE, Howard. *King Stork.*
See Chapter 12, Witchcraft and Sorcery Fantasy.

9-398 PYLE, Katherine. *The Counterpane Fairy.* Gr. 3–5. (Orig. pub. 1898.)
While Teddy is sick in bed, he is entertained by the stories of the Counterpane Fairy.
Illus. by the author, Dutton, 1928, 191 pp., o.p.
(BL 25:174; Mahony 1:40; 2:136)

9-399 QUINDLEN, Anna. *Happily Ever After.* Gr. 1–4.
When a magic baseball mitt transforms 4th-grader Kate into a medieval princess, she befriends a witch, helps slay a dragon, and teaches the female courtiers to play baseball.
Illus. by James Stevenson, Viking, 1997, 43 pp. (0-670-86961-9); Puffin, 1999, pap., 68 pp. (0-14-038706-4)
(BL 93:942; HBG 8:307; Kirkus 65:62; SlJ Mar 1997 p. 164)

9-400 RAWLINGS (Baskin), Marjorie Kinnan. *The Secret River.* Gr. 2–4.
✭ Calpurnia stumbles upon a beautiful river, but it has disappeared by the time she tries to find it again.
Illus. by Leonard Weisgard, Scribner, 1955, 56 pp., o.p; San Marco (repr. of 1955 ed.), 57 pp., o.p.
(CCBB 9:12; BL 51:436; HB 31:254, 258; Kirkus 23:327; LJ 80:1508)

REES, Celia. *City of Shadows.*
See Chapter 10, Time Travel Fantasy.

9-401 REGAN, Dian Curtis. *Monster of the Month Club.* **(Monster of the Month Club quartet, bk. 1).** Gr. 3–5.
Someone is sending Rilla packages from the Monster of the Month Club, and she finds it difficult to keep the little monsters fed and hidden in her attic room. The sequels are *Monsters in the Attic* (1995), *Monsters in Cyberspace* (1997), and *Monsters and My One True Love* (1998).
Illus. by Laura Cornell, Holt, 1994, 152 pp. (0-8050-3443-9)
(BL 91:822; CCBB 48:175; HBG 6:82; SLJ Mar 1995 p. 206)

REIT, Seymour. *Benvenuto.*
See Chapter 8, Humorous Fantasy.

RENDAL, Justine. *A Child of Their Own.*
See Chapter 11, Toy Fantasy.

RHYS, Mimpsey. *Mr. Hermit Crab: A Tale for Children by a Child.*
See Chapter 7, High Fantasy: Travel to Other Worlds.

9-402 RICHEMONT, Enid. *The Glass Bird.* Gr. 3–4. (Orig. British pub. 1990.)
Wishing on a magic chestnut brings Adam a beautiful glass bird and a new friend.
Illus. by Caroline Anstey, Candlewick, 1993, 108 pp. (1-56402-195-5)
(BL 90:443; HBG 5:81; SLJ Oct 1993 p. 128)

9-403 RICHEMONT, Enid. *The Magic Skateboard.* Gr. 3–5. (Orig. British pub. 1992.)
Danny can hardly believe that an old woman has given his skateboard the magical power to transport him wherever he wishes.
Illus. by Jan Ormerod, Candlewick, 1993, 80 pp. (1-56402-132-7), 1995, pap. (1-56402-449-0)
(HBG 4:303; Kirkus 61:378; SLJ May 1993 p. 108)

RIDLEY, Philip. *Krindlekrax; or, How Ruskin Splinter Battled a Horrible Monster and Saved His Entire Neighborhood.*
See Chapter 8, Humorous Fantasy.

RILEY, Louise. *Train for Tiger Lily.*
See Chapter 7, High Fantasy: Travel to Other Worlds.

9-404 RINALDI, Ann. *Millicent's Gift.* Gr. 6–9.
Millicent regrets her inherited gifts of magic and shape-shifting after her new high school friends discover that she will soon be able to grant them a wish.
HarperCollins, 2002, 224 pp. (0-06-029637-2); HarperTrophy, 2004, 224 pp. (0-06-441009-9)
(BL 98:1724; HBG 13:381; Kirkus 70:740; Kliatt May 2002 p. 14; SLJ June 2002 p. 142)

9-405 ROBERTS, Nora. *Key of Light.* **(Key trilogy, bk. 1).** Gr. 10 up.
Invited to a reception at Warrior's Peak, a Pennsylvania estate, three strangers: gallery manager Malory Price, librarian Dana Steele, and hairdresser Zoe McCourt, are offered the chance to search for the keys to a magical glass box imprisoning the souls of three Celtic goddesses. The sequels are *Key of Knowledge* (2003), and *Key of Valor* (2004).
Jove, pap., 2003, 342 pp. (0-515-13628-X)
(BL 100:485; SLJ Mar 2004 p. 252)

9-406 ROBERTS, Willo Davis. *The Magic Book.* Gr. 4–6.
Alex is hopeful that a book called *Magic Spells and Potions for the Beginner* will help him disarm Norm, the neighborhood bully.
Macmillan, 1986, 156 pp., o.p.
(BL 82:1400; CCBB 39:195; Kirkus 54:866; SLJ May 1986 p. 97)

9-407 ROCKWELL, Thomas. *Tin Cans.* Gr. 5–7.
The police begin searching for David and Jane after a magical soup can makes them wealthy.
Illus. by Saul Lambert, Bradbury, 1975, 70 pp., o.p.
(BL 72:240; Kirkus 43:714; SLJ Oct 1975 p. 101)

RODDA, Emily. *The Best-Kept Secret.*
See Chapter 10, Time Travel Fantasy.

RODDA, Emily. *The Charm Bracelet.*
See Chapter 7, High Fantasy: Travel to Other Worlds.

RODDA, Emily. *Finders Keepers.*
See Chapter 7, High Fantasy: Travel to Other Worlds.

9-408 **RODDA, Emily.** *The Pigs Are Flying!* Gr. 4–6. (Orig. Australian pub. 1986, entitled *Pigs Might Fly*.)
After a boring day at home with a cold, Rachel wakes to find herself flying on a unicorn's back through a sky full of pigs. Australian Children's Book of the Year Award, 1987.
Illus. by Noela Young, Greenwillow, 1988, 144 pp., o.p.
(BBL 85:326, 424, 460, 880, 1845; HB 64:784; SLJ Sept 1988 p. 185)

9-409 **RODDA, Emily.** *Something Special.* Gr. 3–5. (Orig. Australian pub. 1984.)
Samantha's imaginary re-creations of the past owners of rummage-sale clothing are startlingly accurate portraits of the shoppers who are buying the clothes.
Illus. by Noela Young, Henry Holt, 1989, 74 pp., o.p., 1991, pap. (0-8050-1641-4)
(BL 86:1009; HBG 1:67; Kirkus 57:1597; SLJ Jan 1990 p. 106)

RODGERS, Mary. *Freaky Friday.*
See Chapter 8, Humorous Fantasy.

ROSALES, Melodye Benson. *Minnie Saves the Day.*
See Chapter 11, Toy Fantasy.

9-410 **ROSS, Tony.** *A Fairy Tale.* Gr. 2–5. (Orig. British pub. 1991.)
Mrs. Leaf, young Bessie's elderly neighbor in an ugly English mill town, tells Bessie that fairyland could be all around them, like a reverse image just below the surface, so neither thinks it odd that Bessie grows older and Mrs. Leaf grows younger as the years go by.
Illus. by the author, Little, Brown, 1992, 28 pp. (0-316-75750-0)
(BL 88:1602; HBG 3:258; Kirkus 60:543; SLJ Aug 1992 p. 147)

ROWLING, J[oanne] K[athleen]. *Harry Potter and the Sorcerer's Stone.*
See Chapter 12, Witchcraft and Sorcery Fantasy.

9-411 **RUBINSTEIN, Gillian.** *Foxspell.* Gr. 6–9. (Oirg. Australian pub. 1994.)
After his father leaves the family, Tod and his sisters move to their grandmother's home in rural Australia, and Tod escapes his problems by transforming himself into a fox. Children's Book Council of Australia Book of the Year Award, 1995.
Simon, 1996, 219 pp. (0-689-80602-7)
(CCBB 50:184; HB 72:746; HBG 8:84; Kirkus 64:1242; VOYA 19:282)

9-412 **RUFF, Matt.** *Fool on the Hill.* Gr. 10 up.
The ordinary life of a Cornell University writer-in-residence is transformed into a romantic saga when he learns to write without paper, finds true love, and slays a dragon.
Atlantic Monthly, 1988, 400 pp., o.p.
(Kirkus 56:1271; LJ Oct 15, 1988 p. 104; VOYA 12:14, 45)

RUFFELL, Ann. *Pyramid Power.*
See Chapter 7, High Fantasy: Travel to Other Worlds.

9-413 **RUPP, Rebecca.** *The Dragon of Lonely Island.* Gr. 4–6.
Hannah, Zackary, and Sarah Emily inherit their great-aunt's house on Lonely Island in Maine, along with an ancient three-headed dragon.

Illus. by Wendell Minor, Candlewick, 1998, 160 pp. (0-7636-0408-9)
(BL 95:975; CCBB 52:145; HBG 10:74; Kirkus 66:1536; SLJ Nov 1998 p. 129)

9-414 **RYLANT, Cynthia.** *The Islander: A Novel.* Gr. 6–8.
✭ Living with his grandfather on a remote British Columbia island, orphaned Daniel finds a mermaid's comb and is rewarded with a magical key enabling him to rescue animals and his future wife.
DK Ink, 1998, 97 pp. (0-7894-2490-8); Laurel Leaf, 1999, pap., 112 pp. (0-440-41542-X)
(BL 94:913; CCBB 51:338; HB 74:349; HBG 9:337; Kirkus 66:200; SLJ Mar 1998 p. 218; VOYA 21:204)

SACHAR, Louis. *Wayside School Is Falling Down.*
See Chapter 8, Humorous Fantasy.

SALSITZ, R(hodi) A. V(ilott). *The Twilight Gate.*
See Chapter 6, High Fantasy: Myth or Legend Fantasy.

9-415 **SANVOISIN, Eric.** *The Ink Drinker.* **(The Ink Drinker series, bk. 1).** Gr. 2–5. (Orig. pub. in France.)
A boy who dislikes reading spies a strange customer sucking the ink out of the books in his father's bookshop, and then becomes a "Draculink" himself. The sequels are *A Straw for Two* (1999), *City of Ink Drinkers* (2002), and *Little Red Ink Drinker* (2002).
Trans. by Georges Morozi, illus. by Martin Matje, Delacorte, 1998, 35 pp., o.p.; Yearling, 2002, 48 pp. (0-440-41485-7)
(BL 95:750; HBG 10:74; Kirkus 66:1123; SLJ Jan 1999 p. 102)

9-416 **SARGENT, Sarah.** *Jonas McFee, A. T. P.* Gr. 4–7.
Lonely Jonas, new kid in fifth grade, is given a mysterious blue marble-sized ball by a frightened girl—a ball with tremendous powers that enable its possessor to take over the world.
Macmillan, 1989, 112 pp., o.p., 1992, pap. (0-689-71579-X)
(BL 85:1471; CCBB 42:180; Kirkus 57:553; SLJ May 1989 p. 112)

9-417 **SARGENT, Sarah.** *Weird Henry Berg.* Gr. 4–6.
✭ Millie Levenson wants to help a Welsh dragon recover its lost baby, but Henry Berg does not want to give up his pet "lizard."
Crown, 1980, 113 pp., o.p.
(BL 77:48; CCBB 34:20; HB 56:642; Kirkus 48:1164; SLJ Sept 1980 p. 78; Suth 3:375)

SAUER, Julia L(ina). *Fog Magic.*
See Chapter 10, Time Travel Fantasy.

9-418 **SAWYER, Ruth.** *The Enchanted Schoolhouse.* Gr. 4–6.
A leprechaun's magic helps the inhabitants of Lobster Cove to build a new school.
Illus. by Hugh Troy, Viking, 1956, 128 pp., o.p.
(BL 53:182; HB 32:450; Kirkus 24:70)

9-419 **SAWYER, Ruth.** *The Year of the Christmas Dragon.* Gr. 3–5.
✭ A little boy and an ancient Chinese dragon enliven a Mexican Christmas fiesta.

Illus. by Hugh Troy, Viking, 1960, 88 pp., o.p.
(BL 57:249; Eakin:283; HB 36:504; Kirkus 28:556; LJ 85:4570)

9-420 SCARBOROUGH, Elizabeth Ann. *The Godmother.* **(The Godmother trilogy, bk. 1).** Gr. 7–12.
Rosalie's frustrated wish for a fairy godmother brings a real fairy godmother to life, in this humorous tale set in Seattle. The sequels are *The Godmother's Apprentice* (1995, 1996) and *The Godmother's Web* (1998, 1999).
Berkley/Ace, 1994, 304 pp. (0-441-00096-7); Ace, 1995, pap. (0-441-00269-2)
(BL 91:28; Kirkus 62:892; VOYA 17:290)

9-421 SCHAEFFER, Susan Fromberg. *The Dragons of North Chittendon.* Gr. 5–7.
Arthur, a dragon who can communicate through dreams with a boy named Patrick, battles the Moon and her Dark Angels, while attempting to win the Queen of Dragons for his wife.
Illus. by Darcy May, Simon & Schuster, 1986, 208 pp., o.p.
(BL 82:1694; SLJ Sept 1986 p. 139)

9-422 SCHEIDL, Gerda Marie. *Loretta and the Little Fairy.* Gr. 2–4. (Orig. Swiss pub. 1992.)
Loretta tries to help a little girl who says she was exiled from fairyland for naughtiness and can make herself invisible.
Illus. by Christa Unzer-Fischer, trans. by J. Alison James, North-South, 1993, 64 pp., o.p.
(HBG 4:290; Kirkus 61:464; SLJ June 1993 p. 88)

9-423 SCHMIDT, Annie M. G. *Minnie.* Gr. 3–6. (Orig. Dutch pub. 1970.)
✶   Minnie, a formerly feline young woman adopted by a timid newspaper reporter, must decide whether to remain human or return to being a cat.
Trans. by Lance Salway, illus. by Kay Sather, Milkweed, 1994, 164 pp., o.p.
(BL 91:44; HB 71:195; HBG 6:304; Kirkus 62:994; SLJ Sep 1994 p. 222)

9-424 SCHOLES, Katherine. *The Landing: A Night of Birds.* Gr. 4–6. (Orig. Australian pub. 1987.)
Annie listens in on the nighttime conversations among dozens of sea birds who have taken shelter from an ocean storm inside her grandfather's boathouse.
Illus. by David Wong, Doubleday, 1989, 65 pp., o.p.
(BL 86:1349; HBG 1:83)

SCIESZKA, Jon. *Knights of the Kitchen Table.*
See Chapter 10, Time Travel Fantasy.

9-425 SEABROOKE, Brenda. *The Dragon That Ate Summer.* Gr. 3–6.
Alistair's scientist Uncle George helps convince the boy's parents that Alistair should be allowed to keep the baby dragon he found. In *The Care and Feeding of Dragons* (1997), Spike the pet dragon, home alone while Alistair is at school, attracts the attention of two strangers in the neighborhood.
Putnam, 1992, 110 pp. (0-399-22115-8); Apple, 1993, pap. (0-590-46986-X)
(BL 88:1281; HBG 3:270; Kirkus 60:544; SLJ Apr 1992 p. 125)

9-426 **SEFTON, Catherine (pseud. of Martin Waddell).** *The Emma Dilemma.*
Gr. 3–5. (Orig. British pub. 1982.)
A bump on the head brings a mischievous transparent twin into Emma's life.
Illus. by Jill Bennett, Faber, 1983, 96 pp., o.p.
(BL 79:1098; CCBB 37:37; SLJ May 1983 p. 77)

9-427 **SELDEN (Thompson), George.** *The Genie of Sutton Place.* Gr. 5–7.
✯ Nothing is quite the same for Tim after Abdulla the genie is released from a
thousand years of captivity in an Arabian carpet.
Farrar, 1973, o.p., 1994, o.p.
(BL 69:861; CC:553; CCBB 26:176; HB 49:382; Kirkus 41:1 16; LJ 98:1398, 1656)

9-428 **SELZNICK, Brian.** *The Houdini Box.* Gr. 2–5.
✯ Ten-year-old Victor dreams of duplicating the incredible escapes of his idol,
Harry Houdini.
Illus. by the author, Knopf, 1991, 64 pp. (0-679-81429-9); Random, 1994, pap.
(0-679-85448-7)
(BL 87:1875; CCBB 44:250; HBG 2:261; Kirkus 59:538; SLJ Sept 1991 p. 241, Oct 1991 p.
104)

9-429 **SELZNICK, Brian.** *The Robot King.* Gr. 3–5.
The Robot King that Lucy creates with a music box heart comes to life and
begins animating other objects at a magical fairgrounds.
Illus. by the author, HarperCollins, 1995, 80 pp. (0-06-024493-3)
(CCBB 49:69; HBG 7:68; Kirkus 63:1030; SLJ Oct 1995 p. 139)

9-430 **SENDAK, Jack.** *The Magic Tears.* Gr. 4–5.
A wizard sends a boy named Yanos to steal the magic tears of a witch girl pro-
tected by a wolf with magical powers.
Illus. by Mitchell Miller, Harper, 1971, 58 pp., o.p.
(CCBB 25:176; Kirkus 39:1213; LJ 97:778)

9-431 **SENDAK, Maurice (Bernard).** *Kenny's Window.* Gr. 1–4.
✯ Kenny must find the answers to seven difficult questions asked by a four-
legged rooster.
Illus. by the author, Harper, 1956, 1964, 1989, 64 pp., o.p., pap. (0-06-443209-
2); DiCapua, 2002, 64 pp. (0-06-028789-6)
(BL 52:393; CCBB 10:13; HB 32:108; Kirkus 24:242; LJ 81:1546)

SEREDY, Kate. *Lazy Tinka.*
See Chapter 1, Allegorical Fantasy and Literary Fairy Tales.

9-432 **SERVICE, Pamela F.** *Being of Two Minds.* Gr. 5–8.
Because Connie, a 14-year-old midwestern girl, and Crown Prince Rudolph of
Thulgaria were born at exactly the same moment, they have always been able
to communicate telepathically during so-called "fainting" episodes.
Macmillan, 1991, 169 pp. (0-689-31524-4); Fawcett, 1992, pap. (0-44970-415-7)
(BL 88:521; CCBB 45:74; HBG 3:72; Kirkus 59:1349; SLJ Oct 1991 p. 128; VOYA 14:387)

SERVICE, Pamela F. *The Reluctant God.*
See Chapter 10, Time Travel Fantasy.

Shape Shifters. **Ed. by Jane (Hyatt) Yolen (Stemple).**
See Chapter 3, Fantasy Collections.

SHEARER, Alex. *The Summer Sisters and the Dance Disaster.*
See Chapter 8, Humorous Fantasy.

9-433   **SHOWELL, Ellen Harvey.** *Cecelia and the Blue Mountain Boy.* Gr. 4–6.
Long ago, the townspeople of Chester began holding an annual music festival
to cheer up a girl named Cecelia who was once enchanted by a fiddler on Blue
Mountain.
Illus. by Margot Tomes, Lothrop, 1983, 76 pp., o.p.
(BL 79:1468; CCBB 36:178; SLJ Aug 1983 p. 70)

SHURA, Mary Francis (pseud. of Mary Francis Craig). *Happles and Cin-namunger.*
See Chapter 4, Ghost Fantasy.

9-434   **SHURA, Mary Francis (pseud. of Mary Francis Craig).** *A Shoe Full of*
☆   *Shamrock.* Gr. 3–5.
Davie O'Sullivan's secret wish comes true when he returns a pouch of fairy
gold to a leprechaun.
Illus. by N(iels) M(ogens) Bodecker, Atheneum, 1965, 64 pp., o.p.
(BL 62:222; CCBB 19:68; Eakin:299; HB 41:500; Kirkus 33:677; LJ 90:4622)

9-435   **SHUSTERMAN, Neal.** *The Eyes of Kid Midas.* Gr. 5–9.
The sunglasses Kevin finds at the top of a mountain are saturated with magic
and will grant him any wish.
Little, Brown, 1992, 185 pp. (0-316-77542-8)
(CCBB 46:157; HBG 4:76; Kirkus 60:1508; SLJ Dec 1992 p. 133; VOYA 15:358)

SHYER, Marlene Fanta. *Ruby, the Red Hot Witch at Bloomingdale's.*
See Chapter 12, Witchcraft and Sorcery Fantasy.

9-436   **SIEGEL, Jan.** *Prospero's Children.* Gr. 10 up. (Orig. British pub. 1999.)
☆   Spending the summer in an old house in Yorkshire, Fern, 16, and her brother
Will, 12, discover that they are descended from ancient Atlanteans, and that
Fern can use thought transference to move objects with her mind. The sequels
are *The Dragon Charmer* (2001, 2002) and *The Witch Queen* (2002, 2003).
Ballantine, 2000, 368 pp., o.p.; Del Rey, 2001, pap., 334 pp. (0-345-44143-5);
Voyager, 2000, new ed., 352 pp. (0-006-51280-1)
(BL 96:1335, 97:860; Kirkus 68:278; LJ April 15, 2000 p. 126, Jan 2001 p. 55)

SILVERSTEIN, Herma. *Mad, Mad Monday.*
See Chapter 4, Ghost Fantasy.

SINGER, Isaac Bashevis. *A Tale of Three Wishes.*
See Chapter 1, Allegorical Fantasy and Literary Fairy Tales.

SINGER, Marilyn. *California Demon.*
See Chapter 12, Witchcraft and Sorcery Fantasy.

SINGER, Marilyn. *Charmed.*
See Chapter 7, High Fantasy: Travel to Other Worlds.

9-437 SINGER, Marilyn. *The Circus Lunicus.* Gr. 4–6.
⭑ Mistreated by his evil stepmother and stepbrothers, 11-year-old Solly sneaks off to the forbidden Circus Lunicus, where he meets singing alligators, a green fairy godmother, and a sinister ringmaster.
Holt, 2000, 168 pp. (0-8050-6268-8)
(BL 97:708; HBG 12:79; Kirkus 68:1364; SLJ Dec 2000 p. 148; VOYA 23:436)

SLADE, Arthur. *Dust.*
See Chapter 12, Witchcraft and Sorcery Fantasy.

9-438 SLATER, Jim. *Grasshopper and the Unwise Owl.* Gr. 3–5. (Orig. British pub. 1979.)
Magic candy makes Graham Hooper small enough to thwart Mr. Groll's plot to cheat the boy's widowed mother out of her home.
Illus. by Babette Cole, Holt, 1980, 88 pp., o.p.
(BL 77:812; CCBB 34:161; SLJ Mar 1981 p. 152)

9-439 SLEIGH, Barbara (de Riemer). *Carbonel: The King of the Cats.* **(Car-**
⭑ **bonel trilogy, bk. 1).** Gr. 4–7. (Orig. British pub. 1955, entitled *Carbonel.*)
Rosemary tries to break a spell on the witch's cat that arrives with her new broom. The sequels are *The Kingdom of Carbonel* (1960) and *Carbonel and Calidor: Being the Further Adventures of a Royal Cat* (1978, 1980).
Illus. by V(iolet) H. Drummond, Bobbs-Merrill, 1956, 253 pp., o.p.; Viking, 1974, o.p.; New York Review, 2004, 216 pp. (1-59017-126-8)
(BL 54:30; CCBB 11:40; Eakin:300; HB 33:408; LJ 82:2702; TLS 1978 p. 765)

SLEPIAN, Jan. *Back to Before.*
See Chapter 10, Time Travel Fantasy.

9-440 SLEPIAN, Jan. *The Mind Reader.* Gr. 5–8.
⭑ Twelve-year-old Connie Leondar must unexpectedly take over his father's vaudeville act and become The Amazing Mind Reader, but Connie knows that he actually can read minds.
Philomel, 1997, 132 pp. (0-399-23150-1)
(BL 94:236; CCBB 51:140; HB 73:580; HBG 9:81; Kirkus 65:1117; SLJ Sep 1997 p. 22)

SMITH, Alison. *Come Away Home.*
See Chapter 2, Animal Fantasy.

SMITH, L(isa) J. *Night of the Solstice.*
See Chapter 7, High Fantasy: Travel to Other Worlds.

9-441 SNYDER, Dianne. *George and the Dragon Word.* Gr. 1–4.
George's "angry word" makes his sister cry and turns Great Aunt Agatha into a dragon.
Illus. by Brian Lies, Houghton, 1991, 56 pp. (0-395-55129-3)
(BL 88:533; HBG 3:61; Kirkus 59:1227; SLJ Jan 1992 p. 98)

9-442 SNYDER, Midori. *Hannah's Garden.* Gr. 7–12.
⭑ Returning to her dying grandfather's farm, Cassie, 17, discovers a family curse and two clans of magical creatures battling for control over her life and the land her grandfather has protected.

Viking, 2002, 208 pp. (0-670-03577-7); Puffin, 2005, pap., 256 pp. (0-14-240135-8)

(BL 99:402; HBG 13:99; Kirkus 70:1401; Kliatt Nov 2002 p. 15; SLJ Oct 2002 p. 172)

9-443 SNYDER, Zilpha Keatley. *Black and Blue Magic.* Gr. 5–7.

☆ Mr. Mazzeek's magic lotion causes Harry Houdini Marco to sprout wings.
Illus. by Gene Holtan, Macmillan, 1966, 1972, 192 pp. (0-689-30075-1);
Aladdin, 1994, pap., 184 pp. (0-689-71848-9)

(BL 62:878; CCBB 20:48; HB 42:308; Kirkus 34:108; LJ 91:2214; Suth:372)

9-444 SNYDER, Zilpha Keatley. *A Season of Ponies.* Gr. 5–7.
Her father's amulet enables Pamela to make friends with a beautiful pastel
pony, and to escape from the pig woman in the swamp.
Illus. by Alton Raible, Macmillan, 1964, 133 pp., o.p.

(CCBB 18:20; HB 40:284; Kirkus 32:108; LJ 89:1862)

9-445 SNYDER, Zilpha Keatley. *The Unseen.* Gr. 5–8.
Seventh-grader Xandra is left with a magical feather after caring for an injured
egret, but is reluctant to accept the help of classmate Belinda and her father,
who understand its power.
Delacorte, 2004, 208 pp. (0-385-73084-5); Yearling, 2005, pap., 208 pp. (0-440-41930-1)

(BL 100:1190; CCBB 57:350; Kirkus 72:277; SLJ April 2004 p. 162;)

SOMMER-BODENBURG, Angela. *My Friend the Vampire.*
See Chapter 8, Humorous Fantasy.

SOMTOW, S. P. (pseud. of Somtow Sucharitkul). *The Wizard's Apprentice.*
See Chapter 12, Witchcraft and Sorcery Fantasy.

9-446 SONENKLAR, Carol. *Bug Boy.* Gr. 3–5.
Charlie was fascinated by insects even before his transformation into one insect
after another by his new Bug-a-View, which promised to give him a bug's-eye-
view of the world. The sequel is *Bug Girl* (1998).
Illus. by Betsy Lewin, Holt, 1997, 100 pp. (0-8050-4794-8); Yearling, 1998,
pap., 112 pp. (0-440-41465-2)

(BL 93:1334; CCBB 50:335; HBG 8:309; Kirkus 65:388; SLJ July 1997 p. 76)

SOTO, Gary. *The Cat's Meow.*
See Chapter 2, Animal Fantasy.

*Spaceships and Spells: A Collection of New Fantasy and Science-Fiction
Stories.* **Ed. by Jane (Hyatt) Yolen (Stemple), Martin H. Greenberg, and
Charles G. Waugh.**
See Chapter 3, Fantasy Collections.

9-447 SPAULDING, Andrea. *The White Horse Talisman.* **(Summer of Magic
Quartet, bk. 1). Gr. 4–7. (Orig. Canadian pub. 2001.)**
The magic talisman Canadians Chantal and Adam find after their arrival in
England involves them in a struggle between an ancient White Horse Wise One
and a dragon. The sequel is *Dance of the Stones* (2003).

Orca, 2002, 160 pp. (1-55143-187-4)
(BL 98:1418; HBG 13:383; SLJ Nov 2002 p. 176; VOYA 25:131)

9-448 **SPINELLI, Jerry.** *The Library Card.* Gr. 4–7.
☆ Four short stories about the power of books to change the lives of a troubled boy named Mongoose, a junkie named Brenda, homeless Sonseray, and lonely April.
Scholastic, 1997, 148 pp. (0-590-46731-X); Apple, 1998, pap., 148 pp. (0-590-38633-6)
(BL 93:942; CCBB 50:257; HB 73:204; HBG 8:309; Kirkus 65:650; VOYA 20:248)

SPRINGER, Nancy. *The Friendship Song.*
See Chapter 7, High Fantasy: Travel to Other Worlds.

SPRINGER, Nancy. *The Hex Witch of Seldom.*
See Chapter 12, Witchcraft and Sorcery Fantasy.

SPRINGER, Nancy. *Red Wizard.*
See Chapter 7, High Fantasy: Travel to Other Worlds.

SPURR, Elizabeth. *Mrs. Minetta's Car Pool.*
See Chapter 8, Humorous Fantasy.

9-449 **STEELE, Mary Q(uintard Govan).** *Wish, Come True.* Gr. 4–6.
The magic ring that Meg finds while she and her brother are staying at Great-Aunt Louise's enables them to miniaturize themselves, breathe underwater, and search for treasure.
Illus. by Muriel Batherman, Greenwillow, 1979, 160 pp., o.p.
(BL 76:47, 1545; Kirkus 48:128; SLJ Sept 1979 p. 148)

9-450 **STERMAN, Betsy, and STERMAN, Samuel.** *Backyard Dragon.* Gr. 3–5.
Owen and his friends are saddled with a hungry medieval Welsh dragon when the wizard who accidentally brought the dragon to New Jersey finds that his magic doesn't work in the 20th century.
Illus. by David Wenzel, Harper, 1993, 192 pp., o.p.
(BL 90:346, 94:475; HBG 4:305; Kirkus 61:792; SLJ Aug 1993 p. 166)

9-451 **STERMAN, Betsy, and STERMAN, Samuel.** *Too Much Magic.* Gr. 3–6.
Bill and his younger brother Jeff try using a magic wish-granting cube, but the consequences are difficult to handle.
Illus. by Judy Glasser, Harper, 1987, 160 pp., o.p., 1994, pap. (0-06-440404-8)
(BL 83:1130; Kirkus 54:1796; SLJ Feb 1987 p. 86)

9-452 **STEVENSON, Jocelyn.** *O'Diddy.* Gr. 2–4.
Boon's outgrown imaginary friend, O'Diddy, is determined not to be forgotten.
Illus. by Sue Truesdell, Random, 1988, 64 pp., o.p.
(BL 84:1842; SLJ Oct 1988 p. 129)

STEVENSON, Robert Louis. *The Bottle Imp.*
See Chapter 1, Allegorical Fantasy and Literary Fairy Tales.

STEWART, Jennifer J. *If That Breathes Fire, We're Toast!*
See Chapter 10, Time Travel Fantasy.

STOLZ, Mary (Slattery). *The Cuckoo Clock.*
See Chapter 1, Allegorical Fantasy and Literary Fairy Tales.

9-453 STORR, Catherine (Cole). *The Magic Drawing Pencil.* Gr. 5–7. (Orig. British pub. 1958, entitled *Marianne Dreams.*)
Everything that Marianne draws comes to life in her dreams, including a boy named Mark.
Illus. by Marjorie-Ann Watts, Barnes, 1960, 191 pp., o.p.
(LJ 86:378; TLS 1958 p. 355)

STORR, Catherine (Cole). *Thursday.*
See Chapter 6, High Fantasy: Myth or Legend Fantasy.

STOVER, Marjorie Filley. *When the Dolls Woke.*
See Chapter 11, Toy Fantasy.

9-454 STRAUSS, Linda Leopold. *A Fairy Called Hilary.* Gr 2–4.
★ Caroline and her parents welcome a fairy named Hilary into their family, even after the two girls make the cat invisible so that it can go to school, in this story published originally in *Cricket* magazine.
Illus. by Sue Truesdell, Holiday, 1999, 113 pp. (0-8234-1418-3); Little Apple, 2001, pap., 128 pp. (0-439-17519-4)
(BL 95:1215; HBG 10:285; Kirkus 68:72; SLJ Mar 1999 p. 185)

9-455 STRICKLAND, Brad. *Dragon's Plunder, or, The Last Voyage of Captain Deadmon: A Fantasy Adventure.* Gr. 6–8.
In this suspenseful adventure story, 12-year-old cabin boy Jamie Falconer uses magic to free Captain Deadmon from his vow to roam the high seas until he can steal a dragon's treasure.
Illus. by Wayne Barlow, Macmillan, 1992, 154 pp. (0-689-31573-2)
(BL 89:892; SLJ Apr 1993 p. 125; VOYA 16:47)

SYKES, Pamela. *Mirror of Danger.*
See Chapter 10, Time Travel Fantasy.

9-456 TAPP, Kathy Kennedy. *Moth-Kin Magic.* Gr. 3–5.
Six tiny people, or Moth-Kins, who were captured by "giants" and imprisoned in a classroom terrarium, carry out a daring escape. The sequel is *Flight of the Moth-Kin* (1987).
Illus. by Michele Chessare, Atheneum, 1983, 122 pp., o.p.
(BL 80:685; CCBB 37:98; Kirkus 51:166; SLJ Mar 1984 p. 166)

9-457 TARN, (Sir) W(illiam) W(oodthorpe). *The Treasure of the Isle of Mist: A Tale of the Isle of Skye.* Gr. 4–7. (Written 1913–1914; orig. British pub. 1919.)
Fiona's search for lost treasure becomes a frantic hunt for a friend held captive in an elfin cave on the Isle of Mist. This story has been said to contain the first real-world villain in children's fantasy literature.
Putnam, 1920, 192 pp., o.p.; illus. by Robert Lawson, Putnam, 1934, 192 pp., o.p.
(BL 17:119, 31:38; HB 10:236, 14:143; LJ 47:814; Mahony 2:298; TLS 1919 p. 740)

9-458 TAYLOR, Cora. *Vanishing Act.* Gr. 4–6. (Orig. pub. in Canada.)
Twins Maggie and Jennifer, 13, and their friend Samuel attempt to use a magic
invisibility spell to find their father, a pilot who disappeared two years earlier.
Orca, 1998, pap., 199 pp. (0-88995-165-9)
(Kliatt May 1998 p. 24; SLJ July 1998 p. 100; VOYA 21:278)

9-459 TAYLOR, G. P. *Shadowmancer.* Gr. 7 up. (Orig. British pub. 2002.)
A shipwrecked African sailor named Raphah helps 13-year-old friends Kate
and Thomas battle mythical creatures while they search for a mysterious icon,
stolen by Vicar Obadiah Demurral, that can stave off the darkness of the end of
time. The sequel is *Wormwood* (2004).
Putnam, 2004, 304 pp. (0-399-24256-2); Puffin, 2005, pap., 288 pp. (0-14-
240341-5)
(BL 100:1451; CCBB 57:486; HB 80:461; Kirkus 72:230; SLJ April 2004 p. 162; VOYA
27:15, 62)

9-460 TAYLOR, Theodore. *The Boy Who Could Fly Without a Motor.* Gr. 3–6.
Jon's lonely life as the son of a California lighthouse keeper improves after he
conjures up the ghost of magician Ling Wu, who teaches him to fly.
Harcourt, 2002, 144 pp. (0-15-216529-0); Harcourt, 2004, pap., 108 pp. (0-15-
204767-0)
(BL 98:1726; HBG 13:384; Kirkus 70:580; SLJ May 2002 p. 161)

THEROUX, Paul. *A Christmas Card.*
See Chapter 1, Allegorical Fantasy and Literary Fairy Tales.

THESMAN, Jean. *The Other Ones.*
See Chapter 12, Witchcraft and Sorcery Fantasy.

THOMPSON, Julian F(rancis). *Herb Seasoning.*
See Chapter 8, Humorous Fantasy.

9-461 THOMPSON, Kate. *Switchers.* (Switchers trilogy, bk. 1). Gr. 6–9. (Orig.
✯ British pub. 1997.)
Tess and Kevin can shape-change into real and mythical animals, and use their
powers to battle an Ice Age and mountainous Krools. In *Midnight's Choice*
(1998, 1999), Tess, nearly 15, must decide whether to stay with her family and
remain human, to assume a permanent animal form, or to become immortal as a
vampire or phoenix. In *Wild Blood* (1999, 2000), Tess, spending the summer in
Ireland, attempts to rescue her cousins after they disappear.
Hyperion, 1998, 221 pp. (0-7868-0380-0), 1999, pap., 224 pp. (0-7868-1396-2)
(BL 94:1245, 1618; CCBB 52:36; HBG 9:339; Kirkus 66:410; SLJ May 1998 p. 148, Jan
2000 p. 74)

9-462 TOLLE, Jean Bashor. *The Great Pete Penney.* Gr. 3–5.
A leprechaun gives Pete (short for Priscilla) Penney a magic ring, enabling her
to throw a curve ball well enough to jump from Little League to major league
baseball.
Atheneum, 1979, 90 pp., o.p.
(BL 76:358; CCBB 33:121; Kirkus 47:1002; SLJ Dec 1979 p. 100)

9-463 TOWNE, Mary (pseud. of Mary Spelman). *Goldenrod.* Gr. 5–7.

A babysitter named Goldenrod can magically transport the Madder children anywhere they choose to go.
Atheneum, 1977, 180 pp., o.p.
(CCBB 31:149; Kirkus 45:852; SLJ Nov 1977 p. 64)

9-464 TOWNSEND, John Rowe. *The Persuading Stick.* Gr. 4–6. (Orig. British
✮ pub. 1986.)
Quiet Sarah, the youngest sister of an angry and depressed older brother, finds a small magical stick that forces people to do whatever she wishes.
Lothrop, 1987, 96 pp., o.p.
(BL 84:486; CCBB 41:38; HB 64:205; Kirkus 55:1398; SLJ Sept 1987 p. 184; Suth 4:414; TLS 1986 p. 1344)

9-465 TOWNSEND, Ralph M. *A Journey to the Garden Gate.* Gr. 2–4.
Prudence-Anne is reduced to insect size after she goes through the small end of a telescope.
Illus. by Milo Winter, Houghton, 1919, 127 pp., o.p.
(BL 16:208; Mahony 2:298)

9-466 TRAVERS, P(amela) L(yndon). *Mary Poppins.* **(Mary Poppins series, bk.**
✮ **1).** Gr. 3–6. (Orig. British and U.S. pub. 1934.)
Mary Poppins blows in on an East Wind to become the Banks children's nanny, suggesting numerous magical adventures. These adventures continue in *Mary Poppins Comes Back* (1935, 1963, 1997), *Mary Poppins Opens the Door* (1943, 1997), *Mary Poppins in the Park* (1952, 1997), *Mary Poppins from A to Z* (1962, 1989), *Mary Poppins in Cherry Tree Lane* (1982, 1999), and *Mary Poppins and the House Next Door* (Delacorte, 1989).
Illus. by Mary Shepard, Harcourt, 1962, 1981 (rev. ed.), 206 pp. (0-15-252408-8); illus. by Mary Shepard, Harcourt, 1997, 203 pp. (0-15-252595-5); pap. (0-15-201719-4)
(BL 31:178, 78:709; Bookshelf 1935 p. 3; HBG 9:340; Mahony 3:212; SLJ Feb 1982 p. 82; TLS 1934 p. 637)

9-467 TROOP, Alan F. *The Dragon DelaSangre.* Gr 10 up.
The lives of Peter and his father, man-eating dragons who can take human form and live on an isolated Florida island, are endangered by a man seeking revenge for his sister's death. *Dragon Moon* (2003) is the sequel.
NAL/Roc, 2002, pap., 292 pp. (0-451-45871-0)
(BL 98:1099, 1939; Kliatt May 2002 p. 31; VOYA 25:299)

TUNNELL, Michael O. *Wishing Moon.*
See Chapter 6, High Fantasy: Myth or Legend Fantasy.

9-468 TURNBULL, Agnes Sligh. *George.* Gr. 3–5.
Is George, the bespectacled rabbit, a figment of the Weaver children's imaginations, or did he really save Tommy from being run over by a car?
Illus. by Trina Schart Hyman, Hale, 1965, 94 pp., o.p.
(CCBB 19:70; Kirkus 33:109)

9-469 TURNER, Ann Warren. *Elfsong.* Gr. 4–6.
Maddy and her Grandpa spend the summer exploring a forest inhabited by elves, one of whom breaks elven tradition to talk to the humans.

Harcourt, 1995, 168 pp. (0-15-200826-8)

(BL 92:321; CCBB 49:141; HBG 7:70; Kirkus 63:1194; SLJ Oct 1995 p. 140)

TURNER, Ann Warren. *Finding Walter.*
See Chapter 11, Toy Fantasy.

TURNER, Ann Warren. *Rosemary's Witch.*
See Chapter 12, Witchcraft and Sorcery Fantasy.

TWOHILL, Maggie. *Jeeter, Mason and the Magic Headset.*
See Chapter 11, Toy Fantasy.

9-470 UPDIKE, David. *An Autumn Tale.* Gr. K–4.
One Halloween night, Homer puts a real jack-o-lantern on as a mask and joins a mysterious procession of walking trees who call him Mr. Pumpkin and won't believe that he is a human boy.
Illus. by Robert Andrew Parker, Pippin, 1988, 40 pp., o.p.
(BL 85:416; CCBB 42:160; SLJ Nov 1988 p. 96)

9-471 UPENSKY, Eduard. *Uncle Fedya, His Dog, and His Cat.* Gr. 2–4. (Orig. Russian pub. 1989.)
After his parents refuse to let him keep a pet, Fedya and his talking cat run away to the country and set up housekeeping with a talking dog.
Illus. by Vladimir Shpitalnik, trans. by Michael Henry Heim, Knopf, 1993, 136 pp., o.p.
(CCBB 47:61; HBG 5:83; Kirkus 61:1530; SLJ Nov 1993 p. 95)

URE, Jean. *The Wizard in the Woods.*
See Chapter 12, Witchcraft and Sorcery Fantasy.

9-472 USPENSKY, Eduard. *The Little Warranty People.* Gr. 3–5. (Orig. pub. in Russia.)
Four tiny Warranty people keep new appliances working until the warranties run out, until they are attacked by resident mice and nearly trapped by a child named Tanya.
Trans. by Nina Iguatowicz, illus. by Vladimir Shpitalnik, Knopf, 1994, 133 pp., o.p.
(BL 91:45; HBG 5:316; Kirkus 62:709; SLJ June 1994 p. 135)

9-473 VAMBA (pseud. of Luigi Bertelli). *The Prince and His Ants.* Gr. 4–6. (Orig. pub. in Italy.)
When he is transformed into an ant, a little Italian boy learns all about the lives of ants, bees, and wasps.
Trans. by S. F. Woodruff, Holt, 1911, o.p.; trans. by Nicola di Pietro, illus. by the author, Crowell, 1935 (entitled *Emperor of the Ants*), 239 pp., o.p.
(BL 7:81; Bookshelf 1921–1922 p. 9, 1935 p. 3; LJ 61:116; Mahony 2:107)

9-474 VAN ALLSBURG, Chris. *Ben's Dream.* Gr. 2–4.
✮   Ben and his friend Margaret find they have had the same dream: sailing across a flooded world in their half-submerged houses.
Illus. by the author, Houghton, 1982, 32 pp. (0-395-32084-4)
(BL 78:1371; CCBB 35:217; HB 58:396; Kirkus 50:487; SLJ May 1982 p. 66; Suth 3:429)

9-475 **VAN ALLSBURG, Chris.** *The Garden of Abdul Gasazi.* Gr. 1–5.

✯   Alan chases Miss Hester's dog, Fritz, into a magician's garden where he finds Fritz transformed into a duck. Boston Globe Horn Book Award for Illustration, 1980; Randolph Caldecott Medal Honor Book, 1980.

Illus. by the author, Houghton, 1979, 32 pp., o.p.

(BL 76:510; CCBB 33:121; HB 56:49; SLJ Jan 1980 pp. 40, 62; Suth 3:429; TLS 1981 p. 1067)

9-476 **VAN ALLSBURG, Chris.** *Jumanji.* Gr. 1–5.

✯✯   A frightening jungle world is unleashed as Peter and Judy play the magical board game they brought home from the park. Boston Globe Horn Book Award Honor Book for Illustration, 1981; Randolph Caldecott Medal, 1982; National Book Award for Graphic Design, 1982. The sequel, *Zathura: A Space Adventure* (2002), is set in outer space.

Illus. by the author, Houghton, 1981, 28 pp. (0-395-30448-2)

(BL 77:1258, 86:790; CCBB 35:18; HB 57:416; Kirkus 49:737; SLJ May 1981 pp. 24, 60; Suth 3:430)

VAN ALLSBURG, Chris. *The Sweetest Fig.*
See Chapter 1, Allegorical Fantasy and Literary Fairy Tales.

VAN ALLSBURG, Chris. *The Widow's Broom.*
See Chapter 12, Witchcraft and Sorcery Fantasy.

VANDE VELDE, Vivian. *Magic Can Be Murder.*
See Chapter 12, Witchcraft and Sorcery Fantasy.

9-477 **VANDE VELDE, Vivian.** *Witch's Wishes.* Gr. 2–5.

✯   An elderly witch fails to foresee the consequences of rewarding 6-year-old Sarah's kindness by transforming her Halloween wand into a magical wish-granting wand.

Holiday, 2003, 112 pp. (0-8234-1789-1)

(BL 100:669; CCBB 57:210; HBG 15:86; Kirkus 71:1184; SLJ Nov 2003 p. 116)

VAN STOCKUM, Hilda (Gerarda). *Kersti and Saint Nicholas.*
See Chapter 8, Humorous Fantasy.

9-478 **VENOKUR, Ross.** *The Amazing Frecktacle.* Gr. 4–7.

Often teased about his abundant freckles, Nicholas Bells discovers their magical powers after Mr. Piddlesticks promises to remove them.

Delacorte, 1998, 136 pp. (0-385-32621-1)

(BL 94:2009; CCBB 52:36; Kirkus 66:974; SLJ Sep 1998 p. 211)

VIVELO, Jackie. *A Trick of the Light: Stories to Read at Dusk.*
See Chapter 3, Fantasy Collections.

WALKER, Gwen. *The Golden Stile.*
See Chapter 7, High Fantasy: Travel to Other Worlds.

9-479 **WALLACE, Barbara Brooks.** *The Barrel in the Basement.* Gr. 3–5.

✯   After their protector, an elderly man named Noah, disappears, three elves living in his house are threatened by an inquisitive 9-year-old boy.

Illus. by Sharon Wooding, Atheneum, 1985, 127 pp., o.p.; Aladdin, 2000, pap., 112 pp. (0-689-83295-8)

(BL 81:1260; CCBB 38:177; HB 61:561; Kirkus 53:14; SLJ Sept 1985 p. 140)

9-480 WALLACE, Barbara Brooks. *The Interesting Thing That Happened at Perfect Acres, Inc.* Gr. 4–6.
Perfecta and her friend Puck use invisibility to outwit the nasty owner of the Perfect Acres housing development.
Illus. by Blanche Sims, Atheneum, 1988, 144 pp., o.p.

(BL 84:1269; CCBB 41:172; Kirkus 56:287; SLJ Apr 1988 p. 105)

9-481 WALLACE, Karen. *Wendy.* Gr. 7–10. (Orig. British pub. 2003.)
In this dark prequel to J. M. Barrie's *Peter Pan* (1904, 1911; see Chapter 7, High Fantasy: Travel to Other Worlds), written for older readers, rebellious 9-year-old Wendy Darling uncovers family secrets, including her father's love affair and drunken firing, and the existence of her mentally disabled older brother.
Simon, 2004, 307 pp. (0-689-86769-7); Simon Pulse, 2005, pap., 208 pp. (1-41690-314-3)

(BL 100:848; CCBB 57:300; HB 80:190; Kirkus 71:1455; SLJ Mar 2004 p. 222; VOYA 27:52)

WANGERIN, Walter, Jr. *Branta and the Golden Stone.*
See Chapter 1, Allegorical Fantasy and Literary Fairy Tales.

WANGERIN, Walter, Jr. *Elisabeth and the Water-Troll.*
See Chapter 1, Allegorical Fantasy and Literary Fairy Tales.

WANGERIN, Walter, Jr. *Potter, Come Fly to the First of the Earth.*
See Chapter 1, Allegorical Fantasy and Literary Fairy Tales.

9-482 WARD, Patricia A(nn). *The Secret Pencil.* Gr. 5–7. (Orig. British pub. 1959, entitled *The Silver Pencil.*)
Spending the summer with her uncle on the coast of Wales, Anna finds a magical silver pencil.
Illus. by Nicole Hornby, Random, 1960, 277 pp., o.p.

(HB 36:217; Kirkus 28:90; LJ 85:2045)

WAUGH, Silvia. *The Mennyms.*
See Chapter 11, Toy Fantasy.

9-483 WEBB, Clifford (Cyril). *The North Pole Before Lunch.* Gr. 2–4. (Orig. U.S. pub. 1936.)
Michael and Jennifer make a fast trip to the North Pole.
Illus. by the author, Warne, 1951, 63 pp., o.p.

(HB 2:349, 27:261; LJ 61:808)

WEISS, Ellen, and FRIEDMAN, Mel. *The Adventures of Ratman.*
See Chapter 8, Humorous Fantasy.

9-484 WELLS, Rosemary. *Through the Hidden Door.* Gr. 5–9.
✶ Eighth-grader Barney Pennimen is reluctant to leave the private school where he's been bullied, after a younger boy shows him a secret cave once inhabited by a miniature ancient civilization.
Illus. by the author, Dial, 1987, 256 pp., o.p.; Puffin, 2002, pap., 264 pp. (0-14-230150-7)
(BL 83:1296; CCBB 40:220; HB 63:474; Kirkus 55:728; SLJ April 1987 p. 114; VOYA 10:284)

WESLEY, Mary. *Haphazard House.*
See Chapter 10, Time Travel Fantasy.

9-485 WESTERFELD, Scott. *The Secret Hour.* **(Midnighters series, bk. 1).** Gr. 7–12.
New at Bixby High, Jessica Day discovers that she is a midnighter, able to explore, each night, a blue-lit 25th hour inhabited by dangerous darklings. The sequel is *Touching Darkness* (2005).
HarperCollins, 2004, 304 pp. (0-06-051952-5); Eos, 2005, pap., 400 pp. (0-06-05195-3-3)
(Kirkus 72:90; Kliatt Mar 2004 p. 16; SLJ June 2004 p. 152; VOYA 27:63)

9-486 WHELAN, Gerard. *Dream Invader.* Gr. 5–7. (Orig. Irish pub. 1997.)
Simon's grandmother and cousin Saskia realize that a mythical creature called a Pooshipaw is causing the boy's nightmares, and ask the local witch for help.
O'Brien, 2002, pap., 176 pp. (0-86278-516-2)
(BL 99:126; Kliatt Sep 2002 p. 28)

WHINNEM, Reade Scott. *Utten and Plumley.*
See Chapter 10, Time Travel Fantasy.

9-487 WHITE, Stewart Edward. *The Magic Forest: A Modern Fairy Story.* Gr. 4–6.
Jimmy Ferris steps off a Canadian Pacific Railroad car into an enchanted forest, where he lives with an Ojibway Indian tribe.
Macmillan, 1903, 1914, 1923, 146 pp., o.p.; Lightyear, 1976, 146 pp., o.p.; Buccaneer, 1991, o.p.
(BL 20:303, 49:209; Bookshelf 1932 p. 12; HB 1[June 1925]:32, 28:422)

9-488 WHITE, T(erence) H(anbury). *Mistress Masham's Repose.* Gr. 5–7.
✶ Maria discovers a group of Lilliputians living on her rundown estate and resolves to save them from her greedy governess, who is plotting to sell them to a circus.
Illus. by Fritz Eichenberg, Putnam, 1946, 255 pp., o.p.; Gregg, 1980, 255 pp., o.p.; illus. by Martin Hargreaves, Antique, 1998, 160 pp. (1-85149-700-5); New York Review of Books, 2004 (1-59017-103-9)
(BL 43:36; HB 57:565, 80:486–487, 490; HBG 10:301; Kirkus 14:529; LJ 71:2107)

WHITEHEAD, Victoria. *The Chimney Witches.*
See Chapter 12, Witchcraft and Sorcery Fantasy.

WICKENDEN, Dan. *The Amazing Vacation.*
See Chapter 7, High Fantasy: Travel to Other Worlds.

WIGNELL, Edel. *Escape by Deluge.*
See Chapter 6, High Fantasy: Myth or Legend Fantasy.

WILLARD, Barbara. *Spell Me a Witch.*
See Chapter 12, Witchcraft and Sorcery Fantasy.

9-489 **WILLARD, Nancy (Margaret).** *The High Rise Glorious Skittle Skat Roar-*
★ *ious Sky Pie Angel Food Cake.* Gr. 2–5.
A magic spell and some angelic help are the missing ingredients needed to
make the glorious angel food cake a young girl's mother requested for her
birthday.
Illus. by Richard Jesse Watson, Harcourt, 1990, 64 pp. (0-15-234332-6); Voyager, 1996, pap., 64 pp. (0-15-201019-X)
(BL 87:52; CCBB 44:105; HBG 2:66; Kirkus 58:1009; SLJ Nov 1990 p. 100)

WILLARD, Nancy (Margaret). *Things Invisible to See.*
See Chapter 1, Allegorical Fantasy and Literary Fairy Tales.

WILLIAMS, Jay. *The Hero from Otherwhere.*
See Chapter 7, High Fantasy: Travel to Other Worlds.

9-490 **WILLIAMS, Jay.** *The Magic Grandfather.* Gr. 4–6.
Sam and his cousin Sarah experiment with magic to bring back their missing
grandfather.
Illus. by Gail Owens, Macmillan, 1979, 149 pp., o.p.
(BL 75:1631; HB 55:418; SLJ Sept 1979 p. 151)

WILLIAMS (John), Ursula Moray. *Castle Merlin.*
See Chapter 4, Ghost Fantasy.

9-491 **WILLIAMS (John), Ursula Moray.** *The Moonball.* Gr. 3–5. (Orig. British
★ pub. 1958.)
The children who find a strange, furry, round creature decide to protect it from
scientific investigations.
Illus. by Jane Paton, Hawthorn, 1967, 138 pp., o.p.
(BL 63:1194; CCBB 21:19; HB 43:344; Kirkus 35:201; LJ 92:2024; Suth:425)

WILLIAMS, Ruth L. *The Silver Tree.*
See Chapter 10, Time Travel Fantasy.

WINDSOR, Patricia (Frances). *How a Weirdo and a Ghost Can Change
Your Entire Life.*
See Chapter 4, Ghost Fantasy.

9-492 **WINTER, Laurel.** *Growing Wings.* Gr. 5–9.
Linnet's mother, Sarah, understands that her daughter's aching shoulders mean
that she's growing wings, because she once grew wings herself.
Houghton, 2000, 195 pp. (0-618-07405-8); Firebird/Penguin, 2002, pap., 195
pp. (0-14-230219-8)
(BL 97:441; CCBB 54:125; HBG 12:81; Kirkus 68:1437; SLJ Oct 2000 p. 174; VOYA
23:280)

WINTHROP (Mahony), Elizabeth. *The Castle in the Attic.*
See Chapter 7, High Fantasy: Travel to Other Worlds.

9-493 **WISEMAN, David.** *Blodwen and the Guardians.* Gr. 5–7. (Orig. pub. in England.)
Blodwen, 10, and Tiddy, her 6-year-old brother, join forces with the fairy "Guardians" of the ancient Grove to save their home from a road-construction project.
Houghton, 1983, 163 pp., o.p.
(BL 80:504; HB 60:58; SLJ Jan 1982 p. 82; VOYA 7:102)

WOLF, Joyce. *Between the Cracks.*
See Chapter 12, Witchcraft and Sorcery Fantasy.

9-494 **WOLFE, Swain.** *The Woman Who Lives in the Earth.* Gr. 10 up. (Orig. pub. Stone Creek, 1995.)
When wells dry up on neighboring farms, young Sarah is accused of witchcraft and a shimmering fox teaches her how to shape-shift.
HarperCollins, 1996, 171 pp. (0-06-017411-0); HarperPerennial, 1997, pap. (0-06-092792-5)
(BL 91:1554, 1558; Kirkus 63:343; VOYA 19:342, 20:13)

9-495 **WOLITZER, Meg.** *The Dream Book.* Gr. 5–7.
Eleven-year-olds Claudia Lemmon and Mindy (Danger) Roth attempt to share each other's dreams in order to find Claudia's missing father.
Greenwillow, 1986, 148 pp., o.p.
(CCBB 40:59; Kirkus 54:1018; SLJ Nov 1986 p. 94; VOYA 9:224)

WOOD, Marcia. *The Secret Life of Hilary Thorne.*
See Chapter 7, High Fantasy: Travel to Other Worlds.

9-496 **WOODRUFF, Elvira.** *Awfully Short for the Fourth Grade.* Gr. 3–6.
Magic powder makes Noah's wish come true: to shrink to the size of his action figures in order to share their adventures. The sequel is *Back in Action* (1991).
Illus. by Will Hillenbrand, Holiday, 1989, 142 pp., o.p.; Dell, 1990, pap. (0-440-40366-9)
(BL 86:922; HBG 1:85; Kirkus 57:1831; SLJ Nov 1989 p. 116)

WOODRUFF, Elvira. *The Disappearing Bike Shop.*
See Chapter 10, Time Travel Fantasy.

9-497 **WOODRUFF, Elvira.** *The Magnificent Mummy Maker.* Gr. 4–6.
The ancient Egyptian mummy case Andy draws after a fifth-grade field trip has the power to grant his wishes.
Scholastic, 1994, pap., 134 pp. (0-590-457-438)
(BL 90:931; CCBB 47:205; HG 70:593; HBG 5:318; Kirkus 62:710; SLJ April 1994 p. 132)

9-498 **WOODRUFF, Elvira.** *The Summer I Shrank My Grandmother.* Gr. 3–6.
To Nelly's shock, the anti-aging formula she secretly applies to her grandmother transforms the elderly woman into a baby.

Illus. by Katherine Coville, Holiday, 1990, 153 pp. (0-8234-0832-9); Dell, 1992, pap. (0-440-40640-4)

(BL 87:1059; HBG 2:76; SLJ Dec 1990 p. 112)

WRIGHT, Betty Ren. *The Ghost of Ernie P.*
See Chapter 4, Ghost Fantasy.

WRIGHT, Betty Ren. *Haunted Summer.*
See Chapter 4, Ghost Fantasy.

9-499   **WRIGHTSON, (Alice) Patricia (Furlonger).** *A Little Fear.* Gr. 6 up. (Orig.
✶   Australian pub. 1983.)
Mrs. Tucker escapes from a nursing home to set up an independent life in a rural cottage, but her peace is disturbed by a mischievous Njimbin, or forest gnome, who wants the cottage for himself. Australian Children's Book of the Year, 1984.
Atheneum, 1983, 111 pp., o.p.
(BL 80:404, 422, 86:907; CCBB 37:60; HB 60:66; Kirkus 51:210; SLJ Nov 1983 p. 98; Suth 3:462; VOYA 7:36)

9-500   **WRIGHTSON, (Alice) Patricia (Furlonger).** *An Older Kind of Magic.* Gr.
4–7. (Australian title: *An Older Form of Magic*, 1972.)
On the night a comet streaks through the sky, aboriginal spirits appear and Rupert, Selina, and Benny save the Botanical Gardens by using ancient spells.
Illus. by Noela Young, Harcourt, 1972, 186 pp., o.p.
(BL 69:247; CCBB 26:35; HB 48:472; Kirkus 40:1100; LJ 97:3458; TLS 1972 p. 1325)

9-501   **WUORIO, Eva-Lis.** *Tal and the Magic Barruget.* Gr. 3–5.
✶   Tal conjures up a bottle-imp, or barruget, to help with the housework.
Illus. by Bettina, World, 1965, 76 pp., o.p.
(BL 62:414; HB 41:630; Kirkus 33:981; LJ 91:430)

YARBRO, Chelsea Quinn. *Monet's Ghost.*
See Chapter 7, High Fantasy: Travel to Other Worlds.

YEP, Laurence M(ichael). *The Ghost Fox.*
See Chapter 4, Ghost Fantasy.

9-502   **YEP, Laurence M(ichael).** *The Imp that Ate My Homework.* Gr. 3–5.
✶   Jim and his grandpop join forces against an ancient magical four-armed imp in this story set in San Francisco's Chinatown.
Illus. by Benrai Huang, HarperCollins, 1998, 86 pp. (0-06-027689-4); Harper-Trophy, 2000, pap., 96 pp. (0-06-440840-X)
(BL 94:698; CCBB 51:302; HB 74:351; HBG 9:342; Kirkus 65:1782; SLJ Mar 1998 p. 190)

9-503   **YEP, Laurence M(ichael).** *The Magic Paintbrush.* Gr. 3–5.
The treasured paintbrush given to recently orphaned Steve by his grandfather makes everything Steve paints come to life, and enables him and his grandfa-ther to travel from San Francisco to the China of the old man's youth.
Illus. by Suling Wang, HarperCollins, 2000, 96 pp. (0-06-028199-5); HarperTrophy, 2003, pap., 96 pp. (0-06-440852-3)
(BL 96:1024; CCBB 53:295; Kirkus 67:1993; SLJ Mar 2000 p. 220)

9-504 **YEP, Laurence M(ichael).** *The Tiger's Apprentice.* **(Tiger's Apprentice series, bk. 1).** Gr. 5–7.
After his grandmother is killed by monsters, San Francisco seventh-grader Tom Lee becomes apprenticed to Mr. Hu, a shape-changing tiger guarding a magical phoenix egg. The sequel is *Tiger's Blood* (2005).
HarperCollins, 2003, 192 pp. (0-06-001014-2); HarperTrophy, 2005, pap., 208 pp. (0-06-001015-0)
(BL 99:1893; HBG 14:378; Kirkus 71:402; SLJ April 2003 p. 170; VOYA 27:148)

YOLEN (Stemple), Jane (Hyatt). *The Faery Flag: Stories and Poems of Fantasy and the Supernatural.*
See Chapter 3, Fantasy Collections.

9-505 **YOLEN (Stemple), Jane (Hyatt).** *The Mermaid's Three Wisdoms.* Gr. 4–6.
Jess comes to terms with her deafness with the help of Melusina, an exiled mermaid who is unable to speak.
Illus. by Laura Rader, Collins+World, 1978, o.p.; Philomel, 1981, 112 pp., o.p.
(BL 74:1738; Kirkus 46:638; SLJ Nov 1978 p. 71)

YOLEN (Stemple), Jane (Hyatt). *The Wizard of Washington Square.*
See Chapter 12, Witchcraft and Sorcery Fantasy.

9-506 **YOLEN (Stemple), Jane (Hyatt).** *The Wizard's Map.* **(Tartan Magic trilogy, bk. 1).** Gr. 4–7.
When an evil wizard imprisons 13-year-old Jennifer Dyer's family, she uses her own magic to summon enchanted creatures to rescue them. In *The Pictish Child* (1999, 2002), a witch gives Jennifer's sister Molly a talisman that connects them to a young Pict girl escaping the violence of ninth-century Britain. In *The Bagpiper's Ghost* (2002, 2003), twins Jennifer and Peter meet the ghost of Mary MacFadden, a young woman thwarted in love by her own twin brother, Andrew.
Harcourt, 1999, 144 pp. (0-15-202067-5); Magic Carpet, 2002, pap. (0-15-216365-4)
(BL 95:1691; HBG 10:301; SLJ May 1999 p. 132; VOYA 22:352)

9-507 **YORK, Carol Beach.** *Miss Know-It-All; A Butterfield Square Story.* Gr. 3–4.
Miss Know-It-All's box of magic chocolates and her marvelous memory create quite a stir in the orphanage at number 18 Butterfield Square. The sequels are *The Christmas Dolls* (1967), *The Ten O'Clock Club* (1970), and *Miss Know-It-All Returns* (1972).
Illus. by Victoria de Larrea, Watts, 1966, 87 pp., o.p.
(CCBB 20:52; LJ 91:4345)

9-508 **ZALBEN, Jane Breskin.** *The Magic Menorah: A Modern Chanukah Tale.* Gr. 2–5.
While Stanley is polishing his grandfather's tarnished menorah, a little old man appears and offers the boy three wishes if he can answer three riddles.
Illus. by Donna Diamond, Simon, 2001, 56 pp. (0-689-82606-0)
(HBG 13:80; Kirkus 69:1436; SLJ Oct 2001 p. 71)

9-509 ZERNER, Amy, and SPICER ZERNER, Jessie. *The Dream Quilt.* Gr. 2–4.

Every night Alex stays at his aunt's house, he dreams of a magic adventure related to his great-grandfather's patchwork quilt, adventures involving princesses, dragons, and Neptune.

Illus. by Jessie Spicer Zerner, Tuttle, 1995, 96 pp. (0-8048-1999-8)

(BL 91:1958; HBG 6:307; SLJ June 1995 p. 98)

9-510 ZOLOTOW, Charlotte S(hapiro). *The Man with Purple Eyes.* Gr. 2–4.

The odd-looking seed Anna is given grows into a beautiful purple plant that helps her invalid father recover from his illness.

Illus. by Joe Lasker, Abelard-Shuman, 1961, 60 pp., o.p.

(CCBB 15:152; HB 37:340; LJ 86:2361)

10

Time Travel Fantasy

Stories about people who step into another time can be the most memorable of fantasy tales. This chapter includes books about travel from our time into the past and into the future, as well as stories in which travelers from the past or future visit the 20th and 21st centuries. A few stories deal with two time periods that somehow touch, permitting glimpses into the past or future, without any actual traveling. In fantasy, the means of time travel must be magical, not scientific. Tales of travelers to other worlds, rather than other times, are found in Chapter 7, Travel to Other Worlds. Stories about people from our world who meet ghosts from the past have been placed in Chapter 4, Ghost Fantasy, if the ghosts, not the human protagonists, do the time traveling.

10-1　**ADKINS, Jan.** *Solstice: A Mystery of the Season.* Gr. 6 up.
Charlie and his father are welcomed into Vern Filson's remote Maine island cabin on Winter Solstice night; but when they return home they discover that Vern and his family died more than 50 years earlier.
Illus. by the author, Walker, 1990, 128 pp., o.p.
(HBG 2:84; Kirkus 58:1389; SLJ Oct 1990 p. 33; VOYA 13:275)

10-2　**ADKINS, Jan.** *A Storm Without Rain.* Gr. 6–9.
While sailing to an island off the coast of Cape Cod, 15-year-old Jack is caught in a storm and finds himself in the year 1904, where he is befriended by young John Swain, his own grandfather.
Little, Brown, 1983, 179 pp., o.p.; Morrow, 1993, pap., 192 pp. (0-688-11852-6)
(BL 79:1089; HB 59:448; Kirkus 51:662; SLJ Oct 1983 p. 155; VOYA 6:212)

AIKEN, Joan (Delano). *The Shadow Guests.*
See Chapter 4, Ghost Fantasy.

10-3　**ALCOCK, Vivien (Dolores).** *The Red-Eared Ghosts.* Gr. 5–9. (Orig. pub. in
✭　England.)
Mary Frewin makes her way across time to learn, from ghosts only she can see, what happened to her great-great-grandmother.
Houghton, 1997, 272 pp. (0-395-81660-2), 1998, pap., 272 pp. (0-395-88350-6)
(BL 93:1160; CCBB 50:270; HBG 8:295; Kirkus 65:548; SLJ April 1997 p. 134; VOYA 20:250)　　**737**

10-4   ALEXANDER, Lloyd (Chudley). *Time Cat: The Remarkable Journeys of Jason and Gareth.* **(British title:** *Nine Lives***, 1963).** Gr. 5–7.
Jason's magic cat Gareth takes him back through time to visit the nine historical periods of his previous lives.
Illus. by Bill Sokol, Henry Holt, 1963, 191 pp., o.p.; Holt, 2003, 216 pp. (0-8050-7270-5); Puffin, 2004, pap., 224 pp. (0-14-240107-2)
(HBG 14:361; LJ 88:2548; TLS 1963 p. 980)

10-5   ALLAN, Mabel E(sther). *Romansgrove.* Gr. 5–7.
Wandering through the ruins of an old manor house called Romansgrove, Clare and Richard find themselves in the year 1902, attempting to save Emily Roman and her family from death by fire.
Illus. by Gail Owens, Atheneum, 1975, 192 pp., o.p.
(BL 72:295; CCBB 29:89; HB 52:54; Kirkus 43:776; SLJ Oct 1975 p. 93)

10-6   ALLAN, Mabel E(sther). *Time to Go Back.* Gr. 5–8.
Sarah reads her late Aunt Larke's poetry and finds herself living in the year 1942, while her friend Larke has a tragic wartime love affair.
Abelard-Schuman, 1972, 134 pp., o.p.
(CCBB 26:70; Kirkus 40:1105; LJ 98:257)

ALLEN, Judy. *The Spring on the Mountain.*
See Chapter 1, Allegorical Fantasy and Literary Fairy Tales.

10-7   ANDERSON, Margaret J(ean). *The Druid's Gift.* Gr. 6–9.
✯   Caitlin, a rebellious girl living on a Scottish isle during the time of the Druids, has visions of herself in three future times as Cathan, Catie, and Catriona.
Knopf, 1989, 192 pp., o.p.
(BL 85:1967, 1970; CCBB 42:188; HB 56:481; Kirkus 57:288; SLJ Mar 1989 p. 175; Suth 4:13)

10-8   ANDERSON, Margaret J(ean). *In the Circle of Time.* **(The Time trilogy, bk. 2).** Gr. 5–8.
A strange fog swirling around an ancient Scottish stone circle sweeps Jennifer and Robert into the year 2179, where they attempt to help a peace-loving tribe escape enslavement by the mechanized Barbaric Ones. This is the sequel to *In the Keep of Time* (Random, 1977) and is followed by *The Mists of Time* (Knopf, 1984).
Knopf, 1979, 181 pp., o.p.
(BL 75:1533; CCBB 32:185; Kirkus 47:635; SLJ Apr 1979 p. 52)

10-9   ANDERSON, Margaret J(ean). *To Nowhere and Back.* Gr. 5–7.
On a path near her home, Elizabeth travels 100 years into the past and becomes a girl named Ann.
Knopf, 1975, 141 pp., o.p.
(BL 71:961; CCBB 28:157; HB 51:379; Kirkus 43:181; SLJ Mar 1975 p. 91)

10-10   ANDERSON, Poul (William). *The Time Patrol.* **(The Time Patrol series).**
✯   Gr. 10 up.
Nine science-fantasy short stories and novellas about Manse Everard, a member of the Time Patrol, a group who travel through time correcting problems in the past to ensure their own future time's safety. This is the sequel to *The*

Shield of Time (1990) and is related to *Guardians of Time* (1960, 1976, 1988) and *Time Patrolman* (1983).

Tor, 1991, 458 pp., o.p.

(BL 88:416, 421; Kirkus 59:1188; LJ Oct 15, 1991 p. 127; SLJ Apr 1992 p. 170; VOYA 15:38)

10-11 ANDREWS, J(ames) S(ydney). *The Green Hill of Nendrum.* Gr. 6–8. (Orig. British pub. 1969, entitled *The Bell of Nendrum.*)

Nial Ross is caught in a storm while sailing and is transported a thousand years back through time to the island monastery of Nendrum.

Hawthorn, 1970, 214 pp., o.p.

(BL 67:266; HB 46:613; TLS 1969 p. 690)

10-12 APPEL, Allen. *Time After Time.* **(Alex Balfour series, bk. 1).** Gr. 10 up.

Alex Balfour, a young history professor, travels back in time to Petrograd in 1917, determined to rescue Czar Nicholas and his family from assassination. In the sequel, *Twice Upon a Time* (1988), Alex helps two Native Americans on display at the 1876 Philadelphia Centennial Exposition escape from their captors, and then finds himself in South Dakota on the eve of the Battle of Little Bighorn. The sequels are *Till the End of Time* (Doubleday, 1990) and *In Time of War* (2003).

Carroll & Graf, 1985, 373 pp., o.p.

(BL 82:179, 215, 83:1117)

ARTHUR, Ruth M(abel). *The Autumn People.*

See Chapter 4, Ghost Fantasy.

10-13 ARTHUR, Ruth M(abel). *On the Wasteland.* Gr. 5–7. (Orig. British pub. 1975.)

When Betony travels into the past, she is transformed from a friendless orphan into Estrith, a Viking chief's daughter engaged to a Saxon prince.

Illus. by Margery Gill, Atheneum, 1975, 159 pp., o.p.

(BL 72:163; HB 51:459; Kirkus 43:710; SLJ Oct 1975 p. 94; TLS 1975 p. 1455)

10-14 ARTHUR, Ruth M(abel). *Requiem for a Princess.* Gr. 6–9. (Orig. British pub. 1967.)

Willow Forrester's upsetting discovery that she is adopted brings on nightmares in which she becomes a 16th-century Spanish girl fated to die by drowning.

Illus. by Margery Gill, Atheneum, 1967, 182 pp., o.p.

(BL 63:1098; CCBB 21:138; HB 43:211; Kirkus 35:61; LJ 92:1744; TLS 1967 p. 1141)

10-15 AVI (Avi Wortis). *Something Upstairs: A Tale of Ghosts.* Gr. 5–9.

☆ The ghost of Caleb, a young black slave murdered nearly 200 years ago in the attic of Kenny's house, convinces Kenny to travel back through time to 18th-century Providence, Rhode Island, to change Caleb's fate.

Orchard, 1988, 120 pp. (0-531-05782-8); HarperTrophy, 1997, pap., 128 pp. (0-380-79086-6)

(BL 85:476; CCBB 42:2; HB 65:65; Kirkus 56:1145; SLJ Oct 1988 p. 138; VOYA 11:293, 12:16)

10-16 BACON, Martha (Sherman). *The Third Road.* Gr. 5–8.
A 20th-century girl named Fox becomes stranded in 17th-century Spain.
Illus. by Robin Jacques, Little, Brown, 1971, 188 pp., o.p.
(Kirkus 39:943; LJ 96:4182)

BANKS, Lynne Reid. *The Indian in the Cupboard.*
See Chapter 9, Magic Adventure Fantasy.

10-17 BARBER, Antonia (pseud. of Barbara Anthony). *The Ghosts.* Gr. 5–7.
✶ Lucy and Jamie move to an old country house where they meet two ghostly
children and make a frightening journey into the past to save the ghosts from a
fiery death.
Farrar, 1969, 189 pp., o.p.; Pocket, 1982, 1989, pap., 224 pp. (0-671-70714-0)
(BL 66:563; CCBB 23:92; HB 45:532; Kirkus 37:854; LJ 95:777; TLS 1969 p. 689)

10-18 BARRON, T(homas) A. *The Ancient One.* Gr. 6–9.
When 13-year-old Kate visits an old-growth redwood forest in the fog-shroud-
ed Lost Crater of Oregon, her owl-headed walking stick takes her hundreds of
years into the past, where a long-vanished Indian tribe is fighting to save the
forest. This is the sequel to the science fiction book *Heartlight* (1990). The
third book in the series is *The Merlin Effect* (Philomel, 1994).
Putnam, 1992, 368 pp., o.p.; Ace, 2003, pap., 320 pp. (0-441-01032-6)
(BL 89:46; CCBB 46:139; HBG 4:79; Kirkus 60:918; SLJ Nov 1992 p. 88; VOYA 15:290,
16:9)

10-19 BELLAIRS, John. *The Trolley to Yesterday.* **(Johnny Dixon series, bk. 6).**
Gr. 5–8.
Professor Childermass takes Johnny and Fergie on a trolley back through time
to Constantinople, in an attempt to change history by preventing a massacre.
The eight other stories in this series are more horror than fantasy: *The Mummy,
the Will and the Crypt* (1983), *The Curse of the Blue Figurine* (1983), *The
Spell of the Sorcerer's Skull* (1984), *The Revenge of the Wizard's Ghost*
(1985), *The Eyes of the Killer Robot* (1986), *The Chessmen of Doom* (1989),
The Secret of the Underground Room (1990), *The Drum, the Doll and the Zombie* (1994; written by Bellairs and Brad Strickland), *The Hand of the Necromancer* (1996; written by Strickland), *The Bell, the Book, and the Spellbinder*
(1997; written by Strickland), and *The Wrath of the Grinning Ghost* (1999;
written by Strickland).
Dial, 1989, 183 pp. (0-8037-0581-6); Puffin, pap., 2004, 183 pp. (0-14-240266-
4)
(BL 85:1719; CCBB 42:217; Kirkus 57:686; SLJ June 1989 p. 102; VOYA 12:219)

10-20 BELLAMY, Edward. *Looking Backward: 2000–1887.* Gr. 10 up. (Orig.
U.S. pub. 1888.)
Wealthy 19th-century Bostonian Julian West awakens in the year 2000, in a
Massachusetts that has become a cooperative utopia, and falls in love with his
fiancée's great-granddaughter. The sequel is *Equality* (1897, 1924, 1970, 1985,
2003).
Houghton, 1915, 1941, 276 pp., o.p.; Harvard University Press, 1967, 314 pp.,
o.p.; Signet, 2000, pap., 222 pp. (0-451-52763-1)
(BL 25:403, 39:141, 42:59)

10-21 BENNETT, Cherie, and GOTTESFELD, Jeff. *Anne Frank and Me.* Gr. 6–11.

Injured while touring an Anne Frank exhibit, 10th-grader Nicole Burns awakens in World War II France within the body of Nicole Bernhardt, a Jewish girl whose family is hiding from the Nazis.

Putnam, 2001, 352 pp. (0-399-23329-6)

(BL 97:1128; CCBB 54:252; HBG 12:320; Kirkus 69:105; Kliatt May 2001 p. 8; SLJ Mar 2001 p. 245)

10-22 BERESFORD, Elizabeth. *Invisible Magic.* Gr. 4–6. (Orig. British pub. 1975.)

Princess Elfrida-of-the-Castle decides she likes life in the 20th century better than in her own time, and welcomes the chance to trade places with Mr. Patrick.

Illus. by Reg Gray, Hart-Davis/Granada, 1977, 158 pp., o.p.

(BL 74:1185; CCBB 32:23; TLS 1975 p. 763)

10-23 BERESFORD, Elizabeth. *Travelling Magic.* Gr. 4–6. (Orig. British pub. 1965.)

Kate and Marcus meet a magician from ancient Britain who has come to the 20th century as part of his studies.

Illus. by Judith Valpy, Granada, 1977, 163 pp., o.p.

(BL 74:1185; TLS 1965 p. 1130)

10-24 BETHANCOURT, T(homas) Ernesto (pseud. of Tom Paisley). *Tune in Yesterday.* Gr. 8–10.

A love of jazz propels two friends back to 1942, but racial prejudice and Nazi plots make life more complicated than they had anticipated. In *The Tomorrow Connection* (1984), Richie and Matty escape their problems by traveling to 1912 and then 1906, but Matty is forced to endure more racial prejudice while they search for a tomorrow gate to take them home.

Holiday, 1978, 156 pp., o.p.

(BL 74:1420, 80:351; HB 54:400; Kirkus 46:311; SLJ May 1978 p. 73)

10-25 BLAIR, Cynthia. *Freedom to Dream.* Gr. 7 up.

An antique ring enables Katy Morris to enter the time of an ancestor in 1787 Philadelphia, just as the U.S. Constitution is about to be written.

Fawcett, 1987, pap., 139 pp., o.p.

(Kliatt Sep 1987 p. 6; VOYA 10:196)

10-26 BOND, Nancy (Barbara). *Another Shore.* Gr. 8–12.

☆ One day she is a summer employee of a Nova Scotia historical park, playing the role of an 18th-century girl, and the next day Lyn Paget awakens to find that she has actually become her "character," 17-year-old Elisabeth Bernard living in the year 1744. This story is disturbing because it ends with Lyn helplessly stranded in a past life she has grown to detest.

Macmillan, 1988, 308 pp., o.p.

(BL 85:67, 70; CCBB 42:26; HB 65:214; Kirkus 56:1400; SLJ Oct 1988 p. 159; Suth 4:39; VOYA 11:246, 12:13)

10-27 BOND, Nancy (Barbara). *A String in the Harp.* Gr. 6–8.

✶ Unhappy over his mother's recent death and the family's move to Wales, Peter Morgan is drawn into the 6th-century period of Taliesin by the tuning key of an ancient harp. Boston Globe Horn Book Award Honor Book for Fiction, 1976; John Newbery Medal Honor Book, 1977; I.R.A. Children's Book Award, 1977; Tir na n-Og Award, 1977.
Macmillan, 1976, 384 pp. (0-689-50036-X); Aladdin/Simon, 1996, pap., 370 pp. (0-689-80445-8)

(BL 72:1108, 80:95; CCBB 29:171; HB 52:287; Kirkus 44:255; SLJ Apr 1976 p. 84; Suth 2:52)

10-28 BOSSE, Malcolm J(oseph). *Cave Beyond Time.* Gr. 7–9.

Bitten by a rattlesnake while on an Arizona archaeological dig, Ben travels back in time to encounter members of two Native American tribes, and his experience helps him adjust to the recent loss of his parents.
Harper, 1980, 187 pp., o.p.

(BL 77:400, 402; CCBB 34:66; HB 57:57; SLJ Nov 1980 p. 83; VOYA 3:37)

BOSTON, L(ucy) M(aria Wood). *The Children of Green Knowe.*
See Chapter 4, Ghost Fantasy.

10-29 BOSTON, L(ucy) M(aria Wood). *The Stones of Green Knowe.* Gr. 4–6.

✶ (Orig. British pub. 1976.)
In the year 1120, a boy named Roger discovers two magical stones at the building site of Green Knowe manor house, and is sent into the future to meet Toby, Linnet, Susan, and Tolly, the protagonists in *The Children of Green Knowe* (1954, 1967; see Chapter 4, Ghost Fantasy). *The River at Green Knowe* (1959, 2002; see Chapter 9, Magic Adventure Fantasy) is a related story.
Illus. by Peter Boston, Atheneum, 1976, 118 pp., o.p.; Harcourt, 2005 (0-15-205560-6)

(BL 73:141; CCBB 30:39; HB 52:623; Kirkus 44:845; SLJ Jan 1977 p. 87; Suth 2:53; TLS 1976 p. 881)

10-30 BOSWORTH, Beth. *Tunneling.* Gr. 10 up.

Asthmatic 12-year-old Rachel Finch is only too happy to leave her life in suburban 1968 New Jersey and travel through time with superhero S-Man, coming to the aid of such famous literary figures as Shakespeare, Voltaire, and Socrates.
Crown, 2003, 304 pp. (0-609-61103-8)

(BL 99:1739; Kirkus 71:766; LJ June 15, 2003 p. 99; SLJ Nov 2003 p. 171)

10-31 BRADBURY, Ray (Douglas). *The Halloween Tree.* Gr. 5–8.

✶ Eight Halloween-costumed boys search ancient Egypt, druidic Britain, medieval Europe, and some Mexican catacombs for a friend who vanished from a haunted house.
Illus. by Joseph Mugnaini, Knopf, 1972, 1988, 160 pp., LB (0-394-92409-6); Knopf, 1996, 150 pp. (0-394-82409-1); Knopf, 1999, pap., 145 pp. (0-375-80301-7)

(BL 69:404; HBG 8:78; Kirkus 40:801; LJ 97:4086; VOYA 12:39)

10-32 BRANDEL, Marc (pseud. of Marcus Beresford). *The Mine of Lost Days.*
✭ Gr. 4–7.
Deep inside an abandoned Irish copper mine, Henry discovers four people who have lived more than 100 years without aging but who would die if they emerged into the modern world.
Illus. by John Verling, Harper, 1974, 185 pp., o.p.
(BL 71:241; Kirkus 42:876; LJ 99:2738)

10-33 BROCK, Darryl. *If I Never Get Back.* Gr. 10 up.
Sam Fowler steps off an Amtrak train into 1869 Ohio, becomes a substitute player for the Cincinnati Red Stockings baseball team, steals gold from the Fenian Army, and falls in love.
Crown, 1990, 425 pp., o.p.
(Kirkus 57:1692; VOYA 13:214)

10-34 BROWN, Rita Mae. *Riding Shotgun.* Gr. 10 up.
Unhappy with her life as a widowed mother of teenagers, Pryor Blackwood follows a magical fox to colonial Virginia, where she becomes her ancestral namesake and lives on a 17th-century plantation.
Bantam, 1996, 336 pp., o.p.
(BL 92:898; Kirkus 64:83)

10-35 BUCHAN, John. *Lake of Gold.* Gr. 5–7. (Orig. Canadian pub. 1941; British title: *The Long Traverse*, 1941.)
Bored by his history lessons, a young boy on a camping trip is given the chance to take part in Canadian history.
Illus. by S. Levenson, Houghton, 1941, 190 pp., o.p.
(HB 17:367, 476; LJ 66:737)

10-36 BUFFIE, Margaret. *The Haunting of Frances Rain.* Gr. 6–9. (Orig. Cana-
✭ dian pub. 1987, entitled *Who Is Frances Rain?*.)
The old spectacles Lizzie finds on Rain Island allow her to glimpse the past life of a reclusive woman named Francis Rain. Young Adult Canadian Book Award, 1988.
Scholastic, 1989, 192 pp., o.p.
(BL 86:273, 344; HBG 1:82; Kirkus 57:1471; SLJ Sept 1989 p. 272; VOYA 12:286)

10-37 BULLETT, Gerald W(illiam). *The Happy Mariners.* Gr. 4–6. (Orig. British pub. 1928, entitled *The Spanish Mariners*.)
The four Robinson children accidentally break a bottle containing a model of an Elizabethan ship, propelling them on an adventure-filled journey involving pirates, buried treasure, and cannibals.
Illus. by C(yril) Walter Hodges, Dodge, 1936, 247 pp., o.p.
(HB 12:355; TLS 1930 p. 805)

10-38 BURFORD, Lolah. *The Vision of Stephen: An Elegy.* Gr. 7 up.
Fleeing a sentence of execution, Prince Stephen escapes from his 7th-century Anglo-Saxon world into Victorian England.
Illus. by Bill Greer, Macmillan, 1972, 192 pp., o.p.
(BL 69:26, 292, 299; Kirkus 40:344; LJ 97:2640, 3473)

10-39 **BURGESS, Melvin.** *An Angel for May.* Gr. 5–9. (Orig. British pub. 1992.)
Tam follows a homeless woman and her dog 50 years into the past, where they meet a disturbed young girl whose guardian is fated to die in a fire.
Simon, 1995, 154 pp. (0-671-89004-2)
(BL 91:1571; CCBB 48:378; HBG 6:294; Kirkus 63:631; SLJ June 1995 p. 108)

10-40 **BUTLER, Octavia E(stelle).** *Kindred.* Gr. 10 up.
Dana, a young black writer living in Los Angeles in 1976, undertakes a series of unexpected and dangerous trips to the year 1819 to rescue Rufus, the young son of a Maryland slaveholder.
Doubleday, 1979, 264 pp., o.p.; Beacon, 1988, 2004, pap., 499 pp. (0-8070-8369-0)
(Kirkus 47:587; LJ 104:1585; VOYA 2:28, 4:47)

10-41 **CAMERON, Eleanor (Frances Butler).** *Beyond Silence.* Gr. 6–10.
✫ Andy is plagued by nightmares and unsettling visits to the past when he and his father visit their ancestral home in Scotland, following his brother's death.
Dutton, 1980, 208 pp., o.p.
(BL 77:205, 207; CCBB 34:88; HB 56:646, 62:616; Kirkus 49:78; SLJ Jan 1981 p. 67; VOYA 4:28)

CAMERON, Eleanor (Frances Butler). *The Court of the Stone Children.*
See Chapter 4, Ghost Fantasy.

10-42 **CAMERON, Eleanor (Frances Butler).** *Time and Mr. Bass: A Mushroom*
✫ *Planet Book.* Gr. 4–6.
Forces of evil reach through Mycetian history to ensnare Tyco Bass and his friends, Chuck and David, after they visit ancient Wales to translate an old scroll. *The Wonderful Flight to the Mushroom Planet* (1954), *Stowaway to the Mushroom Planet* (1956), *Mr. Bass's Planetoid* (1958), and *A Mystery for Mr. Bass* (1960) are science fiction stories that precede this book in the Mushroom Planet series.
Illus. by Fred Meise, Little, Brown, 1967, 247 pp., o.p.
(BL 63:988; HB 43:460; Kirkus 35:56; LJ 92:1314)

CARKEET, David. *I Been There Before.*
See Chapter 8, Humorous Fantasy.

10-43 **CHAMBERLAIN, Penny.** *The Olden Days Locket.* Gr. 5–8. (Orig. Canadian pub. 2002.)
Friendless Jess, a volunteer guide at a historic British Columbia home, goes back in time to 1896 and meets Rose, despondent after her father's death in a streetcar accident.
Sono Nis, 2003, pap., 198 pp. (1-55039-128-3)
(Kliatt Sep 2003 p. 24; SLJ Aug 2003 p. 158; VOYA 26:321)

10-44 **CHASE, Mary (Coyle).** *The Wicked Pigeon Ladies in the Garden.* Gr. 4–6.
✫ Trespassing at the Old Messerman Place, Maureen Swanson finds an unusual bracelet and meets seven evil ghosts who try to trap her in the past.
Illus. by Don Bolognese, Knopf, 1968, 115 pp., o.p.; illus. by Peter Sís (entitled *The Wicked, Wicked Ladies in the Haunted House*) Knopf, 2003, 128 pp. (0-375-92572-4); Yearling, 2005, pap., 144 pp. (0-440-41956-5)

(BL 65:493, 82:682, 99:1428; CCBB 22:90; HB 45:52, 63:491; HBG 15:89; Kirkus 36:1162; LJ 94:293; Suth:69)

10-45 CHETWIN, Grace. *Friends in Time.* Gr. 4–7.
Emma Gibson has always had trouble making friends because her family has moved so often, so she is overjoyed when her heartfelt wish for one true friend brings Abigail Bently to the 20th century from the year 1846.
Macmillan, 1992, 132 pp. (0-02-718318-1)
(BL 88:1936; HBG 3:261; Kirkus 60:716; SLJ July 1992 p. 72; VOYA 15:236)

10-46 CHRISTOPHER, Nicholas. *Veronica.* Gr. 10 up.
Leo's accidental meeting with a young woman named Veronica involves him in her family's search for their missing magician father, lost in time through the interference of a jealous rival.
Dial, 1996, 336 pp., o.p.; Perennial, 2000, pap., 336 pp. (0-380-80657-6)
(BL 92:686; LJ Jan 1996 p. 138)

CHURCH, Richard (Thomas). *The French Lieutenant: A Ghost Story.*
See Chapter 4, Ghost Fantasy.

10-47 CONRAD, Pam. *Stonewords: A Ghost Story.* Gr. 5–9.
★★ Zoe's grandparents think Zoe Louise is only an imaginary friend, but Zoe knows Zoe Louise is the ghost of a little girl who died in a fire on her 11th birthday and Zoe decides to go back in time to save her. Boston Globe Horn Book Award Honor Book, 1990. In the sequel, *Zoe Rising* (1996), 14-year-old Zoe travels in and out of the past, attempting to rescue her mother from danger.
Harper, 1990, 130 pp. (0-06-021316-7)
(BL 86:1338; CCBB 43:211; HB 66:600; HBG 1:254; Kirkus 58:339; SLJ May 1990 p. 103; Suth 4:81; VOYA 13:10)

10-48 COONEY, Caroline B. *Both Sides of Time.* **(Time Quartet, bk. 1).** Gr.
★ 6–10. (Orig. U.S. pub. 1995.)
Sheltering from a storm in a soon-to-be razed Victorian mansion, Annie Lockwood travels 100 years into the past, where she falls in love with Hiram Stratton Jr. and tries to prove the innocence of a maid accused of murder. In *Out of Time* (1996, 1997) Annie returns to the 1890s in an attempt to rescue Strat from an insane asylum and to prevent his sister's marriage to a fortune hunter. Anne Spencer Lindbergh Prize Honor Book 1995–1996. In *Prisoner of Time* (1998, 1999), Strat's younger sister Devonny escapes into the future with Annie's brother Tod. In *For All Time* (2001, 2003), Annie tries to return to Strat's time, but ends up thousands of years in the past.
Delacorte, 2001, 210 pp. (0-385-72948-0); Dell, 2001, pap. (0-440-21932-9)
(BL 92:151; CCBB 49:50; HB 71:745; HBG 7:71, 13:96; Kirkus 63:854; Kliatt Nov 1995 p. 14; SLJ July 1995 p. 95; VOYA 18:168)

10-49 COOPER (Grant), Susan (Mary). *King of Shadows.* Gr. 5–9.
★ Thrilled to be part of an American summer drama troupe performing in London, Nat Field falls ill and awakens as another Nat Field in 1599, an actor in William Shakespeare's new production of "A Midsummer Night's Dream." Boston Globe Horn Book Honor Book, 2000.
McElderry, 1999, 186 pp. (0-689-82817-9); Aladdin/Simon, 2001, pap., 186 pp. (0-689-84445-X)

(BL 96:442, 821; CCBB 53:126; HB 75:735; HBG 11:76; Kirkus 67:1740; Kliatt Nov 1999 p. 10; SLJ Nov 1999 p. 156; VOYA 22:342, 23:11)

CORBETT, Sue. *12 Again.*
See Chapter 9, Magic Adventure Fantasy.

CRESSWELL (Rowe), Helen. *A Game of Catch.*
See Chapter 4, Ghost Fantasy.

10-50 **CRESSWELL (Rowe), Helen.** *Moondial.* Gr. 5–8. (Orig. British pub. 1987.)
✭ Minty Kane feels compelled to travel back through time to rescue the ghosts of two abused children she meets while spending the summer near an old English manor house.
Macmillan, 1987, 208 pp., o.p.
(BL 84:317, 873; CCBB 41:86; HB 66:68; Kirkus 55:1238; SLJ Nov 1987 p. 104; TLS 1987 p. 1285; VOYA 10:243)

CRESSWELL (Rowe), Helen. *The Secret World of Polly Flint.*
See Chapter 9, Magic Adventure Fantasy.

10-51 **CRESSWELL (Rowe), Helen.** *Time Out.* Gr. 3–6. (Orig. British pub. 1990.)
✭ Wilks the butler takes his family on an amazing vacation into the future, from London in 1887 to 1987, where they are astonished by television and automobiles.
Illus. by Peter Ewell, Macmillan, 1990, 80 pp., o.p.
(BL 86:1089; HBG 1:256; Kirkus 58:261:SLJ June 1990 p. 118)

10-52 **CRESSWELL (Rowe), Helen.** *Up the Pier.* Gr. 4–6. (Orig. British pub.
✭ 1971.)
Lonely Carrie meets the invisible Pontifex family, who were unwillingly transported from 1921 to 1971 and need Carrie's help to break the spell that holds them in the wrong time. Carnegie Medal Highly Commended Book, 1971.
Illus. by Gareth Floyd, Macmillan, 1971, 144 pp., o.p.
(BL 68:1002; CCBB 26:40; HB 48:368; Kirkus 40:477; LJ 97:4070; Suth:94; TLS 1971 p. 1516)

10-53 **CRESSWELL (Rowe), Helen.** *The Watchers: A Mystery at Alton Towers.*
✭ Gr. 4–7. (Orig. British pub. 1993.)
Hiding out in Alton Towers, a local amusement park, after running away from a foster home, Katy and Josh discover that they can travel through time and must destroy an evil force that haunts the park.
Macmillan, 1994, 206 pp. (0-02-725371-6)
(BL 91:752; CCBB 48:195; HB 71:192; HBG 6:75; Kirkus 61:1561; SLJ Feb 1995 p. 96; VOYA 18:20)

CROWE, Carole. *Sharp Horns on the Moon.*
See Chapter 4, Ghost Fantasy.

10-54 **CURLEY, Marianne.** *The Named.* **(Guardians of Time trilogy, bk. 1).** Gr. 7 up. (Orig. Australian pub. 2002.)
To become a Guardian of Time, Ethan, 16, must train his schoolmate Isabel as his apprentice and complete a difficult quest by traveling back through time. The sequels are *The Dark* (2003) and *The Key* (2005).

Bloomsbury, 2002, 332 pp. (1-58234-779-4), 2005, pap., 336 pp. (1-58234-913-4)

(BL 99:590; Kirkus 70:1466; SLJ Jan 2003 p. 134; VOYA 25:486)

10-55 CURLEY, Marianne. *Old Magic.* Gr. 6–9. (Orig. Australian pub. 2000.)
Kate reveals her secret witchcraft abilities to help a new classmate whose family is cursed, and the two of them travel through time to medieval England to confront the sorcerer who originally cast the spell.
Bloomsbury, 2000, 316 pp., o.p.; Simon Pulse, 2002, pap., 320 pp. (0-7434-3769-1)

(CCBB 55:276; SLJ May 2002 p. 148; VOYA 25:187)

CURRY, Jane Louise. *The Bassumtyte Treasure.*
See Chapter 4, Ghost Fantasy.

10-56 CURRY, Jane Louise. *Dark Shade.* Gr. 6–10.
✯ Maggie Gilmour, 16, follows her friend Kip into the primeval Pennsylvania Dark Shade Forest of 1758, where she tries to convince Kip to come home and rescues a young Scots soldier.
Simon, 1998, 168 pp. (0-689-81812-2)

(BL 94:1312; HB 74:341; HBG 9:343; Kliatt July 1998 p. 6; SLJ May 1998 p. 141; VOYA 21:207, 22:13)

10-57 CURRY, Jane Louise. *The Daybreakers.* Gr. 5–7.
Researching the history of Apple Lock, Callie, Liss, and Harry are drawn back through time to Abáloc, a primitive village whose people need the children's help to defeat their enemies. The sequel is *The Birdstones* (1977), and both stories are related to *Over the Sea's Edge* (1971; see below).
Illus. by Charles Robinson, Harcourt, 1970, 191 pp., o.p.

(BL 66:1406; HB 46:296; Kirkus 38:452; LJ 95:3626; TLS 1970 p. 1251)

10-58 CURRY, Jane Louise. *Moon Window.* Gr. 5–7.
Climbing through the round attic window in her elderly cousin's New Hampshire home, Joellen finds herself in the 1700s, involved in a mystery surrounding Ellen Macallan, the ancestor who built the house.
Simon, 1996, 170 pp. (0-689-80945-X)

(BL 93:420; CCBB 50:94; HBG 8:64; SLJ Dec 1996 p. 120)

10-59 CURRY, Jane Louise. *Over the Sea's Edge.* Gr. 5–7.
✯ An ancient medallion causes Dave Reese to exchange places with a 12th-century Welsh boy named Dewi. He accompanies the exiled Prince Maduac to the legendary island of Antillia where they are drawn into a struggle between the fairy people of Abáloc and a Native American civilization. *The Daybreakers* (1970; see above) and *The Birdstones* (1977) are related stories.
Illus. by Charles Robinson, Harcourt, 1971, 182 pp., o.p.

(BL 68:333; HB 47:610; Kirkus 39:1079; LJ 96:3474; TLS 1971 p. 1510)

10-60 CURRY, Jane Louise. *Parsley, Sage, Rosemary and Time.* Gr. 3–6.
A herb from her aunt's garden sends Rosemary into Pilgrim times, where she helps a woman accused of witchcraft. The sequel is *The Magical Cupboard* (1976).

Illus. by Charles Robinson, Atheneum, 1975, 108 pp., o.p.
(Kirkus 43:306; SLJ Apr 1975 p. 51)

CURRY, Jane Louise. *Poor Tom's Ghost.*
See Chapter 4, Ghost Fantasy.

CURRY, Jane Louise. *The Sleepers.*
See Chapter 6, High Fantasy: Myth or Legend Fantasy.

10-61   **CURRY, Jane Louise.** *The Watchers.* Gr. 6–8.
☆   Ray Silver joins the family battle against a coal company threatening their land, and when a stone splinter sends him 1,600 years into the past he becomes involved in a tragedy surrounding his ancestors.
Illus. by Trina Schart Hyman, Atheneum, 1975, 235 pp., o.p.
(BL 72:451; CCBB 29:108; Kirkus 43:988; SLJ Nov 1975 p. 73; Suth 2:112; TLS 1976 p. 392)

10-62   **CUTT, W(illiam) Towrie.** *Seven for the Sea.* Gr. 6–8. (Orig. British pub. 1972.)
Two cousins travel 100 years into the past to investigate rumors of selkie ancestors. This is the sequel to the British book *Message from Arkmae* (1972).
Follett, 1974, 96 pp., o.p.
(BL 71:507; HB 50:690; LJ 99:3276)

10-63   **DAVIES, Andrew (Wynford).** *Conrad's War.* Gr. 5–8. (Orig. British pub.
☆☆   1978.)
The tank and the model plane Conrad built allow his "leak" through time to World War II, where he becomes a pilot imprisoned in a German POW camp. Guardian Award for Children's Fiction, 1978; Boston Globe Horn Book Award for Fiction, 1980.
Crown, 1980, 120 pp., o.p.
(BL 76:883; CCBB 33:130; HB 56:171; Kirkus 48:364; SLJ Apr 1980 p. 107; Suth 3:113)

10-64   **DAWSON, Carley.** *Mr. Wicker's Window.* Gr. 5–7.
Chris travels from an antique shop into the Revolutionary War period, where he is sent on a dangerous mission to China. The sequels are *The Sign of the Seven Seas* (1954) and *Dragon's Run* (1955).
Illus. by Lynd Ward, Houghton, 1952, 272 pp., o.p.
(BL 49:160; CCBB 6:31; HB 29:53; LJ 78:68)

10-65   **DEXTER, Catherine.** *Mazemaker.* Gr. 5–8.
☆   After a spray-painted sidewalk maze takes Winnie Brown into the past to Crescent Ridge, she realizes she may be trapped there forever unless she can find the missing maze painter.
Morrow, 1989, 202 pp., o.p.
(BL 85:1820; CCBB 42:192; HB 56:504; Kirkus 57:461; SLJ May 1989 p. 103;VOYA 12:115, 13:14)

10-66   **DOTY, Jean Slaughter.** *Can I Get There by Candlelight?* Gr. 5–7.
Gail's horse, Candlelight, takes her through a long-unused gate to Babylon, a 19th-century estate, where she befriends a girl named Hilary.
Illus. by Ted Lewin, Macmillan, 1980, 111 pp., o.p.
(BL 76:980; HB 56:405; Kirkus 48:364; SLJ Mar 1980 p. 130)

10-67 **DOWNER, Ann.** *Hatching Magic.* Gr. 4–7.

✮ After Wycca, a 13th-century dragon, lays her egg in contemporary Cambridge, Massachusetts, she and her wizard, Gideon, ask a girl named Theodora to protect the newly hatched wyvern from the evil wizard Kobold.

Atheneum, 2003, 242 pp. (0-689-83400-4); Aladdin, 2004, pap., 256 pp. (0-689-87057-4)

(BL 99:1465; CCBB 57:11; HB 79:454; HBG 14:365; Kirkus 71:675; SLJ Aug 2003 p. 158)

10-68 **DUKTHAS, Ann.** *The Prince Lost to Time.* **(Nicholas Segalla Time-Travel Mystery series, bk. 2).** Gr. 10 up.

Time traveler Nicholas Segalla finds a letter written by Marie Antoinette suggesting that her son and heir to the French throne, Louis Charles, survived the Revolution. This book is the sequel to *A Time for the Death of a King* (1994) and is followed by *The Time of Murder at Mayerling* (1996) and *In the Time of the Poisoned Queen* (1998).

St. Martin's, 1995, 240 pp. (0-312-13592-0), 1996, pap. (0-312-95843-9)

(BL 92:536, 541; Kirkus 63:1381; LJ Nov 1, 1995 p. 109)

10-69 **DUNLOP, Eileen (Rhona).** *Elizabeth, Elizabeth.* Gr. 6–9. (Orig. British pub.

✮ 1975, entitled *Robinsheugh*.)

On a lonely visit to her aunt at the Melville manor house, Elizabeth escapes through an old looking glass into the 18th century, but she soon fears for her life.

Illus. by Peter Farmer, Holt, 1977, 185 pp., o.p.

(BL 73:1349; CCBB 30:174; HB 53:314; SLJ May 1977 p. 67; Suth 2:131; TLS 1975 p. 733)

10-70 **DUNLOP, Eileen (Rhona).** *The Maze Stone.* Gr. 6–10. (Orig. British pub.

✮ 1982.)

After Fanny's suspicions about their new drama teacher are aroused by the unusual pendant he wears, she must take quick action to save her sister from a terrifying fate.

Coward, 1983, 159 pp., o.p.

(BL 80:337, 356; CCBB 37:85; Kirkus 51:J173; SLJ Dec 1983 p. 84; TLS 1982 p. 1302; VOYA 7:29)

10-71 **DUNLOP, Eileen (Rhona).** *The Valley of Deer.* Gr. 5–8. (Orig. British pub.

✮ 1989.)

A crystal charm once owned by a deformed 18th-century herbal healer allows Anne Farrar glimpses into the past of the rural Scottish town where her archaeologist parents are excavating a burial mound.

Holiday, 1989, 139 pp., o.p.

(BL 86:456; CCBB 43:54; HB 66:201; HBG 1:86; Kirkus 57:1473; SLJ Jan 1990 103; TLS 1989 p. 560)

10-72 **DUNLOP, Eileen (Rhona).** *Webster's Leap.* Gr. 5–7.

Brother and sister Tad and Jill become involved in the lives of a 16th-century family that once owned their father's Scottish castle.

Holiday, 1995, 168 pp. (0-8234-1193-1)

(BL 92:313; HB 72:205; HBG 7:72; SLJ Oct 1995 p. 133)

10-73 EAGAR, Frances. *Time Tangle.* Gr. 5–7.
Beth spends a lonely Christmas at boarding school until she meets a boy from the 16th century who involves her in a plot to save a hidden cleric.
Nelson, 1977, 172 pp., o.p.
(CCBB 31:45; Kirkus 45:539; SLJ Oct 1977 p. 88)

EAGER, Edward (McMaken). *Time Garden.*
See discussion of *Knight's Castle* in Chapter 7, High Fantasy: Travel to Other Worlds.

10-74 EISENBERG, Lawrence B(enjamin). *The Villa of the Ferromonte.* Gr. 10 up.
While visiting his elderly Aunts Elizabeth and Amy in their run-down Manhattan apartment, Norman Dickens realizes that both he and they can travel into the past.
Simon, 1974, 191 pp., o.p.
(BL 71:22, 34; Kirkus 42:443; LJ 99:1847)

10-75 ENZENSBERGER, Hans Magnus. *Lost in Time.* Gr. 6–9. (Orig. German pub. 1998.)
Various paintings, photographs, television, and movie scenes draw Robert, 15, back through time to Australia in 1946, Russia in 1956, Germany in 1930, and Strasbourg in 1638.
Holt, 2000, 344 pp. (0-8050-6571-7)
(BL 97:634; HBG 12:83; Kirkus 68:1483; SLJ Dec 2000 p. 143; VOYA 23:432)

10-76 ETCHEMENDY, Nancy. *The Power of Un.* Gr. 4–8.
✶ A mysterious old man who "smells like lightning" hands Gib Finney a machine that can send him back in time, and Gib attempts to rewind his life to change the events leading to his 6-year-old sister's accident. Anne Spencer Lindbergh Honor Book, 1999–2000.
Front Street/Cricket, 2000, 148 pp. (0-8126-2850-0); Scholastic, 2000, pap., 148 pp. (0-439-31331-7)
(BL 96:1665; CCBB 53:398; HBG 11:303; Kirkus 68:631; SLJ June 2000 p. 144; VOYA 23:124, 24:11)

10-77 EUBANK, Judith. *Crossover.* Gr. 10 up. (Orig. British pub. 1984.)
American graduate student Meredith Blake is distracted from her studies by ghostly sightings of the Victorian family who once lived in the 17th-century English manor house that is now her university dormitory.
Carroll & Graf, 1992, 224 pp., o.p.
(BL 88:907, 923; Kirkus 59:1436; LJ Dec 1991 p. 196)

EVARTS, Hal G. *Jay-Jay and the Peking Monster.*
See Chapter 8, Humorous Fantasy.

FARMER (Mockridge), Penelope. *A Castle of Bone.*
See Chapter 6, High Fantasy: Myth or Legend Fantasy.

10-78 **FARMER (Mockridge), Penelope.** *Charlotte Sometimes.* Gr. 5–7. (Orig.
✯✯ British pub. 1969.)
Charlotte Makepeace discovers that she has a double named Claire who slept in
the same boarding school bed in the year 1918, and that she and Claire can
exchange places in time. This is the sequel to *The Summer Birds* (1962, see
Chapter 9, Magic Adventure Fantasy) and *Emma in Winter* (1966, see below).
Illus. by Chris Connor, Harcourt, 1969, 192 pp., o.p.; Dell, rev. ed., 1987, pap.
(0-440-41261-7)
(BL 66:457; CCBB 23:158; HB 45:675, 60:223; Kirkus 37:1121; LJ 94:4604; Suth:120; TLS
1969 p. 1190, 1985 p. 348)

10-79 **FARMER (Mockridge), Penelope.** *Emma in Winter.* Gr. 5–7. (Orig. British
pub. 1966.)
Lonely Emma and Bobby find themselves sharing a dream in which they travel
so far back through time that they are in danger of not being able to return to
the real world. This is the sequel to *The Summer Birds* (1962, see Chapter 9,
Magic Adventure Fantasy) and is followed by *Charlotte Sometimes* (1969, see
above).
Illus. by James J. Spanfeller, Harcourt, 1966, 160 pp., o.p.
(BL 63:488:Kirkus 34:835; LJ 91:5747; TLS 1966 p. 1071)

10-80 **FAVOLE, Robert J.** *Through the Wormhole.* Gr. 5–9.
Kate and Michael, both 14, are sent back through time to colonial America to
save the life of one of Michael's ancestors, a free black cavalryman fighting
against the British.
Flywheel, 2001, 192 pp. (1-930826-00-1)
(BL 97:1278; Kirkus 69:52; SLJ April 2001 p. 140; VOYA 24:50)

FFORDE, Jasper. *The Eyre Affair.*
See Chapter 5, High Fantasy: Alternate Worlds or Histories.

10-81 **FINDON, JoAnne.** *When Night Eats the Moon.* Gr. 5–8. (Orig. pub. in
Canada.)
Visiting England from Canada while her parents decide whether to divorce,
Holly is drawn into the past to 600 B.C. Stonehenge, where she is celebrated as
the people's savior from Celtic invaders.
Red Deer, 1999, 176 pp. (0-88995-212-4)
(BL 96:2138; VOYA 23:125;)

10-82 **FINNEY, Jack (pseud. of Walter Branden Finney).** *About Time: Twelve
Stories.* Gr. 10 up. (Orig. pub. separately, 1950–1969.)
Twelve witty and romantic stories about time and time travel, including "Sec-
ond Change," "Of Missing Persons," and "I'm Scared."
Simon, 1986, pap., 224 pp., o.p.
(BL 83:34, 52, 83:777; Kirkus 54:1078; Kliatt 21:16)

10-83 **FINNEY, Jack (pseud. of Walter Branden Finney).** *Time and Again.*
✯ **(Simon Morley series, vol. 1).** Gr. 10 up.
Simon Morley agrees to move into the Dakota apartment building in Manhattan and travel back to the year 1882 as part of a U.S. government project, but
he balks at altering historical events after he falls in love with Julia, a 19th-cen-
tury girl. The sequel is *From Time to Time* (1995).

Simon, 1970, 399 pp., o.p.; Lightyear, 1995 (0-89968-403-3); Touchstone, 1995, pap. (0-684-80105-1)

(BL 67:36, 95, 654; HB 46:502; Kirkus 38:272, 473; LJ 95:3304, 3649)

10-84 FISHER, Leonard Everett. *Noonan: A Novel About Baseball, ESP, and Time Warps.* Gr. 6–9.
In 1896, pitcher Johnny Noonan is hit by a foul ball and sent a hundred years into the future, where his psychokinetic ability to control a baseball leads to stardom.
Doubleday, 1978, 125 pp., o.p.

(BL 74:1733; CCBB 32:60; Kirkus 46:749; SLJ May 1978 p. 87)

10-85 FLEISCHMAN, (Albert) Sid(ney). *The 13th Floor: A Ghost Story.* Gr.
✯ 3–6.
Bud and his older sister Liz are called back in time to colonial Boston to aid Abigail, an ancestor accused of witchcraft.
Illus. by Peter Sís, Greenwillow, 1995, 134 pp. (0-688-14216-8); Dell, 1997, pap., 134 pp. (0-440-41243-9)

(BL 92:314; CCBB 49:53; HB 71:741; HBG 7:61; Kirkus 63:1427; SLJ Oct 1995 p. 133)

10-86 FLINT, Eric. *1632.* Gr. 10 up.
✯ After the West Virginia community of Grantville is transported through time to 1632 Thuringia at the time of the Thirty Years' War, the residents begin the American Revolution nearly 150 years in advance. *1633* (2003; by Flint and David Weber) is the sequel, and *Ring of Fire* (2003) contains stories about the same characters.
Baen, 2000, 512 pp. (0-671-57849-9), 2001, pap., 597 pp. (0-671-39172-8)

(BL 96:887; Kirkus 67:1922; LJ Feb 15, 2000 p. 201; VOYA 23:197, 24:11)

10-87 FREEMAN, Barbara C(onstance). *The Other Face.* Gr. 5–8. (Orig. British pub. 1975.)
A miniature china cottage transports Betony 150 years into the past, where she becomes involved in an ancestor's romance.
Illus. by the author, Dutton, 1976, 151 pp., o.p.

(BL 73:832; Kirkus 44:1169; SLJ Jan 1977 p. 91; TLS 1975 p. 733)

FREEMAN, Barbara C(onstance). *A Pocket of Silence.*
See Chapter 4, Ghost Fantasy.

10-88 FRENCH, Jackie. *Somewhere Around the Corner.* Gr. 5–8. (Orig. pub. in
✯ Australia.)
Running away from a violent demonstration in 1994 Sydney, Australia, Barbara rounds a corner and finds herself 60 years in the past, where she is taken in by a family living in a Depression-era shanty camp. Children's Book Council of Australia Book of the Year Honor Book, 1995.
Holt, 1995, 230 pp. (0-8050-3889-2)

(BL 91:1645; CCBB 48:343; HB 71:599; HBG 6:310; SLJ July 1995 p. 78; VOYA 18:218)

10-89 GABALDON, Diana. *Outlander: A Novel.* **(Outlander series, bk. 1).** Gr.
✯ 10 up.
Touching an ancient Scottish stone circle transports former battlefield nurse Claire Randall back through time from 1945 to 1743, where her medical

knowledge draws accusations of witchcraft. The sequels are *A Dragonfly in Amber* (1992), *Voyager* (1994), *Drums of Autumn* (1997), and *The Fiery Cross* (2002).

Delacorte, 1991, 640 pp. (0-385-30230-4); Dell, 1992, pap., 864 pp. (0-440-21256-1); Delta, 1998, pap., 640 pp. (0-385-31995-9)

(BL 87:2029; Kirkus 59:686; LJ July 1991 p. 134; VOYA 14:311)

10-90   GARCIA Y ROBERTSON, R(odrigo). *Knight Errant.* **(War of the Roses series, bk. 1).** Gr. 11 up.
Robyn Stafford, an American hiking near the Welsh border of England, falls in love with a young knight who says he's from the 15th century, and she convinces a local witches' coven to send her back through time to find him again. The sequels are *Lady Robyn* (2003) and *White Rose* (2004).

Tor, 2001, 480 pp. (0-312-86996-7); Forge, 2003, pap., 560 pp. (0-765-34491-2)

(BL 98:305; Kirkus 69:1314; VOYA 25:126)

GARD, Joyce (pseud. of Joyce Reeves). *Talargain.*
See Chapter 6, High Fantasy: Myth or Legend Fantasy.

10-91   GARNER, Alan. *The Red Shift.* Gr. 8 up. (Orig. British pub. 1973.)
★   The lives of three British teenagers from different time periods—the Roman occupation, the Civil War, and contemporary Britain—are linked by an ancient stone ax.

Macmillan, 1973, 197 pp., o.p.; Collins Voyager, new ed., 2002, pap., 192 pp. (0-00712-786-3)

(BL 70:801; CCBB 27:142; HB 49:580; Kirkus 41:989; TLS 1973 p. 1112)

GARNER, Alan. *The Weirdstone of Brisingamen.*
See discussion of *The Moon of Gomrath* in Chapter 6, High Fantasy: Myth or Legend Fantasy.

GATES, Susan P. *The Burnhope Wheel.*
See Chapter 4, Ghost Fantasy.

10-92   GERROLD, David. *The Man Who Folded Himself.* Gr. 10 up.
Danny Eakins's timebelt shows him numerous versions of himself, occupying many different timelines.

Random, 1973, 148 pp., o.p.; Amereon, 1976 (repr. of 1973 ed.), LB (0-88411-191-1)

(BL 69:835; Kirkus 40:1445; LJ 98:436; TLS 1974 p. 163)

GIFALDI, David. *Gregory, Maw and the Mean One.*
See Chapter 8, Humorous Fantasy.

10-93   GOLDSTEIN, Lisa. *The Dream Years.* Gr. 10 up.
★   A young Parisian surrealist painter living during the 1920s is transported in his dreams to the future of 1968, where he falls in love with a student named Solange and becomes involved in the student protests.

Bantam, 1985, 181 pp., 1989, pap., o.p.

(BL 81:1637; Kirkus 53:678; Kliatt 20:24; LJ Aug 1985 p. 120; SLJ Dec 1985 p. 110)

10-94 GOODWIN, Marie D. *Where the Towers Pierce the Sky.* Gr. 6–9.
Lizzie Patterson is drawn from South Bend, Indiana, to 15th-century France by an astrologer attempting to see Jeanne d'Arc's future.
Macmillan, 1989, 192 pp., o.p.
(BL 86:742; CCBB 43:57; HBG 1:82; Kirkus 57:1403; SLJ Nov 1989 p. 126; VOYA 12:289)

GRANT, Vicki. *The Puppet Wrangler.*
See Chapter 9, Magic Adventure Fantasy.

10-95 GRAY, Luli. *Timespinners.* Gr. 4–7.
Twins Allie and Thaddeus, or Fig, Newton are transported through time from New York City to France in 1913 and then to prehistoric times, where a Neanderthal shaman-in-training helps them return home.
Houghton, 2003, 160 pp. (0-618-16412-X)
(BL 99:1197; HBG 14:366; Kirkus 71:384; SLJ April 2003 p. 162)

10-96 GREAVES, Margaret. *Cat's Magic.* Gr. 5–7. (Orig. British pub. 1980.)
An Egyptian cat goddess rewards Louise for rescuing a drowning kitten by enabling her to travel through time to visit ancient Egypt and Victorian England.
Harper, 1981, 183 pp., o.p.
(BL 77:1028; CCBB 35:9; Kirkus 49:633; SLJ Apr 1981 p. 127; TLS 1980 p. 360; VOYA 3:38)

10-97 GREER, Gerry, and RUDDICK, Bob. *Max and Me and the Time*
★ *Machine.* Gr. 4–7.
Max's doubts about his friend Steve's time machine are dispelled after they find themselves in medieval England—Steve within the body of a famous knight and Max transformed into his horse. The sequel is *Max and Me and the Wild West* (1988).
Harcourt, 1983, 140 pp., o.p.
(BL 79:1465; CCBB 37:28; HB 59:443; Kirkus 51:660; SLJ May 1983 pp. 32, 71; VOYA 6:214)

10-98 GRIFFIN, Peni R(ae). *A Dig in Time.* Gr. 4–7.
Artifacts found by Nan and Tim in their grandmother's San Antonio home allow them to travel into the past to witness their family history firsthand.
Macmillan, 1991, 208 pp. (0-689-50525-6); Puffin, 1992, pap. (0-14-036001-8)
(BL 87:1965; CCBB 45:38; HBG 2:270; Kirkus 59:471; SLJ June 1991 p. 104; VOYA 14:180)

10-99 GRIFFIN, Peni R(ae). *Switching Well.* Gr. 5–9.
★ A wishing well enables 12-year-olds Ada and Amber to trade their 1891 and 1991 lives in San Antonio, Texas, but both girls soon long for their own familiar worlds.
Macmillan, 1993, 224 pp. (0-689-50581-7); Penguin, 1994, pap. (0-14-036910-4)
(BL 89:1812; CCBB 46:345; HBG 4:309; Kirkus 61:529; SLJ June 1993 p. 106; VOYA 16:164; 17:7)

10-100 GROSSER, Morton. *The Snake Horn.* Gr. 5–7.
When Danny blows his antique horn, a 17th-century music master appears and teaches the boy's father music that makes him famous.

Illus. by David Stone, Atheneum, 1973, 131 pp., o.p.
(BL 70:50; CCBB 26:171; Kirkus 41:114; LJ 98:1387; Suth 2:193)

10-101 GUTMAN, Dan. *Honus and Me: A Baseball Card Adventure.* **(Baseball**
⚝ **Card Adventures, bk. 1).** Gr. 4–6.
Joe finds a rare Honus Wagner baseball card that has magical powers, sending
him back in time to the 1909 World Series. The sequels are *Jackie and Me*
(1999), *Babe and Me* (2000), *Shoeless Joe and Me* (2002), and *Mickey and Me*
(2003).
Avon, 1997, 140 pp. (0-380-97350-2); HarperTrophy, 2003, pap., 144 pp. (0-
380-78878-0)
(BL 93:1428; HBG 8:301; Kirkus 65:223; SLJ June 1997 p. 117)

10-102 GUTMAN, Dan. *Qwerty Stevens, Stuck in Time with Benjamin Franklin.*
(Qwerty Stevens, Back in Time series, bk. 2). Gr. 4–7.
After 7th-grader Qwerty Stevens accidentally brings Benjamin Franklin into
the 21st century, Qwerty and his friend Joey follow Franklin back to 18th-cen-
tury Philadelphia where the Declaration of Independence is about to be
approved. The first book in the series is *The Edison Mystery: Qwerty Stevens,
Back in Time* (2001).
Simon, 2002, 183 pp. (0-689-84553-7); Aladdin, 2005, pap., 192 pp. (0-689-
87884-2)
(BL 99:235; HBG 14:81; Kirkus 70:1130; SLJ Aug 2002 p. 188)

10-103 HAHN, Mary Downing. *The Doll in the Garden: A Ghost Story.* Gr. 4–7.
⚝ Ashley finds an old china doll buried in her landlady's rose garden and follows
a ghostly cat through a hedge 80 years into the past, where she meets the little
girl from whom the doll was stolen.
Houghton, 1989, 128 pp. (0-89919-848-1); Avon, 1990, pap. (0-380-70865-5)
(BL 85:1296; CCBB 42:171; HB 65:370; Kirkus 57:546; SLJ May 1989 p. 109)

10-104 HAHN, Mary Downing. *Time for Andrew: A Ghost Story.* Gr. 4–7.
⚝ While staying in his great-aunt's home, Drew trades places in time with a boy
from 1910, his great-great-uncle Andrew who does not have the advantage of
modern medicine to cure his fatal diphtheria.
Clarion, 1994, 167 pp. (0-395-66556-6); HarperTrophy, 1995, pap., 176 pp. (0-
380-72469-3)
(BL 90:1446; CCBB 47:259; HBG 5:310; Kirkus 62:396; SLJ May 1994 p. 114)

HAMILTON (Adoff), Virginia (Esther). *Sweet Whispers, Brother Rush.*
See Chapter 4, Ghost Fantasy.

HAMLETT, Christina. *The Enchanter.*
See Chapter 6, High Fantasy: Myth or Legend Fantasy.

10-105 HAMLEY, Dennis. *Pageants of Despair.* Gr. 6–8. (Orig. British pub. 1974.)
Giles helps the Pageant Master of a medieval English town fight off the devil's
influence on the annual miracle plays.
Phillips, 1974, 180 pp., o.p.
(BL 71:618; Kirkus 42:1065; SLJ Jan 1975 p. 54; TLS 1974 p. 717)

10-106 HANLON, Emily. *Circle Home.* Gr. 5–7.
A Stone Age girl named Mai finds herself in the 20th century, trapped inside the body of a 9-year-old girl who is recovering from a near-fatal automobile accident.
Bradbury, 1981, 237 pp., o.p.
(BL 78:706; CCBB 35:130; Kirkus 50:208; SLJ May 1982 p. 70; VOYA 5[Apr 1982]:39)

10-107 HAUTMAN, Pete. *Mr. Was.* Gr. 7–12.
After his father's alcoholic rage leads to his mother's death, Jack Lund escapes into the past through a door in his grandfather's Minnesota house to start a new life.
Simon, 1996, 216 pp. (0-689-81068-7), 1998, pap. (0-689-81914-5)
(BL 93:230, 1292; CCBB 50:98; HBG 8:80; Kirkus 64:1235; SLJ Oct 1996 p. 147)

HAYNES, Betsy. *The Ghost of the Gravestone Hearth.*
See Chapter 4, Ghost Fantasy.

10-108 HENEGHAN, James. *The Grave.* Gr. 6–9. (Orig. Canadian pub. 2000.)
✯ Tough 13-year-old foster child Tom Mullen falls through a hole in a Liverpool construction site into 19th-century Ireland during the Potato Famine.
Farrar, 2000, 245 pp. (0-374-32765-3); Dell, 2002, pap., 245 pp. (0-440-22948-0)
(BL 97:434; CCBB 54:261; HB 76:754; HBG 12:84; Kirkus 68:1486; SLJ Nov 2000 p. 154; VOYA 23:359, 24:11)

10-109 HILDICK, E(dmund) W(allace). *The Case of the Dragon in Distress: A McGurk Fantasy.* (McGurk Fantasy series, bk. 1). Gr. 4–6.
Jack and the other five members of his McGurk Detective Agency are sent to England in the year 1175 to rescue knights held captive by the literally bloodthirsty Princess Melisande. The sequel is *The Case of the Weeping Witch* (1992), and both books are related to the author's non-fantasy series of McGurk Mysteries.
Macmillan, 1991, 153 pp. (0-02-743931-3)
(BL 87:1716; CCBB 44:264; HBG 2:266; SLJ June 1991 p. 106)

HOFFMAN, Mary. *Stravaganza: City of Masks.*
See Chapter 7, High Fantasy: Travel to Other Worlds.

10-110 HOPPE, Joanne. *Dream Spinner.* Gr. 6–10.
After Mary, 15, her father, and her new stepfamily move into an old Victorian house, she realizes that in her dreams she can visit this house at the turn of the century, becoming a girl called Christabel whose uncle has fallen in love with her.
Morrow, 1992, 240 pp. (0-688-08559-8)
(BL 89:321; CCBB 46:74; HB 69:92; HBG 4:81; Kirkus 60:1309; SLJ Dec 1992 p. 277)

10-111 HOUGHTON, Eric. *Steps Out of Time.* Gr. 5–8.
✯ New in town and lonely, Jonathan is able to step through the dense fog into another time, where he lives in the same house but seems to have a sister who calls him Peter.
Lothrop, 1980, 128 pp., o.p.
(BL 77:405; CCBB 34:12; SLJ Sept 1980 p. 72; Suth 2:119; VOYA 3[Feb 1981]:38)

10-112 HURMENCE, Belinda. *A Girl Called Boy.* Gr. 6–8.

✭ Blanch Overtha Yoncey learns about the hardships of slavery firsthand when she goes back through time to become one of her ancestors, a slave girl named Overtha, in North Carolina during the 1850s.
Houghton, 1982, 180 pp., o.p.
(BL 78:1445; CCBB 36:12; Kirkus 50:490; HB 58:404; SLJ May 1982 p. 63)

10-113 INGOLD, Jeanette. *The Window.* Gr. 7–10.

✭ Coping with her grief after the car accident that blinded her and killed her mother, Mandy discovers that she can "see" her family's unhappy past through a window in her great-aunt's Texas home.
Harcourt, 1996, 181 pp. (0-15-201265-6), 1996, pap. (0-15-201264-8)
(BL 93:490, 1292; CCBB 50:174; HBG 8:80; Kirkus 64:1236; SLJ Dec 1996 p. 136; VOYA 19:270)

10-114 INGRAM, Tom (Thomas Henry). *The Night Rider.* Gr. 5–8.

A cursed golden bracelet lures Laura to pre-Roman Britain where she becomes a girl called Merta, desperate to find the matching necklace and destroy it before the curse kills her.
Bradbury, 1975, 176 pp., o.p.
(BL 71:1128; CCBB 29:47; Kirkus 43:521; SLJ Sept 1975 p. 105)

10-115 JAMES, J. Alison. *Sing for a Gentle Rain.* Gr. 7–10.

Spring Rain, a 13th-century Anasazi Indian girl, fears for her tribe's survival during an endless drought, and hopes that the unexpected arrival of James, a 20th-century teenager, is a good omen for her cliff-dwelling community.
Macmillan, 1990, 211 pp., o.p.
(BL 87:1476; CCBB 44:88; HB 67:74; HBG 2:83; Kirkus 58:1456; SLJ Jan 1991 p. 110; VOYA 13:298)

JONES, Diana Wynne. *Aunt Maria.*
See Chapter 12, Witchcraft and Sorcery Fantasy.

10-116 JONES, Diana Wynne. *Charmed Life.* **(Chrestomanci series, bk. 1).** Gr.

✭ 5–8. (Orig. British pub. 1977.)
After Cat and Gwen Chant are adopted by the mysterious Chrestomanci, Gwen uses witchcraft to change places with a 20th-century girl, leaving Cat to fend for himself. Carnegie Medal Commended Book, 1977; Guardian Award for Children's Fiction, 1978. The prequel is *The Lives of Christopher Chant* (1988; see Chapter 7, High Fantasy: Travel to Other Worlds). *The Magicians of Caprona* (1980; see Chapter 12, Witchcraft and Sorcery Fantasy) and *Witch Week* (1982; see Chapter 12, Witchcraft and Sorcery Fantasy) are related works, and there are short stories about Chrestomanci in *Warlock at the Wheel* (1985; see Chapter 12, Witchcraft and Sorcery Fantasy), *Dragons and Dreams* (ed. by Jane Yolen, Harper, 1986; see Chapter 9, Magic Adventure Fantasy), and *Mixed Magics: Four Tales of Chrestomanci* (2000, 2001; see Chapter 12, Witchcraft and Sorcery Fantasy). The four Chrestomanci novels have been reissued as *The Chronicles of Chrestomanci* (Greenwillow, 2001). Vol. 1 (0-06-447268-X) contains *Charmed Life* and *The Lives of Christopher Chant*. Vol. 2 (0-06-447269-8) contains *Witch Week* and *The Magicians of Caprona*.

Greenwillow, 1978, 217 pp., o.p.; Beechtree, 1998, pap. (0-688-15546-4); Greenwillow, 2001, 261 pp. (0-06-029876-6), 2001, pap. (0-688-15546-4)

(BL 74:1009; CCBB 31:113; HB 54:396; HBG 12:308; Kirkus 46:177; SLJ Apr 1978 p. 94; Suth 2:45; TLS 1977 p. 348)

JONES, Diana Wynne. *A Tale of Time City.*
See Chapter 7, High Fantasy: Travel to Other Worlds.

10-117 JONES, Diana Wynne. *The Time of the Ghost.* Gr. 6–9. (Orig. British pub. 1981.)
Sally Melford, one of four unhappy sisters whose parents run a boys' boarding school, believes she is a ghost enchanted by an evil goddess controlled by the black magic of one of her sisters.
Greenwillow, 1996, 2002, 248 pp. (0-06-029887-1), 2002, pap., 304 pp. (0-06-447354-6)

(BL 92:1894; CCBB 50:65; HB 72:736; HBG 8:68, 14:96; Kirkus 64:969; SLJ Nov 1996 p. 123; VOYA 20:42)

10-118 JORDAN, Sherryl. *The Juniper Game.* Gr. 7–10. (Orig. New Zealand pub. 1991.)
When Dylan agreed to take part in a telepathic experiment with Juniper, he had no idea she would take him back in time to the 15th century to befriend a young woman accused of witchcraft.
Scholastic, 1991, 240 pp. (0-5904-4728-9)

(BL 88:617; HBG 3:79; Kirkus 59:1011; SLJ Oct 1991, p. 145; VOYA 14:313)

10-119 JORDAN, Sherryl. *A Time of Darkness.* Gr. 7 up. (Orig. New Zealand pub. 1990.)
Rocco's nightmares of life in a cave plagued by wolf attacks become reality when he finds himself in a primitive world struggling to be accepted by a cave-dwelling clan.
Scholastic, 1990, 224 pp. (0-590-43363-6), 1992, pap. (0-590-43362-8)

(BL 87:734; HBG 2:85; Kirkus 58:1251; SLJ Jan 1991 p. 110; VOYA 13:298, 14:13)

10-120 JUNG, Reinhardt. *Dreaming in Black and White.* Gr. 5–8. (Orig. German
☆   pub. 1996.)
The disabled narrator travels back through time to 1930s Nazi Germany, where he becomes a boy named Hannes whose teacher threatens him and whose father betrays him for being a "cripple," one of those sentenced to the "elimination of lives not worth living."
Trans. by Anthea Bell, Fogelman, 2003, 112 pp. (0-8037-2811-5); Egmont, 2000, pap. (0-7497-4157-0)

(BL 99:1665; HB 79:612; HBG 15:96; Kirkus 71:805; SLJ Aug 2003 p. 161)

10-121 KASSIRER, Norma. *Magic Elizabeth.* Gr. 4–6.
After Sally's return from the dream-world of a painting depicting one of her ancestors, she searches for Elizabeth, the doll shown in the painting.
Illus. by Joe Krush, Viking, 1966, 173 pp., o.p.

(CCBB 20:44; Kirkus 34:304; LJ 91:3535)

10-122 KATZ, Welwyn Wilton. *Time Ghost.* Gr. 5–8. (Orig. Canadian pub. 1994.)
✯ The threat of ecological disaster takes Sarah, her friend Dani, and Sarah's grandmother, Gwyneth Green, back through time from the mid-21st-century North Pole to 1993, to relive an episode in her activist grandmother's life.
McElderry, 1995, 171 pp. (0-689-80027-4); Groundwood, 2002, pap., 172 pp. (0-88899-275-0)
(BL 91:1573; CCBB 48:312; HBG 6:299; SLJ May 1995 p. 109; VOYA 18:172)

10-123 KENNEMORE, Tim. *Changing Times.* Gr. 7–10. (Orig. British pub. 1984.)
✯ When a 24-hour alarm clock purchased in a junk shop propels Victoria back into her own past—to the ages of 14, 8, and 15 months—she begins to understand the roots of her parents' miserable marriage.
Faber, 1984, 149 pp., o.p.
(BL 81:436, 449; CCBB 38:110; HB 61:58; SLJ Sept 1984 p. 129; Suth 3:229; TLS Nov 1984 p. 1383)

10-124 KEY, Alexander (Hill). *The Sword of Aradel.* Gr. 5–7.
Brian and Merra escape from medieval England into 20th-century Manhattan, searching for the magic sword of Aradel.
Westminster, 1977, 144 pp., o.p.
(BL 73:1728; CCBB 31:35; SLJ Sept 1977 p. 146)

10-125 KIPLING, (Joseph) Rudyard. *Puck of Pook's Hill.* Gr. 5–8. (Orig. British
✯ pub. 1906.)
Puck, the last of the English fairies, takes Don and Una into the past to meet well-known figures from England's history. The sequel is *Rewards and Fairies* (1910; 2001).
Illus. by Arthur Rackham, Doubleday, 1906, 1946, 275 pp., o.p.; Scribners, 1906, 1925, 305 pp., o.p.; Kessinger, 2004, 588 pp. (entitled *Puck of Pook's Hill and Rewards and Fairies*) (1-41791-711-3)
(BL 2:216; HB 61:84; LJ 32:260; TLS 1906 p. 536)

10-126 KITTLEMAN, Laurence R. *Canyons Beyond the Sky.* Gr. 6–8.
While visiting his archaeologist father on a dig, Evan Ferguson falls off a cliff and awakens 5,000 years in the past, where he is befriended by a Native American boy and his people.
Atheneum, 1985, 212 pp., o.p.
(BL 82:810; CCBB 39:111; SLJ Nov 1985 p. 86)

10-127 KOSITSKY, Lynn. *A Question of Will.* Gr. 6–9. (Orig. Canadian pub. 2000.)
On a field trip with her Shakespeare class to London's Globe Theatre, Perin Willoughby is pulled back through time to the 16th century, where she becomes Will Shakespeare's apprentice.
Roussan, 2001, pap., 141 pp. (1-896184-66-9)
(Kliatt Sep 2001 p. 24; SLJ Nov 2001 p. 160; VOYA 24:291)

10-128 KRETZER-MALVEHY, Terry. *Passage to Little Bighorn.* Gr. 6–12.
A mystical blackbird takes 15-year-old Dakota Miles into the past, where he is kidnapped by his own Lakota ancestors, held captive at Sitting Bull's camp, and takes part in the Battle of Little Bighorn.
Northland, 1999, pap., 232 pp. (0-87358-713-8)
(BL 95:1689; HBG 10:304; Kliatt May 1999 p. 26; SLJ June 1999 p. 132; VOYA 22:270)

10-129 LAHEY, Michael. *Quest for Apollo.* Gr. 7–12.
Dell, an American tourist, travels into the past to ancient Rome with the poet Virgil, searching for the trapped spirit of Apollo, whose freedom can prevent the world's destruction.
DAW, 1989, pap., 255 pp., o.p.
(LJ Aug 1989 p. 167; VOYA 12:371, 13:15)

10-130 LAMPLUGH, Lois. *Falcon's Tor.* Gr. 7–10. (Orig. British pub. 1984.)
Aiden Westleigh awakens after a riding accident to find that it is 1915 and he has become Arthur Morchand, son of a wealthy British family experiencing the difficulties of wartime life.
Andre Deutsch, 1984, 121 pp., o.p.
(BL 81:130; CCBB 38:9; SLJ Dec 1984 p. 91; TLS 1984 p. 335)

LAMPMAN, Evelyn Sibley. *Captain Apple's Ghost.*
See Chapter 4, Ghost Fantasy.

LANGTON, Jane (Gillson). *The Diamond in the Window.*
See discussion of *The Astonishing Stereoscope* in Chapter 9, Magic Adventure Fantasy.

10-131 LASKI, Marghanita. *The Victorian Chaise Longue.* Gr. 10 up.
✩ Twentieth-century Melanie Langdon falls asleep on her antique Victorian chaise longue and awakens in 1864, within the body of Milly Baines, a consumptive young mother of an illegitimate child.
Houghton, 1953, 1954, 119 pp., o.p.; Academy Chicago, 1984, pap., 119 pp., o.p.; Persephone, 1999, pap. (0-95347-804-1)
(BL 50:420; Kirkus 22:249; Kliatt 18:14; TLS 1953 p. 705)

10-132 LASKY (Knight), Kathryn. *Blood Secret.* Gr. 6–12.
Mute since her mother's abandonment, 14-year-old Jerry finds a haven in New Mexico with her Great-Aunt Constanza, where she comes across a trunk filled with items that bring on visions of her family's past as persecuted medieval Spanish Jews forced to convert, and to flee Inquisition Spain to the New World.
HarperCollins, 2004, 256 pp. (0-06-000065-1)
(CCBB 58:84; Kirkus 72:689; Kliatt July 2004 p. 8; SLJ Aug 2004 p. 124; VOYA 27:316)

10-133 LASKY (Knight), Kathryn. *Home Free.* Gr. 7 up.
An eagle takes 15-year-old Sam and his supposedly autistic friend Lucy into the past to the time before four Massachusetts towns were abandoned and flooded to create the Quabbin Reservoir, in this story about conservation of wilderness areas and endangered species.
Macmillan, 1985, 244 pp., o.p.
(BL 82:751, 758; CCBB 39:112; Kirkus 53:1198; SLJ Mar 1986, p. 176; VOYA 9:145)

LAWRENCE, Louise (pseud. of Elizabeth Rhoda Holden). *Sing and Scatter Daisies.*
See Chapter 4, Ghost Fantasy.

10-134 LAWSON, John S(hults). *The Spring Rider.* Gr. 5–8.
✶ Jacob and his sister Gray meet the ghost of a Union soldier whose bugle call brings a Civil War battle to life once again. Boston Globe Horn Book Award, 1968.
Crowell, 1968, 147 pp., o.p.; HarperCollins, 1990, 160 pp., o.p.
(BL 65:254; HB 44:564; Kirkus 36:699; Suth:240)

10-135 LEE, Robert C. *Once upon Another Time.* Gr. 7–9.
After a car accident propels Bob Crawford back through time to 1942 when he was 15, he dates the girl he'd once been too shy to approach and draws attention from the military with his knowledge of the future.
Nelson, 1977, 160 pp., o.p.
(CCBB 31:35; Kirkus 45:436; SLJ Mar 1977, p. 152)

10-136 LEE, Robert C. *Timequake.* Gr. 6–8.
Caught in a "timequake" while on a canoe trip, Randy and his cousin Morgan are thrown forward in time to the year 2027. They discover a United States run by state police, where rationed food, computer-designated death, and cannibalism are all part of daily life.
Westminster, 1982, 151 pp., o.p.
(BL 79:907; CCBB 36:128; SLJ Feb 1983 p. 79; VOYA 6:148)

10-137 L'ENGLE, Madeleine. *An Acceptable Time.* Gr. 7–10.
While visiting her grandparents, Dr. and Dr. Murry, in rural Connecticut, Polly O'Keefe suddenly finds herself in a prehistoric time where she is mistaken for a goddess by two warring tribes. This is the sequel to L'Engle's non-fantasy mystery stories *The Arm of the Starfish* (1965), *Dragons in the Waters* (1976), and *A House Like a Lotus* (1984). Polly is the daughter of Meg Murry and Calvin O'Keefe from L'Engle's science fiction books *A Wrinkle in Time* (1962), *A Wind in the Door* (1973), *A Swiftly Tilting Planet* (1978), and *Many Waters* (1986, see below).
Farrar, 1989, 342 pp., o.p.; Dell, 1990, pap. (0-440-20814-9)
(BL 86:902, 918; CCBB 43:87; HBG 1:84; Kirkus 57:1672; SLJ Jan 1990 p. 120; VOYA 13:11, 38)

10-138 L'ENGLE, Madeleine. *Many Waters.* Gr. 6–10.
Twins Sandy and Dennys Murry are stranded in Biblical times, where they become involved in a struggle surrounding Noah and his ark. This is the sequel to *A Wrinkle in Time* (1962), *A Wind in the Door* (1973), and *A Swiftly Tilting Planet* (1978), three "science fantasies" that tend more toward science fiction than fantasy. *A Wrinkle in Time* was the John Newbery Medal winner in 1962.
Farrar, 1986, 310 pp. (0-374-34796-4); Laurel Leaf, 1998, pap., 336 pp. (0-440-22770-4)
(BL 82:1633, 1636, 84:1248; CCBB 40:54; Kirkus 54:1374; SLJ Nov 1986 p. 104; VOYA 9:238)

10-139 LEVIN, Betty (Lowenthal). *Mercy's Mill.* Gr. 6–9.
After her mother and stepfather move to the country to renovate an old mill, Sarah meets a boy named Jethro who was a slave before the Civil War and is searching for his friend Mercy, the daughter of a woman accused of witchcraft in the 1600s.

Greenwillow, 1992, 256 pp. (0-688-11122-X)

(BL 89:670; CCBB 46:182; HB 69:92; HBG 4:72; Kirkus 60:1064; SLJ Dec 1992 p. 278)

10-140 LEVIN, Betty (Lowenthal). *The Sword of Cúlann.* Gr. 6–9.
Claudia and Evan are transported from coastal Maine to Iron Age Ireland, where they are drawn into terrifying mythic battles. The sequels are *A Griffon's Nest* (1975) and *The Forespoken* (1976).
Macmillan, 1973, 288 pp., o.p.

(Kirkus 41:1212; LJ 98:3156)

10-141 LEVY, Elizabeth. *Running Out of Magic with Houdini.* Gr. 4–6.
Three young joggers are swept back through time by a mysterious fog to 1912, where they help save Harry Houdini's life. This is the sequel to *Running Out of Time* (1980), in which the fog takes them back to ancient Rome.
Illus. by Blanche Sims and Jenny Rutherford, Knopf, 1981, 121 pp., o.p.

(BL 78:390; SLJ Dec 1981 p. 86)

10-142 LEWIS, Hilda (Winifred). *The Ship That Flew.* Gr. 5–7. (Orig. British pub. 1939.)
A dwarf-made toy Viking ship takes four modern children to Ancient Egypt, Norman Britain, and Sherwood Forest.
Illus. by Nora Levrin, Phillips, 1958, 246 pp., o.p.; Oxford University Press, new ed., 1998, 256 pp. (0-19-271768-5)

(BL 54:509; CCBB 11:121; HB 34:109; Kirkus 26:77; LJ 83:1286)

10-143 LINDBERGH, Anne Spencer. *The Hunky-Dory Dairy.* Gr. 4–6.
Zannah's old-fashioned horse and buggy dairy wagon enables her to enter a small town "removed" by witchcraft from the 19th to the 20th century, where she befriends a girl named Utopia Graybeal.
Illus. by Julie Brinkloe, Harcourt, 1986, 147 pp. (0-15-237449-3); Avon, 1987, pap. (0-380-70320-3)

(BL 82:1143; CCBB 40:12; Kirkus 54:865; SLJ Aug 1986 p. 95)

10-144 LINDBERGH, Anne Spencer. *Nick of Time.* Gr. 6–9.
Alison and her friend Jericho escape into the future world of 2094 after her mother threatens to remove her from the alternative school run by his parents.
Little, Brown, 1994, 204 pp. (0-316-52629-0)

(BL 90:1804; CCBB 47:225; HB 70:589; HBG 5:312; Kirkus 62:702; SLJ April 1994 p. 128; VOYA 17:38)

LINDBERGH, Anne Spencer. *The People in Pineapple Place.*
See Chapter 4, Ghost Fantasy.

10-145 LINDBERGH, Anne Spencer. *The Shadow on the Dial.* Gr. 5–7.
Marcus and Dawn find a coupon that promises to deliver their heart's desire, and use it to travel back and forth in time trying to fulfill their uncle's dream of becoming a flautist.
Harper, 1987, 160 pp., o.p.

(BL 83:1680; CCBB 40:191; HB 63:463; Kirkus 55:927; SLJ June–July 1987 p. 97; VOYA 10:90)

10-146 LINDBERGH, Anne Spencer. *Three Lives to Live.* Gr. 5–8.
✮ Resentful of her grandmother's easy acceptance of the mysterious arrival of her
"twin," Daisy, Garet discovers that Daisy has actually come from the past.
Little, Brown, 1992, 183 pp. (0-316-52628-2); Aladdin, 1995, pap., 192 pp. (0-
671-86732-6)
(BL 88:1523; CCBB 45:269; HBG 3:266; Kirkus 60:672; SLJ June 1992 p. 121)

10-147 LISSON, Deborah. *The Devil's Own.* Gr. 5–9. (Orig. Australian pub. 1990.)
Bored with cruising on her family's boat, 15-year-old Julie finds herself swept
back through time to the year 1629, where she becomes a shipwrecked passen-
ger struggling to survive.
Holiday, 1991, 169 pp. (0-8234-0871-X), 2000, pap. (0-7344-0128-0)
(BL 87:1956; CCBB 45:15; HBG 2:278; Kirkus 59:319; SLJ Apr 1991 p. 120)

10-148 LITTLE, Jane. *The Philosopher's Stone.* Gr. 4–6.
When a sorcerer named Nyvrem needs a rock from Stephen's collection to con-
vert copper into gold, he accidentally transports Stephen from Indiana to the
12th-century Castle Mordemagne.
Illus. by Robin Hall, Atheneum, 1971, 123 pp., o.p.
(BL 68:367; Kirkus 39:1121; LJ 96:2918)

10-149 LITTLE, Kimberley Griffiths. *The Last Snake Runner.* Gr. 6–9.
Fleeing into the New Mexico desert after his mother's death and his father's
remarriage, Kendall, 14, discovers that he is the last living member of the
Acoma Pueblo Snake clan and is transported back through time to 1598, where
he joins his ancestors' battle against the Spanish conquistadores. This is the
sequel to *Enchanted Runner* (Avon, 1999), which is not a fantasy.
Knopf, 2002, 201 pp. (0-375-81539-2); Laurel Leaf, 2004, 208 pp. (0-440-
23782-3)
(BL 98:1605; HBG 14:84; SLJ Aug 2002 p. 193; VOYA 25:195)

LIVELY, Penelope (Margaret Low). *The Driftway.*
See Chapter 4, Ghost Fantasy.

LIVELY, Penelope (Margaret Low). *The Ghost of Thomas Kempe.*
See Chapter 4, Ghost Fantasy.

10-150 LIVELY, Penelope (Margaret Low). *The House in Norham Gardens.* Gr.
✮ 6–9. (Orig. British pub. 1974.)
A New Guinean ceremonial shield brought home by Clare Mayfield's great-
grandfather has the power to transport Clare from present-day England to the
primitive jungles of New Guinea.
Dutton, 1974, 154 pp., o.p.; Egmont, 1994, pap. (0-7497-0790-9)
(BL 71:767; CCBB 28:96; HB 51:55; Kirkus 42:1161; LJ 99:3273; Suth 2:289; TLS 1974 p.
717)

LIVELY, Penelope (Margaret Low). *A Stitch in Time.*
See Chapter 4, Ghost Fantasy.

LIVELY, Penelope (Margaret Low). *The Whispering Knights.*
See Chapter 6, High Fantasy: Myth or Legend Fantasy.

10-151 LORING, Selden M(elville). *Mighty Magic: An Almost-True Story of Pirates and Indians.* Gr. 3–5.
Granny Matten gives Jack Hollis a magic Indian drum.
Illus. by Brinton (Cassaday) Turkle, Holiday, 1937, 1964, 126 pp., o.p.
(HB 13:151; Kirkus 32:738; LJ 62:564)

Lost Worlds, Unknown Horizons. **Ed. by Robert Silverberg.**
See Chapter 7, High Fantasy: Travel to Other Worlds.

10-152 LUNN, Janet (Louise Swoboda). *The Root Cellar.* Gr. 5–7. (Orig. Canadian
✶ pub. 1981.)
Orphaned Rose escapes from her adoptive relatives by hiding in an old root cellar, where she travels back in time to 1860 and helps a young woman search for her missing lover, a soldier in the American Civil War. Canadian Library Association Best Book of the Year for Children, 1982.
Macmillan, 1983, 256 pp., o.p.; Penguin, 1996, pap. (0-14-038036-1)
(BL 79:1402; HB 59:575; Kirkus 51:661; SLJ Sept 1983 p. 124)

LUNN, Janet (Louise Swoboda). *Twin Spell.*
See Chapter 4, Ghost Fantasy.

LYNCH, Patricia (Nora). *The Turf-Cutter's Donkey.*
See Chapter 9, Magic Adventure Fantasy.

10-153 LYON, George Ella. *Here and Then.* Gr. 5–8.
✶ Playing the role of nurse Eliza Hoskins in a Civil War reenactment, Abby begins hearing Eliza's thoughts and then goes back in time to experience the horrors of war.
Jackson/Orchard, 1994, 114 pp., o.p.
(BL 91:319; CCBB 48:93; HB 71:193; Kirkus 62:1411; VOYA 17:209)

10-154 LYTLE, Robert A. *Three Rivers Crossing.* Gr. 5–8.
The swift current of Story Creek pulls Walker back through time into his pioneer ancestors' early 19th-century Michigan village.
River Road, 2000, 161 pp. (0-938682-55-5)
(BL 96:1744; SLJ June 2000 p. 150)

10-155 MacAVOY, R(oberta) A(nn). *The Book of Kells.* Gr. 10 up.
✶ A professor of Irish history and an unemployed Canadian artist are pulled back through time by the spirals of a Celtic cross to 10th-century Ireland, where the survivors of a Viking raid are yearning for vengeance.
Bantam, 1985, pap., 352 pp., o.p.
(BL 82:195; LJ Aug 1985 p. 120; VOYA 8:364, 394)

10-156 MacDONALD, Reby Edmond. *The Ghosts of Austwick Manor.* Gr. 5–7.
✶ Hilary and Heather MacDonald travel into the past through an exact model of their old family homestead in England and uncover a family curse that threatens their brother's life.
Atheneum, 1982, 144 pp., o.p.; Aladdin, 1991, pap., 144 pp. (0-689-71533-1)
(BL 18:961; HB 58:406; SLJ May 1982 p. 85; VOYA 5[Aug 1982]:34)

10-157 MACE, Elisabeth. *The Ghost Diviners.* Gr. 5–7. (Orig. British pub. 1977.)
Martin's sister Jackie travels back in time to the turn of the century, where she
witnesses a murder on the future site of their house.
Nelson, 1977, 160 pp., o.p.
(BL 74:299; Kirkus 46:3; SLJ Sept 1977 p. 132; TLS 1977 p. 864)

10-158 MACE, Elisabeth. *The Rushton Inheritance.* Gr. 5–7. (Orig. British pub.
1978.)
Two generations of Rushtons search for treasure after Steve visits the 19th century.
Nelson, 1978, 173 pp., o.p.
(BL 75:1093; CCBB 32:179; HB 55:195; Kirkus 42:126; SLJ Dec 1978 p. 54; TLS 1978 p.
1083)

McGRAW, Eloise Jarvis. *A Really Weird Summer.*
See Chapter 4, Ghost Fantasy.

10-159 MacGRORY, Yvonne. *The Secret of the Ruby Ring.* **(Ruby Ring trilogy,
bk. 1).** Gr. 4–6. (Orig. Irish pub. 1991.)
Lucy's birthday ring has the power to grant two wishes, transforming her into a
nursery maid in an 1885 Irish castle. The sequels are *Martha and the Ruby
Ring* (pub. in Ireland), and *Emma and the Ruby Ring* (2002; Irish title: *The
Quest of the Ruby Ring*).
Illus. by Terry Myler, Milkweed, 1994, 192 pp. (0-915943-88-3)
(BL 90:1262; CCBB 47:294; SLJ Mar 1994 p. 223)

10-160 MacHALE, D. J. *Pendragon: The Never War.* **(Pendragon series, bk. 3).**
Gr. 5–8.
Time-traveling friends Bobby Pendragon and Spader use magical "flumes" to
visit Manhattan in 1937, where the universe is threatened by an evil shape-
shifter named SaintDane. This book is preceded by *The Merchant of Death*
(2002) and *The Lost City of Faar* (2003). The sequels are *The Reality Bug*
(2003) and *Black Water* (2004). The author's *Pendragon: A Guide to the Territories of Halla* (2005) is a related work.
Aladdin, 2003, pap., 352 pp. (0-7434-3733-0)
(Kliatt July 2003 p. 33; SLJ July 2003 p. 133; VOYA 26:325, 27:13)

10-161 McKEAN, Thomas. *The Secret of the Seven Willows.* **(Doors into Time
trilogy, bk. 1).** Gr. 4–6.
A magic ring enables Martha and Tad to save their ancestral home by traveling
into the past to the year 1771. The sequel is *The Haunted Circus* (1993).
Simon, 1991, 151 pp. (0-671-72997-7), 1993, pap. (0-671-86690-7)
(HBG 3:69; Kliatt Sept 1993 p. 20; SLJ Oct 1991 p. 125)

MacKELLAR, William. *Alfie and Me and the Ghost of Peter Stuyvesant.*
See Chapter 4, Ghost Fantasy.

MacKELLAR, William. *The Ghost in the Castle.*
See Chapter 4, Ghost Fantasy.

McKILLIP, Patricia A(nne). *The House on Parchment Street.*
See Chapter 4, Ghost Fantasy.

10-162 MacLEOD, Charlotte (Matilda Hughes). *The Curse of the Giant Hogweed.* Gr. 10 up.
Three Massachusetts horticultural professors suddenly find themselves in medieval Wales battling a plant that is taking over the countryside.
Doubleday, 1985, 1986, 168 pp., o.p.
(BL 81:823, 838; Kirkus 52:1170)

10-163 MAGUIRE, Gregory. *Lightning Time.* Gr. 6–8.
Daniel is distressed to learn of construction plans for the mountain where his grandmother lives and where magic occurs whenever lightning strikes. The sequel is *Lights on the Lake* (1981).
Farrar, 1978, 256 pp., o.p.
(BL 74:1680; HB 55:517; Kirkus 46:750; SLJ Sept 1978 p. 143)

10-164 MARZOLLO, Jean. *Halfway Down Paddy Lane.* Gr. 7–10.
Kate awakens to discover that she has gone back in time to 1850 and has become Kate O'Hara, daughter of Irish immigrants who work exhausting 12-hour days in the New England cotton mills.
Dial, 1981, 178 pp. (0-8037-3329-1); Scholastic, 1984, pap. (entitled *Out of Time, Into Love*), o.p.
(BL 77:1198; Kirkus 49:1165; SLJ May 1981 p. 76; VOYA 4:33)

10-165 MATHESON, Richard (Burton). *Bid Time Return.* **(Alternate title:**
✮ *Somewhere in Time*). Gr. 10 up.
Knowing that he is about to die, Richard Collier manages to pull himself back through time from 1971 to 1896 to search for a beautiful girl he once saw in an old photograph. World Fantasy Award, Best Novel, 1976.
Viking, 1975, 278 pp., o.p.; Ballantine, 1976, pap. (entitled *Somewhere in Time*) o.p.; Buccaneer, 1986, 280 pp., o.p.; (entitled *Somewhere in Time*) Tor, 1999, 320 pp. (0-312-86886-3)
(BL 71:1008; Kirkus 42:1320; LJ 100:410; SLJ May 1975 p. 36, Dec 1975 p. 32)

MAYNE, William (James Carter). *Earthfasts.*
See Chapter 6, High Fantasy: Myth or Legend Fantasy.

10-166 MAYNE, William (James Carter). *A Game of Dark.* Gr. 7–10. (Orig.
✮ British pub. 1971.)
Feeling increasingly helpless and guilty over his father's critical illness, Donald finds himself traveling into the past to a land menaced by a huge man-eating worm, or dragon, that only he can destroy. Phoenix Award Honor Book, 1991.
Dutton, 1971, 143 pp., o.p.
(BL 68:629; CCBB 25:61; HB 48:58; Kirkus 39:1022; LJ 97:2490; Suth:274; TLS 1971 p. 1319)

10-167 MAYNE, William (James Carter). *The Hill Road.* Gr. 5–7. (Orig. British
✮ pub. 1968, entitled *Over the Hills and Far Away*.)
Sara, Dolly, and Andrew ride their ponies back through time to post-Roman Britain, where Sara is mistaken for an accused witch.
Dutton, 1968, 144 pp., o.p.
(CCBB 22:161; HB 45:171; Kirkus 37:55; LJ 94:1783)

10-168 MAZER, Norma Fox. *Saturday, the Twelfth of October.* Gr. 6–9.

✶ Furious at her family, Zan Ford wishes so intensely to be elsewhere that she crosses the "river of time" into the Stone Age and is adopted by a tribe of cave dwellers.

Delacorte, 1975, 247 pp., o.p.

(BL 72:44; CCBB 29:67; Kirkus 43:1195; SLJ Nov 1975 p. 93; Suth 2:312)

10-169 MELLING, O(rla) R. *The Singing Stone.* Gr. 6–9. (Orig. Canadian pub. 1986.)

Eighteen-year-old Kay Warrick, abandoned at birth, visits Ireland in hopes of discovering her true identity. There, she is swept back through time to ancient Ireland where she meets an amnesiac young woman named Ahorne and learns that their destinies are intertwined.

Viking, 1987, 206 pp., o.p.

(BL 84:135, 150, 576; CCBB 41:71; SLJ Sept 1987 p. 198)

10-170 MILLER (Mandelkorn), Eugenia. *The Sign of the Salamander.* Gr. 5–7. (Orig. British pub. 1982.)

After he plunges through a French castle floor, 20th-century Henry Carter finds himself within the body of a 16th-century would-be apprentice to Leonardo da Vinci.

Holt, 1967, 233 pp., o.p.

(HB 43:464; Kirkus 35:600; LJ 92:2022)

MOLLOY, Michael. *The Time Witches.*

See Chapter 12, Witchcraft and Sorcery Fantasy.

10-171 MONTES, Marisa. *A Circle of Time.* Gr. 6–9.

In a coma after a car accident, Allison Blair, 14, travels from San Francisco in 1996 to 1906, attempting to change history and help her new friend Becky.

Harcourt, 2002, 261 pp. (0-15-202626-6)

(BL 98:1459; HBG 13:378; Kirkus 70:662; SLJ Aug 2002 p. 195; VOYA 25:130, 26:13)

10-172 MOONEY, Bel. *The Stove Haunting.* Gr. 5–8. (Orig. British pub. 1986.)

An old stove in the house Daniel's family is renovating calls him back to 1835, where he becomes a kitchen boy observing the conflict between privileged English landowners and rising agricultural unions.

Houghton, 1988, 125 pp., o.p.

(BL 83:1677; CCBB 41:185; Kirkus 56:281; SLJ May 1988 p. 99; TLS 1986 p. 898; VOYA 11:96)

10-173 MOORE, Katherine (Davis). *The Little Stolen Sweep.* Gr. 4–6. (Orig. British pub. 1982.)

Staying with relatives in his father's boyhood village, Daniel makes a series of journeys into the past, where he befriends a child chimney sweep named Jim and offers to change places in order to help the boy escape his cruel master.

Illus. by Pat Marriott, Allison, 1982, 121 pp., o.p.

(CCBB 36:131; SLJ Mar 1983 p. 181; TLS 1982 p. 345)

10-174 MORRIS, Gilbert. *The Dangerous Voyage.* **(Time Navigators series, bk. 1).** Gr. 4–6.

Danny and Dixie Fortune travel through time to join the Pilgrims' *Mayflower* voyage from London to the New World in this story emphasizing Christian values. The sequels are *Vanishing Clues* (1996) and *Race Against Time* (1997).
Bethany, 1995, pap., 159 pp. (1-55661-395-4)
(BL 92:835; SLJ Jan 1996 p. 110)

10-175 MOSKIN, Marietta D(unston). *Dream Lake.* Gr. 5–8.
Spending an unhappy summer with her great aunt, Hilary is drawn to a lake she has seen in nightmares, where she is transformed into Margaret Mooney, an 18th-century servant girl.
Atheneum, 1981, 156 pp., o.p.
(BL 77:1024, 1032, 81:1408; CCBB 35:51; Kirkus 49:635; SLJ Mar 1981 p. 149)

10-176 MOWRY, Jess. *Ghost Train.* Gr. 6–8.
When 13-year-old Remi, a recent Haitian immigrant to Oakland, California, realizes that the scene he watches from his window every night is the ghostly re-enactment of a murder, he and his friend Niya enter the past and try to change history.
Holt, 1996, 164 pp. (0-8050-4440-X)
(CCBB 50:145; HBG 8:72; SLJ Dec 1996 p. 139; VOYA 20:330)

MURPHY, Pat. *Points of Departure.*
See Chapter 3, Fantasy Collections.

NATHAN, Robert (Gruntal). *The Elixer.*
See Chapter 6, High Fantasy: Myth or Legend Fantasy.

10-177 NAYLOR, Phyllis Reynolds. *Shadows on the Wall.* **(The York trilogy, bk.**
✫ **1).** Gr. 6–10.
Visiting England with his parents, Dan Roberts makes two disturbing discoveries: that he may have a hereditary illness, Huntington's disease, and that he can see ghostly soldiers from Roman times. In *Faces in the Water* (1981, 2002), Dan and his family have returned home to Pennsylvania, where he continues to worry about his father's illness, and is unexpectedly sent back through time to 14th-century Britain. In *Footprints at the Window* (1981, 2002), Dan returns to medieval Britain, where he tries to help the gypsy girl Orlenda elude the Black Death.
Atheneum, 1980, 165 pp., o.p.; Aladdin, 2002, pap., 174 pp. (0-689-84961-3)
(BL 77:118; CCBB 34:115; HB 56:649; Kirkus 48:1465; SLJ Jan 1981 p. 71; VOYA 4:35)

10-178 NESBIT (Bland), E(dith). *The House of Arden.* Gr. 5–7. (Orig. British pub. 1909; U.S. 1910.)
In the ruins of Arden Castle lives a magical creature called Mouldiwarp, with the power to send Edred and Elfrida into the past in search of lost Arden treasure. The sequel is *Harding's Luck.*
Illus. by H(arold) R. Millar, Coward, 1960, 262 pp., o.p.; illus. by Clarke Hutton, Dutton, 1968, 244 pp., o.p.; Puffin, 1986, pap. (0-14-035073-X); Books of Wonder, 1997, 258 pp. (0-929605-70-5)
(BL 57:32; HB 36:309; LJ 85:3224)

10-179 NESBIT (Bland), E(dith). *The Story of the Amulet.* Gr. 5–7. (Orig. British
☆　　pub. 1906, U.S. 1907.)
In this story, considered to be the first time-travel fantasy with child protagonists, Cyril, Robert, Anthea, and Jane make journeys to ancient Egypt, Babylon, and Rome with the help of their old friend, the Sand Fairy. This is the
sequel to *Five Children and It* (1902, see Chapter 9, Magic Adventure Fantasy)
and *The Phoenix and the Carpet* (1904).
Illus. by J. S. Goodall, Coward, 1949, 367 pp., o.p.; Looking Glass Lib., 1960,
319 pp., o.p.; illus. by H(arold) R. Millar, Puffin, 1996, pap., 304 pp. (0-14-
036752-7); Wildside, 2002, 256 pp. (1-592-24936-1)
(BL 3:206, 27:215, 46:146; CCBB 3:21)

10-180 NICHOLS, (Joanna) Ruth. *Song of the Pearl.* Gr. 7–10. (Orig. Canadian
pub. 1976.)
Margaret Redmond, a withdrawn and troubled young woman, dies in 1900 at
the age of 17 only to regain consciousness and health on a silent island where
she learns about her three previous lives: as the wife of an Elizabethan explorer, as an Indian slave girl, and as a young Sumerian prince.
Macmillan, 1976, 158 pp., o.p.
(CCBB 30:110; HB 53:59; Kirkus 44:740; SLJ Oct 1976 p. 120; VOYA 2:63)

NICHOLS, (Joanna) Ruth. *A Walk out of the World.*
See Chapter 7, High Fantasy: Travel to Other Worlds.

10-181 NIFFENEGGER, Audrey. *The Time Traveler's Wife.* Gr. 10 up.
Henry and Clare Detamble's secret is that Henry is unable to control his travels
through time and is frequently swept away from their Chicago home into the
past and into the future.
MacAdam/Cage, 2003, 518 pp. (1-931561-46-X); Harvest, 2004, pap., 560 pp.
(0-15-602943-X)
(BL 100:59; LJ Aug 2003 p. 134)

NIMMO, Jenny. *Charlie Bone and the Time Twister.*
See *Midnight for Charlie Bone* in Chapter 12, Witchcraft and Sorcery Fantasy.

10-182 NOLAN, Han. *If I Should Die Before I Wake.* Gr. 7–12.
Unconscious in an intensive-care unit following a motorcycle accident, neo-
Nazi follower Hilary Burke slips into the memory of her fellow patient, elderly
Chana Bergman, traveling through time to the Lodz ghetto and to Auschwitz.
Harcourt, 1994, 288 pp. (0-15-238040-X); Harcourt, 2003, pap., 320 pp. (0-15-
204679-8)
(BL 90:1436; CCBB 47:267; HBG 5:322; Kirkus 62:308; SLJ April 1994 p. 152; VOYA
17:88)

10-183 NORTH, Joan. *The Whirling Shapes.* Gr. 7–10. (Orig. pub. in England.)
Liz, 14, enters the past through a house that occasionally appears on the heath
outside her window, in order to save her cousin, aunt, and uncle, trapped in the
whirling fog.
Farrar, 1967, 183 pp., o.p.
(CCBB 21:82; Kirkus 35:1057; LJ 92:3202)

10-184 NORTON, Andre (pseud. of Alice Mary Norton). *Dragon Magic.* Gr. 5–7.
Each of four boys who complete a dragon puzzle is sent into a different time in the past.
Illus. by Robin Jacques, Crowell, 1972, 213 pp., o.p.
(BL 68:1004; CCBB 25:160; HB 48:373; Kirkus 40:485; LJ 97:2244)

10-185 NORTON, Andre (pseud. of Alice Mary Norton). *Lavender Green Magic.*
✶ Gr. 5–7.
A maze at their grandparents' home causes Holly Wade and her brother and sister to travel into the past and meet two witches, one good and one evil.
Illus. by Judith Gwyn Brown, Crowell, 1974, 241 pp., o.p.
(BL 71:101; HB 50:137; LJ 99:2275)

10-186 NORTON, Andre (pseud. of Alice Mary Norton). *Octagon Magic.* Gr. 5–7.
Lorrie enters a doll-sized replica of Octagon House and goes back in time to the era of the Civil War, where she takes part in the Underground Railroad rescue of escaped slaves.
Illus. by Mac Conner, World, 1967, 189 pp., o.p.
(Kirkus 35:610; LJ 92:2656; TLS 1968 p. 584)

10-187 NORTON, Andre (pseud. of Alice Mary Norton). *Red Hart Magic.* Gr. 5–7.
Stepsiblings Charles and Nan are drawn together by mutual dreams of an old English inn as they travel through history and learn to deal with problems in their own lives.
Illus. by Donna Diamond, Crowell, 1976, 179 pp., o.p.
(BL 73:610; CCBB 30:110; HB 53:160; Kirkus 44:974; SLJ Nov 1976 p. 61)

10-188 NORTON, Andre, and EDGHILL, Rosemary. *The Shadow of Albion.*
(Carolus Rex series, bk. 1). Gr. 10 up.
After a dying sorceress brings Sarah Cunningham from the 20th century to early 19th-century Regency England, the girl is told she is the Duchess of Roxbury and must make her way through London society. The sequel is *Leopard in Exile* (2002).
Tor, 1999, 352 pp. (0-312-86427-2), 2000, pap., 416 pp. (0-8125-4539-7)
(BL 95:1389; Kirkus 67:258)

NORTON, Mary (Pearson). *Bedknob and Broomstick.*
See Chapter 9, Magic Adventure Fantasy.

10-189 O'BRIEN, Judith. *Timeless Love.* Gr. 7–10.
An antique necklace and a wish send 16-year-old Sam back through time to Tudor England, where she helps cure the sickly young King Edward VI, brother of the future Queen Elizabeth, and falls in love with Sir Barnaby Fitzpatrick.
Simon, 2002, pap., 232 pp. (0-7434-1921-9)
(Kliatt May 2002 p. 28; SLJ Mar 2002 p. 236)

10-190 ORMONDROYD, Edward. *Time at the Top.* Gr. 4–6.
✶ Susan Shaw takes the elevator to the top floor of her apartment building and steps out into the world of 1881, where she helps two children search for lost treasure. The sequel, *All in Good Time* (1975, 1983), describes what happens when Susan's father follows her into the past.

Illus. by Peggie Bach, Parnassus, 1963, 176 pp., o.p.; Purple House, 2003, 191 pp. (1-930900-19-8)

(BL 60:262; Eakin:251; HB 39:603; LJ 88:4478; TLS 1976 p. 392)

10-191 OSBORNE, Mary Pope. *Dinosaurs Before Dark.* **(Magic Tree House series, bk. 1).** Gr. 1–3.

The books in their magic tree house take Jack and his sister Annie 65 million years into the past for adventures in a world of dinosaurs and volcanoes. The sequels are *Knight at Dawn* (1993), *Mummies in the Morning* (1994), *Pirates Past Noon* (1994), *Afternoon on the Amazon* (1995), *Night of the Ninjas* (1995), *Midnight on the Moon* (1996), *Sunset of the Sabertooth* (1996), *Dolphins at Daybreak* (1997), *Ghost Town at Sundown* (1997), *Day of the Dragon King* (1998), *Hour of the Olympics* (1998), *Lions at Lunchtime* (1998), *Polar Bears Past Bedtime* (1998), *Vacation Under the Volcano* (1998), *Viking Ships at Sunrise* (1998), *Buffalo Before Breakfast* (1999), *Tigers at Twilight* (1999), *Tonight on the Titanic* (1999), *Civil War on Sunday* (2000), *Dingoes at Dinnertime* (2000), *Revolutionary War on Wednesday* (2000), *Christmas in Camelot* (2001), *Earthquake in the Early Morning* (2001), *Twister on Tuesday* (2001), *Stage Fright on a Summer Night* (2002), *Good Morning Gorillas* (2002), *Haunted Castle on Hallows Eve* (2003), *Summer of the Sea Serpent* (2004), *Winter of the Ice Wizard* (2004), *Carnival at Candlelight* (2005), and *Season of the Sandstorms* (2005).

Illus. by Sal Murdocca, Random, 1992, 68 pp. (0-679-92411-6), 1992, pap. (0-679-82411-1)

(BL 89:339; HBG 4:60; Kirkus 60:993; SLJ Sept 1992 p. 209)

10-192 OSTERWEIL, Adam. *The Comic Book Kid.* Gr. 4–6.

Brian's new "Time-Quest" comic book sends him and his friend Paul back and forth through time while searching for a replacement for Brian's father's valuable 1939 "Superman #1."

Illus. by Craig Smith, Front Street, 2001, 151 pp. (1-886910-62-6); Scholastic, 2001, pap., 145 pp. (0-439-41649-3)

(BL 97:1753; HBG 12:313; SLJ Aug 2001 p. 186)

10-193 *The Other Side of the Clock: Stories Out of Time, Out of Place.* **Ed. by Philip Van Doren Stern.** Gr. 10 up.

Twelve stories speculating on the nature of time, whose authors include H. G. Wells and Jack Finney.

Van Nostrand Reinhold, 1969, 192 pp., o.p.

(BL 66:1139, 1157; CCBB 23:152; Kirkus 37:1089; LJ 95:1661)

10-194 OWEN, Gareth. *Rosie No-Name and the Forest of Forgetting.* Gr. 3–6.

(Orig. British pub. 1996.)

Rosie leaves her accident-induced comatose body to chase a mysterious girl into the past of 1916, where she and her new friend Alastair must avoid deadly traps set by a witch.

Holiday, 1996, 109 pp. (0-8234-1266-0)

(BL 93:501; CCBB 50:183; HB 73:65; HBG 8:501; Kirkus 64:1536; SLJ Oct 1996 p. 124)

10-195 PARDOE, M(argaret Mary). *Curtain of Mist.* **(Argle trilogy, bk. 1).** Gr. 6–8. (Orig. British pub. 1956, entitled *Argle's Mist*.)

Three 20th-century children step through a "curtain of mist" into Celtic Britain. The British sequels are *Argle's Causeway* (1958) and *Argle's Oracle* (1959). Illus. by Leslie Atkinson, Funk, 1957, 246 pp., o.p.

(CCBB 11:73; HB 34:38; Kirkus 25:485; LJ 83:652)

10-196 PARK, (Rosina) Ruth (Lucia). *Playing Beatie Bow.* Gr. 5–8. (Orig. Aus-
☆ tralian pub. 1980.)

Angry about her parents' upcoming remarriage and move to Norway, Abigail follows a waif-like girl named Beatie Bow 100 years into the past. Best Australian Children's Book of the Year Award, 1981; Boston Globe Horn Book Award, 1982; Guardian Award, Runner-up, 1982.

Macmillan, 1982, 204 pp., o.p.; Atheneum, 1991, 196 pp., o.p.

(BL 78:1307, 1315, 79:685, 980, 86:790; CCBB 35:156; HB 58:487, 59:331; SLJ May 1982 p. 64; Suth 3:336; TLS 1981 p. 1354; VOYA 5:35)

10-197 PARKER, Richard. *The Old Powder Line.* Gr. 5–8. (Orig. British pub.
☆ 1971.)

Brian Kane embarks on a dangerous journey when he boards an antiquated steam train to rescue his friend Mr. Mincing, who is trapped somewhere in the past. Nelson, 1971, 143 pp., o.p.

(BL 68:676; CCBB 25:78; Kirkus 39:677; Suth:306; TLS 1971 p. 744)

10-198 PARKER, Richard. *A Time to Choose: A Story of Suspense.* Gr. 6–9.
☆ (Orig. British pub. 1973.)

Stephen and Mary are given the choice of staying in a peaceful, unpolluted future world or returning to their unhappy 20th-century lives. Harper, 1974, 151 pp., o.p.

(CCBB 27:183; HB 50:385; Kirkus 42:309; LJ 99:1488; TLS 1973 p. 1434)

10-199 PASCAL, Francine. *Hangin' Out with Cici.* Gr. 7–9.
☆ After Victoria's disruptive behavior gets her expelled from school, a bump on the head transports her to 1944 where she makes friends with a strangely familiar girl.

Viking, 1977, 152 pp., o.p.

(BL 73:1355; HB 53:541; Kirkus 45:99; SLJ Sept 1977 p. 134)

10-200 PATON WALSH, Jill (Gillian Bliss). *A Chance Child.* Gr. 6–9. (Orig.
☆ British pub. 1978.)

Abused by his 20th-century mother, Creep enters an even crueler time, that of the 19th century before child labor laws, where he and two runaways do dangerous work to survive. Phoenix Award, 1998.

Farrar, 1978, 186 pp., o.p.; Sunburst, 1991, pap., 192 pp. (0-374-41174-3)

(BL 75:1215, 1222; CCBB 32:147; HB 55:64; Kirkus 46:1359; SLJ Jan 1979 p. 63)

10-201 PAULSEN, Gary. *The Transall Saga.* Gr. 6–10.

A flash of blue lightning transports Mark to a future world where he is caught in a battle between warring tribes, is enslaved, and eventually escapes to search for the blue light that can lead him home. Delacorte, 1998, 248 pp. (0-385-32196-1); Laurel Leaf, 1999, pap., 256 pp. (0-440-21976-0)

(BL 94:1623; CCBB 51:407; HBG 9:346; Kirkus 66:741; Kliatt May 15, 1998 p. 7; VOYA 21:286)

10-202 PAYNE, Bernal C., Jr. *It's About Time.* Gr. 5–7.
Chris and Gail Davenport travel back through time to the day in 1955 on which their parents first met, but they soon discover that their appearance has altered the past, and they must spend the day trying to ensure their own future existence.
Macmillan, 1982, 170 pp., o.p.; Pocket (entitled *Trapped in Time*), 1984, pap., o.p.
(CCBB 37:210; SLJ Sept 1984 p. 121; VOYA 7:330)

10-203 PEARCE, (Ann) Philippa. *Tom's Midnight Garden.* Gr. 5–8. (Orig. British
✭ pub. 1958.)
When the grandfather clock strikes 13, Tom Long is able to enter an old-fashioned garden to meet Hatty, a mysterious girl who seems to have grown older each time he visits her. Carnegie Medal, 1958.
Lippincott, 1959, 229 pp., o.p.; illus. by Susan Einzig, HarperCollins, 1984, 1992, 240 pp., o.p.
(BL 56:126; CCBB 13:18; Eakin:254; HB 35:478; Kirkus 27:492; LJ 84:3930; TLS Nov 21 1958 p. x)

10-204 PEARSON, Kit. *A Handful of Time.* Gr. 5–8. (Orig. Canadian pub. 1987.)
✭ Spending a lonely summer with unfamiliar cousins while her parents go through a divorce, 12-year-old Patricia finds an old pocket watch that transports her to the time when her mother was 12. Canadian Library Association Best Book of the Year for Children, 1988.
Viking, 1988, 186 pp., o.p.; Puffin, 1991, pap. (0-14-032268-X)
(BL 84:576, 1677; CCBB 41:186; HB 64:391, 497; Kirkus 56:282; SLJ May 1988 p. 100)

10-205 PEASE, (Clarence) Howard. *The Gypsy Caravan; Being the Merry Tale of the Travels of Betty and Joe with the Gypsies—Their Amazing Adventures with Robin Hood—with Richard-the-Lion-Hearted—with Roland—and Sundry Other Great and Famous Persons.* Gr. 5–7. (Orig. pub. in England.)
Two children join a gypsy caravan and embark on a series of adventures with heroes from their history books.
Illus. by Harrie Wood, Doubleday, 1930, 1946, 254 pp., o.p.
(HB 6:331; LJ 56:179; Mahony 3:209)

PECK, Richard (Wayne). *The Ghost Belonged to Me.*
See Chapter 4, Ghost Fantasy.

10-206 PECK, Richard (Wayne). *Voices After Midnight.* Gr. 5–9.
✭ After Heidi, Chad, and Luke discover they can enter the past in the 100-year-old house their family is renting in Manhattan, they try to change history by averting a tragedy that occurred on the night of March 12, 1888.
Delacorte, 1989, 181 pp., o.p.
(BL 86:274, 353; CCBB 43:41; HB 65:776; HBG 1:81; Kirkus 57:1249; SLJ Sept 1989 p. 276; VOYA 12:346)

10-207 PENN, Malka. *The Hanukkah Ghosts.* Gr. 3–5.
By the light of each night's Hanukkah candles, lonely Susan meets the ghosts of Jewish refugee children who lived in her elderly aunt's home during World War II, and she is able to right a 50-year-old wrong.
Holiday, 1995, 76 pp. (0-8234-1145-1)
(BL 92:172; HBG 7:67; SLJ Oct 1995 p. 40)

PEYTON, K. M. *A Pattern of Roses.*
See Chapter 4, Ghost Fantasy.

10-208 PFEFFER, Susan Beth. *Rewind to Yesterday.* Gr. 4–7.
After their grandfather is shot during a robbery, twins Kelly and Scott attempt to change history using a VCR that sends them 24 hours back in time. The sequel is *Future Forward* (1989).
Illus. by Andrew Glass, Delacorte, 1988, 137 pp., o.p.; Dell, pap. (0-440-40474-6)
(CCBB 42:49; Kirkus 56:1154; SLJ Oct 1988 p. 147; VOYA 11:247)

10-209 PHIPSON, Joan (pseud. of Margaret Fitzhardinge). *The Way Home.* Gr. 5–7. (Orig. Australian pub. 1973.)
Prue, Peter, and Richard are thrown over a cliff during a car accident and swept downstream into a world of enormous monsters and volcanic eruptions.
Atheneum, 1973, 184 pp., o.p.
(HB 50:52; Kirkus 41:760; LJ 98:2656; TLS 1973 p. 1114)

10-210 PINKWATER, D(aniel) Manus. *Wingman.* Gr. 4–6.
Wingman flies truant Daniel Chen from the George Washington Bridge into ancient China.
Illus. by the author, Dodd, 1975, 63 pp., o.p.
(Kirkus 43:375; SLJ Sept 1975 p. 109)

10-211 POPE, Elizabeth Marie. *The Sherwood Ring.* Gr. 6 up.
✳ The American Revolutionary period comes alive for Peggy when she meets the ghost of her ancestor, Barbara Grahame, and sympathizes with Barbara's forbidden love affair with a British soldier.
Illus. by Evaline Ness, Houghton, 1958, 266 pp., o.p.; Puffin, 1992, pap. (0-14-034911-1); illus. by Evaline Ness, Houghton, 2001, 266 pp. (0-618-17736-1), 2001, pap. (0-618-15074-9)
(BL 54:567; CCBB 11:22; Eakin:265; HB 34:112, 613, 35:399; Kirkus 26:38; LJ 83:2073)

10-212 POWERS, Tim. *The Anubis Gates.* Gr. 10 up.
A touring group of time travelers are led back to 1810, where they become involved with sorcerers and gypsies.
Ace, 1983, pap., 387 pp., o.p.; Tor, 1997, pap. (0-441-00401-6)
(BL 80:667; VOYA 7:102)

10-213 PRICE, Susan. *The Sterkarm Handshake.* Gr. 7–10. (Orig. British pub.
✳ 1998.)
Andrea Mitchell is torn between the 16th-century Scottish clan that has welcomed her, and her loyalty to the 21st-century English company that has sent her into the past to prepare for colonization and exploitation. Guardian First Book Award, 1999.
HarperCollins, 2000, 428 pp. (0-06-029392-6), 2003, pap., 576 pp. (0-06-447236-1)
(BL 97:332; HBG 12:86; Kirkus 68:1489; SLJ Dec 2000 p. 148; VOYA 23:363, 24:13)

10-214 PRINCE, Maggie. *The House on Hound Hill.* Gr. 7–10. (Orig. British pub.
✶ 1996, entitled *Here Comes a Candle to Light You to Bed.*)
Something odd about her brother's new room in their old London house repeatedly draws Emily, 16, back through time to 1665, the year of the Black Death.
Houghton, 1998, 256 pp. (0-395-90702-0), 2003, pap., 256 pp. (0-618-33124-7)
(BL 95:58; CCBB 52:70; HB 74:739; SLJ Sep 1998 p. 208; VOYA 21:446)

PURTILL, Richard. *Enchantment at Delphi.*
See Chapter 6, High Fantasy: Myth or Legend Fantasy.

RABINOWITZ, Ann. *Knight on Horseback.*
See Chapter 4, Ghost Fantasy.

10-215 RADFORD, Ken. *The Cellar.* Gr. 5–8.
While working at an isolated house in northern Wales, orphaned Sian finds the diary of a girl who was cruelly mistreated by her guardian after her mother's death, and Sian travels into the past to find out what happened to Sarah Jane.
Holiday, 1989, 171 pp., o.p.
(BL 85:1654; CCBB 42:282; SLJ Mar 1989 p. 200; VOYA 12:216)

RADFORD, Ken. *Haunting at Mill Lane.*
See Chapter 4, Ghost Fantasy.

10-216 REES, Celia. *City of Shadows.* **(The Celia Rees Supernatural trilogy, bk. 1).** Gr. 6–8. (Orig. British pub. 1998.)
Siblings Davey and Kate and their cousins Tom and Elinor are trapped in another time by ghosts and make an enemy of the evil Fairy Queen when they rescue another human child. This story was originally published in two volumes: *H Is for Haunting* (1998) and *A Is for Apparition* (1998). The sequels are *A Trap in Time* (2003) and *The Host Rides Out* (2003). The British sequels, all published in 1998, are *U Is for Unbeliever, N Is for Nightmare, T Is for Terror,* and *S Is for Shudder.*
Hodder, 2003, pap., 247 pp. (0-340-81800-X)
(Kirkus 71:65; Kliatt Mar 2003 p. 36)

10-217 REISS, Kathryn. *Dreadful Sorry.* **(Time Travel Mysteries).** Gr. 7–12.
✶ Haunted by nightmares in which she becomes a girl named Clementine who died in 1912, 16-year-old Molly fears that she and her new friend Jared are reliving a tragic love story.
Harcourt, 1993, 272 pp. (0-15-224213-9), 2004, pap., 352 p. (0-15-205087-6)
(BL 89:1959; CCBB 46:293; HBG 4:312; Kirkus 61:603; SLJ June 1993 p. 132; VOYA 16:157)

10-218 REISS, Kathryn. *Paint by Magic: A Time Travel Mystery.* Gr. 5–8.
Connor Chase, 11, is transported through time to 1926, where he discovers that his mother's odd behavior is being controlled by a 15th-century Italian ancestor with dark powers.
Harcourt, 2002, 288 pp. (0-15-216361-1), 2003, pap. (0-15-204925-8)
(BL 98:1418, 1460; CCBB 56:32; HBG 14:87; Kirkus 70:666; SLJ May 2002 p. 158; VOYA 25:131)

10-219 REISS, Kathryn. *Paperquake: A Puzzle.* Gr. 6–9.

☆   After she finds letters and diary pages dating from 1906, Violet, who is terrified of the earthquakes that plague her California home, begins dreaming about three children caught in the big San Francisco quake.

Harcourt, 1998, 264 pp. (0-15-201183-8), 2002, pap., 274 pp. (0-15-201183-8)

(BL 94:1627; CCBB 51:372; HB 74:497; HBG 9:226; Kirkus 66:273; Kliatt May 1998 p. 8; SLJ June 1998 p. 152; VOYA 21:134)

10-220 REISS, Kathryn. *Time Windows.* **(Miranda Browne series, bk. 1).** Gr. 5–9.

☆   When Miranda looks out through the windows of a dollhouse in her attic, she can watch scenes from the lives of three past inhabitants of her house: 8-year-old Dorothy in 1904 and two brothers in the 1940s, all of whom have abusive mothers. The sequel is *Pale Phoenix* (1994, 2003).

Harcourt, 1991, 192 pp. (0-15-288205-7); Harcourt, 2000, pap., 192 pp. (0-15-202399-2)

(BL 88:507; CCBB 45:47; HBG 3:72; Kirkus 59:1407; SLJ Oct 1991 p. 126; VOYA 14:325, 15:11)

10-221 RICHEMONT, Enid. *The Time Tree.* Gr. 4–7. (Orig. British pub. 1989.)

☆   When Anne, a deaf girl from the 16th century, appears in their secret hideaway in a tall tree, Rachel and Joanna teach her to read and write, thus improving her previously unhappy life when she returns to Elizabethan England.

Little, Brown, 1990, 96 pp., o.p.

(BL 86:2179; CCBB 43:224; HBG 1:255; Kirkus 58:654; SLJ June 1990 p. 125; VOYA 13:119)

ROBINSON, Joan (Mary) G(ale Thomas). *When Marnie Was There.*
See Chapter 4, Ghost Fantasy.

10-222 RODDA, Emily. *The Best-Kept Secret.* Gr. 3–6. (Orig. Australian pub.

☆   1988.)

A mysterious carousel takes Jo and some neighbors seven years into the future, and what they see during their one-hour visit affects the choices they make for the rest of their lives.

Illus. by Noela Young, Henry Holt, 1990, 119 pp., o.p.

(BL 87:52; HBG 1:255; Kirkus 58:802; SLJ Jan 1991 p. 79)

10-223 RODOWSKY, Colby F. *Keeping Time.* Gr. 6–9.

Drew Wakeman is drawn into the past to Elizabethan London, where he is befriended by an apprentice minstrel, Symon Ives, who helps Drew learn to communicate with his own taciturn father.

Farrar, 1983, 137 pp., o.p.

(BL 80:419; CCBB 37:116; HB 60:203; SLJ Jan 1984 p. 85)

ROMAIN, Joseph. *The Mystery of the Wagner Whacker.*
See Chapter 4, Ghost Fantasy.

10-224 RUSSELL, Sharman Apt. *The Humpbacked Fluteplayer.* Gr. 5–7.

Touching a Native American pictograph of a flute player sends Arizona classmates May and Evan into the past, where they become slaves of a warring desert tribe.

Knopf, 1994, 150 pp., o.p.

(BL 90:1262; CCBB 47:233; HBG 5:315; Kirkus 62:484; SLJ April 1994 p. 130)

SABERHAGEN, Fred. *Pyramids.*
See Chapter 7, High Fantasy: Travel to Other Worlds.

10-225 ST. GEORGE, Judith. *The Mysterious Girl in the Garden.* Gr. 3–5.
Led back through time into 1805 by a small white dog, Terrie meets Princess Charlotte Augusta. Both girls miss their mothers' companionship and a friendship develops, culminating in a plan to exchange places in time.
Illus. by Margot Tomes, Putnam, 1981, 64 pp., o.p.

(BL 78:599; 81:1408; Kirkus 50:7; SLJ Dec 1981 p. 68)

10-226 ST. GEORGE, Judith. *Who's Scared? Not Me!* Gr. 7–10.
Because the old house Micki finds in New York's Central Park was torn down years ago, she knows she must have gone into the past to visit naturalist John James Audubon.
Putnam, 1987, 174 pp., o.p.

(BL 84:555, 572; Kirkus 55:1397; SLJ Dec 1987 p. 105; VOYA 10:283)

10-227 SAUER, Julia L(ina). *Fog Magic.* Gr. 4–6.
✦ While searching for a friend her own age, Greta Addington wanders through the Nova Scotia fog and enters Blue Cove, a village from a hundred years in the past. John Newbery Medal Honor Book, 1944.
Viking, 1943, 107 pp., o.p.; Viking, 2005, 128 pp. (0-670-06016-X)

(BL 40:83; HB 19:405, 422, 56:548–551; LJ 68:822, 963; TLS 1977 p. 1409)

10-228 SAXTON, Judith. *The Blue and Distant Hills.* Gr. 10 up. (Orig. British pub. 1993.)
Questa's visions of a 1,000-year-old Roman centurion and his family ease her transition from life in Italy during World War II to postwar life in rural Wales.
St. Martin's 1994, 528 pp. (0-312-10944-X)

(BL 90:1424, 1429; Kirkus 62:333; LJ April 1, 1994 p. 134)

10-229 SCHWARTZ, Ellen. *Jesse's Star.* Gr. 2–5. (Orig. Canadian pub. 2000.)
Bored by a third-grade assignment about his family's immigration to Canada, Jesse travels through time to Russia in the 1890s, where his great-great-grandfather's family is suffering through pogroms against the Jews.
Illus. by Kirsti, Orca, 2000, pap., 108 pp. (1-55143-143-2)

(BL 96:2026; SLJ Nov 2000 p. 132; VOYA 23:278)

10-230 SCIESZKA, Jon. *Knights of the Kitchen Table.* (**Time Warp Trio series,**
✦ **bk. 1).** Gr. 3–5.
The Time Warp Trio—Joe, Fred, and Sam—travel through time using a magical book given to Joe by his magician uncle, and save Camelot from a smelly giant. In *The Not-So-Jolly Roger* (1991), the Trio tangles with bloodthirsty Bluebeard the pirate. The sequels are *The Good, the Bad and the Goofy* (1992), *Your Mother Was a Neanderthal* (1993), *2095* (1995), *Tut, Tut* (1996), *Summer Reading Is Killing Me* (1998), *It's All Greek to Me* (1999), *See You Later, Gladiator* (2000), *Sam Samurai* (2001), *Hey Kid, Want to Buy a Bridge?* (2002), *Viking and Liking It* (2002), *Me Oh Maya* (2003), and *Da Wild, Da Crazy, Da Vinci* (2004).

Illus. by Lane Smith, Viking, 1991, 64 pp. (0-670-83622-2)

(BL 87:1716; CCBB 44:274; HBG 2:259; Kirkus 59:609; SLJ Aug 1991 p. 168)

10-231 SCOTT, Deborah. *The Kid Who Got Zapped Through Time.* **Gr. 4–7.**
Touching the wizard's hand in his new computer game sends 7th-grader Flat-top Kincaid back in time to medieval England, where he is taken in by a family of serfs. The sequel is *The California Kid Fights Back* (1998).
Avon, 1997, 160 pp. (0-380-97356-1)

(BL 94:473; SLJ Sep 1997 p. 225)

SELDEN (Thompson), George. *The Genie of Sutton Place.*
See Chapter 9, Magic Adventure Fantasy.

10-232 SERVICE, Pamela F. *The Reluctant God.* **Gr. 6–9.**
Ameni, a young ancient Egyptian king, comes back to life in the 20th century when his body is discovered by apprentice archaeologist Lorna, and together they undertake a dangerous journey to England to recover two sacred urns.
Golden Kite Award Honor Book, 1988.
Macmillan, 1988, 206 pp., o.p.

(BL 84:1186; CCBB 41:167; SLJ June 1988 p. 106; VOYA 11:97, 12:15)

10-233 SERVICE, Pamela F. *Storm at the Edge of Time.* **Gr. 5–7.**
A Neolithic mage enlists the help of three young Scottish descendants from different time periods, asking them to search for three lost staves of power needed to battle the forces of darkness.
Walker, 1994, 192 pp., o.p.

(BL 91:423; HBG 6:83; SLJ Dec 1994 p. 113; VOYA 17:351)

10-234 SERVICE, Pamela F. *Vision Quest.* **Gr. 5–8.**
✮ Two time periods overlap in this story set in Nevada, where Kate's ancient Indian charm stone brings her visions of Wadat, a Native American shaman from long ago whose sacred relic has disappeared.
Macmillan, 1989, 160 pp., o.p.

(BL 85:1471; CCBB 42:236; HB 56:506; Kirkus 57:383; Kliatt Sept 1990 p. 24; SLJ Mar 1989 p. 202)

10-235 SEVERN, David (pseud. of David Unwin). *Dream Gold.* **Gr. 6–8.** (Orig. British pub. 1949.)
Peter and Guy have frightening experiences involving pirates and their "dream gold" while vacationing in Cornwall.
Illus. by Isami Kashiwagi, Viking, 1952, 192 pp., o.p.

(HB 29:53; Kirkus 20:412; LJ 77:2079)

SEVERN, David (pseud. of David Unwin). *The Girl in the Grove.*
See Chapter 4, Ghost Fantasy.

SHECTER, Ben. *The Whistling Whirligig.*
See Chapter 4, Ghost Fantasy.

10-236 SHERBURNE, Zoa (Morin). *Why Have the Birds Stopped Singing?* **Gr. 5–7.**

An epileptic seizure at an ancestor's birthplace sends Katie into the 19th century, where she becomes Kathryn, a girl imprisoned by her uncle.
Morrow, 1974, 189 pp., o.p.
(BL 70:1202; LJ 99:1488)

10-237 SIEGEL, Robert (Harold). *Alpha Centauri.* Gr. 7–9.
Rebecca finds herself in pre-Druid Britain, where she must complete a dangerous quest to save the half-horse, half-human centaurs who have befriended her.
Illus. by Kurt Mitchell, Good News, 1980, 256 pp., o.p.
(BL 77:40, 48; LJ 105:1665)

10-238 SILVERBERG, Robert. *Letters from Atlantis.* Gr. 6–12.
☆ Roy, a 21st-century time-traveler, takes over the mind of Crown Prince Ram on the legendary continent of Atlantis in an attempt to learn its secret history.
Illus. by Robert Gould, Macmillan, 1990, 136 pp., o.p.; Warner, 1992, pap. (0-446-36286-7)
(BL 87:660, 1123; HBG 2:88; Kirkus 58:1460; SLJ Mar 1991 p. 218; VOYA 13:367, 14:11)

10-239 SIMAK, Clifford D(onald). *The Goblin Reservation.* Gr. 10 up.
Time travel permits goblins, trolls, Shakespeare, a Neanderthal man, and a ghost to live together on The Reservation.
Putnam, 1968, 192 pp., o.p.
(BL 65:484, 492; Kirkus 36:722; LJ 94:1164, 2074; SLJ Dec 15, 1968 p. 4740)

10-240 SINYKIN, Sheri Cooper. *A Matter of Time.* Gr. 5–8.
Sixth-grader Jody gets his wish to spend more time with his Dad when he finds himself in the year 1958 and meets his father at his own age.
Cavendish, 1998, 207 pp. (0-7614-5019-X)
(BL 94:1627; HBG 8:338; SLJ May 1998 p. 148)

10-241 SIROF, Harriet. *Bring Back Yesterday.* Gr. 6–9.
Angry and depressed after her parents' accidental deaths, 13-year-old Lisa discovers that she can enter the past, and travels to Elizabethan London to become a theater apprentice.
Atheneum, 1996, 167 pp. (0-689-80638-8)
(BL 93:415; CCBB 50:76; HBG 89:84; SLJ Oct 1996 p. 126; VOYA 19:274)

10-242 SLEATOR, William (Warner III). *The Green Futures of Tycho.* Gr. 5–8.
☆ Tycho's visits to his past and future lives, using an egg-shaped metal object, become frightening as he begins to realize what kind of person his older self has become.
Dutton, 1981, 133 pp., o.p.; Puffin, 1991, pap. (0-14-034581-7)
(BL 77:1108; CCBB 35:58; HB 57:426; Kirkus 49:440; SLJ Apr 1981 p. 133, May 1981 p. 24)

10-243 SLEIGH, Barbara (de Riemer). *Jessamy.* Gr. 5–7. (Orig. British pub. 1967.)
☆ Jessamy travels to the period of World War I to solve a mystery surrounding a missing rare book.
Bobbs-Merrill, 1967, 246 pp., o.p.; Hodder, 1993, pap., 168 pp., o.p.
(BL 63:1195; CCBB 21:33; HB 43:343; Kirkus 35:416; LJ 92:2024; TLS 1967 p. 451)

10-244 SLEPIAN, Jan. *Back to Before.* Gr. 5–7.
Two cousins get their wish to travel one year back through time to the period before Linny's mother dies and before Hilary's father leaves his family, in hopes of making things turn out differently.
Putnam, 1993, 170 pp. (0-399-22011-9); Apple, 1994, pap., 170 pp. (0-590-48459-1)
(BL 90:58; CCBB 47:24; HBG 5:82; Kirkus 61:728; SLJ Oct 1993 p. 130)

SNYDER, Zilpha Keatley. *The Truth About Stone Hollow.*
See Chapter 4, Ghost Fantasy.

10-245 SOBOL, Donald J. *"My Name Is Amelia."* Gr. 5–8.
On a Caribbean island, the evil Doctor Freemont has gathered famous people from many historical periods to create his own world, but a shipwrecked girl named Lisa tries to stop him.
Atheneum, 1994, 105 pp. (0-689-31970-3)
(BL 91:822; CCBB 48:215; HBG 6:84; SLJ Jan 1995 p. 110; VOYA 17:351)

10-246 STEWART, Jennifer J. *If That Breathes Fire, We're Toast!* Gr. 4–6.
Mrs. Yang, a dragon who arrives in a mysterious box, takes Rick and his new friend Natalie on adventures through time.
Holiday, 1999, 118 pp. (0-8234-1430-2)
(BL 95:2053; CCBB 53:32; HBG 10:300; Kirkus 67:728; SLJ Dec 1999 p. 142; VOYA 22:351, 23:13)

10-247 STEWART, Mary (Florence Elinor). *A Walk in Wolf Wood.* Gr. 5–8.
✷ (Orig. British pub. 1980.)
John and Margaret help Mardian, a man forced to become a ferocious wolf each night, to defeat the enchanter who has taken Mardian's place as the king's adviser.
Illus. by Emanuel Schoengut, Morrow, 1980, 1984, 160 pp., o.p.
(BL 77:40, 49; CCBB 34:42; Kirkus 48:1300; SLJ Sept 1980 p. 78; TLS 1980 p. 806)

10-248 STOLZ, Mary (Slattery). *Cat in the Mirror.* Gr. 5–7.
✷ Difficulties in coping with a disinterested mother and unfriendly classmates lead to two lives for Erin Gandy, one in the 20th century and the other in ancient Egypt.
Harper, 1975, 199 pp., o.p.
(BL 72:628; CCBB 29:70; HB 51:597; Kirkus 45:999; SLJ Oct 1975 p. 103; Suth 2:434)

10-249 SYKES, Pamela. *Mirror of Danger.* Gr. 5–7. (Orig. British pub. 1973, enti-
✷ tled *Come Back, Lucy.*)
Orphaned Lucy comes to live with distant cousins and is befriended by Alice, the ghost of a Victorian girl, who tries to trap Lucy permanently in the past. The sequel is *Lucy Beware!* (1984).
Nelson, 1974, 175 pp., o.p.
(BL 70:1007; Kies:170; LJ 99:2742; TLS 1973 p. 1117)

10-250 SYMONS, (Dorothy) Geraldine. *Crocuses Were Over, Hitler Was Dead.*
Gr. 5–7. (Orig. British pub. 1977, entitled *Now and Then.*)
Jassy travels back in time to World War II, where she helps a British solider accomplish a secret mission behind German lines.

Harper, 1978, 158 pp., o.p.
(BL 75:550; CCBB 32:145; Kirkus 46:1308; SLJ Oct 1978 p. 151; TLS 1977 p. 864)

10-251 *Tales out of Time.* **Ed. by Barbara Ireson.** Gr. 7 up.
Fourteen fantasy and science fiction time-travel tales written by John Rowe Townsend, Ray Bradbury, H. G. Wells, and others.
Putnam, 1981, 247 pp., o.p.
(BL 77:1342; CCBB 35:11; SLJ Sept 1981 p. 136)

10-252 TANNEN, Mary. *The Wizard Children of Finn.* Gr. 5–7.
Magic brings Fiona and Bran to ancient Ireland where they help Finn McCool claim his kingdom. The sequel is *The Lost Legend of Finn* (1982).
Illus. by John Burgoyne, Knopf, 1981, 214 pp., o.p.
(BL 77:1157; Kirkus 49:505; SLJ Sept 1981 p. 131)

TAPP, Kathy Kennedy. *The Scorpio Ghosts and the Black Hole Gang.*
See Chapter 4, Ghost Fantasy.

10-253 TARR, Judith, and TURTLEDOVE, Harry. *Household Gods: A Novel of*
✶ *the Depths of Time and the Human Heart.* Gr. 10 up.
After a really bad day, Los Angeles lawyer and single mother Nicole Gunther-Perrin awakens inside the body of Umma, a widowed tavern keeper in an ancient Roman frontier town, where life is also difficult.
Tor, 1999, 512 pp. (0-312-86487-6), 2000, pap., 672 pp. (0-812-56466-9)
(BL 95:1896; Kirkus 67:1000; LJ Aug 1999 p. 147; SLJ Feb 2000 p. 143)

10-254 TEBBETTS, Christopher. *Viking Pride.* **(The Viking saga, bk. 1).** Gr. 4–7.
Fourteen-year-old Zack Gilman goes to the concession stand during a Minnesota Vikings football game, stumbles over a rusty object in the snow, and finds himself in the midst of a 9th-century Viking battle. The sequels are *The Quest for Faith* (2003), *Land of the Dead* (2003), and *The Viking: Hammer of the Gods* (2003).
Penguin/Puffin, 2003, pap., 192 pp. (0-14-250029-1)
(BL 100:124; SLJ Dec 2003 p. 161)

10-255 THOMAS, Jane Resh. *The Princess in the Pigpen.* Gr. 4–6.
Ill with a fever, Elizabeth, daughter of the Duke of Umberland, is transported from England in 1591 to a 20th-century Iowa farm where the McCormick family takes her in but doesn't believe her time-travel story.
Houghton, 1989, 128 pp., o.p.; Harcourt, 1995, pap. (0-15-305231-7)
(BL 86:190; CCBB 43:46; HBG 1:83; Kirkus 57:1537; SLJ Nov 1989 p. 115)

10-256 TOWNSEND, John Rowe. *The Visitors.* Gr. 6–10. (Orig. British pub. 1977,
✶ entitled *The Xanadu Manuscript.*)
Katherine Wyatt and her parents are sent from the world of 2149 A.D. into the 20th century, but they need John Dunham's help to survive and stay out of trouble.
Lippincott, 1977, 221 pp., o.p.
(BL 74:34, 45; CCBB 31:87; HB 53:671; Kirkus 45:856; SLJ Nov 1977 p. 75; Suth 2:454)

10-257 *Trips in Time: Nine Stories of Science Fiction.* **Ed. by Robert Silverberg.**
Gr. 9 up.

Nine time-travel tales by Poul Anderson, Roger Zelazny, Robert Silverberg, and others.

Nelson, 1977, 192 pp., o.p.

(BL 74:369; Kirkus 45:884, 941)

10-258 TWAIN, Mark (pseud. of Samuel Clemens). *A Connecticut Yankee in*
✫ *King Arthur's Court.* **(British title:** *A Connecticut Yankee at the Court of King Arthur***).** Gr. 8 up. (Orig. pub. Harper, 1889.)

An accidental blow to the head sends Hank Morgan 1,300 years back through time to King Arthur's court, where he uses his knowledge of history and modern technology to replace Merlin as Court Magician.

Harper, 1925, 450 pp., o.p.; illus. by Trina Schart Hyman, Morrow, 1988, 384 pp. (0-688-06346-2); Puffin, 1990, pap., 416 pp. (0-14-043064-4); Oxford University Press, 1999, pap., 400 pp. (0-19-283902-0); University of California Press, 2002, pap., 479 pp. (0-520-23576-2); Signet, 2004, pap., 384 pp. (0-45152-958-8)

(BL 22:170, 85:1005; HB 2:30, 60:359)

URE, Jean. *The Children Next Door.*
See Chapter 4, Ghost Fantasy.

10-259 UTTLEY, Alison (Jane [Taylor]). *A Traveler in Time.* Gr. 6–8. (Orig.
✫ British pub. 1939, entitled *A Traveller in Time.*)

While visiting her family's ancient country home, Penelope Cameron is drawn back through time to Elizabethan England, where she becomes involved in an ill-fated plot to save Mary, Queen of Scots.

Illus. by Phyllis Bray, Putnam, 1940, 306 pp., o.p.; illus. by Christine Price, Viking, 1964, 287 pp., o.p.

(BL 61:581; HB 40:612, 58:721; LJ 65:923, 89:4653; SLJ Oct 1981 p. 154; TLS 1939 p. 667)

10-260 VICK, Helen Hughes. *Walker of Time.* **(Walker series, vol. 1).** Gr. 6–10.

A flash of lightning throws Walker, a 15-year-old Hopi, and Tag, the 12-year-old son of an archaeologist, 750 years into the past to save an endangered Sinagua Indian settlement. The sequels are *Walker's Journey Home* (1995) and *Tag Against Time* (1996).

Harbinger, 1993, 192 pp. (0-943173-84-1), pap. (0-943173-80-9)

(BL 90:52; Kliatt Sept 1993 p. 24)

10-261 VOIGT, Cynthia. *Building Blocks.* Gr. 4–7.
✫ A fortress made of children's blocks takes Brann Connell back into the time of his father's boyhood, where he grows to better understand the man he had thought of as a "loser."

Macmillan, 1984, 132 pp., o.p.; Scholastic, 1994, pap. (0-590-47732-3); Aladdin, 2002, pap., 176 pp. (0-689-85105-7)

(BL 80:1350; CCBB 37:157; HB 60:470; Kirkus 52:24; SLJ May 1984 p. 85; Suth 3:435)

WALKER, Mary Alexander. *The Scathach and Maeve's Daughters.*
See Chapter 6, High Fantasy: Myth or Legend Fantasy.

WALLIN, Luke. *The Slavery Ghosts.*
See Chapter 4, Ghost Fantasy.

10-262 WELCH, Ronald (pseud. of Ronald Oliver Felton). *The Gauntlet.* Gr. 7–9.
(Orig. British pub. 1951.)
A medieval gauntlet sends Peter Staunton into the 14th century, where he lives
in his ancestors' castle and takes part in their battles.
Illus. by T. R. Freeman, Oxford University Press, 1952, 248 pp., o.p.
(BL 49:53; HB 29:53; Kirkus 20:456; LJ 77:1522)

10-263 WELDRICK, Valerie. *Time Sweep.* Gr. 5–7. (Orig. Australian pub. 1976.)
Laurie's bed is the means by which he travels from 20th-century Sydney, Aus-
tralia, to 1862 London, where he and his new friend Frank avert a robbery.
Illus. by Ron Brooks, Lothrop, 1978, 157 pp., o.p.
(CCBB 32:127; HB 55:196; Kirkus 47:7; SLJ Jan 1978 p. 58; Suth 2:474)

10-264 WESLEY, Mary. *Haphazard House.* Gr. 6–9. (Orig. British pub. 1983.)
✫ A Panama hat causes the eccentric Fuller family to move from London to an
old country house in a village that seems to be outside time.
Overlook, 1993, 144 pp. (0-87951-470-1)
(BL 90:828; CCBB 47:61; HBG 5:92; Kirkus 61:793; SLJ Aug 1993 p. 190)

10-265 WESTALL, Robert (Atkinson). *The Devil on the Road.* Gr. 8 up. (Orig.
✫ British pub. 1978.)
John Webster becomes convinced of the innocence of Johanna, a 17th-century
girl accused of witchcraft, and makes the mistake of bringing her into the 20th
century. Carnegie Medal Commended Book, 1978.
Greenwillow, 1979, 256 pp., o.p.; Pan Macmillan, 1996, pap., 256 pp., o.p.
(BL 75:1532, 76:1199; CCBB 32:204; HB 55:541; Kirkus 47:860; SLJ May 1979 pp. 36, 76)

WESTALL, Robert (Atkinson). *The Haunting of Chas McGill and Other
Stories.*
See Chapter 4, Ghost Fantasy.

WESTALL, Robert (Atkinson). *The Watch House.*
See Chapter 4, Ghost Fantasy.

10-266 WESTALL, Robert (Atkinson). *The Wind Eye.* Gr. 6–9. (Orig. British pub.
✫✫ 1976.)
A boat that once belonged to a medieval monk carries Mike, Beth, and Sally
across time into the seventh century, where St. Cuthbert changes both their
lives and those of their parents.
Greenwillow, 1977, 213 pp., o.p.; Pan, 2003, pap., 224 pp. (0-330-32234-6)
(BL 74:370, 381; CCBB 31:103; HB 54:56; Kirkus 45:1104; SLJ Nov 1977 p. 77; Suth 2:248;
TLS 1976 p. 1547)

10-267 WHINNEM, Reade Scott. *Utten and Plumley.* Gr. 5–8.
Utten, a magical blue frog-like creature, helps a man named Plumley, and his
dog Corker, travel back through time in an attempt to improve Plumley's
youthful life.
Hampton Roads, 2003, pap., 317 pp. (1-57174-346-4)
(Kliatt Nov 2003 p. 26; SLJ Aug 2003 p. 169; VOYA 26:420)

10-268 WHITMORE, Arvella. *Trapped Between the Lash and the Gun: A Boy's
Journey.* Gr. 5–8.

Just as he's about to pawn his grandfather's watch to buy a gun, gang recruit Jordan Scott is pulled into the past to become Uriah Henning, a young slave working as a field hand who is sold at auction before he can escape on the Underground Railroad.
Dial, 1999, 192 pp. (0-8037-2384-9); Puffin, 2001, pap., 184 pp. (0-14-130319-0)
(BL 95:591; CCBB 52:220; Kirkus 66:1674; SLJ Jan 1999 p. 134; VOYA 22:52)

10-269 WIBBERLEY, Leonard (Patrick O'Connor). *The Crime of Martin Coverly.* Gr. 6–8.
★ Nick Ormsby is drawn into the 18th century for shipboard adventures with his ancestor, pirate Martin Coverly.
Farrar, 1980, 167 pp., o.p.
(BL 76:1538; HB 56:418; Kirkus 48:986; SLJ May 1980 p. 80; VOYA 3:34)

10-270 WILDE, Nicholas. *Down Came a Blackbird.* Gr. 6–9. (Orig. British pub. 1991.)
Angry with his alcoholic mother and his probation officer for sending him to live with his great-uncle, 13-year-old James has vivid dreams about the uncle's tragic childhood.
Henry Holt, 1992, 182 pp. (0-8050-2001-2); HarperCollins, 1993, pap. (0-006-74677-2)
(BL 89:662; CCBB 46:197; Kirkus 60:1450; SLJ Feb 1993 p. 109; VOYA 16:96)

WILLIAMS (John), Ursula Moray. *Castle Merlin.*
See Chapter 4, Ghost Fantasy.

10-271 WILLIAMS, Maiya. *The Golden Hour.* Gr. 5–8.
Exploring an abandoned resort hotel in Maine with their new friends, twins Xanthe and Xavier, motherless Rowan and Nina find themselves in 18th-century Paris during the French Revolution.
Amulet/Abrams, 2004, 272 pp. (0-8109-4823-0)
(BL 100:1307; Kirkus 71:187; SLJ April 2004 p. 163; VOYA 27:148)

10-272 WILLIAMS, Ruth L. *The Silver Tree.* Gr. 5–8.
A beautiful dollhouse in an old toy museum transports Micki Silver 100 years into the past to become her cousin Michelle DeSilver.
Harper, 1992, 243 pp. (0-06-020296-3)
(BL 89:62; HBG 3:272; Kirkus 60:786; SLJ June 1992 p. 126; VOYA 15:116)

10-273 WILLIS, Connie. *Doomsday Book.* Gr. 10 up. (Orig. British pub. 1992.)
Kivrin Engles, a 21st-century Oxford University history student, who is accidentally sent back to medieval England during the Black Death, becomes stranded in the past. This book is set in the same universe as the author's *To Say Nothing of the Dog; or, How We Found the Bishop's Bird Stump at Last* (Bantam, 1998; see below).
Bantam, 1992, 448 pp. (0-553-08131-4); Spectra, 1993, pap., 592 pp. (0-553-56273-8)
(BL 88:1811, 1817, 89:842; Kirkus 60:434; LJ May 15, 1992 p. 123)

WILLIS, Connie. *Fire Watch.*
See Chapter 3, Fantasy Collections.

10-274 WILLIS, Connie. *Lincoln's Dreams.* Gr. 10 up.
Historical researcher Jeff Johnston attempts to help a young woman named Annie who is haunted by the Civil War-ravaged dreams of Robert E. Lee.
Bantam, 1987, o.p., 1992, pap., 224 pp. (0-553-27025-7)
(BL 83:1098, 1117; Kirkus 55:519; LJ Apr 15, 1987 p. 102; VOYA 10:182)

10-275 WILLIS, Connie. *To Say Nothing of the Dog; or, How We Found the*
✶ *Bishop's Bird Stump at Last.* Gr. 10 up. (Orig. British pub. 1997.)
Time-traveler Ned Henry is sent from 2057 to 1888 England in this spoof of a Victorian novel, set in the same universe as the author's *Doomsday Book* (1992; see above).
Bantam, 1998, 448 pp. (0-553-09995-7), 1998, pap., 495 pp. (0-553-57538-4)
(BL 94:786, 1311, 1607; Kirkus 65:1561; LJ Dec 1998 p. 188; VOYA 21:15, 62)

10-276 WILSON, Robert Charles. *A Bridge of Years.* Gr. 10 up.
✶ A tunnel beneath the abandoned cottage Tom Winter buys after his divorce leads back in time to Manhattan in 1962, but he must take care to avoid the murderous 21st-century soldier who patrols the passage.
Doubleday, 1991, 348 pp. (0-385-41936-8); Bantam, 1992, pap. (0-553-29892-5)
(BL 87:2108, 2112; Kirkus 59:829; LJ Aug 1991 p. 150; VOYA 14:388)

10-277 WISEMAN, David. *Adam's Common.* Gr. 5–7. (Orig. pub. in England.)
Peggy uses her ability to glimpse townspeople from the past to solve a mystery and protect the town common from proposed transformation into a shopping mall.
Houghton, 1984, 175 pp., o.p.
(BL 81:592; CCBB 38:97; Kirkus 52:98; SLJ Nov 1984 p. 129)

10-278 WISEMAN, David. *Jeremy Visick.* Gr. 5–8. (Orig. British pub. 1981, entitled
✶✶ *The Fate of Jeremy Visick.*)
Matthew travels back in time in an attempt to save the life of a 12-year-old boy named Jeremy who died in the Cornish mines in 1852.
Houghton, 1981, 170 pp., o.p.; Houghton, 2003, pap., 176 pp. (0-618-34514-0)
(BL 77:1397, 80:96; CCBB 35:20; HB 57:193; Kirkus 49:741; SLJ Apr 1981 p. 134, May 1981 p. 25; Suth 3:456)

10-279 WISEMAN, David. *Thimbles.* Gr. 5–7. (Orig. pub. in England.)
Two old thimbles propel Cathy to Manchester, England, in the year 1819, where she becomes, alternately, two different girls involved in a dangerous demonstration by thousands of workers pleading for the right to vote.
Houghton, 1982, 134 pp., o.p.
(BL 78:965, 980; CCBB 35:219; Kirkus 50:556; SLJ Mar 1982 p. 153; TLS 1983 p. 1318)

10-280 WISEMAN, David. *A Tie to the Past.* Gr. 5–9. (Orig. British pub. 1989.)
Plagued by guilt about having stolen a box of mementos from an elderly friend, Mary has frightening dreams in which she becomes Gladys Mayhew, a militant suffragette in 1909 London.
Houghton, 1989, 160 pp., o.p.
(BL 86:191; CCBB 43:23; HBG 1:74; Kirkus 57:1482; SLJ Sept 1989 p. 258; VOYA 12:285)

10-281 WOOD, Beverly, and WOOD, Chris. *Dogstar.* **(A Sirius Mystery).** Gr.
✴ 5–7. (Orig. Canadian pub. 1997.)
Jeff follows a dog resembling his beloved bull terrier Buddy 60 years into the
past and searches for lost treasure in Juneau, Alaska, in the 1930s.
Polestar, 2000, 256 pp. (1-89609-537-2), 2004, pap. (1-551-92638-5)
(BL 94:1323; Kliatt May 1998 p. 24; SLJ Aug 1998 p. 168; VOYA 21:216)

10-282 WOODRUFF, Elvira. *The Disappearing Bike Shop.* Gr. 5–6.
Tyler and Freckles suspect that Quentin Quigley, a mysterious bike-shop
owner, may actually be the Renaissance genius Leonardo da Vinci, especially
after one of his inventions sends them into the past.
Holiday, 1992, 103 pp. (0-8234-0933-3); Bantam, 1994, pap. (0-440-91007-2)
(BL 88:1380; HBG 3:272; SLJ May 1992 p. 117)

10-283 WOODRUFF, Elvira. *The Orphan of Ellis Island: A Time Travel Adventure.* Gr. 4–7.
Accidentally left behind on a fifth-grade field trip to Ellis Island, Dominic
awakens in a 1908 southern Italian village, where he is taken in by a family
planning to emigrate to America.
Scholastic, 1997, 181 pp. (0-590-48245-9); Scholastic, 2000, pap., 174 pp. (0-
590-48246-7)
(BL 93:1707; CCBB 50:261; HBG 8:311; Kirkus 65:147; SLJ May 1997 p. 140)

YEP, Laurence M(ichael). *The Magic Paintbrush.*
See Chapter 9, Magic Adventure Fantasy.

10-284 YOLEN (Stemple), Jane (Hyatt). *The Devil's Arithmetic.* Gr. 5–9.
✴ Twelve-year-old Hannah, bored by the stories of her Holocaust-survivor relatives, suddenly finds herself in Poland during World War II, within the body of
Chaya, a Jewish girl on her way to a death camp.
Viking, 1988, 160 pp. (0-670-81027-4); Puffin, 2004, pap, 176 pp. (0-14-
2401109-9)
(BL 85:69, 86; CCBB 42:23, 59; Kirkus 56:1248; SLJ Nov 1988 p. 114)

10-285 ZELAZNY, Roger (Joseph Christopher), and SHECKLEY, Robert. *If at*
✴ *Faust You Don't Succeed.* **(Azzie Elbub trilogy, bk. 2).** Gr. 10 up.
A burglar-monk mistaken for Johann Faust is sent back and forth through history, competing in a contest between Light and Dark to determine whether
humanity's fortunes will be shaped by Good or by Evil. This is the sequel to
Bring Me the Head of Prince Charming (1991), and is followed by *A Farce to
Be Reckoned With* (1995).
Bantam, 1993, pap., 336 pp. (0-553-37141-X)
(BL 89:972, 975; Kirkus 60:1542; LJ Feb 15, 1993 p. 196; VOYA 16:172)

11

Toy Fantasy

Tales of toys that talk or exhibit other magical abilities are listed in this chapter. Most of the main characters are dolls, but there are also stories about carousel horses, stuffed animals, toy soldiers, and windup toys.

AAMODT, Donald. *A Name to Conjure With.*
See Chapter 7, High Fantasy: Travel to Other Worlds.

11-1　**AHLBERG, Janet, and AHLBERG, Allan.** *The Bear Nobody Wanted.* Gr. 2–6. (Orig. British pub. 1992.)
A snobbish teddy bear's adventures teach him to be more tolerant and compassionate.
Illus. by Janet Ahlberg, Viking, 1993, 143 pp. (0-670-83982-5)
(CCBB 46:307; HB 69:456; HBG 4:293; Kirkus 61:141; SLJ Sep 1993 p. 248)

AIKEN, Joan (Delano). *The Faithless Lollybird.*
See Chapter 3, Fantasy Collections.

AIKEN, Joan (Delano). *The Kingdom and the Cave.*
See Chapter 5, High Fantasy: Alternate Worlds or Histories.

AIKEN, Joan (Delano). *Smoke from Cromwell's Time and Other Stories.*
See Chapter 3, Fantasy Collections.

AINSWORTH (Gilbert), Ruth (Gallard). *The Bear Who Liked Hugging People and Other Stories.*
See Chapter 3, Fantasy Collections.

11-2　**ALBRECHT, Lillie Vanderveer.** *Deborah Remembers.* Gr. 4–6.
Deborah tells the other museum dolls about the events she witnessed during the American Revolution.
Illus. by Rita Newton, Hastings, 1959, 111 pp., o.p.
(BL 56:246; HB 38:381; Kirkus 27:548)

ALCOCK, Vivien (Dolores). *The Haunting of Cassie Palmer.*
See Chapter 4, Ghost Fantasy.

ALEXANDER, Lloyd (Chudley). *The Cat Who Wished to Be a Man.*
See Chapter 2, Animal Fantasy.

ALEXANDER, Lloyd (Chudley). *The Marvelous Misadventures of Sebastian.*
See Chapter 5, High Fantasy: Alternate Worlds or Histories.

ANASTASIO, Dina. *A Question of Time.*
See Chapter 4, Ghost Fantasy.

ANDERSEN, Hans Christian. *The Steadfast Tin Soldier.*
See Chapter 1, Allegorical Fantasy and Literary Fairy Tales.

11-3   **AVERILL, Esther (Holden).** *The Adventures of Jack Ninepins.* Gr. 3–4.
Jack Ninepins, Charlotte's favorite toy, is determined to follow her across the ocean to France.
Harper, 1944, 63 pp., o.p.
(HB 20:471, 480; Kirkus 12:399; LJ 69:863, 1104)

11-4   **BACON, Martha (Sherman).** *Moth Manor: A Gothic Tale.* Gr. 5–7.
A ghostly moth sparks Monica's interest in the mystery surrounding her great-aunt's dollhouse.
Illus. by Gail Burroughs, Little, Brown, 1978, 160 pp., o.p.
(BL 75:42; CCBB 32:93; Kirkus 46:1188; SLJ Sep 1978 p. 130)

11-5   **BAILEY, Carolyn Sherwin.** *Miss Hickory.* Gr. 3–5.
★   Miss Hickory, a doll with a hickory-nut head, is forgotten by her family and has a winter full of adventure. John Newbery Medal, 1947.
Illus. by Ruth Chrisman Gannett, Viking, 1946, 123 pp., o.p.
(BL 43:74; HB 22:465; Kirkus 14:387; LJ 71:1412, 1544)

11-6   **BAKER, Margaret Joyce.** *The Shoe Shop Bears.* **(The Shoe Shop Bears series, bk. 1).** Gr. 3–5. (Orig. British pub. 1963.)
Three teddy bears leave the shoe shop in search of a truly loving home. The sequels are *Hannibal and the Bears* (1966), *Bears Back in Business* (1967), and *Hi-Jinks Joins the Bears* (1969).
Illus. by C(yril) Walter Hodges, Ariel, 1965, 96 pp., o.p.
(CCBB 19:41; LJ 90:3785; TLS 1964 p. 605)

11-7   **BAKER, Margaret Joyce.** *Victoria Josephine.* Gr. 2–4. (Orig. British pub. 1936, entitled *The Roaming Doll.*)
Freed after 70 years in a box, Victoria Josephine is determined to travel.
Illus. by Mary Baker, Dodd, 1936, 95 pp., o.p.
(HB 12:350; LJ 62:217)

BANKS, Lynne Reid. *The Indian in the Cupboard.*
See Chapter 9, Magic Adventure Fantasy.

11-8   **BARRINGER, Marie.** *Martin the Goose Boy.* Gr. 3–5.
Only Gustel knows that his wooden goose-boy doll, Martin, can talk.

Illus. by Maud Petersham and Miska Petersham, Doubleday, 1932, 1936, 188 pp., o.p.

(BL 29:77; Bookshelf 1932 p. 6; LJ 58:711; Mahony 3:53)

11-9   BARZINI, Luigi (Giorgio, Jr.). *The Little Match Man.* Gr. 4–6. (Orig. Italian pub. 1909.)
A little man made of matchsticks comes to life.
Illus. by Hattie Longstreet, Penn, 1917, 1923, 164 pp., o.p.

(BL 14:202; Bookshelf 1923–1924 p. 8)

11-10   BEMELMANS, Ludwig. *The Happy Place.* Gr. 2–4.
Unsold after Easter, Winthrop the toy rabbit is turned loose in Central Park, where the zoo animals befriend him.
Illus. by the author, Little, Brown, 1952 (c. 1951), 58 pp., o.p.

(Kirkus 20:499; LJ 77:1661)

11-11   BIANCO, Margery (Winifred) Williams. *The Adventures of Andy.* Gr. 4–6.
A doll named Andromeda sets off on an adventurous journey after her owner grows up and gets married.
Illus. by Lech Underwood, Doran, 1927, 227 pp., o.p.

(HB Nov 1927 p. 47; Mahony 2:122; Moore:124)

11-12   BIANCO, Margery (Winifred) Williams. *The Little Wooden Doll.* Gr. 2–4.
A lonely doll found in the attic is transformed into a princess doll.
Illus. by Pamela Bianco, Macmillan, 1925, 65 pp., o.p.; HarperCollins, 2003, pap. (0-06-028277-0)

(BL 22:121; Bookshelf 1928 p. 9; HB 2:18; LJ 51:836; Moore:426)

11-13   BIANCO, Margery (Winifred) Williams. *Poor Cecco: The Wonderful*
✶   *Story of a Wonderful Wooden Dog Who Was the Jolliest Toy in the House Until He Went Out to Explore the World.* Gr. 3–5. (Orig. U.S. and British pubs. 1925.)
Cecco the wooden dog and his friends, Jensina the doll and Bulka the toy rabbit, leave their home in the toy cupboard to search for adventure.
Illus. by Arthur Rackham, Doubleday, 1945, 175 pp., o.p.

(BL 22:121; Bookshelf 1926–1927 p. 5; HB 2:13, 19, 20; Mahony 2:122; Moore:426; TLS 1925 p. 809)

11-14   BIANCO, Margery (Winifred) Williams. *The Velveteen Rabbit; or, How*
✶✶   *Toys Became Real.* Gr. K–4. (Orig. British and U.S. pub. 1922.)
A well-loved toy bunny is transformed into a real rabbit after it has been worn out and discarded. This story is considered to be the first toy animal fantasy novel. The sequel is *The Skin Horse* (orig. British pub. 1927, 1978).
Illus. by William Nicholson, Doubleday, 1958, 1991, 44 pp. (0-385-00913-5); illus. by Michael (R.) Hague, Holt, 1983, 33 pp. (0-8050-0209-X); illus. by Allen Atkinson, Knopf, 1983, 40 pp. (0-394-53221-X); illus. by Ilsa Plume, Harcourt, 1987, 32 pp., o.p.; illus. by Monique Felix, Creative, 1994 (1-56846-093-7); illus. by Loretta Krupinski, Hyperion, 1997, 32 pp. (0-7868-0319-3)

(BL 77:137, 79:1337, 1443, 82:632, 84:401; Bookshelf 1923–1924 p. 7; CCBB 37:2, 39:59; HBG 2:257, 6:64,, 8:295; Kirkus 51:374; Moore:426; SLJ Dec 1981 p. 58, Aug 1983 p. 60; Jan 1986 p. 62)

11-15 BIANCO, Pamela. *Little Houses Far Away.* Gr. 1–4.
Paula explores the teddy bear and doll world she saw from a train window.
Illus. by the author, Oxford University Press, 1951, 87 pp., o.p.
(BL 48:174; CCBB 5:26; HB 27:324; Kirkus 19:614; LJ 76:2009)

11-16 BIANCO, Pamela. *Toy Rose.* Gr. 3–5.
A talking doll named Toy Rose comes between Joy and Jessica, twins who had always been best friends.
Illus. by the author, Lippincott, 1957, 91 pp., o.p.
(CCBB 11:77; HB 33:398; Kirkus 25:479; LJ 82:3241)

11-17 BLOCH, Marie Halun. *The Dollhouse Story.* Gr. 3–5.
Three dollhouse dolls come to life to get rid of a cat who frightened their friend Mouse.
Illus. by Walter Erhard, Walck, 1961, 63 pp., o.p.
(BL 58:488; HB 38:176; LJ 87:329)

BRINK, Carol Ryrie. *Andy Buckram's Tin Men.*
See Chapter 8, Humorous Fantasy.

11-18 BROWN, Abbie Farwell. *The Lonesomest Doll.* Gr. 3–5. (Orig. U.S. pub. 1901.)
The porter's daughter teaches a princess how to play with her lonesome doll.
Illus. by Arthur Rackham, Houghton, 1928, 80 pp., o.p.
(BL 25:173; Bookshelf 1923–1924 p. 12; HB 4:76; Mahony 1:40; Mahony 2:127)

11-19 BUCK, David. *The Small Adventures of Dog.* Gr. 3–5. (Orig. British pub. 1968.)
A discarded leather pig called "Dog" finds he can talk with toys and with real animals.
Illus. by the author, Watts, 1969, 76 pp., o.p.
(CCBB 24:5; LJ 95:778; TLS 1968 p. 1376)

11-20 BUFFETT, Jimmy, and BUFFETT, Savannah Jane. *Trouble Dolls.* Gr. K–4.
Lizzy's tiny Guatemalan Trouble Dolls help her rescue her father, who has become lost in the Florida Everglades.
Illus. by Lambert Davis, Harcourt, 1991, 32 pp. (0-15-290790-4)
(BL 87:1496; HBG 2:260; SLJ June 1991 p. 72)

BURNETT, Frances Hodgson. *Racketty-Packetty House.*
See Chapter 9, Magic Adventure Fantasy.

11-21 BYARS, Betsy (Cromer). *Clementine.* Gr. 3–4.
Clementine, a dragon made from an old green sock, grows dissatisfied with her toy-shelf home and insists on moving to a cave in the country.
Illus. by Charles Wilton, Houghton, 1962, 72 pp., o.p.
(Kirkus 30:280; LJ 87:3199)

CASSEDY, Sylvia. *Behind the Attic Wall.*
See Chapter 4, Ghost Fantasy.

11-22 CLARKE, Judith. *Teddy B. Zoot.* Gr. 2–4.
When Sarah forgets to bring home her math assignment, her teddy bear braves a rainstorm and a vicious dog to find the worksheet and bring it to her.
Illus. by Margaret Hewitt, Henry Holt, 1990, 58 pp. (0-8050-1452-7), 1992, pap. (0-8050-2210-4)
(BL 87:1130; HBG 2:69; SLJ Jan 1991 p. 70)

11-23 CLARKE, Pauline (pseud. of Pauline [Clarke] Hunter Blair). *Five Dolls in a House.* **(Five Dolls series, bk. 1).** Gr. 3–5. (Orig. British pub. 1961.)
After she shrinks to doll-size, Elizabeth sees what life is like for her own five dolls. The sequels are *Five Dolls in the Snow* (1967), *Five Dolls and Their Friends* (British), *Five Dolls and the Duke* (British), and *Five Dolls and the Monkey* (British).
Illus. by Aliki (Brandenberg), Prentice-Hall, 1965, 143 pp., o.p.
(CCBB 19:145; HB 41:627; LJ 91:1696; TLS 1961 p. 451)

11-24 CLARKE, Pauline (pseud. of Pauline [Clarke] Hunter Blair). *The Return*
✮ *of the Twelves.* Gr. 4–7. (Orig. British pub. 1962, entitled *The Twelve and the Genii*.)
Max Morley discovers that his 12 toy soldiers are alive and once belonged to the Brontë children. He helps them return to their ancestral home. Carnegie Medal, 1962.
Illus. by Bernarda Bryson, Coward, 1963, 251 pp., o.p.; Gregg, 1981, 251 pp., o.p.; Trafalgar, 2000, 296 pp. (1-585-79021-4)
(BL 60:701; Eakin:74; HB 39:602, 60:223; LJ 89:390; TLS 1962 p. 901)

11-25 COATSWORTH, Elizabeth (Jane). *All-of-a-Sudden Susan.* Gr. 3–5.
Susan finds that her doll, Emelida, can speak after they are accidentally left behind when her family abandons their house during a flood.
Illus. by Richard Cuffari, Macmillan, 1974, 74 pp., o.p.
(BL 71:506; CCBB 28:128; Kirkus 42:1303; SLJ Mar 1975 p. 86)

11-26 COLLODI, Carlo (pseud. of Carlo Lorenzini). *The Adventures of Pinoc-*
✮ *chio.* Gr. 4–7. (Alternate title *Pinocchio*; written 1880; pub. serially beginning in 1881; orig. Italian pub. in book form, 1883, orig. U.S. pub. 1892.)
A wooden puppet named Pinocchio longs to become a real boy. Five sequels were written by authors other than Collodi and published in the U.S.: *Pinocchio in Africa* (Ginn, 1911) by Eugenio Cherubini, *Pinocchio Under the Sea* (Macmillan, 1913) by Gemma Mongiardini Rembadi, *The Heart of Pinocchio* (Harper, 1919) by Paolo Lorenzini, *Pinocchio in America* (Doubleday, 1928) by Angelo Patri, and *Puppet Parade* (Longmans, 1932) by Carol(yn M.) Delia Chiesa. Roberto Innocenti's illustrations for the 1988 edition of *Pinocchio* won the Kate Greenaway Highly Commended Medal, 1989.
Trans. by Carol(yn M.) Delia Chiesa, illus. by Atillo Mussino, Macmillan, 1925, 1969, 1978, 1989, 310 pp. (0-02-722821-5); adapt. by Neil Morris, illus. by Frank Baber, Macmillan, 1982, 83 pp., o.p.; illus. by Fritz Kredel, Putnam, 1982, 239 pp. (0-448-06001-9); trans. by M. L. Rosenthal, illus. by Troy Howell, Lothrop, 1983, 254 pp., o.p.; adapt. by Stephanie Spinner, illus. by Diane Goode, Random, 1983, 58 pp., o.p.; trans. by James T. Teahan, illus. by Alexa Jaffurs, Schocken, 1985, 206 pp., o.p.; trans. and illus. by Francis Wainwright, Holt, 1986, 96 pp., o.p.; trans. by E. Harden, illus. by Roberto Innocenti,

Knopf, 1988, 144 pp. (0-394-82110-6); adapt. by James Riordan, illus. by Victor G. Ambrus, Oxford University Press, 1988, 96 pp. (entitled *Pinocchio*), o.p.; adapt. and illus. by Chris McEwan, Doubleday, 1990, 32 pp., o.p.; illus. by Lorenzo Mattotti, Lothrop, 1993, 40 pp., LB (0-688-12451-8); adapt. and illus. by Ed Young, Philomel, 1996, 48 pp. (0-399-22941-8); illus. by Victor G. Ambrus, trans. by James Riordan, Oxford, 1997, 91 pp. (0-19-272287-5); (entitled *Pinocchio: A Classic Illustrated Edition*), illus. by multiple illustrators, comp. by Cooper Edens, Chronicle, 2001, 173 pp. (0-8118-2283-4); illus. by Iassen Ghiuselev, Simply Read, 2002, 160 pp. (0-9688768-0-3); (entitled *The Adventures of Pinocchio*) retold by Helen Rossendale and Graham Philpot, illus. by Graham Philpot, Dial, 2003, 96 pp. (0-8037-2919-7); (entitled *The Adventures of Pinocchio*) illus. by Greg Hildebrandt, Courage, 2004, 56 pp. (0-7624-1713-7); illus. by Sara Fanelli, trans. by Emma Rose, Candlewick, 2003, 192 pp. (0-7636-2261-3)

(BL 12:299, 21:238, 60:307, 79:674; 80:856, 85:573, 87:1135, 90:339, 93:586, 98:1328, 100:325 and 664; Bookshelf 1928 p. 9; CCBB 2:4, 4:45, 11:67, 37:105, 144; HB 2:29, 27:260, 59:70, 60:357, 61:588, 65:209, 80:158–159; HBG 2:54, 8:57, 13:83, 14:77, 15:87; Kirkus 37:719, 68:1233; LJ 95:258, June 15, 1985 p. 71; Mahony 2:286; SLJ Feb 1984 p. 56, Feb 1986 p. 72, Mar 1987 p. 156, Feb 1989 p. 68, Jan 1991 p. 78, Oct 1996 p. 85, Dec 2001 p. 133, Dec 2003 p. 148; Suth 3:97)

11-27 COOMBS, Patricia. *The Lost Playground.* Gr. 1–4.
Accidentally left in the park, Mostly, June's homemade stuffed animal, floats off to the Lost Playground where all lost toys go.
Illus. by the author, Lothrop, 1963, 46 pp., o.p.
(CCBB 17:153; HB 39:380)

11-28 DE LEEUW, Adele Louise. *Nobody's Doll.* Gr. 2–5.
Susan Araminta is rescued from the trash by Mr. McHugh, a Scottie who helps her find a new owner.
Illus. by Anne Vaughan, Little, Brown, 1946, 85 pp., o.p.
(BL 42:319; HB 22:268; LJ 71:827)

11-29 DEXTER, Catherine. *The Oracle Doll.* Gr. 5–8. (Paperback title *The Doll Who Knew the Future.*)
When Gabriella, Lucy's talking doll, begins saying things she was not programmed to say, Lucy and her sister realize that Gabby can predict the future, like the ancient Oracle at Delphi.
Macmillan, 1985, 195 pp., o.p.; Morrow, 1994, pap. (entitled *The Doll Who Knew the Future*), 208 pp., o.p.
(BL 82:403; CCBB 39:145; SLJ Feb 1986 p. 84)

11-30 DIAZ, Abby (Morton). *Polly Cologne.* Gr. 3–5. (Orig. pub. 1881.)
A rag doll, named Polly Cologne, goes for a ride in a dog's mouth and gets lost.
Illus. by Morgan J. Sweeney, Lothrop, 1930, 215 pp., o.p.
(BL 27:215; HB 6:332, 7:116; Mahony 1:14)

11-31 DICKS, Terrance. *Sally Ann on Her Own.* **(Sally Ann series, bk. 1).** Gr. 2–4.
Sally Ann, a spunky rag doll, mobilizes the other toys at Mrs. Foster's day-care center to expose the crooked inspectors who are attempting to close the school.

The other books in the series are *Sally Ann at the Ballet* (1990), *Sally Ann: Stella's Wedding* (1990), *Sally Ann Goes to the Hospital* (1990), *Sally Ann - The Pony* (1991), *Sally Ann and the School Show* (1988, 1992), *Sally Ann and the Mystery Picnic* (1990, 1993), and *Nurse Sally Ann* (1994).
Illus. by Blanche Simms, Simon & Schuster, 1992, 64 pp. (0-671-74512-3)
(BL 88:1680; HBG 3:254; Kirkus 60:776; SLJ July 1992 p. 58)

11-32 DILLON, Barbara. *The Teddy Bear Tree.* Gr. 3–5.
A tree full of teddy bears grows where Bertine buries a worn-out teddy bear's glass eye.
Illus. by David S. Rose, Morrow, 1982, 79 pp., o.p.
(BL 79:244; Kirkus 50:734; SLJ Oct 1982 p. 150)

11-33 DILLON, Barbara. *Who Needs a Bear?* Gr. 2–4.
Three old toys leave the safety of their attic home, searching for new owners who really care about them.
Illus. by Diane de Groat, Morrow, 1981, 63 pp., o.p.
(BL 78:104; CCBB 35:84; Kirkus 49:1159; SLJ Nov 1981 p. 90)

11-34 DU BOIS, William (Sherman) Pène. *Gentleman Bear.* Gr. 4–6.
Bayard the gentleman teddy bear accompanies his owner, Sir Billy Browne-Browne, from age 4 through adulthood.
Illus. by the author, Farrar, 1985, 80 pp., o.p.
(BL 82:1080; CCBB 39:145; SLJ Apr 1986 p. 86; Suth 4:103)

DUFFY, James. *The Revolt of the Teddy Bears.*
See Chapter 2, Animal Fantasy.

11-35 ESTERN, Anne Graham. *The Picolinis and the Haunted House.* Gr. 4–6.
The Picolini circus doll family helps Jessica and Peter solve a mystery surrounding the haunted house their parents want to buy. This is the sequel to *The Picolinis* (1988).
Illus. by Hal Frenck, Bantam, 1989, pap., 128 pp., o.p.
(BL 86:1467; SLJ Mar 1990 p. 217)

ESTES, Eleanor (Ruth Rosenfeld). *The Witch Family.*
See Chapter 12, Witchcraft and Sorcery Fantasy.

11-36 FAIRSTAR, Mrs. (pseud. of Richard Henry Home). *Memoirs of a London Doll, Written by Herself.* Gr. 4–6. (Orig. British pub. 1846, U.S. 1852.)
★ Maria Poppet describes her harrowing experiences as she is passed from owner to owner. Considered to be the first talking doll fantasy, this story has been reprinted in *The Silent Playmate* (Macmillan, 1979, 1981), ed. by Naomi Lewis (see this chapter).
Illus. by Emma L(illian) Brock, Macmillan, 1922, 1944, 1951, 173 pp., o.p.; illus. by Margaret Gillies and Richard Smith, Macmillan, 1968, 143 pp., o.p.
(BL 65:257; Bookshelf 1928 p. 16; CCBB 22:79; HB 44:560; Kirkus 36:642; TLS 1967 p. 1143)

11-37 FANCIULLI, Giuseppe. *The Little Blue Man.* Gr. 4–6. (Orig. pub. in Italy.)
The story of the adventures of a small, blue puppet man.

Trans. by May M. Sweet, illus. by H(erman) I(lfeld) Bacharach, Houghton, 1926, 198 pp., o.p.
(BL 23:234; HB 2[Nov 1926]:42; Mahony 2:123)

11-38   **FIELD, Rachel (Lyman).** *Hitty, Her First Hundred Years.* Gr. 4–6. (Orig.
✮   pub. 1929.)
The adventures of a carved-wood doll named Hitty include being shipwrecked while traveling from Maine to the South Seas. John Newbery Medal, 1930. Rosemary Wells has written a revised version of this story entitled *Rachel Field's Hitty, Her First Hundred Years with New Adventures* (Simon, 1999), and Ellen Weiss has written a series of sequels called Hitty's Travels: *Civil War Days* (Simon, 2001), *Gold Rush Days* (Simon, 2001), *Voting Rights Days* (Simon, 2002), and *Ellis Island Days* (Simon, 2002).
Illus. by Dorothy P. Lathrop, Macmillan, 1937, 1969, 207 pp. (0-02-734840-7); adapt. by Rosemary Wells, illus. by Susan Jeffers, Simon, 1999, 106 pp., entitled *Rachel Field's Hitty, Her First Hundred Years with New Adventures* (0-689-81716-9)
(BL 26:125; Bookshelf 1932 p. 12; HB 5:53, 6:22, 76:107; HBG 11:90; LJ 54:986, 55:603, 996; Moore:235, 427; SLJ Jan 2000 p. 112)

11-39 **FOSTER, Elizabeth.** *Gigi: The Story of a Merry-Go-Round Horse.* Gr. 4–6.
A merry-go-round horse has many adventures while traveling from Vienna to Paris, London, and America. The sequel is *Gigi in America: Further Adventures of a Merry-Go-Round Horse* (1946, 1983).
Illus. by Use Bischoff, Houghton, 1943, 118 pp., o.p.; North Atlantic Books, 1983, 124 pp., o.p.
(BL 40:116; HB 19:319; LJ 68:820, 1008)

11-40 **FRANCHI, Anna.** *The Little Lead Soldier.* Gr. 3–5.
Tamburino, a French lead soldier, tells two Italian children the story of his life and adventures.
Illus. by Hattie Longstreet Price, Penn, 1919, 186 pp., o.p.
(BL 16:316; Bookshelf 1923–1924 p. 8)

11-41 **FYLEMAN, Rose (Amy).** *The Dolls' House.* Gr. 2–4. (Orig. British pub. 1930.)
The dollhouse family has a number of adventures while its owner is away.
Illus. by Erick Berry, Doubleday, 1931, 99 pp., o.p.
(BL 28:66; HB 7:220; LJ 56:958; TLS 1930 p. 986)

11-42 **GARDAM, Jane (Pearson).** *Through the Dolls' House Door.* Gr. 4–8.
✮   (Orig. British pub. 1987.)
Forgotten for many years after their playmates have moved away, the "creatures" living in an antique dollhouse (a Dutch doll, a rag doll, a soldier, a little girl doll, and a china cat) despair that they will never be found and played with again.
Greenwillow, 1987, 128 pp. (0-688-07447-2); Dell, 1991, pap. (0-440-40433-9)
(BL 84:318; CCBB 41:48; Kirkus 55:1155; SLJ Oct 1987 p. 125; TLS 1987 p. 751; VOYA 11:39)

11-43 **GARDNER, Sally.** *The Countess's Calamity.* **(Tales from the Box series, bk. 1).** Gr. K–3. (Orig. British pub. 2003.)
Mr. and Mrs. Mouse rescue five dolls abandoned in the park and teach them how to survive. Nestlé Smarties Book Prize, Bronze Award, 2003. The sequel is *Boolar's Big Day Out* (2003).
Illus. by the author, Bloomsbury, 2003, 127 pp. (1-58234-812-X)); Blooms-bury, 2003, pap., 164 pp. (1-58234-855-3)
(HBG 14:354; SLJ Aug 2003 p.128)

11-44 **GODDEN (Dixon), (Margaret) Rumer.** *Candy Floss.* Gr. 1–4. (Orig.
★ British pub. 1959.)
A spoiled little girl named Clementina decides to steal Jack's doll, Candy Floss. This story has been reprinted in *Four Dolls* (Greenwillow, 1984; see below).
Illus. by Adrienne Adams, Viking, 1959, 63 pp., o.p.; illus. by Nonny Hogro-gian, Putnam, 1991, 64 pp. (0-399-21807-6)
(BL 56:633, 88:532; CCBB 13:147; Eakin:141; HB 36:212:HBG 3:58; Kirkus 28:144; LJ 85:247; SLJ Dec 1991 p. 90; TLS Nov 25, 1960 p. iv)

11-45 **GODDEN (Dixon), (Margaret) Rumer.** *The Dolls' House.* Gr. 3–5. (Orig.
★ British pub. 1947.)
Life in a Victorian dollhouse alters dramatically after a haughty new doll arrives.
Illus. by Tasha Tudor, Viking, 1948, 1962, 136 pp., o.p.
(BL 45:53, 59:292; CCBB 2:3, 13:147; Eakin:141; HB 24:347, 457, 39:75; Kirkus 16:363; LJ 73:1097; TLS 1947 p. 636)

11-46 **GODDEN (Dixon), (Margaret) Rumer.** *The Fairy Doll.* Gr. 2–4. (Orig.
★ British pub. 1955.)
The fairy doll atop the Christmas tree helps Elizabeth gain self-confidence. Carnegie Medal Commended Book, 1956. This story has been reprinted in *Four Dolls* (Greenwillow, 1984; see below).
Illus. by Adrienne Adams, Viking, 1956, 67 pp., o.p.; Philomel, 1998, o.p.
(BL 53:51; HB 34:453; Kirkus 24:431; LJ 81:2720; TLS Nov 23, 1956 p. xv)

11-47 **GODDEN (Dixon), (Margaret) Rumer.** *Four Dolls.* Gr. 3–5. (Orig. British
★ pub. in this edition 1983.)
Four timeless tales about spirited little dolls and their resourceful owners, origi-nally published separately as *Impunity Jane* (Viking, 1954; see below), *The Fairy Doll* (Viking, 1956; see above), *The Story of Holly and Ivy* (Viking, 1958; see below), and *Candy Floss* (Viking, 1960; see above).
Illus. by Pauline Baynes, Greenwillow, 1984, o.p.
(BL 81:306; HB 60:615; SLJ Nov 1984 p. 124)

11-48 **GODDEN (Dixon), (Margaret) Rumer.** *Fu-Dog.* Gr. 1–4. (Original British
★ pub. 1989.)
The embroidered satin Fu-Dog her great-uncle sends her from London's China-town enables Li-la to find her Chinese relatives and reconcile the English and Chinese sides of her family.
Illus. by Valerie Littlewood, Viking, 1990, 64 pp., o.p.
(BL 86:1897; HBG 1:237; Kirkus 58:727; SLJ May 1990 p. 86)

11-49   **GODDEN (Dixon), (Margaret) Rumer.** *Home Is the Sailor.* Gr. 3–5. (Orig.
✳   British pub. 1964.)
      A Welsh doll named Curley sets sail for France to search for his older brother
      Thomas.
      Illus. by Jean Primrose, Viking, 1964, 128 pp., o.p.; Pan Macmillan, 1996 (0-
      33306-570-0)
      (CCBB 18:86; Eakin:141; HB 41:56; LJ 90:960; TLS 1964. p. 1081)

11-50   **GODDEN (Dixon), (Margaret) Rumer.** *Impunity Jane: The Story of a*
✳   *Pocket Doll.* Gr. 2–4. (Orig. British pub. 1954.)
      Impunity Jane grows bored sitting on a dollhouse cushion all day and longs to
      take a ride in someone's pocket. This story has been reprinted in *Four Dolls*
      (Greenwillow, 1984; see above).
      Illus. by Adrienne Adams, Viking, 1954, 47 pp., o.p.
      (BL 51:47; CCBB 9:23; Eakin:142; HB 30:330; Kirkus 22:383; LJ 79:1913, 2018)

11-51   **GODDEN (Dixon), (Margaret) Rumer.** *Miss Happiness and Miss Flower.*
✳   Gr. 3–5. (Orig. British pub. 1960.)
      Nona and her cousins build a Japanese-style house for her two Japanese dolls.
      Carnegie Medal Commended Book, 1961. The sequel is *Little Plum* (1962,
      1963).
      Illus. by Jean Primrose, Viking, 1961, 81 pp., o.p.; HarperCollins, 2002 (0-06-
      029193-1), 2002, pap. (0-06-440938-4)
      (BL 57:580; CCBB 14:143; Eakin:142; HB 37:269, 78:430–431; HBG 13:373; Kirkus
      29:328; LJ 86:1983; TLS May 19, 1961 p. iv)

11-52   **GODDEN (Dixon), (Margaret) Rumer.** *The Story of Holly and Ivy.* Gr.
✳   2–4. (Orig. British pub. 1957.)
      The Christmas wishes of an orphaned girl named Ivy, a doll named Holly, and
      a lonely woman named Mrs. Jones are all granted. This story has been reprint-
      ed in *Four Dolls* (Greenwillow, 1984; see this chapter).
      Illus. by Adrienne Adams, Viking, 1958, 64 pp., o.p.; illus. by Barbara Cooney,
      Viking, 1985, 32 pp., o.p.; illus. by Christian Birmingham, Macmillan, 2004,
      new ed., 96 pp. (0-33376-678-4)
      (BL 55:53, 82:261, 417; CCBB 12:47, 39:27; Eakin:143; HB 34:461; Kirkus 26:453; LJ
      83:3572; SLJ Oct 1985 p. 190; TLS Nov 21, 1958 p. xv)

11-53   **GREENWALD, Sheila (pseud. of Sheila Green).** *The Secret Museum.* Gr.
      3–5.
      Jennifer comes upon some antique dolls who agree to perform in plays to earn
      money to help Jennifer's parents.
      Illus. by the author, Lippincott, 1974, 127 pp., o.p.
      (BL 70:1104; CCBB 27:177; Kirkus 42:424; LJ 99:1473)

      GRIFFIN, Peni R(ae). *Margo's House.*
      See Chapter 9, Magic Adventure Fantasy.

11-54   **GRIFFITH, Helen V(irginia).** *Caitlin's Holiday.* Gr. 3–5.
✳   Something compels Caitlin to trade her favorite doll for Holiday, a beautiful
      teenage doll who walks, talks, complains, sulks, and throws tantrums. In the
      sequel, *Doll Trouble* (1993), Caitlin and Jennifer's friendship is tested when
      Holiday is accused of stealing Jennifer's missing doll clothes.

Illus. by Susan Condie Lamb, Greenwillow, 1990, 96 pp. (0-688-09470-8)
(BL 86:2172; CCBB 44:29; HBG 2:74; Kirkus 58:931; SLJ Oct 1990 p. 92)

GRIPE, Maria (Kristina). *Agnes Cecilia.*
See Chapter 4, Ghost Fantasy.

11-55   HISER, Constance. *The Missing Doll.* Gr. 3–4.
Abby and Heather find a missing classmate using rhyming clues supplied by
Abby's talking doll.
Illus. by Marcy Ramsey, Holiday, 1993, 104 pp. (0-8234-1046-3)
(BL 90:623; CCBB 47:123; HBG 5:77; SLJ Feb 1994 p. 102)

HOBAN, Russell C(onwell). *The Mouse and His Child.*
See Chapter 1, Allegorical Fantasy and Literary Fairy Tales.

11-56   HOFFMANN, E(rnst) T(heodor) A(madeus). *The Nutcracker.* Gr. 2 up.
★★   (Orig. German pub. 1819; U.S. pub. 1853, entitled *Nutcracker and Mouse-
King.*)
In a little girl's Christmas Eve dream, her toy nutcracker comes to life and
takes her to a magical world.
Whitman, 1930, o.p.; adapt. and illus. by Warren Chappell, Knopf, 1958, 28
pp., o.p.; adapt. by Janet Schulman, illus. by Kay Chorao, Knopf, 1988 (repr.
of 1978 ed.), 64 pp. (0-394-82018-5); illus. by Rachel Isadora, Macmillan,
1981, 32 pp., o.p.; trans. and adapt. by Anthea Bell, illus. by Lisbeth Zwerger,
Picture Book Studio, 1983, 1987, 28 pp., o.p., 1991, pap. (0-88708-156-8);
trans. by Ralph Manheim, illus. by Maurice Sendak, Crown, 1991, pap., 120
pp. (0-517-58659-2); illus. by Roberto Innocenti, Creative, 1996, 136 pp. (0-
15-100227-4); illus. by Maurice (Bernard) Sendak, trans. by Ralph Manheim,
Crown, 2001 (reissue of 1984 ed.), 102 pp. (0-609-61049-X); illus. by Lisbeth
Zwerger; trans. by Anthea Bell, North-South, 2004, 32 pp. (0-7358-1733-2)
(BL 35:139, 55:78, 56:225, 72:791, 76:452, 78:304, 80:417, 81:146, 101:328; CCBB 32:153,
37:30, 38:67; HB 6:329, 34:460, 35:487, 61:53; HBG 2:46, 8:57, 13:86; Kirkus 26:606,
27:597, 49:1292, 52:75; LJ 55:924; 83:2496, 84:2731; SLJ Oct 1979 p. 118, Oct 1981 p. 155,
Feb 1984 p. 73, Nov 1984 p. 125, Oct 1987 p. 31; Suth 3:194, 195; TLS 1985 p. 75)

11-57   HOWE, Deborah, and HOWE, James. *Teddy Bear's Scrapbook.* Gr. 2–4.
Teddy tells his owner seven adventure-filled tales about his exploits, including
visiting the abominable snowman and becoming a cowboy, a circus performer,
and a movie star.
Illus. by David S. Rose, Macmillan, 1980, 73 pp., o.p., 1988, pap., 80 pp. (0-
689-71168-9)
(BL 76:1424; CCBB 34:13; Kirkus 48:911; SLJ Sep 1980 p. 60)

11-58   HUGHES, Richard (Arthur Warren). *Gertrude's Child.* Gr. K–3.
Mistreated by her owner, Gertrude the wooden doll leaves home and chooses a
new owner, named Annie, but has no idea how to treat the little girl kindly.
Illus. by Rick Schreiter, Harlin Quist, 1966, 42 pp., o.p.
(CCBB 20:123; LJ 91:5740)

11-59   JANE, Pamela. *Noelle of the Nutcracker.* Gr. 3–5.
A ballerina doll who dreams of a dancing career is desperately desired by sec-
ond-graders Ilyana Ingram and her archrival, wealthy Mary Jane Igoe.

Illus. by Jan Brett, Houghton, 1986, 64 pp. (0-395-39969-6); Bantam, 1988, pap. (0-553-15673-X)

(BL 83:132; CCBB 40:28; Kirkus 54:1125; SLJ Oct 1986 p. 112)

11-60 JOHNSON, Crockett (pseud. of David Leisk). *Ellen's Lion: Twelve Stories.* Gr. 2–4.
Ellen and her talking toy lion go on 12 adventures together.
Illus. by the author, Harper, 1959, 62 pp., o.p.

(HB 35:379; Kirkus 27:370; LJ 84:3625)

11-61 JONES, Elizabeth Orton. *Big Susan.* Gr. 2–4.
☆ Big Susan helps the Doll family come to life on Christmas Eve.
Illus. by the author, Macmillan, 1947, 1967, 82 pp., o.p.

(BL 44:138, CCBB 1[Dec 1947]:3; HB 24:39; Kirkus 15:547; LJ 72:1692)

11-62 KARON, Jan. *Jeremy: The Tale of an Honest Bunny.* Gr. 3–5.
A cloth bunny named Jeremy travels from the English village where he was made to his new home in North Carolina.
Illus. by Teri Weidner, Viking, 2000, 82 pp. (0-670-88104-X)

(BL 96:1542; HBG 11:294; Kirkus 67:1886; SLJ Sep 2000 p. 200)

11-63 KENNEDY, (Jerome) Richard. *Amy's Eyes.* Gr. 5–7.
☆ Orphaned Amy's love for her sailor doll, Captain, causes him to grow into a real sailor who runs away from the Home for Girls, vowing to return for Amy once he has made his fortune.
Illus. by Richard Egielski, Harper, 1985, 448 pp., o.p.

(BL 81:1254, 82:1234; CCBB 38:150; HB 61:554; Kirkus 53:42; SLJ May 1985 p. 90; Suth 4:212; VOYA 8:193)

11-64 KING, Beulah. *Ruffs and Pompoms.* Gr. 4–6.
Clown-doll Finney Foo leaves the toyshop and sets out to see the world.
Illus. by Maurice Day, Little, Brown, 1924, 256 pp., o.p.

(HB Oct 1924 pp. 4, 8 and June 1925 p. 32; Mahony 2:282)

11-65 KING-SMITH, Dick. *Lady Daisy.* Gr. 3–6. (Orig. British pub. 1992.)
☆ Hidden away for 89 years, a beautiful Victorian doll is reluctantly "adopted" by 9-year-old Ned, who is teased about her at school before she is stolen.
Illus. by Naimo Jones, Delacorte, 1993, 144 pp. (0-385-30891-4); Yearling, 1995, pap. (0-440-40998-5)

(BL 89:1590; CCBB 46:215; HBG 4:300; Kirkus 61:458; SLJ July 1993 p. 62)

11-66 KNIGHT, Marjorie. *Alexander's Christmas Eve.* **(Alexander trilogy, bk. 1).** Gr. 2–4.
Three Christmas toys escape from Santa's pack and set out to see the world and find their own home. The sequels are *Alexander's Birthday* (1940) and *Alexander's Vacation* (1943).
Illus. by Howard Simon, Dutton, 1938, 93 pp., o.p.

(HB 14:413; LJ 63:798)

11-67 KOONTZ, Dean R(ay). *Oddkins: A Fable for All Ages.* Gr. 7–12.
A stuffed bear and his toy friends battle an evil jack-in-the-box to preserve the toys' magical ability to help children cope with their problems.

Illus. by Phil Parks, Warner, 1988, 180 pp., o.p.
(BL 85:220, 258; Kirkus 56:1200)

11-68   KROEBER, Theodora (Kracow). *Carrousel.* Gr. 2–4.
When Pegason the winged horse falls into a giant city, his friends Gryphon and
Pyggon must rescue him.
Illus. by Douglas Tait, Atheneum, 1977, 91 pp., o.p.
(CCBB 31:97; HB 53:664; Kirkus 45:1198; SLJ Nov 1977 p. 49)

11-69   LATHROP, Dorothy P(ulis). *An Angel in the Woods.* Gr. 2–4.
A toy Christmas angel brings Christmas spirit to the forest animals.
Illus. by the author, Macmillan, 1947, 1955, 42 pp., o.p.
(BL 44:156; HB 24:37; Kirkus 15:578; LJ 72:1784)

LATHROP, Dorothy P(ulis). *The Lost Merry-Go-Round.*
See Chapter 9, Magic Adventure Fantasy.

LAWRENCE, Michael. *The Poppy Kettle Papers.*
See Chapter 5, High Fantasy: Alternate Worlds or Histories.

LISLE, Rebecca. *Copper.*
See Chapter 9, Magic Adventure Fantasy.

11-70   MAHY, Margaret (May). *The Five Sisters.* Gr. 3–5. (Orig. New Zealand
✫   pub. 1996.)
A string of five paper dolls, each drawn by a different person, is blown away
by the hot summer wind and found again many years later.
Illus. by Patricia MacCarthy, Viking, 1997, 80 pp. (0-670-87042-0); Puffin,
1999, pap. (0-14-130334-4)
(BL 93:941; CCBB 50:329; HB 73:201; HBG 8:305; Kirkus 64:1800; SLJ Mar 1997 p. 162)

MARIA, Consort of Ferdinand, King of Rumania. *The Magic Doll.*
See Chapter 9, Magic Adventure Fantasy.

11-71   MARTIN, Ann M(atthews), and GODWIN, Laura. *The Doll People.* Gr.
✫   3–6.
Annabelle Doll tries to use Aunt Sarah Doll's journal to find her aunt, who disappeared in 1955, and is helped by her new friend, Tiffany Funcraft, a modern
plastic doll. In *The Meanest Doll in the World* (2003), Annabelle and Tiffany
ride to school in their human's backpack, but go home with another child, to a
house ruled by Mean Mimi, the meanest doll in the world.
Illus. by Brian Selznick, Hyperion, 2000, 256 pp. (0-7868-0361-4), 2003, pap.,
288 pp. (0-7868-1240-0)
(BL 96:2140; CCBB 54:187; HBG 12:76; Kirkus 68:1200; SLJ Nov 2000 p. 128 and Dec
2000 p. 54)

11-72   MILNE, A(lan) A(lexander). *Winnie-the-Pooh.* Gr. 2–4. (Orig. British and
✫✫   U.S. pub. 1926.)
The adventures of Christopher Robin and his friends—Winnie-the-Pooh, Tig-
ger, Eeyore, Piglet, Rabbit, Owl, Kanga, and Baby Roo—include Pooh's tan-
gles with honeybees and Piglet's encounter with a Heffalump. The sequels are
The House at Pooh Corner (1961; orig. pub. 1928) and *The Hums of Pooh*

(1930). Collections of tales about Pooh include *The World of Pooh* (1957), *The Pooh Story Book* (1965), *The Christopher Robin Story Book* (1966), and *Pooh's Bedtime Book* (1980).

Illus. by Ernest H. Shepard, Dutton, 1926, 1954, 1974, 1988, 161 pp., o.p.; Dell, 1988, pap. (0-440-40116-X); Puffin, 1992, pap., 176 pp. (0-14-036121-9); Penguin, 2001, 40 pp., entitled *Winnie the Pooh and Friends*, o.p.; Dutton, 2001, 557 pp., entitled *The Complete Tales and Poems of Winnie-the-Pooh* (0-5254-6726-2)

(BL 23:137; Bookshelf 1928 p. 9; HB 2:42, 34:122; Kirkus 39:1213; LJ 52:1017; Moore:427; TLS 1926 p. 861, 1971 p. 1614)

11-73 NABB, Magdalen. *The Enchanted Horse.* Gr. 3–6. (Orig. British pub. 1992.)
☆ Lonely Irina's love for Bella, a shabby wooden rocking horse, transforms Bella into a beautiful wild horse who takes Irina on midnight rides.
Illus. by Julek Heller, Orchard, 1993, 90 pp., o.p.; Hyperion, 1995, pap., 90 pp. (0-7868-1029-7)
(BL 90:623; HB 69:744; HBG 5:80; Kirkus 61:1333; SLJ Oct 1993 p. 126)

NESBIT (Bland), E(dith). *The Magic City.*
See Chapter 7, High Fantasy: Travel to Other Worlds.

11-74 O'CONNELL, Jean S. *The Dollhouse Caper.* Gr. 4–6.
☆ Although the Dollhouse family is unable to warn the Humans about an upcoming robbery, they manage to frighten the burglars away by themselves.
Illus. by Erik Blegvad, Crowell, 1976 (c. 1975), 82 pp., o.p.; Harper, 1988 (repr. of 1976 ed.), 96 pp., o.p.
(BL 72:1049; CCBB 29:149; HB 52:291; Kirkus 44:70; SLJ Apr 1976 p. 63; Suth 2:341)

11-75 ODGERS, Sally Farrell. *Drummond: The Search for Sarah.* Gr. 2–4. (Orig. Australian pub. 1990.)
Drummond, a teddy bear bought at a garage sale, tells Sarah and Nicholas that he'd like to be reunited with his original owner.
Illus. by Carol Jones, Holiday, 1990, 112 pp., o.p.
(BL 87:58; HB 66:775; HBG 2:65; SLJ Mar 1991 p. 177)

11-76 PARRISH, Anne. *Floating Island.* Gr. 3–5.
☆ The adventures of a family of dolls who are shipwrecked on a deserted island. John Newbery Medal Honor Book, 1931. This book has been criticized for its stereotypical depiction of Dinah, the black cook doll.
Illus. by the author, Harper, 1930, 265 pp., o.p.
(BL 27:214; Bookshelf 1932 p. 12; HB 6:331, 7:60, 116; Moore:280, 427; TLS 1930 p. 1043)

PELGROM, Els. *Little Sophie and Lanky Flop.*
See Chapter 1, Allegorical Fantasy and Literary Fairy Tales.

PENDERGRAFT, Patricia. *The Legend of Daisy Flowerdew.*
See Chapter 1, Allegorical Fantasy and Literary Fairy Tales.

11-77 PETERSHAM, Maud (Fuller), and PETERSHAM, Miska. *Get A-Way and Hary Janos.* Gr. 2–4.
In a far-off land where old toys become new, a worn-out toy horse and a one-armed wooden soldier doll go on an adventure.

Illus. by the authors, Viking, 1933, 64 pp., o.p.
(BL 30:90; Mahony 3:59)

11-78   PHILLIPS, Ethel Calvert. *Little Rag Doll.* Gr. 3–5.
Mrs. Thimbletop, the doll fairy, befriends a neglected rag doll named Dilly and they go to live with a cat, named Grandma Reddy, inside a child's playhouse.
Illus. by Lois Lenski, Houghton, 1930, 174 pp., o.p.
(BL 27:214; HB 6:322; LJ 55:955, 56:279; Mahony 3:56)

11-79   PHILLIPS, Ethel Calvert. *The Popover Family.* Gr. 2–4.
Ellen meets the Popover doll family living in her Aunt Amelia's old, red dollhouse.
Illus. by E. F. Butler, Houghton, 1927, 132 pp., o.p,
(BL 24:73; HB 3[Nov 1927]:43; LJ 53:1033; Mahony 2:128)

11-80   PHILLIPS, Ethel Calvert. *Pretty Polly Perkins.* Gr. 3–5.
Three little girls each lay claim to an old-fashioned rag doll.
Illus. by E. F. Butler, Houghton, 1925, 122 pp., o.p.
(BL 22:123; HB Nov 1925 p. 17; Mahony 2:128)

11-81   RENDAL, Justine. *A Child of Their Own.* Gr. 3–6. (Orig. British pub. 1990.)
The Darling doll family and two less-elegant dolls, Amanda and Johnsley, are bought in England and shipped to America, where they dream of being loved and played with by real children.
Viking, 1992, 96 pp. (0-670-84418-7)
(BL 88:2014; CCBB 45:276; HBG 4:75; Kirkus 60:854; SLJ Aug 1992 p. 158)

11-82   *Rocking Horse Land and Other Classic Tales of Dolls and Toys.* Comp. by Naomi Lewis. Gr. 4–6. (Orig. British pub. 2000.)
Six stories, including Andersen's "The Steadfast Tin Soldier," Nesbit's "The Town in the Library," and Mrs. Fairstar's "Memoirs of a London Doll."
Illus. by Angela Barrett, Candlewick, 2000, 126 pp. (0-7636-0897-1)
(HBG 12:138; SLJ Apr 2001 p. 115)

11-83   ROSALES, Melodye Benson. *Minnie Saves the Day.* **(The Adventures of Minnie Merriweather, bk. 1).** Gr. 2–4.
Minnie, the brown rag doll sent by Hester's Grandmama, comes to life at night in this story set in Depression-era Chicago.
Illus. by the author, Little, Brown, 2001, 83 pp. (0-316-75605-9)
(BL 97:1553; HBG 12:294; SLJ July 2001 p. 88)

11-84   SHECTER, Ben. *The Stocking Child.* Gr. 2–4.
Sam and his friend Epaphroditus search far and wide for a missing button eye and wind up at Sam's own house.
Illus. by the author, Harper, 1976, 32 pp. o.p.
(BL 73:669; CCBB 30:114; Kirkus 44:1038; SLJ Jan 1977 p. 85)

11-85   SIEBE, Josephine. *Kasperle's Adventures.* Gr. 3–5. (Orig. German pub. 1928.)
Kasperle, a mischievous wooden doll, comes to life as soon as Master Friedolm finishes carving him.

Trans. by Florence Geiser, illus. by Frank Tobias, Macmillan, 1929, 1939, 199 pp., o.p.

(BL 26:126; Bookshelf 1930–1931 p. 9; HB 5:46–47, 49, 7:117; Mahony 3:56)

11-86 *The Silent Playmate: A Collection of Doll Stories.* **Ed. by Naomi Lewis.** Gr. 4–6. (Orig. British pub. 1979.)
Doll stories from various sources, including Mrs. Fairstar's *Memoirs of a London Doll* (1846, 1852; see above).
Illus. by Harold Jones, Macmillan, 1981, 223 pp., o.p.

(BL 78:589; CCBB 35:89; HB 58:44; SLJ Feb 1982 p. 78)

11-87 **SLEATOR, William (Warner III).** *Among the Dolls.* Gr. 3–5.
✶ Vicky learns a painful lesson when she shrinks to doll size and must suffer the ill temper of the dolls she has mistreated.
Illus. by Trina Schart Hyman, Dutton, 1975, 70 pp., o.p.

(BL 72:628; CCBB 29:118; HB 52:53; Kirkus 43:1186; SLJ Dec 1975 p. 55)

11-88 **SLOBODKIN, Louis.** *The Adventures of Arab.* Gr. 3–5. (Orig. pub. 1946.)
Arab is not happy as a merry-go-round horse, so he changes places with a coach horse.
Illus. by the author, Vanguard, 1967, 123 pp., o.p.

(BL 43:148; HB 22:349; Kirkus 14:386; LJ 72:167)

STEARNS, Pamela (Fujimoto). *The Mechanical Doll.*
See Chapter 1, Allegorical Fantasy and Literary Fairy Tales.

11-89 **STOVER, Marjorie Filley.** *When the Dolls Woke.* Gr. 3–6.
Great-Great-Aunt Abigail's dollhouse holds a treasure, if only the doll family can remember where it is hidden in time to help Abigail, now a destitute old woman. The sequel is *Midnight in the Dollhouse* (1990).
Illus. by Karen Loccisano, Whitman, 1985, 128 pp., o.p.

(BL 82:814; SLJ Jan 1986 p. 71)

11-90 **SYMONDS, John.** *Away to the Moon.* Gr. 2–4.
Two dollhouse dolls, named Hetty and Betty, set off to visit the moon.
Illus. by Pamela Bianco, Lippincott, 1956, 64 pp., o.p.

(BL 53:101; HB 32:349; Kirkus 24:571; LJ 81:2723)

11-91 **TOLKIEN, J(ohn) R(onald) R(euel).** *Roverandom.* **Ed. by Christina Scull**
✶ **and Wayne G. Hammond.** Gr. 4–8.
In this posthumously published story begun in 1925, a wizard transforms a dog named Rover into a toy dog who is determined to become real again.
Illus. by the author, Houghton, 1998, 106 pp. (0-395-89871-4), 1999, pap. (0-395-95799-0)

(BL 94:1883; HB 74:240; Kirkus 66:151; LJ Mar 15, 1998 p. 96; SLJ June 1998 p. 153; VOYA 21 p. 290)

11-92 **TREGARTHEN, Enys (pseud. of Nellie Sloggett).** *The Doll Who Came Alive.* Gr. 3–5.
A little girl's great love for her wooden doll brings it to life.
Adapt. by Elizabeth Yates, illus. by Nora S(picer) Unwin, Day, 1942, 1972 (repr. of 1942 ed.), 75 pp., o.p.

(BL 69:911; CCBB 4:51, 26:33; HB 48:596; Kirkus 40:860; LJ 67:884, 98:1009; TLS 1973 p. 387)

11-93 TURNER, Ann Warren. *Finding Walter.* Gr. 3–6.

✯ Angry about an unexpected stay at their grandmother's while their father recovers from an illness, Emily and Rose realize that they can hear the thoughts of a dollhouse doll family trying to find their missing baby.
Harcourt, 1997, 161 pp. (0-15-200212-X), 1997, pap. (0-15-201507-8)
(BL 94:406; CCBB 51:69; HB 74:82; HBG 8:82; Kirkus 65:1230; SLJ Oct 1997 p. 140)

11-94 TWOHILL, Maggie. *Jeeter, Mason and the Magic Headset.* Gr. 3–5.
Ten-year-old Jeeter's Cabbage Patch doll, Morgan, suddenly begins talking to Jeeter through her radio headphones.
Bradbury, 1985, 103 pp., o.p.; Dell, 1986, pap. (0-440-44220-6)
(CCBB 39:18; SLJ Sep 1985 p. 140)

11-95 UPINGTON, Marion. *The Beautiful Culpeppers.* Gr. 2–4.
The Culpepper family, 10 paper dolls, befriends a mouse, two sparrows, and a spider during its adventures in Debby's house.
Illus. by Louis Slobodkin, Watts, 1963, 117 pp., o.p.
(BL 60:266; HB 39:596)

11-96 WAUGH, Silvia. *The Mennyms.* Gr. 4–8. (Orig. British pub. 1993.)

✯✯ The Mennym family—grandparents, parents, and five children—has lived happily together in London for more than 40 years when their Australian landlord suggests paying them a visit, throwing these living, human-sized rag dolls into a panic. Guardian Children's Fiction Prize, 1994. In *The Mennyms in the Wilderness* (1994, 1995), the ghost of Aunt Kate the dollmaker entreats her nephew Albert Pond to befriend the Mennym family and help them fight the proposed highway construction that would destroy their home. In *The Mennyms Under Siege* (1995, 1996), 16-year-old Pilbeam Mennym's visit to the theater draws the curiosity of a neighbor, endangering all of their lives. In *Mennyms Alone* (1996), Sir Magnus Mennym's premonition that he and his family will soon die seems to come true. In *Mennyms Alive* (1996, 1997), the family awakens from a mysterious sleep to find itself in a different house, and plans a mission to rescue the missing brother Soobie.
Greenwillow, 1994, 212 pp. (0-688-13070-4); Avon, 1995, pap., 230 pp. (0-380-72528-2)
(CCBB 47:279; HB 70:456; HBG 5:317; Kirkus 62:311; SLJ Apr 1994 p. 132)

11-97 WILLIAMS (John), Ursula Moray. *Adventures of the Little Wooden Horse.* Gr. 2–4. (Orig. British pub. 1938; orig U.S. pub, 1939.)
A little wooden toy sets out on a series of adventures while searching for his beloved toy-maker master. The sequel is *The Further Adventures of Gobbolino and the Little Wooden Horse* (2002), which is related to the author's *Gobbolino the Witch's Cat* (1942, 2002; see Chapter 2, Animal Fantasy).
Illus. by Joyce L. Brisley, Lippincott, 1939, 204 pp., o.p.; illus. by Peggy Fortnum, Penguin, 1959, o.p.; illus. by Paul Howard, Kingfisher, 2001, 256 pp. (0-7534-5406-8)
(HBG 15:366; Kirkus 7:June 15, 1939; LJ 65:37)

11-98 **WILLIAMS (John), Ursula Moray.** *The Toymaker's Daughter.* Gr. 4–6.
✭   (Orig. British pub. 1968.)
A doll-girl named Marta escapes from Malkin, the evil toy maker, and crosses
the mountains, hoping to become a real girl. The sequels are *The Three Toy-
makers* (1970, 1971) and *Malkin's Mountain* (Nelson, 1971, 1972).
Illus. by Shirley Hughes, Meredith, 1969, 134 pp., o.p.
(CCBB 23:68; HB 45:538; Kirkus 37:507; LJ 94:3209; TLS 1968 p. 1377)

WOODRUFF, Elvira. *Awfully Short for the Fourth Grade.*
See Chapter 9, Magic Adventure Fantasy.

11-99 **WRIGHT, Betty Ren.** *The Dollhouse Murders.* Gr. 4–7.
✭   A miniature version of her great-grandparents' house, complete with dolls,
leads Amy to the conclusion that her great-grandparents were murdered and
that the dolls know who the killer was.
Holiday, 1983, 149 pp. (0-8234-0497-8); Scholastic, 1985, 1989, pap. (0-590-
43461-6)
(BL 80:301; HB 59:713; SLJ Nov 1983 p. 84)

YOUNG, Miriam. *The Witch Mobile.*
See Chapter 12, Witchcraft and Sorcery Fantasy.

12

Witchcraft and Sorcery Fantasy

The books in this chapter are tales of magic as practiced by witches and wizards, enchanters and enchantresses, sorceresses, sorcerers, and magicians. Many have a light-hearted quality that distinguishes them from the darker, more terrifying tales of the occult called horror fiction. Horror fiction has not been included in this guide.

12-1 **ADAMS, Georgie.** *The Three Little Witches Storybook.* Gr. K–2.
Eight very short stories about Zoe, Ziggy, and Zara, three young witches who live in Magic Wood and decide to give a Halloween party.
Illus. by Emily Bolam, Hyperion, 2002, 93 pp. (0-7868-0824-1)
(BL 99:138; HBG 14:64; SLJ Dec 2002 p. 84)

ALEXANDER, Lloyd (Chudley). *The Rope Trick.*
See Chapter 5, High Fantasy: Alternate Worlds or Histories.

12-2 **ALEXANDER, Lloyd (Chudley).** *The Wizard in the Tree.* Gr. 4–6.
★ A firm belief in magic helps Mallory, an overworked, orphaned servant girl, to release a crotchety old wizard from imprisonment in an oak tree.
Illus. by Laszlo Kubinyi, Dutton, 1974, 144 pp., o.p.; Puffin, 1998, pap., 144 pp. (0-14-038801-X)
(BL 71:813; CCBB 28:173; HB 51:377; Kirkus 43:451; SLJ May 1975 pp. 34, 45; Suth 2:9)

12-3 **AMOSS, Berthe.** *Lost Magic.* Gr. 5–9.
Ceridwen, a herbal healer, is accused of witchcraft after she fails to save the life of Lord Robert's wife.
Hyperion, 1993, 184 pp., o.p.
(BL 90:514; HBG 5:72; Kirkus 61:1139; SLJ Sep 1993 p. 248)

12-4 *Ancient Enchantresses.* **Ed. by Kathleen M. Massie-Ferch, Martin H. Greenberg, and Richard Gilliam.** Gr. 10 up.
Nineteen tales about powerful women from around the world, many of whom are sorceresses, written by Melanie Rawn, Andre Norton, Harry Turtledove, and others. *Warrior Enchantresses* (1996) is a companion volume.

DAW, 1995, pap., 352 pp. (0-88677-656-2)

(Kliatt Nov 1995 p. 17; LJ Aug 1995 p. 123; VOYA 18:227, 19:17)

ANDERSEN, Hans Christian. *The Snow Queen.*
See Chapter 1, Allegorical Fantasy and Literary Fairy Tales.

ANTHONY, Piers. *A Spell for Chameleon.*
See Chapter 5, High Fantasy: Alternate Worlds or Histories.

ANTHONY, Piers, and KORNWISE, Robert Ian. *Through the Ice.*
See Chapter 7, High Fantasy: Travel to Other Worlds.

12-5 ARTHUR, Ruth M(abel). *After Candlemas.* Gr. 4–6. (Orig. British pub. 1974.)
Harriet befriends a runaway boy nearly crushed by a rock slide, but fears for his safety after he trespasses on the local witches' meeting ground.
Atheneum, 1974, 122 pp., o.p.

(HB 50:373; Kirkus 42:277; LJ 99:1487)

12-6 ASPRIN, Robert (Lynn). *Hit or Myth.* **(Myth Adventure series, bk. 4).** Gr. 10 up.
In this, the fourth book of Asprin's pun-filled Myth Adventure series, Skeeve, a bumbling apprentice wizard, is left without the aid of his demon-mentor Aahz to fight off numerous magical enemies. The other books in the series are *Another Fine Myth* (1978), *Myth Conceptions* (1980), *Myth Directions* (1982, 1986), *Myth-ing Persons* (1984), *Little Myth Marker* (1985, 1987), *M.Y.T.H. Inc. Link* (1986), *Myth-Nomers and Im-Perfections* (1987), and *Myth Alliances* (by Asprin and Jody Lynn Nye; Meisha Merlin, 2003).
Ed. by Kay Reynolds, Donning, 1983, 172 pp., LB (0-89865-339-8); Ace, 1986, pap. (0-441-33851-8)

(BL 80:715; LJ 108:2174)

AVI (Avi Wortis). *Bright Shadow.*
See Chapter 5, High Fantasy: Alternate Worlds or Histories.

12-7 AVI (Avi Wortis). *Midnight Magic.* Gr. 5–8.
☆ Ten-year-old Princess Teresina tells the King that she has seen the ghost of her missing brother, and the King calls on an ex-magician named Mangus and his servant boy, Fabrizio, to ascertain the truth.
Scholastic, 1999, 256 pp. (0-590-36035-3), 2001, pap. (0-439-24219-3)

(BL 96:256; CCBB 53:121; HB 75:733; HBG 11:73; Kirkus 67:1638; Kliatt Sep 1999 p. 4; SLJ Oct 1999 p. 144; VOYA 22:340, 23:10)

AVI (Avi Wortis). *Tom, Babette, and Simon: Three Tales of Transformation.*
See Chapter 1, Allegorical Fantasy and Literary Fairy Tales.

BACON, Peggy. *The Magic Touch.*
See Chapter 9, Magic Adventure Fantasy.

BALL, Brian. *The Quest for Queenie.*
See Chapter 7, High Fantasy: Travel to Other Worlds.

BALL, Margaret. *Changeweaver.*
See Chapter 5, High Fantasy: Alternate Worlds or Histories.

BANKS, Lynne Reid. *The Farthest-Away Mountain.*
See Chapter 1, Allegorical Fantasy and Literary Fairy Tales.

BARBER, Antonia. *The Enchanter's Daughter.*
See Chapter 1, Allegorical Fantasy and Literary Fairy Tales.

BARKER, Clive. *The Thief of Always: A Fable.*
See Chapter 7, High Fantasy: Travel to Other Worlds.

12-8 **BARNES, Emma.** *Jessica Haggerthwaite: Witch Dispatcher.* Gr. 3–6.
⋆ (Orig. British pub. 2001.)
Jessica's mother turns her interest in witchcraft into a business after Mr. Haggerthwaite loses his job, but Jessica and her brother don't want to be known as the witch's children. The sequel is *Jessica Haggerthwaite: Media Star* (2003).
Illus. by Tim Archbold, Walker, 2001, 168 pp. (0-8027-8794-0); Bloomsbury, 2002, pap. (0-7475-5548-6)
(BL 98:641; CCBB 55:165; HBG 13:367; Kirkus 69:1419; SLJ Mar 2002 p. 225)

BARRON, T(homas) A. *The Lost Years of Merlin.*
See Chapter 6, High Fantasy: Myth or Legend Fantasy.

12-9 **BATO, Joseph.** *The Sorcerer.* Gr. 7–10.
Cro-Magnon Ao'h's sorcery brings him power but eventually causes his downfall.
Ed. by Katherine Donnelly, illus. by the author, McKay, 1976, 171 pp., o.p.
(BL 73:890, 893; HB 53:165; Kirkus 44:1174; SLJ Nov 1976 p. 65)

12-10 **BATTLES, Edith.** *The Witch in Room 6.* Gr. 4–6.
Sean triumphs over his fifth-grade rival with the help of the new girl, an apprentice witch named Cheryl Suzanne.
Harper, 1987, 151 pp., o.p.
(CCBB 40:203; Kirkus 55:854; SLJ June–July 1987 p. 92; VOYA 10:118)

BAUDINO, Gael. *Strands of Starlight.*
See Chapter 5, High Fantasy: Alternate Worlds or Histories.

BAUM, L(yman) Frank. *The Wizard of Oz.*
See Chapter 7, High Fantasy: Travel to Other Worlds.

12-11 **BAXTER, Caroline.** *The Stolen Telesm.* Gr. 4–6. (Orig. British pub. 1975.)
David and Lucy escape on a winged colt from the evil magic of Marada the sorceress.
Lippincott, 1976, 192 pp., o.p.
(Kirkus 44:794; SLJ Oct 1976 p. 104; TLS 1975 p. 1457)

12-12 **BAXTER, Lorna.** *The Eggchild.* Gr. 5–7. (Orig. British pub. 1978.)
Two children with magic powers go up against Doppel the Enchanter to rescue a baby able to transform itself into a glowing egg.
Dutton, 1979, 157 pp., o.p.
(BL 76:663; CCBB 33:126; Kirkus 47:1325; SLJ Jan 1980 p. 65; TLS 1978 p. 1089)

12-13 BEACHCROFT, Nina. *Well Met by Witchlight.* Gr. 4–6. (Orig. British pub. 1972.)
Three children help a good witch fight the evil power of Mrs. Black.
Atheneum, 1973, 137 pp., o.p.
(BL 70:595; Kirkus 41:1199; LJ 99:205)

BEAGLE, Peter S(oyer). *The Folk of the Air.*
See Chapter 6, High Fantasy: Myth or Legend Fantasy.

BEAGLE, Peter S(oyer). *The Innkeeper's Song.*
See Chapter 5, High Fantasy: Alternate Worlds or Histories.

12-14 BEDARD, Michael. *A Darker Magic.* Gr. 6–9. (Orig. Canadian pub. 1987.)
✶   Emily and her elderly teacher, Miss Potts, attempt to thwart the evil plans of Professor Mephisto, whose magic show was responsible for the death of one of Miss Potts's friends in 1936. In the sequel, *Painted Devil* (1994), the sinister magician reappears 28 years later and tries to ensnare Emily's niece, Alice, in his evil plans.
Macmillan, 1987, 208 pp., o.p.
(BL 84:59; CCBB 41:2; Kirkus 55:1235; SLJ Sep 1987 p. 177; VOYA 10:242)

12-15 BEDARD, Michael. *Redwork.* Gr. 6–10. (Orig. Canadian pub. 1990.)
All the neighborhood children are frightened of Cass's landlord, Mr. Magus, and even Cass thinks his vivid dreams of trench warfare, pain, and fear are somehow connected to the strange old man. Governor General's Literary Award for Children's Literature, 1990; Canadian Library Association Best Book of the Year for Children, 1991.
Macmillan, 1990, 261 pp., o.p.
(BL 87:734; HBG 2:87; Kirkus 58:1528; SLJ Oct 1990 p. 139; VOYA 13:1293, 16:34)

BEHN, Harry. *The Faraway Lurs.*
See Chapter 1, Allegorical Fantasy and Literary Fairy Tales.

12-16 BELL, Hilari. *The Goblin Wood.* Gr. 5–9.
✶   Young sorceress Makenna joins forces with goblins to battle the priests of the ruling Hierarch attempting to destroy all magical creatures.
Eros/HarperCollins, 2003, 294 pp. (0-06-051372-1); HarperCollins, pap., 2004, 384 pp. (0-06-051372-1)
(BL 99:1758; CCBB 56:392; HB 79:339; HBG 14:362; Kirkus 71:531; SLJ July 2003 p. 123; VOYA 26:233, 27:10)

12-17 BELLAIRS, John. *The Curse of the Blue Figurine.* **(Johnny Dixon Mysteries, bk. 1).** Gr. 5–7.
✶   Borrowing an ancient Egyptian figurine, Johnny Dixon and his friend, Professor Childermass, are propelled into a suspenseful battle with a sorcerous ghost haunting a local church. The sequels are *The Mummy, the Will, and the Crypt* (1983); *The Spell of the Sorcerer's Skull* (1984); *The Revenge of the Wizard's Ghost* (1985); *The Eyes of the Killer Robot* (1986); *The Chessmen of Doom* (1989); *The Trolley to Yesterday* (1989); *Secret of the Underground Room* (1990); *The Drum, the Doll, and the Zombie* (1994; by Bellairs and Brad Strickland); *The Hand of the Necromancer* (1996; by Strickland); *The Bell, the*

Book, and the Spellbinder (1997; by Strickland); and *The Wrath of the Grinning Ghost* (1999; by Strickland).
Dial, 1983, 198 pp., o.p.; Puffin, 1996, pap. (0-14-038005-1); Puffin, 2004, pap., 200 pp. (0-14-240258-3)
(BL 79:1335; Kirkus 51:578; SLJ May 1983 p. 93; VOYA 7:28)

BELLAIRS, John. *The Dark Secret of Weatherend.*
See Chapter 9, Magic Adventure Fantasy.

12-18   BELLAIRS, John. *The Face in the Frost.* Gr. 8 up.
Two bumbling wizards search for the powerful being causing eerie dreams, terrifying gray shadows, and frost faces to appear on the windows of their land.
Illus. by Marilyn Fitschen, Macmillan, 1969, 174 pp., o.p.; Olmstead, 2000, 174 pp. (1-58754-105-X)
(BL 65:1209; Kirkus 36:1395; LJ 94:776)

BELLAIRS, John. *The House with a Clock in Its Walls.*
See Chapter 4, Ghost Fantasy.

BENARY-ISBERT, Margot. *The Wicked Enchantment.*
See Chapter 1, Allegorical Fantasy and Literary Fairy Tales.

12-19   BENNETT, Anna Elizabeth. *Little Witch.* Gr. 3–5.
✳   Even though she can perform all kinds of exciting and unusual feats, Miniken does not want to be a witch; she wants to go to school like a real little girl.
Illus. by Helen Stone, Harper, 1953, 127 pp., o.p.
(BBC:199; CCBB 7:51; HB 29:356; LJ 78:1855)

BERESFORD, Elizabeth. *Travelling Magic.*
See Chapter 10, Time Travel Fantasy.

BERRY, James R. *The Magicians of Erianne.*
See Chapter 6, High Fantasy: Myth or Legend Fantasy.

BERTIN, Joanne. *The Last DragonLord.*
See Chapter 5, High Fantasy: Alternate Worlds or Histories.

Beware! Beware! Chilling Tales. **Ed. by Jean Richardson.**
See Chapter 4, Ghost Fantasy.

12-20   BISHOP, Anne. *The Pillars of the World.* Gr. 10 up.
Magic and the roads between the human and faery worlds are vanishing as the witches of Sylvalan are slaughtered, and Ari, whose family has always tended one of the Old Places, finds that her life is also in danger. *Shadows and Light* (2002; see below) is a related story.
NAL/Roc, 2001, pap., 420 pp. (0-451-45850-8)
(BL 98:200; Kliatt Jan 2002 p. 15; VOYA 24:442)

12-21   BISHOP, Anne. *Shadows and Light.* Gr. 10 up.
Three of the Fey—the Muse, the Bard, and the Gatherer—search for the Hunter who can convince the other Fey to leave their land of Tir Alainn and enter the human world, in order to save the witches and themselves from destruction. *The Pillars of the World* (2001; see above) is a related story.

NAL, 2002, pap., 432 pp. (0-451-45899-0)
(BL 99:307; VOYA 26:146)

BLACKWOOD, Gary L. *Beyond the Door.*
See Chapter 7, High Fantasy: Travel to Other Worlds.

BLAYLOCK, James P(aul). *The Paper Grail.*
See Chapter 6, High Fantasy: Myth or Legend Fantasy.

BOMANS, Godfried (Jan Arnold). *The Wily Witch and All the Other Fairy Tales and Fables.*
See Chapter 3, Fantasy Collections.

BOSTON, L(ucy) M(aria Wood). *An Enemy at Green Knowe.*
See discussion under *The Children of Green Knowe* in Chapter 4, Ghost Fantasy.

BOYER, Elizabeth H. *The Troll's Grindstone.*
See Chapter 7, High Fantasy: Travel to Other Worlds.

12-22   **BRADBURY, Ray (Douglas).** *Something Wicked This Way Comes.* Gr. 8
✫   up.
Two boys attending a carnival freak show become the targets of an evil magician who imprisons them in the Wax Museum.
Simon, 1962, 317 pp., o.p.; Eos, 1998, pap., 304 pp. (0-380-72940-7), 1999, 293 pp. (0-380-97727-3)
(BL 59:163; TLS 1963 p. 189)

BRADLEY, Marion Zimmer. *The Mists of Avalon.*
See Chapter 6, High Fantasy: Myth or Legend Fantasy.

12-23   **BRADLEY, Marion Zimmer, and McINTYRE, Vonda N.** *Lythande.* Gr.
10 up.
Six tales about the journeys of the magician Lythande.
DAW, 1986, pap., 240 pp., o.p.
(BL 82:1667; VOYA 9:290)

BRADLEY, Marion Zimmer, MAY, Julian, and NORTON, Andre. *Black Trillium.*
See Chapter 5, High Fantasy: Alternate Worlds or Histories.

12-24   **BRENNAN, Herbie.** *Emily and the Werewolf.* Gr. 3–6. (Orig. British pub. 1993.)
Emily tries to learn enough about magic from her grandmother, a witch, to enable her to confront an angry werewolf.
Illus. by David Pace, Macmillan, 1993, 96 pp. (0-689-50593-0)
(HBG 5:73; Kirkus 61:1387; SLJ Nov 1993 p. 76)

BRIGGS, K(atharine) M(ary). *Hobberdy Dick.*
See Chapter 6, High Fantasy: Myth or Legend Fantasy.

BRIGGS, K(atharine) M(ary). *Kate Crackernuts.*
See Chapter 6, High Fantasy: Myth or Legend Fantasy.

BRIN, David. *The Practice Effect.*
See Chapter 7, High Fantasy: Travel to Other Worlds.

12-25 **BRITTAIN, Bill.** *The Devil's Donkey.* **(Coven Tree Saga, bk. 1).** Gr. 3–6.
✰ Turned into a donkey by Old Magda for stealing wood from the witches' tree, Dan'l must confront the devil himself to be freed of the curse. In *The Wish Giver: Three Tales of Coven Tree* (1983), a stranger offers to grant the wishes of four young people from Coven Tree. John Newbery Medal Honor Book, 1984. In *Doctor Dredd's Wagon of Wonders* (1987), orphaned Calvin escapes from bondage to the mysterious rain-maker called Dr. Dredd in time to keep townspeople from trading away their souls. In *Professor Popkin's Prodigious Polish: A Tale of Coven Tree* (1990), Luther Gilpin, a farmer's son, dreams of becoming a salesman for a product that literally brings things to life.
Illus. by Andrew Glass, Harper, 1981, 128 pp., o.p.; HarperCollins, 1990, pap. (0-06-440129-4)
(BL 77:1097, 86:790; HB 57:420; Kirkus 49:503; SLJ Mar 1981 p. 141, May 1981 p. 23)

BROOKS, Terry. *Magic Kingdom for Sale—Sold!*
See Chapter 8, Humorous Fantasy.

12-26 **BROWN, Mary.** *The Unlikely Ones.* **(Summer trilogy, vol. 1).** Gr. 10 up.
Seven human and animal companions, all ensnared in a witch's curse, set out to break the enchantment. The sequels are *Pigs Don't Fly* (1994) and *Master of Many Treasures* (1995).
McGraw-Hill, 1986, 425 pp., o.p.; Baen, 1999, pap., 426 pp. (0-671-57844-8)
(BL 83:191, 217; Kirkus 54:1223; LJ Oct 15, 1986 p. 114)

BRUST, Steven K. (Zoltan). *Taltos.*
See Chapter 5, High Fantasy: Alternate Worlds or Histories.

BUCHWALD, Emilie. *Gildaen: The Heroic Adventures of a Most Unusual Rabbit.*
See Chapter 1, Allegorical Fantasy and Literary Fairy Tales.

BUJOLD, Lois McMaster. *The Spirit Ring.*
See Chapter 5, High Fantasy: Alternate Worlds or Histories.

12-27 **BURCH, Robert.** *The Jolly Witch.* Gr. 2–3.
Cheerful Cluny uses witchcraft to change the lives of an old woman and her son.
Illus. by Leigh Grant, Dutton, 1975, 32 pp., o.p.
(BL 72:512; CCBB 29:92; SLJ Jan 1976 p. 35)

12-28 **BURGESS, Melvin.** *Burning Issy.* Gr. 6–10. (Orig. British pub. 1992.)
Twelve-year-old Issy discovers her own talents for magic and healing while watching other witches persecuted for their religious beliefs.
Simon, 1994, 174 pp. (0-671-89003-4)
(BL 91:816; HB 71:192; SLJ Dec 1994 p. 106; VOYA 18:19)

12-29   BUTLER, Beverly. *Witch's Fire.* Gr. 5–7.
✶   Confined to a wheelchair since the automobile accident that killed her mother and sister, 13-year-old Kirsty resents moving with her father's new family to a house previously owned by a witch.
Dutton, 1993, 135 pp. (0-525-65132-2); Puffin, 1995, pap. (0-14-037614-3)
(BL 89:2056; CCBB 47:40; HBG 5:73; Kirkus 61:998; SLJ Sep 1993 p. 228; VOYA 16:306)

12-30   BYFIELD, Barbara Ninde. *Andrew and the Alchemist.* Gr. 4–6.
✶   Andrew's "easy" job as apprentice to an alchemist goes wrong when he is accused of misusing his power to steal the King's treasure.
Illus. by Deanne Hollinger, Doubleday, 1976, 129 pp., o.p.
(BL 73:128; CCBB 30:172; HB 53:312; Kirkus 44:1264; SLJ Jan 1977 p. 88; Suth 2:71)

CALHOUN, Mary (pseud. of Mary Huiskamp Wilkins). *Magic in the Alley.*
See Chapter 9, Magic Adventure Fantasy.

12-31   CALLANDER, Don. *Aquamancer.* **(Pyromancer quartet, bk. 2).** Gr. 10 up.
Journeyman fire adept Douglas Brightglade and his sea otter companion, Marbleheart, face goblins and black magic while he tries to prove himself worthy of becoming a master magician. This is the sequel to *Pyromancer* (1992) and is followed by *Geomancer* (1994) and *Aeromancer* (1997).
Berkley, 1993, pap., 304 pp. (0-441-02816-0)
(BL 89:718, 722; VOYA 16:36)

CARD, Orson Scott. *Hart's Hope.*
See Chapter 5, High Fantasy: Alternate Worlds or Histories.

CARD, Orson Scott. *Seventh Son.*
See Chapter 5, High Fantasy: Alternate Worlds or Histories.

CARLYON, Richard. *The Dark Lord of Pengersick.*
See Chapter 5, High Fantasy: Alternate Worlds or Histories.

CARPENTER, Christopher. *The Twilight Realm.*
See Chapter 7, High Fantasy: Travel to Other Worlds.

12-32   CARRIS, Joan Davenport. *Witch-Cat.* Gr. 4–6.
Rosetta the witch-cat has trouble making her new mistress understand that she's also a witch.
Illus. by Beth Peck, Harper, 1984, 160 pp., o.p.
(BL 80:1236; SLJ Sep 1984 p. 114)

***Catfantastic: Nine Lives and Fifteen Tales.* Ed. by Andre Norton and Martin H. Greenberg.**
See Chapter 3, Fantasy Collections.

12-33   *A Cavalcade of Magicians.* Ed. by Roger (Gilbert) Lancelyn Green. Gr.
✶   5–7. (Orig. British pub, 1973, entitled *A Book of Magicians*.)
Legends, folktales, and original tales about magic and magicians, including "The Sorcerer's Apprentice" and the story of Merlin.

Illus. by Victor G. Ambrus, Walck, 1973, 274 pp., o.p.
(BL 70:291; HB 49:461; Kirkus 41:645; LJ 98:2664; TLS 1973 p. 1115)

CAYLUS, Anne Claude Philippe, Comte de. *Heart of Ice.*
See Chapter 1, Allegorical Fantasy and Literary Fairy Tales.

CHANT, Joy (pseud. of Eileen Joyce Rutter). *Red Moon and Black Mountain: The End of the House of Kendreth.*
See Chapter 7, High Fantasy: Travel to Other Worlds.

CHAPMAN, Vera. *The Enchantresses.*
See Chapter 6, High Fantasy: Myth or Legend Fantasy.

CHAPMAN, Vera. *The Green Knight.*
See Chapter 6, High Fantasy: Myth or Legend Fantasy.

12-34 CHARNAS, Suzy McKee. *The Bronze King.* **(Sorcery Hall trilogy, bk. 1).** Gr. 5–8.
An elderly man with magical powers needs Tina and Joel's help to defeat a monster hiding in the depths of Manhattan's subway system. The sequels are *The Silver Glove* (Bantam, 1988) and *The Golden Thread* (Bantam, 1989).
Houghton, 1985, 196 pp., o.p.
(CCBB 39:82; Kirkus 53:1087; SLJ Nov 1985 p. 94)

12-35 CHASE, Mary (Coyle). *Mrs. McThing: A Play.* Gr. 5 up.
A witch punishes a wealthy woman who objects to her son's friendship with the witch's daughter.
Illus. by Madeleine Gekiere and Helen Sewell, Oxford University Press, 1952, 141 pp., o.p.
(BL 49:101, 111; CCBB 6:37; HB 28:310, 418; LJ 77:1814)

12-36 CHERRYH, C. J. (pseud. of Carolyn Janice Cherry). *Fortress in the Eye of Time.* **(Fortress series, bk. 1).** Gr. 10 up.
Tristen becomes a pawn in the power struggle between two wizards, but his friendship with Prince Cefwyn helps him to understand his own magic powers. The sequels are *Fortress of Owls* (1998), *Fortress of Eagles* (1998), and *Fortress of Dragons* (2000).
HarperPrism, 1995, 592 pp., o.p., 1999, pap., 773 pp. (0-06-105689-8)
(Kirkus 63:274; LJ May 15, 1995 p. 99; VOYA 18:312, 19:18)

CHERRYH, C. J. (pseud. of Carolyn Janice Cherry). *The Goblin Mirror.*
See Chapter 5, High Fantasy: Alternate Worlds or Histories.

12-37 CHERRYH, C. J. (pseud. of Carolyn Janice Cherry). *Rusalka.* **(Rusalka trilogy, bk. 1).** Gr. 10 up.
Sasha and Pyetr try to convince a wizard to bring a Rusalka, the ghost of a murdered girl, back to life, in this story steeped in Russian legends. The sequels are *Chernevog* (1990) and *Yvgenie* (1991).
Ballantine, 1989, 374 pp. (0-345-35953-4), 1990, pap. (0-345-36934-3)
(BL 86:2, 6, 906; Kirkus 57:1205; LJ Sep 15, 1989 p. 138; VOYA 13:37)

CHESNUTT, Charles Waddell. *Conjure Tales.*
See Chapter 3, Fantasy Collections.

CHETWIN, Grace. *Gom on Windy Mountain.*
See Chapter 5, High Fantasy: Alternate Worlds or Histories.

12-38 CHEW, Ruth (Silver). *No Such Thing as a Witch.* Gr. 2–4.
The fudge made by Nora and Tad's neighbor, Maggie, turns people into animals.
Illus. by the author, Scholastic, 1972, pap., o.p.; illus. by the author, Hastings, 1980, 112 pp., o.p.
(CCBB 33:168; SLJ May 1980 p. 52)

12-39 CHEW, Ruth (Silver). *The Would-Be Witch.* Gr. 3–5.
Miniaturized by a magic cream, Robin and Andy take midnight flights and rescue their friend Zelda from a witches' coven.
Illus. by the author, Hastings, 1977, 112 pp., o.p.
(BL 74:745; SLJ Dec 1977 p. 43)

12-40 CLARK, Douglas W. *Alchemy Unlimited.* Gr. 10 up.
Puns in English and French abound in this humorous story set in an alternate 15th-century France about a sorcerer and a young would-be scholar who discover that foreign-financed water pollution is causing a plague.
Avon, 1990, pap., 310 pp., o.p.
(LJ Aug 1990 p. 147; VOYA 13:294)

12-41 CLARKE, Susanna. *Jonathan Strange and Mr. Norrell.* Gr. 10 up. (Orig.
✭   British pub. 2004.)
As Napoleon conquers Europe, the lost art of English magic comes back to life when two magicians, Gilbert Norrell and Jonathan Strange, join forces to defeat the French armies, and travel to the world of Faerie.
Bloomsbury, 2004, 800 pp. (1-58234-416-7)
(BL 100:1797; Kirkus 72:590; LJ Aug 2004 p. 64)

CLAYTON, Jo. *Moongather.*
See Chapter 5, High Fantasy: Alternate Worlds or Histories.

12-42 COLUM, Padraic. *The Boy Apprenticed to an Enchanter.* Gr. 4–6. (Orig.
✭   pub. 1920.)
Merlin the magician and a girl called Bird of Gold help Eean escape from a wicked enchanter.
Illus. by Edward Leight, Macmillan, 1966, 150 pp., o.p.
(BL 63:493; HB 42:708; LJ 92:333; Mahony 1:39)

COLUM, Padraic. *The Stone of Victory and Other Tales.*
See Chapter 3, Fantasy Collections.

COOK, Glen. *Doomstalker.*
See Chapter 2, Animal Fantasy.

COOK, Glen. *Tower of Fear.*
See Chapter 5, High Fantasy: Alternate Worlds or Histories.

12-43   COOK, Hugh. *The Wizards and the Warriors.* **(Chronicles of an Age of Darkness, no. 1).** Gr. 10 up. (Orig. pub. in New Zealand, 1986.)
Miphon and the other members of the Confederation of Wizards form an uneasy alliance with their ancient enemies, the Warriors of Rovac, to battle a renegade sorcerer threatening to end the world. The sequels are *The Women and the Warlords* (1987), *The Wordsmiths and the Warguild* (1988), *The Wicked and the Witless* (1989), *The Wishstone and the Wonderworkers* (1990), *The Wazir and the Witch* (1990), *The Werewolf and the Wormlord* (1991), *The Worshippers and the Way* (1992), and *The Walrus and the Warwolf* (1992).
Dufour, 1987, 352 pp., o.p.
(BL 83:1252, 1273; LJ Apr 15, 1987 p. 102)

COOKE, Catherine. *Mask of the Wizard.*
See Chapter 5, High Fantasy: Alternate Worlds or Histories.

12-44   COOMBS, Patricia. *Dorrie and the Blue Witch.* **(Dorrie the Witch series,**
★   **bk. 1).** Gr. 2–4.
Shrinking powder enables young Dorrie witch to capture the bad blue witch and win first prize for witch-catching. Other titles in this series are *Dorrie's Magic* (1962), *Dorrie's Play* (1965), *Dorrie and the Weather-Box* (1966), *Dorrie and the Witch Doctor* (1967), *Dorrie and the Wizard's Spell* (1968), *Dorrie and the Haunted House* (1970), *Dorrie and the Birthday Eggs* (1971), *Dorrie and the Goblin* (1972), *Dorrie and the Fortune Teller* (1973), *Dorrie and the Amazing Magic Elixir* (1974), *Dorrie and the Witch's Imp* (1975), *Dorrie and the Halloween Plot* (1976), *Dorrie and the Dreamyard Monsters* (1977), *Dorrie and the Screebit Ghost* (1979), *Dorrie and the Witchville Fair* (1980), *Dorrie and the Witches' Camp* (1983), *Dorrie and the Museum Case* (1986), *Dorrie and the Pin Witch* (1989), and *Dorrie and the Haunted Schoolhouse* (1992).
Illus. by the author, Lothrop, 1964, 42 pp., o.p.
(BL 61:217; CCBB 18:51; HB 40:488; Kirkus 32:595; LJ 89:3458)

COOPER, Gale. *Unicorn Moon.*
See Chapter 1, Allegorical Fantasy and Literary Fairy Tales.

COOPER, Louise. *The Sleep of Stone.*
See Chapter 5, High Fantasy: Alternate Worlds or Histories.

12-45   CORBETT, Scott. *The Great Custard Pie Panic.* **(Dr. Merlin trilogy, bk. 2).** Gr. 2–4.
Nick thwarts Dr. Merlin's diabolical plot to use Nick's dog's brain to create the smartest dog in the world. This is the sequel to *Dr. Merlin's Magic Shop* (1973) and is followed by *The Foolish Dinosaur Fiasco* (1978).
Illus. by Joseph Mathieu, Little, Brown, 1974, 47 pp., o.p.
(BL 70:1252; CCBB 28:26; Kirkus 42:580)

CORLETT, William. *The Steps up the Chimney.*
See Chapter 9, Magic Adventure Fantasy.

COVILLE, Bruce. *The Dragon of Doom.*
See Chapter 5, High Fantasy: Alternate Worlds or Histories.

12-46 *The Crafters.* **Ed. by Christopher Stasheff and Bill Fawcett. (The Crafters series, bk. 1).** Gr. 10 up.
Shared-world stories concerning a family of chemists called the Crafters, set in various historical periods, from Puritan Massachusetts to 19th-century Ireland, written by Katherine Kurtz, Morgan Llewelyn, Ru Emerson, and others. The sequel is *Blessings and Curses* (1992).
Ace, 1991, pap., 246 pp. (0-441-12130-6)
(BL 88:606, 610; Kliatt Apr 1992 p. 16; VOYA 14:380)

CROSS, Gilbert B. *A Witch Across Time.*
See Chapter 4, Ghost Fantasy.

12-47 **CULLUM, Janice A.** *Lyskarion: The Song of the Wind.* **(Chronicles of the Karionin, bk. 1).** Gr. 10 up.
Before he dies, the great wizard Cormer decrees that the wizard Derwin must find the brightest, most talented child in the land of Tamar and train this child to become the next great wizard.
Edge, 2001, pap., 331 pp. (1-894063-02-3)
(BL 98:463; LJ Nov 15, 2001 p. 101; VOYA 25:200)

CURLEY, Daniel. *Billy Beg and the Bull.*
See Chapter 6, High Fantasy: Myth or Legend Fantasy.

CURRY, Jane Louise. *The Sleepers.*
See Chapter 6, High Fantasy: Myth or Legend Fantasy.

12-48 **CUTTER, Leah R.** *Paper Mage.* Gr. 10 up.
Considered an embarrassment to her family after she is apprenticed to an origami magician at her aunt's request, young Xiao Yen meets the goddess Bei Xi while escorting two foreigners on a journey to the Middle Kingdom.
NAL/Roc, 2003, pap., 343 pp. (0-451-45917-2)
(BL 99:1059, 1458; Kliatt May 2003 p. 24)

DAHL, Roald. *George's Marvelous Medicine.*
See Chapter 9, Magic Adventure Fantasy.

12-49 **DAHL, Roald.** *The Witches.* Gr. 4–6. (Orig. British pub. 1983.)
✮ A boy and his grandmother thwart the plans of England's witches to turn all children into mice. Whitbread Literary Award, Children's Book Category, 1983.
Illus. by Quentin Blake, Farrar, 1983, 202 pp., o.p.; Puffin, 2002, pap., 208 pp. (0-14-130110-4); Puffin, new ed., 2004, 208 pp. (0-14-131139-8)
(BL 80:567; CCBB 37:105; HB 60:194; Kirkus 51:190; SLJ Jan 1984 p. 74)

DAWSON, Carley. *Mr. Wicker's Window.*
See Chapter 10, Time Travel Fantasy.

DEAN, Pamela. *The Dubious Hills.*
See Chapter 5, High Fantasy: Alternate Worlds or Histories.

12-50 **DE CHANCIE, John.** *Castle Kidnapped.* **(Castle series, bk. 3).** Gr. 10 up.
One by one, the wizards of Castle Perilous are being kidnapped by the Hosts of
Hell, and those who are left use magic, a time machine, and a computer to save
the universe, in this science-fantasy. This is the sequel to *Castle Perilous*
(1985) and *Castle for Rent* (1989), and is followed by *Castle War!* (1990),
Castle Murders (1991), *Castle Dreams* (1992), *Castle Spellbound* (1992), and
Bride of the Castle (1994).
Ace, 1989, pap., 208 pp., o.p.
(BL 86:265, 273; Kliatt Jan 1990 p. 18)

DE HAVEN, Tom. *Walker of Worlds.*
See Chapter 7, High Fantasy: Travel to Other Worlds.

DE LINT, Charles. *Into the Green.*
See Chapter 5, High Fantasy: Alternate Worlds or Histories.

12-51 **DE LINT, Charles.** *The Little Country.* Gr. 10 up. (Orig. pub. in Canada.)
A rare magical book owned by folk musician Janey Little and her grandfather
draws John Madden and his henchmen to their Cornish village, while inside the
book, a witch transforms a girl named Jodi into a 6-inch-high Small and
imprisons her.
Morrow, 1991, 544 pp. (0-688-10366-9); Tor, 1993, pap. (0-8125-2248-6)
(BL 87:1011, 1049; Kirkus 59:23; LJ Feb 15; 1991 p. 224)

DEL VECCHIO, Gene. *The Pearl of Anton.*
See Chapter 5, High Fantasy: Alternate Worlds or Histories.

12-52 **DEXTER, Catherine.** *A Is for Apple, W Is for Witch.* Gr. 3–6. (Orig. pub. in
England.)
Apple Olson uses her mother's transformation spell on her classmate Barney,
who turns into a frog.
Illus. by Capucine Mazille, Candlewick, 1996, 160 pp. (1-56402-541-1)
(BL 93:238; CCBB 49:188; HBG 8:65; Kirkus 64:687; SLJ July 1996 p. 84)

DIAMOND, Donna, adapt. *Swan Lake.*
See Chapter 1, Allegorical Fantasy and Literary Fairy Tales.

DICKINSON, Peter (pseud. of Malcolm de Brissac). *Merlin Dreams.*
See Chapter 6, High Fantasy: Myth or Legend Fantasy.

DICKINSON, Peter (pseud. of Malcolm de Brissac). *The Ropemaker.*
See Chapter 5, High Fantasy: Alternate Worlds or Histories.

12-53 **DICKINSON, Peter (pseud. of Malcolm de Brissac).** *The Tears of the*
★ *Salamander.* Gr. 6–9. (Orig. British pub. 2003.)
Orphaned Alfredo, taken in by his sorcerer uncle Giorgio, discovers that his
uncle is using black magic to control Mount Etna's volcanic fire, and might
have been responsible for Alfredo's family's deaths.
Random, 2003, 224 pp. (0-385-90125-9); Macmillan, 2004, pap., 240 pp. (0-
330-41540-9)
(BL 99:1659; CCBB 57;148; HB 79:453; HBG 15:90; Kirkus 71:962; Kliatt July 2003 p. 10;
SLJ Aug 2003 p. 158)

DICKINSON, Peter (pseud. of Malcolm de Brissac). *The Weathermonger.*
See Chapter 5, High Fantasy: Alternate Worlds or Histories.

DICKSON, Gordon R(upert). *The Last Dream.*
See Chapter 3, Fantasy Collections.

12-54   DILLON, Barbara. *Mrs. Tooey and the Terrible Toxic Tar.* Gr. 3–6.
While two witches battle over the fate of their town, Margo and Craig Saunders
help destroy a bottle of Terrible Toxic Tar.
Harper, 1988, 96 pp., o.p.
(BL 84:1734; Kirkus 56:759; SLJ Aug 1988 p. 92)

12-55   DILLON, Barbara. *What's Happened to Harry?* Gr. 3–5.
A mischievous witch captures Harry on Halloween, changes him into a poodle,
and takes over his real body.
Illus. by Chris Conover, Morrow, 1982, 125 pp., o.p.
(BL 78:1255; CCBB 36:7; HB 58:399; SLJ Aug 1982, p. 114)

12-56   DIXON, Rachel. *The Witch's Ring.* Gr.3–5.
Amy inadvertently trades lives with Castanetta, granddaughter of a witch who
plans to test her deadly spells on her grandchildren.
Illus. by Jennifer Hewitson, Hyperion, 1994, 117 pp. (1-56282-545-3)
(BL 91:680; HBG 6:75; SLJ Jan 1995 p. 106)

12-57   DOUGLAS, Carole Nelson. *Exiles of the Rynth.* **(Irissa and Kendric trilogy, bk. 2).** Gr. 10 up.
Propelled through a magic gate into the Rynth, Irissa, the last of the Torloc sorceresses, is captured by the wizard Sofistron, and her lover, Kendric, joins a
band of outlaws. This is the sequel to *Six of Swords* (1982) and is followed by
Keepers of Edanvant (Tor, 1987), in which Irissa and Kendric return to Edanvant as a war is beginning between males and females. The latter book also
begins a second trilogy about Irissa and Kendric, called Sword & Circlet,
which continues with *Heir of Rengarth* (1988) and *Seven of Swords* (1989).
Ballantine, 1984, pap., 193 pp., o.p.
(BL 80:1586, 1608, 86:904; LJ 109:1253)

12-58   DOUGLAS, L. Warren. *The Sacred Pool.* **(Sorceress's Tale trilogy, bk.
1).** Gr. 10 up.
Pierrette, disguised and raised as a boy after her mother is accused of witchcraft and killed, devotes herself to learning magic from Christians, Muslims,
and pagans in 8th-century Provence. The sequels are *The Veil of Years* (2001,
2002) and *The Isle Beyond Time* (2003).
Baen, 2001, 416 pp. (0-671-31956-6), 2001, pap., 495 pp. (0-7434-3530-3)
(BL 97:794; Kirkus 68:1651; LJ Jan 2001 p. 163; VOYA 24:212, 25:13)

DOUGLASS, Sara. *Threshold.*
See Chapter 5, High Fantasy: Alternate Worlds or Histories.

12-59   DUANE, Diane (Elizabeth). *The Book of Night with Moon.* Gr. 7–12.
Set in the same universe as the author's Young Wizards series (see *So You
Want to Be a Wizard,* below), this is a story about three feline wizards who are

sent to repair a malfunctioning gate between two worlds. The sequel is *To Visit the Queen* (1999, 2000).
Warner, 1997, 400 pp. (0-446-67302-1), 1999, pap., 446 pp. (0-446-60633-2)
(Kirkus 65:1560; Kliatt Mar 1998 p. 18; VOYA 21:54)

12-60 DUANE, Diane (Elizabeth). *The Door into Fire.* **(The Epic Tales of the Five trilogy, bk. 1).** Gr. 10 up.
Herewiss Hearn's son, a young sorcerer, has difficulty controlling the extra portion of Fire within him until the Goddess helps him to better understand himself. The sequels are *The Door into Shadow* (Bluejay, 1984) and *The Door into Sunset* (1993).
Dell, 1979, 304 pp., o.p.
(BL 75:1482; VOYA 2[Oct 1979]:58)

12-61 DUANE, Diane (Elizabeth). *So You Want to Be a Wizard.* **(Young Wizards series, bk. 1).** Gr. 5–8.
Two novice wizards, Nita and Kit, journey into a frightening alternate Manhattan full of evil machines and terrified people, where they attempt to fight the powers of darkness that are destroying the world. The sequels are *Deep Wizardry* (1985, 1992, 1996, 2001), *High Wizardry* (1990, 1997, 2001), *A Wizard Abroad* (1993, 1997, 2002), *The Wizard's Dilemma* (2001, 2002), in which young wizard Nita travels to other worlds searching for a cure for her mother's malignant brain tumor, and the price she must pay is the loss of her power, *A Wizard Alone* (2002), and *Wizard's Holiday* (2003), a science-fantasy. *Dragons and Dreams* (Harper, 1986; see Chapter 9, Magic Adventure Fantasy) contains a related story. The author's *The Book of Night with Moon* (1997, 1999; see above) and *To Visit the Queen* (1999, 2000) are set in the same universe. The Young Wizards series received the 2001–2002 Anne Spencer Lindbergh Prize in Children's Literature Special Commendation.
Delacorte, 1983, 288 pp. (0-385-29305-4); Dell, 1992, pap., 226 pp. (0-440-40638-2); Harcourt, 2001, pap. (0-15-216250-X), Harcourt, 2003, pap. (0-15-204738-7)
(CCBB 37:106; HB 59:716; Kliatt Fall 1984 p. 26; SLJ Jan 1984 p. 74; VOYA 6:342)

DUNLOP, Eileen (Rhona). *The Valley of Deer.*
See Chapter 10, Time Travel Fantasy.

12-62 DUNSANY, Lord (pseud. of Edward John Morton Drax Plunkett). *The Charwoman's Shadow.* Gr. 10 up. (Orig. British pub. 1926.)
Having sold his shadow to the Magician in exchange for the magical secrets needed to create a dowry and a love potion for his sister, Ramon attempts to use his newfound knowledge to regain his shadow and that of the Magician's kindly charwoman.
Putnam, 1926, 294 pp., o.p.; Del Rey, 1999, pap., 256 pp. (0-345-43192-8)
(BL 23:38; TLS 1926 p. 262)

ECKERT, Allan W. *The Dark Green Tunnel.*
See Chapter 7, High Fantasy: Travel to Other Worlds.

12-63 EDDINGS, David (Carroll). *Queen of Sorcery.* **(Belgariad Saga, bk. 2).** Gr. 10 up.

A sorcerer, his daughter, and a young wizard struggle to keep the Orb of Aldur from being used to revive an evil god. This book is preceded by *Pawn of Prophecy* (1982, 1984), and is followed by *Magician's Gambit* (1983, 1984), *Castle of Wizardry* (1984), and *Enchanter's End Game* (1984). The series is related to the author's Malloreon series, which begins with *Guardians of the West* (1987; see Chapter 5, High Fantasy: Alternate Worlds or Histories). The prequel is *Belgarath the Sorcerer* (1995) by Eddings and Leigh Eddings. *Polgara the Sorceress* (1997) retells the Malloreon and the Belgariad sagas from the point of view of a 3,000-year-old sorceress. *The Rivan Codex: Ancient Texts of the Belgariad and the Malloreon* (1998) is a companion volume.

Ballantine, 1982, 1986, pap., 327 pp., o.p.; Del Rey, 1997, pap. (0-345-41889-1)

(BL 79:714, 86:904; Kliatt Winter 1983 p. 17; SLJ Jan 1983 p. 90)

12-64 EDGERTON, Teresa. *Child of Saturn.* **(Green Lion trilogy, vol. 1).** Gr. 10 up.

Young apprentice wizard Teleri and the Queen's knight, Ceilyn, join forces against the King's sister, Princess Diaspad, who plans to make her own son the heir to the throne. The sequels are *The Moon in Hiding* (1989) and *The Work of the Sun* (1990).

Ace, 1989, pap., 288 pp., o.p.

(BL 85:1095, 1129; VOYA 12:164)

12-65 EDGERTON, Teresa. *Goblin Moon.* **(Goblin trilogy, bk. 1).** Gr. 10 up.

A coffin containing a sorcerer and all of his magical books comes into the possession of a group of river scavengers, in this tale of magic, intrigue, trolls in disguise, goblins, fairies, and romance. The sequels are *The Gnome's Engine* (1991) and *The Queen's Necklace* (2001).

Ace, 1991, pap., 293 pp., o.p.

(BL 87:1011; VOYA 14:41, 15:10)

12-66 EDMONDSON, Madeline. *Anna Witch.* Gr. 2–4.

Angry about her mother's disappointment in Anna's lack of magical prowess, Anna surprises herself by turning her mother into a frog.

Illus. by William (Sherman) Pène du Bois, Doubleday, 1982, 88 pp., o.p.

(BL 79:608; CCBB 36:24; SLJ Dec 1982 p. 64)

12-67 EDMONDSON, Madeline. *The Witch's Egg.* Gr. 2–4.

A crabby witch named Agatha who lives in an abandoned eagle's nest becomes the foster mother of a baby bird.

Illus. by Kay Chorao, Seabury, 1974, 47 pp., o.p.

(BL 70:939; Kirkus 42:182; LJ 99:1465)

12-68 EDWARDS, Dorothy (Brown). *The Witches and the Grinnygog.* Gr. 5–7. (Orig. British pub. 1981.)

Seven children who uncover the history of the last three witches to live in their village bring the old magic to life in time for the Midsummer's Eve festival.

Faber, 1983, 176 pp., o.p.

(BL 79:1400; CCBB 37:47; Kirkus 51:4; SLJ Sep 1983 p. 132)

EGAN, Doris. *The Gate of Ivory.*

See Chapter 5, High Fantasy: Alternate Worlds or Histories.

EISENSTEIN, Phyllis. *Sorcerer's Son.*
See Chapter 5, High Fantasy: Alternate Worlds or Histories.

ELGIN, (Patricia Anne) Suzette Haden. *Twelve Fair Kingdoms.*
See Chapter 5, High Fantasy: Alternate Worlds or Histories.

12-69   **EMBRY, Margaret (Jacob).** *The Blue-Nosed Witch.* Gr. 2–4.
✶   On her way to the witches' Halloween flight meeting, a young witch named Blanche joins a group of trick-or-treating children.
Illus. by Carl Rose, Holiday, 1956, 45 pp., o.p.
(BL 53:154; CCBB 1 1:23; HB 32:366, 63:495; Kirkus 24:514; LJ 81:2720)

ENDE, Michael. *The Night of Wishes, or The Satanarcheolidealcohellish Notion Potion.*
See Chapter 8, Humorous Fantasy.

ERWIN, Betty K. *Aggie, Maggie and Tish.*
See Chapter 9, Magic Adventure Fantasy.

12-70   **ESTES, Eleanor (Ruth Rosenfeld).** *The Witch Family.* Gr. 3–5.
✶   Two girls drawing witches are amazed when their works come to life. Amy has another magic adventure in *The Curious Adventures of Jimmy McGee* (1987).
Illus. by Edward Ardizzone, Harcourt, 1960, 1990, pap., 223 pp. (0-15-298572-7), 2000, 225 pp. (0-15-202604-5)
(BL 57:329; CCBB 14:57; HB 36:395; HBG 12:304; Kirkus 28:817; LJ 85:4558; TLS 1962 p. 393)

FARTHING, Alison. *The Mystical Beast.*
See Chapter 7, High Fantasy: Travel to Other Worlds.

FEIST, Raymond E. *Silverthorn.*
See Chapter 5, High Fantasy: Alternate Worlds or Histories.

12-71   **FIENBERG, Anna.** *The Witch in the Lake.* Gr. 6–8. (Orig. Australian pub. 2001.)
Forbidden to see her lifelong friend Leo because of his wizardly heritage, Merilee meets him secretly until the Wise Woman, Aunt Beatrice, takes her away, in this story set in an alternate 16th-century Italy.
Annick/Firefly, 2002, 220 pp. (1-55037-723-X), 2002, pap. (1-55037-722-1)
(HBG 14:79; Kirkus 70:410; SLJ Aug 2002 p. 183; VOYA 25:201)

FLEISCHMAN, (Albert) Sid(ney). *The 13th Floor: A Ghost Story.*
See Chapter 10, Time Travel Fantasy.

12-72   **FLEISCHMAN, Paul (Taylor).** *The Half-a-Moon Inn.* Gr. 4–6.
✶   Sinister Miss Crackle, thieving innkeeper and dream reader, holds a mute boy named Aaron prisoner after he wanders away from home in search of his mother. Golden Kite Award Honor Book, 1980.
Illus. by Kathy Jacobi, Harper, 1980, 96 pp., LB (0-06-021918-1)
(BL 76:1531; HB 56:294; Kirkus 48:513; SLJ Oct 1980 p. 145)

FLEWELLING, Lynn. *The Bone Doll's Twin.*
See Chapter 5, High Fantasy: Alternate Worlds or Histories.

FLORA, James (Royer). *Grandpa's Ghost Stories.*
See Chapter 4, Ghost Fantasy.

12-73 **FLORA, James (Royer).** *Wanda and the Bumbly Wizard.* Gr. 2–4.
An inept wizard and an orphaned girl named Wanda tame a giant and save the Queen's castle.
Illus. by the author, Atheneum, 1980, 32 pp., o.p.
(BL 76:1056; Kirkus 48:511; SLJ Mar 1980 p. 120)

FREEMAN, Barbara C(onstance). *Broom-Adelaide.*
See Chapter 1, Allegorical Fantasy and Literary Fairy Tales.

12-74 **FRIESNER, Esther M.** *Majyk by Accident.* Gr. 8–12.
Kendar Gangle, an accident-prone student wizard, needs the help of his wise-cracking feline familiar, Scandal, to handle his newly acquired majyk.
Ace, 1993, pap., 288 pp. (0-441-51376-X)
(BL 89:1949, 1953; Kliatt Jan 1994 p. 16; VOYA 16:309)

FRIESNER, Esther M. *Yesterday We Saw Mermaids.*
See Chapter 6, High Fantasy: Myth or Legend Fantasy.

12-75 **FROMAN, Elizabeth Hull.** *Eba, the Absent-Minded Witch.* Gr. 3–5.
Eba the witch is so absent-minded that she has forgotten how to fly.
Illus. by Dorothy Maas, World, 1965, 64 pp., o.p.
(CCBB 20:24; HB 41:491; Kirkus 33:824; LJ 90:5514; TLS 1968 p. 256)

FUNK, Bret M. *Sword of Honor.*
See Chapter 5, High Fantasy: Alternate Worlds or Histories.

12-76 **FURLONG, Monica (Navis).** *Wise Child.* **(Juniper trilogy, bk. 1).** Gr. 6–8.
★ (Orig. British pub. 1987.)
Wise Child, a headstrong young orphan, is taken in by Juniper, a mysterious healer, who teaches the girl the arts of witchcraft. Carnegie Medal Commended Book, 1987. In the prequel, *Juniper* (1991, 2004; orig. British pub. 1990), a girl named Juniper leaves her comfortable castle life to study herb-lore and spell-casting with a harsh mentor named Euny. The final book in the trilogy is *Colman* (2004).
Knopf, 1987, 228 pp., o.p.; Random, 2004 (0-394-89105-8), pap. (0-679-83369-2)
(BL 84:632, 1276, 88:1768; CCBB 41:116; HB 64:206; Kirkus 55:1461; SLJ Sep 1987 p. 195; Suth 4:128; TLS 1987 p. 964)

12-77 **GABHART, Ann.** *The Gifting.* Gr. 6–8.
An old woman passes on her healing powers to 13-year-old Ginny, in this otherwise realistic family story.
Simon & Schuster, 1987, pap., 155 pp., o.p.
(BL 84:714; VOYA 10 234)

GARCIA Y ROBERTSON, R(odrigo). *Knight Errant.*
See Chapter 10, Time Travel Fantasy.

12-78 **GARD, Joyce (pseud. of Joyce Reeves).** *The Mermaid's Daughter.* Gr. 7–9.
Astria, High Priestess of a mystical cult of woman worshippers, travels from
the Scilly Islands to Britain to defeat a Roman plot to destroy her cult.
Holt, 1969, 319 pp., o.p.
(BL 66:564; CCBB 23:176; HB 46:166; LJ 95:1202; Suth:139; TLS 1969 p. 690)

12-79 **GARDNER, Craig Shaw.** *A Disagreement with Death.* **(Ballad of
Wuntvor trilogy, bk. 3).** Gr. 7–12. (Orig. Britsh pub. 1989.)
Death has kidnapped the wizard Ebenezum, causing his apprentice, Wuntvor,
to set out with a witch, three demons, a brownie, a dragon, a unicorn, a giant,
and seven dwarves to save his master, in this humorous conclusion to the trilo-
gy. The preceding volumes are *A Difficulty with Dwarves* (1989) and *An
Excess of Enchantment* (1989).
Ace, 1989, pap., o.p.
(VOYA 12:222)

GARDNER, Craig Shaw. *Dragon Sleeping.*
See Chapter 7, High Fantasy: Travel to Other Worlds.

GARNER, Alan. *The Weirdstone of Brisingamen.*
See Chapter 6, High Fantasy: Myth or Legend Fantasy.

12-80 **GARNER, Alan.** *The Well of the Wind.* Gr. 3–5. (Orig. pub. in England.)
★ An orphaned brother and sister with stars on their foreheads found floating on
the sea in a crystal box are enticed by a sorceress to visit the Well of the Wind
to find a "white bird of perfect feather."
Illus. by Hervé Blondon, DK, 1998, 45 pp. (0-7894-2519-X)
(BL 94:2006; CCBB 52:96; HBG 10:278; Kirkus 66:1284; SLJ Nov 1998 p. 85)

12-81 **GILLILAND, Alexis A(rnaldus).** *Wizenbeak.* **(Wizenbeak trilogy, bk. 1).**
Gr. 10 up.
Wizard Wizenbeak, sent into the outlands to establish a new settlement, is
asked by the Witch-Queen Shaia to protect her two children from their royal
half-brother, and to help them take control of the throne of Cymdulock. The
sequels are *The Shadow Shaia* (1987) and *Lord of the Troll-Bats* (1992).
Bluejay, 1986, 288 pp., o.p.
(BL 82:1361, 1388; Kirkus 54:587; VOYA 9:237)

GILLULY, Sheila. *Greenbriar Queen.*
See Chapter 5, High Fantasy: Alternate Worlds or Histories.

GILMAN, Dorothy. *The Maze in the Heart of the Castle.*
See Chapter 7, High Fantasy: Travel to Other Worlds.

12-82 **GILMORE, Kate.** *Enter Three Witches.* Gr. 6–10.
★★ Sixteen-year-old Bren has a problem: how to keep his new girlfriend from discovering that both his mother and grandmother are practicing witches.
Houghton, 1990, 210 pp. (0-395-50213-6); Scholastic, 1992, pap. (0-590-
44494-8)
(BL 86:1430, 1446, 87:459, 1476; CCBB 43:159; HBG 1:255; Kirkus 58:341; SLJ Apr 1990
p. 139; Suth 4:140; VOYA 13:29)

12-83 GLIORI, Debi. *Pure Dead Magic.* **(Pure Dead trilogy, bk. 1).** Gr. 4–7.
Titus, Pandora, and baby Damp's mother return to Witch's School to better support the family after their father disappears. The sequels are *Pure Dead Wicked* (2002) and *Pure Dead Brilliant* (2003).
Knopf, 2001, 182 pp. (0-375-91410-2); Dell, 2002, pap., 182 pp. (0-440-41849-6)
(BL 97:2118; CCBB 55:204; HBG 13:372; Kirkus 69:1122; SLJ Sep 2001 p. 225; VOYA 24:368)

GLOSS, Molly. *Outside the Gates.*
See Chapter 5, High Fantasy: Alternate Worlds or Histories.

12-84 GOLDSTEIN, Lisa. *The Red Magician.* Gr. 10 up.
✶ Young Kicsi describes the battle between a wonder-working rabbi and a traveling magician who foretells the Holocaust, in this tale set in a small Hungarian Jewish village. American Book Award, Original Paperback Category, 1983.
Pocket, 1982, 1983, pap., 156 pp., o.p.; Tor, 1993, 192 pp. (0-312-85462-5), 1995, pap., 192 pp. (0-312-89007-9)
(BL 78:1004, 1014; VOYA 6:342, 17:19)

GOODKIND, Terry. *Wizard's First Rule.*
See Chapter 5, High Fantasy: Alternate Worlds or Histories.

GORDON, John (William). *The Edge of the World.*
See Chapter 7, High Fantasy: Travel to Other Worlds.

GORDON, John (William). *The Giant Under the Snow.*
See Chapter 6, High Fantasy: Myth or Legend Fantasy.

GOUDGE, Elizabeth (de Beauchamp). *Linnets and Valerians.*
See Chapter 9, Magic Adventure Fantasy.

GRAY, Nicholas Stuart. *Mainly in Moonlight: Ten Stories of Sorcery and the Supernatural.*
See Chapter 3, Fantasy Collections.

GREEN, Kathleen. *Philip and the Pooka and Other Irish Fairy Tales.*
See Chapter 3, Fantasy Collections.

GREEN, Phyllis. *Eating Ice Cream with a Werewolf.*
See Chapter 9, Magic Adventure Fantasy.

12-85 GREGORY, Philippa. *The Wise Woman.* Gr. 10 up. (Orig. British pub. 1992.)
Orphaned Alys, trained in the arts of healing and magic by a healer and witch named Morach, tries to hide in a convent to avoid persecution in 16th-century England.
Pocket, 1993, 438 pp. (0-671-79274-1)
(BL 90:195; LJ Oct 15, 1993 p. 87)

12-86 GRIFFIN, Adele. *Witch Twins.* **(Witch Twins series, bk. 1).** Gr. 3–5.
✶ Only their grandmother knows that fifth-grade twins Claire and Luna are witches, so no one suspects their plans to use magic to ruin their father's sec-

ond wedding. The sequels are *Witch Twins at Camp Bliss* (2002), *Witch Twins and Melody Malady* (2003), and *Witch Twins and the Ghost of Glenn Bly* (2004).

Illus. by Jacqueline Rogers, Hyperion, 2001, 144 pp. (0-7868-0739-3), 2002, pap., 155 pp. (0-7868-1563-9)

(BL 97:1552; HB 77:583; HBG 13:85; Kirkus 69:740; SLJ July 2001 p. 82)

12-87 GRIPE, Maria (Kristina). *The Glassblower's Children.* Gr. 5–7. (Orig.
✶ Swedish pub. 1964.)

Klaus and Klara, kidnapped and imprisoned by the Lord of All Wishes Town, lose all hope of rescue until a sorceress named Flutter Mildweather arrives to help them.

Trans. by Sheila LaFarge, illus. by Harald Gripe, Delacorte, 1973, 170 pp., o.p.

(BL 70:170:CCBB 27:9; HB 62:756; Kirkus 41:515, 1350; LJ 98:2194; Suth 2:192; TLS 1975 p. 365)

12-88 HAHN, Mary Downing. *The Time of the Witch.* Gr. 5–7.
✶ Laura convinces an old woman with sorcerous powers to cast a spell that will reunite her parents, but the spell goes wrong and makes Laura's younger brother very ill.

Houghton, 1982, 160 pp., o.p.

(BL 79:311; HB 59:44; SLJ Nov 1982 p. 84)

12-89 HALDANE, J(ohn) B(urdon) S(anderson). *My Friend Mr. Leakey.* Gr. 3–5. (Orig. British pub. 1937.)

A collection of eerie tales, many of which concern a magician named Mr. Leakey.

Illus. by L. H. Rosoman, Harper, 1938, 179 pp., o.p.

(HB 14:382)

HALDEMAN, Linda (Wilson). *The Lastborn of Elvinwood.*
See Chapter 6, High Fantasy: Myth or Legend Fantasy.

12-90 HALE, F. J. *Ogre Castle.* **(After the Spell Wars trilogy, bk. 1).** Gr. 10 up.

An itinerant wizard hired to exorcise ghostly spells from a castle ends up pursuing a horrible ogre who has kidnapped a princess. The sequel is *In the Sea Nymph's Lair* (1982, 1989).

Crown, 1988, pap., 224 pp., o.p.

(BL 85:42, 68; LJ Sep 15, 1988 p. 96)

12-91 HAMBLY, Barbara. *Dragonsbane.* **(Dragon trilogy, bk. 1).** Gr. 10 up.
✶✶ Mage Jenny Waynest unites her powers with those of the Black Dragon that her lover, John Aversin, has pledged to destroy, in order to defeat an evil sorceress threatening the kingdom. The sequels are *Dragonshadow* (1999, 2000) and *Knight of the Demon Queen* (2000).

Del Rey, 1985, o.p.; Ballantine, 1987, pap., 352 pp., o.p.

(BL 82:851, 860, 83:777, 1118, 86:906; LJ Feb 15, 1986 p. 196, SLJ Sep 1986 p. 152; VOYA 9:162, 10:21)

HAMBLY, Barbara. *The Ladies of Mandrigyn.*
See Chapter 5, High Fantasy: Alternate Worlds or Histories.

12-92 HAMBLY, Barbara. *The Rainbow Abyss.* **(Sun-Cross duology, bk. 1).** Gr. 7–12.

Rhion, apprentice to Master-Wizard Jaldis, must make a perilous journey across the Abyss to a world where all magic has been lost. The sequel is *The Magicians of Night* (1992).

Ballantine/Del Rey, 1991, 295 pp. (0-345-37101-1)

(LJ Sep 15, 1991 p. 117; VOYA 14:382)

HAMBLY, Barbara. *The Silent Tower.*
See Chapter 7, High Fantasy: Travel to Other Worlds.

12-93 HAMBLY, Barbara. *Sisters of the Raven.* Gr. 10 up.

Because the male magicians of King Oryn's realm seem to be losing their powers, the King's consort forms a group of gifted women called Sisters of the Raven, in an attempt to relieve the drought affecting Yellow City.

Warner, 2002, pap., 482 pp. (0-446-67704-3)

(LJ Aug 2002 p. 151; VOYA 25:487)

12-94 HAMBLY, Barbara. *Stranger at the Wedding.* Gr. 7–12.

Apprentice wizard Kyra falls in love with her sister Alix's fiancée while attempting to lift a fatal curse on Alix's life, in this story set in the same world as the author's Windrose Chronicles (see *The Silent Tower* in Chapter 7, High Fantasy: Travel to Other Worlds).

Del Rey, 1994, 341 pp. (0-345-38097-5)

(BL 91:1403; Kliatt Nov 1994 p. 22; VOYA 17:222;)

HAMLETT, Christina. *The Enchanter.*
See Chapter 6, High Fantasy: Myth or Legend Fantasy.

HANSEN, Ron. *The Shadowmaker.*
See Chapter 9, Magic Adventure Fantasy.

12-95 HARDY, Lyndon. *Secret of the Sixth Magic.* **(The Principles of Magic, bk. 2).** Gr. 10 up. **(Orig. British pub. 1984.)**

A bumbling apprentice magician, attempting to master the five magics that govern his world, stumbles upon a demonic sixth magic controlled by the evil Melazar. This is the sequel to *Master of the Five Magics* (1980, 1985), and is followed by *Magic in Triplicate* (1987) and *Riddle of the Seven Realms* (1988).

Ballantine, 1986, pap., 384 pp. (0-345-34500-2)

(BL 81:25, 58; LJ 109:1776; SLJ Jan 1985 p. 92)

12-96 HARRIS, Deborah Turner. *The Burning Stone.* **(Mages of Carillon trilo-**
✶ **gy, bk. 1).** Gr. 10 up.

Young Carodoc Penlluathe seeks revenge against Borthen Berigeld, the man responsible for expelling the young mage from his order. The sequels are *The Gauntlet of Malice* (1988) and *Spiral of Fire* (1989).

Tor, 1987, pap., 307 pp., o.p.

(BL 83:1097, 1116; Kliatt Spring 1987 p. 22; SLJ Sep 1987 p. 204; VOYA 10:90; 11:12)

HARRIS, Deborah Turner. *Caledon of the Mists.*
See Chapter 5, High Fantasy: Alternate Worlds or Histories.

12-97   HARRISON, Mette Ivie. *Mira, Mirror.* Gr. 7–12.
☆   Betrayed by her adopted sister and fellow witch's apprentice, Mira, trans-
formed into a mirror, attempts to free herself by switching the faces of a peas-
ant girl named Ivana and a merchant's daughter.
Viking, 2004, 256 pp. (0-670-05923-4)
(BL 101:106; CCBB 58:124; Kirkus 72:914; Kliatt Sep 2004 p. 10; SLJ Sep 2004 p. 207;
VOYA 27:314;)

12-98   HAYES, Sarah. *Crumbling Castle.* Gr. 2–5. (Orig. British pub. 1989.)
Three stories describing how the newest residents of Crumbling Castle, a wiz-
ard named Zeb and a talking crow named Jason, learn to live with the ghost,
the baby dragon, the mice, the toads, and the beetles already in residence.
Illus. by Helen Craig, Candlewick, 1992, 76 pp., o.p.
(BL 89:737; HBG 4[Spring 1993]:57; Kirkus 60:989; SLJ Oct 1992 p. 88)

12-99   *Hecate's Cauldron.* Ed. by Susan M. Shwartz. Gr. 10 up.
An anthology of fantasy stories based on European, African, and Japanese tales
of witchcraft, written by Katherine Kurtz, C. J. Cherryh, Tanith Lee, and Andre
Norton, among others.
DAW, 1982, pap., 256 pp., o.p.
(BL 78:1299, 1307; Kliatt 16[Spring 1982]:29; VOYA 5[Aug 1982]:39)

12-100 HENDRY, Frances Mary. *Quest for a Maid.* Gr. 6–9. (Orig. British pub.
☆   1988.)
When Meg, a 13th-century shipbuilder's daughter, accompanies an 8-year-old
Norwegian princess on a voyage to Scotland to marry Prince Edward, the ship
is wrecked in a storm caused by Meg's sorceress older sister, Inge, in this his-
torical novel with just a touch of the supernatural.
Farrar, 1990, 273 pp., o.p.
(BL 86:2083, 2089, 87:1229, 1476, 1488; CCBB 44:9; HB 66:601; HBG 2:83; Kirkus 58:875;
SLJ Dec 1990 p. 121; Suth 4:173; VOYA 13:218)

HENRY, Maeve. *The Witch King.*
See Chapter 5, High Fantasy: Alternate Worlds or Histories.

HEWETT, Anita. *The Bull Beneath the Walnut Tree and Other Stories.*
See Chapter 3, Fantasy Collections.

HILL, Douglas (Arthur). *Blade of the Poisoner.*
See Chapter 5, High Fantasy: Alternate Worlds or Histories.

HILL, Elizabeth Starr. *Ever-After Island.*
See Chapter 9, Magic Adventure Fantasy.

HODGES, Margaret, ed. *Comus.*
See Chapter 1, Allegorical Fantasy and Literary Fairy Tales.

HOFFMAN, Nina Kiriki. *A Red Heart of Memories.*
See Chapter 5, High Fantasy: Alternate Worlds or Histories.

HOFFMANN, Eleanor. *Mischief in Fez.*
See Chapter 9, Magic Adventure Fantasy.

12-101 HOLMAN (Valen), Felice. *The Witch on the Corner.* Gr. 3–5.

✶   Miss Pinchon tries to fly on a broomstick but realizes that her magic is meant for gardening.
Illus. by Arnold Lobel, Norton, 1966, 88 pp., o.p.
(CCBB 20:108; Kirkus 34:1101; LJ 92:335; TLS 1967 p. 1133)

HOLT, Tom. *Who's Afraid of Beowulf?*
See Chapter 6, High Fantasy: Myth or Legend Fantasy.

HOOD, Daniel. *Scales of Justice.*
See Chapter 5, High Fantasy: Alternate Worlds or Histories.

HOOKS, William H(arris). *Moss Gown.*
See Chapter 1, Allegorical Fantasy and Literary Fairy Tales.

HOPP, Zinken. *The Magic Chalk.*
See Chapter 9, Magic Adventure Fantasy.

12-102 HOROWITZ, Anthony. *The Devil's Door-Bell.* **(Martin Hopkins trilogy, bk. 1).** Gr. 6–8. (Orig. British pub. 1983.)
The ancient power of a Druidic stone circle, now the site of an abandoned nuclear power plant, awakens orphaned 13-year-old Martin's magical powers to the possibility that his guardian plans to use black magic to murder him. The sequels are *The Night of the Scorpion* (Pacer, 1984) and *The Silver Citadel* (1986).
Henry Holt, 1984, 159 pp., o.p.
(BL 80:814, 1070; Kirkus 52:J15; Kliatt Spring 1985 p. 26; SLJ Apr 1984 p. 124)

12-103 HORWITZ, Elinor Lander. *The Strange Story of the Frog Who Became a Prince.* Gr. 1–4.
A witch who transforms a happy frog into a prince can't understand his dissatisfaction, and can't remember how to change him back.
Illus. by John Heinly, Delacorte, 1971, 45 pp., o.p.
(HB 47:282; Kirkus 39:428; LJ 96:2906)

HOUGH, (Helen) Charlotte (Woodyatt). *Red Biddy and Other Stories.*
See Chapter 3, Fantasy Collections.

12-104 HOUSTON, James A(rchibald). *Spirit Wrestler.* Gr. 10 up.
Shoonah, an orphaned Eskimo boy, longs to become a hunter and lead a normal life, rather than follow in his adoptive mother's footsteps and become the tribal shaman.
Harcourt, 1980, 288 pp., o.p.
(BL 76:700, 713; Kirkus 47:1342, 1382; LJ 10:120)

12-105 HOWARD, Joan (pseud. of Patricia Gordon). *The Witch of Scrapfaggot Green.* Gr. 3–5.
A witch's ghost brings trouble to a small English village.

Illus. by William (Sherman) Pène du Bois, Viking, 1948, 78 pp., o.p.

(BL 44:228; CCBB 1[May 1948]:2; HB 24:191; Kirkus 16:49; LJ 73:609, 657)

12-106 HUFF, Tanya. *The Last Wizard.* **(Wizard of the Grove duology, bk. 1).** Gr. 10 up.

Crystal, a wizard formed from seven goddesses who fused themselves together to defeat evil, joins two brothers searching for the tower of the ancient wizard Aryalan. *Child of the Grove* (DAW, 1988) is the prequel, and *Wizard of the Grove* (DAW, pap., 1999; 0-88677-819-0) contains both books.

DAW, 1989, pap., 288 pp., o.p.; DAW, 1995, pap., 288 pp. (0-88677-331-8)

(VOYA 12:224, 13:14)

12-107 HUGHES, Frieda. *Getting Rid of Aunt Edna.* Gr. 3–5. (Orig. British pub. 1986.)

The peaceful lives of apprentice witch Miranda and her Aunt Agatha are disrupted by the arrival of the third witch in the family, Aunt Edna.

Illus. by Ed Levine, Harper, 1986, 74 pp., o.p.

(BL 82:1612; CCBB 39:211; Kirkus 54:715; SLJ Oct 1986 p. 177; TLS Aug 1, 1986 p. 850)

12-108 HUGHES, Robert Don. *The Faithful Traitor.* **(Wizard and Dragon series, bk. 2).** Gr. 7–12.

After the two-headed dragon he was ordered to create begins destroying the countryside, powershaper Seagryn is branded a traitor. This is the sequel to *The Forging of the Dragon* (1989), and is followed by *The Power and the Prophet* (1985).

Ballantine, 1992, pap., 277 pp. (0-345-36090-7)

(Kliatt Sep 1992 p. 20; VOYA 15:174)

HUNTER, Mollie (pseud. of Maureen Mollie Hunter McVeigh McIlwraith). *The Ferlie.*

See Chapter 9, Magic Adventure Fantasy.

HUNTER, Mollie (pseud. of Maureen Mollie Hunter McVeigh McIlwraith). *The Kelpie's Pearls.*

See Chapter 1, Allegorical Fantasy and Literary Fairy Tales.

HUNTER, Mollie (pseud. of Maureen Mollie Hunter McVeigh McIlwraith). *A Stranger Came Ashore.*

See Chapter 6, High Fantasy: Myth or Legend Fantasy.

12-109 HUNTER, Mollie (pseud. of Maureen Mollie Hunter McVeigh McIl-
✫   **wraith).** *Thomas and the Warlock.* Gr. 4–6. (Orig. British pub. 1967.)

Thomas, the village blacksmith, manages to rescue his wife from an angry warlock and drive all of the witches out of the Scottish lowlands.

Illus. by Joseph Cellini, Funk, 1967, 128 pp., o.p.

(BL 64:450; CCBB 21:60; HB 43:749, 61:84, 63:492; Kirkus 35:808; LJ 92:3850; Suth:204; TLS 1967 p. 451)

12-110 HUNTER, Mollie (pseud. of Maureen Mollie Hunter McVeigh McIl-
✶   **wraith).** *The Walking Stones: A Story of Suspense.* Gr. 4–6. (Orig. British
pub. 1970, entitled *The Bodach.*)
An elderly Bodach, or sorcerer, lets Donald Campbell assume his magical
powers in order to save his stone circle from the waters of a new hydroelectric
plant.
Illus. by Trina Schart Hyman, Harper, 1970, 143 pp., o.p.; Harcourt, 1996,
pap., 168 pp. (0-15-200995-7)
(BL 67:228; CCBB 24:157; HB 47:51; Kirkus 38:800; LJ 95:4375; Suth:204; TLS 1970 p.
1251)

12-111 HUNTINGTON, Geoffrey. *Sorcerers of the Nightwing.* **(The Ravenscliff**
series, vol. 1). Gr. 6–10.
After his adoptive father's death, Devon March, 14, learns that he is descended
from sorcerers who use magic to guard the world from evil. The sequel is
Demon Witch (2003).
Regan, 2002, 279 pp. (0-06-001425-3)
(BL 98:1948; Kirkus 70:1034; SLJ Oct 2002 p. 166; VOYA 25:487, 26:12)

12-112 IBBOTSON, Eva. *Not Just a Witch.* Gr. 4–7. (Orig. British pub. 1989.)
A furrier named Lionel Warthag takes advantage of a feud between witches
Dora and Heckie, former best friends, one of whom can turn evildoers to stone,
and the other who can transform them into animals.
Illus. by Kevin Hawkes, Dutton, 2003, 176 pp. (0-525-47101-4)
(BL 99:1466; CCBB 57:17; HBG 15:80; Kirkus 71:859; SLJ Oct 2003 p. 168)

12-113 IBBOTSON, Eva. *The Star of Kazan.* Gr. 4–8. (Orig. British pub. 2004.)
✶   Wealthy Viennese Annika, 12, lovingly raised by two servants and three pro-
fessors after her abandonment in infancy, is eager to believe that the elegant
woman who takes her away to a remote northern estate is her real mother.
Nestlé Smarties Book Prize, Silver Award, age 9–11 category, 2004.
Illus. by Kevin Hawkes, Dutton, 2004, 405 pp. (0-525-47347-5)
(BL 101:404; CCBB 58:171; HB 80:710; Kirkus 72:915;)

12-114 IBBOTSON, Eva. *Which Witch?* Gr. 5–8. (Orig. British pub. 1979.)
✶   Orphaned Terence convinces Belladonna, a kind white witch, to enter Wizard
Arriman the Awful's competition for a wife. Anne Spencer Lindbergh Prize,
1999-2000.
Illus. by Annabel Large, Dutton, 1999, 231 pp. (0-525-46164-7); Puffin, 2000,
pap., 249 pp. (0-14-130427-8)
(BL 95:2056; CCBB 53:18; HBG 11:80; Kirkus 67:884; SLJ Aug 1999 p. 158)

12-115 *In Celebration of Lammas Night.* **Ed. by Josepha Sherman.** Gr. 10 up.
Nineteen tales by Diana L. Paxson, Ru Emerson, Josepha Sherman, and others,
that re-work a story Mercedes Lackey wrote as a song called "Lammas Night,"
about a traveling wizard haunted by a ghost.
Baen, 1996, 282 pp. (0-671-87713-5)
(Kliatt May 1996 p. 19:VOYA 19:170)

IPCAR, Dahlov (Zorach). *The Queen of Spells.*
See Chapter 6, High Fantasy: Myth or Legend Fantasy.

12-116 IPCAR, Dahlov (Zorach). *The Warlock of Night.* Gr. 5–7.
A young apprentice to the dreaded Warlock of the Land of Night tries to use magic to save his country.
Viking, 1969, 159 pp., o.p.
(Kirkus 37:1195; LJ 95:789, 1911)

JOHNSON, Dorothy M(arie). *Witch Princess.*
See Chapter 6, High Fantasy: Myth or Legend Fantasy.

12-117 JONES, Diana Wynne. *Archer's Goon.* Gr. 6–9. (Orig. British pub. 1984.)
★★ Howard Sykes and his sister, Awful, are determined to discover how their father's writings have kept the mysterious and powerful Archer from leaving their town and taking over the world. Boston Globe Horn Book Award Honor Book in Fiction, 1984.
Greenwillow, 1984, 241 pp., o.p.; Greenwillow, 2003, 336 pp. (0-06-029889-8), 2003, pap., 336 pp. (0-06-447356-2)
(BL 80:1060; CCBB 37:167; HB 60:202; SLJ Mar 1984 p. 160; Suth 3:220; TLS 1984 p. 1198; VOYA 7:101)

12-118 JONES, Diana Wynne. *Aunt Maria.* Gr. 6–9. (Orig. British pub. 1991, enti-
★ tled *Black Maria.*)
Meg seeks help from a magician buried alive for 20 years, after Aunt Maria turns Meg's mother into a virtual slave, transforms her brother into a wolf, and encourages the villagers to hunt him down.
Greenwillow, 1991, 224 pp. (0-688-10611-0); Greenwillow, 2003, 288 pp. (0-06-623742-4)
(BL 88:316; CCBB 45:41; HBG 3:79; Kirkus 59:1223; SLJ Oct 1991 p. 142; TLS July 12, 1991 p. 20; VOYA 15:44, 16:9)

JONES, Diana Wynne. *Charmed Life.*
See Chapter 10, Time Travel Fantasy.

12-119 JONES, Diana Wynne. *Dark Lord of Derkholm.* Gr. 7–10. (Orig. British
★★ pub. 1998.)
The residents of Derkholm are tired after spending 40 years turning themselves and their village into magical creatures and kingdoms to be ravaged as entertainment for Mr. Chesney's annual Pilgrim Party tours, and they hope that their choice of wizard Derk as this year's Dark Lord will put a stop to it. Mythopoeic Fantasy Award for Children's Literature, 1999. In the sequel, *Year of the Griffin* (2000), Derk's griffin daughter, Elda, and her Wizard's University classmates encounter assassins, dwarf forgemasters, gangsters, rogue griffins, and revolutionaries during their year at magic school.
Greenwillow, 1998, 352 pp. (0-688-16004-2); HarperTrophy, 2001, pap., 528 pp. (0-06-447336-8)
(BL 95:110, 1691; CCBB 52:102; HB 74:732; HBG 10:80; Kliatt Nov 1998 p. 6; SLJ Oct 1998 p. 136; VOYA 21:443, 22:14)

12-120 JONES, Diana Wynne. *Deep Secret.* Gr. 10 up. (Orig. British pub. 1997.)
★ Rupert Venables, junior magid in charge of maintaining the Earth's magical balance, attends an English science fiction convention where he hopes to find the missing heir to the Koryfonic Empire and a replacement for the late Chief

Magid. The author's *The Merlin Conspiracy* (2003; see below) is a companion volume.

Tor, 1999, 384 pp. (0-312-86859-6); Starscape, 2002, pap., 384 pp. (0-7653-4247-2)

(BL 95:1293; Kliatt May 2003 p. 26; SLJ Oct 1999 p. 178; VOYA 22:270, 23:12)

12-121 JONES, Diana Wynne. *Fire and Hemlock.* Gr. 7–12. (Orig. British pub.
★★ 1984.)

As Polly's vague memories of the year that she was 10 and first met Thomas Lynn become clearer, she is horrified to realize that someone has erased Tom's existence from both her memory and that of the world at large, and that his life is in her hands.

Greenwillow, 1984, 352 pp., o.p.; Greenwillow, 2002, 432 pp. (0-06-029885-5)

(BL 81:300, 307, 86:906; CCBB 38:68; HB 61:58; HBG 13:392; SLJ Oct 1984 p. 167; Suth 3:221; VOYA 7:266, 8:365)

12-122 JONES, Diana Wynne. *Howl's Moving Castle.* Gr. 7–12. (Orig. British pub.
★★ 1986.)

After a witch turns Sophie into an old woman, she moves into Wizard Howl's moving castle and attempts to tame him, even as she is falling in love with him. Boston Globe Horn Book Award Honor Book in Fiction, 1986. This story is related to the author's *Castle in the Air* (1991; see Chapter 5, High Fantasy: Alternate Worlds or Histories).

Greenwillow, 1986, 224 pp. (0-688-06233-4); Greenwillow, 2001, 329 pp. (0-06-441034-X)

(BL 82:1455, 1461, 83:777, 1118, 1138, 1274, 1592, 86:907, 91:415; CCBB 39:187; HB 62:331; Kirkus 54:868; SLJ Aug 1986 p. 101, Apr 1987 p. 48; Suth 4:207; TLS 1986 p. 1410)

JONES, Diana Wynne. *The Lives of Christopher Chant.*
See Chapter 7, High Fantasy: Travel to Other Worlds.

12-123 JONES, Diana Wynne. *The Magicians of Caprona.* **(Chrestomanci series,**
★ **bk. 4).** Gr. 5–7. (Orig. British pub. 1980.)

When an evil enchantress tries to destroy Caprona by dividing its two families of magicians, two young children and the wizard Chrestomanci join forces to defeat her. This book is related to *Charmed Life* (1978; see Chapter 10, Time Travel Fantasy), *Witch Week* (1982; see below) and *The Lives of Christopher Chant* (1988; see Chapter 7, High Fantasy: Travel to Other Worlds), which is a prequel to this story. Two collections contain short stories about Chrestomanci: *Dragons and Dreams*, ed. by Jane Yolen (Harper, 1986; see Chapter 9, Magic Adventure Fantasy), and *Warlock at the Wheel* by Diana Wynne Jones (Greenwillow, 1985; see below). *Mixed Magics: Four Tales of Chrestomanci* (2000, 2001; see below) is a related work. The four Chrestomanci novels have been reissued as *The Chronicles of Chrestomanci* (Greenwillow, 2001). Vol. 1 (0-06-447268-X) contains *Charmed Life* and *The Lives of Christopher Chant*. Vol. 2 (0-064-47269-8) contains *Witch Week* and *The Magicians of Caprona*.

Greenwillow, 1980, 223 pp., o.p.; Greenwillow, 2001, 269 pp. (0-06-029878-2)

(BL 76:1676; CCBB 33:216; HB 56:407; HBG 12:308; Kirkus 48:1163; SLJ Oct 1980 p. 147; Suth 3:221; TLS 1980 p. 360)

12-124 JONES, Diana Wynne. *The Merlin Conspiracy.* Gr. 6–12. (Orig. pub. in
✫ England.)
Nick Mallory finds his way from England into the alternate world of the
Islands of Blest, where he and Roddy, daughter of the King's weather wizard,
try to prevent the destruction of Blest. *Deep Secret* (1999; see above) is a com-
panion volume.
Greenwillow, 2003, 480 pp. (0-06-052319-0); HarperTrophy, 2004, pap., 480
pp. (0-06-052320-4)
(BL 99:1464; CCBB 56:364; HB 79:359; HBG 14:384; Kirkus 71:469; SLJ May 2001 p. 154;
VOYA 26:236, 27:12)

12-125 JONES, Diana Wynne. *Mixed Magics: Four Tales of Chrestomanci.*
✫ **(Chrestomanci series).** Gr. 5–8. (Orig. British pub. 2000.)
"Warlock at the Wheel," "The Sage of Theare," "Carol Oneir's Hundredth
Dream," and "Stealer of Souls," are four short stories about Chrestomanci, the
enchanter who oversees the magic in a world similar to ours. These stories are
related to *The Lives of Christopher Chant* (1988, 2001; see Chapter 7).
Greenwillow, 2001, 138 pp., o.p.; HarperTrophy, 2003, pap., 208 pp. (0-06-
441018-8)
(BL 97:1558; HB 77:327; HBG 12:309; SLJ July 2001 p. 721; VOYA 24:291)

12-126 JONES, Diana Wynne. *A Sudden Wild Magic.* Gr. 10 up. (Orig. pub. in
England.)
A young woman named Zillah, unaware of the extent of her wild magic pow-
ers, stows away on the Witches' Council mission to the pirate world of Arth, an
all-male society causing environmental disasters, wars, and plagues on Earth.
Morrow, 1992, 416 pp. (0-688-11882-8); Orton, new ed., 1997, pap., 380 pp.
(0-57560-197-3)
(BL 89:492, 496, 842; Kirkus 60:1024; SLJ Mar 1993 p. 234)

JONES, Diana Wynne. *A Tale of Time City.*
See Chapter 7, High Fantasy: Travel to Other Worlds.

12-127 JONES, Diana Wynne. *Warlock at the Wheel and Other Stories.* Gr. 6–8.
(Orig. British pub. 1984.)
Eight stories of fantasy and magic, warlocks and wizards, including one about
Chrestomanci (see the author's *The Magicians of Caprona*, above).
Greenwillow, 1985, 156 pp., o.p.; Mammoth, 1997, pap., 197 pp. (0-74972-
635-0)
(BL 81:1196; CCBB 38:129; HB 61:453; SLJ Apr, 1985 p. 97; Suth 4:207; TLS 1984 p.
1198; VOYA 8:139)

JONES, Diana Wynne. *Wild Robert.*
See Chapter 9, Magic Adventure Fantasy.

12-128 JONES, Diana Wynne. *Witch Week.* **(Chrestomanci series, bk. 3).** Gr. 5–7.
(Orig. British pub. 1982.)
Magical chaos fills Class 6B when a group of witch orphans begins playing
magic tricks. This book is related to *Charmed Life* (1978; see Chapter 10, Time
Travel Fantasy) and *The Magicians of Caprona* (1980; see above). The four
Chrestomanci novels have been reissued as *The Chronicles of Chrestomanci*
(Greenwillow, 2001). Vol. 1 (0-06-447268-X) contains *Charmed Life* and *The*

Lives of Christopher Chant. Vol. 2 (0-064-47269-8) contains *Witch Week* and *The Magicians of Caprona.*
Greenwillow, 1982, 1993, 224 pp., o.p.; Greenwillow, 2001, 270 pp. (0-06-029879-0), pap. (0-688-15545-6)
(BL 79:246; CCBB 36:49; HB 59:44, 70:345; HBG 5:87, 12:308; Kirkus 50:938; SLJ Nov 1982 p. 86; Suth 3:221; TLS 1982 p. 797; VOYA 6:38, 16:382, 17:8)

12-129 JONES, Diana Wynne. *Witch's Business.* Gr. 5–7. (Orig. British pub. 1973, entitled *Wilkin's Tooth.*)
Jess and Frank's "revenge business" runs into competition from a nasty local witch.
Dutton, 1974, 168 pp., o.p.; Greenwillow, 2002, 192 pp. (0-06-008782-X)
(HBG 14:83; Kirkus 42:186; LJ 99:1220; TLS 1973 p. 387)

JORDAN, Robert. *The Eye of the World.*
See Chapter 5, High Fantasy: Alternate Worlds or Histories.

12-130 KATZ, Welwyn Wilton. *Come Like Shadows.* Gr. 9–12. (Orig. Canadian pub. 1993.)
Macbeth's witches seem to have cast an evil spell involving 16-year-old Stratford Festival Theater production assistant Kinny and an ancient mirror.
Viking, 1993, 304 pp. (0-670-84861-1)
(BL 90:685; HBG 5:87; Kirkus 61:1203; SLJ Dec 1993 p. 134; VOYA 16:228)

KAY, Guy Gavriel. *The Summer Tree.*
See Chapter 7, High Fantasy: Travel to Other Worlds.

12-131 KELLEHER, Victor (pseud. of Michael Kitchener). *Master of the Grove.* Gr. 6–8. (Orig. Australian pub. 1982.)
Derin, 14, follows Marna of the Witch people on a dangerous journey to rescue the father he does not remember. Australian Children's Book of the Year Award, 1983.
Puffin, 1983, 1988, pap., 183 pp., o.p.
(BL 85:423; TLS 1982 p. 344)

KELLER, Beverly (Lou). *A Small, Elderly Dragon.*
See Chapter 1, Allegorical Fantasy and Literary Fairy Tales.

KELLER, Gottfried. *The Fat of the Cat and Other Stories.*
See Chapter 3, Fantasy Collections.

12-132 KEMP, Gene. *Mr. Magus Is Waiting for You.* Gr. 4–7. (Orig. British pub. 1987.)
The lives of four young people are endangered when they enter an ancient house surrounded by a strangely beautiful garden.
Illus. by Alan Baker, Faber, 1987, 91 pp., o.p.
(SLJ Sep 1987 p. 180; TLS May 1987 p. 529)

12-133 KERR, Katharine. *Daggerspell.* (Deverry series, bk. 1). Gr. 10 up.
Nevyn, an ancient sorcerer who has become immortal in order to right the wrong he once did to a certain woman, must follow her through several incarnations. The sequels are *Darkspell* (1987; rev. ed. 1994), *The Bristling Wood*

(1989), and *The Dragon Reverant* (1990). The author's Westlands series is also set in Deverry (see *A Time of Exile*, 1991, in Chapter 5, High Fantasy: Alternate Worlds or Histories) as is the Dragon Mage trilogy (see *The Red Wyvern*, 1997, 1998, in the same chapter). All three series are related to the author's *Days of Air and Darkness* (1994).

Doubleday, 1986, 414 pp., o.p.

(BL 82:1667, 1683, 86:905; Kirkus 54:1071; LJ Aug 1986 p. 174; VOYA 9:237, 10:21)

KERR, Katharine. *A Time of Exile.*
See Chapter 5, High Fantasy: Alternate Worlds or Histories.

12-134 KERR, Peg. *Emerald House Rising.* Gr. 10 up.
After Jenna's dreams of following in the footsteps of her father, the best gem-cutter in Piyanthia, are nixed by the gem-cutting Guild, a magical gemstone shows Jenna that she could become a wizard.
Warner, 1997, pap., 325 pp. (0-446-60393-7)
(Kliatt Sep 1997 p. 20; VOYA 20:193, 21:13)

12-135 KIMMEL, Margaret Mary. *Magic in the Mist.* Gr. 2–4.
☆ Although he is studying to be a wizard, young Thomas's spells are unable to warm his own hut until his pet toad, Jeremy, leads him to a tiny dragon.
Illus. by Trina Schart Hyman, Macmillan, 1975, 32 pp., o.p.
(BL 71:867; CCBB 29:28; HB 51:139; Kirkus 43:119; SLJ Apr 1975 p. 46)

12-136 KINDL, Patrice. *Owl in Love.* Gr. 5–10.
☆☆ Owl, a shape-shifting 14-year-old, tries to understand the connection between the science teacher she has a crush on, the starving boy she finds camping in the woods, and the inexperienced young owl she has befriended. Golden Kite Award Fiction Honor Book, 1993; Mythopoeic Fantasy Award for Children's Literature, 1995.
Houghton, 1993, 208 pp. (0-395-66162-5); Graphia/Houghton, 2004, pap., 224 pp. (0-618-43910-2)
(BL 90:51, 94:475; CCBB 47:35, 49; HBG 5:88; Kirkus 61:1276; SLJ Aug 1993 p. 186, Apr 2004 p. 137; VOYA 16:310)

KING, Gabriel. *The Wild Road.*
See Chapter 2, Animal Fantasy.

KING-SMITH, Dick. *The Nine Lives of Aristotle.*
See Chapter 2, Animal Fantasy.

KING, Stephen. *The Gunslinger.*
See Chapter 5, High Fantasy: Alternate Worlds or Histories.

KIRWAN-VOGEL, Anna. *The Jewel of Life.*
See Chapter 5, High Fantasy: Alternate Worlds or Histories.

KLASKY, Mindy L. *Season of Sacrifice.*
See Chapter 5, High Fantasy: Alternate Worlds or Histories.

KOLLER, Jackie French. *A Wizard Named Nell.*
See Chapter 5, High Fantasy: Alternate Worlds or Histories.

12-137 KOOIKER, Leonie (pseud. of Johanna Maria Kooyker-Romijn). *The*
★   *Magic Stone.* Gr. 4–6. (Orig. Dutch pub. 1974.)
Frank's grandmother's magic stone enables his friend Chris to control others'
behavior, but when the witches' association wants the stone back, his grandmother is determined that he keep it. In *Legacy of Magic* (orig. Dutch pub.
1979; U.S. 1981), Chris, now a witch's apprentice, thinks that his friend Alec's
book of magic may help them find buried treasure.
Trans. by Richard Winston and Clara Winston, illus. by Carl Hollander, Morrow, 1978, 224 pp., o.p.
(BL 74:1494; CCBB 32:65; HB 54:396; Kirkus 46:595; SLJ May 1978 p. 68; Suth 2:263)

12-138 KORTUM, Jeanie. *Ghost Vision.* Gr. 5–8.
The visions of a young Greenland Eskimo named Panipaq teach him that he is
becoming an *angakok*, or wise one, with special powers allowing him to see
into other worlds.
Illus. by Dugald Stermer, Sierra Club, 1983, 144 pp., o.p.
(BL 80:814; CCBB 37:110; SLJ Jan 1984 p. 78)

12-139 KRAAN, Hanna. *Tales of the Wicked Witch.* **(Wicked Witch series, bk. 1).**
Gr. 2–5. (Orig. Dutch pub, 1990.)
Fourteen stories about a hare, an owl, a blackbird, and a hedgehog's difficulties
with a neighboring witch, who can't resist trying magic spells on the forest ani-
mals. The sequels are *The Wicked Witch Is At It Again* (1997) and *Flowers for
the Wicked Witch* (1998).
Illus. by Annemarie van Haeringen, Front Street, 1995, 108 pp., o.p.
(BL 92:834; HBG 7:294; Kirkus 63:1772; SLJ Jan 1996 p. 88)

KRENSKY, Stephen (Alan). *A Big Day for Scepters.*
See Chapter 1, Allegorical Fantasy and Literary Fairy Tales.

KRENSKY, Stephen (Alan). *The Dragon Circle.*
See Chapter 9, Magic Adventure Fantasy.

KRENSKY, Stephen (Alan). *The Perils of Putney.*
See Chapter 1, Allegorical Fantasy and Literary Fairy Tales.

KRENSKY, Stephen (Alan). *The Witching Hour.*
See discussion of *The Dragon Circle* in Chapter 9, Magic Adventure Fantasy.

12-140 KURTZ, Katherine (Irene), and HARRIS, Deborah Turner. *The Adept.*
(The Adept series, bk. 1). Gr. 10 up.
Evil magic has been revived in Scotland, causing Sir Adam Sinclair, psychia-
trist and police assistant, to assume his true identity of Adept, a magician
guarding the Light from the forces of Darkness. In the sequel, *The Lodge of the
Lynx* (1992), Sir Adam and his apprentice, Peregrine Lovat, hunt down a broth-
erhood of sorcerers using Hitler's book of black spells. The sequels are *The
Templar Treasure* (1993), *Dagger Magic* (1995; pap. 1996), and *Death of an
Adept* (1996, 1997).
Ace, 1991, pap., 336 pp., o.p.; Severn, 1992 (0-7278-4378-8)
(BL 87:1322, 1374, 88:1670; LJ Mar 15, 1991 p. 119; SLJ Sep 1991 p. 298; VOYA 14:110)

LACKEY, Mercedes. *By the Sword.*
See Chapter 5, High Fantasy: Alternate Worlds or Histories.

LACKEY, Mercedes. *Magic's Pawn.*
See Chapter 5, High Fantasy: Alternate Worlds or Histories.

12-141 LACKEY, Mercedes. *Oathblood.* **(Vows and Honor series, bk. 3).** Gr. 10 up.
A novella and ten short stories featuring White Winds sorceress Kethy and her sword-sister, oath-bound Shin'ain warrior Tarma, who run the schools in Haven. This story is preceded by *The Oathbound* (1988) and *Oathbreakers* (1989), and is set in the same world of Valdemar as many of Lackey's books (see Chapter 5, High Fantasy: Alternate Worlds or Histories: The Heralds of Valdemar trilogy, The Last Herald Mage trilogy; and The Mage Winds trilogy).
DAW, 1998, 394 pp. (0-88677-773-9)
(LJ Apr 15, 1998 p. 119; VOYA 21:368)

12-142 LACKEY, Mercedes. *Sacred Ground.* Gr. 10 up.
✫ Oklahoma Osage shaman and private investigator Jennifer Talldeer's latest case involves an insurance scam and the escape of malevolent ancient magical powers.
Tor, 1994, 384 pp., o.p., 1999, pap., 384 pp. (0-8125-1965-5)
(BL 90:1063, 1068; Kirkus 62:103; Kliatt Sep 1995 p. 23; LJ Feb 15, 1994 p. 188; SLJ Oct 1994 p. 158; VOYA 17:157)

12-143 LACKEY, Mercedes, and DIXON, Larry. *Born to Run.* **(The SERRAted Edge series, bk. 1).** Gr. 10 up.
Tania, a teenage runaway, meets a young mage named Tannim, and both become involved in a battle between good and evil elves. Related books in the series are *Wheels of Fire* (1992), *When the Bough Breaks* (1993; see Chapter 5, High Fantasy: Alternate Worlds or Histories), and *Chrome Circle* (1994). *The Chrome Borne* (1999) contains *Born to Run* and *Chrome Circle. The Otherworld* (2000) contains *Wheels of Fire* and *When the Bough Breaks.*
Baen, 1992, pap., 319 pp., o.p.
(BL 88:1344, 1348; VOYA 15:176)

12-144 LACKEY, Mercedes, and EDGHILL, Rosemary. *Beyond World's End.* **(Knight of Ghosts and Shadows series, bk. 4).** Gr. 10 up.
Juilliard student and elven bard Eric Banyon, on his own in New York City except for a friendly gargoyle named Greystone, is threatened by the lord of the dark elves, who needs a live Bard to help create a gateway for the Wild Hunt. This book is preceded by *Bedlam's Bard* (1998, by Lackey and Ellen Guon; orig. pub. as two novels: *Knight of Ghosts* and *Shadows: An Urban Fantasy*, 1990, 1992, by Lackey, Guon, and Larry Dixon; and *Summoned to Tourney: An Urban Fantasy*, 1992, by Lackey and Guon). *The Chrome Borne* (1999, by Lackey and Larry Dixon) also precedes this story; as does *The Otherworld* (2000, by Lackey and Holly Lisle; containing *Wheels of Fire*, 1992, by Lackey and Mark Shepherd; and *When the Bough Breaks*, 1993, by Lackey and Lisle). The sequels are *Spirits White as Lightning* (2001, by Lackey and Edghill), *Mad*

Maudlin (2003; by Lackey and Edghill), and *Music to My Sorrow* (2004; by Lackey and Edghill).
Baen, 2001, 352 pp. (0-671-31855-1)
(BL 97:928; Kirkus 68:1652; LJ Jan 2001 p. 163; VOYA 24:214)

12-145 LACKEY, Mercedes, and EMERSON, Ru. *Fortress of Frost and Fire.*
(The Bard's Tale series, bk. 2). Gr. 7–12.
Having forsworn the use of dark sorcery, former necromancer Naitachel, his apprentice bard Gawaine, and their traveling companions search for an enchanted valley guarded by an invincible Snow Dragon. This is the sequel to *Castle of Deception* (1992, written by Lackey and Josepha Sherman), and is followed by *Prison of Souls* (1993, written by Lackey and Mark Shepherd), *The Chaos Gate* (1994, written by Sherman), *Thunder of the Captains* (1996, by Holly Lisle and Aaron Allston), *Wrath of the Princes* (1997, by Holly Lisle and Aaron Allston), *Escape from Roksamur* (1997, by Mark Shepherd), and *Curse of the Black Heron* (1998, by Holly Lisle).
Baen, 1993, pap., 297 pp., o.p.
(Kliatt Sep 1993 p. 18; VOYA 16:166, 230)

12-146 LACKEY, Mercedes, and MALLORY, James. *The Outstretched Shadow.*
(The Obsidian trilogy, bk. 1). Gr. 7 up.
Banished by his father, the Arch-Mage of Armethaleih, Kellen Tavadon, 17, seeks to become a Wildmage, and is taken in by an older sister he'd never known.
Tor, 2003, 608 pp. (0-765-30219-5)
(BL 100:218; LJ Aug 2003 p. 140; VOYA 26:414, 27:13)

LARSON, Jean (Russell). *The Silkspinners.*
See Chapter 1, Allegorical Fantasy and Literary Fairy Tales.

12-147 LAUGHLIN, Florence (Young). *The Little Leftover Witch.* Gr. 2–4.
When Felina's broomstick breaks in midair, she falls out of the sky and is stranded on Earth for an entire year.
Illus. by Sheila Greenwald, Macmillan, 1960, 1971, 107 pp., o.p., pap., 1973, 1988, 96 pp. (0-689-71273-1)
(BL 57:362; CCBB 14:82; HB 36:396; Kirkus 28:496; LJ 85:4226; TLS 1967 p. 1153)

LAWHEAD, Stephen R. *In the Hall of the Dragon King.*
See Chapter 5, High Fantasy: Alternate Worlds or Histories.

LAWRENCE, Louise (pseud. of Elizabeth Rhoda Holden). *The Earth Witch.*
See Chapter 6, High Fantasy: Myth or Legend Fantasy.

LEACH, Maria. *The Thing at the Foot of the Bed and Other Scary Tales.*
See Chapter 4, Ghost Fantasy.

12-148 LEE, Josephine. *Joy Is Not Herself.* Gr. 5–7. (Orig. British pub. 1962.)
Melisanda Montgomery discovers that she is part witch.
Illus. by Pat Marriott, Harcourt, 1963, 154 pp., o.p.
(HB 39:174; LJ 88:1768; TLS 1962 p. 393)

LEE, Tanith. *Black Unicorn.*
See Chapter 5, High Fantasy: Alternate Worlds or Histories.

LEE, Tanith. *Cyrion.*
See Chapter 5, High Fantasy: Alternate Worlds or Histories.

LEE, Tanith. *The Dragon Hoard.*
See Chapter 1, Allegorical Fantasy and Literary Fairy Tales.

LEE, Tanith. *Princess Hynchatti and Some Other Surprises.*
See Chapter 1, Allegorical Fantasy and Literary Fairy Tales.

LE GUIN, Ursula K(roeber). *A Wizard of Earthsea.*
See Chapter 5, High Fantasy: Alternate Worlds or Histories.

12-149 LEVINSON, Marilyn. *Rufus and Magic Run Amok.* Gr. 3–5.
Rufus wants to be a normal kid, instead of a wizard from a family of "empowered ones," until he discovers that he can use his magic to help his friends.
Cavendish, 2001, 96 pp. (0-7614-5102-1)
(CCBB 55:177; HBG 13:88; Kirkus 69:1427; SLJ Oct 2001 p. 124)

12-150 LEVOY, Myron. *The Magic Hat of Mortimer Wintergreen.* Gr. 4–7.
Orphaned Joshua and Amy Bains are rescued from the clutches of evil Aunt Vootch by Wizard Mortimer Q. Wintergreen's magic hat.
Illus. by Andrew Glass, Harper, 1988, 211 pp., o.p.
(BL 84:1001; CCBB 41:121; Kirkus 55:1734; SLJ Mar 1988 p. 197)

LEWIS, C(live) S(taples). *The Lion, the Witch, and the Wardrobe.*
See Chapter 7, High Fantasy: Travel to Other Worlds.

12-151 LIFTON, Betty Jean (Kirschner). *Jaguar, My Twin.* Gr. 4–6.
Two shamans battle for the soul of young Shun and his twin animal spirit, a jaguar, in this Zinacantec Indian tale set in Mexico.
Illus. by Ann Legett, Macmillan, 1976, 114 pp., o.p.
(CCBB 30:44; HB 52:625; Kirkus 44:732; SLJ Oct 1976 p. 108)

12-152 LILLINGTON, Kenneth (James). *An Ash-Blond Witch.* Gr. 7 up. (Orig. British pub. 1987.)
A young woman from the 22nd century "beyond the mountains" arrives in the old-fashioned village of Urstwhile and becomes the rival of the local witch.
Faber, 1987, 138 pp., o.p.
(BL 83:776, 1274, 1592; Kirkus 55:60)

LITTLE, Jane. *The Philosopher's Stone.*
See Chapter 10, Time Travel Fantasy.

12-153 LITTLE, Jane. *Sneaker Hill.* Gr. 3 5.
When Matthew's mother, a witch-in-training, forgets to take her owl with her, Matthew and Susan follow her into a magic land.
Illus. by Nancy Grossman, Atheneum, 1967, 176 pp., o.p.
(CCBB 21:29; LJ 92:1738)

12-154 LITTLE, Jane. *Spook.* Gr. 3–5.
Because Grimalda the witch is allergic to cats, she tries to make do with a small dog named Spook, but a boy named Jamie wants Spook too.
Illus. by Suzanne Larsen, Atheneum, 1965, 110 pp., o.p.
(CCBB 19:35; HB 41:492; LJ 90:3812)

LIVELY, Penelope (Margaret Low). *The Ghost of Thomas Kempe.*
See Chapter 4, Ghost Fantasy.

LIVELY, Penelope (Margaret Low). *The Whispering Knights.*
See Chapter 6, High Fantasy: Myth or Legend Fantasy.

12-155 LLYWELYN, Morgan. *The Horse Goddess.* Gr. 10 up. (Orig. pub. in Eng-
✭   land.)
Destined from birth to become the Shaman of her father's Celtic tribe, Epona runs away with Kazhak, leader of a nomadic band of horsemen from Asia Minor.
Houghton, 1982, 417 pp., o.p.; Tor, 1998, pap., 480 pp. (0-8125-5503-1)
(BL 78:1483, 1485, 86:907; Kirkus 50:818; LJ 107:1170; SLJ Dec 1982 p. 87)

LOFTING, Hugh. *The Twilight of Magic.*
See Chapter 9, Magic Adventure Fantasy.

12-156 LOVEJOY, Jack. *The Rebel Witch.* Gr. 4–6.
A magic wand enables Suzie, an apprentice witch, to enter the witch world of Veneficon to search for her teacher, Madame Mengo.
Illus. by Judith Gwyn Brown, Morrow, 1978, 201 pp., o.p.
(BL 75:50; Kirkus 46:1248; SLJ Dec 1978 p. 54)

LUCAS, George, and CLAREMONT, Chris. *Shadow Moon.*
See Chapter 5, High Fantasy: Alternate Worlds or Histories.

12-157 LUENN, Nancy. *Arctic Unicorn.* Gr. 6–10.
Kala, a 13-year-old Eskimo girl, is torn between her attraction to a young hunter who could become her husband, and her visions of arctic unicorns that beckon her to accept her magical powers and become an *angakok*, or shaman.
Atheneum, 1986, 168 pp., o.p.
(CCBB 39:188; Kirkus 54:869; SLJ Oct 1986 p. 179; VOYA 10:38)

LYNN, Elizabeth A. *Dragon's Winter.*
See Chapter 5, High Fantasy: Alternate Worlds or Histories.

12-158 MacAVOY, R(oberta) A(nn). *Damiano.* **(Damiano trilogy, bk. 1).** Gr. 10
✭   up. (Orig. pub. in England.)
Damiano, a 14th-century Italian wizard, is forced by marauders to flee with his wise dog, Macchiata, and his determination for vengeance leads him on an adventurous quest. The sequels are *Damiano's Lute* (1984) and *Raphael* (1984). All three books were collected in *A Trio for Lute* (Science Fiction Book Club, 1985; Bantam, 1988).
Bantam, 1983, pap., 243 pp., o.p.
(BL 80:1099, 1110, 86:905; SLJ Nov 1984 p. 146; VOYA 7:101)

12-159 MacAVOY, R(oberta) A(nn). *The Grey Horse.* Gr. 10 up. (Orig. pub. in
✫   England.)
The Irish village of Carraroe is thrown into turmoil upon the arrival of Ruairi
MacEibhir, a faerie in search of the woman he loves.
Bantam, 1987, pap., 247 pp., o.p.
(BL 83:1655, 1672; LJ Apr 15, 1987 p. 103; VOYA 10:179)

MacDONALD, Greville. *Billy Barnicoat: A Fairy Romance for Young and
Old.*
See Chapter 9, Magic Adventure Fantasy.

12-160 McGARRY, Terry. *Illumination.* **(Illumination trilogy, bk. 1).** Gr. 10 up.
Having passed the mage examination after years of study, Liath is shattered
when she is unable to heal the knife wounds of her first case, but the ruling
mages promise to help her if she will find the Dark mage who threatens to
destroy their world. The sequels are *The Binder's Road* (2003) and *Triad*
(2005).
Tor, 2001, 480 pp. (0-312-87389-1)
(BL 97:2101; Kirkus 69:905; LJ Aug 2001 p. 170)

12-161 McGOWEN, Tom (Thomas E.). *The Magical Fellowship.* **(The Age of
✫   Magic trilogy, bk. 1).** Gr. 5–9.
A troll, a human, and two wizards try to convince the warring races of trolls,
dragons, elves, and humans to join forces to fend off an impending attack on
Earth by forces from another world. In the sequel, *A Trial of Magic* (1992), a
powerful mage uses black magic to disrupt the other mages' unity plan so that
his race will inherit the Earth after the Earthdoom. The final book in the trilogy
is *A Question of Magic* (1993).
Dutton, 1991, 133 pp. (0-525-67339-3)
(BL 87:1377; HBG 2:266; Kirkus 59:396; SLJ Apr 1991 p. 120; VOYA 14:46)

12-162 McGOWEN, Tom (Thomas E.). *The Magician's Apprentice.* **(The Magi-
✫   cian trilogy, bk. 1).** Gr. 5–7.
A wily street urchin named Tigg is befriended by the magician Armindor, who
takes him to the Wild Lands in search of magical artifacts from an earlier civilization. In *The Magician's Company* (1988), Tigg, Armindor, and a girl
named Jilla bring two treasures from the Wild Lands to the counsel of sages
and warn the counsel about a threat to world security. In *The Magician's Challenge* (1989), Tigg and Jilla are captured by the ratlike Reen, who want to
destroy human kind.
Dutton, 1987, 119 pp., o.p.
(BL 83:580, 84:873; CCBB 40:113; Kirkus 54:1649; SLJ Jan 1987 p. 76)

12-163 McGOWEN, Tom (Thomas E.). *Sir Machinery.* Gr. 3–6.
✫   Merlin the wizard joins forces with a physicist to battle an ancient race of
demons bent on taking over the world.
Illus. by Trina Schart Hyman, Follett, 1971, 155 pp., o.p.
(BL 68:367; HB 48:49; Kirkus 39:1071; LJ 96:4191)

12-164 MacKELLAR, William. *The Witch of Glen Gowrie.* Gr. 5–7.
Old Meg's ghost prevents everyone but young Gavin Fraser from finding her treasure.
Illus. by Ted Lewin, Dodd, 1978, 134 pp., o.p.
(BL 74:1109; CCBB 32:34; SLJ May 1978 p. 85)

McKENZIE, Ellen Kindt. *The Golden Band of Eddris.*
See Chapter 5, High Fantasy: Alternate Worlds or Histories.

McKENZIE, Ellen Kindt. *Taash and the Jesters.*
See Chapter 5, High Fantasy: Alternate Worlds or Histories.

McKILLIP, Patricia A(nne). *The Book of Atrix Wolfe.*
See Chapter 5, High Fantasy: Alternate Worlds or Histories.

McKILLIP, Patricia A(nne). *The Changeling Sea.*
See Chapter 5, High Fantasy: Alternate Worlds or Histories.

McKILLIP, Patricia A(nne). *The Cygnet and the Firebird.*
See Chapter 5, High Fantasy: Alternate Worlds or Histories.

McKILLIP, Patricia A(nne). *The Forgotten Beasts of Eld.*
See Chapter 5, High Fantasy: Alternate Worlds or Histories.

McKILLIP, Patricia A(nne). *The Riddle-Master of Hed.*
See Chapter 5, High Fantasy: Alternate Worlds or Histories.

McKILLIP, Patricia A(nne). *The Sorceress and the Cygnet.*
See Chapter 5, High Fantasy: Alternate Worlds or Histories.

12-165 McKINNEY, Meagan. *The Ground She Walks Upon.* Gr. 10 up.
An ancient Irish curse intertwines the lives of Nial Trevallyn, lord of the manor, and Ravenna, granddaughter of the local witch.
Delacorte, 1994, 416 pp., o.p.
(BL 90:1515, 1523; LJ Apr 1, 1994 p. 132)

12-166 MacLACHLAN, Patricia. *Tomorrow's Wizard.* Gr. 3–5.
Tomorrow's Wizard and his apprentice, Murdoch, travel through the kingdom solving problems and fulfilling the wishes of its inhabitants.
Illus. by Kathy Jacobi, Harper, 1982, 80 pp., o.p.; Harcourt, 1996, pap., 66 pp. (0-15-201276-1)
(HB 58:290; SLJ Apr 1982 p. 72)

12-167 McLEOD, Emilie Warren. *Clancy's Witch.* Gr. 2–4.
★   Clancy's next-door neighbor is a witch.
Illus. by Lisl Weil, Little, Brown, 1959, 38 pp., o.p.; Little, Brown, 2000 (0-3165-6201-7)
(BL 55:543; Eakin:224; HB 35:131; Kirkus 26:905; LJ 84:1686)

McMULLAN, Kate. *Under the Mummy's Spell.*
See Chapter 4, Ghost Fantasy.

McNEILL, Janet. *Tom's Tower.*
See Chapter 7, High Fantasy: Travel to Other Worlds.

12-168 MAGUIRE, Gregory. *The Dream Stealer.* Gr. 3–5.
Pasha and Lisette set out to consult the fearsome hag Baba Yaga about their encounter with a Firebird, and about rumors of a marauding demon wolf called the Blood Prince, in this tale involving characters from Russian folklore.
Harper, 1983, 118 pp., o.p.; Clarion, 2002, 133 pp. (0-618-18188-1)
(BL 80:299; HB 59:576; HBG 14:85; Kirkus 51:164; SLJ Feb 1984 p. 75)

12-169 MAGUIRE, Gregory. *Wicked: The Life and Times of the Wicked Witch of the West.* Gr. 10 up.
In this prequel to L. Frank Baum's *The Wonderful Wizard of Oz* (1900; see Chapter 7, High Fantasy: Travel to Other Worlds), three girls named Elphie, Nessie, and Glinda grow up in the land of Oz, where a magic spell assigns each of them a quadrant of their land to rule, and green-skinned Elphaba becomes the wicked witch of the West.
Regan/HarperCollins, 1995, 406 pp., o.p., 2000, pap., 406 pp. (0-06-098710-3), 2004, pap., 448 pp. (0-06-074590-8)
(Kirkus 63:1135; SLJ May 1996 p. 148; VOYA 19:40)

12-170 MAHY, Margaret (May). *Alchemy.* Gr. 7–12. (Orig. New Zealand pub.
✶ 2002.)
Something about a girl named Jess, a nobody in the senior class, awakens popular Roland's childhood memories of a wizard, and his own supernatural powers.
McElderry, 2003, 224 pp. (0-689-85053-0); Simon Pulse, 2004, pap. (0-689-85054-9)
(BL 99:1317; CCBB 56:321; HB 79:352; HBG 14:386; Kirkus 71:391; Kliatt Mar 2003 p. 14; SLJ May 2003 p. 157; VOYA 26:150)

12-171 MAHY, Margaret (May). *The Changeover: A Supernatural Romance.* Gr.
✶✶ 6–10. (Orig. pub. in New Zealand, 1984.)
Laura Chant undergoes a "changeover," a transformation into a witch, to save the life of her brother Jacko, bewitched by a demon. Carnegie Medal, 1984. New Zealand Library Association Esther Glen Award, 1985; Boston Globe Horn Book Award Honor Book in Fiction, 1985.
Macmillan, 1984, 224 pp., o.p.; Penguin, pap., 1994, 224 pp. (0-14-036599-0)
(BL 81:122, 132, 86:790, 91:415; CCBB 38:11; HB 60:764; Kirkus 52:81; SLJ Sep 1984 p. 132; Suth 3:292; TLS 1984 p. 794; VOYA 8:50, 364)

12-172 MAHY, Margaret (May). *The Haunting.* Gr. 5–8. (Orig. pub. in New
✶✶ Zealand, 1982.)
Eight-year-old Barney's frightening messages from a long-lost uncle bring to light a secret family curse. Carnegie Medal, 1982; New Zealand Library Association Esther Glen Award, 1983.
Macmillan, 1982, 144 pp., o.p.
(BL 79:117; CCBB 36:31; HB 59:46; Kirkus 50:1155; SLJ Aug 1982 p. 119; Suth 3:293; TLS 1982 p. 1001)

MAHY, Margaret (May). *A Tall Story and Other Tales.*
See Chapter 9, Magic Adventure Fantasy.

12-173 MARCELLAS, Diana. *Mother Ocean, Daughter Sea.* Gr. 10 up.
Brierley, a Shari'a witch and healer, leaves the safety of her hidden cave to treat the dying wife of Allemani nobleman Melfallen, takes in an orphaned 5-year-old witch, and ultimately falls in love. The sequel is *The Sea Lark's Song* (2002).
Tor, 2001, 416 pp. (0-312-87484-7)
(BL 98:58; LJ Sep 15, 2001 p. 116)

12-174 MARICONDA, Barbara. *Witch Way to the Beach.* Gr. 1–3.
Constance and Drusilla, two witches, spend the day at the beach, where the lifeguard is continually trying to rescue them.
Illus. by Jon McIntosh, Delacorte, 1997, 48 pp. (0-385-32265-8)
(HBG 8:292; SLJ Nov 1997 p.93)

MARTIN, Graham Dunstan. *Giftwish.*
See Chapter 5, High Fantasy: Alternate Worlds or Histories.

MASEFIELD, John (Edward). *The Midnight Folk: A Novel.*
See Chapter 9, Magic Adventure Fantasy.

MAYER, Marianna. *The Sorcerer's Apprentice; A Greek Fable.*
See Chapter 6, High Fantasy: Myth or Legend Fantasy.

MAYNE, William (James Carter). *The Hill Road.*
See Chapter 10, Time Travel Fantasy.

12-175 MAZER, Anne. *The Accidental Witch.* Gr. 3–5.
The experienced witches are too busy to teach Phoebe how to use her accidentally acquired powers, so Bee attempts to test her new talents on her own.
Hyperion, 1995, 123 pp. (0-7868-0088-7)
(BL 92:473; HBG 7:65; SLJ Jan 1996 p. 110)

Merlin. **Ed. by Martin H. Greenberg.**
See Chapter 6, High Fantasy: Myth or Legend Fantasy.

The Merlin Chronicles. **Ed. by Mike Ashley.**
See Chapter 6, High Fantasy: Myth or Legend Fantasy.

12-176 MIAN, Mary (Lawrence Shipman). *Take Three Witches.* Gr. 6–8.
Three sixth-graders, three witches, and a ghost join forces to prevent the town from spraying bird-killing insecticide. The sequel is *The Net to Catch War* (1975).
Illus. by Eric Von Schmidt, Houghton, 1971, 279 pp., o.p.
(HB 47:485; LJ 96:2133)

MIESEL, Sandra. *Shaman.*
See Chapter 7, High Fantasy: Travel to Other Worlds.

MODESITT, L(eland) E(xton), Jr. *Magi'i of Cyador.*
See Chapter 5, High Fantasy: Alternate Worlds or Histories.

MODESITT, L(eland) E(xton), Jr. *The Soprano Sorceress.*
See Chapter 7, High Fantasy: Travel to Other Worlds.

12-177 MOLLOY, Michael. *The Time Witches.* Gr. 5–8.
Witch-in-training Abby chases the evil Night Witch Wolfbane through time to prevent the murder of her ancestor and to rescue Sir Chadwick Street's fiancée, Hilda. This is the sequel to *The Witch Trade* (2001), and is followed by *Wild West Witches* (2003).
Illus. by David Wyatt, Scholastic, 2002, pap., 272 pp. (0-439-42090-3)
(BL 99:892; SLJ Aug 2003 p. 164)

MONTROSE, Anne. *The Winter Flower, and Other Fairy Stories.*
See Chapter 3, Fantasy Collections.

12-178 MORRESSY, John. *A Voice for Princess.* **(Kedrigern Chronicles, bk. 1).** Gr. 10 up.
Disgruntled because the wizards' guild has decided to admit alchemists, Kedrigern quits, sets out to see the world, and meets a mute princess under an enchantment. The sequels are *The Questing of Kedrigern* (1987), *Kedrigern in Wanderland* (1988), *A Remembrance for Kedrigern* (1990), and *Kedrigern and the Charming Couple* (1990). *The Kedrigern Chronicles: The Domesticated Wizard* (Meisha Merlin, 2002), and *The Kedrigern Chronicles: Dudgeon and Dragons* (Meisha Merlin, 2003) contain the author's novels and short stories about Kedrigern.
Ace, 1987, pap., 213 pp., o.p.
(BL 83:1181, 1199, 1592)

MOZART, Wolfgang Amadeus. *The Magic Flute.*
See Chapter 1, Allegorical Fantasy and Literary Fairy Tales.

12-179 MULLARKEY, Lisa Geurdes. *The Witch's Portraits.* Gr. 4–7.
Laura, 12, has trouble believing her best friend Cara's theory that their odd neighbor, Mrs. Blackert, is a witch who holds people hostage inside the portraits she paints.
Dial, 1998, 183 pp. (0-8037-2337-7)
(BL 95:231; Kirkus 66:1289; SLJ Oct 1998 p. 142)

12-180 MURPHY, Jill. *The Worst Witch.* **(The Worst Witch series, bk. 1).** Gr. 2–5. (Orig. British pub. 1974.)
Mildred is the worst student at Miss Cackle's Academy for witches, but she runs away and becomes a heroine when she turns a coven of evil witches into snails. The sequels are *The Worst Witch Strikes Again* (1981, 1989), *A Bad Spell for the Worst Witch* (1982, 1989), and *The Worst Witch at Sea* (1995).
Illus. by the author, Allison, 1980, 1987, 71 pp., o.p.; Viking, 1988, 106 pp., o.p.; Puffin, 1991, pap. (0-14-031108-4)
(CCBB 34:38; HBG 1:85; Kirkus 57:1163; SLJ Sep 1980 p. 62)

MURPHY, Pat. *Points of Departure.*
See Chapter 3, Fantasy Collections.

MURPHY, Shirley Rousseau. *The Catswold Portal.*
See Chapter 7, High Fantasy: Travel to Other Worlds.

12-181 MURPHY, Shirley Rousseau. *The Pig Who Could Conjure the Wind.* Gr. 2–4.

Miss Folly, a flying witch pig, rescues the wind demon's victims.
Illus. by Mark Lefkowitz, Atheneum, 1978, 58 pp., o.p.
(BL 74:1436; HB 54:278; Kirkus 46:239; SLJ Apr 1978 p. 73)

12-182 NAPOLI, Donna Jo. *The Magic Circle.* Gr. 7–12.
☆ A midwife/sorceress called Ugly One, haunted by demons she summoned to aid her in healing, hides away in the forest cottage she decorated with candies in memory of her beloved daughter, in this reworking of the German folktale "Hansel and Gretel," told from the point of view of the witch.
Dutton, 1993, 118 pp. (0-525-45127-7); Penguin, 1995, pap. (0-14-037439-6)
(BL 89:1957, 90:868; CCBB 46:260; HBG 4[Fall 1993]:311; Kirkus 61:789; SLJ Aug 1993 p. 186; VOYA 16:169)

NAPOLI, Donna Jo. *Zel.*
See Chapter 6, High Fantasy: Myth or Legend Fantasy.

12-183 NATHAN, Robert (Gruntal). *The Snowflake and the Starfish.* Gr. 3–4.
A lonely sea-witch takes Vicky and Thomas under the sea with her.
Illus. by Leonard Weisgard, Knopf, 1959, 68 pp., o.p.
(HB 35:478; LJ 84:3930)

NESS, Evaline. *The Girl and the Goatherd, or This and That and Thus and So.*
See Chapter 1, Allegorical Fantasy and Literary Fairy Tales.

NEWMAN, Robert (Howard). *Merlin's Mistake.*
See Chapter 6, High Fantasy: Myth or Legend Fantasy.

NEWMAN, Robert (Howard). *The Shattered Stone.*
See Chapter 5, High Fantasy: Alternate Worlds or Histories.

12-184 NICHOLS, (Joanna) Ruth. *The Left-Handed Spirit.* Gr. 8–10.
Kidnapped by the Chinese ambassador to the Roman Empire, Mariana is expected to use her healing powers to save the life of the ambassador's twin brother.
Atheneum, 1978, 260 pp., o.p.
(BL 75:469; CCBB 32:85; Kirkus 46:1254; SLJ Oct 1978 p. 158; VOYA 1[Dec 1978]:43)

NICHOLS, (Joanna) Ruth. *The Marrow of the World.*
See Chapter 7, High Fantasy: Travel to Other Worlds.

12-185 NIMMO, Jenny. *Midnight for Charlie Bone.* **(Children of the Red King**
☆ **quintet, bk. 1).** Gr. 4–7. (Orig. British pub. 2002.)
Ten-year-old Charlie Bone unexpectedly finds himself enrolled in Bloor's Academy wizardry school, where the magical gifts he inherited from his missing father draw the interest of his evil relatives. In *Charlie Bone and the Time Twister* (2003), Charlie's ancestor, 11-year-old Henry Yewbeam, arrives in the present from 1916 only to be captured by the wicked Ezekiel Bloor, and Charlie must try to rescue him. The third book is *Charlie Bone and the Invisible Boy* (2004; British title: *Charlie Bone and the Blue Boa*).
Orchard, 2003, 416 pp. (0-439-47429-9); Scholastic, 2003, pap. (0-439-54302-9)
(BL 99:892; CCBB 56:373; HBG 14:373; Kirkus 70:1854; SLJ Feb 2003 p. 146; VOYA 26:239)

NIVEN, Larry. *The Magic Goes Away.*
See Chapter 5, High Fantasy: Alternate Worlds or Histories.

12-186 NIX, Garth. *Sabriel.* **(Abhorsen trilogy, bk. 1).** Gr. 7–12. (Orig. Australian
★★ pub. 1995.)
Sabriel, daughter of the mage Abhorsen, enters the Old Kingdom, desperate to
find her father's body and bring his spirit back from Death. In *Lirael: Daughter
of the Clayr* (2001, 2002), Lirael, Second Assistant Librarian to the Clayr, and
Prince Sameth, son of the Abhorsen Sabriel, join forces with the magical Dis-
reputable Dog and an elemental in the body of a cat named Mogget to save the
Old Kingdom. YALSA Top Ten Best Books for Young Adults, 2002. In
Abhorsen (2003, 2004), Lirael, now Abhorsen-in-Waiting, and her nephew
Sameth learn that the evil necromancer Hedge has enslaved Sam's friend Nick,
and is using him and thousands of the newly dead to unearth a powerful Free
Magic being that will destroy all life.
HarperCollins, 1996, 292 pp. (0-06-027322-4); HarperTrophy, 1997, pap., 496
pp. (0-06-447183-7)
(BL 93:350, 1294, 1305, 97:978; CCBB 50:146; HB 73:64; HBG 8:83; SLJ Sep 1996 p. 228;
VOYA 20:12, 44, 84, 86)

NORTON, Andre (pseud. of Alice Mary Norton). *Lavender Green Magic.*
See Chapter 10, Time Travel Fantasy.

NORTON, Andre (pseud. of Alice Mary Norton). *Witch World.*
See Chapter 7, High Fantasy: Travel to Other Worlds.

12-187 NORTON, Andre (pseud. of Alice Mary Norton). *Wizards' Worlds.* Gr. 10
up.
Thirteen of Norton's favorite tales, mostly fantasy, six of which appeared in
Lore of the Witchworld (1980).
Tor, 1989, 288 pp., o.p.
(BL 86:149, 164; Kirkus 57:1437; VOYA 12:373, 13:16)

NORTON, Andre, and EDGHILL, Rosemary. *The Shadow of Albion.*
See Chapter 10, Time Travel Fantasy.

12-188 NORTON, Andre, and LACKEY, Mercedes. *The Elvenbane: An Epic
★ High Fantasy of the Halfblood Chronicles.* **(The Halfblood Chronicles,
bk. 1).** Gr. 10 up.
Half-elven, half-human Shana, raised by dragons, grows up to become the legendary wizard Elvenbane, powerful enough to challenge the tyrannical elves
who rule her world. The sequels are *Elvenblood* (1995, 1996) and *Elvenborn*
(2002, 2003).
Tor, 1991, 384 pp. (0-312-85106-5), 1993, pap. (0-8125-1175-1)
(BL 88:416, 423; Kirkus 59:1123; LJ Oct 15, 1991 p. 127; VOYA 15:45)

NORTON, Andre, and SHWARTZ, Susan. *Imperial Lady: A Fantasy of
Han China.*
See Chapter 6, High Fantasy: Myth or Legend Fantasy.

NORTON, Mary (Pearson). *Bedknob and Broomstick.*
See Chapter 9, Magic Adventure Fantasy.

12-189 OGILVY, Ian. *Measle and the Wrathmonk.* Gr. 4–7. (Orig. British pub. 2004.)

Miniaturized as punishment by his evil guardian, Basil Tramplebone, orphaned Measle Stubbs is imprisoned in the wizard's model railway set, battling hungry creatures while plotting revenge with the other "plastic figures" he meets. The sequel is *Measle and the Dragodon* (2004, 2005).

HarperCollins, 2004, 224 pp. (0-06-058686-9); Oxford University Press, 2004, pap., 206 pp. (0-19-271952-1)

(BL 101:329; CCBB 58:139; Kliatt July 2004 p. 11; SLJ Sep 2004 p. 214;)

O'HANLON, Jacklyn. *The Door.*
See Chapter 7, High Fantasy: Travel to Other Worlds.

12-190 ORR, A. *The World in Amber.* **(World in Amber, bk. 1).** Gr. 10 up.

Court sorcerer Judah Hila transforms Queen Maldive into a palace cat, and transports complacent King Ambrose and his minstrel son, Isme, to magical locations, to improve their ability to rule the land of Phar-Tracil. The sequel is *In the Ice King's Palace* (1986).

Bluejay, 1985, 214 pp., o.p.

(Kirkus 53:679; VOYA 10:105)

O'SHEA, (Catherine) Pat(ricia Shiels). *The Hounds of the Morrigan.*
See Chapter 6, High Fantasy: Myth or Legend Fantasy.

PALMER, David R. *Threshold.*
See Chapter 8, Humorous Fantasy.

PARKER, (James) Edgar (Jr.). *The Enchantress.*
See Chapter 1, Allegorical Fantasy and Literary Fairy Tales.

PARKER, Nancy Winslow. *The Spotted Dog: The Strange Tale of a Witch's Revenge.*
See Chapter 8, Humorous Fantasy.

PAYNE, Joan Balfour (Dicks). *The Piebald Princess.*
See Chapter 2, Animal Fantasy.

PICARD, Barbara Leonie. *The Goldfinch Garden: Seven Tales.*
See Chapter 3, Fantasy Collections.

PICARD, Barbara Leonie. *The Mermaid and the Simpleton.*
See Chapter 3, Fantasy Collections.

PIERCE, Meredith Ann. *The Darkangel.*
See Chapter 5, High Fantasy: Alternate Worlds or Histories.

PIERCE, Meredith Ann. *Treasure at the Heart of the Tanglewood.*
See Chapter 5, High Fantasy: Alternate Worlds or Histories.

PIERCE, Tamora. *Alanna: The First Adventure.*
See Chapter 5, High Fantasy: Alternate Worlds or Histories.

12-191 PIERCE, Tamora. *Magic Steps.* **(The Circle Opens quartet, bk. 1).** Gr.
★ 5–8.

Sandry, 14, interweaves her magic with spells danced by a boy named Pasco to stop the mysterious murders of members of a local merchant family. In *Street Magic* (2001), 14-year-old Briar becomes the reluctant guardian of Evvy, a street urchin in need of protection from a local gang attempting to exploit her stone magic talents. In *Cold Fire* (2002), Daja, visiting a northern empire to study with metal smiths, is dismayed to be assigned as teacher to her host's twin daughters with newly discovered magic powers. In *Shatterglass* (2003), Tris and her glassmaking student mage, Keth, use his magic mixed with lightning to track a killer. This series follows Pierce's Circle of Magic quartet (see *Sandry's Book* below).

Scholastic, 2000, 264 pp. (0-590-39588-2); Point, 2001, pap., 264 pp. (0-590-39605-6)

(BL 96:1236; CCBB 53:253; HB 76:319; HBG 11:310; Kirkus 67:1960; Kliatt Jan 2000 p. 8; SLJ Apr 2000 p. 142; VOYA 23:49)

12-192 PIERCE, Tamora. *Sandry's Book.* **(Circle of Magic quartet, bk. 1).** Gr.
★★ 5–8.

Orphaned lady Sandrilene is one of four misfits rescued from their unhappy lives and brought to Winding Circle Temple to learn the science of magic. In *Tris's Book* (1998), Tris, a weather mage, uses her magic to save the other members of the Winding Circle Temple community from marauding pirates. In *Daja's Book* (1998), Daja accidentally creates a living metal vine while she and her three friends work to eliminate dangerous wildfires threatening the northern communities. In *Briar's Book* (1999), former street urchin Briar and his teacher, Rosethorn, try to find the cause of a virulent plague sweeping through Summersea. This series is followed by a quartet of books called The Circle Opens quartet (see *Magic Steps* above).

Scholastic, 1997, 252 pp. (0-590-55356-9), 1999, pap., 252 pp. (0-590-55408-5)

(BL 94:106, 1618; CCBB 51:97, 292; HBG 9:79; Kirkus 65:1115; SLJ Sep 1997 p. 224; VOYA 20:327, 21:14)

PIERCE, Tamora. *Wild Magic: The Immortals.*
See Chapter 5, High Fantasy: Alternate Worlds or Histories.

12-193 PLACE, Marian T(empleton). *The Resident Witch.* Gr. 3–5.

Living with her aunt while her mother is away, Witcheena is working hard at becoming a Junior Witch when she makes the mistake of befriending some earthlings.

Illus. by Marilyn Miller, Washburn, 1970, 119 pp., o.p.

(CCBB 24:65; Kirkus 38:244; LJ 95:2309)

12-194 PLACE, Marian T(empleton). *The Witch Who Saved Halloween.* Gr. 4–6.

When pollution threatens both witches and humans, Witchard comes up with a plan to save them.

Illus. by Marilyn Miller, Washburn, 1971, 150 pp., o.p.

(BL 75:306; CCBB 25:1281; Kirkus 39:1072; LJ 97:284)

12-195 POOLE, Josephine. *The Visitor: A Story of Suspense.* Gr. 6–9. (Orig. British pub. 1965.)
Mr. Bogle, tutor to 15-year-old Harry, exerts a mysterious power over the villagers of Cormundy, a power connected to the ancient Fury Wood surrounding Harry's house.
Harper, 1972, 148 pp., o.p.
(BL 69:352, 358; Kirkus 40:1153; LJ 97:4087)

POSTMA, Lidia. *The Witch's Garden.*
See Chapter 9, Magic Adventure Fantasy.

12-196 PRANTERA, Amanda. *The Cabalist.* Gr. 10 up. (Orig. British pub. 1985.)
Joseph Kestler, a modern-day Cabalist with a terminal illness, searches for a successor to inherit his magical powers.
Atheneum, 1986, 192 pp., o.p.
(BL 82:1663, 1683; Kirkus 54:966; LJ Aug 1986 p. 172; TLS 1985 p. 1266)

12-197 PREUSSLER, Otfried. *The Little Witch.* Gr. 3–5. (Orig. pub. in Germany.)
Little Witch plots revenge on the older witches who took away her magic broomstick on Walpurgis Night.
Trans. by Anthea Bell, illus. by Winnie Gayler, Abelard-Schuman, 1961, 127 pp., o.p.
(BL 58:450; CCBB 15:84; Kirkus 29:843; LJ 86:4040; TLS May 19, 1961 p. iv)

PREUSSLER, Otfried. *The Robber Hotzenplotz.*
See Chapter 8, Humorous Fantasy.

12-198 PREUSSLER, Otfried. *The Satanic Mill.* Gr. 6–9. (Orig. German pub.
★★ 1971.)
Krabat thinks he has been apprenticed to a miller, but discovers that the mill is actually a school of black magic run by an evil magician.
Trans. by Anthea Bell, Macmillan, 1973, 250 pp., o.p.; Simon Pulse, 1991, pap., 250 pp. (0-02-044775-2)
(BL 69:1073, 70:827, 82:677, 686; CCBB 26:143; HB 49:147; 61:84, 63:492; Kirkus 41:61, 1351; LJ 98:1398, 1655; Suth 2:369; TLS 1972 p. 1489)

12-199 PRICE, Susan. *Ghost Dance: The Czar's Black Angel.* **(Ghost trilogy, bk. 3).** Gr. 6–10. (Orig. British pub. 1994.)
Shape-changing apprentice shaman Shingebiss travels into the ghost world of the dead in order to defeat the evil Czar who calls her his "Black Angel." This book is related to Price's *The Ghost Drum* (1987; see below) and *Ghost Song* (1992; see below).
Farrar, 1994, 217 pp. (0-374-32537-5)
(BL 91:590; HBG 6:313; SLJ Dec 1994 p. 130)

12-200 PRICE, Susan. *The Ghost Drum: A Cat's Tale.* Gr. 5–9. (Orig. British pub.
★ 1987.)
A cat tells the story of the friendship between Chingis, a shaman who lives in a house on chicken legs, and Safa, the Czar's son, who has been imprisoned in a windowless room since birth. Carnegie Medal, 1987. The companion volumes are *Ghost Song* (1992; see below), and *Ghost Dance: The Czar's Black Angel* (1994; see above).

Farrar, 1987, 167 pp., o.p.

(BL 84:152; CCBB 41:36; Kirkus 55:929; SLJ Sep 1987 p. 182, Dec 1987 p. 38; TLS 1987 p. 248; VOYA 10:245)

12-201 PRICE, Susan. *Ghost Song.* Gr. 6–12. (Orig. British pub. 1992.)

✶ The fates of two young men become entangled in this Russian story: Ambrosi, beloved son of two slaves of the Czar, apprenticed to Kuzma, a shaman from the Ghost World; and Fox, a son of the reindeer people, transformed by Kuzma into wolves. This is a companion story to *The Ghost Drum* (1987; see above), and *Ghost Dance: The Czar's Black Angel* (1994; see above).

Farrar, 1992, 160 pp. (0-374-32544-8)

(BL 89:147; CCBB 46:155; HB 69:87; HBG 4:75; Kirkus 60:1133; SLJ Jan 1993 p. 102; VOYA 15:356)

PUSHKIN, Alexander Sergeevich. *The Golden Cockerel and Other Stories.*

See Chapter 3, Fantasy Collections.

12-202 PYLE, Howard. *King Stork.* Gr. 2–4. (Orig. pub. in *The Wonder Clock,*

✶ 1887.)

A beautiful but wicked witch is tamed and won by a poor drummer and King Stork's magic. Boston Globe Horn Book Award for Illustration, 1973.

Illus. by Trina Schart Hyman, Little, Brown, 1973, 48 pp., o.p.; illus. by Trina Schart Hyman, Morrow, 1998, 48 pp. (0-688-15813-7)

(BL 70:174; HB 49:373; Kirkus 41:455; LJ 98:2643)

RAWN, Melanie. *Stronghold.*

See Chapter 5, High Fantasy: Alternate Worlds or Histories.

12-203 REAVES, Michael. *The Shattered World.* Gr. 10 up.

While master-wizard Pandrogas tries to put the world back together a thousand years after it was shattered by an evil sorcerer's spell, his former protégé, Ardatha, sends a master-thief to steal Pandrogas's runestone in order to raise the Necromancer from the dead.

Simon & Schuster, 1984, 349 pp., o.p.

(Kirkus 52:66; LJ 109:599; VOYA 8:212)

REEVES, James (pseud. of John Morris Reeves). *The Cold Flame.*

See Chapter 1, Allegorical Fantasy and Literary Fairy Tales.

REICHERT, Mickey Zucker. *The Last of the Renshai.*

See Chapter 5, High Fantasy: Alternate Worlds or Histories.

REID, Alastair. *Fairwater.*

See Chapter 1, Allegorical Fantasy and Literary Fairy Tales.

REIMANN, Katya. *Prince of Fire and Ashes.*

See Chapter 5, High Fantasy: Alternate Worlds or Histories.

ROACH, Marilynne K(athleen). *Encounters with the Invisible World.*

See Chapter 3, Fantasy Collections.

ROBERSON, Jennifer. *Sword-Breaker.*
See Chapter 5, High Fantasy: Alternate Worlds or Histories.

12-204 ROHAN, Michael Scott. *The Anvil of Ice.* **(Winter of the World trilogy, vol. 1).** Gr. 10 up.
A young magesmith defies his master and attempts to use his growing magical powers to battle the evil Ice Age threatening to destroy the world. The sequels are *The Forge in the Forest* (1987, 1995) and *The Hammer of the Sun* (1993, 1995).
Morrow, 1986, 344 pp., o.p.
(Kirkus 54:1330; LJ Oct 15, 1986 p. 112; SLJ Feb 1987 p. 99)

12-205 ROWLING, J[oanne] K[athleen]. *Harry Potter and the Sorcerer's Stone.*
★★ **(Harry Potter series, bk. 1).** Gr. 4–9. (Orig. British pub. 1997, entitled *Harry Potter and the Philosopher's Stone.*)
Almost 11, and reluctantly raised by his human (or muggle) aunt and uncle, orphaned Harry discovers that he is a wizard when he is invited to attend Hogwarts School of Witchcraft and Wizardry, and that his parents were murdered by the infamous wizard Voldemort. Carnegie Medal Commended Book, 1997; British Book Award Children's Book of the Year, 1997; Nestlé Smarties Book Prize, 1997; Anne Spencer Lindbergh Prize in Children's Literature, 1997–1998. In *Harry Potter and the Chamber of Secrets* (1998, 1999), the second year at Hogwarts is a dangerous one for Harry and his friends Ron and Hermione, particularly after Harry is accused of being the heir of Slytherin, creator of a Chamber of Secrets housing a monster. British Book Award Children's Book of the Year, 1998; Nestlé Smarties Book Prize Gold Award, 1998. In *Harry Potter and the Prisoner of Azkaban* (1999), Harry's life is threatened by the murderer Sirius Black who has escaped from Azkaban prison. Whitbread Children's Book of the Year Award, 1999; Nestlé Smarties Book Prize Gold Award, 1999. In *Harry Potter and the Goblet of Fire* (2000), Harry is selected to participate in a Triwizard Tournament, where students from three rival schools of magic compete in three ordeals involving dragons, water, a maze, and Harry's arch-enemy, Voldemort. Hugo Award for Best Novel, 2001. In *Harry Potter and the Order of the Phoenix* (2003), Harry, now 15, is furious to discover that the Ministry of Magic is discrediting him by declaring that Voldemort has not returned, while the newly revived Order of the Phoenix squabbles about how to protect Harry while fighting for truth and justice. *Harry Potter and the Half-Blood Prince* (2005) is the sixth book in the series. Rowling's *Fantastic Beasts and Where to Find Them* (2001) and *Quidditch Through the Ages* (2001) are related books. The entire series won a 1999–2000 Anne Spencer Lindbergh Prize Special Commendation for making an outstanding contribution to children's fantasy literature.
Illus. by Mary Grandpre, Levine/Scholastic, 1998, 309 pp. (0-590-35340-3); Scholastic, 1999, pap. (0-590-35340-3)
(BL 95:230, 783, 1691; CCBB 52:110; HB 75:71; HBG 10:73; Kirkus 66:1292; SLJ Oct 1998 p. 145, Dec 1998 p. 27; VOYA 21:370, 22:15)

RUSCH, Kristine Kathryn. *The White Mists of Power.*
See Chapter 5, High Fantasy: Alternate Worlds or Histories.

RUSH, Alison. *The Last of Danu's Children.*
See Chapter 6, High Fantasy: Myth or Legend Fantasy.

12-206 RUSSELL, Sean. *The Compass of the Soul.* **(River into Darkness, bk. 2).**
Gr. 10 up.
Anna Fielding has been secretly trained as a mage in a world where magic is vanishing, with the goal of opposing Lord Eldrich, the last mage of Farrland, who refuses to train a successor. This is the sequel to *Beneath the Vaulted Hills* (1997), and is set in an earlier time in the same world as the author's *World Without End* (1995) and *Sea Without a Shore* (1996).
DAW, 1998, 400 pp. (0-88677-792-5)
(Kirkus 66:938; LJ Aug 1998 p. 140; VOYA 21:372)

SABERHAGEN, Fred. *Empire of the East.*
See Chapter 5, High Fantasy: Alternate Worlds or Histories.

12-207 SABIN, E. Rose. *A School for Sorcery.* Gr. 6–12.
Disappointed in her rundown new School for the Magically Gifted, Tria Tesserell finds that she is the only one who can stand against Oryon, a fellow student who has turned to the dark side. The manuscript for this book received the Andre Norton Gryphon Award, 1992. *A Perilous Power* (2004) is the prequel, and *When the Beast Ravens* (2005) is the third book in the trilogy.
Tor, 2002, 320 pp. (0-765-30289-6); Starscape, 2003, pap., 320 pp. (0-765-34219-7)
(BL 99:212; VOYA 25:401, 26:14)

SALSITZ, R(hodi) A. V(ilott). *The Unicorn Dancer.*
See Chapter 5, High Fantasy: Alternate Worlds or Histories.

SALSITZ, R(hodi) A. V(ilott). *Where Dragons Lie.*
See Chapter 5, High Fantasy: Alternate Worlds or Histories.

SALVATORE, R. A. *The Woods Out Back.*
See Chapter 7, High Fantasy: Travel to Other Worlds.

12-208 SAN SOUCI, Robert D., reteller. *Feathertop: Based on the Tale by Nathaniel Hawthorne.* Gr. 2–4.
A witch named Old Mother Rigby transforms her scarecrow into a gentleman to play a trick on Judge Gookin by courting his daughter.
Story by Nathaniel Hawthorne; adapt. and illus. by Daniel San Souci, Doubleday, 1992, 132 pp., o.p.
(HBG 4:61; SLJ Dec 1992 p. 90)

SAN SOUCI, Robert D. *Young Merlin.*
See Chapter 6, High Fantasy: Myth or Legend Fantasy.

12-209 SCALORA, Suza. *The Witches and Wizards of Oberin.* Gr. 6 up.
Geologists discover a magical cave painting in the French Alps, in this photo-collage gallery of mages, each of whom tells his or her own story.
Illus. with photos by the author, HarperCollins, 2001, 48 pp. (0-06-029535-X)
(HBG 13:91; SLJ Oct 2001 p.169; VOYA 24:451, 25:16)

12-210 SCARBOROUGH, Elizabeth Ann. *Phantom Banjo.* **(The Songkiller Saga, vol. 1).** Gr. 10 up.
When devils discover that humans can use music as a weapon against them, they target folk songs as the first type of music to be expunged from the world, begin killing major folksingers, and destroy recording archives. The sequels are *Picking the Ballad's Bones* (1991) and *Strum Again?* (1992).
Bantam, 1991, pap., 272 pp. (0-553-28761-3)
(BL 87:1937; VOYA 14:326)

SCOTT, Evelyn. *Witch Perkins: A Story of the Kentucky Hills.*
See Chapter 7, High Fantasy: Travel to Other Worlds.

12-211 SEDGWICK, Marcus. *The Book of Dead Days.* **(The Book of Dead Days**
☆ **series, vol. 1).** Gr. 6–12. (Orig. British pub. 2003.)
Orphaned Boy follows his master, Valerian the magician, through a dark midwinter city, attempting to help avert the magician's death because of a pact with the devil. The sequel is *Dark Flight Down* (2004, 2005).
Random, 2004, 288 pp. (0-385-90158-5); Orion, 2004, pap., 264 pp. (1-8425-5267-8)
(BL 101:123; CCBB 58:183; HB 80:718; Kirkus 72:968; SLJ Nov 2004 p. 154; VOYA 27:318)

SENDAK, Jack. *The Magic Tears.*
See Chapter 9, Magic Adventure Fantasy.

12-212 SENDAK, Jack. *The Second Witch.* Gr. 3–5.
Andrew tries to save Vivian, an unpopular witch, from the wrath of the villagers of Platzenhausen, in this story written by Maurice Sendak's brother.
Illus. by Uri Shulevitz, Harper, 1965, 94 pp., o.p.
(Kirkus 33:751; LJ 90:4620)

12-213 SERVICE, Pamela F. *When the Night Wind Howls.* Gr. 6–8.
Sid and Joel suspect that Sid's mother's new boyfriend, star of a local theater group, is actually a warlock.
Macmillan, 1987, 153 pp., o.p.
(BL 83:1607; CCBB 40:178; Kirkus 55:224; SLJ Apr 1987 p. 113; VOYA 10:82)

SERVICE, Pamela F. *Winter of Magic's Return.*
See Chapter 6, High Fantasy: Myth or Legend Fantasy.

SERVICE, Pamela F. *Wizard of Wind and Rock.*
See Chapter 6, High Fantasy: Myth or Legend Fantasy.

SHERMAN, Josepha. *Child of Faerie, Child of Earth.*
See Chapter 6, High Fantasy: Myth or Legend Fantasy.

SHERMAN, Josepha. *The Shining Falcon.*
See Chapter 5, High Fantasy: Alternate Worlds or Histories.

12-214 *The Shimmering Door.* **Ed. by Katherine Kerr.** Gr. 7–12.
An anthology of 32 original fantasy stories about sorcerers, written by Esther M. Friesner, Susan Shwartz, Diana Paxson, Josepha Sherman, and others.

HarperPrism, 1996, pap., 134 pp. (0-06-105342-2)
(Kirkus 64:935; LJ Aug 1996 p. 120; VOYA 19:340, 20:12)

12-215 SHINN, Sharon. *The Shape-Changer's Wife.* Gr. 7–12.
Apprentice wizard Aubrey has come to study with master shape-changer Glyrenden, but finds himself falling in love with the magician's wife, Lilith.
Ace, 1995, pap., 208 pp. (0-441-00261-7)
(Kliatt Jan 1996 p. 18; LJ Oct 15, 1995 p. 91; VOYA 18:387, 19:23)

12-216 SHYER, Marlene Fanta. *Ruby, the Red Hot Witch at Bloomingdale's.* Gr. 4–6.
Newly arrived in New York City after their parents' separation, Petra and Thomas meet red-headed Ruby, who claims to be a good witch, on the sixth floor of Bloomingdale's department store.
Viking, 1991, 151 pp. (0-670-83473-4); Puffin, 1993, pap. (0-14-034510-8)
(BL 88:54; CCBB 44:275; HB 67:598; HBG 3:73; Kirkus 59:861; SLJ Oct 1991 p. 130)

SINGER, Isaac Bashevis. *Alone in the Wild Forest.*
See Chapter 1, Allegorical Fantasy and Literary Fairy Tales.

SINGER, Isaac Bashevis. *The Fearsome Inn.*
See Chapter 1, Allegorical Fantasy and Literary Fairy Tales.

12-217 SINGER, Marilyn. *California Demon.* Gr. 4–6.
Rosy Rodriguez, daughter of a practitioner of "the craft" of white magic, accidentally lets loose a demon who stows away to California and causes difficulties for Danny and Laura Pauling.
Hyperion, 1992, 149 pp. LB (1-56282-299-3)
(BL 89:671; CCBB 46:191; HBG 4:76)

12-218 SLADE, Arthur. *Dust.* Gr. 6–12. (Orig. Canadian pub. 2001.)
✫ Eleven-year-old Robert and his Uncle Alden become suspicious of Abram Harsich, newcomer to their Depression-era Saskatchewan town, who convinces the adults to build a "rainmill" and to ignore the disappearance of their children.
Governor General's Award for Children's Literature, 2001.
Wendy Lamb, 2003, 192 pp. (0-385-90093-7); Laurel Leaf, 2004, pap., 192 pp. (0-440-22976-6)
(BL 99:1065; CCBB 56:291; HB 79:217; HBG 14:375; Kirkus 71:540; SLJ Mar 2003 p. 240; VOYA 25:492, 26:14)

SLEIGH, Barbara (de Riemer). *Carbonel: The King of the Cats.*
See Chapter 9, Magic Adventure Fantasy.

SLEIGH, Barbara (de Riemer). *Stirabout Stories, Brewed in Her Own Cauldron.*
See Chapter 3, Fantasy Collections.

SLOBODKIN, Louis. *The Amiable Giant.*
See Chapter 1, Allegorical Fantasy and Literary Fairy Tales.

SMITH, L(isa) J. *Night of the Solstice.*
See Chapter 7, High Fantasy: Travel to Other Worlds.

SMITH, Sherwood. *Wren to the Rescue.*
See Chapter 5, High Fantasy: Alternate Worlds or Histories.

SMITH, Stephanie A. *Snow-Eyes.*
See Chapter 5, High Fantasy: Alternate Worlds or Histories.

SNYDER, Zilpha Keatley. *The Changing Maze.*
See Chapter 1, Allegorical Fantasy and Literary Fairy Tales.

SNYDER, Zilpha Keatley. *A Season of Ponies.*
See Chapter 9, Magic Adventure Fantasy.

12-219 SOMTOW, S. P. (pseud. of Somtow Sucharitkul). *The Wizard's Apprentice.* Gr. 7–10.
Aaron's summer plans are limited to skateboarding, girls, and the mall, until the wizard Anazagoras offers to train Aaron to become his apprentice.
Illus. by Nicholas Jainschigg, Macmillan, 1993, 144 pp. (0-689-31576-7)
(HBG 5:91; Kirkus 61:1398; SLJ Aug 1993 p. 189; VOYA 16:235)

Spells of Wonder. **Ed. by Marion Zimmer Bradley.**
See Chapter 5, High Fantasy: Alternate Worlds or Histories.

12-220 SPRINGER, Nancy. *The Hex Witch of Seldom.* Gr. 7–12.
The powerful black mustang stallion bought for Bobbi Yandro by her grandfather is actually Shane, the Dark Rider, who has been enslaved within the body of a horse.
Baen, 1988, 276 pp., o.p.; Firebird/Penguin, 2002, pap., 276 pp. (0-14-230220-1)
(BL 84:908, 962, 85:863, 86:907; Kirkus 56:169; VOYA 11:196, 12:14)

SPRINGER, Nancy. *Red Wizard.*
See Chapter 7, High Fantasy: Travel to Other Worlds.

STACKPOLE, Michael A. *Fortress Draconis.*
See Chapter 5, High Fantasy: Alternate Worlds or Histories.

STASHEFF, Christopher. *Her Majesty's Wizard.*
See Chapter 7, High Fantasy: Travel to Other Worlds.

STEARNS, Pamela (Fujimoto). *The Fool and the Dancing Bear.*
See Chapter 1, Allegorical Fantasy and Literary Fairy Tales.

STEELE, Mary Q(uintard Govan). *The Owl's Kiss: Three Stories.*
See Chapter 3, Fantasy Collections.

STEELE, Mary Q(uintard Govan). *Wish, Come True.*
See Chapter 9, Magic Adventure Fantasy.

STERMAN, Betsy, and STERMAN, Samuel. *Backyard Dragon.*
See Chapter 9, Magic Adventure Fantasy.

STEWART, Mary (Florence Elinor). *The Crystal Cave.*
See Chapter 6, High Fantasy: Myth or Legend Fantasy.

12-221 STEWART, Mary (Florence Elinor). *The Little Broomstick.* Gr. 3–5.
✮ (Orig. British pub. 1971.)
Mary goes to witch school to learn enough magic to rescue her black cat.
Illus. by Shirley Hughes, Morrow, 1972, 192 pp., o.p.; Hodder, new ed., 2001,
pap., 151 pp. (0-340-79658-8)
(BL 68:822; CCBB 25:146; HB 48:271; Kirkus 40:5; LJ 97:1610; Suth:382)

12-222 STEWART, Mary (Florence Elinor). *Thornyhold.* Gr. 10 up. (Orig. British
pub. 1988.)
Gilly suspects that the animals and people living near her old country house are
under a witch's spell cast by her late cousin Geillis.
Fawcett, 1989, pap., 192 pp. (0-449-21712-4)
(BL 85:186; Kirkus 56:1274; LJ Nov 15, 1988 p. 86)

STEWART, Mary (Florence Elinor). *A Walk in Wolf Wood.*
See Chapter 10, Time Travel Fantasy.

STOCKTON, Frank (Francis) R(ichard). *The Bee-Man of Orn.*
See Chapter 1, Allegorical Fantasy and Literary Fairy Tales.

12-223 STRAUB, Peter (Francis). *Shadowland.* Gr. 10 up.
Tom and Del, two high school students drawn together by an interest in magic,
visit Shadowland, home of renowned magician Coleman Collins, who wants
Tom to be his successor in the practice of black magic.
Coward, 1980, 417 pp., o.p.
(Kirkus 48:1187; LJ 105:2235; SLJ Feb 1981 p. 82; TLS 1981 p. 430)

STRAUSS, Victoria. *The Burning Land.*
See Chapter 5, High Fantasy: Alternate Worlds or Histories.

12-224 STROUD, Jonathan. *The Amulet of Samarkand.* **(The Bartimaeus trilogy,**
✮✮ **bk. 1).** Gr. 5–10. (Orig. British pub. 2003.)
Unhappily apprenticed to a mediocre politician/magician in a magical alternate
London, Nathaniel, 12, secretly studies books of advanced magic and summons
a djinni named Bartimaeus to steal the magical amulet of Samarkand and take
revenge on a magician who humiliated him. YALSA Top Ten Best Books for
Young Adults, 2004; Boston Globe Horn Book Award Fiction Honor Book,
2004. In the sequel, *The Golem's Eye* (2004), set two years later, Bartimaeus is
called back into service to aid Nathaniel in his investigation of a golem who
has destroyed part of the British Museum.
Hyperion, 2003, 462 pp. (0-7868-1859-X), 2004, pap., 464 pp. (0-7868-5255-0)
(BL 100:123; CCBB 57:298; HB 79:757; HBG 15:116; Kirkus 71:1231; SLJ Jan 2004 p. 136;
VOYA 26:419, 27:15)

12-225 STRUGATSKII, Arkadii Natanovich, and STRUGATSKII, Boris
Natanovich. *Monday Begins on Saturday.* Gr. 10 up.
A computer scientist studying witchcraft and magic in a secret laboratory pro-
duces a time-traveling sofa, an unspendable coin, a talking cat, and a house on
hen's legs, in this satire of Russian scientific research.
Trans. by Leonid Renen, DAW, 1977, pap., 220 pp., o.p.
(BL 74:899, 905; Kliatt Winter 1978 p. 11)

SWAHN, Sven. *The Island Through the Gate.*
See Chapter 7, High Fantasy: Travel to Other Worlds.

Sword and Sorceress. **Ed. by Marion Zimmer Bradley.**
See Chapter 5, High Fantasy: Alternate Worlds or Histories.

SYNGE, (Phyllis) Ursula. *Land of Heroes: A Retelling of the Kalevala.*
See Chapter 6, High Fantasy: Myth or Legend Fantasy.

12-226 TARR, Judith. *Devil's Bargain.* Gr. 10 up.
Sioned, half-sister of Richard the Lionheart, uses her magic powers to save her brother's soul and protect his Crusaders' quest for Jerusalem, while he battles the sultan Saladin for control of the Holy Land.
NAL/Roc, 2002, pap., 387 pp. (0-451-45896-6)
(BL 99:309; VOYA 26:69)

12-227 TARR, Judith. *His Majesty's Elephant.* Gr. 6–10.
A stable boy and a princess join forces with Emperor Charlemagne's enchanted elephant to defeat the magic of a Byzantine sorcerer and save her father's life.
Harcourt, 1993, 193 pp. (0-15-200737-7)
(BL 90:817; CCBB 47:170; HBG 5:91; HB 70:76; Kirkus 61:1398; VOYA 16:387)

TENNY, Dixie. *Call the Darkness Down.*
See Chapter 6, High Fantasy: Myth or Legend Fantasy.

TEPPER, Sheri S. *Jinian Footseer.*
See Chapter 5, High Fantasy: Alternate Worlds or Histories.

TEPPER, Sheri S. *Marianne, the Magus, and the Manticore.*
See Chapter 7, High Fantasy: Travel to Other Worlds.

TEPPER, Sheri S. *The Song of Mavin Manyshaped.*
See Chapter 5, High Fantasy: Alternate Worlds or Histories.

TERLOUW, Jan (Cornelis). *How to Become King.*
See Chapter 1, Allegorical Fantasy and Literary Fairy Tales.

12-228 THESMAN, Jean. *The Other Ones.* Gr. 6–10.
✮   Bridget tries to get through high school without revealing her magical powers, until her guardian warns that two of her friends are in imminent danger.
Viking, 1999, 181 pp. (0-670-88594-0); Puffin, 2001, pap., 192 pp. (0-14-131246-7)
(BL 95:1588, 97:1999; CCBB 53:34; HBG 10:308; Kirkus 67:636; Kliatt July 1999 p. 12; SLJ June 1999 p. 138; VOYA 22:196)

12-229 TIERNAN, Cate. *Book of Shadows.* **(Sweep series, bk. 1).** Gr. 8–12.
Cal, new to the high school, thinks that Morgan could be a blood witch as he is, but her parents think Wikka is wrong, and her best friend wants Cal for herself. The sequels are *The Coven* (2001), *Blood Witch* (2001), *Dark Magick* (2001), *Awakening* (2001), *Spellbound* (2001), *The Calling* (2001), *Changeling* (2001), *Strife* (2002), *Seeker* (2002), *Origins* (2002), *Eclipse* (2002), *Reckoning* (2002), *Full Circle* (2002), *Moira's Story* (2003), and *Night's Sweep* (2003).

Penguin/Puffin, 2001, pap., 192 pp. (0-14-131046-4)
(BL 97:1129; VOYA 24:32)

TOLKIEN, J(ohn) R(onald) R(euel). *The Hobbit; Or, There and Back Again.*
See Chapter 5, High Fantasy: Alternate Worlds or Histories.

TOLKIEN, J(ohn) R(onald) R(euel). *Roverandom.*
See Chapter 11, Toy Fantasy.

TOLSTOY, Nikolai. *The Coming of the King: The First Book of Merlin.*
See Chapter 6, High Fantasy: Myth or Legend Fantasy.

TURKLE, Brinton (Cassaday). *Mooncoin Castle; or Skulduggery Rewarded.*
See Chapter 4, Ghost Fantasy.

12-230 **TURNBULL, Ann (Christine).** *The Frightened Forest.* Gr. 4–6. (Orig.
✫ British pub. 1974.)
Responsible for releasing a witch imprisoned in an abandoned tunnel, Gillian and her cousins make a midnight attempt to recapture the malevolent creature.
Illus. by Gillian Gaze, Seabury, 1975, 125 pp., o.p.
(BL 71:1018; HB 51:385; Kirkus 43:460; SLJ May 1975 p. 59; TLS 1974 p. 714)

12-231 **TURNER, Ann Warren.** *Rosemary's Witch.* Gr. 4–8.
✫ Told alternately from the points of view of Mathilda, a witch who was an unloved little girl 150 years ago, and of Rosemary, a contemporary 9-year-old whose family has moved into Mathilde's house, this is the story of an empathetic little girl who reaches out to a lonely, mean, sad old woman.
Harper, 1991, 164 pp., LB (0-06-026128-5)
(BL 87:1569; CCBB 44:230; HBG 2:267; Kirkus 59:400; SLJ May 1991 p. 95)

UNWIN, Nora S(picer). *Two Too Many.*
See Chapter 2, Animal Fantasy.

12-232 **URE, Jean.** *The Wizard in the Woods.* **(Wizard trilogy, bk. 1).** Gr. 3–5.
(Orig. British pub. 1990.)
After his wizard's exam spell goes awry, Ben-Muzzy ends up in our world, where twins Joel and Gemma try to help him get home. The sequels are *Wizard in Wonderland* (1993) and *Wizard and the Witch* (1995).
Illus. by David Anstey, Candlewick, 1992, 176 pp. (1-56402-110-6)
(BL 89:671; HBG 4:78; Kirkus 60:1136; SLJ Oct 1992 p. 122)

VAN ALLSBURG, Chris. *The Garden of Abdul Gasazi.*
See Chapter 9, Magic Adventure Fantasy.

12-233 **VAN ALLSBURG, Chris.** *The Widow's Broom.* Gr. K–3.
✫ A witch gives her broomstick to Widow Shaw, and it proves to be talented at housekeeping, wood-chopping, and even piano playing, to the horror of her neighbors.
Illus. by the author, Houghton, 1992, 32 pp., o.p.
(BL 89:147, 846; CCBB 46:56; HB 69:79; Kirkus 60:1136; SLJ Nov 1992 p. 144, Dec 1992 p. 23)

VANCE, Jack (pseud. of John Holbrook Vance). *Cugel's Saga.*
See Chapter 5, High Fantasy: Alternate Worlds or Histories.

VANDE VELDE, Vivian. *Curses, Inc.: And Other Stories.*
See Chapter 3, Fantasy Collections.

12-234 VANDE VELDE, Vivian. *Magic Can Be Murder.* Gr. 6–10.
✫ Nola, a 17-year-old witch who can spy on others by placing a hair into a bucket of water, witnesses the murder of a silversmith—her mother's former employer—and dons a magical disguise to bring his murderer to justice.
Harcourt, 2000, 208 pp. (0-15-202665-7); Puffin, 2002, pap., 197 pp. (0-14-230210-4)
(BL 97:809; CCBB 54:124; HBG 12:80; Kirkus 68:1366; Kliatt Nov 2000 p. 10; SLJ Nov 2000 p. 164; VOYA 23:364, 24:15)

VANDE VELDE, Vivian. *Witch's Wishes.*
See Chapter 9, Magic Adventure Fantasy.

12-235 VANDE VELDE, Vivian. *Wizard at Work: A Novel in Stories.* Gr. 4–7.
✫ A wizard's plans for a peaceful summer vacation are continually interrupted by the arrival of a prince with a dragon problem, a town with a unicorn problem, a royal family with an unusual daughter, a haunted castle, and a princess who has been bewitched.
Harcourt, 2003, 134 pp. (0-15-204559-7); Harcourt, pap., 2004 (0-15-205309-3)
(BL 99:1466; CCBB 56:465; HBG 14:376; Kirkus 71:401; SLJ May 2003 p. 132)

12-236 VINGE, Joan D(ennison). *Ladyhawke.* Gr. 10 up. (Orig. British pub. 1985.)
✫ Orphaned Philippe escapes death in the Bishop's prison and goes into the service of the mysterious Navarre, whose beautiful lover, Isabeau, has been transformed into a hawk by the evil Bishop.
NAL, 1985, pap., 252 pp., o.p.
(Kliatt Fall 1985 p. 27; TLS 1985 p. 345; VOYA 8:195)

VOLSKY, Paula. *The Luck of Relian Kru.*
See Chapter 5, High Fantasy: Alternate Worlds or Histories.

VOLSKY, Paula. *The Wolf in Winter.*
See Chapter 5, High Fantasy: Alternate Worlds or Histories.

12-237 WALLACE, Barbara Brooks. *Miss Switch to the Rescue.* **(Miss Switch trilogy, bk. 1).** Gr. 3–6.
Miss Switch saves the day after a witch turns Rupert, Amelia, and their entire fifth-grade class into toads. This is the sequel to *The Trouble with Miss Switch* (1981; Simon, pap., 2002), and is followed by *Miss Switch Online* (2002).
Illus. by Kathleen Garry McCord, Abingdon, 1981, 158 pp., o.p.; Simon, 2002, pap., 176 pp. (0-689-85176-6)
(BL 78:760; SLJ Mar 1982 p. 152)

WANGERIN, Walter, Jr. *Thistle.*
See Chapter 1, Allegorical Fantasy and Literary Fairy Tales.

12-238 WARNER, Sylvia Townsend. *Lolly Willowes: Or, the Loving Huntsman.* Gr. 10 up. (Orig. British pub. 1926.)

Laura Willowes leads an uneventful, spinsterly life until the age of 47, when she decides to take up witchcraft and makes a pact with the Devil.

Viking, 1926, 251 pp., o.p.; Academy Chicago, 1978, 1979, pap., 252 pp. (0-915864-91-6); Charles River Books, pap. (0-7043-3824-6); New York Review of Books, 1999, 222 pp. (0-940322-16-1)

(BL 22:332, 25:83; TLS 1926 p. 78, 1978 p. 273)

12-239 WATT-EVANS, Lawrence (pseud. of Richard Watt Evans). *With a Single Spell.* Gr. 10 up.

An inexperienced wizard's apprentice joins a dragon hunt and comes across a magical tapestry linked to another world. This book is set in the same world as *Misenchanted Sword* (1985, 2000).

Ballantine, pap., 1987, 263 pp., o.p.; Wildside, pap., 2003, 206 pp. (1-58715-285-1)

(BL 83:983, 1009; LJ Mar 15, 1987, p. 93)

12-240 WEALES, Gerald (Clifford). *Miss Grimsbee Is a Witch.* Gr. 3–5.

Jimmy is the only one who realizes that Miss Grimsbee is a real witch. The sequel is *Miss Grimsbee Takes a Vacation* (1965).

Illus. by Lita Scheel, Little, Brown, 1957, 123 pp., o.p.

(BL 53:435; CCBB 10:138; HB 33:140; Kirkus 25:74; LJ 82:884)

WEIN, Elizabeth E. *The Winter Prince.*

See Chapter 6, High Fantasy: Myth or Legend Fantasy.

WEIS, Margaret, and HICKMAN, Tracy. *Forging the Darksword.*

See Chapter 5, High Fantasy: Alternate Worlds or Histories.

12-241 WELLS, Martha. *The Death of the Necromancer.* Gr. 10 up.

Obsessed with revenge after his father's execution on the false charge of necromancy, Nicholas Valiarde, alias Donatien the thief, plots to punish Count Mountesq and stumbles upon the existence of a truly malevolent necromancer. This is the sequel to *The Element of Fire* (1993), and is followed by *The Wizard Hunters* (2003; see below) and *The Ships of Air* (2004), which are the first two volumes in The Fall of Ile-Rien series.

Avon, 1998, 368 pp. (0-380-97334-0); Eos, 1999, pap., 544 pp. (0-380-78814-4)

(BL 94:1608; Kirkus 66:621; LJ June 15, 1998 p. 110, Nov 1, 1998 p. 148,, Jan 1999 p. 57)

12-242 WELLS, Martha. *The Wizard Hunters.* **(The Fall of Ile-Rien, vol. 1).** Gr. 10 up.

Playwright Tremaine Valiarde is thrown into another world by the magical sphere she'd hoped would defend her homeland from the black airships of the Gardier. This story is preceded by *The Element of Fire* (1993), and *The Death of the Necromancer* (1998; see above), whose protagonist is Tremaine's father, Nicholas. The sequel is *The Ships of Air* (2004).

Eos/HarperCollins, 2003, 400 pp. (0-380-97788-5); Eos, 2004, pap., 464 pp. (0-380-80798-X)

(BL 99:1586; Kirkus 71:352; LJ Apr 15, 2003 p. 128)

WHITCHER, Susan. *Real Mummies Don't Bleed: Friendly Tales for October Nights.*
See Chapter 3, Fantasy Collections.

WHITE, T(erence) H(anbury). *The Once and Future King.*
See Chapter 6, High Fantasy: Myth or Legend Fantasy.

12-243 WHITEHEAD, Victoria. *The Chimney Witches.* Gr. 4–6. (Orig. British pub. 1986.)
On Halloween Eve, Lucy finally meets the witches she suspected of living in her chimney: Weird Hannah and her bumbling son, Rufus. The sequels are *Chimney Witch Chase* (1987, 1988) and *Chimney Witch Christmas* (1988, 1990).
Illus. by Linda North, Orchard, 1987, 117 pp., o.p.
(BL 84:154; CCBB 41:59; SLJ Nov 1987 p. 107)

WICKENDEN, Dan. *The Amazing Vacation.*
See Chapter 7, High Fantasy: Travel to Other Worlds.

WILDE, Oscar (Fingal O'Flahertie Wills). *The Happy Prince.*
See Chapter 1, Allegorical Fantasy and Literary Fairy Tales.

12-244 WILLARD, Barbara. *Spell Me a Witch.* Gr. 3–5. (Orig. British pub. 1979.)
Belladonna Agrimony, headmistress of the Academy for Young Witches, and Betony, a star student, rescue a young witch who has been transformed into a pig.
Harcourt, 1981, 142 pp., o.p.
(BL 78:313; Kirkus 49:1410; SLJ Nov 1981 p. 99)

WILLEY, Elizabeth. *A Sorcerer and a Gentleman.*
See Chapter 5, High Fantasy: Alternate Worlds or Histories.

WILLEY, Elizabeth. *The Well-Favored Man: The Tale of the Sorcerer's Nephew.*
See Chapter 5, High Fantasy: Alternate Worlds or Histories.

WILLIAMS, Anne. *Secret of the Round Tower.*
See Chapter 1, Allegorical Fantasy and Literary Fairy Tales.

WILLIAMS, Jay. *The Magic Grandfather.*
See Chapter 9, Magic Adventure Fantasy.

WILLIAMS, Jay. *Petronella.*
See Chapter 1, Allegorical Fantasy and Literary Fairy Tales.

WILLIAMS (John), Ursula Moray. *The Toymaker's Daughter.*
See Chapter 11, Toy Fantasy.

12-245 Witches. Ed. by Isaac Asimov, Martin H. Greenberg, and Charles G. Waugh. Gr. 10 up.
Thirteen fantasy and science fiction tales about female witchcraft, including Schmitz's "Witches of Karres" and L'Engle's "Poor Little Saturday." The companion volume is *Wizards* (1983).

NAL, 1984, pap., 350 pp. (0-451-12882-6)

(BL 80:1228, 1234; Kliatt Fall 1984 p. 24; VOYA 7:269)

12-246 *Witches, Witches, Witches.* **Ed. by Helen Hoke.** Gr. 5–8. (Orig. British pub. 1958.)

Twenty-five tales about folktale and fantasy witches, whose authors include Oscar Wilde and Andrew Lang.

Illus. by W. R. Lohse, Watts, 1966, 230 pp., o.p.

(BL 55:190; Kirkus 26:663; LJ 83:3572)

12-247 *The Wizard's Den: Spellbinding Stories of Magic and Magicians.* **Ed. by Peter Haining.** Gr. 5–9. (Orig. pub. in England.)

Fifteen stories of wizardry and magic written by Diana Wynne Jones, E. Nesbit, Joan Aiken, Roald Dahl, Philip Pullman, and others. *The Magician's Circle: More Spellbinding Stories of Wizards and Wizardry* (2003, 2004) is a companion volume.

Souvenir, 2001, 320 pp. (0-285-63628-6)

(SLJ June 2003 p. 143; VOYA 26:242, 17:15)

A Wizard's Dozen: Stories of the Fantastic. **Ed. by Michael Stearns.**
See Chapter 3, Fantasy Collections.

12-248 WOLF, Joyce. *Between the Cracks.* Gr. 6–8.

Eighth-grader Bentley saves her friend Charles from the corrupting influence of Mordicus the magician.

Dial, 1992, 176 pp. (0-8037-1270-7)

(BL 89:432; HBG 4:78; Kirkus 60:1195; SLJ Dec 1992 p. 262; VOYA 15:296)

12-249 WOOD, Frances M. *Becoming Rosemary.* Gr. 5–8.

✭ Twelve-year-old Rosemary Weston's mother and sisters have magical healing and telepathy gifts that must be hidden from the other members of their 1790 North Carolina farming community, and Rosemary longs to know whether she too will have these gifts.

Delacorte, 1997, 247 pp. (0-385-32248-8), pap., 2001, 256 pp. (0-375-89504-3)

(BL 93:846; CCBB 50:338; HBG 8:310; Kirkus 64:1610; SLJ Feb 1997 p. 106; VOYA 20:34)

WREDE, Patricia C(ollins). *The Harp of Imach Thyssel.*
See Chapter 5, High Fantasy: Alternate Worlds or Histories.

WREDE, Patricia C(ollins). *Mairelon the Magician.*
See Chapter 5, High Fantasy: Alternate Worlds or Histories.

WREDE, Patricia C(ollins). *The Seven Towers.*
See Chapter 5, High Fantasy: Alternate Worlds or Histories.

WRIGGINS, Sally. *The White Monkey King: A Chinese Fable.*
See Chapter 6, High Fantasy: Myth or Legend Fantasy.

WRIGHT, Betty Ren. *The Ghost of Ernie P.*
See Chapter 4, Ghost Fantasy.

WRIGHT, Betty Ren. *The Ghost Witch.*
See Chapter 4, Ghost Fantasy.

WRIGHTSON, (Alice) Patricia (Furlonger). *An Older Kind of Magic.*
See Chapter 9, Magic Adventure Fantasy.

WURTS, Janny. *Sorcerer's Legacy.*
See Chapter 5, High Fantasy: Alternate Worlds or Histories.

12-250 WURTS, Janny. *Stormwarden.* **(Cycle of Fire series, bk. 1).** Gr. 10 up.
A brother and sister named Emien and Taen and a young scholar named Jaric
are caught up in a battle between opposing sorceresses. The sequels are *Keeper
of the Keys* (1988) and *Shadowfane* (1988). *The Cycle of Fire* (HarperPrism,
pap., 1999, 695 pp. [0-06-107355-5]) contains all three novels.
Berkley, 1984, pap., 325 pp., o.p.
(BL 81:484, 520; VOYA 8:141)

YEP, Laurence M(ichael). *The Tiger's Apprentice.*
See Chapter 9, Magic Adventure Fantasy.

YOLEN (Stemple), Jane (Hyatt). *Dove Isabeau.*
See Chapter 1, Allegorical Fantasy and Literary Fairy Tales.

12-251 YOLEN (Stemple), Jane (Hyatt). *Here There Be Witches.* Gr. 4–8.
✮ Ten stories and poems about witches, wizards, shamans, and warlocks, includ-
ing one about Merlin and King Arthur. This is a companion volume to Yolen's
Here There Be Angels (1996; see Chapter 3, Fantasy Collections), *Here There
Be Dragons* (1993; see Chapter 3, Fantasy Collections), and *Here There Be
Unicorns* (1994; see Chapter 3, Fantasy Collections).
Illus. by David Wilgus, Harcourt, 1995, 128 pp. (0-15-200311-8), 1997, pap.,
128 pp. (0-15-201657-0)
(BL 92:397, 1296; HBG 7:135; Kirkus 63:1360; SLJ Dec 1995 p. 110; VOYA 18:318, 19:18)

YOLEN (Stemple), Jane (Hyatt). *The Magic Three of Solatia.*
See Chapter 1, Allegorical Fantasy and Literary Fairy Tales.

YOLEN (Stemple), Jane (Hyatt). *Merlin's Booke.*
See Chapter 6, High Fantasy: Myth or Legend Fantasy.

12-252 YOLEN (Stemple), Jane (Hyatt). *The Wizard of Washington Square.* Gr.
4–6.
A tiny wizard is distressed to discover how many children have forgotten that
he exists.
Illus. by Ray Cruz, Collins+World, 1969, 126 pp., o.p.
(CCBB 23:170; Kirkus 37:1150; LJ 95:783)

12-253 YOLEN (Stemple), Jane (Hyatt). *Wizard's Hall.* Gr. 4–7.
✮ Eleven-year-old novice wizard Henry, renamed Thornmallow, can't seem to
master spell-casting and transformations, even though Wizard's Hall needs
help to defeat the evil Master and his Quilted Beast.
Harcourt, 1991, 134 pp. (0-15-298132-2); Harcourt, 1999, pap., 133 pp. (0-15-
202085-3)

(BL 87:1494; CCBB 44:280; HBG 2:270; Kirkus 59:611; SLJ July 1991 p. 75; VOYA 14:184, 15:11)

YOLEN (Stemple), Jane (Hyatt). *The Wizard's Map.*
See Chapter 9, Magic Adventure Fantasy.

12-254 YOUNG, Miriam. *The Witch Mobile.* Gr. 2–4.
Nanette, the smallest witch in the toyshop, does not want to work revengeful spells like her older sisters.
Illus. by Victoria Chess, Lothrop, 1969, 48 pp., o.p.
(Kirkus 37:995; LJ 95:1192)

12-255 *Young Witches and Warlocks.* **Ed. by Isaac Asimov, Martin H. Green-**
✶ **berg, and Charles G. Waugh.** Gr. 6–9.
Ten stories about adolescents with unusual abilities, including "Teregram," "The Entrance Exam," and two by Ray Bradbury and Elizabeth Coatsworth.
Harper, 1987, 207 pp., o.p.
(BL 83:1673, 1683; CCBB 40:202; Kirkus 55:921; SLJ Jan 1988 p. 83; VOYA 10:93)

12-256 ZAMBRENO, Mary Frances. *A Plague of Sorcerers.* Gr. 6–10.
✶ A skunk named Delia becomes apprentice wizard Jermyn's familiar, and the two try to save the city's sorcerers, most of whom have been struck down by a mysterious plague. In the sequel, *Journeyman Wizard: A Magical Mystery* (1994, 1996), Jermyn is accused of murdering his teacher, master-wizard Lady Jane Allons.
Harcourt, 1991, 224 pp. (0-15-262430-9)
(BL 88:626; CCBB 45:53; HBG 3:75; Kirkus 59:1230; SLJ Oct 1991 p. 150; VOYA 14:328, 15:10)

12-257 ZELAZNY, Roger (Joseph Christopher). *Jack of Shadows.* Gr. 10 up.
Jack, a shadow magician from the dark side of the world who was unjustly punished for thievery, is determined to have vengeance.
Walker, 1971, 207 pp., o.p.
(BL 68:320; LJ 97:217)

12-258 ZELAZNY, Roger (Joseph Christopher). *Madwand.* **(The Changeling Saga, bk. 2).** Gr. 10 up.
Pol Detson must use his newly acquired magician's skills to battle a sorcerer bent on ruling the world. This is the sequel to *Changeling* (Ace, 1980), and both books were published together in *Wizard World* (Baen, 1989).
Phantasia Press, 1981, 254 pp., o.p.
(BL 78:850; VOYA 5:41)

ZETTEL, Sarah. *A Sorcerer's Treason.*
See Chapter 7, High Fantasy: Travel to Other Worlds.

ZETTEL, Sarah. *The Usurper's Crown.*
See Chapter 7, High Fantasy: Travel to Other Worlds.

Author and Illustrator Index

This Author and Illustrator Index provides references to the specific works of all authors and editors of books mentioned in Chapters 1 through 12, including out-of-print works. All numbers refer to entry numbers, not page numbers. Authors' and editors' names are followed by a list of specific works. Illustrators are listed with reference to entry number only and do not list specific works.

Bakken, Harald
The Fields and the Hills, 5-42
Balaban, John
The Hawk's Tale, 2-32
Baldwin, Sidney, comp.
Stories by Mrs. Molesworth, 3-212
Ball, Brian
The Quest for Queenie, 7-13
Ball, Duncan
Emily Eyefinger, 9-22
Emily Eyefinger and the Lost Treasure, 9-22
Emily Eyefinger, Secret Agent, 9-22
Selby, 2-33
Selby, Spacedog, 2-33
Selby Speaks, 2-33
Ball, Margaret
Changeweaver, 5-43
Flameweaver, 5-43
No Earthly Sunne, 7-14
The Shadow Gate, 7-15
Bancroft, Alberta
The Goblins of Haubeck, 1-36
Banks, Lynne Reid
The Fairy Rebel, 9-23
The Farthest-Away Mountain, 1-37
Harry the Poisonous Centipede, 2-34
Harry the Poisonous Centipede's Big Adventure, 2-34
I Houdini, 2-35
The Indian in the Cupboard, 9-24
The Key to the Indian, 9-24
The Magic Hare, 2-36
Maura's Angel, 9-25
Melusine, 6-16
The Mystery of the Cupboard, 9-24
The Return of the Indian, 9-24
The Secret of the Indian, 9-24
Banks, Richard
The Mysterious Leaf, 1-38
Barber, Antonia
The Enchanter's Daughter, 1-39
Barber, Antonia (pseud. of Barbara Anthony)
The Ghosts, 10-17
Barker, Clive, 7-16
Abarat, 7-16
Days of Magic, Nights of War, 7-16
The Thief of Always, 7-17
Barker, M(uhammad) A(bd-Al-) R(ahman)
The Man of Gold, 5-44
Barklem, Jill, 2-37
Autumn Story, 2-37
The Four Seasons of Brambly Hedge, 2-37
The High Hills, 2-37
Sea Story, 2-37
The Secret Staircase, 2-37
Spring Story, 2-37
Summer Story, 2-37
Winter Story, 2-37
Barlow, Jennifer
Hamlet Dreams, 7-18

Barlow, Wayne (illus.), 9-455
Barnes, Emma
Jessica Haggerthwaite: Media Star, 12-8
Barnes, John
One for the Morning Glory, 5-45
Barnett, Lisa A.
Point of Dreams, 5-566
Point of Hopes, 5-566
Barney, Maginel (illus.), adapt., 1-285
Barofsky, Seymour, adapt.
In Grandpa's House, 1-294
Barret, Leighton, adapt.
The Adventures of Don Quixote de la Mancha, 1-66
Barrett, Angela (illus.), 1-9, 1-17, 1-23, 4-252, 11-82
Barrett, Neal
The Treachery of Kings, 5-46
Barrett, Nicholas
Fledger, 2-38
Barrett, Ron (illus.), 8-198
Barrett, Tracy
Cold in Summer, 4-24
Barrie, Sir J(ames) M(atthew)
The Little White Bird, 7-19
The Little White Bird; or, Adventures in Kensington Gardens, 1-40
The Lost Girls, 7-19
Peter and the Starcatchers, 7-19
Peter and Wendy, 7-19
Peter Pan, 7-19
Peter Pan and Wendy, 7-19
Peter Pan in Kensington Gardens, 1-40, 7-19
Wendy, 7-19
When Wendy Grew Up, 7-19
Barringer, Marie
Martin the Goose Boy, 11-8
Barron, T(homas) A.
The Ancient One, 10-18
The Fires of Merlin, 6-18
The Great Tree of Avalon, 6-17
Heartlight, 10-18
The Lost Years of Merlin, 6-18
The Merlin Effect, 10-18
The Mirror of Merlin, 6-18
The Seven Songs of Merlin, 6-18
Tree Girl, 5-47
The Wings of Merlin, 6-18
Barry, Dave
Peter and the Starcatchers, 9-26
Peter Pan, 9-26
Bartholomew, Barbara
Child of Tomorrow, 7-20
The Time Keeper, 7-20
The Timekeeper, 7-20
When Dreamers Cease to Dream, 7-20
Bartholomew, Lois Thompson
The White Dove, 5-48

Bartlett, Maurice (illus.), 2-239

Barton, Jill (illus.), 1-177

Barzini, Luigi (Giorgio, Jr.)
  The Little Match Man, 11-9

Base, Graeme
  TruckDogs, 5-49

Baskin, Leonard (illus.), 3-181

Bass, L. G.
  Sign of the Qin, 6-19

Basso, Bill (illus.), 5-456

Batchelor, Joy (illus.), 2-348

Bates, Leo (illus.), 2-31

Bath, K. P.
  The Secret of Castle Cant, 5-50

Batherman, Muriel (illus.), 9-449

Bato, Joseph, 12-9
  The Sorcerer, 12-9

Battles, Edith
  The Witch in Room 6, 12-10

Baudino, Gael
  Strands of Starlight, 5-51

Bauer, Joan
  Thwonk, 8-17

Bauer, Marion Dane
  Ghost Eye, 4-25
  A Taste of Smoke, 4-26
  Touch the Moon, 9-27

Bauer, Steven
  A Cat of a Different Color, 2-39
  Satyrday, 5-52

Baum, Frank Joslyn
  The Laughing Dragon of Oz, 7-22

Baum, L(yman) Frank
  Dorothy and the Wizard in Oz, 7-22
  The Emerald City of Oz, 7-22
  The Enchanted Island of Yew, 5-53
  Glinda of Oz, 7-22
  The Land of Oz, 7-22
  Little Wizard Stories of Oz, 7-22
  The Lost Princess of Oz, 7-22
  The Magic of Oz, 7-22
  The Magical Monarch of Mo, 3-35
  The Marvellous Land of Oz, 7-22
  A New Wonderland, 3-35
  Ozma of Oz, 7-22
  The Patchwork Girl of Oz, 7-22
  Rinki-tink of Oz, 7-22
  The Road to Oz, 7-22
  The Scarecrow of Oz, 7-22
  The Sea Fairies, 7-21
  Sky Island, 7-21
  *The Surprising Adventures of the Magical
    Monarch of Mo and His People*, 3-35
  Tik-Tok of Oz, 7-22
  The Tin Woodman of Oz, 7-22
  The Visitors from Oz, 7-22
  The Wizard of Oz, 7-22
  The Wonderful Wizard of Oz, 7-22

Baum, Roger S.
  Dorothy of Oz, 7-22

Baumgartner, Robert (illus.), 2-275

Baumhauer, H. (illus.), 9-288

Baxter, Caroline
  The Stolen Telesm, 12-11

Baxter, Glen (illus.), 8-157

Baxter, Lorna
  The Eggchild, 12-12

Baynes, Pauline (illus.), 1-104, 1-133, 1-187,
    1-336, 1-337, 7-166, 11-47

Bazilian, Barbara, adapt., 1-16
  The Red Shoes, 1-16

Beachcroft, Nina
  Well Met by Witchlight, 12-13
  The Wishing People, 9-28

Beagle, Peter S(oyer)
  A Dance for Emilia, 4-27
  The Fantasy Worlds of Peter S. Beagle, 3-36
  A Fine and Private Place, 3-36
  A Fine and Private Place, A Novel, 4-28
  The Folk of the Air, 6-20
  Giant Bones, 5-54
  The Innkeeper's Song, 5-55
  The Last Unicorn, 3-36, 5-56
  Peter S. Beagle's Immortal Unicorn, 3-229
  Tamsin, 4-29
  The Unicorn Sonata, 7-23

Bear, Greg(ory Dale)
  The Infinity Concerto, 7-24
  The Serpent Mage, 7-24
  Songs of Earth and Power, 7-24

Beardsley, Aubrey (illus.), 6-265

Beaton-Jones, Cynon
  The Adventures of So Hi, 7-25
  So Hi and the White Horse, 7-25

Beaverson, Aiden
  The Hidden Arrow of Maether, 5-57

Bechdolt, Jack (pseud. of John Ernest Bechdolt)
  Bandmaster's Holiday, 2-40

Becher, Arthur E. (illus.), 9-63

Beck, David Michael (illus.), 5-20

Becker, Eve
  The Love Potion, 9-29
  The Magic Mix-Up, 9-29
  The Popularity Potion, 9-29
  The Sneezing Spell, 9-29
  Thirteen Means Magic, 9-29
  Too Much Magic, 9-29

Becker, Greg (illus.), 7-19

Beckhorn, Susan Williams
  The Kingfisher's Gift, 9-30

Beckman, Kaj (illus.), 1-358

Bedard, Michael
  A Darker Magic, 12-14
  The Nightingale, 1-14
  Painted Devil, 12-14
  Redwork, 12-15

Title Index

This index provides references to all titles mentioned in Chapters 1 through 12. The numbers that follow the titles refer to entry numbers, not page numbers.

1040   *Title Index*

Series Index

The Series Index lists main entry titles that are part of a series. Other titles in the series are noted in the main entry annotation. All references are to entry numbers, not page numbers.

Subject Index

This Subject Index provides topical headings for many areas of interest to children, young adults, and the librarians who serve them—historical periods, ethnic groups, folktales, imaginary beings and worlds, and mythical creatures. Also listed are subjects such as alcoholism, divorce, and other sensitive topics that are not usually tied to the realm of fantasy. Historical periods are listed under specific countries (for example, Revolutionary War can be found under United States—Revolutionary War). General headings such as mythology, folklore, legends, and fantasy are not listed here. All references are to entry numbers within Chapters 1 to 12, not page numbers. Titles listed here are main entry titles. Other titles in a series and sequels are noted in the main entry annotation. Series titles, which were included in the Subject Index in previous editions of this guide, are now listed in a separate Series Index.

Abominable snowman
    Corbalis, Judy. *The Ice Cream Heroes,* 8-49
    Morpurgo, Michael. *King of the Cloud Forests,* 6-284
Aboriginal mythology. *See* Australian Aboriginals—Mythology
Africa. *See also* specific countries and areas, e.g., Ethiopia, Libya, Sahara Desert
    Lofting, Hugh. *The Story of Doctor Dolittle,* 8-183
    Lurie, Morris. *The Twenty-Seventh Annual African Hippopotamus Race,* 2-303
Africa—19th century
    Coville, Bruce. *The Dark Abyss,* 7-65
Africa—Nubia
    Bradshaw, Gillian (Marucha). *The Dragon and the Thief,* 5-79
    Norton, Andre (pseud. of Alice Mary Norton). *Wraiths of Time,* 7-214
Africa, Northern—Folklore
    Myers, Walter Dean. *The Legend of Tarik,* 6-296
    Wellman, Manly Wade. *Cahena,* 6-432
Africa, Northern—Middle Ages
    Coehlo, Paulo. *The Alchemist,* 1-72
    Myers, Walter Dean. *The Legend of Tarik,* 6-296
Africa, Northern—World War II period
    Mellecker, Judith. *Randolph's Dream,* 1-238

African American folklore
    Hamilton (Adoff), Virginia (Esther). *The All Jahdu Storybook,* 8-122
    Hooks, William H(arris). *The Ballad of Belle Dorcas,* 1-156
    McKissack, Patricia C(arwell). *The Dark-Thirty,* 4-209
    Tate, Eleanora E. *Don't Split the Pole,* 3-268
African Americans
    Ansa, Tina McElroy. *Baby of the Family,* 9-10
    Avi (Avi Wortis). *Something Upstairs,* 10-15
    Bethancourt, T(homas) Ernesto (pseud. of Tom Paisley). *Tune in Yesterday,* 10-24
    Bisson, Terry. *Fire on the Mountain,* 5-69
    Brittain, Bill. *All the Money in the World,* 8-29
    Burgess, Barbara Hood. *Oren Bell,* 4-49
    Butler, Octavia E(stelle). *Kindred,* 10-40
    Carew, Jan (Rynveld). *Children of the Sun,* 1-64
    Chesnutt, Charles Waddell. *Conjure Tales,* 3-66
    Faust, Minister. *The Coyote Kings of the Space Age Bachelor Pad,* 9-161
    Favole, Robert J. *Through the Wormhole,* 10-80
    Gray, Genevieve S(tuck). *The Seven Wishes of Joanna Peabody,* 9-197
    Hall, Lynn. *The Mystery of the Caramel Cat,* 4-139

United States—Pacific Northwest Coast
Kesey, Ken. *The Sea Lion,* 6-203
Passey, Helen K. *Speak to the Rain,* 6-326
United States—Prehistoric period
Hanlon, Emily. *Circle Home,* 10-106
Mazer, Norma Fox. *Saturday, the Twelfth of October,* 10-168
United States—Revolutionary War
Alternative Histories, 5-21
Albrecht, Lillie Vanderveer. *Deborah Remembers,* 11-2
Cuyler, Margery. *The Battlefield Ghost,* 4-84
Dawson, Carley. *Mr. Wicker's Window,* 10-64
Favole, Robert J. *Through the Wormhole,* 10-80
Jensen, Dorothea. *The Riddle of Penncroft Farm,* 4-164
Keehn, Sally M. *Moon of Two Dark Horses,* 4-166
Klaveness, Jan O'Donnell. *The Griffin Legacy,* 4-174
Lawson, Robert. *Mr. Revere and I,* 2-286
United States—Southern States
Bisson, Terry. *Fire on the Mountain,* 5-69
Cramer, Alexander. *A Night in Moonbeam County,* 4-74
McKissack, Patricia C(arwell). *The Dark-Thirty,* 4-209
United States—Southern states—19th century
Whitmore, Arvella. *Trapped Between the Lash and the Gun,* 10-268
United States—Southwest—Prehistoric period
Kittleman, Laurence R. *Canyons Beyond the Sky,* 10-126
United States—Western states
King, Stephen. *The Gunslinger,* 5-350
Nixon, Joan Lowery. *Ghost Town,* 4-229
United States—Western states—19th century
Coren, Alan. *Arthur the Kid,* 8-51
Snyder, Midori. *The Flight of Michael McBride,* 6-390
Vande Velde, Vivian. *Ghost of a Hanged Man,* 4-305
Unted States—1960s
Wilson, Robert Charles. *A Bridge of Years,* 10-276

Valdemar
Lackey, Mercedes. *Arrows of the Queen,* 5-365
By the Sword, 5-367
Magic's Pawn, 5-369
Storm Warning, 5-372
Winds of Fate, 5-373
Lackey, Mercedes, and Dixon, Larry. *The Black Gryphon,* 5-374
Owlflight, 5-375
Vampires
Coville, Bruce. *Oddly Enough,* 3-75

De Lint, Charles. *Yarrow,* 7-77
Donaldson, Stephen R(upert). *Reave the Just and Other Tales,* 3-94
Ford, John M. *The Dragon Waiting,* 5-241
Goulart, Ron(ald Joseph). *The Prisoner of Blackwood Castle,* 5-268
Harvey, Jayne. *Great-Uncle Dracula,* 8-125
Jacques, Brian. *Seven Strange and Ghostly Tales,* 4-163
McKinley, (Jennifer Carolyn) Robin (Turrell). *Sunshine,* 5-454
McMullen, Sean. *Voyage of the Shadowmoon,* 5-457
Martin, Ann M(atthews). *Ma and Pa Dracula,* 8-201
Pierce, Meredith Ann. *The Darkangel,* 5-512
Powers, Tim. *The Stress of Her Regard,* 5-520
Sanvoisin, Eric. *The Ink Drinker,* 9-415
Seabrooke, Brenda. *The Vampire in My Bathtub,* 8-255
Sommer-Bodenburg, Angela. *If You Want to Scare Yourself,* 4-283
My Friend the Vampire, 8-263
Weird Tales from Shakespeare, 3-281
Williams, Tad, and Hoffman, Nina Kiriki. *Child of an Ancient City,* 5-680
Zelazny, Roger (Joseph Christopher). *Frost and Fire,* 3-313
Vermont
Anderson, M. T. *The Game of Sunken Places,* 9-8
Lindbergh, Anne Spencer. *Travel Far, Pay No Fare,* 9-303
Maguire, Gregory. *Seven Spiders Spinning,* 8-187
Schaeffer, Susan Fromberg. *The Dragons of North Chittendon,* 9-421
Slepian, Jan. *Back to Before,* 10-244
Vietnam War
Scarborough, Elizabeth Ann. *The Healer's War,* 6-367
Viking Britain. *See* Britain—Viking
Vikings. *See also* Norse mythology
Anderson, Poul (William). *Mother of Kings,* 6-10
War of the Gods, 5-26
Cowell, Cressida. *How to Train Your Dragon,* 8-52
Jones, Terry. *The Saga of Erik the Viking,* 1-168
Jonsson, Runer. *Viki Viking,* 8-153
Marillier, Juliet. *Wolfskin,* 6-267
Tebbetts, Christopher. *Viking Pride,* 10-254
Virginia
Hite, Sid. *Dither Farm,* 9-229
Virginia—17th century
Brown, Rita Mae. *Riding Shotgun,* 10-34
Virginia—19th century
Rucker, Rudy. *The Hollow Earth,* 7-237